D0120025

ORDNANCE SURVEY

STREET ATLAS

Glasgow

& West Central Scotland

Contents

IV   *Key to maps*

VI   *Administrative boundaries*

1   *Street maps*

240   *Index explanation and abbreviations*

241   *Index of towns, villages and rural localities*

242   *Index of street names*

PHILIP'S

Published by

Ordnance Survey   and   Philip's
Romsey Road   an imprint of Reed Books
Maybush   Michelin House, 81 Fulham Road, London, SW3 6RB
Southampton SO16 4GU   and Auckland, Melbourne, Singapore and Toronto

First edition 1995
Reprinted 1996

ISBN 0-540-06183-2 (Philip's, hardback)
ISBN 0-540-06184-0 (Philip's, softback)
ISBN 0-319-00802-9 (Ordnance Survey, hardback)
ISBN 0-319-00803-7 (Ordnance Survey, softback)

To the best of the Publishers' knowledge, the information in this atlas was correct at
the time of going to press. No responsibility can be accepted for any errors or their
consequences.

The representation in this atlas of a road, track or path is no evidence of the existence
of a right of way.

Printed and bound in Great Britain by
The Bath Press, Bath

Key to map symbols

⤨	British Rail station
⊖	Underground station
🚂	Private railway station
◆	Bus or coach station
Ⓗ	Heliport
♦	Police station (may not be open 24 hours)
✚	Hospital with casualty facilities (may not be open 24 hours)
□	Post office
+	Place of worship
◾	Important building
P	Parking
174	Adjoining page indicator
✕	No adjoining page
▬	Motorway
▬	Dual carriageway
▭	Main or through road
A27	Road numbers (Department of Transport)
⊤	Gate or obstruction to traffic (restrictions may not apply at all times or to all vehicles)
- - - -	All paths, bridleways, BOAT's, RUPP's, dismantled railways, etc.
▭	Track

The representation in this atlas of a road, track or path is no evidence of the existence of a right of way

Amb Sta	Ambulance Station	LC	Level crossing
Amb Dpo	Ambulance Depot	Liby	Library
Coll	College	Mus	Museum
FB	Footbridge	Acad	Academy
F Sta	Fire Station	Sch	School
Hospl	Hospital	TH	Town Hall or Town House

0	¼	½	¾	1 mile
0	250 m	500 m	250 m	1 Kilometre

The scale of the maps is 3½ inches to 1 mile (1:18103)

The small numbers around the edges of the maps identify the 1 kilometre National Grid lines

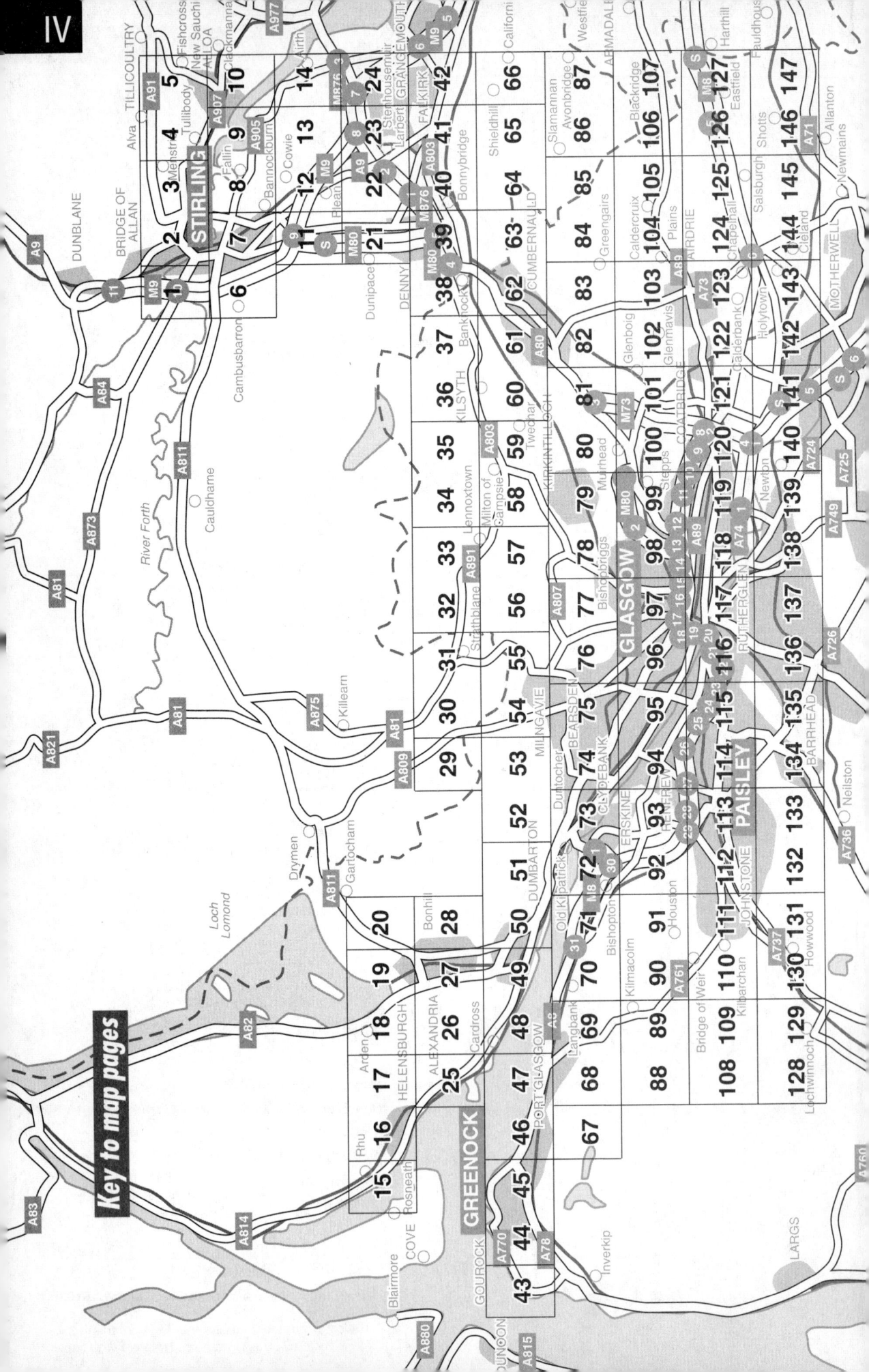

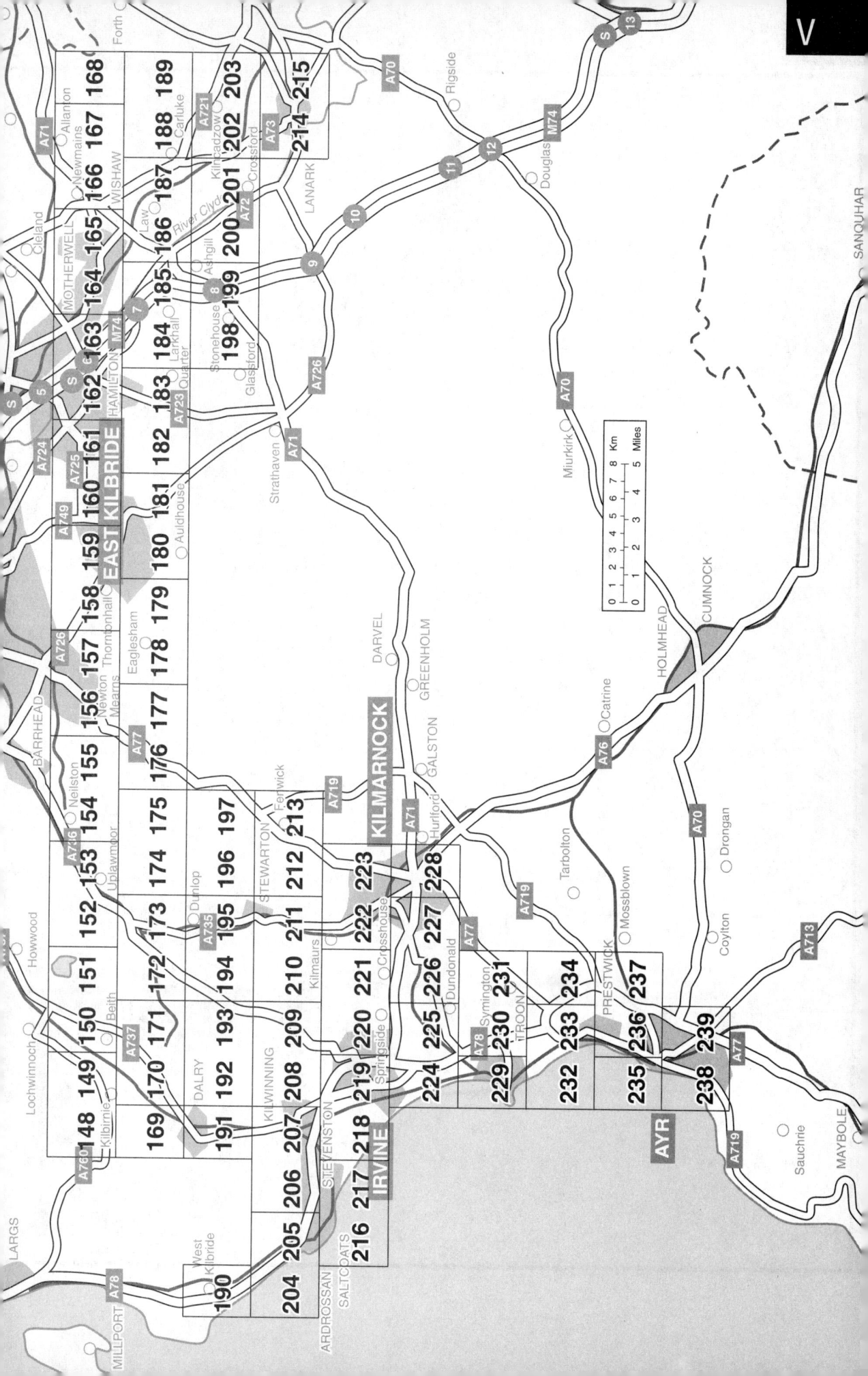

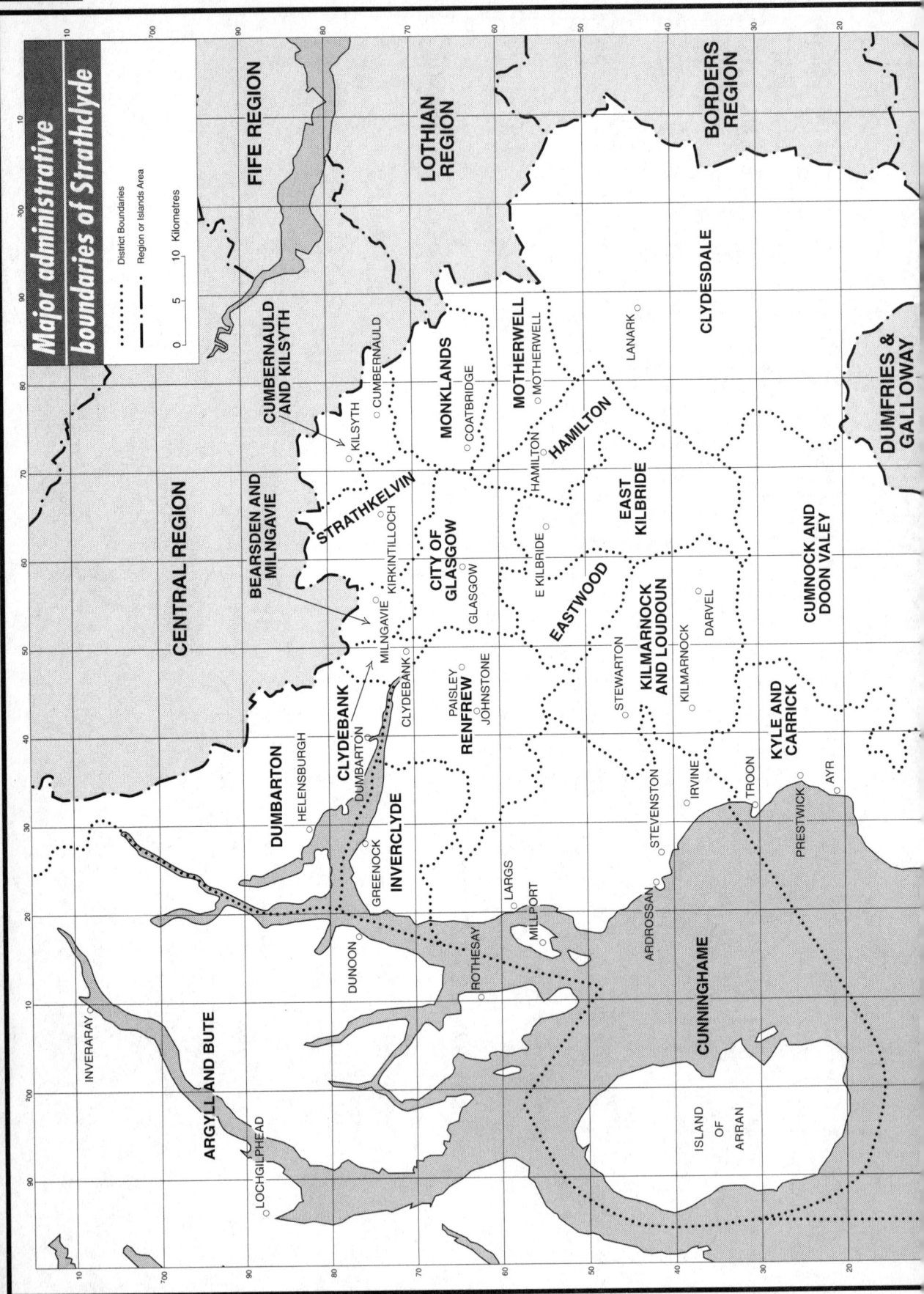

Major administrative boundaries of Strathclyde

District Boundaries
Region or Islands Area

0 5 10 Kilometres

FIFE REGION

LOTHIAN REGION

BORDERS REGION

CENTRAL REGION

DUMFRIES & GALLOWAY

CUMBERNAULD AND KILSYTH

○ KILSYTH

○ CUMBERNAULD

MONKLANDS

○ COATBRIDGE

MOTHERWELL

○ MOTHERWELL

CLYDESDALE

○ LANARK

BEARSDEN AND MILNGAVIE

STRATHKELVIN

MILNGAVIE KIRKINTILLOCH

CITY OF GLASGOW

○ GLASGOW

HAMILTON

○ HAMILTON

EAST KILBRIDE

○ E KILBRIDE

EASTWOOD

KILMARNOCK AND LOUDOUN

○ DARVEL

○ KILMARNOCK

CUMNOCK AND DOON VALEY

CLYDEBANK

○ CLYDEBANK

DUMBARTON

○ DUMBARTON

PAISLEY ○

RENFREW

○ JOHNSTONE

○ STEWARTON

DUMBARTON

HELENSBURGH ○

INVERCLYDE

GREENOCK ○

○ LARGS

○ MILLPORT

○ IRVINE

○ STEVENSTON

○ TROON

KYLE AND CARRICK

○ PRESTWICK

○ AYR

ARGYLL AND BUTE

○ INVERARAY

○ DUNOON

○ ROTHESAY

ARDROSSAN ○

CUNNINGHAME

○ LOCHGILPHEAD

ISLAND OF ARRAN

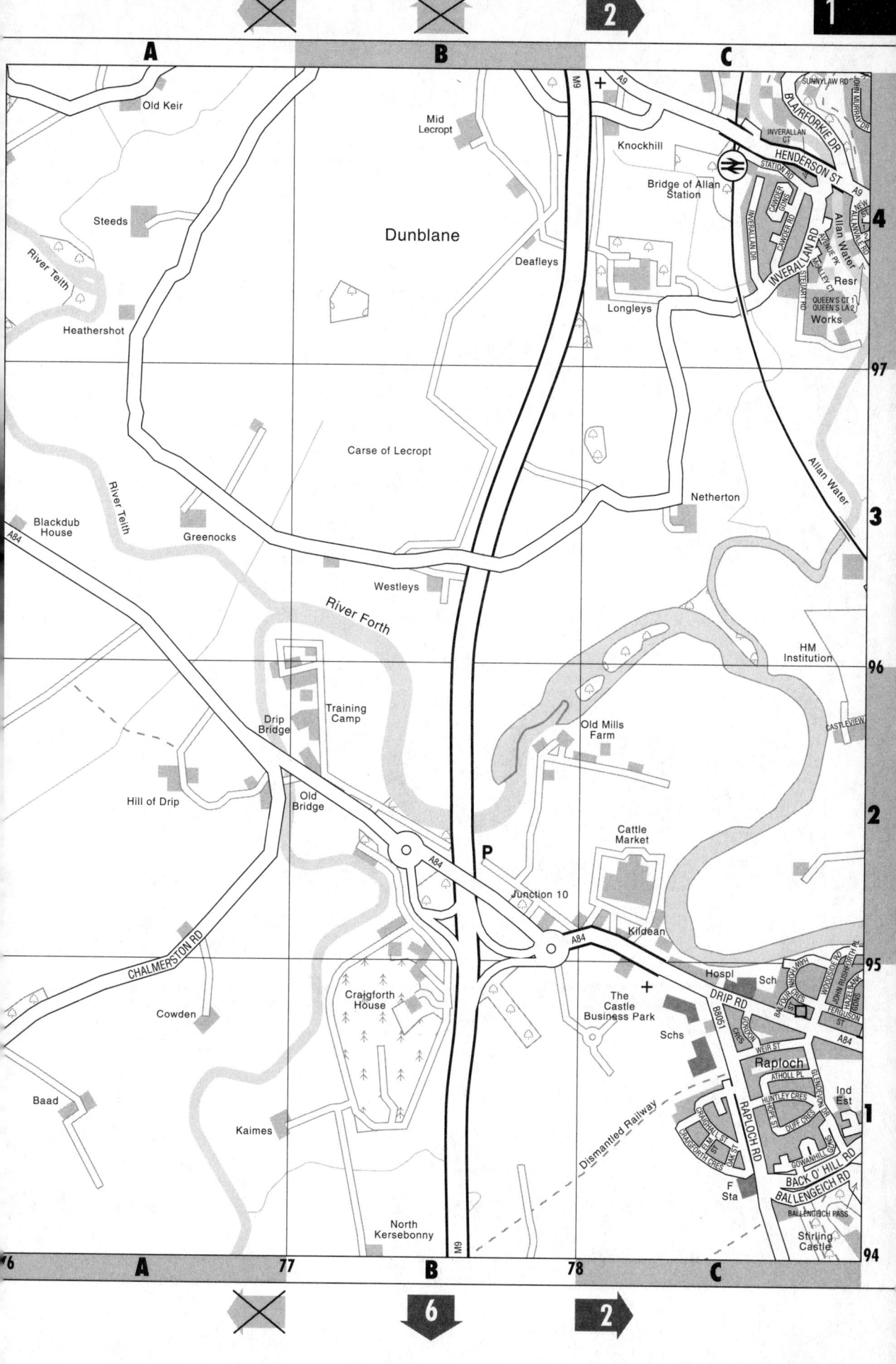

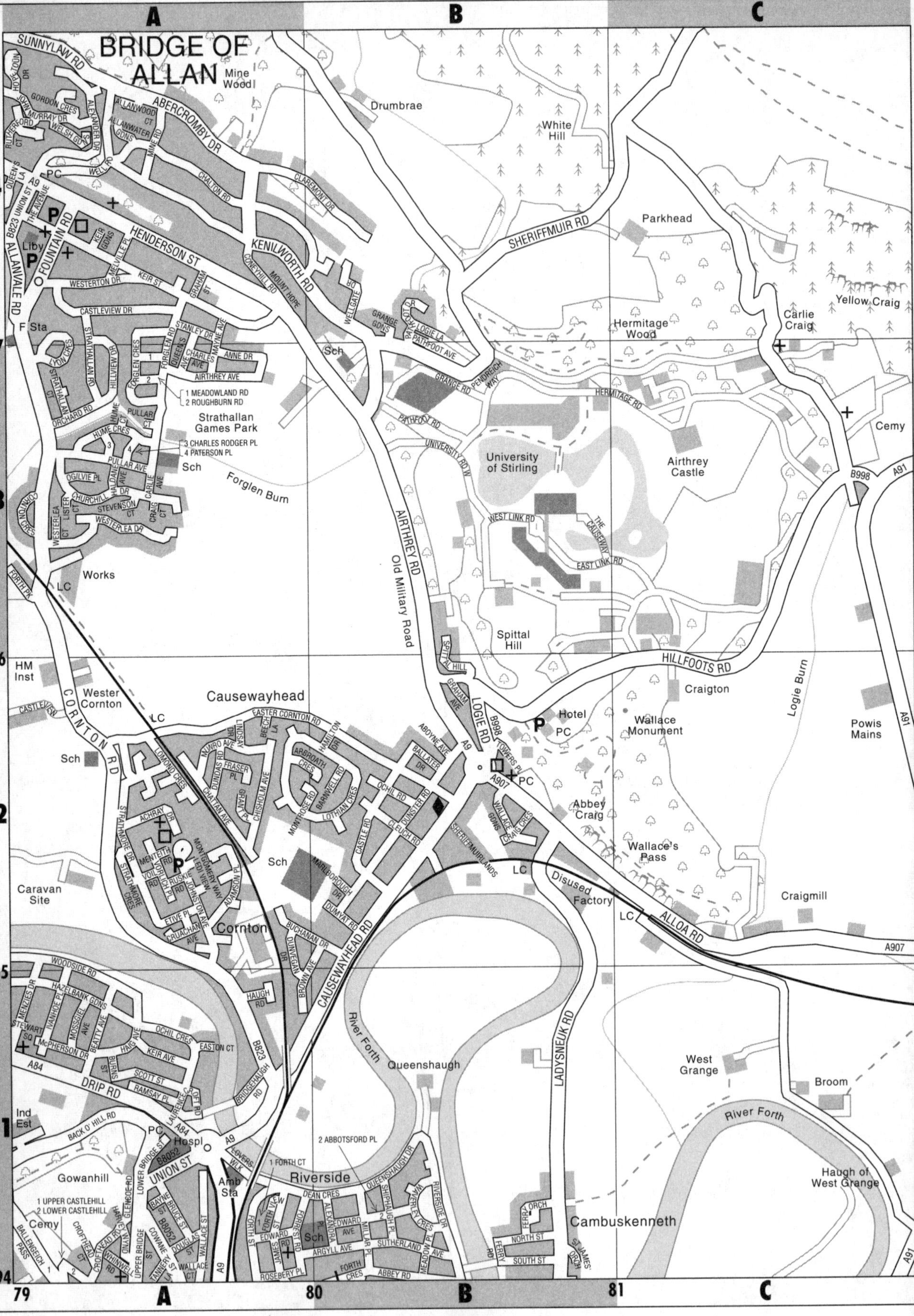

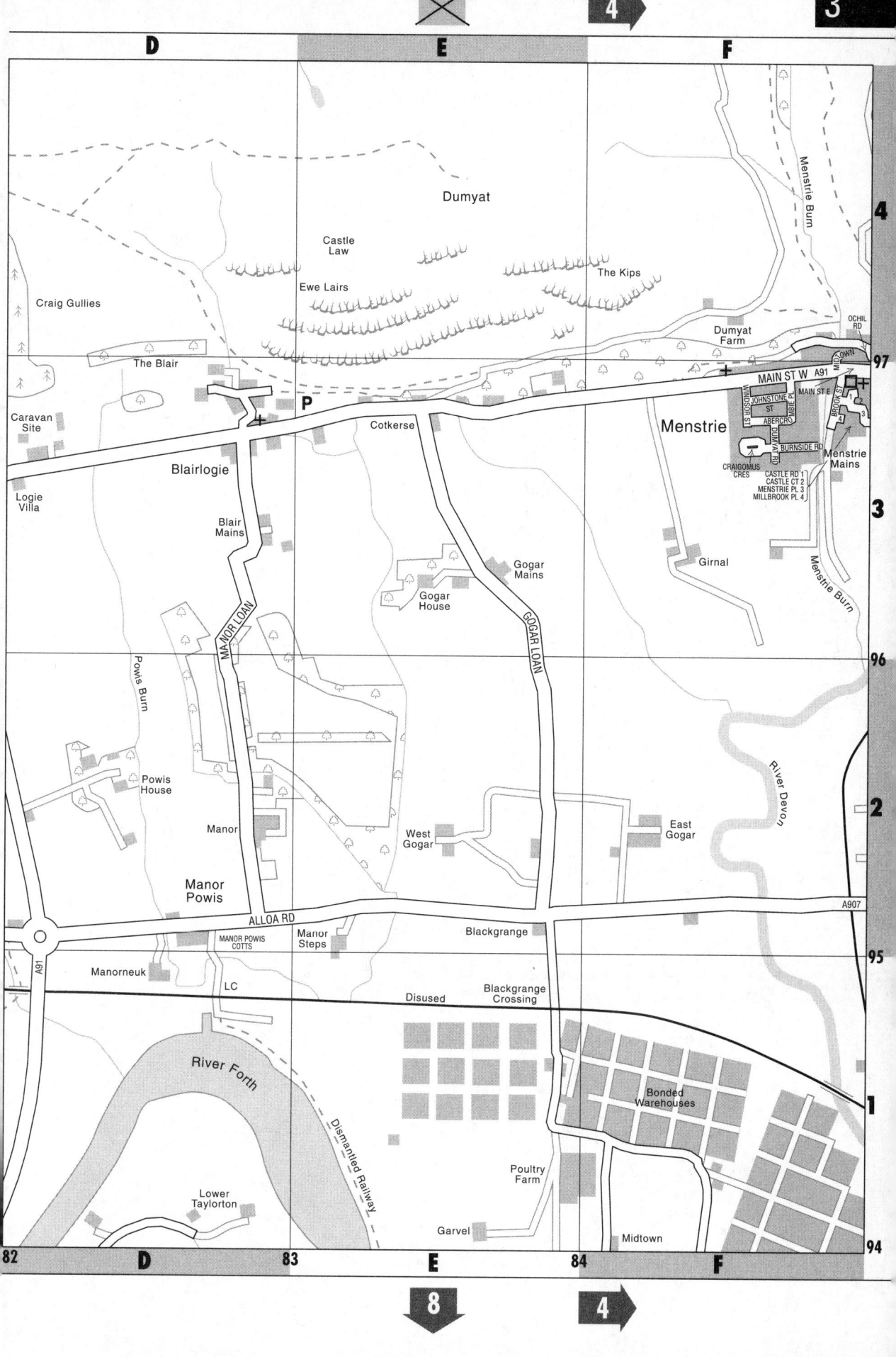

Dumyat

Castle Law

Ewe Lairs

The Kips

Craig Gullies

The Blair

Dumyat Farm

OCHIL RD

MIDTOWN

Caravan Site

MAIN ST W   A91

Menstrie

97

Logie Villa

P

Cotkerse

Blairlogie

Blair Mains

WINDSOR ST
JOHNSTONE ST
ABBEY RD
ABERCRO
DUMYAT RD
BROOK ST

MAIN ST E

Menstrie Mains

BURNSIDE RD

CRAIGOMUS CRES

Girnal

CASTLE RD 1
CASTLE CT 2
MENSTRIE PL 3
MILLBROOK PL 4

3

Powis Burn

Gogar Mains

Gogar House

MANOR LOAN

GOGAR LOAN

Menstrie Burn

96

Powis House

River Devon

Manor

West Gogar

East Gogar

2

Manor Powis

ALLOA RD

A907

Manorneuk

MANOR POWIS COTTS

Manor Steps

Blackgrange

95

A91

LC

Disused

Blackgrange Crossing

River Forth

Dismantled Railway

Bonded Warehouses

1

Lower Taylorton

Poultry Farm

Garvel

Midtown

94

4

8

4

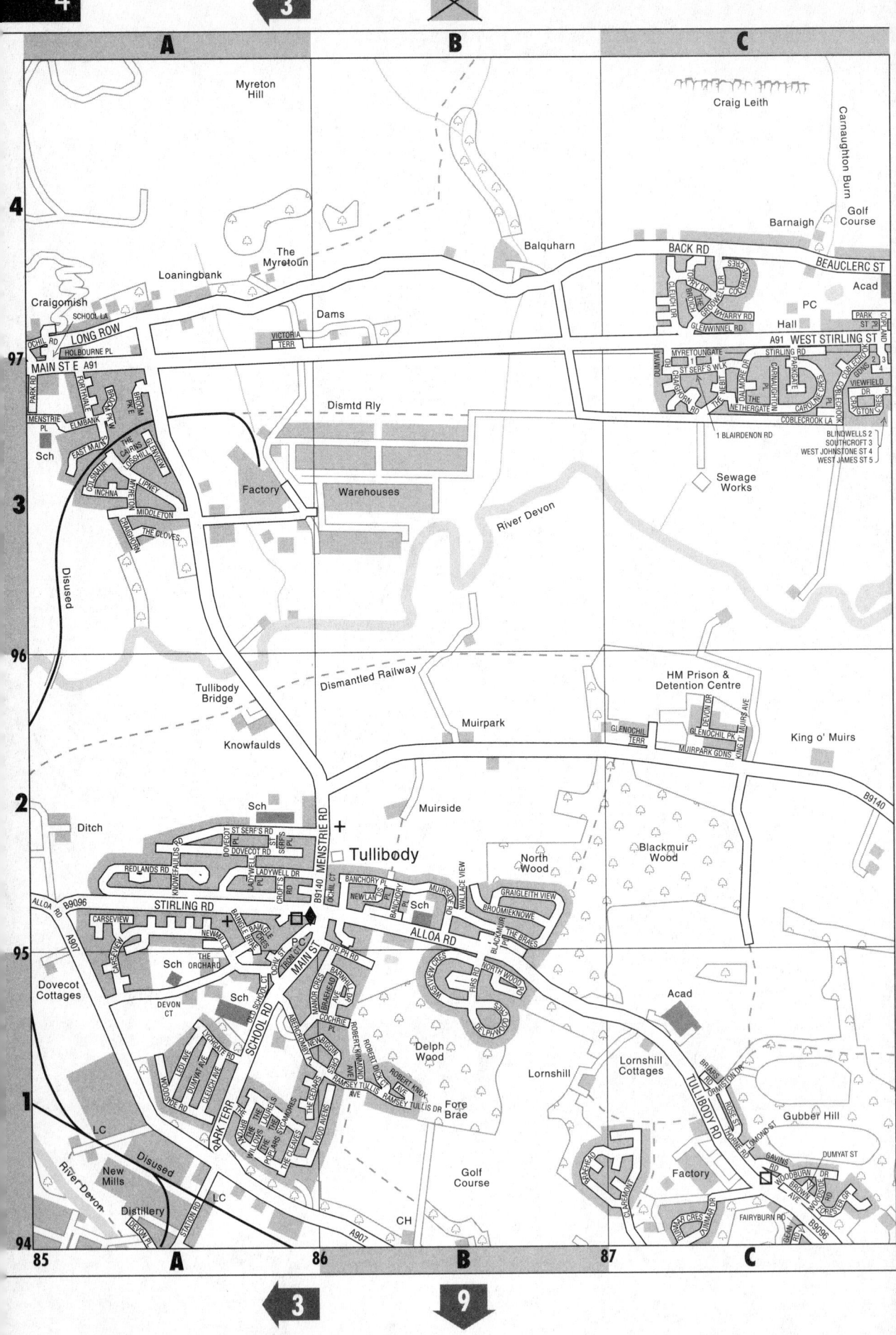

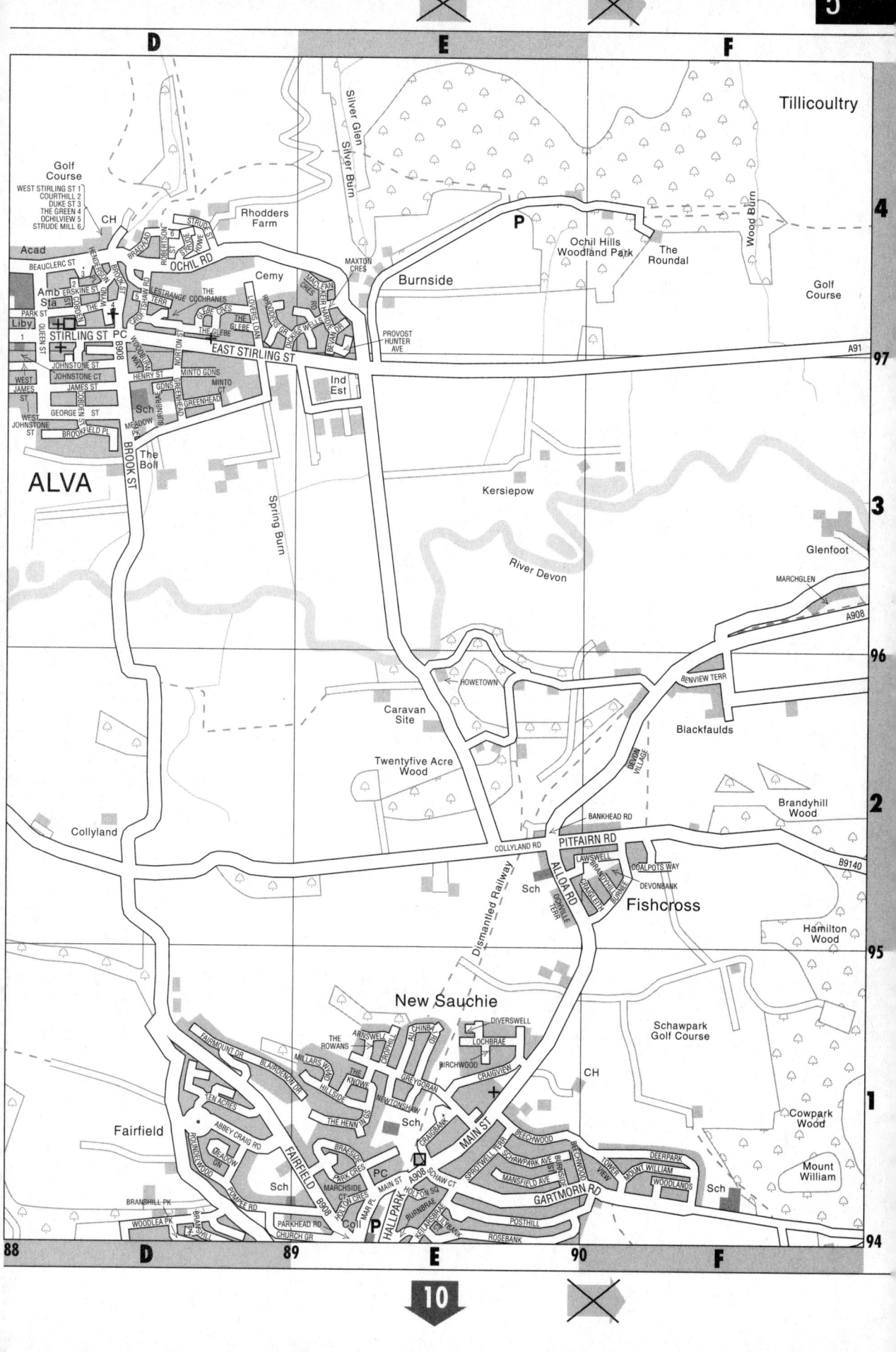

A B C

River Forth

Dismantled Railway

Falleninch

M9

KERSEBONNY RD

DUMBARTON RD

B8051 RAPLOCH RD

King's Knot

4 A811

Polrogan Bridge

Bankend

White House

South Kersebonny

King's Park Farm

Golf Course

CH

BALMORAL PL

A811

QUEEN'S RD

B8051

Raploch Burn

THE HOMESTEADS

King's Park

93

Hillhead

KERSEBONNY RD

Hollandbush

St THOMAS'S WELL

Hayford House

Cemy

ST THOMAS

BROOMHILL PL

DOUGLAS TERR

PARKDYKE

SNOWDON PLACE LA 1
SNOWDON PL 2

PC

PARK AVE

KING'S PK RD

PARK PL

DALMORGLEN PK

Johnny's Bridge

TOUCH RD

Cambusbarron

MILL RD

NORTHEND

DONALDSON PL

STEWART PL

BIRKHILL RD

GRAMPIAN RD

CANEY PARK

Batterflatts

Torbrex

LAURELHILL GDNS

3

Johnny's Burn

MAIN ST

GRIESSON CRES

MILL HILL BRAE

HAYFORD PL

GRAMPIAN RD

KENNINGKNOWES RD

Liby

SCH

QUARRY RD

FIRPARK TERR

OLD DROVE RD

CAULDHAME CRES

THE YETTS

THOMSON PL

MURRAY PL

WOODSIDE

UNDERWOOD COTTS

BRUCE TERR

WALLACE PL

GILLIES HILL

St NINIANS RD

UNDERWOOD RD

Polmaise Farm

POLMAISE RD

SPRINGWOOD AVE

DERORAN PL

LAURELHILL GR

Hospl

SYCAMORE PL

BIRCH AVE

CEDAR PL

ASH TERR

TORBREX LA

TORBREX FARM

ST VALERY DR

DALMORGLEN PK

Gartur

Cambusbarron Quarry

92

Murray's Wood

Gillies Hill

Polmaise Castle

Bearside

TORBREX RD

WELL PARK CRES

Coxet Hill

CULTENHOVE CRES

2

Touchadam Craig

Fir Park

POLMAISE RD

Haggs Wood

CULTENHOVE PL

GATESIDE RD

GRAYSTALE RD

Murrayshall Quarry

91 Castlehill

Murrayshall Farm

Graystale

Wallstale

Chartershall House

1

Sauchie Craig

Moor Burn

Bannock Burn

Middlethird Wood

Cultenhove

Chartershall Farm

CHARTERSHALL RD

90

76 A 77 B 78 C

STIRLING

BANNOCKBURN

D **E** **F**

DEVON PL

STATION RD

FORTH ST

SOUTH ST

MAIN ST

PH

P

Cambus Farm

Cambus

A907

Arnsbrae

DUNMAR DR

Gean House

INGLEWOOD

MT LODGE

B9096 TULLIBODY RD

KENT RD

CROWN RD

GEAN RD

FORTH CRES

INGLEWOOD GDNS

INGLEWOOD RD

IVANHOE

Golf Course

ARNS GR

ACADEMY RD

CLAREMONT

CROWN RD

WINDSOR GDNS

FORTH CRES

CHURCHILL ST

CHARLES ST

OBERON

DAWSON PL

PAVILION VIEW

Acad Sch

CARSE TERR

EDEN RD

NORWOOD AVE

NORWOOD GDNS

STIRLING RD

NORWOOD CRES

ROCKWELL PL

ALEXANDRA DR

LC

A907

Disused

Orchard Farm

Orchard House

DIRLETON LA

DIRLETON GDNS

MITCHELL CRES

SMITHFIELD LOAN

BELLEVUE RD

STANTON AVE

SHIRE WYND

FORBES ST

CALEDONIAN GDNS

CALEDONIAN RD

TOWNS CRES

GRANT ST

MEDWYN

KEVERRAGE PL

MUNRO PL

GRANGE RD

Sch

Works

KELLIEBANK

KELLIEBANK

CRAIGWARD

Pier

Bandeath Ind Est

Tullibody Inch

Rhind Rack

Dismantled Railway

Longcarse

Longcarse Reach

Works

Works

93

3

River Forth

Rhind

Inch

FERRY RD

Works

Pier

South Alloa

92

2

Throsk House

Throsk

KERSIE RD

KERSIE RD

A905

Kersie Mains

KERSIE TERR

91

Mains of Throsk

Poppletrees

Kersie Bridge

Dismantled Railway

South Mains

Willowbank

Meadowfield

South Kersie

A905

1

85 **D** 86 **E** 87 **F** 90

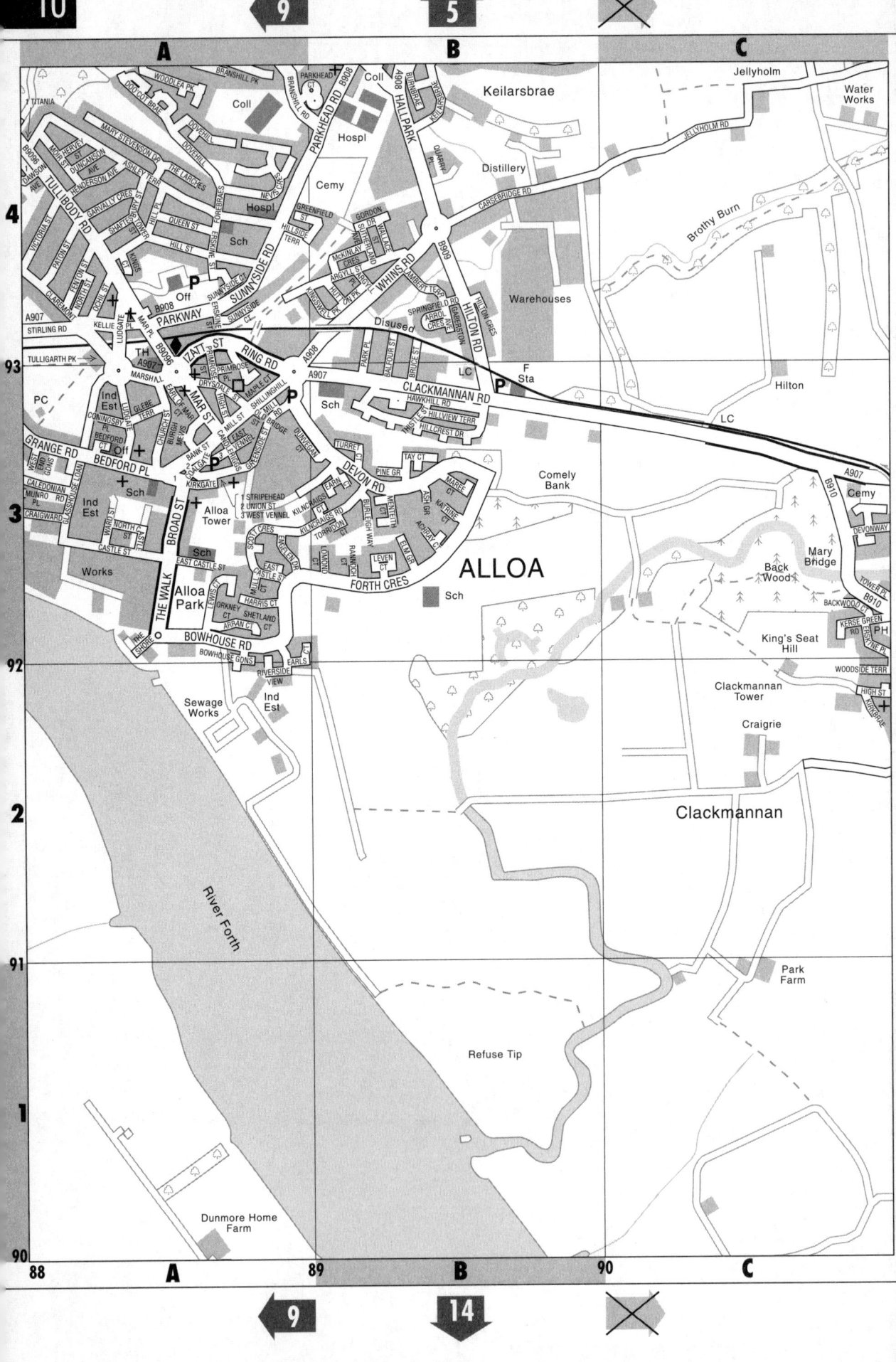

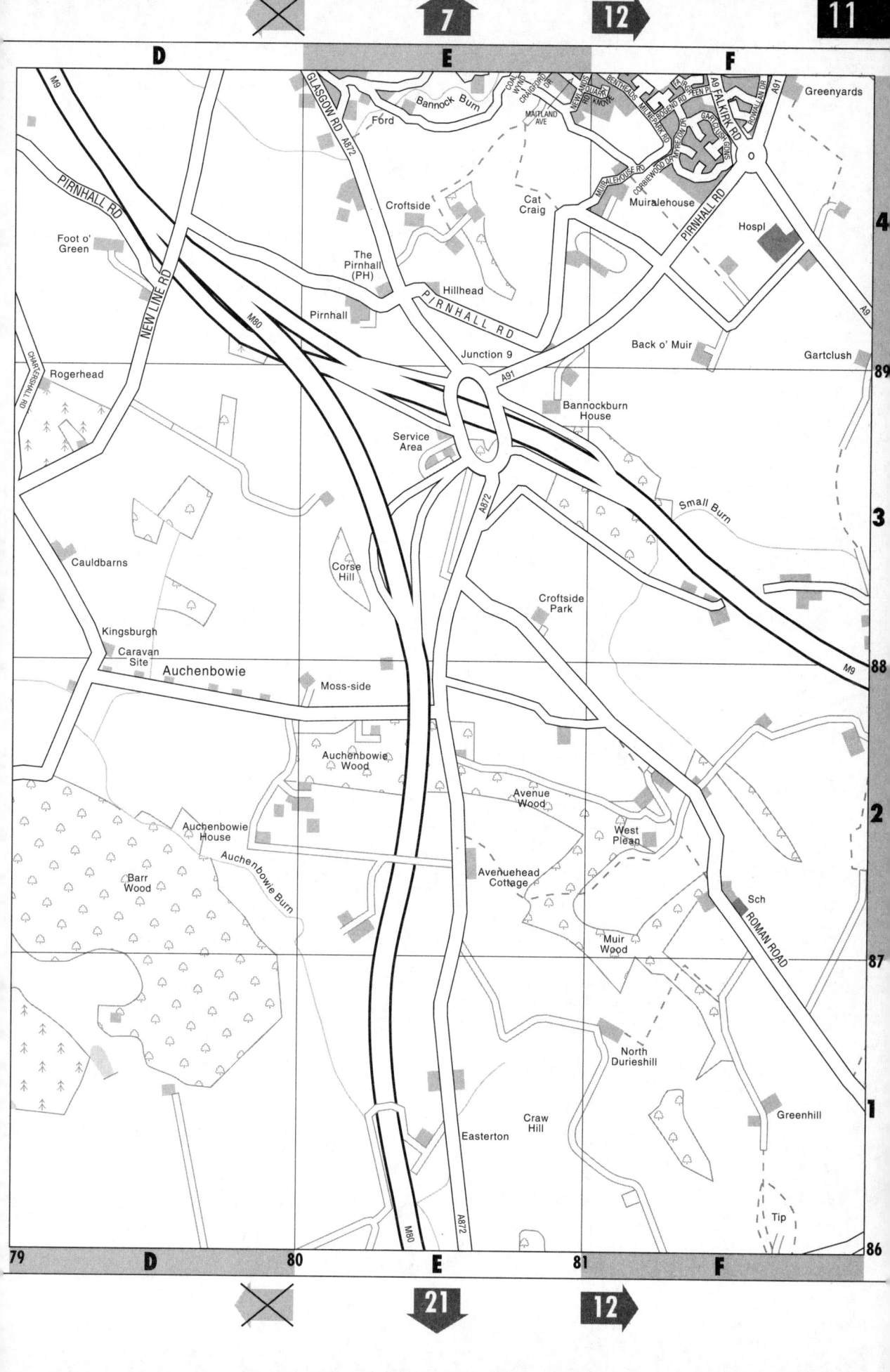

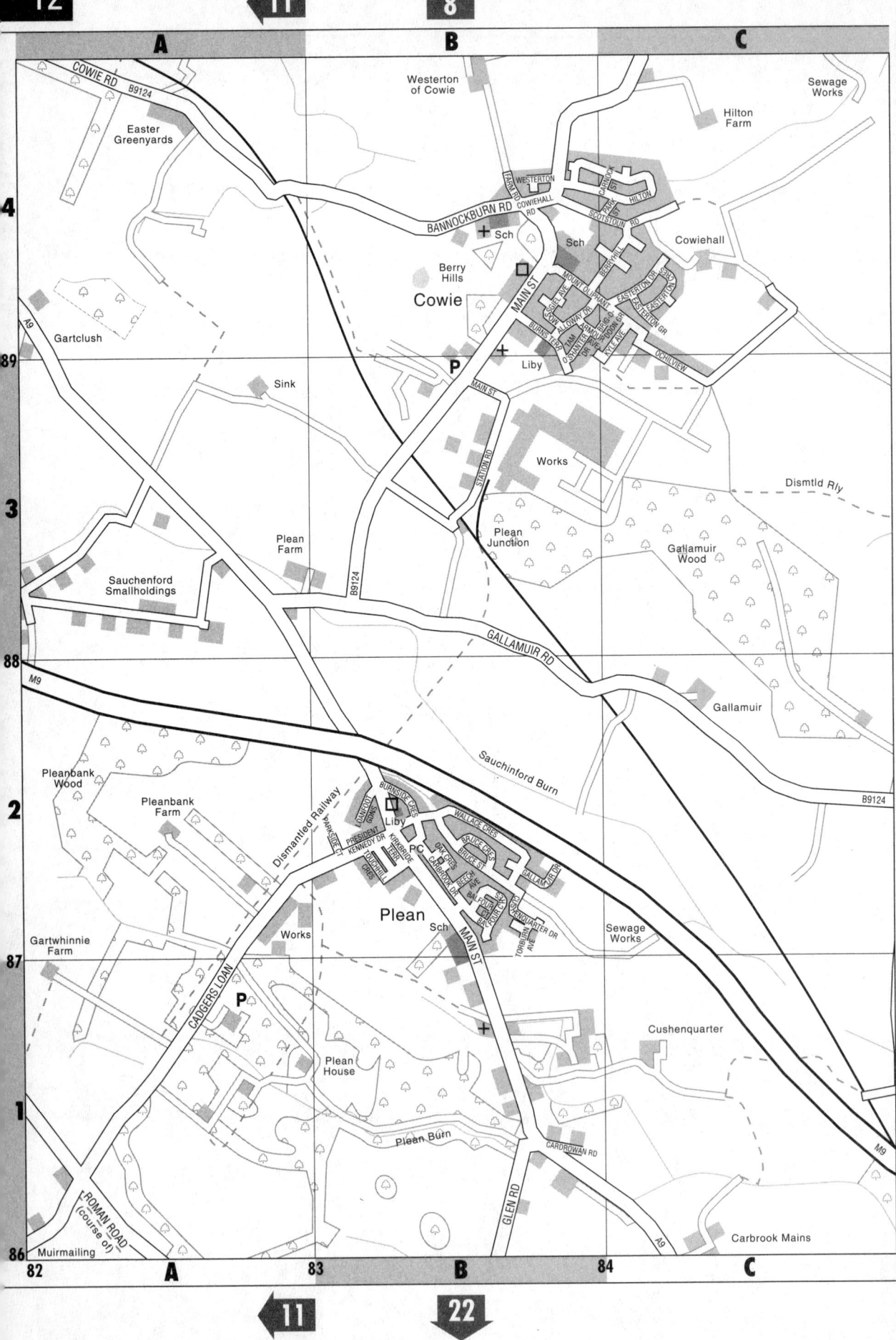

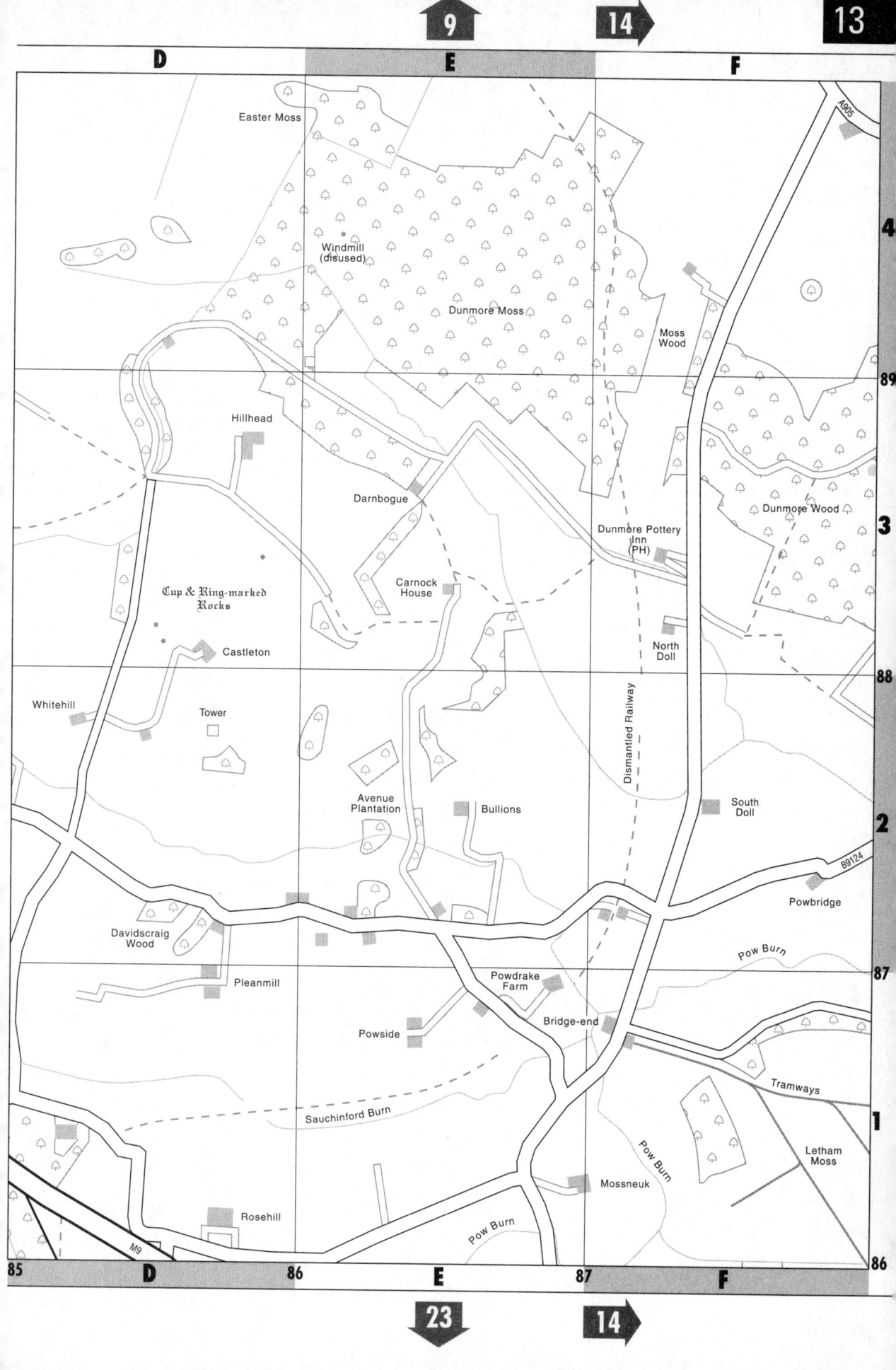

Easter Moss

Windmill
(disused)

Dunmore Moss

Moss
Wood

4

89

Hillhead

Darnbogue

Dunmore Wood

3

Dunmore Pottery
Inn
(PH)

Cup & Ring-marked
Rocks

Carnock
House

Castleton

North
Doll

88

Whitehill

Tower

Avenue
Plantation

Bullions

Dismantled Railway

South
Doll

2

Davidscraig
Wood

B9124

Powbridge

Pleanmill

Pow Burn

87

Powdrake
Farm

Powside

Bridge-end

Tramways

Sauchinford Burn

1

Pow Burn

Letham
Moss

Mossneuk

Rosehill

M9

Pow Burn

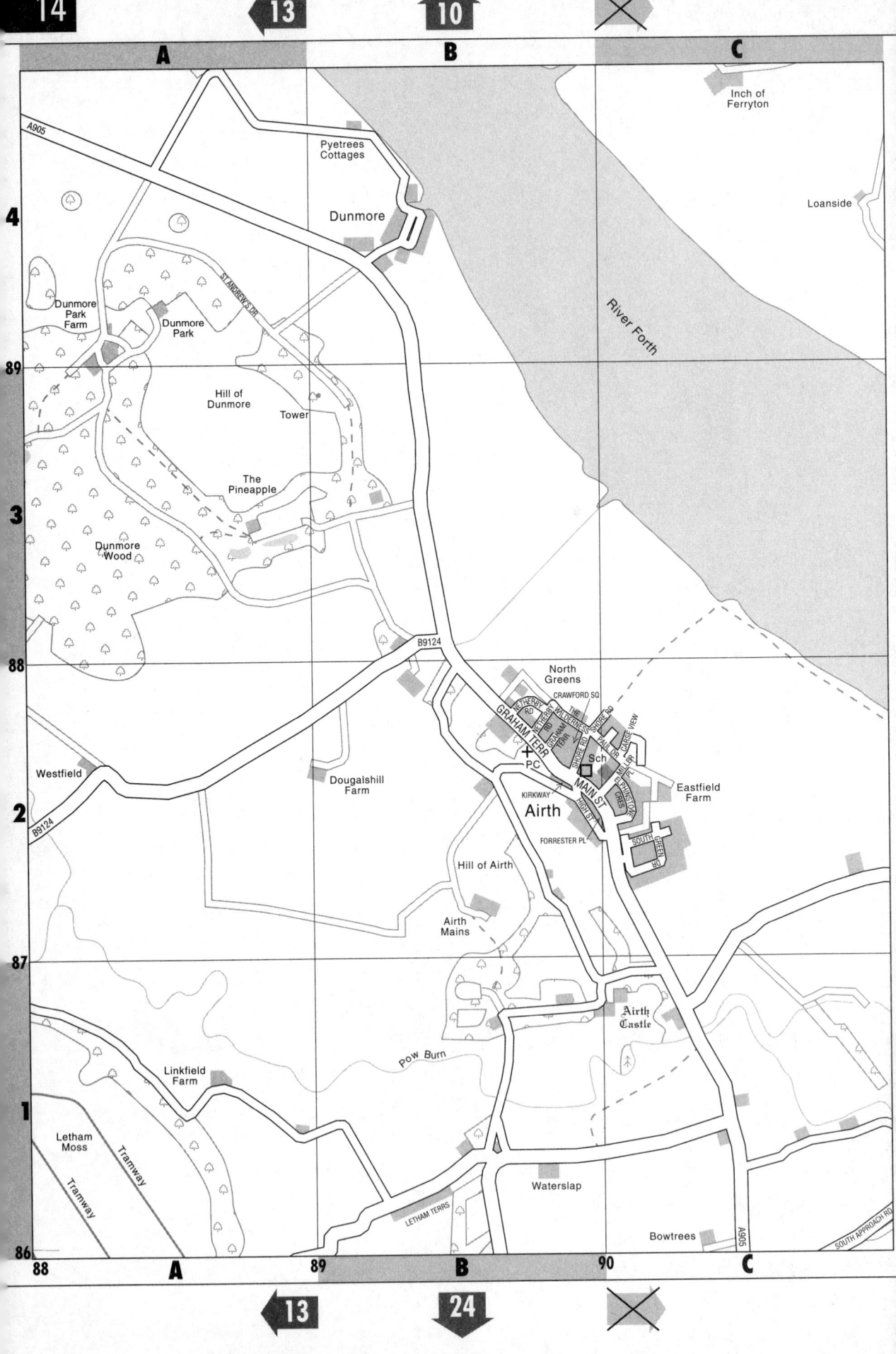

A B C

Inch of
Ferryton

Loanside

4

Pyetrees
Cottages

Dunmore

A905

River Forth

Dunmore
Park
Farm

Dunmore Park

ST ANDREW'S DR

89

Hill of
Dunmore

Tower

The
Pineapple

Dunmore
Wood

B9124

3

88

North
Greens

CRAWFORD SQ

NETHERBY RD

GRAHAM TERR

THE WYND

NETHERBY RD

GRAHAM TERR

SHORE RD

PAUL DR

CRARSE VIEW

SHORE RD

GRANGE VIEW

Westfield

B9124

PC

Dougalshill
Farm

Sch

Eastfield
Farm

KIRKWAY

MAIN ST

ELPHINSTONE CRES

SOUTH GREEN RD

2

Airth

HIGH ST

FORRESTER PL

Hill of Airth

Airth
Mains

87

Airth
Castle

Pow Burn

Linkfield
Farm

1

Letham
Moss

Tramway

Tramway

Waterslap

LETHAM TERRS

Bowtrees

A905

SOUTH APPROACH RD

88 A 89 B 90 C

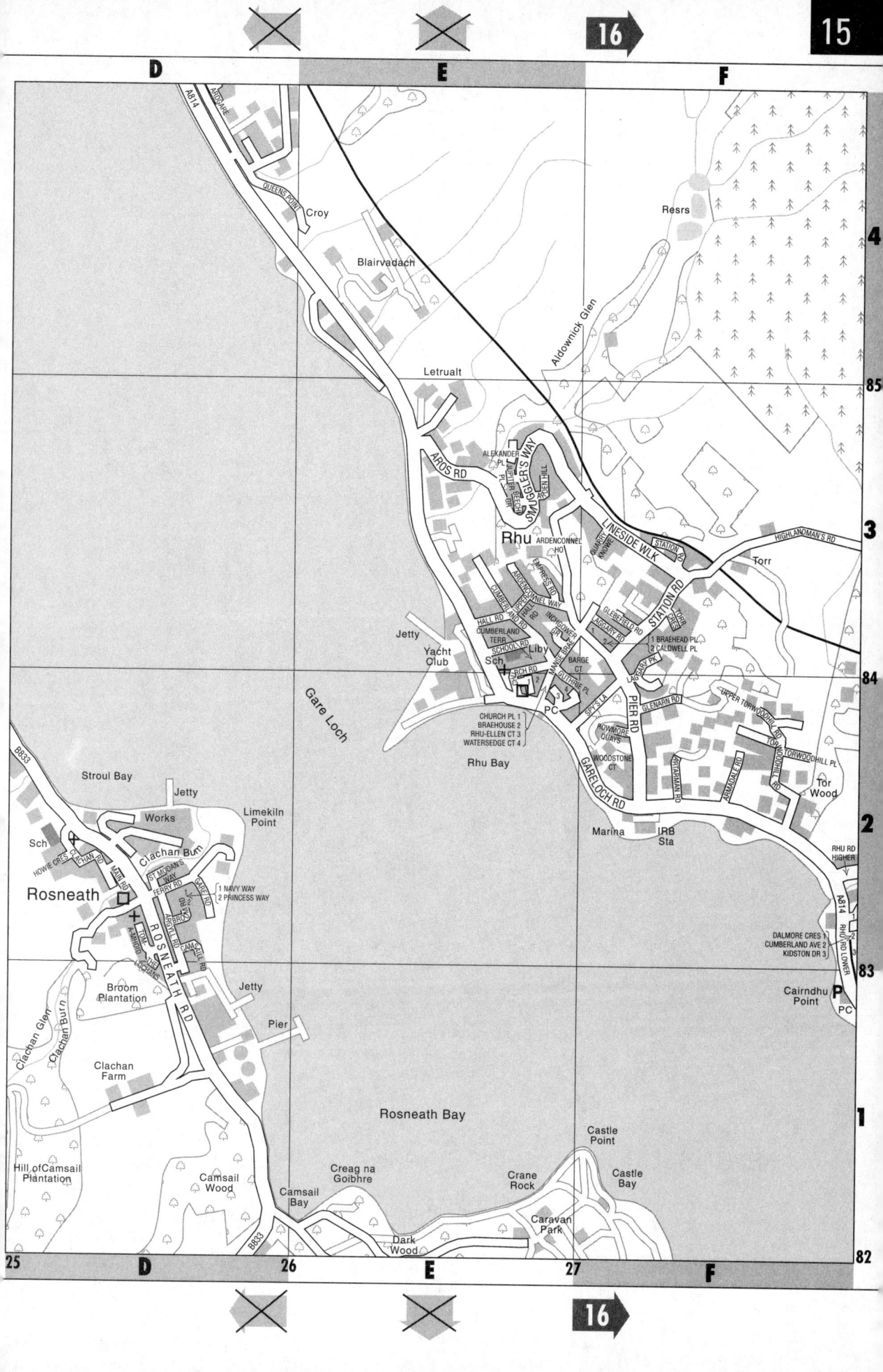

D
E
F

4

A814

QUEENS POINT

Croy

Blairvadach

Resrs

Aldownick Glen

Letrualt

85

AROS RD

SMUGGLER'S WAY

JUPITER BEACH

ALEXANDER PL

ARDEN HILL

LINESIDE WLK

STATION

Highlandman's RD

3

Rhu

ARDENCONNEL HO

QUARRY KNOWE

STATION RD

Torr

CUMBERLAND WAY

AMPRESS RD

ARDENCONNEL WAY

TRIVELL RD

INCHGOWER PL

GLEBEFIELD RD

LAGGARY RD

Jetty

HALL RD
CUMBERLAND
TERR
SCHOOL RD

MANSE BRAE

1 BRAEHEAD PL
2 CALDWELL PL

Yacht
Club

Sch
Liby

BARGE
CT

LAGGARY PK

Gare Loch

CHURCH RD

GUTHRIE PL

SPS LA

PIER RD

GLENARN RD

UPPER TORWOODHILL

84

PC

CHURCH PL 1
BRAEHOUSE 2
RHU-ELLEN CT 3
WATERSEDGE CT 4

ROWMORE
QUAYS

WOODSTONE
CT

ARMADALE RD

TORWOODHILL RD

TORWOODHILL PL

Rhu Bay

GARELOCH RD

ARTARMAN RD

Tor
Wood

Stroul Bay

Jetty

Limekiln
Point

Works

Clachan Burn

Marina

IRB
Sta

2

RHU RD
HIGHER

B833

Sch

HOWIE CRES

CHAN RD

ST MODAN'S
WAY

FERRY RD

CLARE RD

MILL RD

1 NAVY WAY
2 PRINCESS WAY

A814

RHU RD LOWER

Rosneath

ARGYLL RD

CAMSAIL RD

DALMORE CRES 1
CUMBERLAND AVE 2
KIDSTON DR 3

83

ROSNEATH RD

Broom
Plantation

Jetty

Cairndhu
Point

P

PC

Clachan Glen

Clachan Burn

Pier

Clachan
Farm

1

Rosneath Bay

Castle
Point

Hill of Camsail
Plantation

Creag na
Goibhre

Crane
Rock

Castle
Bay

Camsail
Wood

Camsail
Bay

Caravan
Park

B833

Dark
Wood

25
D
26
E
27
F
82

D
E
F

4

Highfields Muir

Kilbride

Highfields

Black
Bull

Cross
Keys

B832

B831

Crosskeys
Wood

85

Inverlauren

Drumfad

Inverlauren Wood

Callendoun

Wester
Bannachra

3

Fruin Water

Daligan

LUSS RD

84

Bannachra
Woods

Old Luss Road

Bannachra
Woods

Golf
Course

Bannachra
Muir

2

Garrawy Glen

83

KENT DR

HORTON PL
GOLFHILL
DR
FISHER
PL
MAL
CHURCH
SQ
CAMPBELL PL
CAMPBELTOWN CT

1 FROBISHER PL
2 RODNEY PL
3 COCHRANE PL
4 BEATTY PL
5 JERVIS PL

COLLINGWOOD PL
GRAHAM

WINSTON RD

Black
Wood

Townhead
Farm

Drumfork
Burn

6 STUCKLECKIE RD

1

BEN BOUIE DR

Sch

Quarry
Wood

Northfield
Wood

7 WILLIAMSON DR
8 OLD LUSS RD

Sch

31
D
32
E
33
F
82

17

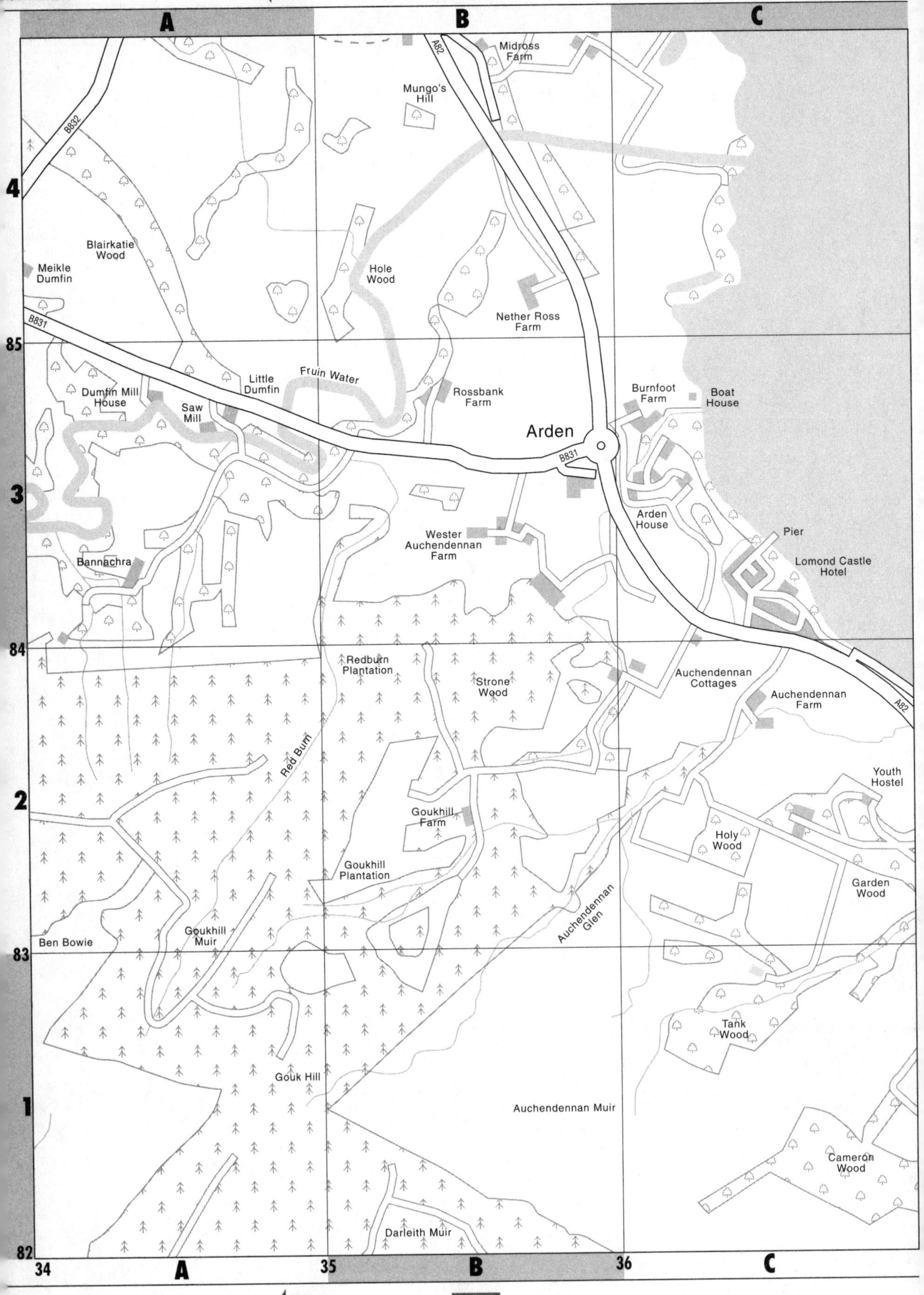

A
B
C

4

Blairkatie
Wood

Meikle
Dumfin

Mungo's
Hill

Midross
Farm

Hole
Wood

Nether Ross
Farm

B831

85

Dumfin Mill
House

Little
Dumfin

Fruin Water

Rossbank
Farm

Burnfoot
Farm

Boat
House

Saw
Mill

Arden

B831

3

Bannachra

Wester
Auchendennan
Farm

Arden
House

Pier

Lomond Castle
Hotel

84

Redburn
Plantation

Strone
Wood

Auchendennan
Cottages

Auchendennan
Farm

A82

Ben Bowie

Red Burn

Goukhill
Plantation

Goukhill
Farm

Auchendennan
Glen

Holy
Wood

Youth
Hostel

2

Goukhill
Muir

Garden
Wood

83

Tank
Wood

Gouk Hill

Auchendennan Muir

1

Cameron
Wood

Darleith Muir

82

34
A
35
B
36
C

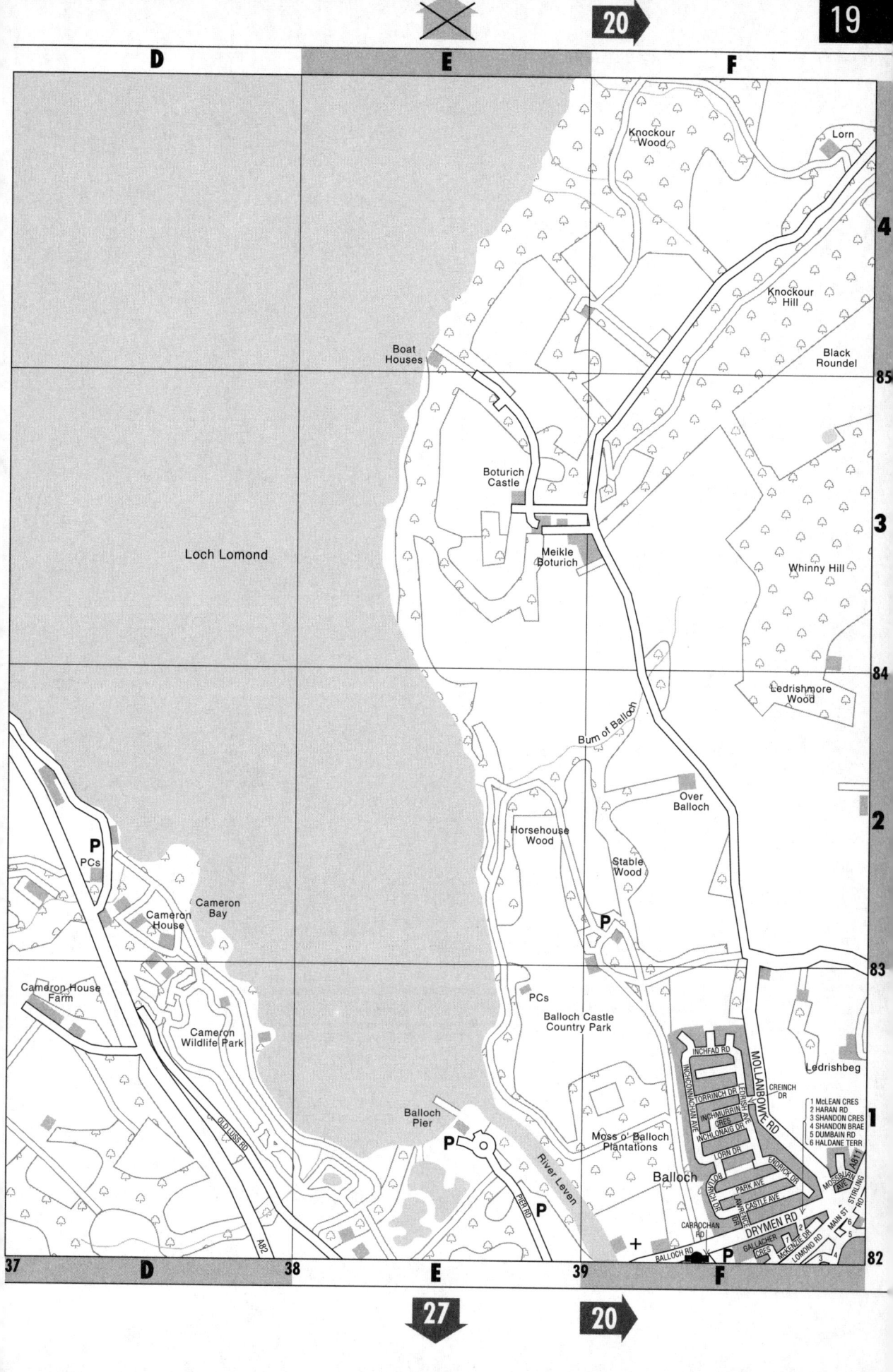

Knockour
Wood

Lorn

Knockour
Hill

Black
Roundel

4

Boat
Houses

85

Boturich
Castle

3

Meikle
Boturich

Whinny Hill

84

Ledrishmore
Wood

Burn of Balloch

Over
Balloch

2

Horsehouse
Wood

Stable
Wood

Loch Lomond

P

PCs

P

Cameron Bay

83

Cameron
House

PCs

Balloch Castle
Country Park

Ledrishbeg

Cameron House
Farm

INCHFAD RD

CREINCH
DR

Cameron
Wildlife Park

Balloch
Pier

Moss o' Balloch
Plantations

1 McLEAN CRES
2 HARAN RD
3 SHANDON CRES
4 SHANDON BRAE
5 DUMBAIN RD
6 HALDANE TERR

1

P

o

Balloch

OLD LUSS RD

River Leven

PIER RD

P

DRYMEN RD

A82

P

BALLOCH RD

82

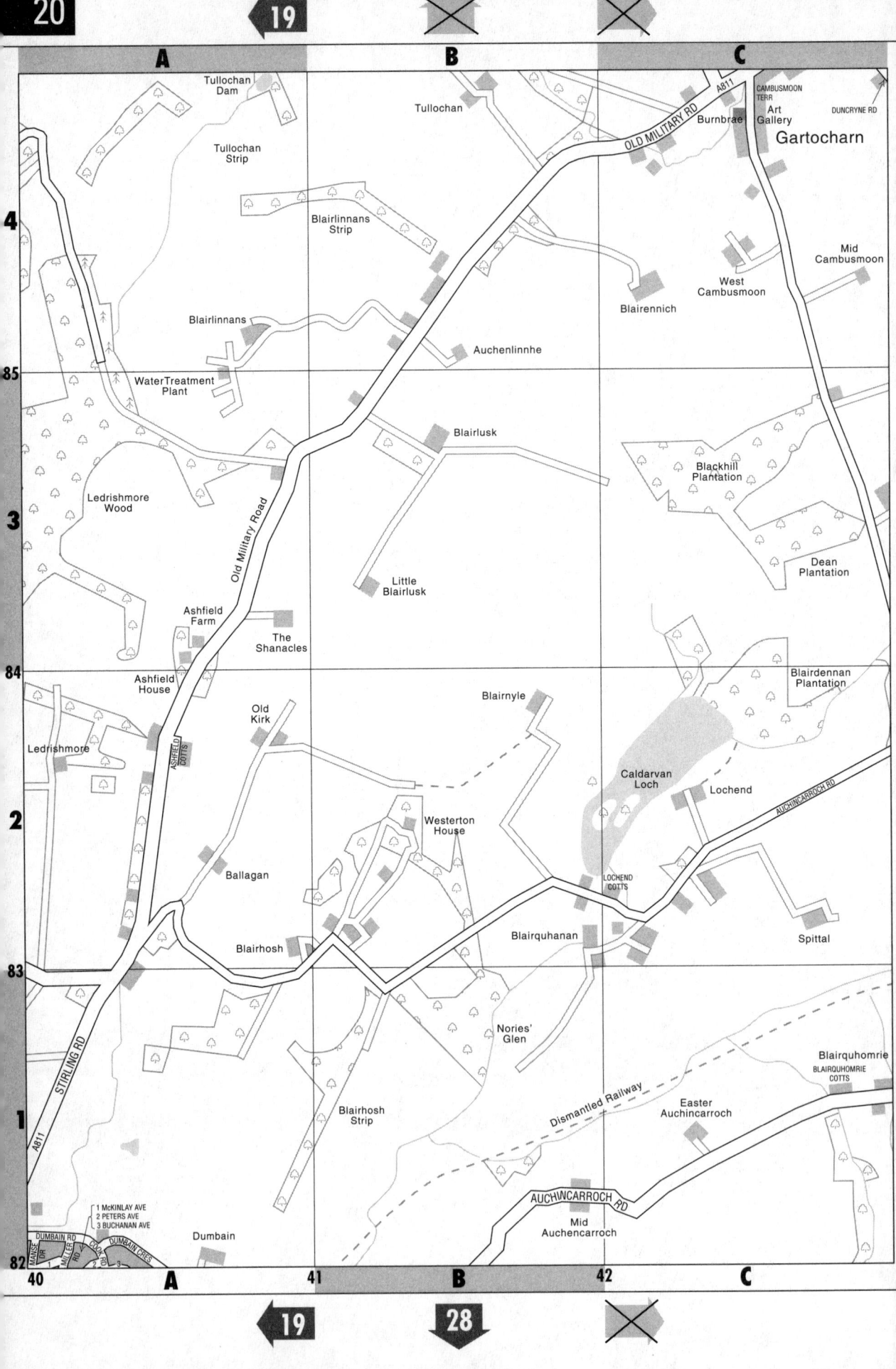

Tullochan
Dam

Tullochan

OLD MILITARY RD

A811

CAMBUSMOON
TERR

Burnbrae

Art
Gallery

DUNCRYNE RD

Gartocharn

Tullochan
Strip

Blairlinnans
Strip

Mid
Cambusmoon

West
Cambusmoon

Blairennich

Blairlinnans

Auchenlinnhe

Water Treatment
Plant

Blairlusk

Blackhill
Plantation

Ledrishmore
Wood

Old Military Road

Dean
Plantation

Little
Blairlusk

Ashfield
Farm

The
Shanacles

Blairdennan
Plantation

Ashfield
House

Old
Kirk

Blairnyle

Ledrishmore

ASHFIELD COTTS

Caldarvan
Loch

Lochend

AUCHINCARROCH RD

Ballagan

Westerton
House

Lochend
Cotts

Blairhosh

Blairquhanan

Spittal

STIRLING RD

Nories'
Glen

Blairquhomrie

BLAIRQUHOMRIE
COTTS

Dismantled Railway

Blairhosh
Strip

Easter
Auchincarroch

A811

1 McKINLAY AVE
2 PETERS AVE
3 BUCHANAN AVE

DUMBAIN RD

MANSE
DR

MILTER RD

DUMBAIN CRES

Dumbain

AUCHINCARROCH RD

Mid
Auchencarroch

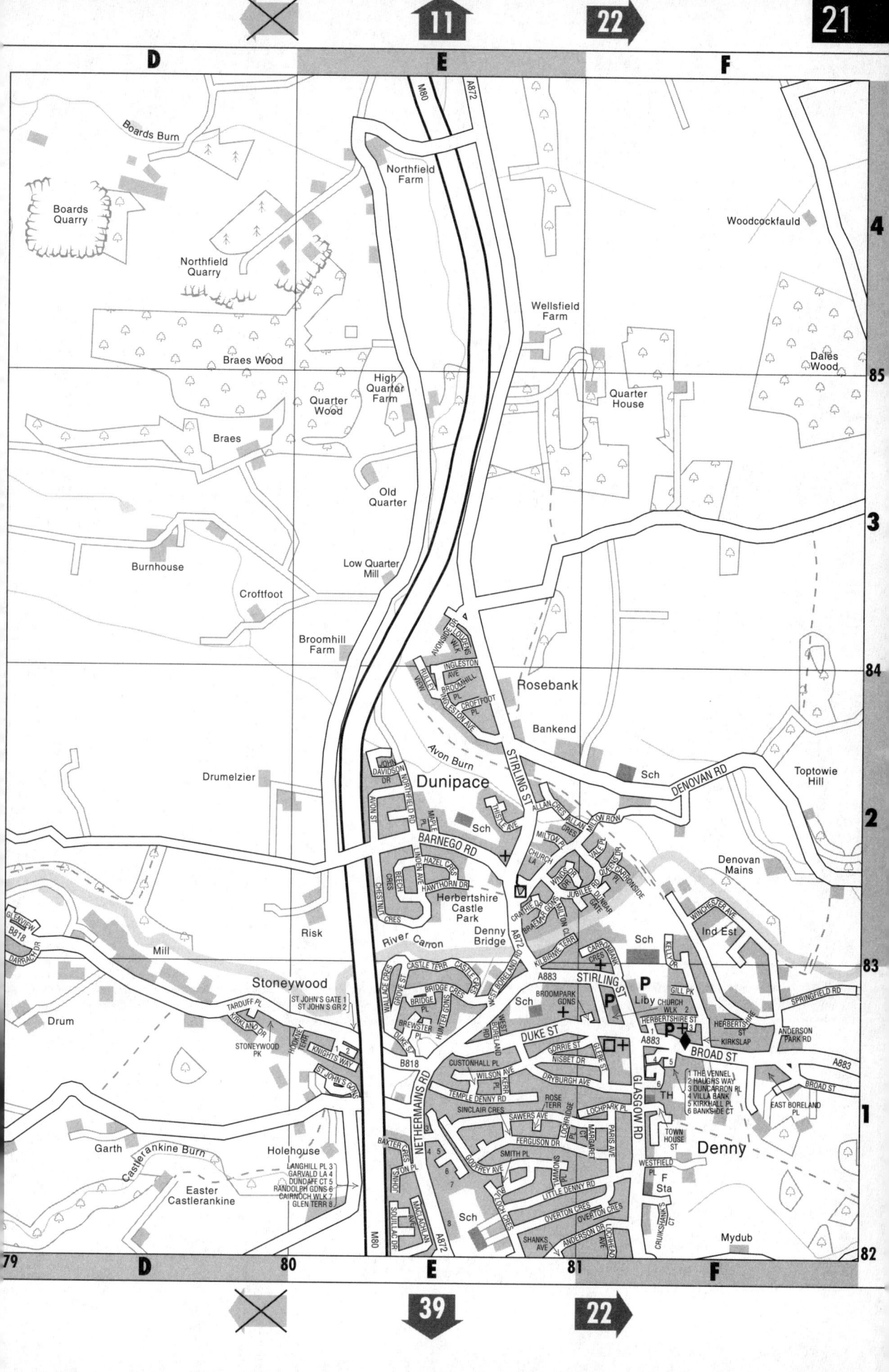

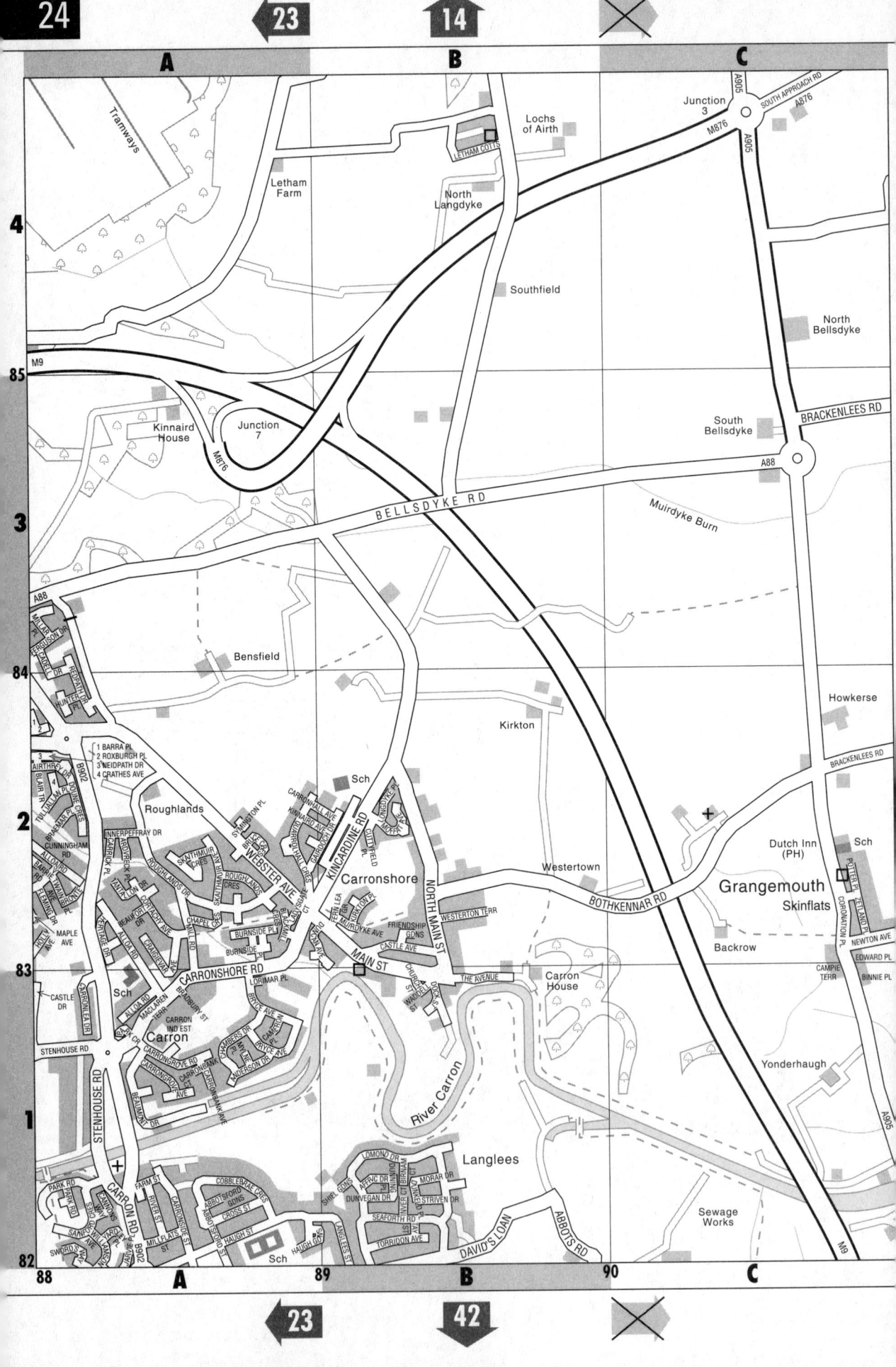

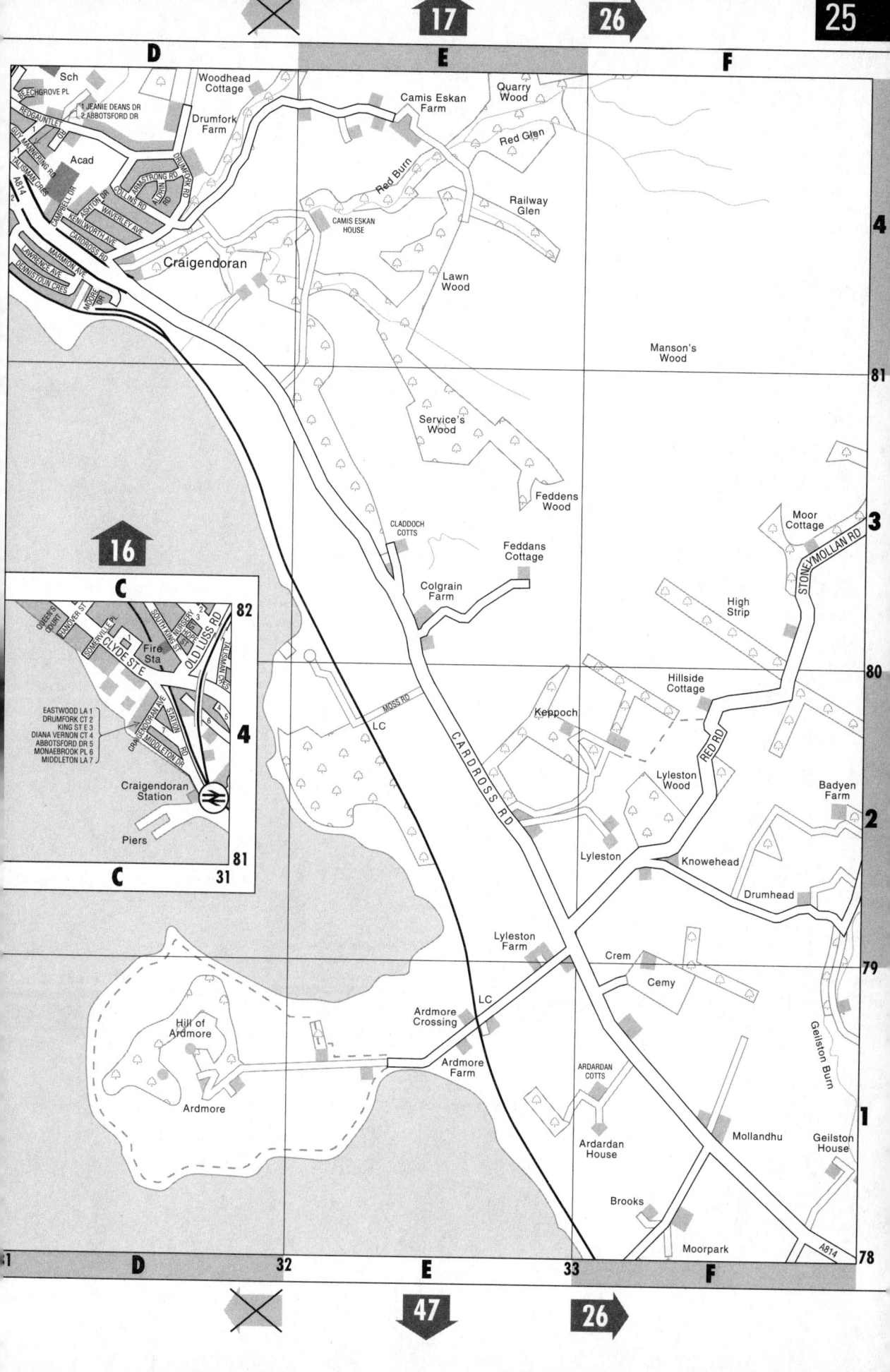

D
E
F

Sch
BEECHGROVE PL
Woodhead
Cottage
Camis Eskan
Farm
Quarry
Wood

REDGAUNTLET
1 JEANIE DEANS DR
2 ABBOTSFORD DR
GUY MANNERING RD
Drumfork
Farm
Red Glen

A814
Acad
CAMPBELL DR
ARMSTRONG RD
ALRTON DR
EASTON DR
COLLINS RD
DRUMFORK RD
Red Burn

KENILWORTH AVE
WAVERLEY AVE
CARDROSS RD
CAMIS ESKAN
HOUSE
Railway
Glen

4

MARMION AVE
LAWRENCE AVE
DENNISTOUN CRES
MOORE DR
Craigendoran
Lawn
Wood

Manson's
Wood

81

Service's
Wood

16

Feddens
Wood

CLADDOCH
COTTS
Moor
Cottage

STONEYMOLLAN RD
3

C
82
Feddans
Cottage
High
Strip

QUEEN'S
COURT
HANOVER ST
SOMERVILLE PL
SOUTH KING ST
NURSERY RD
OLD LUSS RD
Fire
Sta
Colgrain
Farm

CLYDE ST E
TALISMAN CRES

EASTWOOD LA 1
DRUMFORK CT 2
KING ST E 3
DIANA VERNON CT 4
ABBOTSFORD DR 5
MONAEBROOK PL 6
MIDDLETON LA 7
4
STATION RD
CRAIGENDORAN AVE
MIDDLETON RD

MOSS RD

Hillside
Cottage

80

LC

Keppoch

RED RD

Craigendoran
Station
Lyleston
Wood
Badyen
Farm

81
Piers
CARDROSS RD
Lyleston
Knowehead
2

C
31
Drumhead

Lyleston
Farm
Crem

79

Hill of
Ardmore
Ardmore
Crossing
LC
Cemy

Ardmore
Farm
ARDARDAN
COTTS
Geilston Burn

Ardmore
1

Ardardan
House
Mollandhu
Geilston
House

Brooks

A814
78
D
32
E
33
F
Moorpark

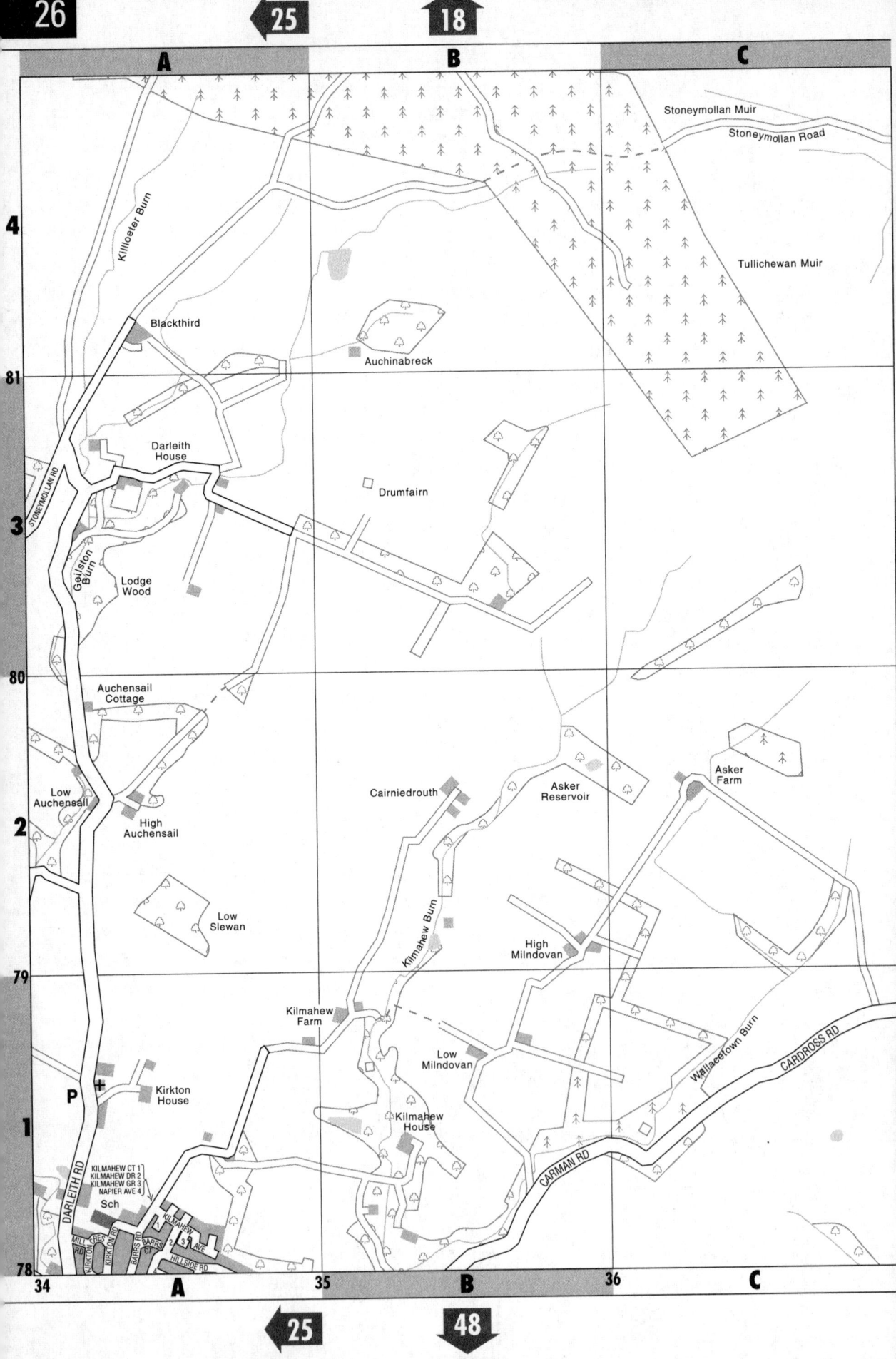

4

81

3

80

2

79

1

78

Killoeter Burn

Blackthird

Auchinabreck

Stoneymollan Muir

Stoneymollan Road

Tullichewan Muir

STONEYMOLLAN RD

Darleith House

Drumfairn

Geilston Burn

Lodge Wood

Auchensail Cottage

Low Auchensail

High Auchensail

Cairniedrouth

Asker Reservoir

Asker Farm

Kilmahew Burn

Low Slewan

High Milndovan

Kilmahew Farm

Low Milndovan

Kilmahew House

Wallacetown Burn

CARDROSS RD

P

+

Kirkton House

DARLEITH RD

KILMAHEW CT 1
KILMAHEW DR 2
KILMAHEW GR 3
NAPIER AVE 4

Sch

CARMAN RD

MILL CRES
KIRKTON RD
KIRKTON RD
BARRS RD
BARRS CT
KILMAHEW AVE
2
3
HILLSIDE RD

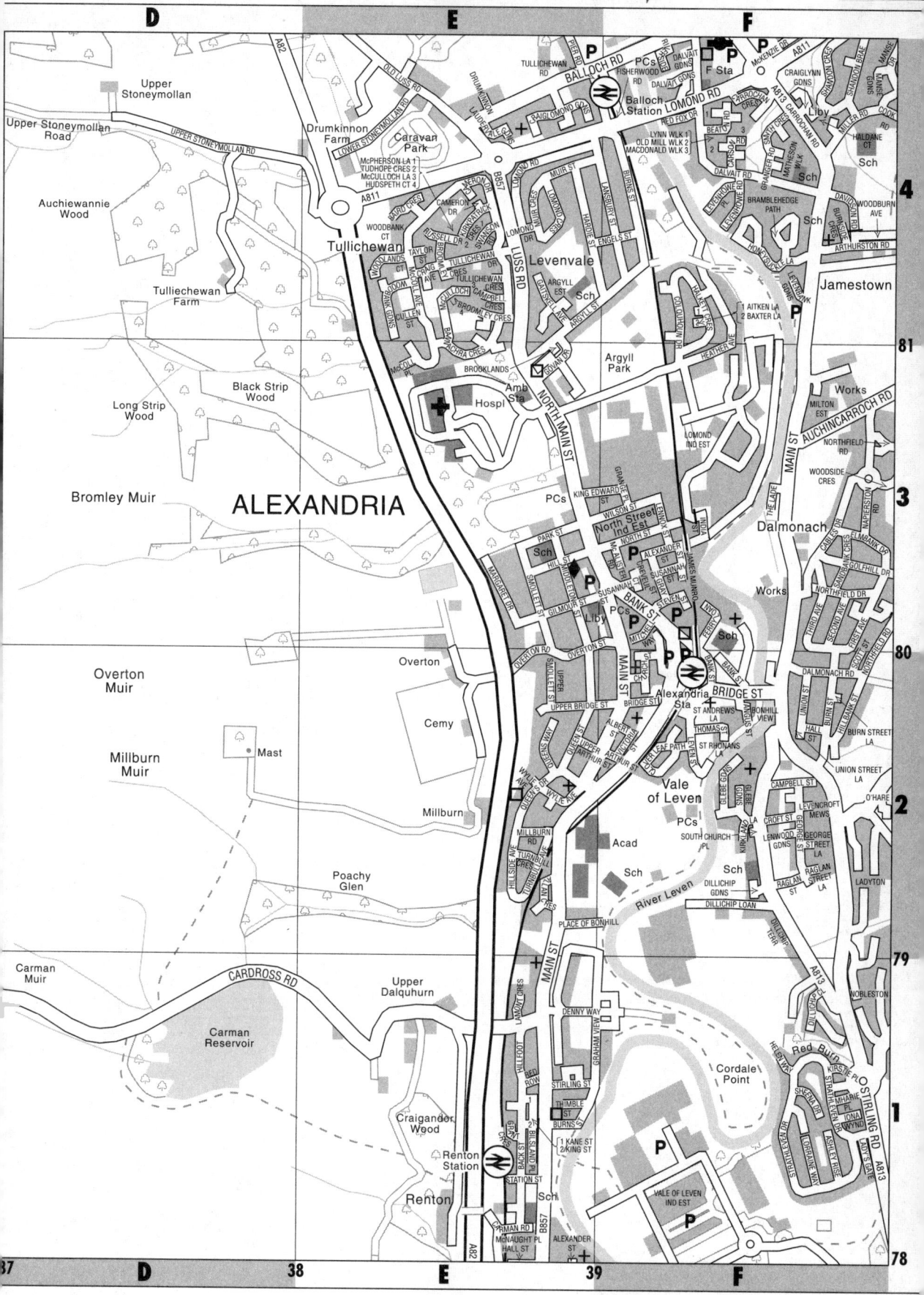

D E F

Upper
Stoneymollan

Upper Stoneymollan
Road

Auchiewannie
Wood

Tulliechewan
Farm

Bromley Muir

Long Strip
Wood

Black Strip
Wood

Drumkinnon
Farm

Caravan
Park

McPHERSON LA 1
TUDHOPE CRES 2
McCULLOCH LA 3
HUDSPETH CT 4

Tullichewan

Levenvale

Argyll
Park

Brooklands

Amb
Sta

Hospl

ALEXANDRIA

BALLOCH RD

TULLICHEWAN
RD

Balloch
Station

LOMOND RD

Jamestown

Dalmonach

Works

Works

Overton
Muir

Millburn
Muir

Mast

Overton

Cemy

Millburn

Poachy
Glen

Carman
Muir

CARDROSS RD

Carman
Reservoir

Upper
Dalquhurn

Craigandor
Wood

Renton
Station

Renton

North Street
Ind Est

Sch

Liby

BANK ST

PCs

MAIN ST

Alexandria
Sta

BRIDGE ST

Vale
of Leven

Acad

Sch

River Leven

PLACE OF BONHILL

MAIN ST

Denny Way

Cordale
Point

VALE OF LEVEN
IND EST

AUCHINCARROCH RD

STIRLING RD

Red Burn

4

81

3

80

2

79

1

A B C

MORE GREG AVE
BROWN RD
MILLS
McINNES ST
PETERS AVE
ROY YOUNG AVE
DUMBAIN CRES
BARTON AVE
COOK RD
CAMO MARTIN AVE
McFARLANE RD
BUCHANAN AVE
Ring Farm
GLEN AVE
TALBOT RD
STEELE CRES
CARDINAL DR
Mill of Haldane
Dismantled Railway

4

STEELE WLK
1 MANSE DR
2 SHEARER QUADRANT
3 SIMPSON QUADRANT
4 LINDSAY QUADRANT
WOODBURN
ARTHURSTON RD
AUCHINCARROCH RD

West Auchencarroch

Auchincarroch Hill

Redcraig
Blairvault Burn

Auchincarroch Muir

81

Woodside

WOODSIDE CRES

3

NORTHFIELD RD
Golf Course

Pappert Hill

GOLFHILL DR

CH

80

Northfield Cottage

2

O'HARE
PAPPERT
LADYTON
Libv Sch
P +
Bonhill
Braehead
BRAEHEAD

Hazel Glen

Auchenreoch

Nobleston Wood

79

NOBLESTON DR
REDBURN
Sch
Sch

Murroch Burn

BEECHWOOD DR
Highdykes
Glendonachy
Auchenreoch

1

Beech Wood
MURROCH CRES
BROOMHILL CRES

Murroch Glen
Spouts Burn

STIRLING RD
Mains
Broomhill Wood
Auchenreoch Glen

A813

78

40 A 41 B 42 C

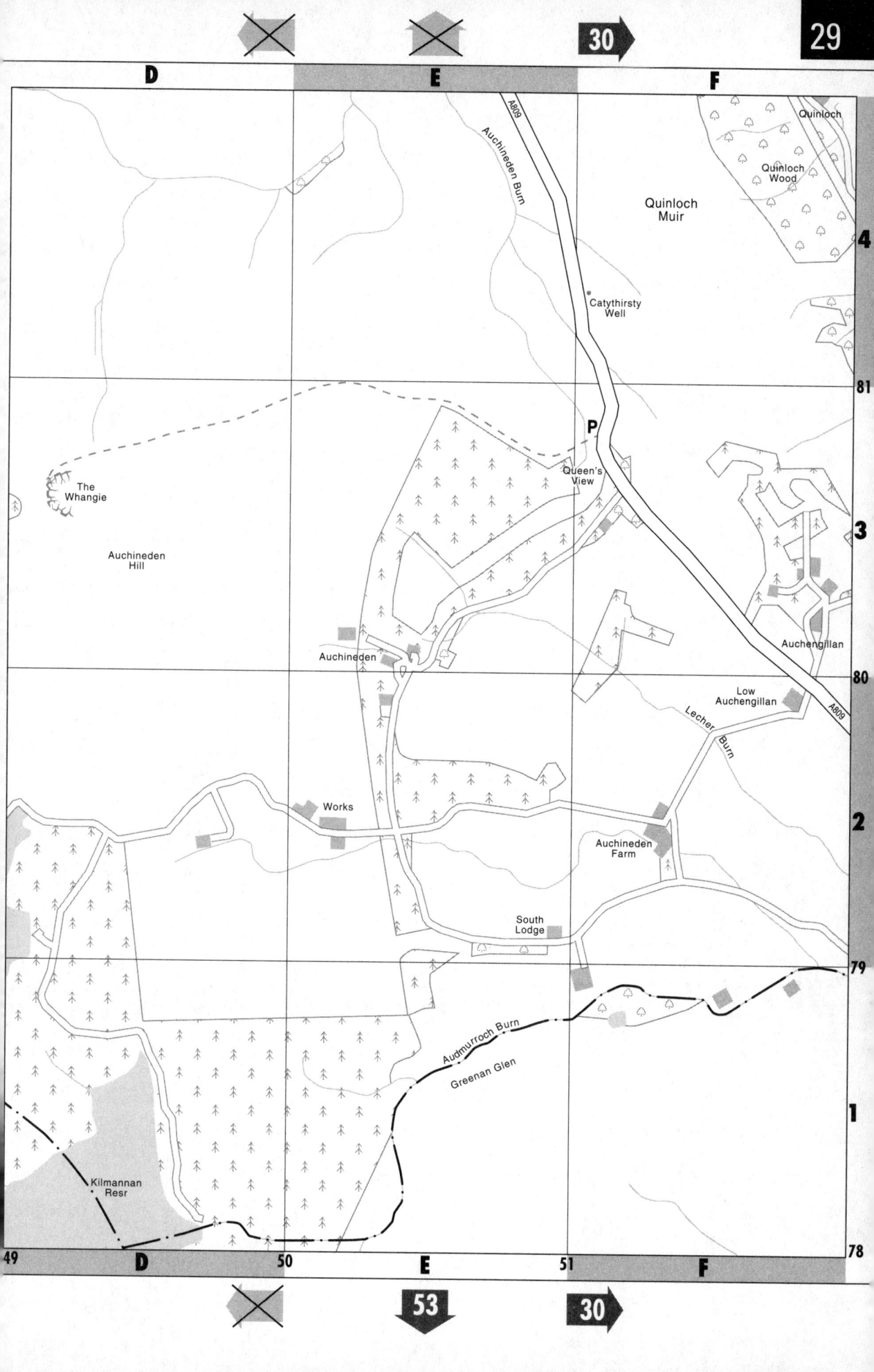

Quinloch

Quinloch
Wood

Quinloch
Muir

A809

Auchineden Burn

Catythirsty
Well

4

81

P

Queen's
View

The
Whangie

Auchineden
Hill

3

Auchengillan

Auchineden

Low
Auchengillan

80

Lecher Burn

A809

Works

Auchineden
Farm

2

South
Lodge

79

Audmurroch Burn

Greenan Glen

1

Kilmannan
Resr

78

D

50

E

51

F

A   B   C

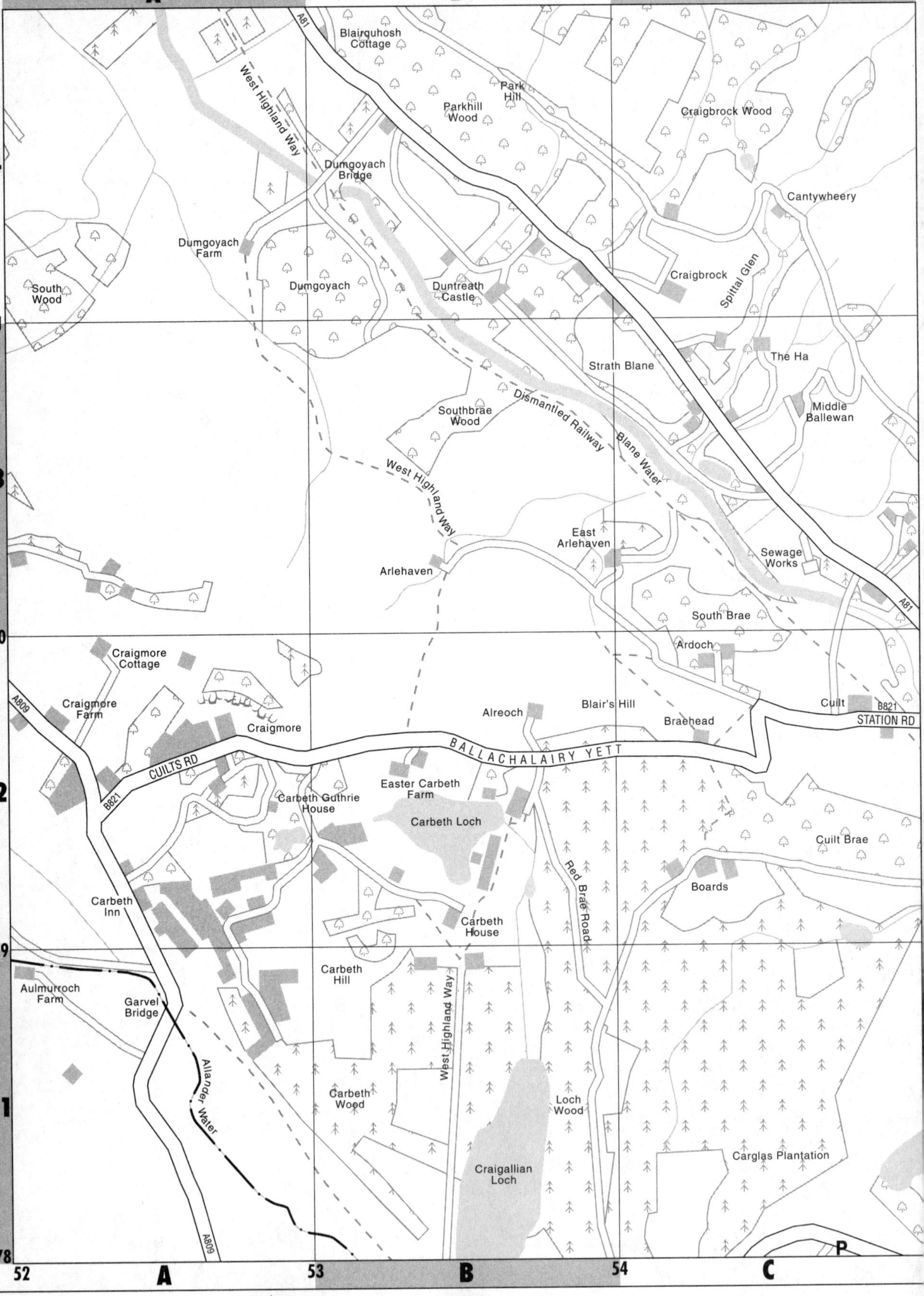

A81

Blairquhosh Cottage

Park Hill

Parkhill Wood

Craigbrock Wood

Cantywheery

4

Dumgoyach Bridge

West Highland Way

Craigbrock

Spittal Glen

Dumgoyach Farm

Dumgoyach

Duntreath Castle

81

Strath Blane

The Ha

South Wood

Southbrae Wood

Dismantled Railway

Blane Water

Middle Ballewan

West Highland Way

3

East Arlehaven

Sewage Works

Arlehaven

South Brae

80

Craigmore Cottage

Ardoch

A809

Craigmore Farm

Alreoch

Blair's Hill

Cuilt

B821

STATION RD

Craigmore

Braehead

BALLACHALAIRY YETT

CUILTS RD

2

B821

Carbeth Guthrie House

Easter Carbeth Farm

Carbeth Loch

Cuilt Brae

Red Brae Road

Boards

Carbeth Inn

Carbeth House

79

Aulmurroch Farm

Garvel Bridge

Carbeth Hill

West Highland Way

Carbeth Wood

Allander Water

1

Loch Wood

Carglas Plantation

Craigallian Loch

P

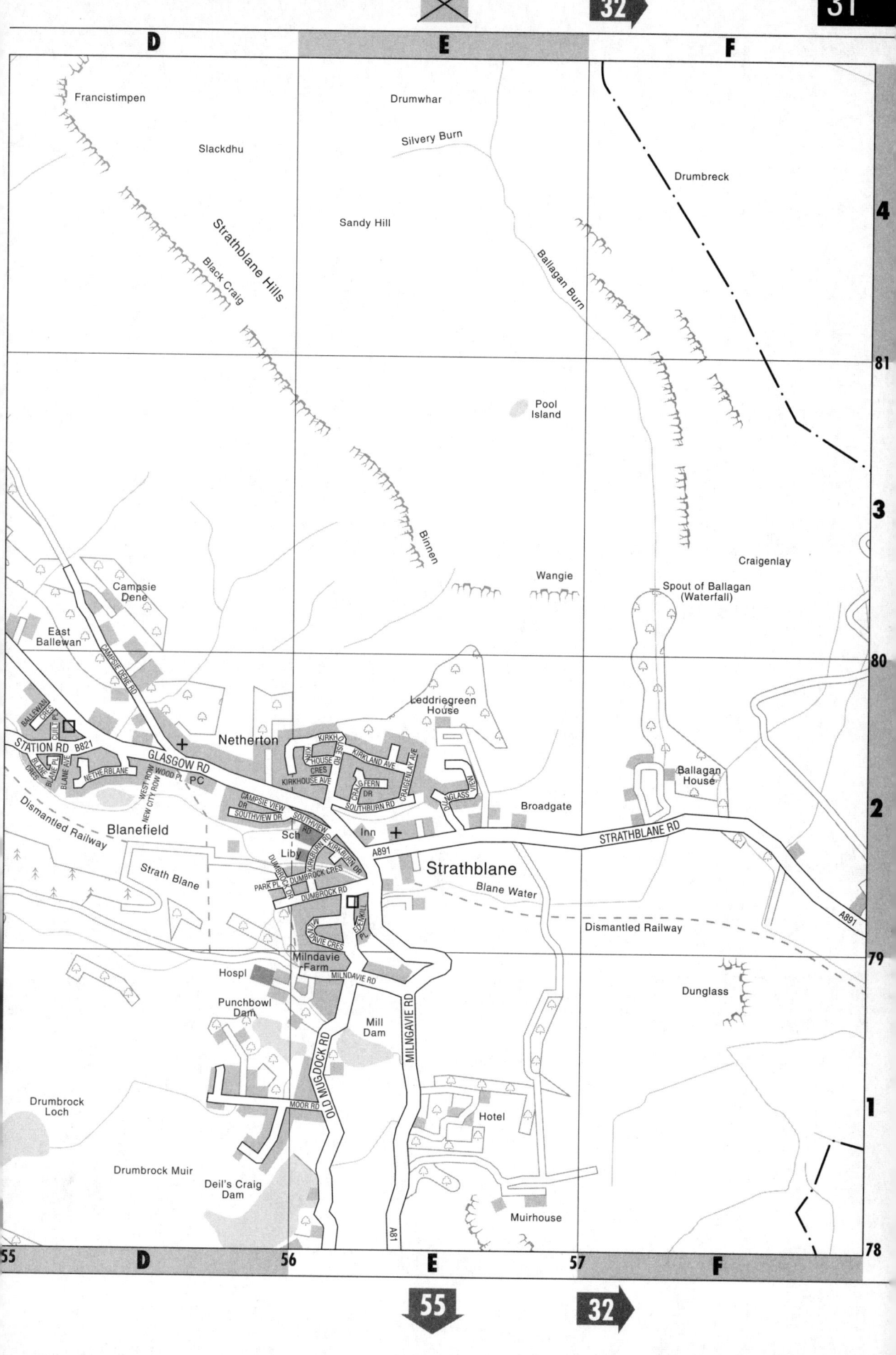

D   E   F

Francistimpen

Drumwhar

Slackdhu

Silvery Burn

Drumbreck

4

Sandy Hill

Strathblane Hills

Black Craig

Ballagan Burn

81

Pool Island

3

Binnen

Craigenlay

Wangie

Spout of Ballagan (Waterfall)

Campsie Dene

East Ballewan

Leddriegreen House

80

CAMPSIE DENE RD

Ballagan House

Netherton

KIRKHOUSE RD

KIRKLAND AVE

BALLEWAN CRES

CULT PL

STATION RD

B821

GLASGOW RD

WEST ROW

NEW CITY ROW

WOOD PL

PC

NETHERBLANE

BLANE AVE

BLANE PL

BLANE CRES

KIRKHOUSE CRES

KIRKHOUSE AVE

CAMPSIE VIEW DR

SOUTHVIEW DR

CRAIGFERN DR

SOUTHBURN RD

CRAIGENLAY AVE

KIRKVIEW

ANGLASS

Broadgate

STRATHBLANE RD

2

Dismantled Railway

Blanefield

Strath Blane

SOUTHVIEW RD

Sch

Liby

KIRKBURN DR

KIRKBURN RD

DUMBROCK RD

PARK PL

DUMBROCK CRES

DUMBROCK RD

MILNDAVIE CRES

PLOVER HILL

Inn

A891

Strathblane

Blane Water

Dismantled Railway

A891

79

Hospl

Milndavie Farm

MILNDAVIE RD

Dunglass

Punchbowl Dam

OLD MUGDOCK RD

Mill Dam

MILNGAVIE RD

Drumbrock Loch

MOOR RD

Hotel

1

Drumbrock Muir

Deil's Craig Dam

A81

Muirhouse

78

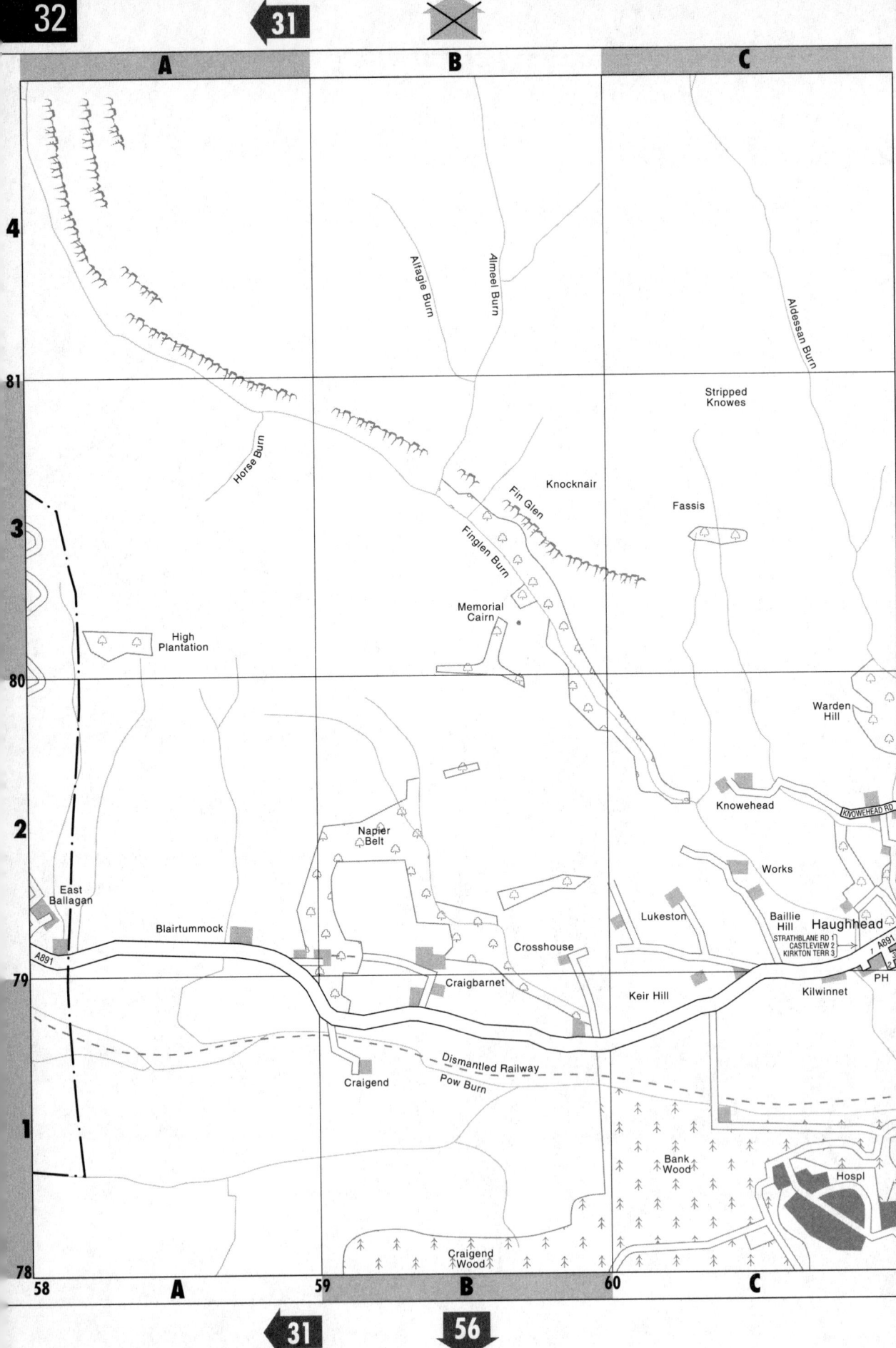

4

Allagie Burn

Almeel Burn

Aldessan Burn

81

Stripped
Knowes

Horse Burn

Fin Glen

Knocknair

Fassis

3

Finglen Burn

Memorial
Cairn

High
Plantation

80

Warden
Hill

Knowehead

KNOWEHEAD RD

2

Napier
Belt

Works

Lukeston

Baillie
Hill

Haughhead

East
Ballagan

Blairtummock

Crosshouse

STRATHBLANE RD 1
CASTLEVIEW 2
KIRKTON TERR 3

A891

A891

PH

79

Craigbarnet

Keir Hill

Kilwinnet

Dismantled Railway

Craigend

Pow Burn

1

Bank
Wood

Hospl

78

Craigend
Wood

D   **E**   **F**

4

81

3

80

2

79

1

78

B822

Moss Maigry

Newhouse Burn

Priest Burn

Nineteentimes Burn

Inner Black Hill

Alvain Burn

Alnwick Burn

Shearer's Burn

Katrine's Burn

Alnwick Bridge

CROW RD

Kirk Burn

Campsie Glen

Jamie Wright's Well

P

Black Craig

Sloughmuclock

Burnel Rannie

KNOWEHEAD RD

CROSSHOUSE RD

Clachan of Campsie

Crosshouse

STRATHBLANE RD

Balcorrach

Hole

CH

Campsie Golf Course

Roughcraig House

Ferrets

Bencloich Mains

GLEN RD

Hospl

NETHERTON OVAL

NETHERTON HILL

D

KINCAID TR

CUMROCH DR

CROFTHEAD DR

LENNOX RD

GEELONG GDNS

CROSSHILL ST B822

WHITEFIELD TERR

SERVICE ST A891

JANEFIELD PL

ST MACHAN'S WAY

QUARRY LA

CHURCH VIEW CT

Sch

BENCLOICH ST

BENCLOICH CRES

BENCLOICH RD

Bencloich Farm

D   62   **E**   63   **F**

33

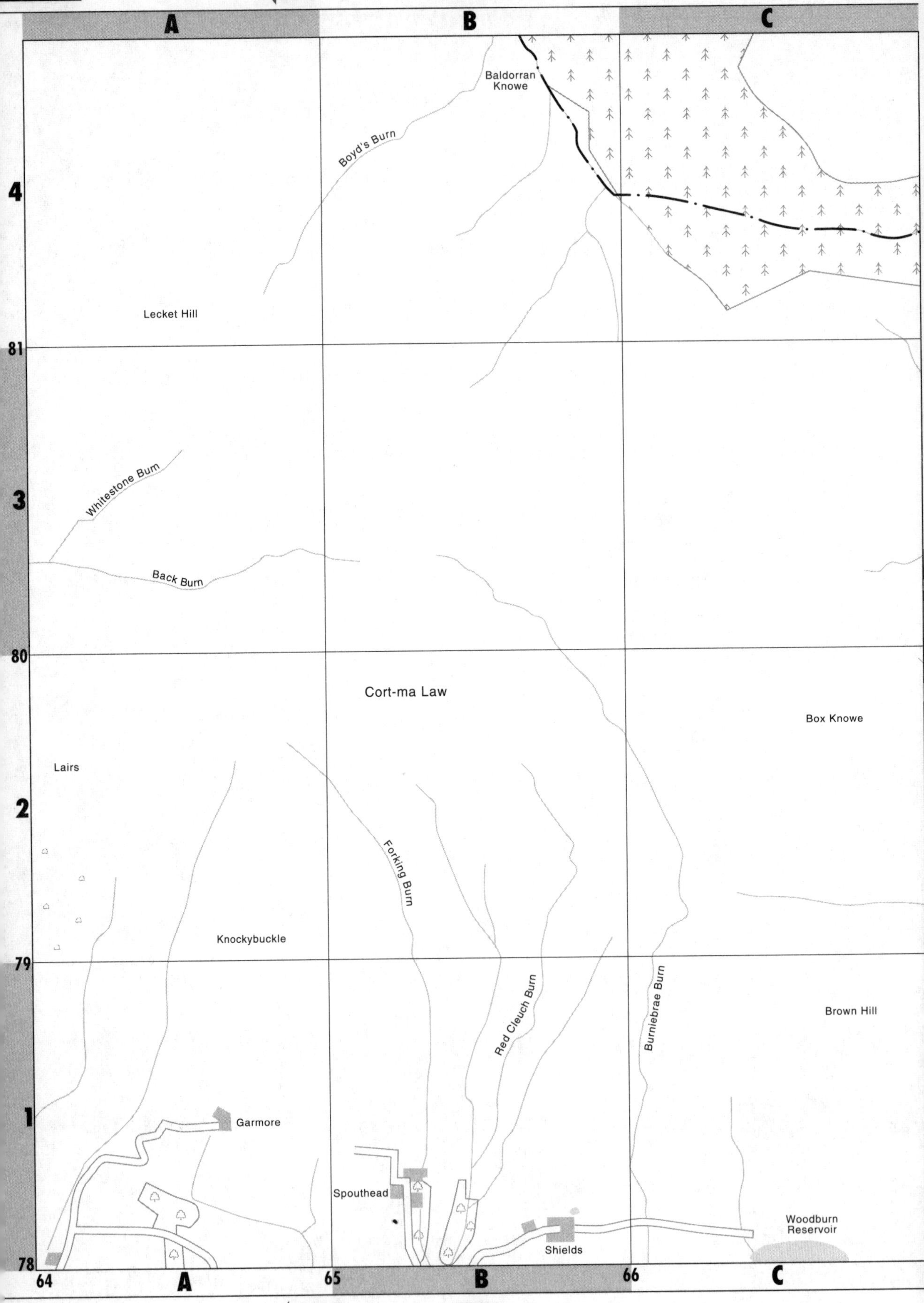
A
B
C
Baldorran Knowe
Boyd's Burn
4
Lecket Hill
81
Whitestone Burn
3
Back Burn
80
Cort-ma Law
Box Knowe
Lairs
2
Forking Burn
Knockybuckle
79
Red Cleuch Burn
Burniebrae Burn
Brown Hill
1
Garmore
Spouthead
Shields
Woodburn Reservoir
78
64
65
66

33
58

36

Black Hill

Birkenburn
Reservoir

4

81

Lunch Knowe

Plea Muir

Birken Burn

3

Laird's Hill

Gray Mare

Kilsyth Hills

White Craig

80

Hailstane Burn

2

The Banns

Corrie
Plantation

Mast

Corrie

79

Drumheldric

Corrie Burn

Stoneree Glen

Cairnbog

1

Burnhead
Farm

Dykehead

WHIN LOAN

DYKEHEAD RD

59

36

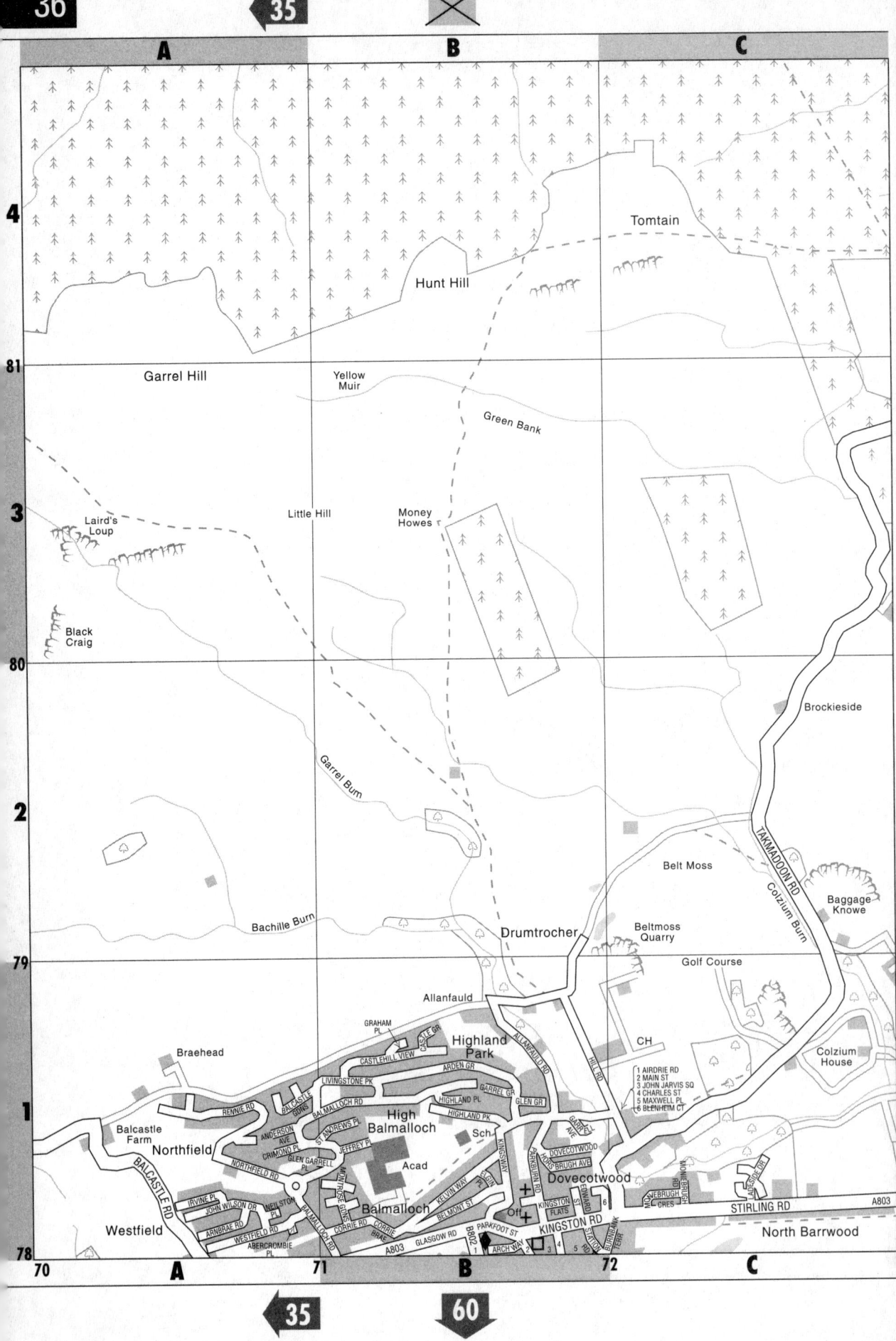

4

Tomtain

Hunt Hill

81

Garrel Hill

Yellow Muir

Green Bank

3

Laird's Loup

Little Hill

Money Howes

Black Craig

80

Brockieside

Garrel Burn

2

Belt Moss

Baggage Knowe

Bachille Burn

Drumtrocher

Beltmoss Quarry

TAKMADOON RD

Colzium Burn

79

Golf Course

Allanfauld

CH

Colzium House

Braehead

Highland Park

GRAHAM PL

CASTLEHILL VIEW

CASTLE GR

ARDEN GR

ALLANFAULD RD

HILL RD

1 AIRDRIE RD
2 MAIN ST
3 JOHN JARVIS SQ
4 CHARLES ST
5 MAXWELL PL
6 BLENHEIM CT

1

Balcastle Farm

Northfield

LIVINGSTONE PK

RENNIE RD

BALCASTLE GDNS

ANDERSON AVE

BALMALLOCH RD

ST ANDREWS PL

CRIMOND PL

JEFFREY PL

High Balmalloch

GARREL GR

GLEN GR

HIGHLAND PL

HIGHLAND PK

Sch

GARREL RD

GABBRO PL

DOVECOTWOOD

KING'S BRUGH AVE

Dovecotwood

MONKEBRUGH CRES

LARKSIDE DR

IRVINE PL

JOHN WILSON DR

NEILSTON

GLEN GARRELL PL

NORTHFIELD RD

MONTROSE GDNS

Acad

KELVIN WAY

KING'S WAY

PARKBURN RD

Westfield

BALCASTLE RD

ARNBRAE RD

WESTFIELD RD

BALMALLOCH RD

Balmalloch

CORRIE PL

BELMONT RD

CONNERBANK

STIRLING RD

A803

North Barrwood

ABERCROMBIE PL

GLASGOW RD

B802

PARKFOOT ST

ARCH WAY

Off

Kingston Flats

KINGSTON RD

BURNBANK TERR

78

D
E
F

4

Doups

81

Craigdouffie Burn

Boiling Glen

3

Drumnessie

Berryhill

Banton Burn

Glenhead

Banton Mains

80

High Banton

Binniemyre

Easter Auchinrivock

Mailings

Meadowside

HIGH BANTON RD

2

Wester Auchinrivock

Slaughter Howe

Drum Burn

HILLVIEW

MILL RD

KELVIN RD

ST MACHANS PL

MAIN ST

MAILINGS RD

HAMMERKNOWES RD

Sch

Auchinvalley

VALLEYBANK

Banton

Riskend

Riskend Strip

79

Riskend

Craigs

Dam Wood

1645

Reservoir

BANTON RD

Dismantled Railway

KELVINHEAD RD

Kelvinhead Farm

A803

Speirs Island

Ruchill

P

Kelvinhead

Craigstone Wood

Castle Hill

Townhead

Gateside

1

Girnal Hill

River Kelvin

Forth and Clyde Canal

Kelvinhead Jetty

STIRLING RD

A803

Bullet Knowes

A803

Back Drain

73
D
74
E
75
F
78

TAKMADOON RD

37

A **B** **C**

Tappetknowe

Leysbent

Castlerankine

Leys

4

Linns

Rashiehill

Castlerankine Burn

Glenhead

Drumbowie Reservoir

81

Bottomhead

Bowridge

Bottomhead Reservoir

3

Whitehill

Easter Wairds

Craigs Plantation

Braeface

80

Cowden Hill

Tomfyne

Wester Thomaston

Brick Works

Junction 4

2

Cloybank

Hotel

Banknock

Doups Burn

HOLLANDBUSH AVE

Dismantled Railway

KILSYTH RD

Sch

HOLLANDBUSH CRES

CONEYPARK CRES

VIEWFIELD RD

BANKIER TERR

CONEYPARK PL

BOG RD

BANKIER RD

BALLINKIER AVE

79

CONEYPARK

JOHN BASSY

Bog

GLENVIEW AVE

LINDEN DR

Orchard Farm

WELLPARK RD

ROWAN DR

MAPLE

HERO AVE

AUCHINCLOCH CRES

CASTLEVIEW TERR

West Auchincloch

Bonny Water

LAUREL SQ

ASH

KELVIN

FOSTER

CUMBERNAULD RD

Auchincloch

Wyndford Lock

CEDAR RD

WILLOW

ALDER

HAWTHORN DR

LARCH DR

HAZEL RD

A803

Netherwood

ALMOND

CHERRY LA

Forth and Clyde Canal

Red Burn

B816

1

WYNDFORD RD

Works

B816

Hirst House

Hotel

CASTLECARY RD

B816

A80

Hirst

78

76 **A** **77** **B** **78** **C**

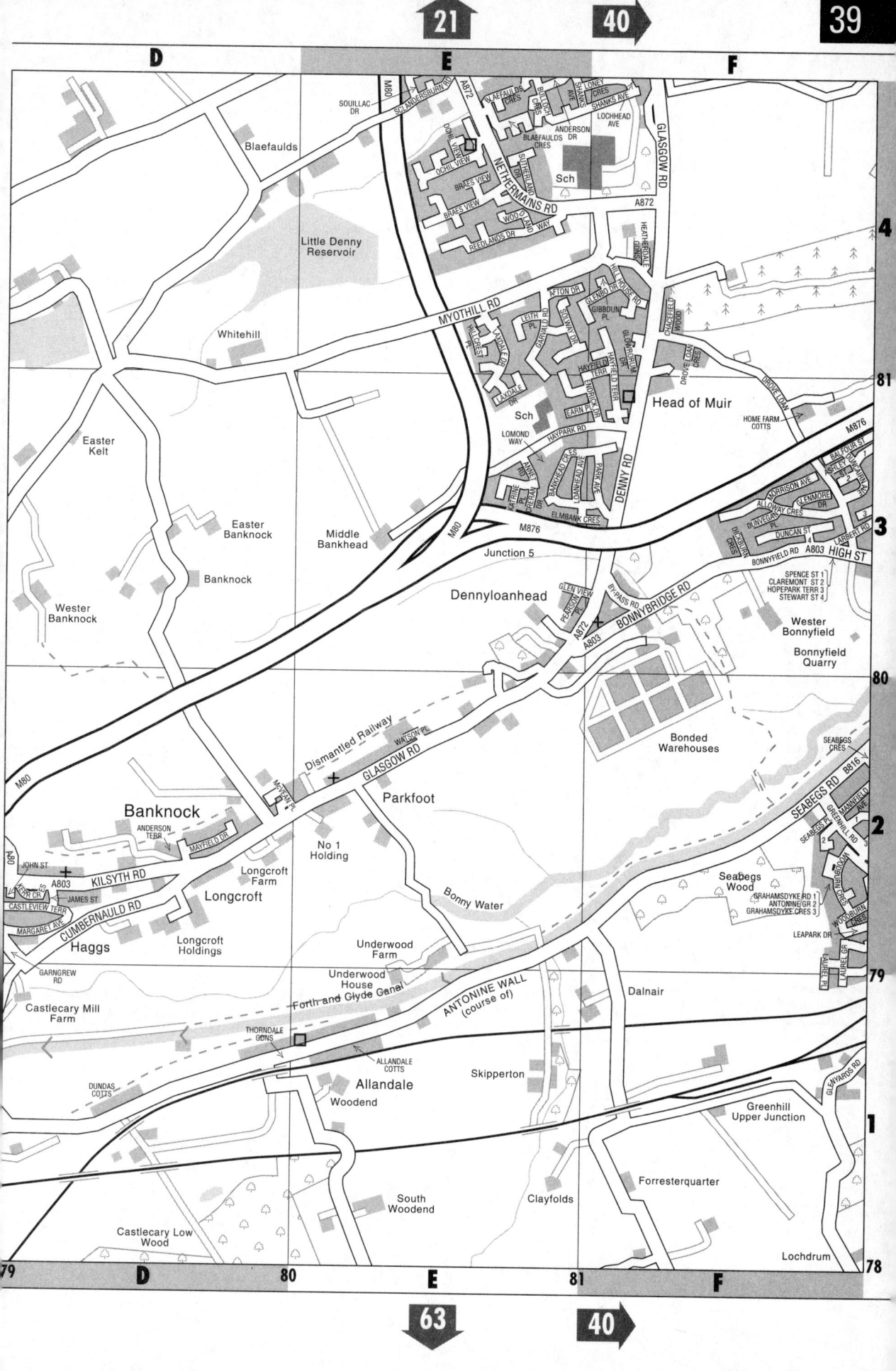

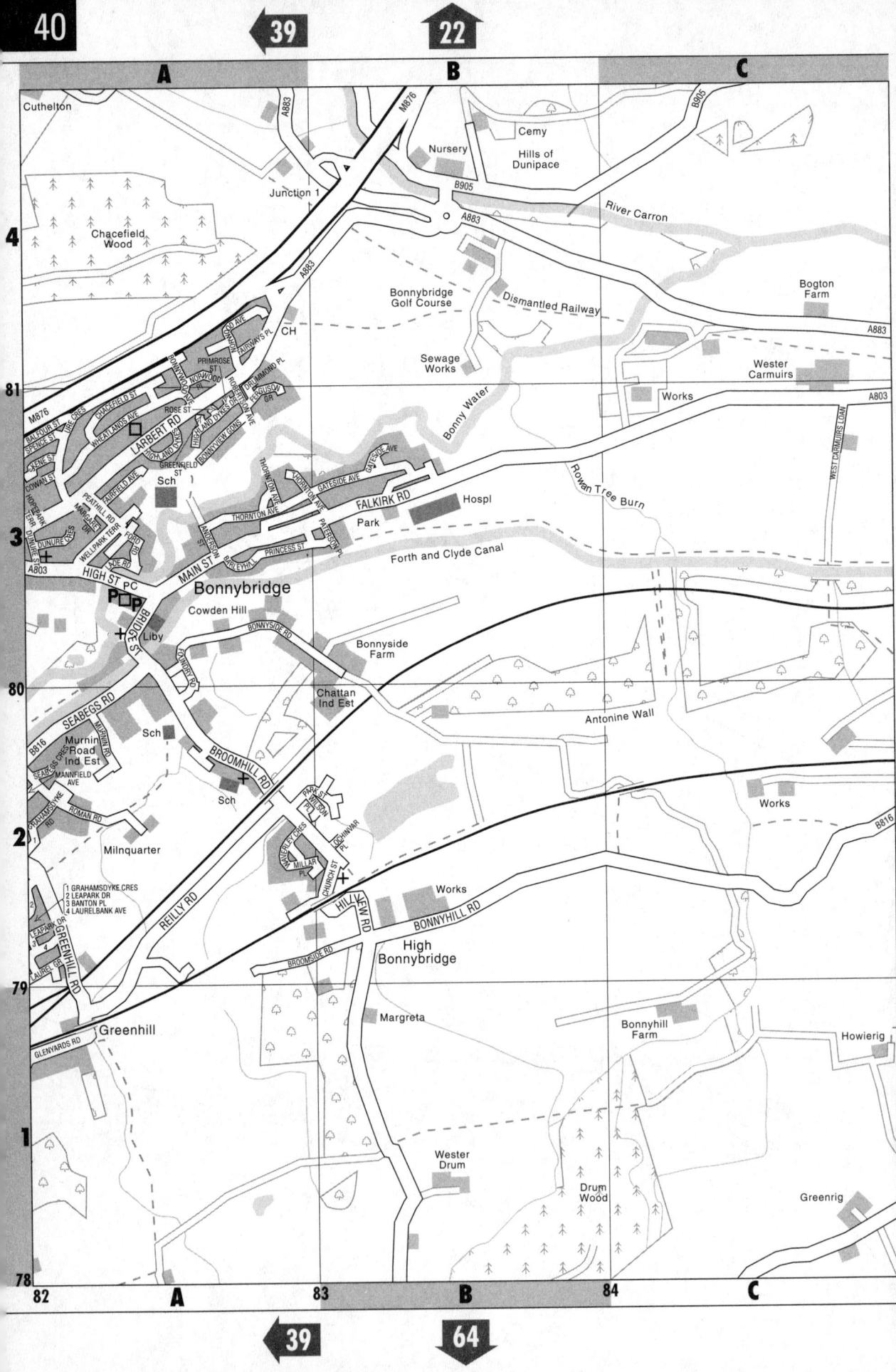

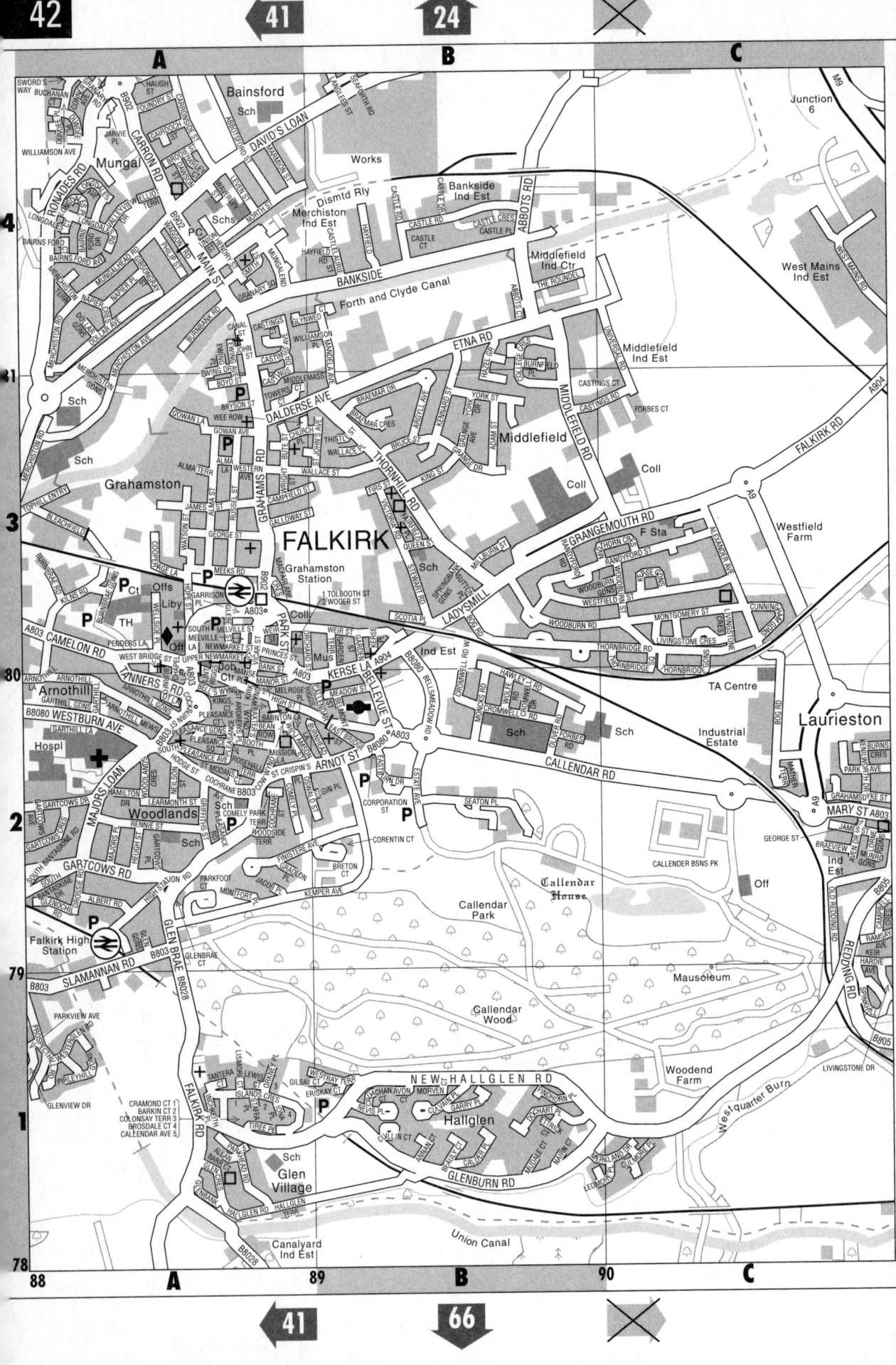

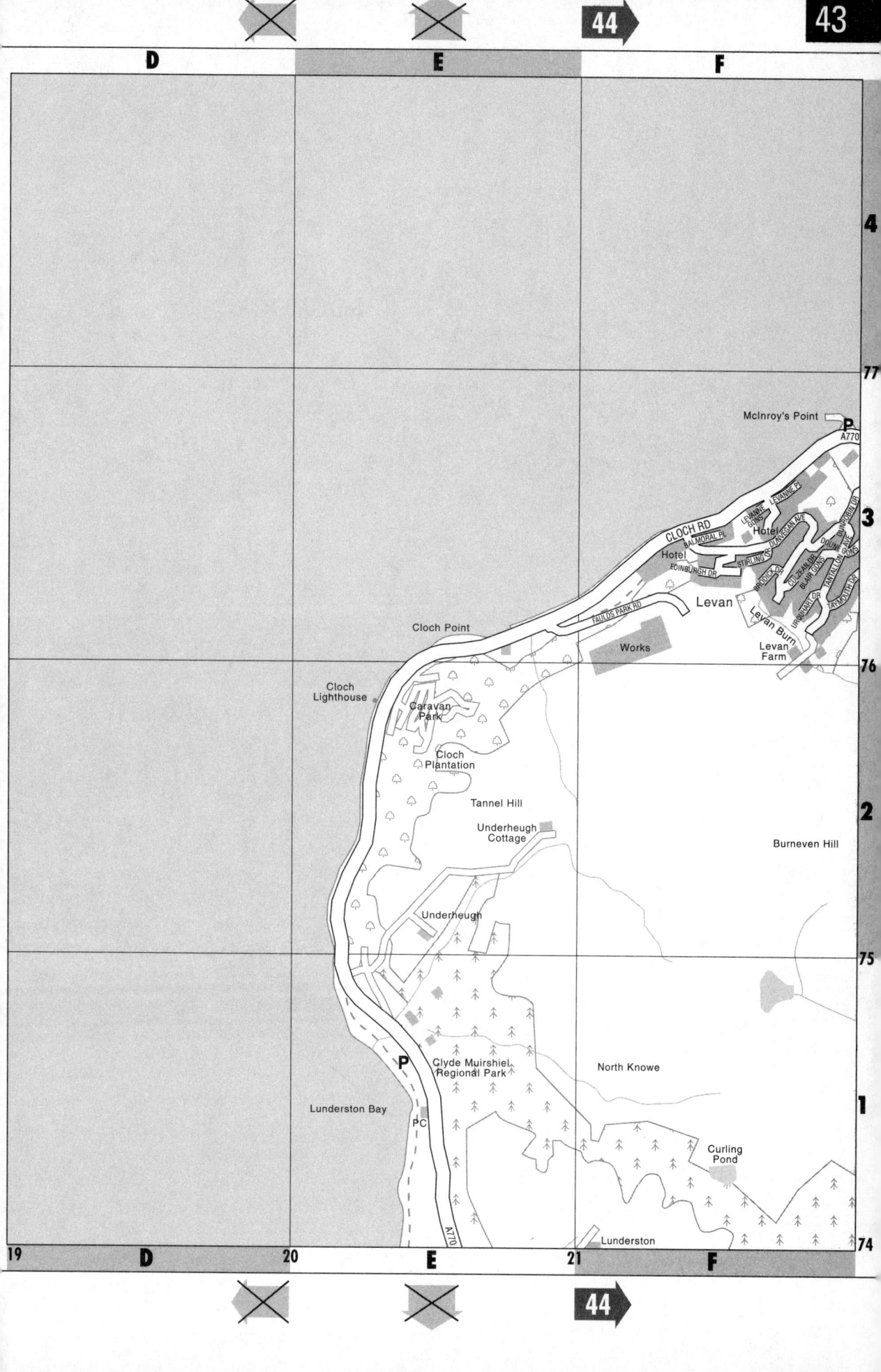

D E F

4

77

McInroy's Point
P
A770

CLOCH RD
Hotel
BALMORAL PL
Hotel
EDINBURGH DR
LEVANNE PL
LEVANNE GDNS
ALVERGEN AVE
STIRLING'S
BRODICK DR
CULZEAN DR
BLAIR GDNS
DRUNE AVE
DUNROBIN DR
TANTALLON GDNS
TRAQUAIR AVE
3

Levan
Cloch Point
FAULDS PARK RD
Works
URQUHART DR
Levan Burn
Levan
Farm
76

Cloch
Lighthouse
Caravan
Park
Cloch
Plantation
Tannel Hill
Underheugh
Cottage
Burneven Hill
2

Underheugh
75

P
Clyde Muirshiel
Regional Park
North Knowe
1

Lunderston Bay
PC
Curling
Pond
A770
Lunderston
74

19 D 20 E 21 F

West Bay

Gourock Bay

Pier

1 CASTLE GDNS
2 ADELAIDE ST

Landing
Stage

KEMPOCK ST

Liby
Off

PC

Gourock Station

SHARP ST 1
MARGARET ST 2

TARGET

SHORE ST

JOHN ST

BROOMBERRY DR

Tower

Tower
Hill

Barr
Hill

DRUMSHANTIE
TERR

GOUROCK

Sch

CARDWELL RD

A770

CALEDONIA CRES

MANOR CRES

ALBERT RD

BARRHILL RD

ASHBURN GATE

PC

ASHGROVE AVE 1
ASHTON TERR 2

Ashton

ASHTON RD

VICTORIA RD

MOORFIELD RD

GOLF RD

PRESTON PL

JACOBS

FINNIE TERR

TOWER DR

BAY VIEW RD

CLYDE RD

ARGYLE RD

GLEN AVE

CLOCH RD

CLOCH BRAE

A770

TURNBERRY AVE

KONAL CRES

DIVERT RD

HAZEL

Midton

ROSE CRES

FIR TERR

ELM TERR

STAFFA ST

GRENVILLE

RESERVOIR RD

OXFORD AVE

COLLINGWOOD
TERR

ST ANDREWS DR

ST ANDREWS LA

BELLEISLE PL

GLENEAGLES DR

CARNOUSTIE AVE

ROSEMOUNT PL

CH

HAWTHORNE PL

MOORFOOT DR

POPLAR PL

BEECH PL

KIRN DR

GEORGE RD

F Sta

MATHIE CRES

Coves
Reservoirs

Trumpethill

Gourock
Golf Course

Mile Burn

LARKFIELD
IND EST

EARNHILL RD

FIFE RD

BANFF RD

Cemy

YORK RD

PLYMOUTH AVE

FALMOUTH DR

BOURNEMOUTH RD

1 AVONMOUTH PL
2 LYNMOUTH PL

LARKFIELD RD

Larkfield

Sch

CAMBRIDGE RD

DORSET RD

OXFORD RD

CHESTER RD

DURHAM RD

Schs

Hospl

14 OBAN TERR
15 MALLAIG TERR
16 PORTREE TERR
17 BROADFORD TERR
18 CUMBERLAND WLK

Coll

FANCY FARM PL 1
NEIL ST 2
GLENNINVER RD 3

BERWICK RD

BURNS SQ

Liby

PEMBROKE RD

CUMBERLAND RD

STAFFORD RD

Branchton
Station

7 KYLEMORE LA
8 BENMORE LA
9 KINLOCH LA
10 MAUCHLINE LA
11 AYR LA
12 CARRICK LA
13 JEAN ARMOUR LA

Stadium

P

Branchton

Banks

Earn Hill

MINERVA LA 1
BRAESIDE LA 2
ATHOLE LA 3
JUNO LA 4
JUPITER LA 5
MERCURY LA 6

Braeside

Sch

INVERKIP RD

Gallow
Hill

WELLYARD LA

WELLYARD

DRUM LAN HILL

CRISSWELL CRES

FLATTERTON LA

Sch

FLATTERTON LA

CRISSWELL CL

Sch

Leitchland
Farm

Flatterton
Farm

Drumillian
Hill

INVERKIP RD

Spango Burn

Spango
Valley

Spango

Howlord Glen

Factory

Hole of Spango

Chrisswell

A78

22 A 23 B 24 C

D E F

ELDON ST

Ind Est

PCs

Battery Park

Cardwell Bay

LYLEFOOT CRES

NEWARK ST

DRUMSLEA

Fort Matilda Station

Fort Matilda Terr

Lyle Hill

LYLE PL

LYLE RD

Craigs

Craigs Top

Tunnel

Mon

Golf Course

Greenock West

Glen Burn

ESPLANADE

SEAFIELD COTTAGE LA

SANDRINGHAM TERR

BROUGHAM ST

UNION ST

NEWTON ST

Acad

Control Tower

Off

PCs

Clydeport Container Terminal

WEST BLACKHALL ST

GREY PL

1 NICOLSON ST
2 WEST BLACKHALL ST
3 WESTBURN BLDGS
4 CHARLES PL
5 HAMILTON GATE
6 HAMILTON WAY
7 CLYDE SQ
8 CATHCART SQ

Sch

Sch

Sch

Liby

Mus

Off

GEORGE SQ

Coll

West Station

Liby

CH

Cemy

Crem

1 AUGHNEAGH FARM LA
2 CUMBRAE CT
3 BUTE CT
4 ARRAN CT

AUGHNEAGH FARM RD

Bow Farm

BOW RD

GRIEVE RD

1 CAWDOR PL
2 FERGUS DR
3 FERGUS PL

Hospl

Smithston

Sch

INVERKIP RD

Cowdenknowes

OLD INVERKIP RD

Reservoirs

Liby

HM Prison

Sch

ORANGEFIELD LA

PCs

Orangefield

HOLMSCROFT ST

BRACHELSTON ST

Acad

ROXBURGH ST

MURDIESTON ST

CORNHADDOCK ST

Sch

Central

Ind Est

DRUMFROCHAR RD

BERRYYARDS RD

LYNEDOCH ST

DUNLOP ST

Sch

PEAT RD

HOLE FARM RD

MAPLE RD

Hospl

Smithston Cotts

KILBRANNS

WOODSTOCK RD

Penny Fern

GLEN DOUGLAS RD

GLEN DOUGLAS WAY

GLEN FRUIN RD

GLEN KINGLAS AVE

GLEN KINGLAS RD

GLEN LUSS RD

GLEN LUSS WAY

Overton

PAPERMILL RD

Murdieston

OLD LARGS RD

CH

Mast

Whin Hill

Black Hill

Cockrobin Hill

Reservoirs

Reservoirs

Whin Hill Golf Course

Whinhill Reservoir

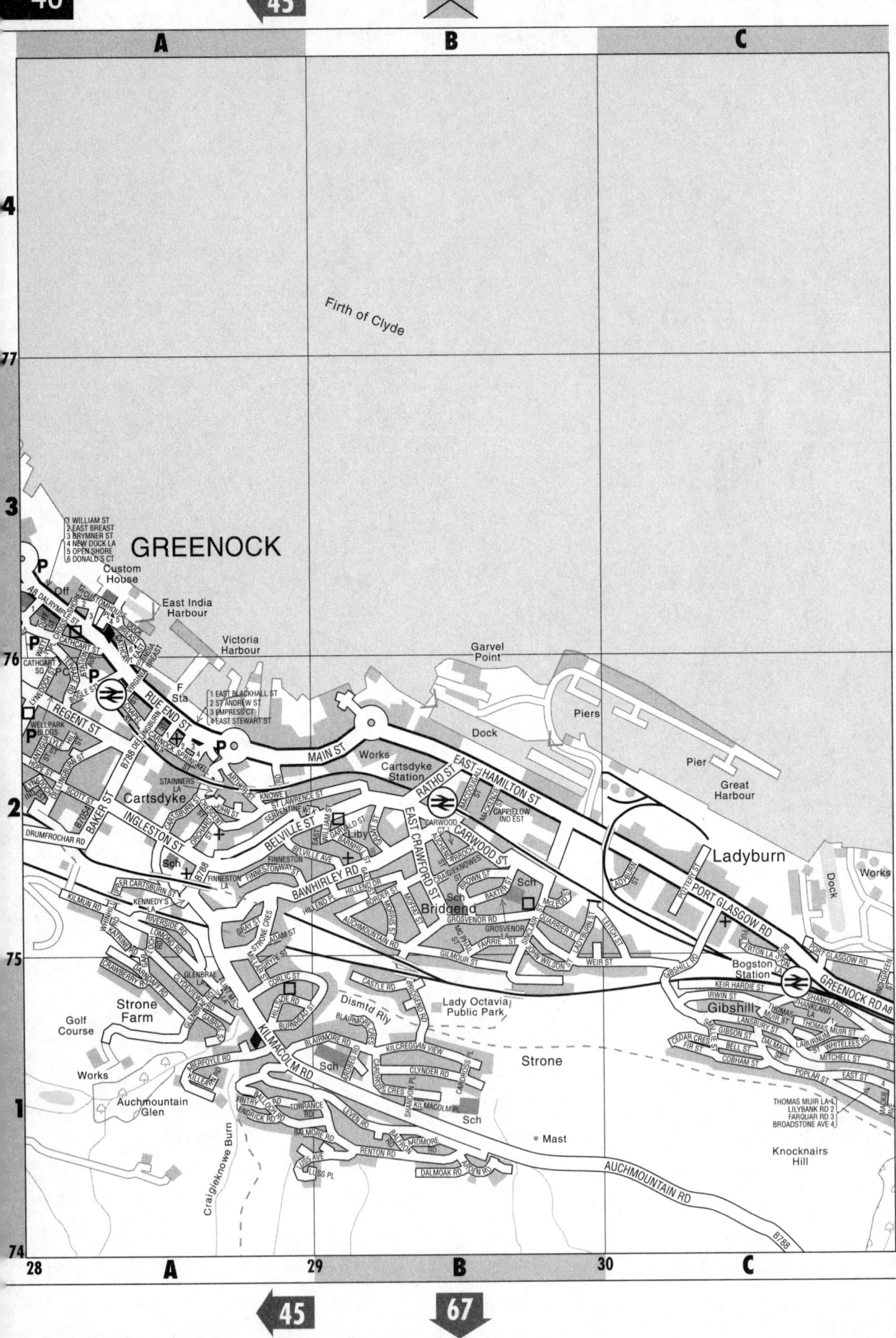

4

Firth of Clyde

77

3

1 WILLIAM ST
2 EAST BREAST
3 BRYMNER ST
4 NEW DOCK LA
5 OPEN SHORE
6 DONALD'S CT

GREENOCK

Custom
House

East India
Harbour

Victoria
Harbour

Garvel
Point

76

1 EAST BLACKHALL ST
2 ST ANDREW ST
3 EMPRESS CT
4 EAST STEWART ST

Piers

Dock

F
Sta

RUE END ST

REGENT ST

WELL PARK
BLDGS

Works

Cartsdyke
Station

MAIN ST

EAST HAMILTON ST

RATHO ST

Pier

Great
Harbour

Cartsdyke

INGLESTON ST

DRUMFROCHAR RD

BAKER ST

STAINNERS LA

ST LAWRENCE ST
SERPENTINE WLK

BELVILLE ST

KNOWE

WILLIAM ST

Liby

Libv

EAST CRAWFORD ST

CARWOOD ST

Carwood
CT

MACKENZIE ST

MACDONALD ST

CAPPIELOW
IND EST

Ladyburn

Works

2

Finneston
FINNESTONWAY

BELVILLE AVE
BARNHILL RD

GARVALD ST

BROWN ST

ARBROCH

CRAIGIEKNOWES

MARTIN ST

PORT GLASGOW RD

Dock

Finneston
LA

BAWHIRLEY RD

HILLEND DR
HILLEND PL

AUCHMOUNTAIN RD

MYFARRIE ST
BAXTER ST

Bridgend

Sch

McLEOD

Sch

LEICH ST

Bogston
Station

GREENOCK RD A8

KILMUN RD

UPPER CARTSBURN ST

KENNEDY'S
LA

RIVERSIDE RD

LOMOND RD

STRONE CRES

ADAM ST

GROSVENOR CT

GROSVENOR

MAC PHAIL
FARRIE ST

SINCLAIR ST

QUARRIER ST
JOHN WILSON

WEIR ST

GIBSHILL RD

MITCHELL ST
PORT GLASGOW RD

KEIR HARDIE ST
IRWIN ST

Port Glasgow RD

75

WHITELEE RD
KATRINE RD

GLENBRAE

BRAY'S PL

BRAESIDE

GORLIC ST
SIDE RD
BURNHEAD ST

Castle RD

BRIDGEND RD

GILMOUR RD

LANSBURY ST

THOMAS MUIR LA

SHANKLAND RD

CEDAR CRES
FIR ST

GIBSON ST
BELL ST

THOMAS MUIR ST

DALMALLY

WHITELEES RD

PORT GLASGOW RD

Golf
Course

Strone
Farm

CRAWBERRY RD

DARNLEY RD

CLYDEVIEW
ST

FANCY FARM RD

GABRIEL

KILMACOLM RD

Dismtd Rly

Lady Octavia
Public Park

COBHAM ST

Gibshill

POPLAR ST

EAST ST

MACKIE

Works

Auchmountain
Glen

ABERFOYLE RD

KILLEARN RD

FINTRY RD

BULLOCH

FENDRICK RD

BLAIRMORE RD

TORRANCE
RD

LEVEN RD

Sch

CARDROSS AVE

KILCREGGAN VIEW

CARDROSS CRES

SHANNON ST
BARR AVE

Sch

CLYNDER RD

KILMACOLM PL

CARDROSS PL

Strone

• Mast

AUCHMOUNTAIN RD

Knocknairs
Hill

THOMAS MUIR LA 1
LILYBANK RD 2
FARQUAR RD 3
BROADSTONE AVE 4

1

BALMORE RD

ARDMORE RD

RENTON RD

DALMOAK RD

ARDEN RD

LISS PL

Craigieknowe Burn

B788

74

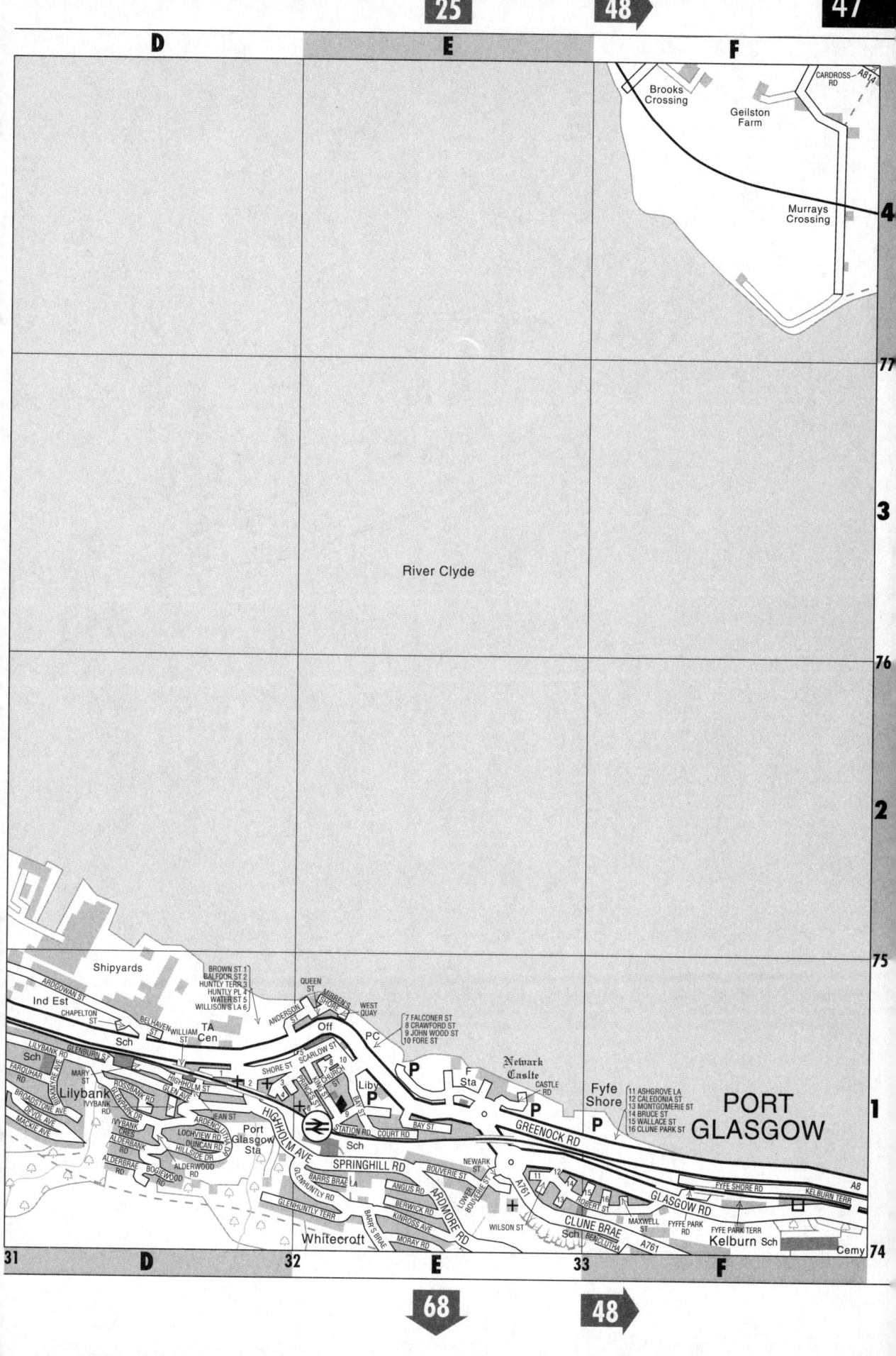

Brooks
Crossing

Geilston
Farm

CARDROSS
RD

A814

Murrays
Crossing

River Clyde

Shipyards

BROWN ST 1
BALFOOR ST 2
HUNTLY TERR 3
HUNTLY PL 4
WATER ST 5
WILLISON'S LA 6

Ind Est

ARDGOWAN ST

CHAPELTON
ST

BELHAVEN
ST

WILLIAM
ST

Sch

TA
Cen

QUEEN
ST

MIRREN'S
SHORE

ANDERSON

Off

WEST
QUAY

PC

7 FALCONER ST
8 CRAWFORD ST
9 JOHN WOOD ST
10 FORE ST

Newark
Castle

Lilybank
Sch

FARQUHAR
RD

GLENBURN ST

MARY
ST

ROSSBANK
RD

FIRPARK DR

HIGHHOLM ST

GLEN AVE

SHORE ST

SCARLOW ST

KING ST

CHURCH ST

Liby

Sta

CASTLE
RD

Fyfe
Shore

11 ASHGROVE LA
12 CALEDONIA ST
13 MONTGOMERIE ST
14 BRUCE ST
15 WALLACE ST
16 CLUNE PARK ST

PORT
GLASGOW

Lilybank

IVYBANK
RD

BROADSTONE AVE

REVOL AVE

MACKIE AVE

IVYBANK
CRES

ALDERBANK

ALDERBRAE

BOGIEWOOD
RD

ALDERWOOD
RD

JEAN ST

ARDENLEA

LOCHVIEW RD

DUNCAN RD

HILLSIDE DR

HIGHHOLM AVE

Port
Glasgow
Sta

STATION RD

COURT RD

BAY ST

Sch

GREENOCK RD

P

P

P

P

P

Whitecraft

GLENHUNTLY TERR

BARR'S BRAE

MORAY RD

SPRINGHILL RD

BARRS BRAE LA

ANGUS RD

BERWICK RD

KINROSS AVE

ARDMORE RD

LOWER
BOUVERIE ST

BOUVERIE ST

NEWARK
ST

Wilson St

A761

CLUNE BRAE

MAXWELL
ST

FYFFE PARK
RD

Sch

BENCLUTHA

A761

ROBERT ST

GLASGOW RD

FYFE SHORE RD

FYFE PARK TERR

KELBURN TERR

A8

Kelburn Sch

Cemy

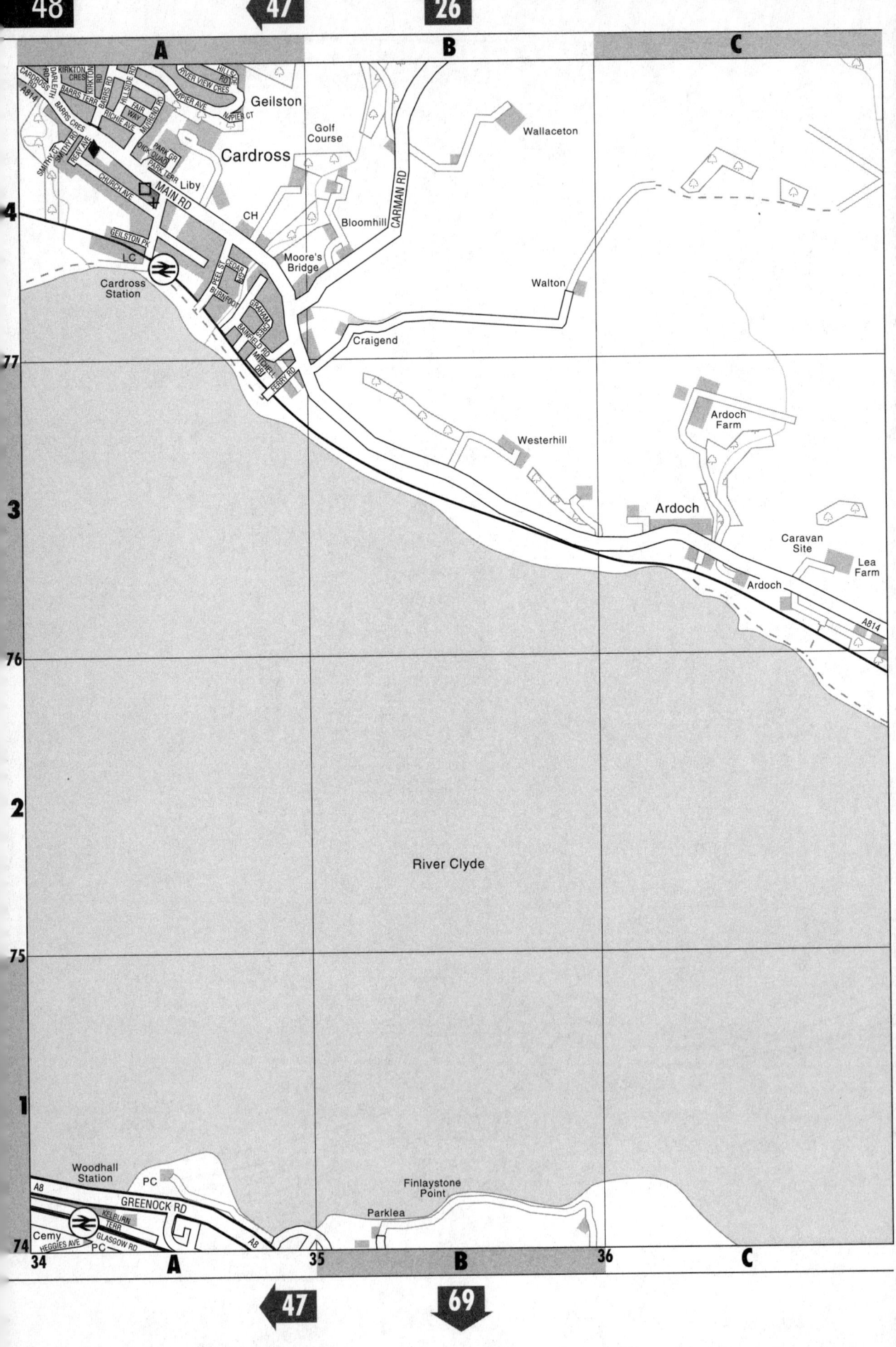

A B C

4

77

3

76

2

75

1

74

34 A 35 B 36 C

Geilston

Cardross

Golf
Course

Wallaceton

Bloomhill

CARMAN RD

CH

Moore's
Bridge

Walton

Cardross
Station

Craigend

Westerhill

Ardoch
Farm

Ardoch

Caravan
Site

Lea
Farm

Ardoch

A814

River Clyde

Woodhall
Station

PC

GREENOCK RD

Finlaystone
Point

Parklea

Cemy

HEGGIES AVE

GLASGOW RD

A8

A8

KELBURN
TERR

PC

River View Cres

Kirkton
Cres

Darleith
Rd

Cardross Rd

Barrs Terr

Barrs Cres

Smiths

Main Rd

Church Ave

Geilston Pk

LC

Park Gdns

Park Terr

Liby

Peel St

Cedar Pl

Burn Foot

Banfield Rd

Mitchell

Ferry Rd

Napier Ave

Napier Ct

Hill St

Hills Rd

Fair
Way

Richie Ave

Dick Quad

Spittal Rd

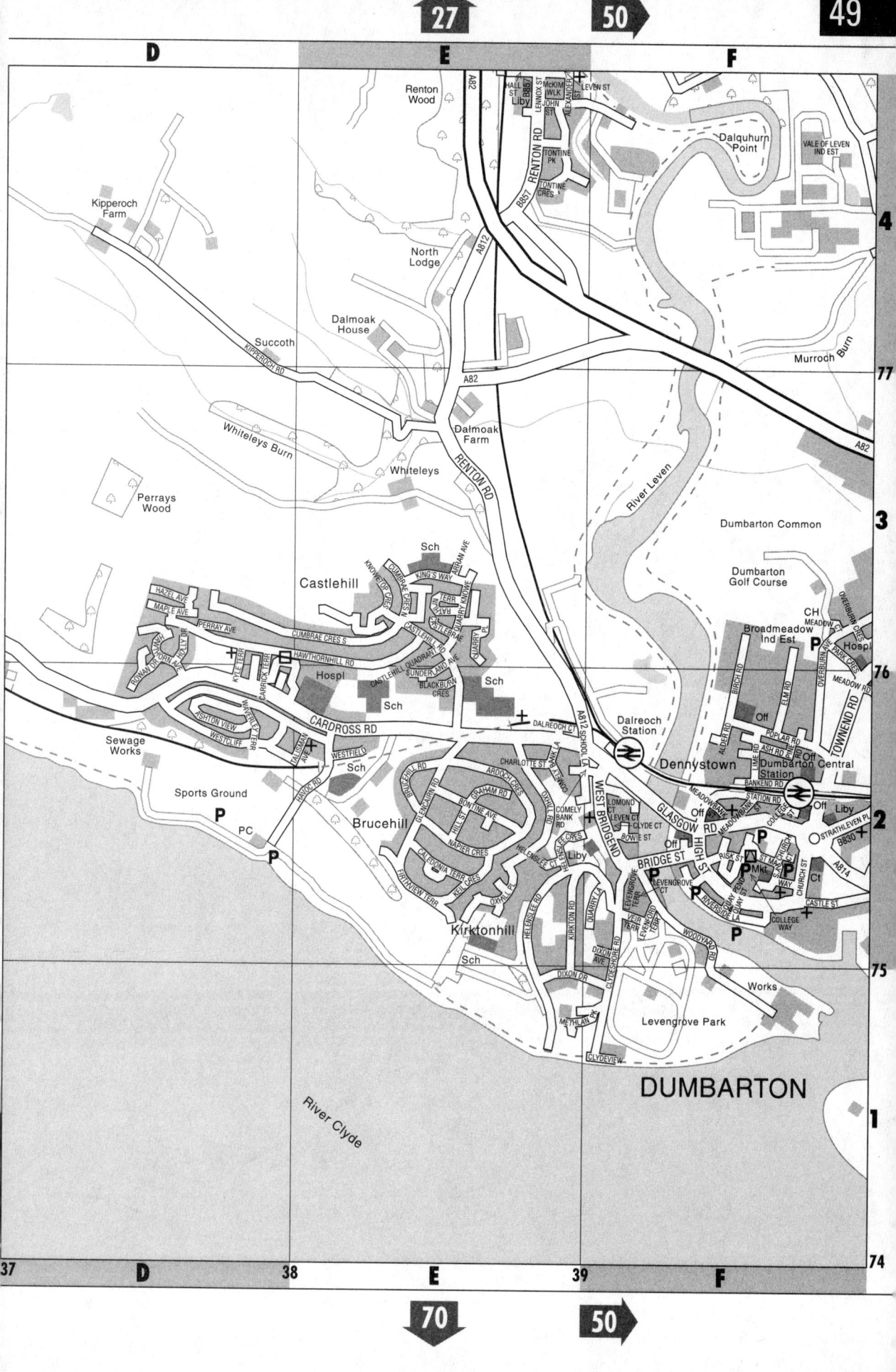

DUMBARTON

River Clyde

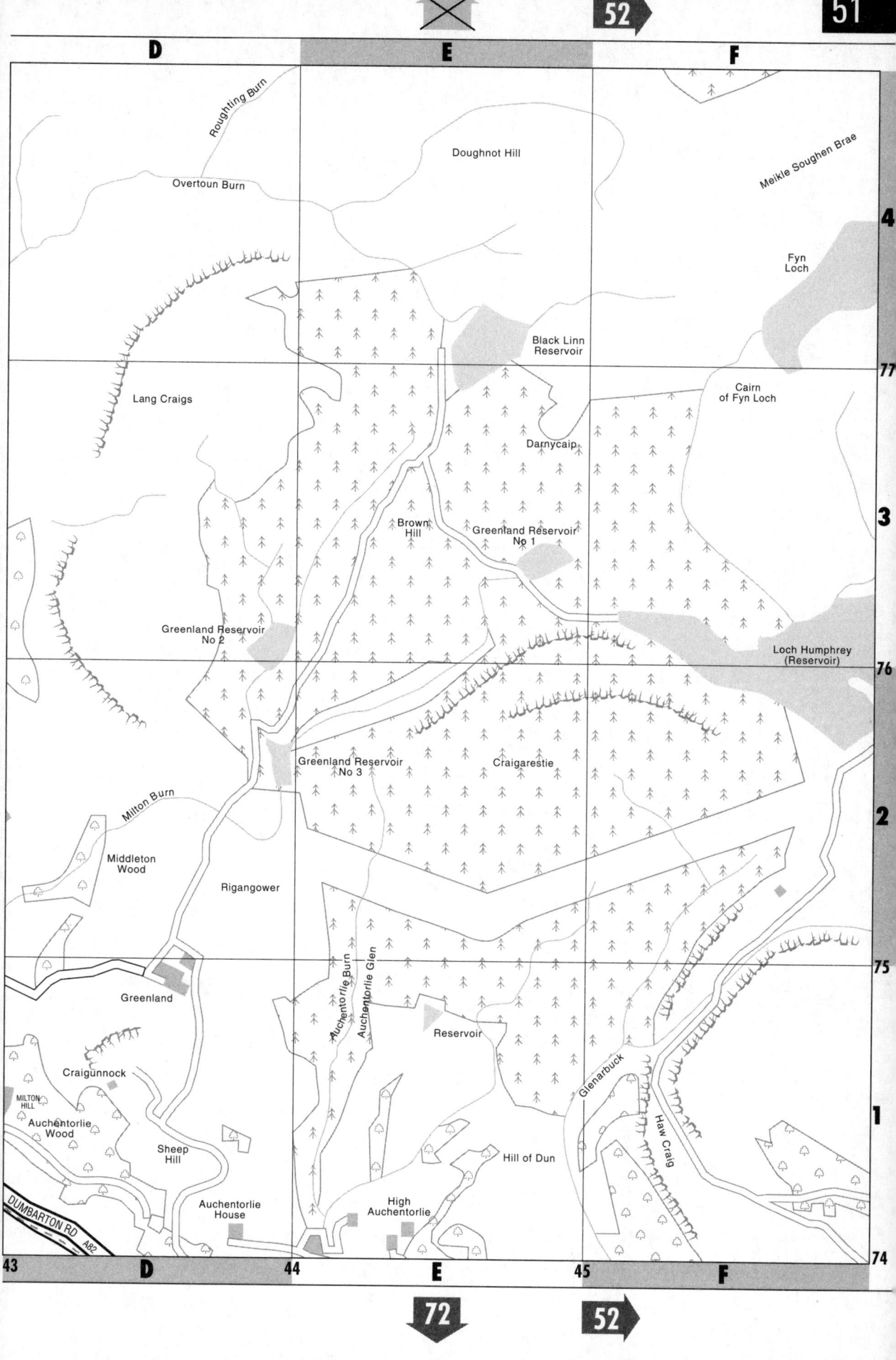

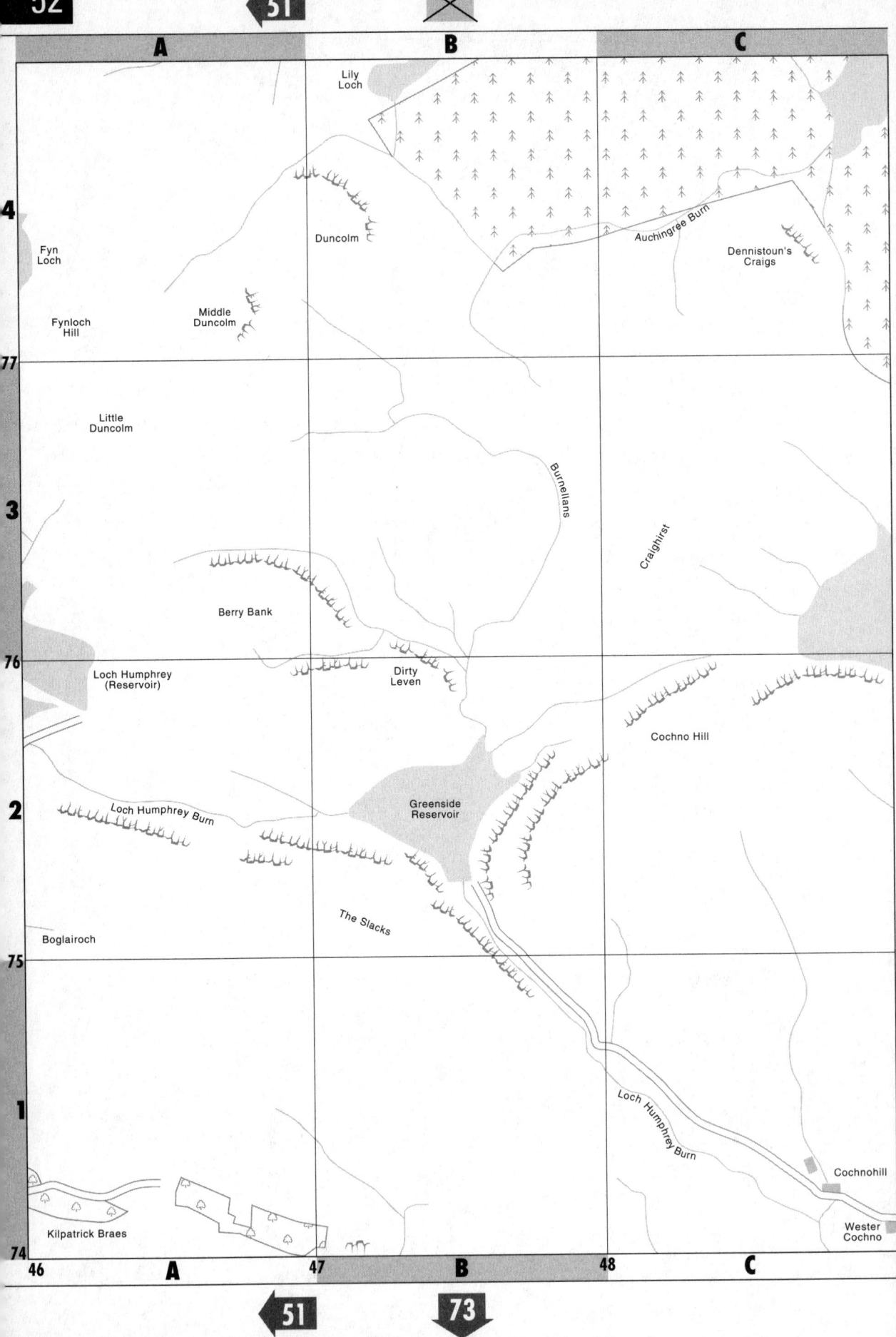

Lily
Loch

4

Fyn
Loch

Duncolm

Auchingree Burn

Dennistoun's
Craigs

Middle
Duncolm

Fynloch
Hill

77

Little
Duncolm

Burnellans

Craighirst

3

Berry Bank

76

Loch Humphrey
(Reservoir)

Dirty
Leven

Cochno Hill

Loch Humphrey Burn

Greenside
Reservoir

2

The Slacks

Boglairoch

75

1

Loch Humphrey Burn

Cochnohill

Kilpatrick Braes

Wester
Cochno

74

D

E

F

Kilmannan Reservoir

Craigton Burn

Craigenkirn Glen

Tomibeg

Meikle Longveggan

Windyedge

Craigbanzeoch

4

Craigmore

Woodie Craigs

Birny Hills

77

Black Loch

3

Dunellan

Cairnhowit

Craigmore

Cochno Loch (Reservoir)

Long Knowe

Jaw Reservoir

76

West Muirhouses

2

East Muirhouses

Todhill Wood

75

Bog Wood

Shield Hill Plantation

Jaw Burn

Auchenduich Wood

Douglas Muir

1

Cochno

Lady's Linn

Cochno Burn

Edinbarnet

A B C

4

A809

CH

Golf
Course

Craigallian
Loch

Boat
House

Scroggy
Hill

Craigallian

Gallow
Hill

Craigend
Castle

Moot
Hill

P

Lower
Craigallian

Kyber
Cottage

77

Craigton Burn

Craigallian
Bridge

West Highland Way

Mugdock
Wood

High
Craigton

Mount
Zion

Allander Water

3

Shank Burn

Golf
Course

Carneddans
Wood

CH

Low
Craigton

CRAIGTON COTTS

Laighpark

76

Wks

Field
Wood

THE OAN

CARNEDDANS RD

Braval

2

Tambowie

Golf
Course

CRAIGTON RD

Little
Balvie

Acad

CH

75

Balviebank

Craigdhu Burn

Sch

HUNTER RD

Crossburn

Douglas
Muir

1

STOCKIEMUIR RD A809

Craigdow

CRAIGDHU RD
B8050

F Sta

Craighead
Knowe
Golf
Course

Mains
Plantation

Old Mains
Farm

Prestonfield

B8050

52 A 53 B 54 C 74

D E F

4

Mugdock Loch

Loch Ardinning

Muirhouse Muir

Black Linn

77

Mugdock Country Park

THE STABLES

Mugdock

Middleton of Mugdock

Easterton Farm

Caigmaddie Loch

Caigmaddie Plantation

Caigmaddie House

Easterton House

3

Bankend

A81

Craigash

Barrachan

76

P

Mugdock Reservoir

Allander Park

DRUMCLOG AVE

CRAIGALLIAN AVE

MUGDOCK RD

Tannock Loch

Craigmaddie Reservoir

Bankell House

Bankell Farm

2

MILNGAVIE

Sch

PC

BLANE DR

SELEA DR

STRATHBLANE RD

CH

Baldernock House

+

75

P

WEST Highland Way

Allander Walk

P

MOOR RD

LYNN DR

Back Wood

Ford

BALDERNOCK RD

Dowan

Kettlehill Farm

DOWAN RD

P

Sch

Golf Course

Stable Wood

Craigmaddie Burn

CRAIGMADDIE RD

1

P

WOODBURN WAY

B8030

Ind Est Milgavie Station

1 NORTH CLAREMONT LA
2 CLAREMONT GDNS
3 SOUTH CLAREMONT

Boghall

VIEWPARK

P

GLASGOW RD

MAIN ST

Lennox Park

DOUGALSTON AVE

DOUGALSTON

Lawn Park

FINLAY RISE

FINLAY RISE

SOUTH MAINS RD

A807

74

5 D 56 E 57 F

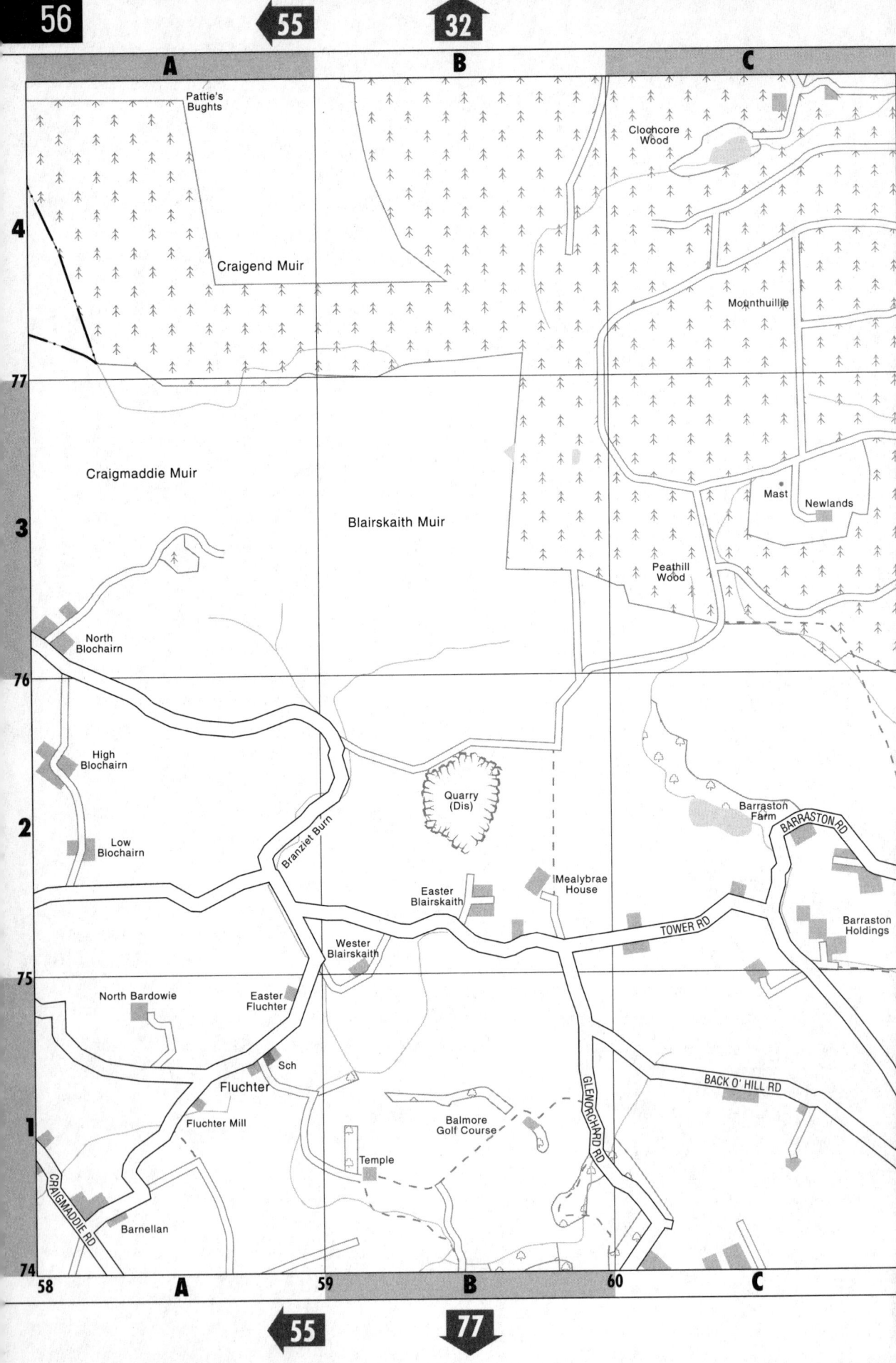

A   B   C

Pattie's
Bughts

Clochcore
Wood

4

Craigend Muir

Mounthuillie

77

Craigmaddie Muir

Blairskaith Muir

Mast

Newlands

3

Peathill
Wood

North
Blochairn

76

High
Blochairn

Quarry
(Dis)

Barraston
Farm

BARRASTON RD

2

Low
Blochairn

Branziet Burn

Mealybrae
House

Barraston
Holdings

Easter
Blairskaith

TOWER RD

Wester
Blairskaith

75

North Bardowie

Easter
Fluchter

GLENORCHARD RD

Sch

BACK O' HILL RD

Fluchter

1

Fluchter Mill

Balmore
Golf Course

CRAIGMADDIE RD

Temple

Barnellan

74

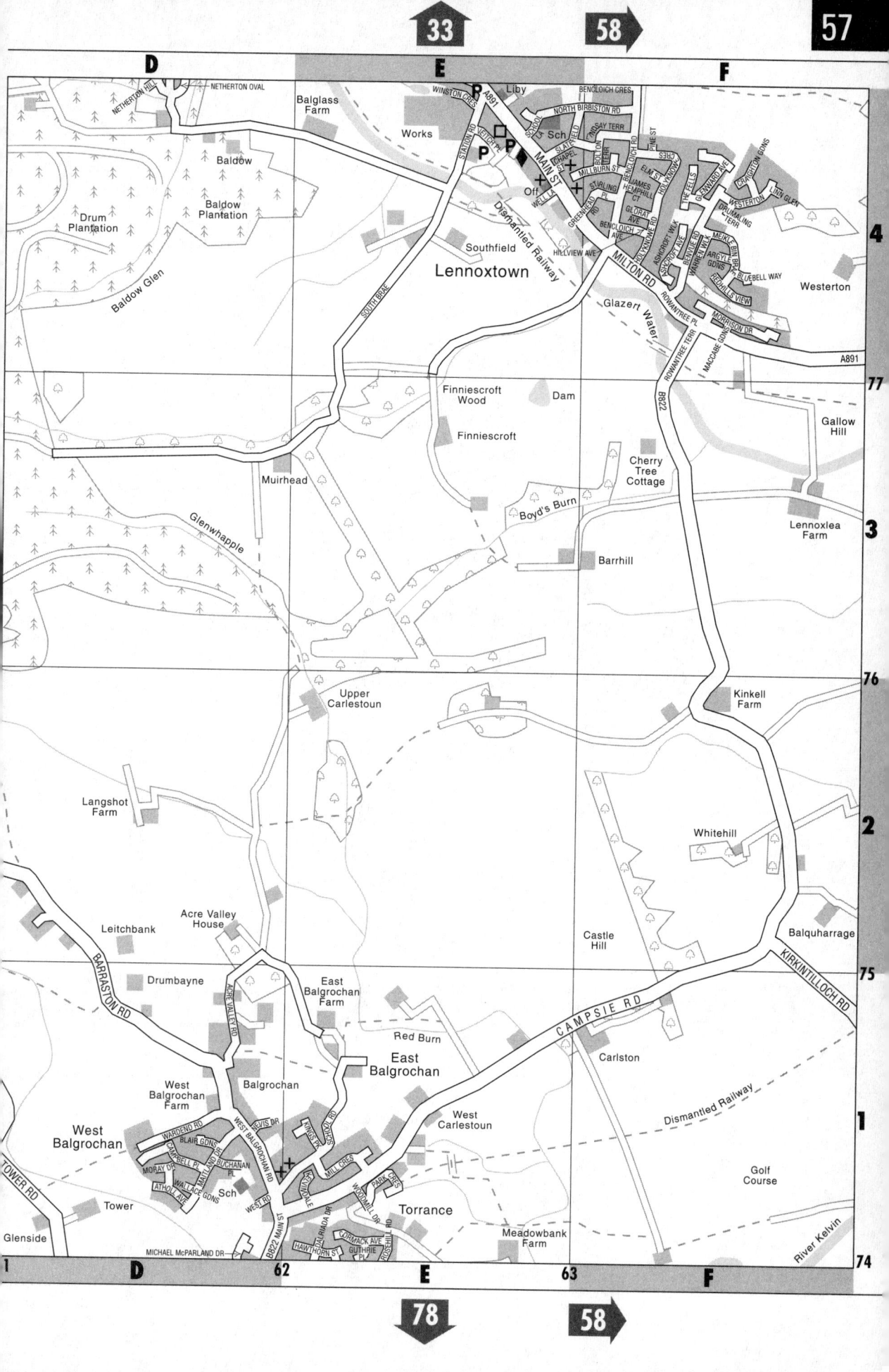

D
E
F

Netherton Hill
Netherton Oval
Balglass Farm
Works
Baldow
Drum Plantation
Baldow Plantation
Baldow Glen
Southfield
Lennoxtown

WINSTON CRES
Liby
A891
P
STATION RD
VEITCH
North Birbiston Rd
BENCLOICH CRES
P
P
Off
WELL LA
Chapel
SLATEFIELD
Sch
Main St
SAY TERR
BOLTON RD
BENCLOICH RD
PINE ST
GREENFIELD RD
MILLBURN ST
STIRLING ST
ELM ST
JAMES HEMPHILL CT
THE FELLS
CROFTHEAD GDNS
GLEN
LINN GLEN
WESTERTON
GLORAT AVE
BENCLOICH AVE
ASHCROFT AVE
GLENYARD AVE
WAVERLEY RD
DRUMELLING TERR
MEIKLE BIN BRAE
ARGYLE GDNS
BLUEBELL WAY
REDHILLS VIEW
MORRISON DR
MILTON RD
Westerton
A891

4

Dismantled Railway
Hillview Ave
Glazert Water
ROWANTREE TERR
B822
ROWANTREE PL
MACCABE GDNS

77

Finniescroft Wood
Dam
Finniescroft
Cherry Tree Cottage
Gallow Hill

Muirhead
Boyd's Burn
Barrhill
Lennoxlea Farm

3

Glenwhapple

Upper Carlestoun
Kinkell Farm

76

Langshot Farm
Whitehill

2

Leitchbank
Acre Valley House
Balquharrage

BARRASTON RD
Drumbayne
East Balgrochan Farm
Castle Hill
KIRKINTILLOCH RD

75

Red Burn
East Balgrochan
CAMPSIE RD
Carlston

ACRE VALLEY RD
West Balgrochan Farm
Balgrochan
West Carlestoun
Dismantled Railway
Golf Course

1

West Balgrochan
WARDEND RD
BLAIR GDNS
NEVIS DR
KINGS LA
SCHAW RD
CAMPBELL PL
MORAY DR
BUCHANAN PL
MILL CRES
WOODHILL DR
PARK CRES
TOWER RD
WALLACE GDNS
ATHOLL AVE
MAITLAND
Sch
FERNDALE
DALRIADA DR
WEST RD
Torrance
Tower
BB22 MAIN ST
HAWTHORN ST
CORMACK AVE
GUTHRIE PL
Meadowbank Farm
River Kelvin
Glenside
MICHAEL McPARLAND DR

74

D
62
E
63
F

Stratford Cottage
Woodburn Reservoir
Ashenwell Dams
Water Works
Spouthead Burn
Shields Cottage

4

Girdle Hill
Cowies Glen
Burniebrae Farm

Alloch Dam

Mount Dam
A891
Antermony Loch

77 Newmill
CAMPSIE RD
VALLEYFIELD
MOUNT PLEASANT CRES
Works
LOCHABER WLK
CRES
LOCHILBO DR
CRAIGHEAD RD
SCOTT AVE
DERRYWOOD RD
Sch
Liby
SCHOOL LA
CRAIGHEAD AVE
Milton of Campsie
Waltry Burn
Alton Holdings
Lochmill Farm

B757
NEWLANDS TERR
GRETA MEEK LA
JAMES LEESON CT
FERGUSSON TERR
Antermony Loch
Lochmill
A891

3
MARGUERITE PL
ARCHIBALD TERR
MARLEY WAY
LABURNUM DR
CHESTNUT CT
IRVING GDNS
HILLSIDE TERR
CAIRNVIEW RD
MURRAY GDNS
ANTERMONY RD
Alton Farm
Alton Holdings
Lochmill

LINDEN LEA
CAMERON CRES
KINCAID WAY
BLAIR DR
MONTGOMERY TERR
HARKNESS AVE
BEECHES RD
LION CRES
GLENBURN CRES
KINCAID FIELD

VIEWFIELD AVE
GLAZERT AVE
REDMOSS RD
MAPLE AVE
HAWTHORN WAY
WILLOW WAY
RUNDELL DR
Redmoss
MUNRO DR
WALNUT LA
CHERRY PL
LIME TREE WLK
PEAR RD
SYCAMORE WAY
ROWAN AVE
POPLAR DR
76
JUNIPER DR
HAZEL BANK
ALDER RD
Glazert Water

Hospl
BIRDSTON RD
Sewage Works

2
Wetshod
Birdstonbank Farm
Birdston
Dismantled Railway
Inchbelle Farm

Birdston Farm
A803

Dismantled Railway
75
Inchbelly Bridge
B8023

Kirkintilloch Golf Course
Hospl
PC
Forth and Clyde Canal
ALLOWAY TERR

Ind Est
Amb Sta
ARRAN
AILSA DR
ALLOWAY GR
LOCH LEA
MOSSGIEL

1
KIRKINTILLOCH RD
CH
Springfield
Goyle Bridge
KILSYTH RD
KENINVAE
BROOMHILL FARM MEWS
GRAHAMSDYKE
Cleddans
WHITEHILL
AFTON
VIEW
LANGMUIR RD

Hayston House
River Kelvin
CAMPSIE RD
ROCHDALE PL 1
BROADCROFT 2
BROADCROFT RD 3
PETER D STIRLING RD 4
HOPKIN'S BRAE 5
Ind Est
MILTON RD B757
Works
Ind Est
BANKS RD
HILLHEAD RD
DANIEL McLAUGHLIN
HARDMUIR GDNS
LANGMUIR AVE
MEIKLEHILL RD
WHITEHILL CRES
MEIKLEHILL CT
HIGHFIELD CT
TINTOCK DR
LANGMUIR RD
Schs

P Liby
GLASGOW RD
A806
EAST HIGH ST
EASTSIDE
LION BANK
CANAL
CATHKIN
REDBRAE RD
LUGGIEBANK
COWAN'S NORTH
WATERLOO GDNS
MEIKLEHILL
HIGHFIELD
NEWFORK RD
P

74
WASHINGTON RD 1
GLASGOW RD 2
A803
WEST HIGH ST
PEEL BRAE
Mus
TH
COWGATE
ELM BANK
CAIRN LA
LION BANK
FELLS RD
1 HIGHFIELD GR
2 RIDGEBANK AVE
3 HIGHFIELD RD
4 LENNOX CT
Merkland

D
E
F

Drumairn

Lossit

Old Place Farm

Kierhill

WHIN LOAN

DYKEHEAD RD

ANDERSON CRES
KILLCREST RD
MEADOWSIDE RD
DUMBRECK TERR
A803

Sch
KILSYTH RD
PH
Queenzieburn

MILL RD

Gallow Hill

Ind Est

4

Dyke Farm

Woodburn

Queenzieburn Farm

Gavell Farm

Gavell

GAVELL RD

77

Inchwood Farm

Wood Burn

Cast Burn

Sewage Works

Queenzie Burn

AUCHENREOCH

Netherinch Farm

Dismtd Rly

3

ANTERMONY RD
Roitfair
A891

Burnside Cottage

Works

Twechar Farm

B8023

76

GLEN SHIRVA RD

MERRYFLATS

MAIN ST

BARHILL LA

1 HILLVIEW COTTS
2 MELROSE GDNS
3 SHIRVA LEA
4 WHITELAW TERR

River Kelvin

ALEXANDER AVE
ANNIESDALE
PARK AVE
WYNDFORD
SUNNYHILL
BURNBRAE

Shirva

Board Burn

2

ANTONINE WALL
(course of)

Sewage Works

Twechar

Sch

Auchendavie Farm

DAVIDSON CRES
KELVIN VIEW
MACDONALD CRES

Bridgend Farm

KELVIN TERR
JOHNSTONE TERR
DIXON TERR
GARTSHORE CRES

75

Forth & Clyde Canal

Mine (dis)

ALLOWAY TERR
ALLOWAY DR
ELLISLAND DR
ELLISLAND DR
BURNS DR

AUCHENDAVIE RD
TINTOCK RD
EASTERMAINS

Tintock

Easterton Moss Plantation

Easterton

Harestanes

MAUCHLINE
MAUCHLINE AVE
KINTYRE
KIRKOSWALD
KINROSS GDNS

ST FLANAN RD

1

CLARIS CRES
BURNS CT
DIXON WAY

Sch
AFTON
TANNOCH CT
ATHOLL

Saddles Brae Farm

Castle Hill

B8048

LANGMUIR RD
Langmuir

BANNOCH RD
MOIDART
APPIN

FOSSIL GR
1 ARMOUR GDNS
2 ALLOWAY QUADRANT
3 ARMOUR PL
4 GLENCONNER WAY
5 MERKLAND PL
6 MERKLAND CT

GRAY
GAIRLOCH GDNS

West Gartclash

East Gartclash

East Lodge

MERKLAND DR

B8048

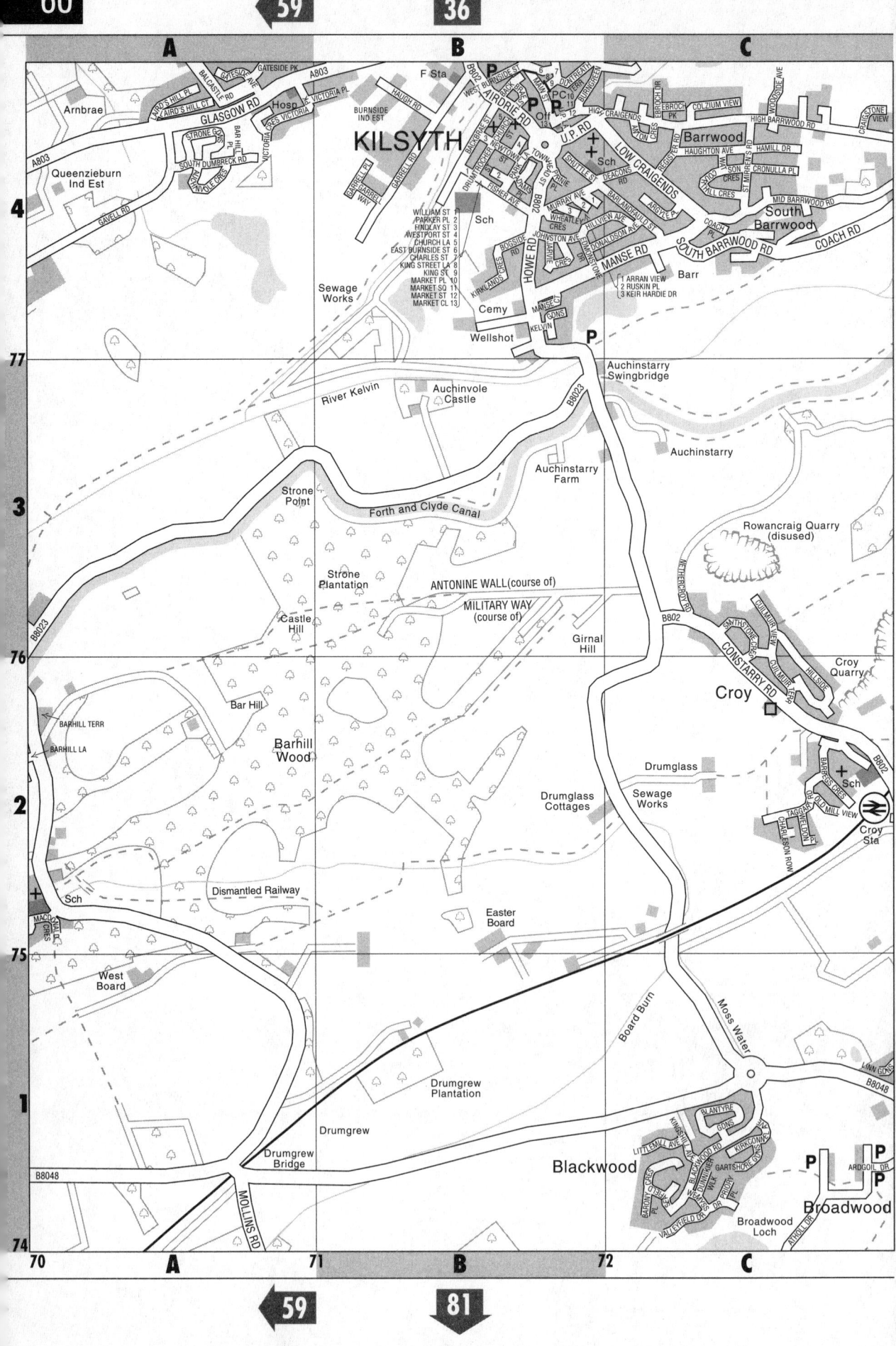

A B C

Arnbrae

Queenzieburn Ind Est

GLASGOW RD

Hosp

BURNSIDE IND EST

F Sta

KILSYTH

AIRDRIE RD

U.P. RD

Barrwood

LOW CRAIGENDS

South Barrwood

COACH RD

SOUTH BARRWOOD RD

MANSE RD

Barr

1 ARRAN VIEW
2 RUSKIN PL
3 KEIR HARDIE DR

WILLIAM ST 1
PARKER PL 2
FINDLAY ST 3
WESTPORT ST 4
CHURCH LA 5
EAST BURNSIDE ST 6
CHARLES ST 7
KING STREET LA 8
KING ST 9
MARKET PL 10
MARKET SQ 11
MARKET ST 12
MARKET CL 13

Sch

Cemy

Wellshot

Kelvin

Sewage Works

Auchinstarry Swingbridge

River Kelvin

Auchinvole Castle

Auchinstarry Farm

Auchinstarry

Strone Point

Forth and Clyde Canal

Rowancraig Quarry (disused)

Strone Plantation

ANTONINE WALL (course of)

MILITARY WAY (course of)

Girnal Hill

Castle Hill

B802

NETHERJOHN RD

CONSTARRY RD

Croy Quarry

Croy

Bar Hill

Barhill Terr

Barhill La

Barhill Wood

Drumglass Cottages

Drumglass

Sewage Works

Sch

Croy Sta

B802

Sch

MACD
SNAIL CL
CRES

Dismantled Railway

Easter Board

West Board

Drumgrew Plantation

Board Burn

Moss Water

B8048

Drumgrew

Drumgrew Bridge

Blackwood

MOLLINS RD

Broadwood

Broadwood Loch

P P P

B8048

70 A 71 B 72 C

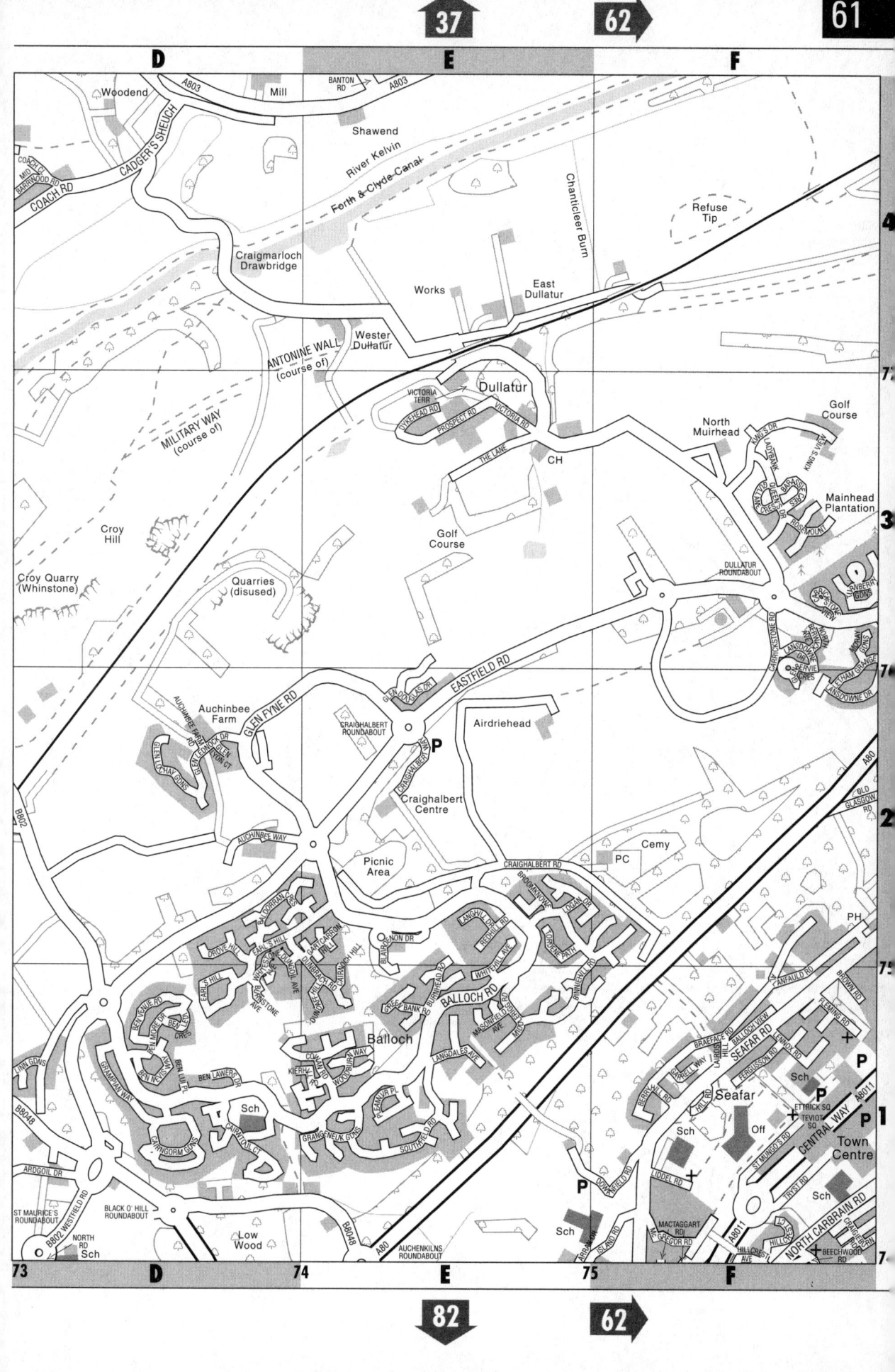

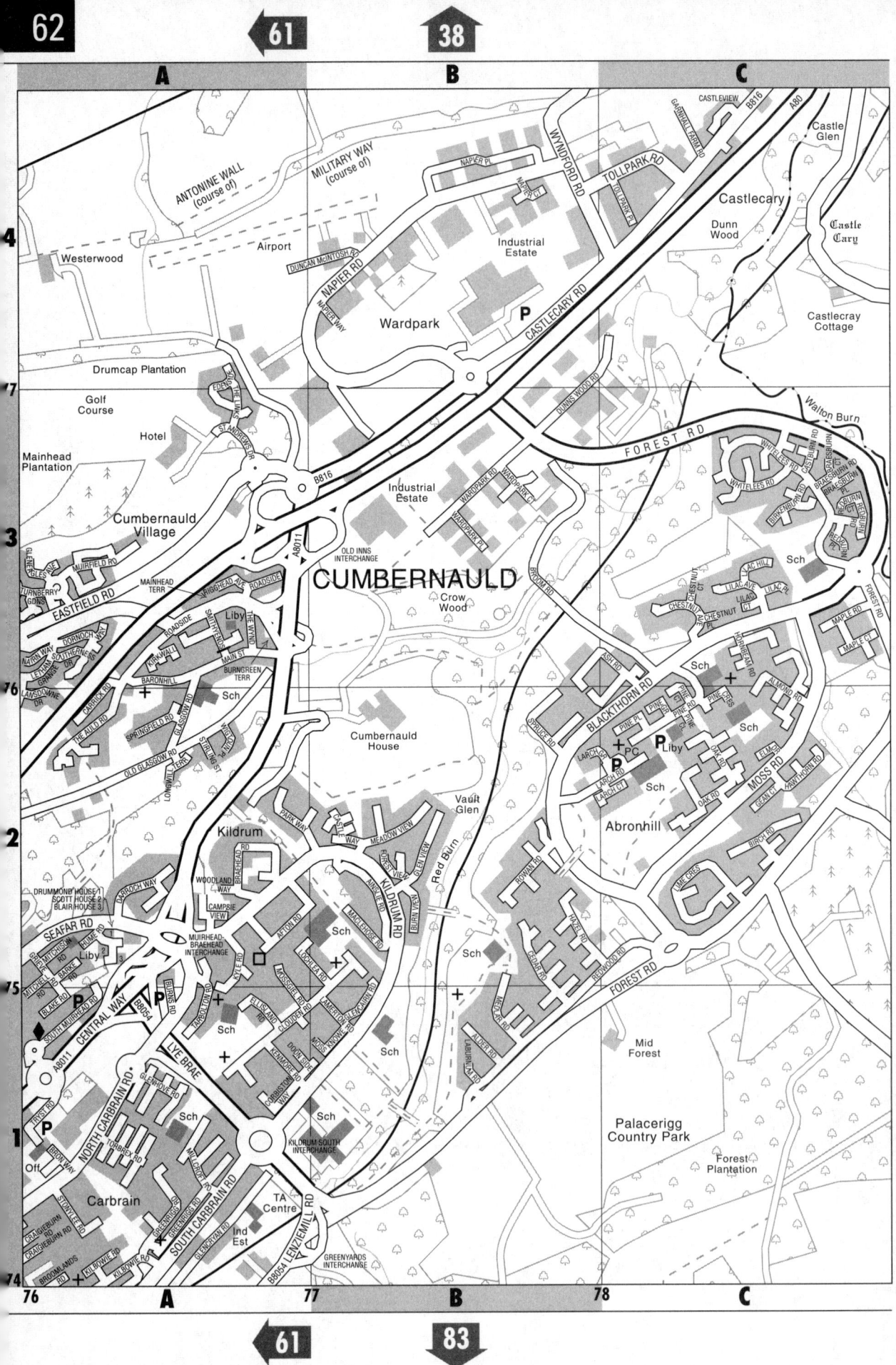

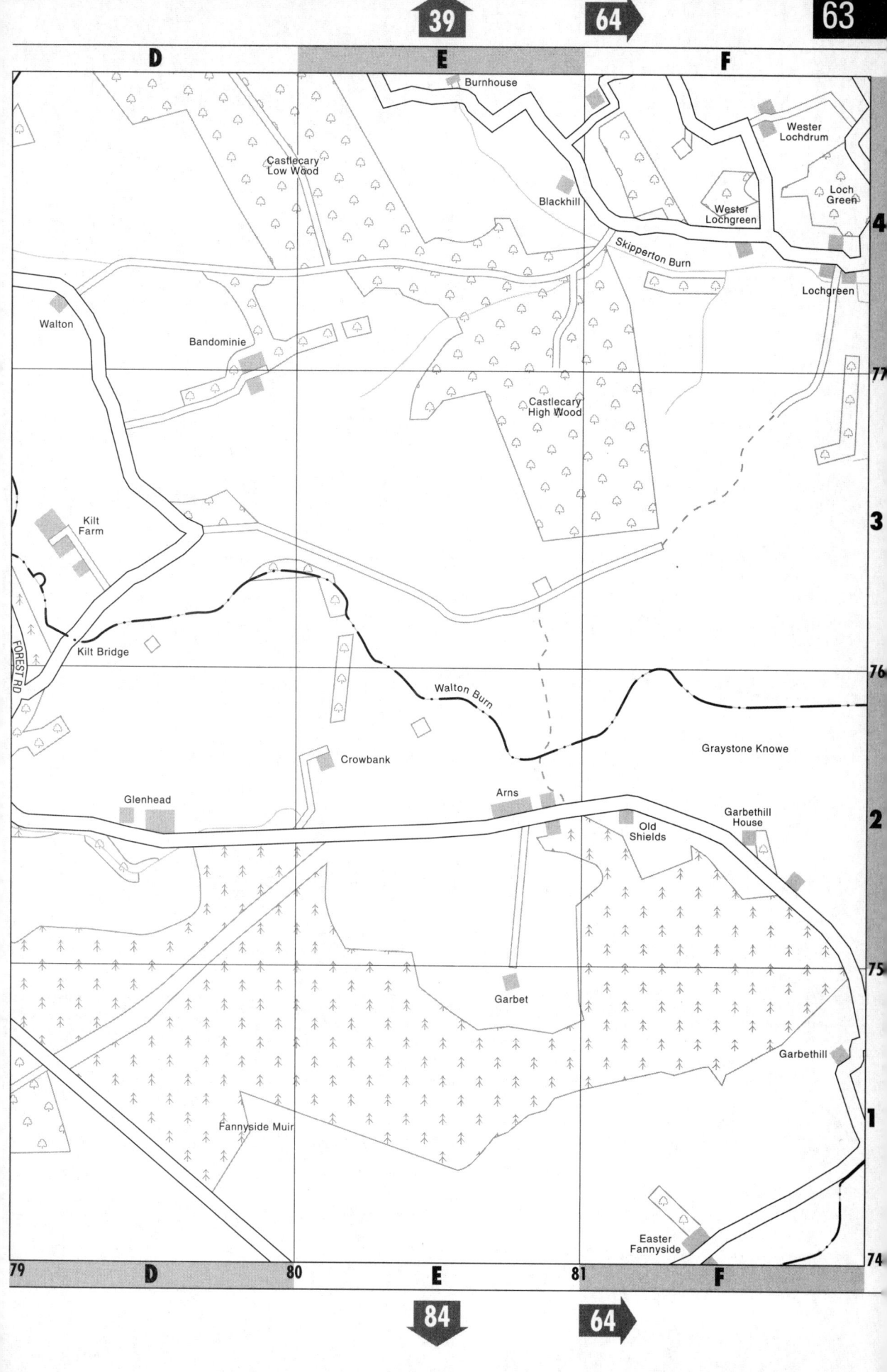

D
E
F

Burnhouse

Castlecary
Low Wood

Wester
Lochdrum

Blackhill

Loch
Green

Wester
Lochgreen

4

Skipperton Burn

Walton

Lochgreen

Bandominie

77

Castlecary
High Wood

3

Kilt
Farm

Kilt Bridge

76

Walton Burn

Graystone Knowe

Crowbank

Arns

Glenhead

Garbethill
House

2

Old
Shields

Garbet

75

Garbethill

Fannyside Muir

1

Easter
Fannyside

74

FOREST RD

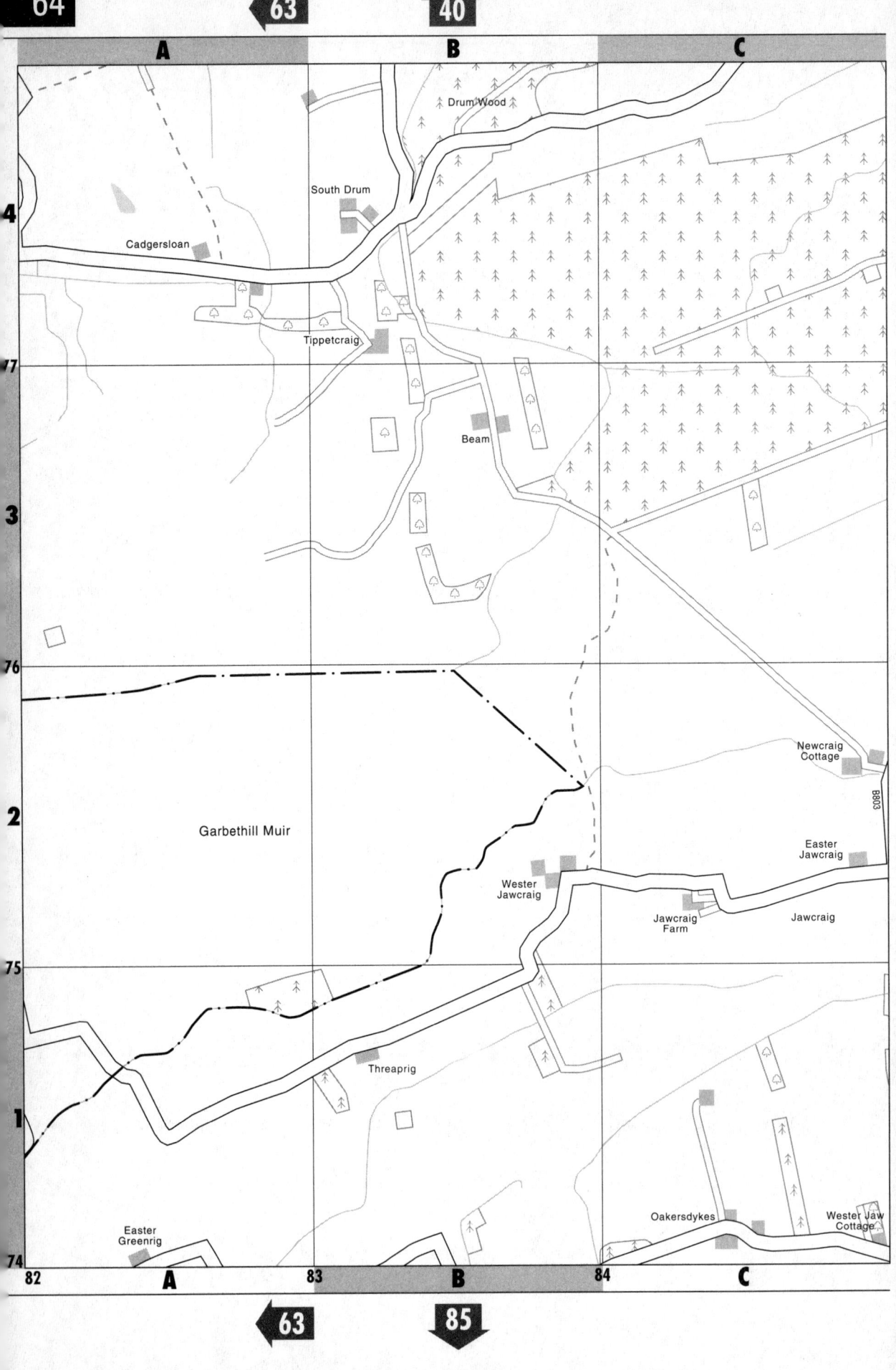

A   B   C

Drum Wood

South Drum

4

Cadgersloan

Tippetcraig

77

Beam

3

76

Newcraig
Cottage

B803

2

Garbethill Muir

Easter
Jawcraig

Wester
Jawcraig

Jawcraig
Farm

Jawcraig

75

Threaprig

1

Oakersdykes

Wester Jaw
Cottage

Easter
Greenrig

74

82   A   83   B   84   C

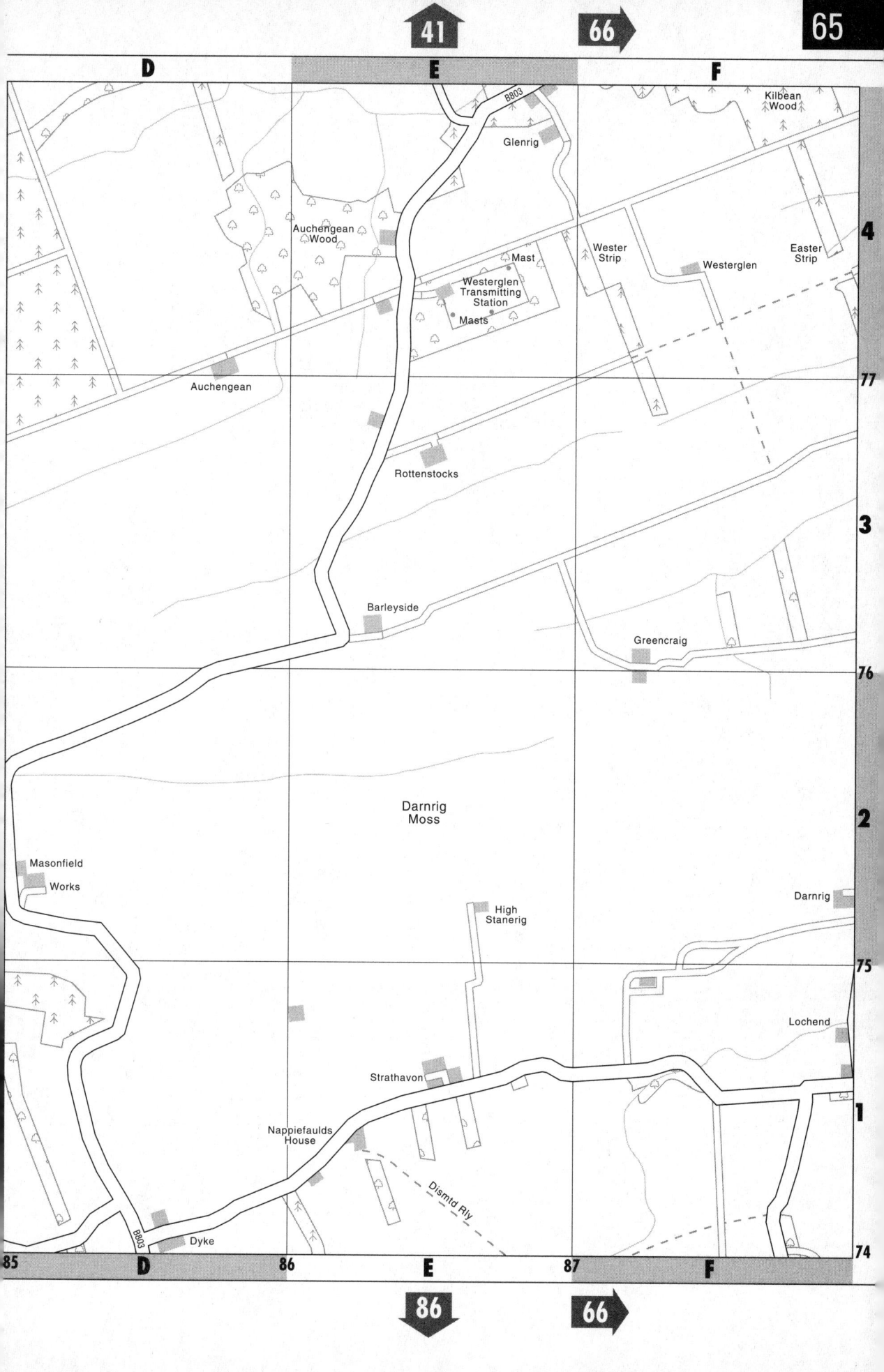

B803
Kilbean
Wood
Glenrig
Auchengean
Wood
Mast
Wester
Strip
Easter
Strip
4
Westerglen
Transmitting
Station
Westerglen
Masts
77
Auchengean
Rottenstocks
3
Barleyside
Greencraig
76
Darnrig
Moss
2
Masonfield
Works
Darnrig
High
Stanerig
75
Lochend
Strathavon
1
Nappiefaulds
House
Dismtd Rly
B803
Dyke

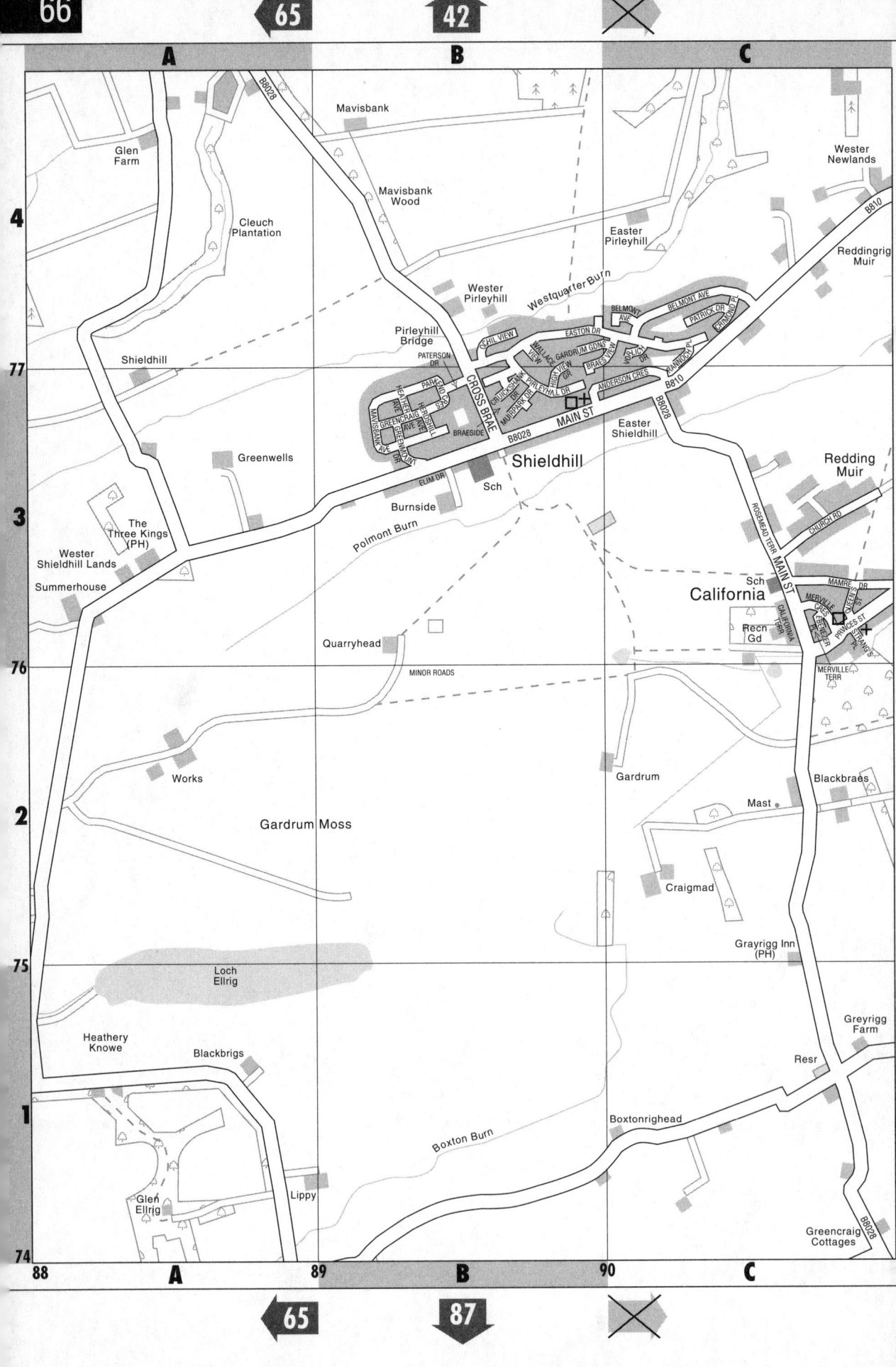

Map labels

Grid references (left): 4, 77, 3, 76, 2, 75, 1, 74
Grid columns (top and bottom): A, B, C
Grid references (bottom): 88, 89, 90

Glen Farm
Mavisbank
Wester Newlands
B810
Cleuch Plantation
Mavisbank Wood
Easter Pirleyhill
Reddingrig Muir
Wester Pirleyhill
Westerquarter Burn
Shieldhill
Pirleyhill Bridge
PATERSON DR
SCHIL VIEW
EASTON DR
BELMONT AVE
BELMONT AVE
PATRICK DR
PRIMROSE PL
WALLACE VIEW
GARDRUM GDNS
BRAES VIEW
VORLICH DR
PARK RD
HEATHER RD
HARDSHILL RD
GREENCRAIG AVE
MAVISBANK AVE
CRUIKSHANK DR
MURDOCH DR
PIRLEYHILL DR
ANDERSON CRES
RANNOCH PL
B810
GREENWELLS INN
BRAESIDE
MAIN ST
B8028
CROSS BRAE
Redding Muir
Greenwells
Easter Shieldhill
CHURCH RD
ELIM DR
Sch
ROSEMEAD TERR
MAIN ST
MAMRE DR
LEES ST
The Three Kings (PH)
Burnside
Polmont Burn
California
Sch
MERVILLE CRES
EBENEZER
PRINCES ST
KINGS ST
Wester Shieldhill Lands
Summerhouse
CALIFORNIA TERR
Recn Gd
MERVILLE TERR
Quarryhead
MINOR ROADS
Works
Gardrum
Blackbraes
Gardrum Moss
Mast
Craigmad
Loch Ellrig
Grayrigg Inn (PH)
Greyrigg Farm
Heathery Knowe
Blackbrigs
Resr
Boxtonrighead
Boxton Burn
Glen Ellrig
Lippy
B8028
Greencraig Cottages
B8028

D
E
F

Burnhead Moor

Lurg Moor

Knocknairs Moor

AUCHMOUNTAIN RD
B788
Devol Burn
DOUGHILL RD

4

Maukinhill Moor

Knocknair'shill
Reservoir

Harelaw
Reservoir

Crawberry
Hill

Devol Burn

73

Corlick
Hill

Burnhead

AUCHENFOIL RD

Devol Moor

3

Glenbrae

72

Gryfe Reservoir No 1

Gryfe Reservoir No 2

Mansfield
Bridge

2

Garshangan
Bridge

Garshangan

Mansfield

Gryfe Neuk
Nursery

Gryfe Water

Gryfe Lea

Auchenfoil
Cottage

B788

Dykefoot

Garshangan Burn

71

Cairncurran
Hill

1

Hillside

28
D
29
E
30
F
70

A B C

DOUGLIEHILL RD

DOUGLIEHILL TERR

DOUGLIEHILL PL

West
Dougliehill

East
Dougliehill

Dougliehill
Reservoir

BARR'S BRAE

MORAY RD

SELKIRK RD

ARDMORE RD

BURNHEAD LA

BURNHEAD RD

AUCHENFOIL LA

AUCHENFOIL RD

BURNBANK TERR

BURNBANK RD

MILLBURN RD

MILLBANK RD

RIDSNEATH

ROSNEATH

NUDALL RD

ISACH LA

MUIRSHIEL LA

McDONALD RD

LANGSIDE TERR

HARELAW AVE

MOORFIELD AV

GOLF FOR

MERRYLEE AVE

MUIRDYKES AVE

GARELOCH LA

GARELOCH RD

GARELOCH RD

LOMOND AV

CLYDEVIEW RD

CARDROSS AVE

BENVIEW RD

BENVIEW
AVE

BRAEHEAD

BRAEHEAD

WEST
AVE

BRIDGEND AVE

BRIDGE AVE

NORTH RD

SOUTH RD

CLUNE BRAE

HIGH CARNEGIE RD

A761

BROOKFIELD RD

PH

Cemy

HEGGIES
AVE

PARKHILL RD

NORTHFIELD RD

WESTFIELD RD

MID AVE

BURNSIDE AVE

Boglestone

BOGLESTONE AVE

DUBBS RD

DEVOL RD

GOLF RD

Ind
Est

Ind Est

Devol

CH

GLENSIDE RD

DENEUK RD

GLENBRAE RD

Golf Course

Mid
Auchinleck

SOUTHFIELD AVE

BARSCUBE
AVE

CROSSHILL

AUCHINLECK RD

AUCHINLECK LA

ALPERSTON

KILMACOLM RD

A761

OAKBANK
RD

Liby

Schs

O Hotel

KILMACOLM RD

MONKTON
PL

Bardrainney

High
Auchenleck

CROSSHILL RD

MAYBOLE RD

MONTROSE RD

MINARD

MOTHART RD

MOSS RD

MILTON RD

METHIL RD

MARKINCH

TEVIOT RD

SIDLAW AVE

FENTLAND AVE

SLAEMUIR
AVE

CULLINS
AVE

MAXWELL
RD

WEST CH

BARMOSS

SAY RD

SAY RD

BARMOSS AVE

WOODSIDE AVE

MARLOCH AVE

Sch

AUCHENBOTHIE RD

Cunston
Cottage

West Kilbride

Dismantled Railway

72 Auchentiber

Devol Moor

Harelaw
Reservoir

Harelaw

Pennytersal

Priestside
Farm

Auchentiber
Bridge

B788

Auchenfoyle

High
Mathernock

Mathernock
Bridge

Gryfe Water

Gryfeside

Strathgryfe

Horsecraigs

Cauldside

Blacksholm
Bridge

Strathgryfe

Faulds

B788

31 A 32 B 33 C

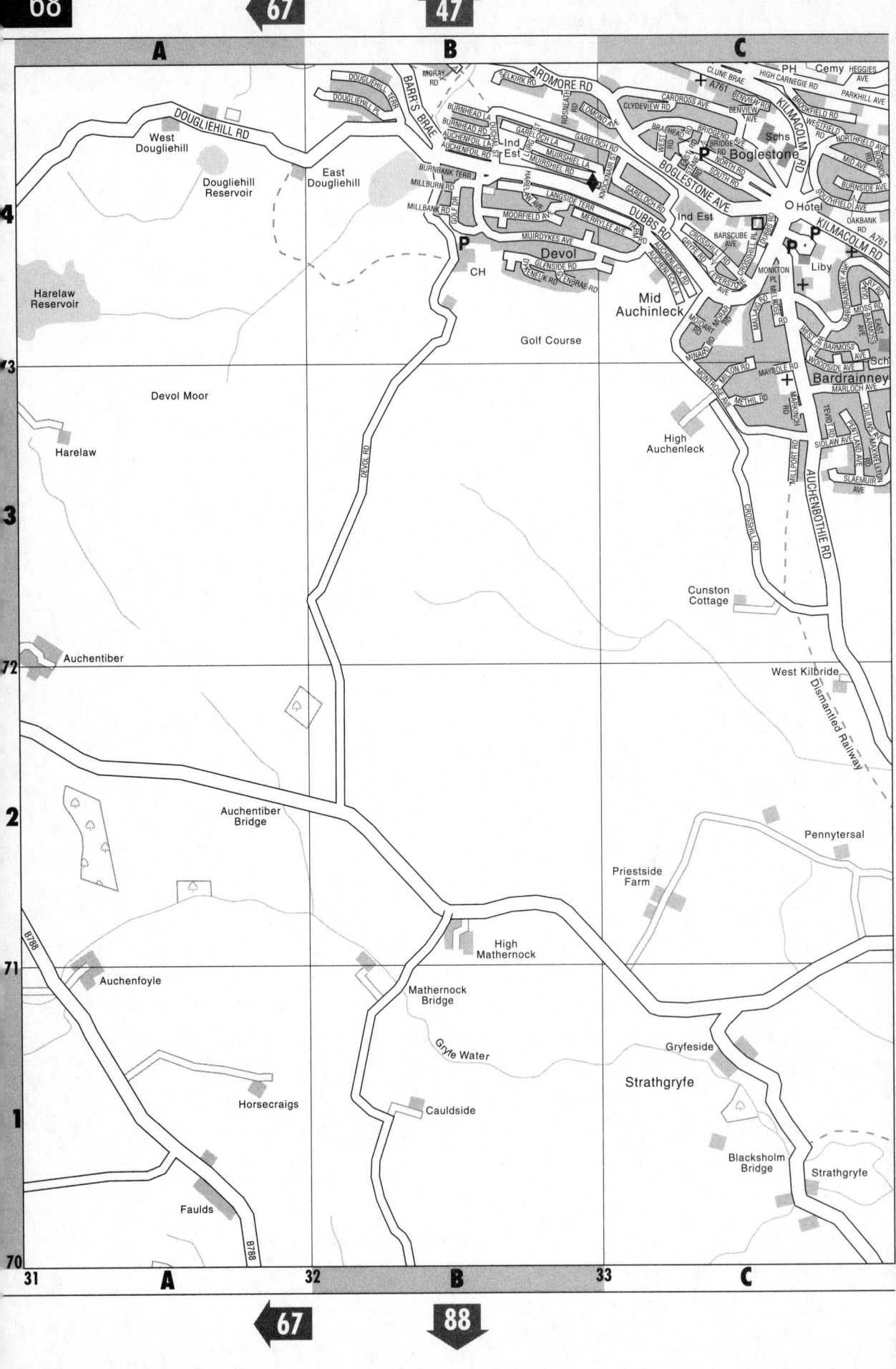

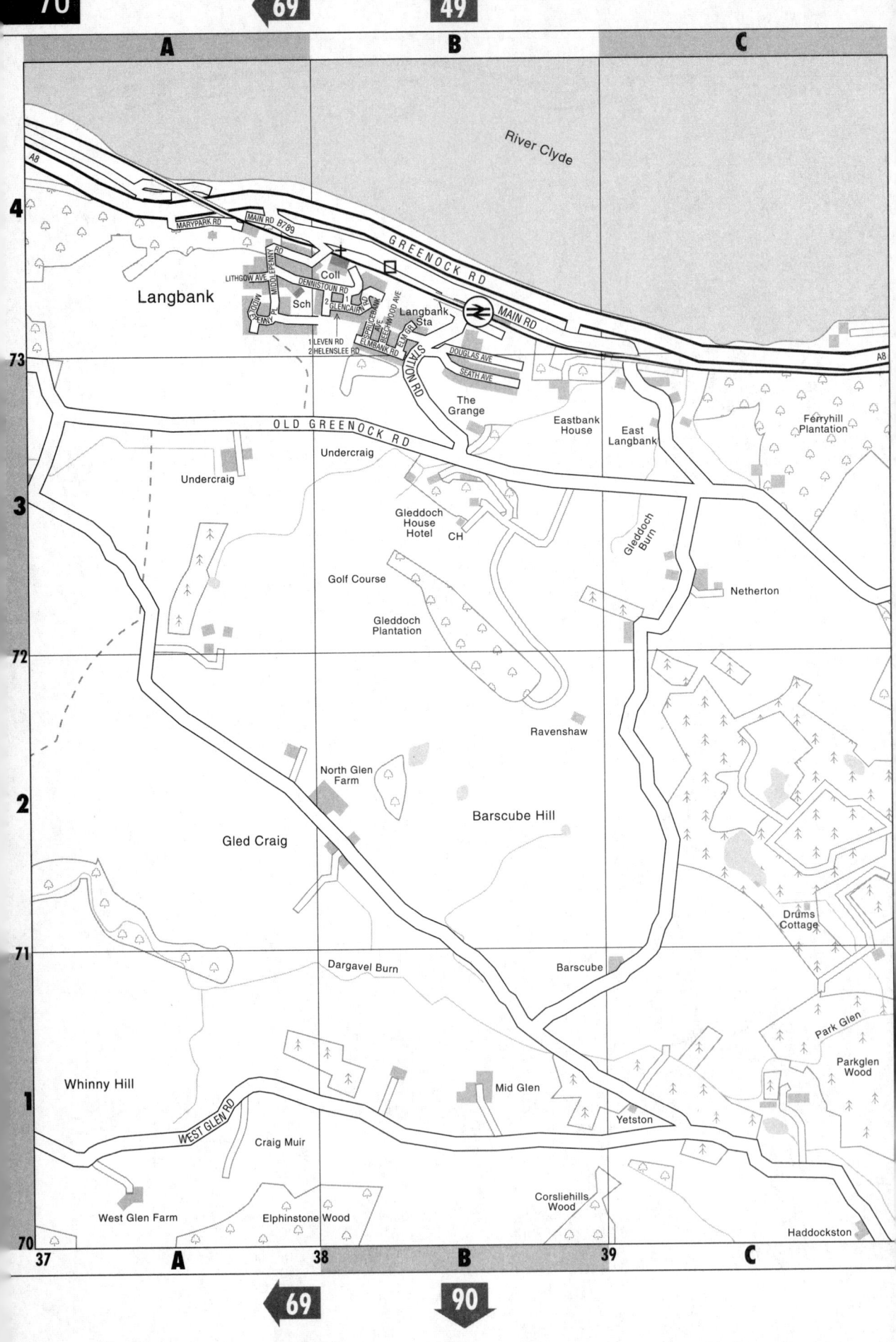

River Clyde

A8

4

MARYPARK RD
MAIN RD B789
GREENOCK RD

LITHGOW AVE
DENNISTOUN RD
Coll
MIDDLEPENNY RD
Sch
GLENCAIRN RD
SPRUCEBANK
BEECHWOOD AVE
ELMBANK RD
ELM GR

Langbank

Langbank Sta

MAIN RD

A8

1 LEVEN RD
2 HELENSLEE RD

STATION RD

73

DOUGLAS AVE
SEATH AVE

The Grange

OLD GREENOCK RD

Undercraig

Eastbank House

East Langbank

Ferryhill Plantation

Undercraig

Undercraig

Gleddoch House Hotel

CH

Gleddoch Burn

3

Golf Course

Netherton

Gleddoch Plantation

72

Ravenshaw

North Glen Farm

Barscube Hill

Gled Craig

2

Drums Cottage

71

Dargavel Burn

Barscube

Park Glen

Whinny Hill

WEST GLEN RD

Mid Glen

Parkglen Wood

1

Yetston

Craig Muir

West Glen Farm

Elphinstone Wood

Corsliehills Wood

Haddockston

70

37
A
38
B
39
C

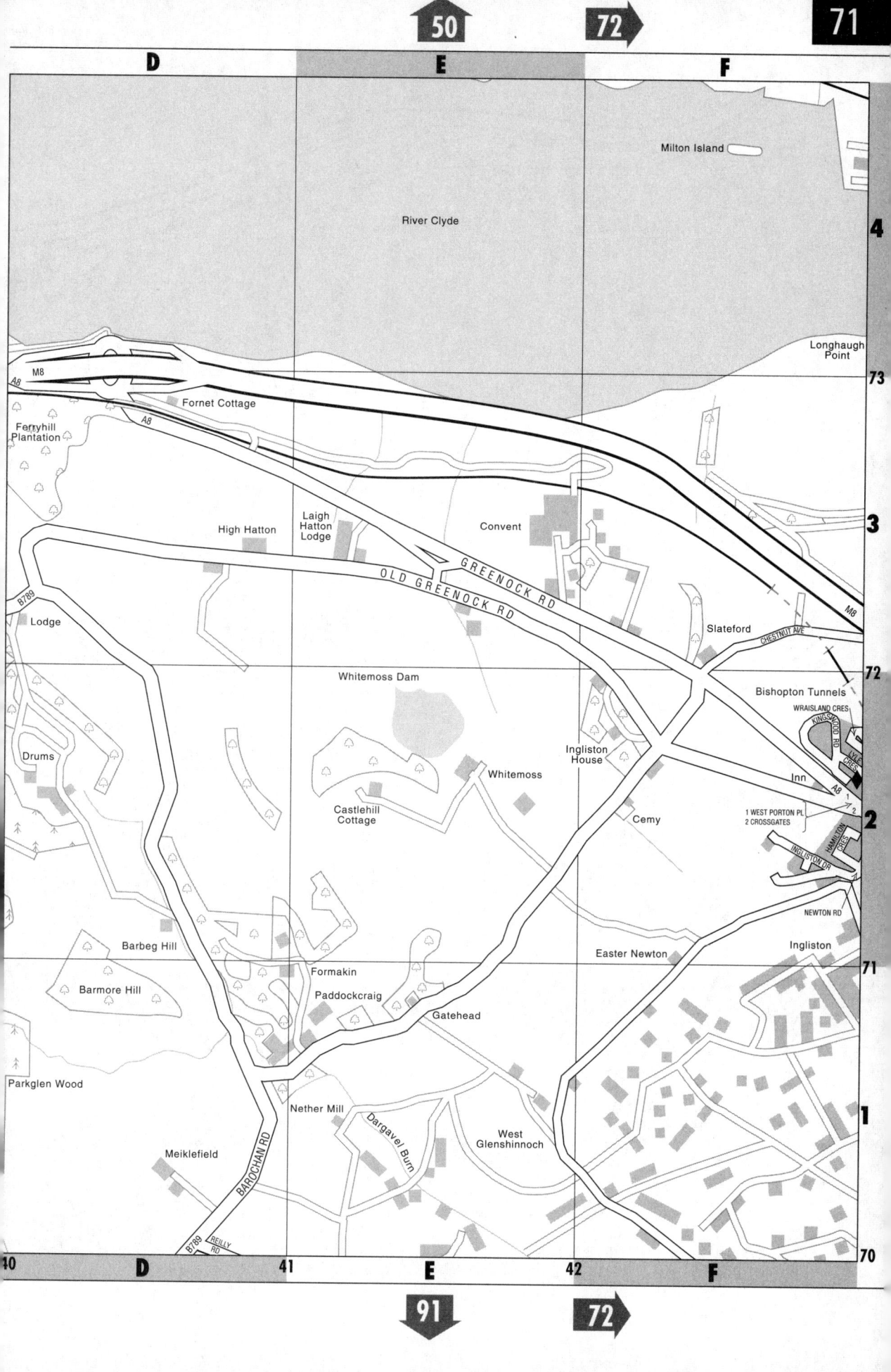

D
E
F

4

Milton Island

River Clyde

Longhaugh
Point

M8
A8

73

Fornet Cottage

Ferryhill
Plantation

A8

High Hatton

Laigh
Hatton
Lodge

Convent

GREENOCK RD

OLD GREENOCK RD

M8

Slateford

CHESTNUT AVE

3

72

B7789

Lodge

Whitemoss Dam

Bishopton Tunnels

WRAISLAND CRES

KINGSWOOD RD

LYLE CRES

Drums

Whitemoss

Ingliston
House

Inn

A8

Castlehill
Cottage

Cemy

1 WEST PORTON PL
2 CROSSGATES

HAMILTON CRES

INGLISTON DR

2

Barbeg Hill

NEWTON RD

Barmore Hill

Formakin

Paddockcraig

Easter Newton

Ingliston

71

Gatehead

Parkglen Wood

BAROCHAN RD

Nether Mill

Dargavel Burn

West
Glenshinnoch

1

Meiklefield

B7789

REILLY RD

40
D
41
E
42
F

70

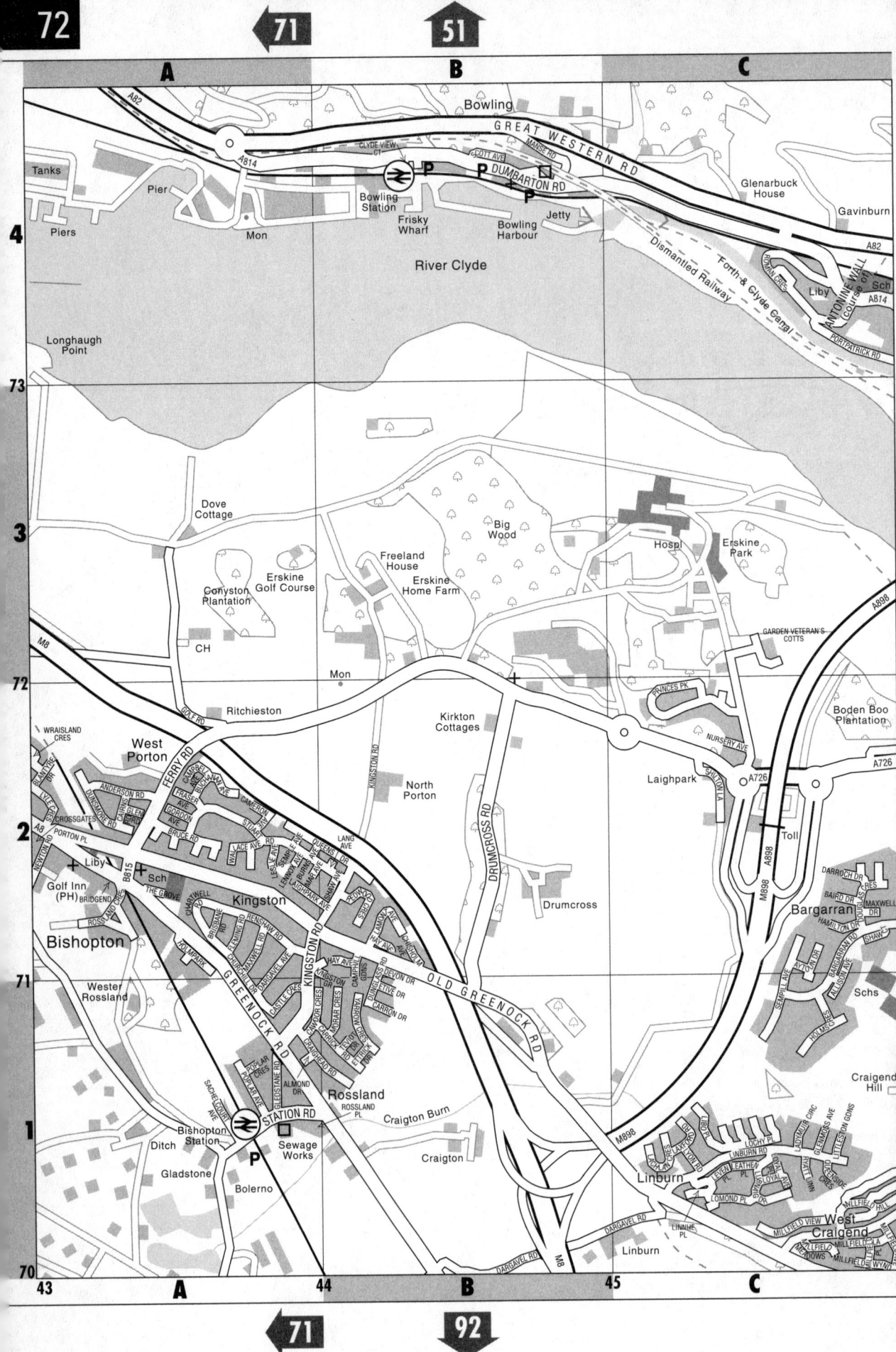

Tanks
Pier
Bowling
GREAT WESTERN RD
A82
A814
CLYDE VIEW CT
SCOTT AVE
MANSE RD
P
DUMBARTON RD
Glenarbuck House
Gavinburn
Piers
Bowling Station
Mon
Frisky Wharf
Bowling Harbour
Jetty
P
P
Dismantled Railway
Forth & Clyde Canal
Course of
ROMAN CRES
ANTONINE WALL
Sch
Liby
A82
A814
PORTPATRICK RD

4

River Clyde

Longhaugh Point

73

Dove Cottage
Big Wood
Hospl
Erskine Park

3

Conyston Plantation
Erskine Golf Course
Freeland House
Erskine Home Farm
GARDEN VETERAN'S COTTS
CH
A898

Mon
Kirkton Cottages
PRINCES PK
NURSERY AVE
Boden Boo Plantation
A726

72

M8
GOLF RD
Ritchieston
KINGSTON RD
Laighpark
SHUTTLE LA
A726
Toll

WRAISLAND CRES
West Porton
FERRY RD
CAMPBELL AVE
CAMERON
North Porton
DRUMCROSS RD
Drumcross
A898
M898
DARROCH DR
RES
BAIRD DR
MAXWELL DR
Bargarran
HAMILTON DR

2

NEWTON RD
A8
CROSSGATES
PORTON PL
B815
Liby
Sch
ANDERSON RD
FRASER AVE
GORDON AVE
BRUCE AVE
STUART RD
WALLACE AVE
LESLIE AVE
LENNOX AVE
BURNS AVE
QUEENS AVE
LANG AVE
SEMPLE AVE
SHAWS
AYTON DR
SEMPLE AVE
Golf Inn (PH)
BRIDGEND
THE GROVE
ROSS
CHARTWELL
BRISBANE RD
RENSHAW RD
LAIGHPARK AVE
MAXWELL AVE
DALE AVE
SPEY AVE
HAY AVE
DARGAVEL AVE
TAY AVE
AVON DR
DEVON DR
DUNGAS CRES
CLYDE DR
Kingston
DARROCH DR
DOUGLAS AVE
HOLMES
HAMILTON DR

Bishopton
Wester Rossland
GREENOCK RD
KINGSTON RD
CASTLE DR
CAMPSIE DR
MAXWELL RD
CHURCHILL AVE
ARGYLE AVE
CAMPSIE CRES
CRAIGHEAD RD
ETIVE DR
CARRON DR
OLD GREENOCK RD
SEMPLE AVE
Schs

71

Ditch
Gladstone
SACHEL COURT AVE
POPLAR DR
ROWANTREE AVE
MYRTLE RD
ALMOND DR
Rossland
ROSSLAND PL
Craigton Burn
M898
Linburn
LADYACRE CIRC
GLENROSS AVE
LINBURN RD
LOYAL PL
LOCHY PL
SEVEN LEATHER
LITTLESON GDNS
Craigend Hill

1

Bishopton Station
STATION RD
P
Sewage Works
Craigton
LOMOND PL
LINNHE PL
West Craigend
MILLFIELD VIEW PL
MILLFIELD
Bolerno
DARGAVEL RD
M8
Linburn
MILLFIELD LA
MILLFIELD WYND

70

D E F

Gavinburn
Cottages

Craigleith

Reservoir

Drums

Mount
Pleasant

Wester
Duntiglennan

Duntocher

KIRK CRES
GAVINBURN GDNS
KIRKTON
PORTPATRICK RD
GAVINBURN PL
THISTLENEUK
ASHTREE CT

Carleith

ANTONINE WALL
(course of)

GREAT WESTERN RD

Crem
Cemy

Old
Kilpatrick

Erskine
View

Station
Rd

A898

Kilpatrick
Station

Cemy

DUMBARTON RD A810
MUNRO CT
GENTLE ROW
BURNCROOKS CT
OLD ST 1
CRAIGENCART CT 2
A82

Erskine
Bridge

Barclay
CT

Dalnottar
Terr
Glen Rd

Erskine Ferry Rd

Golf
Course

Duntocher Burn

Parkhall
POPLAR
DR

Erskine
Harbour

Depot

Freelands
CT

Mountblow
House

Mountblow

MOUNTBLOW RD

SALISBURY PL
CLYDE CT
PARK CT
WEST CT

HORNBEAM DR 1
SYCAMORE DR 2
LIMETREE DR 3

CH

Forth & Clyde Canal

DUMBARTON RD

CANBERRA AVE
LAUREL AVE
CEDAR AVE
LILAC AVE

Clydebank
Public Pk

P

P

Hotel

BARGARRAN RD
BLANTYRE CT

BARRHILL RD

Warehouses

Sch

PCs

Dalmuir

Liby

THE CROSS
STEWART ST
P

North
Barr

Bargarran

North
Barr
Sch

River Clyde

Refuse
Tip

Sewage
works

Ind
Est

Hospl

Rashielee
Schs

Liby
P

Ind Pk
P
PC

Park
Quay

BRIDGEWATER
SHOPPING CTR

BEARDMORE WAY

Off

Craigend
Hill

Rashielee

Rashielee
Plantation

ERSKINE

East
Craigend

Newshot Dr

MAINS RD

1 PARKVALE AVE
2 PARKVALE GDNS
3 GARNIE AVE
4 GARNIE LA
5 GARNIE PL
6 GARNIE OVAL

1 PARK TOR
2 PARK RIDGE

Newshot
Island

1 MILLFIELD DR
2 MILLFIELD WLK

A726

HAWTHORN
CRES

46 D 47 E 48 F 70

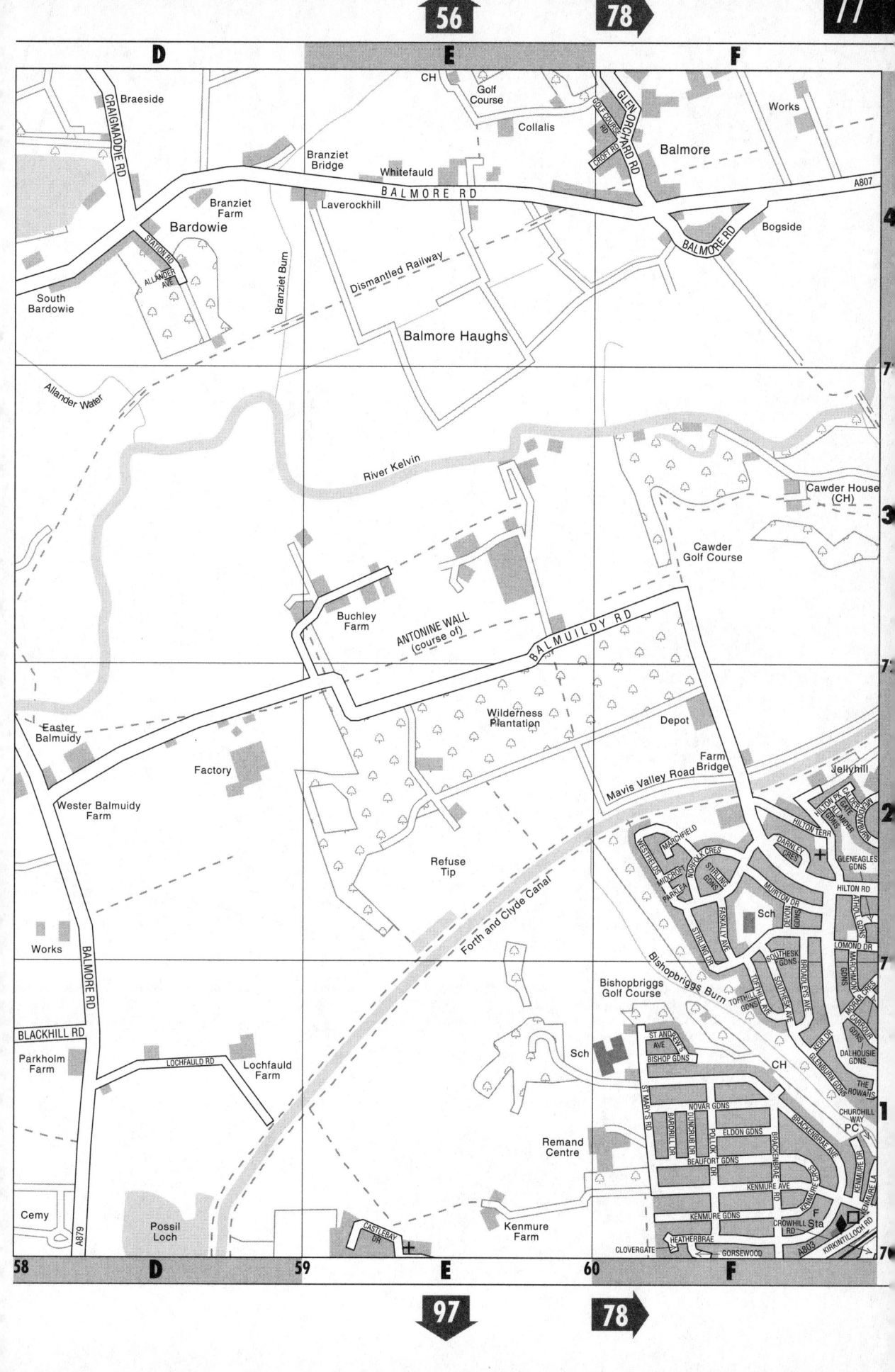

D
E
F

Braeside

CRAIGMADDIE RD

Branziet
Bridge

Branziet
Farm

Bardowie

CH

Golf
Course

Collalis

Whitefauld

Laverockhill

GLEN ORCHARD RD

CROFT RD

GOLF COURSE RD

Works

Balmore

BALMORE RD

A807

Bogside

BALMORE RD

4

South
Bardowie

STATION RD

ALLANDER AVE

Branziet Burn

Dismantled Railway

Balmore Haughs

Allander Water

7

River Kelvin

Cawder House
(CH)

3

Cawder
Golf Course

Buchley
Farm

ANTONINE WALL
(course of)

BALMUILDY RD

7

Wilderness
Plantation

Depot

Easter
Balmuidy

Factory

Farm
Bridge

Jellyhill

HILTON PK
ST
TOWNHEAD AVE

HILTON TERR

Mavis Valley Road

MARCHFIELD

WESTFIELDS

MICROFT
PARK

WYCROFT
GDNS

STIRLING
GDNS

MORTON DR

AVON DR

DARNLEY
CRES

GLENEAGLES
GDNS

+

Wester Balmuidy
Farm

2

STIRLING
DR

FARSKALY AVE

Sch

HILTON RD

ATHOL
GDNS

LOMOND DR

MATCHMILL

Refuse
Tip

SOUTHESK
GDNS

BROADLEY AVE

SOUTHFIELD AVE

TOFTHILL
GDNS

KERR DR

GLENBURN GDNS

MICROFT GDNS

CARSBROOK

DALHOUSIE
GDNS

THE
ROWANS

Works

BALMORE RD

A879

Bishopbriggs
Golf Course

Bishopsbriggs Burn

CH

7

CHURCHILL
WAY

PC

1

BLACKHILL RD

Parkholm
Farm

LOCHFAULD RD

Lochfauld
Farm

Forth and Clyde Canal

Sch

ST ANDREW'S
AVE

BISHOP GDNS

NOVAR GDNS

ST MARY'S RD

BARDRILL DR

DUNCRUB DR

POLLOK

ELDON GDNS

BEAUFORT GDNS

BRACKENBRAE AVE

BRACKENBRAE
RD

KENMURE DR

KENMURE CRES

KENMURE LA

CROWHILL
RD

Crowhill Sta

KIRKINTILLOCH RD

Cemy

Possil
Loch

CASTLEBAY DR

+

Remand
Centre

KENMURE AVE

KENMURE GDNS

Kenmure
Farm

HEATHERBRAE

CLOVERGATE

GORSEWOOD

A803

7

A   B   C

Dismtd Rly
TOWER RD
JOHN McEWAN WAY
Craigmaddie Gdns
Smeaton Ave
DUNDAS AVE
Allander Dr
FORTH RD
Craigbarnet Ave
Craigmarloch Ave
MAIN ST
ROSEHILL RD
VIOLA PL
KELVIN VIEW
DALRIADA RD
CLARK ST
FIRBANK
SNOWDON
PH
B822
A807 BALMORE RD
Sewage Wks
KELVINBRIDGE ROUNDABOUT
Torrance Bridge
Bogton
Meadowbank House
River Kelvin
Sandy Knowes
Sewage Wks
Easter Cadder
The Stables (PH)
A803
TORRANCE RD
Hungryside Bridge
P
Glasgow Bridge
Keir Golf Course
ANTONINE WALL (course of)
A807
Forth & Clyde Canal
Meiklehill Farm
Bishopbriggs Burn
CADDER RD
Cadder
Wks
Cemy
HM Prison
CROSSHILL RD
Bearhill Farm
Cawder Golf Course
High Row
KIRKINTILLOCH RD
Park Burn
B819
Low Moss Ind Est
Low Moss Plantation
Wester Boghead Holdings
LANCASTER
Lochgrog
B819
High Moss Plantation
Works
WESTERHILL RD
F Sta
HILTON RD
BISHOPBRIGGS
Depot
Cadder Yard
P
LOMOND DR
MORAR CRES
Rushyhill
BURRA GDNS
COLA
SELLAR
RONALDSAY DR
Westerhill
WESTER CLEDDENS RD
ROBROYSTON RD
B812
Schs
NESS GDNS 1
MAREE GDNS 2
LOCHY GDNS 3
RANNOCH GDNS 4
SOUTH CROSSHILL RD
Liby
CHURCHILL WAY
KENMURE LA
Sch
1 YOUNGER QUADRANT
2 ARNOLD AVE
3 EMERSON RD W
P
THE LEYS
4 CALLIEBURN RD
5 WOODFIELD AVE
6 ELM BANK
SPRINGFIELD RD
EMERSON RD
AUCHINAIRN RD
B812
A803

61   A   62   B   63   C

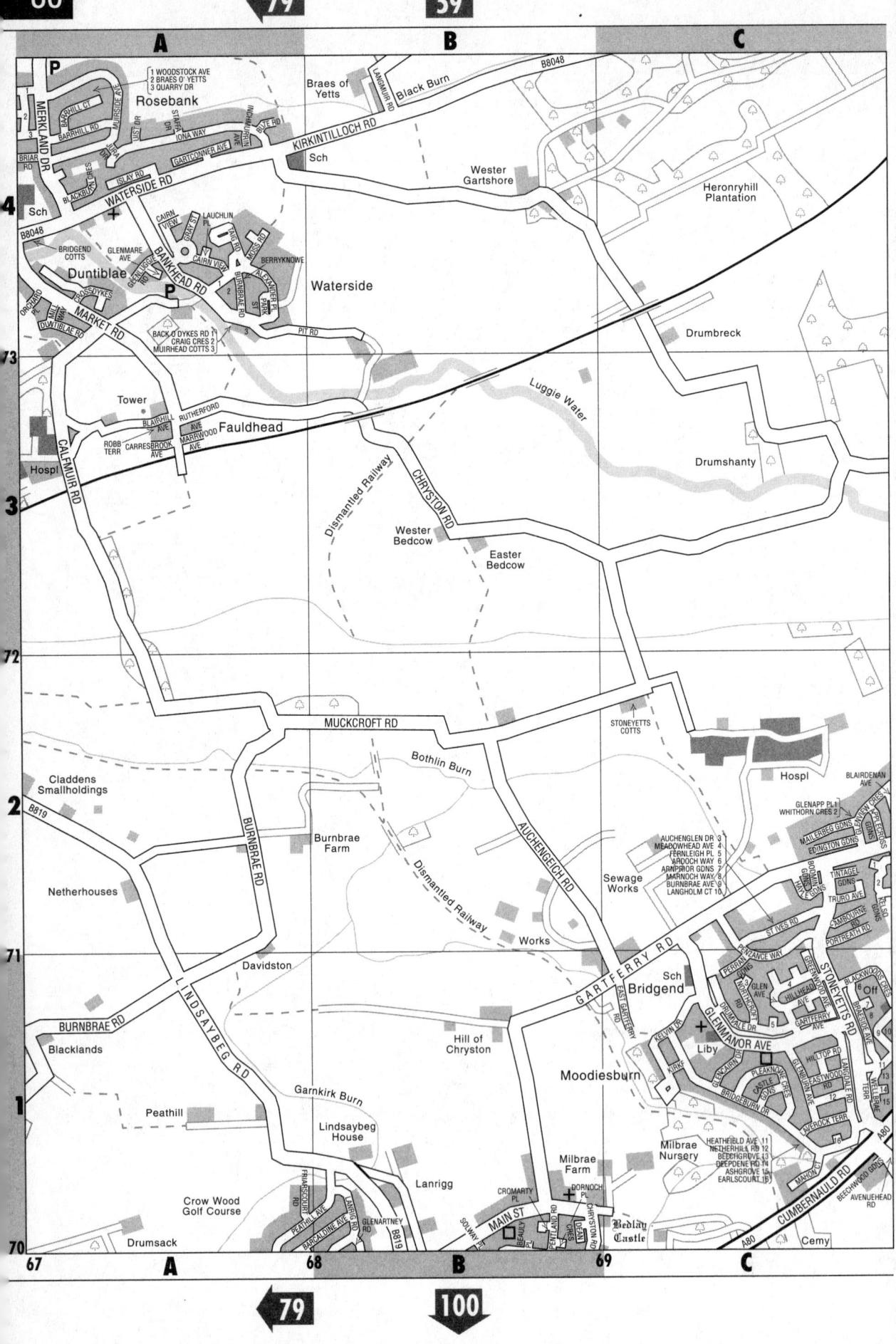

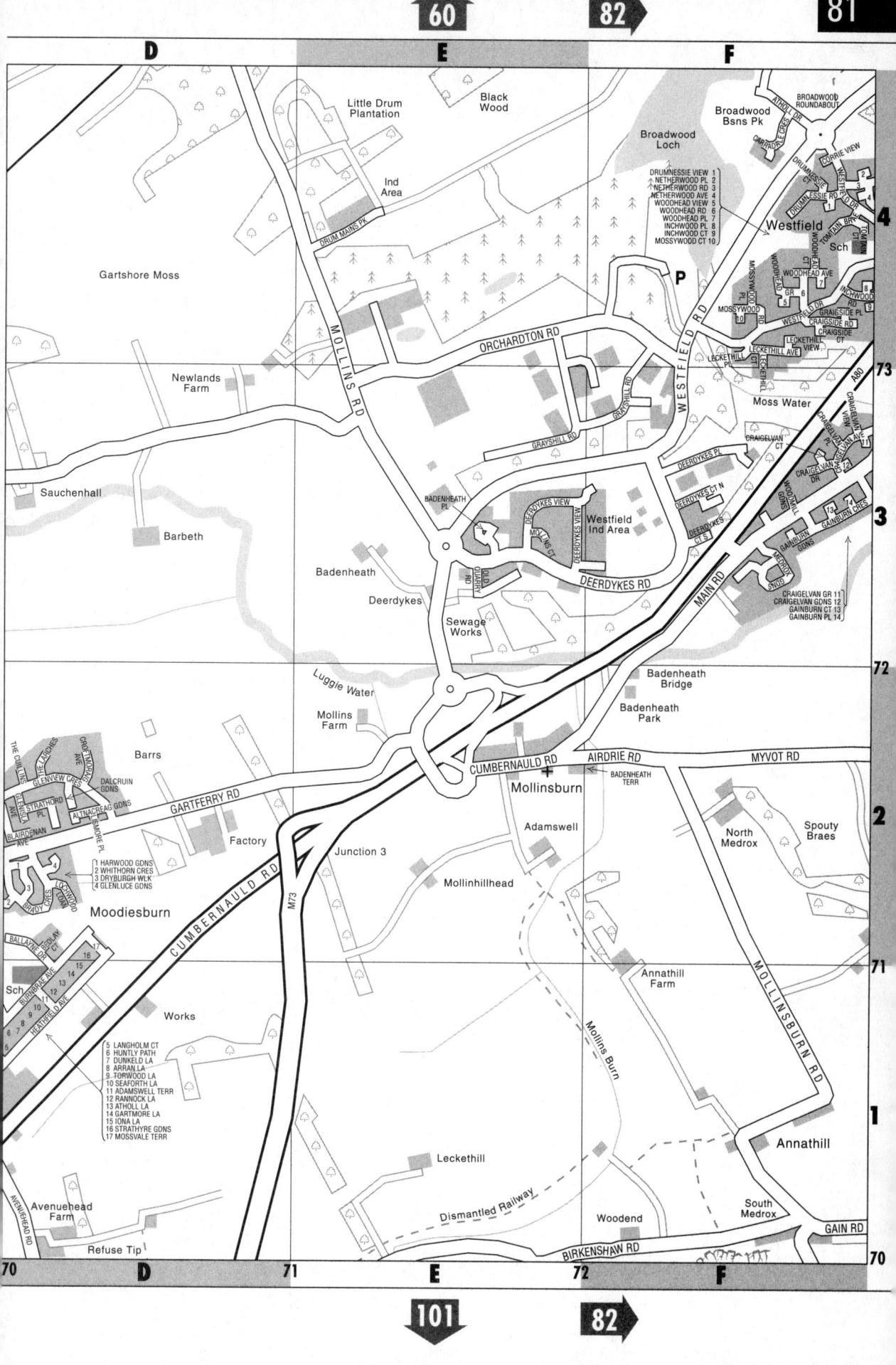

D
E
F

Little Drum
Plantation

Black
Wood

Ind
Area

Broadwood
Loch

Broadwood
Bsns Pk

BROADWOOD
ROUNDABOUT

ATHOLL DR

CORRIE VIEW

DRUMNESSIE VIEW 1
NETHERWOOD PL 2
NETHERWOOD RD 3
NETHERWOOD AVE 4
WOODHEAD VIEW 5
WOODHEAD RD 6
WOODHEAD PL 7
INCHWOOD PL 8
INCHWOOD CT 9
MOSSYWOOD CT 10

DRUM MAINS PK

Gartshore Moss

Westfield
Sch

4

MOLLINS RD

ORCHARDTON RD

P

WOODHEAD AVE

MOSSYWOOD

WESTFIELD RD

INCHWOOD RD

CRAIGSIDE RD
CRAIGSIDE CT

WESTFIELD DR

GRAYSHILL RD

LECKETHILL AVE

A80

73

Newlands
Farm

CRAIGSIDE
VIEW

LECKETHILL
PL

Moss Water

GRAYSHILL RD

CRAIGELVAN
CT

CRAIGELVAN
VIEW

Sauchenhall

BADENHEATH
PL

DEERDYKES PL

CRAIGELVAN
PL

Barbeth

DEERDYKES VIEW

DEERDYKES CT N

CRAIGELVAN
DR

3

MOLLINS CT

Westfield
Ind Area

DEERDYKES
CT S

GAINBURN CRES

GAINBURN
GDNS

Badenheath

DEERDYKES VIEW

WOODHILL GDNS

MEDROX GDNS

Deerdykes

DEERDYKES RD

OLD
QUARRY
RD

Sewage
Works

MAIN RD

CRAIGELVAN GR 11
CRAIGELVAN GDNS 12
GAINBURN CT 13
GAINBURN PL 14

Luggie Water

Badenheath
Bridge

72

Badenheath
Park

Mollins
Farm

CUMBERNAULD RD

AIRDRIE RD

MYVOT RD

THE LARCHES

GLENVIEW CRES

Barrs

BADENHEATH
TERR

The Latches

DALCRUIN
GDNS

STRATHORD
PL

ALTNACREAG GDNS

ELMSMORE PL

North
Medrox

Spouty
Braes

2

STRATHORD
AVE

BLAIRDENAN
AVE

GARTFERRY RD

Mollinsburn

Adamswell

MOLLINSBURN RD

Factory

1 HARWOOD GDNS
2 WHITHORN CRES
3 DRYBURGH WLK
4 GLENLUCE GDNS

Junction 3

Mollinhillhead

BRADY CRES

LOCHWOOD PL

Moodiesburn

M73

CUMBERNAULD RD

Annathill
Farm

71

BALLAIRD PL

16

HEATHERBANK AVE

BURNBRAE AVE

15

Sch

14

13

12

11

Works

10

9

8

5 LANGHOLM CT
6 HUNTLY PATH
7 DUNKELD LA
8 ARRAN LA
9 FORWOOD LA
10 SEAFORTH LA
11 ADAMSWELL TERR
12 RANNOCK LA
13 ATHOLL LA
14 GARTMORE LA
15 IONA LA
16 STRATHYRE GDNS
17 MOSSVALE TERR

Mollins Burn

Annathill

1

Leckethill

Avenuehead
Farm

AVENUEHEAD RD

South
Medrox

Dismantled Railway

Woodend

GAIN RD

Refuse Tip

BIRKENSHAW RD

70

D
71
E
72
F
70

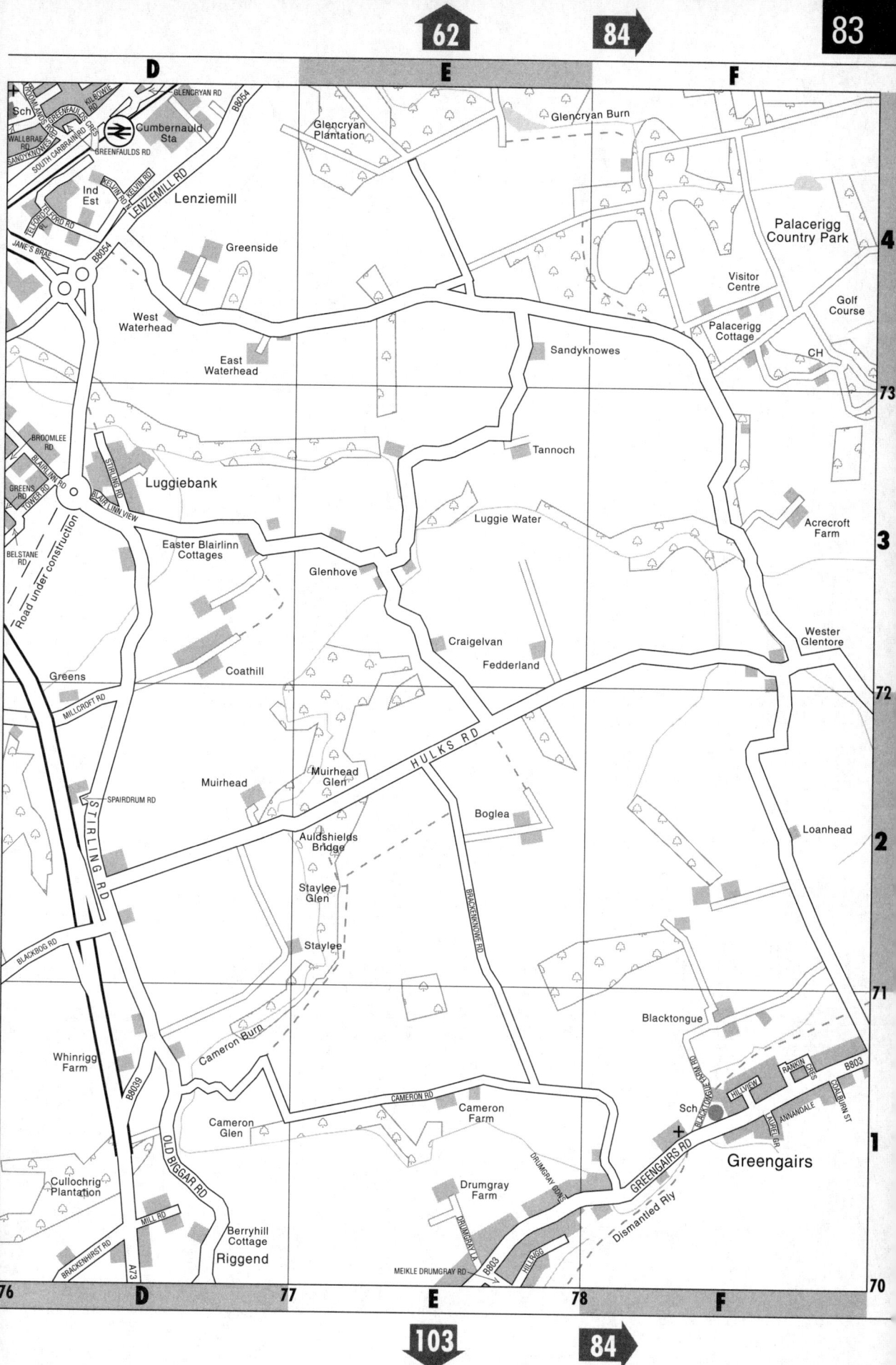

D · E · F

4

73

3

72

2

71

1

70

76 · D · 77 · E · 78 · F

Sch
Cumbernauld Sta
Glencryan Rd
B8054
Ind Est
Lenziemill
Greenfaulds Rd
Jane's Brae
B8054
Greenside
West Waterhead
East Waterhead
Broomlee Rd
Blairlinn Rd
Greens Rd
Tower Rd
Stirling Rd
Luggiebank
Blairlinn View
Belstane Rd
Road under construction
Easter Blairlinn Cottages
Glenhove
Greens
Millcroft Rd
Coathill
Stirling Rd
Spairdrum Rd
Muirhead
Muirhead Glen
Auldshields Bridge
Staylee Glen
Staylee
Blackbog Rd
Whinrigg Farm
B8039
Cameron Burn
Cullochrig Plantation
Old Biggar Rd
Mill Rd
Brackenhirst Rd
A73
Berryhill Cottage
Riggend
Cameron Glen
Cameron Rd
Cameron Farm
Drumgray Farm
Drumgray Burn
Meikle Drumgray Rd
B803
Hillrigg
Dismantled Rly
Greengairs Rd
Blacktongue
Blacktongue Rd
Sch
Greengairs
Hillview
Rankin Cres
Angel Gr
Annandale
Coalburn St
B803
Glencryan Plantation
Glencryan Burn
Sandyknowes
Palacerigg Country Park
Visitor Centre
Palacerigg Cottage
Golf Course
CH
Tannoch
Luggie Water
Acrecroft Farm
Craigelvan
Fedderland
Wester Glentore
Hulks Rd
Brackenknowe Rd
Boglea
Loanhead

A B C

4

Palacerigg Country Park

Golf Course

Fannyside Lochs

Fannyside Lodge

Fannyside Mill

Jawhills

River Avon

Thieves Hill

73

Herd's Hill

West Fannyside

Toddle Knowe

Scar Hill

Bog Bridge

3

Luggie Water

Avon Water

Black Hill

Blackhill

72

Torbrex

Bogside

Netherton of Glentore

Easter Glentore

B803

2

Dismantled Railway

Shielhill Burn

Langdales

Dismantled Railway

GREENGAIRS RD

HM Remand Inst

LUDGE HILL AVE

MERVING LONE

AVON AVE

DRI

SCAMADALE RD

Upperton Farm

Easter Glentore

71

Dismantled Railway

THE CRESCENT

Dismantled Railway

Meadowfield

B803

PH

1

Avalon

Greendykeside

BRIDGE ST

Dismtd Rlwy

70

A B C

River Avon

Wester
Jaw

Redbrae

Northend Bar
(PH)

BALMULZIER RD

Loanrigg

4

Balmulzier

MANSE PL

MOSSCASTLE RD

F
Sta

NEW ST

PH

Hillhead

Sch

HIGH ST

AVONBRIDGE RD

73

Blinkbonnie

BANK ST

Peatrigend

Crossburn

BALQUHATSTONE
GOWANLEA DR

B803

Blinkbonnie
Terr

SOUTHFIELD DR

B8022

Balquhatstone
House

Wester
Crosshill

B8022

THE RUMLIE

WELL RD

OLD HILL TOP

STATION RD

Wester
Arnloss

Crosshill

3

Culloch Burn

Slamannan

Dismantled Railway

Balcastle
House

Binniehill
Farm

Balquhatstone
Mains

North
Arnloss

Binniehill

BINNIEHILL RD

STATION ROW

72

South
Arnloss

Salterhill

2

B825

CAMERON TERR

Easter
Drumclair

THOMPSON PL

The Pine Marten
(PH)

Loch
House

Low
Limerigg

SLAMANNAN RD

71

Limerigg

Little Black
Loch

High
Limerigg

B8022

Barnsmuir

1

LOCHSIDE RD

Sch

Blackloch

Holehousemuir

Stoneridge

B825

CALDERCRUIX RD

Black
Loch

70

85 A 86 B 87 C

D E F

Boxton

Boagstown

North
Bankhead

Balmitchell

Hareburn

4

Windy-yett

Avonview

Avonbridge

Manse

B8028

Dismantled Railway

Whinny
Knowes

South
Bankhead

73

River Avon

Bogo

Neucks

THE NEUCKS

SLAMANNAN RD

AVON PL

B8025

3

Summerhouse

Sch

B8022

Babbithill

Craigend

Crossroads

Bulliondale

72

Dykehead

Holehouse

Redhall

North East
Holehouse

Wester
Holehouse

Lin Mill Burn

Elrigside
Wood

2

Linhouse
Farm

South
Holehouse

Easter
Greenhill

East
Plantation

Wester
Greenhill

71

Drumtassie Burn

Barns

Westfield

North Rhodens
Plantation

1

70

D 89 E 90 F

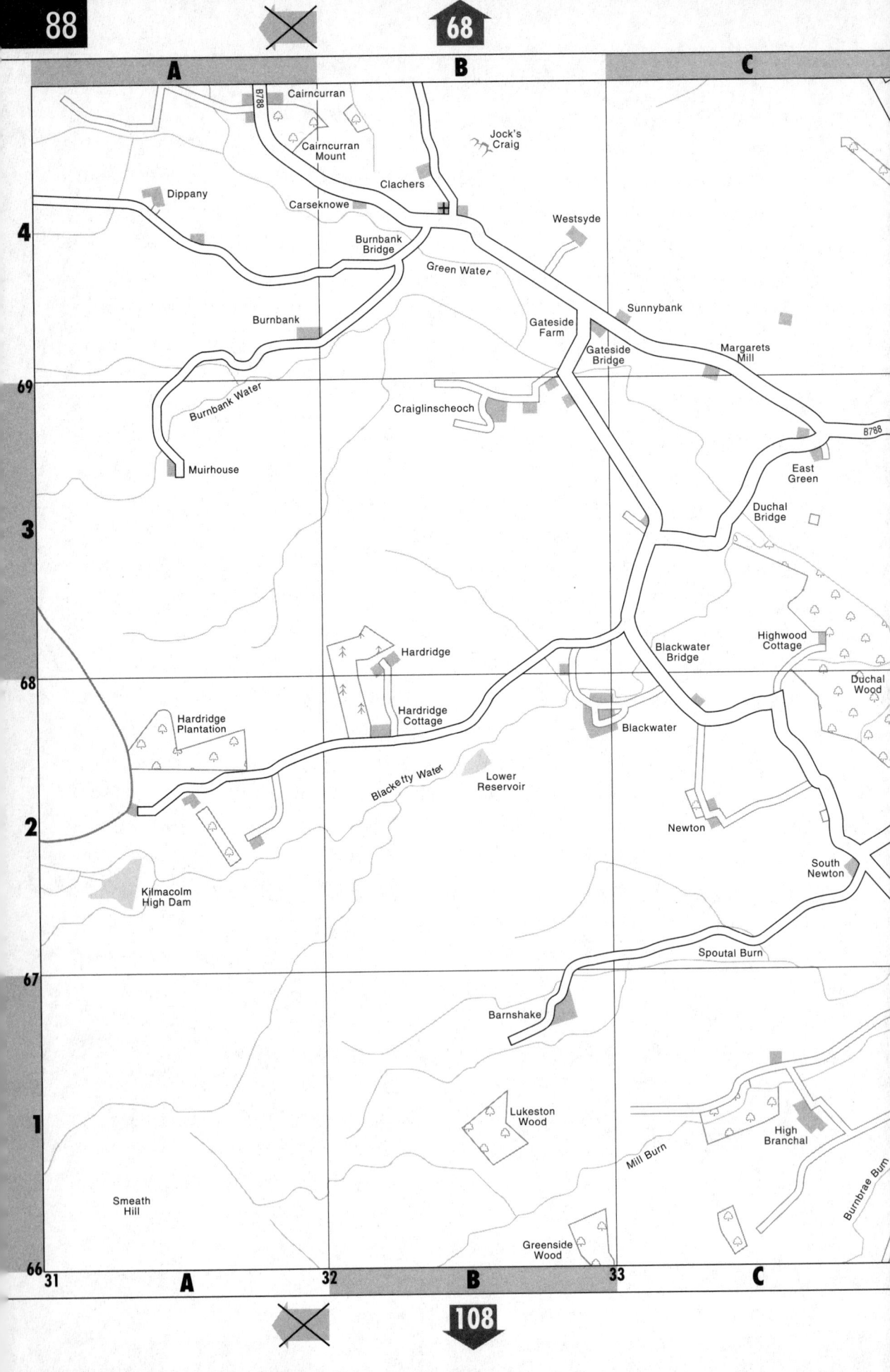

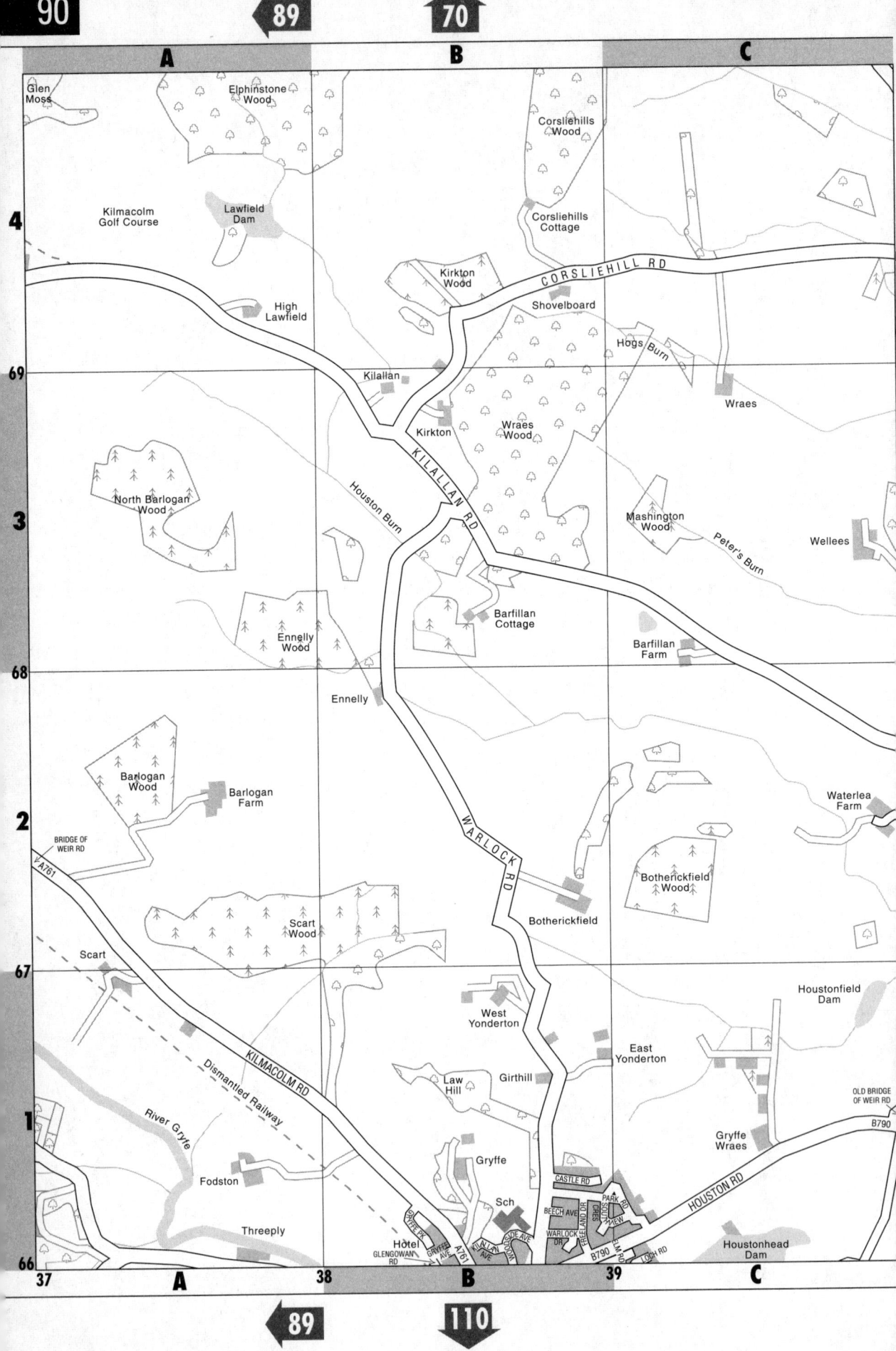

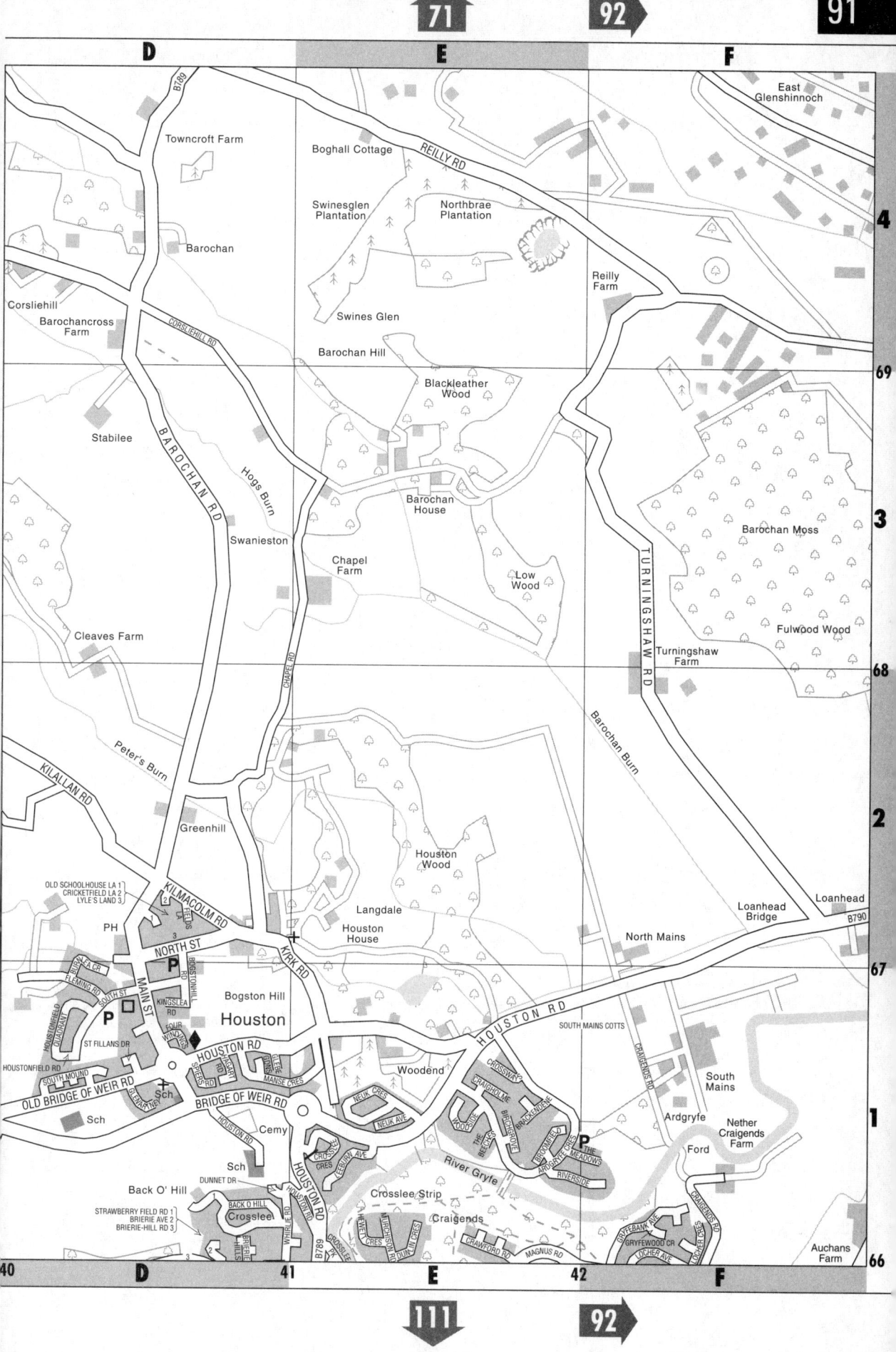

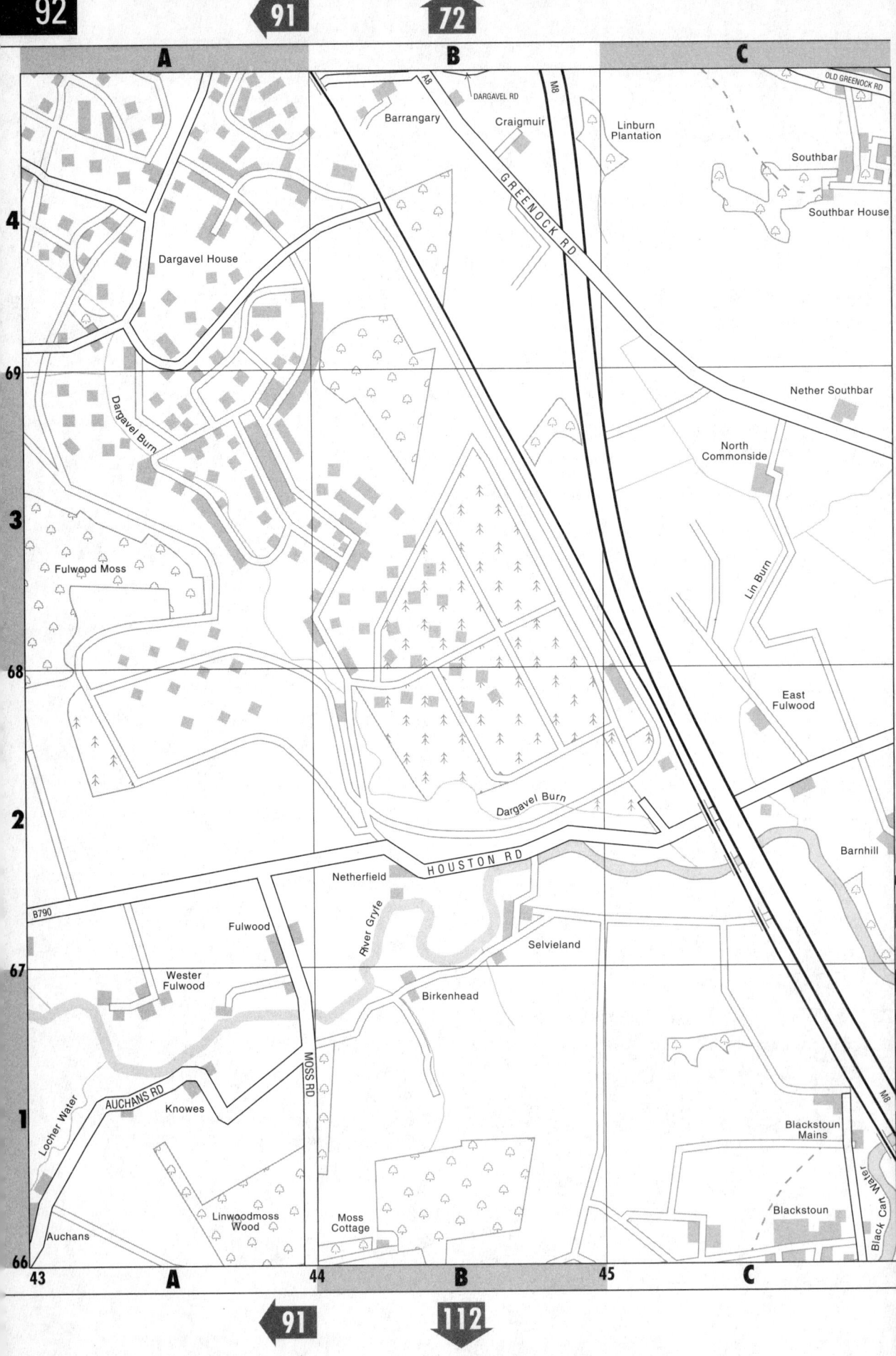

A **B** **C**

OLD GREENOCK RD

DARGAVEL RD

Barrangary

Craigmuir

Linburn
Plantation

Southbar

Southbar House

4

Dargavel House

GREENOCK RD

A8

M8

69

Nether Southbar

Dargavel Burn

North
Commonside

3

Fulwood Moss

Lin Burn

68

East
Fulwood

Dargavel Burn

2

Barnhill

HOUSTON RD

Netherfield

B790

Fulwood

River Gryfe

Selvieland

67

Wester
Fulwood

Birkenhead

MOSS RD

AUCHANS RD

Locher Water

Knowes

1

Blackstoun
Mains

Black Cart Water

M8

Auchans

Linwoodmoss
Wood

Moss
Cottage

Blackstoun

66

43 **A** **44** **B** **45** **C**

D
E
F

1 MILLFIELD WYND
2 MILLFIELD WLK
3 MILLFIELD DR

OLD GREENOCK RD
A726

1 HAWTHORN WAY
2 HAWTHORN RD

PARK RIDGE
PARK BRAE
Sch
Sch
PARK GN
PARK GATE
PARK GATE
MAINS
Park Mains
GARNIE LA
GARNIE AVE
HAWTHORN AVE
BROOMLANDS CRES

4

PARKWAY
Freeland
PARKWAY
PARK SAIL
PARK SAIL
PARK SAIL
PARK SAIL
HIGH PARKSAIL
LOW PARKSAIL
PARKVALE WAY
NEWSHOT DR
Northbar House
Sandieland Wood

SOUTHBAR RD
Wheel Burn
TURNHILL DR
TURNHILL CRES
TURNHILL GDNS
BROOMHILL CRES
FREELAND DR
FERN AVE
CRAIGHALL AVE
Cemy
Sch
LUCKINGSFORD DR
LUCKINGSFORD AVE
GREENHEAD RD
FREELAND DR
BIRCHALL
OLD GREENOCK RD
BRAEMAR RD
BALMORAL CRES

69

Inchinnan
Teucheen Wood
Florish

A8
Broom Hill
GREENOCK RD
PH
BEARDMORE COTTS

3

A726
A8
New Mains
FOUNTAIN CRES
INDIA DR
Town of Inchinnan

NEWMAINS AVE
Inchinnan Ind Est
BROWNSFIELD CRES
BROWNSFIELD RD
ALLANDS AVE
Allands Holdings
Nursery
FOUNTAIN DR

68

Works
HOUSTON RD
B790
BARNSFORD AVE
FOUNTAIN AVE
Black Cart Water

TA Centre
Mast
Ind Est
Brownsfield
CARTSIDE AVE
SOUTH RD

Camp (dis)

Easter Yonderton

2

Wester Yonderton

Barnsford Bridge
BARNSFORD RD
Easter Walkinshaw
WALKINSHAW RD

67

Glasgow Airport

Blackstone Mains
F Sta
Works

ARRAN AVE
ABBOTSINCH RD
White Cart Water
Mill
WRIGHT ST

1

CAMPSIE DR
Douglas Terr
Dismtd Rly

M8
A726
Wester Walkinshaw Farm
CALEDONIA WAY W
BUTE RD
ST ANDREW'S CRES
P
CALEDONIA WAY
Hotel
P
P
P
P
NEVIS WAY
ARGYLL AVE
ST ANDREW'S DR
CALEDONIA WAY E
Sewage Wks
CLYDESDALE AVE 1
SOMERLED AVE 2

46
D
47
E
48
F
66

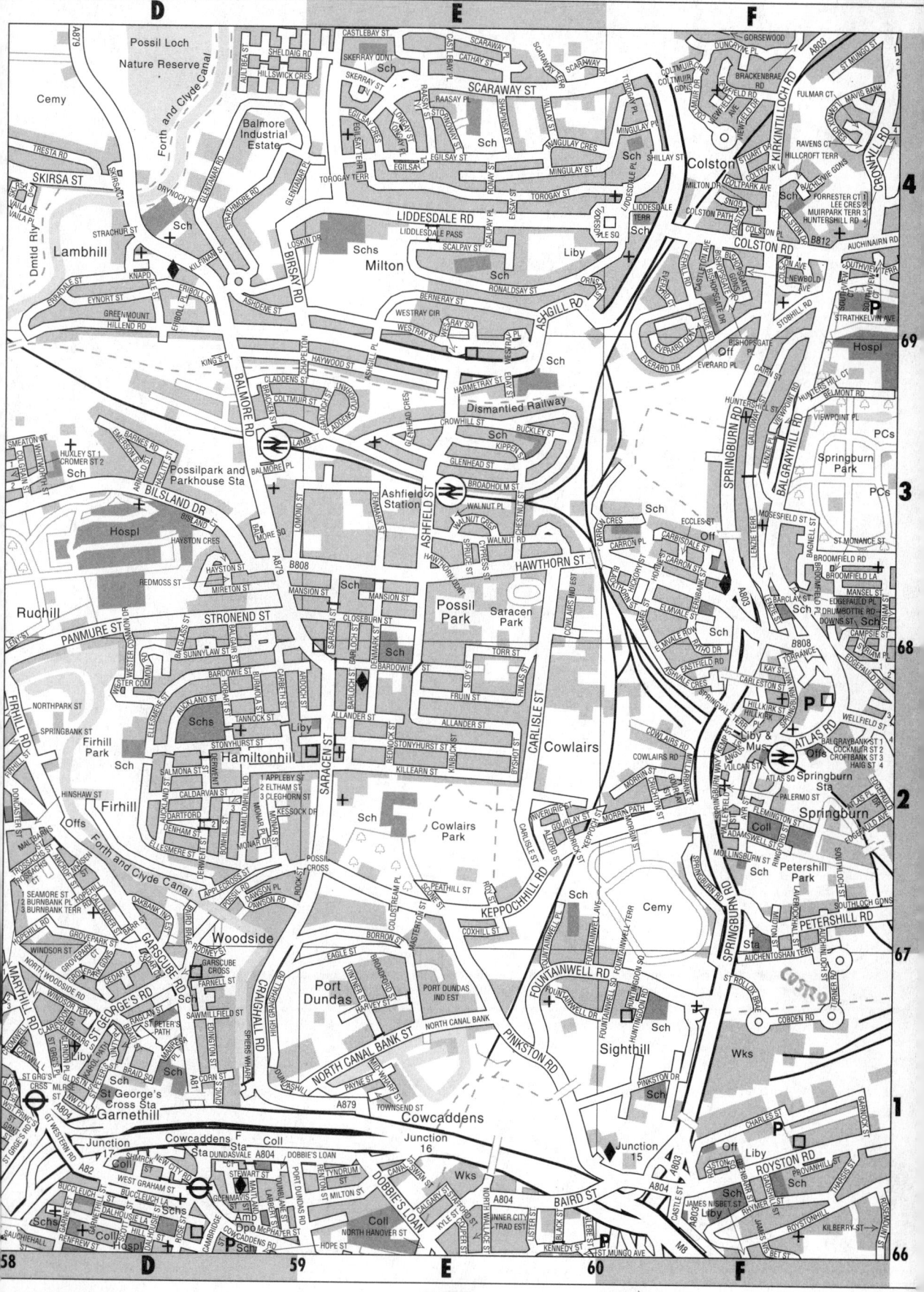

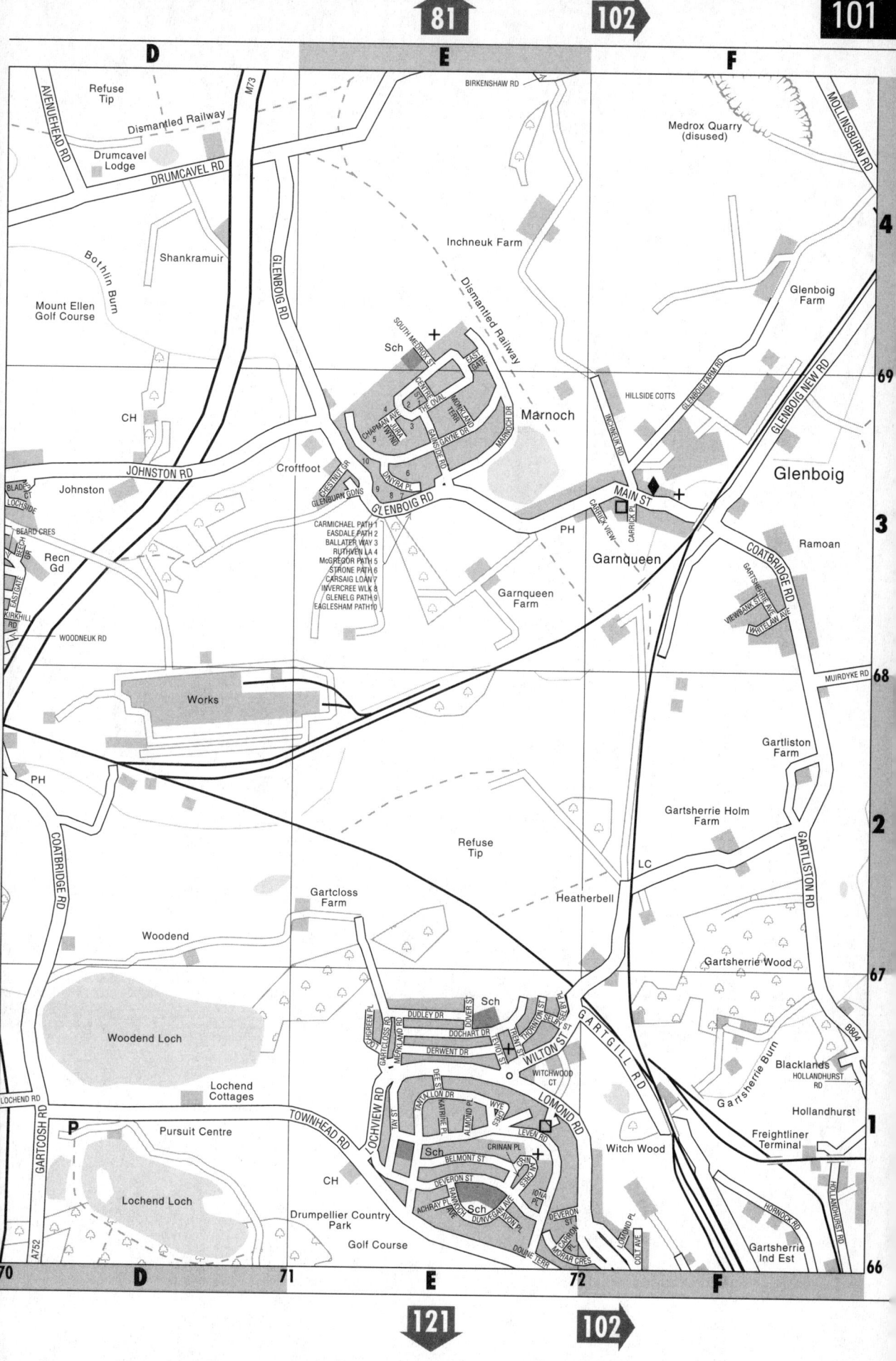

D
E
F

Refuse Tip

MOLLINSBURN RD

Dismantled Railway

Medrox Quarry (disused)

AVENUEHEAD RD

Drumcavel Lodge

DRUMCAVEL RD

M73

GLENBOIG RD

Inchneuk Farm

Glenboig Farm

4

Shankramuir

Bothlin Burn

Mount Ellen Golf Course

Sch

South Medrox St

The Oval

Monkland Terr

Marnoch Dr

Marnoch

Hillside Cotts

GLENBOIG NEW RD

69

CH

JOHNSTON RD

Croftfoot

CHAPMAN AVE
JURA WYND

CENTRE
GAYLE DR

GANSIDE RD

East Gate

Glenboig Farm Rd

Glenboig

CHESTNUT CR
GLENBURN GDNS

10
9 8
7

DINTRA PL

GLENBOIG RD

Carrick View

CARRICK PL

MAIN ST

COATBRIDGE RD

Ramoan

BLADES CT
LOCHSIDE

BEECH GT

Johnston

PH

Garnqueen

GARTSHERRIE AVE
VIEWBANK AVE
WHITELAW AVE

BEARD CRES

Recn Gd

CARMICHAEL PATH 1
EASDALE PATH 2
BALLATER WAY 3
RUTHVEN LA 4
McGREGOR PATH 5
STRONE PATH 6
CARSAIG LOAN 7
INVERCREE WLK 8
GLENELG PATH 9
EAGLESHAM PATH 10

Garnqueen Farm

3

EASTHILL
KIRKHILL RD

WOODNEUK RD

MUIRDYKE RD

68

Works

Gartliston Farm

PH

COATBRIDGE RD

Gartsherrie Holm Farm

2

LC

Refuse Tip

Heatherbell

GARTLISTON RD

Gartcloss Farm

Woodend

Gartsherrie Wood

67

Woodend Loch

Sch

DUDLEY DR
DOVER ST
DOCHART DR
DERWENT DR

GARTCLOSS RD
GLENGREEN RD
MERRYLAND DR

MORTON ST
SELBY ST
ST ALBERT ST
TRENT ST

WILTON ST

GARTGILL RD

B804

Gartsherrie Burn

Blacklands

HOLLANDHURST RD

Lochend Cottages

LOCHEND RD

WITCHWOOD CT

LOMOND RD

Witch Wood

Hollandhurst

P

Pursuit Centre

TOWNHEAD RD

LOCHVIEW RD

TANTALLON DR
DEE ST
AYR ST

MAITRIE ST
ALMOND ST

WYE ST
LEVEN RD

Freightliner Terminal

HORNOCK RD

GARTCOSH RD

CH

Sch

CRINAN PL

BELMONT ST
DEVERON ST
RANNOCH PL

CRINAN ST
IONA ST

DEVERON ST

COLT AVE

HOLLANDHURST RD

A752

Lochend Loch

Drumpellier Country Park

Golf Course

Sch

ACHRAY PL
DUNVEGAN AVE
AVON ST

MOYAR CRES
DOUNE TERR

IONA PL

LOTTONS PL

1

Gartsherrie Ind Est

66

70
D
71
E
72
F

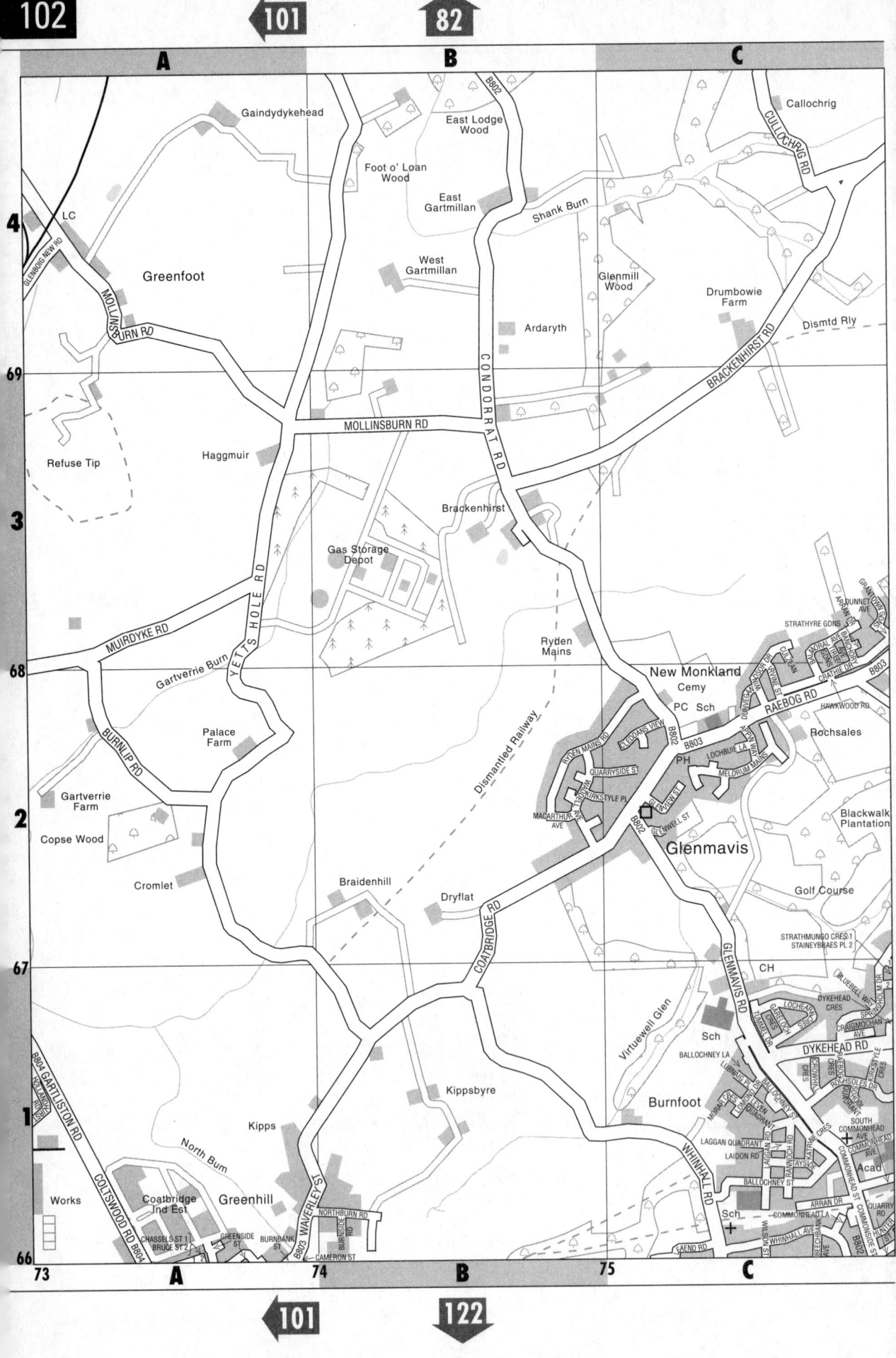

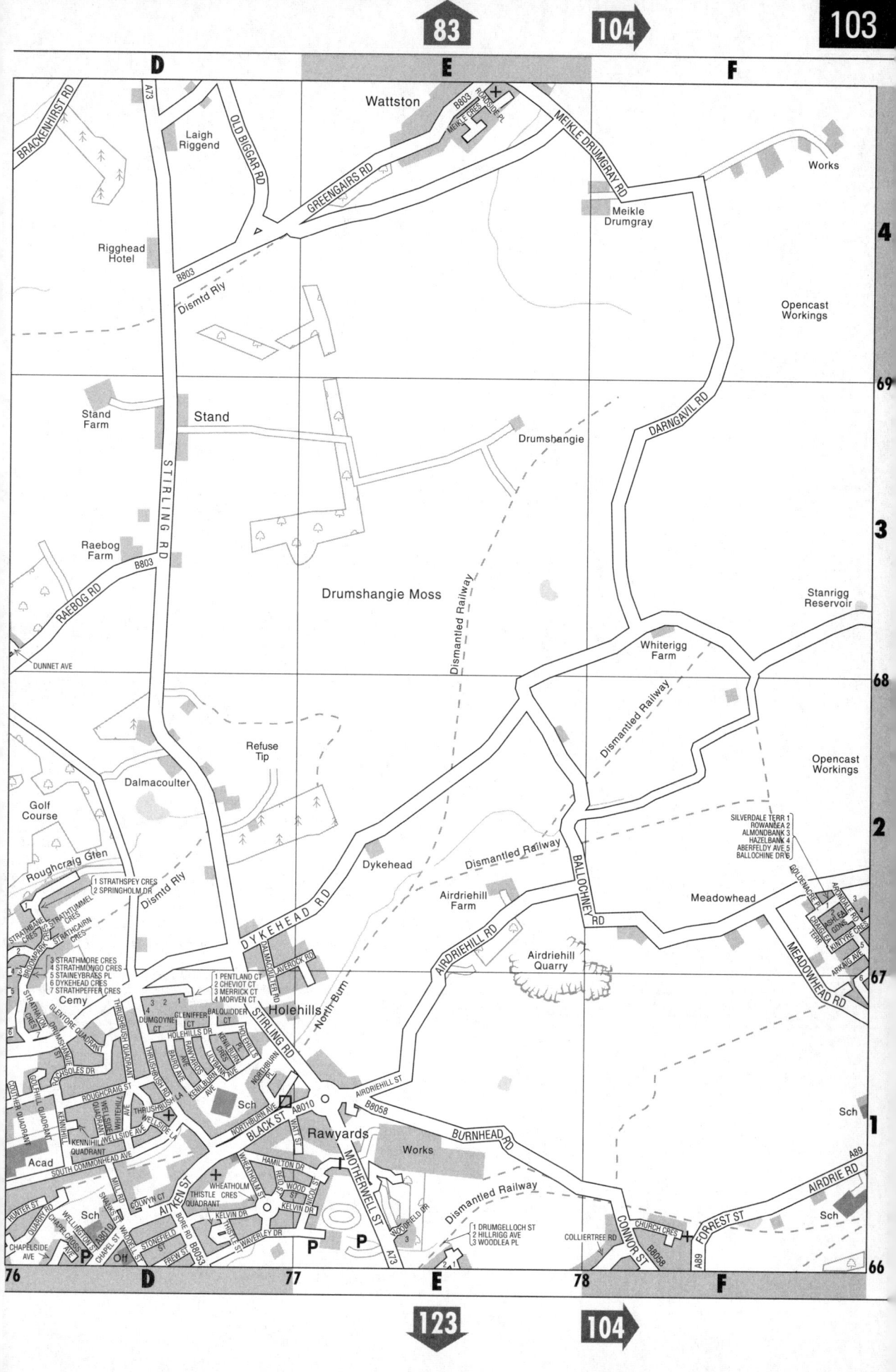

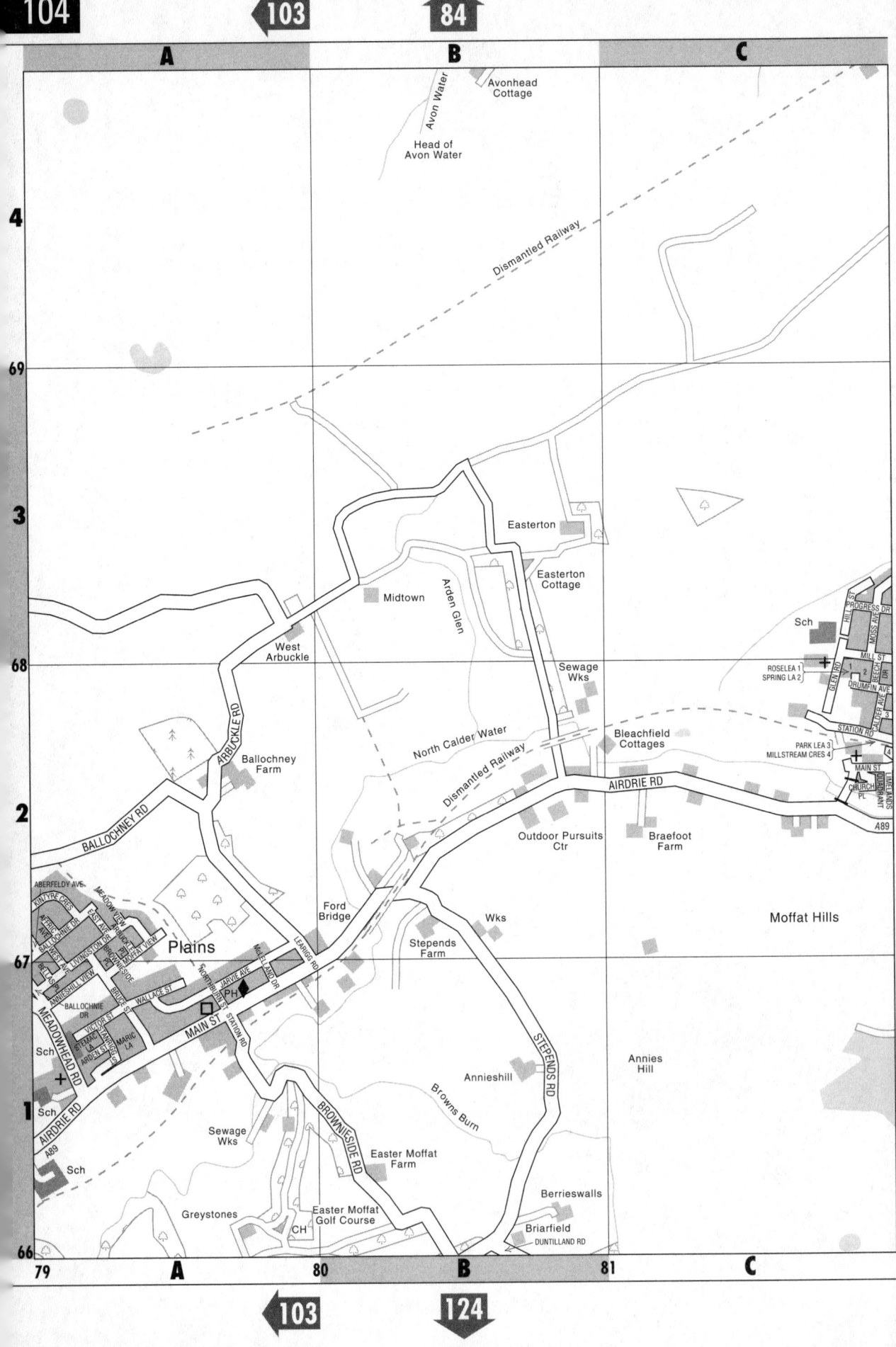

Avon Water

Avonhead
Cottage

Head of
Avon Water

Dismantled Railway

4

69

Easterton

3

Easterton
Cottage

Midtown

Arden Glen

West
Arbuckle

68

Sewage
Wks

Sch

ROSELEA 1
SPRING LA 2

MILL ST

DRUMFIN AVE

GLEN RD

CALDER AVE

BEECH

MISSOURI AVE

PROGRESS DR

HILL

ARBUCKLE RD

Ballochney
Farm

North Calder Water

Bleachfield
Cottages

PARK LEA 3
MILLSTREAM CRES 4

STATION RD

MAIN ST
CHURCH
PL

LIMELANDS
QUADRANT

Dismantled Railway

AIRDRIE RD

A89

2

BALLOCHNEY RD

Outdoor Pursuits
Ctr

Braefoot
Farm

ABERFELDY AVE

MEADOW VIEW

KINTYRE CRES

EAST AVE

MEADOWHEAD DR

LIVINGSTON DR

PARKSIDE

LAUDER VIEW

Plains

Ford
Bridge

Wks

Stepends
Farm

Moffat Hills

67

MCFARLAND DR

LEARIGG RD

NORTHBURN RD

JARVIE AVE

WALLACE ST

PH

ANNIESHILL VIEW

BRUCE ST

BALLOCHNIE
DR

VICTOR ST

STEENAC LA

ARDEN ST

MARIG LA

MAIN ST

STATION RD

Annieshill

STEPENDS RD

Annies
Hill

Sch

Sch

MEADOWHEAD RD

Browns Burn

1

AIRDRIE RD

A89

Sch

Sewage
Wks

BROWNIESIDE RD

Easter Moffat
Farm

Berrieswalls

Greystones

CH

Easter Moffat
Golf Course

Briarfield

DUNTILLAND RD

66

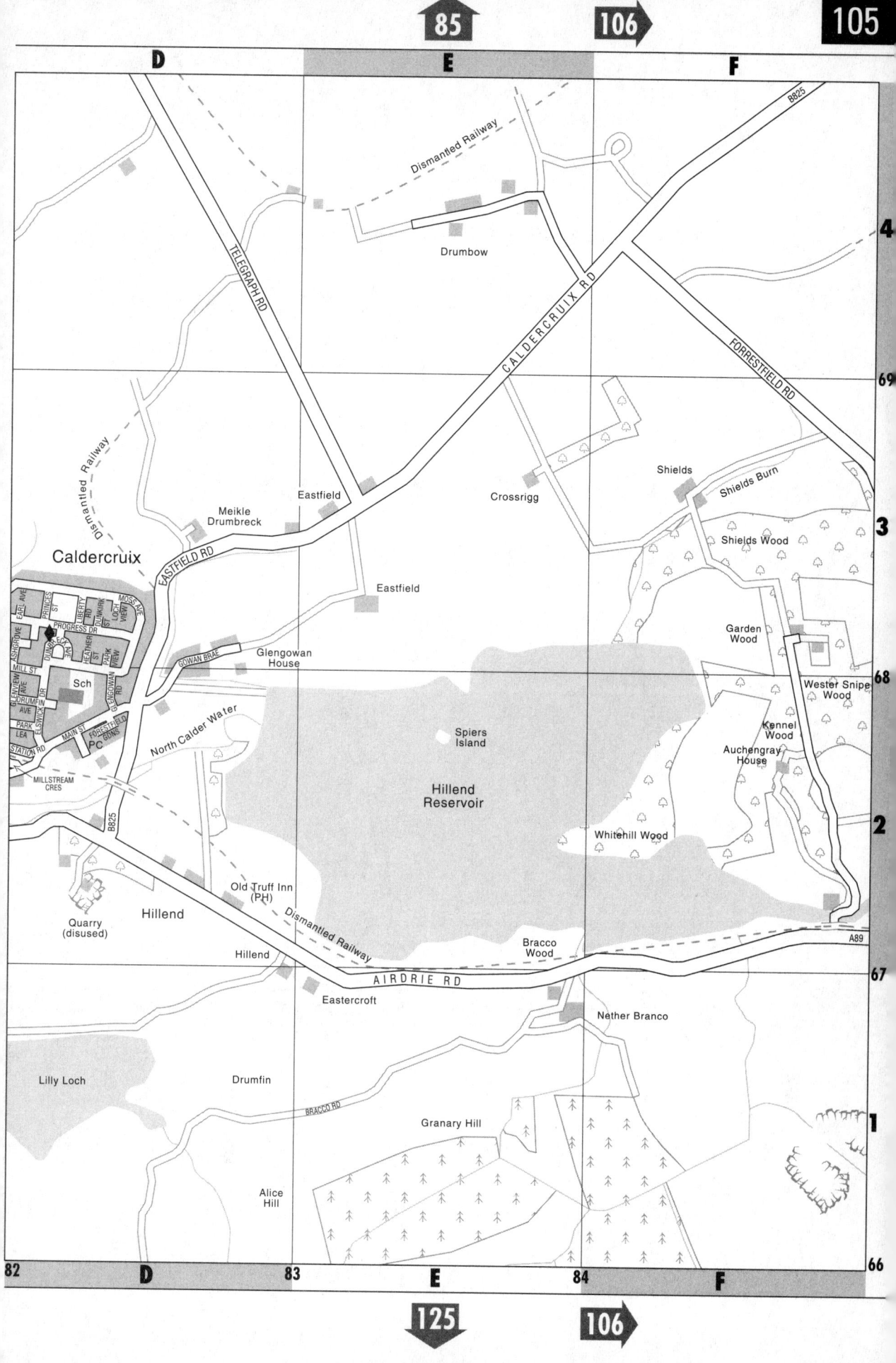

D   E   F

B825

Dismantled Railway

4

Drumbow

CALDERCRUIX RD

FORRESTFIELD RD

69

Dismantled Railway

Shields

Shields Burn

Meikle
Drumbreck

Eastfield

Crossrigg

Shields Wood

3

EASTFIELD RD

Caldercruix

Eastfield

MOSS AVE
EARL AVE
ASHGROVE
PRINCES ST
LIBERTY RD
DUNKIRK
LOCH VIEW
PROGRESS DR
HEATHER RD
PARK VIEW
DRUMBRECK GDNS

Garden
Wood

Wester Snipe
Wood

MILL ST

Sch

GOWAN BRAE

Glengowan
House

68

LOCHVIEW AVE
DRUMFIN AVE
PARK LEA
MAIN ST
STATION RD
FORRESTFIELD GDNS
GLENGOWAN RD

PC

North Calder Water

Spiers
Island

Kennel
Wood

Auchengray
House

MILLSTREAM
CRES

B825

Hillend
Reservoir

Whitehill Wood

2

Old Truff Inn
(PH)

Dismantled Railway

Hillend

Bracco
Wood

A89

Quarry
(disused)

Hillend

AIRDRIE RD

67

Eastercroft

Nether Branco

Lilly Loch

Drumfin

BRACCO RD

Granary Hill

1

Alice
Hill

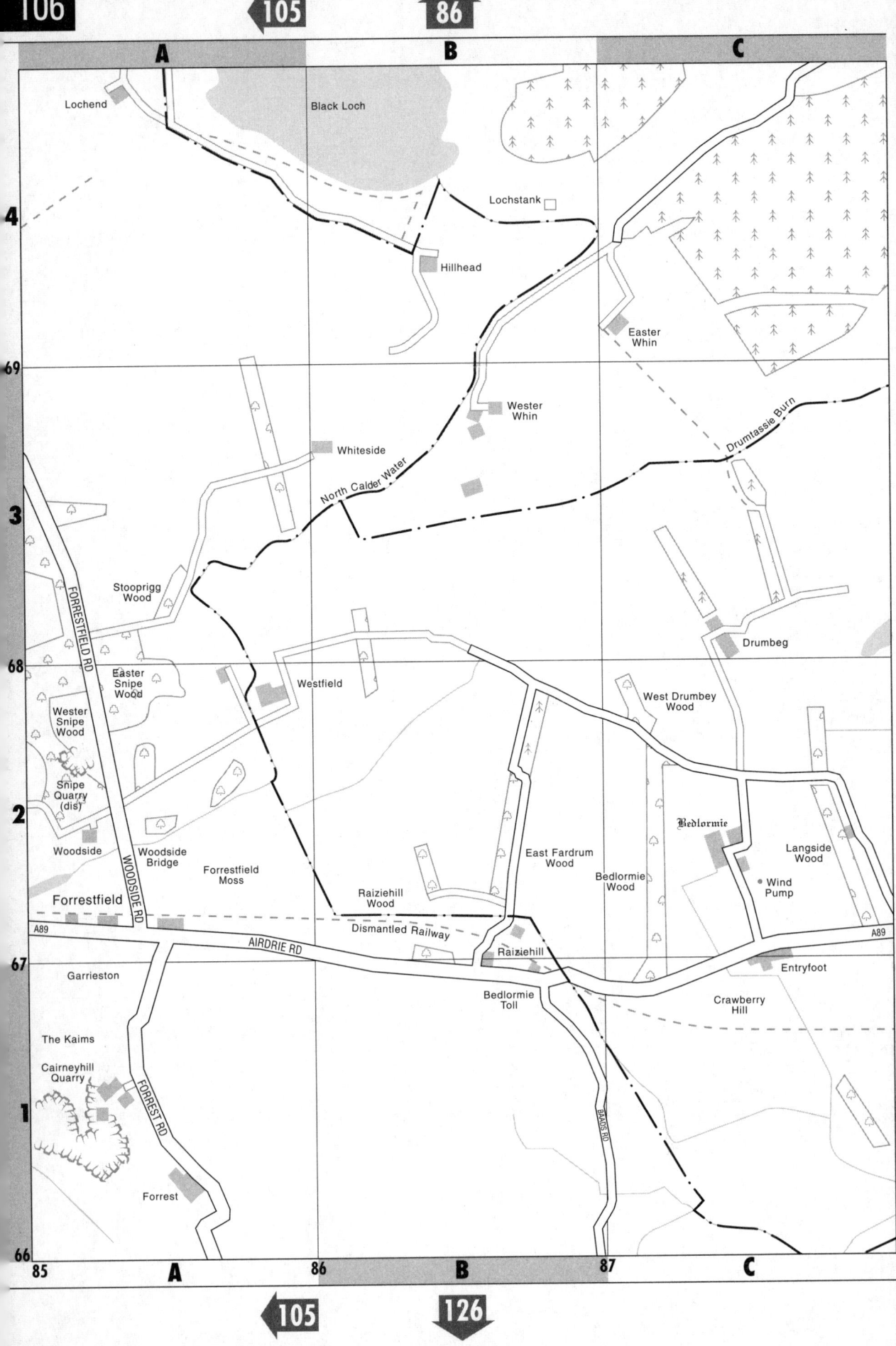

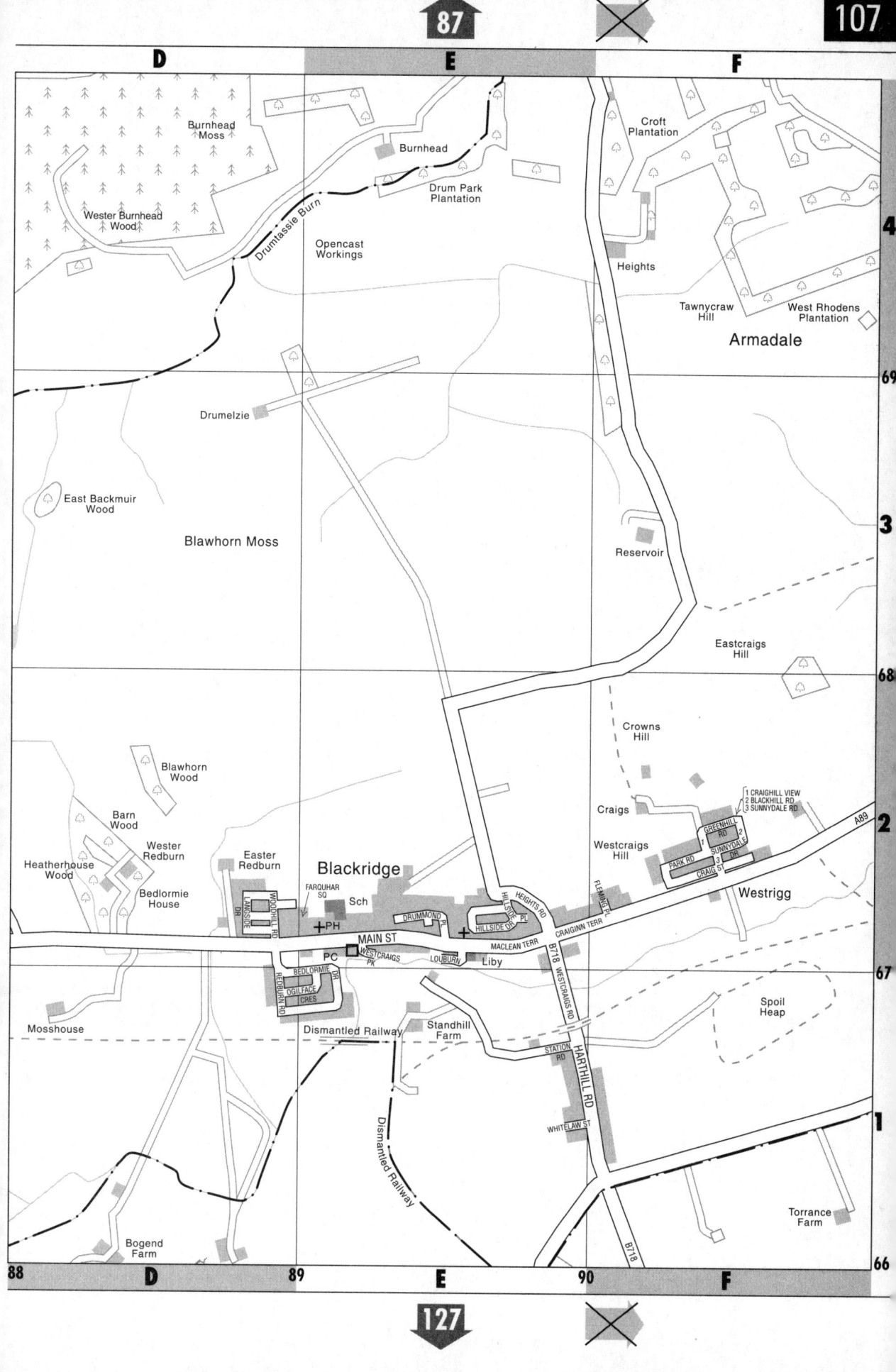

Burnhead Moss

Wester Burnhead Wood

Burnhead

Drum Park Plantation

Drumtassie Burn

Opencast Workings

Croft Plantation

Heights

4

Tawnycraw Hill

West Rhodens Plantation

Armadale

69

Drumelzie

East Backmuir Wood

Blawhorn Moss

Reservoir

3

Eastcraigs Hill

68

Crowns Hill

Blawhorn Wood

Barn Wood

Wester Redburn

Heatherhouse Wood

Bedlormie House

Easter Redburn

Blackridge

FARQUHAR SQ

Sch

LAIRDSIDE DR

WOODHILL RD

DRUMMOND

HILLSIDE DR

HEIGHTS RD

HEIGHTS PL

Craigs

Westcraigs Hill

1 CRAIGHILL VIEW
2 BLACKHILL RD
3 SUNNYDALE RD

GREENHILL RD

SUNNYDALE DR

PARK RD

CRAIG ST

A89

2

Westrigg

Mosshouse

REDBURN RD

BEDLORMIE DR

OGILFACE CRES

PC

WESTCRAIGS PK

PH

MAIN ST

LOUBURN

Liby

MACLEAN TERR

CRAIGINN TERR

FLEMING PL

B718 WESTCRAIGS RD

67

Dismantled Railway

Standhill Farm

Spoil Heap

STATION RD

HARTHILL RD

WHITELAW ST

Dismantled Railway

1

Torrance Farm

B718

Bogend Farm

88

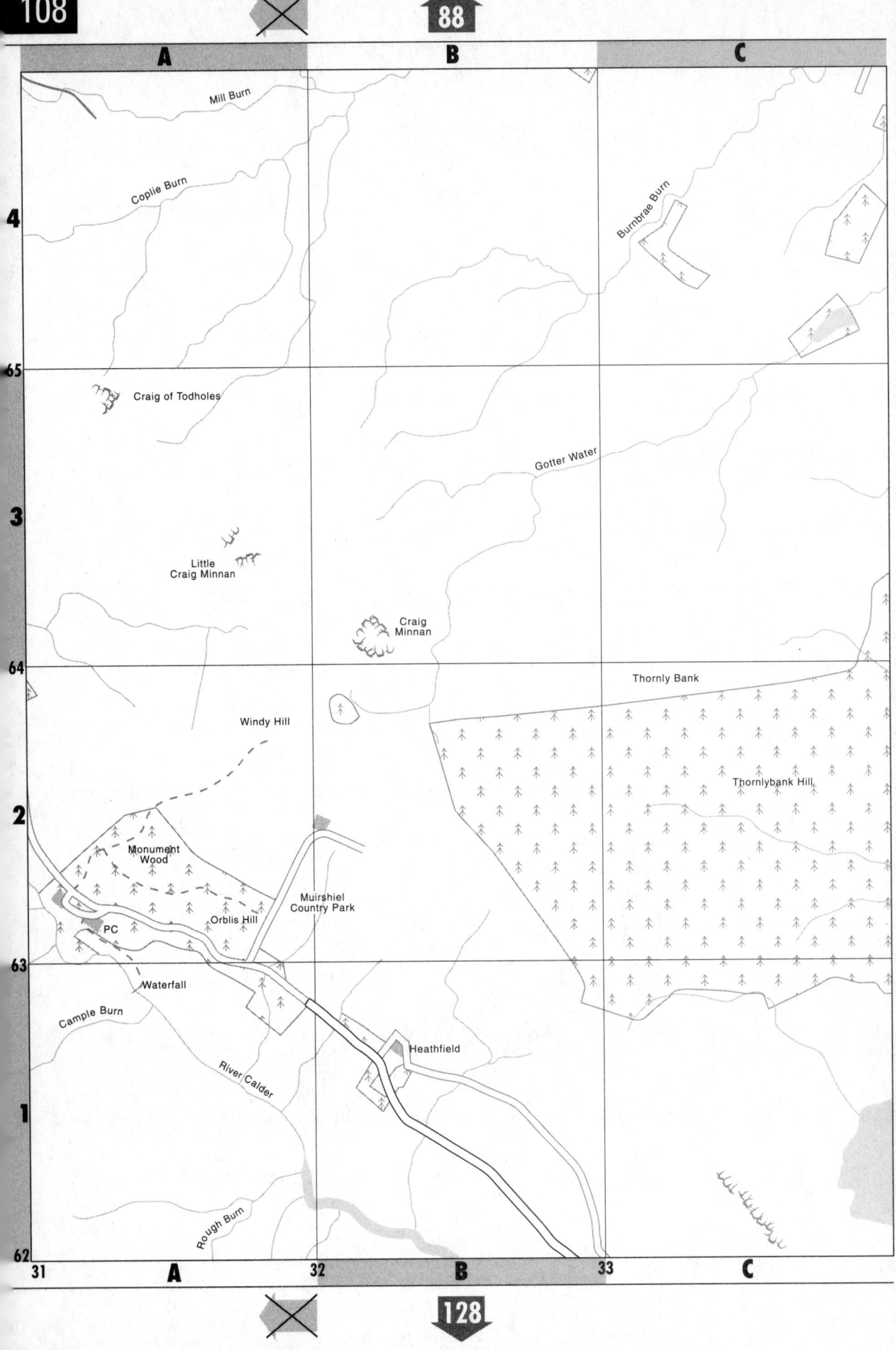

| A | B | C |

4

Mill Burn

Coplie Burn

Burnbrae Burn

65

Craig of Todholes

Gotter Water

3

Little
Craig Minnan

Craig
Minnan

64

Thornly Bank

Windy Hill

Thornlybank Hill

2

Monument
Wood

Muirshiel
Country Park

Orblis Hill

PC

63

Waterfall

Cample Burn

River Calder

Heathfield

1

Rough Burn

62

| 31 | A | 32 | B | 33 | C |

128

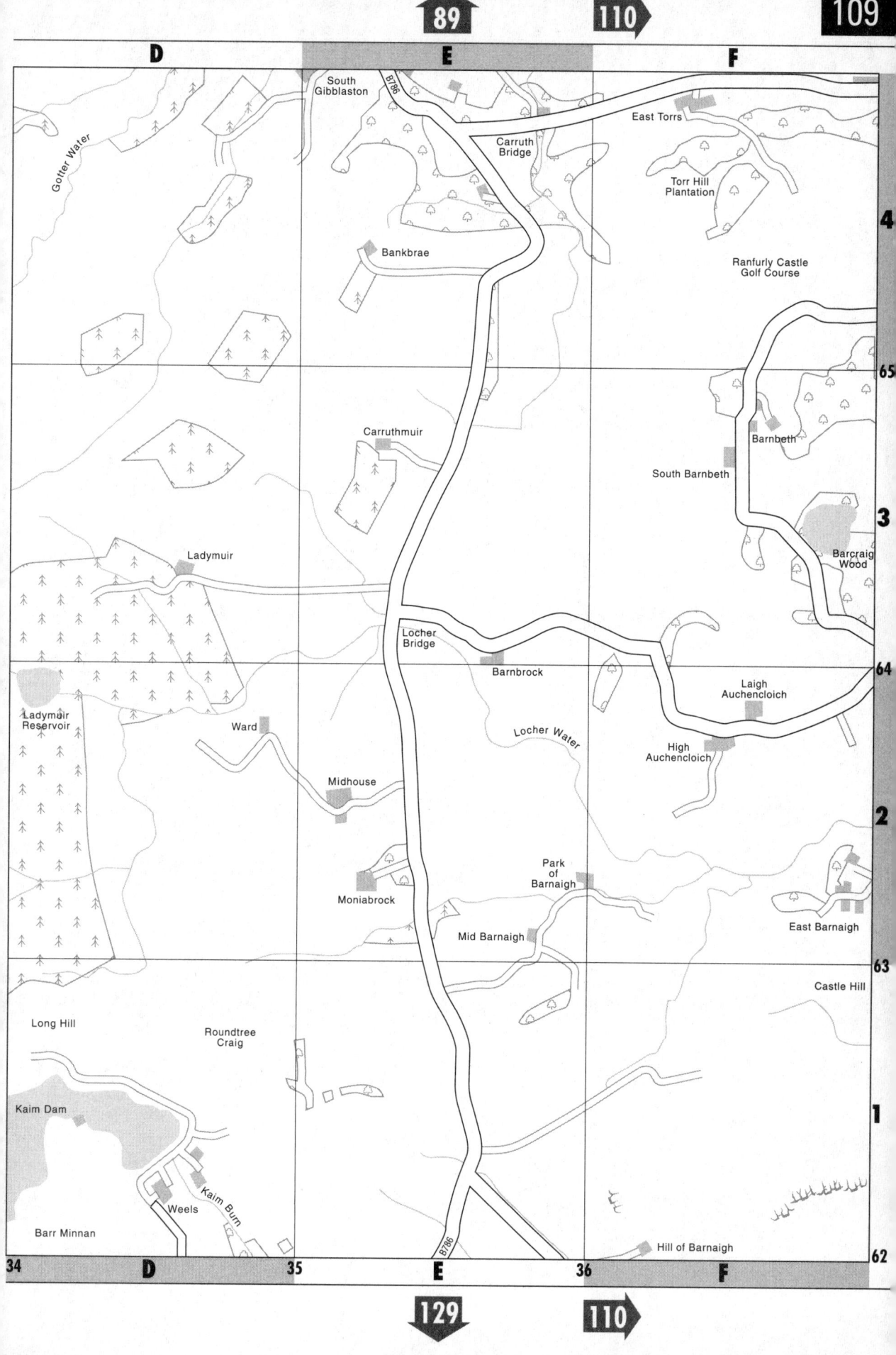

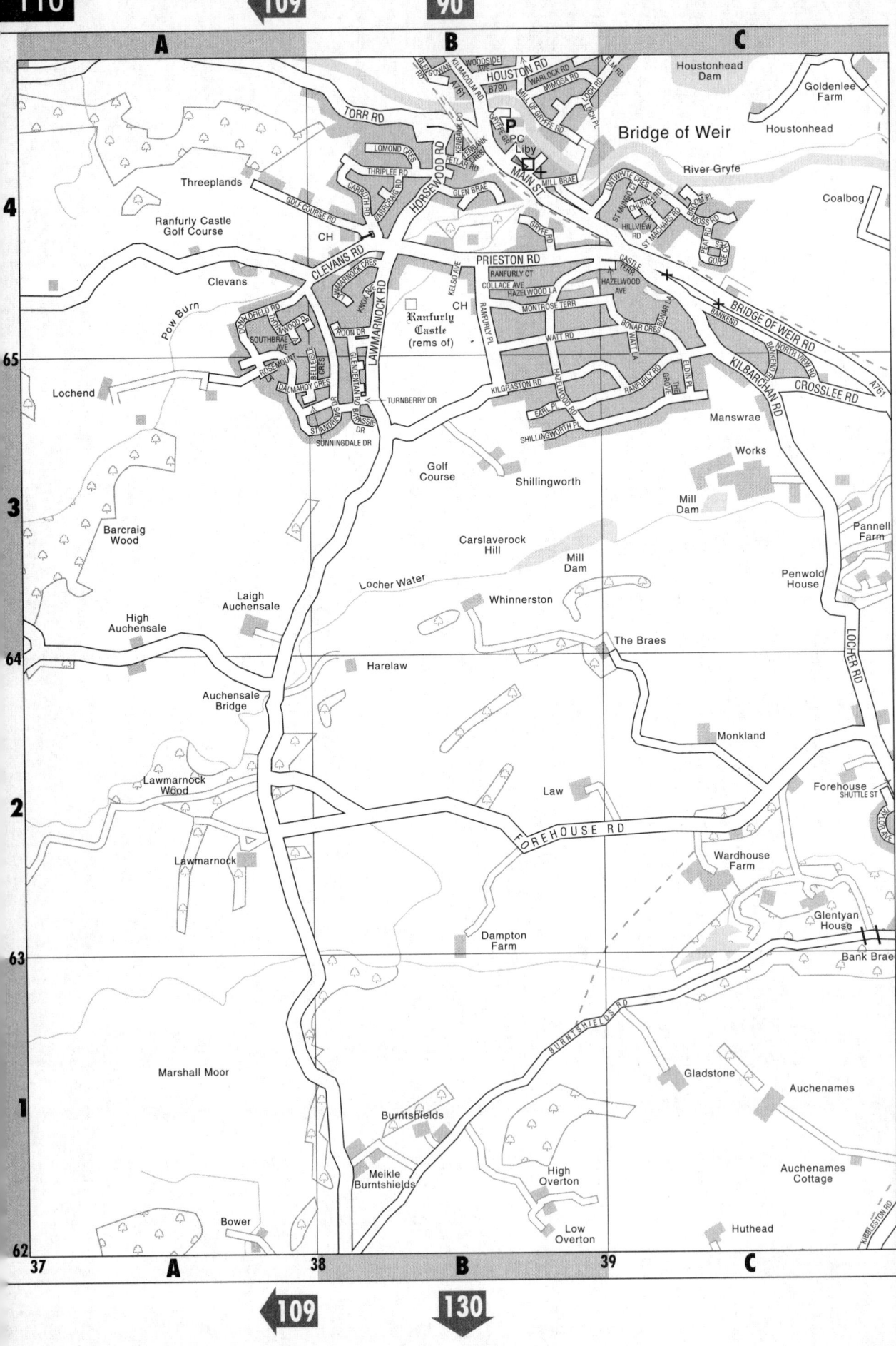

A B C

4

Threeplands

Ranfurly Castle
Golf Course

Clevans

TORR RD

HOUSTON RD

WOODSIDE

GLEN GONAR
KILMACOLM RD
A761
B790
WARLOCK RD
MIMOSA RD
LOCH RD
ELM RD

Houstonhead
Dam

Goldenlee
Farm

Houstonhead

Bridge of Weir

River Gryfe

Coalbog

HORSEWOOD RD

LOMOND CRES
THRIPLEE RD
CABERH RD
HARPCRAIG RD
GOLF COURSE RD

CH

Clevans

CLEVANS RD

GLEN BRAE

P
PC
Liby

MAIN ST

MILL BRAE

GRYFE RD

ST MACHARS RD
LINTWHYTE CRES
CHURCH
HILLVIEW
RD
ST MACHARS RD
BROOM PL
MOSS RD
PEAT RD
GOR
SKEL

PRIESTON RD

Ranfurly Castle
(rems of)

CH

KELSO PL

RANFURLY PL

RANFURLY CT
COLLACE AVE
HAZELWOOD LA
HAZELWOOD
AVE
MONTROSE TERR

CASTLE
TERR
HAZELWOOD
AVE

BONAR CRES

WATT RD

WATT LA

BANKEND

BRIDGE OF WEIR RD

A761

LAWMARNOCK RD

KNOX RD
MARNOCK CRES
MOON DR

SOUTHBRAE
AVE

ROSEMOUNT
LA
DALMAHOY CRES

DOWNFIELD RD
THORNWOOD LA
BELLESLEYE DR
STANDALANE RD
GLENPATRICK RD
BRASSIE
DR

SUNNINGDALE DR

Lochend

65

Turnberry Dr

KILGRASTON RD

HAZELWOOD RD

EARL PL

ELDON PL

SHILLINGWORTH PL

RANFURLY RD
THE GROVE

NORTH VIEW RD
BANKEND RD

KILBARCHAN RD

CROSSLEE RD

A761

Manswrae

Works

Golf
Course

Shillingworth

Mill
Dam

Pannell
Farm

3

Barcraig
Wood

Carslaverock
Hill

Locher Water

Whinnerston

Mill
Dam

Penwold
House

Laigh
Auchensale

The Braes

LOCHER RD

64

High
Auchensale

Harelaw

Monkland

Forehouse
SHUTTLE ST

Auchensale
Bridge

Law

Wardhouse
Farm

PALDEROG

Glentyan
House

2

Lawmarnock
Wood

FOREHOUSE RD

Bank Brae

Lawmarnock

Dampton
Farm

BURNTSHIELDS RD

Gladstone

Auchenames

63

Marshall Moor

Burntshields

High
Overton

Auchenames
Cottage

1

Meikle
Burntshields

Huthead

KIBBLESTON RD

Bower

Low
Overton

62

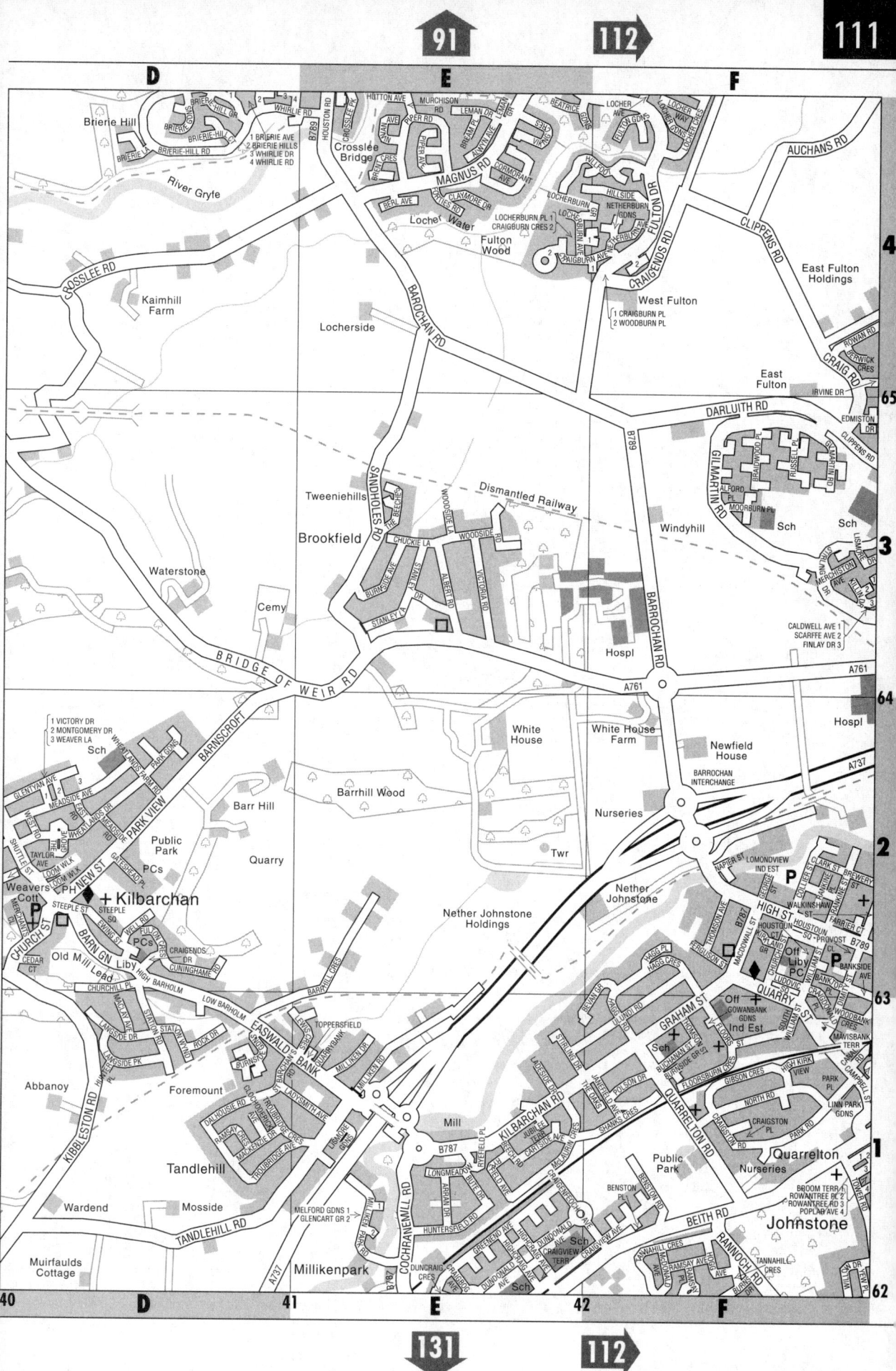

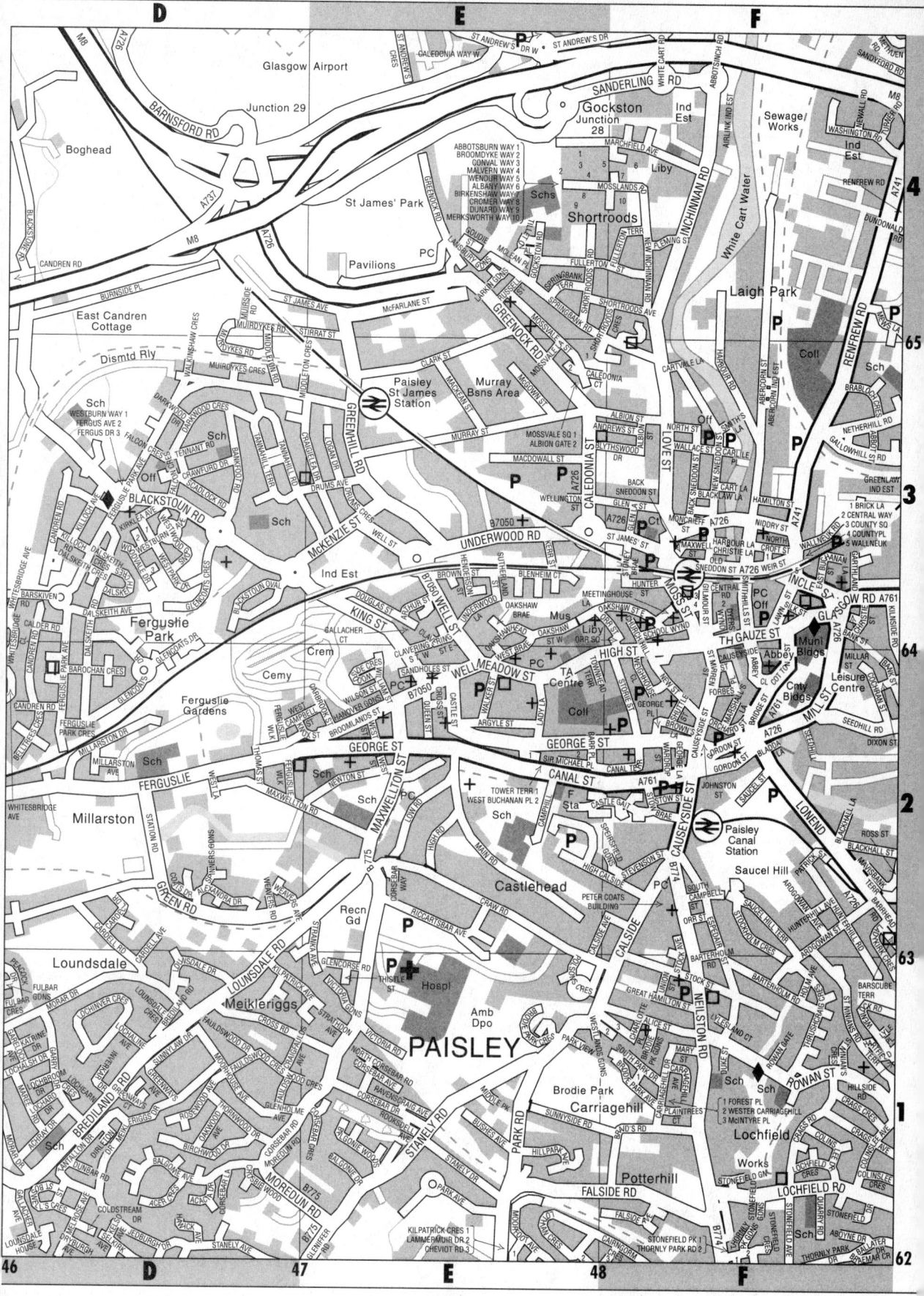

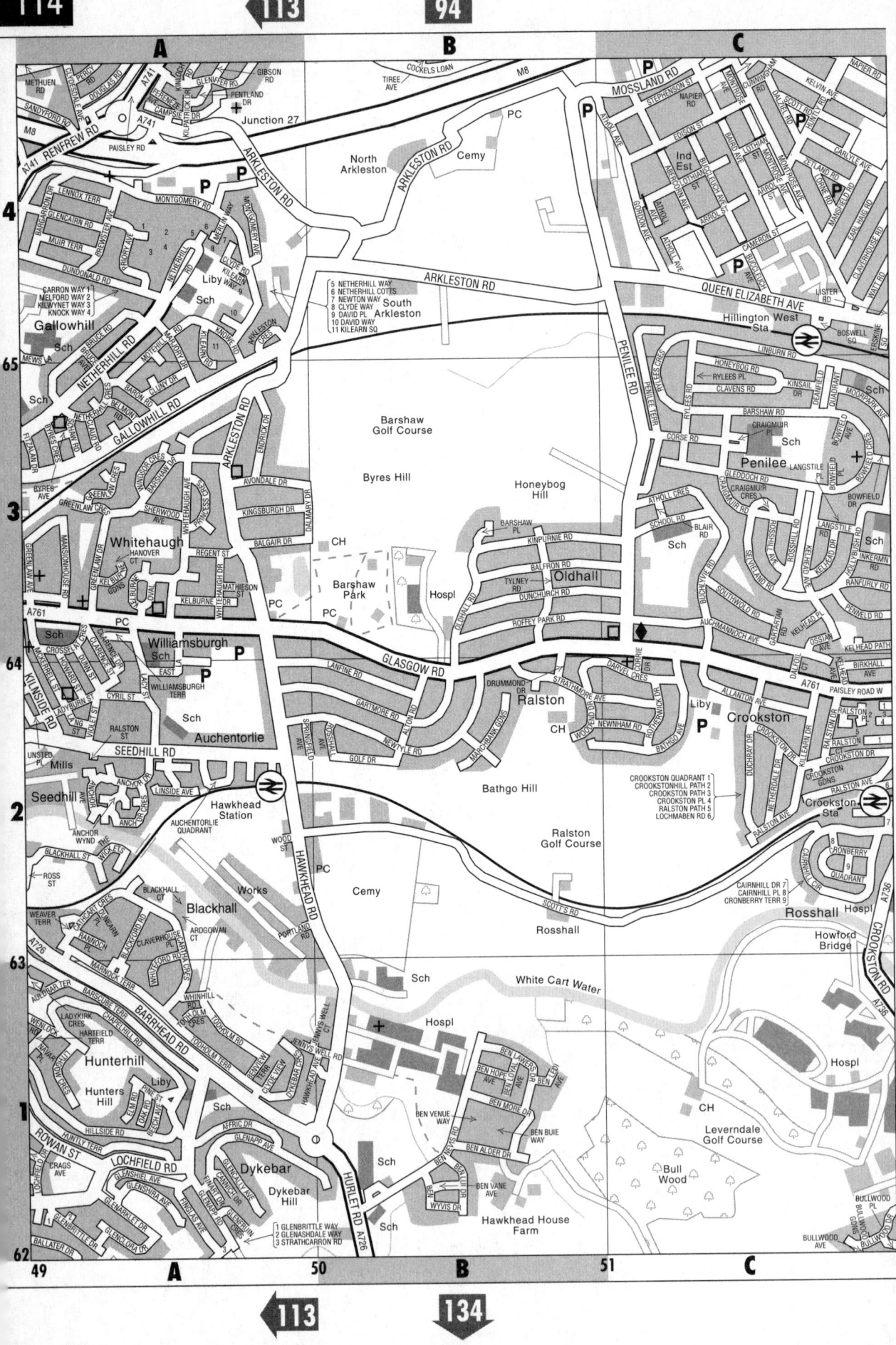

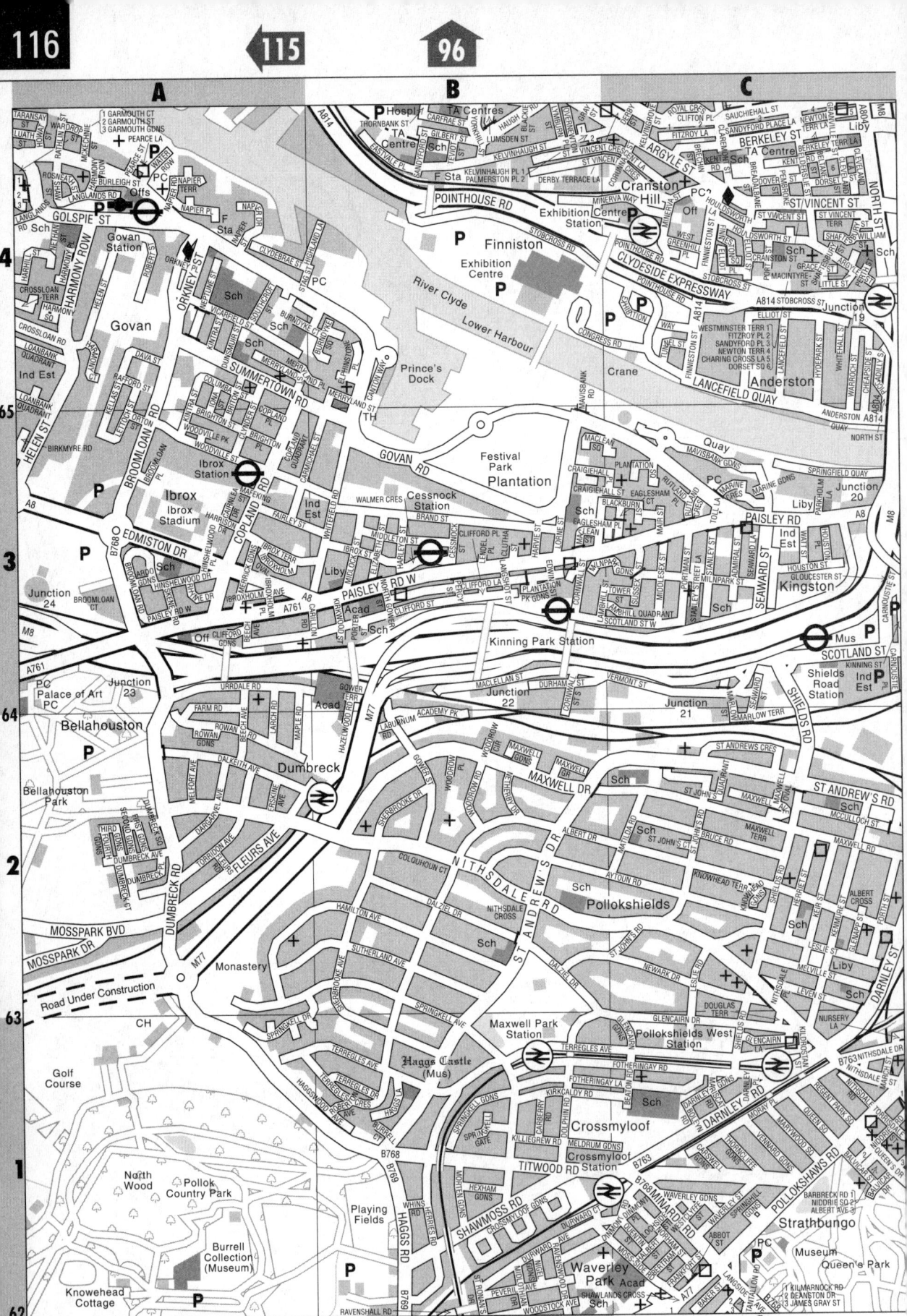

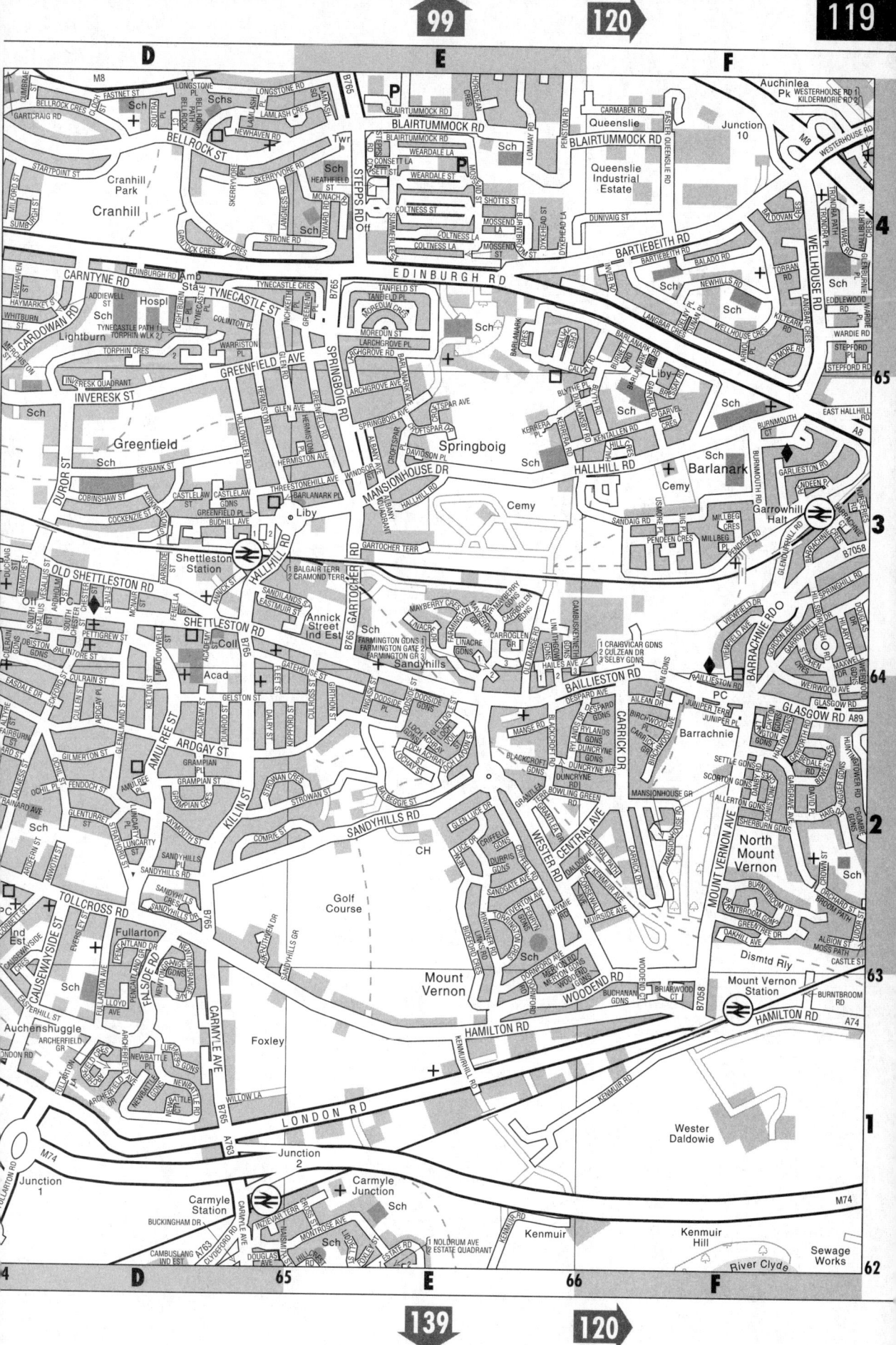

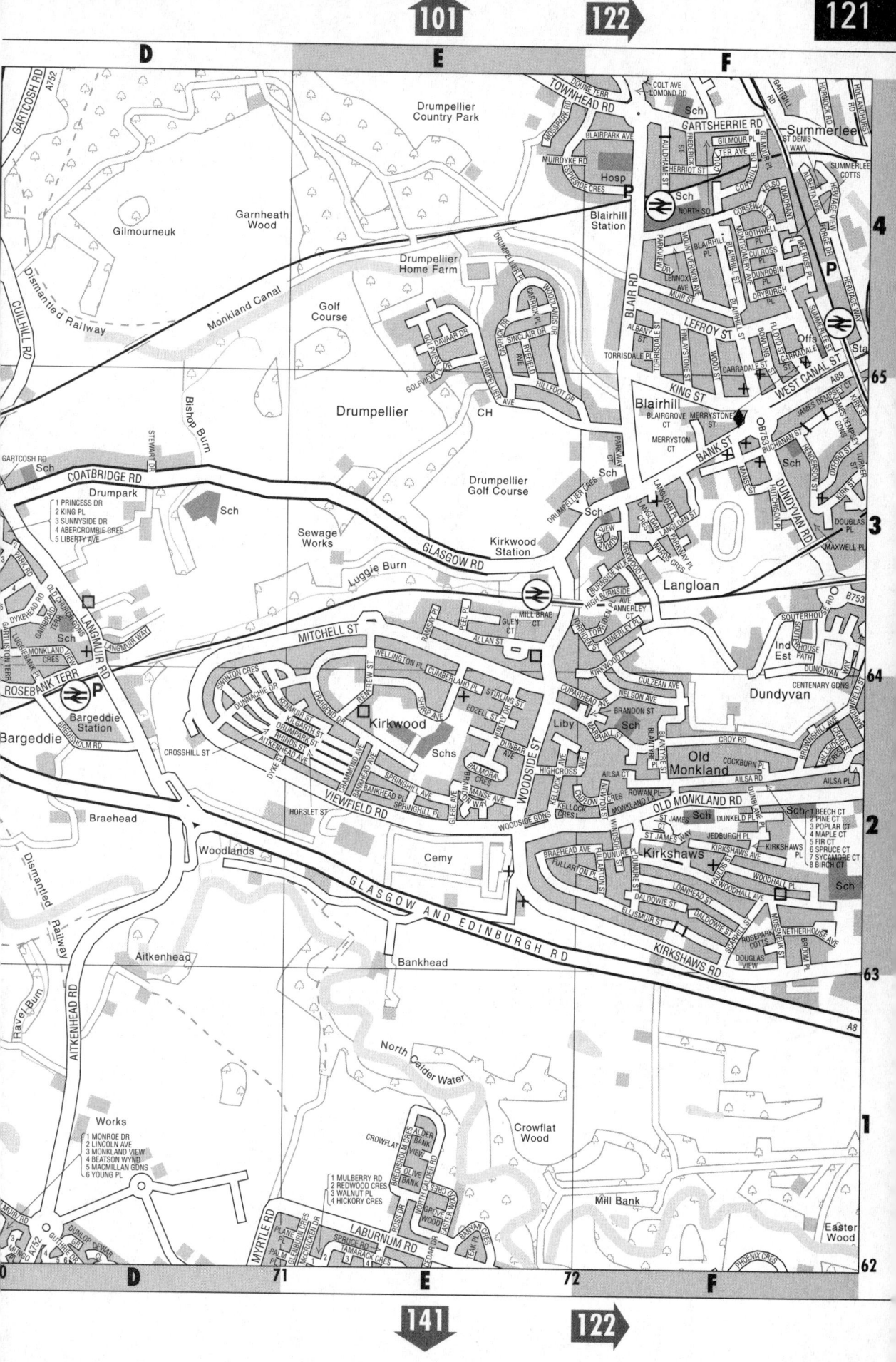

121 102

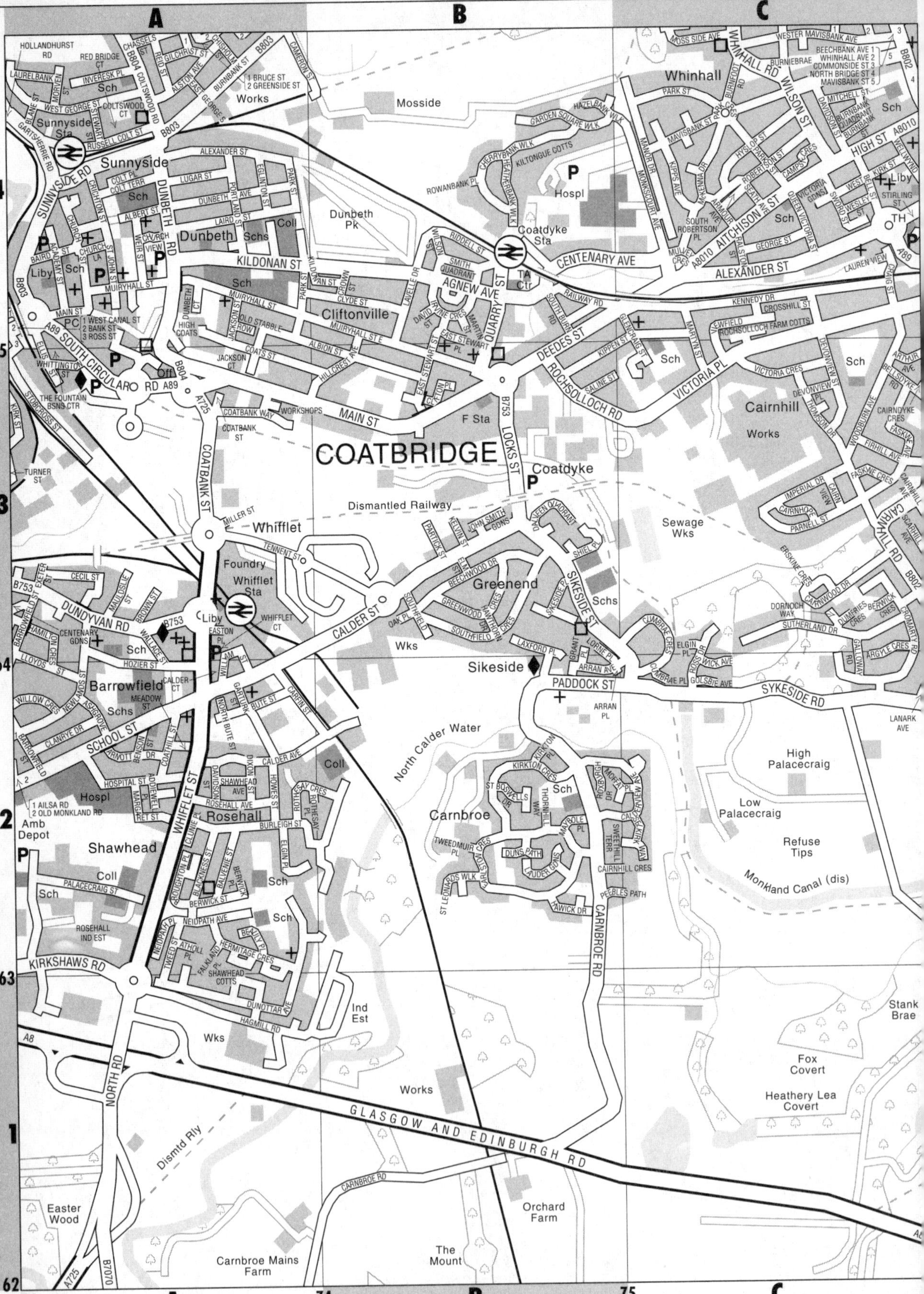

D   E   F

Rawyards Park

AIRDRIE

Off

Sch

Ind Est

8 CAMERON ST
9 GILLIES CT
10 OGILVIE CT
11 FRASER CT
12 ERSKINE CT
13 GORDON CT
14 BRUCE CT

Clarkston

Hospl

North Calder Water

Sch

4

DRUMBATHIE RD

MOTHERWELL RD

COLLIERTREE RD

McAllister Ave

Springfield Rd

Drumgelloch

FORREST ST

Dismtd Rly

Clark St

Hallcraig St

A89 Graham St

Drumgelloch Station

B8058

TOWERS RD

TOWERS PL

65

15 FINLAYSON QUADRANT
16 WESTER MOFFAT CRES

Sch

GIMMERSCROFT CRES

Moffat Mills

INVERVALE AVE

ARDFERN

Craigneuk

Kingston Ave 1
Colston Terr 2
Castle Quadrant 3
Meadowside Pl 4

Carlisle La 5
Cedar La 6
Lime Cres 7

Airdrie Sta

Victoria

Gartlea Rd

HOGG ST

Schs

Gartleahill

Tinto Rd

Gartlea

CRAIGNEUK AVE

PETERSBURN RD

GLEN RD

Glenview

Glenacre Dr

Liby

VARNSDORF WAY

Luing

Islay

Gimmerscroft

ROUGHRIGG RD

3

CRAIGENS RD

Moss Rd

Woodview La

Mossview Cres

Scarhill Ave

Fife Ave

Ind Est

Brown's Burn

BROWNSBURN RD

Viking Rd

CARLISLE RD

Schs

Petersburn

MULL

MINCH WAY

Brownsburn

Gartness

GARTNESS DR

BLACKCROFT

Bowhouse

BOWHOUSE RD

64

Cairnhill Rd

Sykeside Rd

Lanark Ave

B8058

CALDERBANK RD

B802

Hillhead

St Davids Dr

Friars Way

Monkland Bridge

Monkland Canal (disused)

Shotts Burn

BOWHOUSEBRAE RD

Sauchenbog Bridge

MONCRIEFFE RD 1
HOGG RD 2
ABERDEEN RD 3
BURNS RD 4
BURNS LA 5
ROSEBERRY LA 6

Ind Est

BURNIEBRAE RD

2

Faskine Farm

Calderbank

Sch

Main St

MAIN ST

North Calder Water

Queen's Cres

Hotel

Roberton St

LAWHOPE MILL RD

63

New La

Loch St

Faskine Ave

Monkland View

Budshaw Ave

School Rd

BO NESS RD

Sch

Laurel Gdns

Russell St

Chapelhall

BELLSIDE RD

Dismtd Rly

WOODHALL MILL RD

B798

Centre St

Cardell Cres

WOODHALL ST

Charles Path

Kennelburn Rd

Sch

1

GLEN FRUIN PL 1
GLEN ORCHY PL 2
GLEN SHEE CRES 3
GLEN AFFRIC DR 4
GLEN AFFRIC WAY 5

Meadow Path

TIMMONS TERR

WOODNEUK ST

DRUMOAK

Tinbergie Gdns

BIGGAR RD

A73

Bailside Farm

GLASGOW AND EDINBURGH RD A8

WOODHALL COTTAGE RD

B802

62

76   D   77   E   78   F

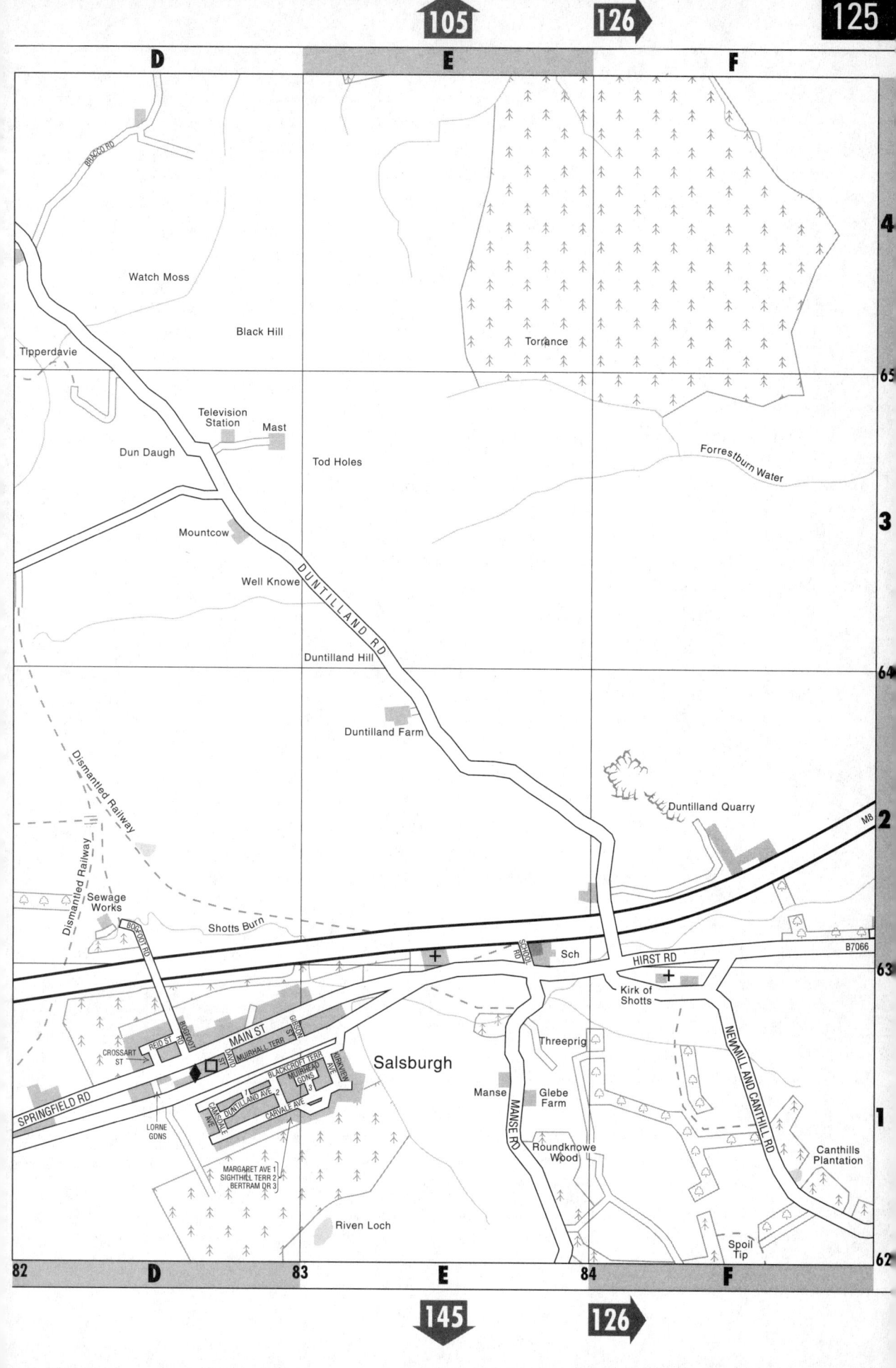

D

E

F

4

Watch Moss

Black Hill

Torrance

Tipperdavie

65

Television Station

Mast

Dun Daugh

Tod Holes

Forrestburn Water

BOXCO RD

Mountcow

3

Well Knowe

DUNTILLAND RD

Duntilland Hill

64

Dismantled Railway

Duntilland Farm

Duntilland Quarry

M8

2

Dismantled Railway

Sewage Works

Shotts Burn

B7066

BOXFOOT RD

SCHOOL RD

Sch

HIRST RD

63

Kirk of Shotts

CROSSART ST

REID ST

BOXFOOT RD

MAIN ST

GIBSON ST

MUIRHALL TERR

Threeprig

DAVID ST

BLACKCROFT TERR

MUIRHEAD GDNS

KIRKVIEW AVE

Salsburgh

Manse

Glebe Farm

SPRINGFIELD RD

CARVALE AVE

DUNTILLAND AVE

CARVALE AVE

MANSE RD

1

LORNE GDNS

Roundknowe Wood

Canthills Plantation

NEWMILL AND CANTHILL RD

MARGARET AVE 1
SIGHTHILL TERR 2
BERTRAM DR 3

Riven Loch

Spoil Tip

62

A   B   C

Baads

Forrestburn Water

4

BLAIRMUCKHOLE AND FORRESTDYKE RD

Works

Forrestburn

Bridgehill

Forrestburn Holding

Forrestburn Water

Papperthill Craigs

FORREST RD

65

Works

Forrestburn Water

Bentfoot

Forrestburn Reservoir

Blairmuckhole

3

Dewshills

Blairmains

M8

64

Mine (dis)

LLYNALLAN RD

B7066

South Blair

DEWSHILL COTTS

TV Station

Junction 5

Welleslea

Mast

HOUSE O' MUIR RD

North Hirst

M8

2

Shotts Burn

HIRSTRIGG COTTS

HIRST RD

SOUTH HIRST RD

South Hirst

Wester Hassockrigg

Easter Hassockrigg

SHOTTS RD

Resr

SHOTTSBURN RD

B7066

63

FORRISET RD

River Almond

Opencast Workings

1

Cant Hills

B7057

WEST BENHAR RD

B717

Easter Baton

NEWMILL AND CANTHILL RD

BENHAR RD

62

85   A   86   B   87   C

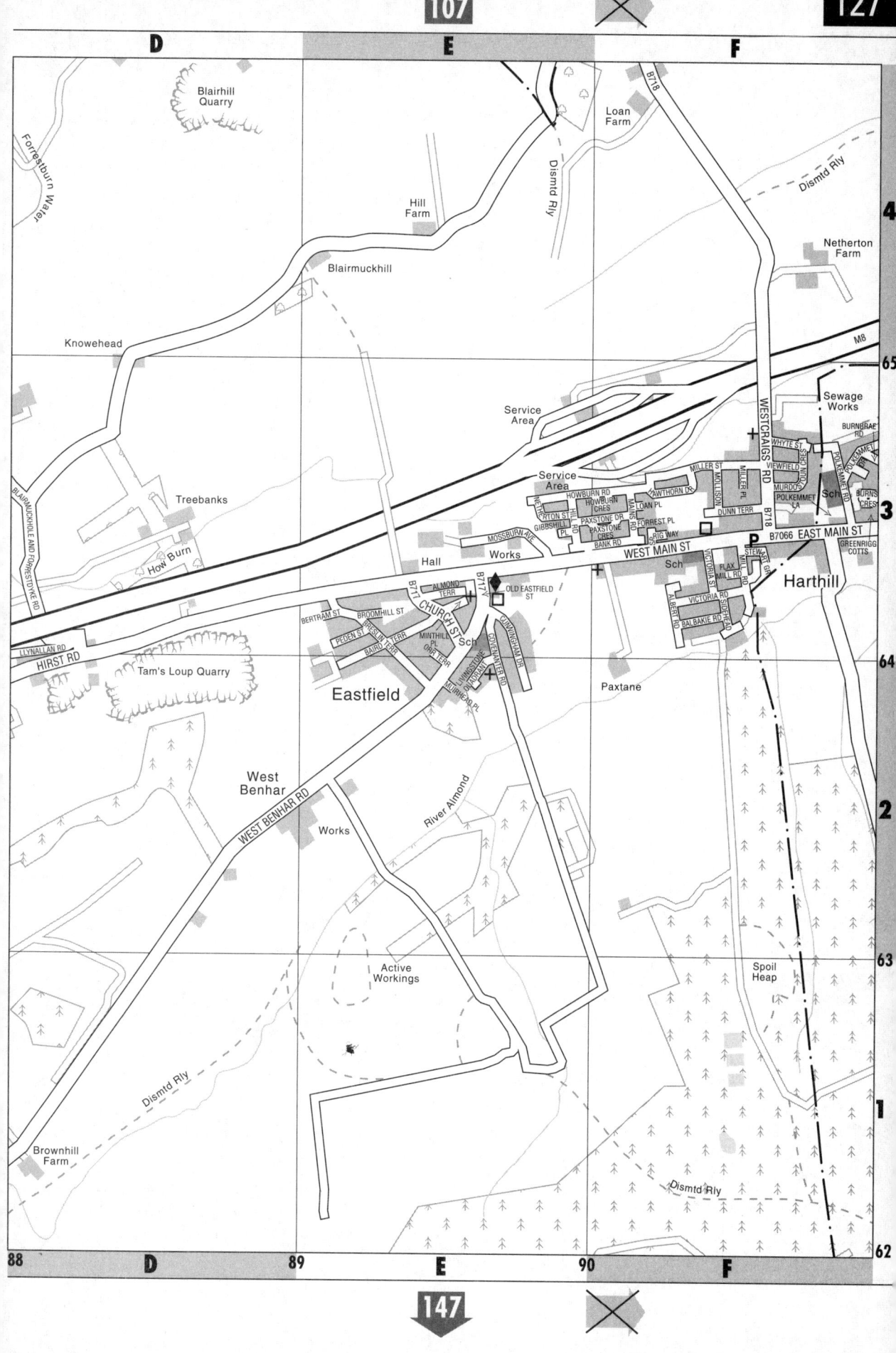

Blairhill Quarry

Forrestburn Water

Dismtd Rly

Loan Farm

B718

Hill Farm

Blairmuckhill

Dismtd Rly

Netherton Farm

Knowehead

4

M8

Service Area

WESTCRAGS RD

Sewage Works

BURNBRAE RD

65

BLAIRMUCKHOLE AND FORRESTDYKE RD

Treebanks

Service Area

WHYTE ST

VIEWFIELD

POLKEMMET

POLKEMMET RD

SCHOOL AVENUE

Sch

BURNS CRES

How Burn

HOWBURN RD
HOWBURN CRES

MILLER ST
MILLER PL
MOLLISON

MURDO

3

NETHERTON ST

PAXSTONE DR
PAXSTONE CRES

HAWTHORN DR
MAINS RD
LOAN PL
FORREST PL

DUNN TERR

GIBBSHILL PL

BANK RD

RIG WAY

WEST MAIN ST

B7066 EAST MAIN ST

GREENRIGG COTTS

MOSSBURN AVE

Works

Sch

P

Harthill

Hall

ALMOND TERR

STEW

VICTORIA RD

FLAX MILL RD

B711

B717

OLD EASTFIELD ST

ALBERT RD

VICTORIA RD

SUIRHEAD

2

BERTRAM ST

BROOMHILL ST

CHURCH ST

Sch

BALBAKIE RD

PEDEN ST

BRESLIN TERR

MINTHILL PL
GHEE TERR

CUNNINGHAM DR

COVENANTER RD

BAIRD TERR

LIVINGSTONE

DUNCAN ST

Paxtane

LLYNALLAN RD

HIRST RD

Tam's Loup Quarry

Eastfield

MUIRHEAD PL

64

West Benhar

WEST BENHAR RD

River Almond

Works

2

Active Workings

Spoil Heap

63

Dismtd Rly

Brownhill Farm

1

Dismtd Rly

62

88   D   89   E   90   F

A **B** **C**

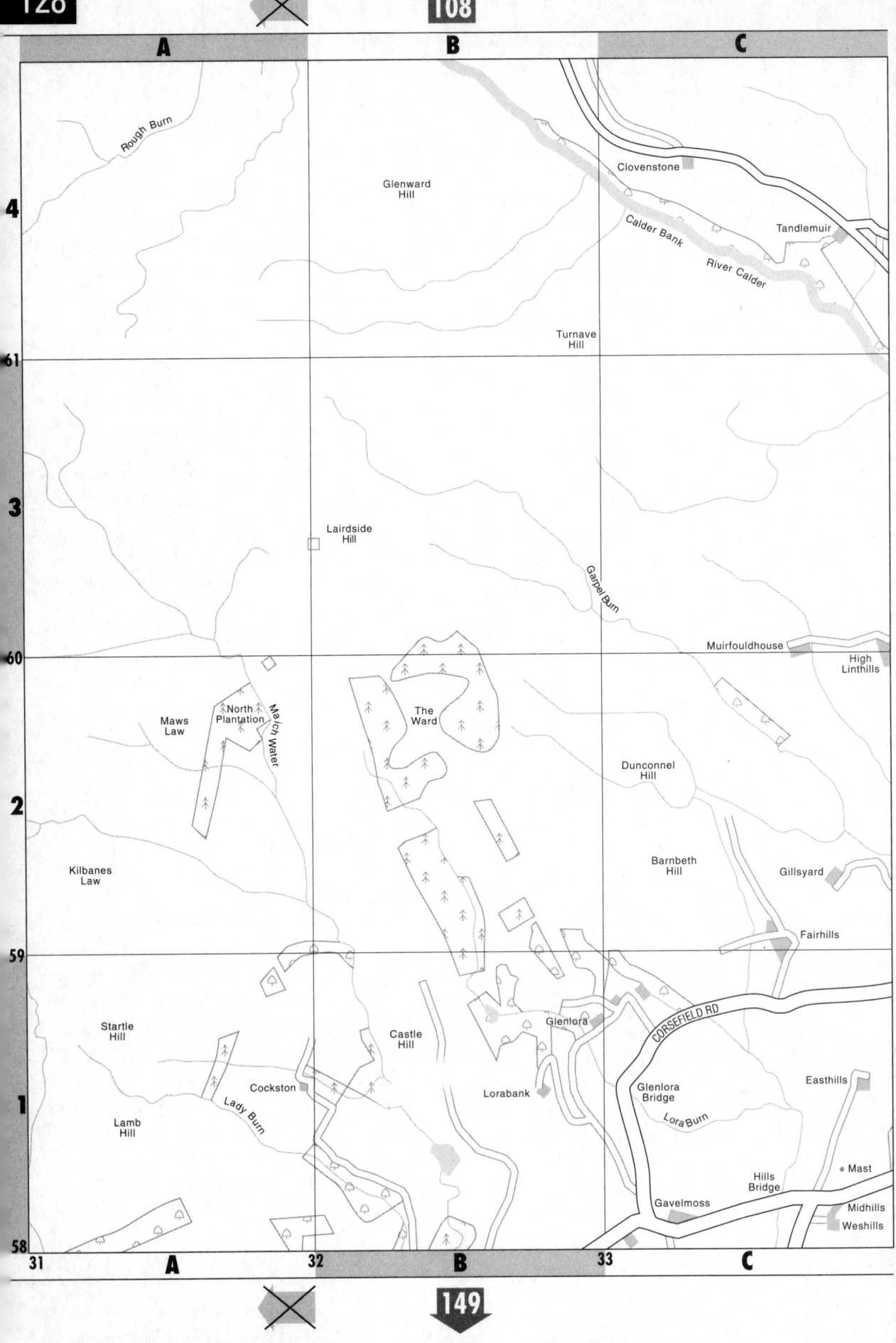

4

Rough Burn

Glenward
Hill

Clovenstone

Calder Bank

Tandlemuir

River Calder

Turnave
Hill

61

3

Lairdside
Hill

Garpel Burn

Muirfouldhouse

High
Linthills

60

Maws
Law

North
Plantation

Maich Water

The Ward

Duncconnel
Hill

Barnbeth
Hill

Gillsyard

Fairhills

2

Kilbanes
Law

59

Startle
Hill

Castle
Hill

Glenlora

CORSEFIELD RD

Easthills

Cockston

Lady Burn

Lorabank

Glenlora
Bridge

Lora Burn

1

Lamb
Hill

Hills
Bridge

Mast

Gavelmoss

Midhills

Weshills

58

31 **A** 32 **B** 33 **C**

D
E
F

Knockmade Hill

How Barnaigh

North Kaim

Kaim Burn

4

West Kaim

The Kaim

Sandieston

Gockstane Wood

East Tandlemuir

Barr Heigh

Kaim Bridge

East Mitchelton

Longcroft

61

Peockstone

West Michelton

Barrs of Cloak

Kaimburn Bridge

Balgreen

Mickle Cloak

East Knockbartnock

Gateside Hill

3

Highlands

River Calder

Boghead

B786

West Knockbartnock

Gateside

Parkhill Wood

Blackditch Burn

Laigh Lainthills

Crooks

60

Park Hill

Courtshaw Hill

Mid Linthills

Cloak Burn

Bridgend Hill

Golf Course

Cemy

Calder Glen Mill

Crook Hill

CRAWFURDS VIEW

WATERSTON WAY

GRAHAM AVE

JOHNSHILL

Beech Burn

Manse

2

Bridgend

Schs

CROOKHILL

CROSS ARDS

CALDERPARK AVE

BRAEHEAD

SEMPLE AVE

EWING RD

MANSFIELD

PARKHILL DR

BEECHBURN CRES

GATES RD

Dismantled Railway

Garpel Burn

Lochwinnoch

SPIERS RD

VIEWFIELD AVE

GARPEL WAY

KILBARCHAN RD

CALDER ST

PALMER RD

CALDERPARK ST

GLENPARK RD

EASTEND

WINNOC RD

P

PC

CORSEFIELD RD

CH

Garpel Bridge

BURNFOOT RD

RAILWAY RD

MCDOWALL RD

LOCHHAGGRIE RD

Library Museum

HIGH ST

SHAW PL

JOHNSTONE DR

MAIN ST

HARVEY TERR

GRANDHOLM ST

PC

Castle Semple Loch

59

Tower

Lochwinnoch Nature Reserve

CHURCH ST

NEWTON

B786 MAIN ST

Lochwinnoch Bridge

LOCHLIP RD

Lade Bridge

Aird Meadow

1

Lochside House

Calder Bridge

Bar Castle (remains of)

Lochall Bridge

A760

A737

Barr Loch

A760

34
D
35
E
36
F
58

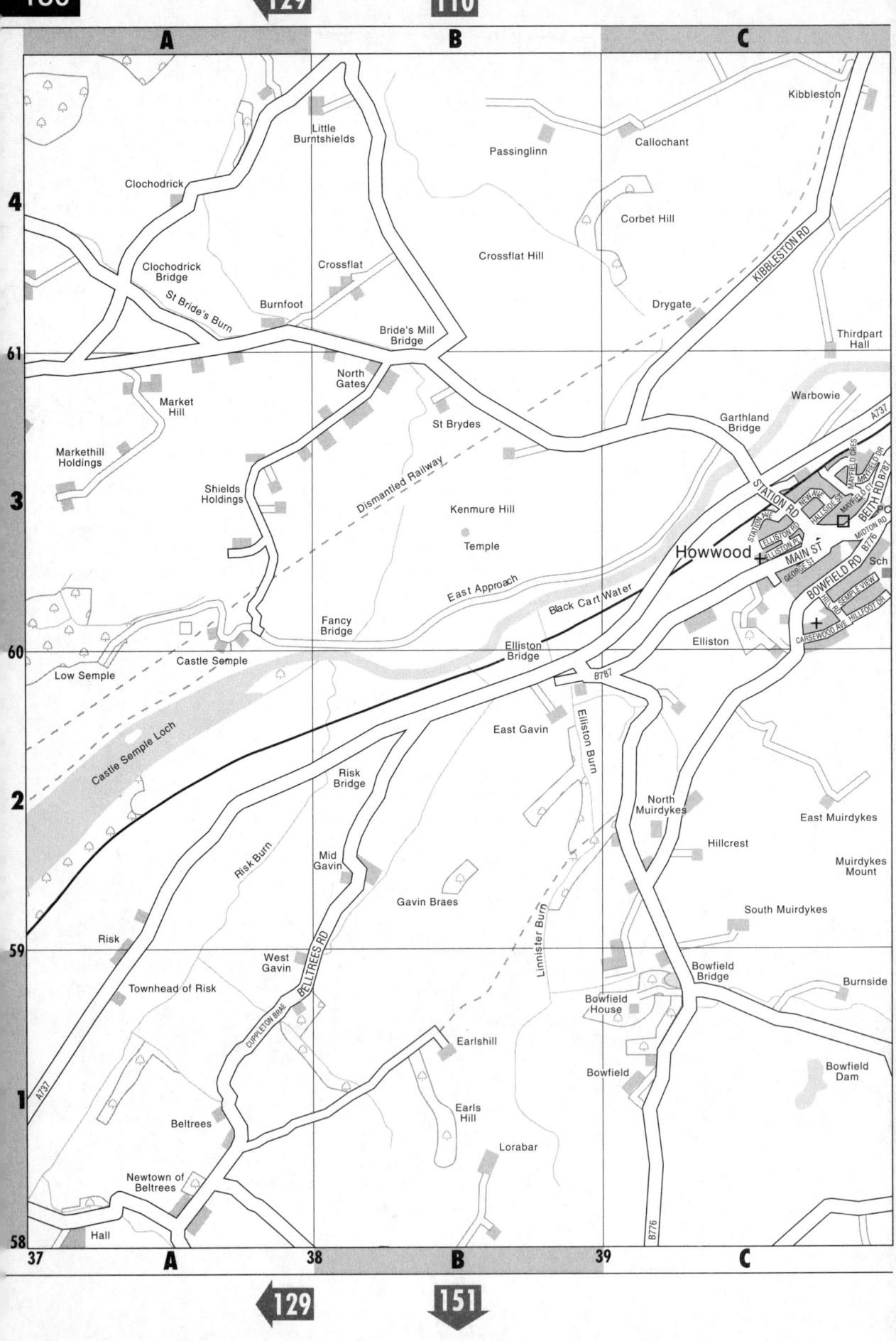

A **B** **C**

4

Kibbleston

Little Burntshields
Clochodrick
Passinglinn
Callochant

Crossflat
Corbet Hill

Clochodrick Bridge
Crossflat Hill

St Bride's Burn
Burnfoot
Drygate

Bride's Mill Bridge
KIBBLESTON RD

61

Thirdpart Hall

North Gates
Warbowie

Market Hill
St Brydes
Garthland Bridge

Markethill Holdings
STATION RD
A737

Shields Holdings
Dismantled Railway
Kenmure Hill
NEW AVE
BEITH RD B787
MAYFIELD CRES
MAYFIELD DR

3

Temple
ELLISTON RD
MIDTON RD
B776

Howwood
MAIN ST
BOWFIELD RD
Sch

East Approach
GEORGE ST
B776

Black Cart Water
SEMPLE VIEW

Fancy Bridge
Elliston
CARSEWOOD AVE
HILLFOOT DR

Elliston Bridge

60

Castle Semple
B787

Low Semple

East Gavin
Elliston Burn

Castle Semple Loch

Risk Bridge
North Muirdykes
East Muirdykes

2

Hillcrest
Muirdykes Mount

Risk Burn

Mid Gavin
South Muirdykes

Gavin Braes

Risk
Linnister Burn
Bowfield Bridge
Burnside

59

West Gavin

Townhead of Risk
BELTTREES RD
Bowfield House
Bowfield Dam

CUPPLETON BRAE
Earlshill
Bowfield

A737

1

Earls Hill

Beltrees
Lorabar

Newtown of Beltrees
B776

58

Hall

37 **A** **38** **B** **39** **C**

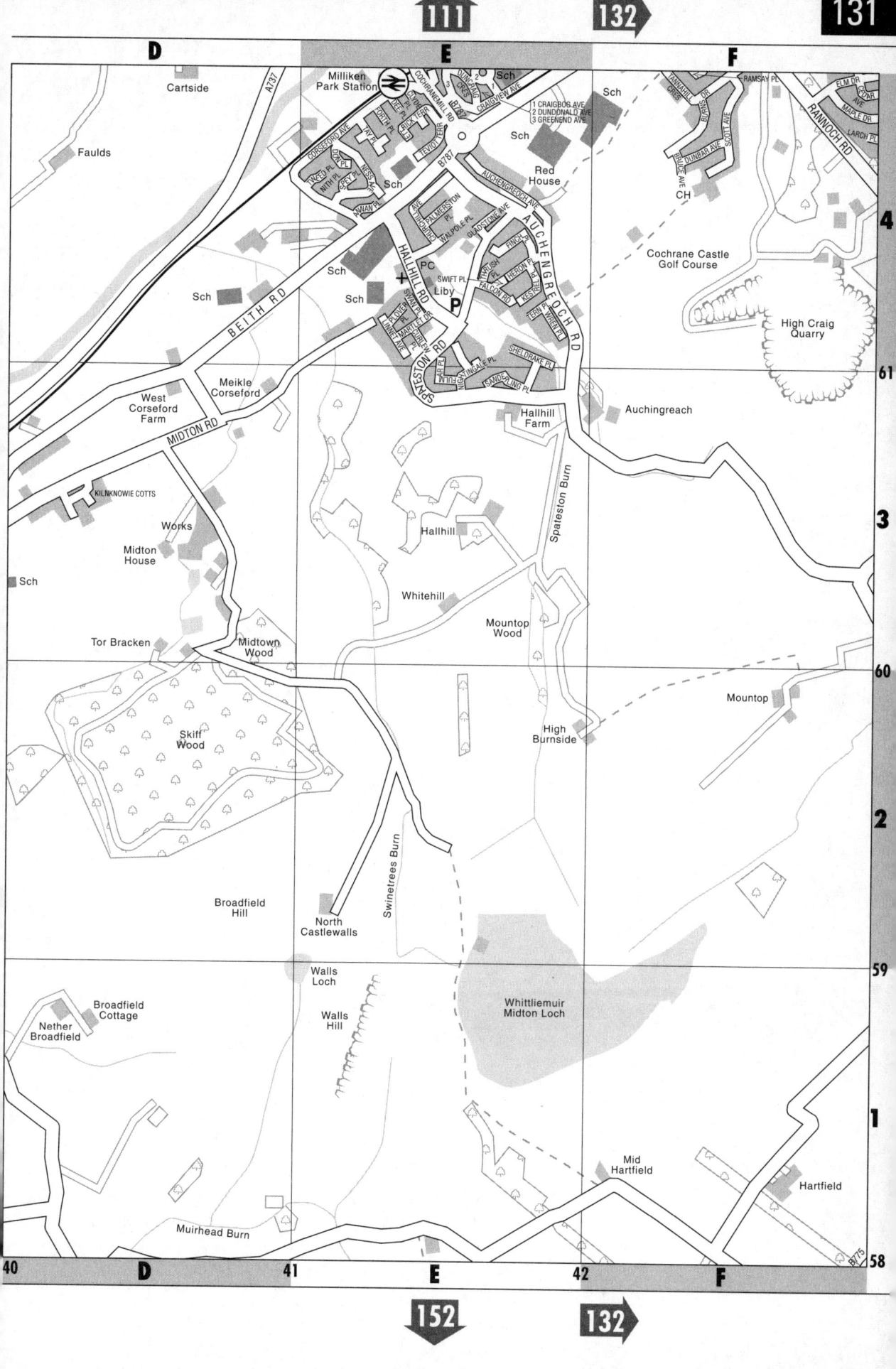

D E F

Cartside

Faulds

A737

Milliken Park Station

Cochranemill Rd

Sch

1 CRAIGBOS AVE
2 DUNDONALD AVE
3 GREENEND AVE

Sch

Red House

Ramsay Pl

Sch

CH

Cochrane Castle Golf Course

RANNOCH RD

ELM DR
MAPLE DR
LARCH PL

4

BEITH RD

Sch

Sch
Sch

Hallhill Rd

PC
Liby
P

AUCHENGREOCH RD

High Craig Quarry

Meikle Corseford

SPATESTON RD

Sheldrake Pl

Sanderling Pl

Hallhill Farm

Auchingreach

61

West Corseford Farm

MIDTON RD

Spateston Burn

KILNKNOWIE COTTS

Works

Hallhill

3

Midton House

Sch

Whitehill

Mountop Wood

Tor Bracken

Midtown Wood

High Burnside

Mountop

60

Skiff Wood

Broadfield Hill

North Castlewalls

Swinetrees Burn

2

Broadfield Cottage

Walls Loch

Nether Broadfield

Walls Hill

Whittliemuir Midton Loch

59

Mid Hartfield

Hartfield

1

Muirhead Burn

B775

58

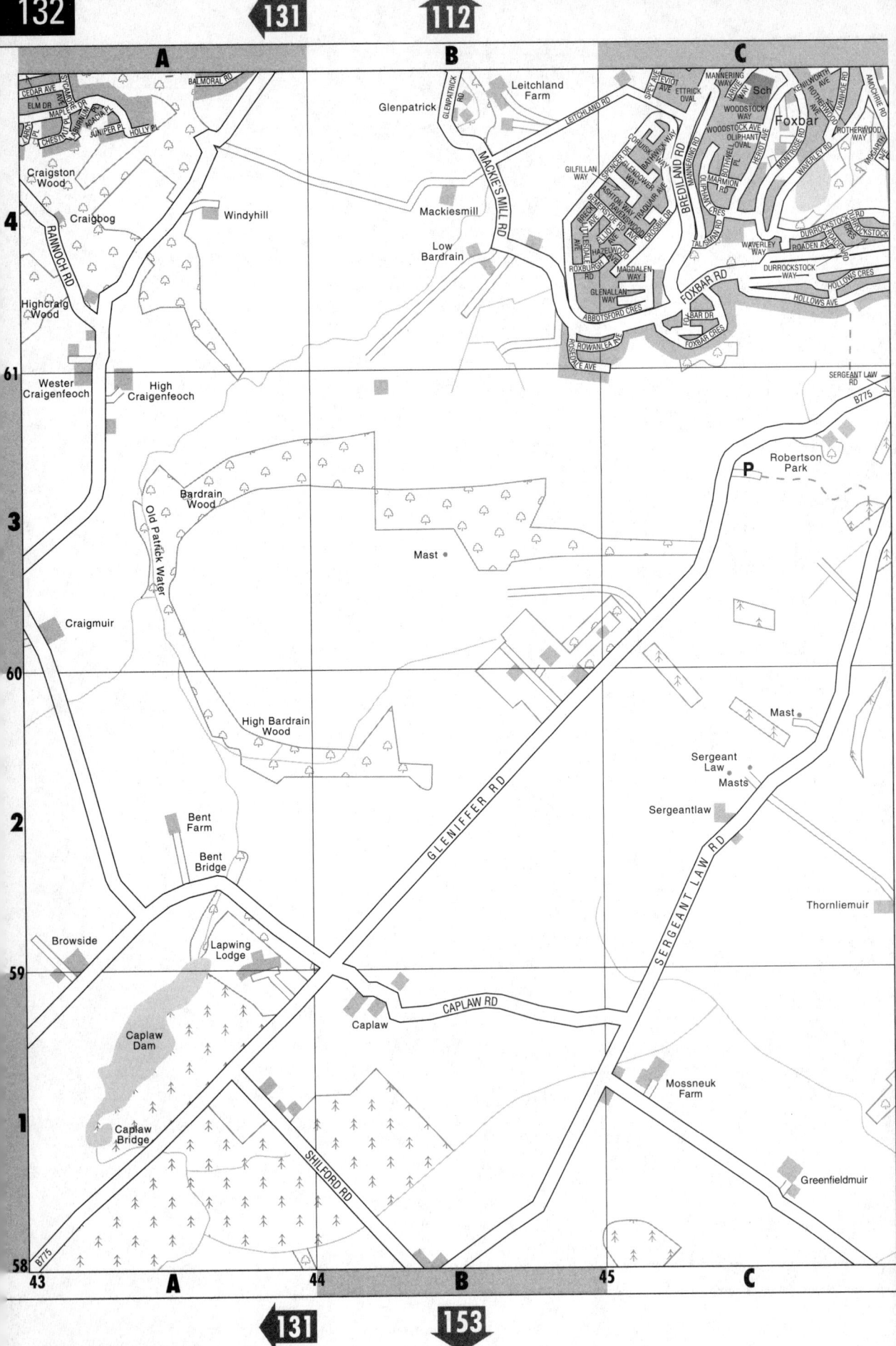

A   **B**   **C**

CEDAR AVE
ELM DR
MAPLE PL
SYCAMORE DR
JUNIPER PL
HOLLY PL
CHESTNUT
ADAM CT
BALMORAL RD

Craigston Wood

Craigbog

Windyhill

Glenpatrick

GLENPATRICK RD

Leitchland Farm

LEITCHLAND RD

SPEY AVE
TEVIOT AVE
ETTRICK OVAL
MANNERING WAY
LUNE WAY
Sch

Foxbar

MANNERING WAY
WOODSTOCK WAY
WOODSTOCK AVE
OLIPHANT OVAL
AMCOURIE RD
KENILWORTH AVE
WAVERLEY RD
ROTHERWOOD WAY

4

RANNOCH RD

Mackiesmill

Low Bardrain

MACKIE'S MILL RD

BREDILAND RD

GILFILLAN WAY

GLENDARROCH WAY
ASHTON WAY
BRICKAN WAY
TINWALD WAY
TRAQUAIR AVE
CROSSBURN

MONTROSE RD

DURROCKSTOCK RD
DURROCKSTOCK RD

ROXBURGH WAY
HAZELWOOD AVE
MAGDALEN WAY
GLENALLAN WAY
ABBOTSFORD CRES
ROWANLEA AVE
ROSEDALE AVE

FOXBAR RD
FOXBAR DR
FOXBAR CRES

WAVERLEY WAY
ROADEN AVE
HOLLOWS CRES
HOLLOWS AVE
DURROCKSTOCK WAY

61

Wester Craigenfeoch

High Craigenfeoch

SERGEANT LAW RD

B775

Highcraig Wood

Old Patrick Water

Bardrain Wood

Mast

P
Robertson Park

3

Craigmuir

High Bardrain Wood

Mast

Sergeant Law
Masts

Sergeantlaw

2

Bent Farm

Bent Bridge

GLENIFFER RD

SERGEANT LAW RD

Thornliemuir

Browside

Lapwing Lodge

59

Caplaw Dam

Caplaw

CAPLAW RD

Mossneuk Farm

1

Caplaw Bridge

SHILFORD RD

Greenfieldmuir

B775

58

43   **A**   **44**   **B**   **45**   **C**

D **E** **F**

Sch

MOGARTH AVE

AMOCHRIE RD

Stanely Reservoir

SELKIRK AVE

STANELY CRES

STANELY AVE

STANELY CT

STANELY AVE

B775

DONALDSWOOD RD

Sch

Glenburn

PARK RD

Sch

MOORFOOT

CAMPSIE DR

Sch

DR

OCHIL

NEILSTON RD

THORNLY PARK DR

THORNLY PARK AVE

SOUTH AVE

4

DURROCKSTOCK RD

HOLLOWS AVE

GLENIFFER RD

FOXBAR RD

CASTLEVIEW DR

CASTLEVIEW PL

1 DURROCKSTOCK CRES
2 HOLLOWS CRES
3 CASTLEVIEW PL

STRAVAIG PATH

STRAVAIG WLK

Works

NETHERCRAIGS RD

4 LIMEVIEW WAY

HOLLYBUSH AVE

CARSEGREEN AVE

NEWARK DR

MOSSNEUK DR

FERENEZE DR

BRAEVIEW AVE

BRAEVIEW

REDHURST LA

LINN CRES

HARELAW CRES

BURNFOOT AVE

DENEWOOD AVE

BRAEHEAD

FAIRWAY AVE

Sch
Liby

SKYE CRES

BUTE CRES

IONA DR

POTTERHILL AVE

ARTHUR

WOODLAND AVE

SOUTHFIELD AVE

TINTY AVE

University of Paisley (Campus)

61

GLENBURN RD

Sch

BRAEMOUNT AVE

HILLCREST

CRAIGMUIR AVE

CRAIGENDOWN

OVAL

Braemount

P

GLENFIELD AVE

GLENFIELD RD

ENFIELD CRES

Thornley Dam

Dismtd Rlys

CAPLEHILL RD

B774

P

PC

Glen Park

Brownside

3

Gleniffer Braes Country Park

SERGEANT LAW RD

Gleniffer Burn

CH

PROCESSION RD

Brownside Braes

Glenburn Reservoir

Paisley Golf Course

Knockindon Burn

Harelaw Burn

Reservoir

Harelaw Reservoir

Fereneze Golf Course

60

2

Mast

Mast

Thornliemuir

Fereneze Hills

59

Woodneuk

HILLSIDE RD

Capellie Farm

Capellie Cottage

Killoch Water

Killoch Hill

Killoch

Reservoir

Gateside

GATESIDE RD

HARPERS VIEW

FERENEZE RD

LOCHLIBO RD

A736

DONNIES BRAE 1
NEILSTON RD 2

1

58

46 **D** 47 **E** 48 **F** 58

133 114

A B C

4

THORNLY PARK AVE
BALLATER DR
SOUTH AVE
STRATHCARRON RD
Tod Burn
ALLOWAY DR
GRAHAMSTON PL
A726
B771
ALLOWAY CRES
GRAHAMSTON CRES
GRAHAMSTON CT
GRAHAMSTON
OLD COTTS
Temple Hill
BULLWOOD CT
Leverndale Ind Ctr
MALBEN
MILLBEG CRES
WINDHOLM CT
MAESWOOD GDNS

Shaw Wood

Hospl

Hurlethill Plantation

HURLET RD

Tongues Hill

Hollybush

Dismtd Rly

Oldbarhills TP Site

Oldbar Hills

Hurlet Hill

Hurlet

FASKIN RD
FASKIN PL
KINARVIE RD
KINARVIE CRES
KINARVIE PL
KINARVIE TER
A736
BARRHEAD RD
KINARVIE GDNS

61

B774
CAPLETHILL RD
GRAHAMSTON RD
Dismtd Rly

Harelaw Burn

Harelaw

Oldbar Burn

West Hurlet House

Raes Wood

BARRHEAD RD
A736
LEVERN RD
HURLET COTTS
NITSHILL RD
A726

3

WINSIDE DR
BROWNSIDE AVE
NOVAR DR
ACACIA DR
GLENIFFER DR
MOSS DR
HEATHER AVE
BRIDGESTONE DR
CROSS AVE
WHIN AVE
B774
B771
LEVEN CT
LINNHE CT
GRAHAMSTON RD
NORTH DR
LOMOND DR
BURNSIDE AVE
FERN DR
PAISLEY RD

F Sta

Blackbyres

Logansraes

Cemy

Nitshill

Waterside

PINMORE ST
PINMOSS ST
DARVEL ST
SEAMILL ST
TAYSIDE
NEILSTON RD
SEAMILL PATH
WOODHEAD RD
WHITEHOPE TER
WHINRIGG
WILLOWFORD
WHITACRES RD

60

QUARRY RD
TREES PARK AVE
BELLFIELD CT
BELLFIELD RD
FERENEZE AVE
CH
Sch
VICTORIA RD
VICTORIA GDNS
CHESTER RD

Quarries (dis)

Wks

Crossmill

Saturland

Bowerwalls

Parkhouse

WEENSMOOR RD 1
WHITACRES PATH 2

BLACKBYRES RD

BLACKBYRES CT
WALLACE AVE
WRAES AVE
STEWART ST
STEWART RD
CROSSMILL AVE
RUFFLEES AVE
MUIRLEA
PL
TAIT AVE
STEWART CT
COMMERCIAL RD
GLASGOW RD
BOWERWALLS ST
SALTERLAND RD

Levern Water

PARKHOUSE RD
B773

2

Fereneze Golf Course

Off Barrhead Sta

GRAHAM ST
GATESIDE RD
HILLSIDE RD
HILLSIDE DR
LAUREL
SAUNDERS CT
ROBERTSON ST
Ind Est
THE CENTRE
CROSS ARTHURLIE ST
B771
CHAPPELL ST
ST GEORGE'S RD
MAXTON
GRANGE AVE
COGAN ST
BARNES RD
GLASGOW RD

Dovecothall

DOVECOTHALL ST
DARNLEY RD
B773
PC
Sch

Cowan Park

Redhall

Tower Rais

Tower Holm

Dubbs

AURS RD
DUBBS RD

CARLIBAR RD
CARLIBAR GDNS
DUNTERLIE CT
CARLIBAR RD
MILLVIEW
WATER RD
GLEN ST
MANSE CT
Sch
Liby
Off
Convent
MAIN ST
MAIN ST
AURSBRIDGE DR
AURSBRIDGE CRES

59

BARRHEAD

West Arthurlie

CRAIGHEAD WAY
STORMYLAND WAY
SUNNYSIDE
KELBURN ST
WRIGHT AVE
DALMENY DR
KERR'S LA
EVANSON ST
BLACKWOOD ST
RALSTON RD
SPRINGHILL RD
CUILLIN WAY
LOMOND
DOUGRAY PL
ALASDAIR CRES
GRAMPIAN AVE
CAMPSIE AVE
SIDLAW AVE
CAIRN AVE
ARTHURLIE AVE
GLANDERSTON AVE

GLANDERSTON AVE

CRAIGTON AVE

North Brae

1

Lochlibo Rd
Arthurlie
A736
LOCHLIBO RD
LOCHLIBO TERR
GATESIDE
Cemy
PC
NEILSTON RD
Kirkton Burn
PARK AVE
PENTLAND DR
TINTO DR
DIVERNIA WAY
NEWTON AVE
FENWICK DR
NEWTON AVE

Auchenback

1 OAKBANK DR
2 SPRINGFIELD RD

58

49 A 50 B 51 C

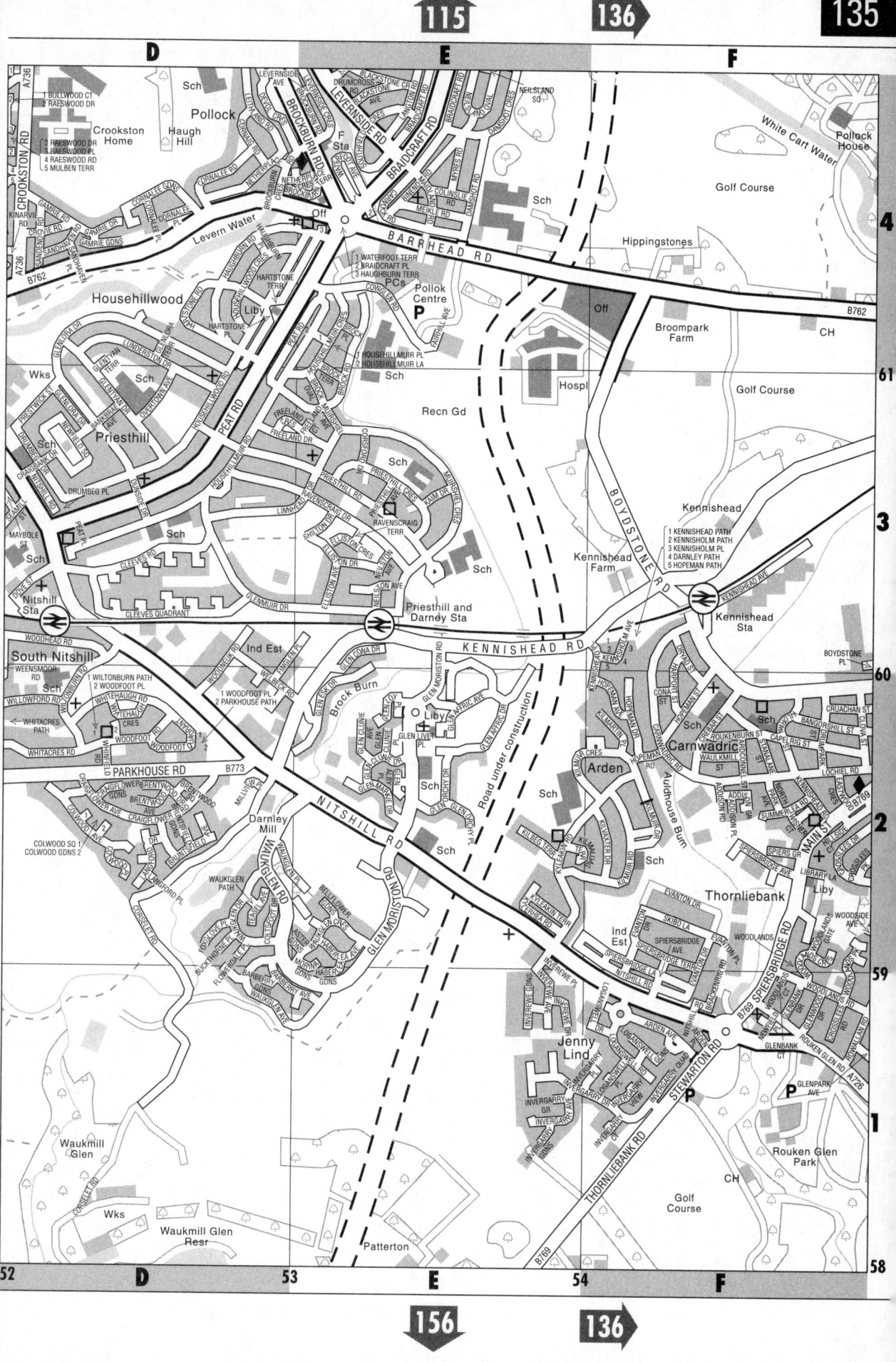

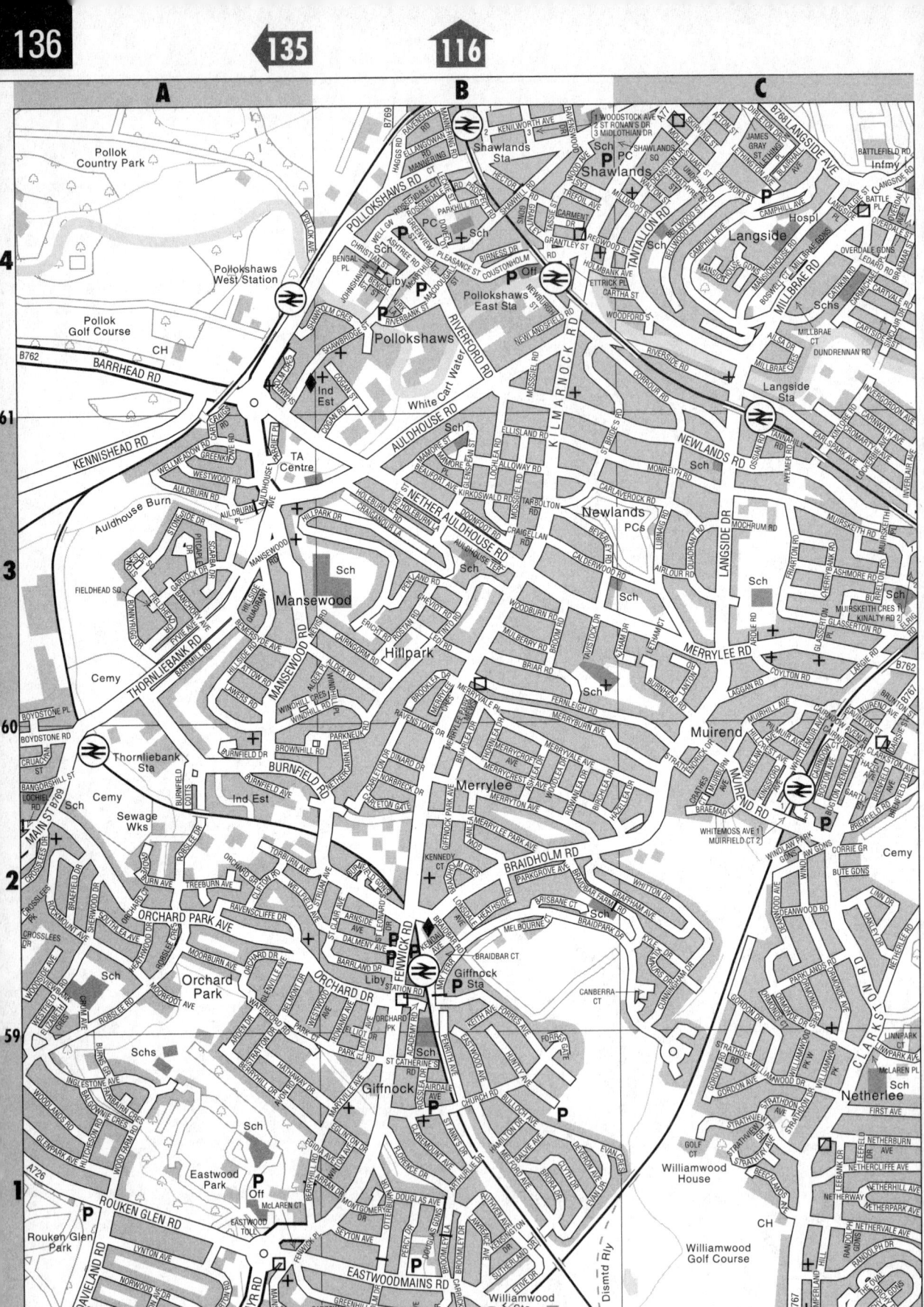

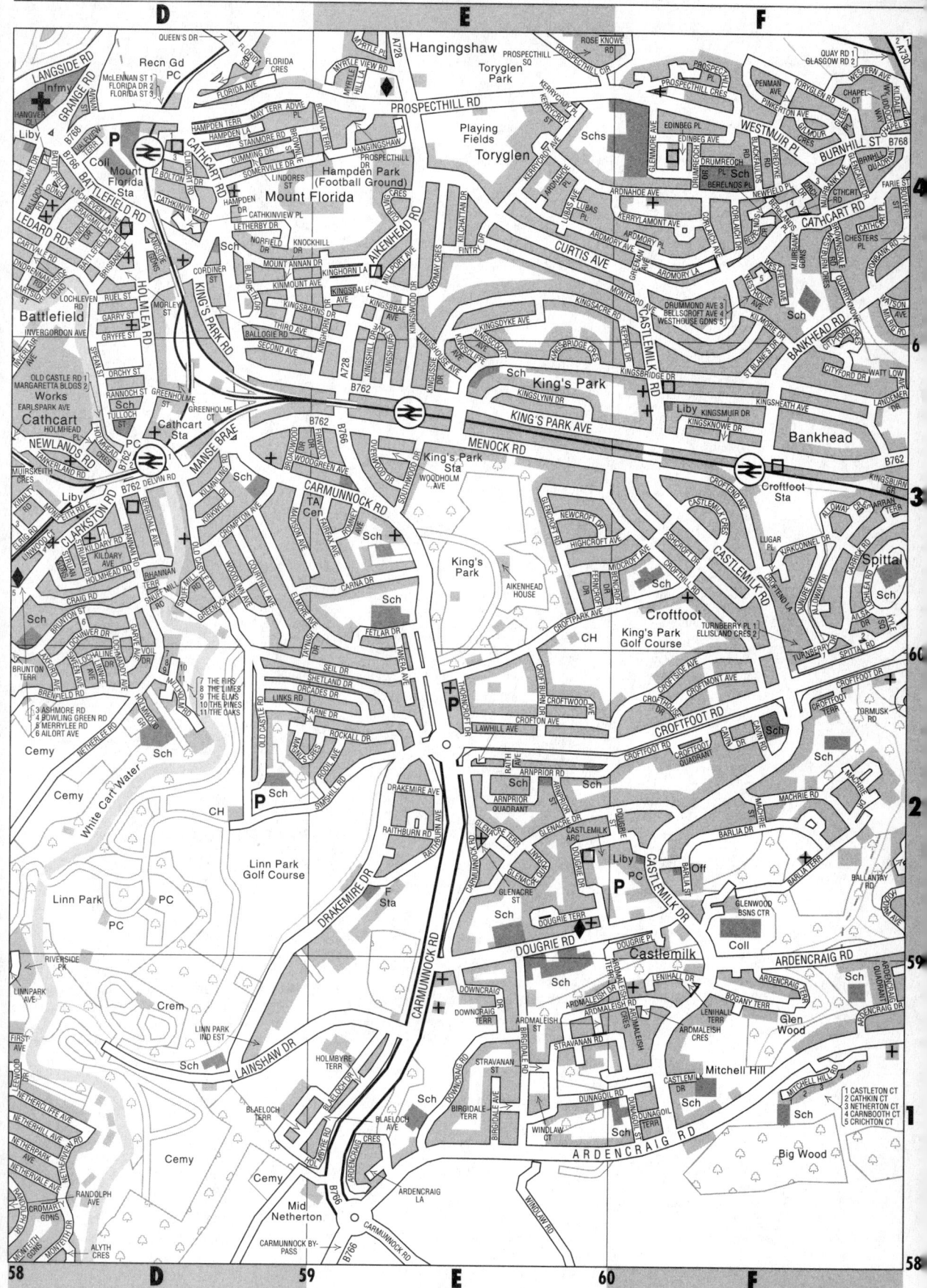

D
E
F

CAMBUSLANG IND EST
CLYDESMILL PL
CLYDESMILL RD
CLYDESMILL DR
CLYDESMILL GR
A763
BUCKINGHAM DR
HILLCREST AVE 1
CATHKIN VIEW 2
BALMORAL PL
GARDENSIDE AVE
BROOMHILLGATE
GARDENSIDE CRES
GARDENSIDE PL
RIVER RD
CARMYLE
CARMYLE AVE

3 HILLCREST RD
4 ROBIN WAY
5 QUEBEC WYND
6 NEUK WAY
7 TORONTO WAY
8 LIDDELL ST
9 NOLDRUM GDNS
10 LAURELBANK RD
11 ARDARGIE GR
12 ARDARGIE PL

River Clyde

Newton Farm

Newton Burn

Cambuslang Bridge
A763
BRIDGE ST
CAMBUSLANG RD
CH
CHURCH VIEW
NEWPARK CRES
THOMSON DR
MITRE GDNS
KINCAID GDNS
KATRINE PL
ORION WAY
Sch
Works
Newton Bridge
Works

61

1 McINTYRE TERR
2 PEEL CT
3 BROWN PL
4 KYLE CT
5 ARNOTT WAY
Westburn Golf Course
WESTBURN RD
Westburn
GREENWOOD AVE
EASTWOOD VIEW
RIVERSIDE PL
LOCKHART AVE
LOCKHART ST
MITCHELL AVE
HENDERSON AVE
McIVER AVE
DUNLOP ST
Sch
PH

MORRISON ST
MONKCASTLE DR
ALLISON DR
MAIN ST
P
P
F Sta
VALLEY VIEW
BIRCH DR
ROWAN PL
FIR PL
ELM DR
QUEEN'S AVE
Dismantled Railway
PC
Cemy
MILL RD
Dismantled Railway
NORTHBANK AVE
WESTBURN RD
NORTHBANK ST
PC
NORTHBANK ST

3

W COATS
BANK ST
B759
Coll
BUSHEYHILL ST
HAMILTON DR
CADZOW DR
CALDER DR
PC
TABERNACLE ST
JOHNSON DR
Sch
VICARS WLK
KING'S CRES
LOCHINVER GR
ANDREW SILLARS AVE
ROBERT TEMPLETON DR
HUGH MURRAY AVE
Spoil Heap
CESSNOCK PL 1
TEITH PL 2
BOWMONT PL 3
EDEN PL 4
HELMSDALE CT 5
TARRAS PL 6
CARRON CT 7
CONAN CT 8
GLENCAIRN GDNS
OLD MILL RD
MILL RD
ARNHAM
ANNICK DR
OLD MILL RD
VISTON ST
CAIRNSIDE
MONTGOMERY ST
MEDWIN ST
GRAHAM AVE
9 EDDLESTON PL
10 TEVIOT PL
11 YARROW CT
12 ETTRICK CT
Newton Station
WORKS AVE
NEWTON BRAE
PH
Hallside

BROWNSIDE RD
Kirkhill Sta
VICARLAND RD
CROFT RD
HOWIESHILL RD
BRAESIDE
COLL
KIRKTON RD
CADOC ST
GLEBE PL
HOWIESHILL AVE
Coll
GATESIDE AVE
OVERTON RD
Village RD
BOWLING GREEN VIEW

60

STEWARTON DR
DOUGLAS DR
GRENVILLE DR
GREENLEES RD
WHITEFORD AVE
MANSFIELD AVE
KIRKBURN AVE
KIRK CLEUGH
HUNTLY DR
KINLOCH DR
JANEBANK AVE
LANGCROFT DR
ROSEBANK AVE
LILYBANK AVE
CAIRNSWELL AVE
CAIRNSWELL PL
IVYBANK AVE
Schs
OAK DR
OVERTON ST
WELFARE AVE
Liby
Halfway
NEW RD
HALLSIDE RD
West Hallside
Sch

Cambuslang
Holmhills Farm
HOLMHILLS GR
Borgie Glen
PC
Kirk Burn
TANZIEKNOWE
TANZIEKNOWE DR
Cambuslang Public Park
HOLLYBANK PL
CAIRNS RD
WOODLAND CRES
DEAN PARK DR
FERNBANK AVE
Wellside
BRANCHOCK AVE
DEANS AVE
CASTLE CHIMMINS AVE
HELENSLEA
LOGAN TOWER
FLEMINGTON IND EST
Works

2

WESTERN RD
KIRKHILL TERR
KIRKHILL AVE
KIRKHILL TERR
Greenlees
EAST GREENLEES RD
EAST GREENLEES DR
EAST GREENLEES AVE
TRINITY DR
AULD KIRK RD
EAST DECHMONT PL
DECHMONT RD
CASTLE CHIMMINS RD
QUARRY RD
HITCHINSON
LIGHTBURN RD
LETTERICKHILLS CRES
DECHMONT COTTS

GLASGOW RD
A749
TURNLAW RD
Light Burn
GILBERT FIELD RD
A724
Sch

59

Gilbertfield
Dechmont Rifle Ranges
Flemington House

1

Turnlaw
Helenslea Cottage
Kirkhill Golf Course
Dechmont Hill
Dechmont Lodge
Quarry Wood
LOANEND COTTS

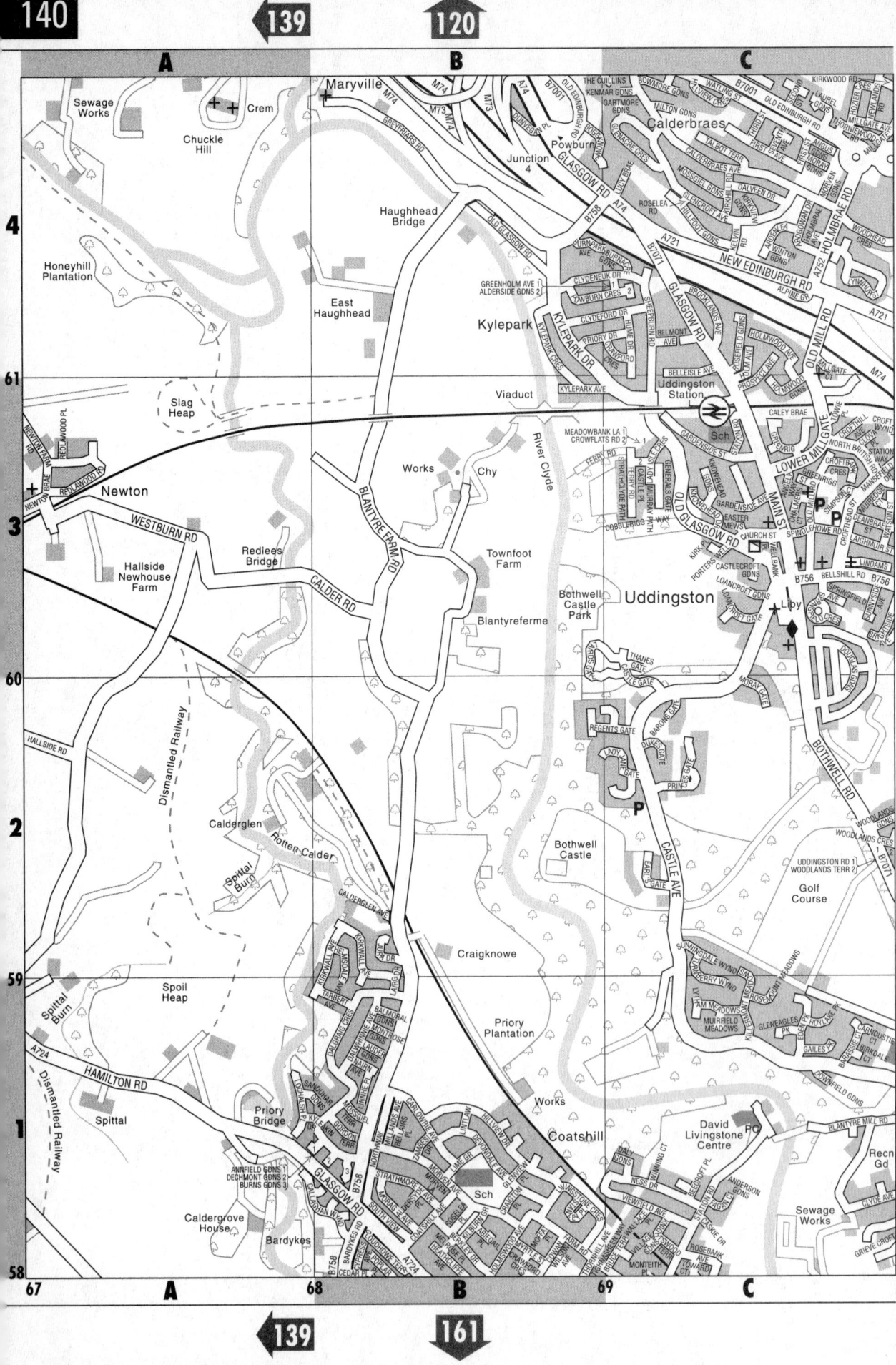

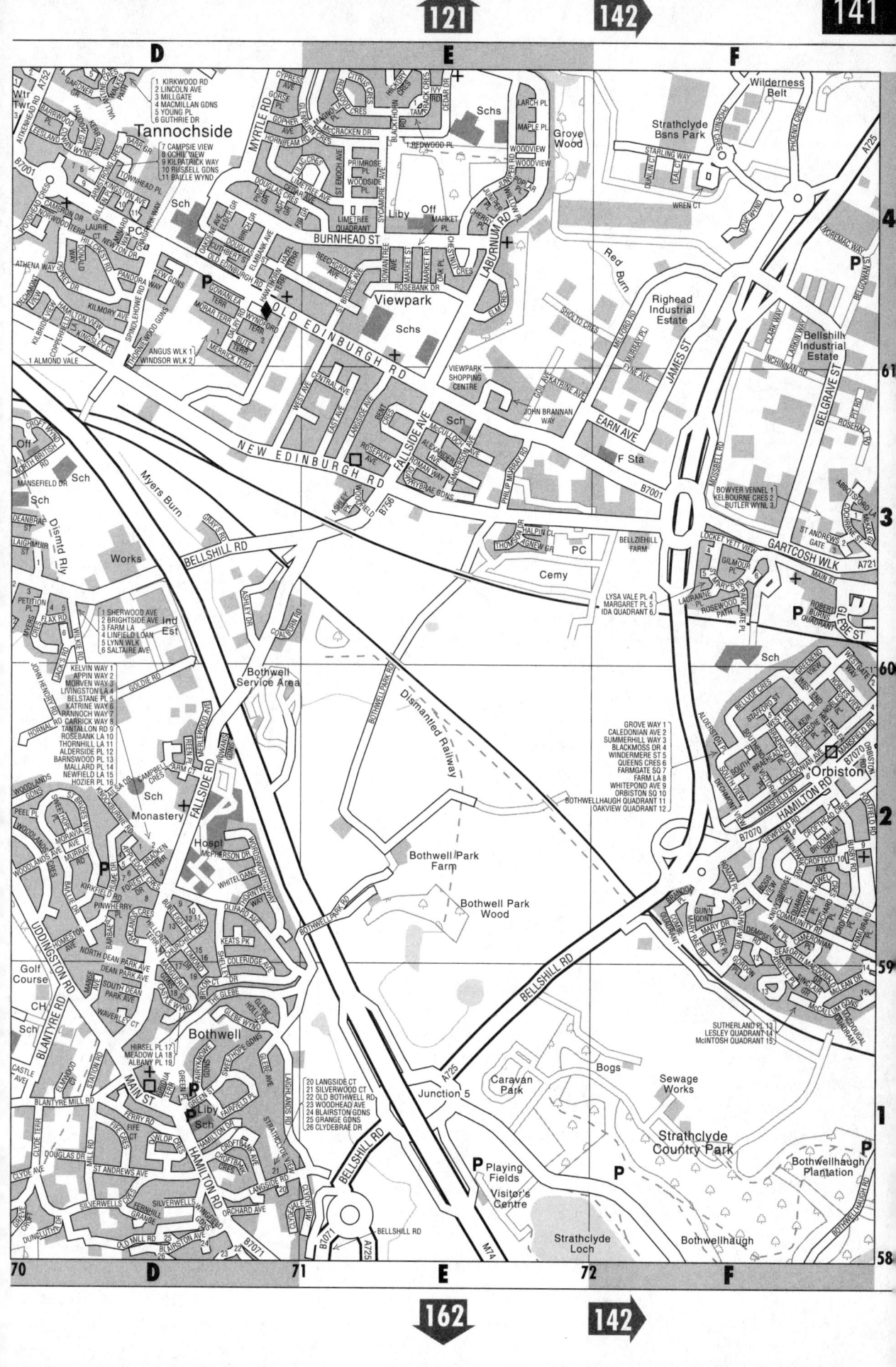

D
E
F

Wtr Twr
A752

1 KIRKWOOD RD
2 LINCOLN AVE
3 MILLGATE
4 MACMILLAN GDNS
5 YOUNG PL
6 GUTHRIE DR

Tannochside

7 CAMPSIE VIEW
8 OCHIL VIEW
9 KILPATRICK WAY
10 RUSSELL GDNS
11 BAILLE WYND

B7001

Sch

1 ALMOND VALE

Laurie
PC

Angus Wlk 1
Windsor Wlk 2

MORAR TERR
WYNDFORD TERR
BUTE TERR
MERRICK TERR

OLD EDINBURGH RD

MYRTLE RD

BURNHEAD ST

Viewpark

Schs

Schs

VIEWPARK SHOPPING CENTRE

Off Market Pl

Liby

Schs

LARCH PL
MAPLE PL

Grove Wood

Red Burn

WOODVIEW
WOODVIEW

Wilderness Belt

Strathclyde Bsns Park

STARLING WAY

WREN CT

Righead Industrial Estate

JAMES ST

Bellshill Industrial Estate

BELGRAVE ST

P

4

61

Off
NORTH BRITISH RD
MANSEFIELD DR
Sch

Sch

LAIGHMUIR ST

Works

Dismtd Rly

Myers Burn

BELLSHILL RD

NEW EDINBURGH RD

FALLSIDE AVE

B756

JOHN BRANNAN WAY

EARN AVE

F Sta

B7001

HALPIN CL
THOMAS AGNEW GR

PC

BELLZIEHILL FARM

Cemy

LYSA VALE PL 4
MARGARET PL 5
IDA QUADRANT 6

GARTCOSH WLK
A721

ST ANDREWS GATE

GILMOUR PL
MAIN ST

ROSEWOOD PARK

Robert Burns Quadrant

GLEBE ST

P

3

1 SHERWOOD AVE
2 BRIGHTSIDE AVE
3 FARM LA
4 LINFIELD LOAN
5 LYNN WLK
6 SALTAIRE AVE

Ind Est

Sch

Dismantled Railway

Bothwell Service Area

GROVE WAY 1
CALEDONIAN AVE 2
SUMMERHILL WAY 3
BLACKMOSS DR 4
WINDERMERE ST 5
QUEENS CRES 6
FARMGATE SQ 7
FARM LA 8
WHITEPOND AVE 9
ORBISTON SQ 10
BOTHWELLHAUGH QUADRANT 11
OAKVIEW QUADRANT 12

Orbiston

B7070

HAMILTON RD

60

KELVIN WAY 1
APPIN WAY 2
MORVEN WAY 3
LIVINGSTON LA 4
BELSTANE PL 5
KATRINE WAY 6
RANNOCH WAY 7
CARRICK WAY 8
TANTALLON RD 9
ROSEBANK LA 10
THORNHILL 11
ALDERSIDE PL 12
BARNSWOOD PL 13
MALLARD PL 14
NEWFIELD PL 15
HOZIER PL 16

Sch

Monastery

Hospl
McPHERSON DR

FALLSIDE RD

BOTHWELLPARK RD

Bothwell Park Farm

Bothwell Park Wood

BELLSHILL RD

B7070

2

Golf Course

CH

Sch

UDDINGTON RD

NORTH DEAN PARK AVE
DEAN PARK AVE
SOUTH DEAN PARK AVE

WAVERLEY CT

THE GLEBE

Bothwell

HIRSEL PL 17
MEADOW LA 18
ALBANY PL 19

KEATS PK
COLERIDGE LA

GLEBE WYND

SUTHERLAND PL 13
LESLEY QUADRANT 14
McINTOSH QUADRANT 15

59

BLANTYRE RD

CASTLE

Blantyre Mill Rd

CLYDE AVE

DOUGLAS DR

ST ANDREWS AVE

Main St

P

Liby

Sch

20 LANGSIDE CT
21 SILVERWOOD CT
22 OLD BOTHWELL RD
23 WOODHEAD AVE
24 BLAIRSTON GDNS
25 GRANGE GDNS
26 CLYDEBRAE DR

A725

Junction 5

HAMILTON RD

Caravan Park

Bogs

Sewage Works

Strathclyde Country Park

P

Bothwellhaugh Plantation

1

SILVERWELLS
FERNHILL GRANGE

HAMILTON RD

ORCHARD AVE

B7071
A725

BELLSHILL RD

BELLSHILL RD

Bellshill Rd

M74

P Playing Fields

Visitor's Centre

Strathclyde Loch

Bothwellhaugh

58

70
D
71
E
72
F

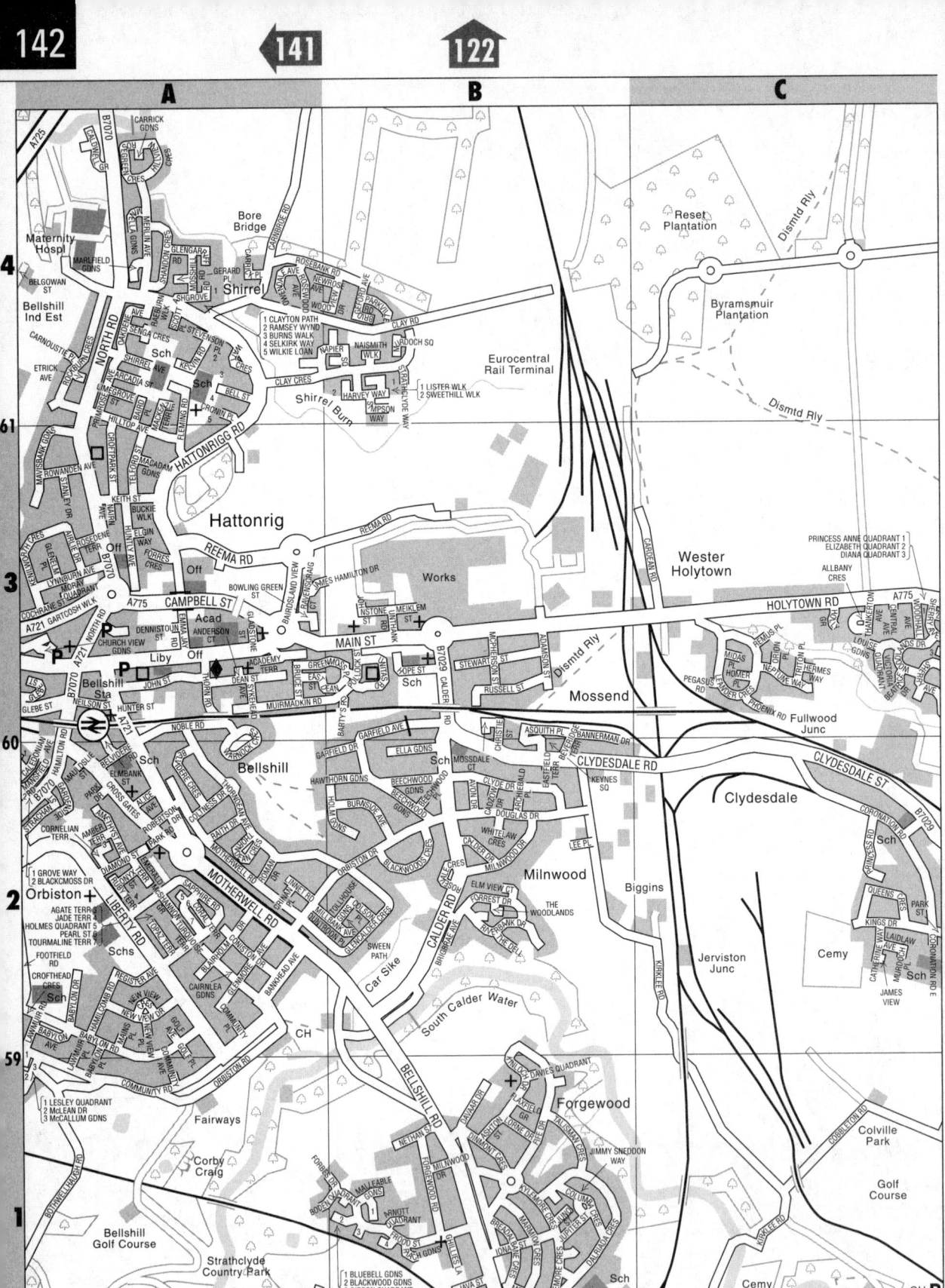

D E F

Dovecote Wood

Blacklands Plantation

Roundel Plantation

Lauchope Mains

Dismtd Rly

A8 M8

GLASGOW AND EDINBURGH RD

B802 WOODHALL MILL RD

B799

4

GLASGOW AND EDINBURGH RD

A775

BIGGAR RD

Townhead

Newhouse Ind Est

ROWANTREE AVE

HOWDEN AVE

SANDYFORD AVE

GLEN RD

MOSSHALL RD

LAUCHOPE RD

SANDYFORD AVE

BODDEN SQ

NICKLAUS WAY

61

O Wood

BEECH RD

BEECH CRES

KIRK RD

BEECH CRES

WESTFIELD RD

WOODLANDS RD

LEGBRANNOCK AVE

WOODBURN RD

EDINBURGH RD

LEGBRANNOCK RD

CASTLE DR

1 ELIZABETH QUADRANT
2 ALBERT QUADRANT
3 DIANA QUADRANT
4 FYNE WAY
5 GOIL WAY
6 LEVEN PATH
7 LOMOND WAY
8 BEECHGROVE QUADRANT
9 BURNSIDE QUADRANT
10 ARD LOAN
11 EARN LA
12 TROSSACHS AVE
13 ECK PATH
14 KATRINE WYND
15 MENTEITH LOAN
16 LUBNAIG WLK
17 NESS WAY
18 TAY LOAN
19 HERMISTON PL
20 MORAY WAY

Holytown

Cemy

Opencast Workings

21 ABBOTSFORD PL
22 BALLANTRAE WYND
23 KENILWORTH CT
24 IVANHOE PL
25 LAMMERMUIR PL
26 JUNIPER WYND
27 HAZELBANK
28 WOOD VIEW
29 OAK PATH
30 LILAC WAY
31 ALMOND PL
32 APOLLO PATH
33 GEMINI GR
34 TWEED LA
35 ASH WLK
36 LARCH GR
37 ALDER LA
38 OLIVE CT

1 ARMINE PATH
2 BURNS WAY
3 VORLICH WYND
4 CARRON WAY
5 MAILIE WLK
6 MORAR WAY
7 CRIFFEL PL
8 LEDI PATH
9 KILBRECK LA
10 ARMOUR PL
11 KYLE QUADRANT
12 BRANNOCK PL
13 BRAEHEAD QUADRANT

Legbrannock

1 ALLOWAY WYND
2 CLOCKERHILL PL

3

MAIN ST

STEVENSTON ST

Sch

Sch

HOLYTOWN RD

CHARLES QUADRANT

CENTENARY QUADRANT

McDONALD

SHERRY AVE

B799

ROWANTREE TERR

CUCKOO WAY

WILLOW GR

MYRTLE DR

ELM RD

POPLAR PL

LIME LOAN

Legbrannock Burn

CLYDE LA

CATRIONA WAY

SPRUCE WAY

LAW DR

SLIOCH SQ

BURNSIDE RD

LITTLE RD

MOSSGIEL WAY

BRANNOCK AVE

LEGBRANNOCK RD

KIRKOSWALD RD

CHURCH ST

HIGH ST

60

New Stevenston

1 BURN LA
2 HEATHER WAY
3 BLUEBELL WLK

HAMILTON PL

KIRK AVE

LAXFORD WAY

LAWERS LA

LOMOND WLK

BROOM RD

BRAESIDE AVE

VALLEYFIELD

CRES

Liby

ROBERT BURNS AVE

MOSSHALL GR

Sch

P

2

CLYDESDALE ST

QUARRY ST

Holytown Station

CEDAR GDNS

SYCAMORE

MAGNOLIA GDNS

CLARINDA PL

SILVER FIRS RD

ELLISLAND WYND

LINTH QUADRANT

GLENMORE RD

LOANHEAD RD

Sch

Liby

Sch

MOSSHALL ST

SPALEHALL DR

TILLANBURN RD

Liby

Sch

PARK AVE

KYLE GR

EARL VIEW

WRIGHT WAY

GREEN LOAN

MOORE ST

5 GROVE WYND

CARFIN ST

STATION RD

WRANGHOLM DR

WRANGHOLM CRES

HAWTHORN

BEECH AVE

SHAFTSBURY CRES 14
BERNADETTE ST 15
WHITTAGREEN CT 16
MELFORT QUADRANT 17
ERIBOL WLK 18

Whittagreen

LOANHEAD CRES

SILVERBIRCH CRES

LAUGHLAND DR

CARFIN RD

Cleland Townhead

CLELAND RD

59

Sch

4 ALDER LA
5 STEVENS LA

ROWAN LA

NORTHAVE

WEST AVE

CENTRAL AVE

EAST AVE

WALLACE RD

BRUCE RD

NEW STEVENSTON RD

Carfin Station

WOODROW AVE

HAMILTON PL

LEVEN PATH

HATTON TERR

NEWARTHILL RD

Sch

TAYLOR AVE

CARDON CT

BEECHWORTH DR

WHITTAGREEN CRES

Golf Course

Coleville Park

HILLHEAD CRES

HILLHEAD DR

HILLHEAD RD

Carfin Ind Est

1 EASTEND AVE
2 NORTHALL QUADRANT
3 JERVISTON CT

GLENBANK TERR

B7066

Carfin

Carfin Lourdes Grotto

Chapelknowe

Westerfield

1

JERVISTON RD

JERVISWOOD

CLAPPERTON RD

COALHALL AVE

MERRY ST

Cleekhimin

B799

LINKSVIEW RD

LOGAN LEA DR

MONTALTO AVE

MOTHERWELL RD

RYRESKNOWE LA

HATTONHILL

CARFIN MILL RD

MARJORY DR

MARION DR

B7029

Carfin Byres

CHAPELKNOWE RD

Playing Fields

B7029

58

76 D 77 E 78 F

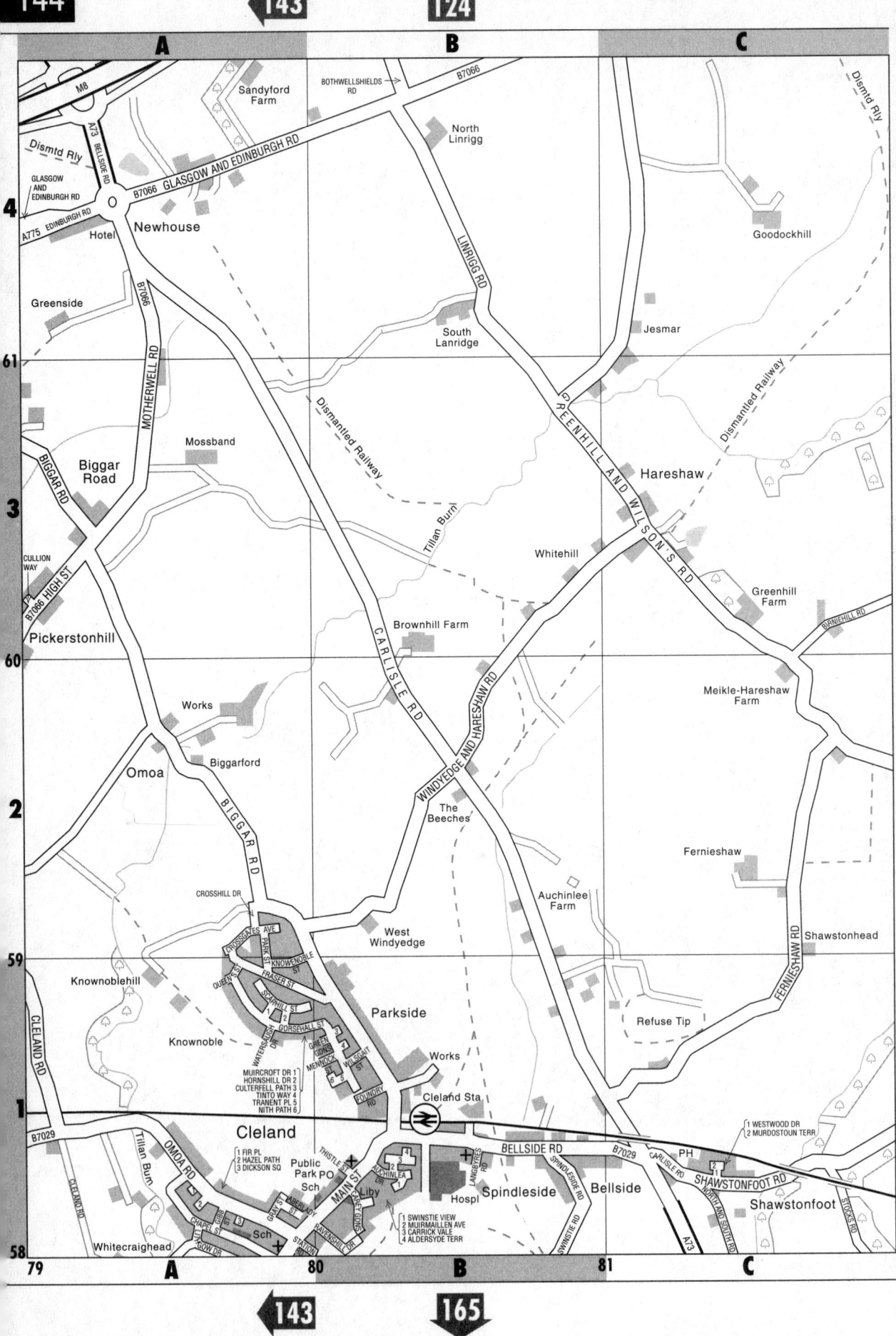

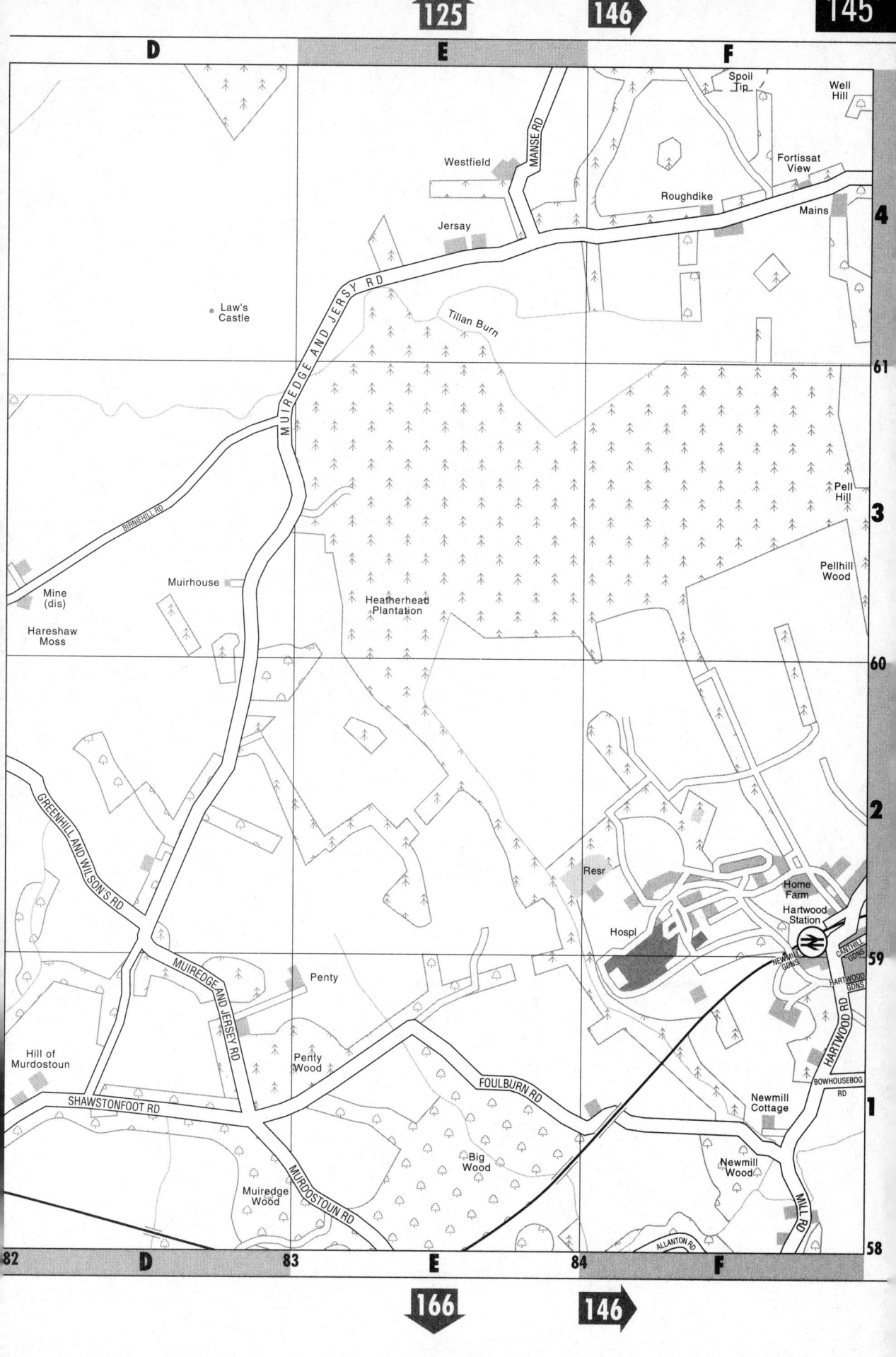

D E F

Spoil Tip
Well Hill

Fortissat View

Westfield
MANSE RD

Roughdike
Mains **4**

Jersay

Law's Castle

Tillan Burn

MUIREDGE AND JERSY RD

61

Pell Hill **3**

BIRNIEHILL RD

Pellhill Wood

Mine (dis)

Muirhouse

Heatherhead Plantation

Hareshaw Moss

60

Resr **2**

Home Farm
Hartwood Station

Hospl

GREENHILL AND WILSON'S RD

Newmill GDNS

CANTHILL GDNS

Hartwood GDNS

59

Penty

MUIREDGE AND JERSEY RD

HARTWOOD RD

Hill of Murdostoun

Penty Wood

FOULBURN RD

Newmill Cottage

BOWHOUSEBOG RD

SHAWSTONFOOT RD **1**

Big Wood

Newmill Wood

Muiredge Wood

MURDOSTOUN RD

MILL RD

ALLANTON RD

82 D 83 E 84 F 58

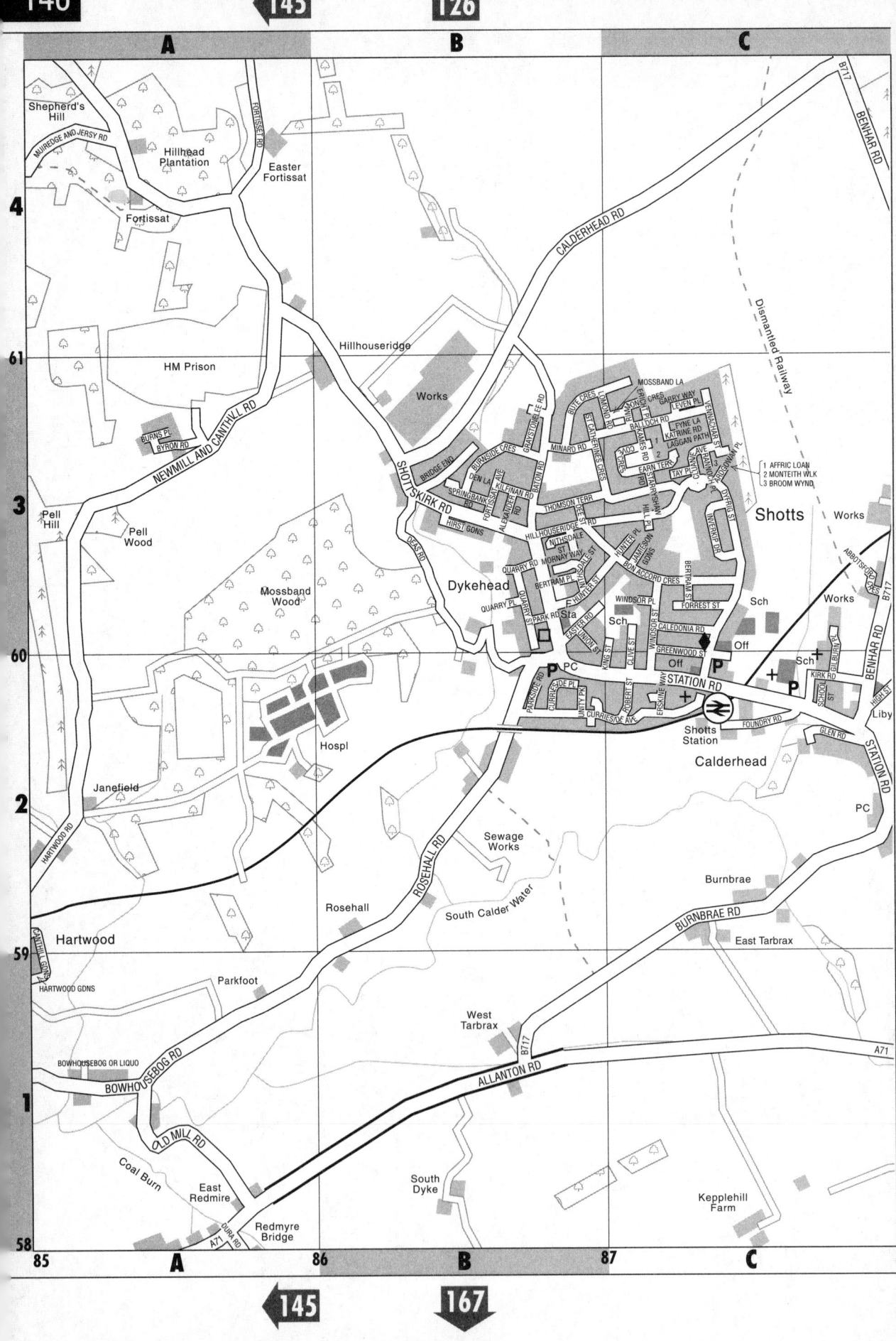

D   E   F

Fauldhouse

4

B717

61

BENHAR RD
CH
Golf Course
Amb Sta
Starryshaw Farm
South Calder Water

3
Spoil Heap
Stanebent
Stane
STABLE RD
Cairneyhead
Torbothie

GRAN ST
HIGH ST
60
ULG WAY
GAIR WYND
DOHRIE'S
TORBOTHIE RD
SOUTHFIELD RD
SOUTHFIELD CRES
CLYDE DR
KELVIN DR
CALDER DR
HAWTHORN DR
Torbothie
Sch
PC
2
CEMETERY RD
MANSE RD
CHARLOTTE ST
NEVIS PL
Cemy
1 ETIVE WAY
2 ULG WAY
3 GAIR WYND
4 BOWMORE WLK
5 TORRIN LOAN
6 DORNIE WYND
7 MORAR WAY
8 COIRE LOAN
9 SUNA PATH
10 SALEN LOAN

B7010
MAIN ST
SANDYVALE PL
Stane
BLINNY CT 1
TARBRAX PATH 2
REDHAWS RD
GARTEN DR
LOCHABER CRES
TULLOCH RD
APPIN TERR
WYVIS PL
MELFORD AVE
LINGT PL
LAGGAN AVE
BRIDGE PL
SHIEL BANK
NAVAR CT
KNOLL CROFT RD
LANSDOWNE CRES
HUNTLY TERR
SPRINGHILL RD
Springhill
B7010
B7010
BLACKHILL ST
BELMONT DR
BERRYHILL PL
BROWN ST
MILTON CT
BRECKONSIDE
STANE RD
LARCHFIELD LA
NORTHFIELD AVE
ELMWOOD RD
59
Works
Springhill
B715
HEADLESSCROSS RD
B715

SPRINGHILL AND LEADLOCH RD
Dismantled Railway
Knowton Farm
Works
Lingore Linn
A71
1

Dismtld Rly

58

88   D   89   E   90   F

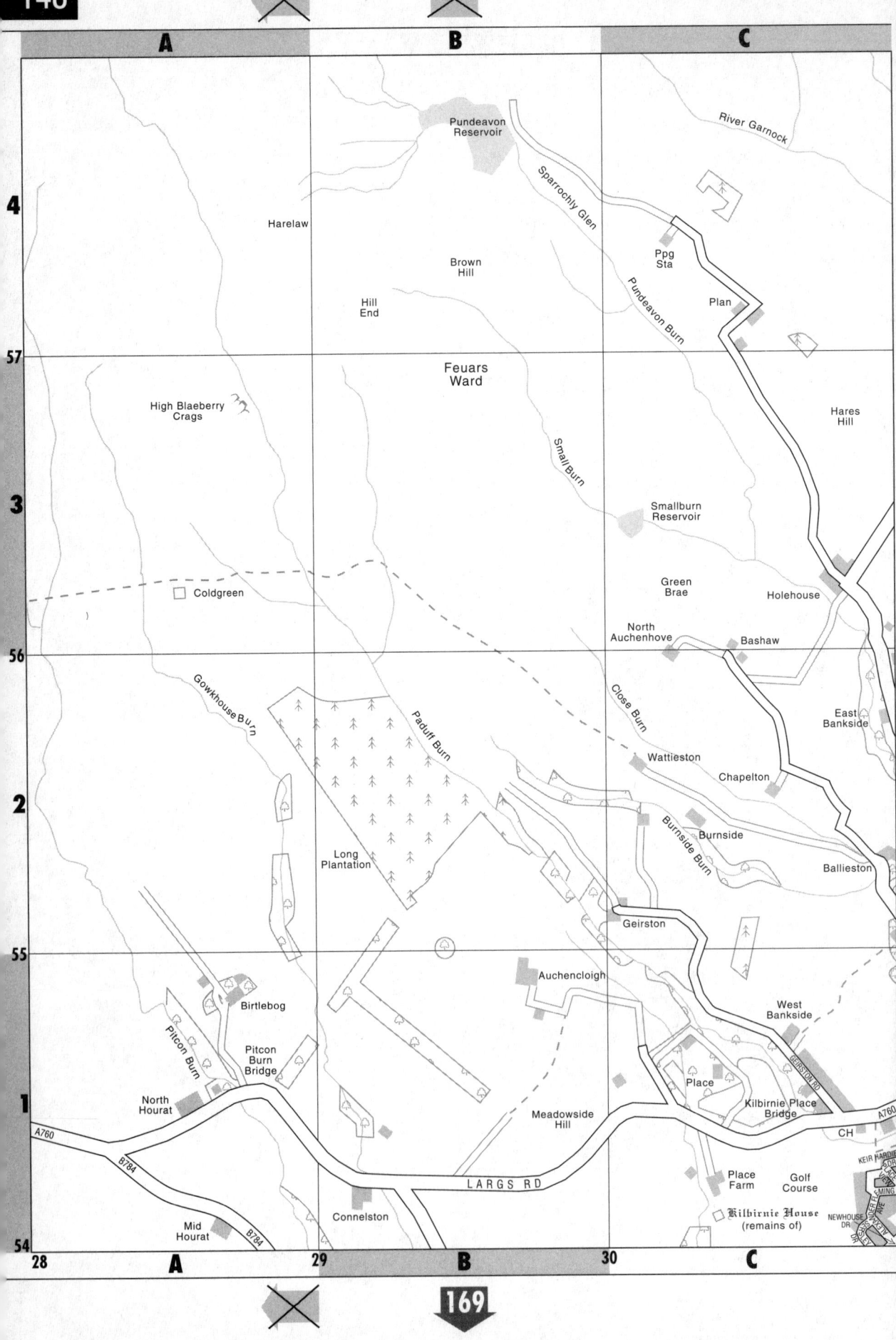

A **B** **C**

4

River Garnock

Pundeavon
Reservoir

Sparrochly Glen

Harelaw

Brown
Hill

Ppg
Sta

Plan

Hill
End

Pundeavon Burn

57

Feuars
Ward

Hares
Hill

High Blaeberry
Crags

Small Burn

3

Smallburn
Reservoir

Green
Brae

Holehouse

Coldgreen

North
Auchenhove

Bashaw

56

East
Bankside

Gowkhouse Burn

Paduff Burn

Close Burn

Wattieston

Chapelton

2

Burnside Burn

Burnside

Ballieston

Long
Plantation

Geirston

55

Auchencloigh

West
Bankside

Birtlebog

GEIRSTON RD

Pitcon Burn

Pitcon
Burn
Bridge

Place

Kilbirnie Place
Bridge

1

North
Hourat

A760

CH

A760

A760

Meadowside
Hill

KEIR HARDIE

B784

LARGS RD

Place
Farm

Golf
Course

NEWHOUSE
DR

Mid
Hourat

B784

Connelston

Kilbirnie House
(remains of)

54

28 **A** 29 **B** 30 **C**

D E F

4

57

3

56

2

55

1

54

Birkhill Wood
Rashlieyett
Ladyland
Smugglers Cave
East Auchenhain
Plantly Moss
Millbank Bridge
Meikle Millbank
Milnside Burn
Ladyland Bridge
West Auchenhain
Kaimhill
Glen Garnock
Blackbarn
High Glengarth
Laigh Glengarth
Langstilly
Jeffreystock
A760
Kaimhill
Whiteridden
Langslie
West Lochhead
Greenridge
Wallace Farm
Dipple Burn
Mach Water
Nervelstone
Langslie Bridge
Newfaulds
North Langlands
Black Burn
Brockly Hill
River Garnock
Barrhill
Kerse
North Kerse
East Kerse
Langlands
Maich Bridge
Black Burn
Bankside Gdns
Redheugh
Wester Kerse
Pundeavon Burn
Dismantled Railway
Lochridge Bridge
Kerse Bridge
Moorpark (Training Centre)
East Lochridge
Sch
Garnock Acad
West Lochridge
Ardloch House
School Rd
Works
Stoneyholm Rd
Kilbirnie Loch
Hotel
Off
PCs
Mains Lodge
Kilbirnie
Paddockholm North Ind Est
Paddockholm South Ind Est
Ind Est
Westfield
Liby

1 D 32 E 33 F 54

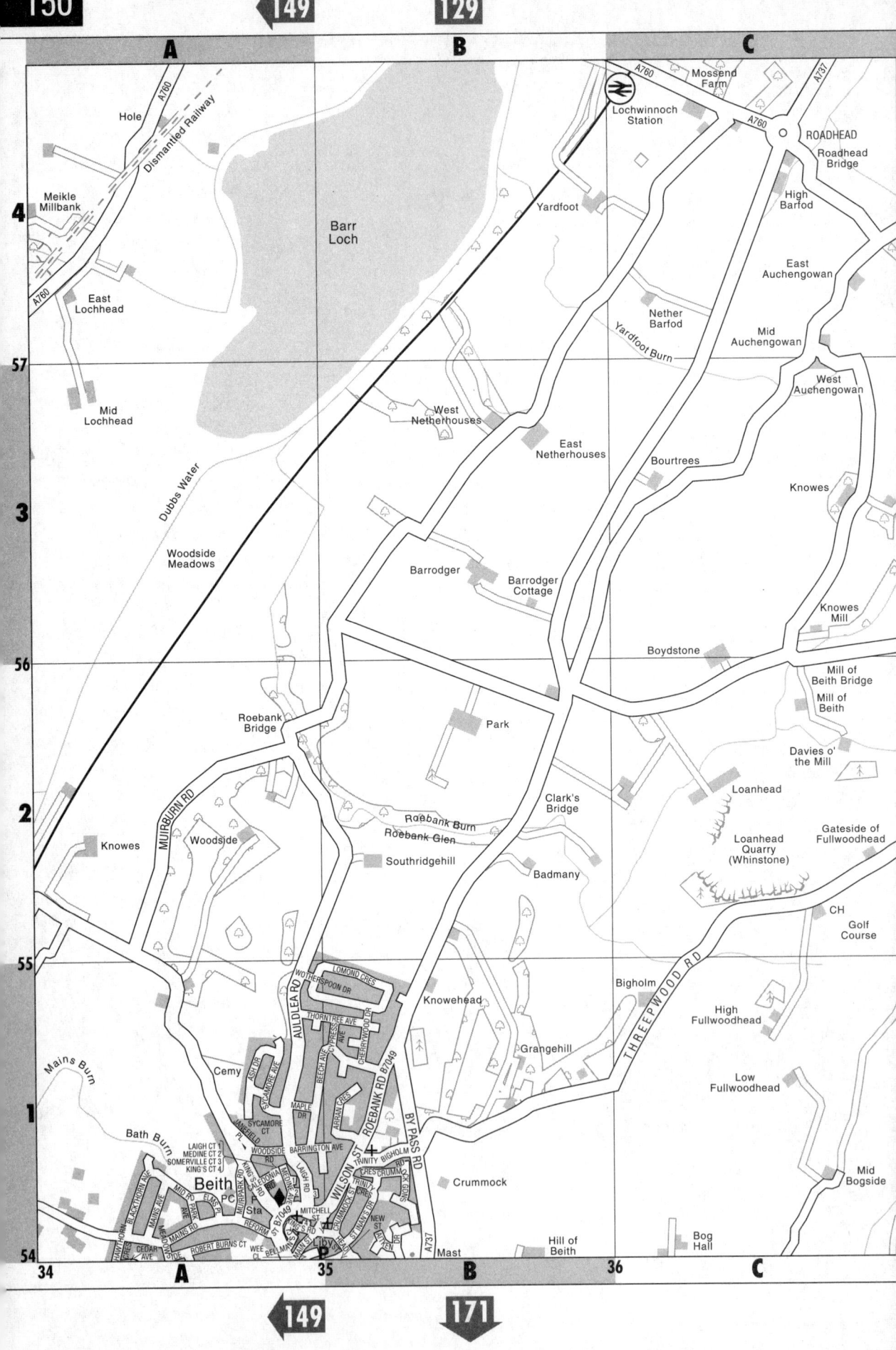

Hole

Dismantled Railway

A760

Meikle
Millbank

4

East
Lochhead

Barr
Loch

Lochwinnoch
Station

Mossend
Farm

A760

ROADHEAD

Roadhead
Bridge

High
Barfod

Yardfoot

East
Auchengowan

Nether
Barfod

Mid
Auchengowan

57

Mid
Lochhead

West
Netherhouses

Yardfoot Burn

West
Auchengowan

East
Netherhouses

Bourtrees

Knowes

Dubbs Water

Woodside
Meadows

3

Barrodger

Barrodger
Cottage

Knowes
Mill

Boydstone

Mill of
Beith Bridge

Mill of
Beith

56

Roebank
Bridge

Park

Davies o'
the Mill

Loanhead

MUIRBURN RD

Knowes

Woodside

Roebank Burn
Roebank Glen

Clark's
Bridge

Loanhead
Quarry
(Whinstone)

Gateside of
Fullwoodhead

2

Southridgehill

Badmany

CH

Golf
Course

55

LOMOND CRES

WOTHERSPOON DR

Knowehead

Bigholm

THREEPWOOD RD

High
Fullwoodhead

AULDLEA RD

THORNTREE AVE

Grangehill

Low
Fullwoodhead

Mains Burn

Cemy

ASH DR

BEECH AVE

CYPRESS AVE

CHERRYWOOD DR

ROEBANK RD B7049

BY PASS RD

1

Bath Burn

SYCAMORE
CT

MAPLE
DR

ARRAN CRES

WOODSIDE RD

BARRINGTON AVE

LAIGH CT 1
MEDINE CT 2
SOMERVILLE CT 3
KING'S CT 4

WILSON ST

BIGHOLM
CRES

CRUMMOCK & SONS

Crummock

Mid
Bogside

Beith

PC

P
Sta

MITCHELL

A737

Mast

Hill of
Beith

Bog
Hall

54

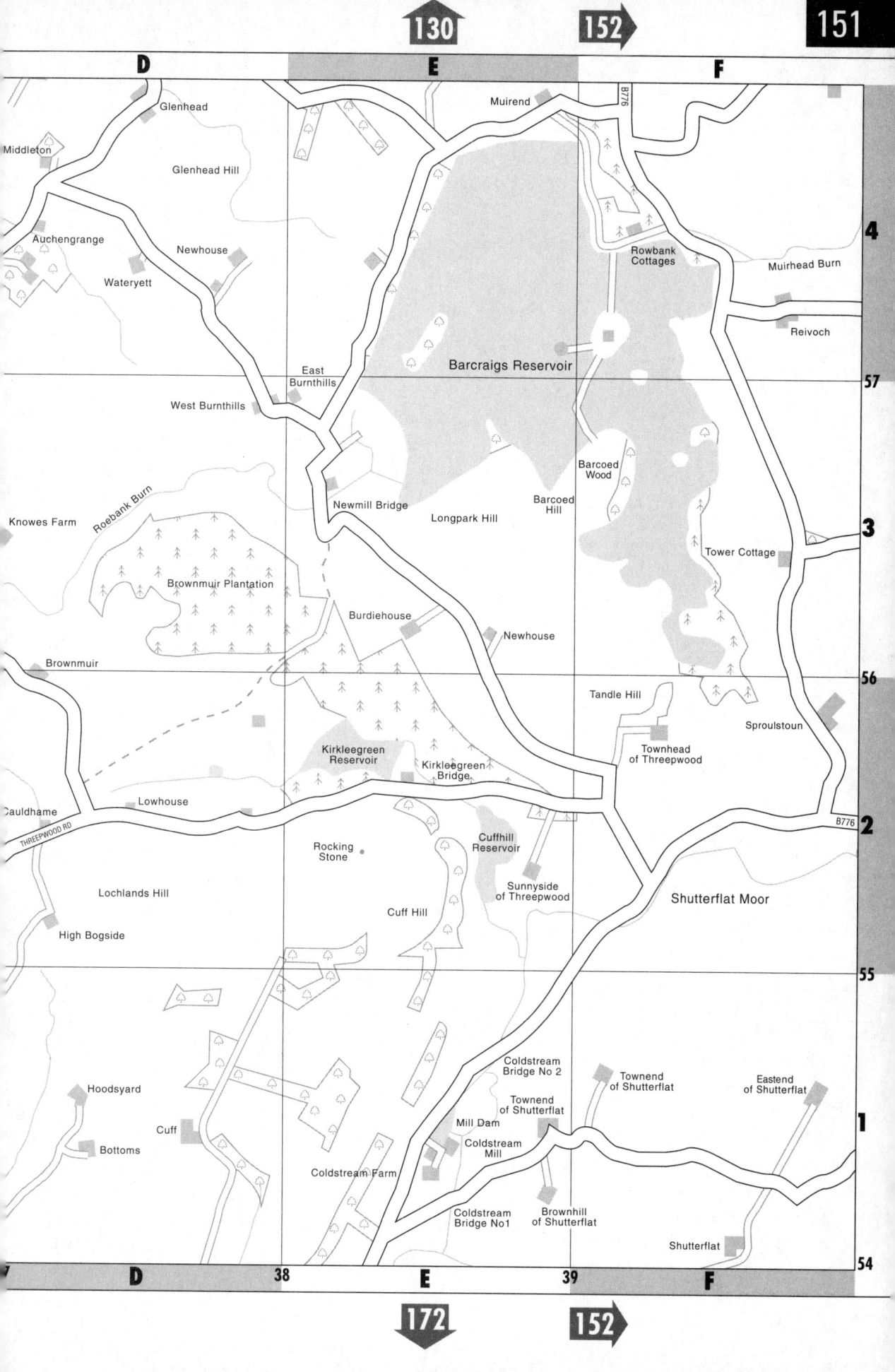

4

Middleton

Glenhead

Glenhead Hill

Auchengrange

Newhouse

Wateryett

Muirend

B776

Rowbank
Cottages

Muirhead Burn

Reivoch

Barcraigs Reservoir

57

East
Burnthills

West Burnthills

Knowes Farm

Roebank Burn

Brownmuir Plantation

Newmill Bridge

Longpark Hill

Barcoed
Wood

Barcoed
Hill

Tower Cottage

3

Burdiehouse

Newhouse

Brownmuir

Tandle Hill

56

Sproulstoun

Kirkleegreen
Reservoir

Kirkleegreen
Bridge

Townhead
of Threepwood

Cauldhame

Lowhouse

THREEPWOOD RD

Rocking
Stone

Cuffhill
Reservoir

B776

2

Lochlands Hill

Cuff Hill

Sunnyside
of Threepwood

Shutterflat Moor

High Bogside

55

Hoodsyard

Coldstream
Bridge No 2

Townend
of Shutterflat

Eastend
of Shutterflat

Townend
of Shutterflat

Cuff

Mill Dam

Bottoms

Coldstream
Mill

1

Coldstream Farm

Coldstream
Bridge No1

Brownhill
of Shutterflat

Shutterflat

54

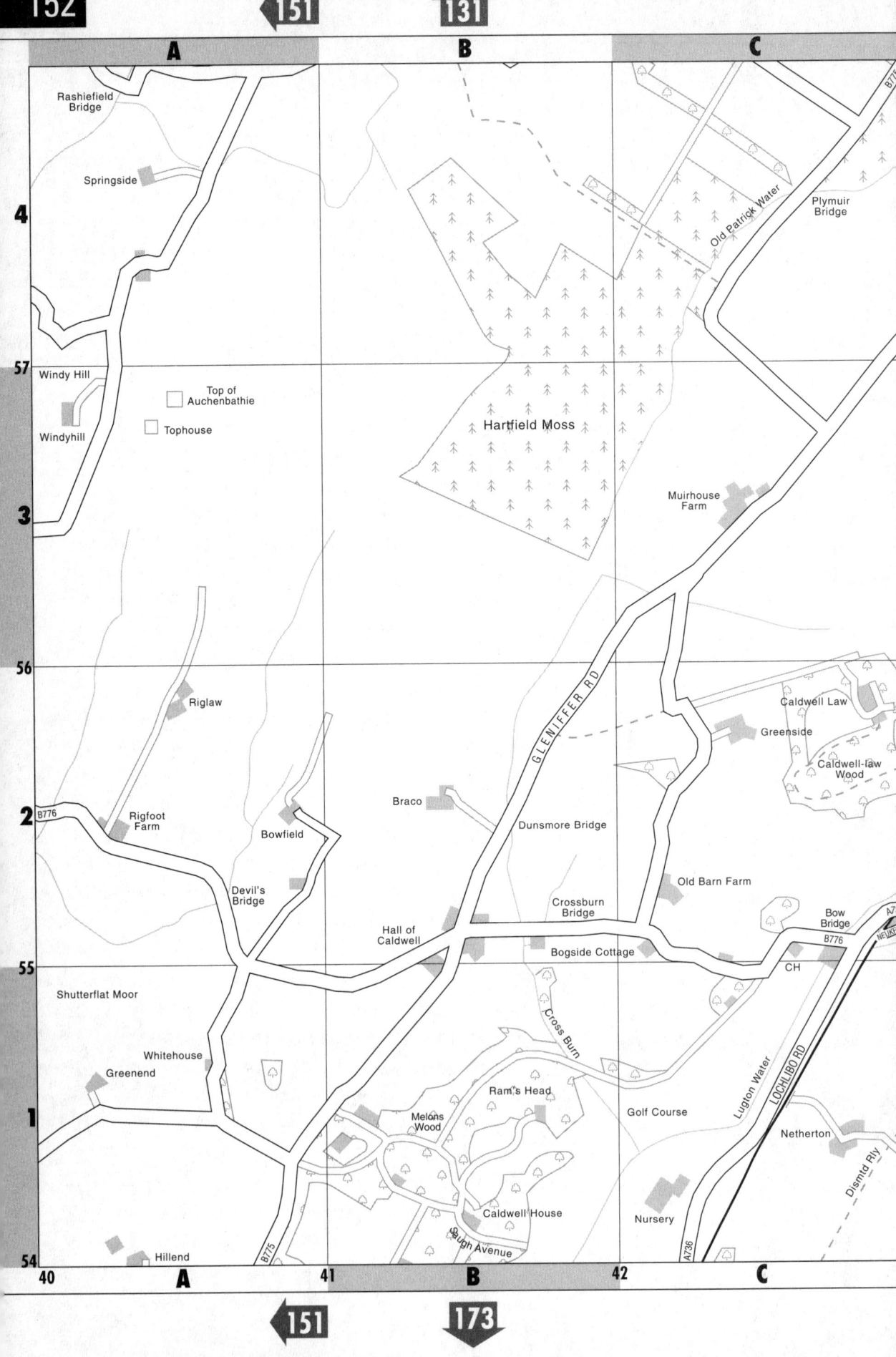

A   **B**   **C**

Rashiefield
Bridge

Springside

4

B775

Old Patrick Water

Plymuir
Bridge

57
Windy Hill

Top of
Auchenbathie

Tophouse

Windyhill

Hartfield Moss

Muirhouse
Farm

3

GLENIFFER RD

56

Riglaw

Caldwell Law

Greenside

Caldwell-law
Wood

Braco

Dunsmore Bridge

2
B776

Rigfoot
Farm

Bowfield

Old Barn Farm

Bow
Bridge

A73

Devil's
Bridge

Crossburn
Bridge

B776

NEUKED

Hall of
Caldwell

Bogside Cottage

CH

55

Shutterflat Moor

Cross Burn

LOCHLIBO RD

Lugton Water

Whitehouse

Greenend

Ram's Head

Golf Course

1

Melons
Wood

Netherton

Dismtd Rly

Caldwell House

Nursery

A736

Hillend

B775

ugh Avenue

54
40   **A**   **41**   **B**   **42**   **C**

Old Patrick Water

Fauldhead

Middleton Farm

Threepgrass Wood

Witch Burn

SERGEANT LAW RD

Lochliboside Hills

4

Caravan Site

Plymuir

FERENEZE RD

Milnthird

57

Corkindale Law

Pattiston Farm

Thorterburn

Side Braes

A736

Banklug

Cowdon Burn

3

Cowdon Mill Bridge

Finniebrae

LOCHLIBO RD

Shillford

UPLAWMOOR RD

56

Caldwell Law

Dismantled Railway

Cowdenmoor

Jaapston Farm

Uplawmoor Wood

Loch Libo

Uplawmoor

Howcraigs Hill

Braeface Farm

2

BIRCHWOOD RD

ARTHURLIE DRIVE

ARTHURLIE AVE

East Uplaw

Muirhead

BRIDGEND WLK

LIBO AVE

EMPIRE PL

NEILSTON RD

Hotel

Mid Uplaw Farm

Aboon the Brae

GLEN LA

Liby

Sch

55

NEUKFOOT LA

TANNOCH RD

POLLOCK CASTLE LA

POLLICK AVE

Cast Bridge

Knockglass

Pollick

Newlands Bridge

Commore Dam

Spunkie

1

Knockenae Plantation

Tennoch Hill

West Uplaw

South Uplaw

153
133

153
175

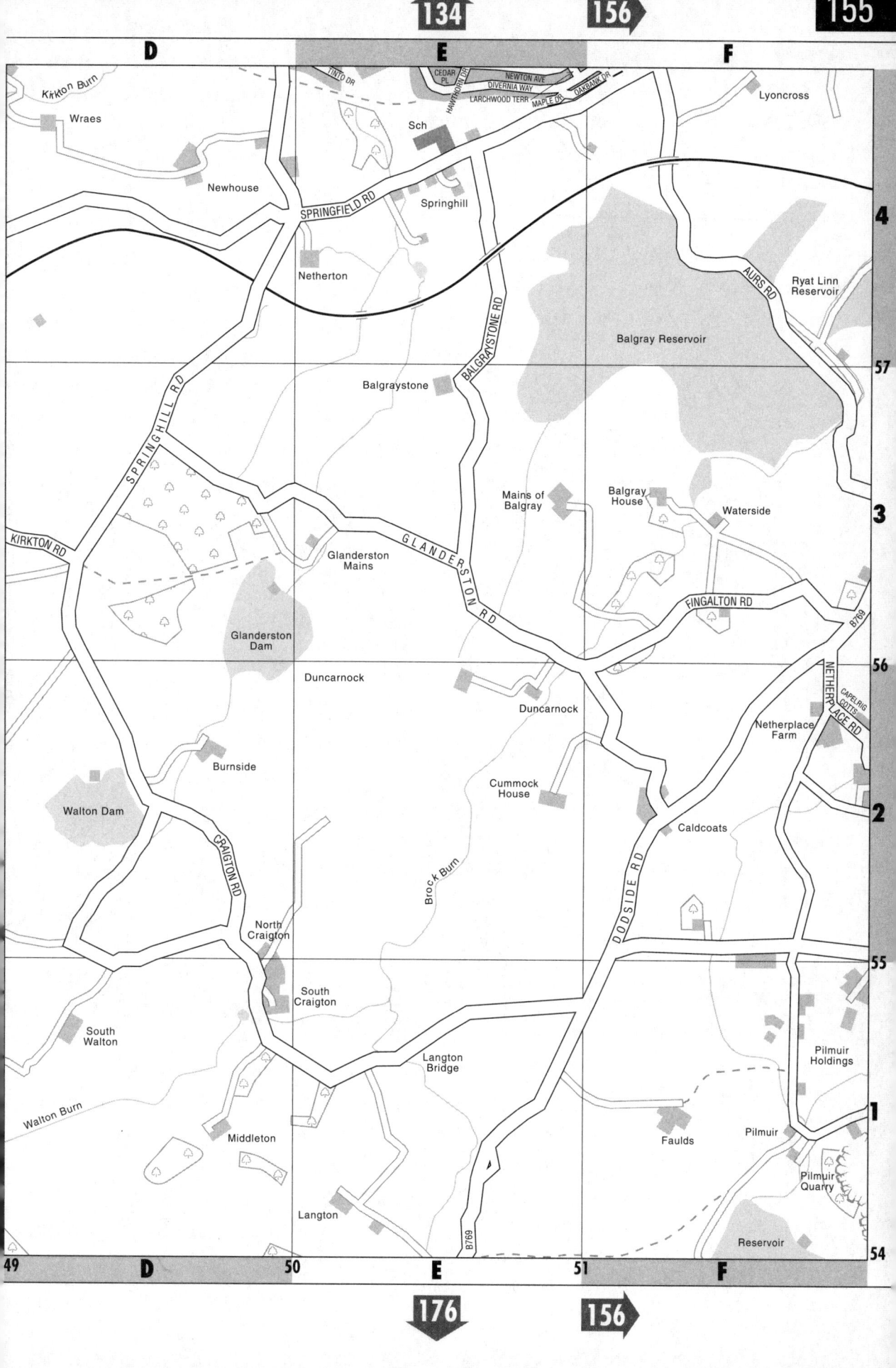

D E F

4

57

3

56

2

55

1

54

Kirkton Burn

Wraes

Newhouse

TINTO DR

CEDAR PL

HAWTHORN DR

NEWTON AVE

DIVERNIA WAY

LARCHWOOD TERR

MAPLE DR

OAKBANK DR

Lyoncross

Sch

SPRINGFIELD RD

Springhill

Netherton

BALGRAYSTONE RD

AURS RD

Ryat Linn
Reservoir

Balgray Reservoir

SPRINGHILL RD

Balgraystone

KIRKTON RD

Mains of
Balgray

Balgray
House

Waterside

GLANDERSTON RD

Glanderston
Mains

FINGALTON RD

B769

Glanderston
Dam

Duncarnock

NETHERPLACE RD

CAPELRIG COTTS

Duncarnock

Netherplace
Farm

Burnside

Cummock
House

Caldcoats

Walton Dam

CRAIGTON RD

Brock Burn

DODSIDE RD

North
Craigton

South
Craigton

South
Walton

Langton
Bridge

Pilmuir
Holdings

Walton Burn

Middleton

Faulds

Pilmuir

Pilmuir
Quarry

Langton

B769

Reservoir

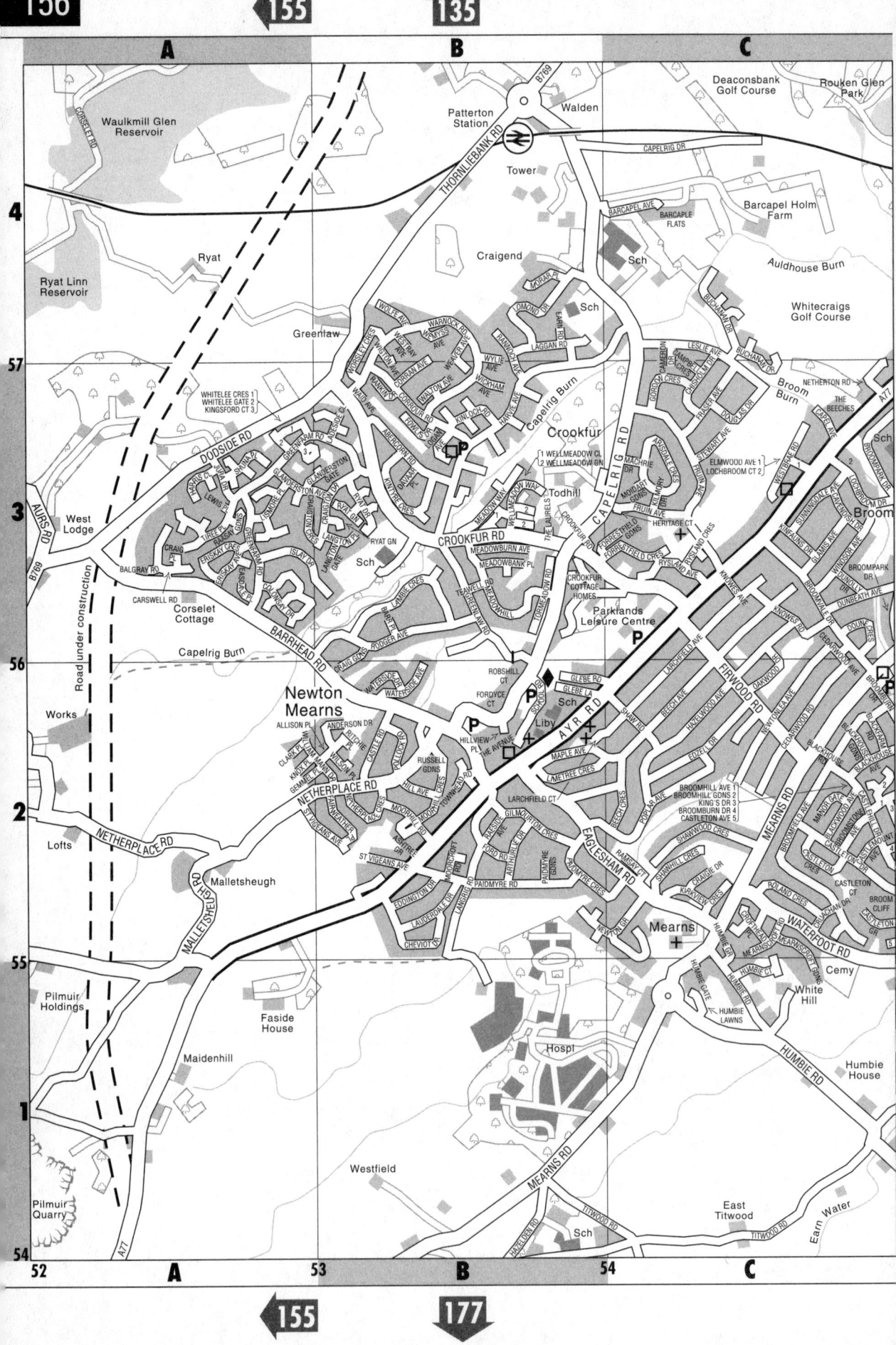

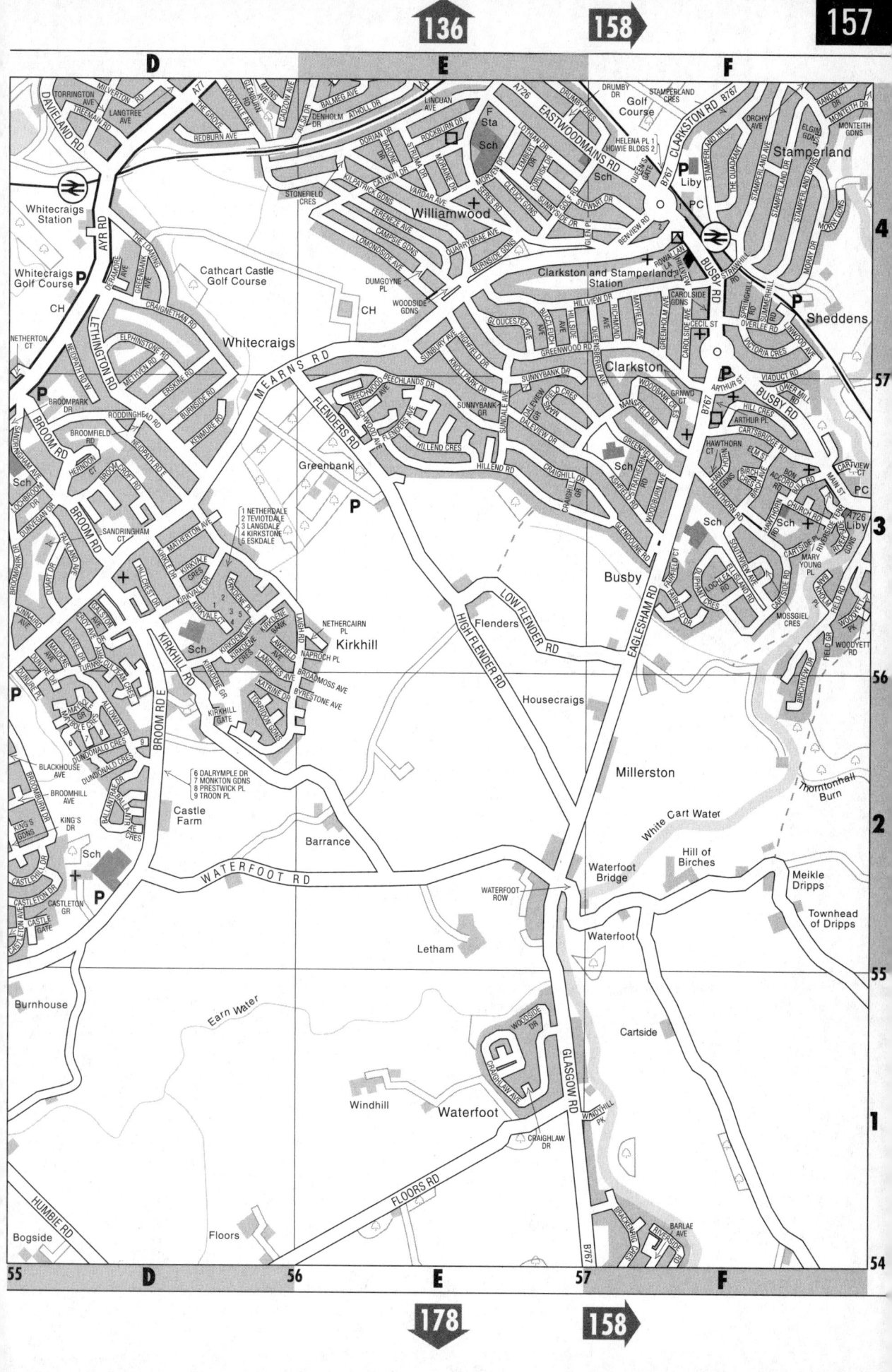

A B C

4

57

3

56

2

55

1

54

58 A 59 B 60 C

Cathkin Braes
Golf Course

B759

CARMUNNOCK RD

White Cart Water

Netherton
Braes

Mast

CARMUNNOCK BY-PASS

Carnbooth
House

Kittoch Water

White Cart Water

Hillcrest

Pedmyre

High Beeches

Greenside RD

CATHKIN RD

Carmunnock

SYCAMORE WAY

BUSBY RD

PEDMYRE LA

Kittoch
Bridge

PICKETLAW FARM RD

Picketlaw

WATERSIDE GDNS

Sch

Parklea

KITTOCHSIDE RD

Easter
Busby

1 GLENVILLE GATE
2 GLENVILLE TERR
3 PRINTERS LAND

CARMUNNOCK RD

WATERSIDE RD

WATERBANK RD

Wester
Kittochside

A726

EAST KILBRIDE RD

Busby
Sta

1 WOODHOUSE CT
2 BELLCRAIG CT

Castle
Hill

The
Peel

Waterside

Kittoch Water

Waterbank

GLEN RD

Dis Rly

Busbyside

Bystone

B766

Sewage
Works

Cemy

CASTLEGLEN RD

Thorntonhall Burn

East Kilbride RD

Philipshill

PHILLPSHILL RD

STEWARTFIELD WAY

Castle
Hill

PEEL RD

Braehead

Braehead RD

Laigh
Braehead

Thorntonhall

BARBANA RD

Hotel

Rough
Hill

GLENBURN WAY

QUEENSWAY

A726

Thorntonhall
Station

WELLKNOWE PL

BISHOPS GATE

WELLKNOWE AVE

THORN AVE

RAVENSCOURT

REDWOOD DR

REDWOOD CRES

REDWOOD PL

Industrial
Estate

PEEL PARK RD

Industrial
Estate

Birkwood

GILMOUR AVE

South Hill
of Dripps

THORNTON RD

Thornton
Farm

Peel
Park

BURLEY PL

North Hill
of Dripps

Southland

Thornton
Farm

Hairmyres
Station

B764

Little
Dripps

Millbrae

HAIRMYRES
ROUNDABOUT

Off

EAGLESHAM RD

Hosp

WESTPORT

Amb
Sta

REDWOOD AVE

REDWOOD CT

B764

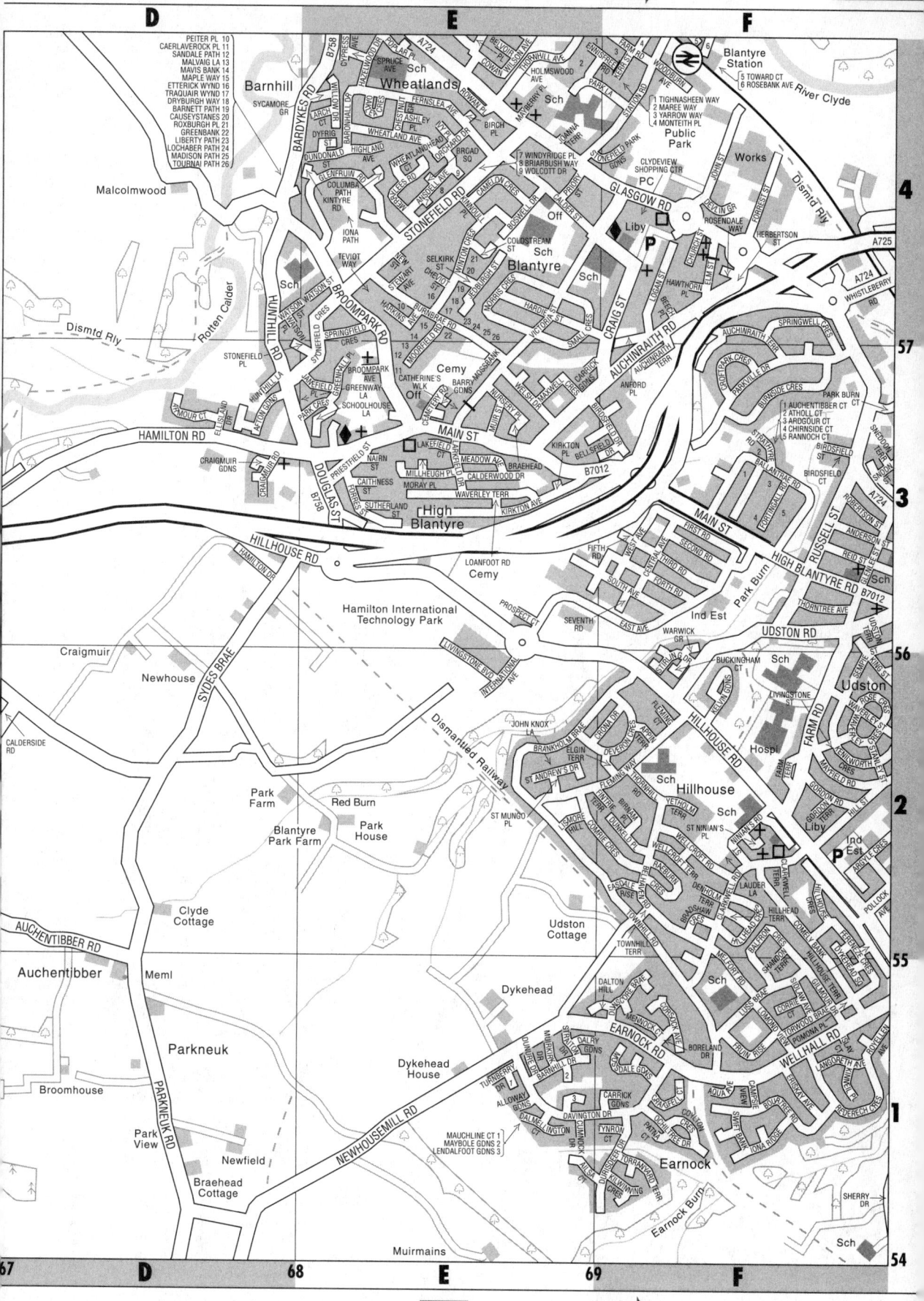

PEITER PL 10
CAERLAVEROCK PL 11
SANDALE PATH 12
MALVAIG LA 13
MAVIS BANK 14
MAPLE WAY 15
ETTERICK WYND 16
TRAQUAIR WYND 17
DRYBURGH WAY 18
BARNETT PATH 19
CAUSEYSTANES 20
ROXBURGH PL 21
GREENBANK 22
LIBERTY PATH 23
LOCHABER PATH 24
MADISON PATH 25
TOURNAI PATH 26

Barnhill
SYCAMORE GR

Malcolmwood

Wheatlands
Sch

Blantyre Station
5 TOWARD CT
6 ROSEBANK AVE

River Clyde

1 TIGHNASHEEN WAY
2 MAREE WAY
3 YARROW WAY
4 MONTEITH PL

Public Park

7 WINDYRIDGE PL
8 BRIARBUSH WAY
9 WOLCOTT DR

CLYDEVIEW
SHOPPING CTR
PC

Works

Dismtd Rly

GLASGOW RD

Liby
P

A725

A724

WHISTLEBERRY RD

Blantyre
Sch

AUCHINRAITH RD

1 AUCHENTIBBER CT
2 ATHOLL CT
3 ARDGOUR CT
4 CHIRNSIDE CT
5 RANNOCH CT

PARK BURN

BIRDSFIELD

57

3

Rotten Calder

Sch

Dismtd Rly

HUNTHILL RD

BROOMPARK RD

Stonefield
PL

MAIN ST

HAMILTON RD

CRAIGMUIR
GDNS

DOUGLAS ST

B758

High
Blantyre

Cemy

LOANFOOT RD

MAIN ST

FIFTH RD

HIGH BLANTYRE RD

RUSSELL ST

B7012

Sch

Craigmuir

Hillhouse Rd

Hamilton International
Technology Park

LIVINGSTONE BLVD

INTERNATIONAL AVE

PROSPECT CT

SEVENTH RD

EAST AVE

WARWICK GR

Ind Est

UDSTON RD

BUCKINGHAM CT

Sch

LIVINGSTONE

Udston

56

Newhouse

SYDES BRAE

HAMILTON DR

Dismantled Railway

JOHN KNOX LA

BRANKHOLM BRAE

ELGIN TERR

ST ANDREW'S DR

St MUNGO PL

HILLHOUSE RD

FARM RD

Hospl

Sch

Hillhouse

Liby
Ind Est
P

2

CALDERSIDE RD

Park Farm

Red Burn

Park House

Blantyre
Park Farm

Udston
Cottage

TOWNHILL RD

Sch

55

Auchentibber

Clyde Cottage

Meml

AUCHENTIBBER RD

PARKNEUK RD

Dykehead

DALTON HILL

EARNOCK RD

WELLHALL RD

Parkneuk

Dykehead
House

NEWHOUSEMILL RD

MAUCHLINE CT 1
MAYBOLE GDNS 2
LENDALFOOT GDNS 3

TURNBERRY DR

ALLOWAY

CARRICK GDNS

Sch

1

Broomhouse

Park
View

Newfield

Braehead
Cottage

Earnock

SHERRY DR

Sch

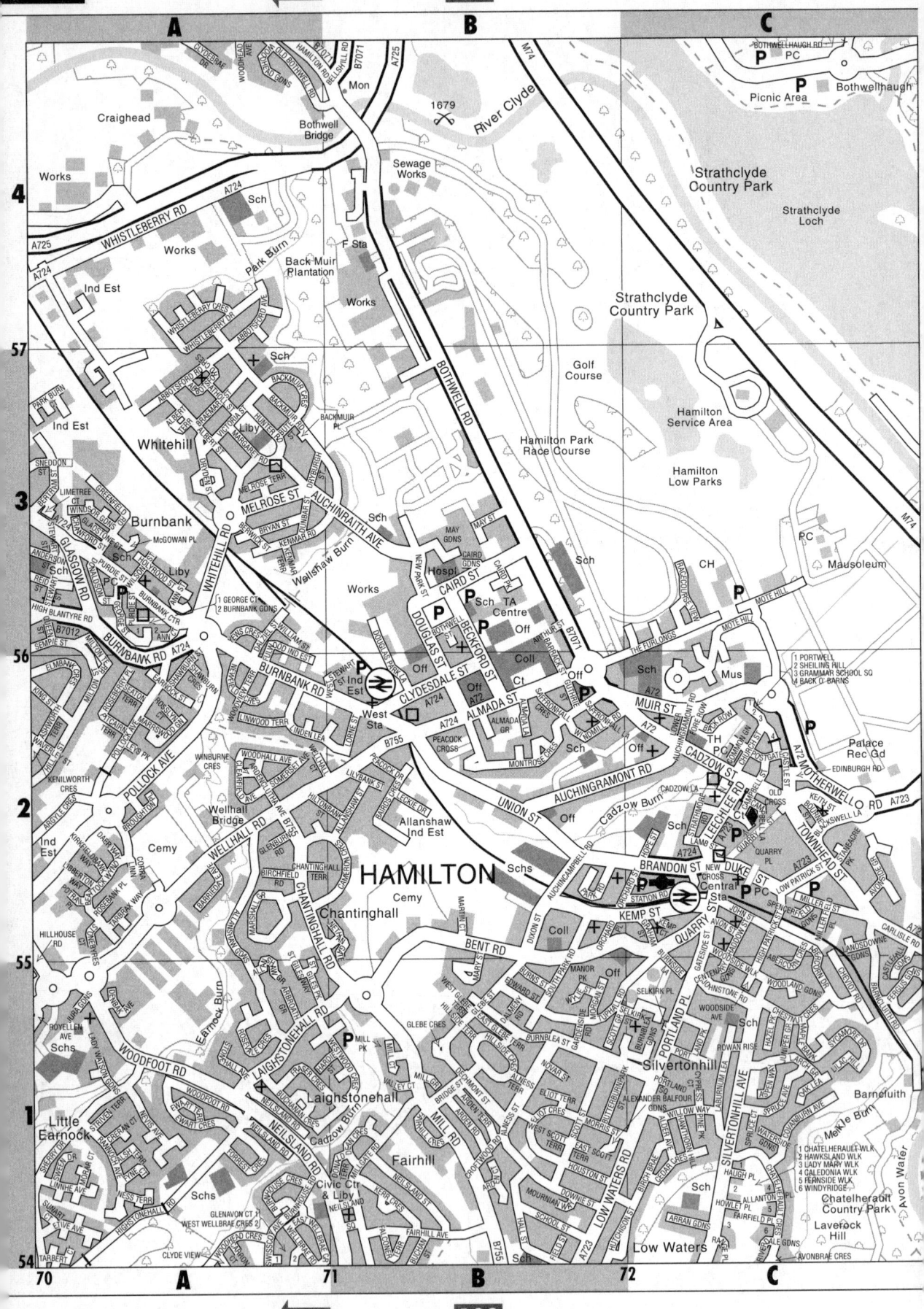

HAMILTON

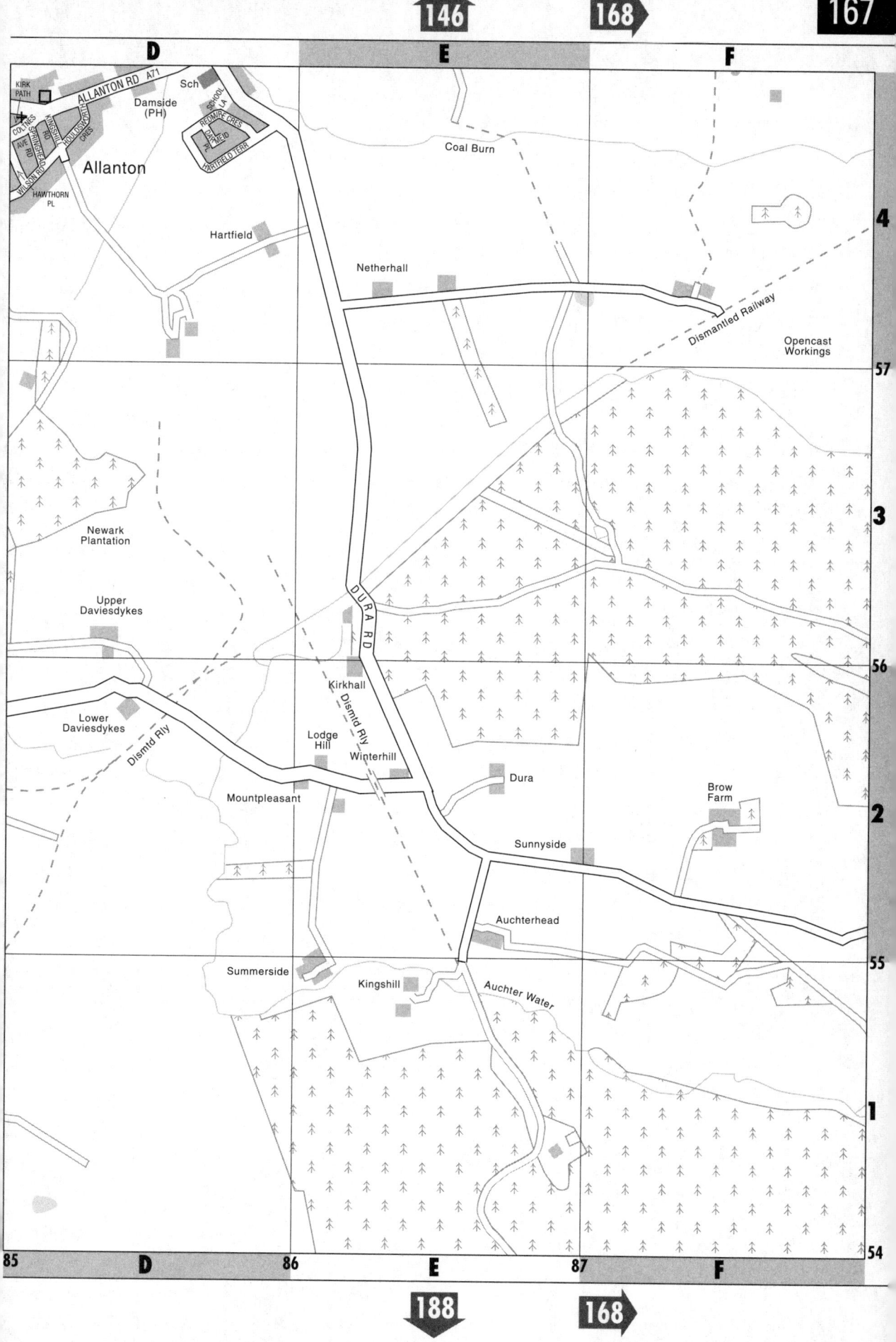

D

E

F

KIRK
PATH
ALLANTON RD A71
COLTNESS
SPRINGFIELD RD
KIRKSHIELD RD
HOLLANDSWORTH RD
WILSON RD
AVE
HAWTHORN PL
Sch
Damside
(PH)
SCHOOL LA
REDMIRE CRES
OAK MEAD
HARTFIELD TERR

Allanton

Hartfield

Coal Burn

Netherhall

4

Dismantled Railway

Opencast
Workings

57

Newark
Plantation

3

Upper
Daviesdykes

DURA RD

56

Kirkhall

Lower
Daviesdykes

Dismtd Rly

Dismtd Rly

Lodge
Hill

Winterhill

Dura

Brow
Farm

2

Mountpleasant

Sunnyside

Auchterhead

55

Summerside

Kingshill

Auchter Water

1

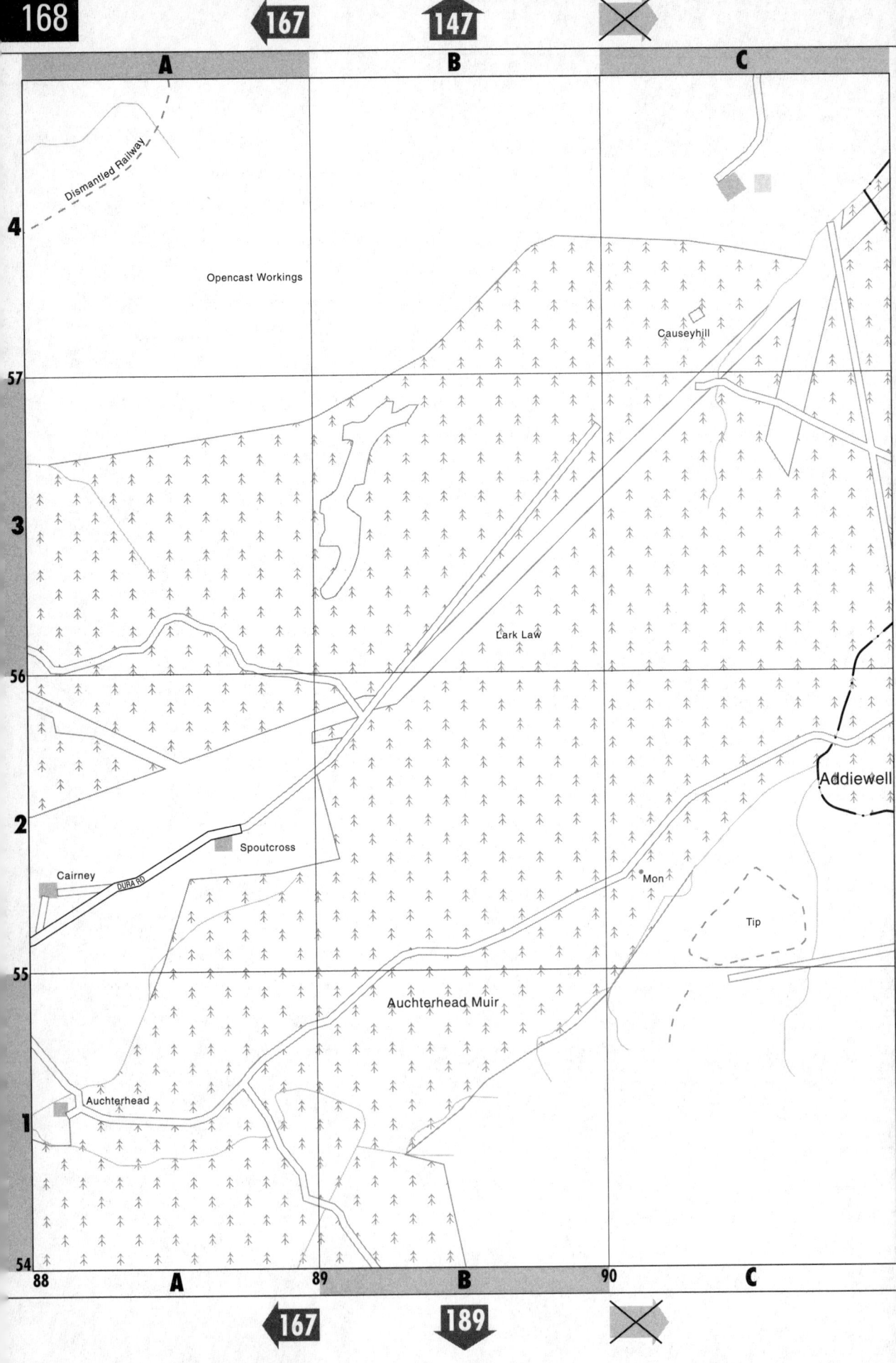

A B C

4

Dismantled Railway

Opencast Workings

Causeyhill

57

3

Lark Law

56

Addiewell

2

Spoutcross

Cairney DURA RD

Mon

Tip

55

Auchterhead Muir

1

Auchterhead

54

88 A 89 B 90 C

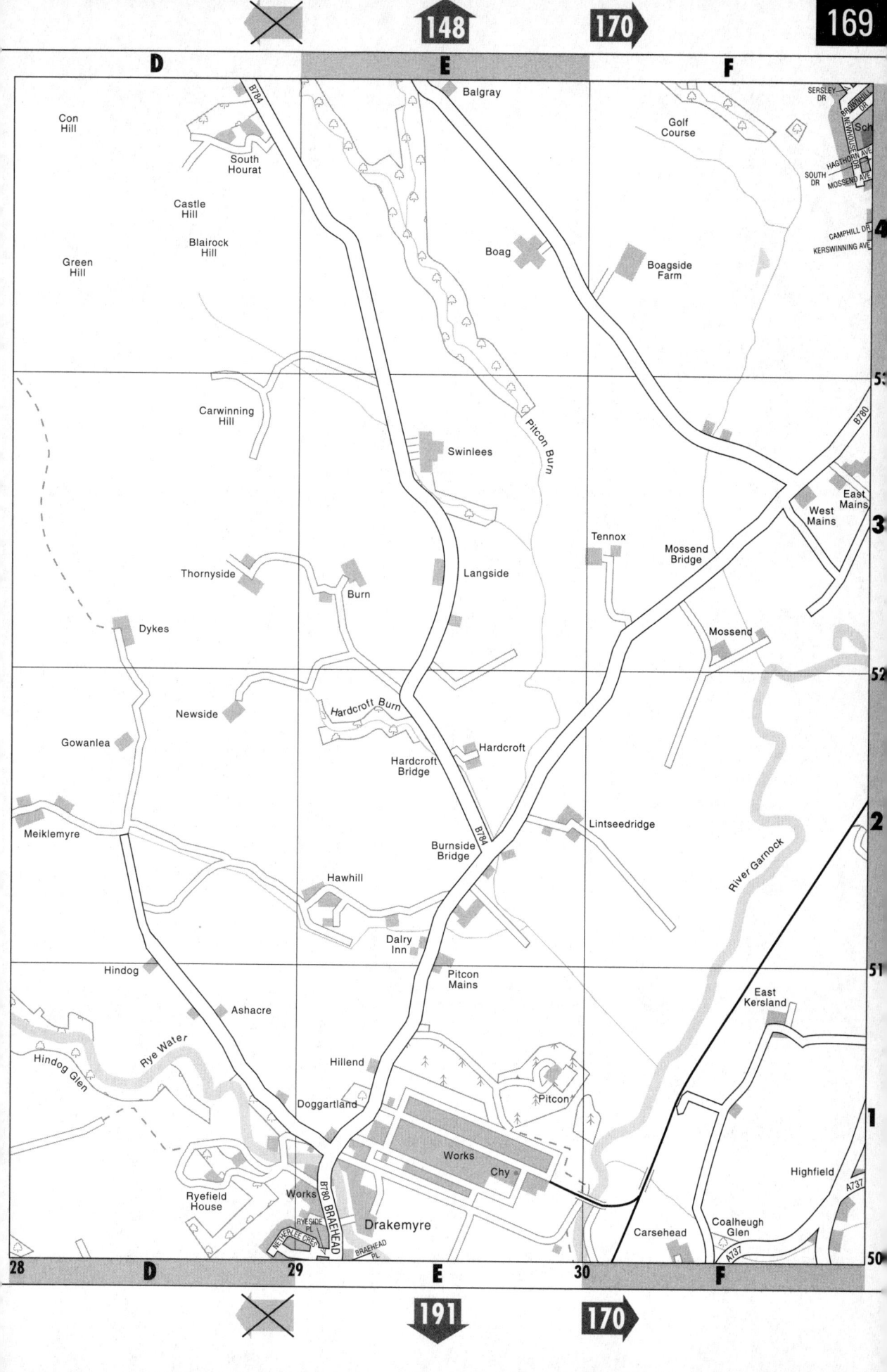

Con
Hill

South
Hourat

Castle
Hill

Blairock
Hill

Green
Hill

Balgray

Golf
Course

Boag

Boagside
Farm

SERSLEY
DR

BROUNHILL
DR

NEWHOUSE DR

Sch

HAGTHORN AVE

SOUTH
DR

MOSSEND AVE

CAMPHILL DR

KERSWINNING AVE

Carwinning
Hill

Swinlees

Pitcon Burn

B780

East
Mains

West
Mains

Thornyside

Burn

Langside

Tennox

Mossend
Bridge

Dykes

Mossend

Newside

Hardcroft Burn

Hardcroft

Gowanlea

Hardcroft
Bridge

Meiklemyre

B784

Burnside
Bridge

Lintseedridge

River Garnock

Hawhill

Dalry
Inn

Hindog

Pitcon
Mains

East
Kersland

Ashacre

Rye Water

Hillend

Pitcon

Hindog Glen

Doggartland

Ryefield
House

Works

B780 BRAEHEAD

RYESIDE
PL

Drakemyre

NETHEREE CRES

BRAEHEAD
PL

Works

Chy

Carsehead

Coalheugh
Glen

Highfield

A737

A737

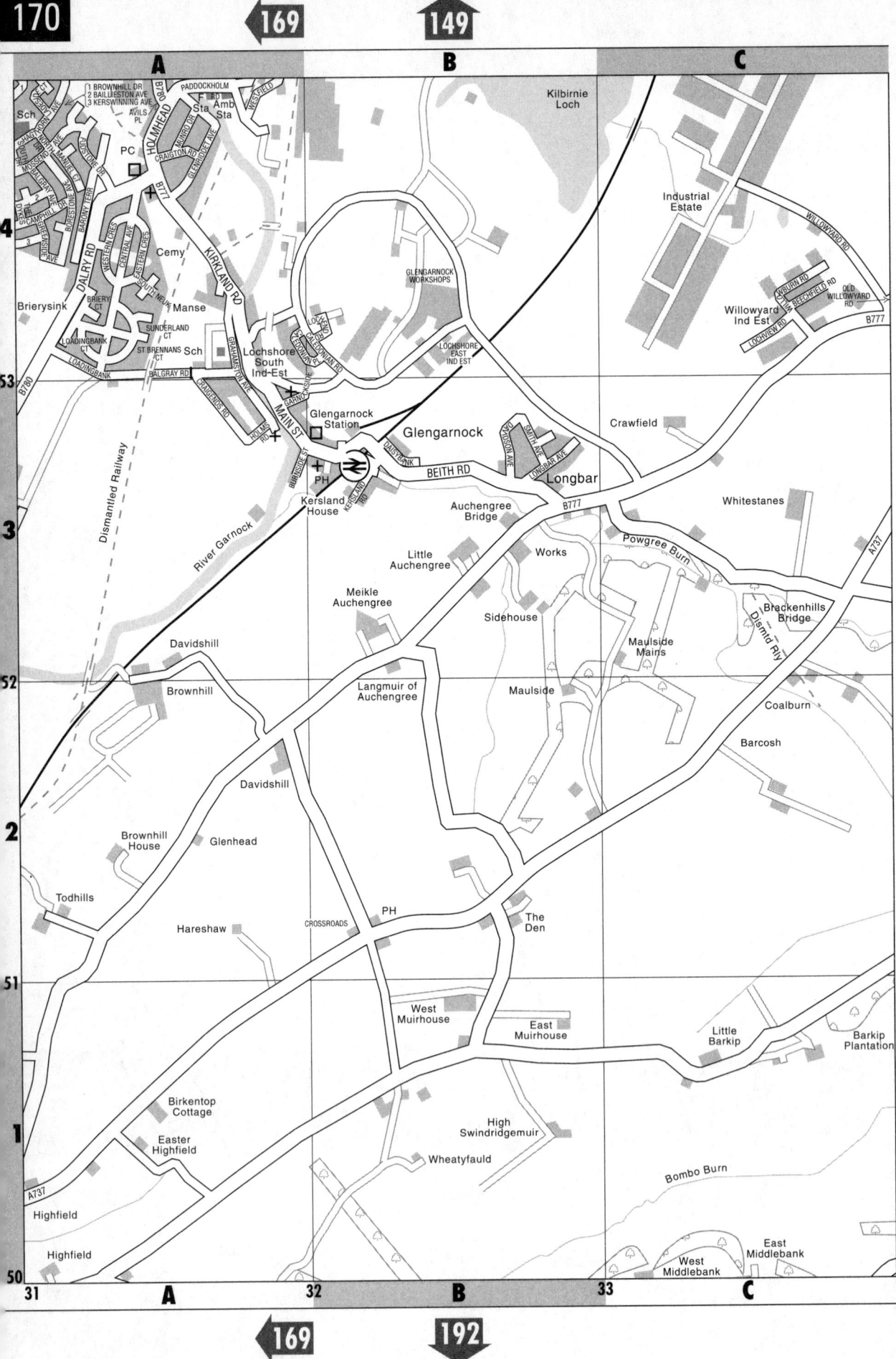

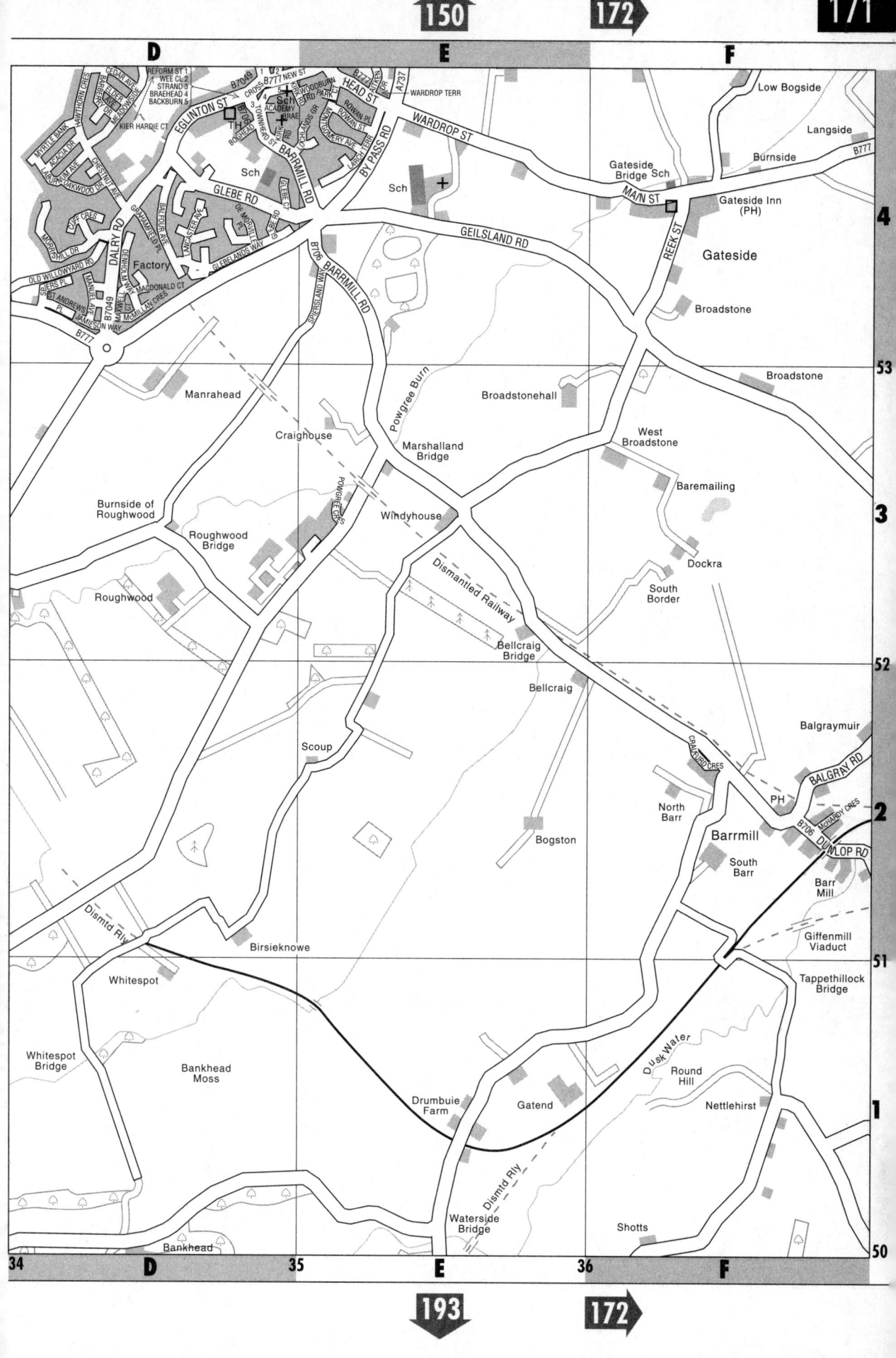

D

E

F

Low Bogside

Langside

Burnside

B777

REFORM ST 1
WEE CL 2
STRAND 3
BRAEHEAD 4
BACKBURN 5

B7049
CROSS
NEW ST
B777
WOODBURN PL

HEAD ST

A737
WARDROP TERR

WARDROP ST

EGLINTON ST

KIER HARDIE CT

Sch

BARRMILL RD

Sch

GLEBE RD

DALRY RD

Factory

B7049

B777

JAMIESON WAY

ST ANDREWS PL

Sch

MAIN ST

REEK ST

Gateside
Bridge Sch

Gateside Inn
(PH)

Gateside

4

GEILSLAND RD

Broadstone

53

Manrahead

Craighouse

Powgree Burn

Broadstonehall

Broadstone

Marshalland
Bridge

West
Broadstone

Baremailing

3

Burnside of
Roughwood

Roughwood
Bridge

Windyhouse

Dockra

South
Border

Roughwood

Dismantled Railway

Bellcraig
Bridge

52

Bellcraig

Balgraymuir

Scoup

CRAIGEND CRES

North
Barr

PH

BALGRAY RD

MCHARDY CRES

B706 DUNLOP RD

2

Bogston

Barrmill

South
Barr

Barr
Mill

Dismtd Rly

Birsieknowe

Giffenmill
Viaduct

Tappethillock
Bridge

51

Whitespot

Whitespot
Bridge

Bankhead
Moss

Drumbuie
Farm

Gatend

DUSK WATER

Round
Hill

Nettlehirst

1

Waterside
Bridge

Dismtd Rly

Shotts

Bankhead

50

34

D

35

E

36

F

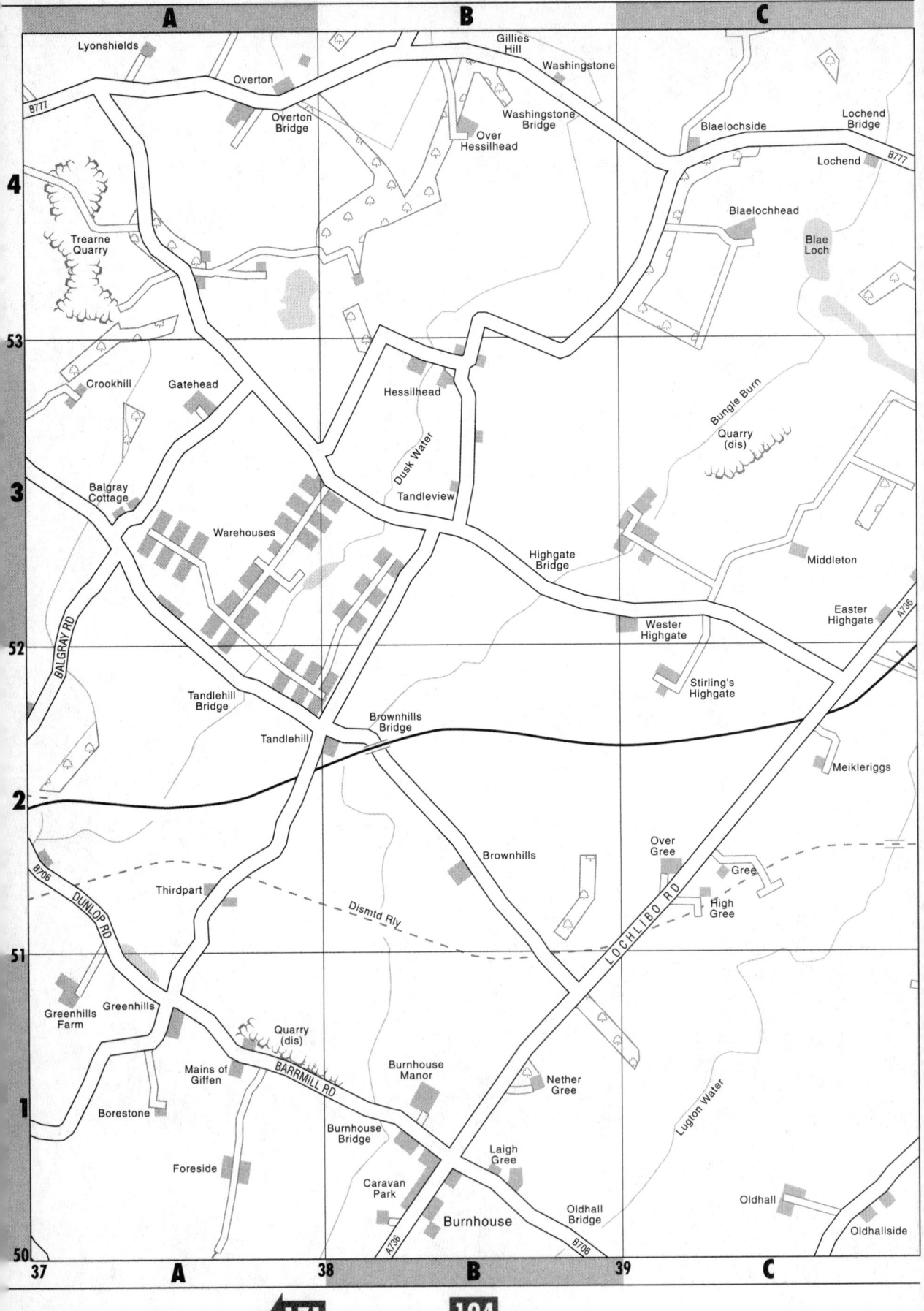

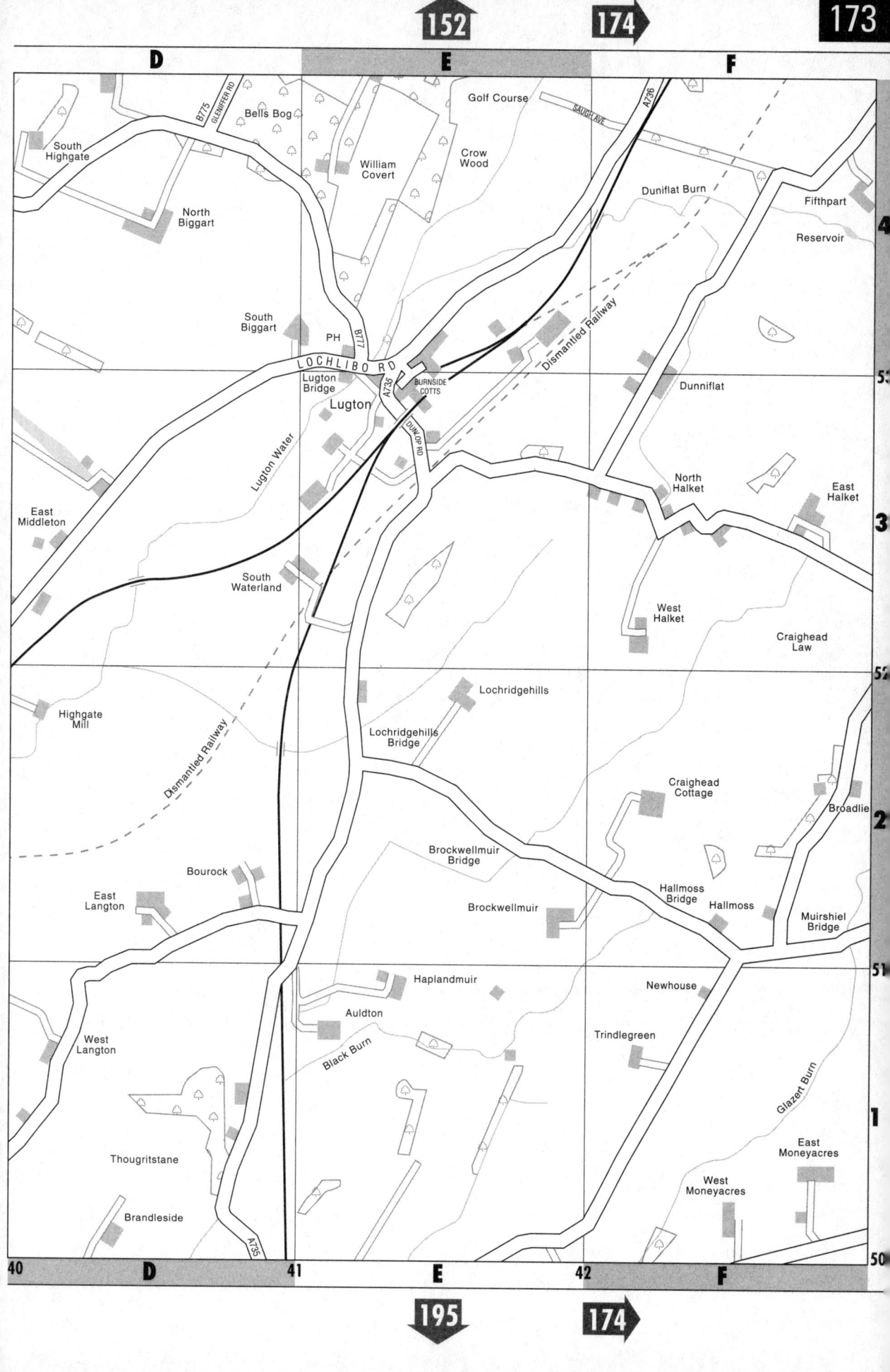

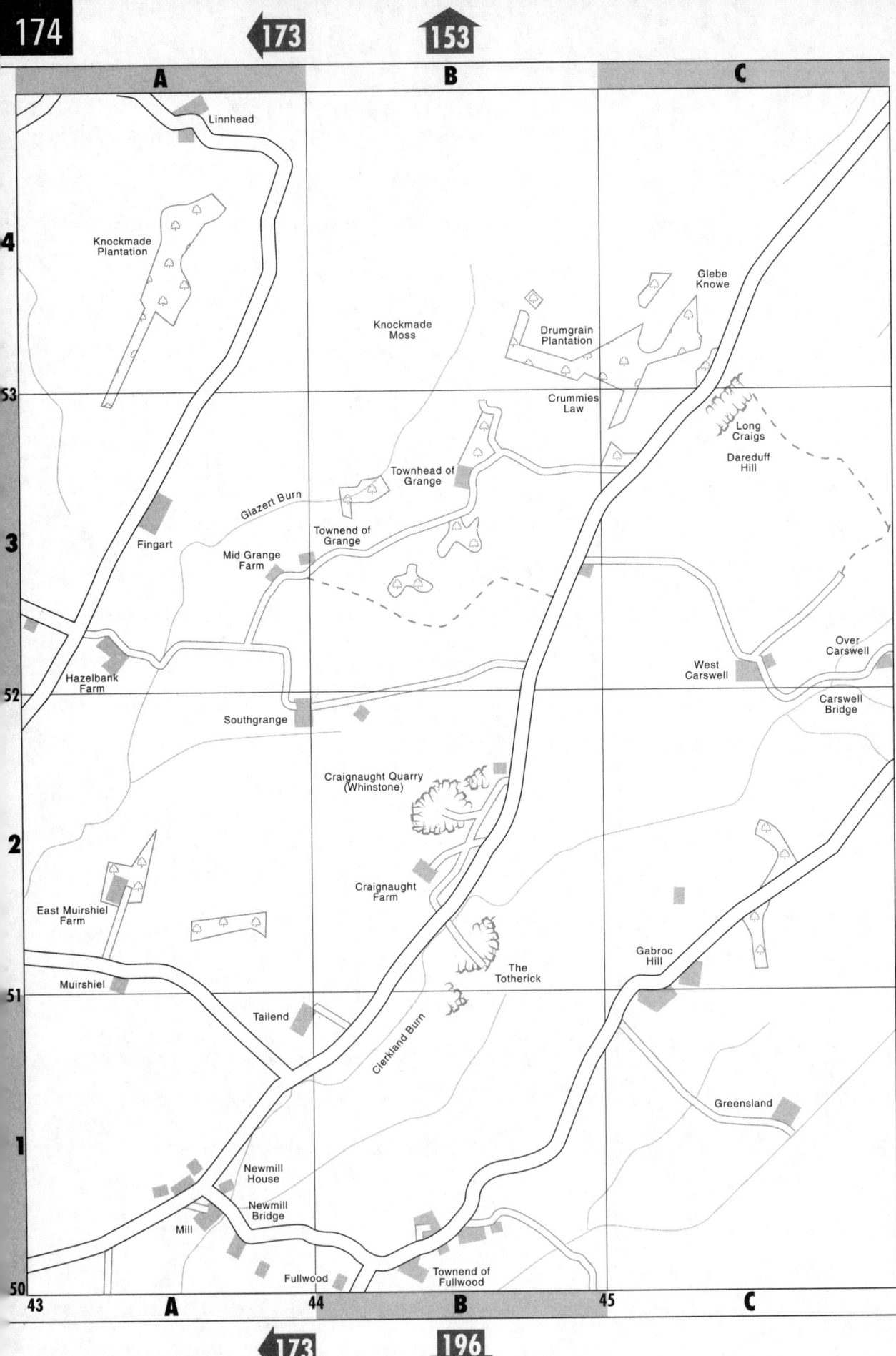

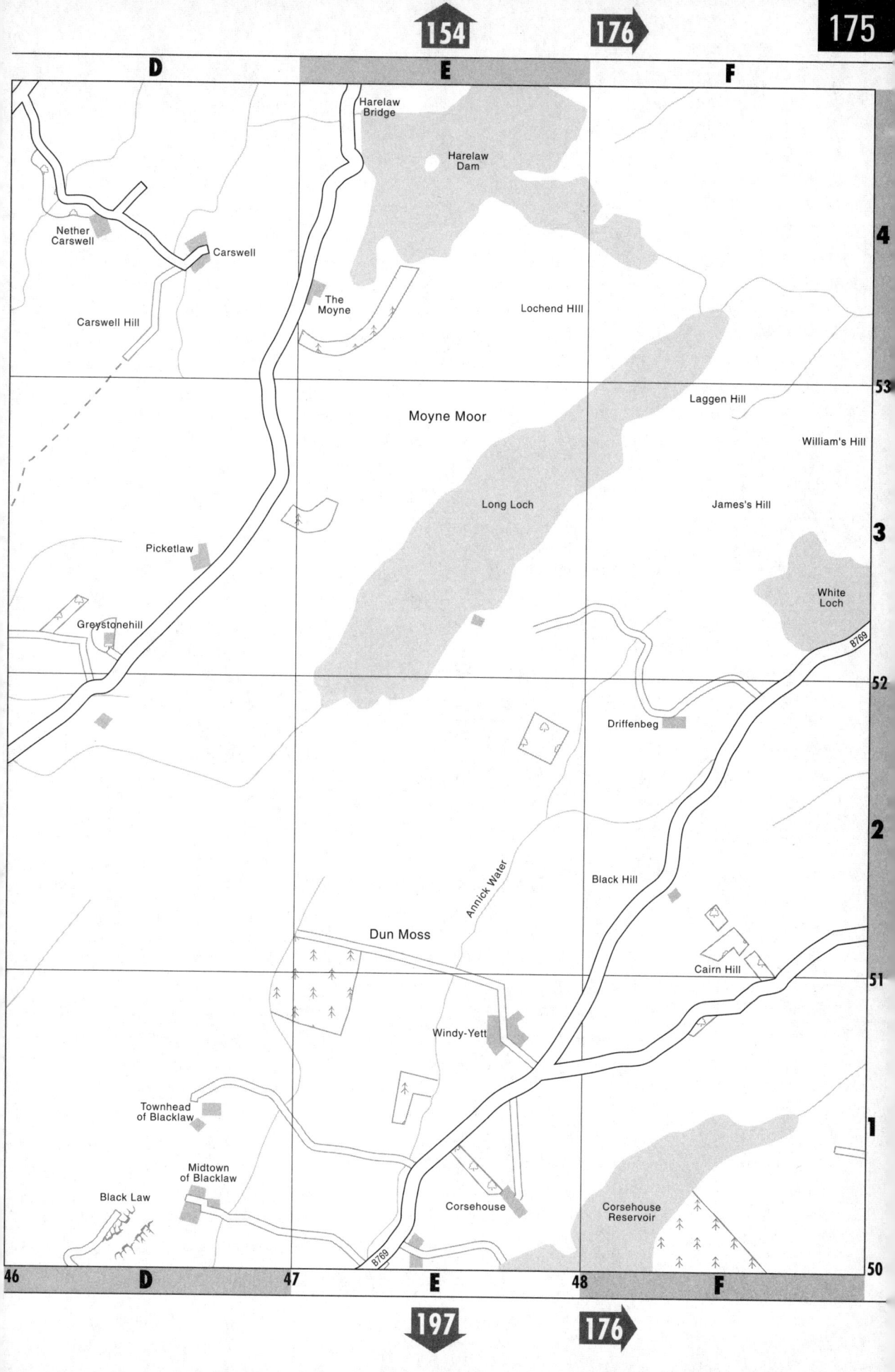

D

Harelaw
Bridge

Harelaw
Dam

Nether
Carswell

Carswell

Carswell Hill

The
Moyne

Lochend Hill

4

Moyne Moor

Laggen Hill

53

William's Hill

Long Loch

James's Hill

Picketlaw

3

White
Loch

Greystonehill

B769

52

Driffenbeg

Annick Water

Black Hill

2

Dun Moss

Cairn Hill

51

Windy-Yett

Townhead
of Blacklaw

1

Midtown
of Blacklaw

Black Law

Corsehouse

Corsehouse
Reservoir

B769

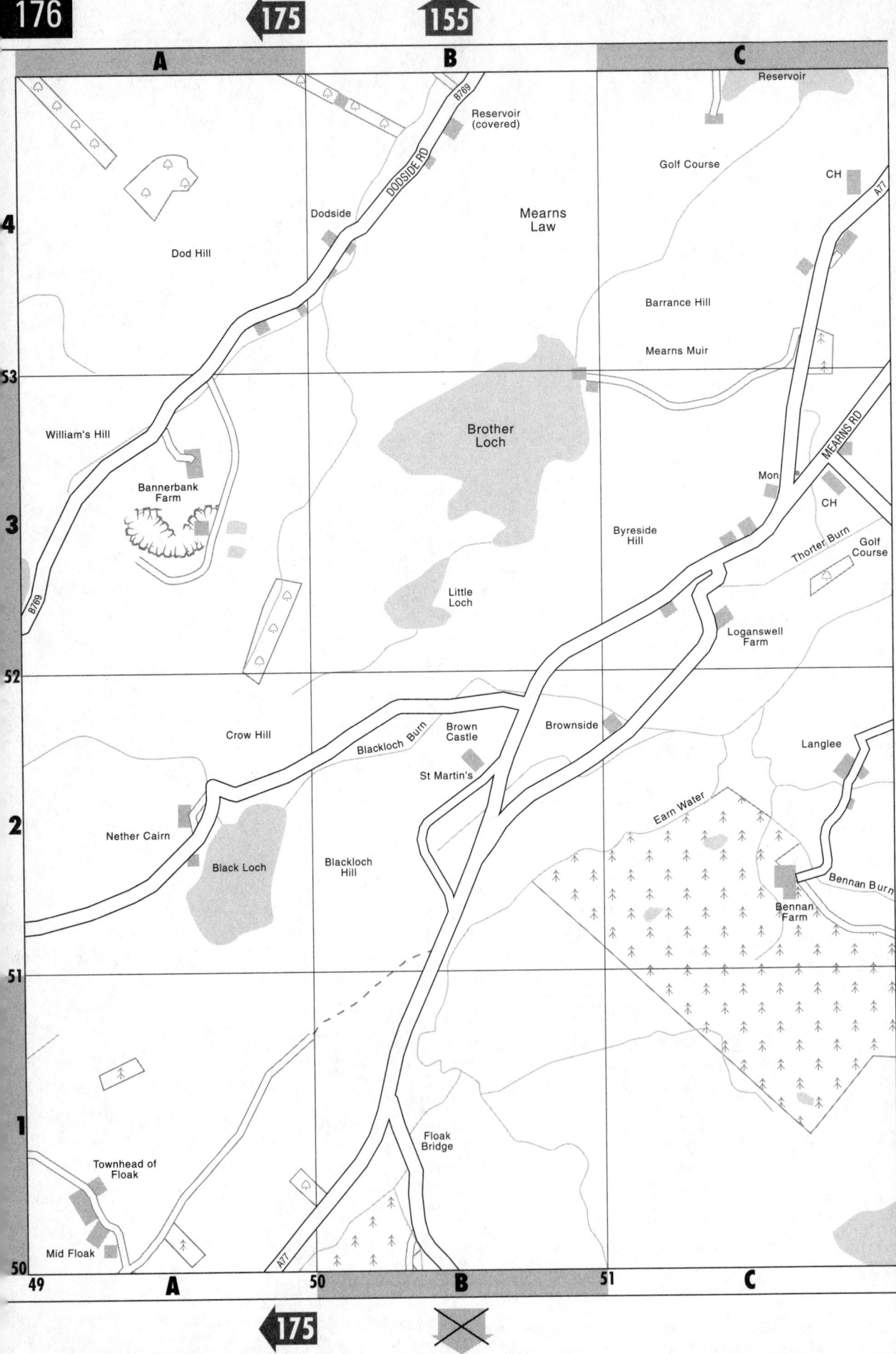

Reservoir

B769

Reservoir
(covered)

DODSIDE RD

Golf Course

CH

A77

4

Dodside

Mearns
Law

Dod Hill

Barrance Hill

53

Mearns Muir

William's Hill

Brother
Loch

Mon

CH

MEARNS RD

Bannerbank
Farm

3

Byreside
Hill

Thorter Burn

Golf
Course

B769

Little
Loch

Loganswell
Farm

52

Crow Hill

Blackloch Burn

Brown
Castle

Brownside

Langlee

St Martin's

Earn Water

Bennan Burn

2

Nether Cairn

Black Loch

Blackloch
Hill

Bennan
Farm

51

1

Floak
Bridge

Townhead of
Floak

A77

Mid Floak

50

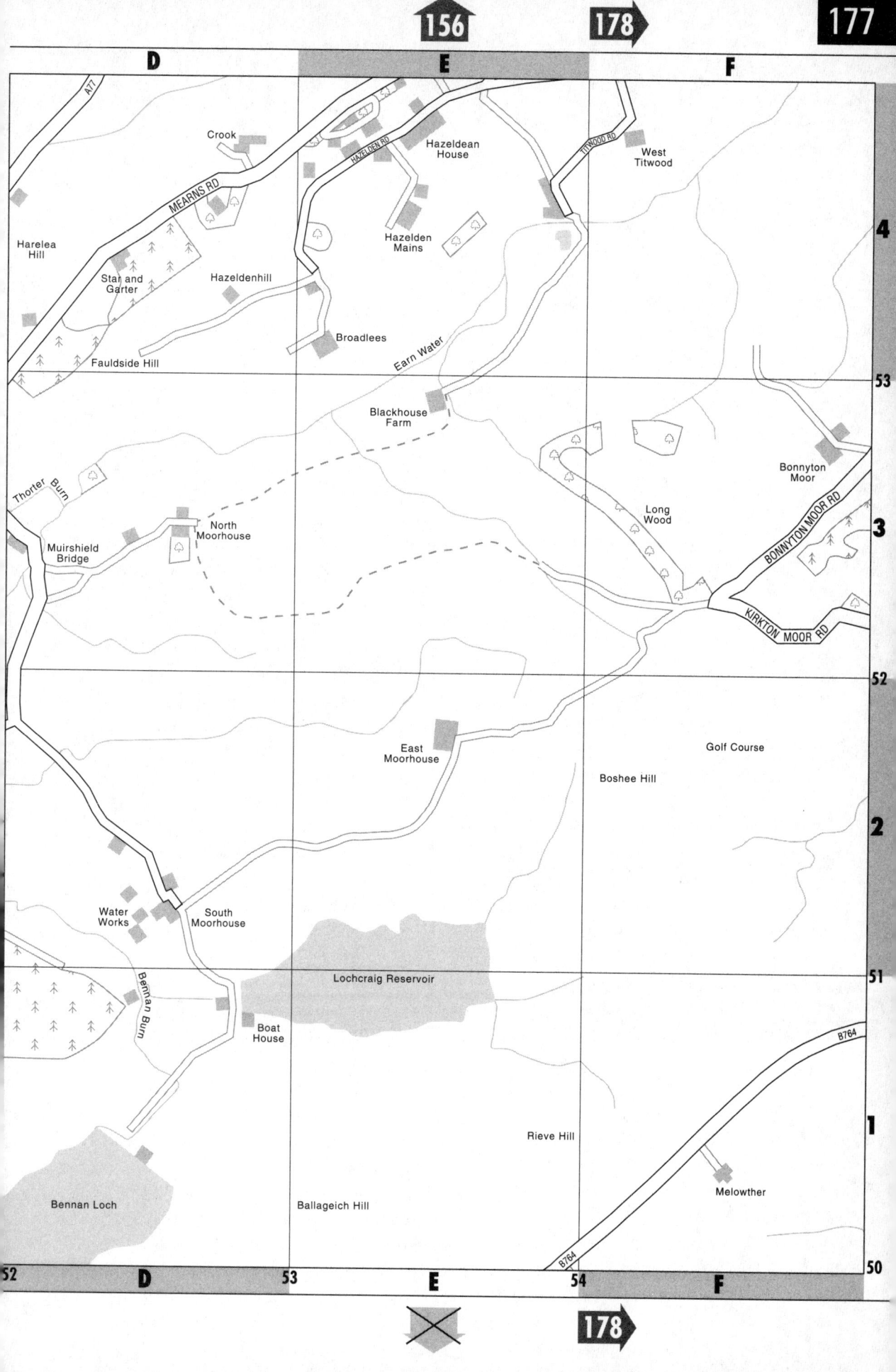

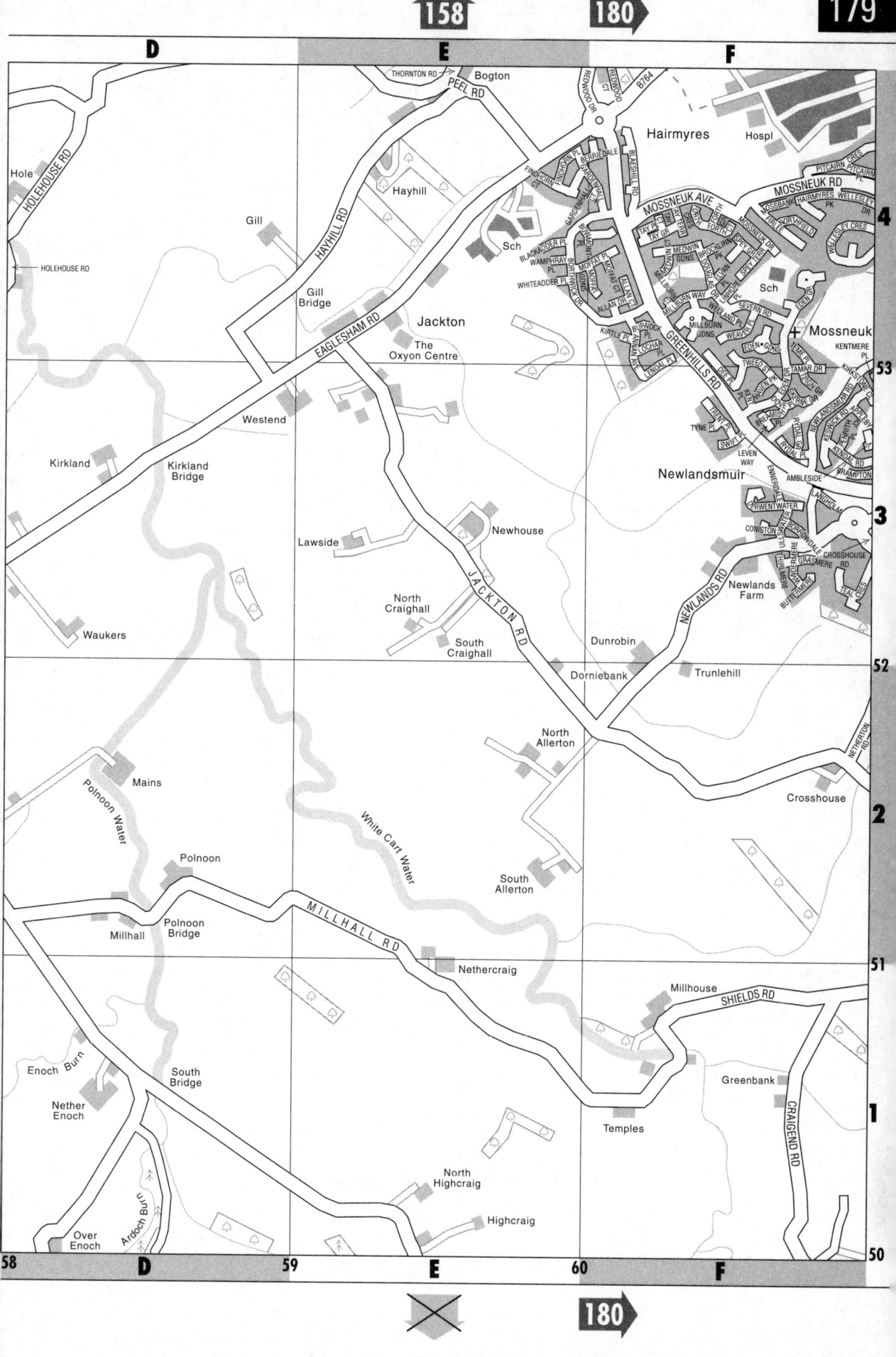

D   E   F

THORNTON RD   Bogton
PEEL RD
Hairmyres   Hospl
Hole
HOLEHOUSE RD
Hayhill   MOSSNEUK RD
Gill   MOSSNEUK AVE   4
Sch   53
HOLEHOUSE RD
Gill Bridge   Sch   Mossneuk
Jackton   KENTMERE PL
The Oxyon Centre   GREENHILLS RD
Westend   Newlandsmuir
AMBLESIDE   3
Kirkland   Newhouse   CROSSHOUSE RD
Kirkland Bridge   Lawside   Newlands Farm
North Craighall   Dunrobin
Waukers   South Craighall   Trunlehill   52
Dorniebank
North Allerton
Mains   Crosshouse   2
Polnoon Water   White Cart Water   South Allerton
Polnoon
MILLHALL RD
Millhall   Polnoon Bridge   Nethercraig   51
Millhouse   SHIELDS RD
Enoch Burn   South Bridge   Greenbank
Nether Enoch   CRAIGEND RD   1
Temples
Ardoch Burn   North Highcraig
Over Enoch   Highcraig

179
159

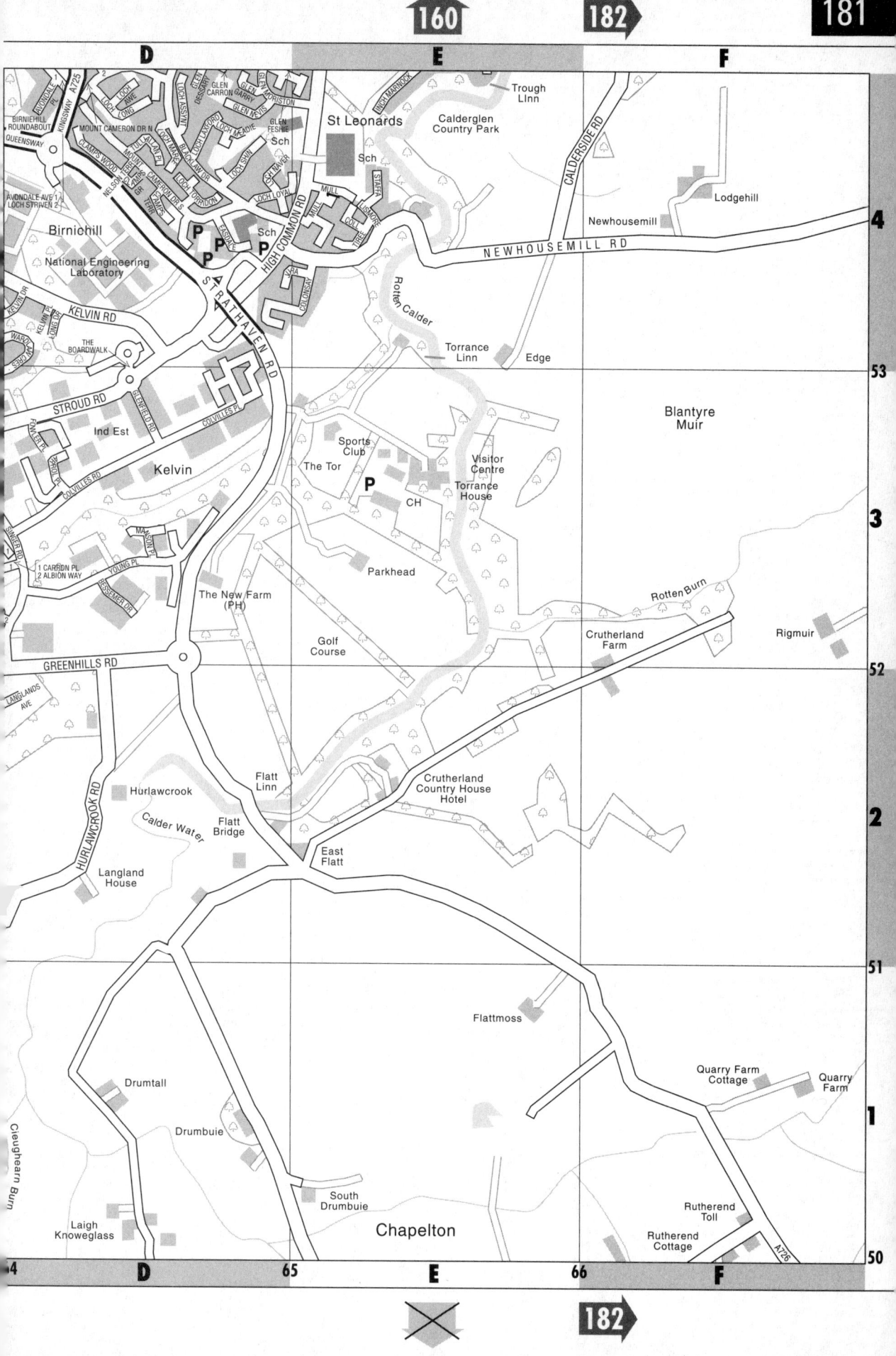

Trough Linn

Calderglen Country Park

St Leonards
Sch

Calderside Rd

Lodgehill

Newhousemill

NEWHOUSEMILL RD

4

Birnichill
National Engineering Laboratory

BIRNIEHILL ROUNDABOUT
QUEENSWAY
AVONDALE A725
KINGSWAY
AVONDALE AVE 1
LOCH STRIVEN 2

MOUNT CAMERON DR N

Sch

HIGH COMMON RD

Rotten Calder

Torrance Linn

Edge

Blantyre Muir

53

KELVIN RD
THE BOARDWALK
STRATHAVEN RD

STROUD RD
Ind Est
Kelvin

COLVILLES RD

1 CARRON PL
2 ALBION WAY
BESSEMER DR
YOUNG PL
MASON PL

The New Farm (PH)

Sports Club
The Tor
P
CH

Visitor Centre
Torrance House

Parkhead

Rotten Burn

Crutherland Farm

Rigmuir

3

Golf Course

GREENHILLS RD

52

LANGLANDS AVE

HURLAWCROOK RD

Hurlawcrook
Calder Water

Flatt Linn
Flatt Bridge

Crutherland Country House Hotel

2

Langland House

East Flatt

51

Cleughearn Burn

Drumtall

Flattmoss

Quarry Farm Cottage
Quarry Farm

Drumbuie

1

South Drumbuie

Chapelton

Rutherend Toll

Rutherend Cottage

A726

50

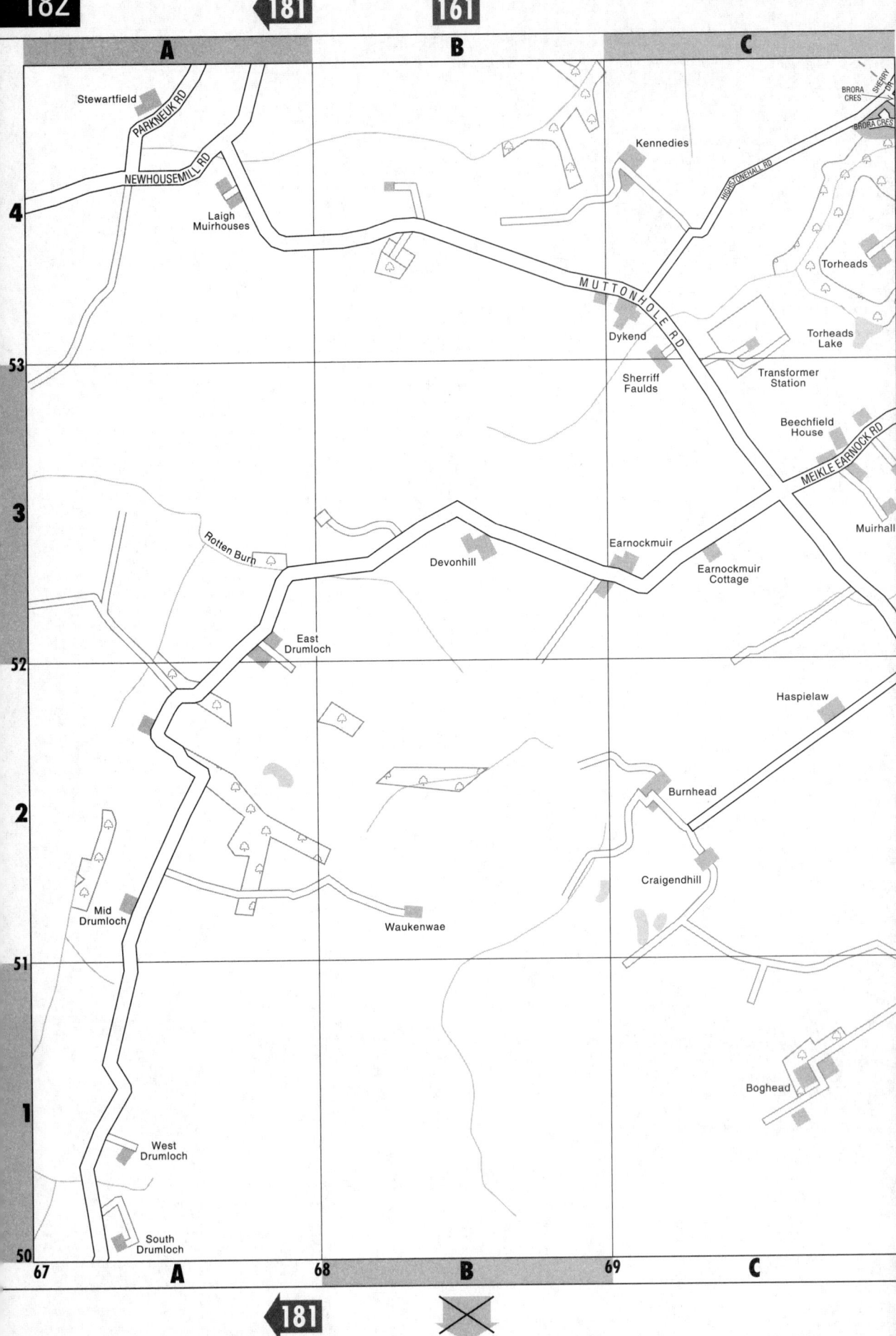

A   **B**   **C**

Stewartfield

PARKNEUK RD

NEWHOUSEMILL RD

Laigh
Muirhouses

4

Kennedies

HIGHSTONEHALL RD

BRORA
CRES

SHERRY DR

BRORA CRES

Torheads

MUTTONHOLE RD

Dykend

Torheads
Lake

Transformer
Station

53

Sherriff
Faulds

Beechfield
House

MEIKLE EARNOCK RD

3

Rotten Burn

Devonhill

Earnockmuir

Earnockmuir
Cottage

Muirhall

East
Drumloch

52

Haspielaw

2

Burnhead

Mid
Drumloch

Waukenwae

Craigendhill

51

1

Boghead

West
Drumloch

South
Drumloch

50

67   **A**   68   **B**   69   **C**

D E F

4

53

3

52

2

51

1

50

Neilsland Park

1 SHERRY DR
2 HIGHSTONEHALL RD
3 BRORA CRES

Woodhead Green

Meikle Earnock

Brackenhill

Broomknowe

Cadzow Burn

Cornhills

Haspie Law

Viewfield

Cedron

MUTTONHOLE RD

Boghead Cottage

Thorniehill

Limekilnburn

Lochlinn Bridge

Browntod

A723

STRATHAVEN RD

Annsfield

Chapel

Lady Mary's Lodge

The Homestead

Station House

Dismantled Railway

LIMEKILNBURN RD

Dismantled Railway

Burnbrae Glen

Darngaber Burn

MEIKLE EARNOCK DR

NEILSLAND RD

Newlands Dr

Eddlewood

Cadzow Burn

B755 MILL RD

Sch

Cadzow Ind Est

Deer Park Ct

Deer Park Pl

Silvertonhill Pl

DEER PARK

Simpsonland Glen

1 THORNTON PL
2 DOUGLAS PL
3 FOREST LA
4 MEADOWSIDE
5 CLYDESDALE PL

Simpsonland

Blackbog

Blackbog Glen

CARSCALLAN RD

Carscallan

Hamilton High Parks

Cadzow House

SILVERTONHILL AVE

Eddlewood Glen

Meikle Burn

Meikle Glen

Kilnhill

Burnbrae

Darngaber

North Crookedstone

Wellbog Plantation

Quarter

Sch

SUNNYSIDE RD

Silverbirch Gr

PH

CASTLE WYND

Cadzow Rd

Station House

D 71 E 72 F

Sewage Works

Randalls Orchard

Carbarns Orchard

Carbarnswood

CALA SONA CT

OLD MANSE RD

B754

GIGHA QUADRANT

ALLERSHAW TOWER 1
BIRKSHAW TOWER 2
CAPLAW TOWER 3

ALLERSHAW RD

MONTGOMERY CRES

Lower Carbarns

Carbarns Wood

North Lodge

Castlehill

CASTLEHILL RD

B754

LINGHOPE PL

4

Junction 7

Upper Carbarns

Hall Gill

Cambusnethan House

53

Highlees

Prince's Lodge

River Clyde

LANARK RD

Highmainshead Wood

SUMMERLEE RD

Whittrick Burn

Skelly Gill

Nursery

3

Tilework Cottage

Sewage Works

Nursery

Cemy

EAST STATION IND EST

Nursery

52

HAMILTON ST

DUKE ST

Meadowhill

GLENORAN LA

EASTWOOD WAY

Skellyton Wood

A72

Skellyton

WELLGATE ST

MONTGOMERY ST

PERCY ST

DRYGATE ST

Skellyton Wood

1 GLENBURN WYND
2 PORTLAND WYND
3 SIGHTHILL LOAN
4 PARKNOOK WAY
5 LOMOND WLK
6 HOZIER LOAN
7 CRAIGIE LA
8 GEORGE WAY
9 ALBANY WYND
10 CRAIGMORE WYND
11 BURNS LOAN
12 ABBEY WLK
13 BANK WAY
14 BRAESIDE LA

Millburn Glen

2

LONDON ST

P

PC

Off

Liby

Larkhall

Golf Course

A71

CORNSILLOCH BRAE

MACNEILL ST

Sch

UNION ST

Sch

BURNSIDE PL

Burnhead

CH

Milburn Cottage

1 LOANING
2 DOON ST
3 LOVAT PATH
4 ALLOWAY ST
5 BALMORAL PATH
6 MILLBURN LA
7 MOSSGIEL LA
8 WINDSOR PATH
9 CARRICK ST
10 GILLBANK LA
11 CATRINE ST
12 LOCHLEE LOAN

Mill Burn

Cornsilloch

51

CHURCH ST

JOHN ST

HARELEESHILL RD

BURNHEAD RD

Milburn

AYR RD

Machan

Charlotte Path

MACHAN RD

SCOTT ST

Sch

13 MAXWELL PATH
14 BRUCE'S LOAN
15 FLEMING WAY
16 ALOA WAY
17 ARRAN PATH
18 DALSERF PATH
19 LOCHNAGAR WAY
20 BLAIR ATHOLL DR
21 TRINITY WAY
22 GLEN FRUIN DR
23 ST ANDREWS PATH
24 LAWRIE WAY
25 KATRIONA PATH
26 CAMERON PATH
27 HAZELDENE LA
28 ROSEMOUNT LA
29 LAUREL LA
30 BRACKEN WAY
31 CAMERONIAN WAY
32 LAMMER WYND

B7019

Shawsburn

1

WHINNIE KNOWE

Sch

Ind Est

KEIR HARDIE RD

Braeside Way

BERTRAM ST

Hareleeshill

Dismtd Rly

ASHGILLHEAD RD

Nurseries

GARRION PL

Stewart Gill

Works

MILLBURN RD

Ashgillhead

50

185
165

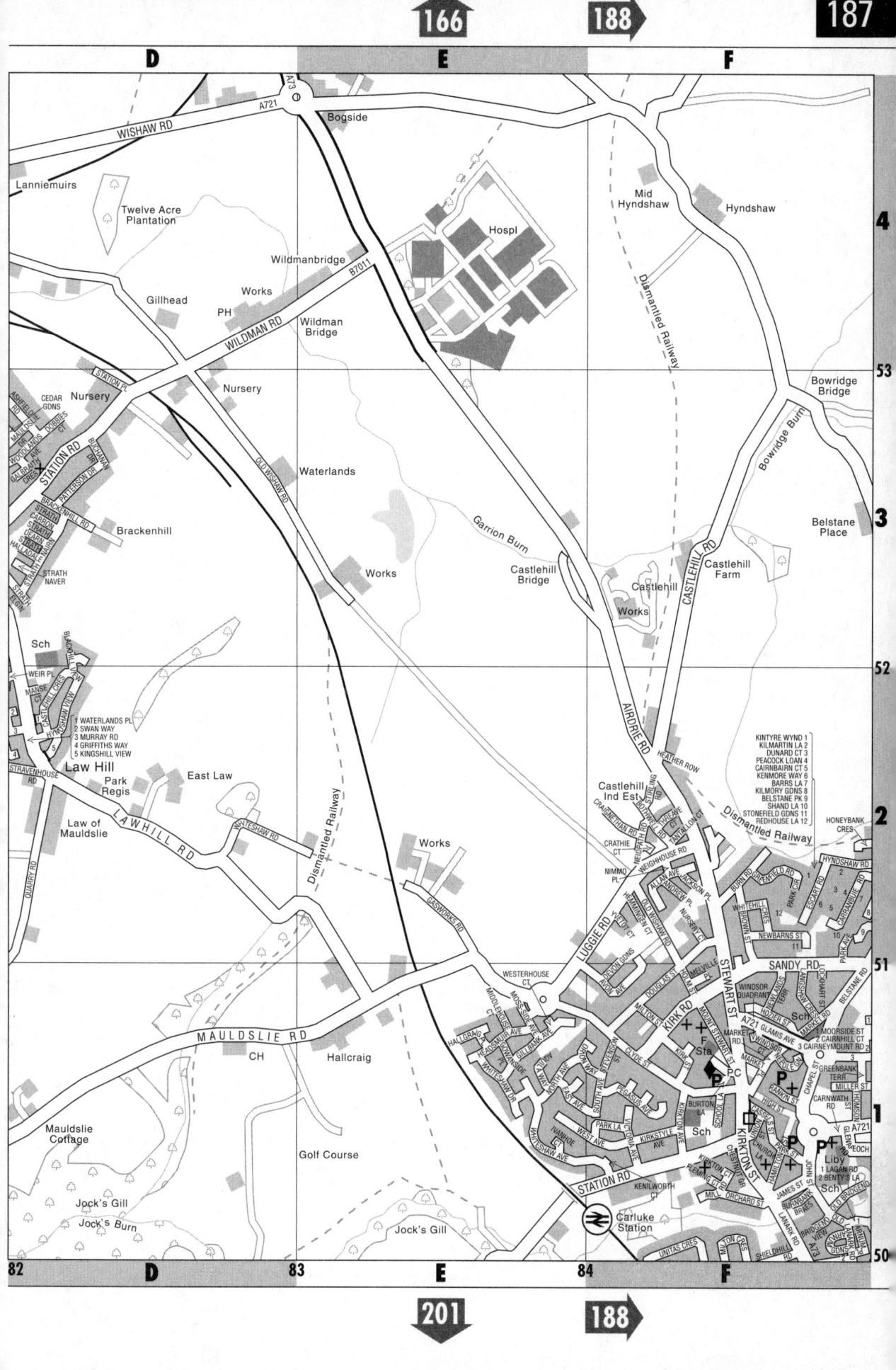

D E F

WISHAW RD
A721
A73
Bogside
Lanniemuirs
Twelve Acre Plantation
Mid Hyndshaw
Hyndshaw
Hospl
Wildmanbridge
Works
B7011
Gillhead
PH
Dismantled Railway
4
WILDMAN RD
Wildman Bridge
53
Bowridge Bridge
STATION PL
CEDAR GDNS
Nursery
Nursery
Bowridge Burn
STATION RD
BUCHANAN
PATTERSON DR
Waterlands
Belstane Place
BRACKENHILL RD
CASTLEHILL RD
Brackenhill
Garrion Burn
3
STRATH NAVER
Works
Castlehill Bridge
Castlehill Works
Castlehill Farm
Sch
WEIR PL
52
MANSE
CASTLEHILL CRES
1 WATERLANDS PL
2 SWAN WAY
3 MURRAY RD
4 GRIFFITHS WAY
5 KINGSHILL VIEW
AIRDRIE RD
HEATHER ROW
KINTYRE WYND 1
KILMARTIN LA 2
DUNARD CT 3
PEACOCK LOAN 4
CAIRNBAIRN CT 5
KENMORE WAY 6
BARRS LA 7
KILMORY GDNS 8
BELSTANE PK 9
SHAND LA 10
STONEFIELD GDNS 11
REDHOUSE LA 12
STRAVENHOUSE RD
Law Hill
Park Regis
East Law
Castlehill Ind Est
Dismantled Railway
HONEYBANK CRES
2
Law of Mauldslie
LAWHILL RD
GATESHAW RD
Works
Dismantled Railway
HYNDSHAW RD
QUARRY RD
GASWORKS RD
CRATHIE CT
NIMMO PL
NEIGHHOUSE RD
LUGGIE RD
WESTERHOUSE CT
MOSSIDE RD
MIDDLEHOUSE CT
SANDY RD
NEWBARNS ST
STEWART ST
51
MAULDSLIE RD
CH
Hallcraig
KIRK RD
Sch
MARKET
MELVILLE PL
A721
WINDSOR QUADRANT
Sch
1 MOORSIDE ST
2 CAIRNHILL CT
3 CAIRNEYMOUNT RD
Mauldslie Cottage
Sch
P PC
BURTON LA
Sch
P
CARNWATH RD
P P
KIRKTON ST
Liby
1 LAGAN RD
2 BENTY LA
Sch
Jock's Gill
Jock's Burn
Golf Course
Jock's Gill
STATION RD
KENILWORTH CT
Carluke Station
1
A721
A73
50

82 D 83 E 84 F

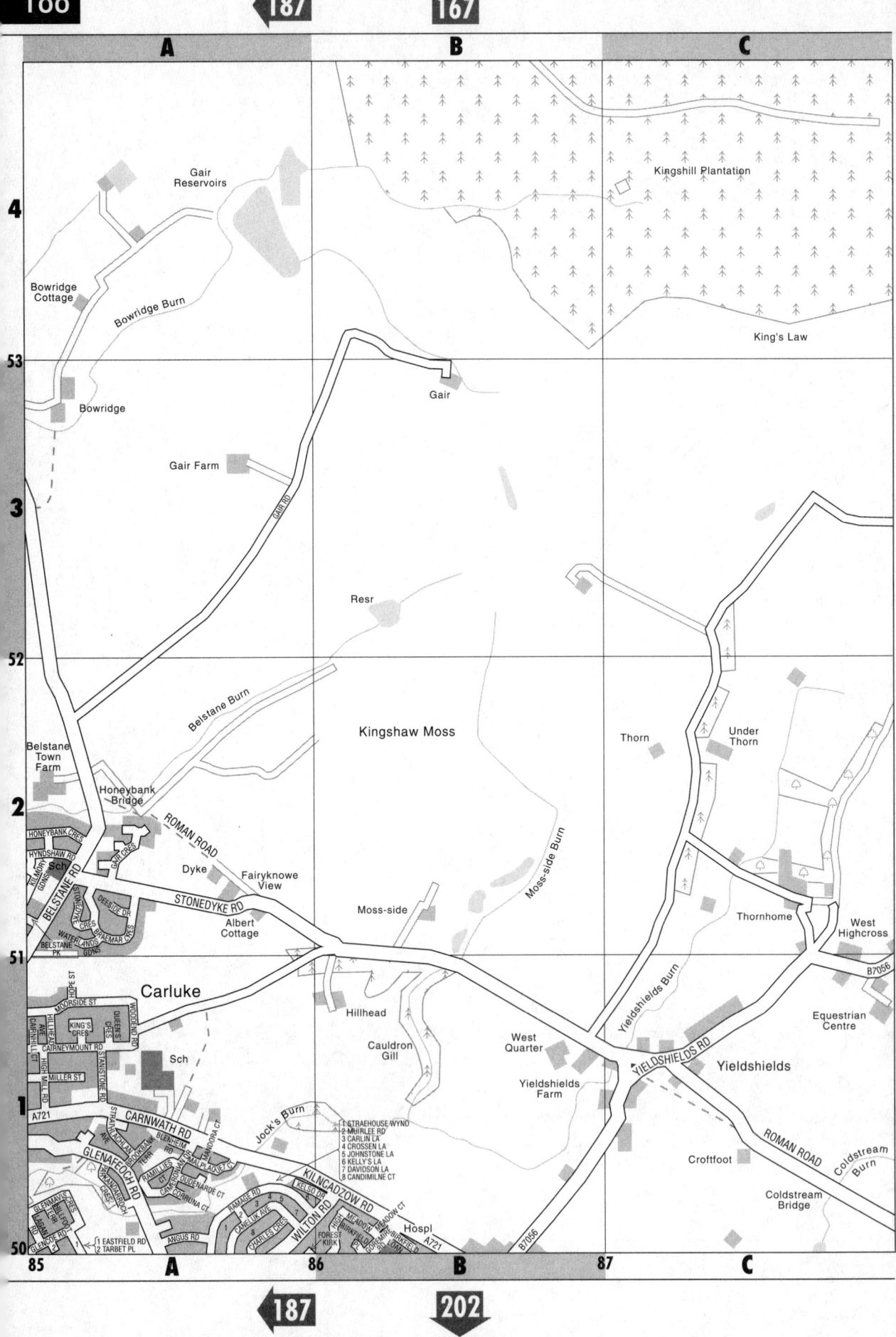

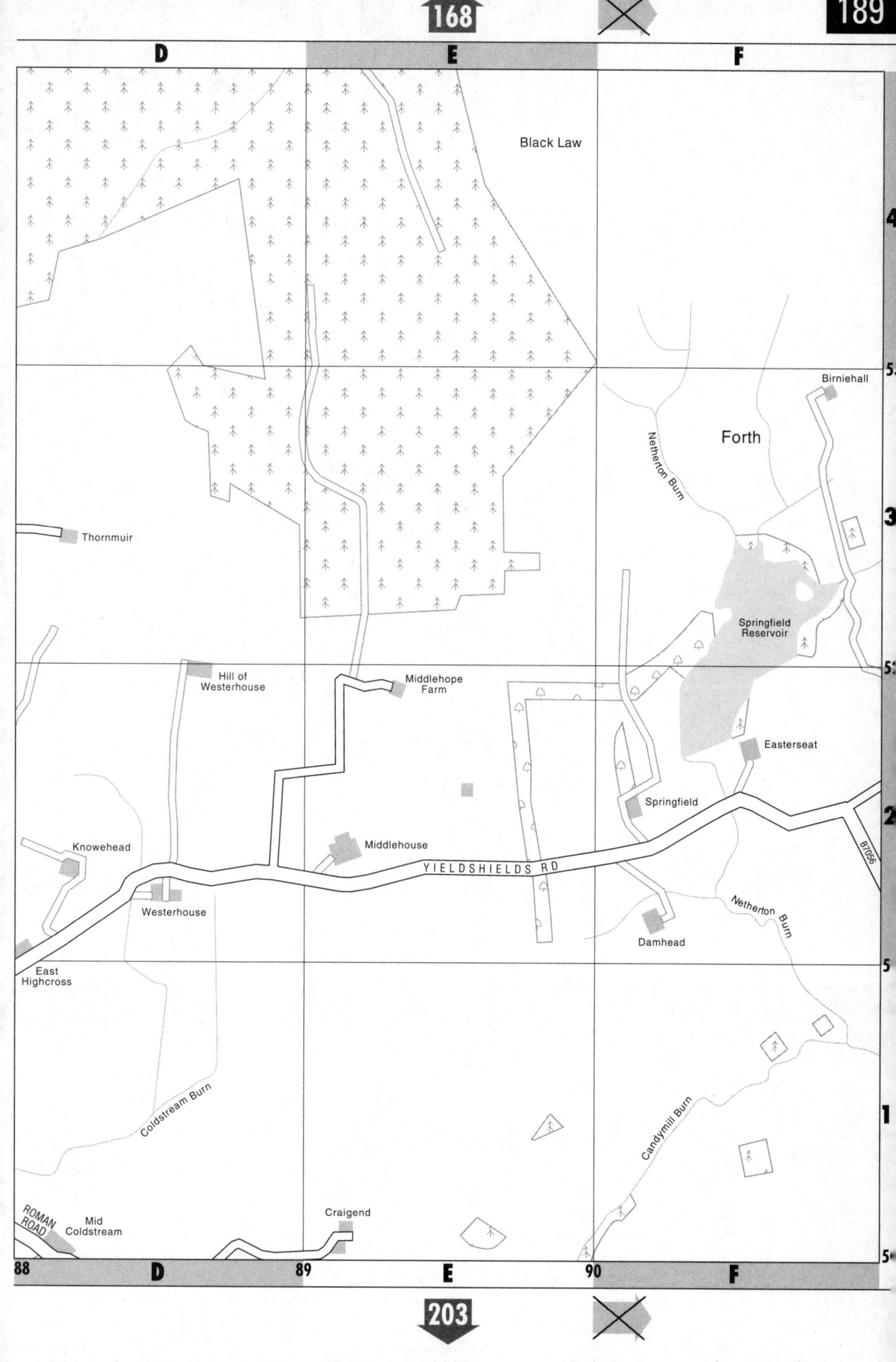

D E F

4

Black Law

5.

Birniehall

Forth

Netherton Burn

3

Thornmuir

Springfield
Reservoir

5:

Hill of
Westerhouse

Middlehope
Farm

Easterseat

Springfield

Knowehead

Middlehouse

YIELDSHIELDS RD

B7056

2

Netherton Burn

Westerhouse

Damhead

East
Highcross

5

Coldstream Burn

Candymill Burn

1

ROMAN
ROAD

Mid
Coldstream

Craigend

5

88 D 89 E 90 F

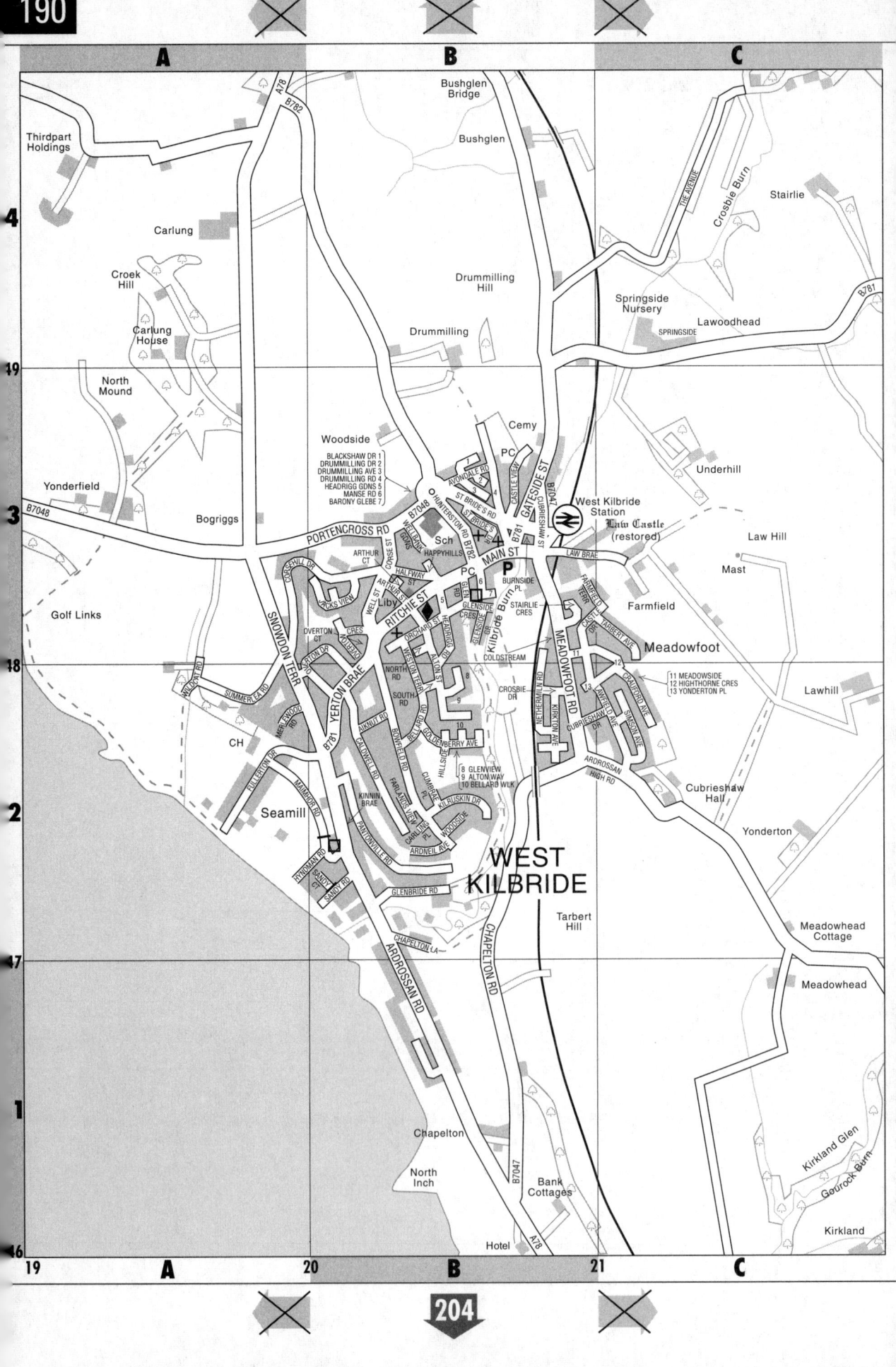

A   **B**   **C**

Thirdpart Holdings

Carlung

Croek Hill

Carlung House

North Mound

Yonderfield

Bogriggs

B7048

Golf Links

Snowdon Terr

CH

Seamill

Bushglen Bridge

Bushglen

Drummilling Hill

Drummilling

Woodside

BLACKSHAW DR 1
DRUMMILLING DR 2
DRUMMILLING AVE 3
DRUMMILLING RD 4
HEADRIGG GDNS 5
MANSE RD 6
BARONY GLEBE 7

PORTENCROSS RD

Cemy

PC

Sch

Happyhills

Library

RITCHIE ST

Arthur Ct

Halfway St

Welll St

Jacks View

Overton Ct

North Rd

South Rd

Yerton Brae

Summerlea Rd

Kinnin Brae

Glenbride Rd

Chapelton La

Ardrossan Rd

Chapelton

North Inch

Hotel

Bank Cottages

B7047

West Kilbride Station

Law Castle (restored)

Law Brae

Main St

Burnside Pl

PC

P

Stairlie Cres

Glenside Cres

Coldstream

Crosbie Dr

8 GLENVIEW
9 ALTON WAY
10 BELLARD WLK

Meadowfoot Rd

High Rd

WEST KILBRIDE

Tarbert Hill

Chapelton Rd

Springside Nursery

Lawoodhead

SPRINGSIDE

Underhill

Law Hill

Mast

Farmfield

Meadowfoot

11 MEADOWSIDE
12 HIGHTHORNE CRES
13 YONDERTON PL

Lawhill

Cubrieshaw Hall

Yonderton

Meadowhead Cottage

Meadowhead

Stairlie

Crosbie Burn

THE AVENUE

B781

Kirkland Glen

Gourock Burn

Kirkland

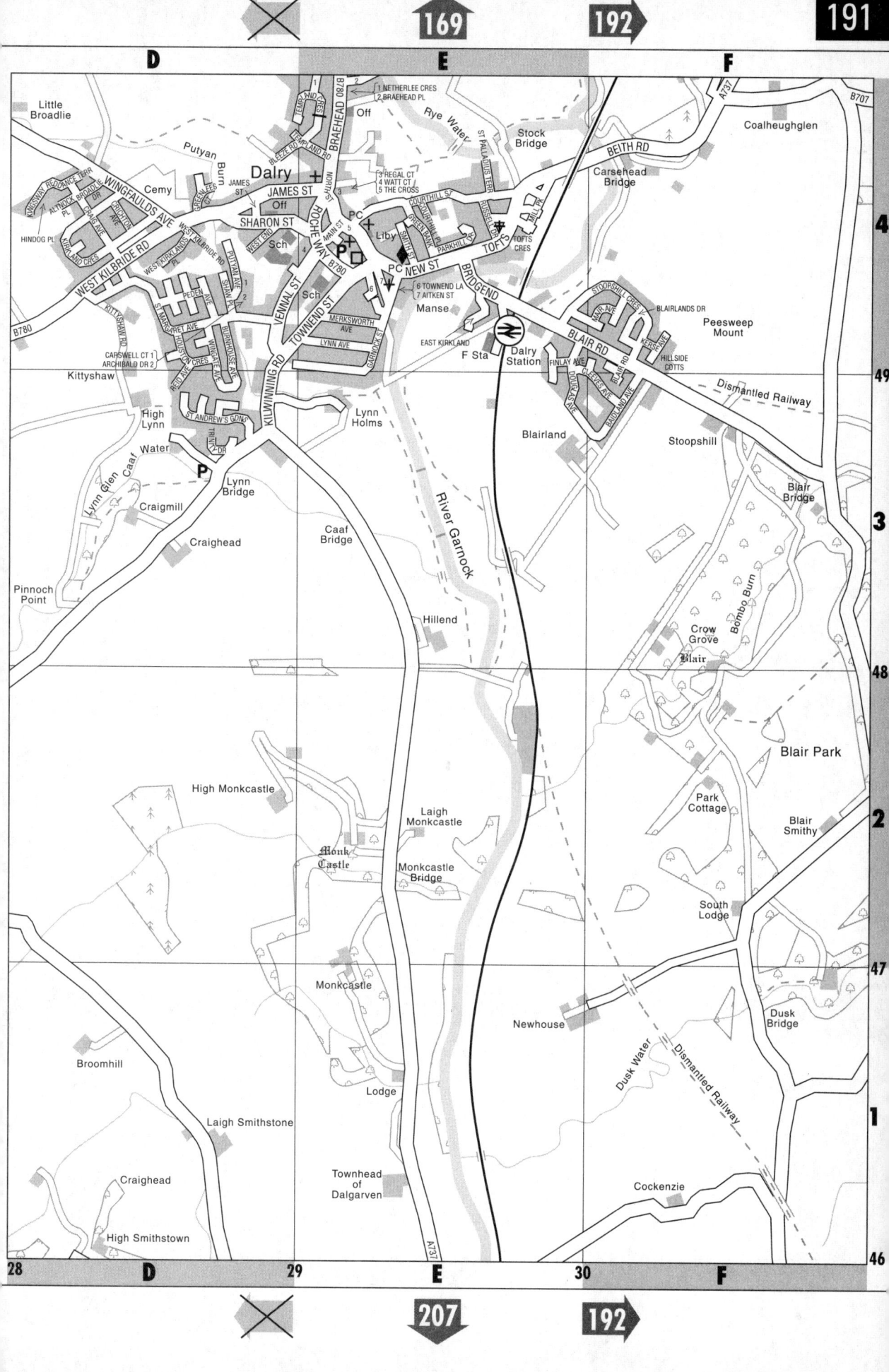

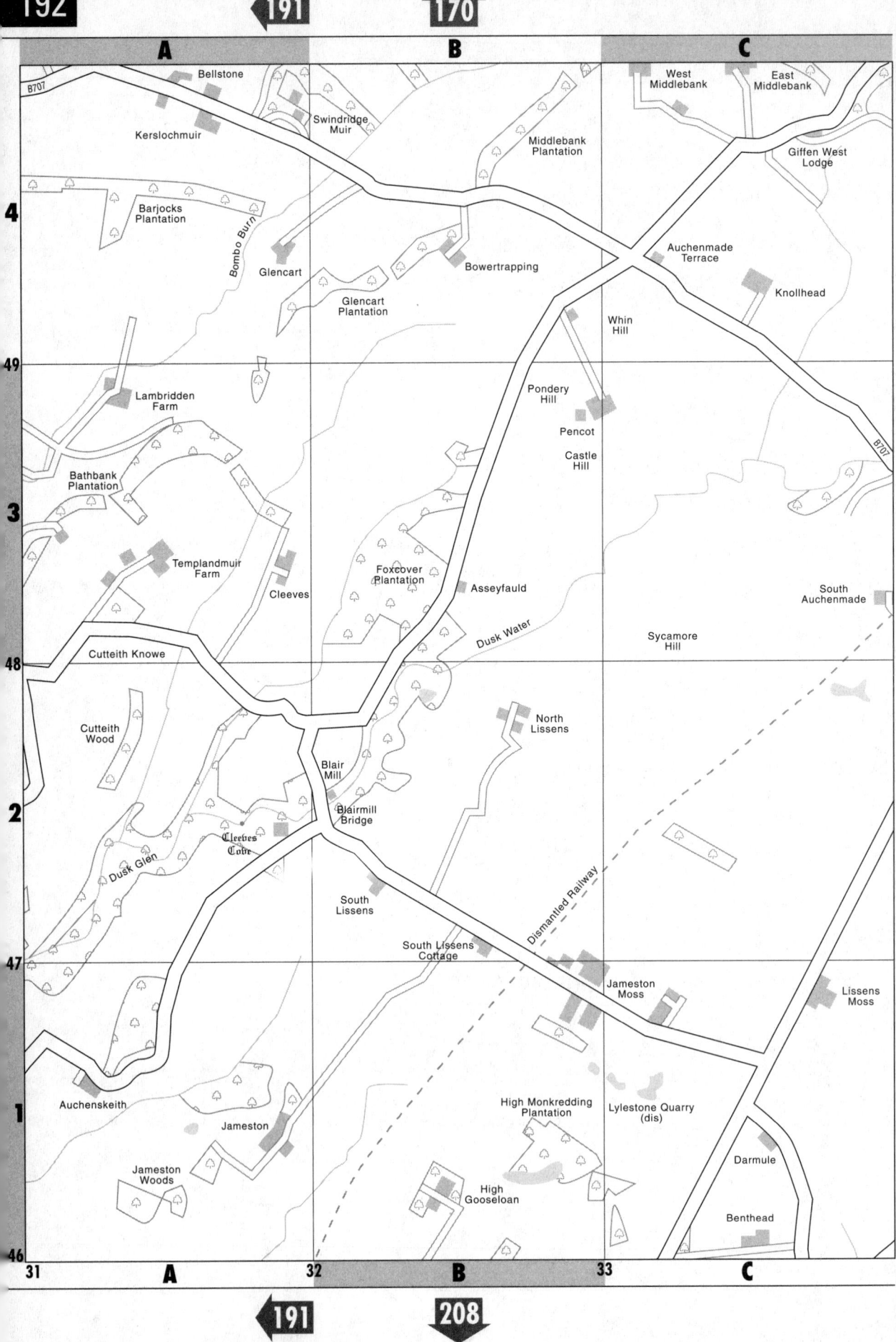

A   **B**   **C**

B707

Bellstone

Kerslochmuir

Swindridge
Muir

Middlebank
Plantation

West
Middlebank

East
Middlebank

Giffen West
Lodge

4

Barjocks
Plantation

Bombo Burn

Glencart

Bowertrapping

Auchenmade
Terrace

Knollhead

Glencart
Plantation

Whin
Hill

49

Pondery
Hill

Lambridden
Farm

Pencot

Castle
Hill

Bathbank
Plantation

South
Auchenmade

3

Templandmuir
Farm

Cleeves

Foxcover
Plantation

Asseyfauld

Dusk Water

Sycamore
Hill

48

Cutteith Knowe

Cutteith
Wood

North
Lissens

2

Blair
Mill

Dusk Glen

Cleeves
Cove

Blairmill
Bridge

South
Lissens

Dismantled Railway

47

South Lissens
Cottage

Jameston
Moss

Lissens
Moss

1

Auchenskeith

Jameston

High Monkredding
Plantation

Lylestone Quarry
(dis)

Darmule

Jameston
Woods

High
Gooseloan

Benthead

46

31   **A**   **32**   **B**   **33**   **C**

B707

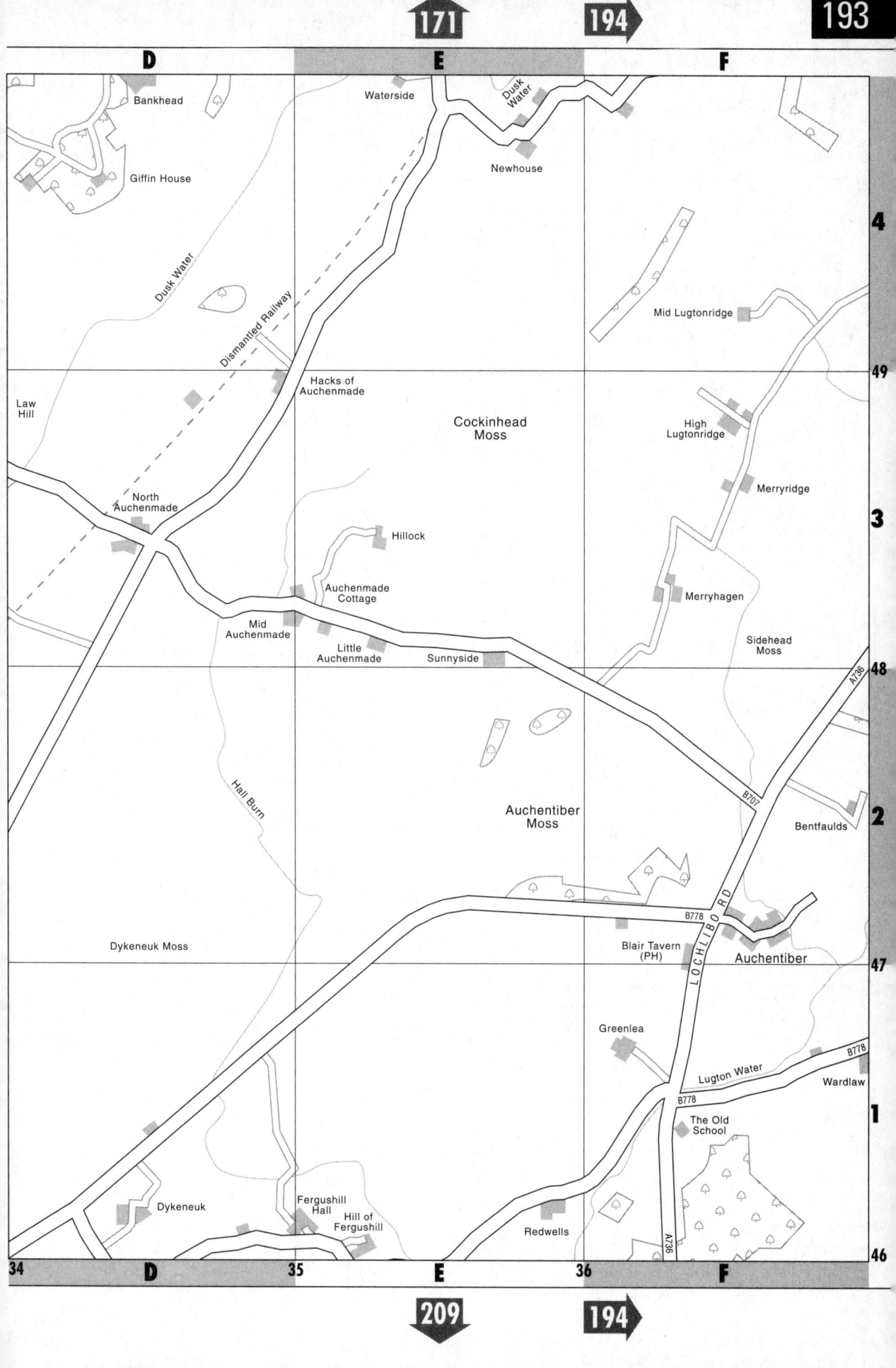

D
E
F

Bankhead

Giffin House

Dusk Water

Waterside

Dusk Water

Newhouse

4

Mid Lugtonridge

Dismantled Railway

Hacks of Auchenmade

49

Law Hill

Cockinhead Moss

High Lugtonridge

North Auchenmade

Merryridge

Hillock

3

Auchenmade Cottage

Merryhagen

Mid Auchenmade

Little Auchenmade

Sunnyside

Sidehead Moss

48

Hall Burn

Auchentiber Moss

B707

A736

Bentfaulds

2

LOCHLIBO RD

Dykeneuk Moss

B778

Blair Tavern (PH)

Auchentiber

47

Greenlea

Lugton Water

B778

Wardlaw

B778

1

The Old School

Dykeneuk

Fergushill Hall

Hill of Fergushill

Redwells

A736

46

34
D
35
E
36
F

193
172

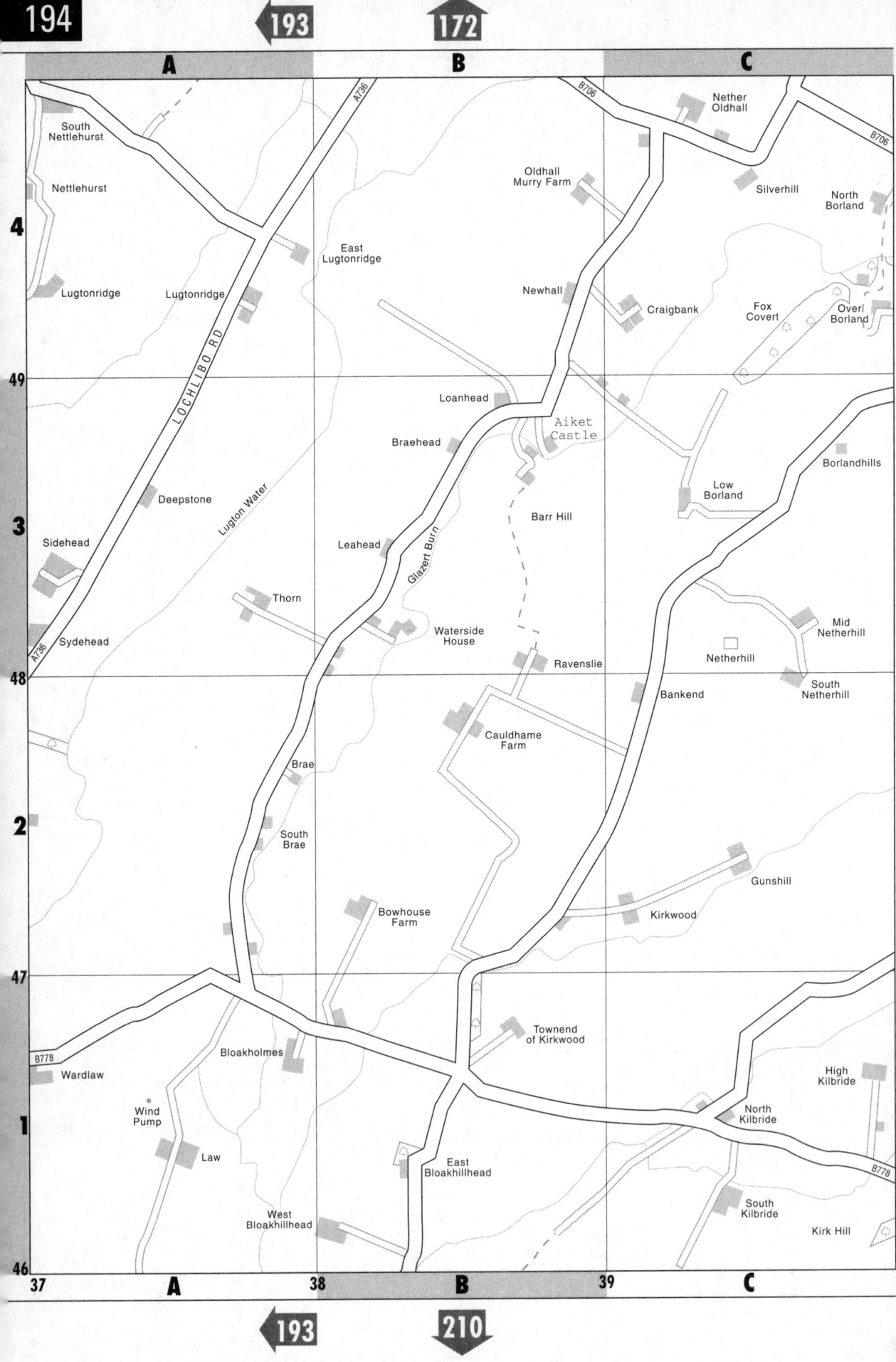

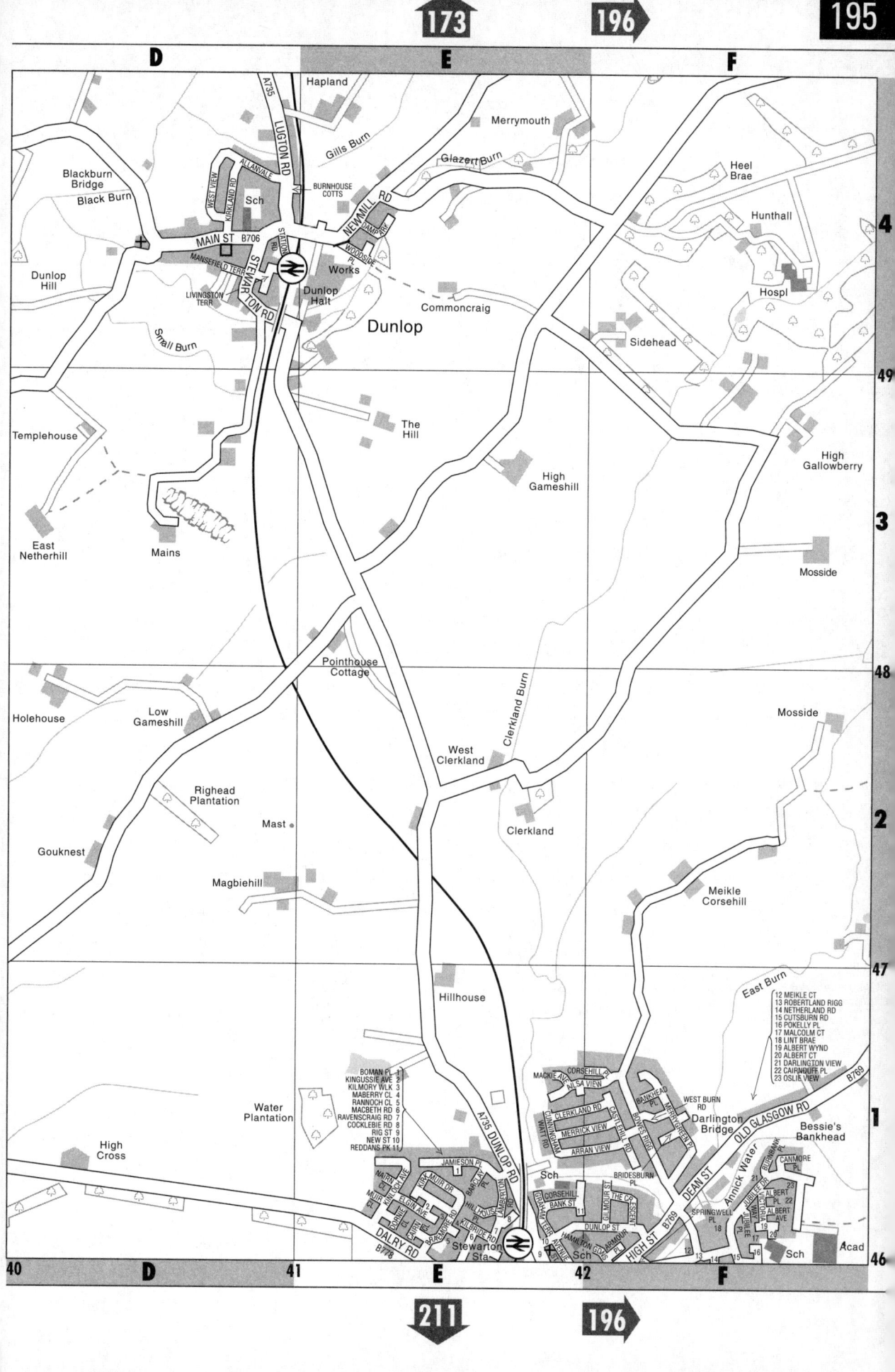

D   E   F

Hapland
Merrymouth
Gills Burn
Glazert Burn
Heel Brae
Blackburn Bridge
Black Burn
WEST VIEW
KIRKLAND RD
ALLANVALE
Sch
BURNHOUSE COTTS
NEWMILL RD
BAMFORD
Hunthall
Dunlop Hill
MAIN ST   B706
MANSEFIELD TERRACE
WOODSIDE PL
Works
Hospl
4
LIVINGSTON TERR
STEWARTON RD
STATION RD
Dunlop Halt
Dunlop
Commoncraig
Sidehead
Small Burn
49
Templehouse
The Hill
High Gameshill
High Gallowberry
3
East Netherhill
Mains
Mosside
Pointhouse Cottage
Holehouse
Low Gameshill
Clerkland Burn
Mosside
48
Righead Plantation
West Clerkland
Gouknest
Mast
Clerkland
Meikle Corsehill
Magbiehill
2
47
East Burn
Hillhouse
Water Plantation
BOMAN PL 1
KINGUSSIE AVE 2
KILMORY WLK 3
MABERRY CL 4
RANNOCH CL 5
MACBETH RD 6
RAVENSCRAIG RD 7
COCKLEBIE RD 8
RIG ST 9
NEW ST 10
REDDANS PK 11
High Cross

12 MEIKLE CT
13 ROBERTLAND RIGG
14 NETHERLAND RD
15 CUTSBURN RD
16 POKELLY PL
17 MALCOLM CT
18 LINT BRAE
19 ALBERT WYND
20 ALBERT CT
21 DARLINGTON VIEW
22 CAIRNDUFF PL
23 OSLIE VIEW

MACKIE AVE
CORSEHILL
AILSA VIEW
BANKHEAD PL
WEST BURN RD
Darlington Bridge
Bessie's Bankhead
OLD GLASGOW RD
B769
CLERKLAND RD
CUNNINGHAM WATTO
CASTLEHILL RD
JONES BRIGG
MERRYHILL
1
A735 DUNLOP RD
Sch
MERRICK VIEW
ARRAN VIEW
BRIDESBURN PL
DEAN ST
SPRINGWELL PL
Amnick Water
CANMORE PL
JAMIESON PL
Sch
CORSEHILL BANK ST
GILMOUR ST
THE CRESCENT
HIGH ST
B769
ALBERT PL
ALBERT AVE
NAIRN
KYLE
MUIR DR
ELGIN AVE
AIRLIE
ALBRIE RD
DUNLOP ST
HAMILTON GD
GILMOUR
PL
Sch
Acad
DALRY RD
B778
Stewarton Sta
Sch
46

40   D   41   E   42   F

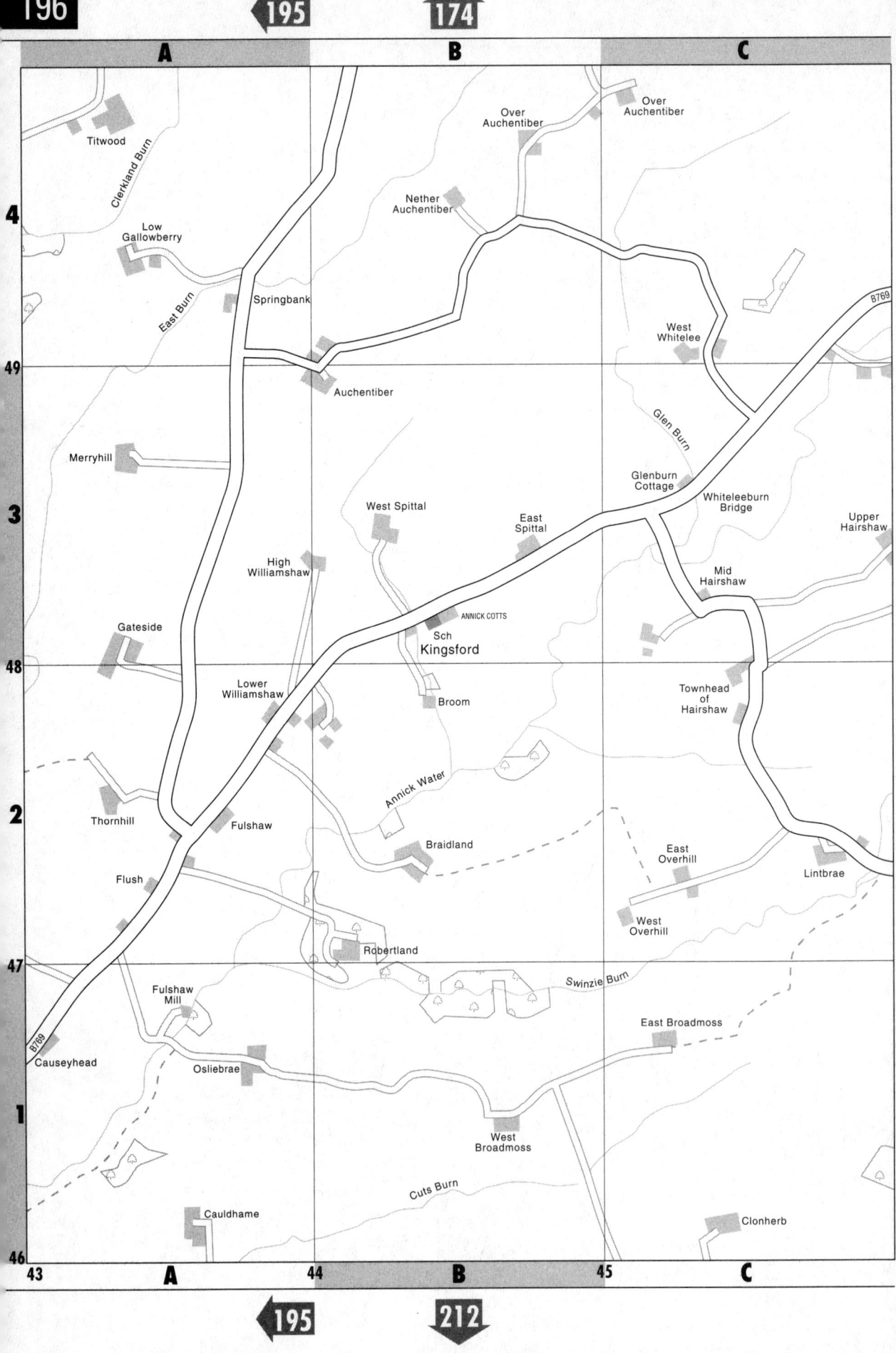

A
B
C

4

Titwood

Clerkland Burn

Low
Gallowberry

East Burn

Springbank

49

Auchentiber

Merryhill

3

West Spittal

High
Williamshaw

East
Spittal

ANNICK COTTS
Sch
Kingsford

Gateside

48

Lower
Williamshaw

Broom

Annick Water

2

Thornhill

Fulshaw

Braidland

Flush

Robertland

47

Fulshaw
Mill

Swinzie Burn

B769

Causeyhead

Osliebrae

East Broadmoss

1

West
Broadmoss

Cauldhame

Cuts Burn

Clonherb

46

43
A
44
B
45
C

Over
Auchentiber

Over
Auchentiber

Nether
Auchentiber

West
Whitelee

B769

Glen Burn

Glenburn
Cottage

Whiteleeburn
Bridge

Upper
Hairshaw

Mid
Hairshaw

Townhead
of
Hairshaw

East
Overhill

Lintbrae

West
Overhill

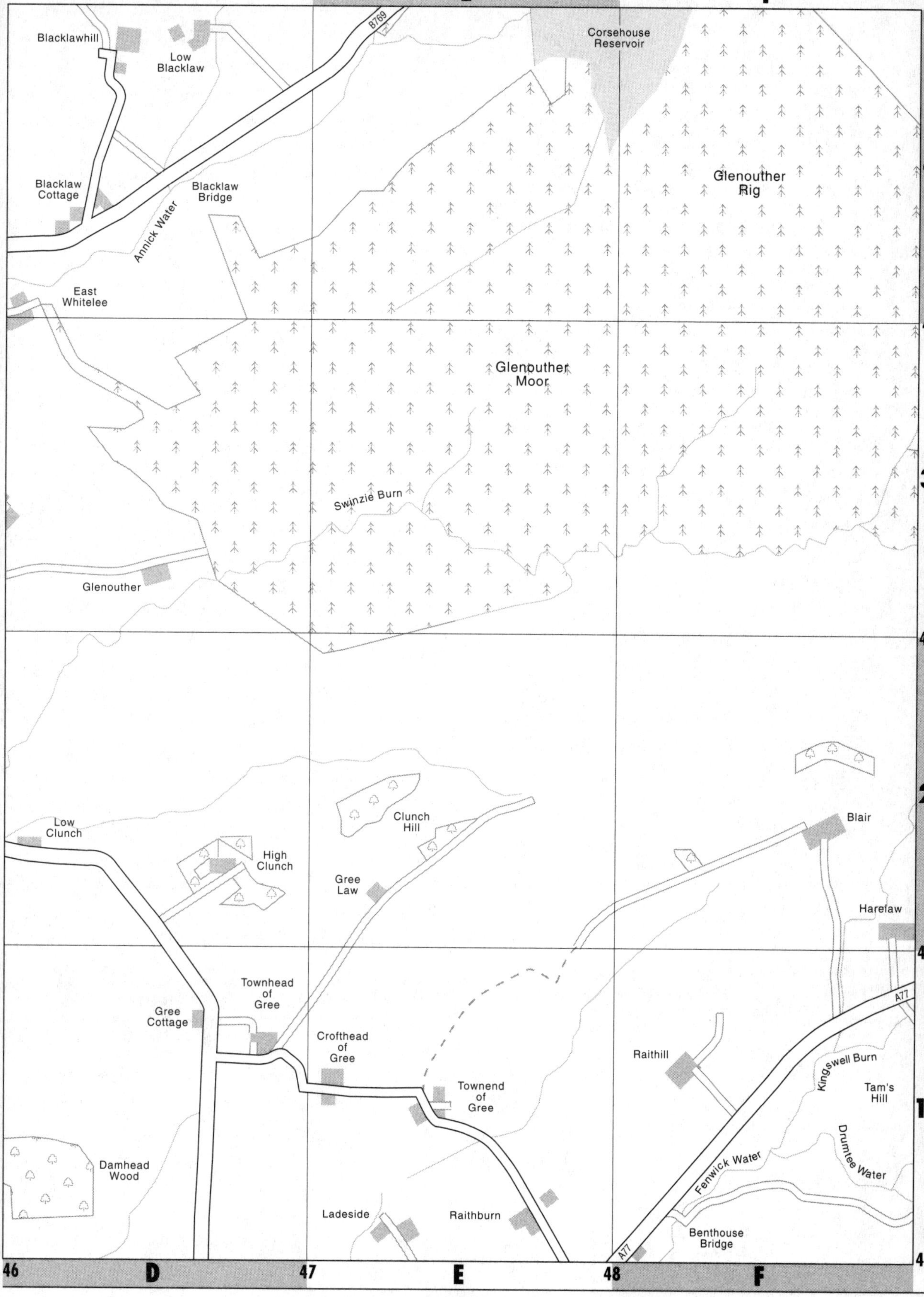

D **E** **F**

Blacklawhill

Low Blacklaw

B769

Corsehouse Reservoir

Blacklaw Cottage

Blacklaw Bridge

Glenouther Rig

4

Annick Water

East Whitelee

49

Glenouther Moor

3

Swinzie Burn

Glenouther

48

Clunch Hill

2

Low Clunch

High Clunch

Blair

Gree Law

Harelaw

47

Townhead of Gree

Gree Cottage

Crofthead of Gree

Raithill

A77

Damhead Wood

Townend of Gree

Kingswell Burn

Tam's Hill

1

Fenwick Water

Drumtee Water

Ladeside

Raithburn

Benthouse Bridge

A77

46 **D** **47** **E** **48** **F** **46**

184

A   B   C

4

Primrose Ave
Glen Ave

Patrickholm

Thinacremuir Lodge
Plotcock Glen
Mafflat
Corslet
Avon Water

East Thinacremuir
Mafflat Orchard

Patrickbrae Cottage

Thinacremuir Muir
Newhouse Farm Cottages
Newhouse
Broomelton Rd
Plotcock Rd
Dismantled Railway

Kittymuirhill

49

Longfaugh
Low Kittymuir

Dismantled Railway

Craigthornhill Rd

3

Craigthornhill
Crofthead
Millheugh Rd

Craigthorn
Kittymuir
Glassford Rd

48

High East Quarter
Howmains

East Quarter

Glassford
Linthaugh Bridge

2

Burnside
Hunterlees Rd
Holm
Linthaugh
Alexander Hamilton Memorial Park

Knowehead
Priest's Burn
Hunterlees
Avon Water
Cemy
A71

Industrial Estate
Lockhart St

47

Manse Whitehill Cottage
Cemy
Manse
Manse Rd
Cemy
McLean Gdns
Lawrie Pl
Green St
Millar St
New St
Cam Nethan St
Murray Dr

Crow Rd
Hill Rd
Vicars Rd
King St
Bogha Pl
Watstone Rd

Whitehill
Tapped Hill
East Mains
Thorndale
Gemmell Way
Crofthead Ct
Queen St
Trongate
Angles

Muirburn Rd
White Hill
Avonholm
Braehead
East Mains Holdings
Dismantled Railway
Townhead St
PC
Stonehouse
Union St

1

West Mains
Homeleigh
A71
Strathaven Rd
Sidehead Rd
Sch

North Lodge
Bankhead
Dismtd Rly
Hospl
Newfield Rd
St Ninians Pl
Spital Rd

1 Davidson Gdns
2 Weavers Way
3 Patrickholm Ave

1 Trongate
2 The Cross

46

73   74   75

A   B   C

184

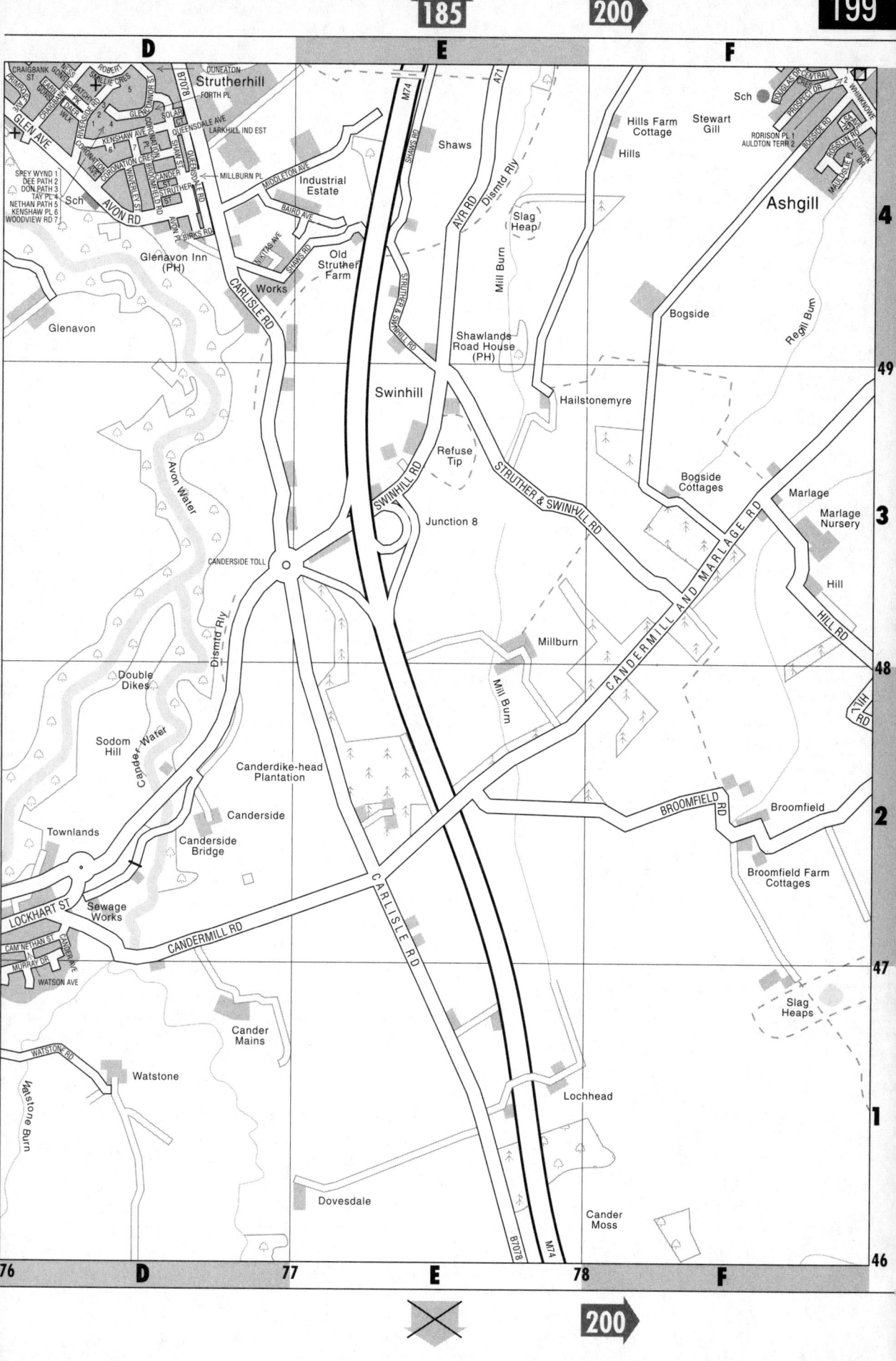

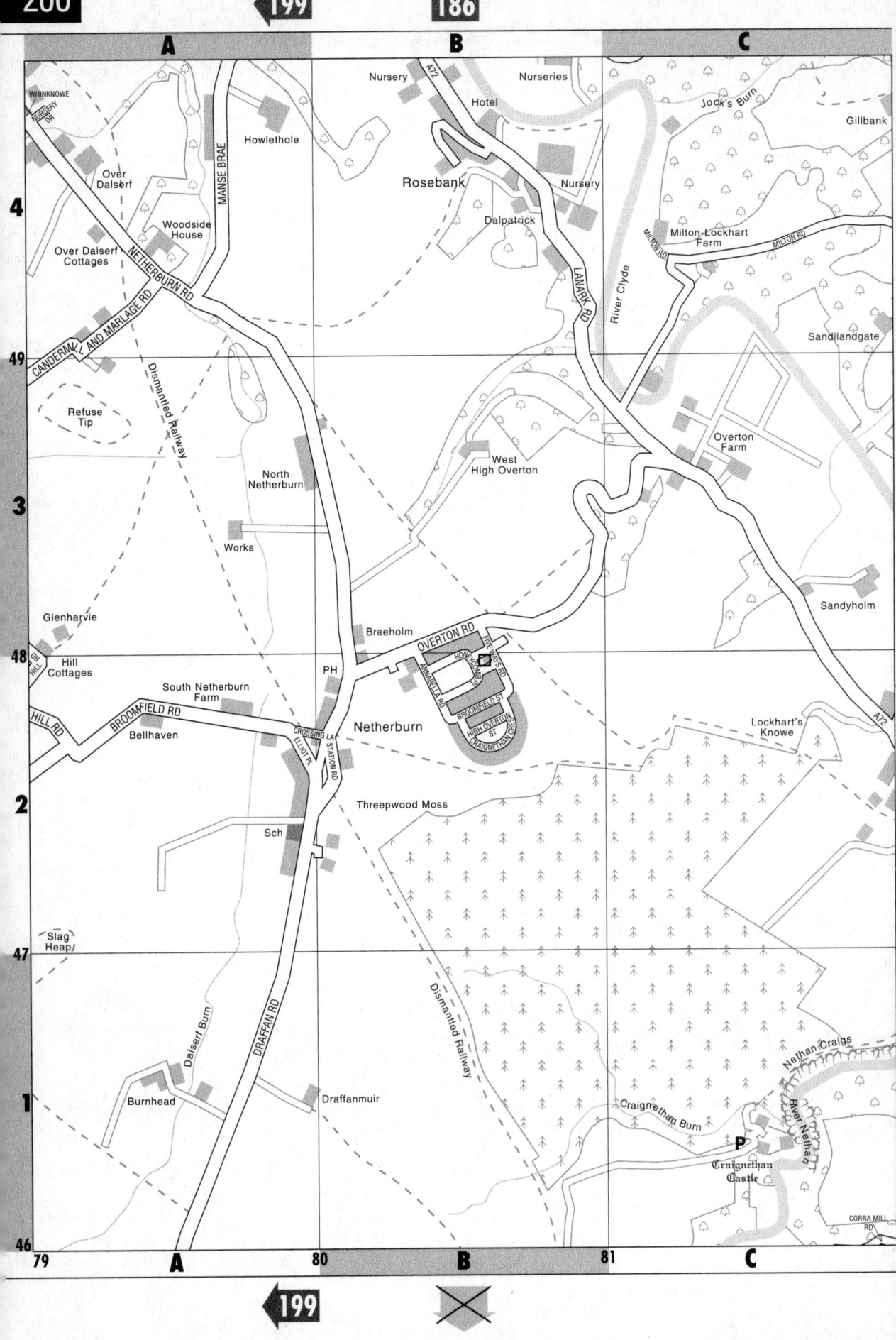

A   B   C

WHINKNOWE
NURSERY DR
Over Dalserf
Howlethole
Nursery
Nurseries
Hotel
Rosebank
Dalpatrick
Nursery
Jock's Burn
Gillbank
Woodside House
Milton-Lockhart Farm
MILTON RD
MILTON RD
NETHERBURN RD
MANSE BRAE
River Clyde
Over Dalserf Cottages
LANARK RD
CANDERMILL AND MARLAGE RD
Sandilandgate
Refuse Tip
Dismantled Railway
West High Overton
Overton Farm
North Netherburn
Works
Sandyholm
Glenharvie
Braeholm
Overton Rd
Hill Cottages
PH
HONEYCOMB?
TINSLEYS RD
OR HILL
South Netherburn Farm
ANNABELLA RD
Lockhart's Knowe
HILL RD
BROOMFIELD RD
Bellhaven
CROSSING LA
ELLIOT PL
STATION RD
Netherburn
BROOMFIELD ST
HIGH OVERTON ST
CRAIGNETHAN CRES
A72
Threepwood Moss
Sch
Slag Heap
Dalserf Burn
DRAFFAN RD
Dismantled Railway
Nethan Craigs
Burnhead
Draffanmuir
Craignethan Burn
River Nethan
P
Craignethan Castle
CORRA MILL RD

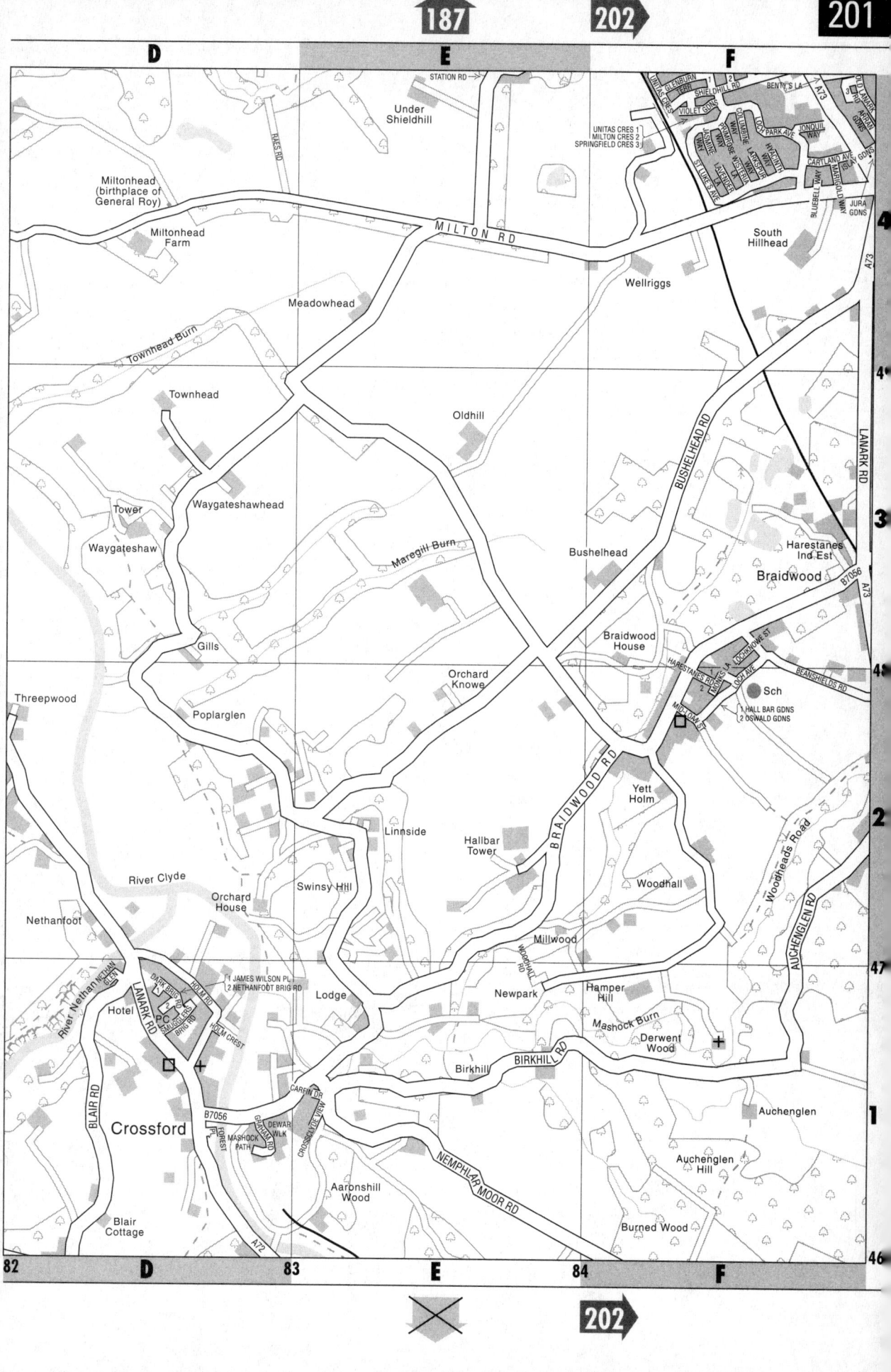

201
188

A   B   C

SAUCHIESMOOR RD
Crawforddyke
Sch
Cemy
Roadmeetings
Hospl
Burnhead
YIELDSHIELDS RD
Burnhead
Bridge
Coldstream
Reservoir
West
Coldstream

WILTON RD
Chy
KILNCADZOW RD

4 CALDWELL RD
5 CAMERON RD
6 CANELUK AVE
7 BRAEHEAD LOAN
8 CHARLES CRES
9 FOREST KIRK

FORRESTLEA
RD

4

Headsmuir
Gowanside

1 GIGHA GDNS
2 ISLAY GDNS
3 JURA GDNS

Langshaw

GOREMIRE RD

BOGHALL RD

Gateside

49

Fiddler Burn

Nursery

Leemuir

3

PH
B7056

Lee
Meadow

A73

Nellfield
House

48

BEANSHIELDS RD

OLD LANARK RD

Crossgates

Cartland Muir
Plantation

Crossgates
Plantation

MEADOW RD

2

AUCHENGLEN RD

Lee Burn

Nursery

Craigen Hill

March
Bridge

LANARK RD

47

Mast

West Wood

Leewood
House

MOOR RD

1

The Lee

New Greentowers
Farm

OLD LANARK RD

Castlehill

Auchenglen Burn

Brocklinn
Glen

Brocklinn Burn

Brocklinn
Bridge

Cartland

GREENTOWERS RD

A73
CARTLAND RD

46

85   A   86   B   87   C

201
214

Glenhead

Kirkland

Gourock Burn

South
Inch

A78

P

P

P

Glenfoot

Boydston
Braes

PC

Scart
Rock

Boydston
Shore

A78

North
Islet

East
Islet

Broad
Rock

Horse
Isle
(Nature Reserve)

North Bay

ARDROSSAN

North Bay

Busbie Bridge

B780

High Boydstone

Little Busbie

Meikle Busbie

Craigspark Plantation

Craigspark

Rashley

Rowanside Burn

Low Boydstone

Caravan Park

Townhead

Stanley Burn

Mill Glen Reservoir

Sorbie

Montfode Burn

Mill Farm

Filter Station

Works

Montfode

A78

Whitlees

Dalry Rd

Stanley Rd

Dykesmains

Sch

Parkhouse Rd

Stanley Burn

Cemy

McDowall

Nursery Pl

Sorbie Rd

B728

Acad

Dismld Rly

Breakwater

Ardrossan Harbour Station

P

Ferry Terminal

Harbour Liby

Off

Montgomerie Pier Rd

Glasgow St

Town Hall

PC

Ardrossan Town Station

LC

South Beach

Promenade

South Crescent Rd

Ardrossan South Beach Station

High Rd

Acad

Jack's Rd

A78

4

Towerlodge

Littlelaught

Meiklelaught

45

West Knockrivoch
Mount

Knockrivoch

East Knockrivoch
Mount

Diddup

Smithstone
Plantation

Quarry

Bankend

Lochwood

AULD CLAY RD

3

South Knockrivoch
Mount

Stevenston or
Ashgrove Loch

The Craigs Loch Craigs

44

Glen
Banks

Ford

Golf
Course

Lochcraigs

Mast

Sharphill

Corsankell

Glen Burn

CH

Filter
Station

Hillhead

2

SHARPHILL
IND EST

Middlepart

Fellie Hill

Greenhead
Holdings

HILLHEAD RD

43

LOCHLEA RD
CARRICK AVE
KELLISLAND
FLEMING
MILGARVIE AVE

1 ISLAY CRES
2 KEIR HARDIE PL
3 JEAN ARMOUR PL
4 ABBOTSFORD PL
5 TALISMAN WLK
6 MUNRO WLK

KENILWORTH
DR

DALRY RD

Schs

Quarrel Burn

MIDDLEPART

MAXWELL PL 1
CLEMENTS PL 2
OAKLAND DR 3
ARDCHOILLE DR 4
ASHGROVE AVE 5
KERELAW AVE 6

Sch

CAMBUSKEITH RD HAWTHORN
DR

HAYOCKS RD

Landsborough PL

Hawkhill

PRIMROSE
PL

SHAW
PL

SANNOX DR

GILFILLAN
AVE

FLECK

7 MIDDLEPART CRES
8 DUGUID DR
9 PROSPECTHILL RD
10 McNAY CRES
11 McKINNON PL
12 CLARK PL
13 ADAMS AVE
14 LOCHRANZA PL

Mayfield

KERELAW RD

Kerelaw
Mains

Stevenston Burn

McGREGOR AVE

WALLACE AVE

Sch

Cemy Sch

A78

1

Priest
Hill

MAYFIELD

SINCLAIR ST

1 JOHN BROGAN PL
2 MARY LOVE PL
3 GOLDIE PL
4 CLYDE VIEW AVE
5 CAPONCRAIG AVE

LOCCARD
RD

GLENCAIRN ST

+

KILWINNING RD

Mount Pleasant

Caravan
Park

HIGH RD

HIGH RD

HIGH RD

THE RIGGS

SCHOOLWELL

AFTON
RD

TOWNHEAD ST

Ardeer Mains

DUBBS RD

ST
LAWRENCE
PL

P GLEBE ST A738 Main St

HILLCRES

B752

12

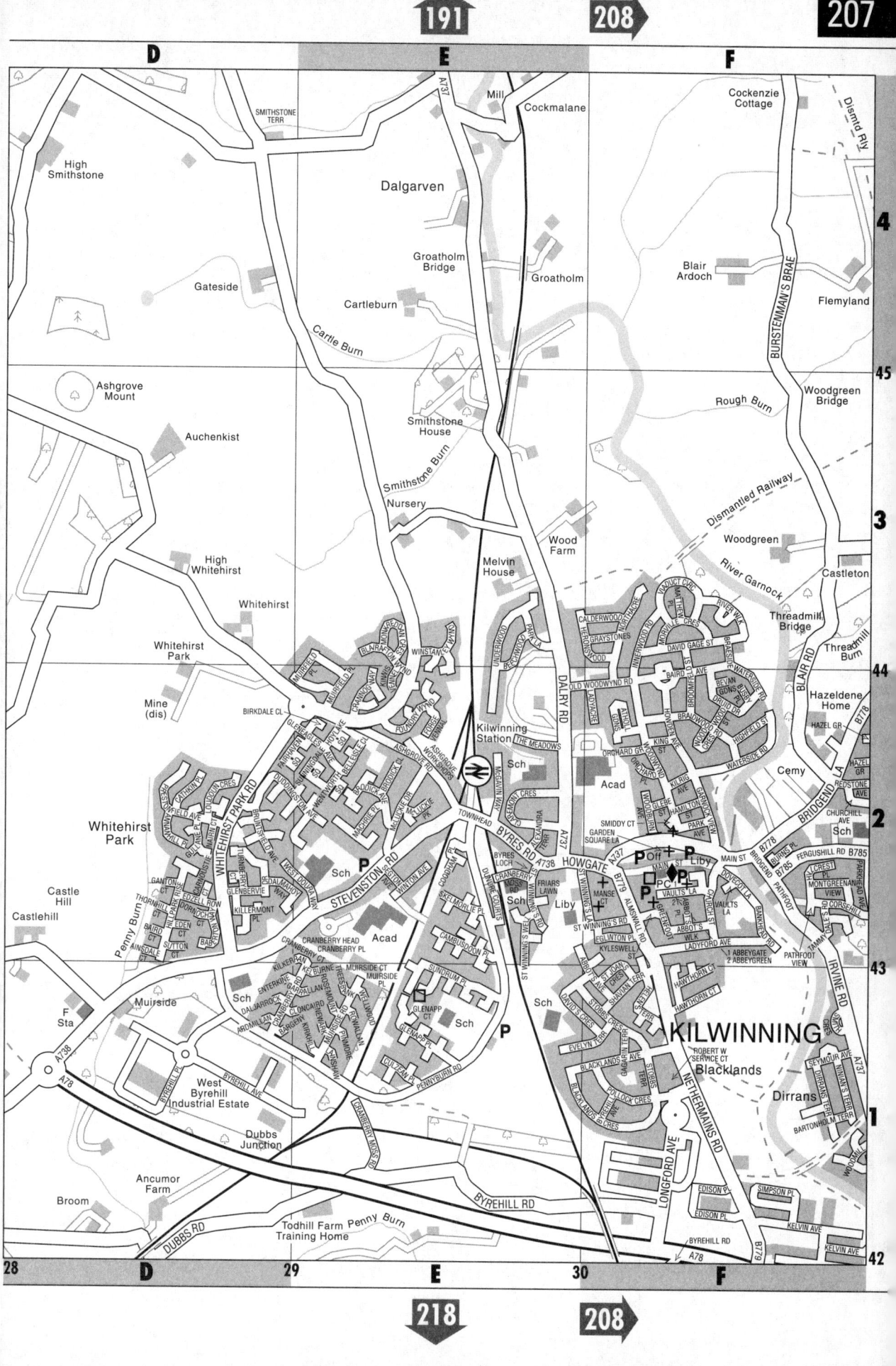

D
E
F

4

Cockenzie
Cottage

Dismtd Rly

SMITHSTONE
TERR

Dalgarven

Mill
Cockmalane

A737

High
Smithstone

Groatholm
Bridge

Groatholm

Blair
Ardoch

Flemyland

Gateside

Cartleburn

Cartle Burn

45

Ashgrove
Mount

Rough Burn

Woodgreen
Bridge

Auchenkist

Smithstone
House

Smithstone Burn

Dismantled Railway

3

Nursery

Wood
Farm

Woodgreen

River Garnock

Castleton

High
Whitehirst

Melvin
House

Threadmill
Bridge

Threadmill
Burn

BLAIR RD

Whitehirst

CALDERWOOD
HERONSWOOD
GRAYSTONES

VIADUCT CIRC
MATHIE CRES
RIVER WLK

Hazeldene
Home

HAZEL GR

44

Whitehirst
Park

UNDERWOOD
PARK LA
RICHMOND

DAVID GAGE ST
BAIRD AVE
BEVAN

HAZEL
GR

Mine
(dis)

BIRKDALE CL

Kilwinning
Station

THE MEADOWS

Sch

OLD WOODWYND RD
ADVAICE

KING
ST

BRAIDWOOD

DRUID DR
HIGHFIELD ST

B778

REDSTONE
AVE

Castle
Hill

Whitehirst
Park

DALRY RD

Acad

ORCHARD GN
ORCHARD

GLEBE ST
HAMILTON ST

Cemy

CHURCHILL
AVE

Sch

2

Castlehill

STEVENSTON RD

Sch

TOWNHEAD

BYRES RD

A737
HOWGATE

SMIDDY CT
GARDEN
SQUARE LA

P Off

P Liby
MAIN ST

B778

FERGUSHILL RD B785

Penny Burn

Cranberry
Byres
Loch

FRIARS
LAWN

MANSE
CT

P
P

P
VAULTS LA

VAULTS
LA

PATHFOOT

Acad

CRANBERRY HEAD
CRANBERRY PL

CAMBUSDOON

ST WINNING'S RD

Liby

ST WINNING'S WY

EGLINTON PL

ABBOT'S
WLK

ABBOT'S
WLK

PATHFOOT
VIEW

43

F
Sta

Muirside

MUIRSIDE CT
MUIRSIDE
PL

GLENAPP
CT

Sch

P

Sch

EVELYN TERR

KYLESWELL

LADYFORD AVE

1 ABBEYGATE
2 ABBEYGREEN

IRVINE RD

A737

KILWINNING

Blacklands

Dirrans

West
Byrehill
Industrial Estate

Dubbs
Junction

BLACKLANDS
CRES

ROBERT W
SERVICE CT

NETHERMAINS RD

BARTONHOLM TERR

1

Ancumor
Farm

LONGFORD AVE

Broom

Todhill Farm Penny Burn
Training Home

DUBBS RD

BYREHILL RD

BYREHILL RD

A78

B779

KELVIN AVE

42

28
D
29
E
30
F

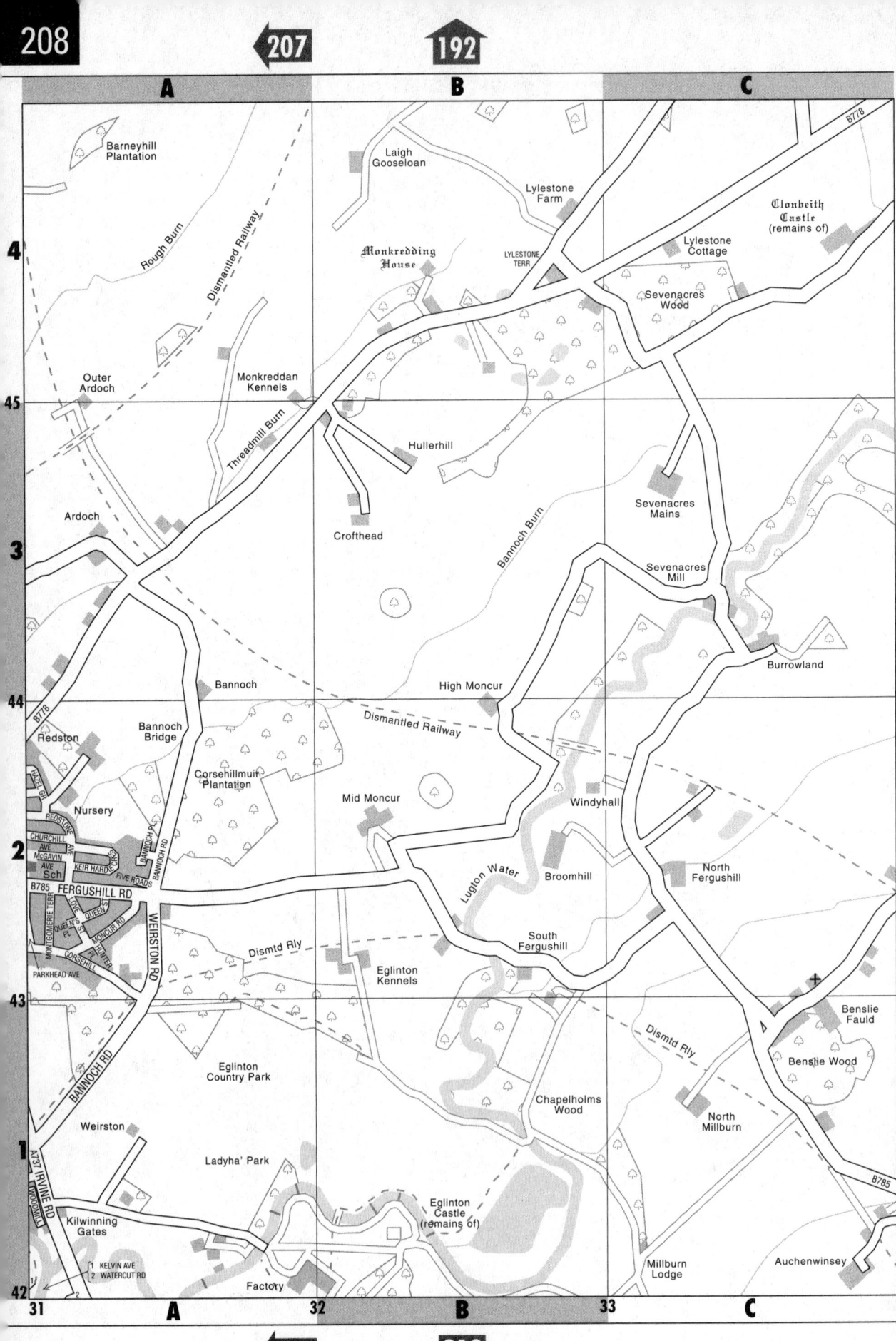

207
192

A   B   C

Barneyhill
Plantation

Laigh
Gooseloan

Lylestone
Farm

Clonbeith
Castle
(remains of)

Rough Burn

Dismantled Railway

Monkredding
House

LYLESTONE
TERR

Lylestone
Cottage

Sevenacres
Wood

4

Outer
Ardoch

Monkreddan
Kennels

45

Threadmill Burn

Hullerhill

Sevenacres
Mains

Ardoch

Crofthead

Bannoch Burn

Sevenacres
Mill

3

Burrowland

Bannoch

High Moncur

44

B778

Redston

Bannoch
Bridge

Dismantled Railway

Nursery

Corsehillmuir
Plantation

Mid Moncur

Windyhall

HAZEL GR

BEASTONS

CHURCHILL
AVE

McGAVIN
AVE

KEIR HARDIE

BANNOCH RD

FIVE ROADS

North
Fergushill

2

Sch

Lugton Water

Broomhill

B785

FERGUSHILL RD

MONTGOMERIE TERR

LOUDON
PL

QUEEN S

MONCUR RD

HUNTER

CORSEHILL

WEIRSTON RD

South
Fergushill

PARKHEAD AVE

Dismtd Rly

Eglinton
Kennels

43

BANNOCH RD

Eglinton
Country Park

Dismtd Rly

Benslie
Fauld

Benslie Wood

Chapelholms
Wood

North
Millburn

Weirston

1

A737 IRVINE RD

WOODMILL

Ladyha' Park

Eglinton
Castle
(remains of)

Millburn
Lodge

B785

Auchenwinsey

Kilwinning
Gates

1 KELVIN AVE
2 WATERCUT RD

42

31   A   **32**   B   **33**   C

Factory

207
219

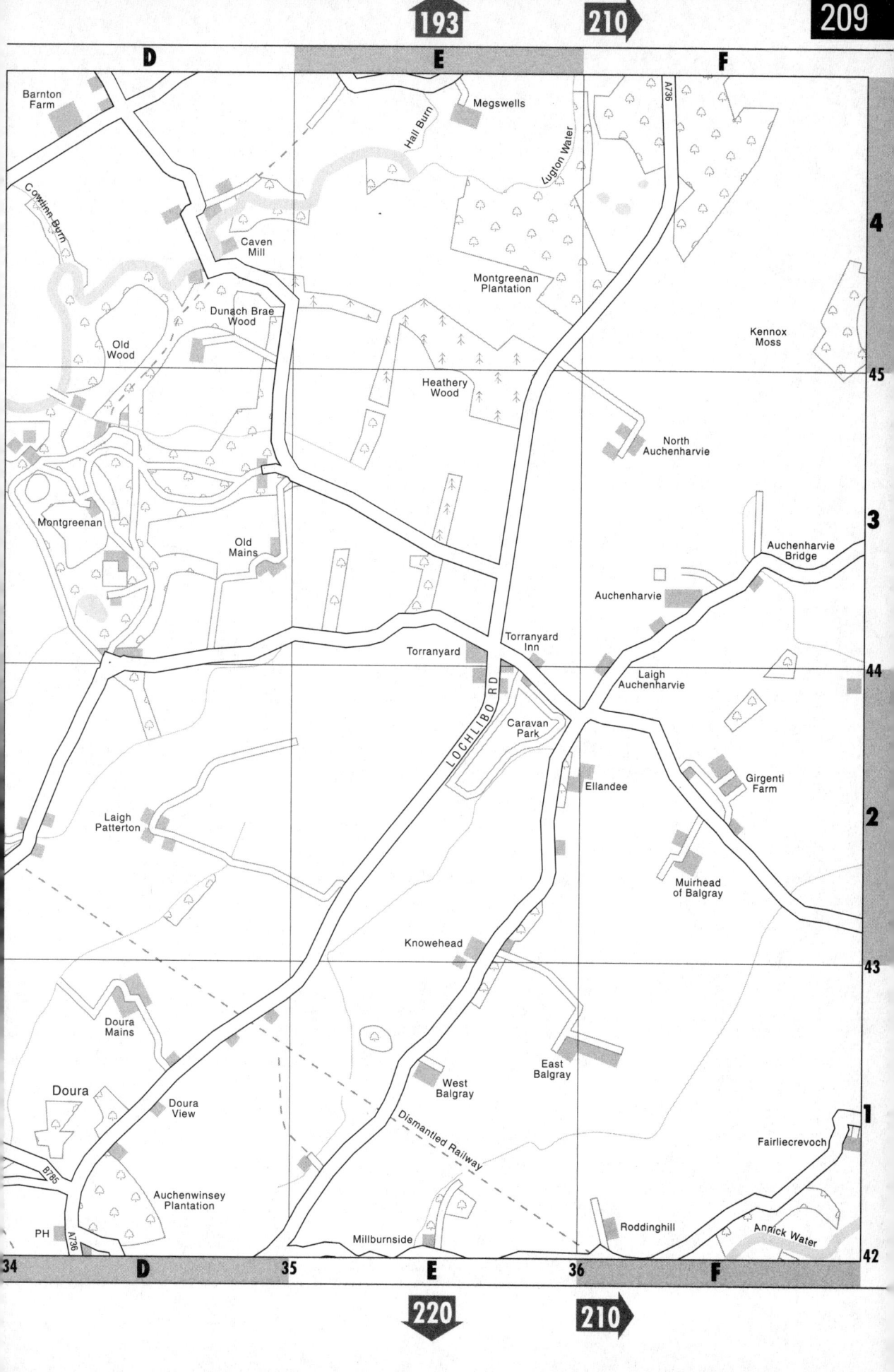

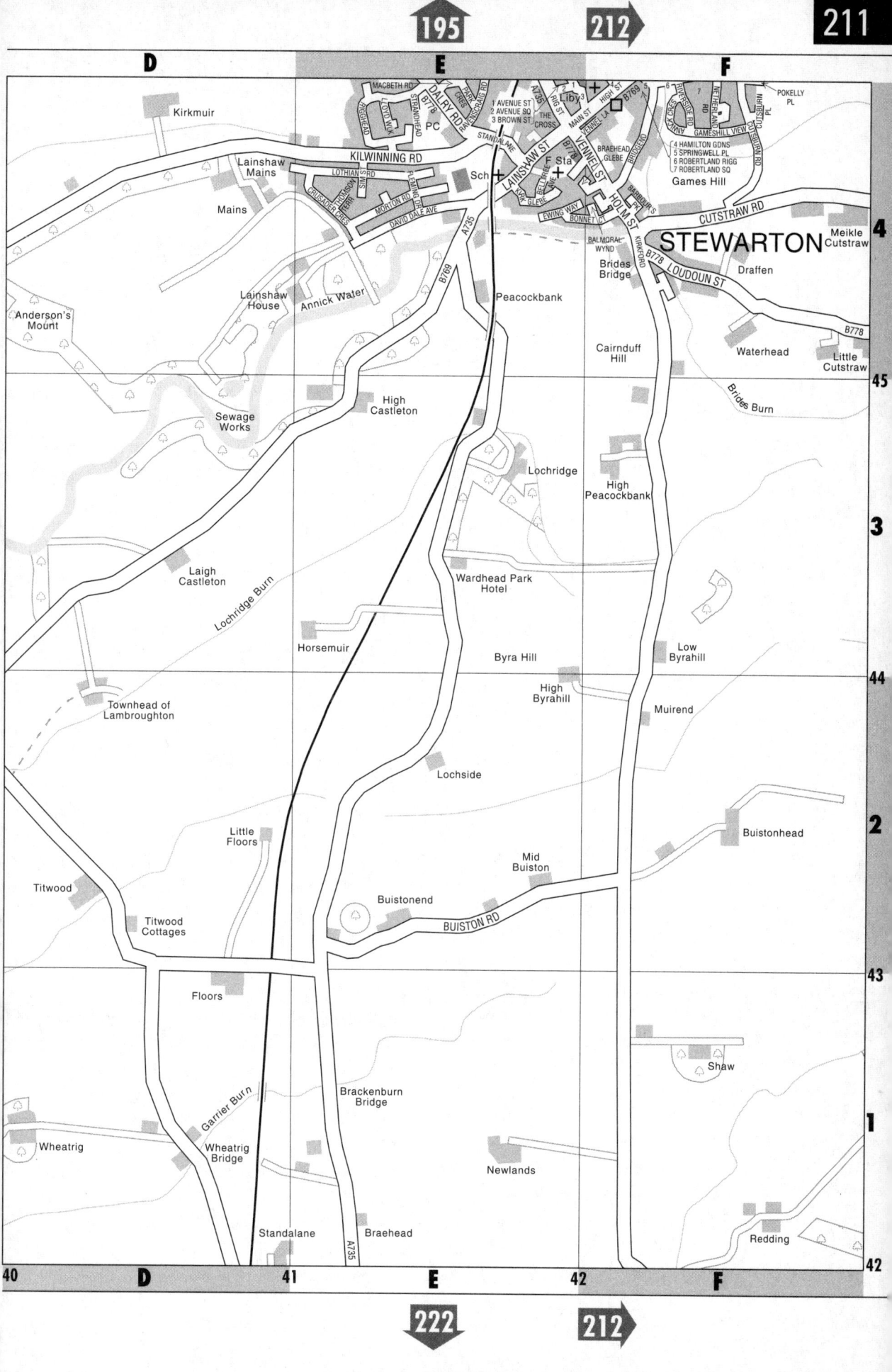

Kirkmuir

Lainshaw
Mains

MACBETH RD
DALRY RD
HIGHFIELD
LLOYD WLK
STRANDHEAD
B778
GREE
RAMSCRAIG RD
PC

A735
1 AVENUE ST
2 AVENUE SQ
3 BROWN ST
RIG ST
MAIN ST
THE
CROSS
HIGH ST
B769
LIBY
NETHERLAND
RD
GAMESHILL VIEW
POKELLY
PL

6
7
RIGFOOT RD
COBURN RD

Mains
KILWINNING RD

LOTHIAN RD
FLEMING DR
SIM
LOTHIAN RD
STANDALANE
LAINSHAW ST
VENNEL LA
BRAEHEAD
GLEBE
4 HAMILTON GDNS
5 SPRINGWELL PL
6 ROBERTLAND RIGG
7 ROBERTLAND SQ

CRUSADER CRES
THOMSON DR
KERR
MORTON CT
DAVID DALE AVE
Sch
BELL CRES
KIRK GLEBE
EWING WAY
BONNET
VENNEL ST
HOLM ST
F Sta
BRAEHEAD
GLEBE
BARBIERI'S
PL
CUTSTRAW RD

Games Hill

Meikle
Cutstraw

Anderson's
Mount

Lainshaw
House

Annick Water

A735
B769
Peacockbank

BALMORAL
WYND
STEWARTON
Brides
Bridge
HOLM ST
KIRKFORD
B778
LOUDOUN ST
B778
Draffen

Waterhead

Little
Cutstraw

4

Sewage
Works

High
Castleton

Cairnduff
Hill

Brides Burn

45

Laigh
Castleton

Lochridge Burn

Lochridge

High
Peacockbank

3

Wardhead Park
Hotel

Horsemuir

Byra Hill

Low
Byrahill

44

Townhead of
Lambroughton

High
Byrahill

Muirend

Lochside

Little
Floors

Buistonhead

2

Titwood

Buistonend

Mid
Buiston

Titwood
Cottages

BUISTON RD

43

Floors

Shaw

Garrier Burn

Brackenburn
Bridge

1

Wheatrig

Wheatrig
Bridge

Newlands

Standalane
A735
Braehead

Redding

211
196

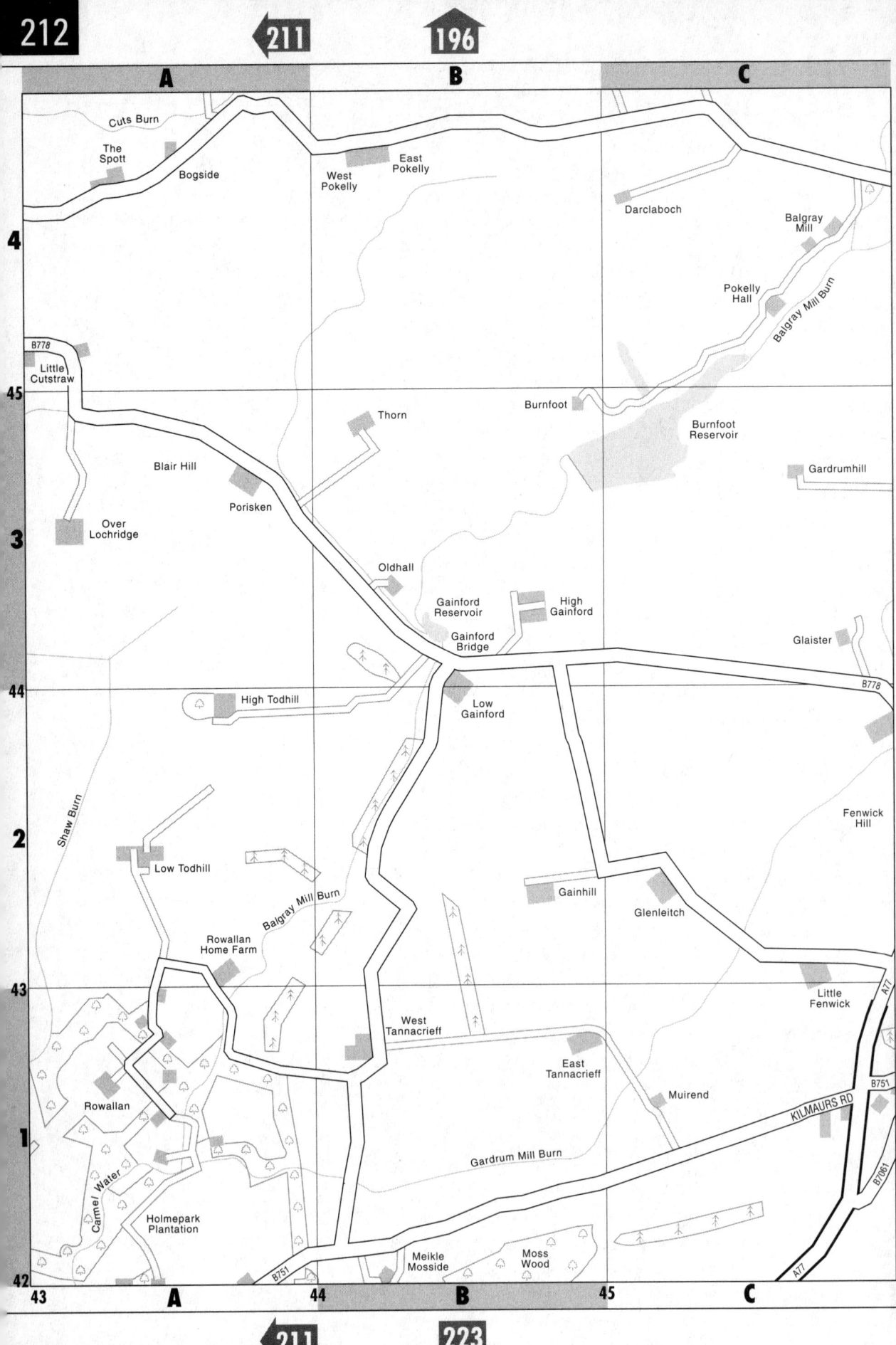

211
223

D   E   F

Damhead

Laighmuir

Glassock Bridge

North Glassock

South Glassock

4

Pokelly Hill

Rigghill

45

Gardrum Mill Burn

Gardrum Mill

High Gardrum

Midton

Water Works

3

Gardrum

Townend

Warnockland

Shelgo Burn

Amlaird

B751

Fenwick Water

Glaister Bridge

BLACKFAULDS GDNS

44

B778

STEWARTON RD

Cemy

Skernieland

McKNIGHT RD

Waterside

Hall PH

Sch

KIRKTON RD

Fenwick

Kirkton Bridge

WEST VIEW

Waterside Bridge

Arness

MAIN RD

Sch

2

MAIN RD

POLES RD

BRAEHEAD

MURCHLAND AVE

Wyllieland

Wyllielandhill

Hareshaw

Hareshaw Mill

43

Laigh Fenwick

WATERSLAP

Bruntland

Bruntland Bridge

Craufurdland Water

Hareshawmuir Water

KILMAURS

B7061

Fenwick Bridge

Midland

Horsehill

Pockinan Bridge

1

Aikenhead

Dalsraith Bridge

Dalsraith

Darwhilling

A719

42

46   D   47   E   48   F

202

A B C

4

Folly Wood

NEMPHLAR MOOR RD

Lochartbank

Rothesbank

Bullions

45

NEMPHLAR RD

Nemphar

HEATHER RD
HALL RD
FOOT OF LONE RD

Chapel Knowe

Burgh Wood

CARTLAND RD
Cartland Mains

A73

LANARK RD

GREENTOWERS RD
OLD LANARK RD
Greentowers

Clencotto

Newsteadings

Lockhart Mill

Woodend

Castle Qua

Mouse Water

Mousebank

Sch

WEST NEMPHLAR RD

Sunnyside Rd

3

Mast

MOUSEMILL RD

Hotel

Hospl

MOUSEBANK RD

SCARLETT

WHEATLANDSIDE
SPRINGFIELD GDNS
CARTLAND VIEW
FLAT HILL
RIDGEPARK DR
GRANGE CT
WELLINGTON TERR
WHEATLANDS DR

Stonebyres Falls

Sunnyside

Caravan Site

44

Hakespie Hill

River Clyde

PC

Sch

KIRKFIELDBANK BRAE

GLASGOW RD

A72

Clydesholm Bridge

PARK PL
WEST PORT A73

Hospl

LANARK RD
A72

Linnmill

B7018

RIVERSIDE RD

Factory

Kirkfieldbank

RAMOTH

Works

St PATRICK'S RD

Castlebank

Castle Hill

2

FAIR VIEW DR
ORCHARD VIEW
LESMAHAGOW RD
HILL VIEW RD Linnville

Kirkfield House

KIRKFIELD RD

Nursery

P

West Kilbank

Kilbank

Braxfield Park

43

B7018

Newhouse

BRAXFIELD TERR
NEW LANARK RD
LONG ROW
ROSEDALE ST

Teaths

Kirkfield Burn

Smithy

BYRETOWN RD

1

GREENRIG RD

Byretown

Greenrig Farm

Over Hall

42

85 A 86 B 87 C

D **E** **F**

Finwood Burn

Jerviswood

Mouse Water

ROMAN ROAD (course of)

Works

A706

LC

4

Mill House

Nursery

Jerviswood Mains

Richland

Cleghorn

HAGHOLM RD

JERVISWOOD DR

AITKEN AVE

ARMOUR AVE

THORNLEA PL

45

Hospl

1 WHEATLANDSIDE
2 WELLINGTON TERR
3 WHEATLAND DR

ST TEILING 4
LEECHFORD 5

STANMORE RD

Stanmore House

Northfaulds

HARDACRES

BELLEFIELD RD

WATERLOO DR

CHAPLAND RD

CLEGHORN RD

BRAEDALE RD

MELVILLE HALL RD

ST NICHOLAS RD

LIMPETLAW

WELLWOOD AVE

ST KENTIGERNS

FORREST

RHYBER AVE

CLEGHORN AVE

STANMORE AVE

QUARRYKNOWE

LAVEROCKHALL

THE MARCHES

POTTERS WYND

RUSSELL

LYING MAINS CT

ST NINIAN'S

WESTCOTT PL

GILROY CL

BELL'S WYND

MARR WYND

STANMORE CRES

MINTO

Stanmore Home Farm

Caldwellside Farm

Ind Est

NORTH FAULDS

YOUNG RD

EAST FAULDS RD

WEST FAULDS RD

A743

3

Gallow Hill

Sch

STUART DR

CLYDE

THE RODDINS

1 RENWICK PL
2 DENNISTON PL
3 LINDSAY LOAN
4 WHITE'S NEUK

Hospl

Ind Est

44

JERVISWOOD RD

A706

F Sta

BAXTER

KILDARE RD

HILLTOP

CAMERONIAN CT

WAVERLEY DR

WOODSTOCK RD

WALLACE PK

SMYLLUM RD

KATE'S MYRE

BRAIDFUTE

WALLACE WAY

Smyllum Park

LC

Wks

Ind Est

ST LEONARD ST

GALLOWHILL RD

Ct

DOVECOT LA

SANDY RD

North Vennel

Liby

P

Lanark Sta

WELLGATE CT

WOODSTOCK DR

KILWORTH RD

VICTORY AVE

KENILWORTH RD

BATHGATE

Sch

Sch

+

Golf Course

2

High St

BANNATYNE ST

ST VINCENT ST

BONNET RD

GLEN PL

BENDIGO PL

WELLGATEHEAD

Off

Off

PC

1 HIGHBURGH CT
2 WOODSTOCK RD

LANARK

WHITELEES RD

Lanark Moor Country Park

Lanark Moor

PC

DELVES RD

PC

WELLGATE

Market

Sch

ALBANY DR

HOME ST

CH

Lanark Loch

43

WHEATPARK RD
GREYSTONE BAULKS
GREENSIDE CL
GREENSIDE LA
AITKEN PL
BLOOMGATE
SHIRLEY'S CL
DUNCAN'S CL
CROSS KEYS CL
RITCHIE'S CL
HUNTER'S CL
BULL'S CL
McKENZIES CL
MARKET END
HYNDFORD PL
BERNARD'S WYND
THOMPSON'S CL

BRIERYBANK AVE

KIRKLANDS RD

BONNINGTON AVE

WELL RD

Sch

Cemy

COUNTY DR

CROSSLAW AVE

NEW LANES ST

Hospl

PC

HYNDFORD RD

PC

P

1

BRAXFIELD RD

BANKHEAD

THE BEECHES

Kingson's Knowe

Dismtd Rly

Cemy

Race Course (dis)

NEW LANARK RD

Sch

BRAXFIELD TERR

Bankhead

P

New Lanark

NEW BUILDINGS
NURSERY BUILDINGS
CAITHNESS ROW

PC

A73

Langloch

42

A

B

C

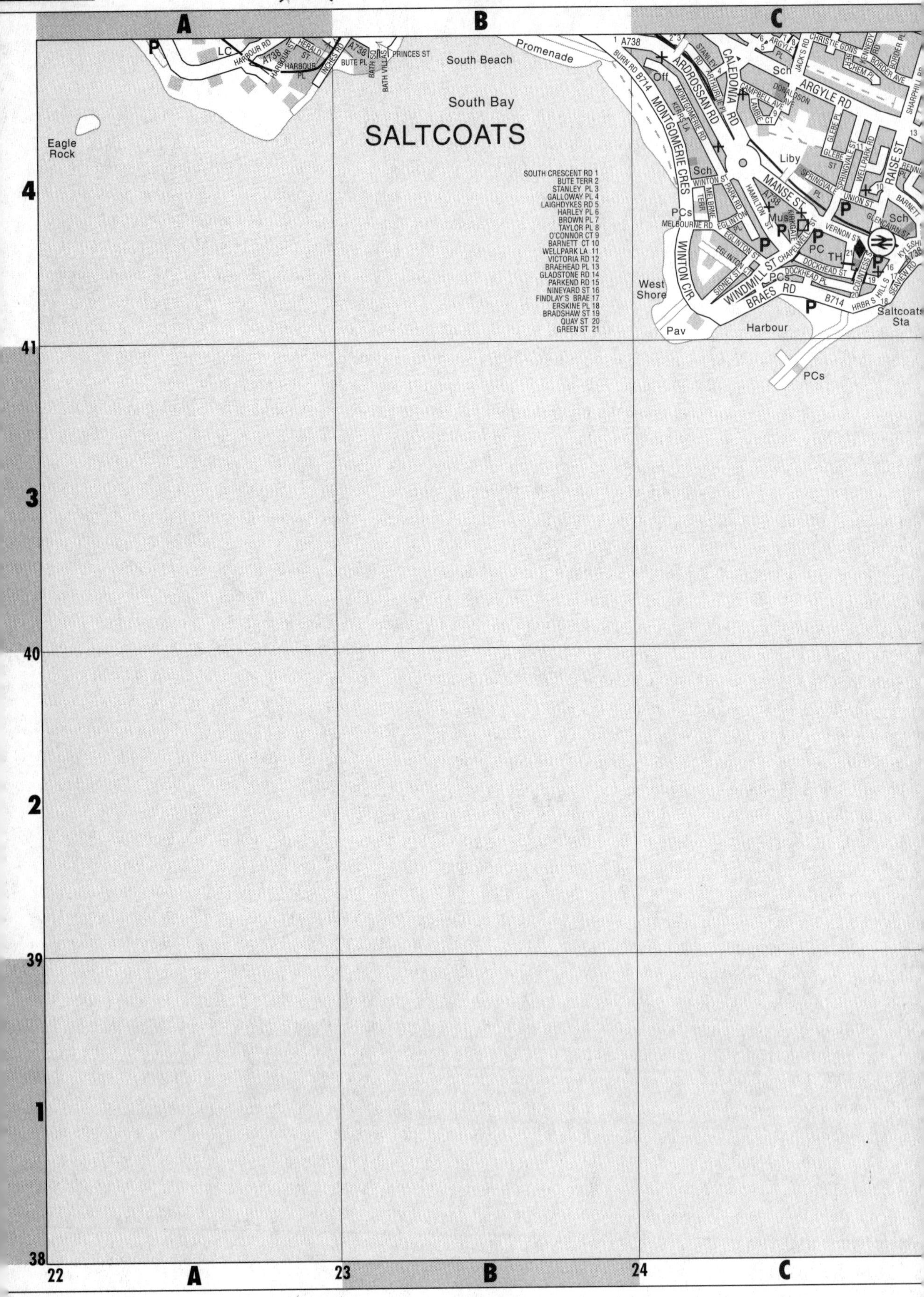

SALTCOATS

South Beach

Promenade

South Bay

Eagle Rock

SOUTH CRESCENT RD 1
BUTE TERR 2
STANLEY PL 3
GALLOWAY PL 4
LAIGHDYKES RD 5
HARLEY PL 6
BROWN PL 7
TAYLOR PL 8
O'CONNOR CT 9
BARNETT CT 10
WELLPARK LA 11
VICTORIA RD 12
BRAEHEAD PL 13
GLADSTONE RD 14
PARKEND RD 15
NINEYARD ST 16
FINDLAY'S BRAE 17
ERSKINE PL 18
BRADSHAW ST 19
QUAY ST 20
GREEN ST 21

West Shore

Pav

Harbour

Saltcoats Sta

PCs

HARBOUR RD
HERALD ST
INCHES RD
BUTE PL
BATH ST
PRINCES ST
BATH VILLAS
A738
HARBOUR PL

BURN RD B714
A738
ARDROSSAN RD
CALEDONIA RD
MONTGOMERIE CRES
MONTGOMERIE RD
CAMPBELL AVE
ARGYLE RD
RAISE ST
MANSE ST
WINTON ST
WINTON CIR
EGLINTON ST
HAMILTON ST
SIDNEY ST
CHAPEL ST
WINDMILL ST
BRAES RD
DOCKHEAD ST
VERNON S
B714

Sch
Mus
Liby
Off
PCs
PC
TH

4
41
3
40
2
39
1
38

22
23
24

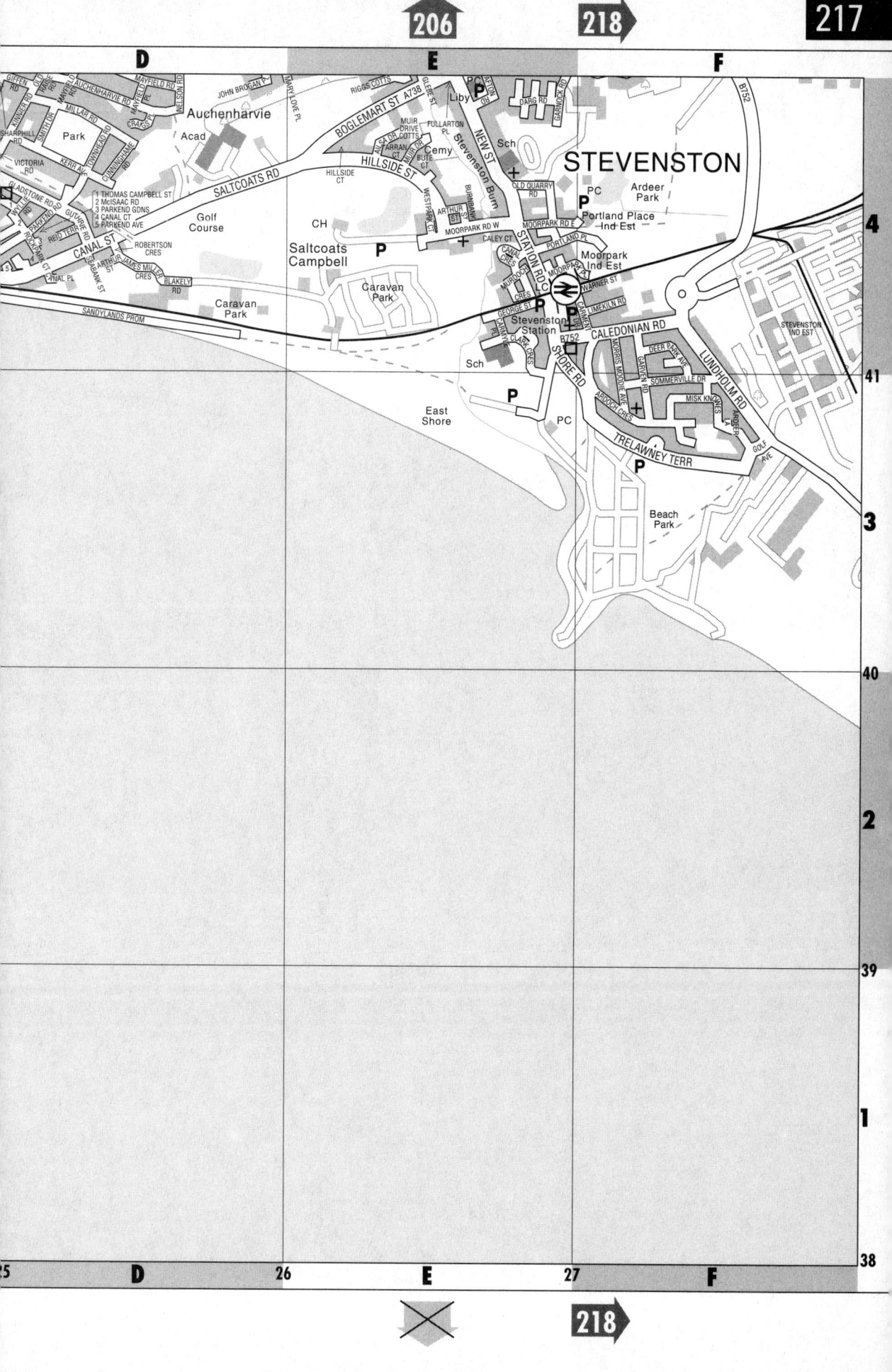

D
E
F

MAYFIELD RD
GIFFEN RD
KINNIER RD
SMITH RD
SHARPHILL RD
AUCHENHARVIE RD
NELSON RD
MILLAR RD
Park
Auchenharvie
Acad
JOHN BROGAN
MARYLANE PL
BOGLEMART ST A738
RIGGS COTTS
GLEBE ST
PC
Liby
P
DARG RD
GARHOCK RD
B752

VICTORIA RD
KERR AV
CUNINGHAME
SALTCOATS RD
HILLSIDE ST
HILLSIDE CT
WESTPARK CT
MUIR DRIVE
SEA DR
FULLARTON PL
FARRAN CT
BUTE CT
Cemy
NEW ST
Sch
Stevenston Burn
STEVENSTON

GLADSTONE RD
WILLIE
PAGEFIELD
RUCKBANK CT
REID TERR
CANAL ST
ROBERTSON CRES
ARTHUR
JAMES MILLER CRES
BLAKELY RD
Golf Course
CH
Saltcoats Campbell
P
ARTHUR ST
MOORPARK RD W
CALEY CT
STATION RD
MURDOCH CRES
PORTLAND PL
MOORPARK RD E
OLD QUARRY RD
PC
P
Portland Place Ind Est
Ardeer Park
Moorpark Ind Est
4

CANAL PL
CANAL ST
Caravan Park
Caravan Park
SANDYLANDS PROM
GEORGE ST
CLARK CRES
CANAL CRES
P
Stevenston Station
B752
P
WARNER ST
LIMEKILN RD
CALEDONIAN RD
DEER PARK AV
GARVEN RD
LUNDHOLM RD
STEVENSTON IND EST
41

Sch
East Shore
P
PC
SHORE RD
ARDOCH CRES
MORRIS MOODIE AV
SOMMERVILLE DR
MISK KNOWES
ARDEER LA
GOLF AV
3

Beach Park
TRELAWNEY TERR
P

40

2

39

1

38

5
D
26
E
27
F

1 THOMAS CAMPBELL ST
2 McISAAC RD
3 PARKEND GDNS
4 CANAL CT
5 PARKEND AVE

A   B   C

DUBBS RD

Penny Burn

BYREHILL RD   A78

B779

Nethermains
Bridge

WATERCUT RD

Refuse
Tip

4

41

Hospl

P

P

PC

Golf
Course

3

Works

CH

Stevenston
Site

Bogside

40

Bogside
Race Course
(disused)

Crooky's
Point

River Irvine

2

39

Bogside
Flats

1

Irvine
Harbour

River Irvine

HARBOUR ST

BEACH DR

P

Leisure
Centre

38

28   A   29   B   30   C

River Garnock

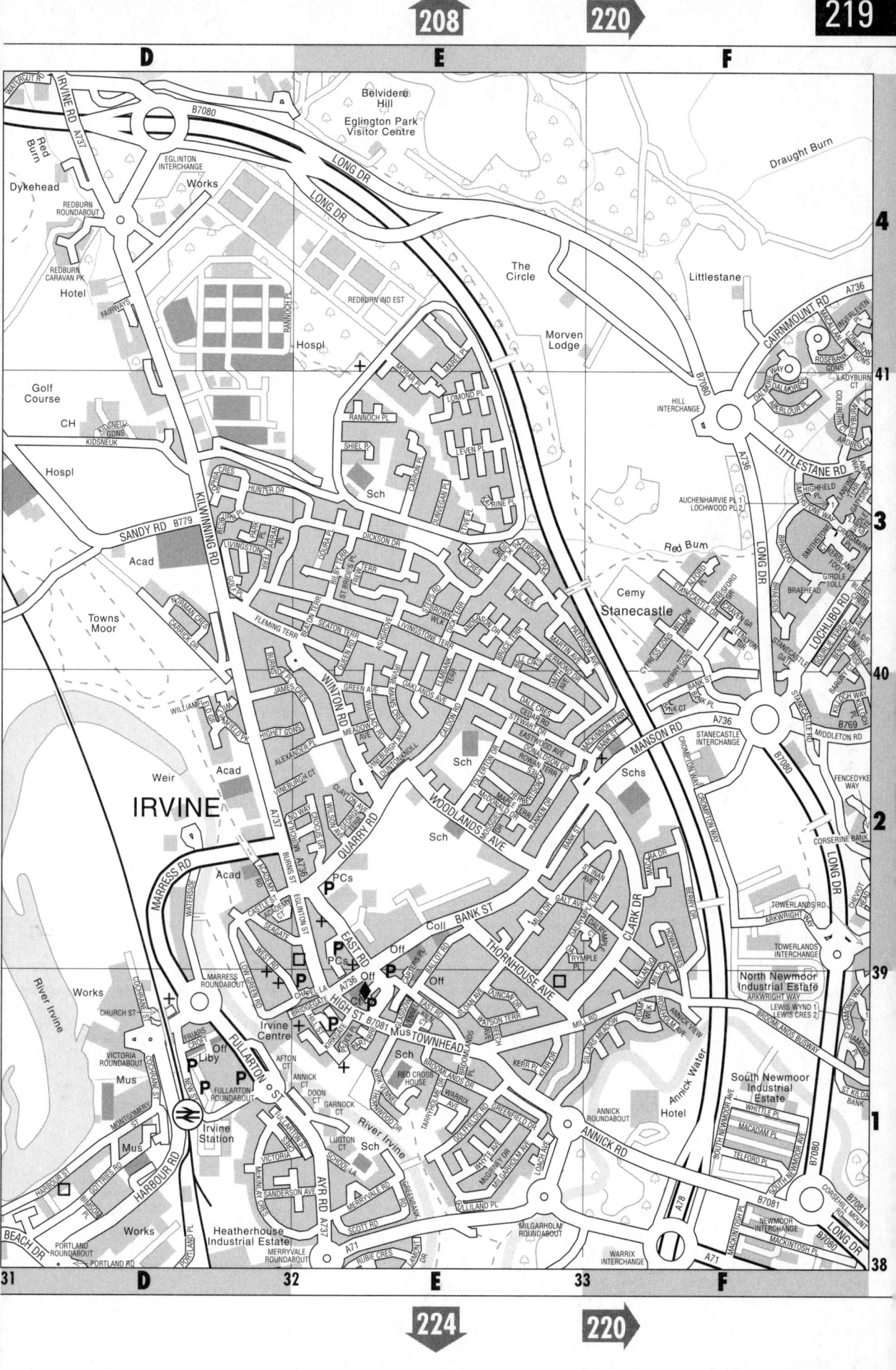

D E F

Belvidere
Hill

Eglington Park
Visitor Centre

LONG DR

Draught Burn

Red
Burn

Dykehead

EGLINTON
INTERCHANGE

Works

LONG DR

The
Circle

Littlestane

4

REDBURN
CARAVAN PK

Hotel

REDBURN IND EST

Morven
Lodge

CAIRNMOUNT RD

A736

ROSEBANK
GDNS

LADYBURN
CT

41

FAIRWAYS

Hospl

HILL
INTERCHANGE

B7080

AUCHENHARVIE PL 1
LOCHWOOD PL 2

HIGHFIELD
PL

Golf
Course

RANNOCH PL

CH

KIDSNEUK
GDNS

SHIEL PL

Sch

KATRINE PL

LEVEN PL

LITTLESTANE RD

A736

3

KIDSNEUK

Hospl

SANDY RD

B779

KILWINNING RD

HUNTER DR

DICKSON DR

Red Burn

Cemy
Stanecastle

LOCHLIBO RD

Acad

Towns
Moor

FLEMING TERR

SEATON TERR

LIVINGSTONE TERR

STANECASTLE DR

40

WILLIAMFIELD

Weir

Acad

IRVINE

GREEN AVE

OAKLANDS AVE

MANSON RD

A736

STANECASTLE
INTERCHANGE

B7080

MIDDLETON RD
B769

FENCEDYKE
WAY

WINTON RD

MEADOW
AVE

DALE CRES
EASTWOOD AVE
ROWAN TERR

Sch

MACKINNON TERR

CROMWELL WAY

CROMPTON WAY

CORSERINE BANK

2

MARRESS RD

Acad

QUARRY RD

WOODLANDS AVE

Sch

Schs

TOWERLANDS RD

ARKWRIGHT WAY

TOWERLANDS
INTERCHANGE

River Irvine

Works

CHURCH ST

Coll

BANK ST

THORNHOUSE AVE

CLARK DR

North Newmoor
Industrial Estate

ARKWRIGHT WAY

LEWIS WYND 1
LEWIS CRES 2

39

EAST RD

PCs

A736

HIGH ST

B7081

TOWNHEAD

Off

Sch

ANNICK RD

South Newmoor
Industrial Estate

ST KILDA
BANK

Victoria
Roundabout

Off
Liby

Irvine
Centre

Mus

FULLARTON
ROUNDABOUT

Annick Water

ANNICK
ROUNDABOUT

Hotel

MACADAM PL

1

Mus

Irvine
Station

VICTORIA

River Irvine

Sch

TELFORD PL

B7080

HARBOUR ST

SANDERSON AVE

AYR RD
A737

A71

MILGARHOLM
ROUNDABOUT

A78

NEWMOOR
INTERCHANGE

B7080

38

BEACH DR

PORTLAND
ROUNDABOUT

PORTLAND RD

Works

Heatherhouse
Industrial Estate

MERRYVALE
ROUNDABOUT

RUBIE CRES

WARRIX
INTERCHANGE

A71

LONG DR
B7081

31 D 32 E 33 F 38

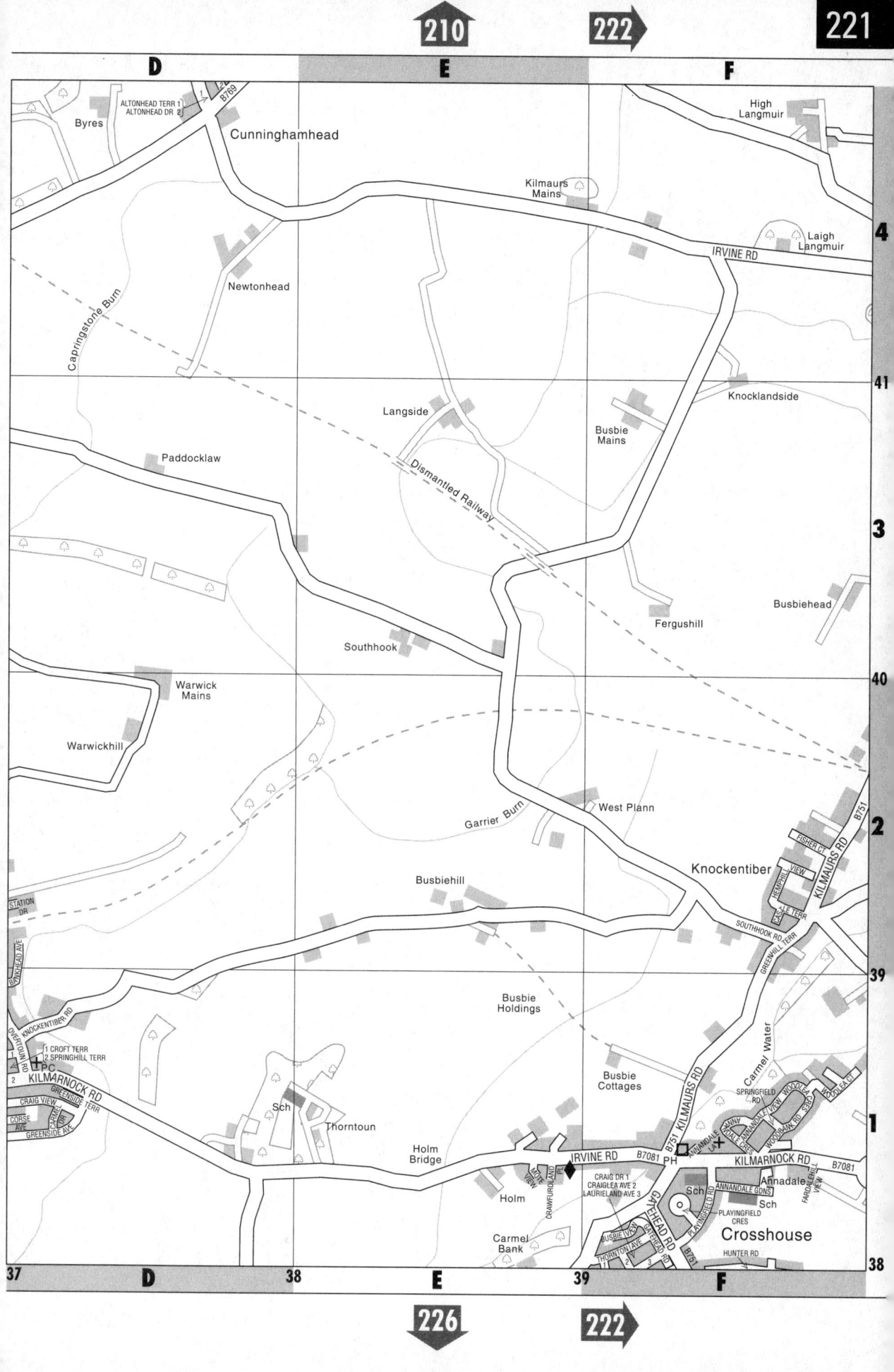

Byres

ALTONHEAD TERR 1
ALTONHEAD DR 2

B769

Cunninghamhead

High Langmuir

Kilmaurs Mains

IRVINE RD

Laigh Langmuir

Newtonhead

Capringstone Burn

Knocklandside

Paddocklaw

Langside

Dismantled Railway

Busbie Mains

Busbiehead

Warwick Mains

Southhook

Fergushill

Warwickhill

Garrier Burn

West Plann

Knockentiber

STATION DR

Busbiehill

FISHER CT

KILMAURS RD

B751

HEMPHILL VIEW

LE TERR

SOUTHHOOK RD TERR

GREESWILL TERR

Busbie Holdings

BACKHEAD AVE

KNOCKENTIBER RD

OVERTOUN RD

1 CROFT TERR
2 SPRINGHILL TERR

PC

KILMARNOCK RD

GREENSIDE TERR

CRAIG VIEW

CORSE AVE

GREENSIDE AVE

Sch

Thorntoun

Busbie Cottages

Carmel Water

SPRINGFIELD RD

WOODSIDE

WOODPARK RD

B751 KILMAURS RD

ANNANDALE VIEW

CANNY

Holm Bridge

Holm

IRVINE RD

B7081

PH

CRAWFURDLAND

STONE VIEW

CRAIG DR 1
CRAIGLEA AVE 2
LAURIELAND AVE 3

Sch

KILMARNOCK RD

B7081

Annadale

ANNANDALE GDNS

Sch

FARQUHARHILL VIEW

GATEHEAD RD

PLAYINGFIELD CRES

Carmel Bank

BUSBIE VIEW

THORNTON AVE

GATEHEAD RD

Sch

B751

Crosshouse

HUNTER RD

A   B   C

Habbie
Auld

Rowallan
Mill

B751

Shaw
Burn

Haghouse
Bridge

Buntonhill

4

Shaw
Bridge

WEST PARK DR

HABBIELAND RD

PARK PARK DR

PARK CRES

STANDALANE

Bellsland

FOUR ACRE DR

VINE PARK

TOWNHEAD

A735

Kilmaurs Mill
Bridge

GLENCAIRN TERR

McNAUGHT

CARMEL PL

HIGH WATT

BOYD ORR CRES

BEAUFIELD GRANGE

EAST PARK DR

FERNING AVE

BELMONT CRES

PARK AVE

ST MAURS GDNS

MILLHILL

MAIN ST

Braehead

Buntonhill
Mount

IRVINE RD

Liby
Sch

B751

FENWICK RD

Kilmaurs

Crofthead

CROFTHEAD RD

HAMILTON CT

SUNNYSIDE

TOWNHEAD

Kilmaurs
Place

MILL AVE

Jocksthorn

41

YARDSIDE RD

Kilmaurs
Station

BRAEHEAD TERR

BRAEHEAD PL

KILMARNOCK RD

KIRKLAND RD

Grassmillside

Towerhill

KIRKLAND GDNS

JOCKSTHORN TERR

TOWERHILL AVE

Cemy

Ind
Est

Carmel Water

Kirkland

3

CROSSHOUSE RD

The
Old Manse

Woodhill Burn

40

North
Woodhill

Altonhill

GLASSOCK RD

GLENCRAIGS DR

BRIGHAM RD

KIRK LN

Sch

Onthank

MILLHILL TERR

NEWLANDS

ARNESS TERR

MACHRIE RD

GORDONS

NEWLANDS PL

KNOCKINLAW RD

Bailliehill
Mount

B751

ALPINECRAIG AVE

ASHDALE PL

INVERCLOY PL

Knockinlaw
Mount

KILMAURS RD

ONTHANK DR

MOSSIDE PL

ARDGOUR PL

2

South
Woodhill

Altonhill

KIRKLAND AVE

WOODHILL CRES

MORVEN AVE

Knockinlaw

ARDGOUR RD

B7064

AFTON

Longpark

INNELLAN DR

Greenhill

West
Hillhead

ALTONHILL AVE

ETTRICK PL 1
LEVEN AVE 2

Schs

HILLHEAD SQ

CAMPBELTOWN DR

FARM RD

HILLBANK
RD

CLAY CRES

WESTERN RDO

A735

HILL ST

Hillhead

39

Greenhill
Smallholdings

Montgomery PL 1
HILLPARK DR 2
NORTHCRAIG RD 3
ORCHARD ST 4
DEAN ST 5
DEAN LA 6
FULTON'S LA 7
MORRIS LA 8
DEAN CT 9
BOYD ST 10

Amb
Sta

LONGPARK AVE

HIGHET ST

BLAIR

Fardalehill

Ind
Est

CRAIGIE RD

WITCH RD

A735

Hospl

BELLEVUE GDNS 1
BONNYTON PL 2

Works

Bonnyton
Ind Est

BURNS PREC 11
FOREGATE SQ 12
THE FOREGATE 13
THE CROSS 14
WEST GEORGE ST 15
LANGLANDS BRAE 16
JOHN DICKIE ST 17
GRANGE ST 18
WOODSTOCK PL 19

Sch

1

SIMPSON ST

LISTER ST

SANNOX RD

SOUTHHOOK RD

BROCK RD

CARMEL AVE

CARMEL TERR

Bonnyton

ROBERT NOBLE PL

BAILLIEHILL

WARWICKHILL RD

North
Hamilton
PL

Kilmarnock
Sta

GRANGE ST

ROBERT CREIGHTON

WELLINGTON ST

Coll

KILMARNOCK RD

B7081

WAVERLEY AVE

ANNANHILL AVE

MUNRO AVE

BONNYTON RD

BUSBIEHILL PL

STEVENSON ST

YORKE PL

DAVIDSON

INKERMAN PL

WEST
LANGLANDS ST

West
Fullarton

GIBSON PL

PARK ST

JOHN FINNIE ST

DUNLOP ST

GREEN ST

P

STIRLING CRES

Annanhill
Golf Course

IRVINE RD

PC

HOLLY PL 1
LOANFOOT AVE 2
GRANGE TERR 3

B7081

PEACE AVE

ARMOUR ST

FULLARTON ST

NORTH HAMILTON ST

MUIRDYKE

Offs

P

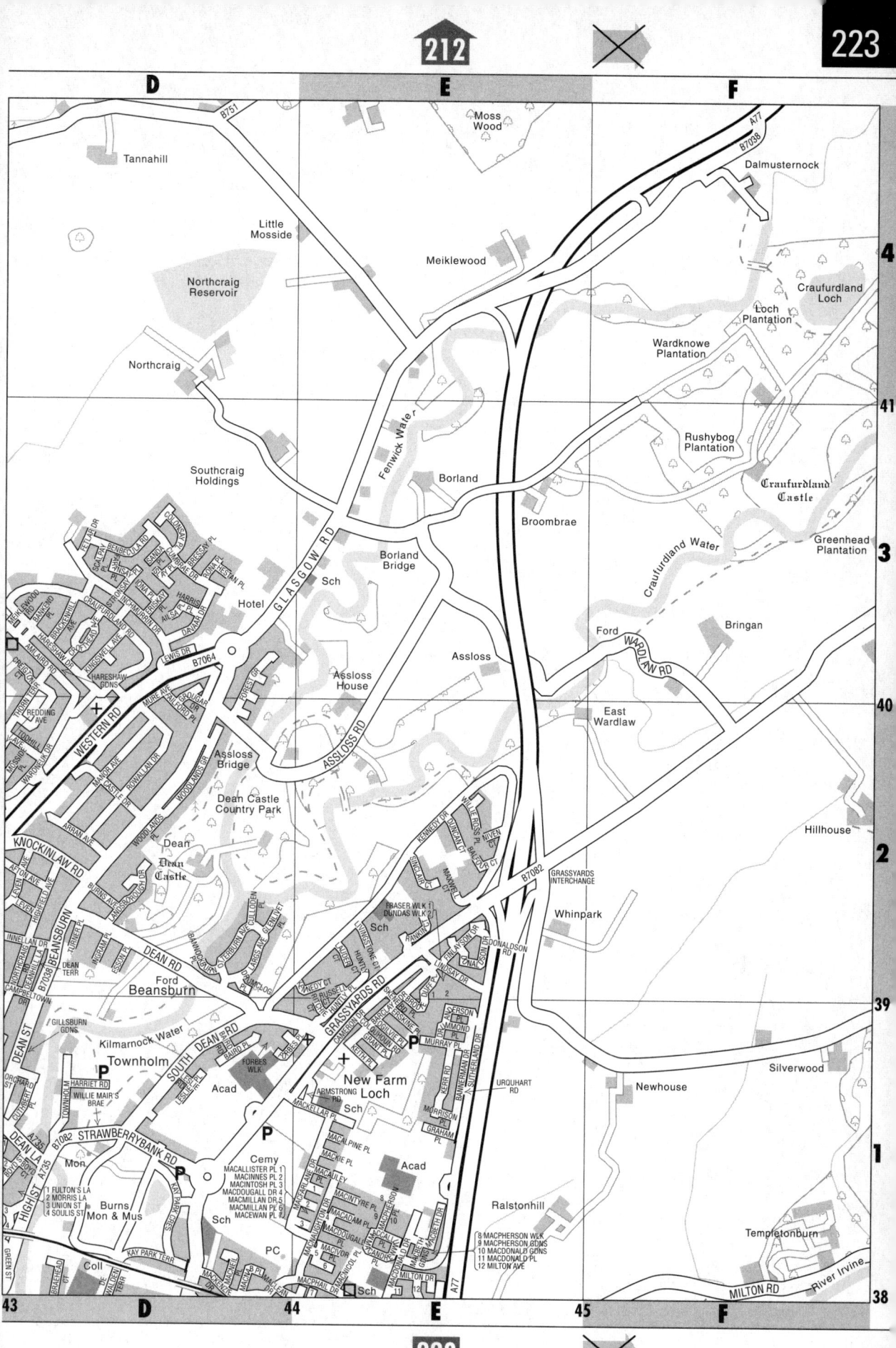

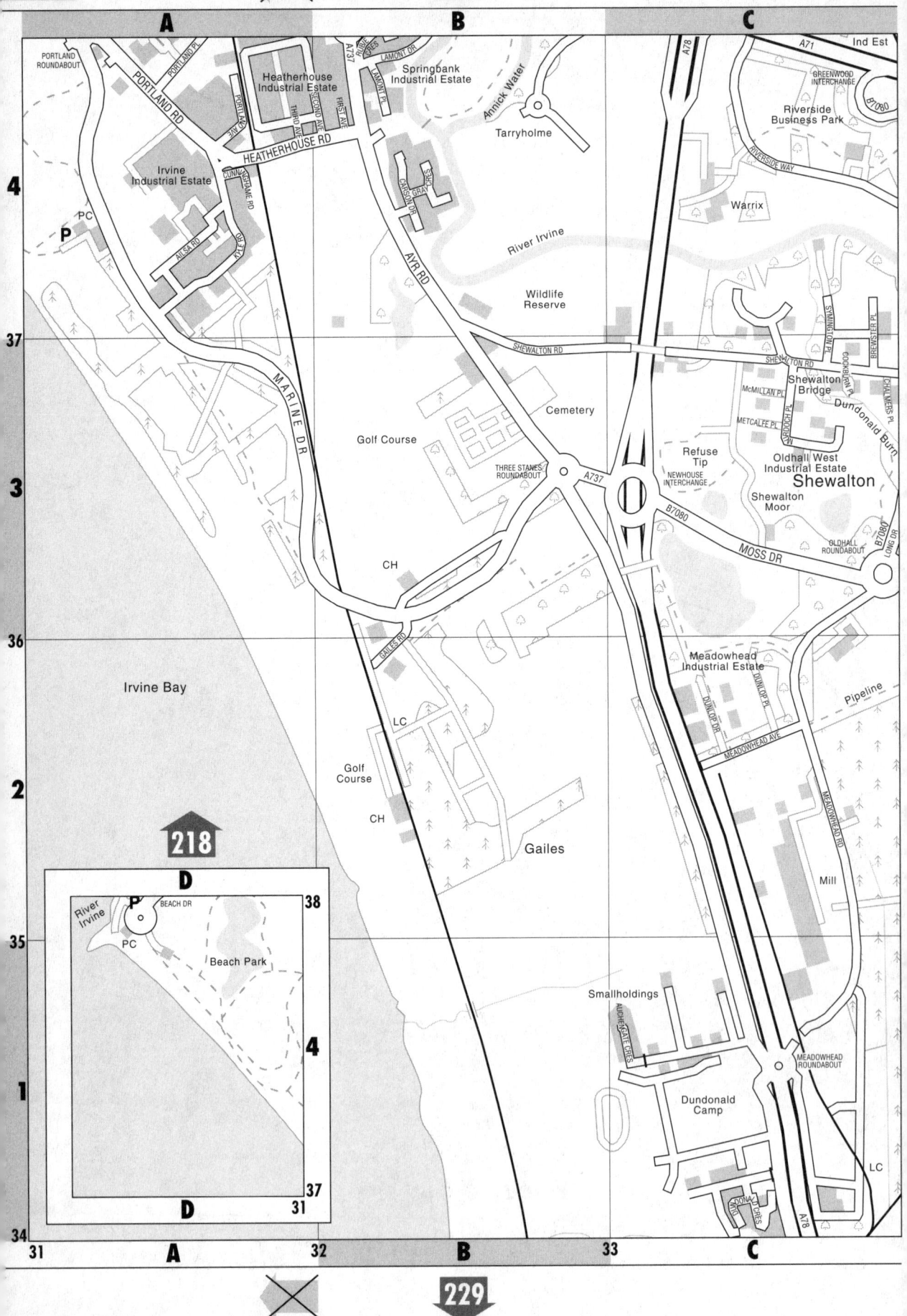

A   B   C

PORTLAND ROUNDABOUT

Ind Est

A71

GREENWOOD INTERCHANGE

Riverside Business Park

PORTLAND RD

PORTLAND PL

Heatherhouse Industrial Estate

Springbank Industrial Estate

Annick Water

A737

LAMONT DR

LAMONT PL

Tarryholme

RIVERSIDE WAY

Warrix

4

Irvine Industrial Estate

HEATHERHOUSE RD

THIRD AVE

SECOND AVE

FIRST AVE

CARSON DR

GRAY

River Irvine

PC

P

ALSA RD

BAY VIEW

CUNNINGHAME RD

AYR RD

Wildlife Reserve

SYMINGTON PL

COCKBURN PL

BREWSTER PL

CHALMERS PL

37

SHEWALTON RD

Shewalton Bridge

McMILLAN PL

MURDOCH

Dundonald Burn

Cemetery

METCALFE PL

Oldhall West Industrial Estate

MARINE DR

Golf Course

Refuse Tip

Shewalton

3

THREE STANES ROUNDABOUT

A737

NEWHOUSE INTERCHANGE

Shewalton Moor

B7080

OLDHALL ROUNDABOUT

LONG DR

CH

B7080

MOSS DR

36

Irvine Bay

GAILES RD

Meadowhead Industrial Estate

Pipeline

LC

DUNLOP DR

DUNLOP PL

218

Golf Course

MEADOWHEAD AVE

2

CH

MEADOWHEAD RD

Gailes

Mill

D

P

BEACH DR

38

River Irvine

PC

35

Beach Park

Smallholdings

AUCHENGATE CRES

4

Dundonald Camp

1

LC

37

DUNDONALD CRES

A78

D

31

34

31   A   32   B   33   C

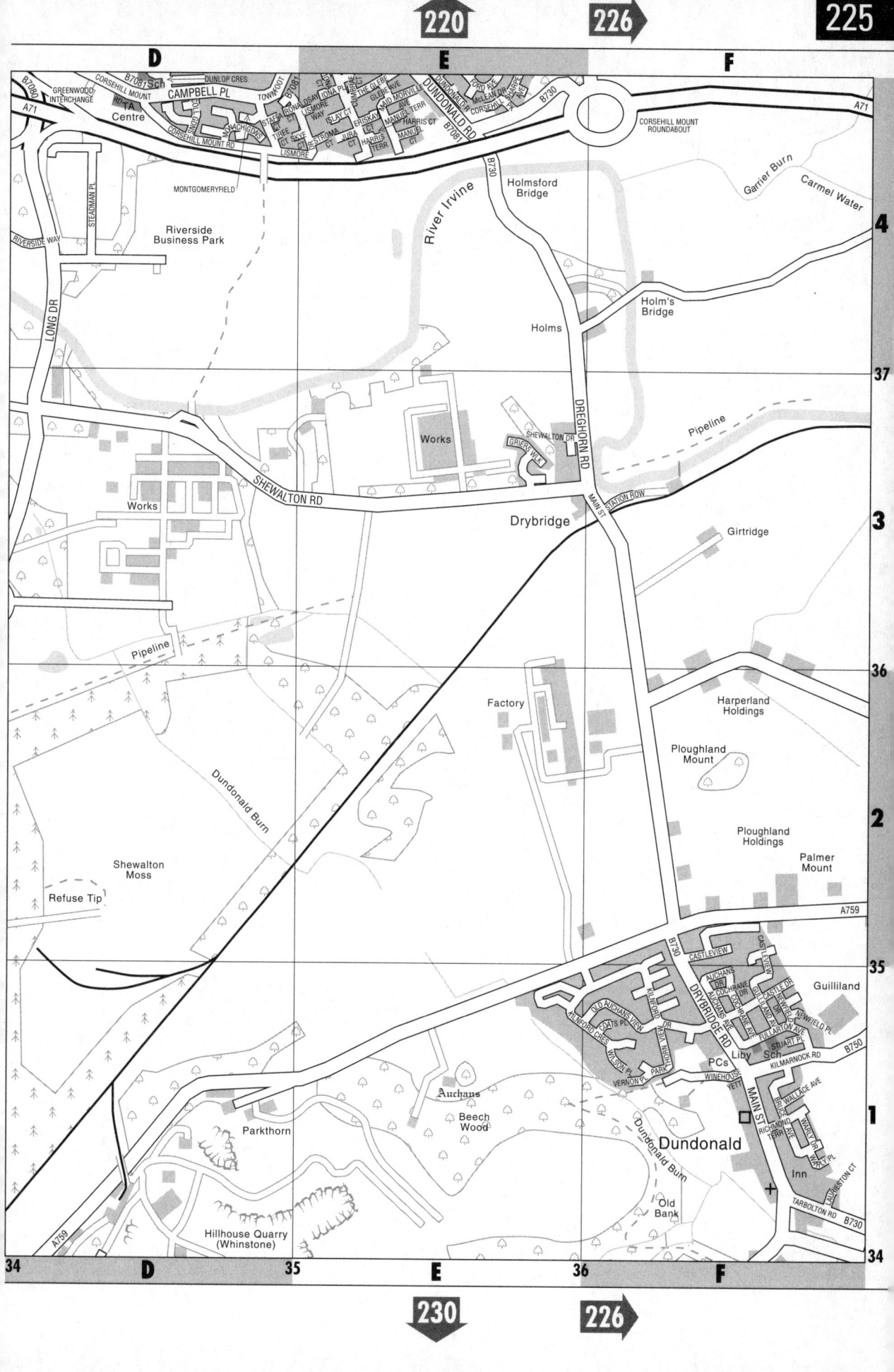

D
E
F

B7081 Sch
B7080
A71
Greenwood
Interchange
Corsehill Mount
CAMPBELL PL
RD TA
Centre
Dunlop Cres
TOWNFOOT
B7081
DUNLOP RD
IONA PL
STAFFA ROW
LISMORE
WAY
TIREE
CT
JURA CT
SLAY CT
ERISKAY
LT
STROMA
CT
IDA SCOLPAY
MULL
THE GLEBE
MID MORVILLE
AVE
SCARP
THE GLEBE
MANUEL TERR
HARRIS CT
MANUEL
CT
DUNDONALD RD
MONTGOMERY
McLEAN PL
CORSEHILL
SHARPE
B730
CORSEHILL MOUNT ROUNDABOUT
A71

Corsehill Mount Rd
LISMORE

MONTGOMERYFIELD

River Irvine
Holmsford Bridge

Garrier Burn
Carmel Water

4

Riverside Business Park

STEADMAN PL

RIVERSIDE WAY

LONG DR

Holms

Holm's Bridge

37

DREGHORN RD

Pipeline

SHEWALTON RD

Works

Shewalton Dr
GRIERS WLK

Works

MAIN ST
STATION ROW

Drybridge

Girtridge

3

Pipeline

36

Factory

Harperland Holdings

Ploughland Mount

Dundonald Burn

Ploughland Holdings

2

Shewalton Moss

Palmer Mount

Refuse Tip

A759

35

Guilliland

CASTLEVIEW
B730
AUCHANS DR
COCHRANE CT
CASTLE DR
CORR PL
GAIL LOAN DR
AFIELD PL

OLD AUCHANSVIEW
KILNFORD DR
CASTLE PL
FULLARTON AVE
KILMARNOCK RD
B750

KILNFORD CRES
COATS PL
KIRK VENNEL
FULLARTON
STUART PL
Liby Sch

WILSON PL
PARK
PCs
WINEHOUSE
YETT

Parkthorn

Auchans

VERNON PL
BRAE
RICHMOND TERR
WARLY DR
WARLY PL

Beech Wood

Dundonald Burn

MAIN ST

WALLACE AVE

1

Dundonald

Inn

AUCHESTON CT

A759

Old Bank

TARBOLTON RD
B730

Hillhouse Quarry (Whinstone)

34

34
D
35
E
36
F
34

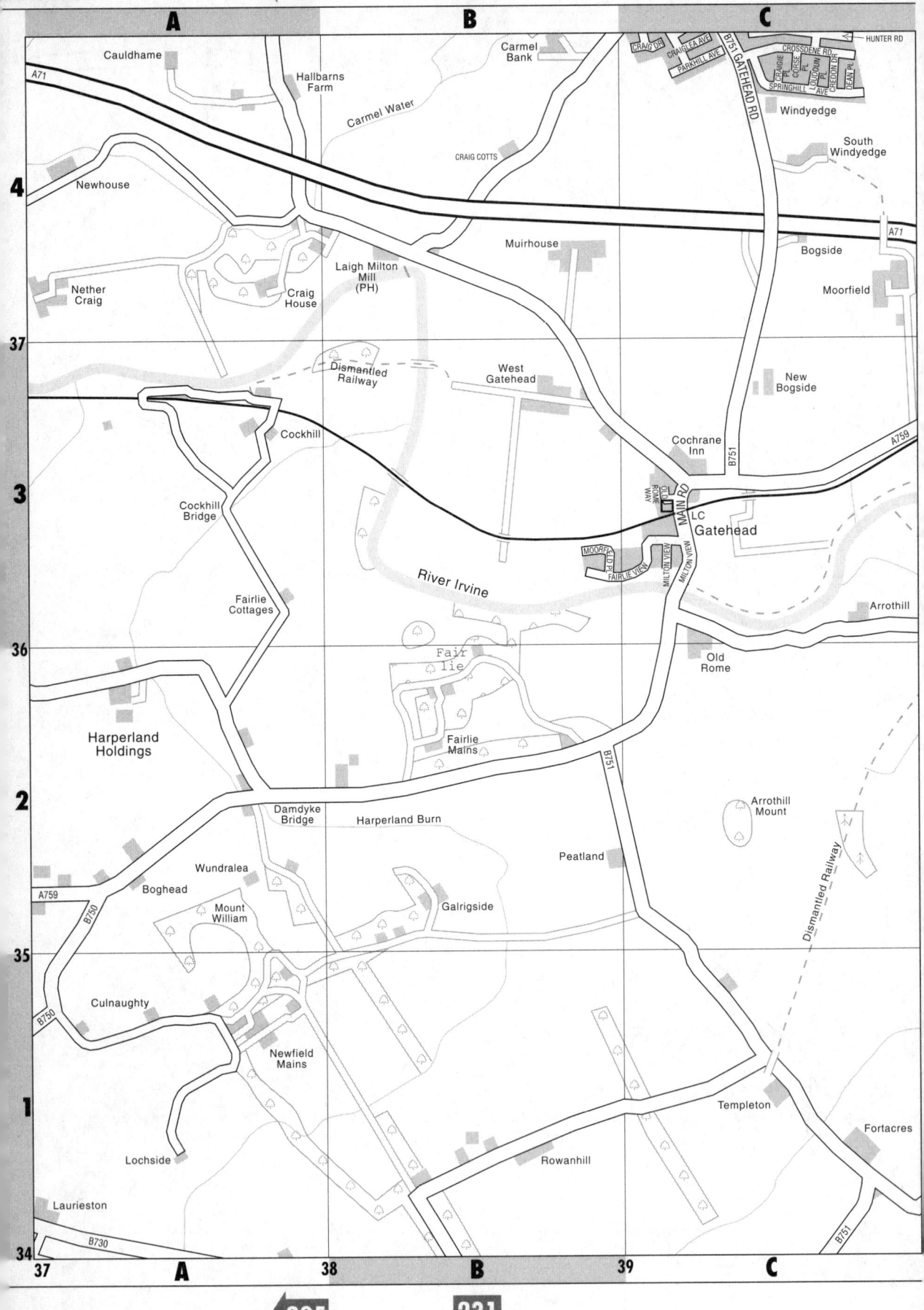

A71
Cauldhame
Hallbarns Farm
Carmel Bank
Carmel Water
CRAIG DR
CRAIGLEA AVE
PARKHILL AVE
B751 GATEHEAD RD
CROSSDENE RD
CRAIGIE PL
GORSE CRES
LODDOUN PL
CREDON DR
DEAN PL
HUNTER RD
SPRINGHILL AVE
Windyedge

CRAIG COTTS
South Windyedge

4

Newhouse
Muirhouse
A71
Bogside
Moorfield

Nether Craig
Laigh Milton Mill (PH)
Craig House

37

Dismantled Railway
West Gatehead
New Bogside

Cockhill
Cochrane Inn
B751
A759

3

Cockhill Bridge
OLD ROME WAY
MAIN RD
LC
Gatehead

MOORFIELD PL
FAIRLIE VIEW
MILTON VIEW
MILTON VIEW

Fairlie Cottages
River Irvine
Arrothill

36

Fair lie
Old Rome

Harperland Holdings
Fairlie Mains
B751
Arrothill Mount

2

Damdyke Bridge
Harperland Burn
Peatland
Dismantled Railway

Wundralea
Galrigside
A759
Boghead
B750
Mount William

35

Culnaughty

Newfield Mains

1

Templeton
Fortacres

Lochside

Laurieston
B730
Rowanhill
B751

34
37
A
38
B
39
C

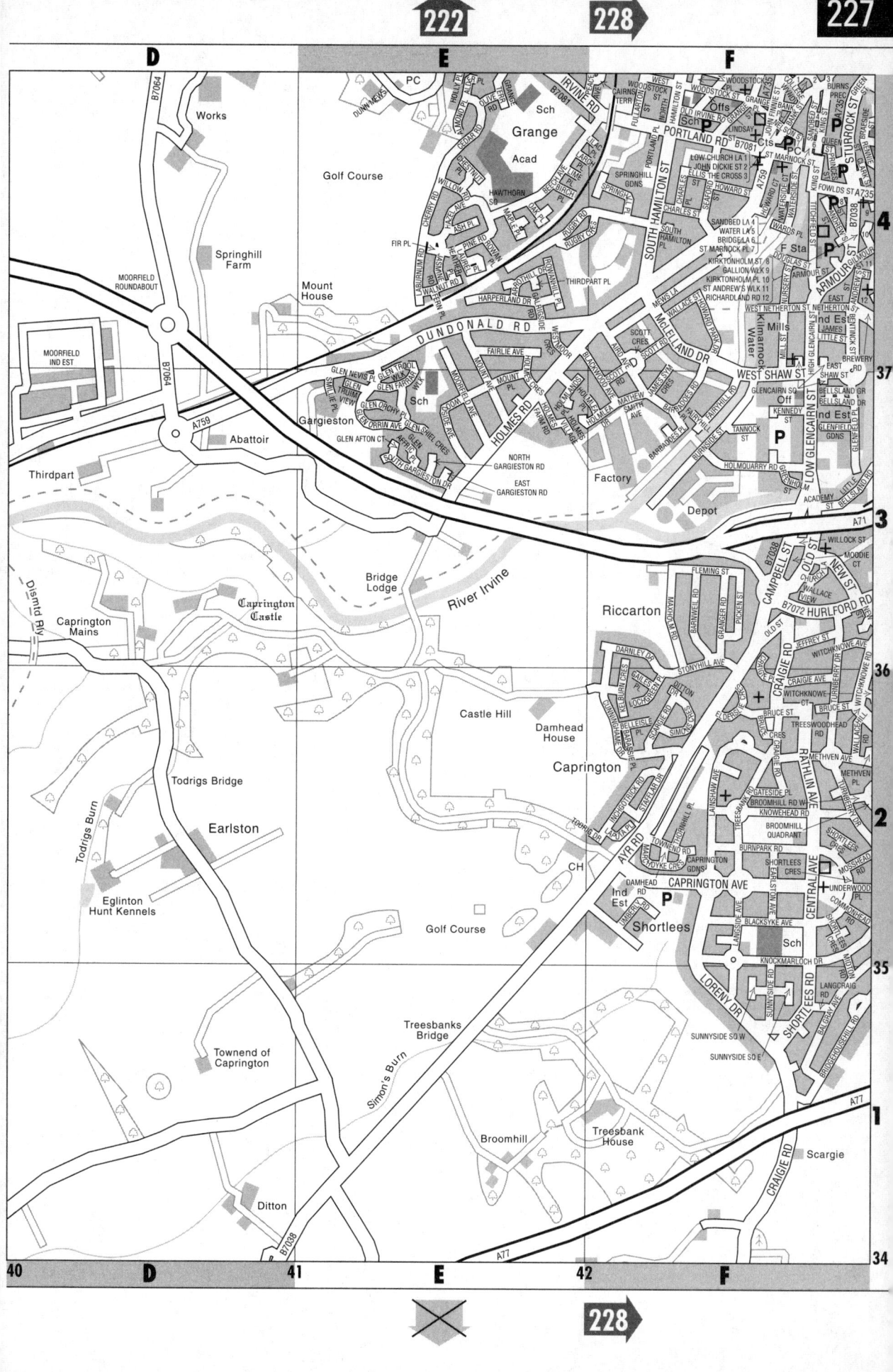

KILMARNOCK

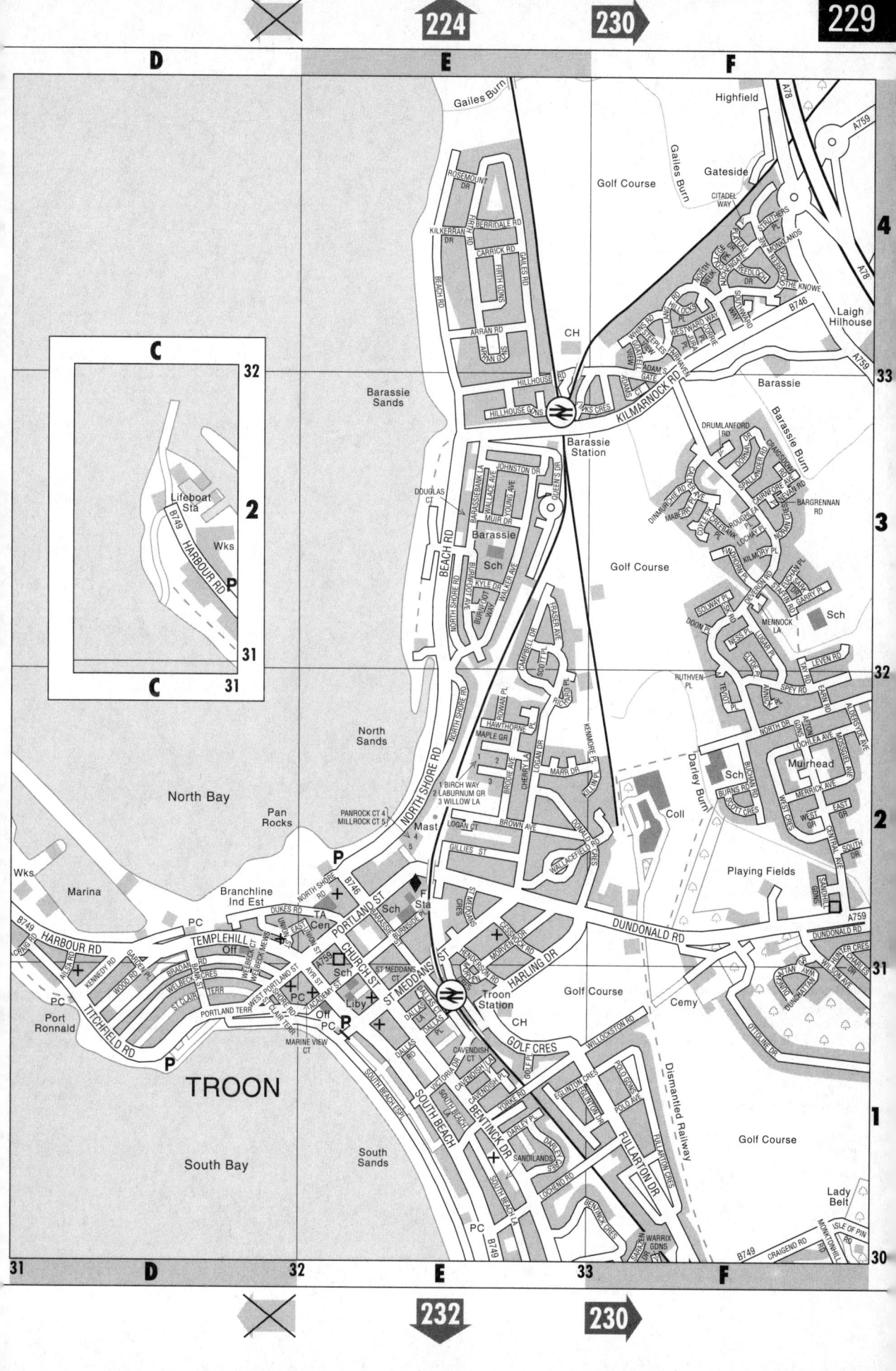

TROON

North Bay

South Bay

South Sands

South Bay

Port Ronnald

Marina

Barassie Sands

North Sands

Barassie

Gailes Burn

Golf Course

Gateside

Highfield

Barassie

Laigh Hilhouse

Golf Course

Muirhead

Playing Fields

Darley Burn

Barassie Station

Troon Station

Golf Course

Golf Course

Golf Cemy

Lady Belt

Map labels

A   B   C

4

33

3

32

2

31

1

30

34   35   36

A   B   C

A759
A78

Hillhouse Quarry
Hillhouse
Chapel Hill

Merkland Loch
Hallyards Quarry
Hallyards
Dundonald Burn
Highlees
Highlees Mount

Works
Aught Wood

Wardlaw Hill
Harpercroft

Collenan Smallholdings

Mast
Works

Highgrove House

Clevance
Langholm

Beattock Burn
Clevance Cottage
Corraith

OLD LOANS RD
SEAVIEW TERR
COLEMAN AVE
CROSSBURN DR
CROSSBURN TERR
BEECHWOOD PADDOCK
STABLE WYND
MAIN ST
PH
HALL
CROSSBURN LA
Loans
CRAIKSLAND PL
COLLING RD
FULLARTON PL
KYLE AREA
TROON RD
B746
Crossburn
Craiksland
Wester Croft

DUNDONALD RD
A759

Darley Burn
B746
Southside
Southside Cottages
High Wexford
Wexford Cottage
KERRIX RD

OTTOLINE DR
LADY MARGARET DR
CHARLES DR
HUNTER CRES
BALCOMIE CRES
WILSON AVE
Darley Plantation
PC
FULLERTON CTYD
Golf Course
Lady Belt
Crosbie House
ISLE OF PIN RD
Fairlees
B746
A78
Rumbling Burn
Crookside

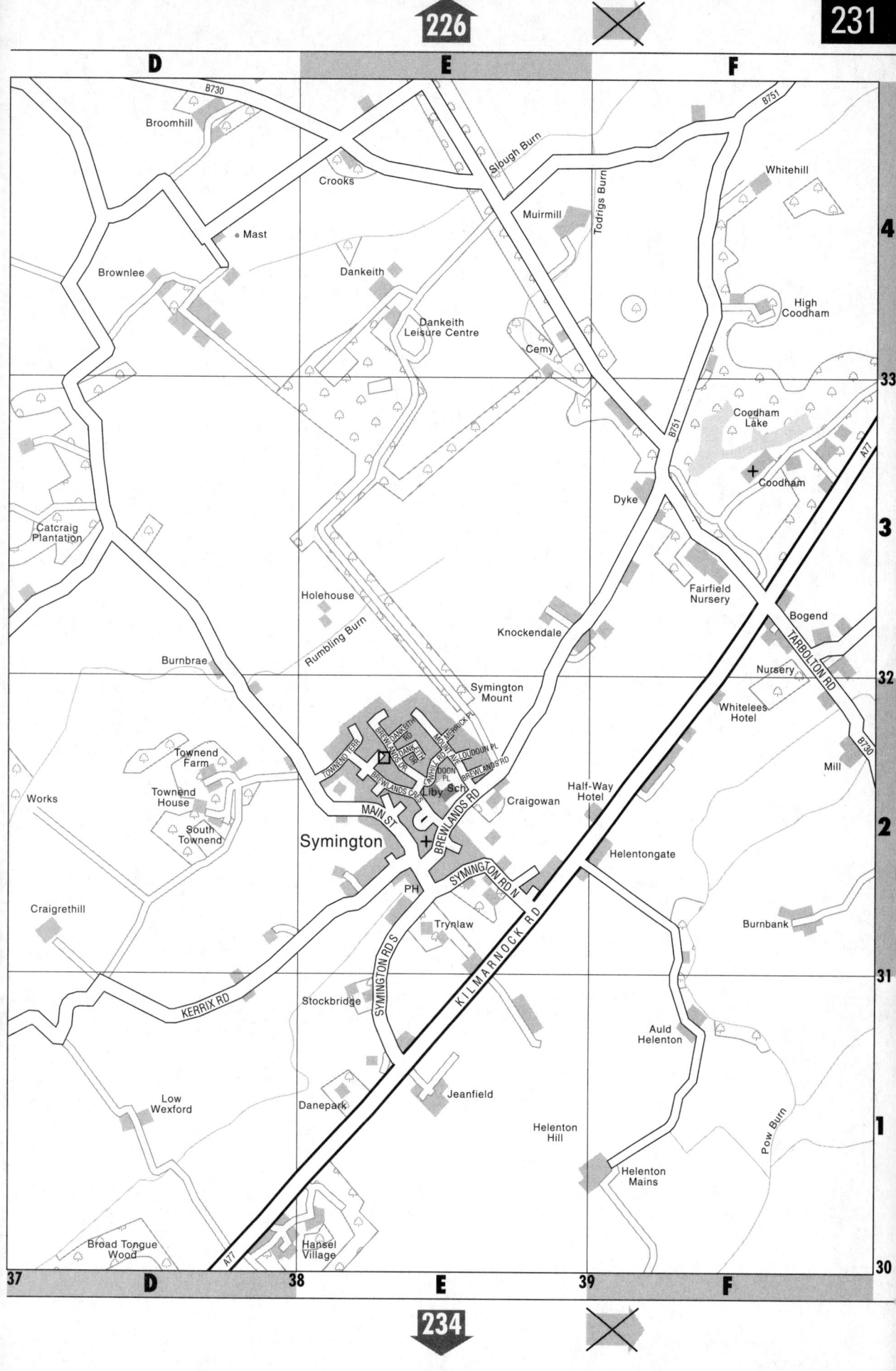

Broomhill

Crooks

Muirmill

Whitehill

Mast

Dankeith

High
Coodham

Brownlee

Dankeith
Leisure Centre

Cemy

Catcraig
Plantation

Coodham
Lake

Coodham

Dyke

Holehouse

Knockendale

Fairfield
Nursery

Bogend

Rumbling Burn

Nursery

Burnbrae

Symington
Mount

Whitelees
Hotel

Mill

Townend
Farm

TOWNEND TERR

BREWLANDS CRES

Liby Schl

BREWLANDS RD

BREWLANDS RD

MERRICK PL

CRAIGHILL RD

DOON PL

LOUDOUN PL

Craigowan

Half-Way
Hotel

Works

Townend
House

MAIN ST

Helentongate

Burnbank

South
Townend

Symington

SYMINGTON RD N

Craigrethill

PH

Trynlaw

KILMARNOCK RD

Auld
Helenton

SYMINGTON RD S

KERRIX RD

Stockbridge

TARBOLTON RD

Pow Burn

Low
Wexford

Danepark

Jeanfield

Helenton
Hill

Helenton
Mains

Broad Tongue
Wood

Hansel
Village

A   B   C

SOUTH BEACH ESPL
B749 SOUTH
GROSBIE CT
BENTINCK DR
BENTINCK CRES
SARAZEN DR
BOX COVE
B749
B749
B749
MONKTONHILL RD
CRAIGEND RD
FULLARTON DR
SOUTHWOOD RD
Dismtd Riv
P
CH
CH
Hotel
Golf Course
GROSBIE RD
Hotel
Golf Course

4

29

3

28

2

27

1

26

31   A   32   B   33   C

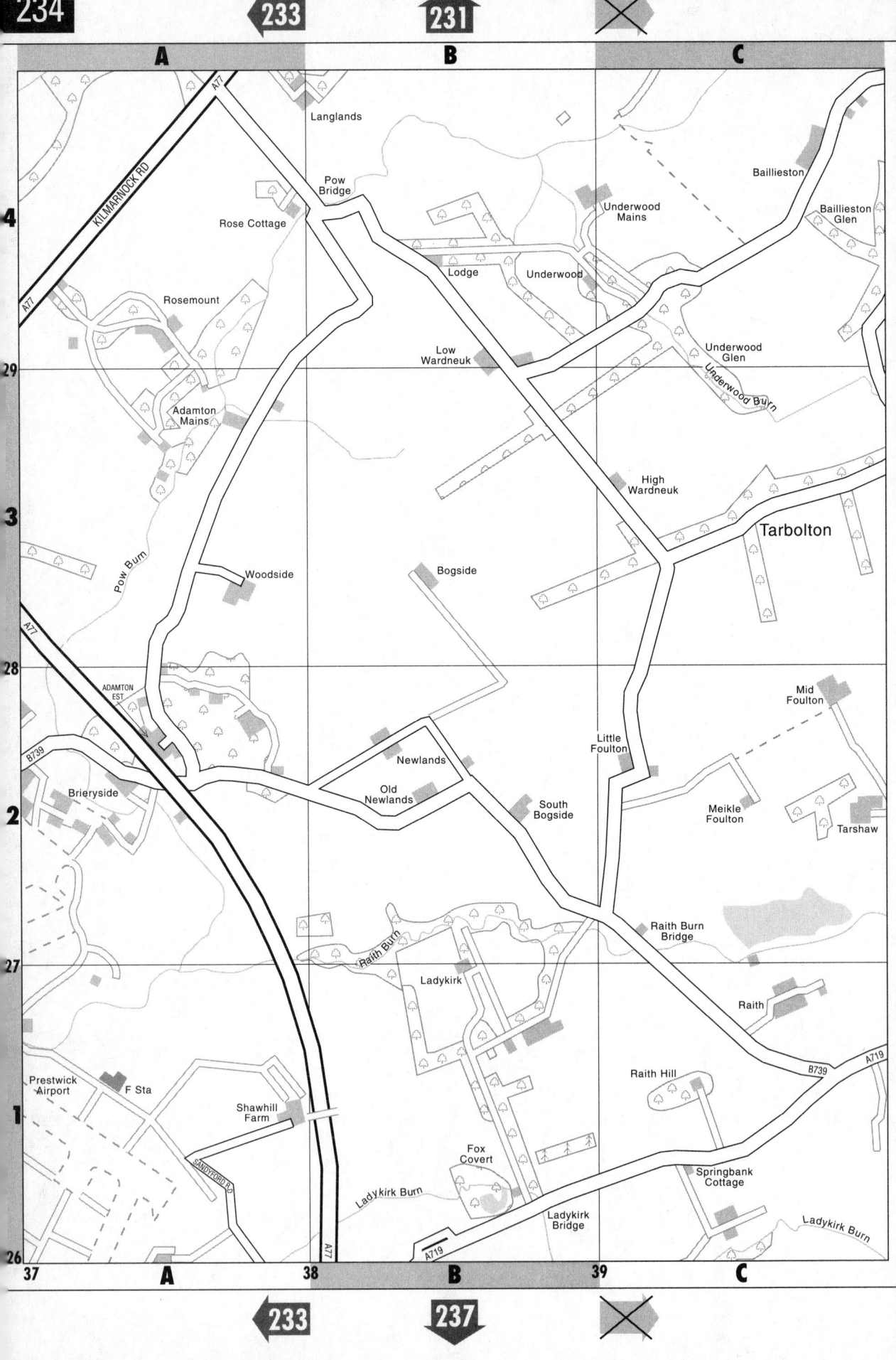

A77

KILMARNOCK RD

Langlands

Pow
Bridge

4

Rose Cottage

A77

Rosemount

Baillieston

Underwood
Mains

Lodge   Underwood

Baillieston
Glen

29

Adamton
Mains

Underwood
Glen

Underwood Burn

Low
Wardneuk

High
Wardneuk

3

Pow Burn

Woodside

Bogside

Tarbolton

28

A77

ADAMTON
EST

Mid
Foulton

Little
Foulton

B739

Newlands

Old
Newlands

South
Bogside

Meikle
Foulton

Tarshaw

2

Brieryside

Raith Burn
Bridge

27

Raith Burn

Ladykirk

Raith

Prestwick
Airport

F Sta

Raith Hill

B739

A719

1

Shawhill
Farm

SANDYFORD RD

Fox
Covert

Springbank
Cottage

Ladykirk Burn

Ladykirk
Bridge

Ladykirk Burn

26

A77

A719

232

236

D E F

4

25

3

24

2

23

1

22

31 D 32 E 33 F 22

238

236

North
Breakwater

Dock

South
Pier

Harbour

ELMBANK ST

WAGGON RD

GREEN ST LA
GREEN ST
BSN'D PK
HALLS
VENNAL

TAYLOR STREET

YORK STREET LA

OSBACADLA

YORK ST

GREEN ST LA

SALTFIELD
LA

BACK PEEBLES ST

PEEBLES ST

NEW RD

SCAVENGER

DAMSIDE

Off

ALLISON
ST

CROWN ST

NORTH HARBOUR ST

GARDEN
CT

Liby

P

P

MAIN ST

KING ST

JOHN ST

River Ayr

B748

A719

ESPLANADE

SOUTH BEACH RD

SEABANK RD

MONTGOMERIE TERR

ARRAN TERR

EGLINTON PL

EGLINTON TERR

FORT ST

BOAT VENNEL

HARBOUR ST

MAIN ST

GEORGE

TH
Bridge

STRATHAYR P

OLD BRIDGE ST

1 BRUCE CRES
2 CATHCART ST
3 ST JOHN ST
4 ACADEMY ST

Acad

P
PC
AILSA
PL

QUEEN'S TERRACE LA

CROMWELL RD

CITADEL PL

SANDGATE

B

NEW BRIDGE ST

SALTPANS RD

LIMEKILN RD

GLEBE CT

WEIR ST

GLEBE CRES

A759

LINCOLN RD

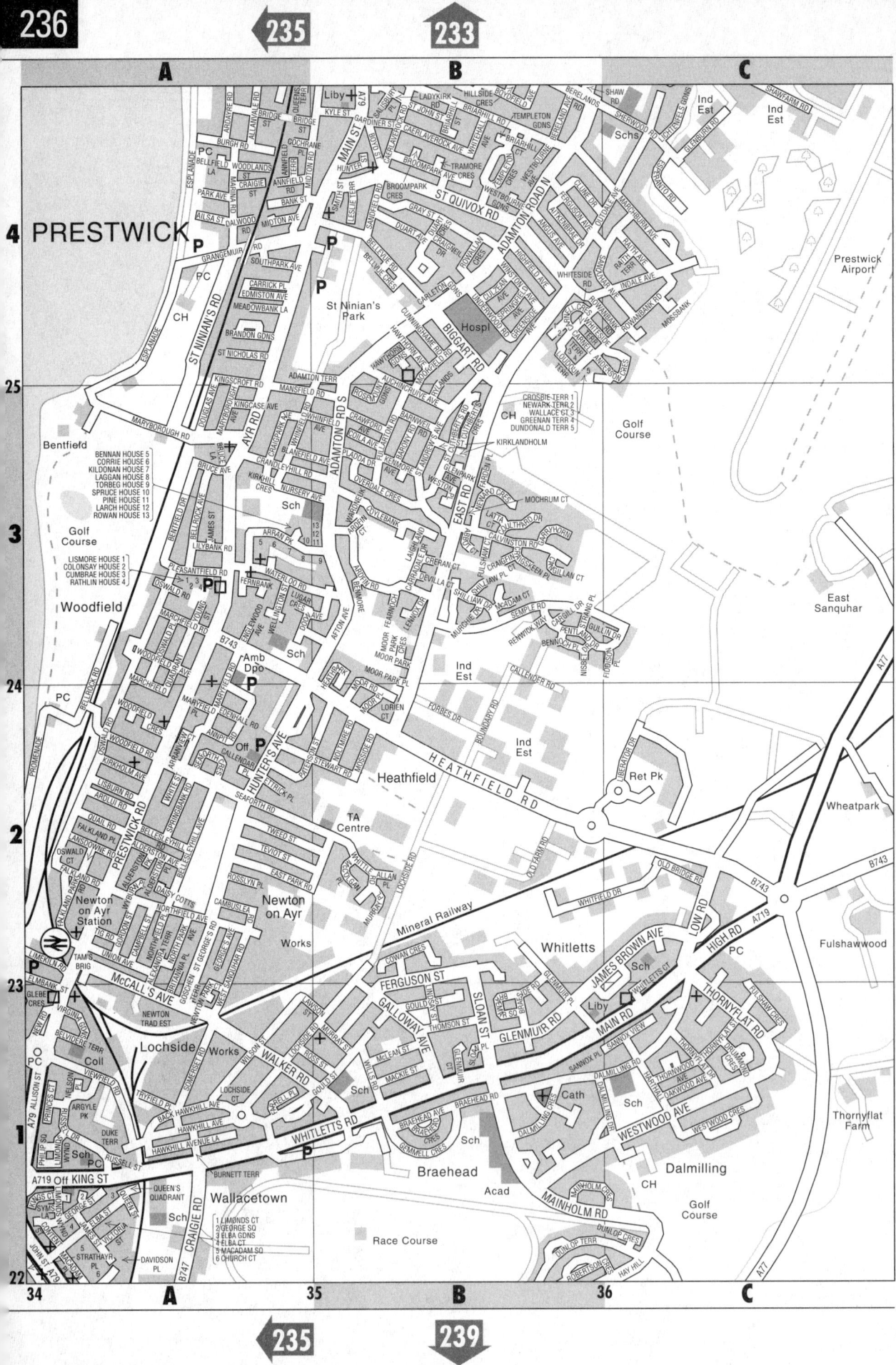

D | **E** | **F**

SANDYFORD RD
A77
A719
A719

Shields

Ladykirk Burn

Ladykirk Burn

Sandyford Smithy
B742

Sandyford

4

Clune

Bogend

Clune Farm Cottage

Dismantled Railway

Raggithill

Mossblown

DRUMLEY AVE

25

Factory

Mossblown Farm

ARGYLL AVE

HILL PARK

Highfield

Kirklandholm Farm

RAGGITHILL AVE 1
SANDYFORD RD 2
BARWHEYS DR 3

B742

B7035
KEVOC COTTS

Barwheys

B743

3

St Quivox

Brickrow Holdings

24

The Hannah Research Institute

B7035

Oswald's Temple

Auchincruive (Agricultural Coll)

Brockle Wood

White Gables

2

River Ayr

Cutting Wood

Pheasant Nook

Oswald's Bridge

Mount Loudoun

Craighall Wood

Mount Charles Wood

Mon

23

Newbarns Wood

Oaklea

Mount Scarburgh

River Ayr

1

Laigland

Craighall

Tarholm Nursery

B744

Mainholm Holdings

Auchincruive Holdings

Stanalane

Mainholm Nursery

B744

22

235

AYR

Low Green
Esplanade
Fairfield Pk
Wellington La
Park Terr
Barns St La
Park Pk
Union Arc 12
Alloway Pl
Dalblair
A70 Miller Rd
Off
Killoch Pl 13
Burns Statue Sq 14
Smith St 15
Parkhouse St 16
Shieling Pk
Craigweil Pl
Savoy Pk
Savoy Ct
Park Circus La
Park Cir
Bellevue St
Bellevue Cres
Bellevue La
Marchmont Rd La
Marchmont
Dornoch Pk
South Lodge Ct
Springvale Pk
Springvale
Bowman Rd
Carrick Road La
Carrick Rd
Balantine Dr
Blackburn Dr
Blackburn Rd
Craigweil
Wheatfield Rd
Westfield Rd
Carrick Ave
Bentfield Ave
Southpark Rd
Airlie Ct
Victoria Pk
Wattfield Rd
Carrick Ave
Carrick Gdns
Broomfield Rd
Broomfield Gdn
Chalmers Rd
Curtecan Pl
Seafield Rd
Seafield Cres
Racecourse View
Seafield Dr
April Dr
Arrol Pk
Rosebank Cres
Corsehill Rd
St Leonard's Dr
Hartfield Rd A79
Rossland Ave
Seafield
Playing Fields
Carwinshoch View
Alchemviek
Alchenmohon Cres
Corsehill View
Corsehill Pl
Corsehill Pk
Bellevale Quadrant
Bellevale Ave
Ewenfield Ave
Chapel Park Rd
Ewenfield Rd
Golf Course
Ewenfield Gdns
Doonfoot Rd
Longbank Rd
Longbank Dr
Slaphouse Burn
Slaphouse
Longlands Rd
Cunning Park
Abercromby Dr
Craigsheil
Gearholm Rd
Belleisle Bridge
Slaphouse Bridge
Knoll Dr
Longhill Point
Castle Wlk
Greenan Pl
Scauld Doon Rd
Cunning Park Dr
Northfield Ave
Argyll
Goudskirk
Belleisle
Hotel
Rozelle Park
Greenan Rd
Lochpark
Greenan Pk
Greenan Way
Belleisle Park
Rozelle
PC
Greenan
Greenan Gr
Abbots Way
Earls Way
Knowholm
Greenfield Ave
Golf Course
Abbots Cres
Kilbrandon Way
Kilbrandon
Nursery
Widow
Str Athdon Pl
Wrightfield
Mus
St Vincent Cres
Longhill
Mill
Charles Cres
Cambusdoon Dr
Cochranhill Park
Cochranhill Rd
The Loaning
The Loaning
Burton Smithy
Dunure Rd
Shalloch Pl
Doonfoot
River Doon
Doonbank Farm
Alloway
Doonholm Rd
High Greenan
Crossburn Dr
Corriebrae Pl
Browncarrick Dr
Glenmuir
Artry
Cairnsmore Dr
Corsehill Pk
Longhill Ave
Lamford Dr
Glenalla Cres
Balminnoch Pk
Doonholm Pl
Sch
Alloway
Liby
Upper Crofts
Laigh Mount
Dismantled Railway
A719
Craigstewart Cres
Portmark Ave
Shanter Way
Heritage Cen
Dismtd Rly
Murdoch's Lone
B7024
River Doon
B7024

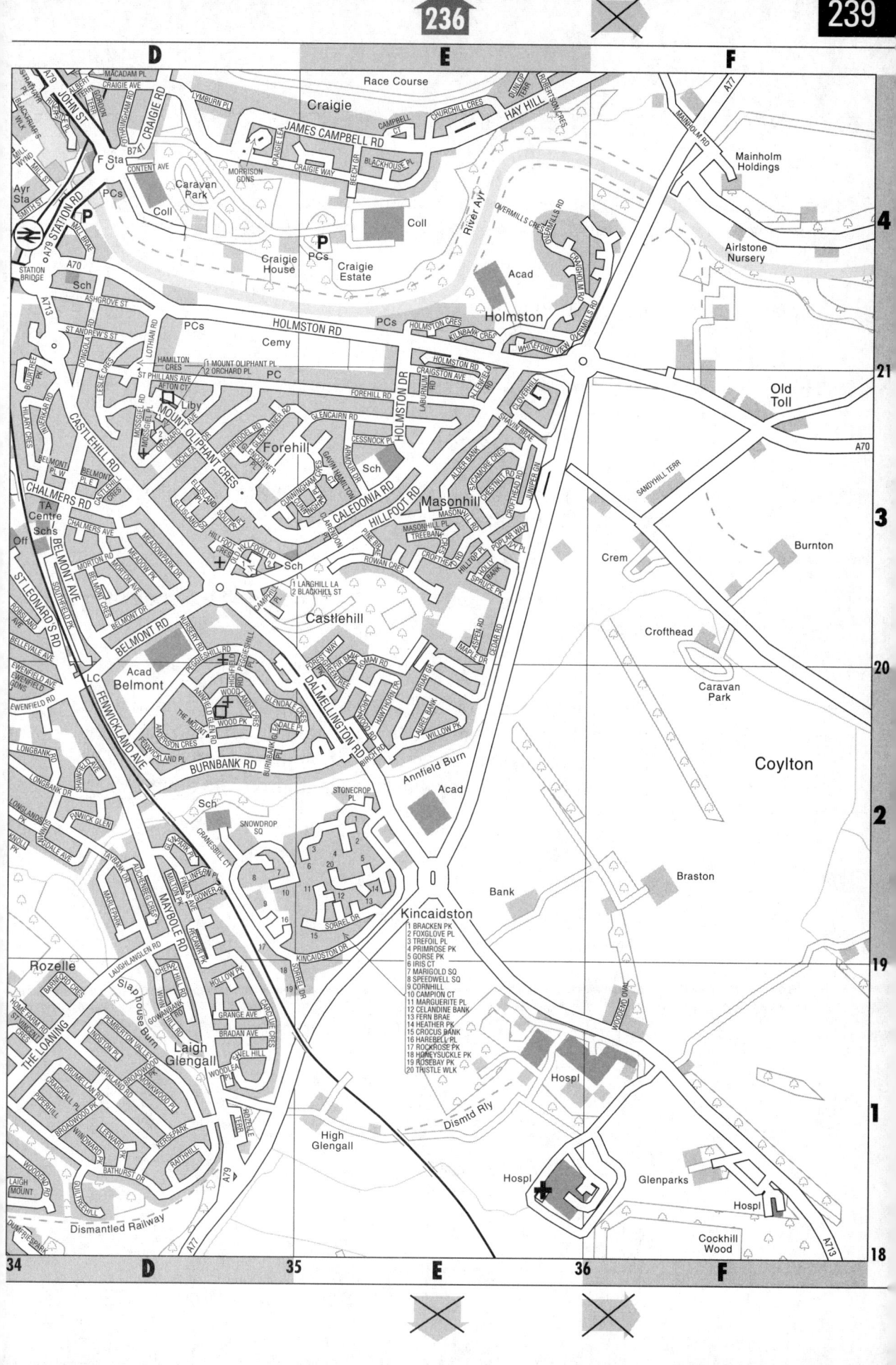

D E F

Race Course

Craigie

MACADAM PL
CRAIGIE AVE
CRAIGIE RD
JOHN ST
LYMBURN PL
JAMES CAMPBELL RD
CAMPBELL CT
CHURCHILL CRES
HAY HILL
DUNLOP CRES
CULBERTSON CRES

MILL WYND
MILL ST
B74

F Sta
CONTENT AVE
CRAIGIE LEA
CRAIGIE WAY
BEECH GR
BLACKHOUSE PL
MORRISON GDNS
OVERMILLS CRES RD
CRAIGHOLM RD
OVERMILLS RD
Mainholm
Holdings

Ayr Sta
SMITH ST
STATION RD
PCs
Caravan
Park
Coll
Coll
River Ayr
Acad
Airlstone
Nursery
4

P
Craigie
House
P
PCs
Craigie
Estate
Holmston
A77

STATION
BRIDGE
A79 STATION RD
A70
Sch
ASHGROVE ST
HOLMSTON RD
PCs
HOLMSTON CRES
KILNBANK CRES
WHITEFORD VIEW
Old
Toll
21

A713
ST ANDREW'S ST
Cemy
PCs
HOLMSTON RD
CRAIGSTON AVE
LABURNUM DR
ALLERTON RD
A70

HAMILTON CRES
ST PHILLANS AVE
AFTON CT
1 Mount Oliphant Pl
2 Orchard Pl
PC
FOREHILL RD
HOLMSTON DR
GLENCAIRN DR
CALDERWOOD RD
SANDYHILL TERR
Burnton

BELMONT
P.W.
CHALMERS RD
MOUNT OLIPHANT CRES
Liby
Forehill
GLENCAIRN RD
GAVIN HAMILTON CT
Sch
CESSNOCK RD
ARMOUR DR
SPRINGBANK
ALDER BANK
CLOVER HILL
3

TA
Centre
Schs
Off
CHALMERS AVE
CASTLEHILL RD
LESLIE CRES
CUNNINGHAME DR
Masonhill
MASONHILL PL
TREBAN
CROFTHEAD
PINE TREE RD
POPLAR WAY
Crem
Crofthead

LC
BELMONT AVE
ST LEONARD'S RD
BELLEVALE AVE
EWENFIELD AVE
Acad
Belmont
BELMONT DR
NURSERY RD
BEGBIESHILL RD
HIGHFIELD RD
FOREST WAY
RMN RD
ASPEN DR
MAPLE DR
CEDAR RD
Caravan
Park
20

EWENFIELD PL
LONGBANK AVE
LONGBANK DR
FENWICK LAND AVE
BURNBANK RD
DALMELLINGTON RD
WOOD PK
GLENDALE CRES
GLENDALE PL
BIRCH RD
WILLOW PK
Annfield Burn
Acad
Coylton

LONGLANDS PK
KNOLL PK
RANWICK GLEN
Sch
STONECROP PL
SNOWDROP SQ
3
5
6
20
14
13
Bank
Braston
2

Rozelle
MAYBOLE RD
CRANESBILL CT
LYNNE PARK
FINCHED PL
BOWER RD
8
7
10
11
12
9
16
15
17
SORREL DR
Kincaidston
1 BRACKEN PK
2 FOXGLOVE PL
3 TREFOIL PL
4 PRIMROSE PK
5 GORSE PK
6 IRIS CT
7 MARIGOLD SQ
8 SPEEDWELL SQ
9 CORNHILL
10 CAMPION CT
11 MARGUERITE PL
12 CELANDINE BANK
13 FERN BRAE
14 HEATHER PK
15 CROCUS BANK
16 HAREBELL PL
17 ROCKROSE PK
18 HONEYSUCKLE PK
19 ROSEBAY PK
20 THISTLE WLK

Slaphouse Burn
Laigh
Glengall
GRANGE AVE
CAROLINE CRES
KINCAIDSTON DR
18
19
SORREL DR
Hospl
MOORFOOT OVAL
19

THE LOANING
HOME FARM RD
WOODLEA
High
Glengall
Dismtd Rly
Hospl
1

LAIGH MOUNT
GUILD HILL
BATHURST DR
Dismantled Railway
Hospl
Glenparks
Hospl

Cockhill
Wood
A713
18

34 D 35 E 36 F

EXPLANATION OF THE STREET INDEX REFERENCE SYSTEM

Street names are listed alphabetically and show the locality, the page number and a reference to the square in which the name falls on the map page.

Example:

Canal St. Pais...113 E2

Canal St

This is the full street name, which may have been abbreviated on the map.

Pais

This is the abbreviation for the town, village or locality in which the street falls.

113

This is the page number of the map on which the street name appears.

E2

The letter and figure indicate the square on the map in which the centre of the street falls..The square can be found at the junction of the vertical column carrying the appropriate letter and the horizontal row carrying the appropriate figure.

ABBREVIATIONS USED IN THE INDEX
Road Names

Approach	App	Green	Gn
Arcade	Arc	Grove	Gr
Avenue	Ave	Heights	Hts
Boulevard	Bvd	Industrial Estate	Ind Est
Buildings	Bldgs	Junction	Junc
Business Park	Bsns Pk	Lane	La
Business Centre	Bsns Ctr	North	N
Broadway	Bwy	Orchard	Orch
Causeway	Cswy	Parade	Par
Centre	Ctr	Park	Pk
Circle	Circ	Passage	Pas
Circus	Cir	Place	Pl
Close	Cl	Precinct	Prec
Common	Comm	Promenade	Prom
Corner	Cnr	Retail Park	Ret Pk
Cottages	Cotts	Road	Rd
Court	Ct	South	S
Courtyard	Ctyd	Square	Sq
Crescent	Cres	Stairs	Strs
Drive	Dr	Steps	Stps
Drove	Dro	Street, Saint	St
East	E	Terrace	Terr
Embankment	Emb	Trading Estate	Trad Est
Esplanade	Espl	Walk	Wlk
Estate	Est	West	W
Gardens	Gdns	Yard	Yd

Key to abbreviations of Town, Village and Rural locality names used in the index of street names.

Addiewell	Add	168	C2
Airdrie	Aird	123	D4
Airth	Air	14	B2
Alexandria	Alex	27	E3
Allanton	Alla	167	D4
Alloa	All	10	B3
Alva	Alva	5	D3
Arden	Arden	18	B3
Ardrossan	Ard	205	D1
Armadale	Arm	107	F4
Ashgill	Ash	199	F4
Auldhouse	Auld	180	B1
Avonbridge	Avon	87	F4
Ayr	Ayr	238	B4
Banknock	Bank	38	C2
Bannockburn	Bann	7	F1
Barrhead	Barr	134	C1
Bearsden	Bear	75	F3
Beith	Beith	150	A1
Bishopbriggs	Bish	78	B2
Bishopton	Bishop	72	A2
Blackridge	Blac	107	E2
Bonhill	Bonh	28	A2
Bonnybridge	Bon	40	A3
Bridge of Allan	B of A	2	A4
Bridge of Weir	B of W	110	C4
Calderbank	Calder	123	D2
Caldercruix	Cald	105	D3
California	Cali	66	C3
Cambus	Camb	9	D4
Cambusbarron	Cam	6	B3
Cardross	Card	48	A4
Carluke	Car	188	A1
Chapelhall	Chap	123	F1
Chapelton	Chapel	181	E1
Clackmannan	Clack	10	C2
Cleland	Cle	144	A1

Clydebank	Clyde	74	A1
Coatbridge	Coat	122	B3
Cowie	Cowie	12	B4
Coylton	Coy	239	F2
Crossford	Cro	201	D1
Crosshouse	Cross	221	F1
Cumbernauld	Cumb	62	B3
Dalry	Dalry	191	D4
Denny	Den	21	F1
Dumbarton	Dumb	49	F1
Dunblane	Dun	1	B4
Dundonald	Dund	225	F1
Dunipace	Duni	21	E2
Dunlop	Dunlop	195	E4
Duntocher	Dunt	74	A4
Eaglesham	Eagle	178	C3
East Kilbride	E Kil	159	E2
Eastfield	East	127	E2
Erskine	Ersk	73	D1
Falkirk	Falk	42	B3
Fallin	Fall	8	B2
Fauldhouse	Fau	147	F4
Fenwick	Fen	213	D2
Fishcross	Fish	5	F2
Forth	For	189	F3
Gartocharn	Gart	20	C4
Glasgow	Glasg	117	E3
Glassford	Glass	198	A2
Glenboig	Glen	101	F3
Glenmavis	Glenm	102	C2
Gourock	Gour	44	B4
Grangemouth	Gran	24	C2
Greengairs	Gree	83	F1
Greenock	Green	46	A3
Hamilton	Ham	162	B2
Harthill	Hart	127	F3
Hattonrig	Hat	142	A3

Helensburgh	Helen	16	A1
Holytown	Holy	143	D3
Houston	Hous	91	D1
Howwood	How	130	C3
Hurlford	Hurl	228	C3
Inchinnan	Inch	93	E3
Irvine	Irvine	219	D2
Johnstone	John	111	F1
Kilbarchan	Kilbar	111	D2
Kilbirnie	Kilb	149	D1
Kilmacolm	Kil	89	E4
Kilmarnock	Kilmk	228	A4
Kilmaurs	Kilm	222	B4
Kilncadzow	Kilnc	203	D3
Kilsyth	Kils	60	B4
Kilwinning	Kilw	207	F1
Kirkintilloch	Kirk	79	F4
Lanark	Lan	215	E2
Langbank	Lang	70	A4
Larbert	Larb	23	D2
Larkhall	Lark	185	D2
Laurieston	Laur	42	C2
Law	Law	186	C3
Lennoxtown	Lennox	57	E4
Linwood	Lin	112	A3
Lochwinnoch	Loch	129	D2
Menstrie	Men	3	F3
Milngavie	Miln	55	D2
Milton of Campsie	M of C	58	B3
Mossblown	Moss	237	F4
Motherwell	Mother	163	E4
Muirhead	Muir	100	B4
Neilston	Neil	154	C3
New Sauchie	N Sau	5	E1
Newmains	New	166	A3
Newton Mearns	Newt M	156	B2
Old Kilpatrick	O Kill	73	D3

Paisley	Pais	113	E1
Plains	Plains	104	A2
Plean	Plea	12	B2
Port Glasgow	P Glasg	47	F1
Prestwick	Pres	236	A4
Quarter	Quart	183	F2
Renfrew	Ren	94	C1
Rhu	Rhu	15	E3
Rosneath	Ros	15	D2
Salsburgh	Sals	125	E1
Saltcoats	Salt	216	B4
Shewalton	Shew	224	C3
Shieldhill	Shi	66	B3
Shotts	Shot	146	C3
Slamannan	Slam	86	A3
Springside	Spring	220	C1
Stenhousemuir	Sten	23	E2
Stepps	Stepps	99	E3
Stevenston	Steven	217	F4
Stewarton	Stew	211	F4
Stirling	Stir	7	E4
Stonehouse	Stone	198	C1
Strathblane	Strath	31	E2
Symington	Sym	231	E2
Tannochside	Tan	141	D4
Tarbolton	Tar	234	C3
Thorntonhall	Thorn	158	B2
Tillicoultry	Till	5	F4
Torwood	Tor	22	C3
Troon	Troon	229	D1
Tullibody	Tull	4	B2
Twechar	Twe	59	F2
Uddingston	Udd	140	C3
Uplawmoor	Uplaw	153	D2
West Kilbride	W Kil	190	B2
Westfield	West	87	F1
Wishaw	Wish	165	D2

Abbey Cl. Pais 113 F2
Abbey Craig Rd. N Sau 5 D1
Abbey Dr. Glasg 95 F2
Abbey Mill. Stir 7 E4
Abbey Pl. Aird 123 E2
Abbey Rd. John 112 B1
Abbey Rd Pl. Stir 7 E4
Abbey Rd. Stir 2 B1
Abbey Wlk. Lark 185 D2
Abbeycraig Rd. Glasg 100 C1
Abbeydale Way. Glasg 138 B2
Abbeygate. Kilw 207 F2
Abbeygreen. Kilw 207 F2
Abbeygreen St. Glasg 100 C1
Abbeyhill St. Glasg 118 C4
Abbeylands Rd. Dunt 74 B3
Abbot Ct. Pres 236 B3
Abbot Dr. Glasg 116 C1
Abbot St. Green 45 E2
Abbot St. Pais 113 F3
Abbot's Ave. Kilw 207 F1
Abbot's Pl. Kilw 207 F2
Abbot's Wlk. Kilw 207 F2
Abbots Cres. Ayr 238 A1
Abbots Ct. Falk 42 B4
Abbots Moss Dr. Falk 41 F1
Abbots Rd. Falk 42 B4
Abbots Terr. Aird 123 E2
Abbots Way. Ayr 238 B2
Abbotsburn Way. Pais 113 F4
Abbotsford Ave. Glasg 138 A4
Abbotsford Ave. Ham 162 A4
Abbotsford Ave. Lark 185 D1
Abbotsford. Bish 78 B1
Abbotsford Brae. E Kil 159 F2
Abbotsford Cres. Ham 162 A3
Abbotsford Cres. Pais 132 C4
Abbotsford Cres. Shot 146 C3
Abbotsford Cres. Wish 165 E2
Abbotsford Ct. Cumb 82 C4
Abbotsford Dr. Helen 25 C1
Abbotsford Dr. Klrk 79 F4
Abbotsford Gdns. Falk 24 A1
Abbotsford La. Hat 141 F3
Abbotsford Pl. Cumb 82 C4
Abbotsford Pl. Glasg 117 D2
Abbotsford Pl. Glasg 117 D3
Abbotsford Pl. Holy 143 D3
Abbotsford Pl. Salt 206 A1
Abbotsford Pl. Stir 2 B1
Abbotsford Rd. Bear 75 E3
Abbotsford Rd. Chap 123 F1
Abbotsford Rd. Clyde 74 A1
Abbotsford Rd. Cumb 82 C4
Abbotsford Rd. Ham 162 A3
Abbotsford Rd. Wish 165 E2
Abbotsford St. Falk 42 A4
Abbotsford Terr. Lan 215 E2
Abbotshall Ave. Glasg 74 C2
Abbotsinch Rd. Inch 93 F1
Abbott Cres. Clyde 94 B4
Aberconway St. Clyde 94 B4
Abercorn Ave. Glasg 114 C4
Abercorn Cres. Ham 162 C1
Abercorn Dr. Ham 162 C1
Abercorn Ind Est. Pais 113 F3
Abercorn Pl. Glasg 76 C1
Abercorn St. Newt M 156 B3
Abercorn St. Dunt 74 C4
Abercorn St. Pais 113 F3
Abercrombie Cres. Coat ... 120 C3
Abercrombie Dr. Bear 75 D4
Abercrombie Pl. Kils 36 A1
Abercrombie Pl. Men 3 F3
Abercrombie St. Falk 41 F3
Abercromby Cres. E Kil 160 A2
Abercromby Cres. Helen ... 16 C2
Abercromby Dr. Ayr 238 B2
Abercromby Dr. B of A 2 A4
Abercromby Dr. Glasg 117 F3
Abercromby Pl. E Kil 160 A2
Abercromby Pl. Stir 7 D4
Abercromby Pl. Tull 4 A1
Abercromby Pl W. Helen ... 16 B2
Abercromby Sq. Glasg 117 F3
Abercromby St E. Helen ... 16 C1
Abercromby St. Glasg 117 F3
Aberdalgie Rd. Glasg 120 A4
Aberdeen Rd. Chap 123 E2
Aberdour St. Glasg 118 B4
Aberfeldy Ave. Plains 103 F2
Aberfeldy St. Glasg 118 B4
Aberfeldy Terr. Irvine 220 A3
Aberfoyle Rd. Green 46 A1
Aberfoyle St. Glasg 118 B4
Aberlady Rd. Glasg 115 F3
Aberlady St. Cle 144 A1
Aberlour Pl. Irvine 219 F3
Abernethy Dr. Lin 112 A3
Abernethy Pk. E Kil 159 E1
Abernethy St. Glasg 118 B4
Abernethy Rd. New 166 A3
Aberuthven Dr. Glasg 119 D2
Abiegail Pl. Udd 140 B1
Aboukir St. Glasg 115 F4
Aboyne Ave. Stir 2 B2
Aboyne Dr. Pais 113 F1

Aboyne St. Glasg 115 F3
Acacia Dr. Barr 134 A3
Acacia Dr. Beith 171 D4
Acacia Dr. Pais 113 D1
Acacia Pl. John 132 A4
Academy Brae. Beith 171 D4
Academy Ct. Hurl 228 C3
Academy Ct. Irvine 219 D2
Academy Pk. Aird 123 D4
Academy Pk. Glasg 116 B2
Academy Pl. Bann 7 F1
Academy Rd. Glasg 136 B1
Academy Rd. Irvine 219 D2
Academy Rd. Stir 7 D4
Academy St. Aird 123 D4
Academy St. All 9 F4
Academy St. Ayr 235 F1
Academy St. Coat 122 A4
Academy St. Glasg 119 D2
Academy St. Glasg 119 D3
Academy St. Hurl 228 C3
Academy St. Kilmk 227 F3
Academy St. Lark 185 D2
Academy St. Troon 229 E1
Academy Terr. Hat 142 A3
Acer Cres. Pais 113 D1
Achamore Rd. Glasg 74 C2
Acherfield Gdns. Glasg 95 D4
Achnasheen Rd. Chap 124 A3
Achray Ct. All 10 B3
Achray Dr. Pais 113 D1
Achray Dr. Stir 2 A2
Achray Pl. Coat 101 E1
Achray Pl. Miln 54 B2
Achray Rd. Cumb 82 B3
Acorn Ct. Glasg 117 F2
Acorn St. Glasg 117 F2
Acre Dr. Glasg 76 A1
Acre Rd. Glasg 76 A1
Acre Valley Rd. Lennox 57 D1
Acredyke Cres. Glasg 98 B4
Acredyke Pl. Glasg 98 B3
Acredyke Rd. Glasg 98 B4
Acredyke Rd. Glasg 137 F4
Acres The. Lark 185 D1
Adair Rd. Salt 205 F1
Adam Ave. Aird 123 D4
Adam Cres. Sten 23 F1
Adam St. Falk 42 B3
Adam St. Green 46 A2
Adam's Gate. Troon 229 F3
Adams Ave. Salt 205 F1
Adams Court La. Glasg 117 D3
Adams Ct. Troon 229 F3
Adams Pl. Kils 60 B4
Adams Wlk. Irvine 219 F1
Adamslie Cres. Klrk 79 D4
Adamslie Dr. Klrk 79 D4
Adamson Pl. Stir 2 A2
Adamson St. Hat 142 B3
Adamswell St. Glasg 97 F2
Adamswell Terr. Muir 81 D1
Adamton Est. Pres 234 B4
Adamton Road N. Pres 236 B4
Adamton Road S. Pres 236 B3
Adamton Terr. Pres 236 B4
Addie St. Mother 163 F4
Addiewell Pl. Coat 122 A2
Addiewell St. Glasg 119 D4
Addison Gr. Glasg 135 F2
Addison Pl. Glasg 135 F2
Addison Rd. Glasg 96 B2
Addison Rd. Glasg 135 F2
Adelaide Rd. E Kil 180 B4
Adelaide St. Gour 44 C4
Adelaide St. Helen 16 C1
Adele St. Mother 163 F2
Adelphi St. Glasg 117 E3
Admiral St. Glasg 116 C3
Admiralty Gdns. Kil 73 D3
Admiralty Gr. O Kill 73 D3
Admiralty Pl. O Kill 73 D3
Advie Pl. Glasg 137 D4
Affric Ave. Plains 104 A2
Affric Dr. Pais 24 B1
Affric Dr. Pais 114 A1
Affric Loan. Shot 146 C3
Afton Ave. Kilmk 223 D2
Afton Ave. Pres 236 B3
Afton Cres. Bear 76 A2
Afton Ct. Ayr 239 D3
Afton Ct. Irvine 219 D1
Afton Ct. Stir 7 E3
Afton Dr. Bank 39 E4
Afton Dr. Ren 94 C1
Afton Gdns. Troon 229 F2
Afton Gdns. Udd 161 D3
Afton Pl. Ard 205 E2
Afton Rd. Cumb 62 A2
Afton Rd. Steven 217 E4
Afton St. Glasg 136 C4
Afton St. Lark 185 E1
Afton View. Kirk 58 C1
Agamemnon St. Clyde 73 F1
Agnew Gr. Tan 141 E3

Agnew La. Glasg 117 D1
Aikenhead House. Glasg .. 137 E3
Aikenhead Rd. Glasg 137 E4
Aikman Pl. E Kil 160 A2
Aikman Rd. Mother 163 D3
Aiknut Rd. W Kil 190 B2
Ailean Dr. Glasg 119 F2
Ailean Gdns. Glasg 119 F2
Aillort Pl. E Kil 159 F2
Ailort Ave. Glasg 137 D3
Ailort Loan. New 165 F3
Ailsa Ave. Ash 199 F4
Ailsa Ave. Mother 163 D4
Ailsa Cres. Mother 163 D4
Ailsa Ct. Coat 121 F2
Ailsa Ct. Ham 161 E1
Ailsa Dr. Dunt 74 B3
Ailsa Dr. Glasg 136 C4
Ailsa Dr. Glasg 137 F3
Ailsa Dr. Glasg 157 A4
Ailsa Dr. Kirk 58 C1
Ailsa Dr. Pais 133 E4
Ailsa Dr. Steven 217 E4
Ailsa Dr. Udd 141 D2
Ailsa Gdns. Ard 205 E2
Ailsa Pl. Ayr 235 F1
Ailsa Pl. Coat 121 F2
Ailsa Pl. Kilmk 223 D3
Ailsa Rd. Bish 78 A1
Ailsa Rd. Coat 121 F2
Ailsa Rd. Gour 44 B3
Ailsa Rd. Irvine 224 A4
Ailsa Rd. Ren 94 B1
Ailsa Rd. Salt 206 A1
Ailsa Rd. Troon 229 D2
Ailsa St. Pres 236 A4
Ailsa Tower. Glasg 138 C2
Ailsa View. Stew 195 F1
Ainsdale Ct. Kilw 207 D2
Ainslie Rd. Cumb 62 B2
Ainslie Rd. Glasg 115 D4
Airbles Cres. Mother 163 E3
Airbles Dr. Mother 163 E3
Airbles Farm Rd. Mother ... 163 E3
Airbles Rd. Mother 163 E3
Airbles St. Mother 163 F3
Aird Ave. Kilmk 227 F4
Aird's La. Glasg 117 E3
Airdale Ave. Glasg 136 B1
Airdrie Rd. Cald 105 E1
Airdrie Rd. Car 187 E2
Airdrie Rd. Cumb 81 F2
Airdrie Rd. Cumb 82 A3
Airdrie Rd. Cumb 82 A4
Airdrie Rd. Kils 60 B4
Airdrie Rd. Law 187 F4
Airdrie Rd. Plains 103 F1
Airdriehill Rd. Aird 103 E2
Airdriehill St. Aird 103 E1
Airgold Dr. Glasg 74 C2
Airlie Ave. Bear 75 F4
Airlie Ct. Ayr 238 C3
Airlie Dr. Hat 142 A3
Airlie Gdns. Glasg 138 B2
Airlie La. Glasg 96 A2
Airlie Rd. Glasg 120 A2
Airlie St. Glasg 96 A2
Airlink Ind Est. Pais 113 F4
Airlour Rd. Glasg 136 C3
Airth Ct. Mother 142 B1
Airth Dr. Glasg 115 F2
Airth Dr. Stir 7 E2
Airth La. Glasg 115 F2
Airthrey Ave. B of A 2 A3
Airthrey Ave. Glasg 95 F2
Airthrey Dr. Sten 24 A2
Airthrey La. Glasg 95 F2
Airthrey Rd. B of A 2 B3
Airthrey Rd. Stir 2 B3
Airyligg Dr. Eagle 178 C3
Aitchison Dr. Lar 23 D2
Aitchison St. Aird 122 C4
Aitken Cres. Stir 7 D1
Aitken Dr. Beith 150 B1
Aitken Dr. Slam 86 A3
Aitken Gdns. Falk 41 F3
Aitken La. Alex 27 F4
Aitken Pl. Lan 215 D2
Aitken Rd. Falk 41 F3
Aitken Rd. Ham 183 F4
Aitken St. Aird 103 D1
Aitken St. Dalry 191 E4
Aitken St. Glasg 118 B4
Aitken Terr. Falk 41 E3
Akarit Rd. Sten 23 F1
Alasdair Ct. Barr 134 A1
Alba Way. Ham 183 E4
Albans Cres. Mother 163 D4
Albany Ave. Glasg 119 E3
Albany Dr. Glasg 138 A3

Albany Dr. Lan 215 D2
Albany. E Kil 160 B2
Albany Pl. Udd 141 D1
Albany Quadrant. Glasg 119 E3
Albany Rd. Ham 183 E4
Albany St. Coat 121 F4
Albany St. Glasg 118 A2
Albany Terr. Glasg 138 C2
Albany Way. Pais 113 F4
Albany Wynd. Lark 185 D2
Albert Ave. Glasg 117 D1
Albert Ave. Stew 195 F1
Albert Cres. Aird 123 D4
Albert Cross. Glasg 116 C2
Albert Ct. Stew 195 F1
Albert Dr. Bear 76 A2
Albert Dr. Glasg 116 B2
Albert Dr. Glasg 138 A3
Albert Dr. Helen 16 C1
Albert Dr. Lark 185 D1
Albert Pl. Aird 123 D4
Albert Pl. Stew 195 F1
Albert Pl. Stir 7 D4
Albert Quadrant. Holy 143 D3
Albert Rd. Clyde 74 A2
Albert Rd. East 127 F3
Albert Rd. Falk 42 A2
Albert Rd. Glasg 117 D1
Albert Rd. Gour 44 B4
Albert Rd. Kilbar 111 E3
Albert Rd. Kils 79 E2
Albert Rd. Ren 94 B2
Albert St. Alex 27 F2
Albert St. Coat 122 A4
Albert St. Ham 162 A3
Albert St. Helen 16 C1
Albert St. Mother 163 F4
Albert Terr. Ham 162 A3
Albert Terr. Ham 239 D4
Albert Barr Ct. Falk 42 A1
Albert Wynd. Stew 195 F1
Alberta Ave. Coat 121 F4
Alberta Ave. E Kil 180 B4
Alberta Cres. E Kil 180 B4
Alberta Pk. E Kil 180 B4
Alberta Pl. E Kil 180 B4
Albion Gate. Glasg 117 E4
Albion Gate. Pais 113 E3
Albion St. Coat 122 B3
Albion St. Glasg 117 E4
Albion St. Mother 163 F3
Albion St. Pais 113 F3
Albion Way. E Kil 180 C3
Alcaig Rd. Glasg 115 F1
Alcath Rd. New 166 A3
Alder Ave. Ham 162 C1
Alder Ave. Klrk 79 D3
Alder Bank. Ayr 239 E3
Alder Bank. Tan 121 E1
Alder Cres. E Kil 180 B3
Alder Ct. Barr 134 B1
Alder Ct. E Kil 180 B3
Alder Gn. Irvine 220 A2
Alder Gn. Holy 143 E3
Alder Pl. E Kil 180 B3
Alder Pl. Glasg 136 B3
Alder Pl. John 112 A1
Alder Pl. Kilmk 227 F4
Alder Rd. Clyde 74 A3
Alder Rd. Cumb 62 B1
Alder Rd. Dumb 49 F2
Alder Rd. Glasg 136 B3
Alder Rd. M of C 58 A2
Alderbank Rd. P Glasg 47 D1
Alderbrae Rd. P Glasg 47 D1
Alderman Pl. Glasg 95 E3
Alderman Rd. Glasg 95 D3
Alderside Ave. Mother 164 B2
Alderside Gdns. Udd 140 C4
Alderside Pl. Udd 141 D2
Alderstocks. E Kil 180 C3
Alderston Ave. Ayr 236 A2
Alderston Pk. Ayr 236 A2
Alderston Pl. Ayr 236 A2
Alderston Pl. Hat 141 F2
Aldersyde Ave. Mother 164 B2
Aldersyde Gdns. Troon 229 F2
Aldersyde Pl. Udd 140 B1
Aldersyde Terr. Cle 144 B1
Alderwood Rd. P Glasg 47 D1
Aldrin Rd. Helen 25 D4
Alexander Ave. Eagle 178 C3
Alexander Ave. Falk 42 C3
Alexander Ave. Steven 206 C1
Alexander Ave. Tan 141 E3
Alexander Ave. Twe 59 F2
Alexander
  Balfour Gdns. Ham 162 B1
Alexander Dr. B of A 2 A4
Alexander
  Fleming Ave. Kilb 148 C1
Alexander Gdns. Ham 163 D1
Alexander Pl. Irvine 219 E2
Alexander Pl. Kirk 80 A4
Alexander Pl. Rhu 15 E3
Alexander Rd. Shot 146 B3
Alexander St. Aird 122 C4
Alexander St. Alex 49 E4

Alexander St. Clyde 74 A1
Alexander St. Coat 122 A4
Alexander St. Dumb 50 A2
Alexander St. Wish 165 D1
Alexander Terr. Neil 154 B3
Alexandra Ave. Klrk 79 E2
Alexandra Ave. Pres 233 E1
Alexandra Ave. Stepps 99 E3
Alexandra Cross. Glasg 118 A4
Alexandra Ct. Glasg 118 A4
Alexandra Dr. All 9 F4
Alexandra Dr. Pais 113 D2
Alexandra Dr. Ren 94 B2
Alexandra Gdns. Klrk 79 E2
Alexandra Par. Glasg 118 A4
Alexandra Park St. Glasg .. 118 A4
Alexandra Pk. Kirk 79 E2
Alexandra Pl. Stir 2 B1
Alexandra St. Klrk 79 E4
Alexandra Terr. Ayr 236 A2
Alexandra Terr. Kilw 207 E2
Alexandria Quadrant. Holy 143 D3
Alford Ave. Kirk 79 D4
Alford Pl. Irvine 219 F3
Alford Pl. Lin 111 F3
Alford Quadrant. Wish 165 D3
Alford St. Glasg 97 E2
Alfred La. Glasg 96 C2
Algie St. Glasg 136 C4
Algoma Pl. E Kil 180 A4
Alice Ave. Hat 142 A2
Alice St. Pais 113 F1
Aline Ct. Barr 134 A2
Alison Lea. E Kil 160 B2
Allan Ave. Car 187 F2
Allan Ave. Ren 94 C1
Allan Cres. Dumb 50 A3
Allan Cres. Duni 21 E2
Allan Ct. E Kil 179 F4
Allan Dr. E Kil 179 F4
Allan Pk. Stir 7 D4
Allan Pl. Ayr 236 B2
Allan Pl. Dumb 50 A2
Allan Pl. Glasg 118 A1
Allan Sq. Irvine 219 F1
Allan St. Coat 121 E3
Allan St. Glasg 118 A1
Allan St. Mother 163 F4
Allanbank Pl. Lar 23 E1
Allanbank St. Alla 166 C4
Allandale Ave. Holy 143 F3
Allandale Cotts. Bon 39 E1
Allander Ave. Bish 77 D4
Allander Dr. Lennox 78 A4
Allander Gdns. Bish 77 F2
Allander Rd. Miln 55 D1
Allander St. Glasg 97 E2
Allands Ave. Inch 93 E3
Allanfauld Rd. Cumb 61 F1
Allanfauld Rd. Kils 36 B1
Allanshaw Gdns. Ham 162 A2
Allanshaw Gr. Ham 162 A1
Allanshaw St. Ham 162 B2
Allanton Ave. Glasg 114 C2
Allanton Dr. Glasg 115 E3
Allanton Gr. Wish 165 D3
Allanton Lea. Ham 183 E4
Allanton Pl. Ham 162 C1
Allanton Rd. Alla 166 C4
Allanton Rd. Shot 146 B1
Allanton Terr. Ham 184 B4
Allanvale. Dunlop 195 D4
Allanvale Rd. B of A 1 C4
Allanvale Rd. Pres 236 A4
Allanwater Gdns. B of A 2 A4
Allanwood Ct. B of A 2 A4
Allbany Cres. Holy 142 C3
Allendale. E Kil 159 E2
Allender Rd. Bear 75 E1
Allenfield Rd. Ayr 239 D3
Allershaw Pl. Wish 185 F4
Allershaw Rd. Wish 185 F4
Allershaw Tower. Wish 185 F4
Allerton Gdns. Glasg 119 E2
Alleysbank Rd. Glasg 118 A1
Allison Ave. Ersk 72 C1
Allison Dr. Glasg 139 D3
Allison Pl. Glasg 117 D1
Allison Pl. Muir 100 C2
Allison Pl. Newt M 156 B2
Allison St. Ayr 236 A1
Allison St. Glasg 117 D1
Allnach Pl. Glasg 120 C4
Alloa Rd. B of A 3 D2
Alloa Rd. N Sau 5 E2
Alloa Rd. Sten 23 F2
Alloa Rd. Sten 24 A2
Alloa Rd. Tull 4 B2
Alloway Ave. Kilmk 228 A4
Alloway. Ayr 238 C1
Alloway Cres. Bon 39 F3
Alloway Cres. Glasg 137 F3
Alloway Cres. Pais 134 B4
Alloway Ct. Kirk 59 D1
Alloway Dr. Clyde 74 B2

243

Alloway Dr. Cowie | Arran Ave. P Glasg

Alloway Dr. Cowie 12 B4
Alloway Dr. Glasg 137 F3
Alloway Dr. Kirk 59 D1
Alloway Dr. Newt M 157 D2
Alloway Dr. Pais 134 A4
Alloway Gdns. Ham 161 E1
Alloway Gdns. Kirk 59 D1
Alloway Gr. Kirk 58 C1
Alloway Pk. Ayr 238 C4
Alloway Pl. Ard 205 E2
Alloway Pl. Ayr 238 C4
Alloway Place La. Ayr 238 C4
Alloway Quadrant. Kirk 59 D1
Alloway Rd. E Kil 160 C2
Alloway Rd. Glasg 136 B3
Alloway St. Ayr 238 C4
Alloway St. Lark 185 E1
Alloway Terr. Kirk 58 C1
Alloway Wynd. Holy 143 F2
Alma La. Falk 42 A3
Alma St. Falk 42 A3
Alma St. Glasg 118 A3
Alma Terr. Falk 42 A3
Almada Gr. Ham 162 B2
Almada La. Ham 162 B2
Almada St. Ham 162 B2
Almond Ave. Ren 94 C1
Almond Cres. Pais 112 C1
Almond Ct. Stir 7 E3
Almond Dr. Bank 38 C1
Almond Dr. Bishop 72 A1
Almond Dr. E Kil 160 A1
Almond Dr. Kirk 79 D3
Almond Pl. Coat 101 E1
Almond Pl. Holy 143 D3
Almond Pl. Kilmk 227 E4
Almond Rd. Bear 75 E1
Almond Rd. Cumb 62 C2
Almond Rd. Stepps 99 E3
Almond St. Glasg 98 B1
Almond Terr. East 127 E3
Almond Vale. Tan 141 D4
Almond Way. Mother 163 F2
Almondbank. Plains 103 F2
Almswall Rd. Kilw 207 F2
Alness Cres. Glasg 115 F2
Alness St. Ham 162 B1
Alness Terr. Ham 162 B1
Alnwick Dr. Eagle 178 B2
Aloa Way. Lark 185 E1
Alpha Ctr. Clyde 94 B4
Alpine Gr. Tan 140 C4
Alsatian Ave. Clyde 74 B1
Alsh Terr. Ham 162 A1
Alston Ave. Coat 122 A4
Alston Gdns. Bear 75 D4
Altnacreag Gdns. Muir 81 D2
Altnock Pl. Dalry 191 D4
Alton Rd. Pais 114 B2
Alton St. W Kil 190 B3
Alton Way. W Kil 190 B2
Altonhead Dr. Spring 210 A1
Altonhead Terr. Spring 221 D4
Altonhill Ave. Kilmk 222 C2
Altry Pl. Ayr 238 A1
Altyre St. Glasg 118 C2
Aluclutha Ave. Dumb 50 A2
Alva Gate. Glasg 115 F2
Alva Gdns. Bear 75 E4
Alva Gdns. Glasg 115 F1
Alva Pl. Kirk 79 F2
Alva Terr. Green 45 D4
Alvord Ave. Pres 233 E1
Alwyn Ave. Hous 111 E4
Alwyn Ct. E Kil 159 F2
Alwyn Dr. E Kil 159 F2
Alyssum Cres. Mother 163 E4
Alyth Cres. Glasg 158 A4
Alyth Gdns. Glasg 115 F2
Alyth Gdns. Glasg 158 A4
Ambassador Way. Ren 94 B1
Amber Terr. Hat 142 A2
Ambleside. E Kil 180 A3
Amethyst Ave. Hat 142 A2
Amisfield St. Glasg 96 C3
Amlaird Rd. Kilmk 223 D3
Amochrie Dr. Pais 133 D4
Amulree Pl. Glasg 119 D2
Amulree St. Glasg 119 D2
Ancaster Dr. Glasg 95 F3
Ancaster La. Glasg 95 F3
Anchor Ave. Pais 114 A2
Anchor Cres. Pais 114 A2
Anchor Dr. Pais 114 A2
Anchor La. Glasg 117 E4
Anchor Wynd. Pais 114 A2
Ancroft St. Glasg 97 D2
Andersen Ct. E Kil 180 C3
Anderside. E Kil 180 C3
Anderson Ave. Kils 36 A1
Anderson Cres. Ayr 239 D2
Anderson Cres. Cali 66 C3
Anderson Cres. Kils 59 F4
Anderson Cres. Pres 236 C4
Anderson Ct. Hat 142 A3
Anderson Dr. Den 21 F1
Anderson Dr. Irvine 219 E3
Anderson Dr. Newt M 156 B2
Anderson Dr. Ren 94 B2
Anderson Dr. Salt 206 A1
Anderson Dr. Sten 24 A1
Anderson Gdns. Udd 140 C1
Anderson La. Aird 123 D4
Anderson Park Rd. Den 21 F1
Anderson Pl. Kilmk 223 E1
Anderson Pl. Stir 7 D2
Anderson Rd. Bishop 72 A2
Anderson St. Aird 123 D4
Anderson St. Bon 40 A3
Anderson St. Glasg 96 A1
Anderson St. Ham 161 F3
Anderson St. Mother 163 F3
Anderson St. P Glasg 47 E1
Anderson Terr. Ard 205 E1
Anderson Terr. Bank 39 D2
Anderston Quay. Glasg 116 C3
Andrew Ave. Kirk 79 E2
Andrew Ave. Ren 94 C2
Andrew Cres. Sten 23 E2
Andrew Dr. Clyde 94 B4
Andrew Pl. Car 187 F2
Andrew Sillars Ave. Glasg 139 E3
Andrew St. E Kil 159 F1
Andrew's La. Glasg 117 E3
Andrews St. Pais 113 F3
Anford Pl. Udd 161 F3
Angela Way. Udd 140 C3
Angle Gate. Glasg 95 E2
Angle St. Stone 198 C1
Angus Ave. Aird 123 D3
Angus Ave. Bish 78 B1
Angus Ave. E Kil 160 A1
Angus Ave. Glasg 115 E2
Angus Ave. Ham 163 D2
Angus Ave. Mother 163 E4
Angus Ave. Pres 236 B4
Angus Gdns. Tan 140 C4
Angus Oval. Glasg 115 D2
Angus Pl. E Kil 160 A1
Angus Pl. Glasg 115 D2
Angus Rd. Car 188 A1
Angus Rd. Gour 44 B2
Angus Rd. P Glasg 47 E1
Angus St. Alex 27 F2
Angus St. Clyde 94 C4
Angus St. Glasg 97 F2
Angus Wlk. Tan 141 D4
Ann Ct. Ham 162 A3
Ann St. Green 45 F2
Ann St. Green 45 F3
Ann St. Ham 162 A3
Ann St. John 112 A2
Annabella Rd. Ash 200 B2
Annan Ave. E Kil 179 F4
Annan Ct. Falk 42 B1
Annan Dr. Bear 75 E2
Annan Dr. Glasg 138 B4
Annan Dr. Pais 112 C1
Annan Glade. Mother 164 A2
Annan Gr. Mother 164 A2
Annan Pl. John 131 E4
Annan Rd. Kilmk 228 A3
Annan St. Glasg 137 D4
Annan St. Mother 164 A2
Annandale Cres. Cross 221 F1
Annandale Gdns. Cross 221 F1
Annandale. Gree 83 F1
Annandale La. Cross 221 F1
Annandale St. Glasg 117 D2
Annandale View. Cross 221 F1
Annandale Way. Irvine 220 A3
Annanhill Ave. Kilmk 222 B1
Annanhill Pl. Kilw 207 D2
Annbank St. Glasg 117 F3
Annbank St. Lark 184 C2
Anne Ave. Ren 94 B2
Anne Cres. Kirk 79 E2
Anne Dr. B of A 2 A3
Anne Dr. Sten 23 F2
Anne St. All 9 F4
Annerley Ct. Coat 121 F3
Annerley Pl. Coat 121 F3
Annes Ct. Glasg 117 F2
Annet Rd. Bank 39 E3
Annette St. Glasg 117 D1
Annfield Dr. Stir 7 E3
Annfield Gdns. Stir 7 D3
Annfield Gdns. Udd 140 B1
Annfield Glen Rd. Ayr 239 D2
Annfield Pl. Glasg 117 F4
Annfield Rd. Pres 236 A4
Annfield Terr. Pres 236 A4
Annick Cotts. Stew 196 B3
Annick Cres. Stew 211 F4
Annick Ct. Irvine 219 E1
Annick Dr. Bear 75 E1
Annick Dr. Irvine 220 A1
Annick Pl. Kilmk 228 A3
Annick Pl. Troon 229 F2
Annick Rd. Irvine 219 F1
Annick Rd. Irvine 220 A1
Annick Roundabout. Irvine 219 E1
Annick St. Glasg 119 D3
Annick St. Glasg 139 E3
Annick View. Irvine 219 F1
Anniesdale Ave. Stepps 99 E3
Anniehill View. Plains 104 A1
Anniesland Cres. Glasg 95 D3
Anniesland Ind Est. Glasg 95 F4
Anniesland Rd. Glasg 95 E3
Annieston. Twe 59 F2
Anniversary Ave. E Kil 180 B4
Annpit Rd. Ayr 236 A2
Annsfield Rd. Ham 183 E4
Ansdell Ave. Udd 161 E4
Anson Ave. Falk 41 F2
Anson St. Glasg 117 F2
Anson Way. Ren 94 B1
Anstruther Ct. Law 186 C3
Anstruther St. Glasg 118 C3
Anstruther St. Law 186 C3
Antermony Rd. M of C 58 C3
Antigua St. Green 46 A2
Antigua Way. E Kil 159 D1
Anton Cres. Kils 60 C4
Antonine Ave. Mother 163 E4
Antonine Gdns. Dunt 74 A3
Antonine Gdns. Falk 41 E3
Antonine Gr. Bon 39 F2
Antonine. Kirk 59 D1
Antonine Rd. Bear 75 D3
Antonine St. Falk 41 E3
Antrim La. Lark 185 D2
Anwoth St. Glasg 119 D2
Apollo Path. Holy 143 D3
Appin Ct. Kirk 59 D1
Appin Rd. Glasg 118 B4
Appin Terr. Glasg 138 B2
Appin Terr. Ham 161 F2
Appin Terr. Shot 147 D2
Appin Way. Glenm 102 C2
Appin Way. Udd 141 D2
Appleby Cl. E Kil 179 F3
Appleby St. Glasg 97 D2
Applecross Gdns. Muir 80 C2
Applecross Quadrant. Wish 165 D3
Applecross Rd. Kirk 59 D1
Applecross St. Glasg 97 D2
Appledore Cres. Udd 141 D2
Apsley La. Glasg 96 A1
Apsley St. Glasg 96 A1
Aqua Ave. Ham 161 F1
Aquila Way. Car 187 E1
Araburn Dr. E Kil 180 C3
Aranthrue Cres. Ren 94 B2
Aranthrue Dr. Ren 94 B2
Aray St. Glasg 96 B3
Arbroath Ave. Glasg 115 D2
Arbroath Cres. Stir 2 A2
Arbroath Gr. Ham 162 A1
Arbuckle Pl. Plains 104 A2
Arbuckle Rd. Cald 104 A2
Arbuckle Rd. Plains 104 A2
Arbuckle St. Kilmk 228 A4
Arbuthnot St. Falk 41 F3
Arcade. Stir 7 D4
Arcadia St. Glasg 117 F3
Arcadia St. Hat 142 A4
Arcan Cres. Glasg 75 D1
Arch Way. Kils 36 B1
Archerfield Ave. Glasg 119 D1
Archerfield Cres. Glasg 119 D1
Archerfield Dr. Glasg 119 D1
Archerfield Gr. Glasg 119 D1
Archerhill Ave. Glasg 95 D4
Archerhill Cotts. Glasg 95 D4
Archerhill Cres. Glasg 95 D4
Archerhill Rd. Glasg 95 D4
Archerhill Sq. Glasg 94 C4
Archerhill Terr. Glasg 95 D4
Archers Ave. Stir 7 E2
Archibald Dr. Dalry 191 D4
Archibald Terr. M of C 58 A3
Archiebald Pl. Hat 142 B2
Archray Rd. Cumb 82 A3
Arcon Ave. Moss 237 F3
Ard La. New 165 F3
Ard Loan. Holy 143 D3
Ard Rd. Ren 94 A2
Ard St. Glasg 119 D2
Ardardan Cotts. Card 25 F1
Ardargie Dr. Glasg 139 E4
Ardargie Gr. Glasg 139 E4
Ardargie Pl. Glasg 139 E4
Ardayre Rd. Pres 236 A4
Ardbeg Ave. Bish 78 B1
Ardbeg Ave. Glasg 138 C2
Ardbeg Ave. Kilmk 222 C2
Ardbeg Ct. Irvine 219 F3
Ardbeg La. Glasg 117 D1
Ardbeg Rd. Green 46 B1
Ardbeg St. Glasg 117 D1
Ardchoille Dr. Steven 206 C1
Ardchoille La. Steven 206 C1
Ardconnel St. Glasg 135 F2
Ardeer La. Steven 217 F3
Arden Ave. Glasg 135 F1
Arden Ct. Ham 162 B1
Arden Dr. Glasg 136 A2
Arden Gr. Kils 36 B1
Arden Hill. Rhu 15 E3
Arden Pl. Glasg 135 F1
Arden Rd. Green 46 B1
Arden Rd. Ham 162 B1
Arden St. Plains 104 A1
Arden Terr. Ham 162 B1
Ardencaple Dr. Helen 16 A1
Ardencaple Quadrant. Helen 16 A1
Ardenclutha Ave. Ham 162 A2
Ardenclutha Dr. P Glasg 47 D1
Ardenconnel Ho. Rhu 15 E3
Ardenconnel Way. Rhu 15 E3
Ardencraig Cres. Glasg 137 E1
Ardencraig Dr. Glasg 138 A1
Ardencraig La. Glasg 137 E1
Ardencraig Quadrant. Glasg 137 F1
Ardencraig Rd. Glasg 137 F1
Ardencraig Rd. Glasg 137 F2
Ardencraig St. Glasg 138 A1
Ardencraig Terr. Glasg 137 F1
Ardenlea St. Glasg 118 A2
Ardenlea. Tan 140 C4
Ardery St. Glasg 96 A1
Ardessie St. Glasg 76 B1
Ardfern Rd. Chap 124 A3
Ardfern St. Glasg 119 D2
Ardfin Ct. Pres 236 B3
Ardfin Rd. Pres 236 B3
Ardgare. Rhu 15 D4
Ardgay Pl. Glasg 119 D2
Ardgay St. Glasg 119 D2
Ardgay Way. Glasg 138 A2
Ardgour Ct. Ham 161 F3
Ardgour Dr. Lin 112 A3
Ardgour Par. Holy 143 E1
Ardgour Pl. Kilmk 222 C2
Ardgour Rd. Kilmk 222 C2
Ardgowan Ave. Pais 113 F2
Ardgowan Ct. Pais 114 A2
Ardgowan Dr. Tan 140 C4
Ardgowan Pl. Shot 146 C3
Ardgowan St. Green 45 F3
Ardgowan St. P Glasg 47 D1
Ardgowan St. Pais 113 F2
Ardgowan Terrace La. Glasg 96 B1
Ardgryfe Cres. Hous 91 E1
Ardholm St. Glasg 119 D3
Ardhu Pl. Glasg 75 D2
Ardlamont Sq. Lin 112 B3
Ardlaw St. Glasg 115 F3
Ardle Ave. Kilmk 228 A3
Ardle Rd. Glasg 136 C3
Ardlui Gdns. Miln 54 B2
Ardlui Rd. Ayr 236 A2
Ardlui St. Glasg 118 C2
Ardmaleish Cres. Glasg 137 F1
Ardmaleish Dr. Glasg 137 E1
Ardmaleish Rd. Glasg 137 F1
Ardmaleish St. Glasg 137 E1
Ardmaleish Terr. Glasg 137 F1
Ardmay Cres. Glasg 137 E4
Ardmillan. Kilw 207 D1
Ardmillan St. Glasg 118 C4
Ardmore Ct. Irvine 220 A3
Ardmore Pl. Green 45 F2
Ardmore Rd. Green 46 B1
Ardmore Rd. P Glasg 47 E1
Ardmore Rd. P Glasg 68 B4
Ardmory Ave. Glasg 137 E4
Ardmory La. Glasg 137 F4
Ardmory Pl. Glasg 137 F4
Ardnahoe Ave. Glasg 137 F4
Ardnahoe Pl. Glasg 137 E4
Ardneil Ave. W Kil 190 B2
Ardneil Ct. Ard 205 D2
Ardneil Rd. Glasg 115 F3
Ardnish St. Glasg 115 F4
Ardo Gdns. Glasg 116 A3
Ardoch Cres. Dumb 49 E2
Ardoch Cres. Steven 217 F3
Ardoch Gdns. Glasg 138 C3
Ardoch Gr. Glasg 138 C3
Ardoch Path. New 165 F3
Ardoch Rd. Bear 76 A3
Ardoch St. Glasg 97 E2
Ardoch Way. Muir 80 C1
Ardochrig. E Kil 180 C3
Ardressie Pl. Glasg 96 B3
Ardrossan High Rd. W Kil 190 C2
Ardrossan Rd. Salt 216 C4
Ardrossan Rd. W Kil 190 B1
Ardshiel Rd. Glasg 115 F4
Ardsloy La. Glasg 95 D2
Ardsloy Pl. Glasg 95 D2
Ardtoe Cres. Stepps 99 F3
Ardtoe Pl. Stepps 99 F3
Arduthie Rd. Glasg 115 F4
Ardvreck Pl. Sten 24 A2
Ardwell Rd. Glasg 115 F2
Argosy Way. Ren 94 B1
Argus Ave. Chap 123 E1
Argyle Cres. Aird 122 C3
Argyle Cres. Ham 161 F2
Argyle Gdns. Lennox 57 F4
Argyle Pk. Ayr 236 A1
Argyle Pl. Kils 60 C4
Argyle Pl. Salt 216 C4
Argyle Rd. Bear 75 F4
Argyle Rd. Gour 44 C3
Argyle Rd. Salt 216 C4
Argyle St E. Helen 16 B1
Argyle St. Glasg 116 C4
Argyle St. Glasg 117 D4
Argyle St. Green 45 F3
Argyle St. Pais 113 E2
Argyle St. Stone 198 C1
Argyle St W. Helen 16 B1
Argyll Arc. Glasg 117 E4
Argyll Ave. Dumb 50 B2
Argyll Ave. Falk 42 B3
Argyll Ave. Inch 93 F1
Argyll Ave. Ren 94 A2
Argyll Ave. Stir 2 B1
Argyll Est. Alex 27 E4
Argyll Gdns. Lark 185 D2
Argyll Pl. All 10 B4
Argyll Pl. Dumb 50 B2
Argyll Pl. E Kil 160 B2
Argyll Pl. Hat 141 F1
Argyll Rd. Clyde 74 B1
Argyll Rd. Ros 15 D2
Argyll St. Alex 27 E4
Argyll St. All 10 B4
Arisaig Dr. Bear 76 A2
Arisaig Dr. Glasg 115 F2
Arisaig Pl. Glasg 115 F2
Arisdale Cres. Newt M 156 C3
Ark La. Glasg 117 F4
Arkaig Ave. Plains 103 F2
Arkaig St. Wish 165 D1
Arkle Terr. Glasg 138 C2
Arkleston Cres. Pais 114 A4
Arkleston Rd. Pais 114 A3
Arkleston Rd. Pais 114 B4
Arkleston Rd. Ren 114 A4
Arklet Rd. Glasg 115 F4
Arkwright Way. Irvine 219 F2
Arlington St. Glasg 96 C1
Armadale Ct. Glasg 118 A4
Armadale Path. Glasg 118 A4
Armadale Pl. Glasg 118 A4
Armadale Pl. Green 45 F2
Armadale Rd. Rhu 15 F2
Armadale St. Glasg 118 A4
Armine Path. Holy 143 E2
Armour Ave. Aird 122 C4
Armour Ave. Cowie 12 B4
Armour Ct. Kirk 59 D1
Armour Ct. Udd 161 D3
Armour Dr. Ayr 239 E3
Armour Dr. Kirk 59 D1
Armour Gdns. Kirk 59 D1
Armour Gr. Mother 164 A2
Armour Pl. Ard 205 E2
Armour Pl. Holy 143 E2
Armour Pl. John 112 A2
Armour Pl. Kirk 59 D1
Armour Pl. Lin 112 B3
Armour Pl. Stew 195 F1
Armour St. Glasg 117 F3
Armour St. John 112 A2
Armour St. Kilmk 227 F4
Armstrong Cres. Tan 141 D4
Armstrong Gr. E Kil 180 B4
Armstrong Rd. Helen 25 D4
Armstrong Rd. Kilmk 223 E1
Arnbrae Rd. Kils 36 A1
Arness Terr. Kilmk 222 C2
Arngask Rd. Glasg 115 F4
Arnhall Pl. Glasg 115 F2
Arnhem St. Glasg 139 E3
Arnholm Pl. Glasg 115 F2
Arnisdale Pl. Glasg 120 A4
Arnisdale Rd. Glasg 120 A4
Arnisdale Way. Glasg 138 A2
Arniston St. Glasg 118 C4
Arnol Pl. Glasg 119 F4
Arnold Ave. Bish 78 A1
Arnold St. Glasg 97 D3
Arnot St. Falk 42 B2
Arnothill Ct. Falk 41 F3
Arnothill. Falk 42 A2
Arnothill Gdns. Falk 42 A2
Arnothill La. Falk 41 F2
Arnothill Mews. Falk 42 A2
Arnott Dr. Coat 122 A2
Arnott Quadrant. Mother 142 B1
Arnott Way. Glasg 139 D3
Arnprior Gdns. Muir 80 C1
Arnprior Pl. Ayr 238 C1
Arnprior Quadrant. Glasg 137 E2
Arnprior Rd. Glasg 137 E2
Arnprior St. Glasg 137 E2
Arns Gr. All 9 F4
Arnside Ave. Glasg 136 B2
Arnswell. N Sau 5 E1
Arnum Gdns. Car 187 F1
Arnum Pl. Car 187 F1
Arnwood Dr. Glasg 96 A3
Aron Terr. Glasg 138 C2
Arondale Rd. Plains 103 F2
Aros Dr. Glasg 115 F1
Aros La. Glasg 115 E1
Aros Rd. Rhu 15 E3
Arran Ave. Coat 122 B2
Arran Ave. Dumb 49 E3
Arran Ave. Inch 93 F1
Arran Ave. Kilmk 223 D2
Arran Ave. P Glasg 69 D4

Arran Cres. Beith	150	B1
Arran Ct. All	10	A3
Arran Ct. Green	45	D3
Arran Ct. Steven	217	E4
Arran Dr. Aird	102	C1
Arran Dr. Cumb	82	B4
Arran Dr. Glasg	115	F2
Arran Dr. Glasg	136	B3
Arran Dr. Glenm	102	C3
Arran Dr. John	111	E1
Arran Dr. Kirk	58	C1
Arran Dr. Pais	133	F4
Arran. E Kil	160	B1
Arran Gdns. Car	201	F4
Arran Gdns. Ham	162	C1
Arran Gdns. Troon	229	E4
Arran La. Muir	81	D1
Arran La. Salt	205	E1
Arran Path. Lark	185	E1
Arran Pk. Pres	236	A3
Arran Pl. Clyde	74	B1
Arran Pl. Coat	122	B2
Arran Pl. Irvine	219	D3
Arran Pl. Lin	112	A3
Arran Pl. Salt	205	E1
Arran Pl. Salt	206	A1
Arran Rd. Gour	44	B3
Arran Rd. Mother	163	E4
Arran Rd. Ren	94	B1
Arran Rd. Troon	229	E4
Arran Terr. Ayr	235	F1
Arran Terr. Falk	41	E2
Arran Terr. Glasg	137	F3
Arran Tower. Glasg	138	C2
Arran View. Kils	60	B4
Arran View. Stew	195	F1
Arranview Ct. Ayr	236	A2
Arranview St. Chap	123	F1
Arrochar Ct. Glasg	96	C4
Arrochar Dr. Glasg	76	B1
Arrochar Path. Glasg	76	B1
Arrochar St. Glasg	76	B1
Arrol Cres. All	10	B4
Arrol Dr. Ayr	238	B3
Arrol Pk. Ayr	238	C3
Arrol Pl. E Kil	181	D3
Arrol Pl. Glasg	118	A2
Arrol St. Glasg	114	C4
Arrothill Dr. Kilmk	227	E4
Arrotshole Rd. E Kil	159	D2
Arrowsmith Ave. Glasg	95	E4
Artarman Rd. Rhu	15	F2
Arthur Ave. Barr	134	A1
Arthur Ct. W Kil	190	B3
Arthur Pl. Newt M	157	F3
Arthur Rd. Pais	133	F4
Arthur St. Alex	27	F2
Arthur St. Ayr	238	C4
Arthur St. Glasg	96	B1
Arthur St. Green	46	A2
Arthur St. Ham	162	B3
Arthur St. Newt M	157	F3
Arthur St. Pais	113	E3
Arthur St. Salt	217	D4
Arthur St. Steven	217	E4
Arthur St. W Kil	190	B3
Arthur's Dr. Sten	23	F1
Arthurlie Ave. Barr	134	B1
Arthurlie Ave. Uplaw	153	E2
Arthurlie Dr. Glasg	136	B1
Arthurlie Dr. Newt M	156	B2
Arthurlie Dr. Uplaw	153	D2
Arthurlie Pl. Salt	216	C4
Arthurlie St. Barr	134	B1
Arthurlie St. Glasg	115	F4
Arthurston Rd. Bonh	28	A4
Arundel Dr. Bish	78	A2
Arundel Dr. Glasg	137	D4
Ascaig Cres. Glasg	115	F1
Ascog Rd. Bear	75	F1
Ascog St. Glasg	117	D1
Ascot Ave. Glasg	95	F3
Ascot. Glasg	96	A3
Ash Ave. E Kil	180	B3
Ash Ct. E Kil	180	B3
Ash Dr. Beith	150	A1
Ash Gr. All	10	B3
Ash Gr. Bish	98	A4
Ash Gr. Klrk	79	D3
Ash Gr. Law	186	C3
Ash Gr. Sten	23	F1
Ash Gr. Tan	141	D4
Ash Pl. Bank	38	C1
Ash Pl. E Kil	180	B3
Ash Pl. John	112	A1
Ash Pl. Kilmk	227	E4
Ash Rd. Clyde	74	A3
Ash Rd. Cumb	62	C3
Ash Rd. Dumb	49	F2
Ash Rd. Glasg	120	A2
Ash Terr. Stir	6	C3
Ash Wlk. Glasg	138	B2
Ash Wlk. Holy	143	D3
Ashbrae Gdns. Stir	7	D1
Ashburn Gate. Gour	44	B4
Ashburn Gdns. Gour	44	B4
Ashburn Gdns. Miln	54	C1
Ashburn Loan. Lark	185	D2
Ashburn Rd. Miln	54	C1
Ashburton La. Glasg	96	A3
Ashburton Pk. E Kil	180	A4
Ashburton Rd. Glasg	96	A3
Ashby Cres. Bear	75	F1
Ashcroft Ave. Lennox	57	F4
Ashcroft Dr. Glasg	137	F3
Ashcroft. E Kil	160	B3
Ashcroft Wlk. Lennox	57	F4
Ashdale Ave. Gour	44	B4
Ashdale Dr. Glasg	115	F2
Ashdale Rd. Kilmk	222	C2
Ashdene St. Glasg	97	D4
Asher Rd. Chap	123	F1
Ashfield. Bish	78	A2
Ashfield Cotts. Gart	20	A2
Ashfield Rd. Law	187	D3
Ashfield Rd. Miln	55	D1
Ashfield Rd. Newt M	157	F3
Ashfield St. Glasg	97	E2
Ashgill Pl. Glasg	97	E3
Ashgill Rd. Glasg	97	E4
Ashgillhead Rd. Ash	185	F1
Ashgrove. Aird	123	E4
Ashgrove Ave. Gour	44	B4
Ashgrove Ave. Steven	206	C1
Ashgrove. Cald	105	D3
Ashgrove. Coat	122	A2
Ashgrove. Irvine	219	E3
Ashgrove La. P Glasg	47	E1
Ashgrove. Muir	80	C1
Ashgrove Rd. Ard	205	E2
Ashgrove Rd. Kilw	207	E2
Ashgrove Rd. Hat	142	A4
Ashgrove St. Ayr	239	D4
Ashgrove St. Glasg	118	A1
Ashgrove Workshops. Kilw	207	E2
Ashiestiel Ct. Cumb	82	C4
Ashiestiel Pl. Cumb	82	C4
Ashiestiel Rd. Cumb	82	C4
Ashkirk Dr. Ash	199	F4
Ashkirk Dr. Glasg	115	F2
Ashland Ave. Ham	183	E3
Ashlea Dr. Glasg	136	B2
Ashlea Gdns. Plains	103	F2
Ashley Dr. Tan	141	D3
Ashley La. Glasg	96	C1
Ashley Pk. Tan	141	E3
Ashley Pl. Udd	161	E4
Ashley Rise. Bonh	39	F3
Ashley St. Bon	39	F3
Ashley St. Glasg	96	C1
Ashley Terr. All	10	A4
Ashmore Rd. Glasg	136	C3
Ashton Dr. Helen	25	D4
Ashton Dr. Hurl	228	C3
Ashton Gn. E Kil	159	F1
Ashton La N. Glasg	96	B1
Ashton Pl. Gour	44	B4
Ashton Rd. Glasg	96	B1
Ashton Rd. Glasg	118	A1
Ashton Rd. Gour	44	B4
Ashton St. Mother	142	B1
Ashton Terr. Gour	44	B4
Ashton View. Dumb	49	D2
Ashton Way. Pais	132	C2
Ashtree Ct. O Kill	73	D3
Ashtree Gr. Newt M	156	B2
Ashtree Rd. Glasg	136	B4
Ashvale Cres. Glasg	97	F2
Ashworth Terr. Ham	162	A2
Aspen Dr. Glasg	98	A2
Aspen Pl. John	112	A1
Aspen Rd. Ayr	239	E3
Aspen Way. Ham	162	C1
Asquith Pl. Hat	142	B3
Assloss Rd. Kilmk	223	E2
Aster Dr. Glasg	138	A2
Aster Gdns. Glasg	135	E2
Aster Gdns. Mother	163	F3
Athelstane Dr. Cumb	82	B4
Athelstane Rd. Glasg	95	E4
Athena Way. Tan	141	D4
Athole Gdns. Glasg	96	B2
Athole La. Glasg	96	B2
Athole La. Gour	44	B4
Athole St. Helen	16	C1
Athole Terr. Gour	44	B2
Atholl Ave. Glasg	114	C4
Atholl Ave. Lennox	57	D1
Atholl Cres. Glasg	114	C3
Atholl Ct. Kirk	59	D1
Atholl Dr. Cumb	81	F4
Atholl Dr. Glasg	157	E4
Atholl Gdns. Bear	75	F4
Atholl Gdns. Bish	77	F2
Atholl Gdns. Glasg	138	C2
Atholl Gdns. Kilw	207	D2
Atholl La. Muir	81	D1
Atholl Pl. Coat	122	A2
Atholl Pl. Lin	112	A3
Atholl Pl. Stir	1	C1
Atholl St. Ham	162	A3
Atholl Terr. Tan	120	C1
Atlas Pl. Glasg	97	F2
Atlas Rd. Glasg	97	F2
Atlas Sq. Glasg	97	F2
Atlas St. Clyde	94	A4
Attercliffe Ave. Wish	164	B1
Attlee Ave. Clyde	74	C1
Attlee Pl. Clyde	74	C1
Attow Rd. Glasg	136	A3
Auburn Dr. Barr	134	B1
Auchans Ave. Dund	225	F1
Auchans Dr. Dund	225	F1
Auchans Pl. Fen	213	D3
Auchans Rd. Lin	92	A1
Auchenbeg Cres. Ayr	239	D2
Auchenbothie Rd. Kil	68	C3
Auchenbothie Rd. P Glasg	68	C3
Auchencar Dr. Kilmk	222	C2
Auchencrow St. Glasg	120	B4
Auchencruive. Miln	76	B4
Auchendarroch St. Green	46	B2
Auchendavie Rd. Kirk	59	D1
Auchendoon Cres. Ayr	238	B2
Auchendores Ave. P Glasg	69	D4
Auchenfoil La. P Glasg	68	B4
Auchenfoil Rd. Kil	67	F3
Auchenfoil Rd. P Glasg	68	B4
Auchengate Cres. Shew	224	C1
Auchengate. Troon	229	F4
Auchengeich Rd. Muir	80	B2
Auchengilloch. E Kil	180	C3
Auchenglen Dr. Muir	80	C1
Auchenglen Rd. Car	201	F2
Auchengreoch Ave. John	131	E4
Auchengreoch Rd. John	131	E3
Auchenharvie Pl. Irvine	219	F3
Auchenharvie Rd. Salt	206	A1
Auchenharvie Rd. Salt	217	D4
Auchenhove Cres. Kilb	149	D2
Auchenhowie Rd. Bish	76	B4
Auchenhowie Rd. Miln	76	B4
Auchenkilns Rd. Cumb	82	B3
Auchenkilns		
Roundabout. Cumb	82	B4
Auchenleck La. P Glasg	68	C4
Auchenleck Rd. P Glasg	68	C4
Auchenlodment Rd. John	112	A1
Auchenreoch Ave. Dumb	50	A3
Auchenreoch. M of C	59	D3
Auchentibber Rd. Ham	161	D2
Auchentorlie Quadrant. Pais	114	A2
Auchentorlie St. Glasg	95	F1
Auchentoshan Ave. Dunt	73	F3
Auchentoshan Terr. Glasg	97	F1
Auchentrae Cres. Ayr	238	B3
Auchinairn Rd. Bish	98	A4
Auchinairn Rd. Glasg	98	B4
Auchinbaird. N Sau	5	E1
Auchinbee Farm Rd. Cumb	61	D2
Auchinbee Way. Cumb	61	D2
Auchincampbell Rd. Ham	162	B2
Auchincarroch Rd. Bonh	28	A4
Auchincarroch Rd. Gart	20	C2
Auchincloch Dr. Bank	38	C1
Auchincruive Ave. Pres	236	B3
Auchingill Pl. Glasg	100	B1
Auchingill Rd. Glasg	100	B1
Auchingramont Rd. Ham	162	B2
Auchinlea Dr. Cle	144	B1
Auchinlea Rd. Glasg	99	F1
Auchinleck Ave. Glasg	98	C3
Auchinleck Cres. Glasg	98	C3
Auchinleck Dr. Glasg	98	C3
Auchinleck Gdns. Glasg	98	C3
Auchinleck Rd. Dunt	74	A4
Auchinleck Rd. Glasg	98	C4
Auchinleck Terr. Dunt	74	A4
Auchinloch Rd. Klrk	79	E2
Auchinloch St. Glasg	97	F2
Auchinraith Ave. Ham	162	B3
Auchinraith Rd. Udd	161	F3
Auchinraith Terr. Udd	161	F3
Auchinvole Cres. Kils	60	A4
Auchmannoch Ave. Glasg	114	C3
Auchmead Rd. Gour	44	C2
Auchmountain Rd. Green	46	B2
Auchmountain Rd. Green	46	C1
Auchmountain Rd. Kil	67	F4
Auchnacraig Rd. Dunt	74	B4
Auchneagh Ave. Green	45	D2
Auchneagh Cres. Green	45	D2
Auchneagh Farm La. Green	45	D3
Auchneagh Farm Rd. Green	45	D3
Auchneagh Rd. Green	45	D2
Auchter Ave. New	166	B3
Auchter Rd. Wish	165	E2
Auchterburn Rd. Alla	166	C4
Auckland Pk. E Kil	159	D1
Auckland Pl. Clyde	73	E2
Auckland St. Glasg	97	D2
Auld Clay Rd. Ard	206	C4
Auld Kirk Rd. Camb	139	E2
Auld Rd The. Cumb	62	A2
Auld St. Clyde	73	F2
Auld's Brae. Aird	123	D4
Auldbar Rd. Glasg	115	F2
Auldbar Terr. Pais	114	A1
Auldburn Rd. Glasg	136	A3
Auldearn Rd. Glasg	98	B4
Auldgirth Rd. Glasg	115	F2
Auldhame St. Coat	121	F4
Auldhouse Ave. Glasg	136	A3
Auldhouse Rd. Auld	180	B1
Auldhouse Rd. Glasg	136	B3
Auldhouse Terr. Glasg	136	B3
Auldlea Rd. Beith	150	A1
Auldton Terr. Ash	185	F1
Aultbea St. Glasg	97	D4
Aultmore Rd. Glasg	119	F4
Aurs Cres. Barr	134	B1
Aurs Dr. Barr	134	B1
Aurs Glen. Barr	134	B1
Aurs Pl. Barr	134	C1
Aurs Rd. Barr	134	C1
Aurs Rd. Newt M	155	F4
Aursbridge Cres. Barr	134	B1
Aursbridge Dr. Barr	134	B1
Austen La. Glasg	95	F3
Austen Rd. Glasg	95	F3
Austine Dr. Ham	183	F4
Aven Dr. Laur	42	C2
Avenel Rd. Glasg	75	F1
Avenue End Rd. Glasg	99	D1
Avenue Oak. Miln	75	F4
Avenue Pk. B of A	1	C4
Avenue Sq. Stew	211	E4
Avenue St. Glasg	118	A1
Avenue St. Glasg	118	A3
Avenue St. Stew	195	E1
Avenue The. B of A	2	A4
Avenue The. Newt M	156	B2
Avenue The. Sten	24	B1
Avenue The. W Kil	190	C4
Avenuehead Rd. Muir	101	D4
Avenuepark St. Glasg	96	C3
Aviemore Gdns. Bear	76	A3
Aviemore Rd. Glasg	115	F2
Avils Hill. Kilb	149	D1
Avils Pl. Kilb	149	D1
Avoch St. Glasg	100	A1
Avon Ave. Bear	76	A2
Avon Ave. Car	187	F1
Avon Ave. Gree	84	B2
Avon Ct. Falk	42	B1
Avon Ct. Irvine	220	A2
Avon Dr. Hat	142	B2
Avon Dr. Lin	112	A3
Avon Pk. Avon	87	F3
Avon Pl. Coat	101	E1
Avon Pl. Kilmk	228	A3
Avon Pl. Lark	199	D4
Avon Rd. Bish	98	A4
Avon Rd. Glasg	136	A1
Avon Rd. Lark	199	D4
Avon St. Duni	21	E2
Avon St. Ham	162	C2
Avon St. Lark	184	C2
Avon St. Mother	163	F3
Avon Tower. Mother	163	F3
Avon Wynd. New	165	F3
Avonbank Cres. Ham	183	F4
Avonbank Rd. Glasg	137	F4
Avonbank Rd. Lark	184	C2
Avonbrae Cres. Ham	183	F4
Avonbridge Rd. Slam	86	A4
Avondale Ave. E Kil	159	F1
Avondale Dr. Pais	114	A3
Avondale Pl. E Kil	181	D4
Avondale Rd. W Kil	190	B3
Avondale St. Glasg	99	D1
Avonhead Ave. Cumb	82	B4
Avonhead. E Kil	180	C3
Avonhead Gdns. Cumb	82	B4
Avonhead Rd. Cumb	82	B4
Avonmouth Pl. Gour	44	C3
Avonside Dr. Duni	21	E3
Avonside Gr. Ham	162	C2
Avonspark St. Glasg	98	A2
Aylmer Rd. Glasg	136	C3
Ayr Dr. Aird	123	D3
Ayr La. Gour	44	C2
Ayr Rd. Ash	185	F1
Ayr Rd. Glasg	157	D4
Ayr Rd. Irvine	224	B4
Ayr Rd. Kilmk	227	C1
Ayr Rd. Newt M	156	B2
Ayr Rd. Pres	236	A3
Ayr Rd. Shew	224	B4
Ayr St. Glasg	97	F2
Ayr St. Troon	229	E1
Ayr Terr. Gour	44	C2
Ayton Pk N. E Kil	160	A2
Ayton Pk S. E Kil	160	A2
Aytoun Dr. Ersk	72	C2
Aytoun Rd. Glasg	116	C2
Baads Rd. Cald	106	B1
Baberton Way. Kilw	207	D2
Babylon Ave. Hat	142	A2
Babylon Dr. Hat	142	A2
Babylon Pl. Hat	142	A2
Babylon Rd. Hat	142	A2
Back Cswy. Glasg	118	B3
Back Hawkhill Ave. Ayr	236	A1
Back O Dykes Rd. Kirk	80	A4
Back O Hill. Hous	91	D1
Back O' Hill Rd. Bish	56	C1
Back O' Hill Rd. Stir	2	A1
Back O'Barns. Ham	162	C2
Back Peebles St. Ayr	235	F1
Back Rd. Alva	4	C4
Back Row. Ham	162	C2
Back Sneddon St. Pais	113	F3
Back St. Alex	27	E1
Backbrae St. Kils	60	B4
Backburn. Beith	171	D4
Backmuir Cres. Ham	162	A3
Backmuir Pl. Ham	162	A3
Backmuir Rd. Glasg	75	D2
Backmuir Rd. Ham	162	A3
Backwood Ct. Clack	10	C3
Badenheath Pl. Cumb	81	E3
Badenheath Terr. Cumb	81	F2
Badenoch Rd. Kirk	59	E1
Bagnell St. Glasg	97	F3
Bahamas Way. E Kil	159	D1
Baidland Ave. Beith	191	D3
Bailie Dr. Bear	75	E4
Bailie Fyfe Way. Falk	186	A4
Bailiehill Pl. Kilmk	222	B1
Bailie Wynd. Tan	141	D4
Baillie Dr. E Kil	160	B2
Baillie Dr. Udd	141	D2
Baillie Gdns. Wish	165	F2
Baillie Pl. E Kil	160	B2
Baillie Waugh Rd. Stir	7	E2
Baillies La. Aird	123	D4
Bailliesmuir Pl. New	166	A3
Baillieston Ave. Kilb	170	A4
Baillieston Rd. Glasg	119	F2
Baillieston Rd. Glasg	120	A1
Bain Cres. Helen	16	C2
Bain St. Glasg	117	F3
Baine St. Green	45	E3
Bainfield Rd. Card	48	A4
Baingle Brae. Tull	4	A2
Baingle Cres. Tull	4	A2
Bainsford St. Glasg	118	C3
Baird Ave. Aird	103	D1
Baird Ave. Glasg	114	C4
Baird Ave. Helen	16	A1
Baird Ave. Kilw	207	F2
Baird Ave. Lark	199	E4
Baird Brae. Glasg	97	D3
Baird Cres. Alex	27	E4
Baird Cres. Cumb	82	A4
Baird Ct. Clyde	74	A1
Baird Ct. Kilw	207	D2
Baird Dr. Bear	75	E3
Baird Dr. Ersk	72	C2
Baird Hill. E Kil	180	C4
Baird Pl. Hat	142	A4
Baird Pl. Kilmk	223	D1
Baird Pl. Pres	233	E2
Baird Pl. Wish	165	F2
Baird Rd. Ayr	238	C1
Baird Rd. Kilmk	223	D1
Baird Rd. Pres	233	E2
Baird St. Coat	122	A4
Baird St. Falk	41	E3
Baird St. Glasg	97	E1
Baird Terr. East	127	E3
Bairds Cres. Ham	162	B2
Bairdsland View. Hat	142	A3
Bairns Ford Ave. Falk	42	A4
Bairns Ford Ct. Falk	42	A4
Bairns Ford Dr. Falk	42	A4
Baker St. Glasg	116	C1
Baker St. Green	46	A2
Baker St. Stir	7	D4
Bakewell Rd. Glasg	120	A3
Balaclava St. Glasg	117	D4
Balado Rd. Glasg	119	F4
Balbakie Rd. East	127	F3
Balbeg St. Glasg	115	F3
Balbeggie St. Glasg	119	E2
Balblair Rd. Glasg	115	F1
Balcarres Ave. Glasg	96	B3
Balcastle Gdns. Kils	36	A1
Balcastle Rd. Kils	36	A1
Balcastle Rd. Slam	86	A3
Balcomie Cres. Troon	230	A1
Balcomie St. Glasg	99	D1
Balcomie Terr. Ham	183	D4
Balcurvie Rd. Glasg	100	A1
Baldernock Rd. Miln	55	E1
Baldinnie Rd. Glasg	120	A4
Baldorran Cres. Cumb	61	D2
Baldovan Cres. Glasg	119	F4
Baldovie Rd. Glasg	115	E2
Baldragon Rd. Glasg	100	B3
Baldric Rd. Glasg	95	E3
Baldwin Ave. Glasg	95	E4
Balerno Dr. Glasg	115	F2
Balfearn Dr. Eagle	178	C3
Balfleurs St. Miln	55	D1
Balfluig St. Glasg	99	F1
Balfour Ave. Beith	171	D4
Balfour Cres. Lar	23	E1
Balfour Cres. Plea	12	B2
Balfour Ct. Kilmk	223	E2
Balfour St. All	10	B4
Balfour St. Bann	7	E1
Balfour St. Bon	39	F3
Balfour St. Glasg	96	B3
Balfour St. P Glasg	47	D1
Balfour St. Stir	1	C1
Balfour Terr. E Kil	180	C4

245

Balfour Wynd. Lark Bearhope St. Green

Balfour Wynd. Lark 185 E1
Balfron Cres. Ham 161 F2
Balfron Rd. Glasg 115 F4
Balfron Rd. Green 46 B1
Balfron Rd. Pais 114 B3
Balgair Dr. Pais 114 A3
Balgair St. Glasg 97 D2
Balgair Terr. Glasg 119 D3
Balglass St. Glasg 97 D3
Balgonie Ave. Pais 113 D1
Balgonie Dr. Pais 113 E1
Balgonie Rd. Glasg 115 F2
Balgonie Woods. Pais 113 E1
Balgownie Cres. Glasg 136 A1
Balgray Ave. Kilb 170 A4
Balgray Ave. Kilmk 227 F1
Balgray Cres. Barr 134 C1
Balgray Rd. Beith 172 A3
Balgray Rd. Kilb 170 A4
Balgray Rd. Newt M 156 A3
Balgray Way. Irvine 220 A3
Balgraybank St. Glasg 98 A2
Balgrayhill Rd. Glasg 97 F3
Balgraystone Rd. Barr 155 E4
Balgraystone Rd. Newt M 155 E4
Balintore St. Glasg 119 D3
Baliol La. Glasg 96 C1
Baliol St. Glasg 96 C1
Baljaffray Rd. Bear 75 D4
Ballachalairy Yett. Strath 30 B2
Ballagan Pl. Miln 54 B1
Ballaig Ave. Bear 75 E3
Ballaig Cres. Stepps 99 E3
Ballantay Quadrant. Glasg 138 A2
Ballantay Rd. Glasg 138 A2
Ballantay Terr. Glasg 138 A2
Ballantine Ave. Glasg 115 D4
Ballantine Dr. Ayr 238 C3
Ballantrae Cres. Newt M 157 D2
Ballantrae Dr. Newt M 157 D2
Ballantrae Rd. Ham 161 F3
Ballater Cres. Wish 165 D3
Ballater Dr. Bear 76 A1
Ballater Dr. Inch 93 E4
Ballater Dr. Pais 114 A1
Ballater Dr. Stir 2 B2
Ballater Pl. Glasg 117 E2
Ballater St. Glasg 117 E2
Ballater Way. Glen 101 E3
Ballayne Dr. Muir 81 D2
Ballengeich Pass. Stir 2 A1
Ballengeich Rd. Stir 1 C1
Ballentrae Wynd. Holy 143 D3
Ballerup Terr. E Kil 180 C3
Ballewan Cres. Strath 31 D2
Ballindalloch Dr. Glasg 118 A4
Ballindalloch La. Glasg 118 A4
Ballinkier Ave. Bank 38 C2
Balloch Gdns. Glasg 115 F2
Balloch Rd. Alex 27 E4
Balloch Rd. Bonh 27 E4
Balloch Rd. Chap 124 A3
Balloch Rd. Cumb 61 E1
Balloch Rd. Green 46 A1
Balloch Rd. Shot 146 C3
Balloch View. Cumb 61 F1
Ballochmill Rd. Glasg 138 B4
Ballochmyle. E Kil 160 B2
Ballochney La. Aird 102 C1
Ballochney Rd. Plains 103 F2
Ballochney St. Aird 102 C1
Ballochnie Dr. Plains 104 A2
Ballogie Rd. Glasg 137 D4
Ballot Rd. Irvine 219 E2
Balmalloch Rd. Kils 36 B1
Balmartin Rd. Glasg 76 B1
Balmedie. Ersk 73 D1
Balmeg Ave. Glasg 157 E4
Balmerino Pl. Bish 98 B4
Balminnoch Pk. Ayr 238 B1
Balmoral Ave. Glenm 102 C3
Balmoral Cres. Coat 121 E2
Balmoral Cres. Inch 93 F3
Balmoral Dr. Bear 76 A1
Balmoral Dr. Falk 41 F2
Balmoral Dr. Glasg 138 C3
Balmoral Dr. Glasg 139 D4
Balmoral Gdns. Tan 120 C1
Balmoral Gdns. Udd 140 B1
Balmoral Path. Lark 185 E1
Balmoral Pl. E Kil 159 E1
Balmoral Pl. Gour 43 F3
Balmoral Pl. Sten 23 F2
Balmoral Pl. Stir 7 D4
Balmoral Rd. John 112 A1
Balmoral Rd. Kilmk 222 C1
Balmoral St. Falk 41 F2
Balmoral St. Glasg 95 D2
Balmoral Wynd. Stew 211 F4
Balmore Ct. Kil 89 E4
Balmore Dr. Ham 183 D4
Balmore Pl. Glasg 97 D3
Balmore Rd. Bish 77 E4
Balmore Rd. Bish 77 F4
Balmore Rd. Glasg 97 D3
Balmore Rd. Green 46 B1
Balmore Sq. Glasg 97 D3
Balmuildy Rd. Bish 77 E3
Balmuildy Rd. Glasg 77 E3
Balmulzier Rd. Slam 86 A4
Balornock Rd. Glasg 98 A3
Balquhatstone Cres. Slam 86 A3
Balquhidderock. Stir 7 E2
Balquidder Ct. Aird 103 D1
Balrossie Dr. Kil 89 D4
Balruddery Pl. Bish 98 B4
Balshagray Ave. Glasg 95 F2
Balshagray Cres. Glasg 95 F1
Balshagray Dr. Glasg 95 F2
Balshagray La. Glasg 95 F2
Balshagray Pl. Glasg 95 F2
Baltic Ct. Glasg 118 A2
Baltic La. Glasg 118 A2
Baltic Pl. Glasg 117 F2
Baltic St. Glasg 118 A2
Balure Cres. Fall 8 B2
Balure St. Glasg 118 B4
Balvaird Cres. Glasg 138 A4
Balvaird Dr. Glasg 138 A4
Balvenie St. Coat 122 A2
Balveny St. Glasg 99 E1
Balvicar Dr. Glasg 116 C1
Balvicar St. Glasg 116 C1
Balvie Ave. Glasg 75 D1
Balvie Ave. Glasg 136 B1
Balvie Cres. Miln 54 C1
Balvie Rd. Miln 54 C1
Banavie Rd. Glasg 96 A2
Banavie Rd. New 165 F3
Banchory Ave. Glasg 136 A3
Banchory Ave. Glenm 102 C3
Banchory Ave. Inch 93 E4
Banchory Cres. Bear 76 A1
Banchory Pl. Tull 4 B2
Banchory Rd. Wish 165 D3
Bandeath Rd. Fall 8 B2
Baneberry Path. E Kil 159 E2
Banff Ave. Aird 123 D2
Banff Pl. E Kil 180 B4
Banff Pl. Gour 44 B3
Banff Quadrant. Wish 165 D3
Banff Rd. Gour 44 B3
Banff St. Glasg 99 D1
Bangorshill St. Glasg 135 F2
Bank Ave. Miln 55 D2
Bank Ct. Irvine 219 F2
Bank Pk. E Kil 180 B4
Bank Pl. Irvine 219 F2
Bank Pl. Kilmk 227 F4
Bank Rd. East 127 F3
Bank Rd. Glasg 139 E4
Bank St. Aird 123 D4
Bank St. Alex 27 F3
Bank St. All 10 A3
Bank St. Barr 134 B1
Bank St. Coat 121 F3
Bank St. Falk 42 A3
Bank St. Glasg 96 C1
Bank St. Glasg 139 D3
Bank St. Green 45 F2
Bank St. Irvine 219 E2
Bank St. Irvine 219 F2
Bank St. Kilb 149 D1
Bank St. Kilmk 227 F4
Bank St. Neil 154 B4
Bank St. Pais 113 F2
Bank St. Pais 113 F3
Bank St. Pres 236 A4
Bank St. Slam 86 A3
Bank St. Stir 7 D4
Bank St. Troon 229 D1
Bank View. Chap 123 E1
Bank Way. Lark 185 D2
Bankbrae Ave. Glasg 135 D3
Bankend. B of W 110 C4
Bankend Pl. Kilmk 223 D3
Bankend Rd. B of W 110 C3
Bankend Rd. Dumb 49 F2
Bankend St. Glasg 99 D1
Bankfaulds Ave. Kilb 149 D1
Bankfield Dr. Ham 183 E4
Bankfoot Dr. Glasg 115 D2
Bankfoot Rd. Glasg 115 D2
Bankfoot Rd. Pais 113 D3
Bankglen Rd. Glasg 75 D2
Bankhall St. Glasg 117 D1
Bankhead Ave. Aird 123 E4
Bankhead Ave. Coat 121 E2
Bankhead Ave. Glasg 95 D3
Bankhead Ave. Hat 142 A2
Bankhead Ave. Spring 221 D1
Bankhead Cres. Bank 39 E3
Bankhead Dr. Glasg 138 A4
Bankhead Pl. Aird 123 E4
Bankhead Pl. Coat 121 E2
Bankhead Pl. Stew 195 F1
Bankhead Rd. E Kil 158 B4
Bankhead Rd. Glasg 137 F4
Bankhead Rd. Hat 207 F2
Bankhead Rd. Kirk 80 A4
Bankhead Rd. N Sau 5 E2
Bankhead Terr. Lan 215 D1
Bankholm Pl. Thorn 157 F3
Bankier Rd. Bank 38 C2
Bankier Terr. Bank 38 C2
Banknock St. Glasg 118 C3
Banks Rd. Kirk 58 B1
Bankside Ave. John 111 F2
Bankside Ct. Den 21 F1
Bankside. Falk 42 B4
Bankside Gdns. Kilb 149 D2
Banktop Pl. John 111 F2
Bankview Cres. Kirk 79 D4
Bankview Dr. Kirk 79 D4
Bannachra Cres. Alex 27 E3
Bannachra Dr. Helen 16 A1
Bannatyne Ave. Glasg 118 A4
Bannatyne St. Lan 215 D2
Banner Dr. Glasg 75 E1
Banner Rd. Glasg 75 E1
Bannercross Ave. Glasg 120 A3
Bannercross Dr. Glasg 120 A3
Bannercross Gdns. Glasg 120 A3
Bannerman Dr. Hat 142 B3
Bannerman Dr. Kilmk 223 E1
Bannerman Pl. Clyde 74 A1
Bannoch Pl. Kilw 208 A2
Bannoch Rd. Kilw 208 A1
Bannoch Rd. Kilw 208 A2
Bannock Rd. Fall 8 B2
Bannockburn Dr. Lark 185 E1
Bannockburn Pl. Kilmk 223 D2
Bannockburn Rd. Cowie 12 B4
Bannockburn Rd. Stir 7 E2
Bannockburn St. Green 45 E2
Bannockburn Station Rd. Fall 8 A2
Bantaskin St. Glasg 96 B4
Bantaskine Dr. Falk 41 F2
Bantaskine Gdns. Falk 41 F2
Bantaskine St. Falk 41 F2
Banton Pl. Bon 40 A2
Banton Pl. Glasg 120 A4
Banton Rd. Kils 37 E1
Banyan Cres. Tan 121 E1
Bar Hill Pl. Kils 60 A4
Barassie Cres. Cumb 61 F3
Barassie Ct. Udd 140 C1
Barassie Dr. B of W 110 B3
Barassie. E Kil 159 E2
Barassie Pl. Kilmk 227 F2
Barassie St. Troon 229 E2
Barassiebank La. Troon 229 E3
Barbadoes Pl. Kilmk 227 F3
Barbadoes Rd. Kilmk 227 F3
Barbados Gn. E Kil 159 D1
Barbae Pl. Udd 141 D2
Barbana Rd. E Kil 158 C1
Barbegs Cres. Kils 60 C2
Barberry Ave. Newt M 135 D1
Barberry Dr. Beith 171 D4
Barberry Gdns. Glasg 135 D1
Barbeth Gdns. Cumb 82 A3
Barbeth Pl. Cumb 82 A3
Barbeth Pl. Irvine 220 A3
Barbeth Rd. Cumb 82 A3
Barbeth Way. Cumb 82 A3
Barbour Ave. Stir 7 E2
Barbour's Pk. Stew 211 F4
Barbreck Rd. Glasg 116 C1
Barcaldine Ave. Muir 80 A1
Barcapel Ave. Newt M 156 C4
Barcaple Flats. Newt M 156 C4
Barclaven Rd. Kil 89 F4
Barclay Ave. John 112 A1
Barclay Ct. O Kill 73 D3
Barclay Dr. Helen 16 B2
Barclay Dr. Kilmk 223 E1
Barclay Pl. Stew 195 E1
Barclay Rd. Mother 163 D3
Barclay Sq. Ren 94 A1
Barclay St. Glasg 97 F3
Barclay St. O Kill 73 D3
Barcraigs Dr. Pais 133 F4
Bard Ave. Glasg 95 D4
Bardowie St. Glasg 97 D2
Bardrain Ave. John 112 B1
Bardrain Rd. Pais 133 E4
Bardrainney Ave. P Glasg 68 C4
Bardrill Dr. Bish 77 F1
Bardykes Rd. Udd 161 D4
Barefield St. Lark 185 D2
Barfillan Dr. Glasg 115 F3
Bargaran Rd. Glasg 115 D2
Bargarran Rd. Ersk 72 C2
Bargarron Dr. Pais 114 A4
Barge Ct. Rhu 15 E3
Bargeddie St. Glasg 98 B1
Bargeny. Kilw 207 D1
Bargrennan Rd. Troon 229 F3
Barhill La. Twe 59 F2
Barhill Rd. Ersk 73 D1
Barhill Terr. Twe 60 A2
Barholm Sq. Glasg 99 E1
Barke Rd. Cumb 62 A2
Barkin Ct. Falk 42 A1
Barkly Terr. E Kil 180 B4
Barlae Ave. Eagle 178 C4
Barlanark Ave. Glasg 119 E3
Barlanark Cres. Glasg 119 E4
Barlanark Pl. Glasg 119 D3
Barlanark Pl. Glasg 119 F4
Barlanark Rd. Glasg 119 F4
Barlandfauld St. Kils 60 C4
Barleith Ct. Hurl 228 C3
Barleyhill. Bon 40 A3
Barlia Dr. Glasg 137 F2
Barlia St. Glasg 137 F2
Barlia Terr. Glasg 137 F2
Barloan Cres. Dumb 50 A3
Barloan Pl. Dumb 50 A3
Barloch Ave. Miln 55 D1
Barloch Rd. Miln 55 D1
Barloch St. Glasg 97 E2
Barlogan Ave. Glasg 115 F3
Barlogan Quadrant. Glasg 115 F3
Barmore Ave. Car 202 A4
Barmouth Ave. Gour 44 C3
Barmulloch Rd. Glasg 98 A2
Barn Gn. Kilbar 111 D2
Barn Rd. Stir 7 D4
Barnard Gdns. Bish 78 A2
Barnbeth Rd. Glasg 115 D1
Barncluith Rd. Ham 162 C1
Barnego Rd. Duni 21 E2
Barnes Rd. Glasg 97 D3
Barnes St. Barr 134 A1
Barnett Cres. Salt 216 C4
Barnett Ct. Salt 216 C4
Barnett Path. Udd 161 E4
Barnflat St. Glasg 118 A1
Barnford Cres. Ayr 239 D1
Barnhill Dr. Ham 161 E1
Barnhill Dr. Tull 4 B1
Barnhill Rd. Dumb 50 B2
Barnhill St. Green 46 B2
Barnkirk Ave. Glasg 75 D2
Barns Cres. Ayr 238 C4
Barns Pk. Ayr 238 C4
Barns St. Ayr 238 C4
Barns St. Clyde 94 B4
Barns Street La. Ayr 238 C4
Barns Terr. Ayr 238 C4
Barns Terrace La. Ayr 238 C4
Barnscroft. Kilbar 111 D2
Barnsdale Rd. Stir 7 D2
Barnsford Ave. Inch 93 D2
Barnsford Rd. Inch 93 D2
Barnswood Pl. Udd 141 D2
Barnton La. Falk 42 A2
Barnton St. Glasg 118 C4
Barnton St. Stir 7 D4
Barnweil Rd. Kilmk 227 F3
Barnweil Rd. Pres 236 B3
Barnweill Dr. Hurl 228 C3
Barnwell Rd. Stir 2 B2
Barnwell Terr. Glasg 115 F4
Barochan Cres. Pais 113 D2
Barochan Rd. Glasg 115 D2
Barochan Rd. Hous 91 D3
Barochan Rd. Hous 111 E4
Barochan Rd. Lang 71 D1
Baron Ct. Ham 163 D1
Baron Rd. Pais 114 A3
Baron St. Ren 94 B1
Baronald Dr. Glasg 96 A3
Baronald Gate. Glasg 96 A3
Baronald St. Glasg 118 A1
Barone Dr. Newt M 157 E4
Baronhall Dr. Udd 161 E4
Baronhill. Cumb 62 A3
Barons Gate. Udd 140 C2
Barons Rd. Mother 164 B1
Baronscourt Dr. Lin 112 C2
Baronscourt Gdns. Lin 112 C2
Baronscourt Rd. Lin 112 C2
Barony Ct. Glasg 120 A3
Barony Ct. Irvine 219 F3
Barony Ct. Salt 205 E1
Barony Dr. Glasg 120 A3
Barony Gdns. Glasg 120 A3
Barony Glebe. W Kil 190 B3
Barony Pl. Cumb 60 C1
Barony Rd. Pres 236 B3
Barony Terr. Kilb 170 A4
Barony Wynd. Glasg 120 A3
Barr Ave. Neil 154 C4
Barr Cres. Dunt 74 A3
Barr Gr. Tan 141 D4
Barr Pl. Newt M 156 B3
Barr Pl. Pais 113 E2
Barr St. Ard 205 E1
Barr St. Glasg 97 D2
Barr St. Mother 163 F4
Barr Terr. E Kil 159 F1
Barr's Brae. Kil 69 E1
Barr's Brae. P Glasg 68 B4
Barra Ave. Ren 94 B1
Barra Ave. Wish 165 F3
Barra Cres. Clyde 73 E3
Barra Cres. Irvine 220 B1
Barra Dr. Aird 123 F3
Barra Gdns. Clyde 73 E3
Barra La. Irvine 220 B1
Barra Pl. Irvine 220 B1
Barra Pl. Sten 24 A2
Barra Rd. Clyde 73 E3
Barra St. Glasg 96 B4
Barra Wynd. Irvine 220 B1
Barrachnie Cres. Glasg 119 F3
Barrachnie Ct. Glasg 119 F3
Barrachnie Rd. Glasg 119 F3
Barrack St. Glasg 117 F3
Barrack St. Ham 162 B2
Barraston Rd. Lennox 57 D1
Barrcraig Rd. B of W 110 B4
Barrhead Rd. Glasg 135 E4
Barrhead Rd. Newt M 156 A3
Barrhead Rd. Pais 114 A1
Barrhill Cres. Kilbar 111 E2
Barrhill Ct. Kirk 80 A4
Barrhill Rd. Ersk 93 D4
Barrhill Rd. Gour 44 B4
Barrhill Rd. Kirk 80 A4
Barrie Quadrant. Clyde 74 A2
Barrie Rd. E Kil 160 B3
Barrie Rd. Glasg 115 D4
Barrie Rd. Sten 23 F2
Barrie St. Mother 163 F3
Barrie Terr. Salt 205 E1
Barriedale Ave. Ham 162 A2
Barrington Ave. Beith 150 A1
Barrington Dr. Glasg 96 C1
Barrisdale Rd. Glasg 96 B4
Barrisdale Rd. New 165 F3
Barrisdale Way. Glasg 138 A2
Barrland Dr. Glasg 136 B2
Barrland St. Glasg 117 D2
Barrmill Rd. Beith 171 E4
Barrmill Rd. Beith 172 A1
Barrmill Rd. Glasg 136 A3
Barrochan Interchange. Lin 111 F2
Barrochan Rd. Lin 111 F3
Barrowfield St. Glasg 118 A3
Barrs Brae La. P Glasg 47 E1
Barrs Cres. Card 48 A4
Barrs Ct. Card 26 A1
Barrs La. Car 187 F2
Barrs Terr. Card 48 A4
Barrwood Pl. Tan 141 D4
Barrwood St. Glasg 98 C1
Barry Gdns. Udd 161 E3
Barscube Ave. P Glasg 68 C4
Barscube Terr. Pais 114 A1
Barshaw Dr. Pais 114 A3
Barshaw Pl. Pais 114 B3
Barshaw Rd. Glasg 114 C3
Barskiven Rd. John 112 C2
Barskiven Rd. Pais 112 C2
Barterholm Rd. Pais 113 F1
Bartholomew St. Glasg 118 A2
Bartiebeith Rd. Glasg 119 F4
Bartlands Pl. Eagle 178 C2
Barton Ave. Bonh 28 A4
Bartonhall Rd. Wish 165 E1
Bartonholm Terr. Kilw 207 F1
Barty's Rd. Hat 142 B3
Barwheys Dr. Moss 237 F3
Barwood Hill. Dumb 50 A3
Bassett Ave. Glasg 95 D4
Bassett Cres. Glasg 95 D4
Bastion Wynd. Stir 7 D4
Bath La. Glasg 117 D4
Bath Pl. Ayr 238 C4
Bath Sq. Salt 216 B4
Bath St. Glasg 117 D4
Bath St. Gour 44 C4
Bath St. Kilmk 222 C1
Bath Villas. Salt 216 B4
Bathgate St. Glasg 118 A3
Bathgo Ave. Pais 114 C2
Bathurst Dr. Ayr 239 D1
Bathville Rd. Kilb 149 D1
Bathwick Way. Pais 132 C4
Baton Rd. Shot 146 B3
Batson St. Glasg 117 D1
Battery Park Ave. Green 45 D4
Battery Park Dr. Green 45 D4
Battismains. Lan 215 E2
Battle Pl. Glasg 136 C4
Battlefield Ave. Glasg 137 D4
Battlefield Gdns. Glasg 137 D4
Battlefield Rd. Glasg 137 D4
Bavelaw St. Glasg 99 E1
Bawhirley Rd. Green 46 B2
Baxter Cres. Den 21 E1
Baxter La. Alex 27 F4
Baxter La. Lan 215 D2
Baxter St. Fall 8 B2
Baxter St. Green 46 B2
Baxter's Wynd. Falk 42 A2
Bay St. P Glasg 47 E1
Bay View Rd. Gour 44 C4
Bayfield Ave. Glasg 75 D2
Bayfield Terr. Glasg 75 D2
Bayne St. Stir 2 A1
Beach Dr. Irvine 218 C1
Beach Rd. Troon 229 E3
Beaconsfield Rd. Glasg 96 A3
Beagle Cres. Ayr 238 B2
Bean Row. Falk 42 A2
Beansburn. Kilmk 223 D2
Beanshields Rd. Car 201 F2
Beard Cres. Muir 100 C3
Beardmore Cotts. Inch 93 F3
Beardmore Pl. Clyde 73 F2
Beardmore St. Clyde 73 F2
Beardmore Way. Ersk 73 E1
Bearford Dr. Glasg 115 D3
Bearhope St. Green 45 F3

246

Bearsden Rd. Glasg

Birnam Cres. Bear

Bearsden Rd. Glasg 95 F4
Bearside Rd. Stir 7 D2
Beaton Ave. Bann 7 E1
Beaton Rd. Bonh 27 F4
Beaton Rd. Glasg 116 C1
Beaton St. Lark 184 C3
Beaton Terr. Irvine 219 E3
Beatrice Dr. Holy 142 C3
Beatrice Gdns. Hous 111 E4
Beattock St. Glasg 118 B3
Beattock Wynd. Ham 162 A2
Beatty Ave. Stir 2 A1
Beatty Pl. Helen 17 D1
Beatty St. Clyde 73 F2
Beauclerc St. Alva 5 D4
Beaufield Gdns. Kilm 222 A4
Beaufort Ave. Glasg 136 B3
Beaufort Dr. Klrk 79 D4
Beaufort Dr. Sten 24 A2
Beaufort Gdns. Bish 77 F1
Beauly Cres. Kil 89 E4
Beauly Cres. Kilmk 228 A3
Beauly Ct. Falk 42 B1
Beauly Dr. Pais 112 C1
Beauly Pl. Coat 122 A2
Beauly Pl. E Kil 159 E1
Beauly Pl. Glasg 96 B3
Beauly Pl. Holy 143 D3
Beauly Pl. Muir 80 B1
Beauly Rd. Glasg 120 A2
Beaumont Dr. Sten 24 A1
Beaumont Gate. Glasg 96 B2
Beckford St. Ham 162 B3
Beda Pl. Fall 8 B3
Bedale Rd. Glasg 119 F2
Bedcow View. Klrk 79 F4
Bedford Ave. Clyde 74 B1
Bedford Ct. All 10 A3
Bedford La. Glasg 117 D3
Bedford Pl. All 10 A3
Bedford St. Glasg 117 D3
Bedford St. Green 45 E4
Bedlay Ct. Muir 81 D2
Bedlormie Dr. Blac 107 E1
Beech Ave. B of W 90 B1
Beech Ave. Bear 76 A4
Beech Ave. Beith 150 A1
Beech Ave. Glasg 116 A2
Beech Ave. Glasg 120 A3
Beech Ave. Glasg 138 B2
Beech Ave. Glasg 138 C3
Beech Ave. Holy 143 D2
Beech Ave. Irvine 219 E1
Beech Ave. John 112 B1
Beech Ave. Kilmk 227 E4
Beech Ave. Lark 185 E1
Beech Ave. Newt M 156 C2
Beech Ave. Pais 114 A1
Beech Ave. Plea 12 B2
Beech Cres. Duni 21 E2
Beech Cres. Holy 143 E4
Beech Cres. Lar 41 E4
Beech Cres. Newt M 156 C2
Beech Ct. Coat 121 F2
Beech Dr. Cald 104 C2
Beech Dr. Clyde 74 A3
Beech Gdns. Glasg 120 A3
Beech Gr. Ayr 239 E4
Beech Gr. E Kil 180 A3
Beech Gr. Law 186 C3
Beech Gr. Muir 101 D3
Beech Gr. Rhu 15 E3
Beech Gr. Wish 165 E4
Beech La. Stir 2 A2
Beech Pl. Bish 98 A4
Beech Pl. Gour 44 B3
Beech Pl. Udd 161 F4
Beech Rd. Bish 98 A4
Beech Rd. Holy 143 E4
Beech Rd. John 111 E1
Beech Rd. Klrk 79 E3
Beech Terr. Lark 185 D1
Beechbank Ave. Aird 102 C1
Beechburn Cres. Loch 129 E2
Beeches Ave. Dunt 73 F3
Beeches Rd. Dunt 73 F3
Beeches Terr. Dunt 74 A3
Beeches The. Hous 91 E1
Beeches The. Kilbar 111 E3
Beeches The. Lan 215 D1
Beeches The. Newt M 156 C3
Beechfield Dr. Car 202 A4
Beechfield Rd. Beith 170 C4
Beechgrove Ave. Tan 141 E4
Beechgrove. Muir 80 C1
Beechgrove Pl. Helen 25 C4
Beechgrove
Quadrant. Holy 143 D3
Beechgrove St. Glasg 118 A1
Beechlands Ave. Glasg 136 C1
Beechlands Dr. Newt M 157 E3
Beechmount Ct. Shot 147 D1
Beechmount Rd. Klrk 79 E2
Beechtree Terr. M of C 58 B3
Beechwood Ave. Glasg 138 B3
Beechwood Ave. Ham 183 D4
Beechwood Ave. Lang 70 B4
Beechwood Ave. Newt M 157 E3
Beechwood Cres. Wish 165 E1
Beechwood Ct. Bear 75 F2
Beechwood Dr. Bonh 28 A1
Beechwood Dr. Coat 122 B3
Beechwood Dr. Glasg 95 F2
Beechwood Dr. Ren 94 B1
Beechwood Gdns. Hat 142 B2
Beechwood Gdns. Muir 80 C1
Beechwood Gr. Barr 134 B1
Beechwood. Kilw 207 E3
Beechwood La. Bear 75 F2
Beechwood. Lark 185 D3
Beechwood. N Sau 5 E1
Beechwood. N Sau 5 F1
Beechwood
Paddock. Troon 230 A2
Beechwood Pl. Glasg 95 F2
Beechwood Pl. Hat 142 B2
Beechwood Rd. Cumb 82 C4
Beechworth Dr. Holy 143 E1
Beecroft Pl. Udd 140 C1
Begg Ave. Falk 41 F2
Beggs Terr. Ard 205 E2
Beil Dr. Clyde 94 C4
Beith Rd. Beith 170 B3
Beith Rd. Beith 191 F4
Beith Rd. Green 45 F1
Beith Rd. How 131 D4
Beith Rd. John 111 F1
Beith St. Glasg 96 A1
Beith St. Glasg 96 B1
Belgowan St. Hat 141 F4
Belgrave La. Glasg 96 C2
Belgrave St. Hat 141 F3
Belhaven Rd. Ham 161 F2
Belhaven Rd. Wish 165 D2
Belhaven St. P Glasg 47 D1
Belhaven Terr. Glasg 96 B2
Belhaven Terr W. Glasg 96 B2
Belhaven Terr. Wish 165 D2
Belhaven Terrace La. Glasg 96 B2
Belhaven
Terrace West La. Glasg 96 B2
Bell Cres. Irvine 219 E3
Bell Gn E. E Kil 180 C4
Bell Gn W. E Kil 180 C4
Bell St. Aird 122 C4
Bell St. Clyde 94 B4
Bell St. Glasg 117 E3
Bell St. Green 46 C1
Bell St. Hat 142 A4
Bell St. Ren 94 B2
Bell St. Wish 165 D2
Bell Trees Rd. How 130 B1
Bell View Ct. Ren 94 B2
Bell's Wynd. Falk 42 A2
Bell's Wynd. Lan 215 E3
Bellahouston Dr. Glasg 115 F2
Bellairs Pl. Udd 140 B1
Bellard Rd. W Kil 190 B2
Bellard Wlk. W Kil 190 B2
Bellas Pl. Plains 104 A1
Bellcraig Ct. Thorn 158 A3
Belleaire Dr. Green 45 E4
Bellefield Rd. Lan 215 D3
Belleisle Ave. Udd 140 C4
Belleisle Ct. Kilw 207 E2
Belleisle Cres. B of W 110 B3
Belleisle Pl. Gour 44 A3
Belleisle Pl. Kilmk 227 F2
Belleisle St. Glasg 117 D1
Bellesleyhill Ave. Ayr 236 A2
Bellesleyhill Rd. Ayr 236 A2
Bellevale Ave. Ayr 239 D3
Bellevale Quadrant. Ayr 238 C3
Bellevue Ave. Klrk 79 D4
Bellevue Cres. Ayr 238 C4
Bellevue Gdns. Kilmk 222 B1
Bellevue La. Ayr 238 C4
Bellevue Rd. All 9 F3
Bellevue Rd. Ayr 238 C4
Bellevue Rd. Kilmk 222 B1
Bellevue Rd. Klrk 79 D4
Bellevue Rd. Pres 236 B4
Bellevue St. Ayr 238 C4
Bellevue St. Falk 42 B2
Bellfield Ave. Hurl 228 B3
Bellfield Cres. Barr 134 A2
Bellfield Ct. Barr 134 A2
Bellfield Ct. Hurl 228 B3
Bellfield Dr. Wish 165 E1
Bellfield La. Pres 236 A4
Bellfield Rd. Bann 7 F1
Bellfield Rd. Klrk 79 D4
Bellfield Rd. Stir 7 D3
Bellfield St. Glasg 118 A3
Bellflower Ct. E Kil 159 E2
Bellflower Gdns. Glasg 135 E2
Bellflower Gr. E Kil 159 E2
Bellgrove St. Glasg 117 F3
Bellisle Terr. Ham 183 D4
Bellrock Ave. Pres 236 A3
Bellrock Cres. Glasg 119 D4
Bellrock Ct. Glasg 119 D4
Bellrock Path. Glasg 119 D4
Bellrock Rd. Ayr 236 A2
Bellrock St. Glasg 119 D4
Bellscroft Ave. Glasg 137 F4
Bellsdyke Rd. Air 24 B3
Bellsdyke Rd. Aird 123 D3
Bellsdyke Rd. Lar 23 E2
Bellsdyke Rd. Sten 23 E2
Bellsfield Dr. Udd 161 F3
Bellshaugh Gdns. Glasg 96 B3
Bellshaugh La. Glasg 96 B3
Bellshaugh Pl. Glasg 96 B3
Bellshaugh Rd. Glasg 96 B2
Bellshill Rd. Hat 141 F2
Bellshill Rd. Mother 142 B1
Bellshill Rd. Tan 141 D3
Bellshill Rd. Tan 141 E1
Bellshill Rd. Udd 141 D3
Bellshill Rd. Udd 141 E1
Bellside Rd. Chap 123 F1
Bellside Rd. Chap 144 A4
Bellside Rd. Cle 144 B1
Bellsland Dr. Kilmk 227 F3
Bellsland Gr. Kilmk 227 F3
Bellsland Pl. Kilmk 228 A4
Bellsmeadow Rd. Falk 42 B2
Bellsmyre Ave. Dumb 50 A3
Belltree Ave. Stew 211 E4
Belltrees Cres. Pais 113 D2
Bellvue Cres. Hat 141 F2
Bellvue Cres. Pres 236 B4
Bellwood St. Glasg 136 C4
Bellziehill Farm. Tan 141 F3
Belman's Cl. Beith 150 A1
Belmont Ave. Ayr 239 D3
Belmont Ave. Shi 66 C4
Belmont Ave. Udd 140 C4
Belmont Cres. Ayr 239 D3
Belmont Cres. Glasg 96 C2
Belmont Cres. Kilm 222 A4
Belmont Ct. Klrk 79 E4
Belmont Dr. Ayr 239 D3
Belmont Dr. Barr 134 B1
Belmont Dr. E Kil 180 A4
Belmont Dr. Glasg 136 A2
Belmont Dr. Glasg 138 A4
Belmont Dr. Shot 147 D1
Belmont La. Glasg 96 C2
Belmont Pl E. Ayr 239 D3
Belmont Pl W. Ayr 239 D3
Belmont Rd. Ayr 239 D3
Belmont Rd. Glasg 97 F3
Belmont Rd. Glasg 138 C2
Belmont Rd. Kil 89 E4
Belmont Rd. Pais 114 A3
Belmont St. Clyde 74 A1
Belmont St. Coat 101 E1
Belmont St. Falk 42 B2
Belmont St. Glasg 96 C2
Belmont St. Kils 36 B1
Belmont St. Wish 186 A3
Belses Dr. Glasg 115 E3
Belstane Pk. Car 187 F2
Belstane Pl. Udd 141 D2
Belstane Rd. Car 188 A2
Belstane Rd. Cumb 82 C3
Belsyde Ave. Glasg 75 D1
Beltane St. Glasg 116 C4
Beltane St. Wish 165 D1
Beltrees Ave. Glasg 115 D1
Beltrees Cres. Glasg 115 D1
Beltrees Rd. Glasg 115 D1
Belvidere Cres. Bish 78 A1
Belvidere Cres. Hat 142 A2
Belvidere Rd. Hat 142 A2
Belvidere Terr. Ayr 236 A1
Belville Ave. Green 46 B2
Belville St. Green 46 A2
Belvoir Pl. Udd 161 E4
Bemersyde Ave. Glasg 136 A3
Bemersyde. Bish 78 B1
Bemersyde Pl. Lark 185 D1
Bemersyde Rd. Pais 132 C4
Ben Alder Dr. Pais 114 B1
Ben Bouie Dr. Helen 16 C1
Ben Buie Way. Pais 114 B1
Ben Hope Ave. Pais 114 B1
Ben Lawers Dr. Cumb 61 D1
Ben Lawers Dr. Pais 114 B1
Ben Ledi Ave. Pais 114 B1
Ben Ledi Cres. Cumb 61 D1
Ben Loyal Ave. Pais 114 B1
Ben Lui Dr. Pais 114 B1
Ben Lui Pl. Cumb 61 D1
Ben More Dr. Cumb 61 D1
Ben More Dr. Pais 114 B1
Ben Nevis Rd. Pais 114 B1
Ben Nevis Way. Cumb 61 D1
Ben Vane Ave. Pais 114 B1
Ben Venue Rd. Cumb 61 D1
Ben Venue Way. Pais 114 B1
Ben Wyvis Dr. Pais 114 B1
Benalder St. Glasg 96 B1
Benarty Gdns. Bish 78 A1
Benbain Pl. Irvine 220 A3
Benbecula. E Kil 160 B1
Benbecula Rd. Kilmk 223 D3
Bencleuch Pl. Irvine 220 A2
Bencloich Ave. Lennox 57 F4
Bencloich Cres. Lennox 33 F1
Bencloich Rd. Lennox 57 F4
Bencloich St. Lennox 33 F1
Benclutha. P Glasg 47 F1
Bencroft Dr. Glasg 137 F3
Bendigo Pl. Lan 215 D2
Benford Ave. Holy 143 E2
Benford Knowe. Holy 143 F2
Bengairn St. Glasg 118 B4
Bengal Pl. Glasg 136 B4
Bengal St. Glasg 136 B4
Benhar Pl. Glasg 118 C4
Benhar Rd. East 126 C1
Benhar Rd. Shot 147 D3
Benholm St. Glasg 118 C2
Benmore La. Gour 44 C2
Benmore. Pres 236 B3
Benmore Tower. Glasg 138 C2
Bennan House. Pres 236 A3
Bennan Sq. Glasg 117 E1
Bennoch Pl. Pres 236 B3
Benrig Ave. Kilm 222 A4
Bensley Ave. Irvine 219 F3
Bensley Rise. Irvine 219 F2
Benson St. Coat 122 A2
Benston Pl. John 111 F1
Benston Rd. John 111 F1
Bent Cres. Tan 141 E3
Bent Rd. Chap 123 E2
Bent Rd. Ham 162 B2
Bentfield Ave. Ayr 238 C3
Bentfield Dr. Pres 236 A3
Bentfoot Rd. Wish 186 B4
Benthall St. Glasg 117 E2
Bentheads. Bann 11 F4
Bentinck Cres. Troon 229 F1
Bentinck Dr. Troon 229 E1
Bentinck St. Glasg 96 C1
Bentinck St. Green 45 E4
Bentinck St. Kilmk 227 F4
Bents Rd. Glasg 120 A3
Benty's La. Car 201 F4
Benvie Gdns. Bish 78 A1
Benview Ave. P Glasg 68 C4
Benview. Bann 7 E1
Benview Rd. Newt M 157 F4
Benview Rd. P Glasg 68 C4
Benview St. Glasg 96 C2
Benview Terr. Fish 5 F2
Benview Terr. Pais 114 A1
Benvue Rd. Lennox 57 F4
Berchem Pl. Salt 216 C4
Bereland Ave. Pres 236 B4
Berelands Cres. Glasg 137 F4
Berelands Gdns. Pres 233 E1
Berelands Pl. Glasg 137 F4
Berelands Rd. Pres 233 E1
Beresford Ave. Glasg 95 F2
Beresford Gr. Irvine 219 F3
Beresford La. Ayr 238 C4
Beresford Terr. Ayr 238 C4
Berkeley St. Glasg 116 C4
Berkeley St. Stir 7 D2
Berkeley
Terrace La. Glasg 116 C4
Berkley Dr. Udd 140 B1
Berl Ave. Hous 111 E4
Bernadette Ave. Holy 143 E1
Bernadette St. Holy 143 E2
Bernard Path. Glasg 118 A2
Bernard St. Glasg 118 A2
Bernard Terr. Glasg 118 A2
Bernard's Wynd. Lan 215 D2
Berneray St. Glasg 97 E4
Berridale Ave. Glasg 137 D3
Berridale Rd. Troon 229 E4
Berriedale Ave. Glasg 120 A2
Berriedale. E Kil 179 F4
Berriedale Quadrant. Wish 165 D3
Berry Dr. Irvine 219 F2
Berryburn Rd. Glasg 98 B2
Berryhill Ave. Irvine 220 A3
Berryhill. Cowie 12 C4
Berryhill Dr. Glasg 136 A1
Berryhill Pl. Shot 147 D1
Berryhill Rd. Cumb 61 F1
Berryhill Rd. Glasg 136 A1
Berryknowe Ave. Muir 100 B4
Berryknowe. Kirk 80 A4
Berryknowes Ave. Glasg 115 E3
Berryknowes La. Glasg 115 E3
Berryknowes Rd. Glasg 115 E3
Berryyards Rd. Green 45 F2
Bertram Dr. Sals 125 E1
Bertram Pl. Shot 146 B3
Bertram St. East 127 E3
Bertram St. Glasg 116 C1
Bertram St. Ham 162 A3
Bertram St. Lark 185 E1
Bertram St. Shot 146 C3
Bervie St. Glasg 115 F3
Berwick Cres. Aird 122 C3
Berwick Cres. Lin 111 F4
Berwick Dr. Glasg 115 D2
Berwick Dr. Glasg 138 B3
Berwick Pl. Coat 122 A2
Berwick Pl. E Kil 160 B2
Berwick Pl. Gour 44 B2
Berwick Rd. Gour 44 B2
Berwick Rd. P Glasg 47 E1
Berwick St. Coat 122 A2
Berwick St. Ham 162 A3
Bessemer Dr. E Kil 181 D3
Beta Ctr. Clyde 94 B4
Betula Dr. Clyde 74 A3
Bevan Ct. Ard 205 D2
Bevan Dr. Alva 5 E4
Bevan Gdns. Kilw 207 F2
Bevan Gr. John 111 F1
Beveridge Terr. Hat 142 B2
Beverley Rd. Glasg 136 B3
Bevin Ave. Clyde 74 B1
Bideford Cres. Glasg 119 E2
Bield The. Wish 165 E1
Biggar Rd. Chap 123 F1
Biggar Rd. Holy 143 F4
Biggar St. Glasg 118 A3
Biggart Rd. Pres 236 B4
Bigholm Rd. Beith 150 B1
Bigton St. Glasg 99 D1
Bilby Terr. Irvine 219 E3
Billings Rd. Mother 163 D3
Bilsland Dr. Glasg 97 D3
Bilsland Pl. Alex 27 E1
Bimson Pl. Irvine 219 D1
Binend Rd. Glasg 135 E4
Binnie La. Gour 44 C4
Binnie Pl. Glasg 117 F3
Binnie Pl. Gran 24 C1
Binnie St. Gour 44 C4
Binniehill Rd. Cumb 61 E1
Binniehill Rd. Slam 85 F2
Binns Rd. Glasg 99 E1
Birch Ave. Newt M 157 F3
Birch Ave. Stir 6 C3
Birch Brae. Ham 162 C1
Birch Cotts. Helen 16 B1
Birch Cres. John 112 A1
Birch Cres. Newt M 157 F3
Birch Ct. Coat 121 F2
Birch Dr. Glasg 139 E3
Birch Dr. Klrk 79 E3
Birch Gr. Lark 185 D3
Birch Gr. Tan 141 D4
Birch Knowe. Bish 98 A4
Birch Pl. Kilmk 227 E4
Birch Pl. Udd 161 E4
Birch Quadrant. Aird 123 E4
Birch Rd. Ayr 239 E2
Birch Rd. Clyde 74 A3
Birch Rd. Cumb 62 C2
Birch Rd. Dumb 49 F2
Birch St. Glasg 117 E2
Birch St. Holy 143 D3
Birch View. Bear 76 A3
Birch Way. Troon 229 E2
Birchfield Dr. Glasg 95 D2
Birchfield Rd. Ham 162 A2
Birchgrove. Hous 91 E1
Birchlea Dr. Glasg 136 B2
Birchview Dr. Thorn 157 F2
Birchwood Ave. Glasg 119 F2
Birchwood Dr. Pais 113 D1
Birchwood. N Sau 5 E1
Birchwood Pl. Glasg 119 F2
Birchwood Rd. Uplaw 153 D2
Birdsfield Ct. Ham 161 F3
Birdsfield Dr. Udd 161 F3
Birdsfield St. Ham 161 F3
Birdston Rd. Glasg 98 B3
Birdston Rd. M of C 58 B2
Birgidale Ave. Glasg 137 E1
Birgidale Rd. Glasg 137 E1
Birgidale Terr. Glasg 137 E1
Birkdale Cl. Kilw 207 E2
Birkdale Ct. Udd 140 C1
Birkdale. E Kil 159 E2
Birken Rd. Klrk 79 F2
Birkenburn Rd. Cumb 62 C3
Birkenshaw Rd. Glen 81 F1
Birkenshaw St. Glasg 118 A4
Birkenshaw Way. Pais 113 F4
Birkfield Loan. Car 188 B1
Birkfield Pl. Car 188 B1
Birkhall Ave. Glasg 115 D2
Birkhall Ave. Inch 93 E4
Birkhall Dr. Bear 75 F1
Birkhill Ave. Bish 78 A1
Birkhill Gdns. Bish 78 A1
Birkhill Rd. Cam 6 C3
Birkhill Rd. Car 201 E1
Birkhill Rd. Ham 183 E4
Birkhill Rd. Stir 6 C3
Birkmyre Ave. P Glasg 47 D1
Birkmyre Rd. Glasg 115 F3
Birks Ct. Law 186 C3
Birks Hill. Irvine 220 A2
Birks Pl. Lan 215 D3
Birks Rd. Lark 199 D4
Birks Rd. Law 186 C2
Birkscairn Pl. Irvine 220 B1
Birkscairn Way. Irvine 220 B1
Birkshaw Brae. Wish 186 A4
Birkshaw Pl. Wish 186 A4
Birkshaw Tower. Wish 185 F4
Birkwood St. Glasg 118 A1
Birmingham Rd. Ren 94 A1
Birnam Ave. Bish 78 A1
Birnam Cres. Bear 76 A3

247
Birnam Ct. Falk
Braehead Rd. Pais

Birnam Ct. Falk 24 B1
Birnam Gdns. Bish 78 A1
Birnam Pl. Ham 161 F2
Birnam Rd. Glasg 118 B2
Birness Dr. Glasg 136 B4
Birnie Ct. Glasg 98 B2
Birnie Rd. Glasg 98 B2
Birniehill Rd. Cle 145 D3
Birniehill Roundabout. E Kil 181 D4
Birniewell Rd. Slam 86 A3
Birnock Ave. Ren 94 C1
Birrell Rd. Miln 54 C2
Birrens Rd. Mother 163 E4
Birsay Rd. Glasg 97 D4
Bishop Gdns. Bish 77 F1
Bishop Gdns. Ham 183 F4
Bishop La. Glasg 117 D4
Bishopdale. E Kil 159 E2
Bishopmill Pl. Glasg 98 B2
Bishopmill Rd. Glasg 98 B2
Bishops Gate. Thorn 158 B2
Bishops Pk. Thorn 158 A2
Bishopsgate Dr. Bish 97 F4
Bishopsgate Gdns. Bish 97 F4
Bishopsgate Pl. Bish 97 F4
Bishopsgate Rd. Bish 97 F4
Bishpobriggs Ind Est. Bish 98 A4
Bisland Ct. Glasg 97 D3
Bissett Cres. Dunt 73 F3
Black O' Hill Roundabout. Cumb 61 D1
Black St. Aird 103 D1
Black St. Glasg 97 E1
Blackadder Pl. E Kil 179 E4
Blackbog Rd. Glenm 82 C1
Blackbraes Rd. E Kil 160 A2
Blackburn Cres. Dumb 49 E2
Blackburn Cres. Kirk 80 A4
Blackburn Dr. Ayr 238 C3
Blackburn Pl. Ayr 238 C3
Blackburn Rd. Ayr 238 C3
Blackburn Sq. Barr 134 B1
Blackburn St. Glasg 116 C3
Blackbyres Ct. Barr 134 B2
Blackbyres Rd. Pais 134 B3
Blackcraig Ave. Glasg 75 D2
Blackcroft Ave. Chap 123 F3
Blackcroft Gdns. Glasg 119 E2
Blackcroft Rd. Glasg 119 E2
Blackcroft Terr. Sals 125 D1
Blackdyke Rd. Klrk 79 F4
Blackfarm Rd. Newt M 156 C2
Blackfaulds Dr. Fen 213 D2
Blackfaulds Gdns. Fen 213 D2
Blackfaulds Rd. Glasg 137 F4
Blackford Cres. Pres 233 F1
Blackford Rd. Pais 114 A2
Blackfriars St. Glasg 117 E4
Blackfriars Wlk. Ayr 238 C4
Blackhall Ct. Pais 114 A2
Blackhall La. Pais 113 F2
Blackhall St. Pais 114 A2
Blackhall St. Shot 147 D2
Blackhill Dr. Helen 16 B2
Blackhill Pl. Glasg 98 B1
Blackhill Rd. Blac 107 F2
Blackhill Rd. Glasg 76 C1
Blackhill St. Ayr 239 D3
Blackhill View. Law 187 D2
Blackhouse Ave. Newt M 156 C2
Blackhouse Gdns. Newt M 156 C2
Blackhouse Pl. Ayr 239 E4
Blackhouse Rd. Newt M 156 C2
Blackie St. Glasg 96 B1
Blacklands Ave. Kilw 207 F1
Blacklands Cres. Kilw 207 F1
Blacklands Pl. Klrk 79 F2
Blacklands Rd. E Kil 159 E1
Blacklaw Dr. E Kil 181 D4
Blacklaw La. Pais 113 F3
Blackmill Cres. Sten 24 A2
Blackmoor Pl. Holy 143 D2
Blackmoss Dr. Hat 142 A2
Blackmuir Pl. Tull 4 B2
Blackness St. Coat 122 A2
Blackshaw Dr. W Kil 190 B3
Blackstone Ave. Glasg 135 E4
Blackstone Cres. Glasg 115 E1
Blackstone Rd. Lin 113 D4
Blackstoun Ave. Lin 112 A3
Blackstoun Oval. Pais 113 D3
Blackstoun Rd. Pais 113 D3
Blackswell La. Ham 162 C2
Blacksyke Ave. Kilmk 227 F2
Blackthorn Ave. Beith 150 A1
Blackthorn Ave. Klrk 79 D3
Blackthorn Gr. Klrk 79 D3
Blackthorn Rd. Cumb 62 C2
Blackthorn Rd. Tan 141 E4
Blackthorn St. Glasg 97 F3
Blacktongue Farm Rd. Gree 83 F1
Blackwood Ave. Kilmk 227 F3
Blackwood Ave. Lin 112 A3
Blackwood Ave. Newt M 156 C2
Blackwood. E Kil 180 B3
Blackwood Gdns. Mother 142 B1
Blackwood Rd. Cumb 60 C1
Blackwood Rd. Miln 54 C2
Blackwood St. Barr 134 A1
Blackwood St. Glasg 95 F4
Blackwoods Cres. Hat 142 B2
Blackwoods Cres. Muir 80 C1
Bladda La. Pais 113 F2
Blades Ct. Muir 101 D3
Bladnoch Dr. Glasg 75 E1
Blaefaulds Cres. Den 39 E4
Blaeloch Ave. Glasg 137 E1
Blaeloch Dr. Glasg 137 E1
Blaeloch Terr. Glasg 137 D1
Blaeshill Rd. E Kil 179 F4
Blair Atholl Dr. Lark 185 E1
Blair Ave. Hurl 228 C3
Blair Cres. Glasg 120 A2
Blair Cres. Hurl 228 C3
Blair Dr. M of C 58 B3
Blair Gdns. Gour 43 F3
Blair Gdns. Lennox 57 D1
Blair House. Cumb 62 A2
Blair Linn View. Cumb 83 D3
Blair Path. Mother 163 F3
Blair Rd. Beith 191 F4
Blair Rd. Coat 121 F4
Blair Rd. Cro 201 D1
Blair Rd. Glasg 114 C3
Blair Rd. Hurl 228 C3
Blair Rd. Kilw 207 F3
Blair St. Glasg 118 C3
Blair St. Kilmk 222 C1
Blair Terr. Sten 24 A2
Blairafton Wynd. Kilw 207 E3
Blairatholl Ave. Glasg 96 A2
Blairatholl Gdns. Glasg 96 A2
Blairbeth Dr. Glasg 137 D4
Blairbeth Pl. Glasg 138 A3
Blairbeth Rd. Glasg 138 B3
Blairbeth Terr. Glasg 138 B3
Blairdardie Rd. Glasg 75 E1
Blairdenan Ave. Muir 81 D2
Blairdenon Cres. Falk 41 F2
Blairdenon Dr. Cumb 61 E2
Blairdenon Dr. N Sau 5 D1
Blairdenon Rd. Alva 4 C3
Blairdenon Way. Irvine 220 A1
Blairforkie Dr. B of A 1 C4
Blairgowrie Rd. Glasg 115 E2
Blairgrove Ct. Coat 121 F3
Blairhall Ave. Glasg 136 C4
Blairhill Ave. Kirk 80 A3
Blairhill Pl. Coat 121 F4
Blairhill St. Coat 121 F4
Blairholm Dr. Hat 142 A2
Blairlands Dr. Beith 191 F4
Blairlinn Rd. Cumb 82 C3
Blairlogie St. Glasg 99 D1
Blairmore Cres. Green 46 B1
Blairmore Rd. Green 46 B1
Blairmuckhole and Forrestdyke Rd. Sals 126 C4
Blairpark Ave. Coat 121 F4
Blairquhomrie Cotts. Bonh 20 C1
Blairston Ave. Udd 141 D1
Blairston Gdns. Udd 141 D1
Blairtum Dr. Glasg 138 A3
Blairtummock Rd. Glasg 119 E4
Blairtummock Rd. Glasg 119 F4
Blake Rd. Cumb 62 A1
Blakely Rd. Salt 217 D4
Blane Ave. Strath 31 D2
Blane Cres. Strath 31 D2
Blane Dr. Miln 55 D2
Blane Pl. Strath 31 D2
Blane St. Coat 122 A4
Blanefield Ave. Pres 236 B3
Blaneview. Stepps 99 E2
Blantyre Cres. Dunt 73 F4
Blantyre Ct. Ersk 73 D2
Blantyre Dr. Bishop 72 A2
Blantyre Farm Rd. Udd 140 B3
Blantyre Gdns. Cumb 60 C1
Blantyre Mill Rd. Udd 141 D1
Blantyre Pl. Coat 121 F2
Blantyre Rd. Udd 141 D1
Blantyre St. Coat 121 F2
Blantyre St. Glasg 96 B1
Blaven Ct. Glasg 120 B2
Blaven Head. Irvine 220 A2
Blawarthill St. Glasg 94 C3
Bleachfield. Falk 42 A3
Bleachfield. Miln 55 D2
Bleeze Rd. Dalry 191 D4
Blenheim Ave. E Kil 180 B4
Blenheim Ave. Stepps 99 F3
Blenheim Ct. Kils 36 C1
Blenheim Ct. Pais 113 E3
Blenheim Pl. Sten 23 F3
Blenheim Rd. Car 188 A1
Blindwells. Alva 4 B2
Blinkbonnie Terr. Slam 86 A3
Blinkbonny Rd. Falk 41 F2
Blinny Ct. Shot 147 D2
Blochairn Rd. Glasg 98 A1
Bloomgate. Lan 215 D2
Bluebell Gdns. Glasg 138 A1
Bluebell Gdns. Mother 142 B1
Bluebell Way. Aird 102 C1
Bluebell Way. Car 201 F4
Bluebell Way. Lennox 57 F4
Bluebell Wlk. Holy 143 D2
Blueknowes Rd. Law 186 C3
Bluevale St. Glasg 118 A3
Blyth Rd. Glasg 119 F3
Blythe Pl. Glasg 119 E3
Blythswood Ave. Ren 94 B2
Blythswood Dr. Pais 113 F3
Blythswood Rd. Ren 94 B2
Blythswood Sq. Glasg 117 D4
Blythswood St. Glasg 117 D4
Bo'ness Rd. Chap 123 E1
Bo'ness Rd. Holy 143 E4
Boardwalk The. E Kil 181 D4
Boat Vennel. Ayr 235 F1
Boclair Ave. Bear 75 F2
Boclair Cres. Bear 76 A2
Boclair Cres. Bish 78 A1
Boclair Rd. Bear 76 B3
Boclair Rd. Bish 78 A1
Boclair Rd. Glasg 76 B3
Boclair St. Glasg 95 F4
Bodden Sq. Holy 143 F4
Boden Quadrant. Mother 142 B1
Boden St. Glasg 118 A2
Bodesbeck Ct. Irvine 220 A2
Bodmin Gdns. Muir 80 C2
Bog Rd. Bank 38 C2
Bog Rd. Falk 42 B3
Bog Rd. Falk 42 C2
Bogany Terr. Glasg 137 F1
Bogbain Rd. Glasg 120 A4
Bogend Rd. Bann 11 F4
Bogend Rd. Lar 23 D4
Bogend Rd. Tor 22 C4
Bogfoot Rd. Sals 125 D1
Boggknowe. Tan 140 B4
Boghall Rd. Car 202 A4
Boghall Rd. Glasg 120 A2
Boghall St. Glasg 99 D1
Boghall St. Stone 198 C1
Boghead Ave. Dumb 50 A2
Boghead. Beith 171 D4
Boghead Rd. Dumb 50 A2
Boghead Rd. Glasg 98 A2
Boghead Rd. Klrk 79 D3
Bogiewood Rd. P Glasg 47 D1
Bogle St. Green 46 A2
Boglemart St. Steven 217 E4
Boglesholе Rd. Glasg 138 C4
Boglestone Ave. P Glasg 68 C4
Bogmoor Rd. Glasg 95 E1
Bogmoor Rd. Glasg 115 E4
Bogs View. Hat 141 F2
Bogside Rd. Ash 199 F4
Bogside Rd. Kils 60 B4
Bogside Rd. P Glasg 68 C4
Bogside Rd. Stepps 99 D3
Bogside St. Glasg 118 A2
Bogston La. Green 46 C1
Bogstonhill Rd. Hous 91 D1
Bogton Ave. Glasg 136 C2
Bogton Avenue La. Glasg 136 C2
Bohun Ct. Bann 7 E2
Boleyn Rd. Glasg 116 C1
Bolingbroke. E Kil 160 B2
Bolivar Terr. Glasg 137 E4
Bolton Dr. Glasg 137 D4
Bolton Terr. Lennox 57 F4
Boman Pl. Stew 195 E1
Bon Accord Cres. Shot 146 C3
Bon Accord Rd. Newt M 157 F3
Bon Accord Sq. Clyde 94 A4
Bonar Cres. B of W 110 C4
Bonar La. B of W 110 C4
Bonar Law Ave. Helen 16 A1
Bonawe St. Glasg 96 C2
Boness St. Glasg 118 A2
Bonhill Rd. Dumb 50 A2
Bonhill St. Glasg 97 D2
Bonkle Gdns. New 166 A3
Bonkle Rd. New 166 A3
Bonnar St. Glasg 118 A2
Bonnaughton Rd. Bear 75 D3
Bonnet Ct. Stew 211 F4
Bonnet Rd. Lan 215 D2
Bonnhill View. Alex 27 F2
Bonnington Ave. Lan 215 D2
Bonnybridge Rd. Bank 39 F3
Bonnybridge Rd. Bon 39 F3
Bonnyfield Rd. Bon 39 F3
Bonnyhill Rd. Bon 40 B2
Bonnyhill Rd. Falk 41 D2
Bonnyholm Ave. Glasg 115 D2
Bonnyrigg Dr. Glasg 136 A3
Bonnyside Rd. Bon 40 A3
Bonnyton Dr. Eagle 178 B3
Bonnyton Foot. Irvine 220 A3
Bonnyton Moor Rd. Eagle 178 A4
Bonnyton Pl. Irvine 220 A3
Bonnyton Pl. Kilmk 222 B1
Bonnyton Rd. Cross 222 B1
Bonnyton Rd. Kilmk 222 B1
Bonnyton Row. Irvine 220 A3
Bonnyview Gdns. Bon 40 A3
Bonnywood Ave. Bon 40 A4
Bontine Ave. Dumb 49 E2
Bonyton Ave. Glasg 94 C3
Boon Dr. Glasg 75 D1
Booth Pl. Falk 42 A2
Boquhanran Pl. Clyde 74 A2
Boquhanran Rd. Clyde 73 F1
Boquhanran Rd. Clyde 74 A2
Borden La. Glasg 95 F3
Borden Rd. Glasg 95 F3
Border Ave. Salt 216 C4
Border Pl. Salt 216 C4
Border St. Green 46 B2
Border Way. Klrk 79 F4
Bore Rd. Aird 123 D4
Boreland Dr. Glasg 95 D3
Boreland Dr. Ham 161 F1
Boreland Pl. Glasg 95 D3
Borestone Ave. Kilb 170 A4
Borestone Cres. Stir 7 D2
Borestone Ct. Stir 7 D1
Borestone Pl. Stir 7 D1
Borgie Cres. Glasg 139 D3
Borland Cres. Eagle 178 C3
Borland Rd. Bear 76 A2
Borron St. Glasg 97 E2
Borrowdale. E Kil 179 F3
Borrowlea Rd. Stir 7 E4
Borrowmeadow Rd. Stir 7 F4
Borthwick Dr. E Kil 179 E4
Borthwick St. Glasg 99 D1
Bosfield Cnr. E Kil 159 F2
Bosfield Pl. E Kil 159 F2
Bosfield Rd. E Kil 159 F2
Boston Dr. Helen 16 C2
Boswell Ct. Glasg 136 C4
Boswell Dr. Udd 161 E4
Boswell Pk. Ayr 238 C4
Boswell Pk. E Kil 160 B2
Boswell Sq. Glasg 114 C4
Bosworth Rd. E Kil 160 A3
Botanic Cres. Glasg 96 B2
Botanic Crescent La. Glasg 96 B2
Bothkennar Rd. Air 24 C2
Bothkennar Rd. Sten 24 C2
Bothlin Dr. Stepps 99 E3
Bothlyn Ave. Klrk 79 F4
Bothlyn Cres. Muir 100 C4
Bothlyn Rd. Muir 100 B4
Bothwell La. Glasg 96 C1
Bothwell La. Glasg 117 D4
Bothwell Pl. Coat 121 F4
Bothwell Pl. Pais 132 C4
Bothwell Rd. Car 187 F2
Bothwell Rd. Ham 162 B3
Bothwell Rd. Udd 140 C2
Bothwell St. Glasg 117 D4
Bothwell St. Glasg 138 C3
Bothwell St. Ham 162 B3
Bothwellhaugh Quadrant. Hat 141 F2
Bothwellhaugh Rd. Hat 142 A1
Bothwellpark Rd. Tan 141 E2
Bothwellshields Rd. Chap 124 B1
Boturich Dr. Bonh 19 F1
Boundary Rd. Pres 236 B2
Bourhill Ct. Wish 164 B1
Bourne Cres. Inch 93 E4
Bourne Ct. Inch 93 E4
Bourne St. Ham 162 C2
Bournemouth Rd. Gour 44 C3
Bourock Sq. Barr 134 C1
Bourtree Pk. Ayr 239 D4
Bourtree Rd. Ham 161 F1
Bouverie St. Clyde 94 C3
Bouverie St. Glasg 137 F4
Bouverie St. P Glasg 47 E1
Bow Rd. Green 45 E2
Bow St. Stir 7 D4
Bowden Dr. Glasg 115 D3
Bowden Pk. E Kil 180 B4
Bower St. Glasg 96 C2
Bowerwalls St. Barr 134 C2
Bowes Cres. Glasg 119 F2
Bowes Rigg. Stew 195 F1
Bowfield Ave. Glasg 114 C3
Bowfield Cres. Glasg 114 C3
Bowfield Dr. Glasg 115 D3
Bowfield Pl. Glasg 114 C3
Bowfield Rd. How 130 C3
Bowfield Rd. W Kil 190 B2
Bowhouse Gdns. All 10 A3
Bowhouse Rd. All 10 A3
Bowhouse Rd. Chap 123 F3
Bowhouse Rise. Irvine 220 A3
Bowhousebog Or Liquo. Shot 146 A1
Bowhousebog Rd. Shot 146 A1
Bowhousebrae Rd. Chap 123 F3
Bowie St. Dumb 49 F2
Bowling Green La. Glasg 95 E2
Bowling Green Rd. Glasg 95 E2
Bowling Green Rd. Glasg 119 E2
Bowling Green Rd. Glasg 137 D3
Bowling Green Rd. Muir 100 B4
Bowling Green St. Hat 142 A3
Bowling Green View. Glasg 139 F2
Bowling St. Coat 121 F4
Bowman Rd. Ayr 238 C3
Bowman St. Glasg 117 D1
Bowmanflat. Lark 185 D2
Bowmont Hill. Bish 78 A2
Bowmont Pl. E Kil 179 E4
Bowmont Pl. Glasg 139 E3
Bowmont Terr. Glasg 96 B2
Bowmore Ct. Irvine 220 A3
Bowmore Gdns. Glasg 138 C2
Bowmore Gdns. Tan 140 C4
Bowmore Rd. Glasg 115 F3
Bowmore Wlk. Shot 147 D2
Bowmount Gdns. Glasg 96 B2
Bowyer Vennel. Hat 141 F3
Boyd Ct. Kilmk 223 D1
Boyd Dr. Mother 163 D4
Boyd Orr Cres. Kilm 222 A4
Boyd Orr Rd. Salt 206 A1
Boyd St. Falk 42 A3
Boyd St. Glasg 117 E1
Boyd St. Kilmk 223 D1
Boyd St. Pres 236 B4
Boydston Rd. Ard 205 E2
Boydstone Pl. Glasg 136 A3
Boydstone Rd. Glasg 135 F3
Boyle St. Clyde 94 B4
Boylestone Rd. Barr 134 A2
Boyndie St. Glasg 120 A4
Brabloch Cres. Pais 113 F3
Bracadale Dr. Glasg 120 B2
Bracadale Gdns. Glasg 120 B2
Bracadale Gr. Glasg 120 B2
Bracadale Rd. Glasg 120 B2
Bracco Rd. Cald 105 E1
Brachelston St. Green 45 E2
Bracken Pk. Ayr 239 E2
Bracken Rd. P Glasg 69 D4
Bracken St. Glasg 97 D3
Bracken St. Holy 143 D2
Bracken Terr. Udd 141 D2
Bracken Way. Lark 185 E1
Brackenbrae Ave. Bish 77 F1
Brackenbrae Rd. Bish 77 F1
Brackendene. Hous 91 E1
Brackenhill Ave. Kilmk 223 D3
Brackenhill Dr. Ham 183 E4
Brackenhill Rd. Law 187 D3
Brackenhirst Rd. Glenm 102 C4
Brackenhurst St. Dumb 50 B3
Brackenknowe Rd. Gree 83 E2
Brackenlees Rd. Air 24 C3
Brackenlees Rd. Gran 24 C2
Brackenrig Cres. Eagle 157 F1
Brackenrig Rd. Glasg 135 F1
Brackla Ave. Clyde 94 C4
Bradan Ave. Ayr 239 D1
Bradan Ave. Clyde 94 C4
Bradan Rd. Troon 229 D1
Bradbury St. Sten 24 A1
Bradda Ave. Glasg 138 B2
Bradfield Ave. Glasg 96 B3
Bradshaw Cres. Ham 161 F2
Bradshaw St. Salt 216 C4
Brady Cres. Muir 81 D2
Brae The. Bann 7 E1
Brae The. Cam 6 B3
Braedale Ave. Aird 123 E4
Braedale Ave. Mother 163 E3
Braedale Cres. New 166 A3
Braedale Pl. New 166 B3
Braedale Rd. Lan 215 D3
Braeface Rd. Cumb 61 F1
Braefield Dr. Glasg 136 A2
Braefoot Ave. Miln 76 A4
Braefoot Cres. Law 186 C3
Braefoot Cres. Pais 133 F4
Braefoot Ct. Law 186 C3
Braefoot. Irvine 219 F3
Braehead. All 4 B1
Braehead. Alva 5 D4
Braehead Ave. Ayr 236 B1
Braehead Ave. Coat 121 E2
Braehead Ave. Dunt 74 A4
Braehead Ave. Lark 184 C1
Braehead Ave. Loch 129 E2
Braehead Ave. Miln 54 C1
Braehead Ave. Neil 154 B4
Braehead Ave. Tull 4 B1
Braehead. Beith 171 D4
Braehead. Bonh 28 A2
Braehead Cres. Ayr 236 B1
Braehead Cres. Dunt 74 A4
Braehead Ct. Kilmk 223 D1
Braehead. Dalry 191 E4
Braehead Dr. Hat 141 F2
Braehead Glebe. Stew 211 F4
Braehead. Irvine 219 F3
Braehead Loan. Car 202 A4
Braehead. Loch 129 E2
Braehead Pl. Dalry 191 E4
Braehead Pl. Hat 141 F2
Braehead Pl. Rhu 15 F3
Braehead Pl. Salt 216 C4
Braehead Quadrant. Holy 143 E2
Braehead Quadrant. Neil 154 B4
Braehead Rd. Ayr 236 B1
Braehead Rd. Cumb 62 A2
Braehead Rd. Dunt 74 A4
Braehead Rd. Fen 213 D2
Braehead Rd. P Glasg 68 C4
Braehead Rd. Pais 133 E4

Braehead Rd. Stir 7 E2
Braehead Rd. Thorn 158 B2
Braehead St. Glasg 117 E2
Braehead St. Kirk 58 B1
Braehead Terr. Kilm 222 B3
Braehead. Udd 161 E3
Braemar Ave. Clyde 73 F2
Braemar Cres. Bear 75 F1
Braemar Cres. Car 188 A2
Braemar Cres. Falk 42 B3
Braemar Cres. Pais 113 F1
Braemar Ct. Glasg 136 C2
Braemar Dr. Falk 42 B3
Braemar Dr. John 112 A1
Braemar Gdns. Duni 21 E2
Braemar Pl. Sten 24 A2
Braemar Rd. Glasg 138 C2
Braemar Sq. Ayr 236 B1
Braemar St. Glasg 136 C4
Braemar St. Ham 162 A3
Braemar View. Clyde 73 F3
Braemore Rd. Stew 195 E1
Braemount Ave. Pais 133 E3
Braes Ave. Clyde 74 B1
Braes O' Yetts. Kirk 80 A4
Braes Rd. Salt 216 C4
Braes The. Tull 4 B2
Braes View. Den 39 E4
Braes View. Shi 66 C3
Braesburn Ct. Cumb 62 C3
Braesburn Pl. Cumb 62 C3
Braesburn Rd. Cumb 62 C3
Braeside Ave. Glasg 138 B4
Braeside Ave. Miln 76 A4
Braeside Ave. Muir 80 C1
Braeside Cres. Barr 134 C1
Braeside Cres. Coat 120 C3
Braeside Dr. Barr 134 C1
Braeside Dr. Dumb 50 A3
Braeside Gdns. Ham 183 F4
Braeside. Irvine 219 F3
Braeside. Kilw 207 F3
Braeside La. Gour 44 B2
Braeside La. Lark 185 D2
Braeside. N Sau 5 E1
Braeside Pl. Glasg 139 D2
Braeside Rd. Ayr 236 B1
Braeside Rd. Gour 44 B2
Braeside Rd. Holy 143 E2
Braeside. Shi 66 B3
Braeside St. Glasg 96 C2
Braeside St. Kilmk 228 A4
Braeside Way. Lark 185 D1
Braeview Ave. Pais 133 D4
Braeview Dr. Pais 133 D4
Braeview Gdns. Pais 133 D4
Braeview. Lar 23 E1
Braeview. Laur 42 C2
Braeview Pl. E Kil 160 A2
Braeview Rd. Pais 133 D4
Braid Sq. Glasg 97 D1
Braid St. Glasg 97 D1
Braid's Rd. Pais 113 F1
Braidbar Ct. Glasg 136 B2
Braidbar Farm Rd. Glasg .. 136 B2
Braidbar Rd. Glasg 136 B2
Braidcraft Pl. Glasg 135 E4
Braidcraft Rd. Glasg 115 E1
Braidcraft Terr. Glasg 115 E1
Braidfauld Gdns. Glasg 118 C2
Braidfauld Pl. Glasg 118 C1
Braidfauld St. Glasg 118 C2
Braidfield Gr. Dunt 74 A3
Braidfield Rd. Dunt 74 A3
Braidfute. Lan 215 E3
Braidholm Cres. Glasg 136 B2
Braidholm Rd. Glasg 136 B2
Braidhurst Ind Est. Mother 142 B1
Braidhurst St. Mother 163 F4
Braidley Cres. E Kil 180 C3
Braidpark Dr. Glasg 136 B2
Braidwood Pl. Lin 111 F3
Braidwood Rd. Car 201 E1
Braidwood Rd. Car 201 F3
Braidwood Rd. Kilw 207 F2
Braidwood St. Wish 165 E4
Bramblehedge Path. Bonh ... 27 F4
Brambling Ct. Wish 165 D1
Bramley Pl. Klrk 79 F2
Brampton. E Kil 179 F3
Branchal Rd. Wish 165 E2
Branchalfield Dr. Wish 165 F2
Branchalmuir Cres. New ... 165 F3
Branchock Ave. Glasg 139 E2
Branchton Rd. Gour 44 C2
Brancumhall Rd. E Kil 160 B2
Brand St. Glasg 116 B3
Brandon Arc. Mother 163 F3
Brandon Dr. Bear 75 F4
Brandon Gdns. Glasg 138 C2
Brandon Gdns. Pres 236 A4
Brandon Par E. Mother 163 F4
Brandon Par S. Mother 163 F3
Brandon Pl. Hat 141 F4
Brandon St. Coat 121 F2
Brandon St. Glasg 117 F3

Brandon St. Ham 162 C2
Brandon St. Mother 163 F3
Brandon Way. Coat 121 F2
Brandyhill. Fish 5 F2
Brankholm Brae. Ham 161 E2
Brannock Ave. Holy 143 E2
Brannock Pl. Holy 143 E2
Brannock Rd. Holy 143 E2
Branshill Pk. N Sau 10 A4
Branshill Rd. N Sau 10 A4
Brassey St. Glasg 96 C3
Braxfield Rd. Lan 215 D1
Braxfield Terr. Lan 214 C1
Breadalbane Cres. Mother 142 B1
Breadalbane Gdns. Glasg . 138 B2
Breadalbane St. Glasg 116 C4
Breadie Dr. Miln 75 F4
Bream Pl. Hous 111 E4
Breamish Pl. E Kil 179 F3
Brechin Rd. Bish 78 B1
Brechin St. Glasg 116 C4
Breck Ave. Pais 132 B4
Brediland Rd. Lin 112 A3
Brediland Rd. Pais 112 C1
Bredin Way. Mother 163 D4
Bredisholm Cres. Tan 121 E1
Bredisholm Dr. Glasg 120 B2
Bredisholm Rd. Coat 120 C2
Bredisholm Rd. Glasg 121 D2
Bredisholm Rd. Glasg 120 B2
Bredisholm Terr. Glasg 120 B2
Brenfield Ave. Glasg 136 C2
Brenfield Dr. Glasg 136 C2
Brenfield Rd. Glasg 137 D2
Brent Cres. Hous 111 E4
Brent Ct. E Kil 159 F2
Brent Rd. E Kil 159 F2
Brentham Ave. Stir 7 D3
Brentham Cres. Stir 7 D3
Brentwood Ave. Glasg 135 D2
Brentwood Dr. Glasg 135 D2
Brentwood Sq. Glasg 135 D2
Brereton St. Glasg 117 E1
Breslin Terr. East 127 E3
Bressay. E Kil 159 F2
Bressay Pl. Kilmk 223 D3
Bressay Rd. Glasg 119 F3
Bressay Wynd. New 165 F3
Breton Cr. Falk 42 B2
Breval Cres. Dunt 74 A4
Brewery Rd. Kilmk 227 F4
Brewery St. John 111 F2
Brewlands Cres. Sym 231 E2
Brewlands Dr. Sym 231 E2
Brewlands Rd. Sym 231 E2
Brewster Ave. Pais 114 A4
Brewster Pl. Den 21 E1
Brewster Pl. Shew 224 C3
Briar Bank. M of C 58 A3
Briar Dr. Clyde 74 A2
Briar Gr. Ayr 239 E2
Briar Neuk. Bish 98 A4
Briar Pl. Gour 44 B3
Briar Rd. Glasg 136 B3
Briar Rd. Klrk 79 F4
Briarbush Way. Udd 161 E4
Briarcroft Pl. Glasg 99 E1
Briarcroft Rd. Glasg 99 E1
Briarhill Ct. Pres 236 B4
Briarhill St. Pres 236 B4
Briarlea Dr. Glasg 136 B2
Briars Rd. All 4 C1
Briarwell La. Miln 55 D1
Briarwell Rd. Miln 55 D1
Briarwood Ct. Glasg 119 F1
Briarwood Rd. Mother 164 C2
Brick La. Pais 113 F3
Bridesburn Pl. Stew 195 F1
Bridge Cres. Den 21 E1
Bridge End. Shot 146 B3
Bridge La. Kilmk 227 F4
Bridge of Weir Rd. B of W . 110 C4
Bridge Of Weir Rd. Hous ... 91 D1
Bridge Of Weir Rd. Kil 89 F3
Bridge Of Weir Rd. Kilbar .. 111 E3
Bridge Of Weir Rd. Lin 112 A3
Bridge Pl. Den 21 E1
Bridge Pl. Miln 55 D1
Bridge Pl. Shot 147 D2
Bridge Rd. P Glasg 68 C4
Bridge St. Alex 27 F2
Bridge St. Cald 84 C1
Bridge St. Clyde 73 F2
Bridge St. Dumb 49 F2
Bridge St. Glasg 139 D3
Bridge St. Ham 162 B4
Bridge St. Kilb 149 D1
Bridge St. Lin 112 B3
Bridge St. Mother 164 C2
Bridge St. Pais 113 F2
Bridge St. Pres 236 A4
Bridgebar St. Barr 134 C2
Bridgeburn Dr. Muir 80 C1
Bridgeford Ave. Hat 142 B4
Bridgegait. Miln 76 B4
Bridgegate. Glasg 117 E3
Bridgegate. Irvine 219 E1

Bridgehaugh Rd. Stir 2 A1
Bridgehousehill Rd. Kilmk . 227 F1
Bridgend Ave. P Glasg 68 C4
Bridgend. Bishop 72 A2
Bridgend Cotts. Kirk 80 A4
Bridgend. Dalry 191 E4
Bridgend. Kilw 207 F2
Bridgend La. Kilw 207 F2
Bridgend Rd. Green 46 B1
Bridgend Rd. Kilb 149 D1
Bridgend. Stew 211 E4
Bridgend View. Car 187 F1
Bridgend Wlk. Uplaw 153 D2
Bridgepark. Salt 205 E1
Bridgewater
    Shopping Ctr. Ersk 73 E1
Bridgeway Ct. Klrk 79 F4
Bridgeway Pl. Klrk 79 F4
Bridgeway Rd. Klrk 79 F4
Bridgeway Terr. Klrk 79 F4
Bridie Terr. E Kil 160 B2
Brierie Ave. Hous 91 D1
Brierie Gdns. Hous 111 D4
Brierie Hills. Hous 91 D1
Brierie La. Hous 111 D4
Brierie-Hill Ct. Hous 111 D4
Brierie-Hill Gr. Hous 111 D4
Brierie-Hill Rd. Hous 111 D4
Briery Ct. Kilb 170 A4
Brierybank Ave. Lan 215 D2
Brig O'Lea Terr. Neil 154 B3
Brig-O-Doon Gr. Cowie 12 C4
Brigbrae Ave. Hat 142 B2
Brigham Pl. Glasg 96 C4
Brighton Pl. Glasg 116 A3
Brighton St. Glasg 116 A3
Brightside Ave. P Glasg 69 D4
Brightside Ave. Udd 140 C3
Brigside Gdns. Ham 163 D1
Bringan Rd. Kilmk 222 C3
Brisbane Ct. Glasg 136 B2
Brisbane Rd. Bishop 72 A2
Brisbane St. Clyde 73 E2
Brisbane St. Glasg 137 D4
Brisbane St. Green 45 E3
Brisbane Terr. E Kil 180 B4
Britannia Pl. Ayr 236 A1
Britannia Way. Ren 94 B1
Briton St. Glasg 116 A4
Broad Sq. Udd 161 E4
Broad St. All 10 A3
Broad St. Den 21 F1
Broad St. Glasg 118 A3
Broad Way. Stir 7 D4
Broad Way The. Mother 164 C2
Broadcroft. Klrk 79 E4
Broadcroft Rd. Klrk 58 B1
Broadfield Ave. P Glasg 69 D4
Broadford St. Glasg 97 E1
Broadford Terr. Gour 44 C2
Broadholm St. Glasg 97 E3
Broadleys Ave. Bish 77 F1
Broadleys Rd. Stir 7 E4
Broadlie Ct. Neil 154 B4
Broadlie Dr. Glasg 135 D3
Broadlie Rd. Neil 154 B4
Broadloan. Ren 94 B1
Broadmoss Ave. Newt M ... 157 E2
Broadstone Ave. P Glasg 47 D1
Broadway. Ard 205 E2
Broadwood Dr. Glasg 137 D3
Broadwood Pk. Ayr 239 D1
Broadwood
    Roundabout. Cumb 81 F4
Brock Oval. Glasg 135 E3
Brock Pl. Glasg 135 E3
Brock Pl. Stir 7 D1
Brock Rd. Glasg 135 E3
Brock Terr. Glasg 135 E3
Brockburn Cres. Glasg 135 D4
Brockburn Rd. Glasg 115 D1
Brockburn Rd. Glasg 135 E4
Brockburn Terr. Glasg 135 E4
Brocklinn Pk. E Kil 179 F4
Brockly View. Kilb 149 D2
Brockville St. Glasg 118 C3
Brodick Ave. Mother 163 D4
Brodick Cl. Kilw 207 E2
Brodick Dr. E Kil 159 E2
Brodick Dr. Gour 43 F3
Brodick Pl. Falk 41 E2
Brodick Rd. Kilmk 222 B1
Brodick St. Glasg 98 A1
Brodie Ave. Troon 229 E2
Brodie Park Ave. Pais 113 F1
Brodie Park Cres. Pais 113 E1
Brodie Park Gdns. Pais 113 F1
Brodie Pl. E Kil 159 E2
Brodie Pl. Kilmk 223 E1
Brodie Pl. Stone 198 C1
Brodie Rd. Glasg 98 B4
Brodie St. Falk 42 A4
Brogan Cres. Mother 163 D4
Broich The. Alva 4 C4
Bron Way. Cumb 62 A1

Bronte Pl. Sten 24 A2
Brook St. Alva 5 D3
Brook St. Clyde 73 F2
Brook St. Glasg 117 F3
Brook St. Men 3 F3
Brookbank Terr. Car 188 A1
Brooke Ave. Bonh 28 A4
Brookfield Pl. Alva 5 D3
Brookfield Rd. P Glasg 68 C4
Brooklands. Alex 27 E3
Brooklands Ave. Udd 140 C4
Brooklands. E Kil 159 D1
Brooklea Dr. Glasg 136 B3
Brooklime Dr. E Kil 159 E2
Brooklyn Pl. Wish 186 A4
Brookside St. Glasg 118 A3
Broom Ave. Inch 93 D4
Broom Cliff. Newt M 156 C2
Broom Cres. Barr 134 A3
Broom Cres. E Kil 180 B3
Broom Ct. Stir 7 E2
Broom Dr. Clyde 74 A2
Broom Dr. Lark 185 D3
Broom Gdns. Klrk 79 D3
Broom Path. Glasg 119 F2
Broom Pk E. Men 4 A3
Broom Pk W. Men 4 A3
Broom Pl. B of W 110 C4
Broom Pl. Coat 121 F2
Broom Pl. Holy 143 E2
Broom Pl. Kilmk 228 A3
Broom Rd. Cumb 62 B3
Broom Rd E. Newt M 157 D2
Broom Rd. Glasg 136 B3
Broom Rd. Newt M 157 D3
Broom Rd. Ros 15 D2
Broom Rd. Stir 7 E2
Broom Terr. John 112 A1
Broom Wynd. Shot 146 C3
Broomage Ave. Lar 23 D2
Broomage Cres. Lar 23 D2
Broomage Dr. Lar 23 D2
Broomage Pk. Lar 23 E1
Broomberry Dr. Gour 44 C4
Broomburn Dr. Newt M 157 D3
Broomcroft Rd. Newt M 157 D3
Broomdyke Way. Pais 113 E4
Broomelton Rd. Quart 184 B1
Broomfield Ave. Glasg 138 B4
Broomfield Ave. Newt M ... 156 C2
Broomfield Gdn. Ayr 238 C3
Broomfield. Hous 91 E1
Broomfield La. Glasg 97 F3
Broomfield Pl. Glasg 97 F3
Broomfield Rd. Ash 199 F2
Broomfield Rd. Ayr 238 C3
Broomfield Rd. Glasg 98 A2
Broomfield Rd. Lark 199 D4
Broomfield Rd. Newt M 157 D3
Broomfield St. Aird 123 D4
Broomfield St. Ash 200 B2
Broomfield St. Kilw 207 F2
Broomfield Terr. Tan 120 C1
Broomfield Wlk. Klrk 79 E4
Broomgate. Lan 215 D2
Broomhill Ave. Glasg 95 F1
Broomhill Ave. Glasg 139 D4
Broomhill Ave. Lar 23 D1
Broomhill Ave. Newt M 157 C2
Broomhill Cres. Bonh 28 A1
Broomhill Cres. Hat 141 F2
Broomhill Cres. Inch 93 D4
Broomhill Dr. Dumb 50 A3
Broomhill Dr. Glasg 95 F2
Broomhill Dr. Glasg 138 A3
Broomhill Farm Mews. Kirk . 58 C1
Broomhill Gate. Lark 185 D1
Broomhill Gdns. Glasg 95 F1
Broomhill Gdns. Newt M ... 156 C2
Broomhill La. Glasg 95 F1
Broomhill Path. Glasg 95 F1
Broomhill Pl. Duni 21 E2
Broomhill Pl. Glasg 95 F1
Broomhill Pl. Stir 6 C3
Broomhill Quadrant. Kilmk 228 A2
Broomhill Rd. Bon 40 A2
Broomhill Rd E. Kilmk 228 A2
Broomhill Rd. Lark 185 D1
Broomhill Rd W. Kilmk 227 F2
Broomhill St. Green 45 E4
Broomhill Terr. Glasg 95 F1
Broomhill View. Lark 184 C1
Broomhill Way. Green 45 E4
Broomieknowe Dr. Glasg .. 138 A3
Broomieknowe Rd. Glasg . 138 A3
Broomieknowe. Tull 4 B2
Broomielaw. Glasg 117 D3
Broomknoll St. Aird 123 D4
Broomknowe. Cumb 61 E2
Broomknowe Rd. Kil 89 E4
Broomknowes Ave. Klrk 79 E2
Broomknowes Rd. Glasg 98 A2
Broomlands Ave. Inch 93 F4
Broomlands
    Busway. Irvine 220 A1
Broomlands Cres. Inch 93 E4
Broomlands Ct. Irvine 220 A1

Broomlands Dr. Irvine 219 E4
Broomlands Gdns. Inch 93 E4
Broomlands Pl. Irvine 219 E1
Broomlands Rd. Cumb 83 D4
Broomlands Rd. Irvine 220 A1
Broomlands St. Pais 113 E2
Broomlea Cres. Inch 93 E4
Broomlee Rd. Cumb 82 C3
Broomley Cres. Alex 27 E4
Broomley Dr. Glasg 136 B1
Broomley La. Glasg 136 B1
Broomloan Ct. Glasg 116 A3
Broomloan Pl. Glasg 116 A3
Broomloan Rd. Glasg 116 A3
Broompark Ave. Pres 236 B4
Broompark Ave. Udd 161 E3
Broompark Cir. Glasg 117 F4
Broompark Cres. Aird 103 D3
Broompark Cres. Pres 236 B4
Broompark Dr. Glasg 117 F4
Broompark Dr. Inch 93 E4
Broompark Dr. Newt M 157 D3
Broompark La. Glasg 117 F4
Broompark Rd. Mother 164 B2
Broompark Rd. Udd 161 E4
Broompark St. Glasg 117 F4
Broomridge Rd. Stir 7 E2
Broomside Cres. Mother ... 163 F2
Broomside Pl. Lar 23 E1
Broomside Rd. Bon 40 A2
Broomside St. Mother 163 F2
Broomstone Ave. Newt M . 156 C2
Broomton Rd. Glasg 98 B4
Broomvale Dr. Newt M 156 C3
Broomward Dr. John 112 A2
Brora Dr. Bear 76 A2
Brora Dr. Glasg 136 B3
Brora Dr. Ren 94 C2
Brora Gdns. Bish 78 A1
Brora Rd. Bish 78 A1
Brora St. Glasg 98 B1
Brosdale Ct. Falk 42 A1
Brougham St. Green 45 F4
Broughton Dr. Glasg 96 C4
Broughton. E Kil 180 C3
Broughton Gdns. Glasg 76 C1
Broughton Pl. Coat 122 A2
Broughton Pl. Ham 162 A2
Broughton Rd. Glasg 76 C1
Brouster Gate. E Kil 159 F1
Brouster Hill. E Kil 159 F1
Brouster Pl. E Kil 159 F1
Brown Ave. All 4 C1
Brown Ave. Dumb 50 A2
Brown Ave. Ren 94 C4
Brown Ave. Stir 2 A1
Brown Ave. Troon 229 E2
Brown Pl. Glasg 139 D3
Brown Pl. Salt 205 F1
Brown Rd. Cumb 61 F1
Brown St. Bonh 28 A4
Brown St. Car 187 F2
Brown St. Coat 122 A3
Brown St. Falk 41 E3
Brown St. Glasg 117 D4
Brown St. Green 46 B2
Brown St. Lark 185 D2
Brown St. Mother 163 F4
Brown St. New 166 A2
Brown St. P Glasg 47 D1
Brown St. Pais 113 E3
Brown St. Ren 94 A2
Brown St. Shot 147 D2
Brown St. Stew 211 E4
Brown Wlk. Irvine 219 E3
Brown's La. Pais 113 F2
Browncarrick Dr. Ayr 238 A1
Brownhill Dr. Kilb 169 F4
Brownhill Rd. Glasg 136 A2
Brownhill View. New 166 A3
Brownieside Pl. Plains 104 A2
Brownieside Rd. Plains 104 B1
Brownlee Rd. Law 186 B2
Brownlie St. Glasg 137 D4
Brownmuir Ave. Eagle 178 C2
Brownsburn Rd. Aird 123 E3
Brownsdale Rd. Glasg 137 F4
Brownsfield Cres. Inch 93 D3
Brownsfield Rd. Inch 93 D3
Brownshill Ave. Coat 121 F2
Brownside Ave. Barr 134 A3
Brownside Ave. Glasg 138 C3
Brownside Cres. Barr 134 A3
Brownside Dr. Barr 134 A3
Brownside Dr. Glasg 94 C3
Brownside Gr. Barr 134 A3
Brownside Mews. Glasg ... 138 C3
Brownside Rd. Glasg 138 C3
Browside Ave. Pais 133 E4
Bruar Way. New 165 F3
Bruart Ave. Sten 23 F2
Bruce Ave. Dund 225 F1
Bruce Ave. John 131 F4
Bruce Ave. Mother 163 E4
Bruce Ave. Pais 114 A3
Bruce Ave. Pres 236 A3

Bruce Cres. Ayr

Bruce Cres. Ayr 238 C4
Bruce Cres. Kilmk 227 F2
Bruce Cres. Plea 12 B2
Bruce Cres. Sten 24 A2
Bruce Ct. Aird 123 F4
Bruce Dr. Fall 8 B3
Bruce Dr. Sten 23 F2
Bruce La. Pres 236 A3
Bruce Pl. E Kil 180 C4
Bruce Rd. Bishop 72 A2
Bruce Rd. Glasg 116 C2
Bruce Rd. Holy 143 D1
Bruce Rd. Pais 114 A4
Bruce Rd. Ren 94 A1
Bruce St. All 10 B4
Bruce St. Bann 7 F1
Bruce St. Clyde 74 A1
Bruce St. Coat 122 A4
Bruce St. Dumb 50 A1
Bruce St. Falk 42 B3
Bruce St. Green 45 F3
Bruce St. Hat 142 A3
Bruce St. Kilmk 227 F2
Bruce St. P Glasg 47 E1
Bruce St. Plains 104 A1
Bruce St. Plea 12 B2
Bruce St. Stir 2 A1
Bruce Terr. Cam 6 B3
Bruce Terr. E Kil 180 C4
Bruce Terr. Irvine 219 E3
Bruce Terr. Udd 140 C1
Bruce's Loan. Lark 185 E1
Brucefield Pl. Glasg 120 B4
Brucehill Rd. Dumb 49 E2
Brunel Way. E Kil 180 C4
Brunstane Rd. Glasg 100 A1
Brunswick La. Glasg 117 E4
Brunswick St. Glasg 117 E4
Brunton St. Glasg 137 D3
Brunton Terr. Glasg 137 D2
Bruntsfield Ave. Glasg 135 D2
Bruntsfield Ave. Kilw 207 D2
Bruntsfield Gdns. Glasg .. 135 D2
Bryan St. Ham 162 A4
Bryce Ave. Sten 24 A1
Bryce Gdns. Lark 185 D2
Bryce Knox Ct. Irvine 220 A3
Bryce Pl. E Kil 180 B3
Brydson Pl. Lin 112 A3
Brymner St. Green 46 A4
Bryon Ct. Udd 141 D1
Bryony The. Tull 4 A1
Bryson Ct. Ham 183 E4
Bryson St. Dunt 74 C4
Bryson St. Falk 42 A3
Buccleuch Ave. Glasg 114 C4
Buccleuch Ave. Newt M 157 E4
Buccleuch Dr. Bear 75 F4
Buccleuch La. Glasg 97 D1
Buccleuch St. Glasg 97 D1
Buccleugh St. Green 45 F3
Buchan Gn. E Kil 160 A2
Buchan Rd. Holy 143 D1
Buchan Rd. Troon 229 F2
Buchan St. Ham 183 E4
Buchan St. Wish 165 D3
Buchan Terr. Glasg 138 C2
Buchanan Ave. Bishop 72 A2
Buchanan Ave. Bonh 28 A4
Buchanan Cres. Bish 98 B4
Buchanan Cres. Ham 162 A1
Buchanan Ct. Falk 42 A4
Buchanan Ct. Stepps 99 F3
Buchanan Dr. Bear 76 A2
Buchanan Dr. Bish 98 B4
Buchanan Dr. Glasg 138 B3
Buchanan Dr. Glasg 138 C3
Buchanan Dr. Klrk 79 E2
Buchanan Dr. Law 187 D3
Buchanan Dr. Newt M 156 C4
Buchanan Dr. Stir 2 A2
Buchanan Gdns. Glasg 119 F1
Buchanan Pl. Kilmk 228 A3
Buchanan Pl. Lennox 57 D1
Buchanan Rd. Helen 17 D1
Buchanan St. Aird 123 D4
Buchanan St. Coat 121 F3
Buchanan St. Dumb 50 A1
Buchanan St. Glasg 117 D4
Buchanan St. Glasg 117 E4
Buchanan St. Glasg 120 A2
Buchanan St. Green 45 D2
Buchanan St. John 111 F1
Buchanan St. Miln 55 D1
Buchandyke Rd. E Kil 160 A2
Buchlyvie Gdns. Bish 97 F4
Buchlyvie Rd. Glasg 114 C3
Buchlyvie St. Glasg 120 A4
Buckie. Ersk 73 D2
Buckie Wlk. Hat 142 A3
Buckingham Ct. Ham 161 F2
Buckingham Dr. Glasg 138 B4
Buckingham Dr. Glasg 139 D4
Buckingham Terr. Glasg 96 B2
Bucklaw Gdns. Glasg 115 E2

Bucklaw Pl. Glasg 115 E2
Bucklaw Terr. Glasg 115 E2
Buckley St. Glasg 97 E3
Bucksburn Rd. Glasg 98 B2
Buckthorne Pl. Glasg 135 D2
Buddon St. Glasg 118 B2
Buddhill Ave. Glasg 119 D3
Budshaw Ave. Chap 123 E1
Buiston Rd. Spring 211 E3
Bull Rd. Newt M 157 F3
Bull's Cl. Lan 215 D2
Bulldale Rd. Glasg 94 C3
Bulldale St. Glasg 94 C3
Bullionslaw Dr. Glasg 138 B3
Bulloch Ave. Glasg 136 B1
Bullwood Ave. Glasg 134 C4
Bullwood Ct. Glasg 115 D1
Bullwood Dr. Glasg 114 C1
Bullwood Gdns. Glasg 114 C1
Bullwood Pl. Glasg 114 C1
Bunbury Terr. E Kil 180 B4
Bunessan St. Glasg 115 F3
Bunhouse Rd. Glasg 96 B1
Buntine Cres. Stir 7 D2
Bunting Pl. Kilmk 228 B4
Burbank. Miln 55 D1
Burbank Terr. P Glasg 68 B4
Burgh Hall La. Glasg 96 A1
Burgh Hall St. Glasg 96 A1
Burgh La. Glasg 96 B2
Burgh Mews. All 10 A1
Burgh Rd. Pres 236 A4
Burgh Wlk. Gour 44 C4
Burghead Dr. Glasg 115 F4
Burghead Pl. Glasg 115 F4
Burgher St. Glasg 118 B3
Burghmuir Rd. Stir 7 D3
Burleigh Rd. Udd 141 D2
Burleigh St. Coat 122 A2
Burleigh St. Glasg 116 A4
Burleigh Way. All 10 B3
Burley Pl. E Kil 158 C1
Burlington Ave. Glasg 96 A3
Burmola St. Glasg 97 D2
Burn Cres. Chap 123 E1
Burn Cres. Holy 143 D2
Burn Dr. Stir 7 E2
Burn La. Holy 143 D2
Burn Rd. Car 187 F2
Burn Rd. Salt 216 B4
Burn St. Alex 27 F2
Burn Street La. Bonh 27 F2
Burn Terr. Glasg 138 C4
Burn View. Cumb 62 B2
Burn's Cres. Aird 123 D3
Burn's Pl. Steven 206 C1
Burnacre Gdns. Udd 140 C4
Burnbank Braes. Car 187 F1
Burnbank Ctr. Ham 162 A3
Burnbank Dr. Barr 134 B1
Burnbank Gdns. Ham 162 A3
Burnbank Pl. Ayr 239 D2
Burnbank Pl. Glasg 97 D1
Burnbank Pl. Stew 195 F1
Burnbank Quadrant. Aird .. 122 C4
Burnbank Rd. Ayr 239 D2
Burnbank Rd. Falk 42 A4
Burnbank Rd. Ham 162 A2
Burnbank St. Aird 122 C4
Burnbank St. Coat 122 A4
Burnbank St. Steven 217 E4
Burnbank Terr. Glasg 97 D1
Burnbank Terr. Kils 36 B1
Burnblea Gdns. Ham 162 C1
Burnblea St. Ham 162 B1
Burnbrae Ave. Bear 76 A4
Burnbrae Ave. Lin 112 B3
Burnbrae Ave. Muir 81 D1
Burnbrae Dr. Glasg 138 B3
Burnbrae Dr. Irvine 220 B3
Burnbrae Dr. John 112 B2
Burnbrae. Dunt 74 A3
Burnbrae Gdns. Alva 5 D3
Burnbrae Gdns. Falk 42 A3
Burnbrae Pl. E Kil 159 E1
Burnbrae Rd. Falk 42 A3
Burnbrae Rd. Hart 127 F3
Burnbrae Rd. John 112 B2
Burnbrae Rd. Kirk 80 A4
Burnbrae Rd. Muir 80 A2
Burnbrae Rd. Shot 146 C2
Burnbrae Rd. Stepps 79 F1
Burnbrae Rd. Udd 161 D4
Burnbrae St. Dunt 74 B4
Burnbrae St. Glasg 98 A2
Burnbrae St. Lark 184 C2
Burnbrae. Tow 59 F2
Burncleuch Ave. Glasg 139 D2
Burncrooks Ave. E Kil 159 E1
Burncrooks Ct. Dunt 73 F3
Burndale La. Kil 89 E4
Burndyke Ct. Glasg 116 B4
Burndyke Sq. Glasg 116 B4
Burnee. Fish 5 F2
Burness Ave. Ayr 238 C1
Burnet Rose Ct. E Kil 159 E2

Burnet Rose Gdns. E Kil ... 159 E2
Burnet Rose Pl. E Kil 159 E2
Burnett Rd. Glasg 119 F4
Burnett Terr. Ayr 236 A1
Burnfield Ave. Glasg 136 A2
Burnfield Cotts. Glasg 136 A2
Burnfield Dr. Glasg 136 A2
Burnfield Gdns. Glasg 136 B2
Burnfield Pl. Falk 42 B4
Burnfield Rd. Glasg 136 A2
Burnfoot Ave. Troon 229 E3
Burnfoot. Card 48 A4
Burnfoot Cres. Glasg 138 B3
Burnfoot Cres. Pais 133 E4
Burnfoot Dr. Glasg 115 D3
Burnfoot La. Ard 205 D2
Burnfoot La. Falk 42 A2
Burnfoot Pl. Kilmk 222 C2
Burnfoot Rd. Aird 122 C4
Burnfoot Rd. Loch 129 D1
Burnfoot Way. Troon 229 E3
Burngreen. Kils 60 B4
Burngreen Terr. Cumb 62 A3
Burnhall Pl. Wish 165 E1
Burnhall Rd. Wish 165 E1
Burnhall St. Wish 165 E1
Burnham Rd. Glasg 95 D2
Burnhaven. Ersk 73 D1
Burnhead La. Falk 42 B2
Burnhead La. P Glasg 68 B4
Burnhead Rd. Aird 103 E1
Burnhead Rd. Cumb 61 D1
Burnhead Rd. Glasg 136 C3
Burnhead Rd. Lar 23 E2
Burnhead Rd. Lark 185 E1
Burnhead Rd. P Glasg 68 B4
Burnhead St. Green 46 A1
Burnhead St. Tan 141 E4
Burnhill Quadrant. Glasg .. 137 F4
Burnhill St. Glasg 137 F4
Burnhouse Ave. Dalry 191 D4
Burnhouse Brae. Chap 123 F2
Burnhouse Cres. Ham 162 A1
Burnhouse Rd. Auld 180 A1
Burnhouse Rd. Ham 162 A1
Burnhouse St. Glasg 96 B3
Burniebrae. Aird 122 C4
Burniebrae Rd. Chap 123 F2
Burnlea Cres. Hous 91 D2
Burnlea Pl. Steven 206 C1
Burnlip Rd. Glen 102 A2
Burnmouth Ct. Glasg 119 F3
Burnmouth Rd. Glasg 119 F3
Burnock Pl. E Kil 179 F4
Burnpark Ave. Tan 140 B4
Burnpark Rd. Kilmk 227 F2
Burns Ave. Bishop 72 A2
Burns Ave. Kilmk 223 D2
Burns Ave. Salt 205 F2
Burns Cres. Hart 127 F3
Burns Cres. Irvine 220 A3
Burns Cres. Laur 42 C2
Burns Ct. Kirk 59 D1
Burns Dr. John 131 F4
Burns Dr. Kirk 59 D1
Burns Gdns. Udd 140 B1
Burns La. Chap 123 E2
Burns Loan. Lark 185 D2
Burns Pk. E Kil 160 A2
Burns Pl. Kilw 207 F2
Burns Pl. Shot 146 A3
Burns Prec. Kilmk 227 F4
Burns Rd. Chap 123 F2
Burns Rd. Cumb 62 A1
Burns Rd. Gour 44 B2
Burns Rd. Kirk 59 D1
Burns Rd. Troon 229 F2
Burns Sq. Ard 205 E2
Burns Sq. Gour 44 B2
Burns St. Alex 27 E1
Burns St. Alex 27 F4
Burns St. Clyde 73 F2
Burns St. Ham 162 B1
Burns St. Irvine 219 D2
Burns St. Stir 2 A1
Burns Statue Sq. Ayr 238 C4
Burns Terr. Ard 205 E2
Burns Terr. Cowie 12 B4
Burns Walk. Hat 142 A4
Burns Way. Holy 143 E2
Burnside Ave. Barr 134 A2
Burnside Ave. Calder 123 D1
Burnside Ave. Hat 142 B2
Burnside Ave. Kilbar 111 D3
Burnside Ave. Klrk 79 D4
Burnside Ave. P Glasg 68 C4
Burnside. Bear 75 E4
Burnside Cotts. Beith 173 E3
Burnside Cres. Bonh 27 F4
Burnside Cres. Dunt 74 A4
Burnside Cres. Ham 161 F3
Burnside Cres. Plea 12 B2
Burnside Cres. Shot 146 B3
Burnside Ct. Bear 75 E4
Burnside Ct. Glasg 138 B3
Burnside Ct. Mother 164 A2
Burnside Gate. Glasg 138 B3

Burnside Gdns. Kilbar 111 D1
Burnside Gdns. Newt M 157 E4
Burnside Gdns. Pres 233 E1
Burnside Gr. John 111 F1
Burnside Ind Est. Kils 60 B4
Burnside La. Ham 162 C1
Burnside Pl. Dumb 50 A1
Burnside Pl. Irvine 219 D2
Burnside Pl. Lark 185 D2
Burnside Pl. Pais 113 D4
Burnside Pl. Sten 24 A2
Burnside Pl. Troon 229 E2
Burnside Pl. W Kil 190 B3
Burnside Quadrant. Holy .. 143 D3
Burnside Rd. Aird 102 B1
Burnside Rd. Glasg 138 B2
Burnside Rd. Gour 44 C3
Burnside Rd. Holy 143 E2
Burnside Rd. John 112 B1
Burnside Rd. Men 3 F3
Burnside Rd. Newt M 157 D3
Burnside Rd. Pres 233 E2
Burnside St. Dumb 50 A1
Burnside St. Kilb 170 A3
Burnside St. Kilmk 227 F3
Burnside St. Mother 164 A2
Burnside St. N Sau 5 E3
Burnside St. Stir 7 E3
Burnside Terr. Falk 41 F3
Burnside View. Coat 121 F3
Burnside Wlk. Coat 121 F3
Burnstone Ave. Cumb 61 D1
Burntbroom Dr. Glasg 119 F2
Burntbroom Gdns. Glasg .. 119 F2
Burntbroom Rd. Glasg 119 F1
Burntbroom St. Glasg 119 E4
Burntshields Rd. Kilbar 110 B1
Burnwood Dr. Chap 124 A3
Burra Gdns. Bish 78 B1
Burrell Ct. Glasg 116 B1
Burrell's La. Glasg 117 F4
Burrelton Rd. Glasg 136 C3
Burstenman's Brae. Beith .. 207 F4
Burton La. Car 187 F1
Burton La. Glasg 117 D1
Busbie View. Cross 221 F1
Busbiehead. Irvine 220 A3
Busbiehill Pl. Kilmk 222 B1
Busby Pl. Kilw 207 F2
Busby Rd. E Kil 158 B4
Busby Rd. Hat 141 F4
Busby Rd. Newt M 157 F3
Busby Rd. Newt M 157 F4
Bush Cres. Wish 165 E1
Bushelhead Rd. Car 201 F3
Bushes Ave. Pais 113 E1
Busheyhill St. Glasg 139 D3
Bute Ave. Mother 163 E4
Bute Ave. P Glasg 69 D4
Bute Ave. Ren 94 B1
Bute Cres. Bear 75 F1
Bute Cres. Pais 133 E4
Bute Cres. Shot 146 B3
Bute Ct. Green 45 D3
Bute Ct. Irvine 220 B1
Bute Ct. Steven 217 E4
Bute Dr. John 111 E1
Bute. E Kil 160 B1
Bute Gdns. Glasg 96 B1
Bute Gdns. Glasg 136 C2
Bute La. Glasg 96 B1
Bute Pl. Ard 205 E1
Bute Rd. Inch 93 E1
Bute Rd. Kirk 80 A4
Bute St. Coat 122 A2
Bute St. Falk 42 A3
Bute St. Gour 44 B3
Bute St. Ham 162 B4
Bute Terr. Glasg 138 A3
Bute Terr. Salt 205 F1
Bute Terr. Tan 141 D4
Bute Tower. Glasg 138 C2
Butt Ave. Helen 16 C2
Butterbiggins Rd. Glasg .. 117 D2
Butterburnpark St. Ham .. 162 B1
Butterfield Pl. Glasg 117 D2
Buttermere. E Kil 179 F3
By Pass Rd. Beith 150 B1
By-Pass Rd. Bank 39 F3
Byars Rd. Klrk 79 D4
Byrebush Rd. Glasg 115 E1
Byrehill Ave. Kilw 207 D1
Byrehill Ave. Kilw 207 D1
Byrehill Pl. Kilw 207 D1
Byrehill Rd. Kilw 207 E1
Byrehill Rd. Kilw 218 C4
Byres Ave. Pais 114 A3
Byres Cres. Pais 114 A3
Byres Loch. Kilw 207 E2
Byres Rd. Glasg 96 B1
Byres Rd. Holy 143 F2
Byres Rd. John 112 B1
Byres Rd. Kilw 207 D1
Byresknowe La. Holy 143 D1
Byrestone Ave. Newt M 157 D2
Byretown Rd. Lan 214 C1
Byron Rd. Shot 146 A3
Byron St. Clyde 74 A2

Byron St. Glasg 95 F1
Byshot St. Glasg 97 E2

Cable Depot Rd. Clyde 73 F1
Cables Dr. Bonh 27 F3
Cabrach Loan. New 165 F3
Cadder Ct. Bish 78 A3
Cadder Pl. Glasg 96 C3
Cadder Rd. Bish 78 A3
Cadder Rd. Glasg 96 C4
Cadder Way. Bish 78 A3
Caddlehill St. Green 45 E3
Cadell Dr. Sten 24 A3
Cadell Gdns. E Kil 160 B3
Cadger's Sheuch. Kils 61 D4
Cadgers Loan. Plea 12 A1
Cadoc St. Glasg 139 D3
Cadogan St. Glasg 117 D4
Cadzow Ave. Glasg 157 D4
Cadzow Cres. Coat 121 F2
Cadzow Dr. Glasg 139 D3
Cadzow Dr. Hat 142 B2
Cadzow Gn. E Kil 159 E1
Cadzow Ind Est. Ham 183 E4
Cadzow La. Ham 162 C2
Cadzow Rd. Quart 183 F2
Cadzow St. Ham 162 C2
Cadzow St. Lark 185 D2
Cadzow St. Mother 163 E3
Caerlaverock Ave. Pres 236 B4
Caerlaverock Pl. Udd 161 E3
Caerlaverock Rd. Pres 236 B4
Caird Ave. Green 45 E4
Caird Dr. Glasg 96 A1
Caird Gdns. Ham 162 B3
Caird Pk. Ham 162 B3
Caird St. Ham 162 B3
Caird Terr. Bear 75 E4
Cairn Ave. Ren 94 C1
Cairn Cl. Stew 195 E1
Cairn Cres. Ayr 238 B1
Cairn Ct. E Kil 159 F2
Cairn Dr. Lin 112 A3
Cairn Pl. E Kil 159 F2
Cairn St. Glasg 97 F3
Cairn View. Aird 122 C3
Cairn View. Kirk 80 A4
Cairnbairn Ct. Car 187 F2
Cairnban St. Glasg 115 E3
Cairnbrook Ind Est. Glasg . 120 B4
Cairnbrook Rd. Glasg 120 B4
Cairncurran Ct. Green 45 F2
Cairndhu Ave. Helen 16 A1
Cairndhu Gdns. Helen 16 A1
Cairndow Ave. Glasg 136 C3
Cairndow
     Avenue La. Glasg 136 C2
Cairndow Ct. Glasg 136 C2
Cairnduff Pl. Stew 195 F1
Cairndyke Cres. Aird 123 D3
Cairney Pl. New 166 B3
Cairneymount Rd. Car 188 A1
Cairnfore Ave. Troon 229 F3
Cairngorm Cres. Barr 134 B1
Cairngorm Cres. Bear 75 D3
Cairngorm Cres. Pais 133 F4
Cairngorm Cres. Wish 164 C2
Cairngorm Ct. Irvine 220 A3
Cairngorm Gdns. Cumb 61 D1
Cairngorm Rd. Glasg 136 B3
Cairngorm Rd. Kilmk 228 A2
Cairnhill Ave. Aird 123 D3
Cairnhill Cir. Glasg 114 C2
Cairnhill Cres. Coat 122 B2
Cairnhill Ct. Car 188 A1
Cairnhill Dr. Glasg 114 C2
Cairnhill Pl. Glasg 114 C2
Cairnhill Rd. Aird 123 D3
Cairnhill Rd. Bear 75 F1
Cairnhope Ave. Aird 122 C3
Cairnlea Dr. Glasg 116 A3
Cairnlea Gdns. Hat 142 A2
Cairnlea Rd. Miln 54 C1
Cairnmount Rd. Irvine 219 F4
Cairnmuir Rd. E Kil 159 E3
Cairnoch Hill. Cumb 61 D1
Cairnoch Way. Bann 7 F1
Cairnoch Wlk. Den 21 E1
Cairnryan. E Kil 159 E2
Cairns Ave. Glasg 139 D3
Cairns Dr. Miln 55 D1
Cairns Rd. Bishop 72 A2
Cairns Rd. Glasg 139 D2
Cairns St. Mother 163 F3
Cairns Terr. Kilmk 222 C1
Cairns The. Men 4 A3
Cairnsgarroch Way. Irvine . 220 A1
Cairnsmore Dr. Ayr 238 B1
Cairnsmore Dr. Bear 75 D3
Cairnsmore Rd. Glasg 74 C1
Cairnsmore Way. Irvine 220 A1
Cairnswell Ave. Glasg 139 E2
Cairnswell Pl. Glasg 139 E2
Cairntoul Ct. Cumb 61 D1
Cairntoul Dr. Glasg 95 D3
Cairntoul Pl. Glasg 95 D3
Cairnview Rd. M of C 58 B3
Cairnwood Dr. Aird 122 C3

Cairnwood Dr. Aird

Caithness Rd. E Kil 160 B2
Caithness Rd. Gour 44 B2
Caithness Row. Lan 215 D1
Caithness St. Glasg 96 C2
Caithness St. Udd 161 E3
Cala Sona Ct. Wish 185 F4
Calcots Path. Glasg 100 B1
Calcots Pl. Glasg 100 B1
Caldarvan St. Glasg 97 D2
Calder Ave. Barr 134 B1
Calder Ave. Cald 104 C2
Calder Ave. Coat 122 A2
Calder Ave. New 166 A3
Calder Ave. Troon 229 F3
Calder Ct. Coat 122 A2
Calder Ct. Stir 7 E3
Calder Dr. Glasg 139 D3
Calder Dr. Hat 142 B2
Calder Dr. Loch 129 E2
Calder Dr. Shot 147 D2
Calder Gate. Bish 77 F2
Calder Pl. Falk 42 B1
Calder Pl. Glasg 120 A2
Calder Pl. Kilmk 228 A3
Calder Rd. Alla 166 C4
Calder Rd. Hat 142 B3
Calder Rd. Pais 113 D3
Calder Rd. Udd 140 B3
Calder St. Calder 123 E1
Calder St. Coat 122 B3
Calder St. Glasg 117 D1
Calder St. Loch 129 E2
Calder St. Udd 161 E4
Calder Tower. Mother 163 F4
Calder View. Ham 183 D4
Calder View. Mother 163 F4
Calderbank Rd. Calder 123 D2
Calderbank Terr. Mother ... 163 F4
Calderbank View. Glasg 120 B2
Calderbraes Ave. Tan 140 C4
Caldercruix Rd. Cald 105 E4
Caldercuilt Rd. Glasg 76 B1
Calderglen Ave. Udd 140 B2
Calderglen Rd. E Kil 160 B1
Caldergrove. Mother 163 F4
Calderhaugh La. Loch 129 D1
Calderhead Rd. Shot 146 B4
Calderpark Ave. Glasg 120 A1
Calderpark Ave. Loch 129 E2
Calderpark Cres. Glasg 120 A1
Calderpark St. Loch 129 E2
Calderrigg Pl. Aird 123 F4
Calderside Rd. Ham 160 C2
Caldervale St. Chap 123 F2
Calderview Ave. Coat 122 C2
Calderwood Ave. Glasg 120 A2
Calderwood Dr. Glasg 120 A2
Calderwood Dr. Udd 161 E3
Calderwood Gdns. E Kil 160 C2
Calderwood Gdns. Glasg .. 120 A2
Calderwood. Kilw 207 F3
Calderwood Rd. E Kil 160 A1
Calderwood Rd. Glasg 136 B3
Calderwood Rd. Glasg 138 B4
Calderwood Sq. E Kil 160 A2
Caldon Rd. Irvine 219 E2
Caldwell Ave. Glasg 95 D3
Caldwell Ave. Lin 112 A3
Caldwell Gr. Hat 142 A4
Caldwell Pl. Rhu 15 F3
Caldwell Quadrant. Mother 163 E3
Caldwell Rd. Car 202 A4
Caldwell Rd. W Kil 190 B2
Caledon La. Glasg 96 B1
Caledon St. Glasg 96 B2
Caledonia Ave. Glasg 117 E2
Caledonia Ave. Glasg 138 A4
Caledonia Cres. Ard 205 E1
Caledonia Cres. Gour 44 C4
Caledonia Cres. Gour 45 D4
Caledonia Ct. Pais 113 E3
Caledonia Dr. Glasg 120 A2
Caledonia Dr. Holy 143 F2
Caledonia Rd. Ard 205 E1
Caledonia Rd. Ayr 239 E3
Caledonia Rd. Beith 150 A1
Caledonia Rd. Glasg 117 E2
Caledonia Rd. Glasg 120 A2
Caledonia Rd. Salt 216 C4
Caledonia Rd. Shot 146 C3
Caledonia St. Clyde 73 C2
Caledonia St. Glasg 117 E2
Caledonia St. P Glasg 47 E1
Caledonia St. Pais 113 E3
Caledonia Terr. Dumb 49 E2
Caledonia Way E. Inch 93 F1
Caledonia Way. Inch 93 E1
Caledonia Way W. Inch 93 E1
Caledonia Wlk. Ham 162 C1
Caledonian Ave. Hat 141 F2
Caledonian Ave. Stone 198 C1
Caledonian Cres. Glasg 96 C1
Caledonian Ct. E Kil 180 C4
Caledonian Gdns. All 9 F3
Caledonian Pl. Kilb 170 A4
Caledonian Rd. All 9 F3
Caledonian Rd. Kilb 170 B4
Caledonian Rd. Lark 185 D2

Caledonian Rd. Steven 217 F4
Caledonian Rd. Wish 165 D1
Caley Brae. Udd 140 C3
Caley Ct. Steven 217 E4
Calfhill Rd. Glasg 115 D1
Calfmuir Rd. Kirk 80 A3
Calgary Pk. E Kil 180 B4
Calgary Pl. E Kil 180 B4
Calgary St. Glasg 97 E1
California Terr. Cali 66 C3
Callaghan Wynd. Udd 140 B1
Callander Dr. Lar 41 E4
Callander St. Glasg 97 D2
Callander Ave. Falk 42 A1
Callandar Pl. Ayr 236 A2
Callendar Pl. Falk 42 B2
Callendar Riggs. Falk 42 B2
Callender Bsns Pk. Falk 42 C2
Callender Rd. Chap 123 E1
Callender Rd. Pres 236 B3
Callieburn Rd. Bish 98 A4
Callon St. Aird 123 D4
Cally Ave. Glasg 75 D2
Calside Ave. Pais 113 F2
Calside. Pais 113 F2
Calton Cres. Stir 7 D2
Calton Entry. Glasg 117 F3
Calvay Cres. Glasg 119 E4
Calvay Rd. Glasg 119 F4
Calvinston Rd. Pres 236 B3
Cam'nethan St. Stone 198 C1
Cambourne Rd. Muir 80 C2
Cambridge Ave. Clyde 74 A2
Cambridge Ave. Gour 45 D4
Cambridge Rd. Gour 44 B2
Cambridge Rd. Ren 94 B1
Cambridge St. Glasg 117 D4
Camburn St. Glasg 118 C3
Cambus Pl. Glasg 99 E1
Cambusdoon Dr. Ayr 238 C1
Cambusdoon Pl. Kilw 207 E2
Cambusdoon Rd. Glasg 99 E1
Cambuskeith Rd. Steven ... 206 C2
Cambuskenneth
   Gdns. Glasg 119 E3
Cambuskenneth Pl. Glasg .. 99 E1
Cambuslang Ind Est. Glasg 139 D4
Cambuslang Rd. Glasg 138 B4
Cambuslang Rd. Glasg 138 C4
Cambuslea Rd. Ayr 236 A2
Cambusmoon Terr. Gart 20 C4
Cambusnethan St. Wish 165 F2
Camden St. Glasg 117 E2
Camelon Cres. Udd 161 E4
Camelon Rd. Falk 41 F3
Camelon St. Glasg 118 C3
Cameron Ave. Bishop 72 A2
Cameron Cres. E Kil 158 C4
Cameron Cres. Ham 162 B2
Cameron Ct. Aird 123 F4
Cameron Ct. Glasg 138 A4
Cameron Dr. Alex 27 E4
Cameron Dr. Bear 76 A2
Cameron Dr. Kilmk 223 E1
Cameron Dr. Newt M 156 C4
Cameron Dr. Tan 141 D4
Cameron Path. Lark 185 E1
Cameron Pl. Sten 24 A1
Cameron Rd. Car 202 A4
Cameron Rd. Gree 83 E1
Cameron Sq. Dunt 74 B3
Cameron St. Clyde 94 B4
Cameron St. Coat 122 A4
Cameron St. Glasg 114 C4
Cameron St. Mother 163 E3
Cameron Terr. Slam 86 A2
Cameronian Ct. Lan 215 E3
Cameronian Dr. Car 188 A1
Cameronian Pl. Hat 141 F2
Cameronian St. Stir 7 D4
Cameronian Way. Lark 185 E1
Camis Eskan House. Card .. 25 E4
Camlachie St. Glasg 118 A3
Camp Rd. Glasg 117 F1
Camp Rd. Glasg 120 A3
Camp Rd. Mother 163 F2
Camp St. Mother 163 F3
Campbell Ave. Bishop 72 A2
Campbell Ave. Dumb 50 B2
Campbell Ave. Miln 55 D1
Campbell Ave. Salt 216 C4
Campbell Ave. Steven 206 B1
Campbell Cres. Alex 27 E4
Campbell Cres. Laur 42 C2
Campbell Cres. Newt M ... 156 C3
Campbell Cres. Udd 141 D2
Campbell Ct. Ayr 239 E4
Campbell Ct. Green 45 F4
Campbell Ct. Stir 6 C2
Campbell Dr. Barr 134 B1
Campbell Dr. Bear 75 E2
Campbell Dr. Dumb 50 B2
Campbell Dr. Helen 25 D2
Campbell Dr. Lar 23 D1
Campbell Dr. Troon 229 E3
Campbell La. Ham 162 C2
Campbell Pl. E Kil 180 C4
Campbell Pl. Irvine 225 D2

Campbell Pl. Lennox 57 D1
Campbell St. Ayr 236 A2
Campbell St. Bonh 27 F2
Campbell St. Glasg 96 C4
Campbell St. Green 45 F3
Campbell St. Ham 162 C2
Campbell St. Hat 142 A3
Campbell St. Helen 16 B2
Campbell St. John 111 F1
Campbell St. Kilmk 227 F3
Campbell St. Ren 94 B3
Campbell St. Wish 165 E1
Campbell Terr. Dumb 50 B2
Campbeltown Dr. Kilmk ... 222 C2
Camperdown Ct. Helen 17 D1
Campfield St. Falk 42 A3
Camphill Ave. Glasg 136 C4
Camphill Ave. Klrk 79 E4
Camphill Dr. Kilb 170 A4
Camphill Gdns. Bishop 72 B2
Camphill. Pais 113 E2
Camphill Pl. Ayr 239 D3
Campie Terr. Gran 24 C1
Camplon Cl. Ayr 239 D2
Campion Rd. Mother 163 F4
Camps Cres. Ren 94 C1
Campsie Ave. Barr 134 B1
Campsie Ave. Irvine 220 A2
Campsie Cres. Aird 122 C4
Campsie Cres. Klrk 79 E3
Campsie Dene Rd. Strath ... 31 D2
Campsie Dr. Bear 75 F4
Campsie Dr. Inch 93 F1
Campsie Dr. Miln 55 D1
Campsie Dr. Pais 133 E1
Campsie Dr. Ren 114 A4
Campsie Gdns. Newt M ... 157 D4
Campsie Pl. Muir 100 B4
Campsie Rd. Kilmk 228 A2
Campsie Rd. Lennox 57 F1
Campsie Rd. Lennox 58 A1
Campsie Rd. M of C 58 A3
Campsie Rd. P Glasg 69 D2
Campsie Rd. Wish 164 C2
Campsie St. Glasg 98 A3
Campsie View. Coat 120 C3
Campsie View. Cumb 62 A2
Campsie View Dr. Strath ... 31 D2
Campsie View. Ham 161 F1
Campsie View. Klrk 79 D4
Campsie View. Muir 100 B4
Campsie View. Stepps 99 E2
Campsie View. Tan 141 D4
Campsie Way. Irvine 220 A2
Campsie Wlk. Irvine 220 A2
Campston Pl. Glasg 99 D1
Camsail Ave. Helen 16 A1
Camsail Rd. Ros 15 D2
Camsbusmore Pl. Glasg 99 E1
Camsdale Ave. Sals 125 D1
Camstradden Dr E. Bear ... 75 E2
Camstradden Dr W. Bear ... 75 E2
Camus Pl. Glasg 74 C2
Canal Ave. John 112 A1
Canal Cres. Steven 217 E4
Canal Ct. Salt 217 D4
Canal La. Kirk 58 B1
Canal Pl. Salt 217 D4
Canal Rd. John 112 A1
Canal St. Falk 41 E3
Canal St. Glasg 97 E1
Canal St. John 112 A2
Canal St. John 112 B2
Canal St. Kirk 58 B1
Canal St. Pais 113 E2
Canal St. Ren 94 B2
Canal St. Salt 217 D4
Canal Terr. Pais 113 F2
Canavan Ct. Stir 7 E2
Canberra Ave. Clyde 73 E2
Canberra Ct. Glasg 136 C2
Canberra Dr. E Kil 180 B4
Cander Ave. Stone 199 D2
Cander Rigg. Bish 78 A2
Cander St. Lark 199 D4
Candermill &
   Marlage Rd. Ash 199 F3
Candermill Rd. Ash 199 D2
Candermill Rd. Stone 199 D2
Canderside Toll. Ash 199 E3
Candimilne Ct. Car 188 A1
Candleriggs. All 10 A3
Candleriggs. Glasg 117 E4
Candren Rd. Lin 112 C3
Candren Rd. Pais 113 D3
Candren Rd. Pais 113 D3
Caneluk Ave. Car 188 A1
Cangillan Ct. Pres 236 B3
Canmore Cres. Green 45 D2
Canmore Dr. Sten 23 F2
Canmore Pl. Glasg 118 B2
Canmore Pl. Stew 195 F1
Canmore St. Glasg 118 B2
Cannerton Cres. M of C 58 A3
Cannich Dr. Pais 114 A1
Cannich Pl. New 165 F3
Canniesburn Rd. Bear 75 D1

Canniesburn Toll. Bear 75 F2
Cannons Way. Falk 24 A1
Canon Ct. Holy 143 E1
Canonbie St. Glasg 100 B1
Canongate. E Kil 160 B2
Canterbury. E Kil 180 B4
Canthill Gdns. Shot 146 A2
Cantieslaw Dr. E Kil 160 A2
Canton Way. Glasg 116 B4
Canyon Rd. Wish 164 B1
Capel Ave. Newt M 156 C3
Capel Gr. E Kil 160 A2
Capel Pl. Irvine 220 A1
Capelrig Cotts. Newt M 155 F2
Capelrig Dr. E Kil 160 A2
Capelrig Rd. Newt M 156 C3
Capelrig St. Glasg 135 F2
Caplaw Pl. Wish 185 F4
Caplaw Rd. Pais 133 E3
Caplaw Rd. Uplaw 132 B1
Caplaw Tower. Wish 185 F4
Caplethill Rd. Barr 134 A3
Caplethill Rd. Paic 133 F4
Caponcraig Ave. Steven 206 B1
Capper View. Pres 233 E1
Cappielow Ind Est. Green ... 46 B2
Capringstone Foot. Irvine ... 220 A3
Caprington Ave. Kilmk 227 F2
Caprington Gdns. Kilmk 227 F2
Caprington St. Glasg 99 D1
Captain St. Green 45 F4
Cara Dr. Glasg 115 F4
Caravelle Way. Ren 94 B1
Carbarns E. Wish 164 B1
Carbarns Rd. Wish 164 B1
Carbarns W. Wish 164 B1
Carbarns. Wish 164 C1
Carberry Rd. Glasg 116 B1
Carbeth Rd. Miln 54 C1
Carbeth St. Glasg 97 D2
Carbisdale St. Glasg 97 F3
Carbost St. Glasg 76 B1
Carbrook Dr. Plea 12 B2
Carbrook St. Glasg 98 A1
Carbrook St. Pais 113 E2
Carcluie Cres. Ayr 239 D1
Cardarrach St. Glasg 98 A2
Cardean Rd. Holy 142 C3
Cardell Ave. Pais 113 D2
Cardell Dr. Pais 113 D2
Cardell Rd. Pais 113 D2
Cardon Pl. Irvine 220 A1
Cardonald Dr. Glasg 115 D2
Cardonald Gdns. Glasg 115 D2
Cardonald Place Rd. Glasg 115 D2
Cardow Cres. Irvine 220 A3
Cardow Rd. Glasg 98 B2
Cardowan Dr. Stepps 99 F3
Cardowan Rd. Glasg 119 D4
Cardowan Rd. Stepps 99 F3
Cardrona St. Glasg 99 D2
Cardross Ave. P Glasg 68 C4
Cardross Cres. Green 46 B1
Cardross Ct. Glasg 117 F4
Cardross Pl. Green 46 B1
Cardross Rd. Alex 27 D1
Cardross Rd. Card 25 D2
Cardross Rd. Card 26 C1
Cardross Rd. Dumb 49 E2
Cardross Rd. Helen 25 D4
Cardross St. Glasg 117 F4
Cardrowan Rd. Plea 12 B1
Cardwell Rd. Gour 44 C4
Cardwell St. Glasg 117 D2
Cardyke St. Glasg 98 A2
Careloch Rd. P Glasg 68 C4
Careston Pl. Bish 78 B1
Carey Gdns. Cle 144 B1
Carey Rd. Salt 205 F2
Carfin Dr. Car 201 E1
Carfin Mill Rd. Holy 143 E1
Carfin Rd. Holy 143 E1
Carfin Rd. Mother 164 B2
Carfin St. Coat 122 A2
Carfin St. Glasg 117 D1
Carfin St. Holy 143 E2
Carfrae St. Glasg 116 B4
Cargil Ave. Kil 89 E4
Cargill Dr. Pres 236 B3
Cargill Sq. Bish 98 B4
Cargill St. Glasg 118 C2
Carham Cres. Glasg 115 E3
Carham Dr. Glasg 115 E3
Caribou Gn. E Kil 180 A4
Carillon Rd. Glasg 116 B3
Carisbrooke Cres. Bish 78 A4
Carlaverock Rd. Glasg 136 C3
Carleith Ave. Dunt 73 F3
Carleith Quadrant. Glasg .. 115 E4
Carleith Terr. Dunt 73 F3
Carleston St. Glasg 97 F2
Carleton Dr. Glasg 136 B2
Carleton Gate. Glasg 136 B2
Carleton Gdns. Pres 236 B4
Carlibar Ave. Glasg 94 C4
Carlibar Dr. Barr 134 B2

Carlibar Gdns. Barr 134 B2
Carlibar Rd. Barr 134 B2
Carlie Ave. B of A 2 A3
Carlile Pl. Pais 113 F3
Carlin La. Car 188 A1
Carlisle La. Aird 123 E4
Carlisle Rd. Aird 123 E3
Carlisle Rd. Ash 199 E2
Carlisle Rd. Chap 123 E3
Carlisle Rd. Chap 144 B3
Carlisle Rd. Cle 144 B1
Carlisle Rd. Ham 163 D1
Carlisle Rd. Lark 184 C4
Carlisle Rd. Lark 199 E2
Carlisle St. Glasg 97 E2
Carlowrie Ave. Udd 140 B1
Carlton Ct. Glasg 117 E3
Carlton Pl. Glasg 117 D3
Carlung Pl. W Kil 190 B3
Carlyle Ave. Glasg 114 C4
Carlyle Dr. E Kil 160 A1
Carlyle Terr. E Kil 160 A1
Carlyle Terr. Glasg 118 A1
Carmaben Rd. Glasg 119 F3
Carman Dr. Alex 27 E1
Carman Rd. Card 48 B3
Carmel Ave. Kilmk 222 B1
Carmel Dr. Spring 221 D1
Carmel Pl. Kilm 222 A4
Carmel Pl. Kilmk 222 B1
Carmel Terr. Kilmk 222 B1
Carmen View. Dumb 50 A3
Carment Dr. Glasg 136 B2
Carment Dr. Steven 217 F4
Carmichael Path. Glen 101 E3
Carmichael Pl. Glasg 136 C4
Carmichael St. Glasg 116 B3
Carmichael St. Green 45 E3
Carmichael St. Law 186 C3
Carmichael Way. Law 186 C3
Carmona Dr. Bonh 28 A4
Carmuirs Ave. Falk 41 E3
Carmuirs Dr. Falk 41 E3
Carmuirs St. Falk 41 E3
Carmunnock
   By-Pass. E Kil 158 B4
Carmunnock Rd. E Kil 159 D2
Carmunnock Rd. E Kil 159 E2
Carmunnock Rd. Glasg 137 E3
Carmunnock Rd. Thorn 158 A3
Carmyle Ave. Glasg 139 D4
Carmyle Pl. Steven 217 E4
Carna Dr. Glasg 137 E3
Carnarvon St. Glasg 96 C1
Carnaughton Pl. Alva 4 C3
Carnbooth Ct. Glasg 137 F1
Carnbroe Rd. Coat 122 B2
Carnbroe Rd. Hat 122 B1
Carneddans Rd. Miln 54 B2
Carnegie Dr. Falk 41 E3
Carnegie Hill. E Kil 180 B4
Carnegie Pl. E Kil 180 B4
Carnegie Rd. Glasg 115 D3
Carnell Cres. Pres 236 B4
Carnell Terr. Pres 236 B4
Carnoch St. Glasg 76 B1
Carnock Cres. Barr 134 A1
Carnock Gdns. Miln 54 C1
Carnock Rd. Glasg 135 E2
Carnock St. Cowie 12 C4
Carnock St. Green 46 A2
Carnoustie Ave. Gour 44 A3
Carnoustie Cres. Bish 78 B1
Carnoustie Cres. E Kil 180 A3
Carnoustie Ct. Kilw 207 D2
Carnoustie Ct. Udd 140 C1
Carnoustie Pl. Glasg 116 C3
Carnoustie Pl. Hat 142 A4
Carnoustie St. Glasg 116 C3
Carntyne Path. Glasg 118 B4
Carntyne Pl. Glasg 118 B4
Carntyne Rd. Glasg 118 C4
Carntynehall Rd. Glasg 118 C3
Carnwadric Rd. Glasg 135 F2
Carnwath Ave. Glasg 136 C3
Carnwath Rd. Car 188 A1
Carnwath Rd. Kilnc 203 E3
Caroline Cres. Alva 4 C3
Caroline St. Glasg 118 C3
Carolside Ave. Newt M ... 157 D3
Carolside Dr. Glasg 75 D2
Carolside Gdns. Newt M ... 157 F4
Carradale Ave. Falk 41 E2
Carradale Cres. Cumb 81 F4
Carradale Dr. Pres 236 B3
Carradale Gdns. Bish 78 B1
Carradale Gdns. Car 202 A4
Carradale Pl. Lin 112 A3
Carradale St. Coat 121 F4
Carranbuie Rd. Car 187 F2
Carrbridge Dr. Glasg 96 B3
Carresbrook Ave. Kirk 80 A3
Carriagehill Ave. Pais 113 F1
Carriagehill Dr. Pais 113 F1
Carrick Ave. Ayr 238 C3
Carrick Ave. Salt 206 A2
Carrick Cres. Glasg 136 B1
Carrick Cres. Wish 165 D2

Carrick Ct. Kirk 59 D1
Carrick Ct. Stir 7 E3
Carrick Dr. Coat 121 E4
Carrick Dr. Glasg 119 F2
Carrick Dr. Glasg 138 A3
Carrick Dr. Irvine 219 D3
Carrick Gdns. Ayr 238 C3
Carrick Gdns. Car 202 A4
Carrick Gdns. Ham 161 F1
Carrick Gdns. Hat 142 A4
Carrick Gdns. Udd 161 E3
Carrick Gr. Glasg 119 F2
Carrick La. Gour 44 C2
Carrick Pk. Ayr 238 C3
Carrick Pl. Ard 205 E2
Carrick Pl. Coat 121 E4
Carrick Pl. Falk 41 E2
Carrick Pl. Glen 101 F3
Carrick Pl. Hat 142 A4
Carrick Pl. Lark 185 D2
Carrick Pl. Pres 236 A4
Carrick Pl. Sten 24 A2
Carrick Rd. Ayr 238 C3
Carrick Rd. Bish 78 B1
Carrick Rd. Bishop 72 B1
Carrick Rd. Cumb 62 A2
Carrick Rd. E Kil 159 F2
Carrick Rd. Glasg 137 F3
Carrick Rd. Troon 229 E4
Carrick Road La. Ayr 238 C3
Carrick St. Ayr 238 C4
Carrick St. Glasg 117 D4
Carrick St. Lark 185 E1
Carrick Terr. Dumb 49 D2
Carrick Vale. Cle 144 B1
Carrick View. Glen 101 F3
Carrick Way. Udd 141 D2
Carrickarden Rd. Bear 75 F2
Carrickstone Rd. Cumb 61 F3
Carrickstone View. Cumb 61 F3
Carrington St. Glasg 96 C1
Carrochan Cres. Bonh 27 F4
Carrochan Rd. Bonh 27 F4
Carrogden Gdns. Glasg 119 E3
Carroglen Gr. Glasg 119 E3
Carron Ave. Kilmk 228 A3
Carron Cres. Bear 75 E2
Carron Cres. Bish 78 A1
Carron Cres. Glasg 97 E3
Carron Cres. Klrk 79 F2
Carron Ct. Glasg 139 E3
Carron Ct. Ham 162 A1
Carron Dr. Bishop 72 B1
Carron Ind Est. Sten 24 A1
Carron Pl. Coat 101 E1
Carron Pl. E Kil 180 C3
Carron Pl. Glasg 97 F3
Carron Pl. Irvine 219 E3
Carron Pl. Stir 7 D1
Carron Rd. Falk 42 A4
Carron St. Glasg 97 F3
Carron St. Wish 165 D1
Carron Way. Holy 143 E2
Carron Way. Pais 114 A4
Carronbank Ave. Sten 24 A1
Carronbank Cres. Den 21 F2
Carronbank St. Sten 24 A1
Carrongrove Ave. Sten 24 A1
Carrongrove Rd. Sten 24 A1
Carronhall Ave. Sten 24 B2
Carronlea Dr. Sten 24 A1
Carronshore Rd. Sten 24 A1
Carronside Pl. Duni 21 F2
Carronside St. Falk 42 A4
Carronvale Ave. Lar 23 E1
Carronvale Rd. Lar 23 E1
Carronview. Lar 23 E1
Carrour Gdns. Bish 77 F1
Carruth Dr. Kil 89 E4
Carruth Rd. B of W 110 B4
Carsaig Dr. Glasg 115 F3
Carsaig Loan. Glen 101 E3
Carscallan Rd. Ham 183 F3
Carscallan Rd. Quart 184 A1
Carse Terr. All 9 F4
Carse View. Air 14 C2
Carsebridge Rd. N Sau 10 B4
Carsegreen Ave. Pais 133 D4
Carseloch Rd. Ayr 238 C1
Carsemeadow. Kil 89 F1
Carseview. Bann 7 F1
Carseview Dr. Bear 76 A3
Carseview. Tull 4 A1
Carsewood Ave. How 130 C3
Carson Dr. Irvine 224 B4
Carson Rd. Bonh 27 F4
Carstairs St. Glasg 118 A1
Carswell Ct. Dalry 191 D4
Carswell Gdns. Glasg 116 C1
Carswell Rd. Newt M 156 A3
Cart La. Pais 113 F3
Cart St. Clyde 94 A4
Cartcraigs Rd. Glasg 136 A3
Carters Pl. Irvine 219 E1
Cartha Cres. Pais 114 A2
Cartha St. Glasg 136 C4
Cartland Ave. Car 201 F4

Cartland Rd. Lan 214 B4
Cartland View. Lan 214 C3
Cartsbridge Rd. Newt M ... 157 F3
Cartsburn St. Green 46 A2
Cartside Ave. Inch 93 D2
Cartside Ave. John 111 E1
Cartside Dr. Thorn 158 A3
Cartside Pl. Newt M 157 F3
Cartside Quadrant. Glasg . 137 D4
Cartside Rd. Newt M 157 F3
Cartside St. Glasg 136 C4
Cartvale La. Pais 113 F3
Cartvale Rd. Glasg 137 D4
Cartview Ct. Newt M 157 F3
Carval Dr. Green 45 E2
Carvale Ave. Sals 125 D1
Carvel Dr. Green 45 E2
Carwinshoch View. Ayr 238 B3
Carwood Ct. Green 46 B2
Carwood St. Green 46 B2
Caskie Dr. Udd 140 C1
Cassels Gr. Mother 142 B1
Cassels St. Car 187 F1
Cassels St. Mother 163 F4
Cassillis St. Ayr 238 C4
Cassley Ave. Ren 94 C1
Castburn Rd. Cumb 62 C3
Castings Ave. Falk 42 A4
Castings Ct. Falk 42 A4
Castings Ct. Falk 42 C3
Castings Dr. Falk 42 A3
Castings St. Falk 42 C3
Castle Ave. Bonh 19 F1
Castle Ave. Helen 16 A1
Castle Ave. Holy 143 D3
Castle Ave. John 112 A1
Castle Ave. Sten 24 B2
Castle Ave. Steven 206 C1
Castle Ave. Udd 140 C2
Castle
Chimmins Ave. Glasg . 139 E2
Castle Chimmins Rd. Glasg 139 E2
Castle Cres. Bishop 72 A1
Castle Cres. Den 21 E1
Castle Cres. Falk 42 B4
Castle Cres. Tor 22 C4
Castle Ct. Falk 42 B4
Castle Ct. Men 3 F1
Castle Ct. Stir 7 D4
Castle Dr. Dund 225 F1
Castle Dr. Falk 42 B4
Castle Dr. Holy 143 D3
Castle Dr. Kilb 149 D1
Castle Dr. Kilmk 223 D2
Castle Dr. Sten 23 F1
Castle Dr. W Kil 190 B3
Castle Gait. Pais 113 F2
Castle Gate. Newt M 157 D2
Castle Gate. Udd 140 C2
Castle Gdns. Gour 44 C4
Castle Gdns. Muir 80 C1
Castle Gr. Kilb 149 D1
Castle Gr. Kils 36 B1
Castle Mains Rd. Miln 54 B1
Castle Pl. Falk 42 B4
Castle Pl. Udd 140 C2
Castle Quadrant. Aird 123 E4
Castle Rd. Aird 123 E4
Castle Rd. Ard 205 E2
Castle Rd. B of W 90 B1
Castle Rd. Dumb 50 A1
Castle Rd. Falk 42 B4
Castle Rd. Green 46 B1
Castle Rd. John 112 B2
Castle Rd. Men 3 F3
Castle Rd. Newt M 156 B2
Castle Rd. P Glasg 47 E1
Castle Rd. Stir 2 B2
Castle Sq. Clyde 73 F2
Castle St. All 10 A3
Castle St. Chap 123 E1
Castle St. Clyde 73 F2
Castle St. Dumb 49 F2
Castle St. Glasg 96 B1
Castle St. Glasg 97 F1
Castle St. Glasg 120 A2
Castle St. Glasg 138 A4
Castle St. Ham 162 C2
Castle St. Irvine 219 D2
Castle St. Pais 113 E2
Castle St. Stir 7 D4
Castle View. Men 166 A3
Castle View. W Kil 190 B3
Castle Way. Cumb 62 B2
Castle Wlk. Ayr 238 B2
Castle Wynd. Quart 183 F2
Castle Wynd. Stir 7 D4
Castle Wynd. Udd 141 D1
Castlebank Cres. Glasg 96 A1
Castlebank Ct. Glasg 95 F3
Castlebank Gdns. Glasg 95 F3
Castlebank St. Glasg 96 A1
Castlebank Villas. Glasg 95 F3
Castlebay Dr. Glasg 77 E1

Castlebay Pl. Glasg 97 E4
Castlebay St. Glasg 97 E4
Castlebrae. Dumb 49 E3
Castlecary Rd. Cumb 62 B4
Castlecroft Gdns. Udd 140 C3
Castlefern Rd. Glasg 138 A2
Castlefield Gdns. E Kil 180 A3
Castlegait. Stir 7 D4
Castlegate. Lan 215 D2
Castleglen Rd. E Kil 159 D2
Castlegreen Cres. Dumb 50 A1
Castlegreen La. Dumb 50 A1
Castlegreen St. Dumb 50 A1
Castlehill Ave. P Glasg 69 D4
Castlehill Ave. Slam 86 A3
Castlehill Cres. Ayr 239 D3
Castlehill Cres. Bank 38 C1
Castlehill Cres. Ham 162 C2
Castlehill Cres. Ham 163 E1
Castlehill Cres. Kil 89 E4
Castlehill Cres. Law 187 E3
Castlehill Cres. Ren 94 B2
Castlehill Dr. Newt M 156 C2
Castlehill Gdns. Ham 162 C1
Castlehill Quadrant. Dumb .. 49 E3
Castlehill Rd. Ayr 239 D3
Castlehill Rd. Bear 75 E3
Castlehill Rd. Car 187 F3
Castlehill Rd. Dumb 49 E3
Castlehill Rd. Kil 89 E4
Castlehill Rd. Stew 195 F1
Castlehill Rd. Wish 186 A4
Castlehill View. Kils 36 B1
Castlelaurie St. Falk 42 B4
Castlelaw Gdns. Glasg 119 D3
Castlelaw St. Glasg 119 D3
Castlemilk Arc. Glasg 137 E2
Castlemilk Cres. Glasg 137 F3
Castlemilk Dr. Glasg 137 F1
Castlemilk Dr. Glasg 137 E2
Castlemilk Rd. Glasg 137 F3
Castlemount Ave. Newt M . 156 C2
Castleton Ave. Bish 97 F4
Castleton Ave. Newt M 157 D2
Castleton Ave. Newt M 156 C2
Castleton Ct. Glasg 137 F1
Castleton Ct. Newt M 156 C2
Castleton Dr. Newt M 156 C2
Castleton Gr. Newt M 156 C2
Castleview Ave. Pais 133 D4
Castleview. B of A 2 A2
Castleview. Cumb 62 C4
Castleview Dr. B of A 2 A4
Castleview. Dund 225 F2
Castleview. Lennox 32 C2
Castleview Pl. Pais 133 D4
Catacol Ave. Salt 205 F1
Cathay St. Glasg 97 E4
Cathburn Rd. New 166 B3
Cathcart Cres. Pais 114 A2
Cathcart Pl. Glasg 137 D4
Cathcart Rd. Glasg 117 D1
Cathcart Rd. Glasg 137 F4
Cathcart Sq. Green 45 F3
Cathcart St. Ayr 235 F1
Cathcart St. Green 46 A3
Cathedral Sq. Glasg 117 E4
Cathedral St. Glasg 117 E4
Catherine Pl. Kilm 222 B3
Catherine St. Bann 7 E1
Catherine St. Klrk 79 E4
Catherine St. Mother 163 F2
Catherine Way. Holy 142 C2
Catherine's Wlk. Udd 161 E3
Cathkin Ave. Glasg 138 B4
Cathkin Ave. Glasg 138 C3
Cathkin By-Pass. Glasg 138 B2
Cathkin Ct. Glasg 137 F1
Cathkin Dr. Newt M 157 E4
Cathkin Gdns. Tan 120 C1
Cathkin Pl. Glasg 138 C3
Cathkin Pl. Kilw 207 D2
Cathkin Rd. Glasg 136 C4
Cathkin Rd. Glasg 138 B1
Cathkin Rd. Tan 120 C1
Cathkin View. Glasg 139 D4
Cathkinview Pl. Glasg 137 D4
Catrine Cres. Mother 164 A2
Catrine. E Kil 159 E1
Catrine St. Lark 185 E1
Catriona Way. Holy 143 D2
Catter Gdns. Miln 54 C2
Cauldhame Cres. Cam 6 B3
Cauldstream Pl. Miln 54 C1
Causeway The. B of A 2 B3
Causewayhead Rd. Stir 2 B2
Causewayside Cres. Glasg 119 D2
Causewayside St. Glasg 119 D1
Causeyfoot Dr. Kilb 149 D1
Causeyside St. Pais 113 F2
Causeystanes. Udd 161 E2
Cavendish Ct. Troon 229 E1
Cavendish Dr. Newt M 156 C3
Cavendish La. Troon 229 E1
Cavendish Pl. Glasg 117 D2

Cavendish Pl. Troon 229 E1
Cavendish St. Glasg 117 D2
Cavin Dr. Glasg 137 F2
Cavin Rd. Glasg 137 F2
Cawder Gdns. B of A 1 C4
Cawder Rd. B of A 1 C4
Cawdor Cres. Bishop 72 A1
Cawdor Cres. Green 45 D2
Cawdor Pl. Green 45 D2
Cawdor Way. E Kil 159 E2
Cayton Gdns. Glasg 119 F2
Cecil St. Coat 122 A3
Cecil St. Glasg 96 B2
Cecil St. Newt M 157 F4
Cecil St. Stir 7 D3
Cedar Ave. Beith 171 D4
Cedar Ave. Clyde 73 E2
Cedar Ave. John 132 A4
Cedar Ave. Stir 6 C3
Cedar Ave. Tan 141 D4
Cedar Cres. Green 46 C1
Cedar Cres. Ham 162 C1
Cedar Ct. E Kil 180 B3
Cedar Ct. Glasg 97 D1
Cedar Ct. Kilbar 111 D2
Cedar Dr. E Kil 180 B3
Cedar Dr. Klrk 79 E3
Cedar Dr. M of C 58 B3
Cedar Dr. Tan 141 E4
Cedar Gdns. Glasg 138 B2
Cedar Gdns. Law 186 C3
Cedar Gr. Card 48 A4
Cedar Gr. Lar 23 E1
Cedar La. Aird 123 E4
Cedar La. Holy 143 D2
Cedar Pl. Barr 155 E4
Cedar Pl. E Kil 180 B3
Cedar Pl. Gour 44 B3
Cedar Rd. Ayr 239 E3
Cedar Rd. Bank 38 C1
Cedar Rd. Bish 98 A4
Cedar Rd. Cumb 62 B2
Cedar Rd. Irvine 219 E2
Cedar Rd. Kilmk 227 E4
Cedar St. Glasg 97 D1
Cedar Wlk. Bish 98 A4
Cedars The. Tull 4 A1
Cedarwood Ave. Newt M .. 156 C3
Cedarwood Rd. Newt M 156 C2
Cedric Pl. Glasg 95 E4
Cedric Rd. Glasg 95 E4
Celandine Bank. Ayr 239 E2
Celtic St. Glasg 96 B4
Cemetery Rd. Glasg 115 F2
Cemetery Rd. Shot 147 D2
Cemetery Rd. Udd 161 E3
Centenary Ave. Aird 122 B4
Centenary Ct. Clyde 74 A1
Centenary Gdns. Coat 122 A3
Centenary Gdns. Ham 162 C1
Centenary Pl. Ard 205 E2
Centenary Quadrant. Holy 143 D3
Central Ave. Ard 205 E2
Central Ave. Clyde 74 A1
Central Ave. Glasg 95 F1
Central Ave. Glasg 119 E2
Central Ave. Glasg 138 C3
Central Ave. Ham 161 F1
Central Ave. Holy 142 C3
Central Ave. Holy 143 D1
Central Ave. Kilb 170 A4
Central Ave. Kilmk 227 F2
Central Ave. Tan 141 E3
Central Ave. Troon 229 F2
Central Cres. Ash 199 F4
Central Dr. Sten 23 F2
Central Path. Glasg 119 F2
Central Quadrant. Ard 205 E2
Central Rd. Pais 113 F3
Central Way. Cumb 61 F1
Central Way. Pais 113 F3
Centre
Roundabout The. E Kil . 159 F1
Centre St. Chap 123 E1
Centre St. Glasg 117 D3
Centre St. Glen 101 E3
Centre The. Barr 134 A1
Ceres Gdns. Bish 78 B1
Cessnock Ave. Hurl 228 C3
Cessnock Dr. Hurl 228 C3
Cessnock Pl. Ayr 239 E3
Cessnock Pl. Glasg 139 E3
Cessnock Rd. Hurl 228 C3
Cessnock Rd. Stepps 99 D2
Cessnock Rd. Troon 229 E2
Cessnock St. Glasg 116 B3
Cessock Pl. Kilmk 228 A3
Chacefield St. Bon 40 A3
Chacefield Wood. Bank 39 F4
Chalmers Ave. Ayr 239 D3
Chalmers Cres. E Kil 180 C4
Chalmers Ct. Glasg 117 F3
Chalmers Dr. E Kil 180 C4
Chalmers Gate. Glasg 117 F3
Chalmers Pl. Glasg 117 F3
Chalmers Pl. Shew 224 C3

Chalmers Rd. Ayr 239 D3
Chalmers St. Clyde 74 A1
Chalmers St. Glasg 117 F3
Chalmers St. Gour 44 C4
Chalmerston Rd. Cam 1 A2
Chalton Rd. B of A 2 A4
Chamberlain La. Glasg 95 F3
Chamberlain Rd. Glasg 95 F3
Chambers Dr. Sten 24 A1
Chancellor St. Glasg 96 B1
Chantinghall Rd. Ham 162 A2
Chantinghall Terr. Ham 162 A2
Chapel Cres. Sten 24 A2
Chapel Ct. Glasg 137 F2
Chapel Dr. Sten 23 F2
Chapel La. Falk 42 A3
Chapel Rd. Dunt 74 A3
Chapel Rd. Hous 91 D2
Chapel Rd. New 166 B1
Chapel St. Aird 123 D4
Chapel St. Car 187 F1
Chapel St. Cle 144 A1
Chapel St. Glasg 96 C3
Chapel St. Glasg 137 F4
Chapel St. Gour 44 C4
Chapel St. Green 46 A2
Chapel St. Lennox 57 E4
Chapelacre Gr. Helen 16 C1
Chapelcross Ave. Aird 103 D3
Chapelgill Pl. Irvine 220 A2
Chapelhill Mount. Ard 205 E3
Chapelhill Rd. Pais 114 A1
Chapelknowe Rd. Holy 143 F1
Chapelpark Rd. Ayr 238 C2
Chapelside Ave. Aird 123 D4
Chapelside Rd. E Kil 160 A3
Chapelton Ave. Bear 75 F2
Chapelton Ave. Dumb 50 A3
Chapelton Gdns. Bear 75 F2
Chapelton Gdns. Dumb 50 A3
Chapelton La. W Kil 190 B2
Chapelton Rd. Cumb 82 B3
Chapelton Rd. W Kil 190 B1
Chapelton St. Glasg 97 D3
Chapelton St. P Glasg 47 D1
Chapeltoun Terr. Spring 210 C2
Chapelwell St. Salt 216 C4
Chapland Rd. Lan 215 D3
Chaplet Ave. Glasg 95 E4
Chapman Ave. Glen 101 E3
Chapman St. Glasg 117 D1
Chapmans Terr. Kilmk 228 A4
Chappell St. Barr 134 A2
Charing Cross La. Glasg ... 116 C4
Charing Cross. Lark 185 D2
Charles Ave. B of A 2 A3
Charles Ave. Pres 233 E3
Charles Ave. Ren 94 B2
Charles Cres. Car 188 A1
Charles Cres. Klrk 79 E3
Charles Dr. Lar 41 E4
Charles Dr. Troon 229 F1
Charles Path. Chap 123 E1
Charles Pl. Green 45 F3
Charles Pl. Kilmk 227 F4
Charles Quadrant. Holy 143 D3
Charles Rodger Pl. B of A 2 A3
Charles St. All 9 F4
Charles St. Glasg 97 F1
Charles St. Kilmk 227 F4
Charles St. Kils 36 B1
Charles St. Mother 164 B2
Charles St. Shot 147 D2
Charles St. Stir 7 D3
Charleson Row. Kils 60 C2
Charlotte Ave. Lennox 78 A4
Charlotte Path. Lark 185 D1
Charlotte Pl. Pais 113 F1
Charlotte St. Ayr 238 C4
Charlotte St. Dumb 49 E2
Charlotte St. Glasg 117 E3
Charlotte St. Helen 16 C1
Charlotte St. Shot 147 D2
Charlotte Street La. Ayr 238 C4
Charter St. Stir 7 D2
Chartershall Rd. Bann 7 D1
Chartershall Rd. Bann 11 D3
Chartwell Rd. Bishop 72 A2
Chassels St. Coat 122 A4
Chateau Gr. Ham 163 D1
Chatelherault Ave. Glasg .. 138 C3
Chatelherault Cres. Ham ... 162 C1
Chatelherault Wlk. Ham ... 162 C1
Chatham. E Kil 180 B4
Chatton St. Glasg 76 B1
Chattan Ave. Stir 2 A2
Cheapside St. Eagle 178 C3
Cheapside St. Glasg 116 C4
Chelmsford Dr. Glasg 96 A3
Cherry Bank. Klrk 79 D3
Cherry Cres. Clyde 74 A2
Cherry Gdns. Irvine 219 F3
Cherry Hill Rd. Ayr 239 D1
Cherry La. Bank 38 C1
Cherry La. Troon 229 E2
Cherry Pl. Bish 98 A4
Cherry Pl. Holy 143 D3

Name	Page	Grid
Cherry Pl. John	112	A1
Cherry Pl. M of C	58	A2
Cherry Pl. Tan	141	E4
Cherry Rd. Kilmk	227	E4
Cherrybank Rd. Glasg	136	C3
Cherrybank Wlk. Aird	122	B4
Cherryhill View. Lark	184	C2
Cherrytree Cres. Lark	185	D3
Cherrywood Dr. Beith	150	B1
Cherrywood Rd. John	112	B1
Chester Rd. Gour	44	C2
Chester St. Glasg	119	D3
Chesterfield Ave. Glasg	96	A3
Chesters Cres. Mother	163	E4
Chesters Pl. Glasg	138	A4
Chesters Rd. Bear	75	E2
Chestnut Ave. Beith	171	D4
Chestnut Ave. Bishop	71	F3
Chestnut Ave. Cumb	62	C3
Chestnut Cres. Duni	21	E2
Chestnut Cres. E Kil	180	B3
Chestnut Cres. Ham	162	C1
Chestnut Cres. Tan	141	E4
Chestnut Ct. Cumb	62	C3
Chestnut Ct. M of C	58	A4
Chestnut Dr. Clyde	74	A3
Chestnut Dr. Klrk	79	D3
Chestnut Gr. Car	187	F1
Chestnut Gr. Glen	101	E3
Chestnut Gr. Lark	185	D3
Chestnut Gr. Mother	163	E2
Chestnut Gr. Sten	23	F2
Chestnut Gr. Udd	161	E4
Chestnut La. Miln	54	C1
Chestnut Pl. Cumb	62	C3
Chestnut Pl. John	132	A4
Chestnut Pl. Kilmk	227	E4
Chestnut Rd. Ayr	239	E3
Chestnut St. Glasg	97	E3
Cheviot Ave. Barr	134	B1
Cheviot Cres. Wish	164	C2
Cheviot Ct. Aird	103	D1
Cheviot Ct. Irvine	220	A2
Cheviot Dr. Newt M	156	B2
Cheviot Gdns. Bear	75	E4
Cheviot Head. Irvine	219	F2
Cheviot Pl. Kilmk	228	A2
Cheviot Rd. Glasg	136	B3
Cheviot Rd. Ham	162	C1
Cheviot Rd. Lark	185	E1
Cheviot Rd. Pais	113	F1
Cheviot St. Udd	161	E4
Cheviot Way. Irvine	220	A2
Chillin Pl. Lark	185	E1
Chirnside Ct. Ham	161	F3
Chirnside Pl. Glasg	115	D3
Chirnside Rd. Glasg	115	D3
Chisholm Ave. Bishop	72	B2
Chisholm Ave. Stir	2	A2
Chisholm Dr. Newt M	156	C3
Chisholm St. Coat	122	A4
Chisolm St. Glasg	117	E3
Chriss Ave. Ham	183	E4
Christchurch Pl. E Kil	180	A4
Christian St. Glasg	136	B4
Christie Gdns. Salt	216	C4
Christie La. Pais	113	F1
Christie St. Hat	142	B3
Christie St. Pais	113	F3
Christopher St. Glasg	98	A1
Chromars Pl. Green	45	F2
Chryston Rd. Kirk	80	B3
Chryston Rd. Muir	100	B4
Chryston Rd. Twe	80	B3
Chuckie La. Kilbar	111	E3
Church Ave. Card	48	A4
Church Ave. Glasg	138	B3
Church Ave. New	166	A2
Church Ave. Stepps	99	E3
Church Cres. Aird	103	F1
Church Cres. Ham	183	E3
Church Ct. Ayr	236	A1
Church Ct. Dumb	49	F2
Church Dr. Klrk	79	E3
Church Gr. N Sau	5	E1
Church Hill. Pais	113	F3
Church La. Car	187	F1
Church La. Coat	122	A4
Church La. Duni	21	E2
Church La. Kilmk	227	F3
Church La. Kils	60	B4
Church Pl. Cald	104	C2
Church Pl. Falk	42	A4
Church Pl. O Kill	73	D3
Church Pl. Rhu	15	E2
Church Pl. Salt	205	E1
Church Rd. B of W	110	C4
Church Rd. Cali	66	C3
Church Rd. Glasg	136	B1
Church Rd. Kil	89	F1
Church Rd. Muir	100	B4
Church Rd. New	166	B3
Church Rd. Newt M	157	F3
Church Rd. Rhu	15	E3
Church St. Alex	27	F2
Church St. All	10	A3
Church St. Bon	40	B2
Church St. Clyde	74	A2
Church St. Coat	122	A4
Church St. Dumb	49	F2
Church St. East	127	E3
Church St. Glasg	96	B1
Church St. Glasg	120	B2
Church St. Gour	44	C4
Church St. Ham	162	C2
Church St. Holy	143	F2
Church St. Irvine	219	D1
Church St. John	111	F2
Church St. Kilbar	111	D2
Church St. Kilmk	222	C1
Church St. Kils	60	B4
Church St. Kilw	207	F2
Church St. Lark	185	D1
Church St. Loch	129	E1
Church St. P Glasg	47	E1
Church St. Sten	23	F2
Church St. Sten	24	B1
Church St. Troon	229	E1
Church St. Udd	140	C3
Church St. Udd	161	F4
Church View. Coat	122	A4
Church View Ct. Lennox	33	E1
Church View Gdns. Hat	142	A3
Church View. Glasg	139	D4
Church Wlk. Den	21	F1
Churchill Ave. E Kil	159	F1
Churchill Ave. John	131	E4
Churchill Ave. Kilw	208	A2
Churchill Cres. Ayr	239	E4
Churchill Cres. Udd	141	D2
Churchill Dr. Ard	205	E2
Churchill Dr. B of A	2	A3
Churchill Dr. Bishop	72	A2
Churchill Dr. Glasg	96	A2
Churchill Pl. Kilbar	111	D2
Churchill Rd. Kil	89	E4
Churchill St. All	9	F4
Churchill Way. Glasg	77	F1
Circus Dr. Glasg	117	F4
Circus Pl. Glasg	117	F4
Circus Place La. Glasg	117	F4
Citadel Pl. Ayr	235	F1
Citadel Pl. Mother	163	E4
Citadel Way. Troon	229	F4
Citizen La. Glasg	117	E4
Citrus Cres. Tan	141	E4
Cityford Cres. Glasg	137	F4
Cityford Dr. Glasg	137	F3
Civic St. Glasg	97	D1
Civic Way. Klrk	79	E4
Clachan Dr. Glasg	115	F4
Clachan Rd. Ros	15	D2
Clachan The. Wish	165	D2
Clackmannan Rd. All	10	B3
Claddens Pl. Klrk	79	F2
Claddens Quadrant. Glasg	97	E3
Claddens St. Glasg	97	D3
Claddoch Cotts. Card	25	E3
Cladence Gr. E Kil	180	C3
Clair Rd. Bish	78	B1
Claire St. New	166	A3
Clairinch Gdns. Ren	94	B1
Clairmont Gdns. Glasg	96	C1
Clamp Rd. Mother	164	B2
Clamps Gr. E Kil	181	D4
Clamps Terr. E Kil	181	D4
Clamps Wood. E Kil	181	D4
Clanrye Dr. Coat	122	A2
Clapperhow Rd. Holy	143	D1
Clare St. Glasg	98	A1
Claremont. All	9	F4
Claremont Ave. Klrk	79	D4
Claremont Cres. Kilw	207	E2
Claremont Dr. B of A	2	B4
Claremont Dr. Miln	55	D1
Claremont Gdns. Miln	55	D1
Claremont Pass. Glasg	96	C1
Claremont Pl. Glasg	96	C1
Claremont St. Bon	39	F3
Claremont St. Glasg	116	C4
Claremont Terr. Glasg	96	C1
Claremont Terrace La. Glasg	96	C1
Claremount Ave. Glasg	136	B1
Clarence Dr. Glasg	96	A2
Clarence Dr. Pais	114	A2
Clarence Gdns. Glasg	96	A2
Clarence La. Glasg	96	A2
Clarence St. Clyde	74	B2
Clarence St. Green	45	F3
Clarence St. Pais	114	A3
Clarendon Pl. Ayr	239	E3
Clarendon Pl. Glasg	97	D1
Clarendon Pl. Stir	7	D4
Clarendon Rd. Stir	7	D4
Clarendon Rd. Wish	164	C1
Clarendon St. Glasg	97	D1
Clarinda Ave. Falk	41	D3
Clarinda Cres. Kirk	59	D1
Clarinda Pl. Holy	143	E2
Clarion Cres. Glasg	95	D4
Clarion Rd. Glasg	95	D4
Clark Cres. Steven	217	E4
Clark Dr. Irvine	219	F2
Clark Pl. Lennox	78	B4
Clark Pl. Newt M	156	A2
Clark Pl. Salt	206	A1
Clark St. Aird	123	D4
Clark St. Clyde	73	F2
Clark St. John	111	F2
Clark St. Kilmk	227	F4
Clark St. New	165	F3
Clark St. Pais	113	E3
Clark St. Ren	94	A2
Clark St. Stir	7	D1
Clark Way. Hat	141	F4
Clarke Ave. Ayr	238	C3
Clarkston Ave. Glasg	136	C2
Clarkston Dr. Aird	123	E4
Clarkston Rd. Glasg	136	C2
Clarkwell Rd. Ham	161	F2
Clarkwell Terr. Ham	161	F2
Clathic Ave. Bear	76	A2
Claud Rd. Pais	114	A3
Claude Ave. Glasg	139	F2
Claude St. Lark	185	D2
Clavens Rd. Glasg	114	C3
Claverhouse Pl. Pais	114	A2
Claverhouse Rd. Glasg	114	C4
Clavering St E. Pais	113	E3
Clavering St W. Pais	113	E2
Clay Cres. Hat	142	B4
Clay Cres. Kilmk	222	C1
Clay Rd. Hat	142	B4
Clayhouse Rd. Stepps	99	F2
Claymore Dr. Bann	7	E2
Claymore Dr. Hous	111	E4
Claypotts Pl. Glasg	99	D1
Claypotts Rd. Glasg	99	D1
Clayslaps Rd. Glasg	96	B1
Clayslaps View. Kilmk	228	A2
Claython Ave. Glasg	117	F3
Claython Cir. Glasg	117	F3
Claython Ct. Glasg	117	F3
Claython Pk. Glasg	117	F3
Claython St. Glasg	117	F3
Claython Terr. Glasg	117	F3
Clayton Ave. Irvine	219	E2
Clayton Path. Hat	142	A4
Clayton Terr. Glasg	117	F4
Clearfield Ave. Ham	162	A2
Cleaves The. Tull	4	A1
Cleddans Cres. Dunt	74	B3
Cleddans Rd. Dunt	74	B3
Cleddans Rd. Kirk	58	C1
Cleddans View. Clyde	74	B2
Cleddans View. Glenm	102	C2
Cleddens Ct. Bish	78	A1
Cleeves Ave. Beith	191	F3
Cleeves Quadrant. Glasg	135	D3
Cleeves Rd. Glasg	135	D3
Cleghorn Ave. Lan	215	D3
Cleghorn Rd. Lan	215	D3
Cleghorn St. Glasg	97	D2
Cleish Ave. Bear	75	E4
Cleland La. Glasg	117	E3
Cleland Pl. E Kil	160	A2
Cleland Rd. Cle	144	A1
Cleland Rd. Holy	143	E1
Cleland Rd. Holy	144	A1
Cleland Rd. Wish	165	D2
Cleland St. Glasg	117	E3
Clelland Ave. Bish	98	A4
Clem Attlee Gdns. Lark	185	D1
Clements Pl. Steven	206	C1
Clerkland Rd. Stew	195	E1
Clerwood St. Glasg	118	B3
Cleuch Ave. Tull	4	A1
Cleuch Dr. Alva	4	C4
Cleuch Gdns. Newt M	157	F3
Cleughearn Rd. Auld	180	B1
Clevans Rd. B of W	110	B4
Cleveden Cres. Glasg	96	A3
Cleveden Crescent La. Glasg	96	A3
Cleveden Dr. Glasg	96	B2
Cleveden Dr. Glasg	138	B3
Cleveden Drive La. Glasg	96	B2
Cleveden Gdns. Glasg	96	B3
Cleveden La. Glasg	96	A3
Cleveden Pl. Glasg	96	A3
Cleveden Rd. Glasg	96	A3
Cleveden Rd. Glasg	96	B3
Cleveland La. Glasg	116	C4
Cleveland St. Glasg	116	C4
Cliff Rd. Glasg	96	C1
Clifford Gdns. Glasg	116	A3
Clifford La. Glasg	116	B3
Clifford Pl. Glasg	116	B3
Clifford Rd. Stir	7	D3
Clifford St. Glasg	116	B3
Clifton Pl. Coat	122	B3
Clifton Pl. Glasg	116	C4
Clifton Rd. Glasg	136	A2
Clifton St. Glasg	96	C1
Clifton Terr. Glasg	138	C2
Clifton Terr. John	112	A1
Climie Pl. Kilmk	228	A4
Clincart Rd. Glasg	137	D4
Clincarthill Rd. Glasg	138	A4
Clippens Rd. Lin	111	F4
Clippens Rd. Lin	112	A3
Clive St. Shot	146	C3
Cloak Rd. Kil	69	E2
Cloan Ave. Glasg	75	D1
Cloan Cres. Bish	78	A2
Clober Farm La. Miln	54	C2
Clober Rd. Miln	55	D1
Cloberfield Gdns. Miln	54	C2
Cloberfield. Miln	54	C2
Cloberhill Rd. Glasg	75	D3
Cloch Brae. Gour	44	A3
Cloch Rd. Gour	43	F3
Cloch St. Glasg	119	D4
Clochbar Ave. Miln	54	C2
Clochbar Gdns. Miln	54	C1
Clochoderick Ave. Kilbar	111	D1
Clochranhill Rd. Ayr	238	C1
Clockerhill Pl. Holy	143	F2
Cloister Ave. Aird	123	E2
Clonbeith St. Glasg	99	F1
Cloncaird. Kilw	207	E1
Closeburn St. Glasg	97	E3
Cloth St. Barr	134	B1
Clouden Rd. Cumb	62	A1
Cloudhowe Terr. Udd	140	B1
Clouston La. Glasg	96	C2
Clouston St. Glasg	96	C2
Clova Pl. Udd	140	C3
Clova St. Glasg	135	F2
Clove Mill Wynd. Lark	184	C1
Clover Leaf Path. Alex	27	F2
Cloverbank St. Glasg	98	A1
Clovergate. Bish	77	F1
Cloverhill. Ayr	239	E3
Cloverhill Pl. Muir	100	B4
Cloverhill Terr. E Kil	159	F1
Cloverhill View. E Kil	159	E1
Cloves The. Men	4	A3
Cluanie Ave. Shot	146	C3
Clune Brae. P Glasg	47	F1
Clune Dr. Pres	236	B4
Clune Park St. P Glasg	47	F1
Clunie Pl. Coat	122	A2
Clunie Pl. New	165	F3
Clunie Rd. Glasg	115	F2
Cluny Ave. Bear	76	A1
Cluny Ave. Dunt	74	B4
Cluny Dr. Bear	76	A1
Cluny Dr. Pais	114	A3
Cluny Dr. Sten	23	F2
Cluny Gdns. Glasg	95	F2
Cluny Gdns. Glasg	120	A2
Cluny Villas. Glasg	95	F2
Clutha Pl. E Kil	180	A4
Clutha St. Glasg	116	B3
Clyde Ave. Barr	134	B1
Clyde Ave. Ham	163	E4
Clyde Ave. Lennox	78	A4
Clyde Ave. Udd	140	C1
Clyde Cres. Lan	215	D3
Clyde Cres. Lar	23	D2
Clyde Ct. Clyde	73	F3
Clyde Ct. Dumb	49	F2
Clyde Dr. Hat	142	B2
Clyde Dr. Shot	147	D2
Clyde La. Holy	143	D2
Clyde Pl. Ard	205	E2
Clyde Pl. Glasg	117	D3
Clyde Pl. Holy	143	D2
Clyde Pl. John	131	E4
Clyde Pl. Kilmk	228	A3
Clyde Pl. Troon	229	F3
Clyde Rd. Gour	44	C3
Clyde Rd. Pais	114	A4
Clyde Shopping Ctr. Clyde	74	A1
Clyde Sq. Green	45	F3
Clyde St. Car	187	F1
Clyde St. Coat	122	B4
Clyde St E. Helen	16	C1
Clyde St E. Helen	25	C1
Clyde St. Falk	41	F3
Clyde St. Glasg	117	E4
Clyde St. Ren	94	B3
Clyde Terr. Ard	205	E2
Clyde Terr. Mother	164	B1
Clyde Terr. Udd	141	D1
Clyde Tower. Mother	163	F3
Clyde Valley Ave. Mother	163	F2
Clyde View Ct. O Kill	72	B4
Clyde View. Ham	162	A1
Clyde View. Pais	114	A1
Clyde Way. Pais	114	A4
Clyde Wynds. Green	45	E2
Clydebrae Dr. Udd	162	A4
Clydebrae St. Glasg	116	A4
Clydeford Dr. Glasg	118	C2
Clydeford Dr. Udd	140	C4
Clydeford Rd. Glasg	139	D4
Clydeholm Rd. Glasg	95	E1
Clydeholm Terr. Clyde	94	B4
Clydeneuk Dr. Udd	140	B4
Clydesdale Ave. Ham	183	E3
Clydesdale Ave. Ren	94	A1
Clydesdale Ave. Wish	166	B3
Clydesdale Pl. Ham	183	E3
Clydesdale Rd. Hat	142	B2
Clydesdale St. Ham	162	C2
Clydesdale St. Holy	142	C2
Clydesdale St. Lark	185	D2
Clydeshore Rd. Dumb	49	F2
Clydeside Expressway. Glasg	116	C4
Clydeside Ind Est. Glasg	95	F1
Clydeside Rd. Glasg	117	F1
Clydesmill Dr. Glasg	139	D4
Clydesmill Gr. Glasg	139	D4
Clydesmill Pl. Glasg	139	D4
Clydesmill Rd. Glasg	139	D4
Clydevale. Udd	141	D1
Clydeview. Dumb	49	F1
Clydeview Rd. Green	46	A1
Clydeview. P Glasg	68	C4
Clydeview Shopping Ctr. Udd	161	F4
Clydeview Terr. Glasg	139	E4
Clydeview. Udd	141	E1
Clynder Rd. Green	46	B1
Clynder St. Glasg	116	A3
Clyth Dr. Glasg	136	B1
Co-Operative Terr. John	112	A2
Coach Cl. Kils	61	D4
Coach Pl. Kils	60	C4
Coach Rd. Kils	60	C4
Coal Wynd. Bann	7	E1
Coalburn Rd. Tan	141	D3
Coalburn St. Gree	83	F1
Coalgate. All	10	A3
Coalhall Ave. Holy	143	D1
Coalhill St. Glasg	118	A3
Coalpots Way. Fish	5	F2
Coatbank St. Coat	122	A3
Coatbank Way. Coat	122	A3
Coatbridge Rd. Aird	102	B2
Coatbridge Rd. Coat	101	D2
Coatbridge Rd. Coat	120	C3
Coatbridge Rd. Glasg	120	C3
Coatbridge Rd. Glen	101	F3
Coatbridge Rd. Glenm	102	B2
Coathill St. Coat	122	A2
Coats Cres. Glasg	120	A3
Coats Dr. Pais	113	D2
Coats Pl. Dund	225	F1
Coats St. Coat	122	A3
Coatshill Ave. Udd	140	B1
Cobbett Rd. Mother	163	D3
Cobblebrae Cres. Falk	24	A1
Cobblerigg Way. Udd	140	C3
Cobbleton Rd. Holy	142	C1
Cobden Rd. Glasg	97	F1
Cobden St. Alva	5	D3
Cobden St. Alva	5	D4
Cobham St. Green	46	C1
Cobington Pl. Glasg	99	D1
Cobinshaw St. Glasg	119	D3
Coblecrook Gdns. Alva	4	C3
Coblecrook La. Alva	4	C3
Coblecrook Pl. Alva	4	C3
Coburg St. Glasg	117	D3
Cochno Dr. Dunt	74	A4
Cochno St. Clyde	74	B1
Cochran St. Pais	113	F2
Cochrane Ave. Dund	225	F1
Cochrane Ave. Falk	42	A2
Cochrane Cres. Alva	4	C4
Cochrane Dr. Miln	76	B4
Cochrane Dr. Dund	225	F1
Cochrane Pl. Helen	17	D1
Cochrane Pl. Pres	236	B4
Cochrane St. Barr	134	A1
Cochrane St. Falk	42	A2
Cochrane St. Glasg	117	E4
Cochrane St. Hat	141	F3
Cochrane St. Irvine	219	D1
Cochrane St. Kilb	149	D1
Cochranemill Rd. John	111	E1
Cochranes The. Alva	5	D4
Cochrie Pl. Tull	4	B1
Cockburn Pl. Coat	121	F2
Cockburn Pl. Shew	224	C3
Cockburn St. Falk	42	A2
Cockels Loan. Ren	94	A1
Cockenzie St. Glasg	119	D3
Cocklebie Rd. Stew	195	E1
Cockmuir St. Glasg	98	A2
Cogan Rd. Glasg	136	B3
Cogan St. Barr	134	A1
Cogan St. Glasg	136	B4
Coila Ave. Pres	236	B3
Coire Loan. Shot	147	D2
Colbert St. Glasg	117	F2
Colbreggan Ct. Dunt	74	B3
Colbreggan Gdns. Dunt	74	B3
Colchester Dr. Glasg	96	A3
Coldgreen Ave. Kilb	149	D1
Coldingham Ave. Clyde	94	C3
Coldstream Cres. Wish	165	E3
Coldstream Dr. Glasg	138	B3
Coldstream Dr. Pais	113	D1
Coldstream Pl. Glasg	97	E2
Coldstream Rd. Clyde	74	A1
Coldstream St. Udd	161	E4
Coldstream. W Kil	190	B3
Colebrooke Pl. Glasg	96	C2
Colebrooke St. Glasg	96	C2
Colebrooke St. Glasg	139	D3

Colebrooke Terr. Glasg	96	C2
Coleburn Ct. Irvine	219	F3
Coleridge Ave. Udd	141	D2
Coleridge. E Kil	180	A4
Colfin St. Glasg	100	B1
Colgrain St. Glasg	97	D3
Colgrave Cres. Glasg	118	C2
Colinbar Circ. Barr	134	A1
Colinslee Ave. Pais	113	F1
Colinslee Cres. Pais	113	F1
Colinslee Dr. Pais	113	F1
Colinslee Rd. Glasg	135	E4
Colinton Pl. Glasg	119	D4
Colintraive Ave. Glasg	98	C2
Colintraive Cres. Glasg	98	C2
Coll Ave. P Glasg	69	D4
Coll Ave. Ren	94	B1
Coll. E Kil	181	E4
Coll Gdns. Irvine	225	D4
Coll Pl. Glasg	98	A1
Coll St. Glasg	98	A1
Coll St. New	165	F3
Colla Gdns. Bish	78	B1
Collace Ave. B of W	110	B4
College Cres. Falk	42	B4
College La. Glasg	117	E4
College Pk. Troon	229	F4
College St. Dumb	49	F2
College St. Glasg	117	E4
College Way. Dumb	49	F2
College Wynd. Kilmk	227	F4
Collenan Ave. Troon	230	A2
Collessie Dr. Glasg	99	E1
Collier St. John	111	F2
Colliertree Rd. Aird	123	E4
Collina St. Glasg	96	B3
Collingwood Ct. Falk	41	F3
Collingwood Pl. Helen	17	D1
Collingwood Terr. Gour	44	C3
Collins Dr. Troon	230	A4
Collins Rd. Helen	25	D4
Collins St. Dunt	74	B3
Collins St. Glasg	117	F4
Collyland Rd. N Sau	5	E2
Collylinn Rd. Bear	75	F2
Colmonell Ave. Glasg	94	C4
Colonsay Ave. P Glasg	69	D4
Colonsay Ave. Ren	94	B1
Colonsay Dr. Newt M	156	A3
Colonsay. E Kil	181	E4
Colonsay House. Pres	236	A3
Colonsay Pl. Kilmk	223	D3
Colonsay Rd. Glasg	115	F3
Colonsay Rd. Pais	133	E4
Colonsay Terr. Falk	42	A1
Colquhoun Ave. Glasg	115	D4
Colquhoun Ct. Glasg	116	B2
Colquhoun Dr. Alex	27	F4
Colquhoun Dr. Bear	75	F3
Colquhoun. Dumb	50	A2
Colquhoun Rd. Dumb	50	C1
Colquhoun Rd. Kilmk	223	E1
Colquhoun Sq. Helen	16	B1
Colquhoun St. Dumb	50	A2
Colquhoun St. Helen	16	B1
Colquhoun St. Stir	7	E3
Colsnaur. Men	4	A3
Colson Pl. Hat	142	B2
Colston Ave. Bish	97	F4
Colston Dr. Bish	97	F4
Colston Gdns. Aird	123	E4
Colston Gdns. Bish	97	F4
Colston Path. Bish	97	F4
Colston Pl. Aird	123	E4
Colston Pl. Bish	97	F4
Colston Rd. Aird	123	E4
Colston Rd. Glasg	97	F4
Colston Terr. Aird	123	E4
Colt Ave. Coat	101	F1
Colt Pl. Coat	122	A4
Colt Terr. Coat	122	A4
Coltmuir Cres. Bish	97	F4
Coltmuir Dr. Bish	97	F4
Coltmuir Gdns. Bish	97	F4
Coltmuir St. Glasg	97	D3
Coltness Ave. Alla	166	C4
Coltness Dr. Hat	142	A2
Coltness La. Glasg	119	E4
Coltness Rd. Wish	165	E4
Coltness St. Glasg	119	E4
Coltpark Ave. Bish	97	F4
Coltpark La. Bish	97	F4
Coltsfoot Dr. Glasg	135	D2
Coltswood Ct. Coat	122	A4
Coltswood Rd. Coat	122	A4
Columba Cres. Mother	142	B1
Columba Path. Udd	161	E4
Columba St. Glasg	116	A4
Columba St. Green	45	E2
Columba St. Helen	16	B1
Columbia Pl. E Kil	180	A4
Columbia Way. E Kil	180	A4
Columbine Way. Car	201	F4
Colvend St. Glasg	117	F2
Colville Dr. Glasg	138	B3
Colvilles Pl. E Kil	181	D3
Colvilles Rd. E Kil	181	D3
Colwood Ave. Glasg	135	D2
Colwood Gdns. Glasg	135	D2
Colwood Pl. Glasg	135	D2
Colwood Sq. Glasg	135	D2
Colwyn Ct. Aird	103	D1
Colzium View. Kils	60	C4
Combe Quadrant. Hat	141	F2
Comedie Rd. Stepps	99	D3
Comely Bank. Ham	161	F2
Comely Park Terr. Falk	42	A2
Comely Pl. Falk	42	A2
Comelybank Pl. Glasg	118	A3
Comelybank Rd. Dumb	49	E2
Comelypark Pl. Glasg	118	A3
Comelypark St. Glasg	118	A3
Commerce St. Glasg	117	D3
Commercial Ct. Glasg	117	E3
Commercial Rd. Barr	134	B2
Commercial Rd. Glasg	117	E3
Common Gn. Ham	162	C2
Commonhead Ave. Aird	102	C1
Commonhead La. Aird	102	C1
Commonhead Rd. Coat	120	C4
Commonhead Rd. Glasg	120	C4
Commonhead Rd. Kilmk	228	A2
Commonhead St. Aird	102	C1
Commonside St. Aird	102	C1
Commore Ave. Barr	134	B1
Commore Dr. Glasg	95	D4
Commore Pl. Neil	154	B3
Community Ave. Hat	142	A1
Community Pl. Hat	142	A2
Community Rd. Hat	142	A1
Comrie Cres. Ham	161	F2
Comrie Rd. Stepps	99	E3
Comrie St. Glasg	119	D2
Cona St. Glasg	135	F2
Conan Ct. Glasg	139	E3
Condorrat Interchange. Cumb	82	B4
Condorrat Rd. Cumb	82	A2
Condorrat Rd. Glen	82	A2
Condorrat Rd. Glenm	102	B3
Condorrat Ring Rd. Cumb	82	B4
Coneyhill Rd. B of A	2	A4
Coneypark Cres. Bank	38	B2
Coneypark Pl. Bank	38	B2
Coneypark. Stir	6	C3
Congress Rd. Glasg	116	B4
Conifer Pl. Klrk	79	D3
Coningsby Pl. All	10	A3
Conisborough Path. Glasg	99	F1
Conisborough Rd. Glasg	100	A1
Coniston Dr. Hat	142	A2
Coniston. E Kil	179	F3
Conistone Cres. Glasg	119	F2
Connal St. Glasg	118	A2
Connell Cres. Miln	55	E1
Connell Ct. Kilb	149	D1
Conner Ave. Falk	42	A4
Conniston St. Glasg	118	C4
Connor Rd. Barr	134	A2
Connor St. Aird	103	F1
Conon Ave. Bear	75	E2
Consett La. Glasg	119	E4
Consett St. Glasg	119	E4
Constable Rd. Stir	7	D3
Constarry Rd. Kils	60	C2
Container Way. Green	45	F3
Content Ave. Ayr	239	D4
Content St. Ayr	236	A1
Contin Pl. Glasg	96	B3
Convair Way. Ren	94	B1
Conval Way. Pais	113	E4
Conway Ct. Falk	41	F2
Coo La. Eagle	178	C3
Coodham Pl. Kilw	207	E2
Cook Rd. Bonh	28	A4
Cook St. Glasg	117	D3
Coolgardie Gn. E Kil	180	B4
Coolgardie Pl. E Kil	180	B4
Cooper's Well St. Glasg	96	B1
Cooperage La. Falk	42	A3
Copenhagen Ave. E Kil	180	C3
Copland Pl. Alva	4	C3
Copland Pl. Glasg	116	A3
Copland Quadrant. Glasg	116	A3
Copland Rd. Glasg	116	A3
Coplaw St. Glasg	117	D2
Copperfield La. Tan	141	D4
Coral Terr. Hat	142	A2
Coralmount Gdns. Klrk	79	F4
Coranbae Pl. Ayr	238	A1
Corbett Pl. Glasg	118	C2
Corbett St. Glasg	119	D2
Corbie Pl. Miln	54	B1
Corbiewood Dr. Bann	11	F4
Corbiston Way. Cumb	62	A3
Cordiner St. Glasg	137	D4
Corentin Ct. Falk	42	B2
Corkerhill Gdns. Glasg	115	F2
Corkerhill Pl. Glasg	115	F1
Corkerhill Rd. Glasg	115	E2
Corlaich Ave. Glasg	137	F4
Corlaich Dr. Glasg	137	F4
Corlic St. Green	46	A1
Corlic Way. Kil	89	E4
Cormack Ave. Lennox	57	E4
Cormorant Ave. Hous	111	E4
Corn Exchange Rd. Stir	7	D4
Corn St. Glasg	97	D1
Cornaig Rd. Glasg	135	D4
Cornalee Gdns. Glasg	135	D4
Cornalee Pl. Glasg	135	D4
Cornalee Rd. Glasg	135	D4
Cornelia St. Mother	142	A1
Cornelian Terr. Hat	142	A2
Cornhaddock St. Green	45	F2
Cornhill. Ayr	239	D2
Cornhill Cres. Stir	7	D2
Cornhill Dr. Coat	121	F4
Cornhill St. Glasg	98	A3
Cornock Cres. Clyde	74	A2
Cornock St. Clyde	74	A2
Cornsilloch Brae. Ash	186	A2
Cornton Cres. B of A	2	A3
Cornton Rd. B of A	2	A2
Cornton Rd. Stir	2	A2
Cornwall Ave. Glasg	138	B3
Cornwall Ct. E Kil	159	F1
Cornwall St. E Kil	159	F1
Cornwall St. Glasg	116	B3
Cornwall St S. Glasg	116	B3
Cornwall Way. E Kil	159	F1
Coronation Ave. Lark	199	D4
Coronation Cres. Lark	199	D4
Coronation Pl. Gran	24	C2
Coronation Pl. Lark	199	D4
Coronation Pl. Muir	100	C4
Coronation Rd E. Holy	142	C2
Coronation Rd. Holy	142	C2
Coronation St. Pres	233	E3
Coronation St. Wish	165	E2
Coronation Way. Bear	76	A1
Corpach Pl. Glasg	100	B1
Corporation St. Falk	42	B2
Corra Linn. Ham	162	A2
Corran Ave. Newt M	156	B3
Corran St. Glasg	118	C4
Correen Gdns. Bear	75	D4
Corrie Ave. Sten	23	F2
Corrie Brae. Kils	36	B1
Corrie Cres. Kilmk	222	C2
Corrie Cres. Salt	205	F1
Corrie Ct. Ham	161	F1
Corrie Dr. Mother	163	D4
Corrie Dr. Pais	114	C2
Corrie Gr. Glasg	136	C2
Corrie Pl. Falk	41	F2
Corrie Pl. Helen	16	C2
Corrie Pl. Klrk	79	F2
Corrie Pl. Troon	229	F4
Corrie Rd. Kils	36	B1
Corrie View. Cumb	81	F4
Corrie Way. Lark	185	D1
Corrour Rd. Glasg	136	C4
Corrour Rd. Newt M	156	B3
Corruna St. Car	188	A1
Corse Ave. Spring	221	D1
Corse Dr. Barr	134	A2
Corse Pl. Cross	226	C4
Corse Rd. Glasg	114	C3
Corse St. W Kil	190	B3
Corsebar Ave. Pais	113	E1
Corsebar Cres. Pais	113	E1
Corsebar Dr. Pais	113	E1
Corsebar La. Pais	113	D1
Corsebar Rd. Pais	113	D1
Corsebar Way. Pais	113	E2
Corsefield Rd. Loch	128	C1
Corseford Ave. John	131	E4
Corsehill Dr. W Kil	190	A3
Corsehill. Kilw	208	A2
Corsehill Mount Rd. Irvine	225	D4
Corsehill Mount Roundabout. Irvine	225	E4
Corsehill Pk. Ayr	238	C3
Corsehill Pk. Irvine	225	D4
Corsehill Pl. Ayr	238	C3
Corsehill Pl. Glasg	120	B4
Corsehill Pl. Stew	195	F1
Corsehill Rd. Ayr	238	C3
Corsehill St. Glasg	120	B4
Corsehill Terr. Spring	220	C1
Corsehillbank St. Stew	195	E1
Corselet Rd. Barr	135	D1
Corselet Rd. Glasg	135	D2
Corserine Bank. Irvine	219	F2
Corserine Rd. Ayr	238	A1
Corsewall Ave. Glasg	119	F2
Corsewall St. Coat	121	F4
Corsford Dr. Glasg	135	E3
Corsliehill Rd. Hous	90	C4
Corsock Ave. Ham	161	F1
Corsock St. Glasg	118	B4
Corston St. Glasg	118	B4
Cortachy Ave. Sten	24	A2
Cortachy Pl. Bish	78	B1
Coruisk Dr. Newt M	157	E4
Corunna St. Glasg	116	C4
Coshneuk Rd. Stepps	99	D2
Cosy Neuk. Lark	185	E1
Cottage Cres. Falk	41	F3
Cottar St. Glasg	96	C4
Cotter Dr. Kilmk	228	B4
Cotton Ave. Lin	112	A3
Cotton St. Glasg	118	A1
Cotton St. Pais	113	F2
Coulport Pl. Helen	16	A1
Coulter Ave. Coat	121	F4
Coulter Ave. Wish	165	E4
Coulthard Dr. Pres	236	B3
Countess St. Salt	216	C4
County Ave. Glasg	138	C4
County Dr. Lan	215	E2
County Pl. Pais	113	F3
County Sq. Pais	113	F3
Couper St. Glasg	97	E1
Coursington Cres. Mother	164	A4
Coursington Gdns. Mother	163	F4
Coursington Pl. Mother	163	F4
Coursington Rd. Mother	163	F4
Coursington Rd. Mother	164	A4
Court Rd. P Glasg	47	E1
Courthill. Alva	5	D4
Courthill Ave. Glasg	137	D3
Courthill. Bear	75	E3
Courthill Cres. Kils	60	C4
Courthill Pl. Dalry	191	E4
Courthill St. Dalry	191	E4
Courtrai Ave. Helen	16	A1
Coustonholm Rd. Glasg	136	B4
Couther Quadrant. Aird	103	D1
Covanburn Ave. Ham	162	C1
Cove Cres. Shot	146	C3
Cove Pl. Helen	16	A1
Cove Rd. Gour	44	C4
Coveland Dr. Glasg	138	A2
Covenant Cres. Lark	185	D1
Covenant Pl. Wish	164	B1
Covenanter Rd. East	127	E2
Covenanters Way. Wish	186	B3
Coventry Dr. Glasg	118	A4
Cow Wynd. Falk	42	A2
Cowal Cres. Gour	44	A3
Cowal Cres. Kirk	59	D1
Cowal Dr. Lin	112	A3
Cowal St. Glasg	96	B4
Cowal View. Gour	44	A3
Cowan Cres. Ayr	236	B2
Cowan Cres. Barr	134	B2
Cowan La. Glasg	96	C1
Cowan Rd. Cumb	61	E1
Cowan St. Bon	40	A3
Cowan St. Glasg	96	C1
Cowan Wilson Ave. Udd	161	E4
Cowan Wynd. Tan	141	D4
Cowan Wynd. Wish	186	B4
Cowane St. Stir	7	D4
Cowans Row. Hurl	228	B4
Cowcaddens Rd. Glasg	97	D1
Cowcaddens St. Glasg	117	D1
Cowden Dr. Bish	78	A2
Cowden St. Glasg	115	E4
Cowdenhill Cir. Glasg	95	E4
Cowdenhill Pl. Glasg	95	E4
Cowdenhill Rd. Glasg	95	E4
Cowdray Cres. Ren	94	B2
Cowgate. Klrk	79	E4
Cowglen Rd. Glasg	135	E4
Cowie Rd. Bann	12	A4
Cowiehall Rd. Cowie	12	B4
Cowlairs Ind Est. Glasg	97	E2
Cowlairs Rd. Glasg	97	F2
Coxdale Ave. Klrk	79	D4
Coxhill St. Glasg	97	E2
Coxithill Rd. Stir	7	D2
Coxton Pl. Glasg	99	E1
Coyle Pk. Troon	229	F3
Coylebank. Pres	236	B3
Coylton Cres. Ham	161	F1
Coylton Rd. Glasg	136	C2
Crabb Quadrant. Mother	142	B1
Cragdale. E Kil	159	E2
Craggan Dr. Glasg	95	D3
Crags Ave. Pais	113	F1
Crags Cres. Pais	113	F1
Crags Rd. Pais	113	F1
Cragwell Pk. E Kil	158	C4
Craig Ave. Alex	27	E4
Craig Ave. Dalry	191	D4
Craig Cotts. Cross	226	B4
Craig Cres. Kirk	80	A4
Craig Cres. Stir	2	B2
Craig Ct. B of A	2	A3
Craig Dr. Cross	226	C4
Craig Gdns. Newt M	156	B3
Craig Hill. E Kil	180	B4
Craig Pl. Newt M	156	A3
Craig Rd. Glasg	137	D3
Craig Rd. Lin	111	F4
Craig Rd. Neil	154	B3
Craig Rd. Troon	229	D2
Craig St. Aird	122	C4
Craig St. Blac	107	F2
Craig St. Coat	121	F4
Craig St. Udd	161	F4
Craig View. Spring	221	D1
Craigallian Ave. Glasg	139	D2
Craigallian Ave. Miln	55	D2
Craiganour La. Glasg	136	B3
Craigard Pl. Glasg	138	B2
Craigash Quadrant. Miln	54	C2
Craigash Rd. Miln	54	C2
Craigbank Cres. Eagle	178	C3
Craigbank Dr. Glasg	135	D3
Craigbank Gr. Eagle	178	C3
Craigbank. N Sau	5	E1
Craigbank St. Lark	185	D1
Craigbanzo St. Dunt	74	B4
Craigbarnet Ave. Lennox	78	A4
Craigbarnet Cres. Stepps	99	D2
Craigbarnet Rd. Miln	54	B1
Craigbet Ave. Kil	89	F1
Craigbet Cres. Kil	89	F1
Craigbet Pl. Kil	89	F1
Craigbo Ave. Glasg	76	B1
Craigbo Ct. Glasg	96	B4
Craigbo Dr. Glasg	76	B1
Craigbo Pl. Glasg	96	B4
Craigbo Rd. Glasg	76	B1
Craigbo St. Glasg	76	B1
Craigbog Ave. John	131	E4
Craigburn Ave. Hous	111	E4
Craigburn Cres. Hous	111	E4
Craigburn Ct. Ash	185	F1
Craigburn Ct. Falk	41	F1
Craigburn Pl. Hous	111	F4
Craigburn St. Ham	183	E4
Craigden Dr. Steven	206	C1
Craigdhu Ave. Miln	54	C1
Craigdhu Rd. Bear	75	F4
Craigdhu Rd. Miln	54	C1
Craigdonald Pl. John	111	F2
Craigelvan Ave. Cumb	81	F3
Craigelvan Ct. Cumb	81	F3
Craigelvan Dr. Cumb	81	F3
Craigelvan Gdns. Cumb	81	F3
Craigelvan Gr. Cumb	81	F3
Craigelvan Pl. Cumb	81	F3
Craigelvan View. Cumb	81	F3
Craigenbay Cres. Klrk	79	F3
Craigenbay Rd. Klrk	79	F3
Craigenbay St. Glasg	98	A2
Craigencart Ct. Dunt	73	F3
Craigend Cres. Miln	54	C1
Craigend Dr. Coat	121	E2
Craigend Dr W. Miln	54	C1
Craigend Pl. Glasg	95	F3
Craigend Rd. Auld	179	F1
Craigend Rd. Stir	7	D2
Craigend Rd. Troon	232	C4
Craigend St. Glasg	95	F3
Craigendmuir Rd. Stepps	99	F2
Craigendmuir St. Glasg	98	B1
Craigendon Oval. Pais	133	E3
Craigendon Rd. Pais	133	E3
Craigendoran Ave. Helen	25	C4
Craigends Ave. Kil	89	F2
Craigends Dr. Kilbar	111	D2
Craigends Pl. Kil	89	F2
Craigends Rd. Hous	111	F4
Craigends Rd. Kilb	170	A3
Craigenfeoch Ave. John	111	E1
Craigenhill Rd. Kilnc	203	D3
Craigenlay Ave. Strath	31	E2
Craigens Rd. Chap	124	B2
Craigfaulds Ave. Pais	113	D1
Craigfell Ct. Ham	161	F1
Craigfin Ct. Pres	236	B3
Craigflower Ave. Glasg	135	D2
Craigflower Gdns. Glasg	135	D2
Craigflower Rd. Glasg	135	D2
Craigford Dr. Bann	7	E1
Craigforth Cres. Stir	1	C1
Craighalbert Rd. Cumb	61	E2
Craighalbert Roundabout. Cumb	61	E2
Craighalbert Way. Cumb	61	E2
Craighall Pl. Ayr	239	D1
Craighall Quadrant. Neil	154	B3
Craighall Rd. Glasg	97	D1
Craighall St. Stir	1	C1
Craighaw St. Dunt	74	B4
Craighead Ave. Glasg	98	B2
Craighead Ave. M of C	58	B3
Craighead Rd. Bishop	72	A1
Craighead Rd. M of C	58	B3
Craighead St. Aird	123	F4
Craighead Way. Barr	134	A1
Craighill Dr. Newt M	157	E3
Craighill Gr. Newt M	157	E3
Craighill View. Blac	107	F2
Craighirst Dr. Dunt	74	A4
Craighirst Rd. Miln	54	B1
Craighlaw Ave. Newt M	157	E1
Craighlaw Dr. Newt M	157	E1
Craigholm Rd. Ayr	239	E4
Craigholme. Hous	91	E1
Craighorn Dr. Falk	41	F1
Craighorn. Men	4	A3
Craighorn Rd. Alva	4	C3
Craighouse St. Glasg	99	D1
Craighton Gdns. Lennox	57	F4
Craigie Ave. Ayr	239	D4
Craigie Ave. Kilmk	227	G2
Craigie Ct. Lar	23	D1
Craigie Dr. Newt M	156	C2
Craigie La. Lark	185	D2

254

Craigie Lea. Ayr Culzean Cres. Glasg

Craigie Lea. Ayr 239 D4
Craigie Pk. Klrk 79 F3
Craigie Pl. Cross 226 C4
Craigie Pl. Kilmk 227 F2
Craigie Rd. Ayr 236 A1
Craigie Rd. Hurl 228 C3
Craigie Rd. Kilmk 227 F1
Craigie Rd. Kilmk 227 F2
Craigie St. Glasg 117 D1
Craigie St. Pres 236 A4
Craigie Way. Ayr 239 E4
Craigiebar Dr. Pais 133 E4
Craigieburn Gdns. Glasg 96 A4
Craigieburn Rd. Cumb 61 F1
Craigiehall Ave. Inch 93 D4
Craigiehall Cres. Inch 93 D4
Craigiehall Pl. Glasg 116 B3
Craigiehall St. Glasg 116 C3
Craigiehall Way. Inch 93 D4
Craigieknowes St. Green 46 B2
Craigielea Cres. Miln 54 C1
Craigielea Dr. Pais 113 E3
Craigielea Pk. Ren 94 B2
Craigielea Rd. Dunt 73 F4
Craigielea Rd. Ren 94 B2
Craigielea St. Glasg 118 A4
Craigielinn Ave. Pais 133 E4
Craigievar Ave. Sten 24 A2
Craigievar St. Glasg 99 F1
Craiginn Terr. Blac 107 E2
Craiglea Ave. Cross 226 C4
Craiglea Pl. Aird 123 E4
Craiglea Terr. Plains 103 F2
Craiglee. E Kil 180 C3
Craigleith Ave. Falk 41 F1
Craigleith. Fish 5 F2
Craigleith St. Glasg 118 C3
Craiglockhart St. Glasg 99 E1
Craiglomond Gdns. Alex 27 E4
Craiglynn Gdns. Bonh 27 F4
Craigmaddie Gdns. Lennox 78 A4
Craigmaddie Rd. Bish 56 A1
Craigmaddie
Terrace La. Glasg 96 C1
Craigmark Pl. Irvine 219 F3
Craigmarloch Ave. Lennox 78 A4
Craigmillar Ave. Miln 55 D2
Craigmillar Pl. Sten 23 F2
Craigmillar Rd. Glasg 137 D4
Craigmochan Ave. Aird 102 C1
Craigmont Dr. Glasg 96 C3
Craigmont St. Glasg 96 C3
Craigmore Rd. Bear 75 D4
Craigmore St. Glasg 118 B3
Craigmore Wynd. Lark 185 D2
Craigmount Ave. Pais 133 E3
Craigmount St. Klrk 79 E4
Craigmuir Cres. Glasg 114 C3
Craigmuir Gdns. Udd 161 D3
Craigmuir Pl. Glasg 114 C3
Craigmuir Rd. Glasg 114 C3
Craigmuir Rd. Udd 161 D3
Craigmuschat Rd. Gour 44 C4
Craignaw Pl. Irvine 220 A1
Craigneil Dr. Pres 236 B4
Craigneil St. Glasg 99 F1
Craignethan Cres. Ash 200 B2
Craignethan Rd. Car 187 F2
Craignethan Rd. Newt M 157 D4
Craigneuk Ave. Aird 123 E3
Craigneuk St. Mother 164 B3
Craignure Rd. Glasg 138 A2
Craigomus Cres. Men 3 F3
Craigpark Ave. Pres 236 A3
Craigpark Dr. Glasg 118 A4
Craigpark. Glasg 118 A4
Craigpark St. Dunt 74 B4
Craigpark Way. Tan 141 D4
Craigs Ave. Dunt 74 B3
Craigs Pl. Salt 217 D4
Craigs The. Green 45 E4
Craigsdow Rd. Troon 229 F3
Craigsheen Ave. E Kil 158 B4
Craigshiel Pl. Ayr 238 B2
Craigside Ct. Cumb 81 F4
Craigside Rd. Cumb 81 F4
Craigskeen Pl. Pres 236 B3
Craigson Pl. Aird 123 F3
Craigspark. Ard 205 E2
Craigstewart Cres. Ayr 238 B1
Craigston Ave. Ayr 239 E3
Craigston Pl. John 111 F1
Craigston Rd. John 111 F1
Craigstone View. Kils 60 C4
Craigthornhill Rd. Glass 198 A3
Craigton Ave. Barr 134 C1
Craigton Ave. Miln 54 C1
Craigton Cotts. Miln 54 B3
Craigton Cres. Alva 4 C3
Craigton Cres. Newt M 156 A3
Craigton Dr. Barr 134 C1
Craigton Dr. Glasg 115 F3
Craigton Dr. Newt M 156 B3
Craigton Gdns. Miln 54 C1
Craigton Pl. Glasg 115 F3
Craigton Pl. Udd 140 B1
Craigton Rd. Glasg 115 F4
Craigton Rd. Kilb 170 A4
Craigton Rd. Miln 54 C2
Craigton Rd. Newt M 155 D2
Craigton St. Dunt 74 B4
Craigvicar Gdns. Glasg 119 E2
Craigview Ave. John 111 F1
Craigview. N Sau 5 E1
Craigview Rd. Mother 163 F4
Craigview Terr. John 111 E1
Craigward. All 10 A3
Craigweil Pl. Ayr 238 C4
Craigweil Rd. Ayr 238 C4
Craigwell Ave. Glasg 138 B3
Craiksland Pl. Troon 230 A2
Crail St. Glasg 118 B3
Cramalt Ct. Irvine 220 A2
Crammond Ave. Coat 121 E2
Cramond Ave. Ren 94 C1
Cramond Ct. Falk 42 A1
Cramond Pl. Irvine 219 F1
Cramond St. Glasg 117 F1
Cramond Terr. Glasg 119 D3
Cramond Way. Irvine 219 F1
Cranberry Moss Rd. Kilw 207 E1
Cranberry Moss Rd. Kilw 207 E2
Cranberry Rd. Kilw 207 D1
Cranborne Rd. Glasg 96 A3
Cranbrooke Dr. Glasg 96 B4
Crandleyhill Rd. Pres 236 A3
Cranesbill Ct. Ayr 239 D2
Crannog Rd. Dumb 50 C1
Crannog Way. Kilw 207 E2
Cranston St. Glasg 116 C4
Cranworth La. Glasg 96 B2
Cranworth St. Glasg 96 B2
Crarae Ave. Bear 75 F1
Crathes Ave. Sten 24 A2
Crathes Ct. Glasg 136 C2
Crathie Ct. Car 187 F2
Crathie Dr. Duni 21 E2
Crathie Dr. Glasg 96 A1
Crathie Dr. Glenm 102 C2
Crathie Dr. Salt 205 E1
Crathie Quadrant. Wish 165 D3
Crathie Rd. Kilmk 222 C1
Crauford Ave. W Kil 190 C2
Craufurd Cres. Beith 171 F2
Craufurdland Rd. Kilmk 223 D3
Craven Gr. Irvine 219 F3
Craw Pl. Loch 129 E1
Craw Rd. Pais 113 E2
Crawberry Rd. Green 46 A1
Crawford Ave. Klrk 79 F2
Crawford Ave. Pres 236 B3
Crawford Cres. Udd 140 B1
Crawford Cres. Udd 140 C4
Crawford Dr. E Kil 160 A1
Crawford Dr. Glasg 75 D1
Crawford Dr. Helen 16 C2
Crawford Gdns. Mother 163 E3
Crawford Hill. E Kil 160 A1
Crawford Rd. Hous 91 E1
Crawford Rd. Miln 54 C2
Crawford Sq. Air 14 B2
Crawford St. Glasg 96 A1
Crawford St. Ham 162 A3
Crawford St. Mother 163 E3
Crawford St. P Glasg 47 E1
Crawfurd Ave. Glasg 138 A3
Crawfurd Dr. Pais 113 D3
Crawfurd Gdns. Glasg 138 B2
Crawfurd Rd. Glasg 138 A2
Crawfurd St. Green 45 F3
Crawfurdland Pl. Cross 221 E1
Crawfurds View. Loch 129 E2
Crawhin Gdns. Green 45 E2
Crawriggs Ave. Klrk 79 E3
Creamery Rd. Wish 165 E1
Crebar Dr. Barr 134 B1
Crebar St. Glasg 135 F2
Credon Dr. Aird 123 D2
Credon Dr. Cross 226 C4
Credon Gdns. Glasg 138 B2
Cree Ave. Bish 78 B1
Cree Gdns. Glasg 118 C3
Cree Pl. E Kil 159 D1
Creebank Pl. Troon 229 F3
Creelshaugh Rd. Fen 213 D2
Creighton Gr. E Kil 159 F1
Creigton Ct. Kilmk 223 D3
Creinch Dr. Bonh 19 F1
Creran Ct. Ham 162 A1
Creran Ct. Pres 236 B3
Creran Dr. Bank 39 E3
Creran Dr. Ren 94 A2
Creran Path. New 165 F3
Crescent Rd. Glasg 95 D3
Crescent St. Green 46 A2
Crescent The. Clyde 73 F2
Crescent The. Gree 84 B1
Crescent The. Stew 195 F1
Crescent The. Thorn 158 A3
Cresswell La. Glasg 96 B2
Cresswell St. Glasg 96 B2
Cressy St. Glasg 115 F4
Crest Ave. Glasg 95 D4
Crestlea Ave. Pais 133 F4
Creveul Ct. Alex 27 F3
Crichton Ave. Dalry 191 D4
Crichton Ct. Glasg 137 F1
Crichton St. Coat 122 A4
Crichton St. Glasg 97 F2
Cricketfield La. Hous 91 D2
Criffel Pl. Holy 143 E2
Criffel Pl. Kilmk 228 A2
Criffell Gdns. Glasg 119 E2
Criffell Rd. Glasg 119 E2
Crimea St. Glasg 117 D4
Crimond Pl. Kils 36 A1
Crimond Pl. Shi 66 C4
Crinan Cres. Coat 101 E1
Crinan Gdns. Bish 78 B1
Crinan Pl. Ard 205 E3
Crinan Pl. Coat 101 E1
Crinan Pl. Hat 142 A2
Crinan Rd. Bish 78 B1
Crinan St. Glasg 118 A4
Crindledyke Cres. New 166 A3
Cringate Gdns. Bann 7 F1
Cripps Ave. Clyde 74 B1
Crisswell Cl. Gour 44 B1
Crisswell Cres. Gour 44 B1
Crocus Bank. Ayr 239 E2
Crocus Gr. Irvine 219 E2
Croe Pl. Kilmk 228 A2
Croft. Lark 184 C1
Croft Pl. Lark 184 C2
Croft Rd. Bish 77 F4
Croft Rd. E Kil 180 C4
Croft Rd. Glasg 139 D3
Croft Rd. Lark 184 C2
Croft St. Bonh 27 F2
Croft St. Kilmk 222 C1
Croft Terr. Spring 220 C1
Croft Wynd. Udd 141 D3
Croft's Rd. Tull 4 A2
Croftbank Ave. Udd 141 D1
Croftbank Cres. Udd 140 C3
Croftbank Cres. Udd 141 D1
Croftbank St. Glasg 97 F2
Croftburn Dr. Glasg 137 E2
Croftcot Ave. Hat 141 F2
Croftcroighn Rd. Glasg 99 D1
Croftend Ave. Glasg 137 F3
Croftend La. Glasg 137 F3
Croftfoot Cres. Glasg 138 A2
Croftfoot Dr. Glasg 137 F2
Croftfoot Pl. Duni 21 E2
Croftfoot Quadrant. Glasg 137 F2
Croftfoot Rd. Glasg 137 F2
Croftfoot St. Glasg 138 A2
Croftfoot Terr. Glasg 137 F2
Crofthead Ave. Kilmk 223 D3
Crofthead Cotts. Neil 154 B4
Crofthead Cres. Hat 141 F2
Crofthead Ct. Irvine 220 A2
Crofthead Ct. Stir 2 A1
Crofthead Ct. Stone 198 C1
Crofthead Dr. Lennox 33 E1
Crofthead. Irvine 220 A2
Crofthead Pl. Hat 141 F2
Crofthead Pl. Newt M 156 C2
Crofthead Rd. Ayr 239 E3
Crofthead Rd. Kilm 222 A4
Crofthead Rd. Pres 233 E1
Crofthead Rd. Stir 2 A1
Crofthead St. Udd 140 C3
Crofthill Ave. Udd 140 C3
Crofthill Rd. Glasg 137 F3
Crofthouse Dr. Glasg 137 F2
Croftmont Ave. Glasg 137 F2
Croftmoraig Ave. Muir 81 D2
Crofton Ave. Glasg 137 E2
Croftpark Ave. Glasg 137 E3
Croftpark Cres. Ham 161 F3
Croftpark Rd. Dunt 74 A4
Croftpark St. Hat 142 A3
Croftshaw Rd. Alva 5 D4
Croftside Ave. Glasg 137 F2
Croftspar Ave. Glasg 119 E3
Croftspar Dr. Glasg 119 E3
Croftspar Pl. Glasg 119 E3
Croftwood Ave. Glasg 137 E2
Croftwood. Bish 78 A2
Croftwood Rd. Ham 162 B1
Crogal Cres. Chap 123 E1
Cromalt Cres. Bear 75 E4
Cromarty Ave. Bish 78 B1
Cromarty Ave. Glasg 136 C3
Cromarty Cres. Bear 75 F4
Cromarty Gdns. Glasg 137 D1
Cromarty Pl. E Kil 160 B2
Cromarty Pl. Muir 80 B1
Cromarty Rd. Aird 122 C3
Crombie Gdns. Glasg 120 A2
Cromdale Rd. Kilmk 228 A2
Cromdale Rd. P Glasg 69 D3
Cromdale St. Glasg 115 F4
Cromer St. Glasg 96 C3
Cromer Way. Pais 113 E4
Crompton Ave. Glasg 137 D3
Crompton Way. Irvine 219 F2
Cromwell Dr. Falk 42 B2
Cromwell La. Glasg 97 D1
Cromwell Rd. Ayr 235 F1
Cromwell Rd. Falk 42 B2
Cromwell Rd W. Falk 42 B2
Cromwell St. Glasg 97 D1
Crona Dr. Ham 161 F2
Cronberry Quadrant. Glasg 114 C2
Cronberry Terr. Glasg 114 C2
Cronin Pl. Hat 142 A4
Cronulla Pl. Kils 60 C4
Crookedshields Rd. E Kil 160 A4
Crookfur Cottage
Homes. Newt M 156 B3
Crookfur Rd. Newt M 156 B3
Crookhill Dr. Loch 129 E2
Crookhill Gdns. Loch 129 E2
Crookston Ave. Glasg 115 D2
Crookston Ct. Glasg 115 D2
Crookston Dr. Glasg 114 C2
Crookston Gdns. Glasg 114 C2
Crookston Gr. Glasg 115 D2
Crookston Path. Glasg 114 C2
Crookston Pl. Glasg 114 C2
Crookston Quadrant. Glasg 115 D2
Crookston Rd. Glasg 135 D4
Crookston Terr. Glasg 115 D2
Crookstonhill Path. Glasg 114 C2
Crophill. N Sau 5 E1
Crosbie Ct. Troon 232 B4
Crosbie Dr. Pais 132 C4
Crosbie Dr. W Kil 190 B2
Crosbie La. Glasg 96 B4
Crosbie Rd. Troon 232 C4
Crosbie St. Glasg 96 B4
Crosbie Terr. Pres 236 B4
Crosbie Wood. Pais 113 D1
Cross Arthurlie St. Barr 134 A2
Cross. Beith 171 D4
Cross Brae. Shi 66 B3
Cross Gates. Hat 142 A2
Cross Key's Cl. Lan 215 D2
Cross Rd. Pais 113 D1
Cross Shore St. Green 46 A3
Cross St. Falk 24 A1
Cross St. Glasg 119 E1
Cross St. Pais 113 E2
Cross The. Dalry 191 E4
Cross The. Glasg 117 E3
Cross The. Kilmk 227 F4
Cross The. Pres 233 E1
Cross The. Stew 211 E4
Cross The. Stone 198 C1
Crossart St. Sals 125 D1
Crossbank Ave. Glasg 117 F1
Crossbank Dr. Glasg 117 E1
Crossbank Rd. Glasg 117 E1
Crossbank Terr. Glasg 117 E1
Crossburn Ave. Miln 54 C1
Crossburn. Ayr 238 A1
Crossburn Dr. Troon 230 A2
Crossburn La. Troon 230 A2
Crossburn Terr. Troon 230 A2
Crossclyde View. Car 201 E1
Crossdene Rd. Cross 226 C4
Crossdykes. Kirk 80 A4
Crossen La. Car 188 A1
Crossflat Cres. Pais 114 A3
Crossford Dr. Glasg 76 C1
Crossgate. Kirk 58 B1
Crossgates Ave. Cle 144 A2
Crossgates. Bishop 72 A2
Crossgates St. Lark 184 C2
Crosshill Ave. Glasg 117 D1
Crosshill Ave. Klrk 79 E3
Crosshill Dr. Cle 144 A2
Crosshill Dr. Glasg 138 A3
Crosshill Pl. P Glasg 68 C4
Crosshill Rd. Bish 78 C3
Crosshill Rd. Klrk 78 C3
Crosshill Rd. P Glasg 68 C3
Crosshill Rd. P Glasg 68 C4
Crosshill St. Aird 122 C4
Crosshill St. Coat 121 D2
Crosshill St. Lennox 33 E1
Crosshill St. Mother 163 F3
Crosshouse Rd. E Kil 180 A3
Crosshouse Rd. Kilm 222 A3
Crosshouse Rd. Lennox 33 D2
Crossing La. Ash 200 A2
Crosslaw Ave. Lan 215 E2
Crosslee Cres. Hous 91 E1
Crosslee Pk. Hous 111 E4
Crosslee Rd. B of W 111 D4
Crosslee St. Glasg 115 E3
Crosslees Dr. Glasg 135 F2
Crosslees Pk. Glasg 135 F2
Crosslees Rd. Glasg 135 F1
Crosslet Ave. Dumb 50 B2
Crosslet Ct. Dumb 50 A2
Crosslet Rd. Dumb 50 A2
Crossloan Rd. Glasg 115 F4
Crossloan Terr. Glasg 116 A4
Crossmill Ave. Barr 134 B2
Crossmyloof Gdns. Glasg 116 B1
Crosspoint Dr. Glasg 76 C1
Crossroads. Beith 170 B2
Crosstobs Rd. Glasg 115 D1
Crossview Ave. Glasg 120 B3
Crossview Pl. Glasg 120 B3
Crossways. Hous 91 E1
Crosveggate. Miln 55 D1
Crovie Rd. Glasg 135 D4
Crow Ave. Holy 143 D3
Crow Rd. Glasg 95 F3
Crow Rd. Glasg 96 A1
Crow Rd. Lennox 33 D3
Crow Rd. Stone 198 C1
Crow Wood Rd. Muir 100 A4
Crow Wood Terr. Muir 100 A4
Crow-Wood Cres. Calder 123 D1
Crow-Wood Rd. Calder 123 D1
Crowflat View. Tan 121 E1
Crowflats Rd. Udd 140 C3
Crowhill Cres. Aird 102 C1
Crowhill Rd. Bish 97 F4
Crowhill St. Glasg 97 E3
Crowlin Cres. Glasg 119 D4
Crown Ave. Clyde 74 A2
Crown Cir. Glasg 96 B2
Crown Gdns. All 9 F4
Crown Gdns. Glasg 96 B2
Crown Rd N. Glasg 96 B2
Crown Rd S. Glasg 96 B2
Crown St. Ayr 235 F1
Crown St. Calder 123 D2
Crown St. Coat 122 B4
Crown St. Glasg 117 E2
Crown St. Glasg 117 E3
Crown St. Glasg 119 F2
Crown St. Green 45 F3
Crown Terr. Glasg 96 B2
Crownest Loan. Lar 23 F1
Crownpoint Rd. Glasg 117 F3
Crowwood Dr. Aird 123 E4
Croy Ave. Newt M 157 D3
Croy. E Kil 159 E2
Croy Pl. Glasg 98 B3
Croy Rd. Coat 121 F2
Croy Rd. Glasg 98 B3
Cruachan Ave. Pais 133 F4
Cruachan Ave. Ren 94 B1
Cruachan Ave. Stir 2 A2
Cruachan Ct. Falk 42 B1
Cruachan Dr. Barr 134 B1
Cruachan Dr. Newt M 156 C2
Cruachan Pl. Kilmk 228 A2
Cruachan Rd. Bear 75 D4
Cruachan Rd. Glasg 138 B2
Cruachan St. Glasg 135 F2
Cruachan Way. Barr 134 B1
Cruden St. Glasg 115 F3
Cruickshank Dr. Shi 66 B3
Cruikshank's Ct. Den 21 F1
Crum Ave. Glasg 136 A2
Crum Cres. Stir 7 E1
Crummock Gdns. Beith 150 B1
Crummock St. Beith 150 B1
Crusader Ave. Glasg 75 E1
Crusader Cres. Stew 211 E4
Cubie St. Glasg 117 F3
Cubrieshaw Dr. W Kil 190 B2
Cubrieshaw St. W Kil 190 B3
Cuckoo Way. Holy 143 D3
Cuff Cres. Beith 171 D4
Cuilhill Rd. Coat 121 D4
Cuillin Ct. Falk 42 B1
Cuillin Pl. Irvine 220 A2
Cuillin Pl. Kilmk 228 A2
Cuillin Way. Barr 134 B1
Cuillins Ave. P Glasg 68 C3
Cuillins The. Muir 81 D2
Cuillins The. Tan 120 C1
Cuilmuir Terr. Kils 60 C2
Cuilmuir View. Kils 60 C3
Cuilt Pl. Strath 31 D2
Cuilts Rd. Strath 30 A2
Culbin Dr. Glasg 94 C4
Culbin Dr. Glasg 95 D4
Cullen. Ersk 73 D2
Cullen La. E Kil 180 C4
Cullen Pl. Tan 141 D4
Cullen Rd. E Kil 180 B4
Cullen Rd. Mother 163 E3
Cullen St. Alex 27 E4
Cullen St. Glasg 119 D2
Cullins Rd. Glasg 138 B2
Cullion Way. Holy 144 A3
Culloch Rd. Bear 75 E4
Culloch Rd. Slam 86 A3
Cullochrig Rd. Glenm 82 C1
Culloden Pl. Kilmk 223 D2
Culloden St. Glasg 118 A4
Culmore Pl. Falk 42 C1
Culrain Gdns. Glasg 119 D3
Culrain St. Glasg 119 D2
Culross Hill. E Kil 159 E1
Culross Pl. Coat 121 F4
Culross Pl. E Kil 159 E1
Culross St. Glasg 119 E2
Cult Rd. Klrk 79 F2
Cultenhove Cres. Stir 6 C2
Cultenhove Pl. Stir 7 D2
Cultenhove Rd. Stir 7 D2
Culterfell Path. Cle 144 B1
Cults St. Glasg 115 F3
Culvain Ave. Bear 75 D4
Culvain Pl. Falk 42 B1
Culzean Ave. Coat 121 F2
Culzean Ave. Pres 236 B4
Culzean Cres. Glasg 120 A2

255

Culzean Cres. Kilmk   Dewar Wlk. Car

Culzean Cres. Kilmk 228 B4
Culzean Cres. Newt M 157 D2
Culzean Dr. E Kil 159 E2
Culzean Dr. Glasg 119 E2
Culzean Dr. Gour 43 F3
Culzean. Glenm 102 C3
Culzean Pl. E Kil 159 E2
Culzean Pl. Kilw 207 E1
Culzean Pl. Sten 23 F2
Culzean Rd. Ayr 238 B2
Cumberland Arc. Glasg 117 E2
Cumberland Ave. Helen 16 A2
Cumberland Pl. Coat 121 E2
Cumberland Pl. Glasg 117 E2
Cumberland Rd. Gour 44 C2
Cumberland Rd. Rhu 15 E3
Cumberland St. Glasg 117 D3
Cumberland St. Glasg 117 E2
Cumberland Terr. Rhu 15 E3
Cumberland Wlk. Gour 44 C2
Cumbernauld Rd. Bank 39 D2
Cumbernauld Rd. Cumb 81 E2
Cumbernauld Rd. Glasg 118 B4
Cumbernauld Rd. Muir 81 D2
Cumbernauld Rd. Muir 100 B4
Cumbernauld Rd. Stepps 99 E3
Cumbrae Ave. P Glasg 69 D4
Cumbrae Cres. Aird 122 C3
Cumbrae Cres N. Dumb 49 E3
Cumbrae Cres S. Dumb 49 E3
Cumbrae Ct. Clyde 74 A1
Cumbrae Ct. Green 45 D3
Cumbrae Ct. Irvine 225 E4
Cumbrae Dr. Falk 41 E2
Cumbrae Dr. Kilmk 223 D3
Cumbrae Dr. Mother 163 E4
Cumbrae. E Kil 160 B1
Cumbrae House. Pres 236 A3
Cumbrae Pl. Aird 122 C2
Cumbrae Pl. Gour 44 B3
Cumbrae Pl. W Kil 190 B2
Cumbrae Rd. Pais 133 F4
Cumbrae Rd. Ren 94 B1
Cumbrae Rd. Salt 205 F1
Cumbrae St. Glasg 119 D4
Cumlodden Dr. Glasg 96 B4
Cumming Dr. Glasg 137 D4
Cumnock Dr. Barr 134 B1
Cumnock Dr. Ham 161 E1
Cumnock Rd. Glasg 98 C3
Cumroch Rd. Lennox 33 E1
Cunard St. Clyde 94 A4
Cuninghame Dr. Salt 206 A1
Cuninghame Rd. Ard 205 E2
Cuninghame Rd. Kilbar 111 D2
Cuninghame Rd. Salt 217 D4
Cunning Park Dr. Ayr 238 B2
Cunningair Dr. Mother 163 F2
Cunningham Cres. Ayr 239 E3
Cunningham Dr. Dunt 73 F3
Cunningham Dr. East 127 E3
Cunningham Dr. Glasg 136 C2
Cunningham Gdns. Falk 42 C3
Cunningham Pl. Ayr 239 E3
Cunningham Rd. Glasg 114 C4
Cunningham Rd. Sten 24 A2
Cunningham Rd. Stir 7 E4
Cunningham St. Mother 163 E3
Cunningham Watt Rd. Stew 195 E1
Cunninghame Dr. Kilmk 227 F2
Cunninghame Rd. E Kil 159 F1
Cunninghame Rd. Glasg 138 B4
Cunninghame Rd. Irvine 224 A4
Cunninghame Rd. Pres 236 B4
Cupar Dr. Green 44 C2
Cuparhead Ave. Coat 121 F2
Cuppleton Brae. How 130 A1
Curfew Rd. Glasg 75 E1
Curle St. Glasg 95 E1
Curlew Cres. Green 45 D2
Curlew La. Green 45 D2
Curlew Pl. John 131 E4
Curling Cres. Glasg 137 E4
Curlinghaugh Cres. Wish 165 E2
Curlingmire. E Kil 180 C4
Curran Ave. Wish 164 C1
Currie Ct. Ard 205 E1
Currie St. Glasg 96 C3
Currieside Ave. Shot 146 C2
Curriesside Pl. Shot 146 B2
Curtecan Pl. Ayr 238 C3
Curtis Ave. Glasg 137 E4
Curzon St. Glasg 96 C3
Cushenquarter Dr. Plea 12 B2
Customhouse Pl. Green 46 A3
Customhall Pl. Den 21 E1
Cuthbert Pl. Kilmk 223 D1
Cuthbert St. Tan 141 D4
Cuthbertson St. Glasg 117 D1
Cuthelton Dr. Glasg 118 C2
Cuthelton St. Glasg 118 B2
Cuthelton Terr. Glasg 118 B2
Cutsburn Pl. Stew 211 F4
Cutsburn Rd. Stew 211 F4
Cutstraw Rd. Stew 211 F4
Cuttyfield Pl. Sten 24 B2
Cypress Ave. Beith 150 B1
Cypress Ave. Tan 141 D4
Cypress Ave. Udd 140 B1
Cypress Cres. E Kil 180 B3
Cypress Ct. E Kil 180 B3
Cypress Ct. Ham 162 C1
Cypress Ct. Kirk 79 D3
Cypress Gdns. Irvine 219 F3
Cypress Pl. E Kil 180 B3
Cypress St. Glasg 97 E3
Cyprus Ave. John 112 A1
Cyril St. Pais 114 A2

Daer Ave. Ren 94 C1
Daer Way. Ham 162 A2
Daer Wlk. Lark 199 D4
Daffodil Way. Mother 163 F4
Dairsie Gdns. Bish 98 B4
Dairsie St. Glasg 136 C2
Daisy Cotts. Ayr 236 A2
Daisy St. Glasg 117 D1
Daisybank. Beith 170 B3
Dakota Way. Ren 94 B1
Dalbeth Pl. Glasg 118 C1
Dalbeth Rd. Glasg 118 C1
Dalblair Arc. Ayr 238 C4
Dalblair Rd. Ayr 238 C4
Dalcharn Pl. Glasg 120 A4
Dalcross St. Glasg 96 B1
Dalcruin Gdns. Muir 81 D2
Dalderse Ave. Falk 42 A3
Daldowie Ave. Glasg 119 E2
Daldowie Rd. Glasg 120 A1
Daldowie St. Coat 121 F2
Dale Ave. E Kil 180 B3
Dale Cres. Irvine 219 E2
Dale Ct. Wish 164 B1
Dale Dr. Holy 143 D2
Dale St. Glasg 117 F2
Dale St. Glasg 118 A2
Dale Way. Glasg 138 A2
Daleview Ave. Glasg 96 A3
Daleview Dr. Newt M 157 E3
Daleview Gr. Newt M 157 E3
Dalfoil Ct. Glasg 114 C2
Dalgain Ct. Irvine 220 A3
Dalgarroch Ave. Clyde 94 C4
Dalgleish Ave. Dunt 73 F3
Dalgleish Ct. Stir 7 D4
Dalgraig Cres. Udd 140 B1
Dalhousie Gdns. Bish 78 A1
Dalhousie La. Glasg 97 D1
Dalhousie Rd. Kilbar 111 D1
Dalhousie St. Glasg 97 D1
Dalilea Dr. Glasg 100 B1
Dalilea Path. Glasg 100 B1
Dalilea Pl. Glasg 100 B1
Dalintober St. Glasg 117 D3
Daljarrock. Kilw 207 D1
Dalkeith Ave. Bish 78 A2
Dalkeith Ave. Glasg 116 A2
Dalkeith Rd. Bish 78 A2
Dallas Ct. Troon 229 E1
Dallas La. Troon 229 E1
Dallas Pl. Troon 229 E1
Dallas Rd. Troon 229 E1
Dalmacoulter Rd. Aird 103 D2
Dalmahoy Cres. B of W 110 B3
Dalmahoy St. Glasg 118 C4
Dalmahoy Way. Kilw 207 D2
Dalmailing Ave. Irvine 220 A1
Dalmailington Ave. Irvine 220 A1
Dalmally St. Glasg 96 C2
Dalmally St. Green 46 C1
Dalmarnock Ct. Glasg 118 A2
Dalmarnock Rd. Glasg 118 A1
Dalmary Dr. Pais 114 A3
Dalmellington Ct. Ham 161 E1
Dalmellington Rd. Ayr 239 E2
Dalmeny Ave. Glasg 136 B2
Dalmeny Dr. Barr 134 A1
Dalmeny Rd. Ham 162 B1
Dalmeny St. Glasg 117 F1
Dalmilling Cres. Ayr 236 B1
Dalmilling Dr. Ayr 236 C1
Dalmilling Rd. Ayr 236 C1
Dalmoak Rd. Green 46 B1
Dalmonach Rd. Bonh 27 F2
Dalmore Cres. Helen 16 A2
Dalmore Dr. Alva 4 C3
Dalmore Pl. Irvine 219 F3
Dalmore Way. Irvine 219 F3
Dalmorglen Pk. Stir 6 C3
Dalnair Pl. Miln 54 B1
Dalnair St. Glasg 96 B1
Dalness St. Glasg 119 D2
Dalnottar Ave. O Kill 73 D3
Dalnottar Dr. O Kill 73 D3
Dalnottar Gdns. O Kill 73 D3
Dalnottar Hill Rd. O Kill 73 D3
Dalnottar Terr. O Kill 73 D3
Dalreoch Ave. Glasg 120 B3
Dalreoch Ct. Dumb 49 E2
Dalreoch Path. Glasg 120 B3
Dalriada Cres. Mother 142 B1
Dalriada Dr. Lennox 78 B4
Dalriada Rd. Gour 44 B2
Dalriada St. Glasg 118 B2
Dalry Gdns. Ham 161 E1
Dalry La. Ard 205 E2
Dalry Rd. Ard 205 E2
Dalry Rd. Beith 171 D4
Dalry Rd. Kilb 170 A4
Dalry Rd. Kilw 207 E2
Dalry Rd. Salt 206 A1
Dalry Rd. Stew 195 E1
Dalry Rd. Tan 141 D4
Dalry St. Glasg 119 D2
Dalrymple Ct. Irvine 219 F2
Dalrymple Dr. E Kil 159 F1
Dalrymple Dr. Irvine 219 F2
Dalrymple Dr. Newt M 157 D2
Dalrymple Pl. Irvine 219 E2
Dalrymple St. Green 45 F3
Dalrymple St. Green 46 A3
Dalserf Cres. Glasg 136 A1
Dalserf Path. Lark 185 E1
Dalserf St. Glasg 118 A3
Dalsetter Ave. Glasg 75 D1
Dalsetter Pl. Glasg 75 D1
Dalshannon Pl. Cumb 82 A4
Dalshannon Rd. Cumb 82 A4
Dalshannon View. Cumb 82 A4
Dalshannon Way. Cumb 82 A4
Dalsholm Rd. Glasg 96 A4
Dalskeith Ave. Pais 113 D3
Dalskeith Cres. Pais 113 D3
Dalskeith Rd. Pais 113 D3
Dalswinton St. Glasg 120 B4
Dalton Ave. Clyde 74 C1
Dalton Hill. Ham 161 F1
Dalton St. Glasg 118 C3
Dalvait Gdns. Bonh 27 F4
Dalvait Rd. Bonh 27 F4
Dalveen Ct. Barr 134 B1
Dalveen Dr. Tan 140 C4
Dalveen Quadrant. Aird 122 B3
Dalveen St. Glasg 118 C3
Dalveen Way. Glasg 138 B2
Dalwhinnie Ave. Udd 140 B1
Dalwood Rd. Pres 236 A4
Daly Gdns. Udd 140 C1
Dalzell Ave. Mother 164 A2
Dalzell Dr. Mother 164 A2
Dalziel Dr. Glasg 116 B2
Dalziel Rd. Glasg 114 C4
Dalziel St. Ham 162 A3
Dalziel St. Mother 163 F4
Damhead Rd. Kilmk 227 F2
Dampark. Dunlop 195 E4
Damshot Cres. Glasg 115 E1
Damshot Rd. Glasg 135 E4
Damside. Ayr 235 F1
Danby Rd. Glasg 119 F2
Danes Cres. Glasg 95 D3
Danes Dr. Glasg 95 E2
Danes La N. Glasg 95 E2
Danes La S. Glasg 95 E2
Daniel McLaughlin Pl. Kirk 58 C1
Dankeith Dr. Sym 231 E2
Dankeith Rd. Sym 231 E2
Darg Rd. Steven 217 E4
Dargarvel Ave. Glasg 116 A2
Dargavel Ave. Bishop 72 A2
Dargavel Rd. Bishop 72 B4
Dargavel Rd. Ersk 72 C1
Dark Brig Rd. Cro 201 D1
Darkwood Cres. Pais 113 D3
Darkwood Dr. Pais 113 D3
Darleith Rd. Card 26 A1
Darleith St. Glasg 118 C3
Darley Cres. Troon 229 E1
Darley Pl. Ham 183 D4
Darley Pl. Troon 229 E1
Darlington View. Stew 195 F1
Darluith Rd. Lin 111 F3
Darmeid Pl. Alla 167 D4
Darnaway Ave. Glasg 99 E1
Darnaway St. Glasg 99 E1
Darndaff Rd. Green 46 A1
Darngaber Gdns. Quart 183 F2
Darngaber Rd. Quart 183 F2
Darngavil Rd. Plains 103 F3
Darnick St. Glasg 98 A1
Darnley Cres. Bish 77 F2
Darnley Dr. Kilmk 227 F3
Darnley Gdns. Glasg 116 C1
Darnley Path. Glasg 135 F3
Darnley Pl. Glasg 116 C1
Darnley Rd. Barr 134 C2
Darnley Rd. Glasg 116 C1
Darnley St. Glasg 116 C2
Darnley St. Stir 7 D4
Darnshaw Cl. Irvine 220 B3
Darrach Dr. Duni 21 D1
Darroch Ave. Gour 44 C4
Darroch Dr. Ersk 72 C2
Darroch Dr. Gour 44 C4
Darroch Way. Cumb 62 A2
Dartford St. Glasg 97 D2
Dartmouth Ave. Gour 44 C3
Darvel Cres. Pais 114 C2
Darvel Dr. Newt M 157 D3
Darvel St. Glasg 134 C3
Darwin Pl. Clyde 73 E2
Darwin Rd. E Kil 180 B4
Dava St. Glasg 116 A4
Davaar Dr. Coat 121 E4
Davaar Dr. Kilmk 223 D3
Davaar Dr. Mother 142 B1
Davaar Dr. Pais 133 F4
Davaar. E Kil 160 B1
Davaar Pl. Newt M 156 B3
Davaar Rd. Gour 44 B2
Davaar Rd. Ren 94 B1
Davaar Rd. Salt 205 F1
Davaar St. Glasg 118 A2
Davan Loan. New 165 F3
Davarr Pl. Falk 41 E2
Daventry Dr. Glasg 96 A3
Davey St. Green 45 E3
David Dale Ave. Stew 211 E4
David Gage St. Kilw 207 F3
David Orr St. Kilmk 222 C1
David Pl. Glasg 119 F2
David Pl. Pais 114 A4
David St. Coat 122 B4
David St. Glasg 118 A3
David St. Sals 125 D1
David Way. Pais 114 A4
David's Cres. Kilw 207 E1
David's Loan. Falk 24 B1
Davidson Ave. Beith 170 B3
Davidson Cres. Twe 59 F2
Davidson Dr. Gour 44 C4
Davidson Gdns. Glasg 95 F2
Davidson La. Car 188 A1
Davidson Pl. Ayr 236 A1
Davidson Pl. Glasg 119 E3
Davidson Quadrant. Dunt 73 F4
Davidson Rd. Bonh 27 F4
Davidson St. Aird 122 C4
Davidson St. Bann 7 E1
Davidson St. Clyde 94 C4
Davidson St. Coat 122 A2
Davidson St. Glasg 118 A2
Davidston Pl. Kirk 79 F2
Davieland Rd. Glasg 136 A1
Davies Quadrant. Mother 142 B1
Davington Dr. Ham 161 E1
Daviot St. Glasg 115 E3
Dawsholm Ind Est. Glasg 96 A4
Dawson Ave. All 9 F4
Dawson Ave. E Kil 159 D1
Dawson Pl. Glasg 97 D2
Dawson Rd. Glasg 97 D2
Dawson St. Falk 42 A4
De Morville Pl. Beith 171 D4
De Walden Terr. Kilmk 223 D1
Deacons Rd. Kils 60 C4
Dealston Rd. Barr 134 A2
Dean Cres. Ham 162 B1
Dean Cres. Muir 80 B1
Dean Cres. Stir 2 B1
Dean Ct. Kilmk 222 C1
Dean La. Kilmk 223 D1
Dean Park Ave. Udd 141 D1
Dean Park Dr. Glasg 139 E2
Dean Park Rd. Ren 94 C1
Dean Pl. Cross 226 C4
Dean Rd. Kilb 149 D1
Dean Rd. Kilmk 223 D2
Dean St. Clyde 74 B1
Dean St. Hat 142 A3
Dean St. Kilmk 223 D1
Dean St. Stew 195 F1
Dean Terr. Kilmk 223 D2
Deanbrae St. Udd 140 C3
Deanfield Quadrant. Glasg 114 C3
Deanhill La. Kilmk 223 D2
Deanpark Gdns. Ren 94 C2
Deans Ave. Glasg 139 E2
Deanside Rd. Glasg 115 D4
Deanston Dr. Glasg 136 C4
Deanwood Ave. Glasg 136 C2
Deanwood Rd. Glasg 136 C2
Deas Rd. Shot 146 B3
Dechmont Ave. Glasg 139 E2
Dechmont Ave. Mother 163 E4
Dechmont Cotts. Glasg 139 F2
Dechmont. E Kil 180 B3
Dechmont Gdns. Udd 140 B1
Dechmont Pl. Glasg 139 E2
Dechmont Rd. Tan 120 C1
Dechmont St. Glasg 118 B2
Dechmont St. Ham 162 B1
Dechmont View. Hat 141 F2
Dechmont View. Tan 141 D4
Dee Ave. Kilmk 228 A2
Dee Ave. Pais 112 C1
Dee Ave. Ren 94 C2
Dee Dr. Pais 112 C1
Dee Path. Holy 143 D3
Dee Path. Lark 199 D4
Dee Pl. E Kil 179 F3
Dee Pl. John 131 E4
Dee St. Coat 101 E1
Dee St. Glasg 118 B4
Dee St. Green 45 D3
Dee St. Shot 146 B3
Dee Terr. Ham 183 D4
Deedes St. Aird 122 B3
Deep Dale. E Kil 159 E2
Deepdene Rd. Bear 75 E1
Deepdene Rd. Muir 80 C1
Deer Park Ave. Steven 217 F4
Deer Park Ct. Ham 183 E4
Deer Park Pl. Ham 183 F4
Deerdykes Ct N. Cumb 81 F3
Deerdykes Ct S. Cumb 81 F3
Deerdykes Pl. Cumb 81 F3
Deerdykes Rd. Cumb 81 F3
Deerdykes View. Cumb 81 E3
Deerpark. N Sau 5 F1
Deeside Dr. Car 188 A2
Delfie Dr. Green 45 D2
Delhi Ave. Clyde 73 E2
Dell The. Hat 142 B2
Dellburn St. Mother 164 A3
Dellingburn St. Green 46 A2
Delny Pl. Glasg 119 F4
Delph Rd. Tull 4 B1
Delphwood Cres. Tull 4 B1
Delves Pk. Lan 215 D2
Delves Rd. Lan 215 D2
Delvin Rd. Glasg 137 D3
Dempsey Rd. Hat 141 F2
Dempster St. Green 45 F2
Den La. Shot 146 B3
Denbak Ave. Ham 162 A1
Denbeck St. Glasg 118 C3
Denbrae St. Glasg 118 C3
Denewood Ave. Pais 133 E4
Denham St. Glasg 97 D2
Denholm Cres. E Kil 180 C4
Denholm Dr. Glasg 136 B1
Denholm Dr. Wish 165 E3
Denholm Gdns. Green 45 E3
Denholm Gdns. Quart 183 F2
Denholm Gn. E Kil 180 C4
Denholm St. Green 45 E3
Denholm Terr. Green 45 E3
Denholm Terr. Ham 161 F2
Denholm Way. Beith 171 D4
Denmark St. Glasg 97 E2
Denmark St. Glasg 97 E3
Denmilne Gdns. Glasg 120 B4
Denmilne Path. Glasg 120 B4
Denmilne Rd. Glasg 120 B4
Denmilne St. Glasg 120 B4
Denniston Pl. Lan 215 E3
Dennistoun Cres. Helen 25 D4
Dennistoun Rd. Lang 70 B4
Dennistoun St. Hat 142 A3
Denny Rd. Bank 39 F3
Denny Rd. Lar 23 D1
Denny Way. Alex 27 E1
Dennyholm Wynd. Kilb 149 D1
Denovan Rd. Duni 21 F2
Denovan Rd. Tor 21 F2
Dentdale. E Kil 159 E2
Deramore Ave. Newt M 157 D4
Derby St. Glasg 116 C4
Derby Terrace La. Glasg 116 C4
Deroran Pl. Stir 6 C3
Derrywood Rd. M of C 58 B3
Dervaig Gdns. Gree 84 B2
Derwent Ave. Falk 41 F2
Derwent Dr. Coat 101 E1
Derwent St. Glasg 97 D2
Derwentwater. E Kil 179 F3
Despard Ave. Glasg 119 F2
Despard Gdns. Glasg 119 F2
Deveron Ave. Glasg 136 B1
Deveron Cres. Ham 161 F2
Deveron Rd. Bear 75 E1
Deveron Rd. E Kil 160 A1
Deveron Rd. Holy 143 D3
Deveron Rd. Kilmk 228 A3
Deveron Rd. Troon 229 F3
Deveron St. Coat 101 E1
Deveron St. Glasg 98 B1
Devilla Ct. Pres 236 B3
Devlin Gr. Udd 161 F4
Devol Ave. P Glasg 47 D1
Devol Cres. Glasg 135 D4
Devol Rd. Kil 68 B3
Devol Rd. P Glasg 68 B3
Devon Ct. Tull 4 A1
Devon Dr. Bishop 72 B2
Devon Dr. Men 4 C2
Devon Gdns. Bish 77 F2
Devon Gdns. Car 187 F1
Devon Pl. Camb 4 A1
Devon Pl. Glasg 117 D2
Devon Rd. All 10 B3
Devon Rd. Gour 44 B2
Devon St. Glasg 117 D2
Devon Village. Fish 5 F2
Devon Way. Mother 163 D3
Devonbank. Fish 5 F2
Devondale Ave. Udd 140 B1
Devonhill Ave. Ham 183 E4
Devonport Pk. E Kil 180 A4
Devonshire Gardens La. Glasg 96 A2
Devonshire Terr. Glasg 96 A2
Devonshire Terrace La. Glasg 96 A2
Devonview Pl. Aird 122 C3
Devonview St. Aird 122 C3
Devonway. Clack 10 C3
Dewar Cl. Tan 121 D1
Dewar Wlk. Car 201 D1

Dewshill Cotts. Sals	126	A2	Donaldson Cres. Klrk	79	E4	Douglas Park Cres. Bear	76	A3	Drumbeg Dr. Glasg	135	D3	Drums Rd. Glasg	115	D2
Dhuhill Dr E. Helen	16	C2	Donaldson Dr. Irvine	219	E2	Douglas Park La. Ham	162	B2	Drumbeg Pl. Glasg	135	D3	Drums Terr. Green	45	D4
Diamond St. Hat	142	A2	Donaldson Dr. Kilmk	223	E2	Douglas Pl. Bear	75	F3	Drumbeg Terr. Miln	54	B1	Drumsack Ave. Muir	100	B4
Diana Ave. Glasg	95	D4	Donaldson Dr. Ren	94	B2	Douglas Pl. Coat	121	F3	Drumbottie Rd. Glasg	98	A3	Drumsargard Rd. Glasg	138	B3
Diana Quadrant. Holy	143	D3	Donaldson Pl. Aird	123	D4	Douglas Pl. Ham	183	E3	Drumbreck Pl. Klrk	79	F2	Drumshangie St. Aird	103	D1
Diana Vernon Ct. Helen	25	C4	Donaldson Pl. Cam	6	B3	Douglas Pl. Klrk	79	E3	Drumbrock Rd. Miln	54	B1	Drumshantie Rd. Gour	44	C3
Dick Cres. Irvine	219	E3	Donaldson Pl. Klrk	79	E4	Douglas Pl. Sten	23	F2	Drumby Cres. Newt M	157	E4	Drumshantie Terr. Gour	44	C4
Dick Ct. Stone	198	C1	Donaldson Rd. Kilmk	223	E2	Douglas Rd. Dumb	50	A2	Drumby Dr. Newt M	157	E4	Drumshaw Dr. Glasg	139	E4
Dick Quad. Card	48	A4	Donaldson Rd. Lark	185	E1	Douglas Rd. Ren	114	A4	Drumcarn Dr. Miln	54	C1	Drumslea. Green	45	E4
Dick Rd. Kilmk	228	A4	Donaldson St. Ham	162	A3	Douglas St. Aird	123	D3	Drumcavel Rd. Muir	100	C4	Drumtrocher St. Kils	60	B4
Dick St. Glasg	96	C2	Donaldson St. Klrk	79	E4	Douglas St. Ayr	238	C4	Drumchapel Gdns. Glasg	75	D1	Drumvale Dr. Muir	80	C1
Dick Terr. Irvine	219	E3	Donaldswood Rd. Pais	133	E4	Douglas St. Bann	7	F1	Drumchapel Pl. Glasg	75	D1	Drunslea. Green	45	D4
Dickburn Cres. Bon	39	F3	Doncaster St. Glasg	97	D2	Douglas St. Car	187	F1	Drumchapel Rd. Glasg	75	D1	Drury St. Glasg	117	D4
Dickens Ave. Clyde	74	A2	Dongola Rd. Ayr	239	D4	Douglas St. Glasg	117	D4	Drumchapel			Dryad St. Glasg	135	F3
Dickies Wells. Alva	5	E4	Donnelly Way. Mother	164	B2	Douglas St. Ham	162	B2	Shopping Ctr. Glasg	74	C2	Drybridge Rd. Dund	225	F1
Dicks Pk. E Kil	180	B4	Donnies Brae. Neil	154	C4	Douglas St. Kilmk	227	F4	Drumclair Ave. Slam	86	A3	Dryburgh Ave. Den	21	E1
Dickson Dr. Irvine	219	E3	Doo'cot Brae. All	10	A4	Douglas St. Lark	185	D2	Drumclair Pl. Aird	123	E4	Dryburgh Ave. Glasg	138	A4
Dickson Sq. Cle	144	A1	Doon Cres. Bear	75	E2	Douglas St. Miln	55	D1	Drumclog Ave. Miln	55	D2	Dryburgh Ave. Pais	113	D1
Dickson St. Lark	185	E1	Doon Cres. Bear	75	E2	Douglas St. Mother	163	E3	Drumclog Gdns. Glasg	98	C3	Dryburgh Gdns. Glasg	96	C2
Diddup Dr. Salt	206	A3	Doon Ct. Irvine	219	E1	Douglas St. Pais	113	E3	Drumclog Pl. Kilmk	223	E1	Dryburgh Hill. E Kil	159	E1
Differ Ave. Twe	59	F1	Doon Pl. Kilmk	228	A2	Douglas St. Stir	2	A1	Drumcross Rd. Bishop	72	B2	Dryburgh La. E Kil	159	E1
Dillchip Terr. Bonh	27	F2	Doon Pl. Kirk	58	C1	Douglas St. Tan	141	D4	Drumcross Rd. Glasg	115	E1	Dryburgh Pl. Coat	121	F4
Dillchip Cl. Bonh	27	F1	Doon Pl. Salt	206	A2	Douglas St. Udd	161	E3	Drumduff. E Kil	180	B3	Dryburgh Pl. Klrk	79	F4
Dillichip Gdns. Bonh	27	F2	Doon Pl. Sym	231	E2	Douglas St. Wish	186	B4	Drumellan Rd. Ayr	239	D1	Dryburgh Rd. Bear	75	E3
Dillichip Loan. Bonh	27	F2	Doon Pl. Troon	229	F3	Douglas Terr. Glasg	116	C1	Drumellan St. Glasg	115	F3	Dryburgh Rd. Wish	165	D2
Dilwara Ave. Glasg	95	F1	Doon Rd. Kirk	59	D1	Douglas Terr. Inch	93	F1	Drumelzier Ct. Irvine	220	A2	Dryburgh St. Ham	162	A3
Dimity St. John	111	F2	Doon Side. Cumb	62	A1	Douglas Terr. Stir	6	C3	Drumfearn Pl. Glasg	118	C1	Dryburgh Way. Udd	161	E4
Dimsdale Cres. Wish	165	E1	Doon St. Clyde	74	B2	Douglas View. Coat	121	F2	Drumfearn Rd. Glasg	118	C1	Dryburgh Wlk. Muir	81	D2
Dimsdale Rd. Wish	165	E1	Doon St. Lark	185	E1	Douglasdale. E Kil	159	E1	Drumfin Ave. Cald	104	C2	Dryburn Ave. Glasg	115	D3
Dinard Dr. Glasg	136	B2	Doon St. Mother	164	A2	Douglashiehill Pl. P Glasg	68	B4	Drumfork Ct. Helen	25	C4	Dryden St. Ham	162	A3
Dinart St. Glasg	98	B1	Doon Way. Kirk	59	D1	Douglashiehill Rd. P Glasg	68	A4	Drumfork Rd. Helen	25	D4	Drygate. Glasg	117	F4
Dinduff St. Glasg	100	B1	Doonfoot Rd. Glasg	136	B3	Douglashiehill Terr. P Glasg	68	B4	Drumfrochar Pl. Green	45	F2	Drygate St. Lark	185	D2
Dingwall Dr. Gour	44	C2	Doonfoot Rd. Glasg	136	B3	Dougray Pl. Barr	134	B1	Drumfrochar Rd. Green	45	F2	Drygrange Rd. Glasg	99	E1
Dinmont Ave. Pais	112	C1	Doonholm Pl. Ayr	238	C1	Dougrie Cres. Glasg	137	E2	Drumgarve Ct. Helen	16	B1	Drymen Pl. Klrk	79	E2
Dinmont Cres. Mother	142	C1	Doonholm Rd. Ayr	238	C1	Dougrie Pl. Glasg	137	F2	Drumgelloch St. Aird	123	E4	Drymen Rd. Bear	75	F2
Dinmont Pl. Glasg	116	C1	Dora St. Glasg	117	F2	Dougrie Rd. Glasg	137	E2	Drumgray Gdns. Gree	83	E1	Drymen Rd. Bonh	19	F1
Dinmont Rd. Glasg	116	B1	Dorain Dr. Newt M	157	E4	Dougrie St. Glasg	137	F2	Drumgray La. Gree	83	E1	Drymen St. Glasg	115	F3
Dinmont Way. Pais	112	C1	Dorchester Ave. Glasg	96	A3	Dougrie Terr. Glasg	137	E2	Drumhead Pl. Glasg	118	C1	Drynoch Pl. Glasg	97	D4
Dinmurchie Rd. Troon	229	F3	Dorchester Ct. Glasg	96	A3	Doune Cres. Bish	78	A2	Drumhead Rd. Glasg	118	C1	Drysdale St. All	10	A3
Dinnet Way. New	165	F3	Dorchester Pl. Glasg	96	A3	Doune Cres. Newt M	156	C3	Drumhill. Kirk	59	D1	Drysdale St. Glasg	94	C3
Dinwiddie St. Glasg	98	B1	Dorian Dr. Newt M	157	E4	Doune Cres. Sten	24	A3	Drumilaw Cres. Glasg	138	A3	Duart Ave. Pres	236	B4
Dinyra Pl. Glen	101	E3	Dorlin Rd. Stepps	99	F3	Doune Gardens La. Glasg	96	C2	Drumilaw Rd. Glasg	138	A3	Duart Cres. Pres	236	B4
Dippin Pl. Salt	205	F1	Dormanside Rd. Glasg	115	E2	Doune Gdns. Glasg	96	C2	Drumilaw Way. Glasg	138	A3	Duart Dr. E Kil	159	E2
Dipple Ct. Kilb	149	D1	Dornal Ave. Clyde	94	C4	Doune Gdns. Gour	44	A3	Drumillan Hill. Gour	44	B1	Duart Dr. John	112	B1
Dipple Pl. Glasg	75	D1	Dornal Dr. Troon	229	F3	Doune Quadrant. Glasg	96	C2	Drumkinnon Rd. Alex	27	E4	Duart Dr. Newt M	157	D3
Dipple Rd. Kilb	149	D2	Dornford Ave. Glasg	119	E2	Doune Terr. Coat	101	E1	Drumlaken Path. Glasg	76	B1	Duart St. Glasg	96	B4
Dipple View. Kilb	149	D2	Dornford Rd. Glasg	119	E2	Doura Dr. Irvine	219	F3	Drumlaken Ct. Glasg	76	B1	Dubbs Rd. Kilw	207	D1
Dirleton Dr. Glasg	136	C4	Dornie Cl. Stew	195	E1	Doura Pl. Irvine	219	E3	Drumlaken St. Glasg	76	B1	Dubbs Rd. P Glasg	68	C4
Dirleton Dr. Pais	113	C1	Dornie Dr. Glasg	139	D4	Dove Pl. E Kil	179	F3	Drumlanford Rd. Troon	229	F3	Dubbs Rd. Steven	206	C1
Dirleton Gate. Bear	75	E1	Dornie Path. New	165	F3	Dove St. Glasg	135	D3	Drumlanrig Pl. Glasg	100	B1	Dubs Rd. Barr	134	C2
Dirleton Gdns. All	9	F4	Dornoch Ave. Glasg	136	B1	Dove Wynd. Tan	141	F4	Drumlanrig Pl. Sten	23	F2	Dubton St. Glasg	100	A1
Dirleton La. All	9	F3	Dornoch Ct. Kilw	207	D2	Dovecot. Glasg	136	B4	Drumlanrig			Duchal Rd. Kil	89	E4
Dirrans Terr. Kilw	207	F1	Dornoch Pk. Ayr	238	C3	Dovecot La. Kilw	207	F2	Quadrant. Glasg	120	B4	Duchal St. P Glasg	68	B4
Ditton Dr. Kilmk	227	F2	Dornoch Pl. Bish	78	B1	Dovecot La. Lan	215	D2	Drumley Ave. Moss	237	F3	Duchall Pl. Glasg	95	D2
Divernia Way. Barr	155	E4	Dornoch Pl. E Kil	159	E1	Dovecot Pl. Tull	4	A2	Drumleyhill Dr. Hurl	228	C3	Duchess Ct. Ham	163	D1
Diverswell. N Sau	5	E1	Dornoch Pl. Muir	80	B1	Dovecot Rd. Tull	4	A2	Drumlin Dr. Miln	76	A4	Duchess Dr. Helen	16	A2
Divert Rd. Gour	44	B3	Dornoch Rd. Bear	75	E1	Dovecote View. Kilmk	79	F4	Drumlochy Rd. Glasg	99	D1	Duchess Palace. Glasg	138	B4
Divert Wlk. Gour	44	B3	Dornoch Rd. Holy	143	D3	Dovecothall St. Barr	134	B2	Drummilling Ave. W Kil	190	B3	Duchess Pk. Helen	16	A2
Dixon Ave. Dumb	49	F2	Dornoch St. Glasg	117	F3	Dovecotwood. Kils	36	B1	Drummilling Dr. W Kil	190	B3	Duchess Rd. Glasg	118	B1
Dixon Ave. Glasg	117	D1	Dornoch Way. Aird	122	C3	Dovehill. All	10	A4	Drummilling Rd. W Kil	190	B3	Duchray Dr. Glasg	114	C2
Dixon Dr. Dumb	49	E1	Dornoch Way. Cumb	62	A3	Doveholm Ave. Dumb	50	A3	Drummond Ave. Glasg	137	F4	Duchray La. Glasg	98	B1
Dixon Pl. E Kil	159	D2	Dorrator Rd. Falk	41	F3	Doveholm. Dumb	50	A3	Drummond Cres. Ayr	236	C1	Duchray St. Glasg	98	B1
Dixon Rd. Glasg	117	E1	Dorset Rd. Gour	44	C2	Dover St. Coat	101	E1	Drummond Dr. Pais	114	B2	Ducraig St. Glasg	119	D3
Dixon Rd. Helen	16	C2	Dorset Sq. Glasg	116	C4	Dover St. Glasg	116	C4	Drummond Dr. Wish	165	D1	Duddingston Ave. Kilw	207	D2
Dixon St. Coat	122	A2	Dorset St. Glasg	116	C4	Dowan Pl. Stir	6	C3	Drummond Hill. E Kil	160	A2	Dudhope St. Glasg	99	E1
Dixon St. Glasg	117	D3	Dosk Ave. Glasg	94	C4	Dowan Rd. Bish	55	F1	Drummond House. Cumb	62	A2	Dudley Dr. Coat	101	E1
Dixon St. Ham	162	B2	Dosk Pl. Glasg	94	C4	Downfield Rd. Cumb	61	F1	Drummond La. Stir	7	D3	Dudley Dr. Glasg	96	A2
Dixon St. Pais	113	F2	Double Edges Rd. Neil	154	B3	Downanfield Rd. Cumb	61	F1	Drummond Pl. Blac	107	E2	Dudley La. Glasg	96	A2
Dobbie Ave. Lar	23	E1	Dougalston Ave. Miln	55	D1	Downanhill St. Glasg	96	B1	Drummond Pl. E Kil	160	A2	Duff Cres. Stir	1	C1
Dobbie's Loan. Glasg	97	E1	Dougalston Cres. Miln	55	D1	Downanside La. Glasg	96	B2	Drummond Pl. Kilmk	223	E1	Duff Pl. Kilmk	223	E2
Dobbies Ct. Law	187	D3	Dougalston Gdns N. Miln	55	D1	Downanside Rd. Glasg	96	B2	Drummond Pl. Stir	7	D3	Duff Pl. Salt	206	A1
Dochart Ave. Ren	94	C1	Dougalston Gdns S. Miln	55	D1	Downcraig Dr. Glasg	137	E1	Drummond Place La. Stir	7	D3	Duff St. Green	46	A4
Dochart Dr. Coat	101	E1	Dougalston Rd. Glasg	76	C1	Downcraig Rd. Glasg	137	E1	Drummond St. Green	45	E2	Duffus Pl. Glasg	139	E4
Dochart Pl. Falk	42	B1	Douglas Ave. Beith	191	E3	Downcraig Terr. Glasg	137	E1	Drummore Rd. Glasg	75	D2	Duffus St. Glasg	100	A1
Dochart St. Glasg	98	C1	Douglas Ave. Glasg	119	D1	Downfield Dr. Ham	183	D4	Drummuir Foot. Irvine	220	A3	Duffus Terr. Glasg	139	E4
Dock Breast. Green	46	A3	Douglas Ave. Glasg	136	B1	Downfield Gdns. Udd	140	C1	Drumnessie Ct. Cumb	81	F4	Duguid St. Salt	206	A1
Dock Rd. Ard	205	D1	Douglas Ave. Glasg	138	B3	Downfield St. Glasg	118	C2	Drumnessie Rd. Cumb	81	F4	Duich Gdns. Glasg	76	D1
Dock St. Clyde	94	B4	Douglas Ave. John	112	A1	Downhill St. Glasg	96	B2	Drumnessie View. Cumb	81	F4	Duisdale Rd. Glasg	139	E4
Dock St. Sten	24	A4	Douglas Ave. Klrk	79	E3	Downie St. Ham	162	B1	Drumore Ave. Chap	123	E1	Duke St. Alva	5	D4
Dockhead Pl. Salt	216	C4	Douglas Ave. Lang	70	B4	Downiebrae Rd. Glasg	118	A1	Drumoyne Ave. Glasg	115	F4	Duke St. Bann	7	E1
Dockhead St. Salt	216	C4	Douglas Ave. Pres	236	A3	Downs Cres. All	9	F3	Drumoyne Cir. Glasg	115	F3	Duke St. Den	21	E1
Dodhill Pl. Glasg	95	D3	Douglas Cres. Aird	123	D3	Downs St. Glasg	97	F3	Drumoyne Dr. Glasg	115	F3	Duke St. Glasg	118	A3
Dodside Gdns. Glasg	119	E2	Douglas Cres. Ersk	72	C2	Dowrie Cres. Glasg	115	D1	Drumoyne Pl. Glasg	115	F3	Duke St. Ham	162	C2
Dodside Pl. Glasg	119	E2	Douglas Cres. Ham	183	E3	Draffan Rd. Ash	200	A1	Drumoyne Quadrant. Glasg	115	F3	Duke St. Lark	185	D2
Dodside Rd. Newt M	155	F2	Douglas Cres. Tan	141	D4	Draffan Rd. Cro	200	A1	Drumoyne Rd. Glasg	115	F4	Duke St. Mother	163	F4
Dodside St. Glasg	119	E2	Douglas Ct. Klrk	79	E3	Draffen Ct. Mother	163	F4	Drumoyne Sq. Glasg	115	F4	Duke St. New	165	F3
Dolan St. Glasg	120	A3	Douglas Ct. Troon	229	E3	Draffen St. Mother	163	F4	Drumpark St. Coat	121	E2	Duke St. Pais	113	F1
Dollar Ave. Falk	42	A4	Douglas Dr. Ash	199	F4	Drake St. Glasg	117	F3	Drumpark St. Glasg	135	F2	Duke Terr. Ayr	236	A1
Dollar Gdns. Falk	42	A4	Douglas Dr E. Helen	16	C2	Drakemire Ave. Glasg	137	E2	Drumpark St. Stir	7	D2	Duke's Rd. Glasg	138	B3
Dollar Pk. Mother	164	A2	Douglas Dr. E Kil	179	F4	Drakemire Dr. Glasg	137	E2	Drumpellier Ave. Coat	121	E3	Dukes Gate. Udd	140	C2
Dollar Terr. Glasg	96	B4	Douglas Dr. Glasg	74	C1	Dreghorn Rd. Shew	225	B3	Drumpellier Ave. Cumb	82	B4	Dukes Pl. Ham	183	E3
Dolphin Rd. Glasg	116	B1	Douglas Dr. Glasg	119	F3	Dreghorn St. Glasg	118	B4	Drumpellier Ave. Glasg	120	A2	Dukes Rd. Coat	120	C3
Dominica Gn. E Kil	159	D1	Douglas Dr. Glasg	138	C3	Dresling Rd. Green	45	F2	Drumpellier Cres. Coat	121	E3	Dukes Rd. Troon	229	D2
Don Ave. Ren	94	C1	Douglas Dr. Hat	142	B2	Drimnin Rd. Stepps	99	F3	Drumpellier Gdns. Cumb	82	B4	Dullatur		
Don Ct. Ham	183	D4	Douglas Dr. Helen	16	B2	Drip Rd. Stir	1	C1	Drumpellier Gr. Cumb	82	B4	Roundabout. Cumb	61	F4
Don Dr. Pais	112	C1	Douglas Dr. Newt M	156	C3	Drive David Gray. Kirk	59	D1	Drumpellier Pl. Coat	121	E4	Dulnain St. Glasg	139	F3
Don Path. Lark	199	D4	Douglas Dr. Stir	7	E2	Drive Rd. Glasg	115	F4	Drumpellier Pl. Cumb	82	B4	Dulsie Rd. Glasg	98	B3
Don Pl. John	131	E4	Douglas Dr. Udd	141	D1	Drochil St. Glasg	100	A1	Drumpellier Pl. Glasg	120	A2	Dumbain Cres. Bonh	28	A3
Don St. Glasg	98	B1	Douglas Gdns. Bear	75	F2	Dromore St. Klrk	79	E1	Drumpellier Rd. Glasg	120	A2	Dumbain Rd. Bonh	20	A1
Don St. Green	45	E3	Douglas Gdns. Glasg	136	B1	Drossie Rd. Falk	42	A2	Drumpellier St. Glasg	98	B1	Dumbarton Rd. Clyde	73	F3
Donald Cres. Troon	229	E2	Douglas Gdns. Klrk	79	E3	Drove Hill. Cumb	61	D2	Drumreoch Dr. Glasg	137	F4	Dumbarton Rd. Clyde	73	F2
Donald Terr. Ham	162	B1	Douglas Gdns. Udd	140	C3	Drove Loan. Bon	39	F3	Drumreoch Pl. Glasg	137	F4	Dumbarton Rd. Clyde	94	C3
Donald Way. Tan	141	D4	Douglas La. Ayr	238	C4	Drove Loan Cres. Bank	39	F4	Drumriggend Rd. Slam	85	E2	Dumbarton Rd. Dumb	50	C1
Donald's Ct. Green	46	A3	Douglas La. Glasg	117	D4	Drove Loan. Den	39	F3	Drumry Rd. Clyde	74	B2	Dumbarton Rd. Dunt	74	A3
Donaldfield Rd. B of W	110	A4	Douglas Muir Dr. Miln	54	B1	Druid Dr. Kilw	207	F2	Drumry Rd E. Glasg	74	C1	Dumbarton Rd. Glasg	96	A1
Donaldson Ave. Kils	60	C4	Douglas Muir Pl. Dunt	74	B4	Drumadoon Dr. Helen	16	C1	Drums Ave. Pais	113	E1	Dumbarton Rd. O Kil	72	B4
Donaldson Ave. Salt	216	C4	Douglas Muir Rd. Miln	54	B1	Drumaling Terr. Lennox	57	F4	Drums Cres. Pais	113	E3	Dumbarton Rd. Stir	6	C4
Donaldson Ave. Steven	206	C1	Douglas Muir Rd. Miln	54	B1	Drumbathie Rd. Aird	123	E4	Drums Cres. Pais	113	E3	Dumbarton Rd. Stir	7	D4

Dumbreck Ave. Glasg 116 A2
Dumbreck Ct. Glasg 116 A2
Dumbreck Pl. Glasg 116 A2
Dumbreck Rd. Glasg 116 A2
Dumbreck Sq. Glasg 116 A2
Dumbreck Terr. Kils 59 F4
Dumbrock Cres. Strath 31 E2
Dumbrock Dr. Strath 31 E2
Dumbrock Rd. Strath 31 E2
Dumbuck Cres. Dumb 50 B1
Dumbuck Rd. Dumb 50 A3
Dumbuck Rd. Dumb 50 B2
Dumbuie Ave. Dumb 50 A2
Dumfries Cres. Aird 122 C3
Dumfriespark. Ayr 239 D1
Dumgoyne Ave. Miln 54 C1
Dumgoyne Ct. Aird 103 D1
Dumgoyne Dr. Bear 75 E4
Dumgoyne Gdns. Miln 54 C1
Dumgoyne Pl. Newt M 157 E4
Dumgoyne Rd. Kilmk 228 A2
Dumyat Ave. Tull 4 A1
Dumyat Dr. Falk 41 F2
Dumyat Rd. Alva 4 C3
Dumyat Rd. Men 3 F3
Dumyat Rd. Stir 2 B2
Dumyat St. All 4 C1
Dunagoil Rd. Glasg 137 E1
Dunagoil St. Glasg 137 F1
Dunagoil Terr. Glasg 137 F1
Dunalastair Dr. Stepps 99 E3
Dunalistair Dr. Stepps 99 D3
Dunan Pl. Glasg 119 F4
Dunard Ct. Car 187 F2
Dunard Rd. Glasg 138 A4
Dunard St. Glasg 96 C2
Dunard Way. Pais 113 E4
Dunaskin St. Glasg 96 B1
Dunbar Ave. Coat 121 F4
Dunbar Ave. Glasg 138 B4
Dunbar Ave. John 131 F4
Dunbar Ave. Sten 23 F2
Dunbar Dr. Mother 164 A2
Dunbar Gate. Duni 21 F2
Dunbar Hill. E Kil 159 E1
Dunbar Pl. E Kil 159 E1
Dunbar Rd. Pais 113 D1
Dunbar St. Ham 162 A3
Dunbeath Pl. Glasg 96 B3
Dunbeith Ave. Coat 122 A4
Dunbeth Ave. Coat 122 A4
Dunbeth Ct. Coat 122 A4
Dunbeth Rd. Coat 122 A4
Dunblane Dr. E Kil 159 F1
Dunblane Pl. Coat 121 F2
Dunblane Pl. E Kil 159 F1
Dunblane St. Glasg 97 D1
Dunbrach Rd. Cumb 61 E1
Dunbreck Ave. Cald 105 D3
Dunbritton Rd. Dumb 50 B2
Duncairn Ave. Bon 39 F3
Duncan Ave. Glasg 95 E2
Duncan Ave. Sten 24 A2
Duncan Ct. Kilmk 223 E2
Duncan Dr. Irvine 219 E1
Duncan Graham St. Lark .. 185 D2
Duncan La. Glasg 95 E2
Duncan La N. Glasg 95 E2
Duncan La S. Glasg 95 E2
Duncan McIntosh Rd. Cumb 62 B4
Duncan Rd. Helen 16 C2
Duncan Rd. P Glasg 47 D1
Duncan St. Bon 39 F3
Duncan St. Clyde 74 A2
Duncan St. Green 45 F3
Duncan's Cl. Lan 215 D2
Duncansby Rd. Glasg 119 E3
Duncanson Ave. All 10 A4
Duncarnock Ave. Neil 154 C4
Duncarnock Cres. Neil 154 C4
Duncarron Pl. Den 21 F1
Dunchattan Gr. Troon 229 F1
Dunchattan Pl. Glasg 117 F4
Dunchattan St. Glasg 117 F4
Dunchattan Way. Troon 229 F1
Dunchurch Rd. Pais 114 B3
Dunclutha Dr. Udd 141 D1
Dunclutha St. Glasg 118 A1
Duncolm Pl. Miln 54 B1
Duncombe Ave. Dunt 74 A4
Duncombe St. Glasg 96 B4
Duncombe View. Clyde 74 B2
Duncraig Cres. John 131 E4
Duncrub Dr. Bish 77 F1
Duncruin St. Glasg 96 B4
Duncruin Terr. Glasg 96 B4
Duncryne Ave. Glasg 119 F2
Duncryne Gdns. Glasg 119 F2
Duncryne Pl. Bish 97 F4
Duncryne Rd. Gart 20 C4
Duncryne Rd. Glasg 119 E2
Dundaff Ct. Den 21 E1
Dundaff Hill. Cumb 61 E1
Dundarroch St. Lar 23 D1
Dundas Ave. Lennox 78 A4
Dundas Cotts. Bon 39 D1
Dundas La. Glasg 117 E4
Dundas Pl. E Kil 159 F1

Dundas Rd. Stir 2 A2
Dundas St. Glasg 117 E4
Dundas Wlk. Kilmk 223 E2
Dundashill. Glasg 97 D1
Dundasvale Ct. Glasg 97 D1
Dundee Dr. Glasg 115 D2
Dundee Pl. Falk 42 A4
Dundonald Ave. John 111 E1
Dundonald Cres. Newt M ... 157 D2
Dundonald Cres. Shew 224 C1
Dundonald Dr. Ham 183 E4
Dundonald Pl. Neil 154 B4
Dundonald Rd. Glasg 96 B2
Dundonald Rd. Irvine 220 B1
Dundonald Rd. Kilmk 227 E4
Dundonald Rd. Pais 114 A4
Dundonald Rd. Troon 229 F2
Dundonald St. Udd 161 E4
Dundrennan Rd. Glasg 136 C4
Dundyvan La. Wish 165 D1
Dundyvan Rd. Coat 121 F3
Dundyvan St. Wish 165 D1
Dundyvan Way. Coat 121 F3
Dunean St. Glasg 96 C1
Dunearn Pl. Pais 114 A2
Duneaton Wynde. Lark 185 D1
Dunedin Ct. E Kil 180 A4
Dunedin Dr. E Kil 180 A4
Dunedin Rd. Lark 185 D1
Dunellan Dr. Dunt 74 A4
Dunellan Rd. Miln 54 B1
Dunellan St. Glasg 115 F3
Dungavel Gdns. Ham 183 F4
Dungavel Rd. Kilmk 228 A2
Dungeonhill Rd. Glasg 120 B4
Dunglass Ave. E Kil 159 F2
Dunglass Ave. Glasg 95 E2
Dunglass La. Glasg 95 E2
Dunglass La N. Glasg 95 E2
Dunglass La S. Glasg 95 E2
Dunglass Pl. Miln 54 C2
Dunglass Rd. Bishop 72 B1
Dunglass Sq. E Kil 159 F2
Dunglass View. Strath 31 E2
Dungoil Ave. Cumb 61 D2
Dungoil Rd. Kirk 79 F2
Dungourney Dr. Green 45 E4
Dungoyne St. Glasg 96 B4
Dunholme Pk. Clyde 73 E2
Dunira St. Glasg 118 C2
Dunivaig St. Glasg 119 F4
Dunkeld Ave. Glasg 138 A4
Dunkeld Dr. Bear 76 A2
Dunkeld Gdns. Bish 78 A1
Dunkeld La. Muir 81 D1
Dunkeld Pl. Coat 121 F2
Dunkeld Pl. Falk 24 B1
Dunkeld Pl. Ham 161 F2
Dunkeld St. Glasg 118 B2
Dunkenny Rd. Glasg 74 C2
Dunkirk St. Cald 105 D3
Dunlin Cres. Hous 91 E1
Dunlin Ct. Tan 141 F4
Dunlin. E Kil 159 F2
Dunlop Cres. Ayr 236 C1
Dunlop Cres. Irvine 220 A1
Dunlop Cres. Ren 94 B2
Dunlop Cres. Udd 141 D1
Dunlop Ct. Ham 183 F4
Dunlop Dr. Shew 224 C2
Dunlop Gr. Tan 121 D1
Dunlop Pl. Miln 54 C2
Dunlop Pl. Shew 224 C2
Dunlop Rd. Beith 172 A2
Dunlop Rd. Dunlop 173 E3
Dunlop Rd. Stew 195 E1
Dunlop St. Fen 213 D2
Dunlop St. Glasg 117 E3
Dunlop St. Glasg 139 F3
Dunlop St. Green 45 E2
Dunlop St. Kilmk 222 C1
Dunlop St. Lin 112 B3
Dunlop St. Ren 94 B2
Dunlop St. Stew 195 F1
Dunlop Terr. Ayr 236 B1
Dunmar Cres. All 4 C1
Dunmar Dr. All 4 C1
Dunmore Dr. Miln 76 B4
Dunmore St. Clyde 94 B4
Dunn Mews. Kilmk 227 E4
Dunn St. Clyde 73 F2
Dunn St. Dunt 73 F3
Dunn St. Glasg 118 A2
Dunn St. Green 45 F2
Dunn St. Pais 114 A2
Dunn Terr. East 127 F3
Dunnachie Dr. Coat 121 D2
Dunnet Ave. Glenm 102 C3
Dunnett Ave. Kilmk 228 A4
Dunnichen Gdns. Bish 78 B1
Dunnikier Wlk. Cumb 60 C1
Dunning Pl. Falk 24 B1
Dunning St. Glasg 118 B2
Dunnotar Wlk. New 165 F3
Dunnottar Cres. E Kil 159 E2
Dunnottar Dr. Sten 23 F2
Dunnottar St. Bish 78 B1
Dunnottar St. Glasg 99 D1

Dunns Wood Rd. Cumb 62 B3
Dunolly Dr. Newt M 156 C3
Dunolly St. Glasg 98 A1
Dunoon Ave. Kilmk 222 C2
Dunottar Ave. Coat 122 A1
Dunphail Dr. Glasg 100 B1
Dunphail Rd. Glasg 120 B4
Dunragit St. Glasg 118 B4
Dunrobin Ave. John 112 B1
Dunrobin Ave. Sten 23 F3
Dunrobin Cres. E Kil 159 E2
Dunrobin Ct. E Kil 159 E2
Dunrobin Dr. E Kil 159 E2
Dunrobin Dr. Gour 43 F3
Dunrobin Pl. Coat 121 F4
Dunrobin Rd. Aird 123 F4
Dunrobin St. Glasg 118 A3
Dunrod Hill. E Kil 159 F2
Dunrod St. Glasg 119 D2
Duns Cres. Wish 165 E4
Duns Path. Coat 122 B2
Dunscore Brae. Ham 161 F1
Dunside Dr. Glasg 135 D3
Dunsiston Rd. Chap 124 A2
Dunskaith St. Glasg 120 B4
Dunsmore Rd. Bishop 72 A2
Dunsmuir St. Glasg 116 A4
Dunster Gdns. Bish 78 A2
Dunster Rd. Stir 2 B2
Dunswin Ave. Clyde 73 F2
Dunsyre Pl. Glasg 76 C1
Dunsyre St. Glasg 118 C4
Duntarvie Cres. Glasg 120 B4
Duntarvie Pl. Glasg 120 A4
Duntarvie Quadrant. Glasg 120 B4
Duntarvie Rd. Glasg 120 A4
Dunterlie Ave. Glasg 95 D3
Dunterlie Ct. Barr 134 B2
Duntiblae Rd. Kirk 80 A4
Duntiglennan Rd. Dunt 74 A3
Duntilland Ave. Sals 125 D1
Duntilland Rd. Chap 124 C4
Duntilland Rd. Sals 125 E3
Duntocher Rd. Bear 75 D3
Duntocher Rd. Clyde 74 A2
Duntocher Rd. Milln 74 C4
Duntonknoll. Irvine 219 E2
Duntreath Ave. Glasg 74 C1
Duntreath Terr. Kils 60 B4
Duntroon Pl. Hat 142 A2
Duntroon St. Glasg 118 A4
Dunure Courts. Kilw 207 E2
Dunure Cres. Bon 40 A3
Dunure Dr. Glasg 137 F3
Dunure Dr. Ham 161 E1
Dunure Dr. Kilmk 228 A4
Dunure Dr. Newt M 157 D3
Dunure Pl. Coat 121 F2
Dunure Pl. Newt M 157 D2
Dunure Rd. Ayr 238 B1
Dunure St. Bon 40 A3
Dunure St. Coat 121 F2
Dunure St. Glasg 96 B4
Dunvegan Ave. Coat 101 E1
Dunvegan Ave. Gour 43 F3
Dunvegan Ave. John 112 B1
Dunvegan Ave. Sten 23 F2
Dunvegan Ct. All 10 A3
Dunvegan Dr. Bish 78 A2
Dunvegan Dr. Falk 24 B1
Dunvegan Dr. Newt M 157 D3
Dunvegan Dr. Stir 2 A2
Dunvegan. Glenm 102 C2
Dunvegan Pl. Bon 39 F3
Dunvegan Pl. E Kil 159 E2
Dunvegan Pl. Irvine 219 E3
Dunvegan Pl. Tan 140 B4
Dunvegan Quadrant. Ren 94 A2
Dunwan Ave. Glasg 94 C4
Dunwan Pl. Glasg 94 C4
Dura Rd. Alla 167 E3
Durban Ave. Clyde 73 E2
Durham Rd. Gour 44 C3
Durham St. Glasg 116 B3
Durisdeer Dr. Ham 161 F1
Durness Ave. Bear 76 A2
Duror St. Glasg 119 D3
Durris Gdns. Glasg 119 E2
Durrockstock Cres. Pais ... 132 C4
Durrockstock Rd. Pais 133 D4
Durrockstock Rd. Pais 132 C4
Durrockstock Way. Pais 132 C4
Durward Ave. Glasg 116 B1
Durward Cres. Pais 112 C1
Durward Ct. Glasg 116 B1
Durward. E Kil 160 C2
Durward Way. Pais 112 C1
Duthie Rd. Gour 45 D4
Duthil St. Glasg 115 D3
Dyce La. Glasg 96 A1
Dyers' Wynd. Pais 113 F3
Dyfring St. Shot 146 C3
Dyfrig St. Udd 161 E4
Dyke Rd. Glasg 95 D4
Dyke St. Coat 121 D4
Dyke St. Glasg 120 B3
Dykebar Ave. Glasg 95 D3
Dykebar Cres. Pais 114 A1

Dykehead Cres. Aird 102 C1
Dykehead Dr. Hurl 228 C3
Dykehead La. Glasg 119 E4
Dykehead Rd. Aird 103 D2
Dykehead Rd. Coat 121 D3
Dykehead Rd. Cumb 61 E3
Dykehead Rd. Kils 59 F4
Dykehead Sq. Ham 161 F2
Dykehead St. Glasg 119 E4
Dykemuir Pl. Glasg 98 A2
Dykemuir Quadrant. Glasg .. 98 A2
Dykemuir St. Glasg 98 A2
Dykeneuk Rd. P Glasg 68 B4
Dykes Pl. Salt 205 F1
Dykes The. Kilb 170 A4
Dykesfield Pl. Salt 205 F1
Dykesmains Rd. Salt 205 F1
Dysart Way. Chap 124 A3

Eagle Cres. Bear 75 D3
Eagle St. Glasg 97 E1
Eaglesham Ct. Glasg 116 C3
Eaglesham Path. Glen 101 E3
Eaglesham Pl. Glasg 116 C3
Eaglesham Rd. E Kil 158 C1
Eaglesham Rd. Eagle 179 E4
Eaglesham Rd. Newt M 156 B2
Eaglesham Rd. Newt M 157 F3
Eaglesham Rd. Thorn 179 E4
Earl Ave. Cald 105 D3
Earl Haig Rd. Glasg 114 C4
Earl La. Glasg 95 E2
Earl Of Mar Ct. All 10 A3
Earl Pl. B of W 110 B3
Earl Pl. Glasg 95 E2
Earl Rd. Kilbar 95 D2
Earl View. Holy 143 D4
Earl's Gate. Udd 140 C2
Earl's Hill. Cumb 61 D2
Earlbank Ave. Glasg 95 E2
Earlbank La N. Glasg 95 E2
Earlbank La S. Glasg 95 E2
Earls Ct. All 10 A3
Earls Way. Ayr 238 B1
Earlsburn Ave. Stir 7 D2
Earlsburn Rd. Klrk 79 F2
Earlscourt. Muir 80 C1
Earlshill Dr. Bann 7 F1
Earlspark Ave. Glasg 136 C3
Earlston Ave. Kilmk 227 F2
Earlston Cres. Coat 122 B2
Earlston St. Wish 165 E3
Earn Ave. Bear 76 A2
Earn Ave. Ren 94 C1
Earn Ave. Tan 141 F3
Earn Cres. Wish 165 D1
Earn Ct. All 10 B3
Earn Gdns. Lark 199 D4
Earn Loan. Holy 143 D3
Earn Pl. Bank 39 E3
Earn Pl. Kilmk 228 A3
Earn Rd. Newt M 156 B4
Earn Rd. Troon 229 F2
Earn St. Glasg 98 C1
Earncraig Gn. Irvine 220 A2
Earnhill Rd. Gour 44 B3
Earnock Ave. Mother 163 E3
Earnock Rd. Ham 161 F1
Earnock St. Glasg 98 B2
Earnock St. Ham 162 A2
Earnside St. Glasg 119 D3
Easdale Dr. Glasg 119 D2
Easdale. E Kil 181 D4
Easdale Path. Glen 101 E3
Easdale Pl. Newt M 156 A3
Easdale Rise. Ham 161 F2
East Academy St. Wish 165 D1
East Ave. Car 187 E1
East Ave. Ham 161 F3
East Ave. Holy 143 D1
East Ave. Plains 104 A2
East Ave. Ren 94 B2
East Ave. Tan 141 E3
East Barmoss Ave. P Glasg 68 C4
East Barns St. Clyde 94 B4
East Bath La. Glasg 117 E4
East Blackhall St. Green ... 46 A2
East Boreland Pl. Den 21 F1
East
  Bowhouse Head. Irvine 220 A3
East
  Bowhouse Way. Irvine . 220 A3
East Breast. Green 46 A3
East Bridge St. Falk 42 B2
East Broomlands. Irvine ... 220 A1
East Buchanan St. Pais 113 F3
East Burnside St. Kils 60 B4
East Campbell St. Glasg ... 117 F3
East Castle St. All 10 A3
East Crawford St. Green 46 B2
East Dean St. Hat 142 A3
East Dr. Lar 23 E1
East Faulds Rd. Lan 215 D2
East Gargieston Ave. Kilmk 227 E3
East Gartferry Rd. Muir 80 C1
East Gate. Glen 101 E4
East Gate. Wish 165 E2

East George St. Coat 122 A4
East Glebe Terr. Ham 162 B1
East Gr. Troon 229 F2
East Greenlees Ave. Glasg 139 E2
East
  Greenlees Cres. Glasg 139 E2
East Greenlees Dr. Glasg . 139 E2
East Greenlees Rd. Glasg . 139 D2
East Greenlees St. Glasg . 139 E2
East Hallhill Rd. Glasg ... 120 B3
East Hamilton St. Green ... 46 B2
East Hamilton St. Wish ... 165 D1
East High St. Aird 123 D4
East High St. Kirk 58 B1
East India Breast. Green .. 46 A3
East Kilbride Rd. E Kil ... 158 C2
East Kilbride Rd. Glasg .. 138 C2
East Kilbride Rd. Thorn .. 158 B2
East Kirkland. Dalry 191 E4
East La. Pais 114 A2
East Lennox Dr. Helen 16 C2
East Link Rd. B of A 2 B3
East Machan St. Lark 185 D1
East Main St. East 127 F3
East Main St. Hart 127 F3
East Mains. Men 4 A3
East Mains Rd. E Kil 159 F2
East Milton Gr. E Kil 159 D1
East Montrose St. Helen ... 16 C1
East Murrayfield. Bann 7 F1
East Netherton St. Kilmk .. 227 F4
East Park Cres. Kilm 222 A4
East Park Dr. Kilm 222 A4
East Park Rd. Ayr 236 A2
East Rd. Irvine 219 E1
East Rd. Kilbar 111 D2
East Rd. P Glasg 68 C4
East Rd. Pres 236 B3
East Rossdhu Dr. Helen 16 C2
East Scott Terr. Ham 162 B1
East Shaw St. Green 45 F3
East Shaw St. Kilmk 227 F3
East Springfield Terr. Bish 98 A4
East Station Ind Est. Lark 185 D2
East Stewart Pl. Coat 122 B4
East Stewart St. Coat 122 B3
East Stewart St. Green 46 A2
East Stirling St. Alva 5 D4
East Thomson St. Clyde 74 A2
East Thornlie St. Wish 165 D1
East Union St. Troon 229 E2
East Vennel. All 10 A3
East St. Green 46 C1
East Wellbrae Cres. Ham .. 162 A1
East Wellington St. Glasg . 118 B3
East William St. Green 46 B2
East
  Woodside Ave. P Glasg . 69 D4
Eastburn Dr. Falk 42 B2
Eastburn Rd. Glasg 98 A3
Eastcote Ave. Glasg 95 F2
Eastcroft. Glasg 138 A4
Eastcroft St. Lar 23 D1
Eastcroft Terr. Glasg 98 A2
Eastend Ave. Holy 143 D1
Eastend. Loch 129 E2
Easter Cornton Rd. Stir 2 A2
Easter Craigs. Glasg 118 A4
Easter Cres. Wish 165 E4
Easter Garngaber Rd. Klrk . 79 F3
Easter Livilands. Stir 7 E2
Easter Mews. Udd 140 C3
Easter Queenslie Rd. Glasg 119 F4
Easter Rd. Shot 146 B3
Easter Rd. Thorn 158 A3
Easter Wood Cres. Tan 121 E1
Eastergreens Ave. Klrk 79 E4
Easterhill Pl. Glasg 118 C2
Easterhill Rd. Helen 16 C2
Easterhill St. Glasg 119 D1
Easterhouse Pl. Glasg 120 B4
Easterhouse
  Quadrant. Glasg 120 B4
Easterhouse Rd. Glasg 120 B4
Eastermains. Kirk 59 D1
Eastern Cres. Kilb 170 A4
Easterton Ave. Thorn 158 A3
Easterton Cres. Cowie 12 C4
Easterton Dr. Cowie 12 C4
Easterton Gr. Cowie 12 C4
Eastfield Ave. Glasg 138 C3
Eastfield Cres. Dumb 50 A1
Eastfield Pl. Dumb 50 A1
Eastfield Rd. Cald 105 D3
Eastfield Rd. Car 202 A4
Eastfield Rd. Cumb 61 E2
Eastfield Rd. Glasg 97 F2
Eastfield Terr. Hat 142 B2
Eastgate. Muir 101 D3
Eastlea Pl. Aird 123 D3
Eastmuir St. Glasg 119 D3
Eastmuir St. Wish 165 F2
Easton Ct. Stir 2 A1
Easton Dr. Shi 66 B4
Easton Pl. Coat 122 A3
Eastside. Kirk 58 B1
Eastvale Pl. Glasg 116 B4
Eastwood Ave. Glasg 136 B1

Eastwood Ave. Glasg	136	B4
Eastwood Ave. Irvine	219	E2
Eastwood Cres. Glasg	135	F2
Eastwood Dr. New	166	A3
Eastwood La. Helen	25	C4
Eastwood Rd. Muir	80	C1
Eastwood Toll. Glasg	136	A1
Eastwood View. Glasg	139	F3
Eastwood Way. Lark	185	D2
Eastwoodmains Rd. Glasg	136	B1
Eastwoodmains Rd. Newt M	157	E4
Easwald Bank. Kilbar	111	E1
Ebenezer Pl. Cali	66	C3
Ebroch Dr. Kils	60	C4
Ebroch Pk. Kils	60	C4
Eccles St. Glasg	97	F3
Eck Path. Holy	143	D3
Eckford St. Glasg	119	D2
Eday St. Glasg	97	E3
Edderton Pl. Glasg	120	A4
Eddington Dr. Newt M	156	B2
Eddleston Pl. Glasg	139	F3
Eddlewood Rd. Glasg	119	F4
Eden Ct. Kilw	207	D2
Eden Dr. E Kil	179	F3
Eden Gdns. E Kil	179	F4
Eden Gr. E Kil	179	F4
Eden La. Glasg	98	B1
Eden Pk. Udd	140	C1
Eden Pl. Glasg	139	E3
Eden Pl. Kilmk	228	A3
Eden Pl. Ren	94	C1
Eden Rd. All	9	F4
Eden St. Glasg	98	B1
Edenhall Rd. Ayr	236	A2
Edenkill Pl. Strath	31	E2
Edenside. Cumb	62	A4
Edenwood St. Glasg	118	C3
Edgam Dr. Glasg	115	E3
Edgefauld Ave. Glasg	97	F2
Edgefauld Dr. Glasg	97	F2
Edgefauld Pl. Glasg	97	F3
Edgefauld Rd. Glasg	98	A2
Edgehill La. Glasg	96	A2
Edgehill Rd. Bear	75	F3
Edgehill Rd. Glasg	96	A2
Edgemont Pk. Ham	183	E4
Edgemont St. Glasg	136	C4
Edinbeg Ave. Glasg	137	F4
Edinbeg Pl. Glasg	137	F4
Edinburgh Dr. Gour	43	F3
Edinburgh Rd. East	127	E3
Edinburgh Rd. Glasg	119	E4
Edinburgh Rd. Ham	162	C2
Edinburgh Rd. Holy	143	E4
Edington Gdns. Muir	80	C2
Edington St. Glasg	97	D1
Edison Pl. Kilw	207	F1
Edison St. Glasg	114	C4
Edmiston Ave. Pres	236	A4
Edmiston Dr. Glasg	116	A3
Edmiston Dr. Lin	112	A3
Edmonstone Dr. Kils	60	B4
Edmonton Terr. E Kil	180	B4
Edmund Kean. E Kil	160	B3
Edrom Ct. Glasg	118	C3
Edrom Path. Glasg	118	C3
Edrom St. Glasg	118	C3
Edward Ave. Ren	94	C2
Edward Ave. Sten	23	F2
Edward Ave. Stir	2	B1
Edward Dr. Helen	16	B2
Edward Pl. Aran	24	C2
Edward Rd. Stir	2	A1
Edward St. Clyde	94	B4
Edward St. Coat	120	C3
Edward St. Ham	162	B1
Edward St. Kils	36	B1
Edward St. Mother	163	F2
Edwin St. Glasg	116	B3
Edzell Ct. Glasg	95	E1
Edzell Dr. John	112	B1
Edzell Dr. Newt M	156	C2
Edzell Gdns. Bish	98	B4
Edzell Pl. Glasg	95	E2
Edzell Row. Kilw	207	D2
Edzell St. Coat	121	E2
Edzell St. Glasg	95	E1
Egidia Ave. Glasg	136	B1
Egilsay Cres. Glasg	97	E4
Egilsay Pl. Glasg	97	E4
Egilsay St. Glasg	97	E4
Egilsay Terr. Glasg	97	E4
Eglinton Cres. Troon	229	E4
Eglinton Ct. Glasg	117	D3
Eglinton Ct. Salt	216	C4
Eglinton Dr. Eagle	178	C2
Eglinton Dr. Glasg	136	B1
Eglinton Dr. Troon	229	F1
Eglinton Interchange. Kilw	219	D4
Eglinton Pl. Ayr	235	F1
Eglinton Pl. Kilw	207	F2
Eglinton Pl. Salt	216	C4
Eglinton Rd. Ard	205	D2
Eglinton Sq. Ard	205	E2
Eglinton St. Beith	171	D4
Eglinton St. Coat	122	A4
Eglinton St. Glasg	117	D2
Eglinton St. Irvine	219	E2
Eglinton St. Salt	216	C4
Eglinton Terr. Ayr	235	F1
Eglinton Wlk. Eagle	178	C2
Egmont Pk. E Kil	180	A4
Eider Ave. E Kil	180	A3
Eider Gr. E Kil	180	A3
Eider Pl. Auld	180	A2
Eighth St. Tan	120	C1
Eildon Dr. Barr	134	B1
Eileen Gdns. Bish	78	A1
Eilt Wlk. New	165	F3
Elcho St. Glasg	117	F3
Elder Ave. Beith	171	D4
Elder Gr. Tan	141	D4
Elder St. Glasg	115	F4
Elderbank. Bear	75	F2
Elderpark Gdns. Glasg	115	F4
Elderpark Gr. Glasg	115	F4
Elderpark St. Glasg	115	F4
Elderslea Rd. Car	202	A4
Elderslie Cres. Kilmk	227	F2
Elderslie St. Glasg	116	C4
Eldin Pl. B of W	110	C3
Eldin Pl. John	112	A1
Eldon Ct. Glasg	96	A1
Eldon Gdns. Bish	77	F1
Eldon Pl. Green	45	E4
Eldon St. Glasg	96	C1
Eldon St. Gour	45	E4
Elgin Ave. E Kil	159	F2
Elgin Ave. Stew	195	E1
Elgin Dr. Stir	7	E2
Elgin Gdns. Glasg	157	F4
Elgin Pl. Aird	122	C3
Elgin Pl. Coat	122	A2
Elgin Pl. E Kil	159	F2
Elgin Pl. Falk	42	B2
Elgin Pl. Kils	36	B1
Elgin Rd. Bear	75	F4
Elgin Terr. Ham	161	F2
Elgin Way. Hat	142	A3
Elibank St. Glasg	99	D1
Elie St. Glasg	96	B1
Eliot Cres. Ham	162	B1
Eliot Terr. Ham	162	B1
Elizabeth Ave. Lar	23	E1
Elizabeth Ave. M of C	58	A3
Elizabeth Cres. Falk	41	D3
Elizabeth Cres. Glasg	136	A2
Elizabeth Quadrant. Holy	142	C3
Elizabeth St. Glasg	116	B3
Elizabeth St. Stir	7	D3
Elizabeth Wynd. Ham	183	E4
Elizabethan Way. Ren	94	B1
Ella Gdns. Hat	142	B2
Ellangowan Rd. Glasg	136	B4
Ellangowan Rd. Miln	55	D1
Ellergreen Rd. Bear	75	F2
Ellerslie St. John	112	A2
Ellesmere St. Glasg	97	D2
Elliot Ave. Pais	132	C4
Elliot Cres. E Kil	160	A1
Elliot Dr. Glasg	136	B2
Elliot Pl. Ash	200	A2
Elliot Pl. Glasg	116	C4
Elliot St. Glasg	116	C4
Elliot Terr. Falk	42	A4
Ellis St. Coat	122	A3
Ellis St. Kilmk	227	F4
Ellis Way. Mother	163	F3
Ellisland Ave. Clyde	74	B2
Ellisland Cres. Glasg	137	F3
Ellisland Dr. Kilmk	228	B4
Ellisland Dr. Kirk	59	D1
Ellisland Dr. Udd	161	D3
Ellisland. E Kil	160	C2
Ellisland. Kirk	59	D1
Ellisland Pl. Ayr	239	D3
Ellisland Pl. Salt	206	A2
Ellisland Rd. Cumb	62	A1
Ellisland Rd. Glasg	136	B3
Ellisland Rd. Newt M	157	F3
Ellisland Sq. Ayr	239	D3
Ellisland Wynd. Holy	143	E2
Ellismuir Farm Rd. Glasg	120	B2
Ellismuir Pl. Glasg	120	B2
Ellismuir Rd. Glasg	120	B2
Ellismuir St. Coat	121	F2
Elliston Ave. Glasg	135	E3
Elliston Cres. Glasg	135	E3
Elliston Dr. Glasg	135	E3
Elliston Pl. How	130	C3
Elliston Rd. How	130	C3
Ellon Dr. Lin	112	A3
Ellrig. E Kil	180	B3
Elm Ave. Klrk	79	E3
Elm Ave. Ren	94	B2
Elm Bank. Bish	78	A1
Elm Bank. Kirk	58	B1
Elm Cres. Tan	141	E4
Elm Dr. Cumb	62	C2
Elm Dr. Glasg	139	E3
Elm Dr. John	112	A1
Elm Dr. Shi	66	B3
Elm Gdns. Bear	75	F3
Elm Gdns. Troon	230	A1
Elm Gr. All	10	B3
Elm Gr. Lang	70	B4
Elm Gr. Lar	23	E1
Elm La E. Glasg	95	E2
Elm La W. Glasg	95	E2
Elm Park. Ard	205	E2
Elm Pl. E Kil	180	B3
Elm Quadrant. Aird	123	E4
Elm Rd. B of W	110	C4
Elm Rd. Clyde	74	A3
Elm Rd. Dumb	49	F2
Elm Rd. Glasg	138	A2
Elm Rd. Holy	143	D3
Elm Rd. Pais	114	A1
Elm St. Coat	122	B3
Elm St. Glasg	95	E2
Elm St. Lennox	57	F4
Elm St. Mother	163	E4
Elm St. Newt M	157	F3
Elm St. Stir	1	C1
Elm St. Udd	161	F4
Elm Terr. Gour	44	C3
Elm View. Cat. Hat	142	B2
Elm Wlk. Bear	75	F3
Elmbank Ave. Kilmk	228	A4
Elmbank Cres. Bank	39	E3
Elmbank Cres. Glasg	117	D4
Elmbank Cres. Ham	162	A2
Elmbank Dr. Bonh	27	F3
Elmbank Rd. Lang	70	B4
Elmbank Rd. Stir	7	D2
Elmbank St. Ayr	236	A2
Elmbank St. Car	202	A4
Elmbank St. Glasg	117	D4
Elmbank Street La. Glasg	117	D4
Elmbank Terr. Irvine	219	E2
Elmfoot St. Glasg	117	E1
Elmhurst. Mother	163	E2
Elmira Rd. Muir	100	B4
Elmore Ave. Glasg	137	D3
Elms Pl. Beith	150	A1
Elms The. Glasg	137	D2
Elmslie Ct. Glasg	120	B2
Elmvale Row. Glasg	97	F3
Elmvale St. Glasg	97	F3
Elmway. Lark	185	D3
Elmwood Ave. Glasg	95	F2
Elmwood Ave. Newt M	156	C3
Elmwood Ct. Udd	141	D1
Elmwood Gdns. Klrk	79	D3
Elmwood La. Glasg	95	F2
Elmwood Rd. Shot	147	D1
Elphin St. Glasg	76	B1
Elphinstone Cres. Air	14	C2
Elphinstone Cres. E Kil	180	C3
Elphinstone Mews. Kil	89	E4
Elphinstone Pl. Glasg	116	B4
Elphinstone Rd. Newt M	157	D4
Elrig Rd. Glasg	137	D3
Elsinore Path. E Kil	180	C3
Elspeth Gdns. Bish	78	B1
Elswick Dr. Cald	105	D2
Eltham St. Glasg	97	D2
Elvan Pl. E Kil	179	F4
Elvan St. Glasg	118	C3
Elvan St. Mother	163	E3
Elvan Tower. Mother	163	F3
Embo Dr. Glasg	95	D3
Emerald Terr. Hat	142	A2
Emerson Rd. Bish	78	A1
Emerson Rd W. Bish	78	A1
Emerson St. Glasg	97	D3
Emily Dr. Mother	163	F2
Emma Jay Rd. Hat	142	A3
Empress Dr. Helen	16	A2
Empress Rd. Rhu	15	E3
Endfield Ave. Glasg	96	A3
Endrick Bank. Bish	78	A2
Endrick Dr. Bank	39	F3
Endrick Dr. Bear	75	F2
Endrick Dr. Bonh	19	F1
Endrick Dr. Pais	114	A3
Endrick Gdns. Miln	54	C1
Endrick Pl. Stir	7	D2
Endrick Rd. Green	46	A1
Endrick St. Glasg	97	E2
Engelen Dr. All	10	A3
Engels St. Alex	27	F4
Englewood Ave. Pres	236	A3
English St. Mother	164	B2
Ennerdale. E Kil	179	F3
Ennisfree Rd. Udd	161	E4
Ensay St. Glasg	97	E4
Enterkin St. Glasg	118	C2
Enterkine. Kilw	207	D1
Eribol Wlk. Holy	143	E2
Eriboll Pl. Glasg	97	D4
Eriboll St. Glasg	97	D4
Ericht Pl. Shot	146	C3
Ericht Rd. Glasg	136	B3
Eriska Ave. Glasg	95	D3
Eriskay Ave. Ham	161	F1
Eriskay Ave. Newt M	156	A3
Eriskay Ave. P Glasg	69	D4
Eriskay Cres. Newt M	156	A3
Eriskay Ct. Falk	42	B1
Eriskay Ct. Irvine	225	E4
Eriskay Pl. Kilmk	223	D3
Erradale St. Glasg	97	D4
Errogie St. Glasg	120	A4
Erskine Ave. Glasg	116	A2
Erskine Cres. Aird	122	C3
Erskine Ct. Aird	123	F4
Erskine Ferry Rd. O Kill	73	D3
Erskine Pl. Clack	10	C3
Erskine Pl. Kilmk	223	E1
Erskine Rd. Newt M	157	D3
Erskine Sq. Glasg	114	C4
Erskine St. All	10	A4
Erskine St. Alva	5	D4
Erskine View. O Kill	73	D3
Erskine Way. Shot	146	C2
Erskinefauld Rd. Lin	112	A3
Ervie St. Glasg	120	B4
Escart Rd. Car	187	F2
Esdaile Ct. Holy	143	D2
Esk Ave. Ren	94	C1
Esk Dale. E Kil	159	E2
Esk Dr. Pais	112	C1
Esk Rd. Kilmk	228	A2
Esk Rd. Troon	229	F3
Esk St. Glasg	94	C3
Esk Way. Pais	112	C1
Eskbank St. Glasg	119	D3
Eskdale Dr. Glasg	138	B4
Eskdale. Newt M	157	D3
Eskdale Rd. Bear	75	E1
Eskdale St. Glasg	117	D1
Esmond St. Glasg	96	B1
Espedair St. Pais	113	F2
Esperanto Rd. Pres	236	C4
Espieside Cres. Coat	121	E4
Esplanade. Ayr	238	C4
Esplanade. Green	45	E4
Esplanade. Pres	233	D1
Esselmont Ave. Glasg	95	E3
Essenside Ave. Glasg	75	E1
Essex Dr. Glasg	95	F2
Essex La. Glasg	95	F2
Essex Rd. Gour	44	C2
Esslemont Ave. Glasg	95	E2
Esson Pl. Kilmk	223	D2
Estate Ave. Falk	42	B2
Estate Quadrant. Glasg	139	E4
Estate Rd. Glasg	119	E1
Etive Ave. Bear	76	A2
Etive Ave. Ham	162	A1
Etive Cres. Bish	78	A1
Etive Cres. Cumb	82	A3
Etive Ct. Cumb	82	A3
Etive Ct. Dunt	74	B3
Etive Dr. Aird	123	E3
Etive Dr. Bishop	72	B1
Etive Dr. Cumb	82	A3
Etive Dr. Glasg	136	B1
Etive Pl. Cumb	82	B3
Etive Pl. Irvine	219	E4
Etive Pl. Stir	2	A2
Etive St. Glasg	119	D3
Etive St. Wish	165	D1
Etive Way. Shot	147	D2
Etna Rd. Falk	42	B4
Etna St. Mother	164	B2
Eton La. Glasg	96	C1
Etrick Ave. Hat	142	A4
Etterick Wynd. Udd	161	E4
Ettrick Ave. Ren	94	C1
Ettrick Cres. Glasg	138	B4
Ettrick Cres. Kilmk	222	C2
Ettrick Ct. Falk	42	B1
Ettrick Ct. Glasg	139	F2
Ettrick Dr. Bear	75	E4
Ettrick Dr. Bishop	72	B1
Ettrick Hill. E Kil	160	A2
Ettrick Oval. Pais	132	C4
Ettrick Pl. Ayr	236	A2
Ettrick Pl. Glasg	136	B4
Ettrick Pl. Kilmk	222	C2
Ettrick Sq. Cumb	61	F1
Ettrick St. Wish	165	D3
Ettrick Terr. John	131	E4
Euchan Pl. Troon	229	F3
Evan Cres. Glasg	136	B1
Evan Dr. Glasg	136	B1
Evans St. Lar	23	E2
Evanton Dr. Glasg	135	F2
Evanton Pl. Glasg	135	F2
Evelyn Terr. Kilw	207	F1
Everard Ct. Bish	97	F4
Everard Dr. Glasg	97	F3
Everard Pl. Bish	97	F4
Everard Quadrant. Bish	97	F4
Everglades The. Muir	100	A4
Eversley St. Glasg	119	D2
Everton Rd. Glasg	115	E1
Ewart Cres. Ham	162	A1
Ewart Terr. Ham	162	A1
Ewenfield Ave. Ayr	239	D2
Ewenfield Gdns. Ayr	239	D2
Ewenfield Pk. Ayr	238	C2
Ewenfield Rd. Ayr	239	D2
Ewing Ave. Falk	42	A4
Ewing Ct. Ham	183	E4
Ewing Ct. Stir	7	E2
Ewing Dr. Falk	42	A4
Ewing Pl. Falk	42	A4
Ewing Pl. Glasg	118	B3
Ewing Rd. Loch	129	E2
Ewing St. Glasg	138	A4
Ewing St. Kilbar	111	D2
Ewing Way. Stew	211	E4
Ewing Wlk. Miln	55	E1
Excelsior St. Mother	164	B2
Exeter Dr. Glasg	96	A1
Exeter La. Glasg	96	A1
Exeter St. Coat	122	A3
Exhibition Way. Glasg	116	C4
Exmouth Pl. Gour	44	C3
Eynort St. Glasg	97	D4
Factory Rd. Mother	163	F3
Fagan Ct. Udd	140	C1
Faifley Rd. Dunt	74	B4
Failford Pl. Kilmk	223	D2
Fair Oaks. E Kil	158	C4
Fair View Dr. Lan	214	A2
Fair Way. Card	48	A4
Fairbairn Cres. Glasg	136	A1
Fairbairn St. Glasg	118	A2
Fairburn St. Glasg	118	C2
Fairfax Ave. Glasg	137	E3
Fairfield Ave. Bon	40	A3
Fairfield Ct. Newt M	157	F3
Fairfield Dr. Newt M	157	F3
Fairfield Gdns. Glasg	115	F4
Fairfield. N Sau	5	E1
Fairfield Pk. Ayr	238	C4
Fairfield Pl. E Kil	159	E1
Fairfield Pl. Falk	42	B3
Fairfield Pl. Glasg	115	F4
Fairfield Pl. Ham	162	C1
Fairfield Pl. Udd	141	D1
Fairfield Rd. Ayr	238	C4
Fairfield St. Glasg	115	F4
Fairford Dr. Cumb	82	B4
Fairgreen Pl. Bann	11	F4
Fairhaven Rd. Glasg	96	C4
Fairhaven Sq. Kilw	207	D2
Fairhaven. Troon	229	F4
Fairhill Ave. Glasg	135	E4
Fairhill Ave. Ham	162	B1
Fairhill Cres. Ham	162	B1
Fairhill Pl. Ham	183	E4
Fairhill Rd. Stir	7	D1
Fairholm Ave. Ham	163	E1
Fairholm St. Glasg	118	C2
Fairholm St. Lark	184	C2
Fairley St. Glasg	116	A3
Fairlie Ave. Kilmk	227	E4
Fairlie Dr. Falk	41	E3
Fairlie. E Kil	159	E2
Fairlie Gdns. Falk	41	E3
Fairlie Park Dr. Glasg	96	A1
Fairlie St. Falk	41	E3
Fairlie View. Cross	226	C3
Fairmount Dr. N Sau	5	D1
Fairrie St. Green	46	B2
Fairview Ct. Miln	55	D1
Fairway Ave. Pais	133	E4
Fairway. Bear	75	E3
Fairways. Irvine	219	D4
Fairways. Lark	185	E2
Fairways Pl. Bon	40	A4
Fairweather Pl. Newt M	156	B2
Fairyburn Rd. All	9	F4
Fairyhill Pl. Kilmk	227	F3
Fairyhill Rd. Kilmk	227	F3
Fairyknowe Gdns. Udd	141	D1
Faith Ave. Kil	89	F1
Falcon Cres. Green	45	D3
Falcon Cres. Pais	113	D3
Falcon Dr. Lar	23	D2
Falcon La. Green	45	D3
Falcon Rd. John	131	E4
Falcon Terr. Glasg	96	B4
Falcon Terrace La. Glasg	96	B4
Falconbridge Rd. E Kil	160	B2
Falconer Ct. Stir	7	E2
Falconer Terr. Ham	162	B1
Falfield St. Glasg	117	D2
Falkirk Rd. Bann	11	F4
Falkirk Rd. Bon	40	B3
Falkirk Rd. Falk	42	A1
Falkirk Rd. Falk	42	C3
Falkirk Rd. Lar	23	D1
Falkirk Rd. Lar	41	E4
Falkland Ave. Newt M	157	D3
Falkland Cres. Bish	98	B4
Falkland Dr. E Kil	159	E1
Falkland La. Glasg	96	A2
Falkland Park Rd. Ayr	236	A2

Falkland Pk. E Kil

Falkland Pk. E Kil 159 E1
Falkland Pl. Ayr 236 A2
Falkland Pl. Coat 122 A2
Falkland Pl. E Kil 159 E1
Falkland Pl. Sten 23 F2
Falkland Rd. Ayr 236 A2
Falkland St. Glasg 96 A2
Falloch Pl. New 165 F3
Falloch Rd. Bear 75 E1
Falloch Rd. Glasg 137 D4
Falloch Rd. Miln 54 C2
Fallside Ave. Tan 141 F3
Fallside Rd. Tan 141 D2
Fallside Rd. Udd 141 D2
Falmouth Dr. Gour 44 C3
Falside Ave. Pais 113 F1
Falside Rd. Glasg 119 D1
Falside Rd. Pais 113 E1
Falstaff. E Kil 160 B3
Fancy Farm Pl. Green 44 C2
Fancy Farm Rd. Green 45 D2
Fara St. Glasg 96 C4
Faraday Ave. Wish 165 E2
Faransay Pl. Kilmk 223 D3
Fardalehill View. Cross 221 F1
Farden Pl. Pres 236 B3
Farie St. Glasg 138 A4
Farlands View. W Kil 190 B2
Farm Cres. Holy 143 F2
Farm Ct. Udd 141 D2
Farm La. Hat 141 F2
Farm Pk. Klrk 79 E2
Farm Rd. Clyde 73 E2
Farm Rd. Cowie 12 B4
Farm Rd. Dunt 74 A4
Farm Rd. Fall 8 B3
Farm Rd. Ham 161 F2
Farm Rd. Kilmk 222 C2
Farm Rd. P Glasg 68 C4
Farm Rd. Udd 140 B1
Farm St. Falk 24 A1
Farm St. Mother 163 E4
Farm Terr. Ham 161 F2
Farme Cross. Glasg 118 A1
Farmeloan Rd. Glasg 138 A4
Farmfield Terr. W Kil 190 B3
Farmgate Sq. Hat 141 F2
Farmington Ave. Glasg 119 E3
Farmington Gate. Glasg 119 E2
Farmington Gdns. Glasg 119 E3
Farmington Gr. Glasg 119 E3
Farndale. E Kil 159 E2
Farne Dr. Glasg 137 E2
Farnell St. Glasg 97 D1
Farquhar Rd. P Glasg 47 D1
Farquhar Sq. Blac 107 E2
Farrell Pl. Ayr 236 A1
Farrier Ct. John 111 F2
Faskally Ave. Bish 77 F2
Faskally Wlk. New 165 F3
Faskin Cres. Glasg 134 C4
Faskin Pl. Glasg 134 C4
Faskin Rd. Glasg 134 C4
Faskine Ave. Aird 122 C3
Faskine Ave. Calder 123 D1
Faskine Cres. Aird 122 C3
Fasque Pl. Glasg 74 C2
Fastnet St. Glasg 119 D4
Fauldhouse St. Glasg 117 E2
Faulds Gdns. Glasg 120 B3
Faulds. Glasg 120 B3
Faulds Park Rd. Gour 43 F3
Faulds St. Coat 121 F2
Fauldshead Rd. Ren 94 B2
Fauldspark Cres. Glasg 120 B3
Fauldswood Cres. Pais 113 D1
Fauldswood Dr. Pais 113 D1
Fearnmore Rd. Glasg 96 B4
Fearnoch. Pres 236 B3
Fells The. Lennox 57 F4
Fellsview Ave. Kirk 58 C1
Fencedyke Way. Irvine 220 A2
Fendoch St. Glasg 119 D2
Fenella St. Glasg 119 D3
Fennsbank Ave. Glasg 138 B2
Fenton St. All 10 A4
Fenwick Dr. Barr 134 B1
Fenwick Dr. Ham 183 F4
Fenwick Pl. Glasg 136 A1
Fenwick Rd. Glasg 136 B2
Fenwick Rd. Kilm 222 B4
Fenwickland Ave. Ayr 239 D2
Fenwickland Pl. Ayr 239 D2
Ferclay St. Dunt 74 B4
Fereneze Ave. Barr 134 A2
Fereneze Ave. Newt M 157 E4
Fereneze Ave. Ren 114 A4
Fereneze Cres. Glasg 95 D4
Fereneze Cres. Ham 161 F2
Fereneze Dr. Pais 133 E4
Fereneze Rd. Neil 154 B4
Fergus Ave. Pais 113 D3
Fergus Dr. Glasg 96 C2
Fergus Dr. Green 45 D2
Fergus Dr. Pais 113 D3
Fergus Gdns. Ham 162 C1
Fergus La. Glasg 96 C2

Fergus Pl. Green 45 D2
Fergus Rd. Green 45 D2
Fergushill Rd. Kilw 208 A2
Ferguslie. Pais 113 D2
Ferguslie Park Ave. Pais ... 113 D3
Ferguslie Park Cres. Pais . 113 D2
Ferguslie Wlk. Pais 113 D2
Ferguson Ave. Miln 55 D1
Ferguson Ave. Pres 236 B4
Ferguson Ave. Ren 94 B2
Ferguson Dr. Den 21 E1
Ferguson Dr. Mother 163 F2
Ferguson Dr. Sten 24 A3
Ferguson Gr. Bon 40 A3
Ferguson St. Ayr 236 B2
Ferguson St. John 111 F2
Ferguson St. Ren 94 B2
Ferguson St. Stir 1 C1
Fergusson Pl. E Kil 160 B3
Fergusson Rd. Cumb 61 F1
Fergusson Terr. M of C 58 B3
Ferguston Rd. Bear 75 F2
Fern Ave. Bish 98 A4
Fern Ave. Inch 93 D4
Fern Ave. Klrk 79 E3
Fern Brae. Ayr 239 E2
Fern Dr. Barr 134 A2
Fern La. Glasg 95 F3
Fern Lea Gr. Sten 24 B2
Fern Pl. Kilmk 227 E4
Fern St. Mother 164 A1
Fernan St. Glasg 118 C3
Fernbank Ave. Glasg 139 E2
Fernbank. Pres 236 A3
Fernbank St. Glasg 97 F3
Fernbrae Ave. Glasg 138 B2
Fernbrae Way. Glasg 138 A2
Ferncroft Dr. Glasg 137 E3
Ferndale Ct. Glasg 96 B4
Ferndale Dr. Glasg 96 B4
Ferndale Gdns. Glasg 96 B4
Ferndale. Lark 185 D1
Ferndale Pl. Glasg 96 B4
Ferness Oval. Glasg 98 B4
Ferness Pl. Glasg 98 B4
Ferness Rd. Glasg 98 B3
Ferngrove Ave. Glasg 96 A3
Fernhill Grange. Udd 141 D1
Fernhill Rd. Glasg 138 A2
Ferniegair Ave. Helen 16 A1
Fernieshaw Rd. Cle 144 C1
Fernlea. Bear 75 C1
Fernleigh Pl. Muir 80 C1
Fernleigh Rd. Glasg 136 B3
Fernside Wlk. Ham 162 C1
Fernslea Ave. Udd 161 E4
Ferry Loan. Alex 27 F3
Ferry Orch. Stir 2 B1
Ferry Rd. Air 9 F2
Ferry Rd. Bishop 72 A2
Ferry Rd. Card 48 A3
Ferry Rd. Ren 94 A1
Ferry Rd. Ros 15 D2
Ferry Rd. Stir 2 B1
Ferry Rd. Udd 140 C3
Ferry Rd. Udd 141 D1
Ferryden Ct. Glasg 95 F1
Ferryden St. Glasg 95 F1
Fersit St. Glasg 136 B3
Fetlar Dr. Glasg 137 E3
Fetlar Dr. Kilmk 223 D3
Fetlar Rd. B of W 110 B4
Fettercairn Ave. Glasg 74 C2
Fettercairn Gdns. Bish 78 B1
Fettes St. Glasg 118 C4
Fiddison Pl. Pres 236 C3
Fiddoch Ct. New 165 F4
Fidra St. Glasg 118 C4
Field Gr. Thorn 157 F3
Field Rd. Dunt 74 B4
Field Rd. Lark 185 D1
Field Rd. Thorn 157 F3
Field St. Ham 162 B1
Fielden Pl. Glasg 118 A3
Fielden St. Glasg 118 A3
Fieldhead Dr. Glasg 136 A3
Fieldhead Sq. Glasg 136 A3
Fields La. Hous 91 D2
Fife Ave. Aird 123 D3
Fife Ave. Glasg 115 C2
Fife Cres. Udd 141 D1
Fife Ct. Udd 141 D1
Fife Dr. Gour 44 B3
Fife Dr. Mother 142 B1
Fife Rd. Gour 44 B3
Fife Way. Bish 98 B4
Fifth Ave. Aird 123 E4
Fifth Ave. Glasg 95 F3
Fifth Ave. Ren 94 B1
Fifth Ave. Stepps 99 D3
Fifth Rd. Ham 161 F3
Finart Dr. Pais 114 A1
Finaven Gdns. Bear 75 D4
Finch Dr. Glasg 96 A4
Finch Pl. John 131 E4
Finch Pl. Kilmk 228 B4
Finch Rd. Green 45 D3
Findhorn Ave. Pais 112 C1

Findhorn Ave. Ren 94 C2
Findhorn Ct. E Kil 179 E4
Findhorn. Ersk 73 D1
Findhorn Pl. E Kil 179 E4
Findhorn Pl. Falk 42 B1
Findhorn Pl. Troon 229 F3
Findhorn Rd. Pres 233 F2
Findhorn St. Glasg 118 B4
Findlay St. Kils 60 B4
Findlay St. Mother 163 F3
Findlay's Brae. Salt 216 C4
Findochty. Ersk 73 D2
Findochty St. Glasg 99 F1
Fingal La. Glasg 96 B4
Fingal St. Glasg 96 B4
Fingalton Rd. Newt M 155 F3
Fingask St. Glasg 119 E2
Finglas Ave. Pais 114 A1
Finglen Gdns. Miln 54 C1
Finglen Pl. Glasg 135 D3
Fingleton Ave. Barr 134 B1
Finhaven St. Glasg 118 C2
Finistere Ave. Falk 42 A2
Finlarig Ct. Sten 23 F2
Finlarig St. Glasg 120 B4
Finlas Ave. Ayr 239 D2
Finlas St. Glasg 97 E2
Finlay Ave. Beith 191 E4
Finlay Dr. Glasg 118 A4
Finlay Dr. Lin 111 F3
Finlay Rise. Miln 76 B2
Finlayson Dr. Aird 123 F4
Finlayson Dr. Kilmk 223 F4
Finlayson Quadrant. Aird .. 123 F4
Finlaystone Cres. Kil 69 E1
Finlaystone Rd. Kil 69 E2
Finlaystone Rd. P Glasg 69 D4
Finlaystone St. Coat 121 F4
Finnart Cres. Gour 44 B3
Finnart Rd. Green 45 D3
Finnart Sq. Glasg 117 F2
Finnart St. Glasg 117 F2
Finnart St. Green 45 E3
Finneston La. Green 46 A2
Finneston St. Green 46 A2
Finneston Way. Green 46 A2
Finnick Glen. Ayr 239 D2
Finnie Terr. Gour 44 B3
Finnie Terr. Spring 220 C1
Finnie Wynd. Mother 164 A2
Finnieston Sq. Glasg 116 C4
Finnieston St. Glasg 116 C4
Finsbay St. Glasg 115 F3
Fintrie Terr. Ham 161 F2
Fintry Ave. Pais 133 F4
Fintry Cres. Barr 134 B1
Fintry Cres. Bish 78 B1
Fintry Dr. Glasg 137 E4
Fintry Gdns. Bear 75 E4
Fintry Pl. Irvine 220 A1
Fintry Rd. Green 46 A1
Fintry Terr. Irvine 220 A2
Fintry Wlk. Irvine 220 A1
Fir Bank Ave. Lark 185 D1
Fir Bank. Ayr 239 E3
Fir Ct. Coat 121 F2
Fir Dr. E Kil 180 A3
Fir Gr. Tan 141 E4
Fir La. Lar 23 E1
Fir Park St. Mother 163 F2
Fir Pl. Cle 144 A1
Fir Pl. Glasg 120 A2
Fir Pl. Glasg 139 E3
Fir Pl. John 112 A1
Fir Pl. Kilmk 227 E4
Fir St. Green 46 C1
Fir Terr. Gour 44 B3
Fir View. Calder 123 D1
Firbank Ave. Lennox 78 A4
Firbank Terr. Barr 134 C1
Firdon Cres. Glasg 75 D1
Firhill Ave. Aird 122 C3
Firhill Rd. Pres 233 E3
Firhill Rd. Glasg 97 D2
Firhill St. Glasg 97 D2
Firlee. E Kil 179 F4
Firpark Rd. Bish 98 A4
Firpark St. Glasg 117 F4
Firpark Terr. Cam 6 B3
Firpark Terr. Glasg 117 F4
Firs Cres. Bann 7 E1
Firs Entry. Bann 7 E1
Firs Rd. Tull 4 B1
Firs St. Falk 42 B3
Firs The. Bann 7 E1
Firs The. Glasg 137 D2
First Ave. Bear 76 A2
First Ave. Bonh 27 F3
First Ave. Dumb 50 B1
First Ave. Glasg 136 C1
First Ave. Irvine 224 B4
First Ave. Ren 94 B1
First Ave. Stepps 79 E1
First Ave. Stepps 99 D2
First Ave. Tan 140 C4
First Gdns. Glasg 116 A2
First Rd. Ham 161 F3
First St. Tan 140 C4

First Terr. Clyde 74 A2
Firth Cres. Gour 44 B3
Firth Gdns. Troon 229 E4
Firth Rd. Troon 229 E4
Firth View Terr. Ard 205 E2
Firthview Terr. Dumb 49 E2
Firtree Pl. New 166 A3
Firtree Rd. New 166 A3
Firwood Dr. Glasg 137 E3
Firwood Rd. Newt M 156 C2
Fischer Gdns. Lin 112 C3
Fisher Ave. Kils 60 B4
Fisher Ave. Lin 112 C2
Fisher Cres. Dunt 74 A3
Fisher Ct. Glasg 117 F4
Fisher Dr. Lin 112 C2
Fisher Pl. Helen 17 D1
Fisher St. Lark 185 D1
Fisher Way. Lin 112 C2
Fishers Rd. Ren 94 B3
Fisherwood Rd. Alex 27 F4
Fishescoates Ave. Glasg .. 138 B3
Fishescoates Gdns. Glasg . 138 B3
Fitzalan Dr. Pais 114 A3
Fitzalan Rd. Ren 94 A1
Fitzroy La. Glasg 116 C4
Fitzroy Pl. Glasg 116 C4
Five Roads. Kilw 208 A2
Five Ways Rd. Ash 200 B2
Flakefield. E Kil 159 D1
Flanders St. Dunt 74 B4
Flatterton La. Gour 44 B1
Flatterton Rd. Gour 44 B1
Flax Mill Rd. East 127 F3
Flax Rd. Udd 141 D3
Flaxfield Gr. Mother 142 B1
Flaxmill Ave. Mother 164 B2
Fleck Ave. Salt 206 A1
Fleet Ave. Ren 94 C1
Fleet St. Glasg 119 D2
Fleming Ave. Clyde 94 B4
Fleming Ave. Muir 100 B4
Fleming Cres. Salt 206 A2
Fleming Ct. Car 187 F1
Fleming Ct. Clyde 74 A1
Fleming Ct. Ham 161 F2
Fleming Ct. Mother 164 A2
Fleming Dr. Sten 24 A2
Fleming Dr. Stew 211 E4
Fleming Gdns. Falk 41 F3
Fleming Pl. Blac 107 F2
Fleming Pl. E Kil 180 C4
Fleming Rd. Bishop 72 A2
Fleming Rd. Cumb 61 F1
Fleming Rd. Hat 142 A4
Fleming Rd. Hous 91 D1
Fleming St. Glasg 118 A3
Fleming St. Kilmk 227 F3
Fleming St. Pais 113 F4
Fleming Terr. Irvine 219 D3
Fleming Way. Ham 161 F2
Fleming Way. Lark 185 E1
Flemington Ind Est. Glasg . 139 F2
Flemington St. Glasg 97 F2
Flenders Ave. Newt M 157 E3
Flenders Rd. Newt M 157 E3
Fletcher Ave. Gour 44 C4
Fleurs Ave. Glasg 116 A2
Fleurs Rd. Glasg 116 A2
Flinders Pl. E Kil 180 A4
Flint Mill La. Green 46 A1
Flloyd St. Coat 121 F4
Floors Rd. Newt M 157 E1
Floors St. John 111 F1
Floorsburn Cres. John 111 F1
Flora Gdns. Bish 78 B1
Florence Dr. Glasg 136 B1
Florence Dr. Kil 89 D4
Florence Gdns. Glasg 138 B2
Florence St. Glasg 117 E2
Florence St. Glasg 117 E3
Florence St. Green 45 D2
Florida Ave. Glasg 137 D4
Florida Cres. Glasg 137 D4
Florida Dr. Glasg 137 D4
Florida Gdns. Glasg 120 A3
Florida Sq. Glasg 137 D4
Florida St. Glasg 137 D4
Flowerdale Pl. Glasg 135 D2
Flowerhill St. Aird 123 D4
Flures Ave. Inch 93 F4
Flures Cres. Inch 93 F4
Flures Dr. Inch 93 F4
Flures Pl. Inch 93 F4
Fochabers Dr. Glasg 115 E3
Fogo Pl. Glasg 96 B3
Foinavon Rd. Quart 183 F2
Foot Of Lone Rd. Lan 214 A3
Footfield Rd. Hat 141 F2
Forbes Cres. Lar 23 E1
Forbes Ct. Falk 42 C3
Forbes Dr. Glasg 117 F3
Forbes Dr. Mother 142 B1
Forbes Pl. Kilmk 223 D1
Forbes Pl. Pais 113 F2
Forbes Rd. Falk 42 B2

Forbes St. All 9 F3
Forbes St. Glasg 117 F3
Forbes Wlk. Kilmk 223 D1
Ford Ave. Irvine 225 E4
Ford Rd. Bon 40 A3
Ford Rd. Glasg 96 B2
Ford Rd. Newt M 156 B2
Forde Cres. Steven 206 C1
Fordneuk St. Glasg 118 A3
Fordoun St. Glasg 120 B4
Fordyce Ct. Newt M 156 B2
Fordyce St. Glasg 96 B1
Fore Row. Ham 162 C2
Fore St. Glasg 95 C2
Fore St. P Glasg 47 E1
Forebraes. All 10 A4
Foregate Sq. Kilmk 222 C1
Foregate The. Kilmk 222 C1
Forehill Rd. Ayr 239 E3
Forehouse Rd. Kilbar 110 B2
Foremount
  Terrace La. Glasg 96 B2
Forest Ave. Ham 183 E3
Forest Dr. Bear 75 D4
Forest Dr. Udd 141 D2
Forest Gdns. Klrk 79 D2
Forest Gr. Kilmk 223 D3
Forest Kirk. Car 202 A4
Forest La. Ham 183 E3
Forest Pl. Cro 201 D1
Forest Pl. Klrk 79 D2
Forest Pl. Pais 113 F1
Forest Rd. Cumb 62 C2
Forest Rd. Cumb 62 C3
Forest Rd. East 185 D2
Forest View. Cumb 62 B2
Forest Way. Ayr 239 E3
Forester Gr. All 4 C1
Forestfield Gdns. Cald 105 D2
Foresthall Dr. Glasg 98 A2
Foresthall Gdns. Glasg 98 A2
Forfar Ave. Glasg 115 D2
Forfar Cres. Bish 98 B4
Forfar Rd. Gour 44 C2
Forgan Gdns. Bish 98 B4
Forge Dr. Coat 121 F4
Forge Pl. Glasg 98 A1
Forge Rd. Aird 123 F3
Forge St. Glasg 98 A1
Forge St. Kilmk 222 C1
Forge Vennal. Kilmk 207 E2
Forgewood Rd. Mother 142 B1
Forglen Cres. B of A 2 A3
Forglen Rd. B of A 2 A3
Forglen St. Glasg 100 A1
Formby Dr. Glasg 76 B1
Forres Ave. Glasg 136 B3
Forres Cres. Hat 142 A3
Forres Gate. Glasg 136 B3
Forres Quadrant. Wish 165 D3
Forres St. Glasg 76 C1
Forres St. Udd 161 E3
Forrest Cres. Ham 162 A1
Forrest Dr. Hat 142 A3
Forrest Pl. East 127 F3
Forrest Rd. Cald 106 A1
Forrest Rd. Lan 215 D3
Forrest Rd. Sals 126 A3
Forrest Rd. Stir 2 A1
Forrest St. Aird 123 E4
Forrest St. Glasg 118 A3
Forrest St. Shot 146 C3
Forrest St. Udd 161 F4
Forrester Ct. Bish 97 F4
Forrester Pl. Air 14 B2
Forrestfield Cres. Newt M .. 156 C3
Forrestfield Gdns. Newt M 156 C3
Forrestfield Rd. Cald 106 A3
Forrestfield St. Glasg 98 A1
Forrestlea Rd. Car 202 A4
Forsyth Gr. Green 45 E3
Forsyth St. Aird 123 D4
Forsyth St. Green 45 E3
Fort Matilda Pl. Green 45 D4
Fort Matilda Terr. Green 45 D4
Fort St. Ayr 235 F1
Fort St. Mother 163 D4
Fort St. Mother 163 E4
Fortacre Pl. Irvine 220 A3
Forteviot Ave. Glasg 120 B3
Forteviot Pl. Glasg 120 B3
Forth Ave. Lar 23 D2
Forth Ave. Pais 112 C1
Forth Cres. All 10 B3
Forth Cres. E Kil 179 F4
Forth Cres. Stir 7 F4
Forth Ct. E Kil 179 F4
Forth Ct. Stir 2 A1
Forth Gr. E Kil 179 F4
Forth Pk. B of A 2 A3
Forth Pl. John 131 E4
Forth Pl. Kilmk 228 A3
Forth Pl. Lark 199 D3
Forth Rd. Bear 75 D1
Forth Rd. Ham 161 F3
Forth Rd. Lennox 78 A4
Forth St. Camb 9 D4
Forth St. Clyde 94 B4

Forth St. Clyde

Forth St. Fall 8 B2
Forth St. Glasg 116 C2
Forth St. Green 45 D3
Forth St. Stir 2 A1
Forth Terr. Ham 183 D4
Forth View. Stir 2 A1
Forthvale. Men 4 A3
Forthview. Bann 7 F1
Forthview Ct. Falk 41 F1
Forties Rd. Hous 111 E4
Fortieth Ave. E Kil 180 C3
Fortingale Ave. Glasg ... 96 B3
Fortingale Pl. Glasg 96 B3
Fortingall Rd. Ham 161 F3
Fortissat Ave. Shot 146 B3
Fortisset Rd. Sals 126 A1
Fortrose St. Glasg 96 A1
Fossil Gr. Kirk 59 D1
Foswell Pl. Glasg 74 C3
Fotheringay La. Glasg 116 C1
Fotheringay Rd. Glasg ... 116 C1
Fothringham Rd. Ayr 239 D4
Foulburn Rd. Cle 145 E1
Foulis La. Glasg 95 F3
Foulis St. Glasg 95 F3
Foulsykes Rd. Wish 165 F2
Foundry La. Barr 134 B1
Foundry Loan. Lar 23 D1
Foundry Rd. Bon 40 A3
Foundry Rd. Cle 144 B1
Foundry Rd. Shot 146 C2
Foundry St. Falk 42 A4
Foundry Wynd. Kilw 207 E2
Fountain Ave. Inch 93 D2
Fountain Cres. Inch 93 E3
Fountain Dr. Inch 93 E2
Fountain Dr. B of A 2 A4
Fountain
  Bsns Ctr The. Coat 122 A3
Fountainwell Ave. Glasg ... 97 E1
Fountainwell Dr. Glasg 97 E1
Fountainwell Pl. Glasg 97 E2
Fountainwell Rd. Glasg 97 E1
Fountainwell Sq. Glasg 97 F1
Fountainwell Terr. Glasg ... 97 F1
Four Acres Dr. Kilm 222 A4
Four Windings. Hous 91 D1
Fourth Ave. Dumb 50 B1
Fourth Ave. Ren 94 B1
Fourth Ave. Stepps 79 E1
Fourth Ave. Stepps 99 D3
Fourth Gdns. Glasg 116 A2
Fourth St. Tan 120 C1
Fowlds St. Kilmk 227 F4
Fowler Pl. E Kil 181 D3
Fowlis Dr. Newt M 156 B3
Fox Gr. Mother 163 D4
Fox St. Glasg 117 D3
Fox St. Green 45 E4
Foxbar Cres. Pais 132 C4
Foxbar Dr. Glasg 95 D3
Foxbar Dr. Pais 132 C4
Foxbar Rd. Pais 132 C4
Foxes Gr. Klrk 79 F3
Foxglove Pl. Ayr 239 E2
Foxglove Rd. Glasg 135 D2
Foxhills Pl. Glasg 76 C1
Foxley St. Glasg 119 E1
Foyers Terr. Glasg 98 A2
Franchi Dr. Sten 23 F3
Francis St. Glasg 117 D2
Frankfield Rd. Stepps 99 F3
Frankfield St. Glasg 98 C1
Frankfort St. Glasg 116 C1
Franklin Pl. E Kil 159 D1
Franklin St. Glasg 117 F2
Fraser Ave. Bishop 72 A2
Fraser Ave. Dumb 50 B2
Fraser Ave. Glasg 138 B4
Fraser Ave. John 112 A1
Fraser Ave. Newt M 156 C3
Fraser Ave. Troon 229 E3
Fraser Cres. Ham 162 A1
Fraser Ct. Aird 123 F4
Fraser Gdns. Klrk 79 D4
Fraser Pl. Stir 2 A2
Fraser St. Cle 144 A1
Fraser St. Glasg 138 C3
Fraser Wlk. Kilmk 223 E2
Frazer Ave. Helen 16 A2
Frazer St. Glasg 118 A3
Frederick St. Coat 121 F4
Freeland Cres. Glasg 135 D3
Freeland Ct. Glasg 135 E3
Freeland Dr. B of W 90 B1
Freeland Dr. Glasg 135 D3
Freeland Dr. Inch 93 E3
Freeland La. E Kil 180 C3
Freeland Pl. Klrk 79 E4
Freeland Rd. Inch 93 D4
Freelands Cres. Clyde 73 E3
Freelands Ct. Clyde 73 E2
Freelands Rd. Clyde 73 E2
Freesia Ct. Mother 163 F3
French St. Clyde 73 F2
French St. Glasg 117 F2
French St. Ren 94 A1

French St. Wish 165 D2
Freuchie St. Glasg 120 A4
Frew Terr. Irvine 219 E3
Friar Ave. Bish 78 A2
Friar's Dene. Lan 214 C2
Friar's La. Lan 214 C2
Friar's Wynd. Lan 214 C2
Friars Croft. Irvine 219 D1
Friars Croft. Klrk 79 F4
Friars Lawn. Kilw 207 E2
Friars Pl. Glasg 95 E4
Friars St. Stir 7 D4
Friars Way. Aird 123 E2
Friarscourt Ave. Glasg 95 E4
Friarscourt Rd. Muir 80 A1
Friarsfield Rd. Lan 214 C2
Friarton Rd. Glasg 136 C3
Friendship Gdns. Sten 24 B2
Friendship Way. Ren 94 B1
Frobisher Ave. Falk 41 F2
Frobisher Pl. Helen 17 D1
Frood St. Mother 142 B1
Fruin Ave. Newt M 156 C3
Fruin Pl. Glasg 74 C1
Fruin Rise. Ham 161 F1
Fruin St. Glasg 97 E2
Fudstone Dr. Kilb 170 A4
Fulbar Ave. Ren 94 B2
Fulbar Cres. Pais 112 C1
Fulbar Ct. Ren 94 B2
Fulbar Gdns. Pais 112 C1
Fulbar La. Ren 94 B2
Fulbar Rd. Glasg 115 E4
Fulbar Rd. Lin 112 C2
Fulbar St. Ren 94 B2
Fullarton Ave. Dund 225 F1
Fullarton Ave. Glasg 119 D1
Fullarton Cres. Troon 229 F1
Fullarton Dr. Troon 229 F1
Fullarton La. Glasg 119 D1
Fullarton Pl. Coat 121 F2
Fullarton Pl. Steven 217 E4
Fullarton Pl. Troon 230 A2
Fullarton Rd. Glasg 119 D1
Fullarton Rndabout. Irvine . 219 D1
Fullarton Rd. Ayr 238 C4
Fullarton Rd. Coat 121 F2
Fullarton Rd. Irvine 219 D1
Fullarton St. Kilmk 222 C1
Fullers Gate. Dunt 74 B4
Fullerton Ctyd. Troon 230 A1
Fullerton Dr. W Kil 190 A2
Fullerton La. Green 46 C2
Fullerton Sq. Ard 205 E1
Fullerton St. Pais 113 E4
Fullerton Terr. Pais 113 F4
Fulmar Ct. Bish 97 F4
Fulmar Pk. E Kil 159 E2
Fulmari. John 131 E3
Fulshaw Cres. Ayr 236 C1
Fulshaw Ct. Pres 236 B3
Fulton Cres. Kilbar 111 D2
Fulton Dr. Hous 111 F4
Fulton Gdns. Hous 111 F4
Fulton Rd. Miln 55 D1
Fulton St. Glasg 95 F4
Fulton's La. Kilmk 222 C1
Fulwood Ave. Glasg 94 C4
Fulwood Ave. Lin 112 A3
Fulwood Ind Est. Ham 162 A3
Fulwood Pl. Glasg 94 C4
Furlongs The. Ham 162 C3
Furnace Rd. Quart 183 F2
Furnace Rd. Hurl 228 C3
Fyfe Park Terr. P Glasg ... 47 F1
Fyfe Shore Rd. P Glasg ... 47 F1
Fyffe Park Rd. P Glasg ... 47 F1
Fyne Ave. Tan 141 F3
Fyne Ct. Ham 162 A1
Fyne La. Shot 146 C3
Fyne Way. Holy 143 D3
Fyneart St. Wish 165 F2
Fynloch Pl. Dunt 73 F4
Fyvie Ave. Glasg 136 A3

Golf Ct. Glasg 136 C1
Gaberston Ave. All 10 B4
Gabriel St. Green 46 A1
Gadie Ave. Ren 94 C1
Gadie St. Glasg 118 B4
Gadloch Ave. Stepps 79 E1
Gadloch Gdns. Klrk 79 E2
Gadloch St. Glasg 97 E3
Gadloch View. Stepps 79 E1
Gadsburn Ct. Glasg 98 B3
Gadshill St. Glasg 97 F1
Gael St. Green 45 E2
Gagarin Terr. Kilw 207 F1
Gailes Pk. Udd 140 C1
Gailes Pl. Kilmk 227 F2
Gailes Rd. Shew 224 B2
Gailes Rd. Troon 229 E4
Gailes St. Glasg 118 A2
Gain and
  Shankburn Rd. Glen ... 82 B1
Gain and
  Shankburn Rd. Glenm ... 82 B1

Gain Rd. Glen 82 A1
Gainburn Cres. Cumb 81 F3
Gainburn Ct. Cumb 81 F3
Gainburn Gdns. Cumb 81 F3
Gainburn Pl. Cumb 81 F3
Gainburn View. Cumb 82 A3
Gainford Pl. Kilmk 222 C2
Gainside Rd. Glen 101 E3
Gair Cres. Car 188 A2
Gair Cres. Wish 165 D1
Gair Rd. Car 188 A3
Gair Wynd. Shot 147 D2
Gairbraid Ave. Glasg 96 B3
Gairbraid Ct. Glasg 96 B3
Gairbraid Pl. Glasg 96 B3
Gairbraid Terr. Coat 121 D3
Gairdoch Dr. Sten 24 B2
Gairdoch St. Falk 42 A4
Gairloch Gdns. Kirk 59 D1
Gaitskell Ave. Alex 27 E4
Gala Ave. Ren 94 C1
Gala Cres. Wish 165 D3
Gala St. Glasg 98 C1
Galbraith Cres. Law 187 D3
Galbraith Dr. Glasg 115 F4
Galbraith Dr. Miln 75 F4
Galdenoch St. Glasg 99 D1
Gallacher Ave. Pais 113 D1
Gallacher Cres. Bonh 19 F1
Gallacher Ct. Pais 113 E3
Gallahill Ave. P Glasg 69 D4
Gallamuir Dr. Plea 12 B2
Gallamuir Rd. Plea 12 B3
Gallan Ave. Glasg 76 C1
Gallion Wlk. Kilmk 227 F4
Galloway Ave. Ayr 236 B1
Galloway Ave. Ham 183 E4
Galloway Dr. Glasg 138 A2
Galloway Dr. Ham 183 E3
Galloway Pl. Salt 216 C4
Galloway Rd. Aird 122 C2
Galloway Rd. E Kil 160 B2
Galloway St. Falk 42 A3
Galloway St. Glasg 97 F3
Gallowflat St. Glasg 138 A4
Gallowgate. Glasg 117 F3
Gallowhill Ave. Klrk 79 E3
Gallowhill Gr. Klrk 79 E4
Gallowhill. Lark 185 D1
Gallowhill Rd. E Kil 158 C4
Gallowhill Rd. Klrk 79 E3
Gallowhill Rd. Lan 215 D2
Gallowhill Rd. Pais 114 A3
Galrigside Rd. Kilmk 227 E4
Galston Ave. Newt M 157 D3
Galston Ct. Ham 183 F4
Galston Rd. Hurl 228 C3
Galston St. Glasg 134 C3
Galt Ave. Irvine 219 E2
Galt Pl. E Kil 180 B4
Galt St. Green 46 B2
Gameshill View. Stew 211 F4
Gamrie Dr. Glasg 135 D4
Gamrie Gdns. Glasg 135 D4
Gamrie Rd. Glasg 135 D4
Gannochy Dr. Bish 78 B1
Gantock Cres. Glasg 119 D4
Ganton Ct. Kilw 207 D2
Garden Ct. Ayr 235 F1
Garden Pl. Troon 229 D2
Garden Square La. Kilw ... 207 F2
Garden Square Wlk. Aird .. 122 B4
Garden St. Ayr 235 F1
Garden St. Falk 42 B3
Garden St. Kilmk 222 C1
Garden Terr. Falk 42 A4
Garden Veteran's Cotts. Ersk72 C3
Gardenhall Ct. E Kil 179 F4
Gardenhall. E Kil 179 F4
Gardenside Ave. Glasg ... 139 D4
Gardenside Ave. Udd 140 C3
Gardenside Cres. Glasg ... 139 D4
Gardenside. Hat 142 A2
Gardenside Pl. Glasg 139 D4
Gardenside Rd. Ham 162 B1
Gardenside St. Udd 140 C3
Gardiner St. Pres 236 B4
Gardner Gr. Tan 141 D4
Gardner St. Glasg 96 A1
Gardrum Gdns. Shi 66 B4
Gardrum Pl. Kilmk 222 C2
Gardyne St. Glasg 100 A1
Gare Rd. Ros 15 D2
Garelet Pl. Irvine 220 A1
Gareloch Ave. Pais 113 D1
Gareloch Cres. Aird 102 C1
Gareloch La. P Glasg 68 A4
Gareloch Rd. Green 46 A2
Gareloch Rd. Helen 15 F2
Gareloch Rd. P Glasg ... 68 C4
Gareloch Rd. Rhu 15 F2
Garfield Ave. Hat 142 B3
Garfield Dr. Hat 142 B2
Garfield St. Glasg 118 A3
Garforth Rd. Glasg 119 F2
Gargrave Ave. Glasg ... 119 F2
Garion Dr. Glasg 95 D3
Garlieston Rd. Glasg ... 119 F3

Garmouth Ct. Glasg 116 A4
Garmouth Gdns. Glasg 116 A4
Garmouth St. Glasg 115 F4
Garnet St. Glasg 97 D1
Garnethill St. Glasg 97 D1
Garngaber Ave. Klrk 79 E3
Garngaber Ct. Klrk 79 F3
Garngrew Rd. Bank 38 C2
Garnhall Farm Rd. Cumb ... 62 C4
Garnie Ave. Inch 93 E4
Garnie La. Inch 93 E4
Garnie Oval. Ersk 73 E1
Garnie Pl. Ersk 73 E1
Garnieland Rd. Ersk 73 E1
Garnieland Rd. Inch 93 E4
Garnkirk La. Stepps 99 F3
Garnock Ct. Irvine 219 E1
Garnock Ct. Kilb 149 D1
Garnock Pk. E Kil 160 A1
Garnock Rd. Kilmk 228 A3
Garnock Rd. Steven 217 E4
Garnock St. Dalry 191 E4
Garnock St. Glasg 97 F1
Garnock St. Kilb 149 D1
Garnock View. Kilw 207 F2
Garnockside. Kilb 170 A3
Garpel Way. Loch 129 D1
Garrallan. Kilw 207 E1
Garrawy Rd. Helen 16 C1
Garrell Av. Kils 36 B1
Garrell Pl. Kils 60 B4
Garrell Rd. Kils 60 B4
Garrell Way. Cumb 61 F1
Garrell Way. Kils 60 B4
Garrier Pl. Kilmk 222 B1
Garrier Rd. Spring 220 C1
Garrioch Cres. Glasg 96 B3
Garrioch Dr. Glasg 96 B3
Garrioch Gate. Glasg 96 B3
Garrioch Quadrant. Glasg ... 96 B3
Garrioch Rd. Glasg 96 B3
Garriochmill Rd. Glasg 96 C2
Garrion Bsns Pk. Wish 186 A4
Garrion Pl. Ash 185 F1
Garrion St. Wish 186 B3
Garrison Pl. Falk 42 A3
Garrowhill Dr. Glasg 119 F3
Garry Ave. Bear 76 A1
Garry Dr. Pais 113 D1
Garry Pl. Falk 42 B1
Garry Pl. Kilmk 228 A3
Garry Pl. Troon 229 F3
Garry St. Glasg 137 D4
Garry Way. Shot 146 C3
Garryhorn. Pres 236 B3
Garscadden Rd. Glasg ... 75 D1
Garscadden Rd S. Glasg ... 94 C4
Garscadden Rd S. Glasg ... 95 D4
Garscadden View. Clyde ... 74 B2
Garscube Cross. Glasg 97 D1
Garscube Rd. Glasg 97 D1
Garshake Ave. Dumb 50 B3
Garshake Rd. Dumb 50 B3
Garshake Rd. Dumb 50 B3
Gartartan Rd. Glasg 114 C3
Gartcarron Hill. Cumb 61 E2
Gartcloss Rd. Coat 101 E1
Gartclush Gdns. Bann 11 F4
Gartconnell Dr. Bear 75 F3
Gartconnell Gdns. Bear ... 75 F3
Gartconnell Rd. Bear 75 F3
Gartconner Ave. Kirk 80 A4
Gartcosh Rd. Coat 101 D1
Gartcosh Rd. Coat 120 C3
Gartcosh Wlk. Hat 141 F3
Gartcows Ave. Falk 42 A2
Gartcows Cres. Falk 42 A2
Gartcows Dr. Falk 42 A2
Gartcows Gdns. Falk 41 F2
Gartcows Pl. Falk 42 A2
Gartcows Rd. Falk 42 A2
Gartcraig Rd. Glasg 118 C4
Garten Dr. Shot 147 D2
Gartferry Ave. Muir 80 C1
Gartferry Rd. Muir 80 C1
Gartferry St. Glasg 98 A2
Gartfield St. Aird 123 D3
Gartgill Rd. Coat 101 F1
Garth St. Glasg 117 E4
Garthamlock Rd. Glasg ... 99 F1
Garthill Gdns. Falk 42 A2
Garthill La. Falk 42 A2
Garthland Dr. Glasg 118 A4
Garthland La. Pais 113 F3
Gartlea Ave. Aird 123 D3
Gartlea Rd. Aird 123 D3
Gartleahill. Aird 123 D3
Gartliston Rd. Glen 101 F2
Gartliston Terr. Coat ... 121 D3
Gartloch Rd. Glasg 99 D1
Gartloch Rd. Glasg 100 B2
Gartly St. Glasg 136 C2
Gartmore Gdns. Tan ... 140 C4
Gartmore La. Muir 81 D1
Gartmore Rd. Pais 114 B2
Gartmore Terr. Glasg ... 138 C2

Gartmorn Rd. N Sau 5 E1
Gartness Dr. Chap 123 F3
Gartness Rd. Chap 124 A2
Gartocher Rd. Glasg 119 E3
Gartocher Terr. Glasg 119 E3
Gartons Rd. Glasg 98 B3
Gartsherrie Ave. Glen 101 F3
Gartsherrie Rd. Coat 121 F4
Gartshore Cres. Twe 59 F1
Gartshore Gdns. Cumb 60 C1
Garturk St. Coat 122 A2
Garturk St. Glasg 117 D1
Garvald Ct. Glasg 118 A2
Garvald Rd. Bank 39 E4
Garvald St. Glasg 118 A2
Garvald St. Green 46 B2
Garvally Cres. All 10 A4
Garve Ave. Glasg 137 D3
Garvel Cres. Glasg 119 F3
Garvel Pl. Miln 54 B1
Garvel Rd. Glasg 119 F3
Garvel Rd. Miln 54 C1
Garven Ct. Kilmk 228 A4
Garven Rd. Steven 217 F3
Garvie Ave. Gour 44 C3
Garvock Dr. Glasg 136 A3
Garvock Dr. Green 45 E2
Garwhitter Dr. Miln 55 D1
Gas St. John 112 A2
Gascoyne. E Kil 180 B4
Gask Pl. Glasg 94 C4
Gaskin Path. Stepps 99 F3
Gasworks Rd. Car 187 E2
Gatehead Rd. Cross 221 F1
Gatehouse St. Glasg ... 119 E2
Gates Rd. Loch 129 E2
Gateshead Pl. Kilbar ... 111 D2
Gateside Ave. Bon 40 B3
Gateside Ave. Glasg ... 139 E3
Gateside Ave. Green ... 45 D2
Gateside Ave. Kils 60 B4
Gateside Cres. Aird ... 123 D4
Gateside Cres. Barr ... 134 A1
Gateside Gdns. Green ... 45 D2
Gateside Gr. Green 45 D2
Gateside. Irvine 219 F3
Gateside Pk. Kils 60 A4
Gateside Pl. Kilmk 227 F2
Gateside Rd. Barr 134 A1
Gateside Rd. Mother ... 164 C2
Gateside Rd. Stir 7 D2
Gateside St. Ham 162 C2
Gateside St. W Kil ... 190 B3
Gateway The. E Kil ... 160 A2
Gauldry Ave. Glasg ... 115 E2
Gauze St. Pais 113 F3
Gavell Rd. Kils 60 A4
Gavin Hamilton Ct. Ayr ... 239 E3
Gavin St. Mother 163 F3
Gavin's Mill Rd. Miln ... 55 D1
Gavinburn Gdns. O Kill ... 73 D4
Gavinburn Pl. O Kill ... 73 D4
Gavinburn St. O Kill ... 73 D4
Gavins Rd. All 4 C1
Gavins Rd. Dunt 74 A3
Gavinton St. Glasg ... 136 C3
Gayne Dr. Glen 101 E3
Gean Ct. Cumb 62 C2
Gean Rd. All 9 F4
Gearholm Rd. Ayr ... 238 B2
Geary St. Glasg 76 B1
Geddes Hill. E Kil ... 160 A2
Geddes Rd. Glasg ... 98 B4
Geelong Gdns. Lennox ... 33 E1
Geils Ave. Dumb 50 B1
Geils Quadrant. Dumb ... 50 B2
Geilsland Rd. Beith ... 171 E4
Geilston Pk. Card 48 A4
Geirston Rd. Kilb 148 C1
Gelston St. Glasg ... 119 D2
Gemini Gr. Holy 143 D3
Gemmell Pl. Newt M ... 156 B2
Gemmell Cres. Ayr ... 236 B1
Gemmell Way. Stone ... 198 C2
General Roy Way. Car ... 202 B4
Generals Gate. Udd ... 140 C3
Gentle Row. Dunt ... 73 F3
George Aitken Ct. Ard ... 205 E2
George Ave. Clyde ... 74 B2
George Cres. Clyde ... 74 B2
George Ct. Ham 162 A3
George Gray St. Glasg ... 138 B4
George La. Pais 113 F2
George Mann Terr. Glasg . 138 A2
George Pl. Pais 113 F2
George Rd. Gour ... 44 C3
George Reith Ave. Glasg ... 95 F3
George Sq. Ayr 236 A1
George Sq. Glasg ... 117 E4
George Sq. Green ... 45 F3
George St. Aird 122 C4
George St. Alva 5 D3
George St. Ayr 235 F1
George St. Ayr 236 A1
George St. Barr 134 A2
George St. Bonh ... 27 F2

261

George St. Chap

Glendevon Pl. Ham

George St. Chap ... 123 E2
George St. Falk ... 42 A3
George St. Glasg ... 117 E4
George St. Glasg ... 120 A2
George St. Ham ... 162 A3
George St. Helen ... 16 C1
George St. Holy ... 143 D2
George St. How ... 130 C3
George St. John ... 111 F2
George St. Lar ... 23 E2
George St. Laur ... 42 C2
George St. Mother ... 163 F2
George St. Pais ... 113 E2
George St. Steven ... 217 E4
George Street La. Bonh ... 27 F2
George Terr. Irvine ... 219 E2
George Way. Lark ... 185 D2
George's Ave. Ayr ... 236 A2
Gerald Terr. Sten ... 23 F2
Gerard Pl. Hat ... 142 A4
Gertrude Pl. Barr ... 134 A1
Ghillies La. Mother ... 142 B1
Gibb St. Chap ... 123 E1
Gibb St. Cle ... 144 A1
Gibbdun Pl. Bank ... 39 F4
Gibbon Cres. E Kil ... 160 B2
Gibbshill Pl. East ... 127 E3
Gibshill Rd. Green ... 46 C1
Gibson Ave. Dumb ... 50 A2
Gibson Cres. John ... 111 F1
Gibson La. Kil ... 69 E1
Gibson Quadrant. Mother .. 142 B1
Gibson Rd. Ren ... 94 A1
Gibson St. Dumb ... 50 A2
Gibson St. Glasg ... 96 C1
Gibson St. Glasg ... 117 F3
Gibson St. Green ... 46 C1
Gibson St. Kilmk ... 222 B1
Gibson St. Sals ... 125 D1
Gibsongray St. Falk ... 42 A4
Giffen Rd. Salt ... 217 D4
Giffnock Park Ave. Glasg .. 136 B2
Gifford Dr. Glasg ... 115 D3
Gigha Cres. Irvine ... 220 A1
Gigha Gdns. Car ... 202 A4
Gigha La. Irvine ... 220 A1
Gigha Pl. Irvine ... 220 A1
Gigha Quadrant. Wish ... 164 C1
Gigha Terr. Irvine ... 220 A1
Gigha Wynd. Irvine ... 220 A1
Gilbert St. Glasg ... 116 B4
Gilbertfield Path ... 99 D1
Gilbertfield Path. Glasg ... 99 D1
Gilbertfield Pl. Glasg ... 99 D1
Gilbertfield Rd. Glasg ... 139 F2
Gilbertfield St. Glasg ... 99 D1
Gilburn Pl. Shot ... 146 C2
Gilchrist Dr. Falk ... 41 F2
Gilchrist St. Coat ... 122 A4
Gilderdale. E Kil ... 159 E1
Gilfillan Ave. Salt ... 206 A1
Gilfillan Pl. Wish ... 186 B4
Gilfillan Way. Pais ... 132 C4
Gilhill St. Glasg ... 96 B4
Gill Pk. Den ... 21 F1
Gill Rd. Wish ... 186 B3
Gill Rd. Wish ... 186 B4
Gillbank Ave. Car ... 187 E1
Gillbank La. Lark ... 185 E1
Gillburn Rd. Kil ... 89 E4
Gillburn St. Wish ... 186 B3
Gillespie Dr. Helen ... 16 B2
Gillespie Pl. Bann ... 7 D1
Gillies Cres. E Kil ... 160 B3
Gillies Ct. Aird ... 123 F4
Gillies Dr. Stir ... 7 E2
Gillies Hill. Cam ... 6 B3
Gillies La. Glasg ... 120 B2
Gillies St. Troon ... 229 E2
Gillsburn Gdns. Kilmk ... 223 D1
Gilmartin Rd. Lin ... 111 F3
Gilmerton St. Glasg ... 119 D2
Gilmour Ave. Dunt ... 74 A3
Gilmour Ave. Thorn ... 158 A1
Gilmour Cres. Eagle ... 178 C3
Gilmour Cres. Glasg ... 137 F4
Gilmour Dr. Ham ... 161 F1
Gilmour Pl. Coat ... 121 F4
Gilmour Pl. Glasg ... 117 E2
Gilmour Pl. Hat ... 141 F3
Gilmour St. Alex ... 27 E3
Gilmour St. Clyde ... 74 B2
Gilmour St. Eagle ... 178 C3
Gilmour St. Green ... 46 B1
Gilmour St. Kilmk ... 228 A4
Gilmour St. Pais ... 113 F3
Gilmour St. Stew ... 195 F1
Gilmourton Cres. Newt M .. 156 B2
Gilroy Cl. Lan ... 215 E3
Gilsay Ct. Falk ... 42 B1
Gimmerscroft Cres. Aird ... 123 F3
Girdle Gate. Irvine ... 219 F3
Girdle Toll. Irvine ... 220 A3
Girthon St. Glasg ... 119 E2
Girvan St. Glasg ... 118 B4
Glade The. Lark ... 185 D1
Gladney Ave. Clyde ... 94 C4
Gladsmuir Rd. Glasg ... 115 D3
Gladstone Ave. Barr ... 134 A1
Gladstone Ave. John ... 131 E4
Gladstone Ct. Ham ... 162 A3
Gladstone Pl. Stir ... 7 D3
Gladstone Rd. Salt ... 217 D4
Gladstone Rd. Sten ... 23 E2
Gladstone St. Glasg ... 97 D1
Gladstone St. Hat ... 142 A3
Glaive Ave. Bann ... 7 E2
Glaive Rd. Glasg ... 75 E1
Glamis Ave. Car ... 187 F1
Glamis Ave. E Kil ... 159 F2
Glamis Ave. John ... 112 A1
Glamis Ave. Newt M ... 156 C3
Glamis Dr. Green ... 45 D3
Glamis Gdns. Bish ... 78 A2
Glamis Pl. Green ... 45 D3
Glamis Rd. Glasg ... 118 B2
Glanderston Ave. Barr ... 134 C1
Glanderston Ave. Newt M . 156 A3
Glanderston Dr. Glasg ... 95 D4
Glanderston Gate. Newt M 156 A3
Glanderston Rd. Newt M ... 155 E3
Glasgow and
Edinburgh Rd. Calder .. 123 D1
Glasgow and
Edinburgh Rd. Chap ... 144 A4
Glasgow and
Edinburgh Rd. Coat ... 121 E2
Glasgow and
Edinburgh Rd. Glasg ... 120 B3
Glasgow and
Edinburgh Rd. Sals ... 125 D1
Glasgow La. Ard ... 205 E1
Glasgow Rd. Bank ... 39 E2
Glasgow Rd. Bann ... 11 E4
Glasgow Rd. Barr ... 134 B2
Glasgow Rd. Clyde ... 94 B4
Glasgow Rd. Coat ... 121 E3
Glasgow Rd. Cumb ... 62 A2
Glasgow Rd. Cumb ... 82 B4
Glasgow Rd. Den ... 21 F1
Glasgow Rd. Dumb ... 50 B1
Glasgow Rd. Dunt ... 74 B3
Glasgow Rd. E Kil ... 160 A4
Glasgow Rd. Eagle ... 178 C4
Glasgow Rd. Falk ... 41 E3
Glasgow Rd. Glasg ... 114 B2
Glasgow Rd. Glasg ... 117 F1
Glasgow Rd. Glasg ... 120 A2
Glasgow Rd. Glasg ... 138 C1
Glasgow Rd. Glasg ... 138 C3
Glasgow Rd. Kilmk ... 223 E3
Glasgow Rd. Kils ... 60 A4
Glasgow Rd. Kirk ... 58 B1
Glasgow Rd. Kirk ... 79 D4
Glasgow Rd. Lan ... 214 C2
Glasgow Rd. Miln ... 55 D1
Glasgow Rd. Mother ... 164 C2
Glasgow Rd. Newt M ... 157 E1
Glasgow Rd. P Glasg ... 47 F1
Glasgow Rd. Ren ... 94 C1
Glasgow Rd. Stir ... 7 D1
Glasgow Rd. Strath ... 31 D2
Glasgow Rd. Tan ... 140 B4
Glasgow Rd. Udd ... 140 C4
Glasgow Rd. Udd ... 161 F4
Glasgow Rd. Wish ... 164 C2
Glasgow St. Ard ... 205 E1
Glasgow St. Glasg ... 96 C1
Glasgow St. Helen ... 16 B1
Glasgow St. Kilb ... 149 D1
Glasgow Vennel. Irvine ... 219 E1
Glassel Rd. Glasg ... 100 B1
Glasserton Pl. Glasg ... 136 C3
Glasserton Rd. Glasg ... 136 C3
Glassford Rd. Stone ... 198 B3
Glassford St. Glasg ... 117 E4
Glassford St. Miln ... 55 D1
Glassford St. Mother ... 164 A2
Glasshouse Loan. All ... 10 A3
Glassock Rd. Kilmk ... 222 C3
Glaudhall Ave. Muir ... 100 C4
Glazert Pl. M of C ... 58 A3
Glebe Ave. Coat ... 121 E2
Glebe Ave. E Kil ... 158 B4
Glebe Ave. Irvine ... 225 E4
Glebe Ave. Kilmk ... 228 A4
Glebe Ave. Stir ... 7 D4
Glebe Ave. Udd ... 141 D1
Glebe Cres. Aird ... 123 E4
Glebe Cres. Alva ... 5 D4
Glebe Cres. Ayr ... 235 F1
Glebe Cres. E Kil ... 159 F1
Glebe Cres. Ham ... 162 B1
Glebe Cres. Stir ... 7 D4
Glebe Ct. Beith ... 171 D4
Glebe Ct. Glasg ... 117 E4
Glebe Ct. Kil ... 89 E4
Glebe Dr. Lan ... 215 D2
Glebe Gdns. Bonh ... 27 F2
Glebe Gdns. Hous ... 91 D1
Glebe Hollow. Udd ... 141 D1
Glebe La. Newt M ... 156 B2
Glebe Pk. Dumb ... 50 A3
Glebe Pl. Glasg ... 137 F4
Glebe Pl. Glasg ... 139 D3
Glebe Pl. Salt ... 216 C4
Glebe Rd. Ayr ... 235 F1
Glebe Rd. Beith ... 171 D4
Glebe Rd. Kil ... 89 E4
Glebe Rd. Kilmk ... 228 A4
Glebe Rd. Newt M ... 156 B2
Glebe St. Den ... 21 F1
Glebe St. E Kil ... 159 F1
Glebe St. Falk ... 42 A3
Glebe St. Glasg ... 97 E1
Glebe St. Glasg ... 117 F4
Glebe St. Ham ... 162 B1
Glebe St. Hat ... 141 F3
Glebe St. Kilw ... 207 F2
Glebe St. Ren ... 94 B2
Glebe St. Salt ... 216 C4
Glebe St. Steven ... 206 B1
Glebe Terr. All ... 10 A3
Glebe Terr. Fen ... 213 D2
Glebe The. Alva ... 5 D4
Glebe The. Irvine ... 225 E4
Glebe The. Lan ... 214 C2
Glebe The. Udd ... 141 D1
Glebe Wynd. Udd ... 141 D1
Glebefield Rd. Rhu ... 15 F3
Glebelands Way. Beith ... 171 D4
Gleddoch Rd. Glasg ... 114 C3
Gledstane Rd. Bishop ... 72 A1
Glen Affric Ave. Glasg ... 135 E2
Glen Affric Dr. Chap ... 123 E1
Glen Affric Dr. Glasg ... 135 E2
Glen Affric. E Kil ... 160 A1
Glen Affric Pl. Kilmk ... 227 E3
Glen Affric Way. Chap ... 123 E1
Glen Afton Ct. Kilmk ... 227 E3
Glen Alby Pl. Glasg ... 135 E2
Glen Almond. E Kil ... 160 B1
Glen Arroch. E Kil ... 160 A1
Glen Ave. Bonh ... 28 A4
Glen Ave. Glasg ... 119 D3
Glen Ave. Gour ... 44 C3
Glen Ave. Muir ... 80 C1
Glen Ave. Neil ... 154 C4
Glen Ave. P Glasg ... 47 D1
Glen Avon Dr. Chap ... 123 E1
Glen Bervie. E Kil ... 160 A1
Glen Brae. B of W ... 110 B4
Glen Brae. Falk ... 42 A2
Glen Cally. E Kil ... 160 A1
Glen Cannich. E Kil ... 160 A1
Glen Carron. E Kil ... 160 A1
Glen Clova. E Kil ... 160 A1
Glen Clunie Ave. Glasg ... 135 E2
Glen Clunie Dr. Glasg ... 135 E2
Glen Clunie. E Kil ... 160 B1
Glen Clunie Pl. Glasg ... 135 E2
Glen Cona Dr. Glasg ... 135 E3
Glen Creran Cres. Neil ... 154 B3
Glen Cres. Clyde ... 94 C4
Glen Cres. Falk ... 42 A1
Glen Ct. Coat ... 121 E3
Glen Ct. Mother ... 164 A2
Glen Derry. E Kil ... 160 B2
Glen Dessary. E Kil ... 181 D4
Glen Devon. E Kil ... 160 B1
Glen Doll. E Kil ... 160 A1
Glen Doll Rd. Neil ... 154 A3
Glen Douglas Dr. Cumb ... 61 E2
Glen Douglas Pl. Green ... 45 E2
Glen Douglas Rd. Green ... 45 E2
Glen Douglas Way. Green ... 45 E2
Glen Dr. Helen ... 16 B2
Glen Dr. Holy ... 143 D3
Glen Dye. E Kil ... 160 A1
Glen Eagles. E Kil ... 160 B1
Glen Esk Dr. Glasg ... 135 E2
Glen Esk. E Kil ... 160 B1
Glen Etive Pl. Glasg ... 138 C1
Glen Falloch Cres. Neil ... 154 B3
Glen Falloch. E Kil ... 160 B1
Glen Farg. E Kil ... 160 B1
Glen Farrar. E Kil ... 160 A1
Glen Farrar Wlk. Kilmk ... 227 E3
Glen Feshie. E Kil ... 181 D4
Glen Finlet Rd. Neil ... 154 B3
Glen Fruin Dr. Lark ... 185 E1
Glen Fruin Pl. Chap ... 123 E1
Glen Fruin Rd. Green ... 45 E2
Glen Fyne Rd. Cumb ... 61 D2
Glen Gairn Cres. Neil ... 154 B3
Glen Gairn. E Kil ... 160 B1
Glen Garrell Pl. Kils ... 36 B1
Glen Garry. E Kil ... 181 D4
Glen Gdns. Falk ... 42 A2
Glen Gdns. John ... 112 B2
Glen Gr. E Kil ... 180 B4
Glen Gr. Kils ... 36 B1
Glen Isla Ave. Neil ... 154 B3
Glen Isla. E Kil ... 160 B1
Glen Kinglas Ave. Green ... 45 E1
Glen Kinglas Rd. Green ... 45 E1
Glen La. Pais ... 113 F3
Glen La. Uplaw ... 153 D2
Glen Lednock Dr. Cumb ... 61 D2
Glen Lee. E Kil ... 160 B1
Glen Lethnot. E Kil ... 160 B1
Glen Livet Pl. Glasg ... 135 E2
Glen Lochay Gdns. Cumb ... 61 D2
Glen Loy Pl. Glasg ... 135 E2
Glen Luce Dr. Glasg ... 119 E2
Glen Luss Rd. Green ... 45 E1
Glen Luss Way. Green ... 45 E1
Glen Lyon Ct. Cumb ... 61 D2
Glen Lyon. E Kil ... 160 B1
Glen Lyon Rd. Neil ... 154 B3
Glen Mallie. E Kil ... 160 B1
Glen Mark. E Kil ... 160 B1
Glen Mark Rd. Neil ... 154 B3
Glen Markie Dr. Glasg ... 135 E2
Glen More. E Kil ... 160 A1
Glen Moriston. E Kil ... 160 A1
Glen Moriston Rd. Glasg ... 135 E2
Glen Moy. E Kil ... 160 B1
Glen Muir Rd. Neil ... 154 B3
Glen Nevis. E Kil ... 181 D4
Glen Nevis Pl. Glasg ... 138 B1
Glen Nevis Pl. Kilmk ... 227 E3
Glen Ochil Rd. Chap ... 123 E1
Glen Ogilvie. E Kil ... 160 B1
Glen Ogle St. Glasg ... 119 E2
Glen Orchy Dr. Glasg ... 135 E2
Glen Orchy Pl. Chap ... 123 E1
Glen Orchy Pl. Glasg ... 135 E2
Glen Orchy Pl. Kilmk ... 227 E3
Glen Orrin Ave. Kilmk ... 227 E3
Glen Pl. Newt M ... 157 E4
Glen Prosen. E Kil ... 160 B1
Glen Quoich. E Kil ... 160 B2
Glen Rannoch Dr. Chap ... 123 E1
Glen Rd. Aird ... 123 F3
Glen Rd. Bishop ... 72 A2
Glen Rd. Cald ... 104 C2
Glen Rd. E Kil ... 158 C3
Glen Rd. Glasg ... 119 D4
Glen Rd. Holy ... 143 E4
Glen Rd. Lennox ... 33 D1
Glen Rd. O Kill ... 73 D3
Glen Rd. Plea ... 12 B1
Glen Rd. Shot ... 146 C2
Glen Rd. Tor ... 22 B4
Glen Rd. W Kil ... 190 B3
Glen Rd. Wish ... 165 D2
Glen Rinnes Dr. Neil ... 154 B3
Glen Roy Dr. Neil ... 154 B3
Glen Sax Dr. Ren ... 94 C1
Glen Shee Ave. Neil ... 154 B3
Glen Shee Cres. Chap ... 123 E1
Glen Shee. E Kil ... 160 B1
Glen Shiel Cres. Kilmk ... 227 E3
Glen Shirva Rd. Twe ... 59 F2
Glen St. Barr ... 134 B2
Glen St. Glasg ... 139 E2
Glen St. Green ... 45 E4
Glen St. Holy ... 143 E2
Glen St. Mother ... 142 C1
Glen St. Pais ... 113 F3
Glen Tanner. E Kil ... 160 B1
Glen Tarbert Dr. Neil ... 154 B3
Glen Tennet. E Kil ... 160 B1
Glen Terr. Den ... 21 E1
Glen Trool Wlk. Kilmk ... 227 E4
Glen Truim View. Kilmk ... 227 E3
Glen Turret. E Kil ... 160 B1
Glen Urquhart. E Kil ... 160 A1
Glen View. Bank ... 39 E3
Glen View. Cumb ... 62 B2
Glen View. Ham ... 183 E4
Glenacre Cres. Tan ... 140 C4
Glenacre Dr. Aird ... 123 E3
Glenacre Dr. Glasg ... 137 E2
Glenacre Quadrant. Glasg 137 E2
Glenacre Rd. Cumb ... 82 C4
Glenacre St. Glasg ... 137 E2
Glenacre Terr. Glasg ... 137 E2
Glenafeoch Rd. Car ... 188 A1
Glenafton View. Ham ... 183 D4
Glenalla Cres. Ayr ... 238 B1
Glenallan Way. Pais ... 132 C4
Glenalmond Rd. Glasg ... 138 B2
Glenalmond St. Glasg ... 119 D2
Glenan Gdns. Helen ... 16 B1
Glenapp Ave. Pais ... 114 A1
Glenapp Ct. Kilw ... 207 E1
Glenapp Pl. Kilw ... 207 E1
Glenapp Pl. Muir ... 80 C2
Glenapp Quadrant. Kilmk .. 228 A4
Glenapp Rd. Pais ... 114 A1
Glenapp St. Glasg ... 116 C2
Glenarklet Dr. Pais ... 114 A1
Glenarn Rd. Rhu ... 15 F2
Glenartney. Hous ... 91 D1
Glenartney Rd. Muir ... 80 B1
Glenashdale Way. Pais ... 114 A1
Glenavon Ct. Ham ... 162 A1
Glenavon Rd. Glasg ... 96 B4
Glenbank Ave. Kirk ... 79 E2
Glenbank Ct. Glasg ... 135 F1
Glenbank Dr. Glasg ... 135 F1
Glenbank. Falk ... 42 A1
Glenbank Rd. Kirk ... 79 E2
Glenbarr St. Glasg ... 97 F1
Glenbervie Ave. Lar ... 23 D2
Glenbervie Cres. Cumb ... 61 F3
Glenbervie Cres. Lar ... 23 D2
Glenbervie Dr. Kilw ... 207 D2
Glenbervie Dr. Lar ... 23 D2
Glenbervie Pl. Glasg ... 76 C1
Glenbervie Pl. Gour ... 44 A3
Glenbo Dr. Bank ... 39 F4
Glenboig Farm Rd. Glen ... 101 F3
Glenboig New Rd. Glen ... 101 F3
Glenboig Rd. Glen ... 101 E3
Glenboig Rd. Muir ... 101 D4
Glenbrae Ct. Falk ... 42 A2
Glenbrae La. Green ... 46 A1
Glenbrae Rd. Green ... 46 A1
Glenbrae Rd. P Glasg ... 68 B4
Glenbride Rd. W Kil ... 190 B2
Glenbrittle Dr. Pais ... 114 A1
Glenbrittle Way. Pais ... 114 A1
Glenbuck Ave. Glasg ... 98 C3
Glenbuck Dr. Glasg ... 98 C3
Glenburn Ave. Glasg ... 120 B3
Glenburn Ave. Glasg ... 138 C3
Glenburn Ave. Holy ... 143 E2
Glenburn Ave. Muir ... 80 C1
Glenburn Cres. M of C ... 58 B3
Glenburn Cres. Pais ... 133 E4
Glenburn Cres. Tan ... 141 E4
Glenburn Dr. Kil ... 69 E1
Glenburn Gdns. Bish ... 77 F1
Glenburn Gdns. Glen ... 101 E3
Glenburn La. Glasg ... 96 C4
Glenburn La. Kil ... 69 E1
Glenburn Rd. Bear ... 75 F3
Glenburn Rd. E Kil ... 159 D2
Glenburn Rd. Falk ... 42 B1
Glenburn Rd. Glasg ... 136 A1
Glenburn Rd. Ham ... 162 A2
Glenburn Rd. Kil ... 69 E1
Glenburn Rd. Pais ... 133 E4
Glenburn Rd. Pres ... 236 C4
Glenburn St. Glasg ... 96 C4
Glenburn St. P Glasg ... 47 D1
Glenburn Terr. Car ... 201 F4
Glenburn Terr. Holy ... 143 E1
Glenburn Way. E Kil ... 158 C2
Glenburn Wlk. Glasg ... 120 B3
Glenburn Wynd. Lark ... 185 D2
Glenburnie Pl. Glasg ... 119 F4
Glencairn Ave. Mother ... 164 B2
Glencairn Dr. Glasg ... 116 C1
Glencairn Dr. Glasg ... 137 F4
Glencairn Dr. Muir ... 80 C1
Glencairn Gdns. Glasg ... 116 C1
Glencairn Gdns. Glasg ... 139 E3
Glencairn La. Glasg ... 116 C1
Glencairn Rd. Ayr ... 239 E3
Glencairn Rd. Cumb ... 62 B1
Glencairn Rd. Dumb ... 49 E2
Glencairn Rd. Gour ... 44 C2
Glencairn Rd. Kil ... 89 F4
Glencairn Rd. Lang ... 70 B4
Glencairn Rd. Pais ... 114 A4
Glencairn Sq. Kilmk ... 227 F3
Glencairn St. Falk ... 41 D3
Glencairn St. Kirk ... 79 E4
Glencairn St. Mother ... 163 F3
Glencairn St. Salt ... 216 C4
Glencairn St. Steven ... 206 C1
Glencairn St. Stir ... 7 D2
Glencairn Terr. Kilm ... 222 A4
Glencalder Cres. Hat ... 142 B2
Glencally Ave. Pais ... 114 A1
Glencart Gr. John ... 111 E1
Glencleland Rd. Mother ... 164 B2
Glenclora Dr. Pais ... 114 A1
Glencloy St. Glasg ... 96 B4
Glenclune Ct. Kil ... 89 E4
Glencoats Dr. Pais ... 113 D2
Glencoe Dr. Holy ... 143 D3
Glencoe Pl. Glasg ... 95 F4
Glencoe Pl. Ham ... 183 D4
Glencoe Rd. Car ... 202 A4
Glencoe Rd. Glasg ... 138 B2
Glencoe Rd. Stir ... 2 A1
Glencoe St. Glasg ... 95 F4
Glenconner Pl. Ayr ... 239 D3
Glenconner Rd. Ayr ... 239 D3
Glenconner Way. Kirk ... 59 D1
Glenconnor St. Lark ... 199 D4
Glencorse Rd. Pais ... 113 E1
Glencorse St. Glasg ... 118 C4
Glencraig St. Aird ... 122 C4
Glencraig Terr. Fen ... 213 D2
Glencraigs Dr. Kilmk ... 222 C3
Glencroft Ave. Tan ... 140 C4
Glencroft Rd. Glasg ... 137 E3
Glencryan Rd. Cumb ... 62 A1
Glendale Ave. Aird ... 123 E3
Glendale Cres. Ayr ... 239 E2
Glendale Cres. Bish ... 98 B4
Glendale Dr. Bish ... 98 B4
Glendale Pl. Ayr ... 239 D2
Glendale Pl. Bish ... 98 B4
Glendale Pl. Glasg ... 118 A3
Glendale St. Glasg ... 118 A3
Glendaruel Ave. Bear ... 76 A2
Glendaruel Rd. Glasg ... 138 C1
Glendee Gdns. Ren ... 94 B1
Glendee Rd. Ren ... 94 B1
Glendentan Rd. B of W ... 110 B3
Glendevon Dr. Stir ... 1 C1
Glendevon Pl. Clyde ... 73 F2
Glendevon Pl. Ham ... 183 D4

262

Glendevon Sq. Glasg Greenhead Rd. Dumb

Glendevon Sq. Glasg 99 D1
Glendinning Pl. Eagle 178 B2
Glendinning Rd. Glasg 75 F1
Glendorch Ave. Wish 165 E4
Glendore St. Glasg 95 F1
Glendoune Rd. Newt M 157 F3
Glendower Way. Pais 132 C4
Glenduffhill Rd. Glasg 119 F3
Gleneagles Ave. Cumb 62 A3
Gleneagles Ave. Kilw 207 E2
Gleneagles Dr. Bish 78 A2
Gleneagles Dr. Gour 44 A3
Gleneagles Gdns. Bish 78 A2
Gleneagles La N. Glasg 95 E2
Gleneagles La S. Glasg 95 E2
Gleneagles Pk. Udd 140 C1
Glenelg Cres. Kirk 59 D1
Glenelg Path. Glen 101 E3
Glenelg Quadrant. Glasg .. 100 B1
Glenelm Pl. Hat 142 A3
Glenfarg Cres. Bear 76 A2
Glenfarg Rd. Glasg 138 A2
Glenfarg Rd. Ham 183 D4
Glenfarg St. Glasg 97 D1
Glenfarm Rd. Holy 143 F2
Glenfield Ave. Pais 133 F4
Glenfield Cres. Pais 133 F3
Glenfield Gdns. Kilmk 227 F3
Glenfield Pl. Kilmk 227 F3
Glenfield Rd. E Kil 181 D3
Glenfield Rd. Pais 133 E3
Glenfinlas St. Helen 16 C1
Glenfinnan Dr. Glasg 76 B2
Glenfinnan Dr. Glasg 96 B3
Glenfinnan Pl. Glasg 96 B3
Glenfinnan Rd. Glasg 96 B3
Glenfruin Cres. Pais 114 A1
Glenfruin Rd. Udd 161 E4
Glenfuir Rd. Falk 41 F3
Glenfuir St. Falk 41 E3
Glengarnock
Workshops. Kilb 170 B4
Glengarriff Rd. Hat 142 A4
Glengarry Dr. Glasg 115 E3
Glengavel Cres. Glasg 98 C3
Glengavel Gdns. Wish 165 E4
Glengowan Rd. B of W 110 B4
Glengowan Rd. Cald 105 D2
Glengyre St. Glasg 100 B1
Glenhead Cres. Dunt 74 A4
Glenhead Cres. Glasg 97 E3
Glenhead Rd. Clyde 74 A3
Glenhead Rd. Klrk 79 E2
Glenhead St. Glasg 97 E3
Glenholme Ave. Pais 113 D1
Glenhove Rd. Cumb 62 A1
Glenhuntly Rd. P Glasg 47 E1
Glenhuntly Terr. P Glasg 47 E1
Gleniffer Ave. Glasg 95 D3
Gleniffer Cres. John 112 B1
Gleniffer Ct. Aird 103 D1
Gleniffer Dr. Barr 134 A3
Gleniffer Rd. John 132 B2
Gleniffer Rd. Pais 133 D4
Gleniffer Rd. Ren 114 A4
Gleniffer Rd. Uplaw 152 B2
Gleniffer View. Clyde 74 B2
Gleniffer View. Neil 154 B4
Gleninver Rd. Green 45 D2
Glenisla Ave. Muir 81 D2
Glenisla St. Glasg 118 B2
Glenkirk Dr. Glasg 75 D1
Glenlee St. Ham 161 F3
Glenleith Pl. Irvine 220 B1
Glenlivet Pl. Kilmk 223 D2
Glenlivet Rd. Neil 154 B3
Glenlora Dr. Glasg 135 D4
Glenlora Terr. Glasg 135 D4
Glenluce Gdns. Muir 81 D2
Glenluce Terr. E Kil 159 E1
Glenluggie Rd. Kirk 80 A4
Glenlui Ave. Glasg 138 A3
Glenlyon Ct. Ham 183 D4
Glenlyon Gr. Irvine 219 F3
Glenlyon Pl. Glasg 138 B2
Glenmalloch Pl. John 112 B2
Glenmanor Ave. Muir 80 C1
Glenmare Ave. Kirk 80 A4
Glenmavis Cres. Car 188 A1
Glenmavis Rd. Aird 102 C1
Glenmavis St. Glasg 97 D1
Glenmore Ave. Glasg 137 F4
Glenmore Ave. Hat 142 A2
Glenmore Dr. Bon 39 F3
Glenmore Rd. Holy 143 E2
Glenmoss Ave. Ersk 72 C1
Glenmosston Rd. Kil 89 F4
Glenmount Pl. Ayr 238 A1
Glenmuir Ct. Ayr 236 B1
Glenmuir Dr. Glasg 135 D3
Glenmuir Pl. Ayr 236 B1
Glenmuir Rd. Ayr 236 B1
Glenochil Pk. Men 4 C2
Glenochil Rd. Falk 42 A2
Glenochil Terr. Men 4 C2
Glenoran La. Lark 185 D2
Glenoran Rd. Helen 16 A2
Glenorchard Rd. Bish 56 B1
Glenorrin Way. Neil 154 B3
Glenpark. Aird 123 F3
Glenpark Ave. Glasg 136 A1
Glenpark Ave. Pres 236 B3
Glenpark Dr. P Glasg 47 D1
Glenpark Gdns. Glasg 138 C4
Glenpark Pl. Ayr 239 D2
Glenpark Rd. Glasg 118 A3
Glenpark Rd. Loch 129 E2
Glenpark St. Glasg 118 A3
Glenpark St. Wish 165 D2
Glenpark Terr. Glasg 138 C4
Glenpath. Dumb 50 B2
Glenpatrick Rd. John 112 B1
Glenraith Path. Glasg 99 D2
Glenraith Rd. Glasg 99 D1
Glenraith Sq. Glasg 99 D2
Glenraith Wlk. Glasg 99 E2
Glenriddel Rd. Ayr 239 D3
Glenriddet Ave. Kilb 170 A4
Glenshee St. Glasg 118 B2
Glenshee Terr. Ham 183 D4
Glenshiel Ave. Pais 114 A1
Glenshira Ave. Pais 114 A1
Glenside Ave. Glasg 115 D1
Glenside Cres. W Kil 190 B3
Glenside Dr. Glasg 138 C3
Glenside Gr. W Kil 190 B3
Glenside Rd. Dumb 50 B3
Glenside Rd. P Glasg 68 B4
Glenspean St. Glasg 136 B3
Glentanar Pl. Glasg 97 D4
Glentanar Rd. Glasg 97 D4
Glentarbert Rd. Glasg 138 B2
Glentore Quadrant. Aird 103 D1
Glenturret St. Glasg 119 D2
Glentyan Ave. Kilbar 111 D2
Glentyan Dr. Glasg 135 D3
Glentyan Terr. Glasg 135 D4
Glentye Gdns. Falk 41 F1
Glenview. Aird 123 E3
Glenview Ave. Bank 38 C2
Glenview Ave. Cald 105 D2
Glenview Cres. Muir 81 D2
Glenview Dr. Falk 41 F1
Glenview. Duni 21 D2
Glenview. Kirk 79 E4
Glenview. Lark 184 C2
Glenview. Men 4 A3
Glenview Pl. Udd 140 B1
Glenview St. Glenm 102 C2
Glenview Terr. Green 45 E2
Glenview. W Kil 190 B2
Glenville Ave. Glasg 136 A2
Glenville Gate. Thorn 158 A3
Glenville Terr. Thorn 158 A3
Glenward Ave. Lennox 57 F4
Glenwell St. Glenm 102 C2
Glenwinnel Rd. Alva 4 C4
Glenwood Ave. Aird 123 E2
Glenwood Bsns Ctr. Glasg 137 F2
Glenwood Ct. Klrk 79 D3
Glenwood Dr. Glasg 135 F1
Glenwood Gdns. Klrk 79 D3
Glenwood Pl. Klrk 79 D3
Glenwood Rd. Klrk 79 D3
Glenyards Rd. Bon 40 A1
Glidden Ct. Wish 186 B4
Glorat Ave. Lennox 57 F4
Gloucester Ave. Glasg 138 B3
Gloucester Ave. Newt M 157 E4
Gloucester St. Glasg 117 D3
Glowrorum Dr. Bank 39 F4
Glynwed Ct. Falk 42 B4
Goatfell View. Troon 229 F4
Gockston Rd. Pais 113 E4
Goddard Pl. New 166 A3
Godfrey Ave. Den 21 E1
Godfrey Cres. Lar 23 E1
Gogar Loan. B of A 3 E3
Gogar Pl. Glasg 118 C4
Gogar Pl. Stir 7 E1
Gogar St. Glasg 118 C4
Goil Ave. Tan 141 E3
Goil Way. Holy 143 D3
Goldberry Ave. Glasg 95 D3
Goldcraig Ct. Irvine 220 A3
Goldenacre Pl. Plains 103 F2
Goldenberry Ave. W Kil 190 B2
Goldie Pl. Steven 206 B1
Goldie Rd. Udd 141 D2
Golf Ave. Hat 142 A2
Golf Ave. Steven 217 F3
Golf Course Rd. B of W 110 B4
Golf Course Rd. Bish 77 F4
Golf Cres. Troon 229 E1
Golf Dr. Glasg 74 C1
Golf Dr. P Glasg 68 B4
Golf Dr. Pais 114 B2
Golf Gdns. Lark 185 E1
Golf Pl. Green 45 E4
Golf Pl. Hat 142 A2
Golf Pl. Helen 17 D1
Golf Pl. Irvine 219 D3
Golf Pl. Troon 229 E1
Golf Rd. Bishop 72 A2
Golf Rd. Glasg 138 A2
Golf Rd. Gour 44 B3
Golf Rd. Newt M 157 E4
Golf View. Clyde 73 F2
Golffields Rd. Irvine 219 E1
Golfhill Dr. Bonh 27 F3
Golfhill Dr. Glasg 118 A4
Golfhill Dr. Helen 16 C1
Golfhill Quadrant. Aird 103 D1
Golfhill Rd. Mother 164 C2
Golfview. Bear 75 E3
Golfview Dr. Coat 121 E4
Golfview Pl. Coat 121 E3
Golsbie Ave. Aird 122 C2
Golspie St. Glasg 116 A4
Goodview Gdns. Lark 185 E1
Goosecroft Rd. Stir 7 D4
Goosedubbs. Glasg 117 E3
Gooseholm Cres. Dumb 50 A3
Gooseholm Rd. Dumb 50 A3
Gopher Ave. Tan 141 D4
Gorbals Cross. Glasg 117 E3
Gorbals Cross. Lark 185 D2
Gorbals St. Glasg 117 E3
Gordon Ave. Bishop 72 A2
Gordon Ave. Glasg 114 C4
Gordon Ave. Glasg 119 F3
Gordon Ave. Glasg 136 C1
Gordon Cres. B of A 2 A4
Gordon Cres. Newt M 156 C3
Gordon Cres. Stir 1 C1
Gordon Ct. Aird 123 F4
Gordon Dr. All 10 B4
Gordon Dr. E Kil 160 A2
Gordon Dr. Glasg 136 C2
Gordon La. Glasg 117 D4
Gordon Pl. Falk 41 F3
Gordon Pl. Hat 141 F1
Gordon Rd. Glasg 136 C1
Gordon Rd. Ham 161 F2
Gordon Rd. Kilmk 222 C2
Gordon St. Ayr 236 A2
Gordon St. Glasg 117 D4
Gordon St. Green 45 F2
Gordon St. Pais 113 F2
Gordon Terr. Ayr 239 D4
Gordon Terr. Ham 161 F2
Gordon Terr. Udd 140 B1
Gorebridge St. Glasg 118 C4
Goremire Rd. Car 202 A4
Gorget Ave. Glasg 75 E1
Gorget Pl. Glasg 75 E1
Gorget Quadrant. Glasg 75 D1
Gorrie St. Den 21 E1
Gorse Cres. B of W 110 C4
Gorse Pk. Ayr 239 E2
Gorse Pl. Tan 141 D4
Gorsehall St. Cle 144 A1
Gorsewood. Bish 77 F1
Gorstan Pl. Glasg 96 B3
Gorstan St. Glasg 96 B4
Goschen Terr. Ayr 236 A1
Gosford La. Glasg 95 D2
Gottries Rd. Irvine 219 D1
Goudie St. Pais 113 E4
Gough St. Glasg 118 B4
Goukscroft Pk. Ayr 238 B2
Gould St. Ayr 236 B1
Gourlay Dr. Wish 186 B3
Gourlay. E Kil 160 B3
Gourlay St. Glasg 97 E2
Gourlay St. Glasg 97 F2
Gourock St. Glasg 117 D2
Govan Dr. Alex 27 E3
Govan Rd. Glasg 115 F4
Govan Rd. Glasg 116 B3
Govanhill St. Glasg 117 D1
Govanhill St. Glasg 117 E1
Gowan Ave. Falk 42 A3
Gowan Brae. Cald 105 D3
Gowan La. Falk 42 A3
Gowanbank Gdns. John ... 111 F1
Gowanbank Rd. Ayr 239 D1
Gowanbrae. Klrk 79 E3
Gowanhill Gdns. Stir 1 C1
Gowanlea Ave. Glasg 75 D1
Gowanlea Dr. Glasg 136 B2
Gowanlea Dr. Slam 86 A3
Gowanlea Terr. Tan 141 D4
Gowanside Pl. Car 187 E1
Gower Pl. Ayr 239 D2
Gower St. Glasg 116 B2
Gower Terr. Glasg 116 B3
Gowkhall Ave. Holy 143 F2
Gowkhouse Rd. Kil 89 F4
Goyle Ave. Glasg 75 E2
Grace Ave. Coat 120 C3
Grace St. Glasg 116 C4
Gracie Cres. Fall 8 B2
Gradlon Pl. Falk 42 A2
Graeme Pl. Falk 41 F1
Graffham Ave. Glasg 136 C2
Grafton Pl. Glasg 117 E4
Graham Ave. Clyde 74 A2
Graham Ave. E Kil 159 F1
Graham Ave. Glasg 139 E3
Graham Ave. Ham 183 E4
Graham Ave. Lar 23 D2
Graham Ave. Stir 2 B2
Graham Cres. Card 48 A4
Graham Dr. Miln 54 C1
Graham Pl. Ash 185 F1
Graham Pl. Helen 17 D1
Graham Pl. Kilmk 223 E1
Graham Pl. Kils 36 B1
Graham Rd. Car 201 D1
Graham Rd. Dumb 49 E2
Graham Sq. Glasg 117 F3
Graham St. Aird 123 D4
Graham St. B of A 2 A4
Graham St. Barr 134 A2
Graham St. Green 45 E3
Graham St. Ham 162 C2
Graham St. Holy 143 D3
Graham St. John 111 F1
Graham St. Wish 165 D1
Graham Terr. Air 14 B2
Graham Terr. Bish 98 A4
Graham Terr. Stew 195 E1
Graham View. Alex 27 F1
Grahamfield Pl. Beith 171 D4
Grahams Ave. Loch 129 E2
Grahams Rd. Falk 42 A3
Grahamsdyke Cres. Bon 40 A2
Grahamsdyke Rd. Bon 40 A2
Grahamsdyke Rd. Kirk 58 C1
Grahamsdyke St. Laur 42 C2
Grahamshill Ave. Aird 123 E4
Grahamshill St. Aird 123 E4
Grahamston Ave. Kilb 170 A4
Grahamston Cres. Pais 134 B4
Grahamston Ct. Pais 134 B4
Grahamston Pk. Barr 134 A3
Grahamston Pl. Pais 134 B4
Grahamston Rd. Barr 134 B3
Grahamston Rd. Pais 134 B3
Graigleith View. Tull 4 B2
Graignestock Pl. Glasg 117 F3
Graignestock St. Glasg 117 F3
Graigside Pl. Cumb 81 F4
Grainger Rd. Bish 78 B1
Grammar School Sq. Ham 162 C2
Grampian Ave. Pais 133 E4
Grampian Cres. Glasg 119 D2
Grampian Ct. Irvine 220 A2
Grampian Pl. Glasg 119 D2
Grampian Rd. Kilmk 228 A2
Grampian Rd. P Glasg 69 D3
Grampian Rd. Stir 6 C3
Grampian Rd. Wish 164 C2
Grampian St. Glasg 119 D2
Grampian Way. Barr 134 B1
Grampian Way. Bear 75 D4
Grampian Way. Bear 75 E4
Grampian Way. Cumb 61 D1
Gran St. Clyde 94 C4
Granary Rd. Falk 42 A4
Granary Sq. Falk 42 A4
Granby La. Glasg 96 B2
Grandtuly Dr. Glasg 96 B3
Grange Ave. Ayr 239 D1
Grange Ave. Falk 42 B3
Grange Ave. Miln 55 D1
Grange Ave. Wish 164 C1
Grange Ct. Lan 214 C3
Grange Dr. Falk 42 B3
Grange Gdns. B of A 2 B4
Grange Gdns. Udd 141 D1
Grange Pl. Alex 27 F3
Grange Pl. Kilmk 227 F4
Grange Rd. All 9 F3
Grange Rd. B of A 2 B3
Grange Rd. Bear 75 F3
Grange Rd. Glasg 137 D4
Grange Rd. Steven 206 B1
Grange St. Kilmk 227 F4
Grange St. Mother 164 A2
Grange Terr. Kilmk 227 E4
Grangemouth Rd. Falk 42 C3
Grangemuir Rd. Pres 236 A4
Grangeneuk Gdns. Cumb ... 61 E1
Granger Rd. Bonh 27 F4
Granger Rd. Kilmk 227 F3
Grangeview. Lar 23 F1
Grant Cres. Alex 27 E1
Grant Ct. Aird 123 F4
Grant Ct. Ham 183 E4
Grant Pl. Coat 122 B2
Grant Pl. Kilmk 223 E1
Grant Pl. Stir 2 A2
Grant St. All 9 F3
Grant St. Glasg 96 C1
Grant St. Green 46 B2
Grant St. Helen 16 B1
Grantholm Ave. Holy 143 D3
Grantlea Gr. Glasg 119 E2
Grantlea Terr. Glasg 119 E2
Grantley Gdns. Glasg 136 B4
Grantley St. Glasg 136 B4
Grantoften Path. E Kil 180 C3
Granton St. Glasg 117 F1
Grantown Gdns. Glenm 102 C3
Granville St. Clyde 74 A2
Granville St. Glasg 116 C4
Granville St. Helen 16 C1
Grasmere. E Kil 179 F3
Grassyards
Interchange. Kilmk 223 E2
Grassyards Rd. Kilmk 223 E1
Grathellen Ct. Mother 164 A4
Gray Cres. Irvine 224 B4
Gray Dr. Bear 75 F2
Gray St. Alex 27 F3
Gray St. Cle 144 A1
Gray St. Glasg 96 C1
Gray St. Green 46 A2
Gray St. Kirk 80 A4
Gray St. Lark 185 D2
Gray St. Pres 236 B4
Gray St. Shot 147 D2
Gray's Cl. Lan 214 B2
Gray's Rd. Tan 141 D3
Grayshill Rd. Cumb 81 F3
Graystale Rd. Stir 7 D2
Graystonelee Rd. Shot 146 B3
Graystones. Kilw 207 F3
Great Dovehill. Glasg 117 E3
Great George La. Glasg 96 B2
Great George St. Glasg 96 B2
Great George St. Glasg 96 C1
Great Hamilton St. Pais 113 F1
Great Kelvin La. Glasg 96 C1
Great Western Rd. Clyde 74 B2
Great Western Rd. Glasg 96 B2
Great Western Rd. Kil 73 E3
Great Western Terr. Glasg .. 96 B2
Great Western
Terrace La. Glasg 96 B2
Green Ave. Irvine 219 E2
Green Bank. Dalry 191 E4
Green Bank Rd. Cumb 61 E1
Green Dale. Wish 165 E3
Green Farm Rd. Lin 112 A3
Green Gdns. Cle 144 B1
Green Loan. Holy 143 D2
Green Pl. Calder 123 D1
Green Pl. Udd 141 D1
Green Rd. Glasg 138 A4
Green Rd. Pais 113 D2
Green St. Ayr 235 F1
Green St. Clyde 74 A2
Green St. Glasg 117 F3
Green St. Salt 216 C4
Green St. Stone 198 C1
Green St. Udd 141 D1
Green Street La. Ayr 235 F1
Green
Street La Bsns Pk. Ayr . 235 F1
Green The. Alva 5 D4
Green The. Glasg 117 F2
Greenacre Ct. Bann 7 F1
Greenacre Pl. Bann 7 F1
Greenacres. Ard 205 F2
Greenacres. Mother 163 E3
Greenacres View. Mother . 163 E3
Greenan Ave. Glasg 137 F4
Greenan Gr. Ayr 238 A2
Greenan Pk. Ayr 238 A2
Greenan Pl. Ayr 238 B2
Greenan Rd. Ayr 238 B2
Greenan Rd. Kilmk 228 A4
Greenan Terr. Pres 236 B4
Greenan Way. Ayr 238 A2
Greenbank Ave. Newt M ... 157 D4
Greenbank Dr. Pais 133 E4
Greenbank Pl. Falk 41 E2
Greenbank Rd. Falk 41 E2
Greenbank Rd. Irvine 219 E1
Greenbank Rd. Wish 165 E2
Greenbank St. Glasg 138 A4
Greenbank Terr. Car 187 F1
Greenbank. Udd 161 E4
Greencraig Ave. Shi 66 B3
Greendyke St. Glasg 117 E3
Greenend Ave. John 111 E1
Greenend Pl. Glasg 119 E4
Greenend View. Hat 141 F3
Greenfarm Rd. Newt M 156 A3
Greenfaulds Cres. Cumb 83 D4
Greenfaulds Rd. Cumb 82 C4
Greenfaulds Rd. Cumb 83 D4
Greenfield Ave. Ayr 238 B1
Greenfield Ave. Glasg 119 D4
Greenfield Cres. Wish 165 E2
Greenfield Dr. Irvine 219 E1
Greenfield Dr. Wish 165 E2
Greenfield Pl. Glasg 119 D3
Greenfield Quadrant. Holy 143 F2
Greenfield Rd. Car 187 F2
Greenfield Rd. Glasg 119 E3
Greenfield Rd. Ham 162 A3
Greenfield Rd. Newt M 157 F3
Greenfield St. All 10 A4
Greenfield St. Bon 40 A3
Greenfield St. Glasg 115 F4
Greenfield St. Wish 165 E2
Greenfoot. Kilw 207 F2
Greengairs Ave. Glasg 115 E4
Greengairs Rd. Gree 83 F1
Greenhall Pl. Udd 161 E3
Greenhead. Alva 5 D3
Greenhead Ave. Dumb 50 A2
Greenhead Ave. Steven 206 C1
Greenhead Gdns. Dumb 50 A2
Greenhead Rd. Bear 75 F2
Greenhead Rd. Dumb 50 B2

Greenhead Rd. Inch 93 E3
Greenhead Rd. Lennox 57 F4
Greenhead Rd. Wish 165 E1
Greenhead St. Glasg 117 F2
Greenhead St. Glasg 117 F3
Greenhill
  and Wilson's Rd. Chap 144 C4
Greenhill
  and Wilson's Rd. Cle 144 C3
Greenhill Ave. Glasg 136 B1
Greenhill Ave. Muir 100 C4
Greenhill. Bish 98 B4
Greenhill Cres. John 112 B1
Greenhill Cres. Lin 112 B3
Greenhill Ct. Glasg 138 A4
Greenhill Ct. Irvine 220 A3
Greenhill Dr. Lin 112 B3
Greenhill Rd. Blac 107 F2
Greenhill Rd. Bon 40 A2
Greenhill Rd. Glasg 138 A4
Greenhill Rd. Pais 113 E3
Greenhill St. Glasg 138 A4
Greenhill Terr. Cross 221 F3
Greenhills Cres. E Kil 180 A3
Greenhills Rd. E Kil 180 B3
Greenholm Ave. Newt M 157 F4
Greenholm Ave. Udd 140 C4
Greenholm St. Kilmk 227 F3
Greenholme Ct. Glasg 137 D3
Greenholme St. Glasg 137 D3
Greenhorn's Well Ave. Falk 41 F2
Greenhorn's Well Cres. Falk 41 F2
Greenhorn's Well Dr. Falk ... 41 F2
Greenknowe Dr. Law 186 C3
Greenknowe Rd. Glasg 136 A3
Greenknowe St. Wish 186 A3
Greenlaw Ave. Pais 114 A3
Greenlaw Ave. Wish 165 E3
Greenlaw Cres. Pais 114 A3
Greenlaw Dr. Pais 114 A3
Greenlaw Ind Est. Pais 113 F3
Greenlaw Rd. Glasg 94 C3
Greenlaw Rd. Newt M 156 B3
Greenlea Rd. Muir 100 A4
Greenlea St. Glasg 95 F3
Greenlees Ct. Dalry 191 D4
Greenlees Gdns. Glasg 138 C2
Greenlees Pk. Glasg 139 D2
Greenlees Rd. Glasg 139 D2
Greenloan Ave. Glasg 115 E4
Greenloan View. Lark 185 D1
Greenmoss Pl. Hat 142 B3
Greenmount Dr. Shi 66 B3
Greenmount. Glasg 97 D4
Greenock Ave. Glasg 137 D3
Greenock Rd. Bishop 71 E3
Greenock Rd. Green 46 C1
Greenock Rd. Hous 92 B4
Greenock Rd. Inch 93 E3
Greenock Rd. Kil 69 E4
Greenock Rd. Lang 70 B4
Greenock Rd. P Glasg 47 E1
Greenock Rd. Pais 113 E4
Greenrig Rd. Lan 214 A1
Greenrig St. Glasg 98 B2
Greenrig. Udd 140 C3
Greenrigg Cotts. Hart 127 F3
Greenrigg Rd. Cumb 62 A1
Greenrigg St. Udd 140 C3
Greens Ave. Klrk 79 E4
Greens Cres. Klrk 79 E4
Greens Rd. Cumb 82 C3
Greenshields Rd. Glasg 120 A3
Greenside Ave. Kilb 170 A4
Greenside Ave. Pres 236 B4
Greenside Ave. Spring 221 D1
Greenside Cl. Lan 215 D2
Greenside Cres. Glasg 98 C2
Greenside. Irvine 220 A2
Greenside La. Lan 215 D2
Greenside Pl. Bear 75 E4
Greenside Rd. Dunt 74 A4
Greenside Rd. E Kil 158 C4
Greenside Rd. Holy 143 E4
Greenside Rd. Wish 165 E1
Greenside St. All 10 A3
Greenside St. Glasg 98 C2
Greenside St. Holy 143 F2
Greenside Terr. Spring 221 D1
Greenside Way. Irvine 220 A2
Greentowers Rd. Lan 214 C4
Greentree Dr. Glasg 119 F2
Greentree Pk. Ayr 239 E2
Greenview St. Glasg 136 B4
Greenville St. Falk 41 F2
Greenway La. Udd 161 E3
Greenways Ave. Pais 113 D1
Greenways Ct. Pais 113 D1
Greenwood Ave. Glasg 139 F3
Greenwood Ave. Muir 80 C1
Greenwood Ave. Stir 7 D4
Greenwood Cres. Coat 122 B3
Greenwood Ct. Newt M 157 F4
Greenwood Dr. Bear 76 A2
Greenwood
  Interchange. Shew 224 C4
Greenwood Quadrant. Clyde 74 B1
Greenwood Rd. Irvine 220 B1

Greenwood Rd. Newt M 157 E4
Greenwood St. Shot 146 C3
Greenyards
  Interchange. Cumb 62 B1
Greer Quadrant. Clyde 74 A2
Grenada Pl. E Kil 159 D1
Grenadier Gdns. Mother 163 E2
Grendon Ct. Stir 7 D3
Grendon Gdns. Stir 7 D3
Grenville Dr. Glasg 138 C2
Grenville Rd. Gour 44 C3
Greta Meek La. M of C 58 B3
Gretna St. Glasg 118 A2
Grey Pl. Green 45 F3
Greyfriars Rd. Udd 140 B4
Greyfriars St. Glasg 118 C4
Greygoran. N Sau 5 E1
Greystone Ave. Glasg 138 B3
Greystone Bauks. Lan 214 C2
Greywood St. Glasg 95 F4
Grier Pl. Lark 184 C1
Grierson Cres. Cam 6 B3
Grierson La. Glasg 118 B4
Grierson St. Glasg 118 B4
Grieve Croft. Udd 140 C1
Grieve Rd. Cumb 62 A2
Grieve Rd. Green 45 D3
Griffiths St. Falk 42 A2
Griffiths Way. Law 186 C2
Griqua Terr. Udd 141 D1
Grodwell Dr. Alva 4 C4
Grogarry Rd. Glasg 75 D2
Grosvenor Cres. Glasg 96 B2
Grosvenor
  Crescent La. Glasg 96 B2
Grosvenor La. Glasg 96 B2
Grosvenor La. Green 46 B2
Grosvenor Rd. Green 46 B2
Grosvenor Terr. Glasg 96 B2
Grougar Dr. Kilmk 223 D2
Grougar Rd. Hurl 228 B4
Grove Cres. Lark 185 E1
Grove Park Gdns. Glasg 97 D1
Grove Pk. Klrk 79 E2
Grove St. Den 21 E1
Grove The. B of W 110 C3
Grove The. Bishop 72 A2
Grove The. Glasg 157 D4
Grove The. Kilbar 111 D2
Grove The. Neil 154 B3
Grove Way. Hat 141 F2
Grove Wood. Tan 121 E1
Grove Wynd. Holy 143 D2
Groveburn Ave. Glasg 136 A2
Grovepark Ct. Glasg 97 D1
Grovepark St. Glasg 97 D2
Grudie St. Glasg 120 A4
Gryfe Rd. B of W 110 B4
Gryfe Rd. P Glasg 68 C4
Gryfe St. Green 46 A1
Gryfebank Ave. Hous 91 F1
Gryfewood Cres. Hous 91 F1
Gryffe Ave. B of W 90 B1
Gryffe Ave. Ren 94 A3
Gryffe Cres. Pais 112 C1
Gryffe Gr. B of W 110 B4
Gryffe Pk. B of W 90 B1
Gryffe Rd. Kil 89 E4
Gryffe St. Glasg 137 D4
Guildford St. Glasg 99 E1
Guiltreehill. Ayr 239 D1
Gullane Cres. Cumb 61 F3
Gullane Ct. Ham 183 D4
Gullane Pl. Kilw 207 D2
Gullane St. Glasg 96 A1
Gulliland Ave. Dund 225 F1
Gulliland Pl. Irvine 219 E1
Gullin Dr. Pres 236 C3
Gunn Quadrant. Hat 141 F2
Guthrie St. Lan 121 D1
Guthrie Pl. E Kil 159 F1
Guthrie Pl. Lennox 57 E1
Guthrie Pl. Rhu 15 E2
Guthrie Rd. Salt 217 D4
Guthrie St. Glasg 96 B3
Guthrie St. Ham 162 B2
Guy Mannering Rd. Helen ... 25 C4

Habbieauld Rd. Kilm 222 A4
Haberlea Ave. Glasg 135 E2
Haberlea Gdns. Glasg 135 E1
Haddington Gdns. Irvine 220 A3
Haddow Gr. Tan 141 D4
Haddow St. Ham 162 C2
Hadrian Terr. Mother 163 E4
Hagart Rd. Hous 91 D1
Hagg Cres. John 111 F2
Hagg Pl. John 111 F1
Hagg Rd. John 111 F1
Haggs La. Glasg 116 B1
Haggs Rd. Glasg 116 B1
Haggswood Ave. Glasg 116 B1
Haghill Rd. Glasg 118 B4
Hagholm Rd. Lan 215 F4
Hagthorn Ave. Kilb 170 A4
Haig Ave. Stir 2 A1

Haig Dr. Glasg 119 F2
Haig St. Glasg 98 A2
Haig St. Green 45 F3
Hailes Ave. Glasg 119 E3
Haining Ave. Kilmk 228 A3
Haining Rd. Ren 94 B2
Haining The. Ren 94 B1
Hairmyres Pk. E Kil 179 F4
Hairmyres
  Roundabout. E Kil 158 C1
Hairmyres St. Glasg 117 E1
Hairst St. Ron 94 B2
Halbeath Ave. Glasg 74 C2
Halbert St. Glasg 116 C1
Halberts Cres. Stir 7 D1
Haldane Ave. B of A 2 A3
Haldane La. Glasg 95 E2
Haldane Pl. E Kil 180 C4
Haldane St. Glasg 95 E2
Haldane Terr. Bonh 19 F1
Halfmerk N. E Kil 160 A1
Halfmerk S. E Kil 160 A1
Halfway St. W Kil 190 B3
Halgreen Ave. Glasg 74 C2
Halifax Way. Ren 94 B1
Halkett Cres. Alex 27 F4
Hall Bar Gdns. Car 201 F2
Hall La. Troon 230 A2
Hall Pl. Lan 215 D2
Hall Rd. Rhu 15 E3
Hall St. Alex 49 E4
Hall St. Bonh 27 F2
Hall St. Clyde 74 A1
Hall St. Ham 162 B1
Hall St. Holy 143 D2
Hallbrae St. Glasg 98 C1
Hallcraig St. Aird 123 D4
Halley Dr. Clyde 94 C4
Halley Pl. Clyde 94 C4
Halley Sq. Clyde 94 C4
Halley St. Clyde 94 C4
Hallforest St. Glasg 99 D1
Hallglen Rd. Falk 42 A1
Hallglen Terr. Falk 42 A1
Hallgraig Pl. Car 187 E1
Hallhill Cres. Glasg 119 F3
Hallhill Rd. Glasg 119 D3
Hallhill Rd. Glasg 119 E3
Hallhill Rd. Glasg 119 F3
Hallhill Rd. Glasg 120 A3
Hallhill Rd. John 131 E4
Halliburton Cres. Glasg 119 F4
Halliburton Terr. Glasg 120 A4
Hallidale Cres. Ren 94 C1
Hallinan Gdns. Wish 164 C1
Hallpark. N Sau 5 B4
Hallrule Dr. Glasg 115 E3
Halls Vennal. Ayr 235 F1
Hallside Ave. Glasg 139 F3
Hallside Cres. Glasg 139 F3
Hallside Dr. Glasg 139 F3
Hallside Gdns. Wish 165 F2
Hallside Pl. Glasg 117 E2
Hallside Rd. Glasg 139 F2
Hallside St. How 130 C3
Hallydown Dr. Glasg 95 E3
Halpin Cl. Tan 141 E3
Halton Gdns. Glasg 119 F2
Hamersley Pl. E Kil 180 A4
Hamilcomb Rd. Hat 142 A2
Hamill Dr. Kils 60 C4
Hamilton Ave. Glasg 116 B2
Hamilton Ave. Sten 23 F2
Hamilton Cres. Ayr 239 D4
Hamilton Cres. Bear 75 F4
Hamilton Cres. Bishop 71 F2
Hamilton Cres. Coat 122 A3
Hamilton Cres. Glasg 139 E3
Hamilton Cres. Ren 94 B3
Hamilton Cres. Steven 206 C1
Hamilton Ct. Kilm 222 A4
Hamilton Dr. Aird 103 D1
Hamilton Dr. Ersk 72 C2
Hamilton Dr. Falk 42 A2
Hamilton Dr. Glasg 96 C2
Hamilton Dr. Glasg 136 B1
Hamilton Dr. Glasg 139 D3
Hamilton Dr. Ham 161 D3
Hamilton Dr. Mother 163 F2
Hamilton Dr. Stir 2 B2
Hamilton Dr. Udd 141 D1
Hamilton Gate. Green 45 F3
Hamilton Gdns. Stew 195 F1
Hamilton Park Ave. Glasg 96 C2
Hamilton Pl. E Kil 180 C4
Hamilton Pl. Ham 183 E3
Hamilton Pl. Holy 143 D2
Hamilton Pl. Holy 143 E2
Hamilton Rd. E Kil 160 B3
Hamilton Rd. Glasg 119 E1
Hamilton Rd. Glasg 118 B4
Hamilton Rd. Glasg 139 E2
Hamilton Rd. Ham 162 A4
Hamilton Rd. Hat 141 F2
Hamilton Rd. Lark 184 C1
Hamilton Rd. Mother 163 E3

Hamilton Rd. Sten 23 E3
Hamilton Rd. Udd 141 D1
Hamilton Rd. Udd 161 D3
Hamilton St. Car 187 F1
Hamilton St. Clyde 94 B4
Hamilton St. Dumb 50 A2
Hamilton St. Falk 41 E3
Hamilton St. Glasg 117 E1
Hamilton St. Kilw 207 F2
Hamilton St. Lark 185 D2
Hamilton St. Pais 113 F3
Hamilton St. Salt 216 C4
Hamilton Terr. Clyde 94 B4
Hamilton View. Tan 141 D4
Hamilton Way. Green 45 F3
Hamilton Way. Pres 233 E1
Hamiltonhill Rd. Glasg 97 D2
Hamlet. E Kil 160 A3
Hampden Dr. Glasg 137 D4
Hampden La. Glasg 137 D4
Hampden Terr. Glasg 137 D4
Hampden Way. Ren 94 B1
Hangingshaw Pl. Glasg 137 E4
Hanover Cl. Glasg 137 D4
Hanover Ct. Glasg 117 E4
Hanover Ct. Pais 114 A3
Hanover Gdns. Bish 78 A1
Hanover Gdns. Pais 114 E2
Hanover St. Glasg 117 E4
Hanover St. Helen 25 C4
Hanson St. Glasg 117 F4
Hapland Ave. Glasg 115 E1
Hapland Rd. Glasg 115 E1
Happyhills. W Kil 190 B3
Haran Rd. Bonh 19 F1
Harbour Ind Est. Ard 205 E1
Harbour La. Pais 113 F3
Harbour Pl. Ard 205 D1
Harbour Rd. Ard 216 A4
Harbour Rd. Irvine 219 D1
Harbour Rd. Pais 113 F3
Harbour Rd. Troon 229 D2
Harbour St. Ard 216 A4
Harbour St. Ayr 235 F1
Harbour St. Irvine 219 D1
Harbour St. Salt 216 C4
Harburn Pl. Ard 205 D1
Harburn Pl. Glasg 76 C1
Harburn Rd. Glasg 94 C3
Harcourt Dr. Glasg 118 A4
Hardacres. Lan 215 D3
Hardgate Dr. Glasg 115 E4
Hardgate Gdns. Glasg 115 E4
Hardgate Pl. Glasg 115 E4
Hardgate Rd. Glasg 115 E4
Hardie Ave. Glasg 138 B4
Hardie Cres. Fall 8 B2
Hardie Ct. Stir 7 E2
Hardie St. Alex 27 E4
Hardie St. Ham 162 A1
Hardie St. Mother 163 F4
Hardie St. Udd 161 E4
Hardmuir Gdns. Kirk 58 C1
Hardmuir Rd. Kirk 58 C1
Hardridge Ave. Glasg 115 F1
Hardridge Pl. Glasg 115 F1
Hardridge Rd. Glasg 115 F1
Hardy Hill. Helen 17 D1
Harebell Pl. Ayr 239 D2
Harefield Dr. Glasg 95 D3
Harelaw Ave. Barr 134 B1
Harelaw Ave. Glasg 136 C2
Harelaw Ave. Neil 154 B3
Harelaw Ave. P Glasg 68 B4
Harelaw Cres. Pais 133 E4
Hareleeshill Rd. Lark 185 E1
Hareshaw Dr. Milnk 223 D3
Hareshaw Gdns. Kilmk 223 D3
Harestanes Gdns. Kirk 59 D1
Harestanes Rd. Car 201 F2
Harestone Cres. Wish 165 E1
Harestone Rd. Wish 165 E1
Harhill St. Glasg 116 A4
Harkins Ave. Udd 161 E4
Harkness Ave. M of C 58 A3
Harland Cotts. Glasg 95 E2
Harland St. Glasg 95 E2
Harlaw Gdns. Bish 78 B1
Harley Cl. Falk 42 A4
Harley Pl. Salt 205 F1
Harley St. Glasg 116 B3
Harling Dr. Troon 229 E1
Harmetray St. Glasg 97 E3
Harmony Ct. Glasg 116 A4
Harmony Pl. Glasg 116 A4
Harmony Row. Glasg 116 A4
Harmony Sq. Glasg 116 A4
Harmsworth St. Glasg 95 F1
Harper Cres. Wish 165 F2
Harperland Dr. Kilmk 227 E4
Harport St. Glasg 135 F2
Harriet Pl. Glasg 136 C1
Harriet Rd. Kilmk 223 D1
Harriet St. Glasg 138 A4
Harrington Rd. E Kil 159 F1
Harris Cl. Newt M 156 A1
Harris Cres. O Kill 73 D3
Harris Ct. All 10 A3
Harris Ct. Irvine 225 E4

Harris Dr. O Kill 73 D3
Harris Gdns. O Kill 73 E3
Harris Pl. Kilmk 223 D3
Harris Quadrant. Wish 165 F3
Harris Rd. Glasg 76 C1
Harris Rd. O Kill 73 E3
Harris Rd. P Glasg 69 D4
Harris Terr. Irvine 225 E4
Harrison Dr. Glasg 116 A3
Harrison Pl. Falk 41 F3
Harrow Ct. Glasg 74 C2
Harrow Pl. Glasg 74 C2
Hart St. Glasg 118 C3
Hart St. Lin 112 A4
Hart Wynd. Bann 7 F1
Hartfield Cres. Neil 154 C4
Hartfield Gdns. Dumb 50 A2
Hartfield Rd. Ayr 238 C3
Hartfield Terr. Alla 167 D4
Hartfield Terr. Pais 114 A4
Harthall. Ayr 236 C1
Harthill Rd. Blac 107 E1
Hartlaw Cres. Glasg 115 D3
Hartree Ave. Clyde 94 C4
Hartstone Pl. Glasg 135 D4
Hartstone Rd. Glasg 135 D4
Hartstone Terr. Glasg 135 D4
Hartwood Gdns. Shot 146 A1
Hartwood Rd. Shot 145 F1
Harvest Dr. Mother 163 E2
Harvey Gdns. Ard 205 E2
Harvey Sq. Loch 129 E1
Harvey St. Ard 205 E2
Harvey St. Glasg 97 E1
Harvey Terr. Loch 129 E1
Harvey Way. Hat 142 B4
Harvey Wynd. Stir 2 A1
Harvie Ave. Newt M 156 B3
Harvie St. Glasg 116 B3
Harwood Gdns. Muir 81 D2
Harwood St. Glasg 118 C4
Hastie St. Glasg 96 B1
Hastings. E Kil 180 A4
Hatfield Ct. Kil 89 E4
Hatfield Dr. Glasg 96 A3
Hathaway Dr. Glasg 136 A1
Hathaway La. Glasg 96 C3
Hathaway St. Glasg 96 C3
Hathersage Ave. Glasg 120 A3
Hathersage Dr. Glasg 120 A3
Hathersage Gdns. Glasg 120 A3
Hatton Gdns. Glasg 115 D2
Hatton Pl. Holy 143 E1
Hatton Terr. Holy 143 E1
Hattonhill. Holy 143 E1
Hattonrigg Rd. Hat 142 A4
Haugh Gdns. Falk 24 A1
Haugh Pl. Ham 162 C1
Haugh Rd. Glasg 116 B4
Haugh Rd. Kils 60 B4
Haugh Rd. Stir 2 A1
Haugh St. Falk 24 A1
Haughburn Pl. Glasg 135 D4
Haughburn Rd. Glasg 135 D4
Haughburn Terr. Glasg 135 E4
Haughton Ave. Kils 60 C4
Haughview Rd. Mother 163 D3
Haupland Rd. Ard 205 D3
Havelock La. Glasg 96 B1
Havelock Pk. E Kil 159 D1
Havelock Pl. Helen 16 C1
Havelock St. Glasg 96 B1
Havelock St. Helen 16 C1
Haven Pk. E Kil 179 F3
Havoc Rd. Dumb 49 E2
Hawbank Rd. E Kil 159 D2
Hawbank
  Roundabout. E Kil 159 D1
Hawick Ave. Pais 113 D1
Hawick Cres. Lark 185 D1
Hawick Dr. Coat 122 B2
Hawick St. Clyde 94 C4
Hawick St. Wish 165 E3
Hawkhead Ave. Pais 114 B1
Hawkhead Rd. Pais 114 A2
Hawkhill Ave. Ayr 236 A1
Hawkhill Avenue La. Ayr ... 236 A1
Hawkhill Dr. Steven 206 C1
Hawkhill Pl. Steven 206 C1
Hawkhill Rd. All 10 B3
Hawksland Wlk. Ham 162 C1
Hawkwood. E Kil 180 B3
Hawkwood Rd. Glenm 102 C2
Hawley Rd. Falk 42 B2
Hawthorn Ave. Bear 76 A4
Hawthorn Ave. Bish 98 A4
Hawthorn Ave. Dumb 49 D3
Hawthorn Ave. Inch 93 F4
Hawthorn Ave. John 112 A1
Hawthorn Ave. Klrk 79 E3
Hawthorn Ave. New 166 B3
Hawthorn Ave. Pres 236 B4
Hawthorn Cres. Beith 171 D4
Hawthorn Cres. Fall 8 B2
Hawthorn Cres. Inch 93 F4
Hawthorn Cres. Stir 1 C1
Hawthorn Ct. Kilw 207 F1

Hawthorn Ct. Newt M	157	F3	Headlesscross Rd. Shot	147	F1	Herma St. Glasg	96	C4	Highfield Dr. Glasg	138	B2
Hawthorn Dr. Aird	123	E3	Headrigg Gdns. W Kil	190	B3	Hermes Way. Holy	142	C3	Highfield Dr. Newt M	157	E4
Hawthorn Dr. Ayr	239	E2	Headrigg Rd. W Kil	190	B3	Hermiston Ave. Glasg	119	E3	Highfield Dr. Steven	206	C1
Hawthorn Dr. Bank	38	C1	Headsmuir Ave. Car	187	E1	Hermiston Pl. Glasg	119	E3	Highfield Gr. Kirk	58	C1
Hawthorn Dr. Barr	155	E4	Heath Ave. Bish	98	A4	Hermiston Pl. Holy	143	D3	Highfield Pl. E Kil	159	F2
Hawthorn Dr. Coat	122	B3	Heath Ave. Klrk	79	E2	Hermiston Rd. Glasg	119	D3	Highfield Pl. Glasg	96	A3
Hawthorn Dr. Duni	21	E2	Heath Rd. Lark	185	D2	Hermitage Ave. Glasg	95	E3	Highfield Pl. Irvine	219	F3
Hawthorn Dr. East	127	F3	Heathcliffe Ave. Udd	140	B3	Hermitage Cres. Coat	122	A2	Highfield Rd. Ayr	239	D2
Hawthorn Dr. Falk	41	F2	Heathcot Ave. Glasg	74	C1	Hermitage Rd. B of A	2	C3	Highfield Rd. Kirk	58	C1
Hawthorn Dr. Fall	8	B2	Heathcot Pl. Glasg	74	C1	Herndon Ct. Newt M	157	D3	Highfield Rd. Lark	185	D2
Hawthorn Dr. Holy	143	D2	Heather Ave. Alex	27	F3	Heron Ct. Dunt	74	A3	Highfield St. Kilw	207	F2
Hawthorn Dr. Shot	147	E2	Heather Ave. Barr	134	A3	Heron Pl. John	131	E4	Highholm Ave. P Glasg	47	D1
Hawthorn Dr. Steven	206	C2	Heather Ave. Bear	75	F4	Heron Rd. Green	45	D2	Highholm St. P Glasg	47	D1
Hawthorn Dr. Wish	165	E2	Heather Ave. Dunt	74	A4	Heron Way. Ren	94	B1	Highland Ave. Udd	161	E4
Hawthorn Gdns. Hat	142	B2	Heather Ave. Holy	143	D3	Heronswood. Kilw	207	F3	Highland Dr. Lar	23	E2
Hawthorn Gdns. Lark	185	E1	Heather Ave. Shi	66	B3	Herries Rd. Glasg	116	B1	Highland Ave. Udd	161	E4
Hawthorn Gdns. Newt M	157	F3	Heather Dr. Klrk	79	D2	Herriet St. Glasg	116	C2	Highland Dykes Cres. Bon	40	A3
Hawthorn Gdns. Pres	236	B4	Heather Gdns. Klrk	79	D2	Herriot Ave. Kilb	149	D2	Highland Dykes Dr. Bon	40	A3
Hawthorn Gr. Law	186	C3	Heather Pk. Ayr	239	E2	Herriot St. Coat	121	F4	Highland La. Glasg	116	B4
Hawthorn Hill. Ham	162	C1	Heather Pl. John	112	A1	Herschell St. Glasg	95	F3	Highland Pk. Kils	36	B1
Hawthorn Pl. Alla	167	D4	Heather Pl. Kilmk	227	E4	Hertford Ave. Glasg	96	A3	Highland Pl. Kils	36	B1
Hawthorn Pl. Troon	229	E2	Heather Pl. Klrk	79	D2	Hervey St. All	10	A4	Highland Rd. Miln	55	D1
Hawthorn Pl. Udd	161	F4	Heather Rd. Lan	214	A3	Hestan Pl. Kilmk	223	D3	Highlandman's Rd. Rhu	15	F3
Hawthorn Quadrant. Glasg	97	E3	Heather Row. Car	187	F2	Heugh St. Falk	42	A2	Highstonehall Rd. Ham	162	A1
Hawthorn Rd. Cumb	62	C2	Heather St. Cald	105	D3	Hewett Cres. Hous	91	E1	Highthorne Cres. W Kil	190	C3
Hawthorn Rd. Inch	93	F4	Heather Way. Holy	143	D2	Hexham Gdns. Glasg	116	B1	Hilary Cres. Ayr	239	D3
Hawthorn Rd. Newt M	157	F3	Heatherbank Wlk. Aird	122	B4	Heyford Pl. Cam	6	B3	Hilary Dr. Glasg	119	F3
Hawthorn Sq. Kilmk	227	E4	Heatherbrae. Bish	77	F1	Heys St. Barr	134	B1	Hilda Cres. Glasg	98	C2
Hawthorn St. Clyde	74	A2	Heatherdale Gdns. Bank	39	F4	Hibernia St. Green	45	E2	Hill Ave. Newt M	156	B2
Hawthorn St. Glasg	97	E3	Heatherhouse Rd. Irvine	224	A4	Hickman St. Glasg	117	E1	Hill Cres. Newt M	157	F3
Hawthorn St. Lennox	57	E1	Heatherstane Bank. Irvine	220	B1	Hickory Cres. Tan	141	E4	Hill Dr. Eagle	178	C2
Hawthorn Terr. E Kil	180	A3	Heatherstane Way. Irvine	220	B1	Hickory St. Glasg	97	F3	Hill House Rd. Bank	39	F4
Hawthorn Terr. Tan	141	D4	Heathery Knowe. E Kil	180	C4	High Avon St. Lark	184	C2	Hill Interchange. Irvine	219	F3
Hawthorn Way. Inch	93	F4	Heathery Rd. Wish	164	C2	High Banton Rd. Kils	37	E2	Hill La. Ard	205	E1
Hawthorn Way. M of C	58	B3	Heatheryknowe Rd. Coat	120	C4	High Barholm. Kilbar	111	D2	Hill Pl. All	10	A4
Hawthorn Wlk. Glasg	138	B3	Heatheryknowe Rd. Glasg	120	C4	High Barrwood Rd. Kils	60	C4	Hill Pl. Ard	205	E1
Hawthornden Gdns. Glasg	76	C1	Heathfield Ave. Muir	81	D1	High Beeches. E Kil	158	C4	Hill Pl. Hat	141	F2
Hawthorne Pl. Gour	44	A3	Heathfield Dr. Miln	55	D2	High Blantyre Rd. Ham	161	F3	Hill Pl. Holy	143	E1
Hawthorne Pl. Lar	23	E1	Heathfield Rd. Ayr	236	B2	High Burnside Ave. Coat	121	F3	Hill Pl. Shot	146	C3
Hawthornhill Rd. Dumb	49	E3	Heathfield St. Glasg	119	E4	High Calside. Pais	113	F2	Hill Rd. Ash	199	F3
Hay Ave. Bishop	72	B2	Heathfield. Wish	186	A4	High Carnegie Rd. P Glasg	68	C4	Hill Rd. Cumb	61	F1
Hay Dr. John	112	A2	Heathpark. Pres	236	B3	High Coats. Coat	122	A4	Hill Rd. East	127	E3
Hay Hill. Ayr	236	C1	Heathside Rd. Glasg	136	B4	High Common Rd. E Kil	181	D4	Hill Rd. How	130	C3
Hay St. Green	45	F2	Heathwood Dr. Glasg	136	A2	High Craigends. Kils	60	C4	Hill Rd. Kils	36	B1
Hayburn Cres. Glasg	96	A3	Hecla Ave. Glasg	74	C2	High Flender Rd. Newt M	157	E3	Hill Rd. Stone	198	C1
Hayburn Gate. Glasg	96	A1	Hecla Pl. Glasg	74	C2	High Glencairn St. Kilmk	227	F4	Hill St. Alex	27	E3
Hayburn La. Glasg	96	A2	Hecla Sq. Glasg	74	C2	High Graighall Rd. Glasg	97	D1	Hill St. All	10	A4
Hayburn St. Glasg	96	A1	Hector Rd. Glasg	136	B4	High Kirk View. John	111	F1	Hill St. Ard	205	E1
Hayfield. Falk	42	B4	Hedges The. Falk	41	F3	High Mains Ave. Dumb	50	B2	Hill St. Cald	104	C3
Hayfield Rd. Falk	42	B4	Heggies Ave. P Glasg	69	D4	High Meadow. Car	188	B1	Hill St. Chap	123	E1
Hayfield St. Glasg	117	E2	Heights Rd. Blac	107	E2	High Mill Rd. Car	188	A1	Hill St. Dumb	49	E2
Hayfield Terr. Bank	39	F4	Helen St. Glasg	116	A3	High Overton St. Ash	200	B2	Hill St. Glasg	97	D1
Hayhill Rd. Thorn	179	E4	Helen St. Bonh	27	F1	High Parks Cres. Ham	183	E3	Hill St. Green	46	A2
Hayle Gdns. Muir	80	C2	Helen's Terr. Kilw	207	F1	High Parksail. Ersk	93	E4	Hill St. Ham	161	F2
Haylnn St. Glasg	95	F1	Helena Pl. Newt M	157	F4	High Patrick St. Ham	162	C2	Hill St. Irvine	219	E1
Haymarket St. Glasg	118	C4	Helensburgh Dr. Glasg	95	F3	High Pleasance. Lark	185	D2	Hill St. Kilmk	222	C1
Hayocks Rd. Steven	206	C1	Helenslea. Glasg	139	F2	High Rd. Ayr	236	C2	Hill St. Lark	185	D1
Haypark Rd. Bank	39	E3	Helenslea Pl. Hat	141	F2	High Rd. Mother	163	F4	Hill St. Salt	216	C4
Haystack Pl. Klrk	79	F2	Helenslee Cres. Dumb	49	E3	High Rd. Pais	113	E2	Hill St. Stir	7	D2
Hayston Cres. Glasg	97	D3	Helenslee Ct. Dumb	49	E2	High Rd. Salt	206	A1	Hill St. Wish	165	D2
Hayston Rd. Klrk	79	D4	Helenslee Rd. Dumb	49	E2	High Rd. Steven	206	B1	Hill Street Ind Est. Ard	205	E1
Hayston St. Glasg	97	D3	Helenslee Rd. Lang	70	B4	High Row. Bish	78	A3	Hill Terr. Holy	143	E1
Haywood St. Glasg	97	E3	Helenvale Ct. Glasg	118	B3	High St. Air	14	B2	Hill View. Dumb	50	C1
Hazel Ave. Ard	205	E2	Helenvale St. Glasg	118	B2	High St. Aird	122	C4	Hill View. E Kil	180	C4
Hazel Ave. Bear	76	A4	Helmsdale Ave. Udd	140	B2	High St. All	10	A3	Hill View Rd. Lan	214	A2
Hazel Ave. Dumb	49	D3	Helmsdale Cl. Glasg	139	E3	High St. Ayr	238	C4	Hillary Ave. Glasg	138	B3
Hazel Ave. Glasg	136	C2	Hemlock St. Glasg	95	F4	High St. Bon	40	A3	Hillary Rd. Lar	23	F1
Hazel Ave. John	112	A1	Hemmingen Ct. Car	187	E2	High St. Car	187	F1	Hillbank Rd. Kilmk	222	C4
Hazel Ave. Kilmk	227	E4	Hemphill View. Cross	221	F2	High St. Clack	10	C2	Hillbank St. Bonh	27	F2
Hazel Ave. Klrk	79	E3	Henderland Rd. Bear	75	F1	High St. Dumb	49	F2	Hillbank St. Glasg	138	A4
Hazel Bank. M of C	58	A2	Henderson Ave. All	10	A4	High St. Falk	42	A2	Hillcrest Ave. Coat	122	B3
Hazel Cres. Duni	21	E2	Henderson Ave. Glasg	139	F3	High St. Glasg	117	E4	Hillcrest Ave. Cumb	82	C4
Hazel Dene. Bish	98	A4	Henderson Pl. Alva	5	D4	High St. Glasg	138	A4	Hillcrest Ave. Glasg	136	C2
Hazel Gdns. Mother	163	F2	Henderson Rd. Troon	229	E1	High St. Green	45	F3	Hillcrest Ave. Glasg	139	D4
Hazel Gr. Falk	42	B4	Henderson St. Aird	123	D4	High St. Holy	143	F2	Hillcrest Ave. Mother	164	C2
Hazel Gr. Kilw	208	A2	Henderson St. B of A	2	A4	High St. Irvine	219	E1	Hillcrest Ave. Pais	133	E3
Hazel Gr. Klrk	79	E3	Henderson St. Clyde	94	C4	High St. John	111	F1	Hillcrest Ct. Cumb	61	F1
Hazel Gr. Law	186	C3	Henderson St. Coat	121	F3	High St. Kil	69	E1	Hillcrest Dr. All	10	B3
Hazel Path. Cle	144	A1	Henderson St. Glasg	96	C2	High St. Kilb	149	D2	Hillcrest Dr. Newt M	157	D3
Hazel Pk. Ham	162	C1	Henderson St. Pais	113	E3	High St. Kilmk	223	D1	Hillcrest Dr. Steven	206	C1
Hazel Rd. Bank	38	C1	Henderson Terr. Gour	44	C3	High St. Lan	215	D2	Hillcrest. E Kil	158	B4
Hazel Rd. Cumb	62	B2	Hendry St. Falk	42	A4	High St. Loch	129	E1	Hillcrest. Muir	100	B4
Hazel Terr. Gour	44	B3	Hennings The. N Sau	5	E1	High St. Neil	154	C4	Hillcrest Pl. Bank	39	E4
Hazel Terr. Tan	141	D4	Henrietta St. Glasg	95	E2	High St. Pais	113	F2	Hillcrest Pl. Kilw	207	F2
Hazelbank Gdns. Stir	2	A1	Henry Bell Gn. E Kil	180	C4	High St. Ren	94	C2	Hillcrest Rd. Bear	75	F2
Hazelbank. Holy	143	D3	Henry Bell St. Helen	16	C1	High St. Shot	146	C2	Hillcrest Rd. Falk	41	F1
Hazelbank. Plains	103	F2	Henry St. Alva	5	D3	High St. Slam	86	A4	Hillcrest Rd. Glasg	139	E4
Hazelbank Wlk. Aird	122	B4	Henry St. Barr	134	A2	High St. Stew	195	F1	Hillcrest Rd. Kils	59	F4
Hazeldean Cres. Wish	165	E3	Hepburn Hill. Ham	183	E4	High Station Rd. Falk	42	A2	Hillcrest St. Miln	55	D1
Hazelden Rd. Newt M	177	E4	Hepburn Rd. Glasg	115	D4	High View Gr. Shi	66	B3	Hillcrest Terr. Udd	141	D2
Hazeldene La. Lark	185	E1	Herald Ave. Glasg	75	E1	High Whitehills Rd. E Kil	180	C3	Hillcrest View. Lark	185	D2
Hazelhead. E Kil	160	A1	Herald Gr. Mother	163	E2	Highburgh Ave. Lan	215	D2	Hillcroft Terr. Bish	97	F4
Hazellea Dr. Glasg	136	C2	Herald St. Ard	216	A4	Highburgh Ct. Lan	215	D2	Hillend Cres. Dunt	73	F4
Hazelmere Rd. Kil	89	D4	Herald Way. Ren	94	B1	Highburgh Dr. Glasg	138	B3	Hillend Cres. Newt M	157	E3
Hazelton. Mother	163	E3	Herbert St. Glasg	96	C2	Highburgh Rd. Glasg	96	B1	Hillend Dr. Green	46	B2
Hazelwood Ave. B of W	110	C4	Herbertson Cres. Irvine	219	E2	Highcraig Ave. John	111	E1	Hillend Pl. Green	46	B2
Hazelwood Ave. Newt M	156	C2	Herbertson St. Glasg	117	D3	Highcroft Ave. Glasg	137	E3	Hillend Rd. Glasg	97	D4
Hazelwood Ave. Pais	132	C4	Herbertson St. Udd	161	F4	Highcross Ave. Coat	121	E2	Hillend Rd. Glasg	138	A3
Hazelwood Dr. Udd	161	E4	Hercules Way. Ren	94	B1	Highet Gdns. Irvine	219	D2	Hillend Rd. Newt M	157	E3
Hazelwood Gdns. Glasg	138	B2	Herdshill Ave. Shi	66	B3	Highet St. Kilmk	222	C1	Hillfoot. Alex	27	E1
Hazelwood La. B of W	110	B4	Heriot Ave. Pais	132	C4	Highfield Ave. Kilmk	223	D2	Hillfoot Ave. Bear	75	F3
Hazelwood Rd. Ayr	238	C3	Heriot Cres. Bish	78	A2	Highfield Ave. Kirk	58	C1	Hillfoot Ave. Dumb	50	B2
Hazelwood Rd. B of W	110	B3	Heriot Rd. Klrk	79	E2	Highfield Ave. Pais	133	E4	Hillfoot Ave. Glasg	138	A4
Hazelwood Rd. Glasg	116	B2	Heritage Ct. Newt M	156	C3	Highfield Ave. Pres	236	B4	Hillfoot Ave. Wish	165	E4
Hazlitt St. Glasg	97	D3	Heritage Dr. Sten	24	A2	Highfield Cres. Mother	164	A4	Hillfoot Cres. Ayr	239	D3
Head St. Beith	171	E4	Heritage View. Coat	121	F4	Highfield Cres. Pais	133	E4	Hillfoot Cres. Wish	165	E4
Headhouse Ct. E Kil	180	B4	Heritage Way. Coat	121	F4	Highfield Dr. Glasg	96	A3	Hillfoot Dr. Bear	75	F3
Headhouse Gn. E Kil	180	C4							Hillfoot Dr. Coat	121	E2

Hillfoot Dr. How	130	C3
Hillfoot Dr. Wish	165	E4
Hillfoot Gdns. Tan	140	C4
Hillfoot Gdns. Wish	165	E4
Hillfoot. Hous	111	F4
Hillfoot Rd. Aird	123	D3
Hillfoot Rd. Ayr	239	E3
Hillfoot St. Glasg	118	A4
Hillfoot Terr. Car	188	A1
Hillfoots Rd. B of A	2	C2
Hillhead Ave. Bank	38	C2
Hillhead Ave. Car	188	A1
Hillhead Ave. Glasg	138	A2
Hillhead Ave. Holy	143	D1
Hillhead Ave. Muir	80	C1
Hillhead Cres. Ham	161	F2
Hillhead Cres. Holy	143	D1
Hillhead Dr. Aird	123	D3
Hillhead Dr. Falk	41	F1
Hillhead Dr. Holy	143	D1
Hillhead Pl. Glasg	138	A2
Hillhead Rd. Glasg	98	B4
Hillhead Rd. Kirk	58	C1
Hillhead Rd. Steven	206	C2
Hillhead Sq. Kilmk	222	C2
Hillhead St. Glasg	96	B1
Hillhead St. Miln	55	D1
Hillhead Terr. Ham	161	F2
Hillhouse Cres. Ham	161	F2
Hillhouse Farm Gate. Lan	214	C3
Hillhouse Farm Rd. Lan	214	C2
Hillhouse Gate. Car	202	B4
Hillhouse Gdns. Troon	229	E3
Hillhouse Pl. Stew	195	E1
Hillhouse Rd. Ham	161	F2
Hillhouse Rd. Troon	229	E3
Hillhouse St. Glasg	98	A3
Hillhouse Terr. Ham	161	F2
Hillhouseridge Rd. Shot	146	B3
Hillington Gdns. Glasg	115	E2
Hillington Park Cir. Glasg	115	E3
Hillington Quadrant. Glasg	115	D3
Hillington Rd. Ren	94	C1
Hillington Rd S. Glasg	115	D3
Hillington Terr. Glasg	115	D3
Hillkirk Pl. Glasg	97	F2
Hillkirk St. Glasg	97	F2
Hillmoss. Kilm	222	A4
Hillneuk Ave. Bear	76	A3
Hillneuk Dr. Bear	76	A3
Hillocks Pl. Troon	229	F4
Hillpark Ave. Pais	113	E1
Hillpark Cres. Bann	7	E1
Hillpark Dr. Bann	7	E1
Hillpark Dr. Glasg	136	B3
Hillpark Dr. Kilmk	222	C1
Hillpark. Moss	237	F3
Hillpark Rise. Kilw	207	D2
Hillrigg Ave. Aird	123	E4
Hillrigg. Gree	83	E1
Hillsborough Rd. Glasg	119	F3
Hillshaw Foot. Irvine	220	B1
Hillshaw Gn. Irvine	220	B1
Hillside Ave. Alex	27	E2
Hillside Ave. Bear	75	F4
Hillside Ave. Kil	69	E1
Hillside Ave. Newt M	157	E4
Hillside Cotts. Beith	191	F4
Hillside Cotts. Glen	101	F3
Hillside Cres. Coat	121	F2
Hillside Cres. Ham	162	B1
Hillside Cres. Holy	143	E3
Hillside Cres. Neil	154	B4
Hillside Cres. Pres	236	B4
Hillside Ct. Glasg	135	F2
Hillside Ct. Steven	217	E4
Hillside Dr. Barr	134	A2
Hillside Dr. Bear	76	A3
Hillside Dr. Bish	78	A1
Hillside Dr. Blac	107	E2
Hillside Dr. P Glasg	47	D1
Hillside Gr. Barr	134	A1
Hillside Gr. Bish	98	B4
Hillside. Hous	111	F4
Hillside. Kils	60	C2
Hillside. N Sau	5	E1
Hillside Pk. Dunt	74	A3
Hillside Pl. Blac	107	E2
Hillside Pl. Holy	143	E2
Hillside Quadrant. Glasg	136	A3
Hillside Rd. Barr	134	A2
Hillside Rd. Card	26	A1
Hillside Rd. Glasg	136	A3
Hillside Rd. Gour	44	B4
Hillside Rd. Green	46	A1
Hillside Rd. Neil	154	B4
Hillside Rd. Pais	114	A1
Hillside Rd. Steven	217	E4
Hillside Terr. All	10	A4
Hillside Terr. Ham	162	B1
Hillside Terr. M of C	58	A3
Hillside. W Kil	190	B2
Hillswick Cres. Glasg	97	D4
Hilltop Ave. Hat	142	A4
Hilltop Cres. Gour	44	C3
Hilltop Pl. Ayr	239	E2
Hilltop Rd. Gour	44	C3

265
Hilltop Rd. Muir
Invercloy Pl. Kilmk

Hilltop Rd. Muir 80 C1
Hillview Ave. Kils 60 C4
Hillview Ave. Lennox 57 F4
Hillview Cotts. Twe 59 F2
Hillview Cres. Hat 142 A4
Hillview Cres. Lark 185 D1
Hillview Cres. Tan 140 C4
Hillview Dr. B of A 2 A3
Hillview Dr. Helen 16 B2
Hillview Dr. Newt M 157 F4
Hillview Dr. Udd 140 B1
Hillview Gdns. Bish 98 A4
Hillview. Gree 83 F1
Hillview. Kils 37 E2
Hillview Pl. Fall 8 B2
Hillview Pl. Newt M 156 B2
Hillview Pl. Newt M 157 F4
Hillview Rd. B of W 110 C4
Hillview Rd. Bon 40 B2
Hillview Rd. John 112 B1
Hillview Rd. Lar 23 E2
Hillview St. Glasg 118 C3
Hillview Terr. All 10 B3
Hilton. Cowie 12 C4
Hilton Cres. All 10 B4
Hilton Ct. Bish 78 A2
Hilton Gdns. Glasg 95 F4
Hilton Pk. Bish 77 F2
Hilton Rd. All 10 B4
Hilton Rd. Bish 78 A2
Hilton Rd. Miln 54 C1
Hilton Terr. Bish 77 F2
Hilton Terr. Fall 8 B2
Hilton Terr. Glasg 95 F4
Hilton Terr. Glasg 138 C2
Hiltonbank St. Ham 162 A2
Hindog Pl. Dalry 191 D4
Hindsland Rd. Lark 185 D1
Hinshaw St. Glasg 97 D2
Hinshelwood Dr. Glasg 116 A3
Hinshelwood Pl. Glasg 116 A3
Hirsel Pl. Udd 141 D1
Hirst Gdns. Shot 146 B3
Hirst Rd. East 126 B2
Hirst Rd. Sals 126 B2
Hirstrigg Cotts. Sals 126 A2
Hobart Cres. Clyde 73 E3
Hobart Quadrant. Wish 165 F2
Hobart Rd. E Kil 180 B4
Hobart St. Glasg 97 D2
Hobden St. Glasg 98 A2
Hoddam Ave. Glasg 138 A2
Hoddam Terr. Glasg 138 A2
Hodge St. Falk 42 A2
Hoey Dr. Wish 186 B4
Hogan Ct. Dunt 73 F3
Hogarth Ave. Glasg 118 B4
Hogarth Ave. Salt 205 F1
Hogarth Cres. Glasg 118 B4
Hogarth Dr. Glasg 118 B4
Hogarth Gdns. Glasg 118 B4
Hogg Ave. John 111 F1
Hogg Rd. Chap 123 E2
Hogg St. Aird 123 D4
Hogganfield St. Glasg 98 B1
Holbourne Pl. Men 4 A4
Hole Farm Rd. Green 45 E2
Holeburn La. Glasg 136 B3
Holeburn Rd. Glasg 136 B3
Holehills Dr. Aird 103 D1
Holehills Pl. Aird 103 D1
Holehouse Brae. Neil 154 B4
Holehouse Dr. Glasg 95 D3
Holehouse Dr. Kilb 149 D2
Holehouse Rd. Eagle 178 C3
Holehouse Rd. Kilmk 228 A4
Holehouse Rd. Thorn 179 D4
Holehouse Terr. Neil 154 B4
Holland St. Glasg 117 D4
Hollandbush Ave. Bank 38 C2
Hollandbush Cres. Bank 38 C2
Hollandhurst Rd. Coat 101 F1
Hollinwell Rd. Glasg 76 B1
Hollow Pk. Ayr 239 D1
Hollowglen Rd. Glasg 119 D3
Hollows Ave. Pais 132 C4
Hollows Cres. Pais 132 C4
Holly Ave. M of C 58 A3
Holly Ave. Sten 23 F2
Holly Bank. Ayr 239 E3
Holly Dr. Dumb 49 D3
Holly Dr. Glasg 98 A2
Holly Gr. Bank 38 C1
Holly Gr. Holy 142 C3
Holly Pl. John 132 A4
Holly Pl. Kilmk 222 B1
Holly St. Aird 123 E3
Holly St. Clyde 74 A2
Hollybank Pl. Glasg 139 D2
Hollybank St. Glasg 98 A1
Hollybrook St. Glasg 117 D1
Hollybush Ave. Pais 133 D4
Hollybush Rd. Glasg 114 C3
Hollymount. Bear 75 F1
Holm Ave. Pais 113 F1
Holm Ave. Udd 140 C4
Holm Cres. Fen 213 D2
Holm Crest. Cro 201 D1
Holm Gdns. Hat 142 B2
Holm La. E Kil 159 F1
Holm Pl. Lark 184 C1
Holm Pl. Lin 112 A4
Holm Place. Lark 184 C1
Holm Rd. Cro 201 D1
Holm St. Car 187 F1
Holm St. Glasg 117 D4
Holm St. Holy 143 D2
Holm St. Stew 211 F4
Holmbank Ave. Glasg 136 B4
Holmbrae Ave. Tan 140 C4
Holmbrae Rd. Tan 140 C4
Holmbyre Rd. Glasg 137 E1
Holmbyre Terr. Glasg 137 E1
Holmes Ave. Ren 94 B1
Holmes Cres. Kilmk 227 E3
Holmes Farm Rd. Kilmk 227 E3
Holmes Quadrant. Hat 142 A2
Holmes Rd. Kilmk 227 E3
Holmes Village. Kilmk 227 E3
Holmfauld Rd. Glasg 95 F1
Holmfauldhead Dr. Glasg 115 F4
Holmfauldhead Pl. Glasg 115 F4
Holmfield. Kirk 79 F4
Holmhead Cres. Glasg 137 D3
Holmhead. Kilb 170 A4
Holmhead Pl. Glasg 137 D3
Holmhead Rd. Glasg 137 D3
Holmhill Ave. Glasg 139 D2
Holmhills Dr. Glasg 138 C2
Holmhills Gdns. Glasg 138 C2
Holmhills Gr. Glasg 138 C2
Holmhills Pl. Glasg 138 C2
Holmhills Rd. Glasg 138 C2
Holmhills Terr. Glasg 138 C2
Holmlands Pl. Kilmk 227 E3
Holmlea Dr. Kilmk 227 F3
Holmlea Pl. Kilmk 227 F3
Holmlea Rd. Glasg 137 D4
Holmpark. Bishop 72 A2
Holmquarry Rd. Kilmk 227 F3
Holms Ave. Irvine 220 B1
Holms Cres. Ersk 72 C1
Holms Pl. Muir 100 C4
Holms Rd. Kilb 170 A3
Holmscroft Ave. Green 45 F2
Holmscroft St. Green 45 F3
Holmscroft Way. Green 45 F2
Holmston Cres. Ayr 239 E4
Holmston Dr. Ayr 239 E3
Holmston Rd. Ayr 239 E4
Holmswood Ave. Udd 140 B1
Holmwood Ave. Udd 140 C4
Holmwood Gdns. Udd 140 C3
Holmwood Gr. Glasg 137 D2
Holton Cres. N Sau 5 E1
Holton Sq. N Sau 5 E1
Holyknowe Cres. Lennox 57 F4
Holyknowe Rd. Lennox 57 F4
Holyoake Ct. Hurl 228 C4
Holyrood Cres. Glasg 96 C1
Holyrood Pl. Sten 23 F2
Holyrood Quadrant. Glasg 96 C1
Holyrood St. Ham 162 A3
Holytown Rd. Holy 142 C3
Holywell St. Glasg 118 A3
Home Farm Cotts. Den 39 F3
Home Farm Rd. Ayr 239 D1
Home St. Lan 215 E2
Homer Pl. Holy 142 C3
Homesteads The. Stir 6 B4
Homeston Ave. Udd 141 D2
Honeybank Cres. Car 188 A2
Honeybog Rd. Glasg 114 C3
Honeycomb Pl. Ash 200 B2
Honeysuckle La. Bonh 27 F4
Honeysuckle Pk. Ayr 239 D1
Honeywell Cres. Chap 123 F1
Hood Ct. Helen 16 A1
Hood St. Clyde 74 B1
Hood St. Green 45 F3
Hookney Terr. Den 21 E1
Hope Ave. Kil 89 F1
Hope Cres. Lark 185 D2
Hope St. Ayr 238 C4
Hope St. Car 188 A1
Hope St. Falk 42 A3
Hope St. Glasg 117 D4
Hope St. Green 45 F2
Hope St. Ham 162 C2
Hope St. Hat 142 B3
Hope St. Helen 25 C4
Hope St. Lan 215 D2
Hope St. Mother 163 F4
Hope St. New 166 A2
Hope St. Stir 1 C1
Hopefield Ave. Glasg 96 B3
Hopehill Rd. Glasg 97 D2
Hopeman Ave. Glasg 135 F2
Hopeman Dr. Glasg 135 F2
Hopeman. Ersk 73 D2
Hopeman Path. Glasg 135 F3
Hopeman Rd. Glasg 135 F2
Hopeman St. Glasg 135 F2
Hopepark Terr. Bon 39 F3
Hopetoun Bank. Irvine 220 B1
Hopetoun Dr. B of A 2 A4
Hopetoun Pl. Glasg 76 C1
Hopkin's Brae. Kirk 58 B1
Horatius St. Mother 142 A1
Hornal Rd. Udd 141 D2
Hornbeam Dr. Clyde 74 A2
Hornbeam Rd. Cumb 62 C3
Hornbeam Rd. Tan 141 D4
Horndean Cres. Glasg 99 E1
Horndean Ct. Bish 78 A2
Horne St. Glasg 97 F3
Hornock Rd. Coat 101 F1
Hornshill Dr. Cle 144 A1
Hornshill Farm Rd. Stepps 99 F3
Hornshill St. Glasg 98 A2
Horsbrugh Ave. Kils 36 B1
Horsburgh St. Glasg 99 E1
Horse Shoe Rd. Bear 75 F2
Horsewood Rd. B of W 110 B4
Horslet St. Coat 121 E2
Horslethill Rd. Glasg 96 B2
Horsley Brae. Wish 186 A2
Horton Pl. Helen 17 D2
Hospital Rd. Wish 186 A4
Hospital St. Coat 122 A2
Hospital St. Glasg 117 D2
Hospitland Dr. Lan 215 E2
Hotspur St. Glasg 96 C2
Houldsworth Cres. Alla 167 D4
Houldsworth La. Glasg 116 C4
Houldsworth St. Glasg 116 C4
House O' Muir Rd. Sals 126 A2
Househillmuir Cres. Glasg 135 E4
Househillmuir La. Glasg 135 E4
Househillmuir Pl. Glasg 135 E4
Househillmuir Rd. Glasg 135 D3
Househillwood Cres. Glasg 135 D4
Househillwood Rd. Glasg 135 D3
Housel Ave. Glasg 95 D4
Houston Cres. Dalry 191 D4
Houston Pl. Glasg 116 C3
Houston Pl. John 112 B1
Houston Rd. B of W 90 B1
Houston Rd. Hous 91 D1
Houston Rd. Inch 92 B2
Houston Rd. Kil 89 F4
Houston St. Glasg 116 C3
Houston St. Green 45 F3
Houston St. Ham 162 B1
Houston St. Ren 94 B2
Houston St. Wish 165 E1
Houston Terr. E Kil 159 E1
Houstonfield Quadrant. Hous 91 D1
Houstonfield Rd. Hous 91 D1
Houstoun Ct. John 111 F2
Houstoun Sq. John 111 F2
Howacre. Lan 214 C3
Howard Ave. E Kil 160 A3
Howard Ct. E Kil 160 A3
Howard Ct. Kilmk 227 F4
Howard Park Dr. Kilmk 227 F4
Howard St. Falk 41 F2
Howard St. Glasg 117 E3
Howard St. Kilmk 227 F4
Howard St. Lark 185 E1
Howard St. Pais 114 A2
Howat Cres. Irvine 219 F2
Howat St. Glasg 116 A4
Howatshaws Rd. Dumb 50 A3
Howburn Cres. East 127 F3
Howburn Rd. East 127 E3
Howden Ave. Holy 143 E4
Howden Ave. Kilw 207 F2
Howden Dr. Lin 112 A3
Howden Pl. Holy 143 D3
Howe Rd. Kils 60 B4
Howes St. Coat 122 A2
Howetown. Fish 5 E2
Howford Rd. Glasg 115 D2
Howgate Ave. Glasg 74 C2
Howgate. Kilw 207 E2
Howgate Rd. Ham 183 E4
Howie Bldgs. Newt M 157 F4
Howie Cres. Ros 15 D2
Howie St. Lark 185 D1
Howie's Pl. Falk 41 D2
Howieshill Ave. Glasg 139 D3
Howieshill Rd. Glasg 139 D3
Howlands Rd. Stir 7 D2
Howlet Pl. Ham 162 C1
Howletnest Rd. Aird 123 E3
Howson View. Mother 163 D4
Howth Dr. Glasg 95 F4
Howth Terr. Glasg 95 F4
Hoylake Pk. Udd 140 C1
Hoylake Pl. Glasg 76 C1
Hoylake Sq. Kilw 207 E2
Hozier Cres. Tan 140 C4
Hozier Loan. Lark 185 D2
Hozier Pl. Udd 141 D2
Hozier St. Car 187 F1
Hozier St. Coat 122 A2
Hudson Terr. E Kil 180 B4
Hudson Way. E Kil 180 B4
Hudspeth Ct. Alex 27 E4
Hugh Murray Dr. Glasg 139 E3
Hugh Watt Pl. Kilm 222 A4
Hughenden Dr. Glasg 96 A2
Hughenden Gdns. Glasg 96 A2
Hughenden La. Glasg 96 A2
Hughenden Rd. Glasg 96 A2
Hugo St. Glasg 96 C3
Hulks Rd. Gree 83 E2
Humbie Ct. Newt M 156 C1
Humbie Gate. Newt M 156 C1
Humbie Gr. Newt M 156 C2
Humbie Lawns. Newt M 156 C1
Humbie Rd. Eagle 178 B4
Humbie Rd. Newt M 156 C1
Hume Cres. B of A 2 A3
Hume Ct. B of A 2 A3
Hume Dr. Udd 140 C4
Hume Dr. Udd 141 D2
Hume Pl. E Kil 180 B4
Hume Rd. Cumb 62 A2
Hume St. Clyde 74 A1
Hunter Ave. Salt 205 E1
Hunter Cres. Troon 230 A1
Hunter Dr. Irvine 219 D3
Hunter Gdns. Den 21 E1
Hunter Pl. Kilbar 111 D1
Hunter Pl. Kilw 208 A2
Hunter Pl. Miln 54 C1
Hunter Pl. Shot 146 C3
Hunter Pl. Sten 24 A2
Hunter Rd. Cross 221 F1
Hunter Rd. Glasg 118 B1
Hunter Rd. Ham 162 A3
Hunter Rd. Miln 54 C1
Hunter St. Aird 103 D1
Hunter St. E Kil 159 F1
Hunter St. Glasg 117 F3
Hunter St. Glasg 117 F4
Hunter St. Hat 142 A3
Hunter St. Pais 113 F3
Hunter St. Pres 236 B4
Hunter St. Shot 146 B3
Hunter's Ave. Ayr 236 A2
Hunter's Ave. Dumb 50 B2
Hunter's Cl. Lan 215 D2
Hunterfield Dr. Glasg 138 C3
Hunterhill Ave. Pais 113 F2
Hunterhill Rd. Pais 113 F2
Hunterlees Rd. Glass 198 A2
Hunters Hill Ct. Glasg 97 F3
Hunters Pl. Green 45 F3
Huntersfield Rd. John 111 E1
Huntershill Rd. Bish 97 F4
Huntershill St. Glasg 97 F3
Hunterston Rd. W Kil 190 B3
Hunthill La. Udd 161 D3
Hunthill Pl. Thorn 158 A3
Hunthill Rd. Udd 161 D4
Hunting Lodge Gdns. Ham 163 D1
Huntingdon Rd. Glasg 97 F1
Huntingdon Sq. Glasg 97 F1
Huntingtower Rd. Glasg 119 F2
Huntley Cres. Stir 1 C1
Huntley Gdns. Glasg 96 B2
Huntly Ave. Glasg 136 B1
Huntly Ave. Hat 142 A3
Huntly Ct. Bish 98 A4
Huntly Ct. Kilmk 223 E2
Huntly Dr. Bear 75 F4
Huntly Dr. Coat 121 E2
Huntly Dr. Glasg 139 D2
Huntly Dr. Gour 44 C2
Huntly Path. Muir 81 D1
Huntly Pl. Kilmk 223 E1
Huntly Pl. P Glasg 47 D1
Huntly Quadrant. Wish 165 D3
Huntly Rd. Glasg 96 B2
Huntly Rd. Glasg 114 C4
Huntly Terr. P Glasg 47 D1
Huntly Terr. Pais 114 A1
Huntly Terr. Shot 147 D2
Hurlawcrook Rd. Chapel 180 C1
Hurlawcrook Rd. E Kil 181 D2
Hurlet Cotts. Glasg 134 C3
Hurlet Rd. Pais 134 B4
Hurlford Ave. Glasg 94 C4
Hurlford Rd. Kilmk 228 A3
Hurly Hawkin. Bish 98 B4
Hurworth St. Falk 41 F2
Hutcheson Rd. Glasg 136 A1
Hutcheson St. Glasg 117 E4
Hutchinson Pl. Glasg 139 F2
Hutchinson St. Wish 186 B4
Hutchinson Town Ct. Glasg 117 E2
Hutchison Dr. Bear 76 A1
Hutchison Pl. Coat 121 F3
Hutchison St. Ham 162 B1
Hutton Ave. Hous 111 E4
Hutton Dr. Glasg 115 F4
Hutton Pk. All 10 B4
Huxley St. Glasg 96 C3
Hyacinth Way. Car 201 F4
Hydepark St. Glasg 116 C4
Hyndal Ave. Glasg 115 E1
Hyndford Pl. Lan 215 D2
Hyndford Rd. Lan 215 E1
Hyndland Ave. Glasg 96 A1
Hyndland Rd. Glasg 96 A2
Hyndland St. Glasg 96 B1
Hyndlee Dr. Glasg 115 E3
Hyndman Rd. W Kil 190 B2
Hyndshaw Rd. Car 188 A2
Hyndshaw View. Law 187 D2
Hyslop Pl. Clyde 74 A2
Hyslop Rd. Steven 206 C1
Hyslop St. Aird 122 C4

Iain Dr. Bear 75 E3
Iain Rd. Bear 75 E3
Ian Smith Ct. Clyde 94 B4
Ibrox St. Glasg 116 B3
Ibrox Terr. Glasg 116 A3
Ibroxholm Ave. Glasg 116 A3
Ibroxholm Oval. Glasg 116 A3
Ibroxholm Pl. Glasg 116 A3
Ida Quadrant. Hat 141 F3
Iddesleigh Ave. Miln 55 D1
Ilay Ave. Glasg 96 A4
Ilay Ct. Glasg 96 A4
Ilay Rd. Glasg 96 A4
Imperial Dr. Aird 122 C3
Inch Garve. E Kil 160 B1
Inch Keith. E Kil 160 B1
Inch Marnock. E Kil 160 B1
Inch Murrin. E Kil 160 B1
Inchbrae Rd. Glasg 115 E2
Inchcolm Pl. E Kil 159 E1
Inchconnachan Ave. Bonh 19 F1
Inches Rd. Ard 216 A4
Inches Rd. Salt 205 E1
Inchfad Dr. Glasg 74 C2
Inchfad Rd. Bonh 19 F1
Inchgotrick Rd. Kilmk 227 F2
Inchgower Gr. Rhu 15 E3
Inchgreen St. Green 46 C1
Inchholm La. Glasg 95 F1
Inchholm St. Glasg 95 F1
Inchinnan Rd. Hat 141 F4
Inchinnan Rd. Pais 113 F4
Inchinnan Rd. Ren 94 A2
Inchkeith Pl. Falk 42 A1
Inchkeith Pl. Glasg 119 D4
Inchlee St. Glasg 95 F2
Inchlonaig Dr. Bonh 19 F1
Inchmurrin Ave. Kirk 80 A4
Inchmurrin Cres. Bonh 19 F1
Inchmurrin Dr. Glasg 138 B1
Inchmurrin Dr. Kilmk 223 D3
Inchmurrin Gdns. Glasg 138 B1
Inchmurrin Pl. Glasg 138 B1
Inchna. Men 4 A3
Inchneuk Rd. Glen 101 F3
Inchoch St. Glasg 99 F1
Inchrory Pl. Glasg 74 C2
Inchwood Ct. Cumb 82 A4
Inchwood Pl. Cumb 81 F4
Inchwood Rd. Cumb 82 A4
Incle St. Pais 113 F3
Indale Ave. Pres 236 C4
India Dr. Inch 93 E3
India St. Alex 27 F3
India St. Glasg 117 D4
Industry St. Klrk 79 E4
Inga St. Glasg 96 C4
Ingerbreck Ave. Glasg 138 B2
Ingleby Dr. Glasg 118 A4
Ingleby Pl. Neil 154 C4
Inglefield Ct. Aird 123 D4
Inglefield St. Glasg 117 D1
Ingleneuk Ave. Stepps 99 D3
Ingleside. Klrk 79 E3
Ingleston Ave. Duni 21 E3
Ingleston St. Green 46 A2
Inglestone Ave. Glasg 136 A1
Inglewood. All 9 F4
Inglewood Cres. E Kil 180 A4
Inglewood Rd. All 9 F4
Inglis Pl. E Kil 180 C4
Inglis St. Glasg 118 A3
Inglis St. Wish 164 B1
Ingliston Dr. Bishop 71 F2
Ingram Pl. Kilmk 223 D2
Ingram St. Glasg 117 E4
Inishail Rd. Glasg 99 E1
Inkerman Pl. Kilmk 222 C1
Inkerman Rd. Glasg 114 C3
Innellan Dr. Kilmk 222 C2
Inner City Trad Est. Glasg 97 E1
Innerleithen Dr. Wish 165 E3
Innermanse Quadrant. Holy 143 F3
Innerpeffray Dr. Sten 24 A2
Innerwick Dr. Glasg 115 D3
Innerwood Rd. Kilw 207 F3
Innes Ct. E Kil 159 F2
International Ave. Ham 161 E2
Inver Ct. Falk 24 B1
Inver Rd. Glasg 119 F4
Inverallan Ct. B of A 1 C4
Inverallan Dr. B of A 1 C4
Inverallan Rd. B of A 1 C4
Inveraray Dr. Bish 78 A2
Inverary Dr. Sten 23 F3
Inveravon Dr. Mother 163 E3
Inverbervie. Ersk 73 D1
Invercanny Dr. Glasg 75 D2
Invercanny Pl. Glasg 75 D2
Invercargill. E Kil 180 A4
Invercloy Pl. Kilmk 222 C2

Inverclyde Gdns. Glasg

Inverclyde Gdns. Glasg 138 C2
Invercree Wlk. Glen 101 E3
Inveresk Pl. Coat 122 A4
Inveresk Quadrant. Glasg . 119 D3
Inveresk St. Glasg 119 D3
Inverewe Ave. Glasg 135 E1
Inverewe Dr. Glasg 135 E1
Inverewe Gdns. Glasg 135 E1
Inverewe Pl. Glasg 135 E2
Invergarry Ave. Glasg 135 E1
Invergarry Ct. Glasg 135 F1
Invergarry Dr. Glasg 135 E1
Invergarry Gdns. Glasg 135 E1
Invergarry Gr. Glasg 135 E1
Invergarry Pl. Glasg 135 F1
Invergarry Quad. Glasg 135 F1
Invergarry View. Glasg 135 F1
Inverglas Ave. Ren 94 C1
Invergordon Ave. Glasg 136 C4
Invergyle Dr. Glasg 115 E3
Inverkar Dr. Pais 113 D1
Inverkar Rd. Ayr 239 D3
Inverkip Dr. Shot 146 C3
Inverkip Rd. Gour 44 B1
Inverkip Rd. Green 45 E2
Inverkip St. Green 45 F3
Inverlair Ave. Glasg 136 C3
Inverleith St. Glasg 118 C4
Inverleven Pl. Irvine 219 F4
Inverlochy St. Glasg 99 E1
Inverness St. Glasg 115 E3
Inveroran Dr. Bear 76 A2
Invershiel Rd. Glasg 76 C1
Invershin Dr. Glasg 96 B3
Inverurie St. Glasg 97 E2
Invervale Ave. Aird 123 F3
Inzievar Terr. Glasg 119 D1
Iona. Aird 123 E3
Iona Ave. E Kil 160 A2
Iona Cres. Clyde 73 E3
Iona Cres. Gour 44 B3
Iona Ct. Irvine 225 E4
Iona Dr. Pais 133 E4
Iona Gdns. Clyde 73 E3
Iona La. Muir 81 D1
Iona Path. Udd 161 E4
Iona Pl. Clyde 73 E3
Iona Pl. Coat 101 E1
Iona Pl. Falk 42 A1
Iona Pl. Irvine 225 E4
Iona Pl. Kilmk 223 D3
Iona Quadrant. Wish 165 F3
Iona Rd. Glasg 138 C2
Iona Rd. New 165 F3
Iona Rd. P Glasg 69 D4
Iona Rd. Ren 94 B1
Iona Ridge. Ham 161 F1
Iona St. Glasg 116 A4
Iona St. Green 45 E2
Iona St. Mother 142 B1
Iona Way. Kirk 80 A4
Iona Way. Stepps 99 F2
Iona Wlk. Gour 44 B3
Iona Wynd. Bonh 27 F1
Iris Ave. Glasg 138 A2
Iris Ct. Ayr 239 E2
Irongray St. Glasg 118 B4
Irvine Cres. Coat 122 B4
Irvine Gdns. M of C 58 A3
Irvine Mains Cres. Irvine ... 219 E2
Irvine Pl. Kils 36 A1
Irvine Pl. Kil 7 D4
Irvine Rd. Cross 221 F1
Irvine Rd. Kilm 222 A4
Irvine Rd. Kilmk 222 B1
Irvine Rd. Kilw 207 F1
Irvine Rd. Kilw 219 D4
Irvine St. Glasg 118 A2
Irvine St. Glenm 102 C2
Irvine Terr. Ham 183 E4
Irving Ave. Dunt 74 A3
Irving Ct. Dunt 74 A3
Irving Ct. Falk 41 F3
Irving Quadrant. Dunt 74 A3
Irwin St. Green 46 C1
Isabella Gdns. Ham 163 E1
Isla Ave. New 165 F3
Island Rd. Cumb 82 B4
Island View. Ard 205 D2
Islands Cres. Falk 42 A1
Islay. Aird 123 F3
Islay Ave. Glasg 138 C2
Islay Ave. P Glasg 69 D4
Islay Cres. Clyde 73 E3
Islay Cres. Pais 133 E4
Islay Cres. Salt 205 F1
Islay Ct. Ham 161 F1
Islay Ct. Irvine 225 E4
Islay Dr. Clyde 73 E3
Islay Dr. Newt M 156 A3
Islay Gdns. Car 202 A4
Islay Gdns. Lark 185 D2
Islay Pl. Kilmk 223 D3
Islay Quadrant. Wish 164 C1
Islay Rd. Kirk 80 A4
Isle Of Pin Rd. Troon 230 A1
Ivanhoe Cres. Wish 165 E2
Ivanhoe Ct. Car 187 E1

Ivanhoe Dr. Klrk 79 F4
Ivanhoe Dr. Salt 206 A1
Ivanhoe. E Kil 160 B2
Ivanhoe Pl. Holy 143 D3
Ivanhoe Pl. Stir 2 A1
Ivanhoe Rd. Cumb 82 C4
Ivanhoe Rd. Glasg 95 E4
Ivanhoe Way. Pais 112 C1
Ivy Cres. Gour 44 C3
Ivy Pl. Ayr 239 E3
Ivy Pl. Holy 143 D2
Ivy Pl. Udd 161 E4
Ivy Rd. Tan 141 E4
Ivy Terr. Holy 143 D3
Ivybank Ave. Glasg 139 E2
Ivybank Cres. P Glasg 47 D1
Ivybank Rd. P Glasg 47 D1
Izatt St. All 10 A4

Jack St. Ham 183 E4
Jack St. Mother 164 A2
Jack's Rd. Salt 205 F1
Jack's Rd. Udd 141 D3
Jacks View. W Kil 190 B3
Jackson Ct. Coat 122 A3
Jackson Pl. Car 187 F2
Jackson St. Coat 122 A4
Jackton Rd. Auld 179 E3
Jackton Rd. Thorn 179 E3
Jacob Pl. Falk 42 A2
Jacob's Ladder Way. Wish .. 186 B3
Jacobs Dr. Gour 44 B3
Jagger Gdns. Glasg 119 F2
Jail Wynd. Stir 7 D4
Jamaica Dr. E Kil 159 D1
Jamaica La. Green 45 F3
Jamaica St. Glasg 117 D3
Jamaica St. Green 45 F3
James Brown Ave. Ayr 236 C2
James Campbell Rd. Ayr 239 E4
James Cres. Irvine 219 E2
James Croft Dr. Falk 41 F1
James Dempsey Ct. Coat ... 121 F3
James
     Dempsey Gdns. Coat ... 121 F3
James Dunlop Gdns. Bish .. 98 A4
James Gray St. Glasg 136 C4
James Hamilton Dr. Hat 142 A3
James Healy Dr. Ham 183 E4
James Hemphill Ct. Lennox 57 F4
James Leeson Ct. M of C 58 B3
James Little St. Kilmk 227 F4
James Miller Cres. Salt 217 D4
James Morrison St. Glasg . 117 E4
James Nisbet St. Glasg 97 F1
James St. Alex 27 F3
James St. Alva 5 D3
James St. Ayr 236 A1
James St. Bank 39 D2
James St. Bann 7 E1
James St. Car 187 F1
James St. Dalry 191 D4
James St. Falk 42 A3
James St. Glasg 117 D3
James St. Helen 16 B1
James St. Lar 23 E1
James St. Laur 42 C2
James St. Mother 163 E4
James St. Pres 236 A3
James St. Stir 2 A1
James St. Tan 141 F4
James Sym Cres. Kilmk 227 F3
James View. Holy 142 C2
James Watt La. Glasg 117 D3
James Watt Pl. E Kil 159 D2
James Watt Rd. Miln 54 C2
James Watt St. Glasg 117 D4
James Wilson Pl. Cro 201 D1
Jamieson Ct. Dunt 74 A4
Jamieson Ct. Glasg 117 D1
Jamieson Dr. E Kil 160 A1
Jamieson Gdns. Shot 146 C3
Jamieson Pl. Stew 195 E1
Jamieson St. Glasg 117 D1
Jamieson St. Glasg 117 D1
Jamieson Way. Beith 171 D4
Jane Ct. Lark 185 D1
Jane's Brae. Cumb 82 C4
Jane's
     Brae Interchange. Cumb 82 C4
Janebank Ave. Glasg 139 E2
Janefield Ave. John 111 F1
Janefield Pl. Beith 150 A1
Janefield Pl. Lennox 33 E1
Janefield Pl. Udd 161 E3
Janefield St. Glasg 118 B3
Janesmith St. Mother 164 B2
Janetta St. Clyde 74 A2
Jardine St. Glasg 96 C2
Jardine Terr. Green 45 F4
Jardine Terr. Muir 100 C3
Jarvie Ave. Plains 104 A3
Jarvie Cres. Kils 60 B4
Jarvie Pl. Falk 42 A1
Jarvie Way. Pais 132 C4
Jasmine Pl. Cumb 82 A3
Jasmine Rd. Kilmk 227 E4

Jasmine Way. Car 201 F4
Java St. Mother 142 B1
Jean Armour Dr. Clyde 74 B2
Jean Armour La. Gour 44 C2
Jean Armour Pl. Salt 206 A1
Jean Armour Terr. Gour 44 C2
Jean St. P Glasg 47 D1
Jeanette Ave. Ham 183 E4
Jeanie Deans Dr. Helen 25 D4
Jedburgh Ave. Glasg 138 A4
Jedburgh Dr. Pais 113 D1
Jedburgh Gdns. Glasg 96 C2
Jedburgh Pl. Coat 121 F2
Jedburgh Pl. E Kil 159 F1
Jedburgh St. Wish 165 E3
Jedworth Ave. Glasg 75 E2
Jedworth Ct. Bear 75 F3
Jedworth Rd. Glasg 75 D2
Jeffrey Pl. Kils 36 B1
Jeffrey St. Kilmk 227 F3
Jellicoe Pl. Helen 17 D1
Jellicoe St. Clyde 73 F2
Jellyholm Rd. N Sau 10 C4
Jennie Lee Dr. Wish 186 A4
Jennys Well Ct. Pais 114 A1
Jennys Well Rd. Pais 114 A1
Jermond Dr. Irvine 219 E3
Jervis Pl. Helen 17 D1
Jervis Terr. E Kil 180 A4
Jerviston Ct. Holy 143 D1
Jerviston Rd. Glasg 99 E1
Jerviston Rd. Holy 143 D1
Jerviston St. Holy 143 D2
Jerviston St. Mother 163 F4
Jerviswood Dr. Lan 215 F4
Jerviswood. Holy 143 D1
Jerviswood Rd. Lan 215 D2
Jessie St. Glasg 117 E1
Jessiman Sq. Ren 94 A1
Jimmy
     Sneddon Way. Mother . 142 B1
Joanna Terr. Udd 161 E4
Jocelyn Sq. Glasg 117 E3
Jocksthorn Terr. Kilm 222 B3
John Bassy Dr. Bank 38 B2
John Brannan Way. Tan 141 E3
John Brogan Pl. Salt 217 D4
John Brown Pl. Muir 100 B4
John Burnside Dr. Dunt 74 B4
John Davidson Dr. Duni 21 E2
John Dickie St. Kilmk 222 C1
John Ewing Gdns. Lark 185 D2
John Finnie St. Kilmk 227 F4
John Gregor Pl. Loch 129 E1
John Hendry Rd. Udd 141 D2
John Jarvis Sq. Kils 36 B1
John Knox La. Ham 161 E2
John Knox St. Clyde 94 B4
John Knox St. Glasg 117 F4
John Lang St. John 112 A2
John
     McEwan Way. Lennox .. 78 A4
John Murray Ct. Mother 163 F2
John Murray Dr. B of A 2 A4
John Rushforth Pl. Stir 1 C2
John St. Alex 49 E4
John St. Ayr 239 D4
John St. Bank 39 D2
John St. Barr 134 A2
John St. Car 187 F1
John St. Falk 42 A4
John St. Glasg 117 E4
John St. Gour 44 C4
John St. Green 46 A2
John St. Ham 162 C2
John St. Hat 142 A3
John St. Helen 16 B1
John St. Kirk 58 B1
John St. Lark 185 D1
John St. Mother 164 B2
John St. Stir 7 D4
John St. Udd 161 F4
John Street La. Helen 16 B1
Johnson Dr. Glasg 139 D3
Johnshaven. Ersk 73 D1
Johnshaven St. Glasg 136 B4
Johnshill. Loch 129 E2
Johnson Ct. Helen 16 C1
Johnson Dr. Glasg 139 D3
Johnston Ave. Clyde 94 B4
Johnston Ave. Kils 60 B4
Johnston Ave. Sten 23 F2
Johnston Ave. Stir 2 A2
Johnston Dr. Troon 229 E3
Johnston Pl. Den 21 E1
Johnston Rd. Muir 101 D3
Johnston St. Aird 123 D4
Johnston St. Bann 7 E1
Johnston St. Green 45 E4
Johnston St. Pais 113 F2
Johnston Terr. Green 45 E4
Johnstone Ave. Glasg 115 D4
Johnstone Dr. Glasg 138 A4
Johnstone Dr. Loch 129 E1
Johnstone La. Car 188 A1

Johnstone Rd. Ham 162 C1
Johnstone St. Alva 5 D3
Johnstone St. Hat 142 B3
Johnstone St. Men 3 F3
Johnstone Terr. Twe 59 F2
Jones Ave. Lar 41 E4
Jonquil Way. Car 201 F4
Joppa St. Glasg 118 C4
Jordan St. Glasg 95 E1
Jordanhill Cres. Glasg 95 E3
Jordanhill Dr. Glasg 95 E3
Jordanhill La. Glasg 95 F3
Jordanvale Ave. Glasg 95 E1
Jowitt Ave. Clyde 74 B1
Jubilee Bank. Kirk 79 E2
Jubilee Dr. Stew 195 F1
Jubilee Gdns. Bear 75 F2
Jubilee Pl. Stew 195 F1
Jubilee Rd. Duni 21 F2
Jubilee Terr. John 111 E1
Julian Ave. Glasg 96 B2
Julian La. Glasg 96 B2
Juniper Ct. Klrk 79 D3
Juniper Dr. M of C 58 A2
Juniper Gn. Ayr 239 E3
Juniper Pl. Glasg 119 F2
Juniper Pl. John 132 A4
Juniper Pl. Tan 141 E4
Juniper Rd. Tan 141 E4
Juniper Terr. Glasg 119 F2
Juniper Wynd. Holy 143 D3
Juno La. Gour 44 B2
Juno St. Mother 142 B1
Juno Terr. Gour 44 B2
Jupiter La. Gour 44 B2
Jupiter Pl. Rhu 15 E3
Jupiter St. Mother 142 B1
Jupiter Terr. Gour 44 B2
Jura Ave. Ren 94 B1
Jura Ct. Irvine 225 E4
Jura Dr. Clyde 73 E3
Jura Dr. Kirk 80 A4
Jura Dr. Newt M 156 A3
Jura Dr. Udd 140 B2
Jura. E Kil 181 D4
Jura Gdns. Car 202 A4
Jura Gdns. Clyde 73 E3
Jura Gdns. Ham 162 A1
Jura Gdns. Lark 185 E2
Jura Pl. Clyde 73 E3
Jura Pl. Troon 229 F4
Jura Quadrant. Wish 164 C1
Jura Rd. Clyde 73 E3
Jura Rd. Pais 133 E4
Jura St. Glasg 115 F3
Jura St. Green 45 E2
Jura Wynd. Glen 101 E3
Jutland Ct. Helen 16 A2

Kaim Dr. Glasg 135 E3
Kames Dr. Irvine 220 A3
Kames Rd. Shot 146 C3
Kane Pl. Stone 198 C1
Kane St. Alex 27 E1
Karadale Gdns. Lark 185 D2
Karol Path. Glasg 97 D1
Karriemuir Rd. Bish 78 B1
Katewell Ave. Glasg 74 C2
Katherine St. Aird 123 F4
Kathleen Pk. Helen 16 A2
Katrine Ave. Bish 78 A1
Katrine Ave. Tan 141 E3
Katrine Cres. Aird 102 C1
Katrine Ct. All 10 B3
Katrine Ct. Kilmk 228 A3
Katrine Dr. Newt M 157 D2
Katrine Dr. Pais 113 D1
Katrine Pl. Bank 39 E3
Katrine Pl. Coat 101 E1
Katrine Pl. Glasg 139 D3
Katrine Pl. Irvine 219 E3
Katrine Rd. Green 46 A2
Katrine Rd. Shot 146 C3
Katrine Way. Udd 141 D2
Katrine Wynd. Holy 143 D3
Katriona Path. Lark 185 E1
Kay Gdns. Mother 163 D3
Kay Park Cres. Kilmk 223 D1
Kay Park Terr. Kilmk 223 D1
Kay St. Glasg 97 F2
Kaystone Rd. Glasg 75 D1
Keal Ave. Glasg 95 D4
Keal Cres. Glasg 95 D4
Keal Dr. Glasg 95 D4
Keal Pl. Glasg 95 D4
Kearn Ave. Glasg 75 D1
Kearn Pl. Glasg 75 D1
Keats Pk. Udd 141 D2
Keil Cres. Dumb 49 E2
Keilarsbrae. N Sau 5 E1
Keir Ave. Stir 2 A1
Keir Cres. Wish 165 D2
Keir Dr. Bish 77 F1
Keir Gdns. B of A 2 A4
Keir Hardie Ave. Holy 143 D3
Keir Hardie Ave. Laur 42 C2

Keir Hardie Cres. Kilw 208 A2
Keir Hardie Ct. Bish 78 A1
Keir Hardie Dr. Ard 205 D2
Keir Hardie Dr. Hat 141 F2
Keir Hardie Dr. Kilb 149 D1
Keir Hardie Dr. Kils 60 B4
Keir Hardie Pl. Hat 141 F2
Keir Hardie Pl. Salt 206 A1
Keir Hardie Rd. Alva 5 E4
Keir Hardie Rd. Lark 185 E1
Keir Hardie Rd. Steven 206 C1
Keir Hardie St. Green 46 C1
Keir St. B of A 2 A4
Keir St. Glasg 116 C2
Keir's Wlk. Glasg 139 D3
Keith Ave. Glasg 136 B2
Keith Ct. Glasg 96 B1
Keith Pl. Kilmk 223 E1
Keith Quadrant. Wish 165 D3
Keith St. Glasg 96 B1
Keith St. Hat 142 A3
Kelbourne Cres. Hat 141 F3
Kelbourne St. Glasg 96 C2
Kelburn Cres. Kilmk 227 F2
Kelburn St. Barr 134 A1
Kelburn Terr. P Glasg 48 A1
Kelburne Dr. Pais 114 A3
Kelburne Gdns. Glasg 120 A2
Kelburne Gdns. Pais 114 A3
Kelburne. Kilw 207 E1
Kelburne Oval. Pais 114 A3
Kelhead Ave. Glasg 114 C2
Kelhead Ave. Glasg 114 C3
Kelhead Dr. Glasg 114 C3
Kelhead Path. Glasg 114 C3
Kelhead Pl. Glasg 114 C3
Kellas St. Glasg 116 A4
Kellie Gr. E Kil 159 E2
Kellie Pl. All 10 A4
Kelliebank. All 9 F3
Kellock Ave. Coat 121 E2
Kellock Cres. Coat 121 E2
Kells Pl. Glasg 74 C2
Kelly Dr. Den 21 F2
Kelly St. Green 45 E3
Kelly's La. Car 188 A1
Kelso Ave. B of W 110 B4
Kelso Ave. Glasg 138 A4
Kelso Ave. Pais 113 D1
Kelso Cres. Wish 165 D3
Kelso Dr. Car 188 B1
Kelso Dr. E Kil 160 A2
Kelso Gdns. Muir 80 C2
Kelso Pl. Clyde 94 C3
Kelso Quadrant. Coat 121 F4
Kelso St. Glasg 94 C4
Kelton St. Glasg 119 D2
Kelvin Ave. Glasg 114 C4
Kelvin Ave. Kilw 207 F1
Kelvin Cres. Bear 75 F1
Kelvin Ct. Glasg 96 A3
Kelvin Dr. Aird 103 D1
Kelvin Dr. Barr 134 B1
Kelvin Dr. Bish 78 A1
Kelvin Dr. E Kil 180 C4
Kelvin Dr. Glasg 96 B2
Kelvin Dr. Klrk 79 D4
Kelvin Dr. Muir 80 C1
Kelvin Dr. Shot 147 D2
Kelvin Gdns. Ham 161 F2
Kelvin Gdns. Kils 60 B4
Kelvin Pl. E Kil 181 D4
Kelvin Rd. Cumb 83 D4
Kelvin Rd. E Kil 181 D4
Kelvin Rd. Miln 54 C2
Kelvin Rd N. Cumb 83 D4
Kelvin Rd. Tan 140 C2
Kelvin St. Coat 122 B3
Kelvin Terr. Twe 59 F2
Kelvin View. Lennox 78 B4
Kelvin View. Twe 59 F2
Kelvin Way. Glasg 96 C1
Kelvin Way. Kils 36 B1
Kelvin Way. Klrk 79 D4
Kelvin Way. Udd 141 D2
Kelvinbridge
     Roundabout. Lennox ... 78 A4
Kelvindale Gdns. Glasg 96 B3
Kelvindale. Lennox 57 E1
Kelvindale Pl. Glasg 96 B3
Kelvindale Rd. Glasg 96 B3
Kelvingrove St. Glasg 116 C4
Kelvinhaugh Pl. Glasg 116 B4
Kelvinhaugh St. Glasg 116 B4
Kelvinhead Rd. Kils 37 F1
Kelvinside Ave. Glasg 96 C2
Kelvinside Cres. Kils 37 F2
Kelvinside Dr. Glasg 96 C2
Kelvinside
     Gardens La. Glasg 96 C2
Kelvinside Gdns E. Glasg ... 96 C2
Kelvinside Gdns. Glasg 96 C2
Kelvinside Terr S. Glasg 96 C2
Kelvinside Terr W. Glasg ... 96 C2
Kelvinvale. Kirk 58 B1
Kelvinview Ave. Bank 38 C1

Kemp Ave. Ren 94 A1
Kemp Ct. Ham 162 C2
Kemp St. Glasg 97 F2
Kemp St. Ham 162 C2
Kemper Ave. Falk 42 B2
Kempock Pl. Gour 44 C4
Kempock St. Glasg 118 B2
Kempock St. Gour 44 C4
Kempsthorn Cres. Glasg 115 D1
Kempsthorn Rd. Glasg 115 D1
Ken Rd. Kilmk 228 A3
Kenbank Cres. B of W 110 B4
Kenbank Rd. B of W 110 B4
Kendal Ave. Glasg 96 A3
Kendal Ave. Glasg 136 B2
Kendal Dr. Glasg 96 A3
Kendal Rd. E Kil 179 F3
Kendoon Ave. Glasg 74 C2
Kenilburn Ave. Aird 103 D1
Kenilburn Cres. Aird 103 D1
Kenilworth Ave. Glasg 136 B4
Kenilworth Ave. Helen 25 D4
Kenilworth Ave. Pais 132 C4
Kenilworth Ave. Wish 165 D2
Kenilworth Cres. Bear 75 E3
Kenilworth Cres. Green 45 E2
Kenilworth Cres. Ham 161 F2
Kenilworth Cres. Hat 142 A3
Kenilworth Ct. Holy 143 D3
Kenilworth Dr. Aird 123 E4
Kenilworth Dr. Laur 42 C2
Kenilworth Dr. Salt 206 A1
Kenilworth. E Kil 160 C2
Kenilworth Rd. B of A 2 A4
Kenilworth Rd. Klrk 79 F4
Kenilworth Rd. Lan 215 D2
Kenilworth Way. Pais 112 C1
Kenmar Gdns. Tan 140 C4
Kenmar Rd. Ham 162 A3
Kenmar Terr. Ham 162 A3
Kenmore Ave. Pres 236 B3
Kenmore Gdns. Bear 76 A3
Kenmore Pl. Troon 229 F2
Kenmore Rd. Cumb 62 A1
Kenmore Rd. Kil 89 E4
Kenmore St. Glasg 119 D3
Kenmore Way. Car 187 F2
Kenmuir Ave. Glasg 119 F2
Kenmuir Rd. Glasg 119 F1
Kenmuir Rd. Glasg 139 E4
Kenmuir St. Coat 121 E2
Kenmuir St. Falk 41 D3
Kenmuiraid Pl. Hat 141 F2
Kenmuirhill Rd. Glasg 119 E1
Kenmure Ave. Bish 77 F1
Kenmure Cres. Bish 77 F1
Kenmure Dr. Bish 77 F1
Kenmure Gdns. Bish 77 F1
Kenmure La. Bish 77 F1
Kenmure Pl. Sten 23 F2
Kenmure Rd. Newt M 157 D3
Kenmure St. Glasg 116 C2
Kenmure Way. Glasg 138 A2
Kennard St. Falk 42 B3
Kennedar Dr. Glasg 115 F4
Kennedy Ct. Glasg 136 B2
Kennedy Ct. Kilmk 223 E2
Kennedy Dr. Aird 122 C4
Kennedy Dr. Helen 16 B2
Kennedy Dr. Kilmk 223 E2
Kennedy Gdns. Wish 186 A4
Kennedy Rd. Salt 205 F1
Kennedy Rd. Troon 229 D1
Kennedy St. Kilmk 227 F3
Kennedy St. Wish 165 E2
Kennedy's La. Green 46 A2
Kennelburn Rd. Chap 123 E1
Kenneth Rd. Mother 163 E2
Kennihill. Aird 103 D1
Kennihill Quadrant. Aird 103 D1
Kenningknowes Rd. Stir 6 C3
Kennishead Ave. Glasg 135 F3
Kennishead Path. Glasg 135 F3
Kennishead Pl. Glasg 135 F3
Kennishead Rd. Glasg 135 E3
Kennishead Rd. Glasg 135 F2
Kennisholm Ave. Glasg 135 F3
Kennisholm Path. Glasg 135 F3
Kennisholm Pl. Glasg 135 F3
Kennoway Dr. Glasg 95 F1
Kennyhill Sq. Glasg 118 A4
Kenshaw Ave. Lark 199 D4
Kenshaw Pl. Lark 199 D4
Kensington Dr. Glasg 136 B1
Kensington Gate. Glasg 96 B2
Kensington Gate La. Glasg . 96 B2
Kensington Rd. Glasg 96 B2
Kent Ct. Helen 17 D2
Kent Dr. Glasg 138 B3
Kent Dr. Helen 17 D2
Kent Pl. E Kil 179 F3
Kent Rd. All 9 F4
Kent Rd. Glasg 116 C4
Kent Rd. Stir 7 D4
Kent St. Glasg 117 F3
Kentallen Rd. Glasg 119 F3
Kentigern Terr. Bish 98 A4

Kentmere Cl. E Kil 180 A3
Kentmere Dr. E Kil 180 A3
Kentmere Pl. E Kil 180 A3
Keppel Dr. Glasg 137 F3
Keppoch St. Glasg 97 E2
Keppochhill Rd. Glasg 97 E2
Ker Rd. Miln 54 C2
Ker St. Green 45 F3
Kerelaw Ave. Steven 206 C1
Kerelaw Rd. Steven 206 B1
Kerfield Pl. Glasg 74 C2
Kerr Ave. Salt 217 D4
Kerr Cres. Bank 39 D2
Kerr Cres. Ham 162 B1
Kerr Dr. Irvine 219 E1
Kerr Dr. Mother 163 E3
Kerr Gdns. Tan 141 D4
Kerr Pl. Den 21 E1
Kerr Pl. Glasg 117 F3
Kerr Pl. Irvine 219 E1
Kerr Rd. Kilmk 223 E1
Kerr St. Barr 134 A1
Kerr St. Glasg 117 F3
Kerr St. Klrk 79 E4
Kerr St. Pais 113 E3
Kerr St. Udd 161 F4
Kerrera Pl. Glasg 119 E3
Kerrera Rd. Glasg 119 E3
Kerrix Rd. Sym 231 D1
Kerrmuir Ave. Hurl 228 C3
Kerrs La. Salt 216 C4
Kerry Pl. Glasg 74 C2
Kerrycroy Ave. Glasg 137 E4
Kerrycroy Pl. Glasg 137 E4
Kerrycroy St. Glasg 137 E4
Kerrydale St. Glasg 118 A2
Kerrylamont Ave. Glasg 137 F4
Kerse Ave. Beith 191 F4
Kerse Gdns. Falk 42 C3
Kerse Gn Rd. Clack 10 C3
Kerse La. Falk 42 B3
Kerse Pl. Falk 42 B3
Kerse Rd. Fal 7 F3
Kerse Rd. Stir 7 E3
Kersebonny Rd. Cam 6 B4
Kershaw St. Wish 186 B4
Kersie Rd. Fall 9 D2
Kersie Terr. Air 9 F2
Kersland Cres. Hurl 228 C3
Kersland Dr. Miln 55 D1
Kersland Foot. Irvine 219 F3
Kersland La. Glasg 96 B2
Kersland La. Miln 55 D1
Kersland Rd. Beith 170 B3
Kersland St. Glasg 96 B2
Kerswinning Ave. Kilb 170 A4
Kessington Dr. Bear 76 A2
Kessington Rd. Bear 76 A2
Kessock Dr. Glasg 97 D2
Kestrel Cres. Green 45 D3
Kestrel Ct. Dunt 74 A3
Kestrel Pl. Green 45 D3
Kestrel Pl. John 131 E4
Kestrel Rd. Glasg 95 E3
Keswick Rd. E Kil 179 F3
Kethers La. Mother 163 E4
Kethers St. Mother 163 E3
Keverkae. All 9 F3
Kevoc Cotts. Moss 237 D3
Kew Gdns. Tan 141 D4
Kew La. Glasg 96 B2
Kew Terr. Glasg 96 B2
Keynes Sq. Hat 142 B2
Keystone Ave. Miln 76 A4
Keystone Quadrant. Miln 76 A4
Keystone Rd. Miln 76 A4
Kibbleston Rd. Kilbar 130 C4
Kidsneuk Gdns. Irvine 219 D3
Kidsneuk. Irvine 219 D3
Kidston Dr. Helen 16 A1
Kidston St. Glasg 117 E2
Kier Hardie Ct. Beith 171 D4
Kierhill Rd. Cumb 61 E1
Kilallan Ave. B of W 90 B1
Kilallan Rd. Hous 90 B3
Kilbarchan Rd. B of W 110 C3
Kilbarchan Rd. John 111 E1
Kilbarchan St. Glasg 117 D3
Kilbean Dr. Falk 41 F1
Kilbeck Gdns. Bear 75 E4
Kilbeg Terr. Glasg 135 E2
Kilberry St. Glasg 98 A1
Kilbirnie Pl. Glasg 117 D2
Kilbirnie St. Glasg 117 D2
Kilbirnie Terr. Den 21 E2
Kilblain St. Green 45 F3
Kilbowie Rd. Clyde 74 A2
Kilbowie Rd. Cumb 62 A1
Kilbowie Rd. Dunt 74 A3
Kilbrandon Cres. Ayr 238 A1
Kilbrandon Way. Ayr 238 A1
Kilbrannan Ave. Salt 205 F1
Kilbrannan Dr. Green 45 D2
Kilbreck Dr. Falk 41 D2
Kilbrennan Dr. Mother 163 D4
Kilbrennan Rd. Lin 112 A3

Kilbride Dr. Helen 16 C2
Kilbride Rd. Stew 195 E1
Kilbride St. Glasg 117 E1
Kilbride View. Tan 141 D4
Kilburn Gr. Udd 140 B1
Kilburn Pl. Glasg 95 D3
Kilchattan Dr. Glasg 137 E4
Kilchoan Rd. Glasg 99 E1
Kilcloy Ave. Glasg 75 D2
Kilcreggan View. Green 46 B1
Kilda Dr. Glasg 95 F2
Kildale Rd. Loch 129 D1
Kildale Way. Glasg 137 F4
Kildare Dr. Lan 215 D2
Kildare Pl. Lan 215 D2
Kildare Rd. Lan 215 D2
Kildary Ave. Glasg 137 D3
Kildary Rd. Glasg 137 D3
Kildermorie Rd. Glasg 120 A4
Kildonan Ct. New 165 F4
Kildonan Dr. Glasg 96 A1
Kildonan Dr. Helen 16 C1
Kildonan House. Pres 236 A3
Kildonan Pl. Mother 163 E4
Kildonan Pl. Salt 205 F1
Kildonan St. Coat 122 A4
Kildrostan St. Glasg 116 C1
Kildrum Rd. Cumb 62 B2
Kildrum South
   Interchange. Cumb 62 A1
Kildrummy Ave. Sten 23 F2
Kildrummy Pl. E Kil 159 E2
Kilearn Rd. Pais 114 A4
Kilearn Sq. Pais 114 A4
Kilearn Way. Pais 114 A4
Kilfinan Rd. Shot 146 B3
Kilfinan St. Glasg 97 D4
Kilgarth St. Coat 121 E2
Kilgraston Rd. B of W 110 B3
Kilkerran Dr. Glasg 98 C3
Kilkerran Dr. Troon 229 E4
Kilkerran. Kilw 207 D2
Killearn Dr. Glasg 114 C2
Killearn Rd. Green 46 A1
Killearn St. Glasg 97 E2
Killermont Ave. Bear 76 A1
Killermont Ct. Bear 76 A1
Killermont Meadows. Udd . 140 C1
Killermont Pl. Kilw 207 D2
Killermont Rd. Bear 76 A1
Killermont St. Glasg 117 E4
Killermont View. Glasg 76 A1
Killiegrew Rd. Glasg 116 B1
Killin Dr. Lin 111 F3
Killin Pl. Troon 229 F2
Killin St. Glasg 119 D2
Killoch Ave. Pais 113 D3
Killoch Dr. Barr 134 B1
Killoch Dr. Glasg 95 D3
Killoch Pl. Irvine 219 F2
Killoch Rd. Pais 113 D3
Killoch Way. Irvine 219 F2
Kilmacolm Pl. Green 46 B1
Kilmacolm Rd. B of W 90 A2
Kilmacolm Rd. Green 46 A1
Kilmacolm Rd. Hous 91 D2
Kilmacolm Rd. Kil 69 D3
Kilmacolm Rd. P Glasg 69 D3
Kilmahew Ave. Card 26 A1
Kilmahew Ct. Card 26 A1
Kilmahew Dr. Card 26 A1
Kilmahew Gr. Card 26 A1
Kilmailing Rd. Glasg 137 D3
Kilmair Pl. Glasg 96 B3
Kilmaluag Terr. Glasg 135 E2
Kilmannan Gdns. Miln 54 C2
Kilmany Ct. Salt 205 E1
Kilmany Dr. Glasg 118 C3
Kilmany Gdns. Glasg 118 C3
Kilmardinny Ave. Bear 75 F3
Kilmardinny Cres. Bear 76 A3
Kilmardinny Dr. Bear 75 F3
Kilmardinny Gate. Bear 75 F3
Kilmardinny Gr. Bear 75 F3
Kilmarnock Rd. Cross 222 A1
Kilmarnock Rd. Dund 225 F1
Kilmarnock Rd. Glasg 136 B4
Kilmarnock Rd. Kilm 222 B3
Kilmarnock Rd. Pres 233 F3
Kilmarnock Rd. Spring 221 D1
Kilmarnock Rd. Sym 231 E2
Kilmarnock Rd. Troon 229 F3
Kilmartin La. Car 187 F2
Kilmartin Pl. Glasg 135 F2
Kilmaurs Dr. Glasg 136 C2
Kilmaurs Rd. Cross 221 F1
Kilmaurs Rd. Fen 212 C1
Kilmaurs Rd. Kilmk 222 C2
Kilmaurs Rd. Stew 212 C1
Kilmaurs St. Glasg 115 F3
Kilmeny Cres. Wish 165 E3
Kilmeny Terr. Salt 205 E1
Kilmichael Ave. New 166 A3
Kilmorie Dr. Glasg 137 F4
Kilmory Ave. Tan 141 D4
Kilmory Ct. Falk 41 E2
Kilmory Dr. Newt M 156 C3

Kilmory Gdns. Car 188 A2
Kilmory Pl. Kilmk 222 C2
Kilmory Pl. Troon 229 F3
Kilmory Rd. Car 202 A4
Kilmory Rd. Salt 205 F1
Kilmory Wlk. Stew 195 E1
Kilmuir Cres. Glasg 135 E2
Kilmuir Dr. Glasg 135 F2
Kilmuir Rd. Glasg 135 F2
Kilmuir Rd. Tan 120 C1
Kilmun Rd. Green 46 A2
Kilmun St. Glasg 96 B4
Kiln Ct. Irvine 219 E1
Kilnbank Cres. Ayr 239 E4
Kilnburn Rd. Mother 163 E4
Kilncadzow Rd. Car 188 B1
Kilncadzow Rd. Kilnc 202 C4
Kilncraigs Ct. All 10 B3
Kilncraigs Rd. All 10 B3
Kilnford Cres. Dund 225 E1
Kilnford Dr. Dund 225 F1
Kilnknowie Cotts. How 131 D3
Kilns Pl. Falk 41 F3
Kilns Rd. Falk 42 A3
Kilnside Rd. Pais 114 A2
Kilnwell Quadrant. Mother . 163 E4
Kiloran St. Glasg 135 F2
Kilpatrick Ave. Pais 113 D1
Kilpatrick Cres. Pais 133 E4
Kilpatrick Ct. Irvine 220 A2
Kilpatrick Ct. O Kill 73 D3
Kilpatrick Dr. Bear 75 E4
Kilpatrick Dr. Ren 114 A4
Kilpatrick Gdns. Newt M 157 E4
Kilpatrick Pl. Irvine 220 A1
Kilpatrick View. Dumb 50 A2
Kilpatrick Way. Tan 141 D4
Kilrig Ave. Kilw 207 F2
Kilruskin Dr. W Kil 190 B2
Kilsyth Cres. Irvine 220 A2
Kilsyth Rd. Bank 38 B2
Kilsyth Rd. Kils 59 F4
Kilsyth Rd. Kirk 58 C1
Kilsyth Wlk. Irvine 220 A2
Kiltarie Cres. Aird 123 F3
Kiltearn Rd. Glasg 119 F4
Kiltongue Cotts. Aird 122 B4
Kilvaxter Dr. Glasg 135 F2
Kilwinning Cres. Ham 161 F1
Kilwinning Rd. Dalry 191 D4
Kilwinning Rd. Irvine 219 D3
Kilwinning Rd. Steven 206 C1
Kilwinning Rd. Stew 211 E4
Kilwynet Way. Pais 114 A4
Kimberley Gdns. E Kil 180 B4
Kimberley St. Clyde 73 F3
Kimberley St. Mother 164 B2
Kinalty Rd. Glasg 137 D3
Kinarvie Cres. Glasg 134 C4
Kinarvie Pl. Glasg 134 C4
Kinarvie Rd. Glasg 134 C4
Kinarvie Terr. Glasg 134 C4
Kinbuck St. Glasg 97 E2
Kincaid Dr. Lennox 33 E1
Kincaid Field. M of C 58 B3
Kincaid Gdns. Glasg 139 D3
Kincaid St. Green 45 D4
Kincaid Way. M of C 58 B3
Kincaidston Dr. Ayr 239 E2
Kincardine Dr. Bish 98 B4
Kincardine Pl. Bish 98 B4
Kincardine Pl. E Kil 160 B2
Kincardine Rd. Sten 24 B2
Kincardine Sq. Glasg 99 E1
Kincath Ave. Glasg 138 B2
Kinclaven Ave. Glasg 75 D2
Kincraig St. Glasg 115 E3
Kinellan Rd. Bear 75 F1
Kinellar Dr. Glasg 95 D3
Kinfauns Dr. Glasg 75 D2
Kinfauns Dr. Newt M 156 C3
King Edward La. Glasg 95 F3
King Edward Rd. Glasg 95 F3
King Edward St. Alex 27 D1
King O' Muirs Ave. Men 4 C2
King Pl. Coat 121 D3
King St. Alex 27 E1
King St. Ayr 236 A1
King St. Clyde 94 B4
King St. Coat 121 F3
King St E. Helen 16 C1
King St E. Helen 25 C4
King St. Falk 42 B3
King St. Fall 8 B2
King St. Glasg 117 E3
King St. Glasg 138 A4
King St. Gour 44 C4
King St. Green 45 F3
King St. Ham 162 A2
King St. Kilb 58 B4
King St. Kils 60 B4
King St. Kilw 207 F2
King St. Lark 185 D2
King St. New 166 A3
King St. P Glasg 47 E1
King St. Pais 113 E3
King St. Shot 146 C2

Kilmory Gdns. Car 188 A2

King St. Sten 23 E1
King St. Sten 23 F2
King St. Stir 7 D4
King St. Stone 198 C1
King St. Wish 165 D1
King Street La. Glasg 138 A4
King Street La. Kils 60 B4
King's Cres. Car 188 A1
King's Cres. Glasg 139 D3
King's Cres. Helen 16 C1
King's Ct. Beith 150 A1
King's Dr. Cumb 61 F3
King's Dr. Glasg 117 F2
King's Dr. Newt M 157 D2
King's Gdns. Newt M 157 D2
King's Inch Rd. Ren 94 C2
King's Park Ave. Glasg 137 E3
King's Park Rd. Glasg 137 D4
King's Park Rd. Stir 7 D4
King's Pk Rd. Stir 6 C3
King's Pl. Glasg 97 D3
King's Rd. Beith 150 A1
King's Rd. John 112 A1
King's View. Cumb 61 F3
King's Way. Dumb 49 E3
Kingarth La. Glasg 117 D1
Kingarth St. Glasg 117 D1
Kingarth St. Ham 183 E4
Kingcase Ave. Pres 236 A3
Kinghorn Dr. Glasg 137 E4
Kinglas Rd. Bear 75 E1
Kings Cres. John 112 B2
Kings Ct. All 10 A4
Kings Ct. Ayr 236 A1
Kings St. Falk 42 A3
Kings Dr. Holy 142 C2
Kings Myre. Lan 215 E2
Kings Pk. Lennox 57 E1
Kingsacre Rd. Glasg 137 E4
Kingsbarns Dr. Glasg 137 D4
Kingsborough Gate. Glasg . 96 A2
Kingsborough Gdns. Glasg . 96 A2
Kingsborough La E. Glasg . 96 A2
Kingsborough La. Glasg 96 A2
Kingsbrae Ave. Glasg 137 E3
Kingsbridge Cres. Glasg 137 E3
Kingsbridge Dr. Glasg 137 E3
Kingsburgh Dr. Pais 114 A3
Kingsburn Dr. Glasg 138 A3
Kingsburn Gr. Glasg 138 A3
Kingscliffe Ave. Glasg 137 E3
Kingscourt Ave. Glasg 137 E3
Kingscroft Rd. Pres 236 A4
Kingsdale Ave. Glasg 137 E4
Kingsdyke Ave. Glasg 137 E4
Kingseat Pl. Falk 41 F2
Kingsford Ave. Glasg 136 C2
Kingsford Ct. Newt M 156 B3
Kingsgate Ret Pk. E Kil 160 A3
Kingsheath Ave. Glasg 137 F3
Kingshill Ave. Cumb 60 C3
Kingshill Dr. Glasg 137 E3
Kingshill Rd. Alla 167 D3
Kingshill View. Law 187 D2
Kingshouse Ave. Glasg 137 E3
Kingshurst Ave. Glasg 137 E3
Kingsknowe Dr. Glasg 137 F3
Kingsland Cres. Glasg 115 D3
Kingsland Dr. Glasg 115 E3
Kingsland La. Glasg 115 E3
Kingslea Rd. Hous 91 D1
Kingsley Ave. Glasg 117 D1
Kingsley Ave. Sten 23 F2
Kingsley Ct. Tan 141 D4
Kingslynn Dr. Glasg 137 E3
Kingsmuir Dr. Glasg 137 F3
Kingstables La. Stir 7 D4
Kingston Ave. Aird 123 E4
Kingston Ave. Neil 154 B3
Kingston Ave. Tan 141 D4
Kingston Flats. Kils 36 B1
Kingston Gr. Bishop 72 A2
Kingston Pl. Clyde 73 E2
Kingston Rd. Bishop 72 B2
Kingston Rd. Bishop 72 B2
Kingston Rd. Neil 154 B3
Kingston St. Glasg 117 D3
Kingsway Ct. Glasg 95 D3
Kingsway. Dalry 191 D4
Kingsway. E Kil 160 A2
Kingsway. Glasg 95 D3
Kingsway. Gour 44 B3
Kingsway. Kils 36 B1
Kingsway. Kirk 59 D1
Kingswell Ave. Kilmk 223 D3
Kingswell Pk. All 10 B4
Kingswood Dr. Glasg 137 E3
Kingswood Rd. Bishop 71 F2
Kingussie Ave. Stew 195 E1
Kingussie Dr. Glasg 137 E3
Kiniver Dr. Glasg 75 D1
Kinkell Gdns. Kirk 59 D1
Kinloch Ave. Glasg 139 D2
Kinloch Ave. Lin 112 A3
Kinloch Ave. Stew 195 E1
Kinloch Dr. Mother 142 B1

Kinloch La. Gour 44 C2
Kinloch Rd. Kilmk 228 A3
Kinloch Rd. Newt M 156 B3
Kinloch Rd. Ren 94 A1
Kinloch St. Glasg 118 B2
Kinloch Terr. Gour 44 C2
Kinloss Pl. Glasg 159 F1
Kinmount Ave. Glasg 137 D4
Kinnaird Ave. Newt M 157 D3
Kinnaird Cres. Bear 76 A2
Kinnaird Dr. Lin 112 A3
Kinnaird Dr. Sten 23 F2
Kinnaird Pl. Bish 98 A4
Kinnear Rd. Glasg 118 A2
Kinneil Pl. Ham 161 F1
Kinnell Ave. Glasg 115 E2
Kinnell Cres. Glasg 115 E2
Kinnell Pl. Glasg 115 E2
Kinnier Rd. Salt 217 D4
Kinnin Brae. W Kil 190 B2
Kinninoul Ave. Bear 75 E4
Kinnoull Pl. Udd 161 E4
Kinnoull Rd. Kilmk 228 A2
Kinpurnie Rd. Pais 114 B3
Kinross Ave. Glasg 115 D2
Kinross Ave. P Glasg 47 E1
Kinross Pk. E Kil 160 B2
Kinsail Dr. Glasg 114 C3
Kinstone Ave. Glasg 95 D3
Kintail Gdns. Kirk 59 D1
Kintessack Pl. Bish 78 B1
Kintillo Dr. Glasg 95 D3
Kintore Pk. Ham 183 D4
Kintore Rd. Glasg 136 C3
Kintore Tower. Glasg 138 C2
Kintra St. Glasg 116 A4
Kintyre Ave. Lin 112 A2
Kintyre Cres. Newt M 156 B3
Kintyre Cres. Plains 104 A2
Kintyre Gdns. Kirk 59 D1
Kintyre Pl. Falk 41 E2
Kintyre Rd. Udd 161 E4
Kintyre St. Glasg 98 A1
Kintyre Terr. Gour 44 B2
Kintyre Wynd. Car 187 F2
Kippen Dr. Thorn 158 A3
Kippen St. Aird 122 C4
Kippen St. Glasg 97 E3
Kipperoch Rd. Alex 49 D4
Kipperoch Rd. Card 49 D4
Kipperoch Rd. Dumb 49 D4
Kippford St. Glasg 119 E2
Kipps Ave. Aird 122 C4
Kirk Ave. Sten 23 F1
Kirk Cres. Kil 73 D4
Kirk Glebe. Neil 154 C4
Kirk Glebe. Stew 211 E4
Kirk La. Bear 75 F3
Kirk La. Glasg 136 B4
Kirk Path. Alla 167 D4
Kirk Pl. Bear 75 F3
Kirk Pl. Cumb 82 A4
Kirk Pl. Udd 140 C3
Kirk Port. Ayr 238 C4
Kirk Rd. Ash 186 A1
Kirk Rd. Bear 75 F3
Kirk Rd. Beith 171 D4
Kirk Rd. Car 187 F1
Kirk Rd. E Kil 158 B4
Kirk Rd. Holy 143 E4
Kirk Rd. Hous 91 E1
Kirk Rd. Shot 146 C2
Kirk Rd. Wish 165 E2
Kirk St. Car 187 F1
Kirk St. Coat 121 F3
Kirk St. Miln 54 C1
Kirk St. Mother 163 F4
Kirk St. Pres 233 E1
Kirk St. Stone 198 C1
Kirk Vennel. Irvine 219 E1
Kirk Wynd. Falk 42 A2
Kirk Wynd. Stir 7 D2
Kirkaig Ave. Ren 94 C1
Kirkbean Ave. Glasg 138 A2
Kirkbrae. Clack 10 C2
Kirkbride Terr. Plea 12 B2
Kirkbriggs Gdns. Glasg 138 A3
Kirkbriggs Way. Glasg 138 A3
Kirkburn Ave. Glasg 139 D2
Kirkburn Dr. Strath 31 E2
Kirkburn Rd. Strath 31 E2
Kirkburn. Slam 86 A4
Kirkcaldy Rd. Glasg 116 B1
Kirkconnel Ave. Cumb 60 C1
Kirkconnel Ave. Glasg 94 C3
Kirkconnel Dr. Glasg 137 F3
Kirkcudbright Pl. E Kil 160 B2
Kirkdale Dr. Glasg 115 F2
Kirkdene Ave. Newt M 157 D3
Kirkdene Bank. Newt M 157 D3
Kirkdene Cres. Newt M 157 D3
Kirkdene Gr. Newt M 157 D3
Kirkdene Pl. Newt M 157 D3
Kirkfield Bank Way. Ham 162 A2
Kirkfield Rd. Lan 214 B2

Kirkfield Rd. Udd 141 D2
Kirkfield Terr. Wish 165 E2
Kirkfieldbank Brae. Lan 214 C2
Kirkford Rd. Muir 80 C1
Kirkford. Stew 211 F4
Kirkgate. All 10 A3
Kirkgate. Irvine 219 E1
Kirkgate. Salt 216 C4
Kirkhall Gdns. Ard 205 E3
Kirkhall Pl. Den 21 F1
Kirkhall Rd. Holy 143 E2
Kirkhill Ave. Glasg 139 D2
Kirkhill Cres. Neil 154 C4
Kirkhill Cres. Pres 236 A3
Kirkhill Dr. Glasg 96 B3
Kirkhill Gate. Newt M 157 D2
Kirkhill Gdns. Glasg 139 D2
Kirkhill Gr. Glasg 139 D2
Kirkhill. Kilw 207 E1
Kirkhill Pl. Glasg 96 B3
Kirkhill Pl. Wish 164 B1
Kirkhill Rd. Muir 100 C3
Kirkhill Rd. Newt M 157 D3
Kirkhill Rd. Tan 140 C4
Kirkhill Rd. Wish 164 B1
Kirkhill St. Wish 164 B1
Kirkhill Terr. Glasg 139 D2
Kirkholm Ave. Ayr 236 A2
Kirkhope Dr. Glasg 75 D1
Kirkhouse Ave. Strath 31 E2
Kirkhouse Cres. Strath 31 E2
Kirkhouse Rd. Strath 31 E2
Kirkinner Rd. Glasg 119 E2
Kirkintilloch Rd. Bish 78 B3
Kirkintilloch Rd. Kirk 78 B3
Kirkintilloch Rd. Kirk 80 B4
Kirkintilloch Rd. Lennox 58 A1
Kirkland Ave. Kilmk 222 C2
Kirkland Ave. Strath 31 E2
Kirkland Cres. Dalry 191 D4
Kirkland Dr. Duni 21 D1
Kirkland Gdns. Kilm 222 B3
Kirkland Gr. John 111 F2
Kirkland La. Bonh 27 F2
Kirkland Rd. Dunlop 195 D4
Kirkland Rd. Kilb 170 A4
Kirkland St. Glasg 96 C2
Kirkland St. Mother 163 E4
Kirkland Terr. Spring 220 C1
Kirklandholm. Pres 236 B3
Kirklandneuk Rd. Ren 94 A2
Kirklands Cres. Kils 60 B4
Kirklands Cres. Udd 141 D2
Kirklands Rd. Lan 215 D2
Kirkle Dr. Newt M 157 D3
Kirklea Ave. Pais 113 D3
Kirklee Cir. Glasg 96 B2
Kirklee Gardens La. Glasg .. 96 B2
Kirklee Gdns. Glasg 96 B2
Kirklee Pl. Glasg 96 B2
Kirklee Quadrant. Glasg 96 B2
Kirklee Quadrant La. Glasg . 96 B2
Kirklee Rd. Glasg 96 B2
Kirklee Terr. Glasg 96 B2
Kirklee Terrace La. Glasg .. 96 B2
Kirklee Terrace Rd. Glasg .. 96 B2
Kirkliston St. Glasg 118 C3
Kirkmichael Ave. Glasg 96 A2
Kirkmichael Gdns. Glasg 96 A2
Kirkmichael Rd. Helen 16 C1
Kirkmuir Dr. Glasg 138 A2
Kirkmuir Dr. Stew 195 E1
Kirkness St. Aird 123 D4
Kirknethan. Wish 164 B1
Kirknewton St. Glasg 119 D3
Kirkoswald Dr. Clyde 74 B2
Kirkoswald. E Kil 160 B2
Kirkoswald Rd. Glasg 136 B3
Kirkoswald Rd. Holy 143 F2
Kirkpatrick Cres. Alex 27 E4
Kirkpatrick St. Glasg 118 A3
Kirkriggs Ave. Glasg 138 A3
Kirkshaws Ave. Coat 121 F2
Kirkshaws Pl. Coat 121 F2
Kirkshaws Rd. Coat 121 F2
Kirkslap. Den 21 F1
Kirkstall Gdns. Bish 78 A2
Kirkstone Cl. E Kil 179 F3
Kirkstone. Newt M 157 D3
Kirkstyle Ave. Car 187 F1
Kirkstyle Cres. Aird 102 C1
Kirkstyle Cres. Neil 154 B4
Kirkstyle Ct. Irvine 220 A3
Kirkstyle La. Neil 154 C4
Kirkstyle Pl. Glenm 102 B2
Kirksyde Ave. Klrk 79 F4
Kirkton Ave. Barr 134 A1
Kirkton Ave. Car 187 F1
Kirkton Ave. Glasg 95 D3
Kirkton Ave. Udd 161 E3
Kirkton Ave. W Kil 190 B4
Kirkton Cres. Card 26 A1
Kirkton Cres. Coat 122 C2
Kirkton Cres. Glasg 95 D3
Kirkton Cres. M of C 58 B3
Kirkton Ct. Car 187 F1
Kirkton Ct. Eagle 178 C2

Kirkton Dr. Eagle 178 C3
Kirkton. Ersk 73 D2
Kirkton Gate. E Kil 159 F1
Kirkton Moor Rd. Eagle 178 A2
Kirkton. O Kill 73 D4
Kirkton Pk. E Kil 159 F1
Kirkton Pl. Coat 122 B2
Kirkton Pl. E Kil 159 F1
Kirkton Pl. Fen 213 D2
Kirkton Pl. Sten 24 B2
Kirkton Pl. Udd 161 E3
Kirkton Rd. Card 26 A1
Kirkton Rd. Dumb 49 D2
Kirkton Rd. Fen 213 D2
Kirkton Rd. Glasg 139 D3
Kirkton Rd. Kilm 222 B3
Kirkton Rd. Kilmk 222 C3
Kirkton Rd. Neil 154 C3
Kirkton St. Car 187 F1
Kirkton Terr. Lennox 32 C2
Kirktonfield Rd. Neil 154 C4
Kirktonholm Pl. Kilmk 227 F4
Kirktonholm St. Kilmk 227 F4
Kirktonholme Cres. E Kil 159 E1
Kirktonholme Rd. E Kil 159 E1
Kirktonside. Barr 134 A1
Kirkvale Cres. Newt M 157 D3
Kirkvale Ct. Newt M 157 D3
Kirkvale Dr. Newt M 157 D3
Kirkview. Cumb 82 A3
Kirkview Ct. Cumb 82 A3
Kirkview Gdns. Tan 140 C4
Kirkville Pl. Glasg 75 D1
Kirkwall Ave. Udd 140 B2
Kirkwall. Cumb 62 A3
Kirkwall Rd. Gour 44 C2
Kirkway. Air 14 B2
Kirkwell Rd. Glasg 137 D3
Kirkwood Ave. Clyde 74 C1
Kirkwood Pl. Coat 121 F3
Kirkwood Quadrant. Clyde .. 74 B1
Kirkwood Rd. Tan 140 C4
Kirkwood St. Coat 121 F3
Kirkwood St. Glasg 116 B3
Kirkwood St. Glasg 138 A4
Kirn Dr. Gour 44 B3
Kirn Rd. Kilmk 222 C1
Kirriemuir Ave. Glasg 115 E2
Kirriemuir. E Kil 160 B3
Kirriemuir Gdns. Bish 78 B1
Kirriemuir Pl. Glasg 115 E2
Kirriemuir Rd. Bish 78 B1
Kirstie Pl. Bonh 27 F1
Kirtle Dr. Ren 94 C1
Kirtle Pl. E Kil 179 F4
Kishorn Pl. Glasg 99 E1
Kitchener St. Wish 165 D2
Kittoch Pl. E Kil 159 F1
Kittoch St. E Kil 159 F1
Kittochside Rd. E Kil 158 C3
Kittybrewster Rd. Dalry 191 D4
Knapdale St. Glasg 97 D4
Knights Way. Den 21 E1
Knightsbridge St. Glasg 95 E4
Knightscliffe Ave. Glasg 95 E4
Knightswood Rd. Glasg 95 E4
Knightswood Terr. Udd 140 C1
Knivysbridge Pl. Hat 141 F2
Knock Way. Pais 114 A4
Knockbuckle Ave. Kil 69 D1
Knockbuckle Rd. Kil 89 E4
Knockburnie Rd. Udd 141 D2
Knockentiber Rd. Spring 221 D1
Knockhall St. Glasg 99 E1
Knockhill Dr. Glasg 137 D4
Knockhill Rd. Ren 94 A1
Knockinlaw Mount. Kilmk .. 222 C2
Knockinlaw Rd. Kilmk 222 C2
Knockmarloch Dr. Kilmk 227 F2
Knocknair St. P Glasg 68 C2
Knockrivoch Pl. Ard 205 F2
Knockrivoch Wynd. Ard 205 F2
Knockside Ave. Pais 133 E4
Knoll Croft Rd. Shot 147 D2
Knoll Pk. Ayr 238 C2
Knollpark Dr. Newt M 157 E3
Knowe Cres. Holy 143 E2
Knowe Rd. Green 46 A2
Knowe Rd. Muir 100 B4
Knowe Rd. Pais 114 A4
Knowe St. Miln 54 C1
Knowe The. N Sau 5 E1
Knowe The. Troon 229 E4
Knowefaulds Rd. Tull 4 A2
Knowehead Dr. Udd 140 C3
Knowehead Gdns. Udd 140 C3
Knowehead Rd. Hurl 228 C3
Knowehead Rd. Kilmk 227 F2
Knowehead Rd. Lennox 32 C2
Knowehead Rd. Wish 165 E1
Knoweholm. Ayr 238 B1
Knowenoble St. Cle 144 A1
Knowes Ave. Newt M 156 C3
Knowes Rd. Newt M 156 C3
Knowetap St. Glasg 96 C4
Knowetop Ave. Mother 163 F2

Knowetop Cres. Dumb 49 E3
Knowhead Gdns. Glasg 116 C2
Knowhead Terr. Glasg 116 C2
Knox Ave. B of W 110 B4
Knox Pl. Newt M 156 A2
Knox Pl. Salt 206 A1
Knox St. Aird 123 D4
Knox St. Pais 113 E2
Knoxland Sq. Dumb 50 A1
Knoxland St. Dumb 50 A1
Knoxville Rd. Kilb 149 D1
Kronborg Way. E Kil 180 C3
Kyle Ave. Cowie 12 C4
Kyle Ave. Spring 220 C1
Kyle Cres. Troon 230 A2
Kyle Ct. Glasg 139 D3
Kyle Ctr. Ayr 238 C4
Kyle Dr. Glasg 136 C2
Kyle Dr. Troon 229 E3
Kyle Gr. Holy 143 D2
Kyle Quadrant. Holy 143 E2
Kyle Quadrant. Wish 164 C1
Kyle Rd. Cumb 62 A2
Kyle Rd. Irvine 224 A4
Kyle Sq. Glasg 137 F3
Kyle St. Ayr 238 C4
Kyle St. Glasg 97 E1
Kyle St. Mother 163 D4
Kyle St. Pres 236 B4
Kyle Terr. Dumb 49 D3
Kyleakin Dr. Udd 140 A1
Kyleakin Rd. Glasg 135 E2
Kyleakin Terr. Glasg 135 E2
Kylemore Cres. Mother 142 B1
Kylemore La. Gour 44 C2
Kylemore Terr. Gour 44 C2
Kylepark Ave. Udd 140 B3
Kylepark Cres. Udd 140 B4
Kylepark Dr. Udd 140 B4
Kylerhea Rd. Glasg 135 E2
Kyleshill. Salt 216 C4
Kyleswell St. Kilw 207 F2

La Belle Allee. Glasg 96 C1
La Belle Pl. Glasg 96 C1
Laburnum Ave. Beith 171 D4
Laburnum Ave. E Kil 180 B3
Laburnum Cres. Wish 165 D3
Laburnum Ct. E Kil 180 B3
Laburnum Dr. M of C 58 A3
Laburnum Gdns. Klrk 79 D3
Laburnum Gr. Klrk 79 D3
Laburnum Gr. Stir 6 C3
Laburnum Gr. Troon 229 E2
Laburnum Lea. Ham 162 C1
Laburnum Pl. John 132 A4
Laburnum Rd. Ayr 239 E3
Laburnum Rd. Bank 38 C1
Laburnum Rd. Cumb 62 B1
Laburnum Rd. Glasg 116 B2
Laburnum Rd. Kilmk 227 E4
Laburnum Rd. Tan 141 E4
Laburnum St. Green 46 C1
Lachlan Cres. Ersk 72 C1
Lacy St. Pais 114 A2
Lade Dr. Lar 41 E4
Lade Rd. Bon 40 A3
Lade Terr. Glasg 115 D2
Lade The. Bonh 27 F3
Ladeside Cl. Newt M 156 B3
Ladeside Cres. Lar 23 F1
Ladeside Ct. Kilb 170 A4
Ladeside Dr. John 111 E1
Ladeside Dr. Kils 36 C1
Ladeside. Kilm 222 B4
Ladeside Rd. Kilm 222 B4
Ladhope Pl. Glasg 94 C4
Lady Ann Cres. Aird 123 E3
Lady Anne St. Glasg 94 C3
Lady Isle Cres. Udd 140 C3
Lady Jane Gate. Udd 140 C2
Lady La. Pais 113 E2
Lady Margaret Dr. Troon 230 A1
Lady Mary Wlk. Ham 162 C1
Lady Watson Gdns. Ham 162 A1
Lady Wilson St. Aird 123 D4
Lady's Gate. Bonh 27 F1
Ladyacre. Kilw 207 F2
Ladyacre Rd. Lan 215 D2
Ladyacres. Inch 93 E3
Ladybank Ct. E Kil 159 F1
Ladybank. Cumb 61 F3
Ladybank Dr. Glasg 115 F2
Ladybank Gdns. E Kil 159 F1
Ladybank Pl. E Kil 159 F1
Ladyburn Ct. Irvine 219 F3
Ladyburn St. Green 46 B2
Ladyburn St. Pais 114 A2
Ladyford Ave. Kilw 207 F2
Ladyha Ct. Irvine 220 A3
Ladyhill Dr. Glasg 140 A1
Ladykirk Cres. Glasg 115 D3
Ladykirk Cres. Pais 113 F2
Ladykirk Dr. Glasg 115 D3
Ladykirk Rd. Pres 236 B4
Ladyland Dr. Kilb 149 D2
Ladyloan Ave. Glasg 74 C2

Ladymuir Circ. Ersk 72 C1
Ladymuir Cres. Glasg 115 E1
Ladysgate Ct. Sten 24 A2
Ladysmill. Falk 42 B3
Ladysmith Ave. Kilbar 111 E1
Ladysmith Rd. Kilb 149 D1
Ladysmith St. Mother 164 B2
Ladysneuk Rd. Stir 2 B1
Ladyton. Bonh 27 F2
Ladywell Ct. Lar 23 D2
Ladywell Dr. Tull 4 A2
Ladywell Pl. Tull 4 A2
Ladywell Rd. Mother 163 E4
Ladywell St. Glasg 117 F4
Ladywood. Miln 55 D1
Lagan Rd. Car 188 A1
Laggan Ave. Shot 147 D2
Laggan House. Pres 236 A3
Laggan Path. Shot 146 C3
Laggan Quadrant. Aird 102 C1
Laggan Rd. Aird 102 C1
Laggan Rd. Bish 78 A1
Laggan Rd. Glasg 136 C3
Laggan Rd. Newt M 156 B4
Laggan Terr. Ren 94 A2
Laggan Way. New 165 F4
Laggary Pk. Rhu 15 F3
Laggary Rd. Rhu 15 F3
Laidlaw Ave. Holy 142 C2
Laidlaw Gdns. Tan 120 C1
Laidlaw St. Glasg 117 D3
Laidon Rd. Aird 102 C1
Laidon Wlk. New 165 F3
Laigh Ct. Beith 150 A1
Laigh Mount. Ayr 238 C1
Laigh Rd. Beith 150 A1
Laigh Rd. Newt M 157 E3
Laighcartside St. John 112 A2
Laighdykes Rd. Salt 205 F1
Laighland. Pres 236 B3
Laighlands Rd. Udd 141 D1
Laighmuir St. Udd 140 C3
Laighpark Ave. Bishop 72 A3
Laighstonehall Rd. Ham 162 A1
Laightoun Ct. Cumb 82 A3
Laightoun Dr. Cumb 82 A3
Laightoun Gdns. Cumb 82 A3
Lainshaw Ave. Kilmk 227 F2
Lainshaw Dr. Glasg 137 D1
Lainshaw. Kilw 207 E1
Lainshaw St. Stew 211 E4
Laird Pl. Glasg 117 F2
Laird St. Coat 122 A4
Laird St. Green 45 F3
Laird Weir. Ard 205 E2
Laird's Hill Ct. Kils 60 A4
Laird's Hill Pl. Kils 60 A4
Lairds Gate. Udd 140 B3
Lairds Hill. Cumb 61 F1
Lairg Dr. Udd 140 B2
Lairhills Rd. E Kil 180 C4
Lake Ave. Lan 215 E1
Lakefield Ct. Udd 161 E3
Lamb St. Glasg 97 D3
Lamb St. Ham 162 C2
Lambert Terr. All 10 B4
Lamberton Ave. Stir 7 E2
Lamberton Dr. Glasg 115 E3
Lamberton Gdns. Irvine 220 B3
Lamberton Rd. Stew 195 E1
Lambhill Quadrant. Glasg .. 116 C3
Lambhill St. Glasg 116 B3
Lambie Cres. Newt M 156 B3
Lambie Ct. Salt 216 C4
Lamerton Rd. Cumb 62 B1
Lamford Dr. Ayr 238 B3
Lamington Rd. Glasg 115 D3
Lamlash Cres. Glasg 119 D4
Lamlash Pl. Glasg 119 D4
Lamlash Pl. Helen 16 C1
Lamlash Pl. Mother 163 E4
Lamlash Sq. Glasg 119 D4
Lammer Wynd. Lark 185 E1
Lammerknowes Rd. Kils 37 F2
Lammermoor Ave. Glasg .. 115 E2
Lammermoor Cres. Klrk 79 F4
Lammermoor Dr. Cumb 82 C4
Lammermoor. E Kil 160 C2
Lammermoor Gdns. Klrk 79 F4
Lammermoor Rd. Klrk 79 F4
Lammermoor Terr. Wish 165 D2
Lammermuir Ct. Irvine 220 A2
Lammermuir Dr. Pais 133 F4
Lammermuir Gdns. Bear 75 E4
Lammermuir Pl. Holy 143 D3
Lammermuir Rd. Kilmk 228 A2
Lamond View. Lar 23 E1
Lamont Ave. Bishop 72 B2
Lamont Cres. Alex 27 E1
Lamont Cres. Fall 8 B3
Lamont Dr. Irvine 224 B4
Lamont Pl. Irvine 224 B4
Lamont Rd. Glasg 98 A3
Lanark Ave. Aird 123 D2
Lanark Rd. Ash 200 B4
Lanark Rd. Car 187 F1
Lanark Rd. Kilnc 202 A2
Lanark Rd. Lark 185 E3

Lanark St. Glasg 117 E3
Lancaster Ave. Beith 171 D4
Lancaster Ave. Calder ... 123 E1
Lancaster Cres. Glasg 96 B2
Lancaster
  Crescent La. Glasg 96 B2
Lancaster Rd. Bish 78 A2
Lancaster Terr. Glasg 96 B2
Lancaster
  Terrace La. Glasg 96 B2
Lancaster Way. Ren 94 B1
Lancefield Quay. Glasg 116 C4
Lancefield St. Glasg 116 C4
Landemer Dr. Glasg 138 A3
Landressy Pl. Glasg 117 F2
Landressy St. Glasg 117 F2
Landsborough Dr. Kilmk 223 D2
Landsborough Pl. Steven .. 206 C1
Landsdowne Gdns. Ham .. 162 C2
Landsdowne Rd. Lark 185 E1
Lane Gdns. Glasg 96 A2
Lane The. Cumb 61 E3
Lanfine Rd. Pais 114 B2
Lanfine Terr. Irvine 219 F3
Lanfine Way. Irvine 220 A3
Lang Ave. Bishop 72 B2
Lang Ave. Ren 94 B1
Lang Rd. Troon 229 F4
Lang St. Pais 114 A2
Langa St. Glasg 96 C4
Langbank Dr. Kil 69 F1
Langbank Rise. Kil 69 F1
Langbank St. Glasg 117 D3
Langbar Cres. Glasg 119 F4
Langbyres Rd. Cle 144 B1
Langcraig Rd. Kilmk 227 F1
Langcraigs Ct. Pais 133 E4
Langcraigs Dr. Pais 133 E3
Langcraigs Terr. Pais 133 E3
Langcroft Ave. Pres 233 F1
Langcroft Dr. Glasg 139 E2
Langcroft Pl. Glasg 115 E4
Langcroft Rd. Glasg 115 E4
Langcroft Terr. Glasg 115 E4
Langdale Ave. Glasg 98 C2
Langdale. E Kil 159 E2
Langdale. Newt M 157 D3
Langdale Rd. Muir 80 C1
Langdale St. Glasg 98 C2
Langdales Ave. Cumb 61 E1
Langfaulds Cres. Dunt 74 B3
Langford Dr. Glasg 135 D2
Langford Pl. Glasg 135 D2
Langhill Dr. Cumb 61 E2
Langhill Pl. Den 21 E1
Langholm Cres. Wish 165 E3
Langholm Ct. Muir 81 D1
Langholm Dr. Lin 112 B3
Langholm. E Kil 179 F3
Langlands Ave. E Kil 180 C2
Langlands Ave. Glasg 115 E4
Langlands Brae. Kilmk 222 C1
Langlands Ct. E Kil 180 C2
Langlands Dr. E Kil 180 C2
Langlands Dr. Glasg 115 E4
Langlands Pl. E Kil 180 C2
Langlands Rd. Auld 180 C2
Langlands Rd. Glasg 115 F4
Langlands St. Kilmk 222 C1
Langlands Terr. Dumb 50 A3
Langlands-seafar
  Interchange. Cumb 82 C4
Langlea Ave. Glasg 138 C2
Langlea Gr. Glasg 138 C2
Langlea Rd. Glasg 138 C2
Langlees Ave. Newt M 157 D3
Langlees St. Falk 24 B1
Langley Ave. Glasg 95 D4
Langloan Cres. Coat 121 F3
Langloan Pl. Coat 121 F3
Langloan St. Coat 121 F3
Langmuir Ave. Irvine 220 B3
Langmuir Ave. Kirk 58 C1
Langmuir Ct. Irvine 220 B3
Langmuir Rd. Coat 121 D3
Langmuir Rd. Kirk 59 D1
Langmuir Way. Coat 121 D3
Langmuirhead Rd. Stepps .. 79 E1
Langness Rd. Glasg 119 D4
Langoreth Ave. Ham 161 F1
Langrig Rd. Glasg 98 A2
Langrig Rd. Newt M 156 B2
Langshaw Cres. Car 187 F1
Langshot St. Glasg 116 B3
Langside Ave. Glasg 136 C4
Langside Ave. Kilmk 227 F2
Langside Ave. Tan 141 E3
Langside Ct. Udd 141 D1
Langside Dr. Blac 107 D2
Langside Dr. Glasg 136 C3
Langside Dr. Kilbar 111 D1
Langside Gdns. Glasg 137 D4
Langside La. Glasg 117 D1
Langside Pk. Kilbar 111 D1
Langside Pl. Glasg 136 C4
Langside Pl. Kilb 149 D1
Langside Rd. Glasg 137 D4
Langside Rd. Udd 141 D1

Langside St. Dunt 74 C3
Langside Terr. P Glasg 68 B4
Langstile Pl. Glasg 114 C3
Langstile Rd. Glasg 114 C3
Langton Cres. Barr 134 B1
Langton Cres. Glasg 115 E1
Langton Gate. Newt M 156 B3
Langton Gdns. Glasg 119 F2
Langton Pl. Newt M 156 B3
Langton Rd. Glasg 115 E1
Langtree Ave. Glasg 136 A1
Lanrig Pl. Muir 100 B4
Lanrig Rd. Muir 100 B4
Lansbury Gdns. Pais 113 E4
Lansbury St. Alex 27 F4
Lansbury Terr. Lark 185 E1
Lansdowne Cres. Glasg 96 C1
Lansdowne Cres. Shot 147 D2
Lansdowne
  Crescent La. Glasg 96 C1
Lansdowne Dr. Cumb 61 F3
Lansdowne Dr. Cumb 61 F3
Lansdowne Rd. Ayr 236 A2
Lanton Dr. Glasg 115 D3
Lanton Rd. Glasg 136 C3
Lappin St. Clyde 94 B4
Laputa Pl. Kilmk 227 F2
Larbert Rd. Bon 40 A3
Larbert St. Glasg 97 D1
Larch Ave. Bish 98 A4
Larch Ave. Klrk 79 E3
Larch Cres. Klrk 79 E3
Larch Ct. Cumb 62 C2
Larch Ct. E Kil 180 A3
Larch Ct. Udd 161 E4
Larch Dr. Bank 38 C1
Larch Dr. E Kil 180 A3
Larch Gr. Cumb 62 C2
Larch Gr. Holy 143 D3
Larch Gr. Ham 162 C1
Larch Gr. M of C 58 A3
Larch Gr. Sten 23 F2
Larch House. Pres 236 A3
Larch Pl. E Kil 180 A3
Larch Pl. John 132 A4
Larch Pl. Kilmk 227 E4
Larch Pl. Tan 141 E4
Larch Rd. Cumb 62 C2
Larch Rd. Glasg 116 A2
Larch Terr. Beith 171 E4
Larches The. All 10 A4
Larches The. Muir 81 D2
Larchfield Ave. Glasg 95 D3
Larchfield Ave. Newt M 156 C3
Larchfield Cres. Wish 165 E3
Larchfield Ct. Newt M 156 B2
Larchfield Dr. Glasg 138 B2
Larchfield Gdns. Wish 165 E3
Larchfield Gr. Wish 165 E4
Larchfield La. Shot 147 D1
Larchfield Pl. Glasg 95 D2
Larchfield Pl. Wish 165 E3
Larchfield Rd. Bear 75 F1
Larchgrove Ave. Glasg 119 E3
Larchgrove Pl. Glasg 119 E4
Larchgrove Rd. Glasg 119 E4
Larchwood Rd. Ayr 239 E2
Larchwood Terr. Barr 155 E4
Larghill La. Ayr 239 D3
Largie Rd. Glasg 136 C3
Largo Pl. Glasg 115 F4
Largs Ave. Kilmk 223 D2
Largs Rd. Kilb 148 B1
Larkfield Dr. Udd 161 E3
Larkfield Gr. Gour 44 C2
Larkfield Ind Est. Gour 44 B3
Larkfield Rd. Gour 44 C2
Larkfield Rd. Gour 44 C3
Larkfield Rd. Klrk 79 F3
Larkfield St. Glasg 117 D2
Larkhill Ind Est. Lark 199 D4
Larkin Gdns. Pais 113 E4
Larkin Way. Hat 141 F4
Larksfield Dr. Car 202 A4
Larkspur Dr. E Kil 159 E2
Larkspur Way. Car 201 F4
Lashley Gr. Wish 186 B4
Lasswade St. Clyde 94 C3
Latherton Dr. Glasg 96 B3
Latimer Gdns. Glasg 115 D2
Latta Ct. Pres 236 B3
Latta St. Dumb 50 A2
Lauchlin Pl. Kirk 80 A4
Lauchope Rd. Holy 143 E4
Lauchope St. Chap 123 F1
Laudedale La. Glasg 96 A2
Lauder Cres. Wish 165 D3
Lauder Ct. Kilmk 223 E2
Lauder Dr. Glasg 138 B3
Lauder Dr. Lin 112 A3
Lauder Gdns. Coat 122 B2
Lauder Gdns. Udd 140 B1
Lauder Gn. E Kil 160 A2
Lauder La. Ham 161 F2
Lauder St. Glasg 117 D2
Lauderdale Dr. Newt M 156 B2
Lauderdale Gdns. Glasg ... 96 A2
Laudervale Gdns. Alex 27 E4

Laughland Dr. Holy 143 E2
Laughlanglen Rd. Ayr 239 D2
Laundry La. Stepps 99 E3
Lauranne Pl. Hat 141 F3
Laurel Ave. Clyde 73 E2
Laurel Ave. Klrk 79 E3
Laurel Bank. Ayr 239 E2
Laurel Bank. Ham 183 E4
Laurel Ct. E Kil 180 B3
Laurel Ct. Falk 41 E3
Laurel Dr. E Kil 180 B3
Laurel Dr. Lark 185 E1
Laurel Dr. Mother 164 C2
Laurel Gdns. Chap 123 F1
Laurel Gdns. Tan 140 C4
Laurel Gr. Bon 39 F2
Laurel Gr. Gree 83 F1
Laurel La. Lark 185 E1
Laurel Pl. Bon 39 F2
Laurel Pl. E Kil 180 B3
Laurel Pl. Glasg 96 A1
Laurel Pl. Kilmk 227 E4
Laurel Sq. Bank 38 C1
Laurel St. Glasg 96 A1
Laurel Way. Barr 134 A2
Laurel Wlk. Glasg 138 B2
Laurelbank Ave. Bon 40 A4
Laurelbank. Coat 122 A4
Laurelbank Rd. Glasg 139 E4
Laurelbank Rd. Muir 100 A4
Laurelhill Gdns. Stir 6 C3
Laurelhill Pl. Stir 7 D3
Laurels The. Newt M 156 B3
Laurels The. Tull 4 A1
Lauren View. Aird 122 C4
Laurence Dr. Bear 75 D4
Laurencecroft Rd. Stir 2 A1
Laurenstone Terr. E Kil ... 160 A2
Laurie Ct. Tan 141 D4
Laurieland Ave. Cross 221 F1
Laurieston Ct. Dund 225 F1
Laurieston Way. Glasg 138 A2
Lauriston Ct. Salt 205 E1
Lavelle Dr. Coat 122 B4
Lavender Dr. E Kil 180 B3
Lavender La. Car 201 F4
Laverock Ave. Green 45 E2
Laverock Ave. Ham 163 D1
Laverock Rd. Aird 103 D2
Laverock Terr. Muir 80 C1
Laverockhall St. Glasg 97 F2
Law Brae. W Kil 190 B3
Law Dr. Holy 143 E2
Law Pl. E Kil 159 F3
Law Roundabout. E Kil ... 159 F2
Law St. Glasg 118 A3
Law View. Wish 186 B3
Lawer Pl. Irvine 220 A2
Lawers Cres. Kilmk 228 A2
Lawers Dr. Bear 75 E4
Lawers La. Holy 143 E4
Lawers Rd. Glasg 136 A3
Lawers Rd. Kilmk 228 A2
Lawers Rd. Ren 94 B1
Lawfield Ave. Newt M 157 D3
Lawfield Ave. W Kil 190 C2
Lawhill Ave. Glasg 137 E2
Lawhill Rd. Law 187 D2
Lawhill Rd. Sym 231 E2
Lawhope Mill Rd. Chap ... 123 F2
Lawmarnock Cres. B of W .. 110 B4
Lawmarnock Rd. B of W ... 110 B4
Lawmoor Ave. Glasg 117 E2
Lawmoor Pl. Glasg 117 E1
Lawmoor Rd. Glasg 117 E2
Lawmoor St. Glasg 117 E2
Lawmuir Cres. Dunt 74 C4
Lawmuir Pl. Hat 142 A1
Lawmuir Rd. Hat 142 A2
Lawmuir Rd. Law 186 C3
Lawn Pk. Miln 55 E1
Lawn St. Pais 113 F3
Lawrence Ave. Glasg 136 B1
Lawrence Ave. Helen 25 D4
Lawrence Dr. Bonh 19 D1
Lawrence St. Glasg 96 B1
Lawrie St. Glasg 96 A1
Lawrie St. New 165 F3
Lawrie St. Stone 198 C1
Lawrie Way. Lark 185 E1
Lawson Ave. Mother 163 F2
Lawson Dr. Ard 205 E2
Lawson St. Ayr 236 A1
Lawson St. Kilmk 228 A4
Lawswell. Fish 5 F2
Lawthorn
  Roundabout. Irvine 220 A3
Laxdale Dr. Bank 39 E4
Laxford Ave. Glasg 137 D2
Laxford Pl. Coat 122 B2
Laxford Rd. Ersk 72 C1
Laxford Way. Holy 143 E2
Laxton Dr. Klrk 79 F2
Le Froy Gdns. E Kil 180 A3
Le Froy La. E Kil 180 A3
Lea Ave. Neil 154 B4
Leabank Ave. Pais 133 F4

Leadburn Rd. Glasg 98 B2
Leadburn St. Glasg 118 C4
Leader St. Glasg 98 B1
Leadhills Rd. Kilmk 228 A2
Leaend Rd. Aird 102 C1
Leander Cres. Holy 142 C3
Leander Cres. Ren 94 C1
Learigg Rd. Plains 104 A2
Learmont Pl. Miln 54 C1
Learmonth St. Falk 42 A2
Leathem Pl. Wish 164 B1
Leathen Pl. Ersk 72 C1
Leaveret Lea. Hurl 228 B4
Leckethill Ave. Cumb 81 F4
Leckethill Ct. Cumb 81 F4
Leckethill Pl. Cumb 81 F4
Leckethill View. Cumb 81 F4
Leckie Dr. Ham 162 B2
Leckie St. Glasg 136 B4
Ledaig St. Glasg 118 B4
Ledard Rd. Glasg 137 D4
Ledcameroch Cres. Bear ... 75 F2
Ledcameroch Pk. Bear 75 E2
Ledcameroch Rd. Bear 75 F2
Ledgate. Kirk 58 B1
Ledgowan Pl. Glasg 96 B4
Ledi Ave. Tull 4 A1
Ledi Dr. Bear 75 D4
Ledi Path. Holy 143 E2
Ledi Rd. Glasg 136 B3
Ledi View. Stir 2 A2
Ledmore Dr. Glasg 74 C2
Ledmore Pl. Falk 42 C1
Lednock Rd. Glasg 115 D3
Lednock Rd. Stepps 99 E3
Ledrish Ave. Bonh 19 F1
Lee Ave. Glasg 98 C1
Lee Cres. Bish 98 A4
Lee Pl. Hat 142 B2
Leebank Dr. Glasg 136 C1
Leeburn Ave. Hous 91 E1
Leeburn Ave. Hous 91 E1
Leechford. Lan 215 D3
Leechlee Rd. Ham 162 C2
Leefield Dr. Glasg 136 C1
Leehill Rd. Bish 97 F4
Leesburn Pl. E Kil 159 F2
Leeside Rd. Bish 97 F4
Leesland. Tan 141 D4
Leeward Circ. E Kil 159 D1
Leeward Pk. Ayr 239 D1
Leewood Dr. Glasg 137 D1
Lefroy St. Coat 121 F4
Legbrannock Ave. Holy 143 E3
Legbrannock Cres. Holy ... 143 E2
Legbrannock Rd. Holy 143 F3
Leicester Ave. Glasg 96 A3
Leighton St. Glasg 96 C3
Leighton St. Wish 165 D1
Leitch St. Green 46 C2
Leitchland Rd. John 132 B4
Leitchland Rd. Pais 132 B4
Leith Pl. Bank 39 E4
Leith St. Glasg 118 B4
Leithland Ave. Glasg 115 D1
Leithland Rd. Glasg 115 D1
Leman Dr. Hous 111 E4
Leman Gr. Hous 111 E4
Lembert Dr. Newt M 157 E4
Lemmon St. Green 45 E2
Lendal Pl. E Kil 179 F3
Lendale La. Bish 78 A2
Lendalfoot Gdns. Ham 161 E1
Lendel Pl. Glasg 116 B3
Lenihall Dr. Glasg 137 F1
Lenihall Terr. Glasg 137 F1
Lennox Ave. Bishop 72 A2
Lennox Ave. Coat 121 F4
Lennox Ave. Glasg 95 E2
Lennox Ave. Miln 55 D1
Lennox Ave. Stir 7 D2
Lennox Cres. Bish 97 F4
Lennox Cres. Kilmk 222 B1
Lennox Dr. Bear 75 F3
Lennox Dr. Dunt 74 B4
Lennox Dr. Pres 236 B3
Lennox Gdns. Glasg 95 E2
Lennox La E. Glasg 95 E2
Lennox La W. Glasg 95 E2
Lennox Pl. Clyde 73 F2
Lennox Rd. Cumb 61 F1
Lennox Rd. Dumb 50 A2
Lennox Rd. Dumb 50 C1
Lennox Rd. Lennox 33 E1
Lennox St. Alex 27 F3
Lennox St. Alex 49 E4
Lennox St. Dumb 50 A2
Lennox St. Glasg 96 B4
Lennox St. Wish 165 F2
Lennox Terr. Pais 114 A4
Lentran St. Glasg 120 B4
Lenwood Gdns. Bonh 27 F4
Leny St. Glasg 96 C2
Lenzie Pl. Glasg 97 F3
Lenzie Rd. Klrk 79 E3
Lenzie Rd. Stepps 99 E3
Lenzie St. Glasg 97 F3
Lenzie Terr. Glasg 97 F3

Lenziemill Rd. Cumb 83 D4
Leperstone Ave. Kil 69 E1
Leperstone Ave. P Glasg ... 68 C4
Leperstone Rd. Kil 69 E1
Lesley Pl. Steven 206 C1
Lesley Quadrant. Hat 142 A1
Leslie Ave. Bishop 72 A2
Leslie Ave. Newt M 156 C4
Leslie Cres. Ayr 239 D3
Leslie Pl. Kilmk 223 D1
Leslie Rd. Glasg 116 C2
Leslie Rd. Kilmk 223 D1
Leslie St. Glasg 116 C2
Leslie St. Mother 163 F4
Leslie Terr. Pres 236 B4
Lesmahagow Rd. Lan 214 A2
Lesmuir Dr. Glasg 95 D3
Lesmuir Pl. Glasg 94 C3
Lestrange Terr. Alva 5 D4
Letham Cotts. Air 24 B4
Letham Ct. Glasg 136 C3
Letham Dr. Bish 98 B4
Letham Dr. Glasg 136 C3
Letham Grange. Cumb 62 A3
Letham Oval. Bish 98 B4
Letham Terrs. Air 14 B1
Lethamhill Cres. Glasg 98 C1
Lethamhill Pl. Glasg 98 C1
Lethamhill Rd. Glasg 98 C1
Lethbridge Pl. E Kil 180 B4
Letherby Dr. Glasg 137 D4
Letheron Dr. Wish 165 D3
Lethington Ave. Glasg 136 C4
Lethington Pl. Glasg 136 C4
Lethington Rd. Newt M 157 D4
Letterfearn Rd. Glasg 76 C1
Letterickhills Cres. Glasg .. 139 F2
Lettoch St. Glasg 116 A3
Levanne Gdns. Gour 43 F3
Levanne Pl. Gour 43 F3
Leven Ave. Bish 78 A1
Leven Ave. Kilmk 223 D2
Leven Ct. All 10 B3
Leven Ct. Barr 134 C4
Leven Ct. Dumb 49 F2
Leven Ct. Hurl 228 C3
Leven Dr. Bear 75 F2
Leven Dr. Ham 183 D4
Leven Dr. Hurl 228 C3
Leven Path. Holy 143 D3
Leven Pl. Ersk 72 C1
Leven Pl. Green 46 B1
Leven Pl. Irvine 219 E3
Leven Pl. Kilmk 223 D2
Leven Pl. Shot 146 C3
Leven Quadrant. Aird 102 C1
Leven Rd. Coat 101 E1
Leven Rd. Green 46 B1
Leven Rd. Lang 70 B4
Leven Rd. Troon 229 F3
Leven Sq. Ren 94 A2
Leven St. Alex 27 F2
Leven St. Alex 49 E4
Leven St. Dumb 50 A2
Leven St. Falk 42 A4
Leven St. Glasg 116 C2
Leven St. Mother 163 F4
Leven Terr. Holy 143 E1
Leven Way. E Kil 179 F3
Leven Way. Pais 112 C1
Levenbank Gdns. Bonh 27 F4
Levencroft Mews. Bonh 27 F2
Levenford Terr. Dumb 49 F2
Levengrove Ct. Dumb 49 F2
Levengrove Terr. Dumb 49 F2
Levenhowe Pl. Bonh 27 F4
Levenhowe Rd. Bonh 27 F4
Lever Rd. Helen 16 C2
Levern Cres. Barr 134 A1
Levern Gdns. Barr 134 A2
Levern Rd. Barr 134 A1
Levernside Ave. Barr 134 A1
Levernside Ave. Glasg 135 E4
Levernside Cres. Glasg 135 E4
Levernside Rd. Glasg 135 E4
Lewis Ave. Ren 94 B1
Lewis Ave. Wish 165 F3
Lewis Cres. Irvine 219 F1
Lewis Cres. Kilbar 111 E1
Lewis Cres. O Kill 73 E3
Lewis Ct. All 10 A3
Lewis Ct. Falk 42 A1
Lewis Ct. Kilmk 223 D3
Lewis Dr. O Kill 73 D3
Lewis Gdns. Bear 75 D3
Lewis Gdns. O Kill 73 E3
Lewis Gr. O Kill 73 E3
Lewis Pl. Newt M 156 A3
Lewis Pl. O Kill 73 E3
Lewis Rd. Green 45 E2
Lewis Rd. P Glasg 69 D2
Lewis Rise. Irvine 220 A1
Lewis Terr. Irvine 220 A1
Lewis Wynd. Irvine 220 A1
Lewiston Dr. Glasg 76 B1
Lewiston Pl. Glasg 76 B1
Lewiston Rd. Glasg 76 B1
Lexwell Ave. John 112 B2

Lexwell Rd. Pais	112	C1
Leyden Ct. Glasg	96	C3
Leyden Gdns. Glasg	96	C3
Leyden St. Glasg	96	C3
Leys Pk. Ham	162	A2
Leys The. Bish	78	A1
Libberton Way. Ham	162	A2
Liberator Dr. Pres	236	C2
Liberton St. Glasg	118	C4
Liberty Ave. Coat	121	D3
Liberty Path. Udd	161	E4
Liberty Rd. Cald	105	D3
Liberty Rd. Hat	142	A2
Libo Ave. Glasg	115	E1
Libo Ave. Uplaw	153	D2
Libo Pl. Ersk	72	C1
Library La. Glasg	135	F2
Lichtenfels Gdns. Pres	236	C4
Lickprivick Rd. E Kil	180	A3
Liddel Rd. Cumb	61	F1
Liddell Gr. E Kil	180	B4
Liddell St. Glasg	119	E1
Liddells Ct. Bish	98	A4
Liddesdale Pl. Bish	97	F4
Liddesdale Rd. Glasg	97	E4
Liddesdale Sq. Bish	97	F4
Liddesdale Terr. Bish	97	F4
Liddesdale Pass. Glasg	97	F4
Liddoch Way. Glasg	137	F4
Liff Gdns. Bish	98	B4
Liff Pl. Glasg	100	B1
Lifnock Ave. Hurl	228	C3
Lightburn Pl. Glasg	119	D4
Lightburn Rd. Glasg	118	B3
Lightburn Rd. Glasg	139	F2
Lilac Ave. Clyde	73	E3
Lilac Ave. Cumb	62	C3
Lilac Cres. Tan	141	E4
Lilac Ct. Cumb	62	C3
Lilac Gdns. Bish	98	A4
Lilac Hill. Cumb	62	C3
Lilac Hill. Ham	162	C1
Lilac Pl. Cumb	62	C3
Lilac Pl. Kilmk	227	F4
Lilac Way. Holy	143	D2
Lillyburn Pl. Glasg	74	C3
Lily St. Glasg	118	A2
Lilybank Ave. Aird	103	D1
Lilybank Ave. Glasg	139	E2
Lilybank Ave. Muir	100	B4
Lilybank Ct. N Sau	5	E1
Lilybank Gardens La. Glasg	96	B1
Lilybank Gdns. Glasg	96	B1
Lilybank La. Glasg	96	B1
Lilybank Rd. P Glasg	47	D1
Lilybank Rd. Pres	236	A3
Lilybank St. Ham	162	B2
Lilybank Terr. Glasg	96	B1
Lilybank Terrace La. Glasg	96	B1
Lime Cres. Aird	123	E4
Lime Cres. Cumb	62	C2
Lime Gr. Klrk	79	E3
Lime Gr. Lar	23	E1
Lime Gr. Mother	163	F2
Lime Gr. Udd	140	B1
Lime La. Glasg	95	E2
Lime Loan. Holy	143	D2
Lime Pl. Kilmk	227	E4
Lime Rd. Dumb	49	F2
Lime Rd. Falk	41	D2
Lime St. Glasg	95	E2
Lime St. Green	45	F2
Limecraigs Ave. Pais	133	E4
Limecraigs Cres. Pais	133	E4
Limecraigs Rd. Pais	133	E4
Limegrove St. Hat	142	A4
Limekiln Rd. Ayr	236	A2
Limekiln Rd. Steven	217	F4
Limekilns Rd. Cumb	82	C3
Limekilns St. Dunt	74	B4
Limelands Quadrant. Cald	104	C2
Limes The. Glasg	137	D2
Limeside Ave. Glasg	138	B4
Limeside Gdns. Glasg	138	B4
Limetree Ave. Tan	141	E4
Limetree Cres. Newt M	156	B2
Limetree Ct. Ham	162	A3
Limetree Dr. Clyde	74	A2
Limetree Quadrant. Tan	141	E4
Limetree Wlk. M of C	58	A2
Limeview Ave. Pais	133	D4
Limeview Cres. Pais	133	D4
Limeview Rd. Pais	133	D4
Limeview Way. Pais	133	D4
Limonds Ct. Ayr	236	A1
Limonds Wynd. Ayr	236	A1
Limpetlaw. Lan	215	D3
Linacre Dr. Glasg	119	E3
Linacre Gdns. Glasg	119	E3
Linburn Pl. Glasg	115	D3
Linburn Rd. Ersk	72	C1
Linburn Rd. Glasg	114	C3
Linclive Interchange. Lin	112	B3
Linclive Terr. Lin	112	B3
Lincoln Ave. Glasg	95	E3
Lincoln Ave. Tan	120	C1
Lincoln Rd. Gour	44	B2

Lincuan Ave. Glasg	157	E4
Lindams. Udd	140	C3
Linden Ave. Duni	21	E2
Linden Ave. Stir	7	E3
Linden Ave. Wish	165	E3
Linden Dr. Bank	38	C1
Linden Dr. Dunt	74	A3
Linden Lea. Ham	162	A2
Linden Lea. M of C	58	A3
Linden Pl. Glasg	95	F4
Linden St. Glasg	95	F4
Linden Way. Glasg	95	F4
Lindores Ave. Glasg	138	B4
Lindores Dr. E Kil	159	E1
Lindores Pl. E Kil	159	E1
Lindores St. Glasg	137	D4
Lindrick Dr. Glasg	76	C1
Lindsay Ave. Glasg	96	A3
Lindsay Dr. Glasg	96	A3
Lindsay Dr. Kilmk	223	E2
Lindsay Dr. Stir	2	A2
Lindsay Gr. E Kil	159	F1
Lindsay Loan. Lan	215	E3
Lindsay Pl. E Kil	160	A1
Lindsay Pl. Glasg	96	A3
Lindsay Pl. John	112	A2
Lindsay Pl. Klrk	79	E2
Lindsay Quadrant. Bonh	28	A3
Lindsay Rd. E Kil	159	F1
Lindsay Rd. Salt	205	F1
Lindsay St. Ayr	236	B1
Lindsay St. Kilmk	227	F4
Lindsay Terr. Lennox	57	F4
Lindsaybeg Rd. Muir	80	A1
Lindston Pl. Ayr	239	D1
Lindum Cres. Mother	163	D4
Lindum St. Mother	163	D4
Lineside Wlk. Rhu	15	F3
Linfern Ave E. Kilmk	228	B4
Linfern Ave. Kilmk	228	B4
Linfern Ave W. Kilmk	228	B4
Linfern Pl. Ayr	239	D2
Linfern Rd. Glasg	96	B2
Linfield Loan. Udd	141	D3
Linghope Pl. Wish	185	F4
Lingley Ave. Aird	123	D3
Linhope Pl. E Kil	179	F4
Links Cres. Troon	229	F3
Links Rd. Glasg	119	E2
Links Rd. Glasg	137	E2
Links Rd. Pres	233	D1
Links Rd. Salt	205	F1
Links The. Cumb	62	A3
Links View. Lark	185	E1
Linksview Rd. Holy	143	D1
Linkwood Ave. Glasg	74	C2
Linkwood Cres. Glasg	75	D2
Linkwood Ct. Irvine	220	A3
Linkwood Dr. Glasg	75	D2
Linkwood Pl. Glasg	74	C2
Linkwood Pl. Irvine	220	A3
Linlithgow Gdns. Glasg	119	E3
Linlithgow Pl. Sten	23	F2
Linn Cres. Lan	214	A2
Linn Cres. Pais	133	E4
Linn Dr. Glasg	136	C2
Linn Gdns. Cumb	61	D1
Linn Glen. Lennox	57	F4
Linn Park Gdns. John	112	A1
Linn Park Ind Est. Glasg	137	D1
Linn Rd. Ard	205	E2
Linnburn Terr. Ard	205	D2
Linnet Ave. John	131	E4
Linnet Rd. Green	45	D2
Linnet Rd. Hat	142	A2
Linnhe Ave. Bish	78	A1
Linnhe Ave. Glasg	137	D2
Linnhe Ave. Ham	162	A1
Linnhe Cres. Wish	165	D1
Linnhe Dr. Barr	134	A3
Linnhe Pl. Ersk	72	C1
Linnhe Pl. Udd	140	B1
Linnhead Dr. Glasg	135	E3
Linnhead Pl. Glasg	95	D2
Linnpark Ave. Glasg	136	C1
Linnpark Ct. Glasg	136	C1
Linnwell Cres. Pais	133	E4
Linrigg Rd. Chap	144	B4
Linside Ave. Pais	114	A2
Lint Brae. Stew	195	F1
Lint Riggs. Falk	42	A3
Linthaugh Rd. Glasg	115	E2
Linthaugh Terr. Glasg	115	E1
Linthill. Lan	215	D3
Linthouse Bldgs. Glasg	115	F4
Linthouse Rd. Glasg	95	F1
Lintie Rd. Holy	143	E2
Lintlaw Dr. Glasg	115	D3
Lintlaw. Udd	140	B1
Lintmill Terr. Neil	154	B3
Linton St. Glasg	118	C3
Lintwhite Cres. B of W	110	C4
Linwood Ave. E Kil	159	D1
Linwood Ave. Newt M	157	F4
Linwood Ct. Glasg	137	D3
Linwood Rd. Lin	112	C2
Linwood Terr. Ham	162	A2
Lion Bank. Kirk	58	B1

Lionthorn Rd. Falk	41	F1
Lipney. Men	4	A3
Lisburn Rd. Ayr	236	A2
Lismore Ave. Mother	163	D4
Lismore Ave. P Glasg	69	D4
Lismore Ave. Ren	94	B1
Lismore Ct. Falk	42	A1
Lismore Dr. Irvine	225	D4
Lismore Dr. Lin	111	F3
Lismore Dr. Pais	133	E4
Lismore. E Kil	181	E4
Lismore Gdns. Kilbar	111	E1
Lismore Hill. Ham	161	E2
Lismore House. Pres	236	A3
Lismore Pl. Muir	81	D2
Lismore Pl. Newt M	156	A3
Lismore Rd. Glasg	96	A3
Lismore Way. Irvine	225	E4
Lister Ct. B of A	2	A3
Lister Gdns. Thorn	158	A3
Lister Pl. Glasg	115	D4
Lister Rd. Glasg	115	D4
Lister St. Cross	222	A1
Lister St. Glasg	97	E1
Lister Wlk. Hat	142	B4
Lithgow Ave. Klrk	79	F4
Lithgow Ave. Lang	70	A4
Lithgow Cres. Pais	114	A1
Lithgow Dr. Cle	144	A1
Lithgow Pl. E Kil	159	D1
Little Bellsland Rd. Kilmk	228	A3
Little Denny Rd. Den	21	E1
Little Dovehill. Glasg	117	E3
Little John Gdns. New	165	F2
Little St. Glasg	116	C4
Littlehill St. Glasg	98	A2
Littleholm Pl. Clyde	73	F2
Littlemill Ave. Cumb	60	C1
Littlesdale Ave. Pais	132	B4
Littlestane Rd. Irvine	220	A3
Littlestane Rise. Irvine	220	A3
Littlestane		
Roundabout. Irvine	220	A3
Littleston Gdns. Ersk	72	C1
Littleton Dr. Glasg	76	B1
Littleton St. Glasg	76	B1
Livilands Ct. Stir	7	D3
Livilands Gate. Stir	7	D3
Livilands La. Stir	7	D3
Livingston Dr. Plains	104	A2
Livingston La. Udd	141	D2
Livingston Terr. Dunlop	195	D4
Livingstone Ave. Glasg	115	D4
Livingstone Bvd. Ham	161	E2
Livingstone Cres. E Kil	180	B4
Livingstone Cres. Falk	42	C3
Livingstone Cres. Udd	140	B1
Livingstone Ct. Kilmk	223	E2
Livingstone Dr. E Kil	180	C4
Livingstone Dr. Laur	42	C1
Livingstone Gdns. Lark	185	D2
Livingstone Pk. Kils	36	B1
Livingstone Pl. Aird	123	D4
Livingstone Quadrant. East	127	E2
Livingstone St. Clyde	74	B1
Livingstone St. Ham	161	F2
Livingstone Terr. Irvine	219	E3
Livinstone Pk. Kils	36	A1
Lloyd Ave. Glasg	119	D1
Lloyd Dr. Holy	143	D1
Lloyd St. Glasg	118	A1
Lloyd St. Glasg	118	A4
Lloyd St. Holy	143	D1
Lloyd Wlk. Stew	211	E4
Lloyds St. Coat	122	A2
Llynallan Rd. East	127	D3
Loach Ave. Irvine	219	E1
Loadingbank Ct. Kilb	170	A4
Loadingbank. Kilb	170	A4
Loan Lea Cres. Lark	185	D1
Loan Pl. East	127	F3
Loan The. Miln	54	B2
Loanbank Quadrant. Glasg	115	F4
Loancroft Ave. Glasg	120	B2
Loancroft Gate. Udd	140	C3
Loancroft Gdns. Udd	140	C3
Loancroft Pl. Glasg	120	A2
Loanend Cotts. Glasg	139	F1
Loanfoot Ave. Glasg	95	D4
Loanfoot Ave. Kilmk	222	B1
Loanfoot Ave. Neil	154	B3
Loanfoot Gdns. Plea	12	B2
Loanfoot Rd. Udd	161	E3
Loanhead Ave. Bank	39	E3
Loanhead Ave. Holy	143	E2
Loanhead Ave. Lin	112	A3
Loanhead Ave. Ren	94	B2
Loanhead Cres. Holy	143	E2
Loanhead La. Lin	112	A3
Loanhead Rd. Holy	143	E2
Loanhead Rd. Lin	112	A3
Loanhead Rd. Salt	205	E1
Loanhead St. Coat	121	F2
Loanhead St. Glasg	118	C4
Loanhead St. Kilmk	228	A4
Loaning. Lark	185	E1
Loaning The. Ayr	239	D1
Loaning The. Klrk	79	E4

Loaning The. Mother	163	E4
Loaning The. Newt M	157	D4
Loaninghead Dr. Dumb	50	A3
Lobnitz Ave. Ren	94	B2
Loccard Rd. Steven	206	B1
Loch Achray Gdns. Glasg	119	E2
Loch Achray St. Glasg	119	E2
Loch Assynt. E Kil	181	D4
Loch Ave. Car	201	F2
Loch Awe. E Kil	181	D4
Loch Dr. Helen	16	A1
Loch Goil. E Kil	160	A1
Loch Laidon St. Glasg	119	E2
Loch Laxford. E Kil	181	D4
Loch Lea. Kirk	58	C1
Loch Long. E Kil	181	D4
Loch Loyal. E Kil	181	D4
Loch Maree. E Kil	181	D4
Loch Meadie. E Kil	181	D4
Loch Naver. E Kil	181	D4
Loch Park Ave. Car	201	F4
Loch Park Pl. Lark	185	D1
Loch Pl. B of W	110	B4
Loch Rd. B of W	110	B4
Loch Rd. Chap	123	E4
Loch Rd. Klrk	79	F4
Loch Rd. Miln	55	D2
Loch Rd. Stepps	99	E2
Loch Shin. E Kil	181	D4
Loch St. Calder	123	D1
Loch Striven. E Kil	160	A1
Loch Torridon. E Kil	181	D4
Loch View. Cald	105	D3
Loch View. Calder	123	D4
Loch Voil St. Glasg	119	E2
Lochaber Cres. Shot	147	D2
Lochaber Dr. Glasg	138	B2
Lochaber Dr. Sten	23	F2
Lochaber Path. Udd	161	E4
Lochaber Pl. E Kil	159	F2
Lochaber Rd. Bear	76	A1
Lochaber Wlk. M of C	58	B4
Lochaline Ave. Pais	113	D1
Lochaline Dr. Glasg	137	D2
Lochalsh Cres. M of C	58	A4
Lochalsh Dr. Pais	113	D1
Lochalsh Pl. Udd	140	A1
Lochans The. Ros	15	D2
Lochar Cres. Glasg	115	E1
Lochar Pl. E Kil	179	F4
Lochard Dr. Pais	113	D1
Lochay Pl. Troon	229	F3
Lochay St. Glasg	119	E2
Lochbrae Dr. Glasg	138	B2
Lochbrae. N Sau	5	E1
Lochbridge Rd. Glasg	120	A4
Lochbroom Ct. Newt M	156	C3
Lochbroom Dr. Newt M	156	C3
Lochbroom Dr. Pais	113	D1
Lochbuie La. Glenm	102	C2
Lochburn Cres. Glasg	96	C4
Lochburn Gr. Glasg	96	C4
Lochburn Pass. Glasg	96	C4
Lochburn Rd. Glasg	96	C4
Lochcraig Ct. Irvine	220	A2
Lochdochart Rd. Glasg	120	B4
Lochearn Cres. Aird	102	C1
Lochearn Cres. Pais	113	D1
Lochearnhead Rd. Stepps	99	E2
Lochend Ave. Muir	100	C4
Lochend Cotts. Gart	20	C2
Lochend Cres. Bear	75	D2
Lochend Dr. Bear	75	F2
Lochend Rd. Bear	75	F2
Lochend Rd. Coat	101	D1
Lochend Rd. Glasg	100	B1
Lochend Rd. Kilb	170	B4
Lochend Rd. Troon	229	E1
Lochend St. Mother	163	F3
Locher Ave. Hous	91	F1
Locher Cres. Hous	111	F4
Locher Gdns. Hous	111	F4
Locher Rd. Kilbar	110	C2
Locher Way. Hous	111	F4
Locherburn Ave. Hous	111	F4
Locherburn Gr. Hous	111	F4
Locherburn Pl. Hous	111	F4
Lochfauld Rd. Glasg	77	D1
Lochfield Cres. Pais	113	F1
Lochfield Dr. Pais	114	A1
Lochfield Rd. Pais	114	A1
Lochgilp St. Glasg	96	B4
Lochgoin Ave. Glasg	74	C2
Lochgreen Ave. Troon	229	F4
Lochgreen Pl. Coat	101	E1
Lochgreen Pl. Ham	183	D4
Lochgreen Pl. Kilmk	227	F2
Lochgreen Rd. Falk	41	F1
Lochgreen St. Glasg	98	B2
Lochhead Ave. Den	21	F1
Lochhead Ave. Lin	112	A3
Lochiel Dr. M of C	58	B3
Lochiel La. Glasg	138	B2
Lochiel Rd. Glasg	135	F2
Lochinvar Pl. Bon	40	B2
Lochinvar Rd. Cumb	82	C4
Lochinver Cres. Pais	113	D1
Lochinver Dr. Glasg	137	D3
Lochinver Gr. Glasg	139	D3

Lochknowe St. Car	201	F3
Lochlands Gr. Beith	171	E4
Lochlands Ind Est. Falk	41	D4
Lochlea Ave. Clyde	74	B2
Lochlea Ave. Troon	229	F2
Lochlea Dr. Ayr	239	D3
Lochlea. E Kil	160	B2
Lochlea Rd. Cumb	62	B2
Lochlea Rd. Glasg	136	B3
Lochlea Rd. Glasg	137	F3
Lochlea Rd. Newt M	157	F3
Lochlea Rd. Salt	206	A2
Lochlea Way. Holy	143	F2
Lochlee Loan. Lark	185	E1
Lochleven La. Glasg	137	D4
Lochleven Rd. Glasg	137	D4
Lochlibo Ave. Glasg	94	C4
Lochlibo Cres. Barr	134	A1
Lochlibo Ct. Irvine	220	A3
Lochlibo Rd. Barr	134	A1
Lochlibo Rd. Beith	172	C2
Lochlibo Rd. Kilw	209	E2
Lochlibo Rd. Neil	154	C4
Lochlibo Rd. Stew	209	E4
Lochlibo Rd. Uplaw	152	C1
Lochlibo Terr. Barr	134	A1
Lochlie Pl. Steven	206	C1
Lochlip Rd. Loch	129	E1
Lochmaben Dr. Sten	23	F2
Lochmaben Rd. Glasg	114	C2
Lochmaddy Ave. Glasg	137	D2
Lochnagar Dr. Bear	75	D4
Lochnagar Rd. Kilmk	228	A2
Lochnagar Way. Lark	185	E1
Lochpark. Ayr	238	B2
Lochpark Pl. Den	21	F1
Lochranza Dr. Helen	16	C1
Lochranza Pl. Salt	206	A1
Lochridge Pl. Den	21	E1
Lochshore		
East Ind Est. Kilb	170	B4
Lochside. Bear	75	F2
Lochside Ct. Ayr	236	A1
Lochside. Muir	100	C3
Lochside Rd. Ayr	236	A1
Lochside Rd. Slam	86	B1
Lochside St. Glasg	116	C1
Lochview Ave. Gour	45	D4
Lochview Cres. Glasg	98	C2
Lochview Dr. Glasg	98	C2
Lochview Gdns. Glasg	98	C2
Lochview Pl. Glasg	98	C2
Lochview Rd. Bear	75	F2
Lochview Rd. Beith	170	C4
Lochview Rd. Coat	101	E1
Lochview Rd. P Glasg	47	D1
Lochview Terr. Muir	100	C3
Lochwinnoch Rd. Kil	89	E4
Lochwood Gdns. Glasg	120	B4
Lochwood Loan. Muir	81	D2
Lochwood Pl. Irvine	219	F3
Lochwood St. Glasg	98	C1
Lochy Ave. Ren	94	C1
Lochy Gdns. Bish	78	A1
Lochy Pl. Ersk	72	C1
Lochy St. Wish	165	D1
Lock Sixteen. Falk	41	E3
Lockerbie Ave. Glasg	136	C3
Locket Yett View. Hat	141	F3
Lockhart Ave. Glasg	139	E3
Lockhart Ave. Lan	214	C3
Lockhart Dr. Glasg	139	E3
Lockhart Pl. Stone	198	C2
Lockhart Pl. Wish	165	F4
Lockhart St. Car	187	F1
Lockhart St. Glasg	98	A1
Lockhart St. Ham	183	E3
Lockhart St. Stone	199	D2
Lockhart Terr. E Kil	160	A1
Locks St. Coat	122	B3
Locksley Ave. Cumb	82	C4
Locksley Ave. Glasg	95	E4
Locksley Cres. Cumb	82	C4
Locksley Ct. Cumb	82	C3
Locksley Pl. Cumb	82	C3
Locksley Rd. Cumb	82	C3
Locksley Rd. Pais	112	C1
Lodge Cres. Kil	89	F4
Lodge Dr. Sten	23	F1
Lodge Gdns. Kil	69	F1
Lodge Gr. Kil	69	F1
Lodge Pk. Kil	69	F1
Logan Ave. Newt M	156	B3
Logan Ct. Troon	229	E2
Logan Dr. Cumb	61	D2
Logan Dr. Pais	113	E3
Logan Dr. Troon	229	E2
Logan Gdns. Cle	165	D4
Logan St. Glasg	117	E2
Logan St. Udd	161	F4
Logan Tower. Glasg	139	F2
Logandale Ave. New	165	F3
Loganlea Dr. Holy	143	D1
Logans Rd. Mozther	163	E4
Loganswell Dr. Glasg	135	F1
Loganswell Gdns. Glasg	135	F1
Loganswell Pl. Glasg	135	F1
Loganswell Rd. Glasg	135	F1

Logie Dr. Lar 23 D2
Logie La. B of A 2 B4
Logie Pk. E Kil 160 A2
Logie Rd. Stir 2 B2
Logie Sq. E Kil 160 A2
Lomax St. Glasg 118 B4
Lomond Ave. Hurl 228 C3
Lomond Ave. P Glasg 68 C4
Lomond Ave. Ren 94 A1
Lomond Cres. Alex 27 E4
Lomond Cres. Beith 150 B1
Lomond Cres. B of W 110 B4
Lomond Cres. Cumb 82 B4
Lomond Cres. Pais 133 E4
Lomond Cres. Sten 23 F2
Lomond Cres. Stir 2 A2
Lomond Ct. All 10 B3
Lomond Ct. Barr 134 B1
Lomond Ct. Cumb 82 B4
Lomond Ct. Dumb 49 F2
Lomond Ct. Helen 16 C1
Lomond Dr. Aird 102 C1
Lomond Dr. Alex 27 E4
Lomond Dr. Bann 7 F1
Lomond Dr. Barr 134 A2
Lomond Dr. Bish 78 A2
Lomond Dr. Cumb 82 A4
Lomond Dr. Dumb 50 A3
Lomond Dr. Falk 24 B1
Lomond Dr. Newt M 156 B4
Lomond Dr. Udd 141 D2
Lomond Dr. Wish 165 D1
Lomond. E Kil 180 C3
Lomond Gdns. John 112 B1
Lomond Gr. Cumb 82 B4
Lomond Ind Est. Alex 27 F3
Lomond Pl. Coat 101 F1
Lomond Pl. Cumb 82 A4
Lomond Pl. Ersk 72 C1
Lomond Pl. Irvine 219 E4
Lomond Pl. Stepps 99 F2
Lomond Rd. Alex 27 E4
Lomond Rd. Bear 75 F1
Lomond Rd. Bonh 27 F4
Lomond Rd. Coat 101 E1
Lomond Rd. Green 46 A2
Lomond Rd. Kilmk 228 A2
Lomond Rd. Klrk 79 E3
Lomond Rd. Shot 146 C3
Lomond Rd. Tan 120 C1
Lomond St. All 4 C1
Lomond St. Glasg 97 D3
Lomond St. Helen 16 C1
Lomond View. Cumb 82 B4
Lomond View. Ham 161 F1
Lomond Way. Bank 39 E3
Lomond Way. Holy 143 D3
Lomond Way. Irvine 220 A2
Lomond Wlk. Holy 143 E2
Lomond Wlk. Lark 185 D2
Lomondside Ave. Newt M .. 157 E4
Lomondview Ind Est. John .. 111 F2
London Rd. Glasg 118 C1
London Rd. Glasg 119 E1
London Rd. Hurl 228 A4
London Rd. Kilmk 228 A4
London St. Lark 185 D2
London St. Ren 94 B3
Lonend. Pais 113 F2
Loney Cres. Den 39 F4
Long Crags View. Dumb 50 B3
Long Dr. E Kil 181 D4
Long Dr. Irvine 219 F2
Long Dr. Kilw 219 E4
Long Dr. Shew 225 D4
Long Row. Glasg 120 B3
Long Row. Lan 214 C1
Long Row. Men 4 A4
Longay Pl. Glasg 97 E4
Longay St. Glasg 97 E4
Longbank Dr. Ayr 239 D2
Longbank Rd. Ayr 239 D2
Longbar Ave. Beith 170 B3
Longcraigs Ave. Ard 205 E3
Longcroft Dr. Ren 94 B2
Longdales Ave. Falk 42 A4
Longdales Ct. Falk 42 A4
Longdales Pl. Falk 42 A4
Longdales Rd. Falk 42 A4
Longden St. Clyde 94 B4
Longdyke Pl. Sten 24 B2
Longfield Ave. Salt 205 F1
Longfield Pl. Salt 205 F1
Longford Ave. Kilw 207 F1
Longford St. Glasg 118 B4
Longhill Ave. Ayr 238 B1
Longlands Pk. Ayr 238 C2
Longlee. Glasg 120 A2
Longmeadow. John 111 E1
Longpark Ave. Kilmk 222 C1
Longriggend Rd. Cald 85 E1
Longrow Gdns. Irvine 219 F4
Longstone Pl. Glasg 119 D4
Longstone Rd. Glasg 119 D4
Longwill Terr. Cumb 62 A2
Lonmay Rd. Glasg 119 E4
Lonsdale Ave. Glasg 136 B2
Loom Wlk. Kilbar 111 D2

Lora Dr. Glasg 115 F2
Loreny Dr. Kilmk 227 F1
Loretto Pl. Glasg 118 C4
Loretto St. Glasg 118 C4
Lorien Ct. Pres 236 B2
Lorimer Pl. Sten 24 A1
Lorimer Cres. E Kil 180 B4
Lorn Ave. Muir 100 B4
Lorn Dr. Bonh 19 F1
Lorn Pl. Kirk 59 E1
Lorne Arc. Ayr 238 C4
Lorne Cres. Bish 78 B1
Lorne Dr. Lin 112 A3
Lorne Dr. Mother 142 B1
Lorne Gdns. Laur 42 C2
Lorne Gdns. Sals 125 D1
Lorne Pl. Coat 122 B3
Lorne Rd. Glasg 114 C4
Lorne Rd. Lar 23 E1
Lorne St. Glasg 116 B3
Lorne St. Ham 162 B2
Lorne St. Helen 16 B1
Lorne Terr. Glasg 138 C2
Lornshill Cres. All 9 F4
Lorraine Gardens La. Glasg .. 96 B2
Lorraine Gdns. Glasg 96 B2
Lorraine Rd. Glasg 96 B2
Lorraine Way. Bonh 27 F1
Loskin Dr. Glasg 97 D3
Losshill. Men 4 A3
Lossie Cres. Ren 94 C1
Lossie St. Glasg 98 B1
Lothian Cres. Pais 113 E1
Lothian Cres. Stir 2 B2
Lothian Dr. Newt M 157 E4
Lothian Gdns. Glasg 96 C2
Lothian Rd. Ayr 239 D4
Lothian Rd. Gour 44 B2
Lothian Rd. Stew 211 E4
Lothian St. Glasg 114 C4
Lothian Way. E Kil 160 B2
Louburn. Blac 107 E2
Louden St. Aird 123 D4
Loudens Wlk. Duni 21 E3
Loudon. E Kil 180 C3
Loudon Gdns. John 112 A2
Loudon Rd. Stepps 99 D2
Loudon St. Wish 165 D3
Loudon Terr. Bear 75 E4
Loudonhill Ave. Ham 183 F4
Loudoun Ave. Kilmk 228 A2
Loudoun Cres. Kilw 207 D2
Loudoun Pl. Cross 226 C4
Loudoun Pl. Sym 231 E2
Loudoun St. Stew 211 E4
Loudoun Terr. Pres 236 B4
Louise Gdns. Holy 142 C3
Louisville Ave. Wish 165 E3
Lounsdale Cres. Pais 113 D1
Lounsdale Dr. Pais 113 D1
Lounsdale House. Pais 113 D1
Lounsdale Pl. Glasg 95 D2
Lounsdale Rd. Pais 113 D1
Lourdes Ave. Glasg 115 E2
Lourdes Ct. Glasg 115 E2
Lovat Ave. Miln 75 F4
Lovat Dr. Klrk 79 D4
Lovat Path. Lark 185 E1
Lovat Pl. Glasg 138 B2
Love Ave. Kil 89 F1
Love St. Kilw 208 A2
Love St. Pais 113 F3
Lovers Loan. Alva 5 D4
Lovers Wlk. Stir 2 A1
Low Barholm. Kilbar 111 D1
Low Broadlie Rd. Neil 154 B4
Low Church La. Kilmk 227 F4
Low Craigends. Kils 60 C4
Low Cres. Clyde 94 C4
Low Flender Rd. Newt M ... 157 E3
Low Glencairn St. Kilmk ... 227 F3
Low Green Rd. Irvine 219 D1
Low Parksail. Ersk 93 E4
Low Patrick St. Ham 162 C2
Low Pleasance. Lark 185 D2
Low Rd. Ayr 236 C2
Low Rd. Pais 113 E2
Low Waters Rd. Ham 162 B1
Lower Auchingramont
    Rd. Ham 162 C2
Lower Bourtree Dr. Glasg . 138 B2
Lower Bouverie St. Port 47 E1
Lower Bridge St. Stir 2 A1
Lower Castlehill. Stir 2 A1
Lower Mill Rd. Newt M 157 F3
Lower Millgate. Udd 140 C3
Lower
    Stoneymollan Rd. Alex ... 27 E4
Lower
    Sutherland Cres. Helen .. 16 A2
Lowndes St. Barr 134 B1
Lowther Ave. Bear 75 E4
Lowther Bank. Irvine 220 B1
Lowther Pl. Kilmk 228 A2
Lowther Terr. Glasg 96 B2
Loyal Ave. Ersk 72 C1
Loyal Gdns. Bear 75 D4
Loyal Pl. Ersk 72 C1

Loyne Dr. Ren 94 C1
Luath St. Glasg 116 A4
Lubas Ave. Glasg 137 E4
Lubas Pl. Glasg 137 E4
Lubnaig Dr. Ersk 72 C1
Lubnaig Gdns. Bear 75 E4
Lubnaig Pl. Aird 102 C1
Lubnaig Rd. Glasg 136 C3
Lubnaig Wlk. Holy 143 D3
Luce Ave. Kilmk 228 A3
Luckenhill Dr. Gree 84 B2
Luckiesfauld. Neil 154 B3
Luckingsford Ave. Inch 93 E4
Luckingsford Dr. Inch 93 E4
Luckingsford Rd. Inch 93 E4
Lucy Brae. Tan 140 C4
Ludgate. All 10 A3
Ludovic Sq. John 111 F2
Luffness Gdns. Glasg 119 D1
Lugar Ave. Irvine 220 A3
Lugar Cres. Pres 236 A3
Lugar Dr. Glasg 115 F2
Lugar Pl. Glasg 137 F3
Lugar Pl. Troon 229 F3
Lugar St. Coat 122 A4
Luggie Rd. Car 187 F2
Luggie View. Cumb 82 A4
Luggiebank Pl. Coat 121 D2
Luggiebank Rd. Kirk 58 B1
Luggiebank Rd. Klrk 79 E4
Lugton Ct. Irvine 219 E1
Lugton Rd. Dunlop 195 D4
Luing. Aird 123 F3
Luing Rd. Glasg 115 F3
Lumloch St. Glasg 98 A1
Lumsden La. Glasg 96 B1
Lumsden Pl. Steven 206 C1
Lumsden St. Glasg 96 B1
Lunan Dr. Bish 98 B4
Lunan Pl. Glasg 115 F4
Luncarty Pl. Glasg 119 D2
Luncarty St. Glasg 119 D2
Lunderston Dr. Glasg 135 D4
Lundholm Rd. Steven 217 F4
Lundie Gdns. Bish 98 B4
Lundie St. Glasg 118 C2
Lurg St. P Glasg 68 B4
Luss Ave. Green 46 A1
Luss Brae. Ham 161 F1
Luss Pl. Green 46 A1
Luss Rd. Alex 27 E4
Luss Rd. Glasg 115 F4
Luss Rd. Helen 17 D3
Lusset Gdn. O Kill 73 D3
Lusset Rd. O Kill 73 D3
Lusshill Terr. Glasg 120 A1
Lybster Cres. Glasg 138 B2
Lychgate Rd. Tull 4 A1
Lyell Ct. E Kil 159 F2
Lyell Gr. E Kil 159 F2
Lyle Cres. Bishop 72 A2
Lyle Gr. Green 45 D4
Lyle Pl. Green 45 D4
Lyle Pl. Pais 113 F1
Lyle Rd. Aird 123 F4
Lyle Rd. Green 45 D4
Lyle Rd. Kil 89 E4
Lyle Sq. Miln 54 C1
Lyle St. Green 45 F2
Lyle St. Green 46 A2
Lylefoot Cres. Green 45 D4
Lylefoot Pl. Green 45 D4
Lylesland Ct. Pais 113 F1
Lylestone Terr. Kilw 208 B4
Lyman Dr. Wish 165 E4
Lymburn Pl. Ayr 239 D4
Lymburn St. Glasg 116 B4
Lymekilns Rd. E Kil 159 E2
Lyndale Pl. Glasg 96 B4
Lyndale Rd. Glasg 96 B4
Lyndhurst
    Gardens La. Glasg 96 C2
Lyndhurst Gdns. Glasg 96 C2
Lyne Croft. Bish 78 A2
Lyne St. Wish 165 D3
Lynedoch Cres. Glasg 96 C1
Lynedoch
    Crescent La. Glasg 96 C1
Lynedoch Ind Est. Green ... 46 A2
Lynedoch Pl. Glasg 96 C1
Lynedoch St. Glasg 96 C1
Lynedoch St. Green 45 F2
Lynedoch Terr. Glasg 96 C1
Lynmouth Pl. Gour 44 C3
Lynn Ave. Dalry 191 E4
Lynn Ct. Lark 185 D1
Lynn Dr. Eagle 178 C3
Lynn Dr. Kilb 149 D2
Lynn Dr. Miln 55 E1
Lynn Wlk. Bonh 27 F4
Lynn Wlk. Udd 141 D3
Lynnburn Ave. Hat 142 A3
Lynne Dr. Glasg 76 C1
Lynnhurst. Tan 140 C4
Lynnwood Rd. New 166 B3
Lynton Ave. Glasg 136 A1
Lyon Cres. B of A 2 A3

Lyon Rd. Ersk 72 C1
Lyon Rd. John 112 A2
Lyon Rd. Pais 112 C1
Lyoncross Ave. Barr 134 B2
Lyoncross Cres. Barr 134 B2
Lyoncross Rd. Glasg 115 D1
Lyons Quadrant. Mother .. 164 B2
Lysa Vale Pl. Hat 141 F3
Lysander Way. Ren 94 B1
Lytham Dr. Glasg 76 C1
Lytham Meadows. Udd 140 C1
Lythgow Way. Lan 215 E3
Lyttelton. E Kil 180 A4

Mabel St. Mother 163 F3
Macadam Gdns. Hat 142 A3
Macadam Pl. Ayr 236 A1
Macadam Pl. E Kil 180 C4
Macadam Pl. Irvine 219 F1
Macadam Pl. Kilmk 223 E1
Macadam Place. Falk 41 E3
Macadam Sq. Ayr 236 A1
Macallan Pl. Irvine 219 F4
Macallister Pl. Kilmk 223 E1
Macalpine Pl. Kilmk 223 E1
Macandrew Pl. Kilmk 223 E1
Macara Dr. Irvine 219 F2
Macarthur Ave. Glenm 102 B2
Macarthur Cres. E Kil 159 E2
Macarthur Ct. E Kil 159 E2
Macarthur Dr. E Kil 159 E2
Macarthur Gdns. E Kil 159 E2
Macaulay Pl. Helen 16 A1
Macauley Pl. Helen 16 A1
Macbeth Dr. Kilmk 223 E1
Macbeth. E Kil 160 A3
Macbeth Gdns. Kilmk 223 E1
Macbeth Pl. Glasg 118 B2
Macbeth Pl. Kilmk 223 E1
Macbeth Rd. Green 45 D3
Macbeth Rd. Stew 211 E4
Macbeth St. Glasg 118 B2
Maccabe Gdns. Lennox 57 F4
Maccallum Pl. Kilmk 223 E1
Maccrimmon Pk. E Kil 159 D2
Macdairmid Dr. Ham 183 D4
Macdonald Ave. E Kil 159 D2
Macdonald Cres. Twe 60 A2
Macdonald Ct. Beith 171 D4
Macdonald Dr. Kilmk 223 E1
Macdonald Dr. Stir 7 D2
Macdonald Gdns. Kilmk ... 223 E1
Macdonald Gr. Hat 141 F1
Macdonald Pl. Kilmk 223 E1
Macdonald St. Glasg 138 A4
Macdonald St. Mother 163 F3
MacDonald Wlk. Bonh 27 F4
Macdougal Quadrant. Hat . 141 F1
Macdougall Dr. Kilmk 223 E1
Macdougall St. Glasg 136 B4
Macdougall St. Green 46 B2
Macdowall St. John 111 F2
Macdowall St. Pais 113 E3
Macduff. Ersk 73 D1
Macduff Pl. Glasg 118 B2
Macduff St. Glasg 118 B2
Mace Ct. Bann 7 E2
Mace Rd. Glasg 75 E1
Macewan Pl. Kilmk 228 B4
Macfarlane Cres. Falk 42 A3
Macfarlane Dr. Kilmk 223 E1
Macfarlane Rd. Bear 76 A2
Macfie Pl. E Kil 159 D2
Macgregor Dr. Kilmk 228 B4
Machan Ave. Lark 185 D2
Machan Rd. Lark 185 D1
Machanhill. Lark 185 D1
Machanhill View. Lark 185 D1
Machrie Ct. Falk 41 E2
Machrie Dr. Glasg 137 F2
Machrie Dr. Helen 16 C2
Machrie Dr. Newt M 156 C3
Machrie Pl. Kilw 207 E2
Machrie Rd. Glasg 137 F2
Machrie Rd. Kilmk 222 C1
Machrie Rd. Mother 163 D4
Machrie St. Glasg 137 F2
Macinnes Pl. Kilmk 223 E1
Macintosh Pl. E Kil 180 B4
Macintosh Pl. Kilmk 223 E1
Macintyre Pl. Kilmk 223 E1
Macintyre Rd. Pres 233 E1
Macintyre St. Glasg 116 C4
Macivor Cres. E Kil 159 D2
Macivor Pl. Kilmk 223 E1
Mack St. Aird 123 D4
Mackean St. Pais 113 E3
Mackeith St. Glasg 117 F2
Mackellar Pl. Kilmk 223 E1
Mackendrick Pl. Kilmk 228 B4
Mackenzie Dr. Kilbar 111 D1
Mackenzie Dr. Kilmk 223 E1
Mackenzie Gdns. E Kil 159 D2
Mackenzie St. Green 46 B2
Mackenzie Terr. Hat 142 A4
Mackie Ave. Green 46 C2
Mackie Ave. P Glasg 47 D1

Mackie Ave. Stew 195 E1
Mackie Pl. Kilmk 223 E1
Mackie St. Ayr 236 B1
Mackie's Mill Rd. John 132 B4
Mackinlay Pl. Kilmk 228 A4
Mackinlay St. Glasg 117 D2
Mackinnon Dr. Kilmk 228 B4
Mackinnon Terr. Irvine 219 F2
Mackintosh Pl. Irvine 219 F1
Maclachlan Ave. Den 21 E1
Maclachlan Pl. Helen 16 C2
Maclachlan Rd. Helen 16 C2
Maclaren Pl. Kilmk 228 B4
Maclaren Terr. Sten 24 A1
Maclay Ave. Kilbar 111 D1
Maclean Cres. Alva 5 E4
Maclean Ct. E Kil 159 D2
Maclean Ct. Stir 7 E2
Maclean Dr. Kilmk 223 D1
Maclean Gr. E Kil 159 D2
Maclean Pl. E Kil 159 D2
Maclean Sq. Glasg 116 C3
Maclean St. Clyde 94 C4
Maclean St. Glasg 116 B3
Maclean Terr. Blac 107 E4
Maclehose Rd. Cumb 62 B2
Maclellan Rd. Neil 154 C1
Maclellan St. Glasg 116 B3
Macleod Cres. Helen 16 A2
Macleod Dr. Helen 16 B3
Macleod Dr. Kilmk 228 B4
Macleod Pl. E Kil 160 A2
Macleod Pl. Kilmk 228 B4
Macleod St. Glasg 117 F4
Macmillan Dr. Gour 44 B3
Macmillan Dr. Kilmk 223 E1
Macmillan Gdns. Tan 121 D1
Macmillan Pl. Kilmk 223 E1
Macmillan St. Lark 184 C1
Macnab Pl. Kilmk 223 E1
Macnaughton Dr. Kilmk ... 223 E1
Macneil Pl. Kilmk 223 D1
Macneil Dr. E Kil 159 D2
Macneill Gdns. E Kil 159 D2
Macneill St. Lark 184 C2
Macneish Way. E Kil 159 E2
Macnicol Ct. E Kil 159 D2
Macnicol Pk. E Kil 159 D2
Macnicol Pl. E Kil 159 D2
Macphail Dr. Kilmk 223 E1
Macpherson Gdns. Kilmk . 223 E1
Macpherson Pk. E Kil 159 E2
Macpherson Pl. Kilmk 223 E1
Macpherson Wlk. Kilmk ... 223 E1
Macphie Rd. Dumb 50 B2
Macrae Dr. Pres 233 E1
Macrae Gdns. E Kil 159 E2
Macrimmon Pl. E Kil 180 C4
Macrobert Ave. Irvine 220 A1
Mactaggart Rd. Cumb 82 C4
Madeira La. Green 45 E4
Madeira St. Green 45 E4
Madill Pl. Sten 23 F2
Madison Ave. Glasg 137 D3
Madison Path. Udd 161 E4
Madras Pl. Neil 154 C4
Madras St. Glasg 117 F2
Mafeking Pl. Glasg 116 A3
Mafeking St. Mother 164 B2
Mafeking Terr. Neil 154 B4
Magdalen Way. Pais 132 C4
Maggie Wood's Loan. Falk . 41 F3
Magna St. Mother 163 D4
Magnolia Gdns. Holy 143 E2
Magnolia Pl. Tan 141 E4
Magnolia St. Wish 165 D3
Magnus Cres. Glasg 137 D2
Magnus Rd. Hous 111 E4
Mahon Ct. Muir 80 C1
Maid Morville Ave. Irvine . 225 D2
Maidens Ave. Newt M 157 D3
Maidens. E Kil 159 E2
Maidland Rd. Glasg 135 E4
Mailerbeg Gdns. Muir 80 C2
Mailie Wlk. Holy 143 E2
Mailing Ave. Bish 78 B1
Mailings Rd. Kils 37 F2
Maimhor Rd. W Kil 190 B2
Main Rd. Ayr 236 C1
Main Rd. Card 48 A4
Main Rd. Cross 226 C3
Main Rd. Cumb 82 A4
Main Rd. Fen 213 D2
Main Rd. Fen 213 F2
Main Rd. Hurl 228 C4
Main Rd. John 112 B2
Main Rd. Kilb 149 D1
Main Rd. Lang 70 B4
Main Rd. Pais 113 E2
Main Rd. Ros 15 D2
Main Rd. Spring 220 C1
Main St. Air 14 B2
Main St. Alex 27 F2
Main St. Ayr 235 F1
Main St. B of W 110 B4
Main St. Bann 7 E1
Main St. Barr 134 B2

272

Main St. Beith

Maxwell St. P Glasg

Main St. Beith 150 A1
Main St. Blac 107 E2
Main St. Bon 40 A3
Main St. Bonh 19 F1
Main St. Bonh 27 F3
Main St. Cald 85 D1
Main St. Cald 105 D2
Main St. Calder 123 E1
Main St. Cali 66 C3
Main St. Cam 6 B3
Main St. Camb 9 D4
Main St. Chap 123 F2
Main St. Cle 144 B1
Main St. Coat 122 B3
Main St. Cowie 12 B4
Main St. Cumb 62 A3
Main St. Dalry 191 E4
Main St. Dund 225 F1
Main St. Dunlop 195 D4
Main St. E Kil 159 F1
Main St E. Men 4 A3
Main St. Falk 41 F3
Main St. Falk 42 A4
Main St. Fall 8 C2
Main St. Glasg 117 F2
Main St. Glasg 120 B2
Main St. Glasg 135 F2
Main St. Glasg 138 A4
Main St. Glasg 139 D3
Main St. Glen 101 F3
Main St. Green 46 B2
Main St. Ham 161 F3
Main St. Hat 142 A3
Main St. Holy 143 D3
Main St. Hous 91 D1
Main St. How 130 C3
Main St. Irvine 220 B1
Main St. Kilb 170 A3
Main St. Kilm 222 B4
Main St. Kils 37 E2
Main St. Kils 60 B4
Main St. Kilw 207 F2
Main St. Lar 23 E1
Main St. Lennox 57 E4
Main St. Lennox 78 A4
Main St. Loch 129 E1
Main St. Miln 76 A4
Main St. Muir 80 B1
Main St. N Sau 5 E1
Main St. Neil 154 B4
Main St. New 166 A2
Main St. Newt M 157 F3
Main St. Plains 104 A1
Main St. Plea 12 B2
Main St. Pres 233 E2
Main St. Pres 236 B4
Main St. Sals 125 D1
Main St. Shew 225 E3
Main St. Shi 66 B3
Main St. Shot 147 D2
Main St. Slam 86 A4
Main St. Sten 23 F1
Main St. Sten 24 B2
Main St. Steven 206 B1
Main St. Stew 211 E4
Main St. Stir 7 D2
Main St. Sym 231 E2
Main St. Troon 230 A2
Main St. Tull 4 A1
Main St. Twe 59 F2
Main St. Udd 140 C3
Main St. Udd 141 D1
Main St. Udd 161 E3
Main St. W Kil 190 B3
Main St W. Men 3 F3
Main St. Wish 165 D2
Main St. Wish 186 B3
Mainhead Terr. Cumb 62 A3
Mainhill Ave. Glasg 120 B3
Mainhill Dr. Glasg 120 B3
Mainhill Pl. Glasg 120 B3
Mainhill Rd. Coat 120 C3
Mainholm Cres. Ayr 236 B1
Mainholm Rd. Ayr 236 B1
Mainholm Rd. Moss 239 F4
Mains Ave. Beith 150 A1
Mains Ave. Glasg 136 A1
Mains Ave. Helen 16 A2
Mains Ct. Lan 215 E3
Mains Dr. Ersk 73 E1
Mains Hill. Ersk 73 D1
Mains Pl. Hat 142 A2
Mains Rd. Beith 150 A1
Mains Rd. E Kil 159 F3
Mains Rd. East 127 F3
Mains River. Ersk 73 E1
Mains Wood. Ersk 73 E1
Mainscroft. Ersk 73 E1
Mainshill Ave. Ersk 73 D1
Mainshill Gdns. Ersk 73 D1
Mair Ave. Beith 191 F4
Mair St. Glasg 116 C3
Maitland Ave. Bann 7 E1
Maitland Bank. Lark 185 E2
Maitland Cres. Stir 7 D2
Maitland Ct. Helen 16 B1
Maitland Dr. Lennox 57 D1
Maitland Pl. Ren 94 A1
Maitland St. Glasg 97 D1
Maitland St. Helen 16 B1
Majors Loan. Falk 42 A2
Majors Pl. Falk 42 A2
Malcolm Ct. Stew 195 F1
Malcolm Dr. Sten 23 F2
Malcolm Pl. Helen 17 D1
Malcolm St. Mother 163 E3
Malin Pl. Glasg 118 C4
Mallaig Pl. Glasg 115 E4
Mallaig Rd. Glasg 115 F4
Mallaig Rd. P Glasg 68 C4
Mallaig Terr. Gour 44 C2
Mallard Cres. E Kil 180 A3
Mallard Cres. Green 45 D3
Mallard La. Green 45 D3
Mallard La. Udd 141 D2
Mallard Pl. E Kil 180 A3
Mallard Rd. Dunt 74 A3
Mallard Terr. E Kil 180 A3
Malleable Gdns. Mother 142 B1
Malletsheugh Rd. Newt M 156 A2
Malloch Cres. John 112 A1
Malloch Pl. E Kil 160 A1
Malloch St. Glasg 96 C3
Malov Ct. E Kil 180 C3
Malplaquet Ct. Car 188 A1
Maltbarns St. Glasg 97 D2
Malvaig La. Udd 161 E3
Malvern Ct. Glasg 118 A3
Malvern Way. Pais 113 E4
Mambeg Dr. Glasg 115 F4
Mamore Pl. Glasg 136 B3
Mamore St. Glasg 136 B3
Mamre Dr. Cali 66 C3
Manchester Dr. Glasg 96 A3
Mandela Ave. Falk 42 B4
Mandora Ct. Car 188 A1
Manitoba Cres. E Kil 159 D1
Mannering Ct. Glasg 136 B4
Mannering. E Kil 160 B2
Mannering Rd. Glasg 136 B4
Mannering Rd. Pais 132 C4
Mannering Way. Pais 112 C1
Mannfield Ave. Bon 39 F2
Mannofield. Bear 75 E2
Manor Ave. Kilmk 223 D2
Manor Cres. Gour 44 C4
Manor Cres. Tull 4 A1
Manor Dr. Aird 122 C4
Manor Gate. Newt M 156 C2
Manor Loan. B of A 3 D2
Manor Pk. Ham 162 B1
Manor Powis Cotts. B of A 3 D2
Manor Rd. Glasg 74 C1
Manor Rd. Glasg 95 F2
Manor Rd. Muir 100 C3
Manor Rd. Pais 112 C1
Manor St. Falk 42 A2
Manor View. Calder 123 D1
Manor View. Lark 185 E1
Manor Way. Glasg 138 B2
Manresa Pl. Glasg 97 D1
Manse Ave. Bear 75 F3
Manse Ave. Coat 121 E2
Manse Ave. Udd 141 D1
Manse Brae. Ash 200 A4
Manse Brae. Glasg 137 D3
Manse Brae. Rhu 15 E3
Manse Cres. Hous 91 D1
Manse Cres. Stir 7 D2
Manse Ct. Barr 134 B2
Manse Ct. Kils 60 B4
Manse Ct. Kilw 207 F2
Manse Ct. Law 187 D2
Manse Dr. Bonh 27 F4
Manse Garden's. Bonh 27 F4
Manse Pl. Aird 123 D4
Manse Pl. Bann 7 F1
Manse Pl. Falk 42 A2
Manse Pl. Slam 86 A4
Manse Rd. Bear 75 F3
Manse Rd. Coat 120 C3
Manse Rd. E Kil 158 B4
Manse Rd. Glasg 119 E2
Manse Rd. Glasg 120 C3
Manse Rd. Kils 60 C4
Manse Rd. Lan 214 C2
Manse Rd. Mother 163 F2
Manse Rd. Neil 154 C4
Manse Rd. New 166 A2
Manse Rd. O Kill 72 B4
Manse Rd. Sals 125 E1
Manse Rd. Shot 147 D2
Manse Rd. Stone 198 B1
Manse Rd. W Kil 190 B3
Manse St. Coat 121 F3
Manse St. Kil 89 F4
Manse St. Kilmk 228 A4
Manse St. Ren 94 B2
Manse St. Salt 216 C4
Manse View. Holy 143 F3
Mansefield Ave. Glasg 139 D2
Mansefield Cres. O Kill 73 D3
Mansefield Dr. Udd 140 C3
Mansefield Rd. Newt M 157 E3
Mansefield Terr. Dunlop 195 D4
Mansel St. Glasg 98 A3
Manseview. Lark 185 D1
Manseview Terr. Eagle 178 C3
Mansewood Ct. Glasg 120 B2
Mansewood Dr. Dumb 50 A3
Mansewood Rd. Glasg 136 A3
Mansfield Ave. N Sau 5 E1
Mansfield Cres. Newt M 157 E3
Mansfield Rd. Glasg 114 C4
Mansfield Rd. Ham 183 F3
Mansfield Rd. Hat 141 F2
Mansfield Rd. Loch 129 E2
Mansfield Rd. Newt M 157 F3
Mansfield Rd. Pres 236 A3
Mansfield St. Glasg 96 B1
Mansfield Way. Irvine 220 A3
Mansion Ave. P Glasg 69 D4
Mansion Ct. Glasg 139 D3
Mansion St. Glasg 97 E3
Mansion St. Glasg 139 D3
Mansionhouse Ave. Glasg 139 E4
Mansionhouse Dr. Glasg 119 E3
Mansionhouse Gdns. Glasg 136 C4
Mansionhouse Gr. Glasg 119 F2
Mansionhouse Rd. Falk 41 E3
Mansionhouse Rd. Glasg 119 F2
Mansionhouse Rd. Glasg 136 C4
Mansionhouse Rd. Pais 114 A3
Manson Ave. Pres 233 E1
Manson Pl. E Kil 181 D3
Manson Rd. Irvine 219 F2
Manuel Ave. Beith 171 D4
Manuel Ct. Irvine 225 E4
Manuel Ct. Kilb 170 A4
Manuel Terr. Irvine 225 E4
Maple Ave. Dumb 49 D3
Maple Ave. M of C 58 A3
Maple Ave. Newt M 156 B2
Maple Ave. Sten 23 F2
Maple Bank. Ham 162 C1
Maple Ct. All 10 A3
Maple Ct. Coat 121 F2
Maple Ct. Cumb 62 C3
Maple Dr. Ayr 239 E3
Maple Dr. Barr 155 E4
Maple Dr. Beith 150 A1
Maple Dr. Clyde 74 A3
Maple Dr. John 132 A4
Maple Dr. Klrk 79 D3
Maple Dr. Lark 185 D3
Maple Gr. E Kil 180 A3
Maple Gr. Troon 229 E2
Maple Pl. Bank 38 C1
Maple Pl. Duni 21 E2
Maple Pl. E Kil 180 A3
Maple Pl. Kilmk 227 E4
Maple Pl. Tan 141 E4
Maple Quadrant. Aird 123 E3
Maple Rd. Cumb 62 C3
Maple Rd. Glasg 116 A2
Maple Rd. Green 45 D2
Maple Rd. Holy 143 D3
Maple Terr. E Kil 180 A3
Maple Terr. Irvine 219 E2
Maple Way. Udd 161 E4
Mar Ave. Bishop 72 A2
Mar Dr. Bear 75 F4
Mar Gdns. Glasg 138 B2
Mar Pl. All 10 A4
Mar Pl. N Sau 5 E1
Mar Pl. Stir 7 D4
Mar St. All 10 A3
Marble Ave. Irvine 220 B1
March St. Glasg 116 C1
Marchbank Gdns. Pais 114 B2
Marchburn Ave. Pres 236 C4
Marchdyke Cres. Kilmk 227 F2
Marches The. Lan 215 D3
Marchfield Ave. Pais 113 F4
Marchfield. Bish 77 F2
Marchfield Quadrant. Ayr 236 A3
Marchfield Rd. Ayr 236 A3
Marchglen. Fish 5 F3
Marchglen Pl. Glasg 115 E4
Marchmont Ct. Hurl 228 C4
Marchmont Gdns. Bish 77 F1
Marchmont Rd. Ayr 238 C3
Marchmont Road La. Ayr 238 C4
Marchmont Terr. Glasg 96 B2
Marchside Ct. N Sau 5 E1
Mardale. E Kil 159 E2
Maree Ct. All 10 B3
Maree Dr. Cumb 82 A4
Maree Dr. Glasg 115 F2
Maree Gdns. Bish 78 A1
Maree Pl. Irvine 219 E4
Maree Rd. Pais 113 D1
Maree Way. Udd 161 E4
Maree Wlk. New 165 F3
Marfield St. Glasg 118 C3
Margaret Ave. Bank 39 D2
Margaret Ave. Sals 125 D1
Margaret Ct. Den 21 F1
Margaret Dr. Alex 27 E3
Margaret Dr. Bon 40 A3
Margaret Pl. Hat 141 F3
Margaret Rd. Bann 7 E1
Margaret Rd. Ham 162 A3
Margaret St. Coat 122 A2
Margaret St. Gour 44 C4
Margaret St. Green 45 E4
Margaret Terr. Sten 23 F2
Margaret's Pl. Lark 185 D2
Margaretta Bldgs. Glasg 137 D3
Margaretvale Dr. Lark 185 D1
Marguerite Ave. Klrk 79 E3
Marguerite Dr. Klrk 79 E3
Marguerite Gdns. Klrk 79 E3
Marguerite Gdns. Udd 141 D1
Marguerite Gr. Klrk 79 E3
Marguerite Pl. Ayr 239 E2
Marguerite Pl. M of C 58 A3
Marian Dr. Holy 143 E1
Marigold Ave. Mother 163 F4
Marigold Sq. Ayr 239 D2
Marigold Way. Car 201 F4
Marina Rd. Pres 236 A4
Marine Cres. Glasg 116 C3
Marine Dr. Shew 224 A3
Marine Gdns. Glasg 116 C3
Marine View Ct. Troon 229 E1
Mariner Ave. Falk 41 D3
Mariner Dr. Falk 41 D3
Mariner Gdns. Falk 41 E3
Mariner Rd. Falk 41 E3
Mariner St. Falk 41 D3
Mariscat Rd. Glasg 116 C1
Marjory Dr. Pais 114 A4
Marjory Rd. Ren 94 A1
Market Cl. Kils 60 B4
Market End. Lan 215 D2
Market Pl. Car 187 F1
Market Pl. Kil 89 E4
Market Pl. Kils 60 B4
Market Pl. Tan 141 E4
Market Rd. Car 187 F1
Market Rd. Kirk 80 A4
Market Rd. Tan 141 E4
Market Sq. Kils 60 B4
Market St. Aird 123 D4
Market St. Kils 60 B4
Market St. Tan 141 E4
Markethill Rd. E Kil 159 F2
Markethill Rd. E Kil 159 F3
Markethill Roundabout. E Kil 159 F2
Markinch Rd. P Glasg 68 C3
Marlborough Ave. Glasg 95 F2
Marlborough Dr. Stir 2 B2
Marlborough La N. Glasg 95 F2
Marlborough La S. Glasg 95 F2
Marlborough Pk. E Kil 180 A4
Marldon La. Glasg 95 F2
Marlepark. Ayr 239 D2
Marley Way. M of C 58 A3
Marlfield Gdns. Hat 142 A4
Marloch Ave. P Glasg 69 D3
Marlow St. Glasg 116 C3
Marlow Terr. Glasg 116 C2
Marmion Ave. Helen 25 D4
Marmion Cres. Mother 142 B1
Marmion Dr. Klrk 79 F4
Marmion Pl. Cumb 82 C4
Marmion Rd. Cumb 82 C4
Marmion Rd. Pais 132 C4
Marmion St. Falk 42 A4
Marne St. Glasg 118 A4
Marnoch Dr. Glen 101 E3
Marnoch Way. Muir 80 C1
Marnock Terr. Pais 114 A1
Marr Dr. Troon 229 E2
Marr's Wynd. Lan 215 E3
Marress Rd. Irvine 219 D2
Marress Roundabout. Irvine 219 D1
Marrswood Gn. Ham 162 A2
Marrwood Ave. Kirk 80 A3
Mars Rd. Gour 44 B1
Marschal Ct. Bann 7 E2
Marshall Gr. Ham 162 A2
Marshall La. Wish 165 D2
Marshall St. Coat 121 F2
Marshall St. Lark 185 D1
Marshall St. Wish 164 C1
Marshall's La. Pais 113 F2
Marshill. All 10 A3
Marsmount Rd. Pres 233 F1
Mart St. Glasg 117 E3
Martha St. Glasg 117 E4
Martin Ave. Bonh 28 A4
Martin Ave. Irvine 219 E3
Martin Cres. Glasg 120 B3
Martin Ct. Ham 162 B2
Martin Pl. Holy 143 E2
Martin Sq. Salt 206 A1
Martin St. Coat 122 B4
Martin St. Glasg 117 F2
Martinside. E Kil 180 C3
Martlet Dr. John 131 E4
Martyn St. Aird 122 C3
Martyrs Pl. Bish 98 A4
Marwick St. Glasg 118 A4
Mary Dr. Hat 141 F2
Mary Love Pl. Salt 206 A1
Mary Rae Rd. Hat 141 F2
Mary Sq. Coat 120 C3
Mary St. Green 45 E2
Mary St. Ham 162 B1
Mary St. John 112 A2
Mary St. Laur 42 C2
Mary St. P Glasg 47 D1
Mary St. Pais 113 F1
Mary Stevenson Dr. All 10 A4
Mary Young Pl. Newt M 157 F3
Maryborough Ave. Pres 236 A3
Maryborough Rd. Pres 236 A3
Maryfield Pl. Ayr 236 A2
Maryfield Pl. Falk 41 D2
Maryfield Rd. Ayr 236 A2
Maryhill Rd. Bear 76 A1
Maryhill Rd. Glasg 96 B3
Maryknowe Rd. Holy 143 E1
Maryland Dr. Glasg 115 F3
Maryland Gdns. Glasg 115 F3
Maryland Rd. Dumb 50 B3
Marypark Rd. Lang 70 A4
Maryston St. Glasg 98 B1
Maryville Ave. Glasg 136 B1
Maryville View. Tan 120 B1
Marywood Sq. Glasg 116 C1
Mashock Path. Car 201 D1
Mason La. Mother 163 F3
Mason St. Lark 185 E1
Mason St. Mother 163 F3
Masonfield Ave. Cumb 61 E1
Masonhill Pl. Ayr 239 E3
Masonhill Rd. Ayr 239 E3
Masterton St. Glasg 97 E2
Mather Terr. Laur 42 C2
Matherton Ave. Newt M 157 D3
Matheson Wlk. Bonh 27 F4
Mathew Smith Ave. Kilmk 227 F3
Mathie Cres. Gour 44 C3
Mathieson Rd. Glasg 118 B1
Mathieson St. Pais 114 A3
Matilda Rd. Glasg 116 C2
Matthew McWhirter Pl. Lark 185 D2
Matthew Pl. Kilw 207 F3
Mauchline Ave. Kirk 59 D1
Mauchline Ct. Ham 161 E1
Mauchline Ct. Kirk 59 D1
Mauchline. E Kil 160 C2
Mauchline La. Gour 44 C2
Mauchline Rd. Hurl 228 C3
Mauchline St. Glasg 117 D2
Mauchline Terr. Gour 44 C2
Maukinfauld Ct. Glasg 118 B2
Maukinfauld Rd. Glasg 118 C2
Mauldslie Dr. Law 187 D3
Mauldslie Pl. Ash 199 F4
Mauldslie Rd. Car 187 D1
Mauldslie Rd. Law 186 C1
Mauldslie St. Coat 122 A3
Mauldslie St. Glasg 118 A2
Mauldslie St. Hat 142 A2
Maule Dr. Glasg 96 A1
Maunsheugh Rd. Fen 213 D2
Maurice Ave. Bann 7 E2
Mavis Bank. Bish 97 F4
Mavis Bank. Udd 161 E4
Mavis Rd. Green 45 D2
Mavisbank Ave. Shi 66 B3
Mavisbank Gdns. Glasg 116 C3
Mavisbank Gdns. Hat 142 A3
Mavisbank Rd. Glasg 116 B3
Mavisbank St. Aird 122 C4
Mavisbank St. New 166 B3
Mavisbank Terr. John 111 F1
Mavisbank Terr. Pais 113 F2
Mavor Ave. E Kil 160 A2
Mavor Roundabout. E Kil 159 F2
Maxholm Rd. Kilmk 227 F3
Maxton Ave. Barr 134 A2
Maxton Cres. Alva 5 E4
Maxton Cres. Wish 165 E3
Maxton Terr. Glasg 138 C2
Maxwell Ave. Bear 75 F1
Maxwell Ave. Glasg 116 C2
Maxwell Ave. Glasg 120 A3
Maxwell Cres. Udd 161 E3
Maxwell Ct. Beith 171 D4
Maxwell Ct. Kilmk 223 E2
Maxwell Dr. Ersk 72 C2
Maxwell Dr. Glasg 116 B2
Maxwell Dr. Glasg 120 A3
Maxwell Gdns. Glasg 116 B2
Maxwell Gdns. Hurl 228 C3
Maxwell Gn. Irvine 220 A2
Maxwell Gr. Glasg 116 B2
Maxwell Oval. Glasg 116 C2
Maxwell Path. Lark 185 E1
Maxwell Pl. Coat 121 F3
Maxwell Pl. Glasg 117 D2
Maxwell Pl. Kils 36 B1
Maxwell Pl. Steven 206 C1
Maxwell Pl. Stir 7 D4
Maxwell Rd. Bishop 72 A2
Maxwell Rd. Glasg 117 D2
Maxwell St. Clyde 73 F2
Maxwell St. Glasg 117 E3
Maxwell St. Glasg 117 E4
Maxwell St. Glasg 120 A2
Maxwell St. P Glasg 47 F1

Maxwell St. Pais 113 F3
Maxwell Terr. Glasg 116 C2
Maxwellton Ave. E Kil 160 A2
Maxwellton Pl. E Kil 160 A2
Maxwellton Rd. E Kil 160 B2
Maxwellton Rd. P Glasg 68 C3
Maxwellton St. Pais 113 D2
Maxwellton St. Pais 113 E2
Maxwood Pl. Irvine 220 A3
May Gdns. Ham 162 B3
May Rd. Pais 133 F4
May St. Ham 162 B3
May Terr. Glasg 136 B2
May Terr. Glasg 137 D4
Maybank La. Glasg 117 D1
Maybank St. Glasg 117 D1
Mayberry Cres. Glasg 119 E3
Mayberry Gdns. Glasg 119 E3
Mayberry Gr. Glasg 119 E3
Mayberry Pl. Udd 161 E4
Maybole Cres. Newt M 157 D2
Maybole Gdns. Ham 161 E1
Maybole Gr. Newt M 157 D2
Maybole Pl. Coat 122 B2
Maybole Rd. Ayr 239 D2
Maybole St. Glasg 134 C3
Mayfield Ave. Hurl 228 C3
Mayfield Ave. Newt M 157 F4
Mayfield Cres. How 130 C3
Mayfield Cres. Steven 206 B1
Mayfield Ct. How 130 C3
Mayfield Ct. Stir 7 D2
Mayfield Dr. Bank 39 D2
Mayfield Dr. How 130 C3
Mayfield Gr. Steven 206 B1
Mayfield Mews. Falk 41 F2
Mayfield Pl. Car 202 A4
Mayfield Pl. Salt 217 D4
Mayfield Rd. Ham 161 F2
Mayfield Rd. Salt 206 B1
Mayfield Rd. Salt 217 D4
Mayfield Rd. Steven 206 B1
Mayfield St. Glasg 96 C3
Mayfield St. Stir 7 D2
Mayne Ave. B of A 2 A3
Mayville St. Steven 206 B1
Mc Donald Ave. John 111 F1
Mc Laurin Cres. John 111 E1
Mc Phail St. Green 46 B2
McAdam Ct. Pres 236 B3
McAlister Rd. Alex 27 F3
McAlley Ct. B of A 1 C4
McAllister Ave. Aird 123 E4
McAllister Ct. Bann 7 E1
McAlpine St. Glasg 117 D4
McAlpine St. Wish 165 D1
McArdle Ave. Mother 163 D4
McArthur Pk Kirk 79 E4
McArthur St. Glasg 136 B4
McAslin Ct. Glasg 117 E4
McAslin St. Glasg 117 E4
McAuslan Pl. Helen 16 C1
McCall's Ave. Ayr 236 A1
McCallum Ave. Glasg 138 A4
McCallum Cres. Gour 44 C4
McCallum Ct. E Kil 159 D2
McCallum Gdns. Hat 141 F1
McCallum Gr. E Kil 159 D2
McCallum Pl. E Kil 159 D2
McCallum Rd. Lark 185 D1
McCASH PL. Kirk 79 E4
McClue Ave. Ren 94 A2
McClue Rd. Ren 94 B2
Mcclurg Ct. Mother 163 F3
McColgan Pl. Ayr 236 B2
McColl Ave. Alex 27 E3
McColl Pl. Alex 27 E3
McConnell Rd. Loch 129 D1
McCormack Gdns. Holy 143 F2
McCracken Ave. Ren 94 A1
McCracken Dr. Tan 141 E4
McCreery St. Clyde 94 B4
McCulloch Ave. Tan 141 E3
McCulloch La. Alex 27 E4
McCulloch St. Glasg 116 C2
McDonald Cres. Clyde 94 B4
McDonald Dr. Irvine 219 D2
McDonald Pl. Holy 143 D2
McDonald Pl. Neil 154 C4
McDowall Ave. Ard 205 E1
McDowall Pl. Ard 205 E1
McEwan Dr. Helen 16 C2
McEwan Gdns. E Kil 159 D2
McEwans Way. Stone 198 B1
McFarlane Rd. Bonh 28 A4
McFarlane St. Glasg 117 F3
McFarlane St. Pais 113 E4
McGavin Ave. Kilw 208 A2
McGavin Way. Kilw 207 E2
McGhee St. Clyde 74 A2
McGibney Dr. Irvine 219 E1
McGillivray Ave. Salt 205 F1
McGowan Pl. Ham 162 A3
McGown St. Pais 113 E3
McGregor Ave. Aird 123 E4

McGregor Ave. Bonh 28 A4
McGregor Ave. Ren 94 A1
McGregor Ave. Steven 206 B1
McGregor Dr. Dumb 50 B2
Mcgregor Path. Glen 101 E3
McGregor Rd. Cumb 61 F1
McGregor St. Clyde 94 B4
McGregor St. Glasg 115 F3
McGregor St. Mother 164 B2
McGrigor Rd. Miln 54 C2
McGrigor Rd. Stir 7 D2
McHardy Cres. Beith 171 F2
McInnes Ct. Wish 165 D1
McInnes Pl. Wish 186 A4
McInnes St. Bonh 28 A4
McIntosh Ct. Glasg 117 F4
McIntosh Quadrant. Hat 141 F1
McIntosh St. Glasg 117 F4
McIntosh Way. Mother 163 E3
McIntyre Pl. Pais 113 F1
McIntyre Terr. Glasg 139 D3
McIsaac Rd. Salt 217 D4
McIver St. Glasg 139 F3
McKay Cres. John 112 A1
McKay Gr. Hat 141 F3
McKay Pl. E Kil 159 D2
McKechnie St. Glasg 116 A4
McKellar Ave. Ard 205 E1
McKenna Dr. Aird 122 C4
McKenzie Ave. Clyde 74 A2
McKenzie Dr. Bonh 19 F1
McKenzie St. Pais 113 E3
McKenzie's Cl. Lan 215 D2
McKerrell St. Pais 114 A3
McKillop Pl. Salt 205 F1
McKim Wlk. Alex 49 E4
McKinlay Ave. Bonh 20 A1
McKinlay Cres. All 10 B4
McKinlay Cres. Irvine 219 D1
Mckinnon Pl. Salt 206 A1
McKnight Ave. Fen 213 F2
McLachlan Ave. Stir 7 D1
McLachlan St. Lar 23 E1
McLaren Ave. Ren 94 B1
Mclaren Ct. Glasg 136 A1
McLaren Ct. Lar 23 E1
McLaren Gr. E Kil 159 D2
Mclaren Pl. Glasg 136 C1
McLaren Terr. Stir 7 D2
McLean Cres. Bonh 19 F1
McLean Dr. Hat 141 F1
McLean Dr. Irvine 225 E4
Mclean Gdns. Stone 198 C1
McLean Pl. Pais 113 E4
McLean St. Ayr 236 B1
McLees La. Mother 163 D4
McLelland Dr. Kilmk 227 F4
McLennan St. Glasg 137 D4
McLeod Rd. Dumb 50 B2
McLeod St. Green 46 B2
McLuckie Dr. Kilw 207 E2
McLuckie Pk. Kilw 207 E2
McMillan Ave. Beith 171 D4
McMillan Dr. Ard 205 D2
McMillan Pl. Shew 224 C3
McMillan Rd. Wish 164 B1
McMillan Way. Law 186 C3
McNair St. Glasg 119 D3
McNaught Pl. Alex 27 E1
McNaught Pl. Kilm 222 A4
McNay Cres. Salt 206 A1
McNeil Ave. Clyde 74 C1
McNeil Pl. Wish 186 A4
McNeil St. Glasg 117 E2
McNeill Ave. Pres 233 E1
McPhail St. Glasg 117 F2
McPhater St. Glasg 97 D1
McPherson Cres. Chap 123 F1
McPherson Dr. Gour 44 B4
McPherson Dr. Stir 2 A1
McPherson Dr. Udd 141 D2
McPherson La. Alex 27 E4
McPherson St. Hat 142 B3
McShannon Gr. Hat 142 A2
McVean Pl. Bank 39 D2
Meadow Ave. Irvine 219 E2
Meadow Ave. Udd 161 E3
Meadow Ct. Car 188 B1
Meadow Ct. Dumb 49 F3
Meadow Gn. N Sau 5 D1
Meadow La. Ren 94 B3
Meadow La. Udd 141 D1
Meadow Path. Chap 123 E1
Meadow Pk. Alva 5 D3
Meadow Pk. Ayr 239 D3
Meadow Pl. Stir 2 B1
Meadow Rd. Dumb 50 A2
Meadow Rd. Glasg 96 A1
Meadow Rd. Kilnc 202 A2
Meadow Rd. Mother 164 A3
Meadow St. Coat 122 A2
Meadow St. Falk 42 B2
Meadow View. Cumb 62 B2
Meadow View. Plains 104 A2
Meadow Way. Newt M 156 B3
Meadowbank La. Pres 236 A4
Meadowbank La. Udd 140 C3
Meadowbank Pl. Newt M 156 B3

Meadowbank St. Dumb 49 F2
Meadowburn Ave. Klrk 79 F3
Meadowburn Ave. Newt M 156 B3
Meadowburn. Bish 78 A2
Meadowburn Rd. Wish 165 E2
Meadowfield Pl. New 166 B3
Meadowfoot Rd. W Kil 190 B2
Meadowforth Rd. Stir 7 E4
Meadowhead Ave. Muir 80 C1
Meadowhead Ave. Shew 224 C2
Meadowhead Rd. Mother 164 B2
Meadowhead Rd. Plains 103 F1
Meadowhead Rd. Shew 224 C2
Meadowhead
   Roundabout. Shew 224 C1
Meadowhill. Newt M 156 B3
Meadowhill St. Lark 185 D2
Meadowland Rd. B of A 2 A3
Meadowpark Dr. Ayr 239 D3
Meadowpark St. Glasg 118 A4
Meadows Ave. Lark 185 D2
Meadows The. Hous 91 F1
Meadows The. Kilw 207 E2
Meadowside Ave. John 112 B1
Meadowside Gdns. Aird 123 E4
Meadowside. Ham 183 E3
Meadowside. Hurl 228 C4
Meadowside Pl. Aird 123 E4
Meadowside Rd. Kils 59 F4
Meadowside St. Glasg 96 A1
Meadowside St. Ren 94 B3
Meadowside. W Kil 190 B3
Meadowwell St. Glasg 119 D3
Meadside Ave. Kilbar 111 D2
Meadside Rd. Kilbar 111 D2
Mealkirk St. Dunt 74 B4
Mearns Ct. Ham 183 F4
Mearns Rd. Mother 163 E4
Mearns Rd. Newt M 156 B1
Mearns St. Green 45 F2
Mearns St. Green 45 F3
Mearns Way. Bish 78 B1
Mearnscroft Gdns. Newt M ... 156 C2
Mearnscroft Rd. Newt M 156 C2
Medine Ave. Beith 150 A1
Medine Ct. Beith 150 A1
Medlar Rd. Cumb 62 B1
Medrox Gdns. Cumb 81 F3
Medwin Ct. E Kil 179 F4
Medwin Gdns. E Kil 179 F4
Medwin St. Glasg 139 F3
Medwyn Pl. All 9 F3
Medwyn St. Glasg 95 G2
Medwyn St. Glasg 95 F1
Meek Pl. Glasg 139 D3
Meeks Rd. Falk 42 A3
Meetinghouse La. Pais 113 F3
Megan St. Glasg 117 F2
Meikle Ave. Ren 94 B1
Meikle Bin Brae. Lennox 57 F4
Meikle Cres. Gree 103 E4
Meikle Cres. Ham 183 E4
Meikle Ct. Stew 195 F1
Meikle Drumgray Rd. Gree ... 103 F4
Meikle Earnock Rd. Ham .. 183 D4
Meikle Rd. Glasg 135 D4
Meiklehill Ct. Kirk 58 C1
Meiklehill Rd. Kirk 58 C1
Meiklem St. Hat 142 B3
Meiklerig Cres. Glasg 115 E1
Meikleriggs Dr. Pais 113 D1
Meiklewood Ave. Pres 233 E1
Meiklewood Rd. Glasg 115 E3
Meiklewood Rd. Kilmk 222 C3
Melbourne Ave. Clyde 73 E3
Melbourne Ave. E Kil 180 A4
Melbourne Ct. Glasg 136 B2
Melbourne Gn. E Kil 180 A4
Melbourne Rd. Salt 216 C4
Melbourne St. Glasg 117 F3
Melbourne Terr. Salt 216 C4
Meldon Pl. Glasg 115 E4
Meldrum Gdns. Glasg 116 B1
Meldrum Mains. Glenm 102 C2
Meldrum St. Clyde 94 B4
Melford Ave. Glasg 136 B1
Melford Ave. Klrk 79 D4
Melford Ave. Shot 147 D2
Melford Gdns. John 111 E1
Melford Rd. Tan 141 F4
Melford Way. Pais 114 A4
Melfort Ave. Clyde 74 B2
Melfort Ave. Glasg 116 A2
Melfort Dr. Stir 7 D2
Melfort Path. New 165 F4
Melfort Quadrant. Holy 143 E2
Melfort Rd. Ham 161 F1
Mellerstain Dr. Glasg 94 C3
Mellock Gdns. Falk 41 F1
Melness Pl. Glasg 115 E4
Melrose Ave. Chap 123 E1
Melrose Ave. Coat 120 C3
Melrose Ave. Holy 143 D1
Melrose Ave. Lin 112 A4
Melrose Ave. Pais 113 D1
Melrose Cres. Wish 165 D3

Melrose Ct. Glasg 138 A4
Melrose Gdns. Glasg 96 C2
Melrose Gdns. Tan 120 C1
Melrose Gdns. Twe 59 F2
Melrose Pl. Coat 121 F4
Melrose Pl. Falk 42 A2
Melrose Pl. Lark 185 D1
Melrose Pl. Udd 140 B1
Melrose Rd. Cumb 82 C4
Melrose Rd. P Glasg 68 C4
Melrose St. Glasg 97 D1
Melrose St. Ham 162 A3
Melrose Terr. E Kil 159 F2
Melrose Terr. Ham 162 A3
Melvaig Pl. Glasg 96 B3
Melvick Pl. Glasg 115 E4
Melville Cres. Glasg 117 E3
Melville Dr. Mother 163 F3
Melville Gdns. Bish 78 A1
Melville Pk. E Kil 160 A2
Melville Pl. B of A 2 A4
Melville Pl. Car 187 F1
Melville St. Glasg 116 C2
Melville St. Kilmk 228 A4
Melville Terr. Stir 7 D3
Melvinhall Rd. Lan 215 D3
Memel St. Glasg 97 F3
Memus Ave. Glasg 115 E2
Mennock Ct. Ham 161 F1
Mennock Dr. Bish 78 A2
Mennock La. Troon 229 F3
Mennock St. Cle 144 B1
Menock Rd. Glasg 137 E3
Menstrie Pl. Men 4 A3
Menteith Ave. Bish 78 A1
Menteith Ct. All 10 B3
Menteith Dr. Glasg 138 B1
Menteith Gdns. Bear 75 E4
Menteith Loan. Holy 143 D3
Menteith Pl. Glasg 138 B1
Menteith Rd. Mother 163 F4
Menteith Rd. Stir 2 A2
Menzies Dr. Glasg 98 A3
Menzies Dr. Stir 2 A1
Menzies Pl. Glasg 98 A3
Menzies Rd. Glasg 98 A3
Merchant La. Glasg 117 E3
Merchants Cl. Kilbar 111 D2
Merchiston Ave. Falk 42 A4
Merchiston Ave. Lin 111 F3
Merchiston Gdns. Falk 42 A3
Merchiston Rd. Falk 42 A4
Merchiston St. Glasg 118 C4
Merchiston Terr. Falk 42 A4
Mercury La. Gour 44 B2
Meredith Dr. Sten 23 F2
Merino Rd. Green 45 F2
Merkins Ave. Dumb 50 A3
Merkland Ct. Glasg 96 A1
Merkland Ct. Kirk 59 D1
Merkland Dr. Falk 42 C1
Merkland Dr. Kirk 80 A4
Merkland Pl. Kirk 59 D1
Merkland Rd. Ayr 239 D1
Merkland Rd. Coat 101 E1
Merkland St. Glasg 96 A1
Merksworth Ave. Dalry 191 E4
Merksworth Way. Pais 113 F4
Merlewood Rd. W Kil 190 A2
Merlin Ave. Green 45 D3
Merlin Ave. Hat 142 A4
Merlin La. Green 45 D3
Merlin Way. Pais 114 A4
Merlinford Ave. Ren 94 C2
Merlinford Cres. Ren 94 C2
Merlinford Way. Ren 94 C2
Merrick Ave. Pres 233 E1
Merrick Ave. Troon 229 F2
Merrick Ct. Aird 103 D1
Merrick Gdns. Bear 75 E4
Merrick Gdns. Glasg 116 A3
Merrick Gdns. Quart 183 F2
Merrick Pl. Irvine 220 A1
Merrick Pl. Sym 231 E2
Merrick Rd. Kilmk 228 A2
Merrick Terr. Tan 141 D4
Merrick View. Stew 195 F1
Merrick Way. Glasg 138 A2
Merry St. Holy 143 D1
Merry St. Mother 163 F4
Merryburn Ave. Glasg 136 B2
Merrycrest Ave. Glasg 136 B2
Merrycroft Ave. Glasg 136 B2
Merryflats. Twe 59 F2
Merrygreen Pl. Stew 195 F1
Merryland Pl. Glasg 116 B4
Merryland St. Glasg 116 A4
Merryland St. Glasg 116 A4
Merrylee Ave. P Glasg 68 C4
Merrylee Cres. Glasg 136 B3
Merrylee Park Ave. Glasg ... 136 B2
Merrylee Park Mews. Glasg 136 B3
Merrylee Pk. Glasg 136 B3
Merrylee Rd. Glasg 136 C3
Merrylees Rd. Udd 161 E4
Merryston Ct. Coat 121 F3

Merrystone St. Coat 121 F4
Merryton Ave. Glasg 75 D2
Merryton Ave. Glasg 136 B2
Merryton Pl. Glasg 75 D2
Merryton Rd. Lark 184 C3
Merryton Rd. Mother 164 B1
Merryton St. Lark 184 C3
Merryvale Ave. Glasg 136 B2
Merryvale Pl. Glasg 136 B3
Merryvale Rd. Irvine 219 E1
Merryvale
   Roundabout. Irvine 219 E1
Merton Dr. Glasg 115 D3
Merville Cres. Cali 66 C3
Merville Terr. Cali 66 C3
Meryon Gdns. Glasg 119 E1
Meryon Rd. Glasg 119 E2
Metcalfe Pl. Shew 224 C3
Methil Rd. P Glasg 68 C3
Methil St. Glasg 95 E2
Methlan Pk. Dumb 49 E1
Methuen Rd. Ren 93 F1
Methuen Rd. Ren 114 A4
Methven Ave. Bear 76 A3
Methven Ave. Kilmk 227 F2
Methven Pl. E Kil 159 E1
Methven Rd. Kilmk 227 F2
Methven Rd. Newt M 157 D4
Methven St. Clyde 73 F2
Methven St. Glasg 118 B2
Metropole La. Glasg 117 E3
Mews La. Ayr 238 C2
Mews La. Green 45 E4
Mews La. Kilmk 227 F4
Mews La. Pais 113 F4
Mharie Pl. Bonh 27 F1
Michael
   McParland Dr. Lennox ... 78 A4
Michael Terr. Chap 123 E1
Micklehouse Oval. Glasg 120 A3
Micklehouse Pl. Glasg 120 A3
Micklehouse Rd. Glasg 120 A3
Micklehouse Wynd. Glasg 120 A3
Mid Ave. P Glasg 68 C4
Mid Barrwood Rd. Kils 60 C4
Mid Carbarns. Wish 164 B3
Mid Dykes Rd. Salt 205 F1
Mid Pk. E Kil 180 C4
Mid Rd. Beith 150 A1
Mid Rd. Cumb 82 C3
Mid Rd. Eagle 178 C2
Mid Rig. Irvine 220 A2
Mid-Loan St. Car 201 F2
Mid-Wharf St. Glasg 97 E1
Midas Pl. Holy 142 C3
Midcroft Ave. Glasg 137 F3
Midcroft. Bish 77 F2
Middle Pk. Pais 113 E1
Middle Ward St. Dunt 74 B4
Middlefield. E Kil 180 C3
Middlefield Rd. Falk 42 B3
Middlehouse Ct. Car 187 E1
Middlemass Ct. Falk 42 A3
Middlemass St. Kilmk 228 A4
Middlemuir Ave. Klrk 79 E3
Middlemuir Rd. Klrk 79 E3
Middlemuir Rd. Stir 7 E3
Middlepart Cres. Salt 206 A1
Middlepart. Steven 206 B1
Middlepenny Pl. Lang 70 A4
Middlepenny Rd. Lang 70 A4
Middlerigg Rd. Cumb 61 E1
Middlesex St. Glasg 116 C3
Middleton Cres. Lark 199 D4
Middleton Cres. Pais 113 D3
Middleton Dr. Helen 25 C4
Middleton Dr. Miln 55 E1
Middleton La. Helen 25 C4
Middleton. Men 4 A3
Middleton Pk. Irvine 220 A2
Middleton Rd. Irvine 220 A2
Middleton Rd. Lin 112 B4
Middleton Rd. Pais 113 D3
Middleton St. Alex 27 E3
Middleton St. Glasg 116 B3
Midland St. Glasg 117 D4
Midlem Dr. Glasg 115 E3
Midlem Oval. Glasg 115 E3
Midlock St. Glasg 116 B3
Midlothian Dr. Glasg 116 B1
Midthorn Cres. Falk 42 C3
Midton Ave. Pres 236 A4
Midton Ave. Ayr 238 C3
Midton Rd. How 131 D3
Midton Rd. Kilmk 227 F1
Midton Rd. Pres 236 B4
Midton St. Glasg 97 F2
Midtown. Men 3 F3
Migvie Pl. Glasg 96 B3
Milford. E Kil 180 A4
Milford St. Glasg 119 D4
Milgarholm Ave. Irvine 219 E1
Milgarholm
   Roundabout. Irvine 219 E1
Mill Ave. Kilm 222 B4
Mill Brae. Ayr 239 D4
Mill Brae. B of W 110 B4
Mill Brae Ct. Coat 121 E3

Mill Cres. Glasg

Street	Page	Grid
Mill Cres. Glasg	117	F2
Mill Cres. Irvine	219	F2
Mill Cres. Lennox	57	E1
Mill Ct. Glasg	138	A4
Mill Ct. Ham	162	B1
Mill Ct. Kilmk	228	A4
Mill Gr. Ham	162	B1
Mill Hill. Cam	6	B3
Mill Loan. Aird	123	D4
Mill of Gryffe Rd. B of W	110	B4
Mill Pk. Dalry	191	E4
Mill Pk. Ham	162	B1
Mill Pl. Lin	112	A3
Mill Rd. Aird	103	D1
Mill Rd. All	10	A3
Mill Rd. Cam	6	B3
Mill Rd. Car	187	F1
Mill Rd. Card	26	A1
Mill Rd. Cle	145	F1
Mill Rd. Clyde	94	B4
Mill Rd. East	127	F3
Mill Rd. Glasg	139	E3
Mill Rd. Ham	162	B1
Mill Rd. Irvine	219	F1
Mill Rd. Kilb	149	D1
Mill Rd. Kils	37	E2
Mill Rd. Kils	59	F4
Mill Rd. Mother	163	F4
Mill Rd. New	166	C3
Mill Rd. Sten	24	A2
Mill Rd. Udd	141	D1
Mill Rig. E Kil	180	B3
Mill Rise. Klrk	79	E2
Mill St. All	10	A3
Mill St. Ayr	239	D4
Mill St. Cald	104	C3
Mill St. Glasg	138	A3
Mill St. Green	45	F2
Mill St. Kilmk	227	F4
Mill St. Pais	113	F2
Mill Way. Ayr	80	A4
Mill Wynd. Ayr	238	C4
Millands Ave. Udd	140	B1
Millar Pl. Bon	40	A2
Millar Pl. Sten	24	A3
Millar Rd. Stir	2	B1
Millar Rd. Salt	217	D4
Millar St. Green	46	A1
Millar St. Pais	113	F3
Millar St. Stone	198	C1
Millar Terr. Glasg	118	A1
Millarbank St. Glasg	97	F2
Millars Pl. Klrk	79	E2
Millars Wynd. N Sau	5	E1
Millarston Ave. Pais	113	D2
Millarston Dr. Pais	113	D2
Millbank Ave. Hat	142	B2
Millbank Rd. P Glasg	68	B4
Millbank Rd. Wish	164	C1
Millbeg Cres. Glasg	119	F3
Millbeg Pl. Glasg	119	F3
Millbrae Ave. Muir	100	B4
Millbrae Cres. Clyde	94	B4
Millbrae Cres. Glasg	136	C4
Millbrae Ct. Glasg	136	C4
Millbrae Gdns. Glasg	136	C4
Millbrae Rd. Glasg	136	C4
Millbrix Ave. Glasg	95	D3
Millbrook. E Kil	159	D1
Millburn Ave. Clyde	94	C4
Millburn Ave. Glasg	138	A3
Millburn Ave. Ren	94	C2
Millburn Cres. Dumb	50	A2
Millburn Ct. E Kil	179	F4
Millburn Dr. Kil	89	D4
Millburn Dr. Ren	94	C2
Millburn Gdns. E Kil	179	F4
Millburn La. Lark	185	E1
Millburn Pl. Lark	199	D4
Millburn Rd. Alex	27	E2
Millburn Rd. Ash	186	A1
Millburn Rd. Dumb	50	A2
Millburn Rd. P Glasg	68	B4
Millburn Rd. Ren	94	B2
Millburn St. Falk	42	B3
Millburn St. Glasg	98	A1
Millburn St. Lennox	57	F4
Millburn St. Mother	163	F4
Millburn Terr. Irvine	220	A3
Millburn Way. E Kil	179	F4
Millburn Way. Ren	94	C2
Millcroft Rd. Cumb	62	A1
Millcroft Rd. Glasg	117	F1
Millcroft Rd. Glenm	82	C2
Millcroft Rd. Glenm	83	D2
Milldam Rd. Dunt	74	B4
Milldown Pl. Irvine	220	B1
Miller Ct. Dumb	50	A2
Miller Field Pl. Ham	162	C2
Miller Pl. Air	14	C2
Miller Pl. Ard	205	D2
Miller Pl. East	127	F3
Miller Rd. Ayr	238	C4
Miller St. Bonh	27	F4
Miller St. Car	188	A1
Miller St. Clyde	74	A1
Miller St. Coat	122	A3
Miller St. Dumb	50	A2
Miller St. East	127	F3
Miller St. Glasg	117	E4
Miller St. Glasg	120	A2
Miller St. Ham	162	C2
Miller St. John	112	A2
Miller St. Lark	185	D2
Miller St. Wish	165	D2
Miller's Pl. Aird	123	D4
Millerfield Pl. Glasg	118	A2
Millerfield Rd. Glasg	118	A2
Millerslea Gdns. Helen	16	C1
Millersneuk Ave. Klrk	79	E2
Millersneuk Cres. Stepps	99	D3
Millersneuk Dr. Klrk	79	E2
Millersneuk Rd. Klrk	79	E2
Millerston St. Glasg	118	A3
Millfield Ave. Ersk	72	C1
Millfield Ave. Mother	163	F4
Millfield Cres. Ersk	73	D1
Millfield Dr. Ersk	73	D1
Millfield Gdns. Ersk	73	D1
Millfield Hill. Ersk	72	C1
Millfield La. Ersk	72	C1
Millfield Meadows. Ersk	72	C1
Millfield Pl. Ersk	72	C1
Millfield View. Ersk	72	C1
Millfield Wlk. Ersk	73	D1
Millfield Wynd. Ersk	72	C1
Millflats St. Falk	24	A1
Millford Dr. Lin	112	A3
Millfore Ct. Irvine	220	A2
Millgate Ave. Tan	140	C4
Millgate. Udd	140	C4
Millgate Rd. Ham	162	B1
Millglen Pl. Ard	205	E2
Millglen Rd. Ard	205	E2
Millhall Rd. Eagle	179	E2
Millhall Rd. Stir	7	E3
Millheugh Brae. Lark	184	C1
Millheugh. Lark	184	C1
Millheugh Pl. Udd	161	E3
Millheugh Rd. Stone	198	C3
Millhill Ave. Kilm	222	B4
Millhill Terr. Kilmk	222	C2
Millholm Rd. Glasg	137	D2
Millhouse Cres. Glasg	96	B4
Millhouse Dr. Glasg	96	B4
Millichen Rd. Glasg	76	C3
Millig St. Helen	16	B2
Milliken Dr. Kilbar	111	E1
Milliken Park Rd. John	111	E1
Milliken Rd. Kilbar	111	E1
Millport Ave. Glasg	137	E4
Millport Rd. P Glasg	68	C3
Millroad Dr. Glasg	117	F3
Millroad Gdns. Glasg	117	F3
Millroad St. Glasg	117	F3
Millrock Ct. Troon	229	E2
Millstream Cres. Cald	105	D2
Millview. Barr	134	B2
Millview Pl. Glasg	135	D2
Millview Terr. Neil	154	B4
Millwood St. Glasg	136	C4
Milnbank St. Glasg	118	A4
Milncroft Pl. Glasg	99	D1
Milncroft Rd. Glasg	99	D1
Milndavie Cres. Strath	31	E2
Milndavie Rd. Strath	31	E1
Milnepark Rd. Bann	11	F4
Milner La. Glasg	95	F3
Milner Rd. Glasg	95	F3
Milngavie Rd. Bear	75	F2
Milngavie Rd. Bear	76	A3
Milngavie Rd. Strath	31	E1
Milnpark Gdns. Glasg	116	C3
Milnpark St. Glasg	116	C3
Milnwood Dr. Hat	142	B2
Milnwood Dr. Mother	142	B1
Milovaig Ave. Glasg	76	B1
Milovaig St. Glasg	76	B1
Milrig Rd. Glasg	138	A4
Milton Ave. Glasg	138	C3
Milton Ave. Kilmk	223	E1
Milton Brae. Dumb	50	C1
Milton Brae. Stir	7	D1
Milton Cl. Duni	21	E2
Milton Cres. Bann	7	E1
Milton Cres. Car	187	F1
Milton Cres. Irvine	220	B1
Milton Cres. Dumb	50	C1
Milton Ct. Irvine	220	B1
Milton Douglas Rd. Dunt	74	A3
Milton Dr. Bish	97	F4
Milton Dr. Kilmk	223	E1
Milton Est. Bonh	27	F3
Milton Gdns. Bann	7	E1
Milton Gdns. Tan	140	C4
Milton Hill. Dumb	50	C1
Milton Mains Rd. Clyde	74	A3
Milton Pk. Ayr	239	D2
Milton Pk. Kilb	149	D1
Milton Pl. Duni	21	E2
Milton Quadrant. Kilb	149	D2
Milton Rd. Bann	7	E1
Milton Rd. Car	201	E4
Milton Rd. E Kil	159	D1
Milton Rd. Hurl	223	F1
Milton Rd. Irvine	220	B1
Milton Rd. Kilb	149	D2
Milton Rd. Kilmk	228	B4
Milton Rd. Kirk	58	B1
Milton Rd. Lennox	57	F4
Milton Rd. P Glasg	68	C3
Milton Row. Duni	21	F2
Milton St. Aird	123	D4
Milton St. Car	187	F1
Milton St. Glasg	97	E1
Milton St. Ham	162	A2
Milton St. Mother	163	F4
Milton Terr. Bann	7	D1
Milton Terr. Ham	162	A3
Milton View. Cross	226	C3
Milverton Ave. Bear	75	E3
Milverton Rd. Glasg	136	A1
Mimosa Rd. B of W	110	B4
Minard Rd. Glasg	116	C1
Minard Rd. P Glasg	68	C4
Minard Rd. Shot	146	B3
Minard Way. Tan	141	D4
Minch Way. Aird	123	E3
Mincher Cres. Mother	163	F2
Mine Rd. B of A	2	A4
Minella Gdns. Hat	142	A4
Minerva La. Gour	44	B2
Minerva St. Glasg	116	C4
Minerva Terr. Gour	44	B2
Minerva Way. Glasg	116	C4
Mingarry La. Glasg	96	C2
Mingarry St. Glasg	96	C2
Mingulay Cres. Glasg	97	E4
Mingulay Pl. Bish	97	F4
Mingulay St. Glasg	97	E4
Minmoir Rd. Glasg	134	C4
Minster Wlk. Coat	120	C3
Minstrel Rd. Glasg	75	E1
Minthill Pl. East	127	E3
Minto Ave. Glasg	138	B2
Minto Cres. Glasg	115	F3
Minto Ct. Alva	5	D3
Minto Gdns. Alva	5	D3
Minto Pk. Wish	165	E3
Minto St. Glasg	115	F3
Minto St. Green	45	E2
Mireton St. Glasg	97	D3
Mirren Dr. Dunt	73	F4
Mirren's Shore. P Glasg	47	E1
Mirrlees Dr. Glasg	96	B2
Mirrlees La. Glasg	96	B2
Misk Knowes. Steven	217	F3
Mission La. Falk	42	A2
Mitchell Ave. Glasg	139	F3
Mitchell Ave. Ren	94	A1
Mitchell Cres. All	9	F4
Mitchell Ct. Kilmk	228	A4
Mitchell Dr. Card	48	A3
Mitchell Dr. Miln	55	E1
Mitchell Hill Rd. Glasg	137	F1
Mitchell La. Glasg	117	D4
Mitchell Pl. Falk	41	F1
Mitchell Pl. Salt	205	F1
Mitchell Rd. Cumb	62	A2
Mitchell St. Aird	122	C4
Mitchell St. Beith	150	B1
Mitchell St. Coat	121	E3
Mitchell St. Glasg	117	D4
Mitchell St. Green	46	C1
Mitchell Way. Alex	27	F3
Mitchison Rd. Cumb	62	A2
Mitre Ct. Glasg	95	F2
Mitre La. Glasg	95	F2
Mitre La W. Glasg	95	E2
Mitre Rd. Glasg	95	F2
Moat Ave. Glasg	95	E4
Mochrum Ct. Pres	236	B3
Mochrum Rd. Glasg	136	C3
Modan Rd. Stir	7	D2
Moffat Ave. Sten	24	B2
Moffat Ct. E Kil	179	F4
Moffat Gdns. E Kil	179	F4
Moffat Pl. Coat	122	C2
Moffat Pl. E Kil	179	F4
Moffat Pl. Udd	140	B1
Moffat Rd. Aird	123	F4
Moffat St. Glasg	117	E2
Moffat St. Green	46	B2
Moffat View. Plains	104	A2
Moffathill. Chap	123	F3
Mogarth Ave. Pais	132	C4
Moidart Ave. Ren	94	A2
Moidart Cres. Glasg	115	F3
Moidart Ct. Barr	134	A2
Moidart Gdns. Kirk	59	D1
Moidart Gdns. Newt M	156	C3
Moidart Pl. Glasg	115	F3
Moidart Rd. Glasg	115	F3
Moidart Rd. P Glasg	68	C4
Moir St. All	10	A4
Moir St. Glasg	117	E3
Molendinar St. Glasg	117	E3
Molendinar Terr. Neil	154	B3
Mollanbowie Rd. Bonh	19	F1
Mollins Ct. Cumb	81	E3
Mollins Rd. Cumb	81	E3
Mollinsburn Rd. Glen	81	F1
Mollinsburn Rd. Glenm	102	B3
Mollinsburn St. Glasg	97	F2
Mollison Ave. East	127	F3
Monach Gdns. Irvine	225	D4
Monach Rd. Glasg	119	E4
Monach Rd. P Glasg	69	D4
Monaebrook Pl. Helen	25	C4
Monar Dr. Glasg	97	D2
Monar Pl. Glasg	97	D2
Monar St. Glasg	97	D2
Monar Way. New	165	F3
Monart Pl. Glasg	96	C2
Moncur St. Kilw	208	A2
Moncur St. Glasg	117	F3
Moness Dr. Glasg	115	F2
Moniebrugh Cres. Kils	36	C1
Moniebrugh Rd. Kils	36	C1
Monifieth Ave. Glasg	115	E2
Monikie Gdns. Bish	78	B1
Monkcastle Dr. Glasg	139	D3
Monkland Ave. Klrk	79	E3
Monkland La. Coat	121	F2
Monkland St. Aird	123	D4
Monkland Terr. Glen	101	E3
Monkland View. Calder	123	D1
Monkland View Cres. Coat	121	D3
Monkland View. Tan	121	D1
Monklands. Troon	229	F4
Monkreddan Cres. Kilw	207	E3
Monks La. Car	201	F2
Monks Rd. Aird	123	E2
Monksbridge Ave. Glasg	75	E1
Monkscourt Ave. Aird	122	C4
Monkscroft Ave. Glasg	96	A1
Monkscroft Ct. Glasg	96	A1
Monkscroft Gdns. Glasg	96	A1
Monkton Ct. Pres	233	E1
Monkton Dr. Glasg	75	E1
Monkton Gdns. Newt M	157	D2
Monkton Pl. P Glasg	68	C4
Monkton Rd. Pres	233	E1
Monktonhill Rd. Pres	233	D4
Monktonhill Rd. Troon	233	D4
Monkwood Pl. Ayr	239	D1
Monmouth Ave. Glasg	96	A3
Monreith Ave. Bear	75	E1
Monreith Rd E. Glasg	137	D3
Monreith Rd. Glasg	136	C3
Monroe Dr. Tan	120	C1
Monroe Pl. Tan	120	C1
Montague La. Glasg	96	A2
Montague St. Glasg	96	C1
Montalto Ave. Holy	143	D1
Montclair Pl. Lin	112	A3
Montego Gn. E Kil	159	D1
Monteith Dr. Glasg	158	A4
Monteith Gdns. Glasg	157	F4
Monteith Pl. Glasg	117	F3
Monteith Pl. Udd	161	F4
Monteith Row. Glasg	117	F3
Monteith St. Wish	146	C3
Montfode Ct. Ard	205	E2
Montfode Dr. Ard	205	D2
Montford Ave. Glasg	137	F4
Montfort Pl. Falk	42	A2
Montgomerie Cres. Salt	216	C4
Montgomerie Pier Rd. Ard	205	D1
Montgomerie Rd. Pres	233	D1
Montgomerie Rd. Salt	216	C4
Montgomerie St. Ard	205	E1
Montgomerie St. P Glasg	47	E1
Montgomerie Terr. Ayr	235	F1
Montgomery Ave. Beith	171	E4
Montgomery Ave. Coat	121	F4
Montgomery Ave. Pais	114	A4
Montgomery Cres. Wish	185	F4
Montgomery Ct. Eagle	178	C2
Montgomery Ct. Kilb	149	D1
Montgomery Dr. Glasg	136	B1
Montgomery Dr. Kilbar	111	D2
Montgomery Pl. E Kil	159	F1
Montgomery Pl. Kilmk	222	C1
Montgomery Pl. Lark	185	D1
Montgomery Pl. Pais	114	A4
Montgomery Sq. Eagle	178	C2
Montgomery St. E Kil	159	F1
Montgomery St. Eagle	178	C2
Montgomery St. Falk	42	C3
Montgomery St. Glasg	118	A2
Montgomery St. Glasg	139	F3
Montgomery St. Irvine	219	D1
Montgomery St. Kilmk	222	C1
Montgomery St. Lark	185	D2
Montgomery Terr. Kilw	208	A2
Montgomery Terr. M of C	58	B3
Montgomery Way. Stir	2	A2
Montgomeryfield. Irvine	225	D4
Montgreenan View. Kilw	207	F2
Montraive St. Glasg	118	B1
Montrave St. Glasg	115	E2
Montreal Pk. E Kil	159	D1
Montrose Ave. Glasg	114	C4
Montrose Ave. Glasg	119	E1
Montrose Ave. P Glasg	68	C3
Montrose Cres. Ham	162	B2
Montrose Dr. Bear	75	F4
Montrose Gdns. Kils	36	B1
Montrose Gdns. Miln	55	D2
Montrose Gdns. Udd	140	B1
Montrose Pl. Lin	112	A3
Montrose Rd. Pais	132	C4
Montrose Rd. Stir	2	B2
Montrose St. Clyde	74	B1
Montrose St. Glasg	117	E4
Montrose St. Mother	142	B1
Montrose Terr. B of W	110	B4
Montrose Terr. Bish	98	B4
Monument Cres. Pres	233	F1
Monument Rd. Ayr	238	C2
Monymusk Gdns. Bish	78	B1
Monymusk Pl. Glasg	74	C3
Moodie Ct. Kilmk	227	F3
Moodiesburn St. Glasg	98	C1
Moor Park Cres. Pres	236	B3
Moor Park Pl. Pres	236	B3
Moor Pk. Pres	236	B3
Moor Pl. Pres	236	B2
Moor Rd. Eagle	178	B2
Moor Rd. Lan	202	C1
Moor Rd. Miln	55	D1
Moor Rd. Pres	236	B3
Moor Rd. Strath	31	E1
Moorburn Ave. Glasg	136	A2
Moorburn Pl. Lin	111	F3
Moorcroft Rd. Newt M	156	B2
Moore Dr. Bear	75	F2
Moore Dr. Helen	25	D4
Moore Gdns. Ham	183	F4
Moore St. Glasg	117	F3
Moore St. Holy	143	D2
Moorfield Ave. Kilmk	227	E3
Moorfield Ave. P Glasg	68	B3
Moorfield Ind Est. Cross	227	D4
Moorfield La. Gour	44	B3
Moorfield Pl. Cross	226	B3
Moorfield Rd. Gour	44	B4
Moorfield Rd. Pres	236	B4
Moorfield Rd. Udd	161	E3
Moorfield Roundabout. Cross	227	D4
Moorfoot Ave. Glasg	136	A2
Moorfoot Ave. Pais	113	E1
Moorfoot. Bish	78	B1
Moorfoot Dr. Gour	44	B3
Moorfoot Dr. Wish	164	C2
Moorfoot Path. Pais	133	E4
Moorfoot Pl. Irvine	220	A2
Moorfoot St. Glasg	118	C3
Moorfoot Way. Bear	75	D4
Moorhill Cres. Newt M	156	B2
Moorhill Rd. Newt M	156	B2
Moorhouse Ave. Glasg	94	C3
Moorhouse Ave. Pais	113	D1
Moorhouse St. Barr	134	B1
Moorpark Ave. Glasg	115	D3
Moorpark Ave. Muir	100	B4
Moorpark Pl. Steven	217	E4
Moorpark Rd E. Steven	217	E4
Moorpark Rd W. Steven	217	E4
Moorpark Sq. Ren	94	A1
Moorside St. Car	188	A1
Morag Ave. Udd	140	B1
Moraine Ave. Glasg	75	D1
Moraine Cir. Glasg	75	D1
Moraine Dr. Glasg	75	D1
Moraine Dr. Newt M	157	E4
Moraine Pl. Glasg	75	D1
Morar Ave. Clyde	74	A2
Morar Cres. Aird	102	C1
Morar Cres. Bish	77	F1
Morar Cres. Bishop	72	B1
Morar Cres. Clyde	74	A2
Morar Cres. Coat	101	E1
Morar Cres. Clyde	74	A2
Morar Ct. Cumb	82	A4
Morar Ct. Ham	162	A1
Morar Dr. Bear	76	A2
Morar Dr. Clyde	74	A2
Morar Dr. Cumb	82	A4
Morar Dr. Falk	24	B1
Morar Dr. Glasg	133	D2
Morar Dr. Lin	112	A3
Morar Dr. Pais	113	D1
Morar Pl. E Kil	159	F2
Morar Pl. Irvine	219	E3
Morar Pl. Newt M	156	B4
Morar Pl. Ren	94	A2
Morar Rd. Clyde	74	A2
Morar Rd. Glasg	115	F3
Morar Rd. P Glasg	68	C4
Morar St. Wish	165	D1
Morar Terr. Glasg	138	B2
Morar Terr. Tan	141	D4
Morar Way. Holy	143	D2
Morar Way. Shot	147	D2
Moravia Ave. Udd	141	D2

Moray Ave. Aird

Moray Ave. Aird 123 D3
Moray Dr. Glasg 157 F4
Moray Dr. Lennox 57 D1
Moray Gate. Udd 140 C2
Moray Gdns. Cumb 61 F3
Moray Gdns. Glasg 157 F4
Moray Gdns. Tan 140 C4
Moray Pl. Bish 78 B1
Moray Pl. Glasg 116 C1
Moray Pl. Kirk 59 D1
Moray Pl. Lin 112 A3
Moray Pl. Muir 100 B4
Moray Pl. Udd 161 E3
Moray Quadrant. Hat 142 A3
Moray Way. P Glasg 47 E1
Mordaunt St. Glasg 118 A2
Moredun Cres. Glasg 119 E4
Moredun Rd. Pais 113 D1
Moredun St. Glasg 119 E4
Morefield Rd. Glasg 115 E4
Morgan Ct. Stir 7 E2
Morgan Mews. Glasg 117 D2
Morgan St. Ham 162 B1
Morgan St. Lark 184 C2
Morina Gdns. Glasg 135 E2
Morion Rd. Glasg 95 E4
Moriston Ct. New 165 F3
Morland. E Kil 160 B2
Morley Cres. Stir 7 D2
Morley St. Glasg 137 D4
Morna La. Glasg 95 F1
Mornay Way. Shot 146 B3
Morningside Rd. New 166 B2
Morningside St. Glasg 118 C4
Morrin Path. Glasg 97 F2
Morrin St. Glasg 97 F2
Morris Cres. Hurl 228 C3
Morris Cres. Udd 161 E4
Morris La. Kilmk 223 D1
Morris
  Moodie Ave. Steven 217 F4
Morris Rd. Pres 233 E1
Morris St. Green 46 B2
Morris St. Ham 162 B1
Morris St. Lark 185 E1
Morris Terr. Stir 7 D4
Morrishall Rd. E Kil 160 B2
Morrishill Dr. Beith 171 D4
Morrison Ave. Bon 39 F3
Morrison Ave. Steven 206 C1
Morrison Dr. Bann 7 E1
Morrison Dr. Lennox 57 F4
Morrison Gdns. Ayr 239 D4
Morrison Gdns. Lennox 78 B4
Morrison Pl. Kilmk 223 E1
Morrison Quadrant. Clyde 74 C1
Morrison St. Dunt 73 F3
Morrison St. Glasg 117 D3
Morriston Cres. Ren 94 C1
Morriston Park Dr. Glasg 139 D3
Morriston St. Glasg 139 D3
Morten Gdns. Glasg 116 B1
Morton Ave. Ayr 239 D3
Morton Pl. Kilmk 222 C1
Morton Rd. Ayr 239 D3
Morton Rd. Stew 211 E4
Morton St. Mother 163 F4
Morven Ave. Bish 78 B1
Morven Ave. Kilmk 222 C2
Morven Ave. Pais 133 E4
Morven Ave. Udd 140 B1
Morven Cres. Troon 229 E1
Morven Ct. Aird 103 D1
Morven Ct. Falk 42 B1
Morven Dr. Lin 112 A3
Morven Dr. Newt M 157 E4
Morven Dr. Troon 229 E2
Morven Gdns. Tan 140 C4
Morven La. Udd 140 B1
Morven Rd. Bear 75 F3
Morven Rd. Glasg 138 C2
Morven St. Coat 122 A4
Morven St. Glasg 115 F3
Morven Way. Udd 141 D2
Morville Cres. Kilw 207 F3
Mosesfield St. Glasg 97 F3
Moss Ave. Cald 105 D3
Moss Ave. Lin 112 A3
Moss Dr. Barr 134 A3
Moss Dr. Inch 93 D4
Moss Dr. Shew 224 C3
Moss Heights Ave. Glasg 115 E3
Moss Knowe. Cumb 62 B1
Moss Path. Glasg 119 F2
Moss Rd. Aird 123 D3
Moss Rd. Auld 180 B2
Moss Rd. B of W 110 C4
Moss Rd. Card 25 E2
Moss Rd. Cumb 62 C2
Moss Rd. Fall 8 B2
Moss Rd. Glasg 115 E4
Moss Rd. Kil 89 E4
Moss Rd. Klrk 79 D3
Moss Rd. Kirk 80 A4
Moss Rd. Lin 112 B4
Moss Rd. Muir 100 B4
Moss Rd. P Glasg 68 C4

Moss Rd. Wish 165 F2
Moss Side Ave. Aird 122 C4
Moss St. Pais 113 F3
Moss-Side Rd. Glasg 116 C1
Mossacre Rd. Wish 165 E2
Mossband La. Shot 146 C3
Mossbank Ave. Glasg 98 C2
Mossbank Cres. Holy 143 F2
Mossbank Dr. Glasg 98 C2
Mossbank. E Kil 179 F4
Mossbank. Pres 236 C4
Mossbank Rd. Wlsh 165 E2
Mossbank. Udd 161 E3
Mossbell Rd. Hat 141 F3
Mossblown St. Lark 184 C2
Mossburn Ave. Bonh 19 F1
Mossburn Ave. East 127 E4
Mossburn Rd. Wish 165 E2
Mossburn St. Wish 165 E1
Mosscastle Rd. Glasg 99 E1
Mosscastle Rd. Slam 86 A4
Mossdale Ct. Hat 142 B3
Mossdale. E Kil 159 E2
Mossdale Gdns. Ham 161 F1
Mossend Ave. Helen 16 C1
Mossend Ave. Kilb 170 A1
Mossend La. Glasg 119 E4
Mossend Pl. Helen 16 C1
Mossend St. Glasg 119 E4
Mossgiel Ave. Cowie 12 B4
Mossgiel Ave. Glasg 138 A3
Mossgiel Ave. Kilmk 228 B4
Mossgiel Ave. Stir 2 A1
Mossgiel Ave. Troon 229 F2
Mossgiel Cres. Newt M 157 F3
Mossgiel Dr. Clyde 74 B2
Mossgiel Dr. Irvine 219 E2
Mossgiel. E Kil 180 A4
Mossgiel Gdns. Kirk 58 C1
Mossgiel Gdns. Tan 140 C4
Mossgiel La. Lark 185 E1
Mossgiel Pl. Ayr 239 D3
Mossgiel Pl. Glasg 138 A3
Mossgiel Pl. Steven 206 C1
Mossgiel Rd. Ard 205 E2
Mossgiel Rd. Ayr 239 D3
Mossgiel Rd. Cumb 62 A1
Mossgiel Rd. Glasg 136 B3
Mossgiel Rd. Glasg 136 B4
Mossgiel Rd. Salt 206 A2
Mossgiel St. Falk 41 D3
Mossgiel Terr. Udd 140 B1
Mossgiel Way. Holy 143 F2
Mosshall Gr. Holy 143 F2
Mosshall Rd. Holy 143 E4
Mosshall St. Holy 143 F2
Mosshead Rd. Bear 76 A4
Mosshead Rd. Kilmk 228 A2
Mosshill Rd. Hat 142 A4
Mosside Pl. Kilmk 222 C2
Mosside Rd. Ayr 236 B2
Mossland Dr. Wish 165 E2
Mossland Rd. Glasg 114 C4
Mosslands Rd. Pais 113 F4
Mosslingal. E Kil 180 C3
Mossmulloch. E Kil 180 C3
Mossneuk Ave. E Kil 179 F4
Mossneuk Cres. Wish 165 E2
Mossneuk Dr. E Kil 179 F4
Mossneuk Dr. Pais 133 E4
Mossneuk Dr. Wish 165 E2
Mossneuk Pk. Wish 165 E2
Mossneuk Rd. E Kil 180 A4
Mossneuk St. Coat 121 F2
Mosspark Ave. Glasg 115 F2
Mosspark Ave. Miln 55 D2
Mosspark Bvd. Glasg 115 F2
Mosspark Dr. Glasg 115 F2
Mosspark La. Glasg 115 F2
Mosspark Oval. Glasg 115 F2
Mosspark Rd. Coat 121 E4
Mosspark Rd. Miln 55 D2
Mosspark Sq. Glasg 115 F2
Mossvale Cres. Glasg 99 E1
Mossvale La. Pais 113 E3
Mossvale Path. Glasg 99 E2
Mossvale Rd. Glasg 99 E1
Mossvale Sq. Glasg 99 D1
Mossvale Sq. Pais 113 E3
Mossvale St. Pais 113 E4
Mossvale Terr. Muir 81 D2
Mossvale Way. Glasg 99 E1
Mossvale Wlk. Glasg 99 E1
Mossview Cres. Aird 123 D3
Mossview La. Glasg 115 E3
Mossview Quadrant. Glasg 115 E3
Mossview Rd. Stepps 99 F3
Mosswell Rd. Miln 55 D2
Mossyde Ave. P Glasg 69 D4
Mossywood Ct. Cumb 81 F4
Mossywood Pl. Cumb 81 F4
Mossywood Rd. Cumb 81 F4
Mote Hill. Ham 162 C3
Mote View. Cross 221 E1
Motehill Rd. Pais 114 A4
Motherwell Rd. Chap 144 A3
Motherwell Rd. Ham 163 D2

Motherwell Rd. Hat 142 A2
Motherwell Rd. Holy 143 E1
Motherwell St. Aird 123 E4
Moulin Cir. Glasg 115 D2
Moulin Pl. Glasg 115 D2
Moulin Rd. Glasg 115 D2
Moulin Terr. Glasg 115 D2
Mount Annan Dr. Glasg 137 D4
Mount Ave. Kilmk 227 E3
Mount Ave. Sym 231 E2
Mount Cameron Dr N. E Kil 181 D4
Mount Cameron Dr S. E Kil 181 D4
Mount Charles Cres. Ayr 238 B1
Mount Harriet Ave. Stepps 99 F3
Mount Harriet Dr. Stepps 99 F3
Mount Hope. B of A 2 B4
Mount Oliphant. Cowie 12 B4
Mount Oliphant Cres. Ayr 239 D3
Mount Oliphant Pl. Ayr 239 D3
Mount Pl. Kilmk 227 E3
Mount
  Pleasant Cres. M of C 58 A3
Mount Pleasant Dr. O Kill 73 D3
Mount Pleasant St. Green 45 F2
Mount St. Glasg 96 C2
Mount Stewart St. Car 187 F1
Mount Stuart St. Glasg 136 C4
Mount The. Ayr 239 D2
Mount Vernon Ave. Coat 121 F4
Mount Vernon Ave. Glasg 119 F2
Mount View. Irvine 220 B1
Mount William. N Sau 5 F1
Mountainblue St. Glasg 118 A3
Mountblow Rd. Clyde 73 E3
Mountgarrie Rd. Glasg 115 E4
Mountherrick. E Kil 180 C3
Mournian Way. Ham 162 B1
Mousebank La. Lan 214 C2
Mousebank Rd. Lan 214 C3
Mousemill Rd. Lan 214 B3
Mowbray Ave. Muir 100 C3
Mowbray Ct. Bann 7 E2
Mowbray. E Kil 160 B2
Moy Path. New 165 F3
Moyne Rd. Glasg 115 D1
Muckcroft Rd. Muir 80 B2
Mudale Ct. Falk 42 B1
Mugdock Rd. Miln 55 D2
Muir Cl. Stew 195 E1
Muir Cres. Alex 27 E4
Muir Dr. Irvine 219 E2
Muir Dr. Steven 217 E4
Muir. Dr. Troon 229 E3
Muir Drive Cotts. Steven 217 E4
Muir Rd. Dumb 50 B3
Muir St. Alex 27 E4
Muir St. Bish 78 A1
Muir St. Coat 121 F4
Muir St. Ham 162 C2
Muir St. Lar 23 E1
Muir St. Lark 185 D2
Muir St. Law 186 C3
Muir St. Mother 163 E4
Muir St. Ren 94 B2
Muir St. Udd 161 E3
Muir Terr. Pais 114 A4
Muiralehouse Rd. Bann 11 F4
Muirbank Ave. Glasg 137 F4
Muirbank Gdns. Glasg 137 F4
Muirbrae Rd. Glasg 138 A2
Muirbrae Way. Glasg 138 A2
Muirburn Ave. Glasg 136 C2
Muirburn Rd. Beith 150 A2
Muirburn Rd. Glass 198 A1
Muircroft Dr. Cle 144 A1
Muirdrum Ave. Glasg 115 E2
Muirdyke Ave. Sten 24 B2
Muirdyke Rd. Coat 121 E4
Muirdyke Rd. Glen 102 A3
Muirdykes Ave. Glasg 115 D3
Muirdykes Cres. Pais 113 D3
Muirdykes Ave. P Glasg 68 B4
Muirdykes Rd. Glasg 115 D3
Muirdykes Rd. Pais 113 D3
Muiredge
  and Jersey Rd. Cle 145 D1
Muiredge
  and Jersy Rd. Sals 145 E4
Muiredge Ct. Udd 140 C3
Muiredge Terr. Glasg 120 A2
Muirend Ave. Glasg 136 C3
Muirend Rd. Card 48 A4
Muirend Rd. Glasg 136 C2
Muirend Rd. Kilmk 222 C3
Muirend Rd. Stir 7 D3
Muirend St. Kilb 149 D1
Muirfield Cres. Glasg 76 C1
Muirfield Ct. Glasg 136 C2
Muirfield Meadows. Udd 140 C1
Muirfield Pl. Kilw 207 E2
Muirfield Rd. Cumb 62 A3
Muirfield Rd. Lar 23 F1
Muirhall Pl. Lar 23 E2
Muirhall Rd. Lar 23 E2
Muirhall Terr. Sals 125 D1
Muirhead Cotts. Kirk 80 A4
Muirhead Dr. Holy 143 F2
Muirhead Dr. Lin 112 A3

Muirhead Gdns. Glasg 120 B2
Muirhead Gdns. Sals 125 D1
Muirhead Pl. East 127 E2
Muirhead Rd. East 127 E2
Muirhead Rd. Glasg 120 A2
Muirhead Rd. Sten 23 F2
Muirhead St. Klrk 79 E4
Muirhead St. Loch 129 E1
Muirhead Terr. Mother 163 F2
Muirhead Way. Bish 78 B1
Muirhead-Braehead
  Interchange. Cumb 62 A2
Muirhill Ave. Glasg 136 C3
Muirhill Cres. Glasg 95 D4
Muirhouse Ave. Mother 164 A2
Muirhouse Ave. New 166 A3
Muirhouse Dr. Mother 164 B1
Muirhouse La. E Kil 180 C4
Muirhouse Rd. Mother 164 A1
Muirhouse St. Glasg 117 D2
Muirkirk Dr. Glasg 95 F4
Muirkirk Dr. Ham 161 E1
Muirlee Rd. Car 188 A1
Muirlees Cres. Miln 54 C1
Muirmadkin Rd. Hat 142 A3
Muirmaillen Ave. Cle 144 B1
Muirpark Ave. Ren 94 B1
Muirpark Dr. Bish 98 A4
Muirpark Dr. Shi 66 B3
Muirpark Gdns. Men 4 C2
Muirpark Rd. Beith 150 A1
Muirpark St. Glasg 96 A1
Muirshiel Ave. Glasg 135 E3
Muirshiel Cres. Glasg 135 E3
Muirshiel La. P Glasg 68 B4
Muirshiel Rd. P Glasg 68 B4
Muirshot Rd. Lark 185 D2
Muirside Ave. Glasg 119 F2
Muirside Av. Kirk 80 A4
Muirside Ct. Kilw 207 E1
Muirside Pl. Kilw 207 E1
Muirside Pl. New 165 F3
Muirside Rd. Glasg 120 A2
Muirside Rd. Kilw 207 E1
Muirside Rd. Pais 113 D4
Muirside Rd. Tull 4 B2
Muirside St. Glasg 120 A2
Muirskeith Cres. Glasg 137 D3
Muirskeith Pl. Glasg 136 C3
Muirskeith Rd. Glasg 136 C3
Muirton Dr. Bish 77 F2
Muirton Rd. Fal 7 D4
Muiryfauld Dr. Glasg 118 C3
Muiryhall St. Coat 122 A4
Muiryhall St E. Coat 122 B4
Mulben Cres. Glasg 134 C4
Mulben Pl. Glasg 134 C4
Mulben Terr. Glasg 134 C4
Mulberry Dr. E Kil 180 B3
Mulberry Rd. Glasg 136 B3
Mulberry Rd. Tan 121 E1
Mulberry Way. E Kil 180 B3
Muldron Terr. Shot 147 D1
Mulgrew Ave. Salt 206 A1
Mull. Aird 123 E3
Mull Ave. P Glasg 69 D4
Mull Ave. Pais 133 F4
Mull Ave. Ren 94 B1
Mull Cres. Irvine 220 A1
Mull Ct. All 10 A3
Mull Ct. Irvine 220 A1
Mull. E Kil 181 E4
Mull Pl. Irvine 220 A1
Mull Quadrant. Wish 165 F3
Mull St. Glasg 98 A1
Mull Terr. Irvine 220 A1
Mullardoch St. Glasg 76 B1
Mulvey Cres. Aird 122 C4
Mungalend. Falk 42 A4
Mungalhead Rd. Falk 42 A4
Mungo Pk. E Kil 180 B4
Mungo Pl. Tan 121 D1
Munlochy Rd. Glasg 115 E4
Munnoch Cres. Ard 205 D3
Munro Ave. Glasg 222 B1
Munro Ave. Stir 2 A2
Munro Ct. Dunt 73 F3
Munro Dr. Kilb 170 A4
Munro Dr. M of C 58 A3
Munro Gdns. Laur 42 C2
Munro La E. Glasg 95 F3
Munro La. Glasg 95 F3
Munro Pl. All 9 F3
Munro Pl. E Kil 160 A2
Munro Pl. Glasg 95 F3
Munro Pl. Kilmk 222 C1
Munro Pl. Salt 206 A1
Munro Rd. Fal 7 D4
Munro Rd. Glasg 95 F3
Munro St. Alex 27 F3
Munro St. Steven 45 D2
Munro St. Sten 23 F2
Munro Wlk. Salt 206 A1
Murano St. Glasg 96 C2
Murchie Dr. Pres 236 B3
Murchison Dr. E Kil 180 A4

Murchison Rd. Hous 91 E1
Murchland Ave. Fen 213 D2
Murchland Way. Irvine 219 E2
Murdieston St. Green 45 E2
Murdoch Cres. Steven 217 E4
Murdoch Dr. Miln 76 B4
Murdoch Pl. Holy 142 C2
Murdoch Pl. Shew 224 C3
Murdoch Rd. E Kil 180 C4
Murdoch Sq. Hat 142 B4
Murdoch's Lone. Ayr 238 C1
Murdostoun Cres. East 127 F3
Murdostoun Gdns. Wish 165 D3
Murdostoun Terr. Cle 144 C1
Murdostoun View. New 165 F3
Mure Ave. Kilmk 223 D3
Mure Pl. Uplaw 153 D2
Muriel La. Barr 134 B2
Muriel St. Barr 134 B2
Murnin Ct. Stir 7 E2
Murnin Rd. Bon 40 A2
Murray Ave. Kils 60 B4
Murray Ave. Salt 205 F1
Murray Dr. Stone 198 C1
Murray Gdns. M of C 58 B3
Murray Gr. Bear 75 D4
Murray Path. Udd 140 C3
Murray Pl. Ayr 236 B2
Murray Pl. Barr 134 B2
Murray Pl. Cam 6 B3
Murray Pl. Dumb 50 B2
Murray Pl. Gour 44 C3
Murray Pl. Kilmk 223 E1
Murray Pl. Stir 7 D4
Murray Pl. Tan 141 F4
Murray Rd. Law 186 C2
Murray Rd The. E Kil 180 C4
Murray Rd. Udd 141 D2
Murray
  Roundabout The. E Kil 180 C4
Murray Sq The. E Kil 180 C4
Murray St. Ayr 236 B1
Murray St. Green 45 E3
Murray St. Pais 113 E3
Murray St. Ren 94 B2
Murray Terr. Mother 163 D4
Murrayfield. Bish 78 A2
Murrayfield Dr. Bear 75 F1
Murrayfield Pl. Bann 7 E1
Murrayfield St. Glasg 118 C4
Murrayfield Terr. Bann 7 E1
Murrayhill. E Kil 180 B4
Murrayshall Rd. Stir 7 D2
Murrayside. Stone 198 B3
Murrin Ave. Bish 78 B1
Murroch Ave. Dumb 50 B3
Murroch Cres. Bonh 28 A1
Murroes Rd. Glasg 115 D4
Musgrove Pl. E Kil 180 B4
Muslin St. Glasg 117 F2
Muttonhole Rd. Ham 182 C4
Muttonhole Rd. Quart 183 D2
Mybster Pl. Glasg 115 E4
Myers Cres. Udd 141 D3
Mylne Pl. Sten 24 A1
Myothill Rd. Bank 39 E4
Myres Rd. Glasg 135 E4
Myreside Pl. Glasg 118 B3
Myreside St. Glasg 118 C3
Myreton Ave. Kil 89 E4
Myreton Dr. Bann 11 F4
Myreton Way. Falk 41 F2
Myretoungate. Alva 4 C3
Myrie Gdns. Bish 78 A1
Myroch Pl. Glasg 100 B3
Myrtle Ave. Klrk 79 E3
Myrtle Bank. Beith 171 D4
Myrtle Dr. Holy 143 D3
Myrtle Dr. Mother 164 B2
Myrtle Hill La. Glasg 137 E4
Myrtle La. Lark 185 E1
Myrtle Pk. Glasg 117 E1
Myrtle Pl. Glasg 137 E4
Myrtle Rd. Clyde 73 E2
Myrtle Rd. Tan 141 D4
Myrtle Sq. Bish 98 A4
Myrtle St. Udd 140 B1
Myrtle View Rd. Glasg 137 E4
Myrtle Wlk. Glasg 138 C3
Myvot Ave. Cumb 82 A3
Myvot Rd. Cumb 82 A3

Nailer Rd. Falk 41 F3
Nailer Rd. Stir 7 E4
Nairn Ave. Hat 142 A3
Nairn Ave. Udd 140 B1
Nairn Cl. Stew 195 E1
Nairn Cres. Aird 123 D3
Nairn Ct. Falk 42 B1
Nairn Ct. Kilw 207 D2
Nairn Dr. Gour 44 B3
Nairn Pl. Clyde 73 F2
Nairn Pl. E Kil 160 B2
Nairn Quadrant. Wish 165 D3
Nairn Rd. Gour 44 B2
Nairn St. Clyde 73 F2
Nairn St. Glasg 96 B1

Nairn St. Lark 184 C1
Nairn St. Udd 161 E3
Nairn Way. Cumb 62 A3
Nairnside Rd. Glasg 98 B4
Naismith Ct. Stone 198 C1
Naismith St. Glasg 139 E4
Naismith Wlk. Hat 142 B4
Nansen St. Glasg 97 D2
Napier Ave. Card 48 A4
Napier Cres. Dumb 49 E2
Napier Cres. Falk 42 A4
Napier Ct. Card 48 A4
Napier Ct. Clyde 73 E3
Napier Ct. Cumb 62 B4
Napier Dr. Glasg 116 A4
Napier Gdns. Lin 112 B3
Napier Hill. E Kil 180 C4
Napier La. E Kil 180 C4
Napier Pl. Clyde 73 E3
Napier Pl. Cumb 62 B4
Napier Pl. Falk 42 A4
Napier Pl. Glasg 116 A4
Napier Rd. Cumb 62 B4
Napier Rd. Glasg 114 C4
Napier Rd. Glasg 116 A4
Napier Sq. Hat 142 B4
Napier St. Clyde 94 B4
Napier St. Glasg 116 A4
Napier St. John 111 F2
Napier St. Lin 112 B3
Napier Terr. Glasg 116 A4
Napier Way. Cumb 62 B4
Napiershall La. Glasg 96 C1
Napiershall Pl. Glasg 96 C1
Napiershall St. Glasg 96 C1
Napierston Rd. Bonh 27 F3
Naproch Pl. Newt M 157 E3
Naseby Ave. Glasg 95 F2
Naseby La. Glasg 95 F2
Nasmyth Pl. Bear 75 D4
Nasmyth Rd. Glasg 115 D4
Nasmyth Rd N. Glasg 115 D4
Nasmyth Rd S. Glasg 115 D4
Nassau Pl. E Kil 159 D1
Navar Ct. Shot 147 D2
Navar Pl. Pais 114 A1
Naver St. Glasg 98 C1
Navy Way. Ros 15 D2
Naylor La. Aird 123 D4
Naysmyth Bank. E Kil 180 C4
Nebit The. Alva 4 C3
Needle Gn. Car 187 F1
Neidpath Ave. Coat 122 A2
Neidpath Dr. Sten 23 F2
Neidpath. Glasg 120 A2
Neidpath Pl. Coat 122 A2
Neidpath Rd. Car 187 F2
Neidpath Rd E. Newt M 157 D3
Neidpath Rd W. Newt M 157 D4
Neil Ave. Irvine 219 E3
Neil St. Green 45 D2
Neil St. Ren 94 B3
Neilsland Dr. Ham 183 E4
Neilsland Dr. Mother 163 D3
Neilsland Oval. Glasg 115 E1
Neilsland Rd. Ham 183 E4
Neilsland Sq. Glasg 115 E1
Neilsland St. Ham 162 B1
Neilsland St. Ham 162 B1
Neilson St. Falk 42 A2
Neilson St. Hat 142 A3
Neilston Ave. Glasg 135 E3
Neilston Pl. Kils 36 A1
Neilston Rd. Neil 154 C4
Neilston Rd. Pais 113 F1
Neilston Rd. Uplaw 153 D2
Neilvaig Dr. Glasg 138 B2
Nelson Ave. Coat 121 F2
Nelson Cres. Mother 164 A2
Nelson Mandela Pl. Glasg . 117 E4
Nelson Pl. Ayr 236 A1
Nelson Pl. Glasg 120 A2
Nelson Pl. Helen 17 D1
Nelson Pl. Stir 7 E3
Nelson Rd. Gour 44 C3
Nelson Rd. Salt 217 D4
Nelson St. Glasg 117 D3
Nelson St. Glasg 120 A2
Nelson St. Green 45 F3
Nelson St. Kilmk 227 F4
Nelson Terr. E Kil 181 D4
Nemphlar Moor Rd. Car 201 E1
Nemphlar Moor Rd. Lan 214 A4
Nemphlar Rd. Lan 214 A3
Nemphlat Hill. Lan 214 C3
Neptune St. Glasg 116 A4
Neptune Way. Holy 142 C3
Nerston Rd E. Kil 159 F3
Ness Ave. John 131 E4
Ness Dr. E Kil 160 A1
Ness Dr. Udd 140 C1
Ness Gdns. Bish 78 A1
Ness Gdns. Lark 199 D4
Ness Pl. Troon 229 F3
Ness Rd. Green 45 E3
Ness Rd. Ren 94 A2
Ness St. Glasg 98 C1
Ness St. Wish 186 A4

Ness Terr. Ham 162 A1
Ness Way. Holy 143 D3
Nethan Ave. Wish 164 B1
Nethan Gate. Ham 162 B2
Nethan Glen. Cro 201 D1
Nethan Path. Lark 199 D4
Nethan Pl. Ham 183 E3
Nethan St. Glasg 116 A4
Nethan St. Mother 142 B1
Nethanfoot Brig Rd. Cro 201 D1
Nether
    Auldhouse Rd. Glasg ... 136 B3
Netherbank Rd. Wish 164 B1
Netherblane. Strath 31 D2
Netherbog Ave. Dumb 50 A2
Netherbog Rd. Dumb 50 A2
Netherburn Ave. Glasg 136 C1
Netherburn Gdns. Hous 111 F4
Netherburn Rd. Ash 200 A4
Netherby Dr. Glasg 116 B2
Netherby Rd. Air 14 B2
Nethercairn Pl. Newt M 157 E3
Nethercairn Rd. Glasg 136 B2
Nethercliffe Ave. Glasg 136 C1
Nethercraigs Dr. Pais 133 E4
Nethercraigs Rd. Pais 133 D4
Nethercroy Rd. Kils 60 C3
Netherdale Cres. Wish 164 B1
Netherdale Dr. Glasg 114 C2
Netherdale. Newt M 157 D3
Netherdale Rd. Wish 164 C1
Netherfield St. Glasg 118 B3
Netherhall Rd. Wish 164 B1
Netherhill Ave. Glasg 137 D1
Netherhill Cotts. Pais 114 A4
Netherhill Cres. Pais 114 A3
Netherhill Rd. Muir 80 C1
Netherhill Rd. Pais 114 A4
Netherhill Way. Pais 114 A4
Netherhouse Ave. Coat 121 F2
Netherhouse Ave. Klrk 79 F2
Netherhouse Pl. Glasg 120 C4
Netherhouse Rd. Glasg 120 C4
Netherland Rd. Stew 211 F4
Netherlee Cres. Dalry 169 D1
Netherlee Rd. Glasg 137 D2
Nethermains Rd. Den 21 E1
Nethermains Rd. Kilw 207 F1
Nethermains Rd. Miln 76 A4
Nethermiln Rd. W Kil 190 B2
Netherpark Ave. Glasg 137 D1
Netherplace Cres. Glasg 135 D4
Netherplace Cres. Newt M ... 156 B2
Netherplace Rd. Glasg 135 D4
Netherplace Rd. Newt M 156 A2
Netherton Ave. P Glasg 69 D4
Netherton Ct. Glasg 137 F1
Netherton Ct. Newt M 157 D3
Netherton Dr. Barr 134 C1
Netherton Hill. Lennox 57 D4
Netherton Oval. Lennox 33 D1
Netherton Rd. E Kil 180 A2
Netherton Rd. E Kil 180 B4
Netherton Rd. Glasg 95 F4
Netherton Rd. Newt M 156 C3
Netherton Rd. Wish 164 C1
Netherton St. East 127 E3
Netherton St. Glasg 95 F4
Netherton St. Wish 164 C1
Nethervale Ave. Glasg 136 C1
Netherview Rd. Glasg 137 D1
Netherway. Glasg 136 C1
Netherwood Ave. Cumb 81 F4
Netherwood Ct. Cumb 82 A4
Netherwood Gr. Cumb 82 A4
Netherwood Pl. Cumb 81 F4
Netherwood Rd. Cumb 81 F4
Netherwood Rd. Mother 164 B2
Netherwood Way. Cumb 82 A4
Nethy Way. Ren 94 C1
Neucks The. Slam 87 D3
Neuk Ave. Hous 91 E1
Neuk Ave. Muir 100 B4
Neuk Cres. Hous 91 E1
Neuk The. Mother 164 C2
Neuk Way. Glasg 139 E4
Neukfoot La. Uplaw 153 D2
Nevan Rd. Troon 229 F3
Neville. E Kil 160 B2
Nevis Ave. Ham 162 A1
Nevis Cres. All 10 A4
Nevis Ct. Barr 134 B1
Nevis Dr. Lennox 57 D1
Nevis Pl. Falk 42 B1
Nevis Pl. Kilmk 228 A2
Nevis Pl. Shot 147 D2
Nevis Rd. Bear 75 D4
Nevis Rd. Glasg 136 A3
Nevis Rd. Ren 94 A1
Nevis Way. Inch 93 F1
Nevis Way. Irvine 220 A2
Nevison St. Lark 185 D1
New Ashtree St. Mother 164 C2
New Ave. How 130 C3
New Bridge St. Ayr 235 F1
New Buildings. Lan 215 D1

New City Rd. Glasg 97 D1
New City Row. Strath 31 D2
New Cross. Ham 162 C2
New Dock La. Green 46 A3
New Edinburgh Rd. Tan 141 E3
New England Rd. Salt 206 A1
New Hallglen Rd. Falk 42 B1
New Inchinnan Rd. Pais 113 F4
New Kirk Rd. Bear 75 F3
New La. Calder 123 D2
New Lairdsland Rd. Klrk 79 E4
New Lanark Rd. Lan 214 C1
New Line Rd. Bann 11 D4
New Luce Dr. Glasg 119 E2
New Mill Rd. Kilmk 228 A4
New Park St. Ham 162 B3
New Plymouth. E Kil 180 A4
New Rd. Ayr 235 F1
New Rd. Bann 7 E1
New Rd. Glasg 139 F2
New Sneddon St. Pais 113 F3
New St. B of A 1 C4
New St. Beith 171 D4
New St. Dalry 191 E4
New St. Dunt 74 A3
New St. Irvine 219 D1
New St. Kilbar 111 D2
New St. Kilmk 227 F3
New St. Loch 129 E1
New St. Pais 113 F2
New St. Slam 86 A4
New St. Steven 217 E4
New St. Stew 195 E1
New St. Stone 198 C1
New St. Udd 161 E4
New Stevenston Rd. Holy 143 D1
New View Cres. Hat 142 A2
New View Dr. Hat 142 A2
New View Pl. Hat 142 A2
New Wynd. Glasg 117 E3
Newall Rd. Pais 113 F4
Neward Cres. Pres 236 B3
Newark Ave. Green 45 E4
Newark Cres. Ayr 238 A1
Newark Dr. Glasg 116 C2
Newark Dr. Pais 133 E4
Newark Dr. Wish 165 E3
Newark. Kilw 207 E1
Newark Pl. Wish 165 E3
Newark St. Green 45 E4
Newark St. P Glasg 47 E1
Newark Terr. Pres 236 B4
Newarthill Rd. Holy 143 E1
Newbarns St. Car 187 F2
Newbattle Ave. Calder 123 D1
Newbattle Ct. Glasg 119 D1
Newbattle Gdns. Glasg 119 D1
Newbattle Pl. Glasg 119 D1
Newbattle Rd. Glasg 119 D1
Newbiggin Cres. Tull 4 B1
Newbold Ave. Bish 97 F4
Newburgh. Ersk 73 D2
Newburgh St. Glasg 136 B4
Newcastleton Dr. Glasg 76 C1
Newcroft Dr. Glasg 137 E3
Newdyke Ave. Klrk 79 F4
Newdyke Rd. Klrk 79 F4
Newdykes Farm Rd. Pres . 233 E1
Newdykes Rd. Pres 233 E1
Newfield Cres. Ham 162 A2
Newfield Dr. Dund 225 F1
Newfield La. Udd 141 D2
Newfield Pl. Dund 225 F1
Newfield Pl. Glasg 135 F1
Newfield Pl. Glasg 137 F4
Newfield Pl. Irvine 220 A3
Newfield Rd. Stone 198 C1
Newfield Sq. Glasg 135 D3
Newhall St. Glasg 117 F2
Newhaven Rd. Glasg 119 D4
Newhaven St. Glasg 119 D4
Newhills Rd. Glasg 119 F4
Newhouse Dr. Falk 41 F1
Newhouse Dr. Kilb 169 F2
Newhouse
    Interchange. Shew 224 C3
Newhouse. Stir 7 D1
Newhouse Way. Irvine 220 A3
Newhousemill Rd. E Kil 181 E4
Newhousemill Rd. Ham 182 A4
Newhouses Rd. Brox 61 D2
Newhut Rd. Mother 142 B1
Newington St. Glasg 118 C3
Newlands Dr. Ham 183 E4
Newlands Dr. Kilmk 222 C3
Newlands Gdns. John 112 B1
Newlands Pl. E Kil 159 F1
Newlands Pl. Kilmk 222 C2
Newlands Pl. Tull 4 B2
Newlands Rd. Bann 11 E4
Newlands Rd E. Kil 179 F3
Newlands Rd. E Kil 180 A4
Newlands Rd. Glasg 136 C3
Newlands Rd. Tan 140 C4
Newlands St. Coat 122 A2
Newlands St. Lan 215 E2
Newlands Terr. Car 187 F1
Newlands Terr. M of C 58 B3

Newlandsfield Rd. Glasg ... 136 B4
Newlandsmuir Rd. E Kil 180 A3
Newmains Ave. Inch 93 D3
Newmains Rd. Ren 94 B1
Newmarket. Bann 7 F1
Newmarket St. Ayr 238 C4
Newmarket St. Falk 42 A3
Newmill
    and Canthill Rd. Shot . 146 A3
Newmill Gdns. Shot 145 F2
Newmill Rd. Dunlop 195 E4
Newmill Rd. Glasg 98 B3
Newmill-Canthill Rd. Shot . 146 A3
Newmills. Tull 4 A2
Newmoor
    Interchange. Irvine 219 F1
Newnham Rd. Pais 114 C2
Newpark Cres. Glasg 139 D4
Newpark Cres. Stir 7 D1
Newpark Rd. Stir 7 D1
Newrose Ave. Hat 142 B4
Newshot Dr. Ersk 73 E1
Newstead Gdns. Glasg 76 C1
Newton Ave. Glasg 139 E3
Newton Ave. Gran 24 C2
Newton Ave. John 112 C2
Newton Brae. Glasg 139 F3
Newton Brae. Udd 140 A3
Newton Dr. John 112 C2
Newton Dr. New 166 A3
Newton Dr. Tan 141 D4
Newton Gr. Newt M 156 C2
Newton Of Barr. Loch 129 D1
Newton Park Ct. Ayr 236 A1
Newton Pl. Glasg 96 C1
Newton Rd. Bishop 72 A2
Newton Rd. Klrk 79 F2
Newton St. Coat 121 F2
Newton St. Glasg 117 D4
Newton St. Green 45 E3
Newton St. Kilb 149 D1
Newton St. Pais 113 E2
Newton St. Tan 141 D4
Newton Terr. Glasg 116 C4
Newton Terr. Green 45 E3
Newton Terr. John 112 C2
Newton Terrace La. Glasg ... 116 C4
Newton Trad Est. Ayr 236 A1
Newton Way. Pais 114 A4
Newton Wlk. Kilmk 228 A4
Newtongrange Ave. Glasg ... 119 D1
Newtongrange
    Gdns. Glasg 119 D2
Newtonhead. Irvine 220 A3
Newtonlea Ave. Newt M 156 C2
Newtonshaw. N Sau 5 E1
Newtown St. Kils 60 B4
Newtyle Pl. Bish 78 B1
Newtyle Rd. Pais 114 B2
Nicholas St. Glasg 117 E4
Nicholson St. Glasg 117 D3
Nicklaus Way. Holy 143 F4
Nicol St. Aird 103 E1
Nicol St. Green 45 D2
Nicolson Dr. Stepps 99 F3
Nicolson St. Green 45 F3
Niddrie Rd. Glasg 117 D1
Niddrie Sq. Glasg 116 C1
Niddry St. Pais 113 F3
Nigel Gdns. Glasg 116 B1
Nigel St. Mother 163 E3
Nigg Pl. Glasg 120 A4
Nightingale Pl. John 131 E3
Nikitas Ave. Lark 199 D4
Nile Ct. Ayr 238 C4
Nile St. Green 45 F2
Nimmo Dr. Glasg 115 F4
Nimmo Pl. Car 187 F2
Nimmo Rd. Green 45 E4
Nimmo St. Green 45 E2
Nineyard St. Salt 216 C4
Ninian Ave. Hous 111 E4
Ninian Rd. Aird 123 E3
Ninian's Rise. Klrk 79 F4
Ninian's Terr. Kilw 207 F1
Nisbet Dr. Den 21 E1
Nisbet Dr. Pres 236 B3
Nisbet St. Glasg 118 B3
Nisbet Pl. Chap 123 F1
Nisbett St. Chap 123 F1
Nith Ave. Pais 112 C1
Nith Dr. Ham 183 D4
Nith Dr. Ren 94 C1
Nith La. New 165 F3
Nith Path. Cle 144 A1
Nith Pl. John 131 E4
Nith Pl. Kilmk 228 A3
Nith Quadrant. Holy 143 E2
Nith St. Glasg 98 B1
Nithsdale Cres. Bear 75 E3
Nithsdale Cross. Glasg 116 B2
Nithsdale Dr. Glasg 116 C1
Nithsdale. E Kil 160 B2
Nithsdale Pl. Glasg 116 C2
Nithsdale Rd. Ard 205 D4
Nithsdale Rd. Glasg 116 B2
Nithsdale Rd. Glasg 116 C1
Nithsdale St. Glasg 116 C1
Nithsdale St. Shot 146 B3
Nitshill Rd. Glasg 135 D3

Nitshill Rd. Glasg 135 E2
Niven Ct. Kilmk 223 E2
Niven St. Glasg 96 B3
Noble Rd. Hat 142 A3
Nobles Pl. Hat 141 F2
Nobles View. Hat 141 F2
Nobleston. Bonh 27 F1
Noldrum Ave. Glasg 139 E4
Noldrum Gdns. Glasg 139 E4
Noltmire Rd. Ayr 236 B2
Noran Cres. Troon 229 F3
Norbreck Dr. Glasg 136 B2
Norby Rd. Glasg 95 F2
Noremac Way. Hat 141 F4
Norfield Dr. Glasg 137 D4
Norfolk Cres. Bish 77 F2
Norfolk Ct. Glasg 117 D3
Norfolk House. E Kil 159 F1
Norfolk Rd. Gour 44 C2
Norfolk St. Glasg 117 D3
Norham St. Glasg 116 C1
Norman Cres. Irvine 219 D3
Norman St. Glasg 117 F2
Norse La. N. Glasg 95 E2
Norse La S. Glasg 95 E2
Norse Rd. Glasg 95 E2
North and South Rd. Cle 144 C1
North Ave. Car 187 E1
North Ave. Clyde 74 A1
North Ave. Glasg 138 C3
North Ave. Holy 143 D1
North Bank Pl. Clyde 94 B4
North Bank St. Clyde 94 B4
North Barr Ave. Ersk 73 D1
North Barr. Ersk 73 D2
North Berwick Ave. Cumb 61 F3
North Berwick Cres. E Kil .. 180 A3
North Biggar Rd. Aird 123 D4
North Bridge St. Aird 122 C4
North British Rd. Udd 140 C3
North Bute St. Coat 122 A2
North Calder Dr. Aird 123 E3
North Calder Rd. Tan 121 E1
North Campbell Ave. Miln 54 C1
North Canal Bank. Glasg 97 D3
North Canal Bank St. Glasg . 97 E1
North Carbrain Rd. Cumb 61 F1
North Castle St. All 10 A3
North Claremont La. Miln 55 D3
North Claremont St. Glasg .. 96 C1
North Corsebar Rd. Pais 113 E1
North Court La. Glasg 117 E4
North Crescent Ave. Ard 205 E2
North Crescent Rd. Ard 205 D2
North Croft St. Pais 113 F3
North Ct. Glasg 117 E4
North Dean Park Ave. Udd .. 141 D1
North Douglas St. Clyde 94 B4
North Dr. Kilb 170 A4
North Dr. Lin 112 A3
North Dr. Troon 229 F2
North Dryburgh Rd. Wish 165 D3
North Dumgoyne Ave. Miln .. 54 C2
North Elgin Pl. Clyde 94 B4
North Elgin St. Clyde 94 B4
North Erskine Pk. Bear 75 E3
North Faulds Rd. Lan 215 F3
North Frederick St. Glasg .. 117 E4
North Gardner St. Glasg 96 A2
North
    Gargieston Rd. Kilmk .. 227 E3
North Gower St. Glasg 116 B3
North Grange Rd. Bear 75 F3
North Hamilton Pl. Kilmk 222 C1
North Hamilton St. Kilmk 222 C1
North Hanover St. Glasg 117 E4
North Harbour St. Ayr 235 F1
North
    Iverton Park Rd. John .. 112 A2
North Kilmeny Cres. Wish . 165 E3
North La. Lin 112 B3
North Lodge Ave. Mother .. 163 F2
North Lodge Rd. Ren 94 B2
North Main St. Alex 27 E3
North Main St. Sten 24 B2
North Moraine La. Glasg 75 E1
North Neuk. Troon 229 F4
North Orchard St. Mother ... 163 E4
North Park Ave. Ayr 236 A2
North Park Ave. Glasg 135 F2
North Portland St. Glasg 117 E4
North Rd. Coat 122 A1
North Rd. Cumb 82 A4
North Rd. Hat 142 A4
North Rd. John 111 F1
North Rd. P Glasg 68 C2
North Rd. W Kil 190 B3
North Shore Rd. Troon 229 E2
North Shore Rd. Troon 229 E3
North Sq. Coat 121 F4
North St. Alex 27 E3
North St. All 10 A4
North St. Dalry 191 E4
North St. Falk 42 A4
North St. Glasg 116 C4
North St. Green 45 E4
North St. Hous 91 D2

North St. Lark 185 D2
North St. Mother 163 F4
North St. Pais 113 F3
North St. Stir 2 B1
North Vennel. Irvine 220 A2
North Vennel. Lan 215 D2
North View. Bear 75 E1
North View Rd. B of W 110 C3
North Wallace St. Glasg 97 E1
North Wood Rd. Tull 4 B1
North Woodside Rd. Glasg .. 96 C2
Northacre. Kilw 207 F3
Northall Quadrant. Holy 143 D1
Northampton Dr. Glasg 96 A3
Northampton La. Glasg 96 A3
Northbank Ave. Glasg 139 E3
Northbank Ave. Klrk 79 E4
Northbank St. Glasg 139 E3
Northbrae Pl. Glasg 95 D3
Northburn Ave. Aird 103 D1
Northburn Pl. Aird 103 D1
Northburn Rd. Aird 102 B1
Northburn St. Plains 104 A1
Northcraig Rd. Kilmk 223 D2
Northcroft Rd. Muir 80 C1
Northdoon Pl. Ayr 238 B2
Northend. Cam 6 B3
Northfield Ave. Ayr 236 A2
Northfield Ave. P Glasg 68 C4
Northfield Ave. Shot 147 D1
Northfield Dr. Bonh 27 F3
Northfield. E Kil 179 F4
Northfield Pl. Ayr 236 A2
Northfield Rd. Bonh 28 A3
Northfield Rd. Duni 21 E2
Northfield Rd. Kils 36 A1
Northfield St. Mother 163 F4
Northgate Quadrant. Glasg 98 B3
Northgate Rd. Glasg 98 B4
Northinch Ct. Glasg 95 E1
Northinch St. Glasg 95 E1
Northland Dr. Glasg 95 E3
Northland La. Glasg 95 E2
Northmuir Dr. Wish 165 E2
Northmuir Rd. Glasg 75 D2
Northpark St. Glasg 96 C2
Northumberland St. Glasg 96 C2
Northway. Udd 140 B1
Northwood Dr. New 166 A3
Norton St. Alva 5 D4
Norval St. Glasg 96 A1
Norwich Dr. Glasg 96 A3
Norwood Ave. All 9 F4
Norwood Ave. Bon 40 A4
Norwood Ave. Klrk 79 D4
Norwood Cres. All 9 F4
Norwood Dr. Glasg 136 A1
Norwood Gr. All 9 F4
Norwood Pk. Bear 75 F2
Norwood Pl. Bon 40 A4
Norwood Terr. Tan 141 D4
Nottingham Ave. Glasg 96 A3
Nottingham La. Glasg 96 A3
Novar Dr. Glasg 96 A2
Novar Gdns. Bish 77 F1
Novar St. Ham 162 B1
Nuneaton St. Glasg 118 A2
Nurseries Rd. Glasg 119 F3
Nursery Ave. Ersk 72 C2
Nursery Ave. Kilmk 228 A4
Nursery Ave. Pres 236 A3
Nursery Buildings. Lan 215 D1
Nursery Ct. Car 187 F2
Nursery Dr. Ash 200 A4
Nursery Gr. Kil 69 E1
Nursery La. Glasg 117 D1
Nursery La. Kil 69 E1
Nursery Pl. Ard 205 E1
Nursery Pl. Udd 161 E2
Nursery Rd. Ayr 239 D3
Nursery Rd. Falk 41 F2
Nursery St. Glasg 117 D2
Nursery St. Helen 25 C4
Nursery St. Kilmk 227 F4
Nutberry Ct. Glasg 117 D1

O'Connor Ct. Salt 216 C4
O'Hare. Bonh 28 A2
O'Neil Ave. Bish 98 A4
O'Wood Ave. Holy 143 D4
Oak Ave. Bear 75 F4
Oak Ave. E Kil 180 A3
Oak Cres. Glasg 120 A2
Oak Cres. Plea 12 B2
Oak Dr. Fall 8 B2
Oak Dr. Glasg 139 E2
Oak Dr. Klrk 79 D3
Oak Dr. Lar 23 E1
Oak Fern Dr. E Kil 159 E2
Oak Fern Gr. E Kil 159 E2
Oak Lea. Ham 162 C1
Oak Path. Holy 143 D3
Oak Pk. Bish 78 A1
Oak Pk. Mother 163 E2
Oak Pl. Coat 122 B3
Oak Pl. E Kil 180 A3
Oak Pl. Kilmk 227 E4

Oak Pl. Tan 141 E4
Oak Rd. Ard 205 E2
Oak Rd. Clyde 73 F3
Oak Rd. Cumb 62 C2
Oak Rd. Pais 114 A1
Oak St. Stir 1 C1
Oakbank Ave. Wish 164 C1
Oakbank Dr. Barr 155 F4
Oakbank Ind Est. Glasg 97 D2
Oakbank Rd. P Glasg 68 C4
Oakbank St. Aird 123 E4
Oakburn Ave. Miln 54 C1
Oakburn Cres. Miln 54 C1
Oakdene Ave. Hat 142 A4
Oakdene Ave. Tan 141 D4
Oakdene Cres. Holy 143 E2
Oakfield Ave. Glasg 96 C1
Oakfield Dr. Mother 163 F3
Oakfield La. Glasg 96 C1
Oakfield Rd. Mother 163 F3
Oakhill Ave. Glasg 119 F2
Oakland Dr. Steven 206 C1
Oaklands Ave. Irvine 219 E2
Oaklea Cres. Udd 161 E4
Oakleigh Dr. Green 45 E4
Oakley Dr. Glasg 136 C2
Oakley Terr. Glasg 117 F4
Oaks The. Glasg 137 D2
Oaks The. John 111 F1
Oakshaw Brae. Pais 113 E3
Oakshaw St E. Pais 113 F3
Oakshaw St W. Pais 113 E3
Oakshawhead. Pais 113 E3
Oakview Quadrant. Hat 141 F2
Oakwood Ave. Ayr 236 C1
Oakwood Ave. Pais 113 D1
Oakwood Dr. Beith 171 D4
Oakwood Dr. Newt M 156 C2
Oates Gdns. Mother 164 A2
Oatfield St. Glasg 98 A2
Oban Dr. Glasg 96 C2
Oban La. Glasg 96 C2
Oban Terr. Gour 44 C2
Oberon. All 9 F4
Obiston Gdns. Glasg 119 D3
Observatory La. Glasg 96 B2
Observatory Rd. Glasg 96 B2
Ochil Cres. Stir 2 A1
Ochil Ct. Irvine 220 A1
Ochil Dr. Barr 134 B1
Ochil Dr. Pais 133 F4
Ochil Dr. Sten 23 F2
Ochil Pl. Glasg 119 D2
Ochil Pl. Kilmk 228 A2
Ochil Rd. Alva 5 D4
Ochil Rd. Bear 75 D4
Ochil Rd. Bish 78 B1
Ochil Rd. Men 4 A4
Ochil Rd. Ren 94 A1
Ochil Rd. Stir 2 B2
Ochil St. All 10 A4
Ochil St. Fall 8 B2
Ochil St. Glasg 119 D2
Ochil St. Tull 4 A2
Ochil St. Wish 164 C2
Ochil View. Den 39 E4
Ochil View. Shi 66 B4
Ochil View. Tan 141 D4
Ochilmount. Bann 7 F1
Ochiltree Ave. Glasg 95 F4
Ochiltree Dr. Ham 161 F1
Ochiltree Terr. Falk 41 D3
Ochilview. Alva 5 D4
Ochilview. Cowie 12 C3
Ochville Terr. Fish 5 E2
Octavia Terr. Green 45 E4
Odense Ct. E Kil 180 C3
Ogilface Cres. Blac 107 E1
Ogilvie Ct. Aird 123 F4
Ogilvie Pl. B of A 2 A3
Ogilvie Pl. Glasg 118 B2
Ogilvie Pl. Kilmk 223 E1
Ogilvie Rd. Stir 7 D3
Ogilvie St. Glasg 118 B2
Old Aisle Rd. Klrk 79 F4
Old Avon Rd. Ham 163 D1
Old Bellsdyke Rd. Lar 23 D2
Old Biggar Rd. Gree 83 D1
Old Bore Rd. Aird 123 F4
Old Bothwell Rd. Udd 162 A4
Old Bridge
of Weir Rd. B of W 90 C1
Old Bridge
of Weir Rd. Hous 91 D1
Old Bridge Rd. Ayr 236 C2
Old Bridge St. All 10 A3
Old Bridge St. Ayr 235 F1
Old Bridgend. Car 187 F1
Old Castle Rd. Glasg 137 D3
Old Church Gdns. Coat 121 D3
Old Coach Rd. E Kil 159 F2
Old Cotts. Pais 134 B4
Old Cross. Aird 123 D4
Old Cross. Ham 162 C2
Old Dalmarnock Rd. Glasg 117 F2

Old Dalnottar Rd. O Kill 73 E3
Old Denny Rd. Lar 23 D2
Old Drove Rd. Cam 6 B2
Old Dumbarton Rd. Glasg ... 96 B1
Old Eastfield St. East 127 E3
Old Edinburgh Rd. Tan 140 C4
Old Edinburgh Rd. Tan 141 D4
Old Edinburgh Rd. Tan 141 E4
Old Farm Rd. Ayr 236 B2
Old Gartloch Rd. Muir 100 C3
Old Glasgow Rd. Cumb 62 A2
Old Glasgow Rd. Stew 195 F1
Old Glasgow Rd. Udd 140 B4
Old Glasgow Rd. Udd 140 C3
Old Govan Rd. Ren 94 C2
Old Greenock Rd. Bishop 71 E3
Old Greenock Rd. Ersk 72 C1
Old Greenock Rd. Lang 70 B3
Old Hillfoot Rd. Ayr 239 D3
Old Inns Interchange. Cumb 62 B3
Old Inverkip Rd. Green 45 D2
Old Irvine Rd. Kilmk 227 F4
Old Lanark Rd. Car 202 A4
Old Lanark Rd. Kilnc 202 A2
Old Lanark Rd. Lan 202 C1
Old Largs Rd. Green 45 F1
Old Loans Rd. Troon 230 A2
Old Luss Rd. Alex 19 D1
Old Luss Rd. Helen 16 C1
Old Luss Rd. Helen 25 C4
Old Manse Rd. Glasg 119 E3
Old Manse Rd. Wish 164 C1
Old Military Rd. Gart 20 C4
Old Mill Rd. Alla 146 A1
Old Mill Rd. Dunt 74 A3
Old Mill Rd. E Kil 159 F1
Old Mill Rd. Glasg 139 E3
Old Mill Rd. Kilmk 228 A4
Old Mill Rd. Udd 140 C3
Old Mill Rd. Udd 141 D1
Old Mill View. Kils 60 C2
Old Mill Wlk. Bonh 27 F4
Old Monkland Rd. Coat 121 F2
Old Playfield Rd. E Kil 158 B4
Old Quarry Rd. Cumb 81 E3
Old Quarry Rd. Steven 217 E4
Old Raise Rd. Salt 206 A1
Old Rd. John 112 B2
Old Redding Rd. Laur 42 C2
Old Renfrew Rd. Glasg 95 D1
Old Rome Way. Cross 226 C3
Old Rutherglen Rd. Glasg 117 E2
Old School Ct. Tull 4 A1
Old Schoolhouse La. Hous .. 91 D2
Old Shettleston Rd. Glasg 119 D3
Old Sneddon St. Pais 113 F3
Old St. Dunt 73 F3
Old St. Kilmk 227 F3
Old Stable Row. Coat 122 A4
Old Town. Bann 7 E1
Old Union St. Aird 123 D4
Old Willowyard Rd. Beith 171 D4
Old Wishaw Rd. Car 187 F2
Old Wishaw Rd. Law 187 D3
Old Wood Rd. Glasg 120 A2
Old Woodwynd Rd. Kilw 207 F2
Old Wynd. Glasg 117 E3
Oldbarhills TP Site. Pais 134 B4
Oldhall Dr. Kil 69 E1
Oldhall Rd. Pais 114 B3
Oldhall Roundabout. Shew 224 C3
Olifard Ave. Udd 141 D2
Oliphant Cres. Newt M 157 F3
Oliphant Cres. Pais 132 C4
Oliphant Dr. Kilmk 228 B4
Oliphant Oval. Pais 132 C4
Olive Bank. Tan 121 E1
Olive Ct. Holy 143 D3
Olive Rd. Kilmk 227 E4
Olive St. Glasg 98 B2
Oliver Rd. Falk 42 B2
Olympia Arcade. E Kil 180 C4
Olympia Ct. E Kil 180 C4
Olympia St. Glasg 117 F3
Olympia The. E Kil 180 C4
Olympia Way. E Kil 159 F1
Omoa Rd. Cle 144 A1
Onich Pl. Shot 147 D2
Onslow Dr. Glasg 118 A4
Onslow. E Kil 180 B4
Onslow Rd. Clyde 74 B1
Onslow Sq. Glasg 118 A4
Ontario Pk. E Kil 159 D1
Ontario Pl. E Kil 159 D1
Onthank Dr. Kilmk 222 C2
Onyx St. Hat 142 A2
Open Shore. Green 46 A3
Oran Gate. Glasg 96 C3
Oran Gdns. Glasg 96 C3
Oran Pl. Glasg 96 C2
Oran St. Glasg 96 C2
Orangefield Dr. Pres 233 E1
Orangefield. Green 45 F3
Orangefield Ind Est. Pres .. 233 E1
Orangefield La. Green 45 F3
Orbiston Ct. Mother 164 A3
Orbiston Dr. Dunt 74 B4

Orbiston Dr. Hat 142 B2
Orbiston Pl. Dunt 74 B4
Orbiston Rd. Hat 141 F2
Orbiston Rd. Hat 142 A1
Orbiston Sq. Hat 141 F2
Orbiston St. Mother 163 F3
Orcades Dr. Glasg 137 E2
Orchard Ave. Ayr 239 D3
Orchard Ave. Udd 141 D1
Orchard Brae. Klrk 79 F2
Orchard Ct. Glasg 136 A2
Orchard Ct. Glasg 139 D4
Orchard Ct. Glasg 136 A2
Orchard Dr. Glasg 137 F4
Orchard Dr. Udd 161 E4
Orchard Field. Klrk 79 F2
Orchard Gate. Lark 185 D1
Orchard Gn. E Kil 160 A2
Orchard Gr. Glasg 136 A2
Orchard Gr. Kil 89 E4
Orchard Gr. Kilw 207 F2
Orchard Park Ave. Glasg .. 136 A2
Orchard Pk. Glasg 136 B2
Orchard Pl. Ayr 239 D3
Orchard Pl. Ham 162 B2
Orchard Pl. Hat 141 F2
Orchard Pl. Kilw 207 F2
Orchard Pl. Kirk 80 A4
Orchard St. B of A 2 A3
Orchard St. Car 187 F1
Orchard St. Falk 42 A3
Orchard St. Glasg 119 F2
Orchard St. Green 46 A2
Orchard St. Ham 162 C2
Orchard St. Kilmk 222 C1
Orchard St. Mother 163 E4
Orchard St. Pais 113 F2
Orchard St. Ren 94 B2
Orchard St. W Kil 190 B3
Orchard St. Wish 186 A3
Orchard The. Tull 4 A1
Orchard View Dr. Lan 214 A2
Orchardcroft. Stir 7 D4
Orchardton Rd. Cumb 81 E4
Orchy Ave. Glasg 136 C1
Orchy Cres. Aird 123 E2
Orchy Cres. Bear 75 E1
Orchy Cres. Pais 112 C1
Orchy Ct. Dunt 74 B3
Orchy Dr. Glasg 136 C1
Orchy Gdns. Glasg 136 C1
Orchy St. Glasg 137 D3
Orchy Terr. E Kil 160 A1
Orefield Pl. E Kil 159 F2
Oregon Pl. Glasg 117 E2
Orion Pl. Holy 142 C3
Orion Way. Car 187 E1
Orion Way. Glasg 139 D3
Orkney Ct. All 10 A3
Orkney Pl. Glasg 116 A4
Orkney Quadrant. Wish 165 E2
Orkney St. Glasg 116 A4
Orlando. E Kil 160 B3
Orleans Ave. Glasg 95 F2
Orleans La. Glasg 95 F2
Ormiston Ave. Glasg 95 E2
Ormiston Dr. All 4 C1
Ormiston Dr. Ham 183 E4
Ormiston La. Glasg 95 E2
Ormiston La N. Glasg 95 E2
Ormiston La S. Glasg 95 E2
Ormonde Ave. Glasg 136 C2
Ormonde Cres. Glasg 136 C2
Ormonde Ct. Glasg 136 C2
Ormonde Dr. Glasg 136 C2
Ornsay St. Glasg 97 E4
Oronsay Ave. P Glasg 69 D3
Oronsay Cres. Bear 76 A2
Orr Sq. Pais 113 F3
Orr St. Glasg 117 F3
Orr St. Pais 113 F2
Orr St. Pais 113 E3
Orr Terr. East 127 E2
Orr Terr. Neil 154 B3
Orton St. Glasg 116 A3
Osborne Cres. Thorn 158 A2
Osborne Gdns. Falk 41 F2
Osborne St. Clyde 74 A2
Osborne St. Falk 41 F2
Osborne St. Glasg 117 E3
Oslie View. Stew 195 F1
Osprey Dr. Kilmk 228 B4
Osprey Dr. Tan 141 D4
Osprey Rd. Green 45 D2
Ossian Ave. Glasg 114 C3
Ossian Rd. Glasg 136 C3
Oswald Ct. Ayr 236 A2
Oswald Dr. Pres 233 E1
Oswald Gdns. Car 201 F2
Oswald La. Ayr 235 F1
Oswald Pl. Ayr 236 A3
Oswald Rd. Ayr 236 A2
Oswald St. Falk 42 A1
Oswald St. Glasg 117 D4
Oswald Wlk. Miln 76 B4

Otago Pk. E Kil 159 D1
Otago St. Glasg 96 C1
Othello. E Kil 160 A3
Ottawa Cres. Clyde 73 E2
Otterburn Ave. Kilmk 223 D2
Otterburn Dr. Glasg 136 B1
Otterswick Pl. Glasg 99 E1
Ottoline Dr. Troon 229 F1
Oudenarde Ct. Car 188 A1
Outdale Ave. Pres 236 C4
Oval The. Glasg 136 C1
Oval The. Glen 101 E3
Overbrae Pl. Glasg 74 C3
Overburn Ave. Dumb 49 F3
Overburn Cres. Dumb 49 F3
Overburn Terr. Dumb 50 A3
Overdale Ave. Glasg 136 C4
Overdale Cres. Pres 236 B3
Overdale Gdns. Glasg 136 C4
Overdale Pl. Wish 186 B3
Overdale St. Glasg 136 C4
Overjohnstone Dr. Mother .. 164 B2
Overlea Ave. Glasg 138 B3
Overlee Rd. Newt M 157 F4
Overmills Cres. Ayr 239 E4
Overmills Rd. Ayr 239 E4
Overnewton Pl. Glasg 116 B4
Overnewton Sq. Glasg 96 B1
Overnewton St. Glasg 96 B1
Overton Cres. Den 21 E1
Overton Cres. Green 45 E2
Overton Cres. John 112 A2
Overton Cres. W Kil 190 B3
Overton Ct. W Kil 190 B3
Overton Dr. W Kil 190 B3
Overton Gdns. Kil 69 F1
Overton Gr. Kil 69 F1
Overton Pl. Irvine 220 A3
Overton Rd. Alex 27 E2
Overton Rd. Ash 200 B3
Overton Rd. Glasg 139 E2
Overton Rd. John 112 A1
Overton St. Alex 27 E2
Overton St. Glasg 139 E2
Overtoun Ave. Dumb 50 A2
Overtoun Dr. Clyde 73 F2
Overtoun Dr. Glasg 138 A4
Overtoun Rd. Clyde 73 F2
Overtown Ave. Glasg 135 D3
Overtown Rd. New 165 F1
Overtown Rd. Wish 165 F1
Overtown St. Glasg 118 A3
Overwood Dr. Dumb 50 A2
Overwood Dr. Glasg 137 E3
Overwood Gr. Dumb 50 A2
Owen Ave. E Kil 180 B4
Owen Kelly Pl. Salt 205 F1
Owen Pk. E Kil 180 B4
Owen St. Mother 163 F4
Owendale Ave. Hat 142 A4
Oxford Ave. Gour 45 D3
Oxford Dr. Lin 112 A3
Oxford La. Glasg 117 D3
Oxford Rd. Gour 44 B2
Oxford Rd. Ren 94 B2
Oxford St. Coat 121 F3
Oxford St. Glasg 117 D3
Oxford St. Klrk 79 E4
Oxgang Pl. Klrk 79 F4
Oxhill Pl. Dumb 49 E2
Oxhill Rd. Dumb 49 E2
Oxton Dr. Glasg 115 D3

Pacemuir La. Kil 89 D4
Pacemuir Rd. Kil 89 E4
Paddock The. Coat 122 B2
Paddock The. Irvine 220 B3
Paddock The. Thorn 158 A3
Paddockholm
North Ind Est. Kilb 149 D1
Paddockholm Rd. Kilb 149 D1
Paddockholm
South Ind Est. Kilb 149 D1
Paduff Pl. Kilb 149 D1
Paidmyre Cres. Newt M 156 B2
Paidmyre Gdns. Newt M 156 B2
Paidmyre Rd. Newt M 156 B2
Paisley Rd. Barr 134 C4
Paisley Rd. Glasg 116 C3
Paisley Rd. Ren 94 B1
Paisley Rd W. Glasg 115 E2
Paisley St. Ard 205 E1
Palacecraig St. Coat 122 A2
Paladin Ave. Glasg 95 D4
Palermo St. Glasg 97 F2
Palladium Pl. Glasg 95 E2
Palm Pl. Tan 121 E3
Palmer Ave. Glasg 75 E1
Palmerston. E Kil 180 A4
Palmerston Pl. Glasg 116 B4
Palmerston Pl. John 131 E4
Pandora Way. Tan 141 D4
Pankhurst Pl. E Kil 159 F1
Panmure St. Glasg 97 D3
Panrock Ct. Troon 229 E2
Pantonville Rd. W Kil 190 B2
Papermill Rd. Green 45 D4
Pappert. Bonh 28 A2

Pardovan Pl. Falk 41 F3
Paris Ave. Den 21 F1
Park Ave. Bank 39 F3
Park Ave. Barr 134 A1
Park Ave. Beith 150 A1
Park Ave. Bish 78 A2
Park Ave. Bonh 19 F1
Park Ave. Car 187 F2
Park Ave. Dumb 50 A2
Park Ave. Glasg 96 C1
Park Ave. Gour 45 D4
Park Ave. Holy 143 D3
Park Ave. John 112 B1
Park Ave. Kilw 207 F2
Park Ave. Klrk 79 E4
Park Ave. Lar 23 E1
Park Ave. Laur 42 C2
Park Ave. Miln 55 D1
Park Ave. Pais 113 E1
Park Ave. Pres 236 A4
Park Ave. Stir 7 D3
Park Ave. Twe 59 F2
Park Bank. Ersk 73 D1
Park Brae. Ersk 93 E4
Park Burn Ct. Ham 162 A3
Park Cir. Ayr 238 C4
Park Cir. Car 187 F2
Park Cir. Glasg 96 C1
Park Circus La. Ayr 238 C4
Park Circus La. Glasg 96 C1
Park Circus Pl. Glasg 96 C1
Park Cres. Aird 122 C4
Park Cres. Bann 7 E1
Park Cres. Bear 75 E3
Park Cres. Bish 78 A1
Park Cres. Dumb 49 F3
Park Cres. Eagle 178 C3
Park Cres. Inch 93 E4
Park Cres. Lennox 57 E1
Park Cres. N Sau 5 E1
Park Cres. Sten 24 A1
Park Cres. Stew 211 E4
Park Cres. Udd 161 E3
Park Ct. Beith 171 E4
Park Ct. Bish 78 A2
Park Ct. Clyde 73 F2
Park Ct. Glasg 136 A2
Park Ct. Mother 163 E3
Park Dr. Bann 7 E1
Park Dr. Ersk 93 D4
Park Dr. Ersk 93 E4
Park Dr. Glasg 96 C1
Park Dr. Glasg 138 A4
Park Dr. Ham 163 E1
Park Dr. Hat 142 A2
Park Dr. Lan 214 C2
Park Dr. Lar 23 E1
Park Dr. New 166 A3
Park Dr. Thorn 158 B2
Park Gardens La. Glasg 96 C1
Park Gate. Ersk 93 D4
Park Gate. Glasg 96 C1
Park Gate Pl. Hat 141 F3
Park Gdns. Bann 7 E1
Park Gdns. Glasg 96 C1
Park Gdns. Kilbar 111 D2
Park Glade. Ersk 93 D4
Park Gn. Ersk 93 D4
Park Gr. Card 48 A4
Park Gr. Ersk 93 E4
Park Hill. Ersk 73 D1
Park La. Ard 205 E2
Park La. Car 187 F1
Park La. Glasg 117 F3
Park La. Kils 60 B4
Park La. Kilw 207 E3
Park La. Stir 7 D4
Park La. Udd 161 F4
Park Lea. Cald 105 D2
Park Moor. Ersk 93 D4
Park Pl. All 10 B4
Park Pl. Hat 141 F2
Park Pl. Irvine 219 D3
Park Pl. John 111 F1
Park Pl. Lan 214 C2
Park Pl. Stir 6 C3
Park Pl. Strath 31 D2
Park Pl. Thorn 158 B2
Park Quadrant. Glasg 96 C1
Park Quadrant. Wish 164 C1
Park Rd. Ard 205 E1
Park Rd. B of W 90 B1
Park Rd. Bish 78 A1
Park Rd. Blac 107 F2
Park Rd. Calder 123 D2
Park Rd. Clyde 73 F2
Park Rd. Coat 121 D3
Park Rd. Falk 24 A1
Park Rd. Glasg 96 C1
Park Rd. Glasg 136 B1
Park Rd. Glasg 139 E4
Park Rd. Ham 162 B2
Park Rd. Hat 142 A2
Park Rd. Holy 143 D1
Park Rd. Inch 93 E4
Park Rd. John 111 F1
Park Rd. Kil 89 E4
Park Rd. Men 4 A3

Park Rd. Miln 55 D1
Park Rd. Muir 100 B4
Park Rd. Pais 113 C1
Park Rd. Salt 216 C4
Park Rd. Shot 146 B3
Park Ridge. Ersk 93 E4
Park St. Aird 122 C4
Park St. Alex 27 E3
Park St. Alva 5 D4
Park St. Bon 40 B2
Park St. Car 187 F1
Park St. Cle 144 A2
Park St. Coat 122 A4
Park St. Cowie 12 C4
Park St. Dumb 50 A2
Park St. Falk 42 A3
Park St. Holy 143 D2
Park St. Kilmk 222 C1
Park St. Kirk 80 A4
Park St. Mother 163 F3
Park St S. Glasg 96 C1
Park Terr. Ayr 238 C4
Park Terr. Card 48 A4
Park Terr. E Kil 159 F1
Park Terr. Glasg 96 C1
Park Terr. Gour 44 C4
Park Terr. Stir 7 D3
Park Terr. Tull 4 A1
Park
  Terrace East La. Glasg .. 96 C1
Park Terrace La. Glasg 96 C1
Park Top. Ersk 73 E1
Park View. Ard 205 E2
Park View. Cald 105 D3
Park View. Kilb 149 D1
Park View. Kilbar 111 D2
Park View. Lark 185 D1
Park View. Pais 113 E1
Park Way. Cumb 62 A2
Park Winding. Ersk 93 E4
Park Wood. Ersk 73 E1
Parkandarroch Cres. Car .. 188 A1
Parkburn Ave. Klrk 79 E4
Parkburn Rd. Kils 36 B1
Parkdyke. Stir 6 C3
Parkend Ave. Salt 217 D4
Parkend Cres. Shi 66 B3
Parkend Gdns. Salt 217 D4
Parkend Rd. Salt 217 D4
Parker Pl. Kils 60 B4
Parker Pl. Lark 185 D2
Parkfield. E Kil 180 C3
Parkfoot Ct. Falk 42 A2
Parkfoot St. Kils 36 B1
Parkgate. Alva 4 C3
Parkgrove Ave. Glasg 136 B2
Parkgrove Terr. Glasg 96 C1
Parkgrove
  Terrace La. Glasg 96 C1
Parkhall Rd. Clyde 73 F2
Parkhall St. E Kil 159 F1
Parkhall Terr. Clyde 73 F3
Parkhead Ave. Kilw 207 F2
Parkhead Cross. Glasg 118 B3
Parkhead St. N Sau 10 B4
Parkhead La. Aird 123 D4
Parkhead Rd. Falk 42 A1
Parkhead Rd. N Sau 10 B4
Parkhead St. Aird 123 D4
Parkhead St. Mother 163 F3
Parkhill Ave. Cross 226 C4
Parkhill Ave. P Glasg 69 D4
Parkhill Dr. Dalry 191 E4
Parkhill Dr. Glasg 138 A4
Parkhill Dr. Loch 129 E2
Parkhill Rd. Glasg 136 B4
Parkholm La. Glasg 116 C3
Parkhouse Dr. Kilb 149 D1
Parkhouse Gdns. Salt 205 E1
Parkhouse Rd. Ard 205 E1
Parkhouse Rd. Glasg 135 D2
Parkhouse St. Ayr 238 C4
Parkinch. Ersk 93 E4
Parklands Rd. Glasg 136 C2
Parklea. Bish 77 F2
Parklee Dr. E Kil 158 C4
Parkneuk Rd. Glasg 136 B2
Parkneuk Rd. Ham 161 D1
Parkneuk St. Mother 163 E4
Parknook Way. Lark 185 D2
Parks View. Ham 183 E3
Parksail Dr. Ersk 93 E4
Parksail. Ersk 93 E4
Parkside Ct. Plea 12 B2
Parkside Rd. Mother 163 D3
Parkside Rd. Shot 146 B2
Parkthorn View. Dund 225 F1
Parkvale Ave. Ersk 93 E4
Parkvale Cres. Ersk 93 F4
Parkvale Dr. Ersk 93 E4
Parkvale Gdns. Ersk 93 E4
Parkvale Pl. Ersk 93 E4
Parkvale Way. Ersk 93 E4
Parkview Ave. Falk 41 F1
Parkview Ave. Klrk 79 E4
Parkview. Ayr 238 C1
Parkview Cres. New 166 A2
Parkview Ct. Klrk 79 E4

Parkview Dr. Coat 121 F4
Parkview Dr. Stepps 99 F3
Parkville Dr. Ham 161 F3
Parkville Rd. Hat 142 B4
Parkway. All 10 A4
Parkway Ct. Coat 121 F3
Parkway. Ersk 93 D4
Parkway Pl. Coat 121 F3
Parnell St. Aird 122 C3
Parnie St. Glasg 117 E3
Parry Terr. E Kil 159 D1
Parsonage Row. Glasg 117 E4
Parsonage Sq. Glasg 117 E3
Parterre. Irvine 219 E1
Partick Bridge St. Glasg 96 B1
Partickhill Ave. Glasg 96 A2
Partickhill Ct. Glasg 96 A2
Partickhill Rd. Glasg 96 A1
Partridge Rd. Green 45 D3
Patchy Pk. Lark 199 D4
Paterson Ave. Irvine 219 F3
Paterson Cres. Irvine 219 E3
Paterson Dr. Helen 16 A2
Paterson Dr. Shi 66 B3
Paterson Pl. B of A 2 A3
Paterson Pl. Bear 75 E4
Paterson Pl. Bon 40 B3
Paterson St. Ayr 236 A2
Paterson St. Glasg 117 D3
Paterson St. Mother 163 F4
Paterson Terr. E Kil 180 B4
Path The. Bann 7 E1
Pather St. Wish 165 D1
Pathfoot Ave. B of A 2 B4
Pathfoot Dr. B of A 2 B4
Pathfoot. Kilw 207 F2
Pathfoot Rd. B of A 2 B3
Pathfoot View. Kilw 207 F2
Pathhead Gdns. Glasg 98 C3
Pathhead Rd. E Kil 158 B4
Patna Ct. Ham 161 F1
Patna St. Glasg 118 A2
Paton St. All 10 A4
Paton St. Glasg 118 A4
Paton St. Green 45 E3
Patrick Ave. Steven 206 B1
Patrick Dr. Shi 66 C4
Patrick St. Green 45 F3
Patrick St. Pais 113 F2
Patterson Dr. Law 187 D3
Patterton Dr. Barr 134 B1
Pattison St. Clyde 73 F2
Paul Dr. Air 14 C2
Pavilion Pl. Salt 205 E1
Pavilion View. All 9 F4
Paxstone Cres. East 127 F3
Paxstone Dr. East 127 F3
Paxton Pl. Kilmk 228 A4
Payne St. Glasg 97 E1
Peace Ave. Kil 89 F1
Peace Ave. Kilmk 222 B1
Peacock Ave. Pais 112 C1
Peacock Cross. Ham 162 B2
Peacock Dr. Ham 162 B2
Peacock Dr. Pais 112 C1
Pearce La. Glasg 116 A4
Pearce St. Glasg 116 A4
Pearl St. Hat 142 A2
Pearson Dr. Ren 94 B2
Pearson Pl. Bank 39 E3
Pearson Pl. Lin 112 A3
Peat Pl. Glasg 135 D3
Peat Rd. B of W 110 C4
Peat Rd. Glasg 135 D3
Peat Rd. Green 45 E2
Peathill Ave. Muir 100 A4
Peathill Rd. Bon 40 A3
Peathill St. Glasg 97 E2
Peatland Quadrant. Kilmk . 228 A2
Peatland Rd. Kilmk 228 A2
Pebbles Dr. Glasg 138 B4
Peden Ave. Dalry 191 D4
Peden Pl. Irvine 219 E1
Peden St. East 127 E3
Pedmyre La. E Kil 158 B4
Peebles Path. Coat 122 B2
Peebles St. Ayr 235 F1
Peel Brae. Kirk 58 B1
Peel Ct. Glasg 139 D3
Peel Glen Rd. Bear 75 D3
Peel Glen Rd. Glasg 75 D3
Peel La. Glasg 96 A1
Peel Park Pl. E Kil 158 C1
Peel Pl. Coat 121 E3
Peel Pl. Udd 141 D2
Peel Rd. Thorn 158 A1
Peel St. Card 48 A4
Peel St. Glasg 96 A1
Peel View. Clyde 74 B2
Pegasus Ave. Car 187 F1
Pegasus Rd. Holy 142 C3
Peggieshill Pl. Ayr 239 D3
Peggieshill Rd. Ayr 239 D3
Peile St. Green 45 E3
Peiter Pl. Udd 161 E4
Pelstream Ave. Stir 7 D2

Pemberton Valley. Ayr 239 D1
Pembroke. E Kil 160 B2
Pembroke Rd. Gour 44 B2
Pembroke St. Glasg 116 C4
Pembroke St. Lar 23 E2
Penbreck Ct. Irvine 220 A3
Pencaitland Dr. Glasg 119 D2
Pencaitland Gr. Glasg 119 D2
Pencaitland Pl. Glasg 76 C1
Pendeen Cres. Glasg 119 F3
Pendeen Pl. Glasg 119 F3
Pendeen Rd. Glasg 119 F3
Penders La. Falk 42 A3
Pendicle Cres. Bear 75 E2
Pendicle Rd. Bear 75 F2
Pendreich Way. Stir 2 A2
Penfold Cres. E Kil 180 B4
Penicuik St. Glasg 118 B3
Penilee Rd. Glasg 114 C3
Penilee Terr. Glasg 114 C3
Peninver Dr. Glasg 115 F4
Penman Ave. Glasg 137 F4
Pennan. Ersk 73 D2
Pennan Pl. Glasg 95 D3
Penneld Rd. Glasg 114 C3
Penniecroft Ave. Dumb 50 B3
Pennyburn Rd. Kilw 207 E1
Pennyfern Dr. Green 45 D2
Pennyfern Rd. Green 45 D2
Pennyroyal Ct. E Kil 159 E2
Pennyvenie Way. Irvine 220 A3
Penrith Ave. Glasg 136 B1
Penrith Dr. Glasg 96 A3
Penrith Pl. E Kil 179 F3
Penryn Gdns. Glasg 119 E2
Penston Rd. Glasg 119 E4
Pentland Ave. Lin 112 A3
Pentland Ave. P Glasg 68 C3
Pentland Cres. Pais 133 E4
Pentland Ct. Aird 103 D1
Pentland Ct. Barr 134 B1
Pentland Dr. Barr 134 B1
Pentland Dr. Bish 78 B1
Pentland Dr. Pres 236 B3
Pentland Dr. Ren 114 A4
Pentland Pl. Bear 75 D4
Pentland Pl. Irvine 220 A2
Pentland Rd. Glasg 136 B3
Pentland Rd. Kilmk 228 A2
Pentland Rd. Muir 100 B4
Pentland Rd. Wish 164 C2
Penzance Way. Muir 80 C1
Peockland Gdns. John 112 A2
Peockland Pl. John 112 A2
Peploe Dr. E Kil 160 B3
Perceton
  Roundabout. Irvine 220 A3
Perceton Row. Irvine 220 B2
Percy Dr. Glasg 136 B1
Percy Rd. Ren 94 A1
Percy St. Glasg 116 B3
Percy St. Lark 185 D2
Perran Gdns. Muir 80 C1
Perray Ave. Dumb 49 D3
Perth Ave. Aird 123 D2
Perth Cres. Clyde 73 E3
Perth St. Glasg 116 C4
Peter Coats Building. Pais ... 113 F2
Peter D.Stirling Rd. Kirk 58 B1
Peters Ave. Bonh 20 A1
Petersburn Pl. Aird 123 E3
Petersburn Rd. Aird 123 E3
Petershill Dr. Glasg 98 B2
Petershill Pl. Glasg 98 A2
Petershill Rd. Glasg 98 A2
Peterson Dr. Clyde 94 C4
Peterson Gdns. Clyde 94 C4
Petition Pl. Udd 141 D3
Pettigrew St. Glasg 119 D3
Peveril Ave. Glasg 116 B1
Peveril Ave. Glasg 138 B3
Peveril Ct. Glasg 138 B3
Pharonhill St. Glasg 118 B3
Philip Dr. Lar 23 E1
Philip Murray Rd. Tan 141 E3
Philip Sq. Ayr 236 A1
Philip St. Falk 42 A4
Philipshill Rd. E Kil 158 C2
Phoenix Cres. Tan 141 F4
Phoenix Pl. Holy 143 D2
Phoenix Pl. John 112 B2
Phoenix Rd. Holy 142 C3
Piccadilly St. Glasg 116 C4
Picken St. Kilmk 227 F3
Pickerstonhill. Holy 143 F2
Picketlaw Dr. E Kil 158 B4
Picketlaw Farm Rd. E Kil ... 158 B4
Pier Rd. Alex 19 E1
Pier Rd. Rhu 15 F2
Piershill St. Glasg 99 D4
Piersland Pl. Irvine 220 A3
Pikeman Rd. Glasg 95 E4
Pilmuir Ave. Glasg 136 C2
Pilrig St. Glasg 118 C4
Pilton Rd. Glasg 75 D2
Pine Brae. Ayr 239 E3
Pine Cl. Cumb 62 C2
Pine Cres. Cumb 62 C2

Pine Cres. E Kil 180 A3
Pine Cres. John 112 A1
Pine Ct. Coat 121 F2
Pine Ct. Cumb 62 C2
Pine Ct. E Kil 180 B3
Pine Gr. All 10 B3
Pine Gr. Calder 123 D1
Pine Gr. Cumb 62 C2
Pine Gr. Holy 143 D3
Pine Gr. Tan 141 D4
Pine House. Pres 236 A3
Pine Lawn. Wish 165 E3
Pine Pk. Ham 162 C1
Pine Pl. Cumb 62 C2
Pine Pl. Glasg 117 E2
Pine Rd. Clyde 73 E2
Pine Rd. Cumb 62 C2
Pine Rd. Dumb 49 F2
Pine Rd. Kilmk 227 E4
Pine St. Aird 123 E4
Pine St. Green 45 F2
Pine St. Lennox 57 F4
Pine St. Pais 114 A1
Pine Wlk. Lar 23 E1
Pinelands. Bish 78 A2
Pines The. Glasg 137 D2
Pinewood Ave. Klrk 79 D3
Pinewood Ct. Dumb 50 B3
Pinewood Ct. Klrk 79 D3
Pinewood Pl. Klrk 79 D3
Pinkerton Ave. Glasg 137 F4
Pinkston Dr. Glasg 97 F1
Pinkston Rd. Glasg 97 E1
Pinmore. Kilw 207 E1
Pinmore Pl. Glasg 134 C3
Pinmore St. Glasg 134 C3
Pinwherry Pl. Udd 141 D2
Piper Ave. Hous 111 E4
Piper Rd. Aird 123 E4
Piper Rd. Hous 111 E4
Piperhill. Ayr 239 D1
Pirleyhill Dr. Shi 66 B3
Pirleyhill Gdns. Falk 42 A1
Pirnhall Rd. Bann 11 D3
Pirnhall Rd. Bann 11 E4
Pirnie Pl. Kils 60 B4
Pirnmill Ave. Mother 163 D4
Pirnmill Pl. Helen 16 C1
Pirnmill Rd. Salt 205 F1
Pit Rd. Hat 141 F3
Pit Rd. Kirk 80 B4
Pitcairn Cres. E Kil 179 F4
Pitcairn Gr. E Kil 180 A3
Pitcairn Pl. E Kil 179 F4
Pitcairn St. Glasg 118 C2
Pitcairn Terr. Ham 162 A2
Pitcaple Dr. Glasg 136 A3
Pitfairn Rd. Fish 5 F2
Pitlochry Dr. Glasg 115 E2
Pitlochry Dr. Lark 185 E1
Pitmedden Rd. Bish 78 B1
Pitmilly Rd. Glasg 75 E2
Pitreavie Ct. Ham 183 D4
Pitreavie Pl. Glasg 99 E1
Pitt St. Glasg 117 D4
Pitt Terr. Stir 7 D3
Place Of Bonhill. Alex 27 E2
Place View. Kilb 149 D1
Pladda Ave. Irvine 220 A1
Pladda Ave. P Glasg 69 D3
Pladda Cres. Irvine 220 A1
Pladda Ct. Irvine 220 A1
Pladda Dr. Pres 236 B3
Pladda Rd. Ren 94 B1
Pladda Rd. Salt 205 F1
Pladda St. Mother 163 D4
Pladda Terr. Irvine 220 A1
Pladda Way. Helen 16 C1
Pladda Wynd. Irvine 220 A1
Plaintrees Ct. Pais 113 F1
Plan View. Kilb 149 D2
Plane Pl. Tan 121 E1
Planetree Pl. John 112 A1
Planetree Rd. Clyde 74 A3
Plant St. Glasg 118 B3
Plantation Ave. Holy 143 D3
Plantation
  Park Gdns. Glasg 116 B3
Plantation Sq. Glasg 116 C3
Plateau Dr. Troon 229 F4
Platthorn Dr. E Kil 159 F1
Platthorn Rd. E Kil 159 F1
Playfair St. Glasg 118 A2
Playingfield Cres. Cross 221 F1
Playingfield Rd. Cross 221 F1
Plaza The. E Kil 159 F1
Pleaknowe Cres. Muir 80 C1
Pleamuir Pl. Cumb 61 E1
Plean St. Glasg 95 D3
Pleasance Ct. Falk 42 A4
Pleasance. Falk 42 A4
Pleasance Gdns. Falk 42 A4
Pleasance Sq. Falk 42 A4
Pleasance St. Glasg 136 B4
Pleasantfield Rd. Pres 236 A3
Pleasantside Ave. P Glasg 69 D4
Plotcock Rd. Quart 198 B4

Name	Page	Grid
Plotcock Rd. Stone	198	B4
Plover Dr. E Kil	180	A3
Plover Pl. John	131	E4
Plusgarten Loan. New	165	F4
Plymouth Ave. Gour	44	C3
Poet's View. Klrk	79	F4
Poindfauld Terr. Dumb	50	A2
Pointhouse Rd. Glasg	116	B4
Pokelly Pl. Stew	195	F1
Polbae Cres. Eagle	178	C3
Poles Rd. Fen	213	D2
Polkemmet Dr. Hart	127	F3
Polkemmet La. Hart	127	F3
Polkemmet Rd. Hart	127	F3
Pollick Ave. Uplaw	153	D2
Pollick Farm La. Dunlop	153	D1
Pollock Ave. Eagle	178	C3
Pollock Ave. Ham	162	A2
Pollock Cres. Kilw	207	F1
Pollock Rd. Bear	76	A2
Pollock Rd. Newt M	156	B2
Pollock St. Hat	142	B3
Pollock St. Mother	163	F4
Pollok Ave. Glasg	136	A4
Pollok Dr. Bish	77	F1
Pollok La. E Kil	160	A2
Pollok Pl. E Kil	160	A2
Pollokshaws Rd. Glasg	116	C1
Pollokshaws Rd. Glasg	117	D2
Polmadie Ave. Glasg	117	E1
Polmadie Rd. Glasg	117	E1
Polmadie St. Glasg	117	E1
Polmaise Ave. Stir	7	D2
Polmaise Cres. Fall	8	B3
Polmaise Ct. Stir	7	D2
Polmaise Rd. Cam	6	C2
Polmaise Rd. Stir	6	C3
Polnoon Ave. Glasg	95	D4
Polnoon Dr. Eagle	178	C3
Polnoon St. Eagle	178	B2
Polo Ave. Troon	229	F1
Polo Gdns. Troon	229	F1
Polson Dr. John	111	F1
Polsons Cres. Pais	113	E1
Polwarth La. Glasg	96	A2
Polwarth St. Glasg	96	A2
Pomona Pl. Ham	161	F1
Pompee Rd. N Sau	5	D1
Poplar Ave. Bishop	72	A1
Poplar Ave. Glasg	95	F2
Poplar Ave. John	112	A1
Poplar Ave. Newt M	156	C2
Poplar Cres. Bishop	72	A1
Poplar Ct. Coat	121	F2
Poplar Dr. Clyde	73	F3
Poplar Dr. Klrk	79	D3
Poplar Dr. M of C	58	B3
Poplar Gdns. E Kil	180	B3
Poplar Pl. Gour	44	B3
Poplar Pl. Holy	143	D2
Poplar Pl. Tan	141	E4
Poplar Pl. Udd	140	B1
Poplar Rd. Dumb	49	F2
Poplar St. Aird	123	E4
Poplar St. Green	46	C1
Poplar Way. Glasg	239	E3
Poplars The. Bear	75	E4
Poplars The. Tull	4	B1
Poplin St. Glasg	118	A2
Porchester St. Glasg	99	E1
Port Dundas Ind Est. Glasg	97	E1
Port Dundas Pl. Glasg	117	E4
Port Dundas Rd. Glasg	97	E1
Port Glasgow Rd. Green	46	C2
Port Glasgow Rd. Kil	69	D1
Port St. Glasg	116	C4
Port St. Stir	7	D4
Portal Rd. Glasg	95	E4
Portdownie. Falk	41	E3
Portencross Rd. W Kil	190	B3
Porter St. Glasg	116	B3
Porterfield Rd. Kil	89	F4
Porterfield Rd. Ren	94	A2
Porters La. Chap	123	E1
Porters Well. Udd	140	C2
Portessie. Ersk	73	D1
Porthlethen. Ersk	73	D1
Portland Ave. Irvine	224	A4
Portland Brae. Hurl	228	C3
Portland Ct. Hurl	228	C3
Portland Pk. Ham	162	C1
Portland Pl. Ham	162	C1
Portland Pl. Irvine	224	A4
Portland Pl. Kilmk	227	F4
Portland Pl. Lan	215	D2
Portland Pl. Steven	217	E4
Portland Rd. Irvine	224	A4
Portland Rd. Kilmk	227	F4
Portland Rd. Pais	114	A2
Portland Roundabout. Irvine	219	D1
Portland Sq. Ham	162	C1
Portland St. Coat	122	A4
Portland St. Kilmk	222	C1
Portland St. Troon	229	E2
Portland Terr. Troon	229	D1
Portland Wynd. Lark	185	D2
Portman St. Glasg	116	C3
Portmark Ave. Ayr	238	B1
Portmarnock Dr. Glasg	96	C4
Porton Pl. Bishop	72	A2
Portpatrick Rd. O Kill	72	C4
Portreath Rd. Muir	80	C2
Portree Terr. Gour	44	C2
Portsmouth Dr. Gour	44	C3
Portsoy Ave. Glasg	94	C4
Portsoy. Ersk	73	D1
Portsoy Pl. Glasg	94	C4
Portugal St. Glasg	117	D3
Portwell. Ham	162	C2
Possil Cross. Glasg	97	E2
Possil Rd. Glasg	97	D2
Postgate. Ham	162	C2
Posthill. N Sau	5	E1
Potassels Rd. Muir	100	B4
Potrail Pl. Ham	162	A2
Potter Cl. Glasg	118	C2
Potter Gr. Glasg	118	C2
Potter Pl. Glasg	118	C2
Potter Pl. Gran	24	C2
Potter St. Glasg	118	C2
Potterhill Ave. Pais	133	F4
Potterhill Rd. Glasg	115	D1
Potters Wynd. Lan	215	E3
Pottery Pl. Kilmk	222	C1
Pottery St. Green	46	C2
Pottis Rd. Bann	7	E2
Potts Way. Mother	142	B1
Powbrone. E Kil	180	C3
Powburn Cres. Udd	140	B4
Powfoot St. Glasg	118	B3
Powforth Cl. Lark	184	C2
Powgree Cres. Beith	171	E3
Powmill Rd. Pres	233	E1
Powrie St. Glasg	99	E2
Prentice Rd. Mother	163	D3
President Kennedy Dr. Plea	12	B2
Preston Pl. Glasg	117	D1
Preston St. Glasg	117	D1
Preston St. Glasg	117	D1
Prestonfield Ave. Kilw	207	D2
Prestonfield. Miln	54	C1
Prestwick Pl. Newt M	157	D2
Prestwick Rd. Ayr	236	A2
Prestwick St. Glasg	135	D3
Pretoria Rd. Lar	23	D1
Priestfield St. Udd	161	E3
Priesthill Ave. Glasg	135	E3
Priesthill Cres. Glasg	135	E3
Priesthill Rd. Glasg	135	E3
Priestknowe Roundabout. E Kil	159	F1
Prieston Rd. B of W	110	B4
Primrose Ave. Hat	142	A4
Primrose Ave. Lark	199	D4
Primrose Cres. Mother	163	F3
Primrose Ct. Glasg	95	E2
Primrose Pk. Ayr	239	E2
Primrose Pl. All	10	A3
Primrose Pl. Cumb	82	A3
Primrose Pl. Kilmk	222	B1
Primrose Pl. Salt	206	A1
Primrose Pl. Tan	141	E4
Primrose St. All	10	A4
Primrose St. Bon	40	A3
Primrose St. Glasg	95	E2
Primrose Way. Car	201	F4
Prince Albert Rd. Glasg	96	B2
Prince Albert Terr. Helen	16	B1
Prince Edward St. Glasg	117	D1
Prince of Wales Gdns. Glasg	96	B4
Prince Pl. New	166	A3
Prince's Gdns. Glasg	96	A2
Prince's Pl. Glasg	96	B2
Prince's Terr. Glasg	96	B2
Princes Ct. Ayr	236	A1
Princes Gate. Glasg	138	A4
Princes Gate. Udd	140	C2
Princes Mall. E Kil	159	F1
Princes Pk. Ersk	72	C2
Princes Pl. Ard	205	D1
Princes Sq. Barr	134	B2
Princes Sq. E Kil	159	F1
Princes Square Shop Ctr. Glasg	117	E4
Princes St. Ard	205	D1
Princes St. Cald	105	D3
Princes St. Cali	66	C3
Princes St E. Helen	16	C1
Princes St. Falk	42	A3
Princes St. Glasg	138	A4
Princes St. Green	45	F3
Princes St. Kilmk	227	F4
Princes St. Mother	163	F4
Princes St. P Glasg	47	E1
Princes St. Salt	216	B4
Princes St. Stir	7	D4
Princess Anne Quadrant. Holy	142	C3
Princess Cres. Pais	114	A3
Princess Ct. Helen	16	B1
Princess Ct. Kilmk	228	A2
Princess Dr. Coat	121	D3
Princess Rd. Holy	142	C2
Princess Sq. New	165	F3
Princess St. Bon	40	A3
Princess Way. Ros	15	D2
Printers Land. Thorn	158	A3
Priory Ave. Pais	114	A4
Priory Dr. Udd	140	B4
Priory Gate. Wish	186	A4
Priory Pl. Cumb	60	C1
Priory Pl. Glasg	95	E4
Priory Rd. Glasg	95	E4
Priory St. Udd	161	E4
Priory Terr. Wish	164	B1
Procession Rd. Pais	133	E3
Professors' Sq. Glasg	96	B1
Progress Dr. Cald	105	D3
Promenade. Ayr	236	A2
Prosen St. Glasg	118	C2
Prospect Ave. Glasg	138	C3
Prospect Ave. Udd	140	C4
Prospect Ct. Ham	161	E3
Prospect Dr. Ash	199	F4
Prospect Rd. Cumb	61	E3
Prospect Rd. Glasg	136	B4
Prospect St. Falk	41	F3
Prospecthill Cir. Glasg	117	E1
Prospecthill Cres. Glasg	137	F4
Prospecthill Dr. Glasg	137	E4
Prospecthill Pl. Glasg	137	F4
Prospecthill Pl. Green	45	F2
Prospecthill Rd. Falk	42	A1
Prospecthill Rd. Glasg	137	E4
Prospecthill Rd. Salt	206	A1
Prospecthill Sq. Glasg	137	E4
Prospecthill St. Green	45	F2
Provan Rd. Glasg	118	B4
Provand Hall Cres. Glasg	120	A3
Provanhill St. Glasg	97	F1
Provanmill Rd. Glasg	98	C1
Provost Cl. John	111	F2
Provost Gate. Lark	185	D2
Provost Hunter Ave. Alva	5	E4
Pullar Ave. B of A	2	A3
Pullar Ct. B of A	2	A3
Pundeavon Ave. Kilb	149	D2
Purdie. E Kil	160	B3
Purdie St. Ham	162	A3
Purdon St. Glasg	96	A1
Putyan Ave. Dalry	191	D4
Pyatshaw Rd. Lark	185	D1
Quadrant Rd. Glasg	136	C3
Quadrant The. Glasg	157	F4
Quail Rd. Ayr	236	A2
Quakerfield. Bann	7	F1
Quarrelton Rd. John	111	F1
Quarrier St. Green	46	B2
Quarrolhall Cres. Sten	24	A2
Quarry Ave. Glasg	139	F2
Quarry Dr. Kil	69	E1
Quarry Dr. Klrk	79	F4
Quarry Knowe. Bann	11	F4
Quarry Knowe Pl. Hat	141	F2
Quarry Knowe. Rhu	15	F3
Quarry La. Dumb	49	F2
Quarry La. Eagle	178	B2
Quarry La. Lennox	33	E1
Quarry Pk. E Kil	180	C4
Quarry Pl. Dumb	49	E3
Quarry Pl. Glasg	138	C3
Quarry Pl. Ham	162	C2
Quarry Pl. N Sau	10	B4
Quarry Pl. Shot	146	B3
Quarry Rd. Aird	103	D1
Quarry Rd. Barr	134	A2
Quarry Rd. Cam	6	B3
Quarry Rd. E Kil	180	B3
Quarry Rd. Irvine	219	E2
Quarry Rd. Lark	185	D1
Quarry Rd. P Glasg	68	C4
Quarry Rd. Pais	113	F1
Quarry Rd. Shot	146	B3
Quarry St. Coat	122	B4
Quarry St. Ham	162	C2
Quarry St. Holy	143	D2
Quarry St. John	111	F1
Quarry St. Lark	185	D1
Quarry St. Shot	146	B3
Quarry St. Wish	165	D2
Quarrybank. Kilbar	111	E1
Quarrybrae Ave. Newt M	157	E4
Quarrybrae Gdns. Tan	141	E3
Quarrybrae St. Glasg	118	C3
Quarryknowe. Glasg	137	F4
Quarryknowe St. Dunt	74	C4
Quarryknowe St. Glasg	118	C3
Quarryside St. Glenm	102	C2
Quarrywood Ave. Glasg	98	B2
Quarrywood Rd. Glasg	98	B2
Quay Pend. Dumb	49	F2
Quay Rd. Glasg	118	A1
Quay Road N. Glasg	118	A1
Quay St. Dumb	49	F2
Quay St. Salt	216	C4
Quebec Dr. E Kil	159	E1
Quebec Gn. E Kil	159	E1
Quebec Wynd. Glasg	139	E4
Queen Elizabeth Ave. Glasg	114	C4
Queen Elizabeth Ct. Mother	163	E4
Queen Elizabeth Sq. Glasg	117	E2
Queen Margaret Dr. Glasg	96	C2
Queen Mary Ave. Clyde	74	B1
Queen Mary Ave. Glasg	117	D1
Queen Mary St. Glasg	118	A2
Queen Rd. Irvine	219	E3
Queen Sq. Glasg	116	C1
Queen St. Alex	27	E2
Queen St. All	10	A4
Queen St. Alva	5	D4
Queen St. Ayr	236	A1
Queen St. Bann	7	E1
Queen St. Falk	42	B3
Queen St. Fall	8	B2
Queen St. Glasg	117	E4
Queen St. Glasg	138	A4
Queen St. Ham	162	A3
Queen St. Helen	16	B2
Queen St. Kilmk	227	F4
Queen St. Kilw	208	A2
Queen St. Klrk	79	E4
Queen St. Mother	163	F4
Queen St. New	165	F3
Queen St. P Glasg	47	E1
Queen St. Pais	113	E2
Queen St. Ren	94	B2
Queen St. Stir	7	D4
Queen St. Stone	198	C1
Queen Victoria Dr. Glasg	95	E2
Queen Victoria Gate. Glasg	95	E3
Queen Victoria St. Aird	122	C4
Queen's Ave. B of A	2	A3
Queen's Ave. Glasg	139	D3
Queen's Court. Helen	25	C4
Queen's Cres. Car	188	A1
Queen's Cres. Chap	123	E2
Queen's Cres. Coat	120	C3
Queen's Cres. Falk	41	F3
Queen's Cres. Glasg	97	D1
Queen's Ct. B of A	1	C4
Queen's Ct. Miln	76	A4
Queen's Dr. Alex	27	E2
Queen's Dr. Ard	205	E2
Queen's Dr. Cumb	61	F3
Queen's Dr. Glasg	117	D1
Queen's Dr. Kilmk	228	A3
Queen's Dr. Lar	23	E1
Queen's Dr. Pres	233	E3
Queen's Dr. Troon	229	E3
Queen's Drive La. Glasg	117	D1
Queen's Gate. Newt M	157	F4
Queen's Gdns. Glasg	96	B2
Queen's La. B of A	2	A4
Queen's Pl. Glasg	96	B2
Queen's Pl. Kilw	208	A2
Queen's Quadrant. Ayr	236	A1
Queen's Rd. John	112	B1
Queen's Rd. Stir	6	C4
Queen's St. Cali	66	C3
Queen's St. Cle	144	A1
Queen's Terr. Ayr	238	C4
Queen's Terrace La. Ayr	238	C4
Queens Cres. Hat	141	F2
Queens Dr. Bishop	72	B2
Queens Dr. Duni	21	F2
Queens Dr. Falk	41	F3
Queens Dr. Ham	183	E3
Queens Point. Rhu	15	D4
Queens Terr. Pres	233	D1
Queens Way. Alex	27	E2
Queens Way. Lennox	78	A4
Queensbank Ave. Muir	100	C4
Queensberry Ave. Bear	75	F4
Queensberry Ave. Newt M	157	F4
Queensborough Gdns. Glasg	96	A2
Queensby Ave. Glasg	120	A3
Queensby Dr. Glasg	120	A3
Queensby Pl. Glasg	120	B3
Queensby Rd. Glasg	120	B3
Queensdale Ave. Lark	199	D4
Queensdale Rd. Lark	199	D4
Queensferry St. Glasg	117	F1
Queenshaugh Dr. Stir	2	B1
Queensland Ct. Glasg	115	E3
Queensland Dr. Glasg	115	E3
Queensland Gdns. Glasg	115	E3
Queensland La E. Glasg	115	E3
Queensland La W. Glasg	115	E3
Queenslie St. Glasg	98	B1
Queensway. E Kil	159	E1
Queensway. Gour	44	B3
Queenzieburn Ind Est. Kils	60	A4
Quendale Dr. Glasg	118	C2
Quentin St. Glasg	116	C1
Quinton Gdns. Glasg	120	A3
Raasay Cres. Aird	123	F3
Raasay Dr. Pais	133	E4
Raasay Gdns. Newt M	156	A3
Raasay Pl. Glasg	97	E4
Raasay St. Glasg	97	E4
Racecourse Rd. Ayr	238	C3
Racecourse View. Ayr	238	C3
Racecourse View. Ham	162	C3
Rachan St. Glasg	100	B1
Radnor St. Clyde	74	A2
Rae St. Sten	23	E2
Raeberry St. Glasg	96	C2
Raeburn Ave. E Kil	160	A2
Raeburn Cres. Ham	161	F2
Raeburn Pl. E Kil	160	A2
Raeburn Wlk. Hat	142	A4
Raes Rd. Car	201	D4
Raeside Ave. Newt M	156	B2
Raeswood Dr. Glasg	134	C4
Raeswood Pl. Glasg	135	D4
Raeswood Rd. Glasg	134	C4
Raewell Cres. Hat	141	F2
Rafford St. Glasg	116	A4
Raggithill Ave. Moss	237	F3
Raglan St. Bonh	27	F2
Raglan St. Glasg	97	D1
Raglan Street La. Bonh	27	F2
Railway Rd. Aird	122	B4
Raise St. Salt	216	C4
Raith Ave. Glasg	137	E2
Raith Ave. Pres	236	C4
Raith Dr. Hat	142	A2
Raith Rd. Fen	213	D2
Raith Terr. Pres	236	C4
Raithburn Ave. Glasg	137	E2
Raithburn Ave. Kilmk	222	C2
Raithburn Rd. Glasg	137	E2
Raithhill. Ayr	239	D1
Raleigh Ct. Falk	41	F3
Ralston Ave. Glasg	114	C2
Ralston Ct. Glasg	114	C2
Ralston Dr. Hurl	228	B4
Ralston Path. Glasg	114	C2
Ralston Pl. Glasg	114	C2
Ralston Rd. Barr	134	B1
Ralston Rd. Bear	75	F3
Ralston St. Aird	122	C4
Ralston St. Pais	114	A2
Ralstonyards Rd. Hurl	228	C4
Ram St. Glasg	118	C3
Ramage Rd. Car	188	A1
Ramillies Ct. Car	188	A1
Ramoth. Lan	214	B2
Rampart Ave. Glasg	95	D4
Ramsay Ave. John	111	F1
Ramsay Ave. Laur	42	C2
Ramsay Cres. Kilbar	111	D1
Ramsay Ct. Newt M	156	C2
Ramsay Hill. E Kil	160	A2
Ramsay Pl. Coat	121	E3
Ramsay Pl. John	111	F1
Ramsay Pl. Stir	2	A1
Ramsay St. Clyde	73	F2
Ramsey Tullis Ave. Tull	4	B1
Ramsey Tullis Dr. Tull	4	B1
Ramsey Wynd. Hat	142	A4
Ramstane Pl. Irvine	220	B3
Ranald Gdns. Glasg	138	B2
Randolph Ave. Glasg	137	D1
Randolph Cres. Bann	7	E1
Randolph Ct. Stir	7	D3
Randolph Dr. Glasg	136	C1
Randolph Gdns. Den	21	E1
Randolph Gdns. Glasg	136	C1
Randolph La. Glasg	95	F2
Randolph Pl. Bann	7	E1
Randolph Rd. Glasg	95	F2
Randolph Rd. Glasg	96	A2
Randolph Rd. Stir	7	D3
Randolph Terr. Stir	7	D2
Randyford Rd. Falk	42	B3
Randyford St. Falk	42	C3
Ranfurly Ct. B of W	110	B4
Ranfurly Pl. B of W	110	C3
Ranfurly Rd. B of W	110	C3
Ranfurly Rd. Glasg	114	C3
Range Ave. Mother	164	C1
Range Pl. Ham	162	C1
Range Rd. Mother	164	C1
Range St. Mother	164	A2
Rangerhouse Rd. E Kil	180	C3
Ranken Dr. Irvine	219	E2
Rankin Cres. Gree	83	F1
Rankin Ct. Kilmk	223	E2
Rankin Dr. Newt M	156	B3
Rankin Rd. Wish	165	E1
Rankin St. Car	187	F1
Rankin St. Green	45	E2
Rankine Pl. John	111	F2
Rankine St. John	111	F2
Rannoch Ave. Bish	78	A1
Rannoch Ave. Coat	101	E1
Rannoch Ave. Ham	162	A1
Rannoch Ave. Newt M	156	B4
Rannoch Cl. Stew	195	F1
Rannoch Ct. All	10	B3
Rannoch Ct. Cumb	82	A3
Rannoch Ct. Ham	161	F2
Rannoch Dr. Bear	76	A2

Rannoch Dr. Cumb	82	A3
Rannoch Dr. Kirk	59	D1
Rannoch Dr. Ren	94	B2
Rannoch Dr. Wish	165	D1
Rannoch Gdns. Bish	78	B1
Rannoch Gn. E Kil	159	F2
Rannoch Pl. Irvine	219	D4
Rannoch Pl. Irvine	219	E3
Rannoch Pl. Pais	114	A2
Rannoch Pl. Shi	66	C4
Rannoch Pl. Shot	146	C3
Rannoch Pl. Sten	23	F2
Rannoch Rd. Aird	102	C1
Rannoch Rd. John	131	F4
Rannoch Rd. Kil	89	E4
Rannoch Rd. Tan	120	C1
Rannoch St. Glasg	137	D3
Rannoch Terr. Lark	185	E1
Rannoch Way. Udd	141	D2
Rannock La. Muir	81	D1
Raploch Ave. Glasg	95	D2
Raploch Cres. Dunt	74	B4
Raploch La. Glasg	95	D2
Raploch Rd. Lark	184	C2
Raploch Rd. Stir	1	C1
Raploch St. Lark	184	C2
Rashieburn. Ersk	73	D1
Rashieglen. Ersk	73	D1
Rashiehill. Ersk	73	D1
Rashiehill Rd. Slam	86	A3
Rashielee Ave. Ersk	73	D1
Rashielee Rd. Ersk	73	D1
Rashiewood. Ersk	73	D1
Rashley Sq. Ard	205	E2
Rathlin Ave. Kilmk	227	F2
Rathlin House. Pres	236	A3
Rathlin St. Glasg	116	A4
Rathlin Terr. Dumb	49	E3
Ratho Dr. Glasg	97	F2
Ratho Pk. Ham	183	D4
Ratho St. Green	46	B2
Rattray. Ersk	73	D2
Rattray St. Glasg	118	C2
Ravel Row. Glasg	118	B3
Ravelston Rd. Bear	75	F1
Ravelston St. Glasg	118	C3
Raven Rd. Green	45	D3
Ravens Ct. Bish	97	F4
Ravenscliffe Dr. Glasg	136	A2
Ravenscourt. Thorn	158	B1
Ravenscraig Ave. Pais	113	E1
Ravenscraig Ct. Hat	142	A3
Ravenscraig Dr. Glasg	135	E3
Ravenscraig Rd. Stew	211	E4
Ravenscraig Terr. Glasg	135	E3
Ravenshall Rd. Glasg	136	B4
Ravenshill Dr. Cle	144	B1
Ravenstone Dr. Glasg	136	B3
Ravenswood Ave. Pais	132	C4
Ravenswood Dr. Glasg	116	B1
Ravenswood Rd. Glasg	120	B3
Rawyards Ave. Aird	103	D1
Raymond Pl. E Kil	159	E1
Rayne Pl. Glasg	75	D2
Ream Ave. Aird	123	F3
Reay Ave. Card	48	A4
Recawr Pk. Ayr	239	D2
Red Bridge Ct. Coat	122	A4
Red Deer Rd. E Kil	180	B4
Red Fox Dr. E Kil	27	F4
Red Gables Sq. Ard	205	D2
Red Rd. Card	25	F2
Red Rd. Glasg	98	A2
Red Road Ct. Glasg	98	A2
Red Row. Alex	27	E1
Redan St. Glasg	117	F3
Redbrae Rd. Klrk	79	F4
Redburn Ave. Glasg	157	D4
Redburn. Bonh	28	A1
Redburn		
Caravan Pk. Irvine	219	D4
Redburn Ct. Cumb	62	C3
Redburn Ind Est. Irvine	219	E4
Redburn Pl. Cumb	62	C3
Redburn Pl. Irvine	219	D3
Redburn Rd. Blac	107	D1
Redburn Rd. Cumb	62	C3
Redburn		
Roundabout. Irvine	219	D4
Redcastle Sq. Glasg	99	E1
Redcliffe Dr. E Kil	180	A4
Redclyffe Gdns. Helen	16	B2
Reddance Terr. Dalry	191	D4
Reddans Pk. Stew	195	E1
Redding Ave. Kilmk	222	C2
Redding Rd. Laur	42	C2
Rederech Cres. Ham	161	F1
Redford St. Glasg	118	B4
Redgate Pl. Glasg	95	D2
Redgauntlet Rd. Helen	25	C4
Redgrave. E Kil	160	B3
Redhaws Rd. Shot	147	D2
Redhill Rd. Cumb	61	E2
Redhills View. Lennox	57	F4
Redhouse La. Car	187	F2
Redhurst Cres. Pais	133	E4
Redhurst La. Pais	133	E4
Redhurst Way. Pais	133	E4
Redlands La. Glasg	96	B2
Redlands Rd. Glasg	96	B2
Redlands Rd. Tull	4	A2
Redlands Terr. Glasg	96	B2
Redlands Terrace La. Glasg	96	B2
Redlawood Pl. Glasg	140	A3
Redlawood Rd. Glasg	140	A3
Redmire Cres. Alla	167	D4
Redmoss Rd. Dunt	73	F4
Redmoss Rd. M of C	58	A3
Redmoss St. Glasg	97	D3
Rednock St. Glasg	97	E2
Redpath Dr. Glasg	115	E3
Redpath Dr. Sten	24	A2
Redstone Ave. Kilw	208	A2
Redwell Pl. All	9	F4
Redwing Gdns. Wish	165	D1
Redwood Ave. E Kil	158	C1
Redwood Cres. Bishop	72	B2
Redwood Cres. E Kil	158	C1
Redwood Cres. Tan	141	E4
Redwood Ct. E Kil	179	F4
Redwood Dr. E Kil	158	C1
Redwood Dr. Glasg	98	A2
Redwood Pl. E Kil	158	C1
Redwood Pl. Klrk	79	D3
Redwood Pl. Tan	141	E4
Redwood Rd. Cumb	62	C2
Redwood Rd. Holy	143	D3
Reedlands Dr. Den	39	E4
Reedloch Dr. Troon	229	F4
Reek St. Beith	171	F4
Reelick Ave. Clyde	94	C4
Reelick Quadrant. Clyde	94	C4
Reema Rd. Hat	142	A3
Reen Pl. Udd	141	D2
Reform St. Beith	150	A1
Regal Ct. Dalry	191	E4
Regency Way. Ham	163	D1
Regent Moray St. Glasg	96	B1
Regent Park Sq. Glasg	116	C1
Regent Pl. Clyde	73	F2
Regent Sq. Klrk	79	E2
Regent St. Clyde	73	F2
Regent St. Green	45	F2
Regent St. Klrk	79	E4
Regent St. Pais	114	A3
Regents Gate. Udd	140	B2
Register Ave. Hat	142	A2
Register Rd. Kils	60	C4
Regwood St. Glasg	136	B4
Reid Ave. Bear	76	A3
Reid Ave. Dairy	191	D3
Reid Ave. Lin	112	A3
Reid Gr. Mother	164	A2
Reid Pl. Glasg	117	F2
Reid St. Aird	103	D1
Reid St. Coat	122	A4
Reid St. Glasg	117	F2
Reid St. Glasg	138	A4
Reid St. Ham	161	F3
Reid St. Sals	125	D1
Reid Terr. Salt	217	D4
Reid's Ave. Steven	206	B1
Reidvale St. Glasg	118	A3
Reilly Rd. Bon	40	A2
Reilly Rd. Hous	91	E4
Reith Dr. E Kil	180	B4
Remus Pl. Holy	142	C3
Renfield La. Glasg	117	D4
Renfield St. Glasg	117	D4
Renfield St. Ren	94	B2
Renfrew Ct. Glasg	117	E4
Renfrew La. Glasg	117	D4
Renfrew Rd. Glasg	95	D1
Renfrew Rd. Pais	113	F4
Renfrew St. Coat	121	E2
Renfrew St. Glasg	117	D4
Rennie Pl. E Kil	159	D2
Rennie Pl. Salt	216	C4
Rennie Rd. Kils	36	A1
Rennie St. Falk	42	A2
Rennie St. Kilmk	228	A4
Renshaw Dr. Glasg	115	D3
Renshaw Rd. Bishop	72	A2
Renshaw Rd. John	112	B1
Renton St. Alex	49	E3
Renton Rd. Dumb	49	E3
Renton Rd. Green	46	B1
Renton St. Glasg	97	E1
Renwick Pl. Lan	215	E3
Renwick Way. Pres	236	B3
Reservoir Rd. Gour	44	C3
Resipol Rd. Stepps	99	F3
Reston Dr. Glasg	115	D3
Reuther Ave. Glasg	138	A4
Revoch Dr. Glasg	95	D4
Reynolds Path. Wish	165	E1
Rhannan Rd. Glasg	137	D3
Rhannan Terr. Glasg	137	D3
Rhindhouse Pl. Glasg	120	B3
Rhindhouse Rd. Glasg	120	B3
Rhindmuir Ave. Glasg	120	B3
Rhindmuir Cres. Glasg	120	B3
Rhindmuir Ct. Glasg	120	B3
Rhindmuir Dr. Glasg	120	B3
Rhindmuir Gdns. Glasg	120	B3
Rhindmuir Gr. Glasg	120	B3
Rhindmuir Path. Glasg	120	B3
Rhindmuir Pl. Glasg	120	B3
Rhindmuir Rd. Glasg	120	B3
Rhindmuir View. Glasg	120	B3
Rhindmuir Wynd. Glasg	120	B3
Rhinds St. Coat	121	E2
Rhindsdale Cres. Glasg	120	B3
Rhodders Gr. Alva	5	D4
Rhu Quad. Wish	186	B3
Rhu Rd Lower. Helen	16	A1
Rhu Rd Lower. Ros	15	F1
Rhu Road Higher. Helen	16	A2
Rhu-Ellen Ct. Rhu	15	E2
Rhyber Ave. Lan	215	D3
Rhymer St. Glasg	97	F1
Rhymie Rd. Glasg	119	E2
Rhymiebank. Stone	198	B1
Rhynie Dr. Glasg	116	A3
Riach Gdns. Mother	142	B1
Ribblesdale. E Kil	159	E2
Riccarton. E Kil	180	A4
Riccarton Rd. Hurl	228	B3
Riccarton St. Glasg	117	E1
Riccartsbar Ave. Pais	113	E2
Richard Pl. Troon	229	E2
Richardland Pl. Kilmk	228	A4
Richardland Rd. Kilmk	227	F4
Richardson Ave. Hurl	228	C3
Richie Ave. Card	48	A4
Richmond Ave. Newt M	157	F4
Richmond Ct. Glasg	138	B4
Richmond Dr. Bish	78	A2
Richmond Dr. Glasg	138	B4
Richmond Dr. Glasg	138	C3
Richmond Dr. Lin	112	A4
Richmond Gdns. Muir	100	A4
Richmond Gr. Glasg	138	B4
Richmond Pl. Glasg	138	B4
Richmond Rd. Glasg	138	B4
Richmond St. Clyde	74	B1
Richmond St. Glasg	117	E4
Richmond Terr. Dund	225	F1
Riddell St. Clyde	74	B2
Riddell St. Coat	122	B4
Riddon Ave. Clyde	94	C4
Riddon Pl. Clyde	94	C4
Riddrie Cres. Glasg	118	C4
Riddrie Knowes. Glasg	118	C4
Riddrievale Ct. Glasg	98	C1
Riddrievale St. Glasg	98	C1
Ridgepark Dr. Lan	214	C3
Ried Ct. Hurl	228	C4
Rig St. Stew	211	E4
Rigby St. Glasg	118	C3
Rigfoot. Irvine	220	A3
Rigghead Ave. Cumb	62	A3
Rigghead. Stew	211	E4
Riggs The. Miln	55	D2
Riggs The. Pres	233	E1
Riggs The. Steven	206	B1
Riggside Rd. Glasg	99	E1
Righead Gate. E Kil	159	F1
Righead Roundabout. E Kil	159	E1
Rigland Way. Ren	94	B2
Riglaw Pl. Glasg	95	D4
Rigmuir Rd. Glasg	115	E3
Rimmon Cres. Shot	146	C3
Rimsdale St. Glasg	118	A3
Ring Rd. All	10	A4
Ringford St. Glasg	97	F2
Ripon Dr. Glasg	96	A3
Risk St. Clyde	73	F2
Risk St. Dumb	49	F2
Ristol Rd. Glasg	95	D3
Ritchie Cres. John	112	B2
Ritchie Ct. Kilmk	223	E1
Ritchie Pk. John	112	A2
Ritchie Pl. Newt M	156	B2
Ritchie St. Glasg	117	D2
Ritchie St. Mother	164	B2
Ritchie St. W Kil	190	B3
Ritchie's Cl. Lan	215	D2
River Pl. Kilb	149	D1
River Rd. Glasg	139	D4
River St. Ayr	235	F1
River St. Falk	24	A1
River Terr. Ayr	235	F1
River View Cres. Card	48	A4
River Wlk. Kilw	207	F3
Riverbank Dr. Hat	142	B2
Riverbank Pl. Kilmk	228	A4
Riverbank St. Glasg	136	B4
Riverbank View. Stir	7	D4
Riverdale Gdns. Ham	162	C1
Riverford Rd. Glasg	118	B1
Riverford Rd. Glasg	136	B4
Riversdale La. Glasg	95	D2
Riverside. Bonh	27	F4
Riverside Dr. Stir	2	B1
Riverside Gdns. Newt M	157	F3
Riverside. Hous	91	E1
Riverside La. Dumb	49	F2
Riverside. Miln	55	D1
Riverside Pk. Glasg	137	D1
Riverside Pl. Ayr	239	D4
Riverside Pl. Glasg	139	F3
Riverside Rd. Eagle	178	C4
Riverside Rd. Glasg	136	C4
Riverside Rd. Green	46	A2
Riverside Rd. Irvine	220	B1
Riverside Rd. Kilb	149	D1
Riverside Rd. Lan	214	B2
Riverside Rd. Lark	199	D4
Riverside Rd. Stew	211	F4
Riverside Terr. Newt M	157	F3
Riverside View. All	10	A2
Riverside Way. Shew	224	C4
Riverview Dr. Glasg	117	D3
Riverview Gdns. Glasg	117	D3
Riverview Pl. Glasg	117	D3
Roaden Ave. Pais	132	C4
Roaden Rd. Pais	132	C4
Roadhead. How	150	C4
Roadside. Cumb	62	A3
Roadside Pl. Gree	103	E4
Robb Terr. Kirk	80	A3
Robert Bruce Ct. Lar	23	D1
Robert Burns Ave. Clyde	74	B2
Robert Burns Ave. Holy	143	F2
Robert Burns Ct. Beith	150	A1
Robert		
Burns Quadrant. Hat	141	F3
Robert Creighton Pl. Kilmk	222	C1
Robert Dick Ct. Tull	4	B1
Robert Kinmond Ave. Tull	4	B1
Robert Knox Ave. Tull	4	B1
Robert Noble Pl. Kilmk	222	B1
Robert Smillie Cres. Lark	185	D1
Robert St. Glasg	116	A4
Robert St. P Glasg	47	F1
Robert St. Shot	146	C2
Robert		
Templeton Dr. Glasg	139	D3
Robert W Service Ct. Kilw	207	F1
Robertland Rigg. Stew	195	F1
Robertland Sq. Stew	211	F4
Roberton Ave. Glasg	116	B1
Roberton St. Chap	123	F2
Roberts St. Clyde	73	F2
Roberts St. Wish	165	D2
Robertson Ave. Bon	40	A3
Robertson Cres. Ayr	236	B1
Robertson Cres. Neil	154	B4
Robertson Cres. Salt	217	D4
Robertson Dr. E Kil	160	A1
Robertson Dr. Hat	142	A2
Robertson La. Glasg	117	D4
Robertson Pl. Kilmk	228	A4
Robertson Pl. Stir	7	D2
Robertson St. Aird	122	C4
Robertson St. Alva	5	D4
Robertson St. Barr	134	A1
Robertson St. Glasg	117	D4
Robertson St. Green	45	F3
Robertson St. Ham	161	F3
Robertson Terr. Glasg	120	B3
Robin Rd. Green	45	D3
Robin Way. Glasg	139	E4
Robroyston Ave. Glasg	98	C2
Robroyston Rd. Bish	78	C1
Robroyston Rd. Glasg	98	B2
Robroyston Rd. Glasg	98	C3
Robroyston Rd. Stepps	79	D2
Robshill Ct. Newt M	156	B2
Robsland Ave. Ayr	238	C3
Robslee Cres. Glasg	136	A2
Robslee Dr. Glasg	136	A2
Robslee Rd. Glasg	136	A2
Robson Gr. Glasg	117	D2
Rochdale Pl. Kirk	79	E4
Roche Way. Dalry	191	E4
Rochsoles Dr. Aird	103	D1
Rochsolloch		
Farm Cotts. Aird	122	C4
Rochsolloch Rd. Aird	122	B3
Rock Dr. Kilbar	111	D1
Rock St. Glasg	97	D2
Rockall Dr. Glasg	137	E2
Rockbank Pl. Dunt	74	B3
Rockbank Pl. Glasg	118	A3
Rockbank St. Glasg	118	A3
Rockburn Cres. Hat	142	A4
Rockburn Dr. Newt M	157	E4
Rockcliffe St. Glasg	117	F2
Rockfield Pl. Glasg	98	B3
Rockfield Rd. Glasg	98	B3
Rockhampton Ave. E Kil	180	A4
Rockmount Ave. Barr	134	A1
Rockmount Ave. Glasg	136	A2
Rockpark Ct. Salt	217	D4
Rockrose Pk. Ayr	239	D2
Rockwell Ave. Pais	133	E4
Rodding The. Lan	215	D3
Roddinghead Rd. Newt M	157	D2
Rodger Ave. Newt M	156	B3
Rodger Dr. Glasg	138	A3
Rodger Pl. Glasg	138	A3
Rodil Ave. Glasg	137	E2
Rodney Pl. Helen	17	D1
Rodney Rd. Gour	44	C3
Rodney St. Glasg	97	D1
Roebank Dr. Barr	134	B1
Roebank Rd. Beith	150	B1
Roebank St. Glasg	118	A4
Roffey Park Rd. Pais	114	B3
Rogart St. Glasg	117	F3
Rogerfield Rd. Glasg	120	B4
Rogers Ct. Stone	198	B1
Rokeby La. Glasg	96	C2
Roland Cres. Newt M	156	C2
Roman Ave. Bear	75	F3
Roman Ave. Glasg	75	D1
Roman Cres. O Kill	72	C4
Roman Ct. Bear	75	F3
Roman Ct. Lan	215	C4
Roman Dr. Bear	75	F3
Roman Dr. Falk	41	E3
Roman Dr. Hat	142	A2
Roman Gdns. Bear	75	F3
Roman Hill Rd. Dunt	74	A4
Roman Pl. Hat	141	F2
Roman Rd. Ayr	239	E3
Roman Rd. Bear	75	F3
Roman Rd. Bon	40	A2
Roman Rd. Dunt	74	A3
Roman Rd. Klrk	79	D4
Roman Rd. Mother	163	F4
Roman Way. Tan	141	E3
Romney Ave. Glasg	137	E3
Rona Ave. P Glasg	69	D4
Rona Pl. Kilmk	223	D3
Rona St. Glasg	98	A1
Rona Terr. Glasg	138	C2
Ronades Rd. Falk	42	A4
Ronald Cres. Lar	23	D1
Ronald Pl. Stir	7	D4
Ronaldsay Dr. Irvine	225	D4
Ronaldsay Dr. Bish	78	B1
Ronaldsay Pl. Cumb	82	B4
Ronaldsay St. Glasg	97	E4
Ronaldshaw Pk. Ayr	238	C3
Ronay St. Glasg	97	E4
Ronay St. Wish	165	F3
Rook Rd. Green	45	D3
Rooksdell Ave. Pais	113	E1
Ropework La. Glasg	117	E3
Rorison Pl. Ash	185	F1
Rosa Pl. Salt	206	A3
Rose Cres. Gour	44	B3
Rose Cres. Ham	161	F2
Rose Dale. Bish	98	A4
Rose Knowe Rd. Glasg	137	E4
Rose Mount Ct. Aird	123	D4
Rose St. All	4	C1
Rose St. Bon	40	A3
Rose St. Cumb	82	A3
Rose St. Glasg	97	D1
Rose St. Green	45	E2
Rose St. Klrk	79	E4
Rose St. Mother	164	A3
Rose Terr. Den	21	E1
Rose Terr. Sten	23	F2
Rosebank Ave. Klrk	79	F4
Rosebank Ave. Udd	140	C1
Rosebank Cres. Ayr	238	C3
Rosebank Dr. Glasg	139	E2
Rosebank Dr. Tan	141	E4
Rosebank Gdns. Irvine	219	F4
Rosebank La. Udd	141	D2
Rosebank. N Sau	5	E1
Rosebank Pl. Falk	41	F3
Rosebank Pl. Ham	162	A4
Rosebank Pl. Kilmk	222	C1
Rosebank Rd. Hat	142	A4
Rosebank Rd. Wish	186	A4
Rosebank St. Aird	123	F4
Rosebank Terr. Coat	121	D2
Rosebank Terr. Kil	89	E4
Rosebay Pk. Ayr	239	D1
Roseberry La. Chap	123	F2
Roseberry Pl. Ham	162	A2
Roseberry Rd. Chap	123	F2
Roseberry St. Glasg	117	F1
Rosebery Pl. Stir	2	A1
Rosedale Ave. Pais	132	B4
Rosedale Dr. Glasg	120	A2
Rosedale. E Kil	159	E2
Rosedale Gdns. Glasg	96	B4
Rosedale Gdns. Helen	16	C1
Rosedale St. Lan	214	C1
Rosedene Terr. Hat	142	A4
Rosefield Gdns. Udd	140	C4
Rosegreen Cres. Hat	142	A2
Rosehall Ave. Coat	122	A2
Rosehall Ind Est. Coat	122	A2
Rosehall Rd. Hat	141	F3
Rosehall Rd. Shot	146	B2
Rosehall Terr. Falk	41	F1
Rosehall Terr. Wish	164	C1
Rosehill Dr. Cumb	82	A3
Rosehill Rd. Lennox	78	B4
Roseholm Ave. Irvine	219	F1
Roselea. Cald	104	C2
Roselea Dr. Miln	55	D2
Roselea Gdns. Glasg	95	F4
Roselea Pl. Udd	140	B1
Roselea Rd. Tan	140	C4
Roselea St. Lark	185	D2
Rosemead Terr. Cali	66	C3
Rosemount. Cumb	61	D3
Rosemount Dr. Troon	229	E4

Rosemount Gdns. Pres

Saline St. Coat

Rosemount Gdns. Pres 236 B3
Rosemount. Kilw 207 E1
Rosemount La. B of W 110 A3
Rosemount La. Lark 185 E1
Rosemount
  Meadows. Udd 140 C1
Rosemount Pl. Gour 44 A3
Rosemount St. Glasg 97 F1
Rosendale Way. Udd 161 F4
Roseneath Dr. Helen 16 A1
Roseneath St. Green 45 E4
Rosenheath Gate. E Kil 159 E1
Rosepark Ave. Tan 141 E3
Rosepark Cotts. Coat 121 F2
Rosevale Cres. Ham 162 A1
Rosevale Cres. Hat 142 B2
Rosevale Rd. Bear 75 F2
Rosevale St. Glasg 96 A1
Rosewood Ave. Hat 142 A4
Rosewood Ave. Pais 113 D1
Rosewood Path. Hat 141 F3
Rosewood St. Glasg 95 F4
Roslea Dr. Glasg 118 A4
Roslin Ct. Kil 89 E4
Roslin St. Green 45 F3
Roslin Tower. Glasg 138 C2
Roslyn Dr. Coat 120 C3
Rosneath Rd. P Glasg 68 B4
Rosneath St. Glasg 116 A4
Ross Ave. Klrk 79 F4
Ross Ave. Ren 94 A1
Ross Cres. Falk 41 E3
Ross Cres. Mother 163 E3
Ross Ct. Stir 7 D2
Ross Dr. Aird 122 C2
Ross Dr. Mother 163 E3
Ross Dr. Tan 121 E1
Ross Gdns. Mother 163 E3
Ross Hall Pl. Ren 94 B2
Ross Pl. Glasg 138 B2
Ross Rd. Salt 205 F1
Ross St. Ayr 236 B1
Ross St. Coat 122 A4
Ross St. Glasg 117 E3
Ross St. Pais 114 A2
Ross Terr. Ham 163 E1
Rossbank Rd. P Glasg 47 D1
Rossendale Ct. Glasg 136 B4
Rossendale Rd. Glasg 136 B4
Rosshall Ave. Pais 114 B2
Rosshill Ave. Glasg 114 C3
Rosshill Rd. Glasg 114 C3
Rossie Cres. Bish 98 B4
Rossland Cres. Bishop 72 A2
Rossland Pl. Bishop 72 B1
Rosslea Dr. Glasg 136 B1
Rosslyn Ave. E Kil 160 A2
Rosslyn Ave. Glasg 138 B4
Rosslyn Ct. Ham 162 A2
Rosslyn Pl. Ayr 236 A2
Rosslyn Rd. Ash 199 F4
Rosslyn Rd. Bear 75 D2
Rosslyn Terr. Glasg 96 B2
Rostan Rd. Glasg 136 B3
Rosyth Rd. Glasg 117 F1
Rosyth St. Glasg 117 F1
Rotherwick Dr. Pais 114 C2
Rotherwood Ave. Glasg 75 E1
Rotherwood Ave. Glasg 75 F1
Rotherwood Ave. Pais 132 C4
Rotherwood La. Glasg 75 E1
Rotherwood Pl. Glasg 95 E4
Rotherwood Way. Pais 132 C4
Rothes Dr. Glasg 96 B4
Rothes Pl. Glasg 76 B1
Rothesay Cres. Coat 122 A2
Rothesay Pl. Coat 122 A2
Rothesay Pl. E Kil 159 F1
Rothesay Pl. Kilmk 222 C1
Rothesay Rd. Gour 44 C2
Rothesay St. E Kil 180 C4
Rottenrow E. Glasg 117 E4
Rottenrow. Glasg 117 E4
Rottenrow. Glasg 117 F4
Roughburn Rd. B of A 2 A3
Roughcraig St. Aird 103 D1
Roughlands Cres. Sten 24 A2
Roughlands Dr. Sten 24 A2
Roughlea Pl. Troon 229 F3
Roughrigg Rd. Chap 124 B3
Rouken Glen Rd. Glasg 136 A1
Roukenburn St. Glasg 135 F2
Round Riding Rd. Dumb 50 A2
Roundel The. Falk 42 B4
Roundel The. Wish 165 E1
Roundelwood. N Sau 5 D1
Roundhill Dr. John 112 C2
Roundknowe Rd. Glasg 120 B1
Rowallan Cres. Pres 236 B4
Rowallan Dr. Bann 11 F4
Rowallan Dr. Kilmk 223 D2
Rowallan Gdns. Glasg 96 A2
Rowallan. Kilw 207 E1
Rowallan La. Glasg 96 A2
Rowallan La. Newt M 157 F4
Rowallan Rd. Glasg 135 F1
Rowallan St. Helen 16 A2

Rowallan Terr. Stepps 99 D2
Rowallen Dr. Bann 11 F4
Rowan Ave. M of C 58 B3
Rowan Ave. Ren 94 B2
Rowan Cres. Ayr 239 E3
Rowan Cres. Falk 41 D2
Rowan Cres. Klrk 79 E3
Rowan Ct. Bann 7 F1
Rowan Ct. Wish 164 B1
Rowan Dr. Bank 38 C1
Rowan Dr. Bear 76 A4
Rowan Dr. Clyde 73 F2
Rowan Dr. Dumb 49 D2
Rowan Gate. Pais 113 F1
Rowan Gdns. Glasg 116 A2
Rowan House. Pres 236 A3
Rowan La. Holy 143 D1
Rowan Pl. Beith 171 E4
Rowan Pl. Coat 121 F2
Rowan Pl. Glasg 139 E3
Rowan Pl. Kilmk 227 E4
Rowan Pl. Troon 229 E4
Rowan Pl. Udd 161 E4
Rowan Rd. Cumb 62 B2
Rowan Rd. Glasg 116 A2
Rowan Rd. Lin 111 F4
Rowan Rise. Ham 162 C1
Rowan St. Beith 171 E4
Rowan St. Green 45 E3
Rowan St. Pais 113 F1
Rowan St. Wish 165 D3
Rowan Terr. Irvine 219 E2
Rowanbank Pl. Aird 122 B4
Rowanbank Rd. Pres 236 C4
Rowand Ave. Glasg 136 B2
Rowandale Ave. Glasg 120 A2
Rowanden Ave. Hat 142 A3
Rowanhill Pl. Kilmk 227 E4
Rowanlea Ave. Pais 132 C4
Rowanlea Dr. Glasg 136 B2
Rowanlea. Plains 103 F2
Rowanpark Dr. Barr 134 A3
Rowans Gdns. Udd 141 D2
Rowans The. Bish 77 F1
Rowans The. N Sau 5 E1
Rowanside Terr. Ard 205 E2
Rowantree Ave. Glasg 138 A3
Rowantree Ave. Holy 143 E4
Rowantree Ave. Tan 141 E4
Rowantree Gdns. Glasg 138 A3
Rowantree Gdns. Irvine 220 A3
Rowantree Pl. John 111 F1
Rowantree Pl. Lark 185 E1
Rowantree Pl. Lennox 57 F4
Rowantree Rd. John 112 A1
Rowantree Terr. Holy 143 D3
Rowantree Terr. Lennox 57 F4
Rowantreehill Rd. Kil 89 F4
Rowena Ave. Glasg 75 E1
Rowmore Quays. Rhu 15 F2
Roxburgh Ave. Green 45 F2
Roxburgh Dr. Bear 75 F4
Roxburgh Dr. Coat 122 B2
Roxburgh Pk. E Kil 159 F1
Roxburgh Pl. Sten 23 F2
Roxburgh Pl. Udd 161 E4
Roxburgh Rd. Hurl 228 C3
Roxburgh Rd. Pais 132 B4
Roxburgh St. Glasg 96 B2
Roxburgh St. Green 45 F2
Roxburgh St. Green 45 F3
Roxburgh Way. Green 45 F2
Roy St. Glasg 97 E2
Roy Young Ave. Bonh 28 A4
Royal Cres. Glasg 116 C4
Royal Dr. Ham 163 D1
Royal Exchange Ct. Glasg 117 E4
Royal Exchange Sq. Glasg 117 E4
Royal Gdns. Stir 7 D4
Royal Inch Terr. Ren 94 B3
Royal St. Gour 44 C4
Royal Terr. Glasg 96 C1
Royal Terr. Wish 165 E4
Royal Terrace La. Glasg 96 C1
Royellen Ave. Ham 161 F1
Royston Rd. Glasg 98 B2
Royston Sq. Glasg 97 F1
Roystonhill. Glasg 97 F1
Rozelle Ave. Glasg 75 D2
Rozelle Terr. Ayr 239 D1
Rubie Cres. Irvine 219 E1
Rubislaw Dr. Bear 75 F2
Ruby St. Glasg 118 A2
Ruchazie Pl. Glasg 118 C4
Ruchazie Rd. Glasg 118 C4
Ruchill Pl. Glasg 96 C3
Ruchill St. Glasg 96 C3
Rue End St. Green 46 A2
Ruel St. Glasg 137 D4
Rufflees Ave. Barr 134 B2
Rugby Ave. Glasg 95 D4
Rugby Cres. Kilmk 227 E4
Rugby Rd. Kilmk 227 E4
Rulley View. Duni 21 E2
Rullion Pl. Glasg 118 C4
Rumford St. Glasg 117 F2
Rumlie The. Slam 86 A3
Runciman Pl. E Kil 160 A2

Rundell Dr. M of C 58 B3
Rupert St. Glasg 96 C1
Rushyhill St. Glasg 98 A2
Ruskie Rd. Stir 2 A2
Ruskin La. Glasg 96 C2
Ruskin Pl. Glasg 96 C2
Ruskin Pl. Kils 60 B4
Ruskin Sq. Bish 78 A1
Ruskin Terr. Glasg 96 C2
Russel St. Falk 42 A3
Russell Colt St. Coat 122 A4
Russell Ct. Kilmk 223 E2
Russell Dr. Alex 27 E4
Russell Dr. Ayr 236 A1
Russell Dr. Bear 75 F3
Russell Dr. Dalry 191 E4
Russell Gdns. Newt M 156 B2
Russell La. Wish 165 D1
Russell Pl. E Kil 180 B4
Russell Pl. Lin 111 F3
Russell Pl. Thorn 158 A3
Russell Rd. Dunt 73 F4
Russell Rd. Lan 215 D3
Russell St. Ayr 236 A1
Russell St. Chap 123 F1
Russell St. Ham 161 F3
Russell St. Hat 142 B3
Russell St. John 112 A2
Russell St. Pais 113 E4
Russell St. Wish 165 D1
Rutherford Ave. Bear 75 D4
Rutherford Ave. Kirk 80 A3
Rutherford Ct. B of A 2 A4
Rutherford Ct. Clyde 74 A1
Rutherford La. E Kil 180 C4
Rutherford Sq. E Kil 180 C4
Rutherglen Rd. Glasg 117 F1
Ruthven Ave. Glasg 136 B1
Ruthven La. Glasg 96 B2
Ruthven La. Glen 101 E3
Ruthven Pl. Bish 98 B4
Ruthven Pl. Troon 229 F2
Ruthven St. Glasg 96 B2
Rutland Cres. Glasg 116 C3
Rutland Pl. Glasg 116 C3
Ryan Rd. Bish 78 A1
Ryan Way. Glasg 138 B2
Ryat Dr. Newt M 156 B3
Ryat Gn. Newt M 156 B3
Ryatt Linn. Ersk 72 C1
Rydal Gr. E Kil 179 F3
Rydal Pl. E Kil 179 F3
Ryde Rd. Wish 165 E2
Ryden Mains Rd. Glenm 102 B2
Rye Cres. Glasg 98 A3
Rye Rd. Glasg 98 B3
Rye Way. Pais 112 C1
Ryebank Rd. Glasg 98 B3
Ryecroft Dr. Glasg 120 A3
Ryedale Pl. Glasg 75 D2
Ryefield Ave. Coat 121 E4
Ryefield Ave. John 111 E1
Ryefield Pl. John 111 E1
Ryefield Rd. Glasg 98 A3
Ryehill Pl. Glasg 98 B3
Ryehill Rd. Glasg 98 B3
Ryemount Rd. Glasg 98 B3
Ryeside Pl. Dalry 169 E1
Ryeside Rd. Glasg 98 A2
Rylands Dr. Glasg 119 E2
Rylands Gdns. Glasg 119 F2
Rylands. Pres 236 B3
Rylees Cres. Glasg 114 C3
Rylees Pl. Glasg 114 C3
Rylees Rd. Glasg 114 C3
Rysland Ave. Newt M 156 C3
Rysland Cres. Newt M 156 C3
Rysland Dr. Fen 213 D2
Ryvra Rd. Glasg 95 E3

Sachelcourt Ave. Bishop 72 A1
Sackville Ave. Glasg 95 F3
Sackville La. Glasg 95 F3
Saddell Rd. Glasg 75 D2
Saffronhall Cres. Ham 162 B2
Saffronhall La. Ham 162 B2
Sainford Cres. Falk 24 A1
St Abb's Dr. Pais 113 D1
St Andrew St. Green 46 A2
St Andrew's Ave. Bish 77 F1
St Andrew's Ave. Pres 236 B3
St Andrew's Brae. Dumb 50 A3
St Andrew's Cres. Dumb 50 A3
St Andrew's Cres. Pais 113 E4
St Andrew's Cross. Glasg 117 D2
St Andrew's Ct. Lar 23 D2
St Andrew's Dr. Air 14 A4
St Andrew's Dr. Glasg 116 B2
St Andrew's Dr. Ham 161 E2
St Andrew's Dr. Inch 113 E4
St Andrew's Dr W. Inch 93 E1
St Andrew's Gdns. Aird 123 D4
St Andrew's Gdns. Dalry 191 D3
St Andrew's Pl. Steven 206 C1
St Andrew's Rd. Ard 205 E2
St Andrew's Rd. Glasg 116 C2
St Andrew's Rd. Ren 94 B1

St Andrew's Sq. Glasg 117 E3
St Andrew's St. Ayr 239 D4
St Andrew's St. Glasg 117 E3
St Andrew's St. Kilmk 227 F4
St Andrew's Wlk. Kilmk 227 F4
St Andrews Ave. Udd 141 D1
St Andrews Cres. Glasg 116 C2
St Andrews Ct. E Kil 180 B3
St Andrews Ct. Holy 143 D3
St Andrews Dr. B of W 110 B3
St Andrews Dr. Cumb 62 A3
St Andrews Dr. Gour 44 A3
St Andrews Gate. Hat 141 F3
St Andrews La. Alex 27 F2
St Andrews La. Gour 44 A3
St Andrews Path. Lark 185 E1
St Andrews Pl. Beith 171 D4
St Andrews Pl. Falk 42 A2
St Andrews Pl. Kils 36 B1
St Andrews St. Holy 143 D3
St Andrews Wynd. Helen 16 C2
St Ann's Dr. Glasg 136 B1
St Anne's Cres. Bann 7 F1
St Barchan's Rd. Kilbar 111 D1
St Blane's Dr. Glasg 137 F3
St Boswell's Cres. Pais 113 D1
St Boswells Rd. Coat 122 B2
St Brennans Ct. Kilb 170 A4
St Bride's Ave. Tan 141 E4
St Bride's Dr. W Kil 190 B3
St Bride's Rd. Glasg 136 B3
St Bride's Rd W Kil 190 B3
St Brides Way. Udd 141 D2
St Bryde St. E Kil 159 F1
St Catherine's Rd. Glasg 136 B1
St Catherines Cres. Shot 146 C3
St Clair Ave. Glasg 136 B2
St Clair Terr. Troon 229 D1
St Columba Dr. Klrk 79 F4
St Columba Pl. Steven 206 C1
St Crispin's Pl. Falk 42 A2
St Cuthbert's Cres. Pres 236 B3
St Cuthbert's Rd. Pres 236 B3
St Cyrus Gdns. Bish 78 B1
St Cyrus Rd. Bish 78 B1
St David's Ct. Lar 23 D1
St David's Pl. Lark 185 D2
St Davids Dr. Aird 123 E2
St Denis Way. Coat 121 F4
St Edmunds Gr. Miln 55 D2
St Enoch Ave. Tan 141 E4
St Enoch Pl. Glasg 117 D4
St Enoch
  Shopping Ctr. Glasg 117 E3
St Enoch Sq. Glasg 117 D3
St Fillans Dr. Hous 91 D1
St Fillans Rd. Stepps 99 E3
St Flanan Rd. Twe 59 E1
St George's Cross. Glasg 97 D1
St George's Ct. Lar 23 D1
St George's Pl. Glasg 97 D1
St George's Rd. Ayr 236 A2
St George's Rd. Glasg 97 D1
St Germains. Bear 75 F2
St Giles Pk. Ham 162 A1
St Giles Sq. Falk 41 D3
St Giles Way. Falk 41 D3
St Giles Way. Ham 162 A1
St Helena Cres. Dunt 74 B3
St Inan Ave. Irvine 219 E2
St Inan's Dr. Beith 150 B1
St Ives Rd. Muir 80 C2
St James Ave. Pais 113 D4
St James Ct. Coat 121 F2
St James' Orch. Stir 2 B1
St James' Pl. Steven 206 C1
St James Rd. Glasg 117 E4
St James' St. Pais 113 F3
St James Terr. Kil 89 E4
St James Way. Coat 121 F2
St Joan's Cres. Kilw 207 F1
St John St. Ayr 235 F1
St John St. Coat 122 A4
St John St. Pres 236 B4
St John St. Stir 7 D4
St John's Ave. Falk 42 B3
St John's Ct. Glasg 116 C2
St John's Gate. Den 21 E1
St John's Gdns. Den 21 E1
St John's Pl. Steven 206 C1
St John's Quadrant. Glasg ... 116 C2
St John's Rd. Glasg 116 C2
St John's Rd. Gour 44 C4
St Kenneth Dr. Glasg 115 F4
St Kentigerns Rd. Lan 215 D3
St Kilda Bank. Irvine 220 A1
St Kilda Ct. Irvine 220 A1
St Kilda Pl. Irvine 220 A1
St Kilda Way. Wish 165 F3
St Laurence Cres. Slam 86 A3
St Lawrence Pk. E Kil 159 E1
St Lawrence Pl. Salt 206 A1
St Lawrence St. Green 46 A2
St Leonard St. Lan 215 D3
St Leonard's Dr. Glasg 136 B2
St Leonard's Rd. Ayr 239 D3

St Leonard's Rd. Lan 215 D2
St Leonards Rd. E Kil 160 B1
St Leonards Wlk. Coat 122 B2
St Luke's Ave. Car 201 F4
St Machan's Way. Lennox 33 E1
St Machars Rd. B of W 110 C4
St Margaret Ave. Dalry 191 D4
St Margaret's Ave. Kils 37 F2
St Margaret's Dr. Wish 164 C1
St Margaret's Pl. Glasg 117 E3
St Margaret's Rd. Ard 205 E2
St Mark Gdns. Glasg 118 C3
St Mark St. Glasg 118 C3
St Marnock Pl. Kilmk 227 F4
St Marnock St. Glasg 118 A3
St Marnock St. Kilmk 227 F4
St Mary's Cres. Barr 134 B1
St Mary's Ct. Wish 165 D1
St Mary's La. Glasg 117 D4
St Mary's Pl. Salt 205 F1
St Mary's Rd. Bish 77 F1
St Mary's Rd. Hat 141 F3
St Mary's Way. Dumb 49 F2
St Mary's Wynd. Stir 7 D4
St Marys Gdns. Barr 134 B1
St Maur's Cres. Kilmk 222 C2
St Maur's Pl. Kilmk 222 C2
St Maurice's
  Roundabout. Cumb 61 D1
St Maurs Gdns. Kilm 222 B4
St Meddan's Cres. Troon 229 E2
St Meddans Ct. Troon 229 E1
St Meddans St. Troon 229 E1
St Michael Dr. Helen 16 C1
St Michael Rd. Wish 164 B1
St Mirren St. Pais 113 F2
St Mirren's Rd. Kils 60 C4
St Modan's Way. Ros 15 D2
St Modans Ct. Falk 42 A2
St Monach's Pl. Steven 206 C1
St Monance St. Glasg 97 F3
St Mungo Ave. Glasg 117 E4
St Mungo Ct. B of W 110 C4
St Mungo Pl. Glasg 117 E4
St Mungo Pl. Ham 161 F2
St Mungo St. Bish 97 F4
St Mungo's. Lan 215 D2
St Mungo's Rd. Cumb 61 F1
St Nicholas Rd. Lan 215 D3
St Nicholas Rd. Pres 236 A4
St Ninian St. Glasg 117 E3
St Ninian's Cres. Pais 113 F1
St Ninian's. Lan 215 D3
St Ninian's Pl. Ham 161 F2
St Ninian's Rd. Ham 161 F2
St Ninian's Rd. Pres 236 A4
St Ninians Pl. Stone 198 C1
St Ninians Rd. Pais 113 F1
St Ninians Rd. Stir 6 C3
St Ninians Rd. Stir 7 D3
St Palladius Terr. Dalry 191 E4
St Patrick's Ct. Lan 214 C2
St Patrick's Rd. Lan 214 C2
St Peter's La. Glasg 117 D4
St Peter's Path. Glasg 97 D1
St Peter's St. Glasg 97 D1
St Phillans Ave. Ayr 239 D1
St Quivox Rd. Pres 236 B4
St Rhonans La. Alex 27 E4
St Rollox Brae. Glasg 97 F1
St Ronan's Dr. Glasg 136 B4
St Ronan's Dr. Ham 183 E4
St Ronans Dr. Glasg 138 B3
St Serf's Pl. Tull 4 A2
St Serf's Rd. Tull 4 A2
St Serf's Wlk. Alva 4 C3
St Stephen's Cres. Glasg 138 C2
St Stephen's Pl. Steven 206 C1
St Stephens Ave. Glasg 138 B2
St Teiling. Lan 215 D3
St Thomas's Pl. Stir 6 C3
St Thomas's Well. Stir 6 B4
St Valery Dr. Stir 7 D2
St Vigeans Ave. Newt M 156 B2
St Vincent Cres. Ayr 239 D1
St Vincent Cres. Glasg 116 C4
St Vincent
  Crescent La. Glasg 116 C4
St Vincent La. Glasg 117 D4
St Vincent Pl. E Kil 180 A4
St Vincent Pl. Glasg 117 E4
St Vincent Pl. Lan 215 D2
St Vincent Pl. Mother 163 F4
St Vincent St. Glasg 116 C4
St Vincent St. Glasg 117 D4
St Vincent Terr. Glasg 116 C4
St Winifred's Way. Wish 165 D2
St Winning's La. Kilw 207 E2
St Winning's Rd. Kilw 207 E2
St Winning's Rd. Kilw 207 E2
St Winning's Well. Kilw 207 E2
St Winnoc Rd. Loch 129 E2
Salamanca St. Glasg 118 B3
Salen Loan. Shot 147 E4
Salen St. Glasg 115 F3
Saline St. Coat 122 B3

Salisbury Ave. Hurl 228 C3
Salisbury Cres. Mother 163 D4
Salisbury. E Kil 160 B2
Salisbury Pl. Clyde 73 E3
Salisbury Pl. Pres 236 B4
Salisbury St. Glasg 117 D2
Salkeld St. Glasg 117 D3
Salmon Dr. Falk 41 F1
Salmon St. Green 45 F3
Salmona St. Glasg 97 D2
Saltaire Ave. Udd 141 D3
Saltcoats Rd. Salt 217 D4
Saltcoats Rd. Steven 217 E4
Salterland Rd. Barr 134 C2
Saltfield La. Ayr 235 F1
Saltire Cres. Lark 185 E1
Saltmarket. Glasg 117 E3
Saltmarket Pl. Glasg 117 E3
Saltoun La. Glasg 96 B2
Saltoun St. Glasg 96 B2
Saltpans Rd. Ayr 235 F2
Salvia St. Glasg 138 C3
Samson Ave. Kilmk 228 A4
Sanda Pl. Kilmk 223 D3
Sanda Pl. Salt 205 F1
Sanda St. Glasg 96 C2
Sandaig Rd. Glasg 119 F3
Sandale Path. Udd 161 E3
Sandalwood Ave. E Kil 159 E2
Sandbank Ave. Glasg 96 B3
Sandbank Cres. Bonh 27 F3
Sandbank Cres. Glasg 96 B3
Sandbank Dr. Glasg 96 B4
Sandbank St. Glasg 96 B4
Sandbank Terr. Glasg 96 B4
Sandbed La. Kilmk 227 F4
Sandbed St. Kilmk 227 F4
Sandend. Ersk 73 D2
Sandend Rd. Glasg 135 D4
Sanderling Pl. John 131 E3
Sanderling Rd. Pais 113 F4
Sanderson Ave. Irvine 219 D1
Sanderson Ave. Tan 141 E3
Sandfield Ave. Miln 55 D2
Sandfield Rd. Pres 236 B4
Sandfield St. Glasg 96 C3
Sandford Gdns. Glasg 120 A3
Sandgate Ave. Glasg 119 E2
Sandgate. Ayr 238 C4
Sandhaven Pl. Glasg 135 D4
Sandhaven Rd. Glasg 135 D4
Sandhill Gdns. Troon 229 F2
Sandholes St. Kilbar 111 E3
Sandholes St. Pais 113 E2
Sandholm Pl. Glasg 94 C3
Sandholm Terr. Glasg 94 C3
Sandiefield Rd. Glasg 117 E2
Sandielands Ave. Inch 93 E4
Sandilands Cres. Mother .. 163 D3
Sandilands St. Glasg 119 E3
Sandilands. Troon 229 E1
Sandmill St. Glasg 98 A1
Sandpiper Dr. E Kil 180 A3
Sandpiper Pl. E Kil 180 A3
Sandpiper Rd. Loch 129 E1
Sandra Rd. Bish 78 B1
Sandray Ave. P Glasg 69 D4
Sandringham Ave. Newt M 157 D3
Sandringham Ct. Newt M .. 157 D3
Sandringham Dr. John 112 A1
Sandringham La. Glasg 96 B2
Sandringham Terr. Green .. 45 F4
Sandwood Cres. Glasg 115 D3
Sandwood Rd. Glasg 115 D3
Sandy Ct. W Kil 190 B2
Sandy Rd. Car 187 F1
Sandy Rd. Glasg 96 A1
Sandy Rd. Irvine 219 D3
Sandy Rd. Ren 94 B1
Sandy Rd. W Kil 190 B2
Sandyfaulds Sq. Glasg 117 E2
Sandyfaulds St. Glasg 117 E2
Sandyford Ave. Holy 143 E4
Sandyford Pl. Glasg 116 C4
Sandyford Pl. Holy 143 E4
Sandyford Place La. Glasg 116 C4
Sandyford Rd. Holy 143 E4
Sandyford Rd. Pres 234 A1
Sandyford Rd. Ren 114 A4
Sandyford St. Glasg 116 B4
Sandyhill Ave. Shot 147 D2
Sandyhill Terr. Coy 239 F3
Sandyhills Cres. Glasg 119 D2
Sandyhills Dr. Glasg 119 D2
Sandyhills Gr. Glasg 119 D1
Sandyhills Pl. Glasg 119 D2
Sandyhills Rd. Glasg 119 E2
Sandyknowes Rd. Cumb .. 83 D4
Sandylands Cres. Mother .. 163 E3
Sandylands Prom. Salt 217 D4
Sandyvale Pl. Shot 147 D2
Sannox Dr. Mother 163 D4
Sannox Dr. Salt 206 A1
Sannox Gdns. Glasg 118 A4
Sannox Pl. Ayr 236 B1
Sannox Pl. Helen 16 C2
Sannox Rd. Kilmk 222 B1
Sannox View. Ayr 236 C1

Sanquhar Ave. Pres 236 B4
Sanquhar Gdns. Udd 140 A1
Sapphire Rd. Hat 142 A2
Saracen Head Rd. Glasg .. 117 F3
Saracen St. Glasg 97 E2
Sardinia La. Glasg 96 B2
Sark Dr. Troon 229 F3
Saskatoon Pl. E Kil 159 D1
Saucel Hill Terr. Pais 113 F2
Saucel St. Pais 113 F2
Sauchie Ct. Bann 7 F1
Sauchiehall La. Glasg 117 D4
Sauchiehall St. Glasg 117 D4
Sauchiesmoor Rd. Car 202 A4
Saugh Ave. Uplaw 173 E4
Saughs Ave. Glasg 98 C3
Saughs Dr. Glasg 98 C3
Saughs Gate. Glasg 98 C3
Saughs Pl. Glasg 98 C3
Saughs Rd. Glasg 98 C3
Saughs Rd. Glasg 99 D3
Saughs Rd. Stepps 99 D3
Saughton St. Glasg 118 C4
Saughtree Ave. Salt 205 F1
Saunders Ct. Barr 134 A2
Saunterne Rd. Pres 233 E1
Savoy Ct. Ayr 238 C4
Savoy Pk. Ayr 238 C4
Savoy St. Glasg 117 F2
Sawers Ave. Den 21 E1
Sawmill Rd. Glasg 95 F1
Sawmillfield St. Glasg 97 D1
Saxon Rd. Glasg 95 E4
Scadlock Rd. Pais 113 D3
Scalpay E Kil 160 B1
Scalpay Pl. Glasg 97 E4
Scalpay Pl. Kilmk 223 D3
Scalpay St. Glasg 97 E4
Scamadale Rd. Gree 84 B2
Scapa St. Glasg 96 C4
Scaraway Dr. Glasg 97 E4
Scaraway Pl. Glasg 97 E4
Scaraway St. Glasg 97 E4
Scaraway Terr. Glasg 97 E4
Scarba Dr. Glasg 136 A3
Scarba Quadrant. Wish 164 C1
Scarffe Ave. Lin 111 F3
Scargie Rd. Kilmk 227 F2
Scarhill Ave. Aird 122 C3
Scarhill La. Aird 123 D3
Scarhill St. Cle 144 A1
Scarhill St. Coat 121 F2
Scarletmuir. Lan 214 C3
Scarlow St. P Glasg 47 E1
Scarrel Dr. Glasg 138 A2
Scarrel Rd. Glasg 138 A2
Scarrel Terr. Glasg 138 A2
Scaur O' Doon Rd. Ayr 238 B2
Schaw Ct. Bear 75 F3
Schaw Ct. N Sau 5 E1
Schaw Dr. Bear 75 F3
Schaw Dr. Dunt 74 C4
Schaw Rd. Pais 114 A3
Schawpark Ave. N Sau 5 E1
Schiltron Way. Bann 7 E2
Scholar's Gate. E Kil 180 B3
School Ave. Glasg 139 D3
School La. Alla 167 D4
School La. Car 187 F1
School La. Dumb 49 E2
School La. Irvine 219 E1
School La. Lennox 57 E4
School La. M of C 58 B3
School La. Men 4 A4
School Quadrant. Aird 102 C1
School Rd. Glasg 114 C3
School Rd. Kilb 149 D1
School Rd. Lennox 57 E1
School Rd. New 166 A2
School Rd. Newt M 156 B2
School Rd. Rhu 15 E3
School Rd. Sals 125 E2
School Rd. Stepps 99 F3
School Rd. Tull 4 A1
School St. Chap 123 E1
School St. Coat 122 A2
School St. Ham 162 B1
School St. Shot 146 C2
School Wlk. Sten 23 E2
School Wynd. Kilb 149 D1
School Wynd. Pais 113 F3
Schoolhouse La. Udd 161 E3
Schoolwell St. Steven 206 B1
Scioncroft Ave. Glasg 138 B4
Sclandersburn Rd. Den 39 E4
Scone Pl. E Kil 159 E2
Scone St. Glasg 97 E2
Sconser St. Glasg 76 C1
Scorton Gdns. Glasg 119 F2
Scotia Cres. Lark 185 D1
Scotia Gdns. Ham 183 E4
Scotia Pl. Falk 42 B3
Scotia St. Mother 163 E4
Scotland St. Glasg 116 C3
Scotland St W. Glasg 116 C3
Scotsblair Ave. Klrk 79 E4
Scotsburn Rd. Glasg 98 B2
Scotstoun Rd. Cowie 12 C4

Scotstoun St. Glasg 95 E2
Scott Ave. John 131 F4
Scott Ave. M of C 58 B3
Scott Ave. O Kill 72 B4
Scott Cres. All 10 A3
Scott Cres. Cumb 82 B4
Scott Cres. Kilmk 227 F4
Scott Cres. Troon 229 F2
Scott Ct. Helen 16 B1
Scott Dr. Bear 75 E3
Scott Dr. Cumb 82 B4
Scott Gr. Ham 162 B1
Scott Hill. E Kil 160 A2
Scott House. Cumb 62 A2
Scott Pl. Hat 142 A4
Scott Pl. Salt 205 F1
Scott Pl. Troon 229 E3
Scott Rd. Glasg 114 C4
Scott Rd. Irvine 219 E1
Scott Rd. Kilmk 227 F4
Scott St. Bonh 27 F2
Scott St. Clyde 73 F2
Scott St. Glasg 97 D1
Scott St. Glasg 120 A2
Scott St. Green 46 A2
Scott St. Ham 162 B1
Scott St. Lark 185 D1
Scott St. Mother 163 F4
Scott St. Stir 2 A1
Scott's Pl. Aird 123 D4
Scott's Rd. Pais 114 B2
Seabank Rd. Ayr 235 F1
Seabank St. Salt 217 D4
Seabegs Cres. Bon 40 A2
Seabegs Pl. Bon 39 F2
Seabegs Rd. Bon 39 F2
Seafar Rd. Cumb 61 F1
Seafield Ave. Bear 75 F4
Seafield Cottage La. Green . 45 E4
Seafield Cres. Ayr 238 C3
Seafield Cres. Cumb 60 C1
Seafield Ct. Ard 205 D2
Seafield Ct. Falk 41 F1
Seafield Dr. Ard 205 D2
Seafield Dr. Ayr 238 B3
Seafield Dr. Glasg 138 B2
Seafield Rd. Ayr 238 C3
Seaford St. Kilmk 227 F4
Seaforth Cres. Ayr 236 A2
Seaforth Cres. Barr 134 A2
Seaforth La. Muir 81 D1
Seaforth Pl. Hat 141 F2
Seaforth Pl. Stir 7 D4
Seaforth Rd. Ayr 236 A2
Seaforth Rd. Clyde 74 A1
Seaforth Rd. Falk 24 B1
Seaforth Rd. Glasg 115 D4
Seaforth Rd N. Glasg 115 D4
Seaforth Rd S. Glasg 115 D4
Seagate. Irvine 219 D2
Seagate. Pres 233 E1
Seagrove St. Glasg 118 B3
Seamill Path. Glasg 134 C3
Seamill St. Glasg 134 C3
Seamore St. Glasg 97 D1
Seath Ave. Aird 122 C4
Seath Ave. Lang 70 B3
Seath Rd. Glasg 118 A1
Seath St. Glasg 117 E1
Seaton Pl. Falk 42 B2
Seaton Terr. Ham 162 A2
Seaton Terr. Irvine 219 E3
Seaview Rd. Salt 216 C4
Seaview Terr. Troon 230 A2
Seaward La. Glasg 116 C3
Seaward St. Glasg 116 C3
Second Ave. Bear 76 A2
Second Ave. Bonh 27 F3
Second Ave. Clyde 74 A2
Second Ave. Dumb 50 B1
Second Ave. Glasg 137 D3
Second Ave. Irvine 224 B4
Second Ave. Ren 94 B1
Second Ave. Stepps 79 E1
Second Ave. Stepps 99 D2
Second Ave. Tan 120 C1
Second Gdns. Glasg 116 A2
Second Rd. Ham 161 F3
Second St. Tan 140 C4
Seedhill. Pais 113 F2
Seedhill Rd. Pais 114 A2
Seggielea La. Glasg 95 E3
Seggielea Rd. Glasg 95 E3
Segton Ave. Kilw 207 E2
Seil Dr. Glasg 137 E2
Selborne Pl. Glasg 95 F3
Selborne Place La. Glasg . 95 F3
Selborne Rd. Glasg 95 F3
Selby Gdns. Glasg 119 E3
Selby Pl. Coat 101 E1
Selby St. Coat 101 E1
Selkirk Ave. Glasg 115 E2
Selkirk Ave. Pais 133 D4
Selkirk Dr. Glasg 138 B4
Selkirk Pl. E Kil 160 B2
Selkirk Pl. Ham 162 C1
Selkirk Rd. P Glasg 68 B4
Selkirk St. Ham 162 B1

Selkirk St. Udd 161 E4
Selkirk St. Wish 165 E3
Selkirk Way. Coat 122 C2
Selkirk Way. Hat 142 A4
Sella Rd. Bish 78 B1
Selvieland Rd. Glasg 114 C3
Semphill Gdns. E Kil 160 A1
Sempie St. Ham 161 F2
Sempill Ave. Ersk 72 C1
Semple Ave. Bishop 72 A2
Semple Ave. Loch 129 E2
Semple Pl. Lin 112 A4
Semple Rd. Pres 236 B3
Semple View. How 130 C3
Senga Cres. Hat 142 A4
Seres Rd. Newt M 157 E4
Sergeant Law Rd. Pais 132 C2
Sergeant Law Rd. Uplaw . 132 D3
Sergeant Law Rd. Uplaw . 153 D2
Seright Cres. Hurl 228 B4
Seright Sq. Hurl 228 B4
Serpentine Wlk. Green 46 B2
Sersley Dr. Kilb 148 C1
Service St. Lennox 33 E1
Seton Dr. Stir 7 E2
Seton La. Ard 205 E1
Seton St. Ard 205 E1
Seton Terr. Glasg 117 F4
Settle Gdns. Glasg 119 F2
Seven Sisters. Klrk 79 F3
Seventh Ave. Tan 140 C4
Seventh Rd. Ham 161 F3
Severn Rd. E Kil 179 F4
Seymour Ave. Kilw 207 F1
Seymour Gn. E Kil 180 A4
Seyton La. E Kil 159 F2
Seyton La. E Kil 136 B1
Shaftesbury St. All 10 A4
Shaftesbury St. Glasg 116 C4
Shafton Pl. Glasg 95 F4
Shafton Rd. Glasg 95 F4
Shaftsbury Ave. Clyde 73 F1
Shaftsbury Cres. Holy 143 E2
Shakespeare Ave. Clyde .. 73 F2
Shakespeare St. Glasg 96 C3
Shalloch Pk. Ayr 238 B1
Shalloch Pl. Irvine 220 A1
Shamrock St. Glasg 97 D1
Shamrock St. Klrk 79 E4
Shand La. Car 187 F2
Shand St. Wish 165 E1
Shandon Brae. Bonh 27 F4
Shandon Cres. Bonh 27 F4
Shandon Cres. Hat 142 A4
Shandon Pl. Green 46 B1
Shandon Terr. Ham 161 F2
Shandwick St. Glasg 120 A4
Shankland La. Green 46 C1
Shankland Rd. Green 46 C1
Shanks Ave. Barr 134 B1
Shanks Ave. Den 39 F4
Shanks Cres. John 111 F1
Shanks Ct. Kilmk 222 C1
Shanks St. Aird 103 D1
Shanks St. Glasg 96 C3
Shannon Dr. Falk 41 F2
Shannon St. Glasg 96 C3
Shanter Pl. Kilmk 228 B4
Shanter Way. Ayr 238 C1
Shapinsay St. Glasg 97 E4
Sharon St. Dalry 191 D4
Sharp Ave. Coat 121 E2
Sharp St. Gour 44 C4
Sharp St. Mother 163 F4
Sharpe Ave. Irvine 220 B1
Sharphill Ind Est. Salt 206 A2
Shavian Terr. Kilw 207 F1
Shavin Brae. Ayr 239 E3
Shaw Ave. Bishop 72 B2
Shaw Ct. Ersk 72 C2
Shaw Pl. Dalry 191 D4
Shaw Pl. Green 45 F3
Shaw Pl. Lin 112 A3
Shaw Pl. Salt 206 A1
Shaw Rd. Miln 76 A4
Shaw Rd. Newt M 156 C2
Shaw Rd. Pres 233 F1
Shaw St. Glasg 116 A4
Shaw St. Lark 199 D4
Shawbank Pl. Kilmk 228 A4
Shawbridge St. Glasg 136 B4
Shawburn Cres. Ham 162 A2
Shawburn St. Ham 162 A2
Shawfarm Ct. Pres 233 E1
Shawfield Ave. Ayr 239 D2
Shawfield Cres. Law 186 C3
Shawfield Dr. Glasg 117 F1
Shawfield Rd. Glasg 117 F2
Shawhead Ave. Coat 122 A2
Shawhead Cotts. Coat 122 A2
Shawhill Rd. Glasg 136 B4
Shawholm Cres. Glasg 136 A4
Shawhill Cres. Newt M 156 C2
Shawlands Cross. Glasg .. 116 C1
Shawlands Sq. Glasg 136 C4
Shawmoss Rd. Glasg 116 B1
Shawpark St. Glasg 96 C3
Shawrigg Rd. Lark 185 E1

Shaws Rd. Lark 199 E4
Shawstonfoot Rd. Cle 145 D1
Shawwood Cres. Newt M .. 156 C2
Shearer Dr. Ham 183 E4
Shearer Quadrant. Bonh .. 28 A4
Sheddens Pl. Glasg 118 C3
Sheena Dr. Bonh 27 F1
Sheepburn Rd. Udd 140 C4
Sheila St. Glasg 98 C2
Sheildhill. E Kil 180 C4
Sheiling Hill. Ham 162 C2
Sheldaig Rd. Glasg 97 D4
Sheldrake Pl. John 131 E3
Shellbridge Way. Ard 205 E1
Shelley Ct. Glasg 96 A3
Shelley Dr. Clyde 74 A2
Shelley Dr. Udd 141 D1
Shelley Rd. Glasg 96 A3
Shells Rd. Kirk 58 C1
Sherbrooke Ave. Glasg .. 116 B2
Sherbrooke Dr. Glasg 116 B2
Sherbrooke Pl. E Kil 159 E1
Sherburn Gdns. Glasg 119 F2
Sherdale Ave. Chap 123 E1
Sheriff Park Ave. Glasg .. 138 A4
Sheriffmuir Rd. B of A 2 B4
Sheriffmuirlands. Stir 2 B4
Sherriff La. Sten 23 F2
Sherry Dr. Ham 162 A3
Sherwood Ave. Pais 114 A3
Sherwood Ave. Udd 141 D3
Sherwood Dr. Glasg 136 A2
Sherwood Pl. Glasg 75 D2
Sherwood Rd. Hurl 228 C3
Sherwood Rd. Pres 236 C4
Shetland Ct. All 10 A3
Shetland Dr. Glasg 137 E2
Shettleston Rd. Glasg 119 D3
Shettleston
  Sheddings. Glasg 118 C3
Shewalton Dr. Shew 225 E3
Shewalton Rd. Shew 224 B3
Shewalton Rd. Shew 225 D3
Shiel Ave. E Kil 159 F2
Shiel Ct. Barr 134 A4
Shiel Gdns. Falk 24 B1
Shiel Gdns. Shot 147 D2
Shiel Hill. Ayr 239 D1
Shiel Pl. Aird 122 B3
Shiel Pl. E Kil 159 F2
Shiel Pl. Irvine 219 E3
Shiel Rd. Bish 78 A1
Shiel Terr. New 165 F3
Shielbridge Gdns. Glasg .. 76 C1
Shieldaig Dr. Glasg 138 A2
Shieldburn Rd. Glasg 115 E4
Shieldhall Gdns. Glasg .. 115 E4
Shieldhall Rd. Glasg 115 E4
Shieldhill Rd. Car 201 F4
Shieldmuir St. Mother 164 B2
Shields Dr. Mother 164 A2
Shields Loan. Lan 214 C3
Shields Rd. Auld 180 A2
Shields Rd. Glasg 116 C2
Shields Rd. Mother 164 A2
Shielhope Ct. Irvine 220 A2
Shieling Pk. Ayr 238 C4
Shilford Ave. Glasg 95 D4
Shilford Rd. Uplaw 132 A3
Shillay St. Bish 97 F4
Shilliaw Pl. Pres 236 B3
Shilliaw Pl. Pres 236 B3
Shillinghill. All 10 A3
Shillingworth Pl. B of W .. 110 B3
Shilton Dr. Glasg 135 E3
Shilton La. Ersk 72 C2
Shinwell Ave. Clyde 74 B1
Shipbank La. Glasg 117 E3
Shiphaugh Pl. Stir 2 B1
Shira Terr. E Kil 160 A1
Shire Way. All 9 F3
Shirley Quadrant. Mother .. 163 E2
Shirley's Cl. Lan 215 D2
Shirra's Brae Rd. Stir 7 E2
Shirrel Ave. Hat 142 A4
Shirrel Rd. Holy 143 D2
Shirva Lea. Twe 59 F2
Shiskine Dr. Glasg 96 B4
Shiskine Dr. Kilmk 222 C2
Shiskine Pl. Glasg 96 B4
Shiskine Pl. Helen 16 C1
Shiskine St. Glasg 96 B4
Sholto Cres. Tan 141 E4
Shore Rd. Air 14 B2
Shore Rd. Steven 217 E4
Shore Rd. Stir 7 D4
Shore Rd. Troon 229 D1
Shore St. Glasg 118 A1
Shore St. Gour 44 C4
Shore St. P Glasg 47 D1
Shore The. All 10 A3
Shortlees Cres. Kilmk 227 F2
Shortlees Rd. Kilmk 227 F1
Shortridge St. Glasg 96 C3
Shortroods Ave. Pais 113 F4
Shortroods Cres. Pais 113 F4
Shortroods Rd. Pais 113 E4
Shotts Rd. Sals 126 C1

Shotts St. Glasg 119 E4
Shottsburn Rd. Sals 126 A2
Shottskirk Rd. Shot 146 B3
Shuna Pl. Glasg 96 C3
Shuna Pl. Newt M 156 A3
Shuna St. Glasg 96 C3
Shuttle St. Glasg 117 E4
Shuttle St. Kilbar 111 D2
Shuttle St. Kils 60 B4
Shuttle St. Pais 113 F2
Sidehead Rd. East 127 F3
Sidehead Rd. Stone 198 C1
Sidland Rd. Glasg 98 B3
Sidlaw Ave. Barr 134 B1
Sidlaw Ave. Ham 161 F1
Sidlaw Ave. P Glasg 68 C3
Sidlaw Dr. Wish 164 C2
Sidlaw Foot. Irvine 220 B1
Sidlaw Pl. Kilmk 228 A2
Sidlaw Rd. Bear 75 D4
Sidney St. Salt 216 C4
Sielga Pl. Glasg 120 A4
Siemens Pl. Glasg 98 A1
Siemens St. Glasg 98 A1
Sievewright St. Glasg 118 B1
Sighthill Loan. Lark 185 D2
Sighthill Terr. Sals 125 D1
Sikeside Pl. Coat 122 B3
Sikeside St. Coat 122 B3
Silk St. Pais 113 F3
Sillars Meadow. Irvine 219 F1
Silvan Pl. Thorn 158 A3
Silver Firs. Holy 143 E2
Silverbirch Gr. Quart 183 F2
Silverburn St. Glasg 118 C4
Silverdale Cres. Holy 143 E2
Silverdale. E Kil 159 E2
Silverdale Gr. Lan 214 C2
Silverdale St. Glasg 118 B2
Silverdale Terr. Plains 103 F2
Silverfir St. Glasg 117 E2
Silvergrove St. Glasg 117 F3
Silvermuir Ave. Lan 215 F4
Silverton Ave. Dumb 50 A2
Silvertonhill Ave. Ham 162 C1
Silvertonhill La. Dumb 50 A2
Silvertonhill Pl. Ham 183 E4
Silverwells Cres. Udd 141 D1
Silverwells. Udd 141 D1
Silverwood Ct. Udd 141 D1
Silverwood Rd. Hurl 228 B4
Sim St. Stew 211 E4
Simons'Cres. Kilmk 227 F2
Simons Cres. Ren 94 B3
Simpson Ct. Clyde 74 A1
Simpson Ct. Udd 140 C3
Simpson Dr. E Kil 180 B4
Simpson Dr. Salt 205 F2
Simpson Pl. E Kil 180 B4
Simpson Pl. Kilw 207 F1
Simpson Quadrant. Bonh .. 28 A4
Simpson St. Cross 222 A1
Simpson St. Falk 41 F3
Simpson St. Glasg 96 C2
Simpson Way. Hat 142 B4
Simshill Rd. Glasg 137 E2
Simson Ave. W Kil 190 C2
Sinclair Ave. Bear 75 F3
Sinclair Cres. Den 21 E1
Sinclair Ct. Bann 7 F1
Sinclair Ct. Kilmk 223 E2
Sinclair Dr. Coat 121 E4
Sinclair Dr. Fall 8 B2
Sinclair Dr. Glasg 136 C4
Sinclair Dr. Helen 16 C1
Sinclair Gdns. Bish 98 A4
Sinclair Gr. Hat 141 F1
Sinclair La. Helen 16 C1
Sinclair Pk. E Kil 180 C4
Sinclair Pl. E Kil 180 C4
Sinclair St. Clyde 94 B4
Sinclair St. Green 46 B2
Sinclair St. Helen 16 B1
Sinclair St. Miln 55 D1
Sinclair St. Steven 206 B1
Singer Rd. Clyde 73 F2
Singer Rd. E Kil 181 D3
Singer St. Clyde 74 A2
Sir Michael Pl. Green 45 F3
Sir Michael Pl. Pais 113 E2
Sir Michael St. Green 45 F3
Sixth Ave. Ren 94 B1
Sixth St. Tan 120 C1
Skaethorn Rd. Glasg 96 A4
Skaethorn St. Glasg 96 A4
Skaithmuir Ave. Sten 24 A2
Skaithmuir Cres. Sten 24 A2
Skara Wlk. New 165 F4
Skaterigg Dr. Glasg 95 F3
Skaterigg Gdns. Glasg 95 F3
Skaterigg La. Glasg 95 F3
Skelbo Pl. Glasg 100 B1
Skellyton Cres. Lark 185 D1
Skelmorlie Pl. Kilw 207 E4
Skelmorlie Pl. Sten 23 F2
Skene Rd. Glasg 116 A3

Skene Rd. Kilmk 223 E2
Skene St. Bon 40 A3
Skerne Gr. E Kil 179 F3
Skernieland Rd. Fen 213 D2
Skerray Quadrant. Glasg 97 E4
Skerray St. Glasg 97 E4
Skerryvore Pl. Glasg 119 D4
Skerryvore Rd. Glasg 119 D4
Skibo La. Glasg 135 F2
Skipness Ave. Car 202 A4
Skipness Dr. Glasg 115 E4
Skirsa Ct. Glasg 97 D4
Skirsa Pl. Glasg 96 C4
Skirsa Sq. Glasg 97 D4
Skirsa St. Glasg 96 C4
Skirving St. Glasg 136 C4
Skovlunde Way. E Kil 180 C3
Skye Ave. Ren 94 B1
Skye Cres. Clyde 73 E3
Skye Cres. Gour 44 B3
Skye Cres. Pais 133 E4
Skye Ct. Irvine 225 D4
Skye Dr. Clyde 73 E3
Skye Dr. Cumb 82 B4
Skye. E Kil 160 B1
Skye Gdns. Bear 75 D3
Skye Pl. Cumb 82 B4
Skye Quadrant. Wish 165 F3
Skye Rd. Cumb 82 B4
Skye Rd. Glasg 138 B2
Skye Rd. P Glasg 69 D3
Skye Rd. Pres 233 F1
Skye St. Green 45 E2
Skyeside Rd. Aird 122 C2
Skythorn Way. Falk 41 F1
Slaemuir Ave. P Glasg 68 C3
Slakiewood Ave. Muir 100 C4
Slatefield Ct. Glasg 118 A3
Slatefield. Lennox 57 E4
Slatefield St. Glasg 118 A3
Sleaford Ave. Mother 163 E2
Slenavon Ave. Glasg 138 B2
Slessor Dr. E Kil 180 C4
Slioch Sq. Holy 143 E2
Sloan Ave. Irvine 219 E1
Sloan Pl. Ayr 236 B1
Sloan St. Ayr 236 B1
Sloy St. Glasg 97 E2
Sloy St. Wish 165 D1
Small Cres. Udd 161 E4
Smeaton Ave. Lennox 78 A4
Smeaton St. Glasg 96 C3
Smiddy Ct. Kilw 207 F2
Smiddy Ct. Lan 215 D2
Smillie Pl. Kilmk 227 E3
Smillie St. Green 46 C1
Smith Ave. Beith 170 B3
Smith Ave. Irvine 219 E2
Smith Ave. Wish 186 A4
Smith Cres. Bonh 27 F4
Smith Cres. Dunt 74 A3
Smith Cres. Kilw 207 F1
Smith Dr. Salt 217 D4
Smith Pl. Den 21 E1
Smith Quadrant. Coat 122 B4
Smith St. Ayr 239 D4
Smith St. Dairy 191 E4
Smith St. Falk 42 A4
Smith St. Glasg 95 F1
Smith St. Green 45 F3
Smith St. Pres 236 B4
Smith Terr. Glasg 118 A1
Smith's La. Pais 113 F3
Smithfield Loan. All 9 F3
Smithhills St. Pais 113 F3
Smithson Cotts. Green 45 D2
Smithstone Cres. Kils 60 C3
Smithstone Ct. Irvine 219 F3
Smithstone Terr. Kilw 207 D4
Smithstone Way. Irvine ... 219 F3
Smithview. Wish 186 B4
Smithy Brae. Kil 89 E4
Smithy Ct. Card 48 A4
Smithy Rd. Card 48 A4
Smithycroft. Ham 163 D1
Smithycroft Rd. Glasg 98 C1
Smithyends. Cumb 62 A3
Smollett St. Alex 27 E3
Smollett Rd. Dumb 50 A2
Smuggler's Way. Rhu 15 E3
Smugglers Brig Rd. Cro 201 D1
Smyllum Pk. Lan 215 E2
Smyllum Rd. Lan 215 E2
Snaefell Ave. Glasg 138 B2
Snaefell Cres. Glasg 138 B3
Sneddon Ave. Wish 165 E1
Sneddon St. Ham 161 F3
Sneddon Terr. Ham 161 F3
Snowdon Pl. Glasg 117 E2
Snowdon Pl. Stir 7 D3
Snowdon Place La. Stir 7 D3
Snowdon St. Glasg 117 E2
Snowdon Terr. W Kil 190 A3
Snowdrop Sq. Ayr 239 D2

Snuff Mill Rd. Glasg 137 D3
Society St. Glasg 118 A3
Solar Ct. Lark 199 D4
Sollas Pl. Clyde 94 C4
Solway Ct. Ham 183 D4
Solway Pl. Kilmk 228 A2
Solway Pl. Muir 80 B1
Solway Pl. Troon 229 F3
Solway Rd. Bish 78 B1
Solway St. Glasg 117 F1
Somerford Rd. Bear 75 F1
Somerled Ave. Ren 94 A1
Somerset Ave. Ham 162 A2
Somerset Pl. Glasg 96 C1
Somerset
  Place Meuse. Glasg 96 C1
Somerset Rd. Ayr 236 A1
Somervell St. Glasg 138 C3
Somerville Ct. Beith 150 A1
Somerville Dr. E Kil 180 C4
Somerville Dr. Glasg 137 D4
Somerville La. E Kil 180 C4
Somerville Pl. Helen 25 C4
Somerville Terr. E Kil 180 C4
Sommerville Dr. Steven ... 217 F3
Sophia Cres. Irvine 219 D3
Sorbie Dr. Stone 198 C1
Sorbie Rd. Ard 205 F2
Sorbie Rd. Salt 205 F1
Sorby St. Glasg 118 B3
Sorley St. Glasg 95 F1
Sorn St. Glasg 118 A2
Sorrel Dr. Ayr 239 E2
Souillac Dr. Den 21 E1
Soulis St. Kilmk 223 D1
Sourlie Roundabout. Irvine 220 A4
Sourlie Terr. Irvine 219 F3
Souter Dr. Kilmk 228 B4
Souter Pl. Ayr 239 D3
Souterhouse Path. Coat ... 121 F3
Souterhouse Rd. Coat 121 F3
South Annandale St. Glasg 117 D1
South Approach Rd. Air 24 C4
South Ave. Car 187 F1
South Ave. Clyde 74 A1
South Ave. Ham 161 F3
South Ave. Pais 133 F4
South Ave. Ren 94 B2
South Bank St. Clyde 94 B4
South Bantaskine Dr. Falk .. 42 A2
South Bantaskine Rd. Falk .. 42 A2
South Barrwood Rd. Kils 60 C4
South Beach La. Troon 229 E1
South Beach Rd. Ayr 235 F1
South Beach Rd. Salt 205 E1
South Beach. Troon 229 E1
South Biggar Rd. Aird 123 D4
South Brae. Lennox 57 E4
South Bridge St. Aird 123 D4
South Broomage Ave. Lar .. 23 E1
South Burn Rd. Aird 122 B2
South Campbell St. Pais ... 113 F2
South Carbrain Rd. Cumb ... 62 A2
South Chester St. Glasg ... 119 D3
South Church Pl. Bonh 27 F2
South Circular Rd. Coat ... 122 A3
South Claremont La. Miln ... 55 D1
South
  Commonhead Ave. Aird 103 D1
South Crescent Rd. Salt ... 205 E1
South Crosshill Rd. Bish 78 A1
South Dean Park Ave. Udd 141 D1
South Dean Rd. Kilmk 223 D1
South Douglas St. Clyde 94 B4
South Dr. Kilb 170 A4
South Dr. Lin 112 A3
South Dr. Troon 229 F2
South Dumbreck Rd. Kils ... 60 A4
South Elgin Pl. Clyde 94 B4
South Elgin St. Clyde 94 B4
South Erskine Pk. Bear 75 E3
South Exchange Ct. Glasg 117 E4
South Frederick St. Glasg . 117 E4
South Gargieston Dr. Kilmk 227 E2
South Glassford St. Miln 55 D1
South Green Dr. Air 14 C2
South Hamilton Pl. Kilmk .. 227 F4
South Hamilton St. Kilmk .. 227 F4
South Hirst Rd. Sals 126 B2
South Isle Rd. Ard 205 E3
South King St. Helen 25 C4
South Loan. Muir 100 B4
South Lodge Ct. Ayr 238 C3
South Mains Cotts. Hous 91 F1
South Mains Rd. Miln 54 C1
South Medrox St. Glen 101 E4
South Melville La. Falk 42 A3
South Moraine La. Glasg 75 E3
South Mound. Hous 91 D1
South Muirhead Rd. Cumb .. 62 A1
South Neuk. Kilb 170 A4
South
  Newmoor Ave. Irvine ... 219 F1
South Nimmo St. Aird 123 D4
South Park Dr. Pais 113 F1
South Park Rd. Ham 162 B1

South Pl. Hat 141 F2
South Pleasance Ave. Falk . 42 A2
South Portland St. Glasg .. 117 D3
South Rd. P Glasg 68 C4
South Rd. Thorn 158 A3
South Rd. W Kil 190 B2
South Robertson Pl. Aird .. 122 C4
South Scott St. Glasg 120 A2
South St. Camb 9 D4
South St. Glasg 95 E2
South St. Green 45 E2
South St. Hous 91 D1
South St. Inch 93 D2
South St. Stir 2 B1
South Vennel. Irvine 220 A2
South Vennel. Lan 215 D2
South Vesalius St. Glasg .. 119 D3
South View. Clyde 73 F2
South View. Hat 141 F2
South View. Lar 23 E1
South View. Udd 140 B1
South William St. John 111 F1
South Woodside Rd. Glasg . 96 C1
South Woodside Rd. Glasg . 96 C2
Southampton Dr. Glasg 96 A3
Southampton La. Glasg 96 A3
Southbank Dr. Klrk 79 E4
Southbank Rd. Klrk 79 E4
Southbank St. Glasg 118 B3
Southbar Ave. Glasg 95 D4
Southbar Rd. Inch 93 D4
Southbrae Ave. B of W 110 A4
Southbrae Dr. Glasg 95 E2
Southbrae La. Glasg 95 F3
Southburn Rd. Strath 31 E2
Southcroft. Alva 4 C3
Southcroft Rd. Glasg 117 F1
Southcroft St. Glasg 116 A4
Southdeen Ave. Glasg 75 D2
Southdeen Rd. Glasg 75 D2
Southend Pl. Hat 141 F2
Southend Rd. Dunt 74 A3
Southern Ave. Glasg 138 A3
Southerness Dr. Cumb 62 A3
Southesk Ave. Bish 77 F1
Southesk Gdns. Bish 77 F2
Southfield Ave. P Glasg 68 C4
Southfield Ave. Pais 133 F4
Southfield Ave. Shot 147 D2
Southfield. Coat 122 B3
Southfield Cres. Coat 122 B3
Southfield Cres. Glasg 135 E4
Southfield Cres. Shot 147 D2
Southfield Cres. Stir 7 D3
Southfield Dr. Slam 86 A3
Southfield Pk. Ayr 239 D3
Southfield Rd. Cumb 61 E1
Southfield Rd. Shot 147 D2
Southgate. E Kil 159 F1
Southgate. Miln 55 D1
Southhill Ave. Glasg 138 B3
Southhook Rd. Cross 221 E2
Southhook Rd. Kilmk 222 B1
Southinch Ave. Clyde 94 C3
Southinch La. Clyde 94 C3
Southlea Ave. Glasg 136 A2
Southloch Gdns. Glasg 97 F2
Southloch St. Glasg 97 F2
Southmuir Pl. Glasg 96 B3
Southook Row. Irvine 220 A3
Southpark Ave. Glasg 96 C1
Southpark Ave. Pres 236 A4
Southpark La. Glasg 96 C1
Southpark Rd. Ayr 238 C3
Southpark Terr. Glasg 96 C1
Southview Ave. Newt M ... 157 F3
Southview. Bear 75 E3
Southview Cres. B of W 90 B1
Southview Ct. Bish 97 F4
Southview Dr. Strath 31 D2
Southview Pl. Muir 100 C3
Southview Rd. Strath 31 E2
Southview Terr. Bish 97 F4
Southward Way. Troon 229 F4
Southwold Rd. Glasg 114 C3
Southwood Dr. Glasg 137 E3
Southwood Rd. Troon 233 D3
Soutra Pl. Glasg 119 D4
Spairdrum Rd. Glenm 82 C2
Spairdrum Rd. Glenm 83 D2
Spalehall Dr. Holy 143 F2
Spallander Rd. Troon 229 F4
Sparrow Gdns. Kilmk 228 B4
Spateston Rd. John 131 E4
Spean Ave. E Kil 160 A1
Spean St. Glasg 137 D3
Speedwell Sq. Ayr 239 D2
Speirs Pl. Lin 112 B4
Speirs Rd. Bear 76 A1
Speirsfield Gdns. Pais 113 F2
Speirshall Cl. Glasg 94 C3
Speirshall Terr. Glasg 94 C3
Spence St. Bon 40 A3
Spence St. Glasg 96 B4
Spencer Dr. Pais 132 C4
Spencer St. Clyde 74 A2
Spencer St. Glasg 95 F4
Spencerfield Gdns. Ham ... 162 C2

Spey Ave. Kilmk 228 A3
Spey Ave. Pais 112 C1
Spey Ct. Aird 123 E3
Spey Ct. New 165 F3
Spey Ct. Stir 7 E3
Spey Dr. Ren 94 C1
Spey Gdns. Ham 183 D4
Spey Gr. E Kil 179 F4
Spey Pl. John 131 E4
Spey Rd. Bear 75 E1
Spey Rd. Pres 233 E1
Spey Rd. Troon 229 F2
Spey St. Glasg 118 C4
Spey Terr. E Kil 179 F4
Spey Wlk. Holy 143 D3
Spey Wynd. Lark 199 D4
Speyburn Pl. Irvine 219 F3
Speyburn Pl. Irvine 219 F3
Spiers Gr. Glasg 135 F2
Spiers Pl. Beith 171 D4
Spiers Rd. Hous 91 D1
Spiers Rd. John 112 A2
Spiers Rd. Loch 129 D2
Spiers Wharf. Glasg 97 D1
Spiersbridge Ave. Glasg .. 135 F1
Spiersbridge Ave. Glasg .. 135 F2
Spiersbridge La. Glasg 135 F2
Spiersbridge Rd. Glasg ... 135 E4
Spiersbridge Terr. Glasg .. 135 F2
Spiersland Way. Beith 171 E4
Spindlehowe Rd. Tan 141 D4
Spindlehowe Rd. Udd 140 C3
Spindleside Rd. Cle 144 B1
Spinkhill. Laur 42 C1
Spinners Gdns. Pais 113 D2
Spinners La. Dunt 74 A4
Spinningdale. Stone 198 B1
Spital Rd. Stone 198 C1
Spittal Hill. B of A 2 B2
Spittal Rd. Glasg 137 F3
Spittal St. Stir 7 D4
Spoutmouth. Glasg 117 E4
Sprig Way. East 127 F3
Spring La. Cald 104 C2
Springbank Rd. Ayr 236 A2
Springbank Rd. Pais 113 E4
Springbank Rd. Shot 146 B3
Springbank Rd. Stir 7 E3
Springbank St. Glasg 97 D2
Springbank Terr. Pais 113 E4
Springboig Rd. Glasg 119 E3
Springboig Rd. Glasg 119 E3
Springburn Pl. E Kil 159 D2
Springburn Rd. Glasg 97 F2
Springburn Way. Glasg 97 F2
Springcroft Ave. Glasg 120 A3
Springcroft Gdns. Glasg .. 120 B3
Springcroft Rd. Glasg 120 A4
Springfield Ave. Bish 98 A4
Springfield Ave. Pais 114 A2
Springfield Ave. Pres 236 B4
Springfield Ave. Udd 140 C3
Springfield Cres. Bish 98 A4
Springfield Cres. Car 201 F4
Springfield Cres. Udd 140 C3
Springfield Cres. Udd 161 E4
Springfield Ct. Glasg 117 E4
Springfield Dr. Barr 134 C1
Springfield Dr. Falk 41 F2
Springfield Gdns. Lan 214 C3
Springfield Park Rd. Glasg 138 C3
Springfield Pk. John 112 A1
Springfield Quay. Glasg ... 116 C3
Springfield Rd. Aird 123 F4
Springfield Rd. All 10 B4
Springfield Rd. Barr 155 E4
Springfield Rd. Bish 78 A1
Springfield Rd. Cross 221 F1
Springfield Rd. Cumb 62 A2
Springfield Rd. Den 21 F1
Springfield Rd. Glasg 118 A2
Springfield Rd. Sals 125 D1
Springfield Rd. Stir 7 E3
Springfield Sq. Bish 98 A4
Springfield Woods. John .. 112 A1
Springhead Rd. Alla 167 D4
Springhill
  and Leadloch Rd. Shot 147 F1
Springhill Ave. Aird 123 D4
Springhill Ave. Coat 121 E2
Springhill Ave. Cross 226 C4
Springhill Gdns. Glasg 116 C1
Springhill Gdns. Kilmk 227 F4
Springhill Pl. Coat 121 E2
Springhill Pl. Kilmk 227 F4
Springhill Rd. Barr 134 A1
Springhill Rd. Glasg 120 A3
Springhill Rd. Newt M 155 D3
Springhill Rd. Newt M 157 F4
Springhill Rd. P Glasg 47 E1
Springhill Rd. Shot 147 D2
Springhill Terr. Spring 220 C1
Springholm Dr. Aird 102 C1
Springkell Ave. Glasg 116 B1
Springkell Dr. Glasg 116 A1
Springkell Gate. Glasg 116 B1
Springkell Gdns. Glasg 116 B1
Springkell St. Green 46 A2

Springkerse Rd. Stir

Springkerse Rd. Stir 7 E3
Springside Pl. Glasg 75 D2
Springside Terr. Spring 220 C1
Springside. W Kil 190 C4
Springvale Pk. Ayr 238 C3
Springvale Pl. Salt 216 C4
Springvale Rd. Ayr 238 C3
Springvale St. Salt 216 C4
Springvale Terr. Glasg 97 F2
Springwell Cres. Ham 161 F4
Springwell Pl. Stew 195 F1
Springwells Ave. Aird 123 E4
Springwells Cres. Aird 123 E4
Springwood Ave. Stir 6 C3
Springwood Dr. Kil 69 E1
Sprotwell Terr. N Sau 5 E1
Spruce Ave. Ham 162 C1
Spruce Ave. John 112 A1
Spruce Ave. Udd 161 E4
Spruce Ct. Coat 121 F2
Spruce Ct. Ham 162 C1
Spruce Dr. Klrk 79 D3
Spruce House. Pres 236 A3
Spruce Pk. Ayr 239 E3
Spruce Rd. Cumb 62 B2
Spruce Rd. Tan 121 E1
Spruce St. Glasg 97 E3
Spruce Way. Holy 143 D2
Sprucebank Ave. Lang 70 B4
Spy's La. Rhu 15 F2
Spynie Pl. Bish 78 B1
Spynie Way. New 165 F3
Square The. Fall 8 B2
Squire St. Glasg 95 F1
Stable Pl. Miln 54 C2
Stable Rd. Miln 54 C2
Stable Rd. Shot 147 D3
Stable Wynd. Troon 230 A2
Stables The. Strath 55 D3
Staffa Ave. P Glasg 69 D4
Staffa Ave. Ren 94 B1
Staffa Ct. Irvine 225 D4
Staffa Dr. Aird 123 F4
Staffa Dr. Kirk 80 A4
Staffa Dr. Pais 133 F4
Staffa. E Kil 181 E4
Staffa Pl. Falk 42 A1
Staffa Rd. Glasg 138 C2
Staffa St. Glasg 118 A4
Staffa St. Gour 44 C3
Staffin Dr. Glasg 76 B1
Staffin Rd. Troon 229 F3
Staffin St. Glasg 76 C1
Stafflar Dr. Kilmk 227 F2
Stafford Cres. Gour 44 C2
Stafford Rd. Gour 44 C2
Stafford St. Glasg 97 E1
Stafford St. Hat 141 F2
Stafford St. Helen 16 B1
Stafford St. Kilmk 222 C1
Stafford St W. Helen 16 B2
Staffordway S. Gour 44 C2
Stag St. Glasg 116 A4
Staig Wynd. Mother 164 A2
Staikhill. Lan 214 C3
Stain

Stairlie Cres. W Kil 190 B3
Stalker St. Mother 164 B2
Stamford St. Glasg 118 A3
Stamperland Ave. Glasg 157 F4
Stamperland Cres. Glasg .. 157 F4
Stamperland Dr. Glasg 157 F4
Stamperland Gdns. Glasg . 157 F4
Stamperland Hill. Glasg 157 F4
Stanalane St. Glasg 135 F2
Standalane. Kilm 222 B4
Standalane. Stew 211 E4
Standburn Rd. Glasg 98 B3
Stane Rd. P Glasg 68 C4
Stane Rd. Shot 147 D1
Staneacre Pk. Ham 162 C2
Stanecastle Dr. Irvine 219 F3
Stanecastle Gate. Irvine ... 219 F3
Stanecastle
  Interchange. Irvine 219 F2
Stanecastle Rd. Irvine 219 F2
Stanecraigs Pl. New 165 F3
Stanefield Dr. Holy 143 F2
Stanely Cres. Pais 133 D4
Stanely Ct. Pais 133 D4
Stanely Dr. Pais 113 E1
Stanely Rd. Pais 113 E1
Stanford St. Clyde 74 B1
Stanhope Dr. Glasg 138 B3
Stanhope Pl. Wish 186 A4
Stanistone Rd. Car 188 A1
Stanley Ave. Ard 205 E2
Stanley Ave. Pais 113 D1
Stanley Dr. Ard 205 E2
Stanley Dr. B of A 2 A4
Stanley Dr. Bish 78 A1
Stanley Dr. Hat 142 A3
Stanley Dr. Kilbar 111 E3
Stanley La. Kilbar 111 E3
Stanley Pk. Aird 123 D4
Stanley Pl. Salt 205 F1
Stanley Pl. Udd 140 B1
Stanley Rd. Ard 205 E2

Stanley Rd. Salt 216 C4
Stanley St. Glasg 116 C3
Stanley St. Ham 161 F2
Stanley Street La. Glasg ... 116 C3
Stanmore Ave. Lan 215 D3
Stanmore Cres. Lan 215 E3
Stanmore Rd. Glasg 137 D4
Stanmore Rd. Lan 215 E3
Stanners La. Green 46 A2
Stanrigg St. Plains 104 A1
Stanton Ave. All 9 F3
Stark Ave. Dunt 73 F3
Stark Ave. Falk 41 E3
Starling Way. Tan 141 F4
Starryshaw Rd. Shot 146 C3
Startpoint St. Glasg 119 D4
Station Ave. Green 46 A2
Station Ave. How 130 C3
Station Brae. Irvine 220 B1
Station Brae. Neil 154 B4
Station Bridge. Ayr 239 D4
Station Cres. Ren 94 C2
Station Dr. Hurl 228 B3
Station Dr. Pres 233 E1
Station Dr. Spring 221 D2
Station Pl. Law 187 D3
Station Rd. Aird 123 F4
Station Rd. Ash 200 B2
Station Rd. B of A 1 C4
Station Rd. Bann 7 F1
Station Rd. Bear 75 E2
Station Rd. Bish 77 D4
Station Rd. Bishop 72 A1
Station Rd. Blac 107 E1
Station Rd. Cald 104 C2
Station Rd. Camb 4 A1
Station Rd. Car 187 F1
Station Rd. Cle 144 A1
Station Rd. Cowie 12 B3
Station Rd. Dumb 49 F2
Station Rd. Dunlop 195 D4
Station Rd. Glasg 96 B4
Station Rd. Glasg 120 B2
Station Rd. Glasg 136 B2
Station Rd. Gour 44 C4
Station Rd. Helen 25 C4
Station Rd. Holy 143 D2
Station Rd. How 130 C3
Station Rd. Kilbar 111 D1
Station Rd. Kils 36 B1
Station Rd. Lang 70 B3
Station Rd. Lark 185 D2
Station Rd. Law 187 D3
Station Rd. Lennox 57 E4
Station Rd. Miln 55 D1
Station Rd. Muir 100 B3
Station Rd. Neil 154 B4
Station Rd. O Kill 73 D3
Station Rd. Pais 113 D2
Station Rd. Plains 104 A1
Station Rd. Pres 233 E1
Station Rd. Pres 233 E2
Station Rd. Ren 94 C2
Station Rd. Rhu 15 F3
Station Rd. Shot 146 C2
Station Rd. Slam 86 A3
Station Rd. Spring 220 C1
Station Rd. Stepps 99 D3
Station Rd. Steven 217 E4
Station Rd. Stir 7 D4
Station Rd. Strath 31 D2
Station Rd. Thorn 158 A3
Station Rd. Tull 4 A1
Station Rd. Udd 140 C1
Station Rd. Udd 140 C3
Station Rd. Udd 141 D1
Station Rd. Wish 165 D1
Station Rise. Loch 129 E1
Station Row. Shew 225 F3
Station Row. Slam 86 A3
Station St. Alex 27 E1
Station Way. Udd 140 C3
Station Wynd. Kilbar 111 D1
Steading The. Wish 165 D3
Steadman Pl. Irvine 225 D4
Steel St. Glasg 117 E3
Steel St. Wish 165 D1
Steele Cres. Bonh 28 A4
Steele Wlk. Bonh 28 A4
Steeple Sq. Kilbar 111 D2
Steeple St. Kilbar 111 D2
Steeples View. Troon 229 F4
Stein Sq. Bann 7 F1
Stenhouse Ave. Muir 100 B4
Stenhouse Rd. Sten 23 F1
Stenton Cres. Wish 164 B1
Stenton Pl. Wish 164 B1
Stenton St. Glasg 118 C4
Stepends Rd. Chap 124 B4
Stepends Rd. Plains 104 B1
Stepford Pl. Glasg 119 F4
Stepford Rd. Glasg 120 A4
Stephen Cres. Glasg 119 F3
Stephenson Pl. E Kil 180 B4

Stephenson Sq. E Kil 180 B4
Stephenson St. Glasg 114 C4
Stephenson Terr. E Kil 180 B4
Stepps Rd. Glasg 119 E4
Stepps Rd. Stepps 79 F1
Steps Rd. Irvine 219 E3
Steps St. Sten 23 F2
Steuart Rd. B of A 1 C4
Steven St. Alex 27 F3
Stevens La. Holy 143 D2
Stevens Pl. Gour 44 C3
Stevenson Ct. B of A 2 A3
Stevenson Pl. Hat 142 A4
Stevenson St. Car 187 F1
Stevenson St. Clyde 73 F2
Stevenson St. Glasg 117 F3
Stevenson St. Kilmk 222 B1
Stevenson St. Pais 113 F2
Stevenson Ct. Holy 143 D2
Stevenston Ind Est. Steven 217 F4
Stevenston Rd. Kilw 207 E2
Stevenston St. Holy 143 D2
Stewart Ave. Newt M 156 C3
Stewart Ave. Ren 94 A1
Stewart Ave. Udd 161 E4
Stewart Cres. New 166 A3
Stewart Ct. Barr 134 B2
Stewart Ct. Glasg 138 B4
Stewart Dr. Coat 121 D3
Stewart Dr. Dunt 74 A3
Stewart Dr. Irvine 219 E2
Stewart Dr. Newt M 157 F4
Stewart Gr. East 127 F3
Stewart Quadrant. Holy 143 D3
Stewart Rd. Ayr 236 B2
Stewart Rd. Falk 42 B3
Stewart Rd. Pais 133 F4
Stewart Sq. Stir 2 A1
Stewart St. Barr 134 B2
Stewart St. Bon 39 F3
Stewart St. Cam 6 B3
Stewart St. Car 187 F1
Stewart St. Clyde 73 F2
Stewart St. Coat 122 A4
Stewart St. Glasg 97 D1
Stewart St. Ham 162 A3
Stewart St. Mil 142 B3
Stewart St. Miln 55 D1
Stewartfield Cres. E Kil 159 E2
Stewartfield Dr. E Kil 159 E2
Stewartfield Rd. E Kil 159 E2
Stewartfield Way. E Kil 159 E2
Stewartgill Pl. Ash 185 F1
Stewarton Dr. Glasg 138 C3
Stewarton Rd. Dunlop 195 D4
Stewarton Rd. Fen 213 D2
Stewarton Rd. Glasg 135 F1
Stewarton St. Wish 165 E1
Stewarton Terr. Wish 165 E1
Stewartville St. Glasg 96 A1
Stinchar St. Pres 233 E1
Stirling Ave. Bear 75 F1
Stirling Ave. E Kil 160 A2
Stirling Ave. Kilmk 222 B1
Stirling Cres. Kilmk 222 B1
Stirling Dr. Bear 75 E3
Stirling Dr. Bish 77 F2
Stirling Dr. Glasg 138 A3
Stirling Dr. Gour 43 F3
Stirling Dr. Ham 161 F2
Stirling Dr. John 111 E1
Stirling Dr. Lin 112 A3
Stirling Gdns. Bish 77 F2
Stirling Pl. Lennox 57 F4
Stirling Rd. Aird 103 D1
Stirling Rd. All 9 F4
Stirling Rd. Alva 4 C4
Stirling Rd. Bonh 20 A1
Stirling Rd. Bonh 27 F1
Stirling Rd. Car 187 F2
Stirling Rd. Chap 123 E2
Stirling Rd. Cumb 83 D2
Stirling Rd. Dumb 50 B2
Stirling Rd. Falk 41 E4
Stirling Rd. Fall 8 B2
Stirling Rd. Glasg 117 E4
Stirling Rd. Glenm 83 D3
Stirling Rd. Glenm 103 D3
Stirling Rd. Kils 36 C1
Stirling Rd. Lar 22 C3
Stirling Rd. Lar 23 D1
Stirling Rd. Tor 22 C3
Stirling Rd. Tull 4 A2
Stirling St. Aird 123 D4
Stirling St. Alex 27 E1
Stirling St. Alva 5 D4
Stirling St. Coat 121 E2
Stirling St. Cumb 62 A2
Stirling St. Den 21 F1
Stirling St. Duni 21 E2
Stirling St. Mother 164 B1
Stirling Way. Glasg 120 A2
Stirling Way. Ren 94 B1
Stirlingfauld Pl. Glasg 117 D3
Stirrat St. Glasg 96 B3
Stirrat St. Pais 113 E4
Stobbs Cres. Kilw 207 F1
Stobbs Terr. Kilw 207 F1

Stobcross Rd. Glasg 116 B4
Stobcross St. Coat 122 A3
Stobcross St. Glasg 116 C4
Stobhill Cotts. Glasg 98 A4
Stobhill Rd. Bish 97 F4
Stobo Ct. E Kil 160 B2
Stobo. E Kil 160 B2
Stobo St. Wish 165 E3
Stobs Dr. Barr 134 A2
Stobs Pl. Glasg 100 B1
Stock Ave. Pais 113 F2
Stock St. Pais 113 F1
Stockbridge Cres. Kilb 149 D2
Stockholm Cres. Pais 113 F2
Stockiemuir Ave. Bear 75 F4
Stockiemuir Ct. Bear 75 F4
Stockiemuir Rd. Bear 75 E4
Stockiemuir Rd. Miln 54 B1
Stocks Rd. Cle 144 C1
Stockwell Pl. Glasg 117 E3
Stockwell St. Glasg 117 E3
Stoddard Sq. John 112 B2
Stonebyres Ct. Ham 162 A2
Stonecraig Rd. Wish 165 E1
Stonecrop Pl. Ayr 239 E2
Stonedyke Cres. Car 188 A2
Stonedyke Gr. Car 188 A2
Stonefield Ave. Glasg 96 B3
Stonefield Ave. Pais 113 F1
Stonefield Cres. Newt M .. 157 E4
Stonefield Cres. Pais 113 F1
Stonefield Cres. Udd 161 E3
Stonefield Dr. Pais 113 F1
Stonefield Gdns. Car 187 F2
Stonefield Gdns. Pais 113 F1
Stonefield Green. Pais 113 F1
Stonefield Park Gdns. Udd 161 F4
Stonefield Pk. Ayr 238 B1
Stonefield Pk. Pais 133 F4
Stonefield Pl. Udd 161 E3
Stonefield Rd. Udd 161 E4
Stonefield St. Aird 103 A1
Stonehall Ave. Ham 162 A1
Stonehaven Rd. Gour 44 C2
Stonelaw Dr. Glasg 138 A3
Stonelaw Rd. Glasg 138 A4
Stonelaw Towers. Glasg ... 138 B3
Stoneleigh Pl. Green 45 E4
Stoneleigh Rd. Green 45 E4
Stoneside Dr. Glasg 136 A3
Stoneside Sq. Glasg 136 A3
Stoney Brae. Pais 113 F3
Stoneyetts Cotts. Muir 80 C2
Stoneyetts Rd. Muir 80 C1
Stoneyholm Rd. Kilb 149 D1
Stoneyhurst St. Glasg 97 D2
Stoneyhurst St. Glasg 97 E2
Stonelee Rd. Cumb 62 A1
Stoopshill Cres. Beith 191 F4
Storie St. Pais 113 F2
Stormyland Way. Barr 134 B1
Stornoway Cres. Wish 165 F3
Stornoway St. Glasg 97 E4
Stow Brae. Pais 113 F2
Stow St. Pais 113 F2
Strachan St. Falk 41 F2
Strachan St. Hat 142 A2
Strachur St. Glasg 97 D4
Straehouse Wynd. Car 188 A1
Strain Cres. Aird 123 D3
Straiton Dr. Ham 161 E1
Straiton St. Glasg 118 C4
Strand. Beith 171 D4
Strand St. Kilmk 222 C1
Strandhead. Stew 211 E4
Strang Pl. Pres 236 B3
Strang's Pl. Cali 66 C3
Stranka Ave. Pais 113 E2
Stranraer Dr. Glasg 75 E1
Stratford. E Kil 160 B3
Stratford St. Glasg 96 C3
Strath Carron. Law 187 D3
Strath Dearn. Law 187 D3
Strath Elgin. Law 187 D3
Strath Halladale. Law 187 D3
Strath Nairn. Law 187 D3
Strath Naver. Law 187 D3
Strathallan Ct. B of A 2 A3
Strathallan Gdns. Klrk 79 E4
Strathallan Rd. B of A 2 A3
Strathallon Pl. Glasg 138 B2
Strathaven Rd. E Kil 181 D4
Strathaven Rd. Eagle 178 C2
Strathaven Rd. Ham 183 E3
Strathaven Rd. Stone 198 C1
Strathavon Cres. Aird 103 D1
Strathayr Pl. Ayr 239 D4
Strathblane Cres. Aird 103 D2
Strathblane Rd. Lennox 32 C2
Strathblane Rd. Miln 55 E2
Strathbran St. Glasg 118 B2
Strathcairn Cres. Aird 103 D2

Strathcarron Pl. Glasg 96 B3
Strathcarron Rd. Pais 114 A1
Strathclyde Ave. Ard 205 E2
Strathclyde Ct. Helen 16 A2
Strathclyde Path. Udd 140 C3
Strathclyde Pl. Helen 16 A1
Strathclyde Rd. Dumb 50 A3
Strathclyde Rd. Mother ... 163 D3
Strathclyde St. Glasg 118 A1
Strathclyde View. Udd 141 D1
Strathclyde Way. Hat 142 B4
Strathcona Dr. Glasg 96 A4
Strathcona Gdns. Glasg 96 A4
Strathcona La. E Kil 180 C4
Strathcona Pl. E Kil 180 C4
Strathcona Pl. Glasg 138 B2
Strathcona St. Glasg 95 F3
Strathclyde Dr. Glasg 138 A3
Strathdee Ave. Dunt 74 A3
Strathdee Rd. Glasg 136 C1
Strathdon Ave. Glasg 136 C1
Strathdon Ave. Pais 113 E1
Strathdon Dr. Glasg 136 C1
Strathdoon Pl. Ayr 238 B1
Strathearn Gr. Kirk 59 D1
Strathearn Rd. Newt M 157 F3
Strathendrick Dr. Glasg ... 136 C2
Strathfillan Rd. E Kil 159 E1
Strathkelvin Ave. Bish 97 F4
Strathlachlan Ave. Car 188 A1
Strathleven Dr. Bonh 27 F1
Strathleven Pl. Dumb 49 F2
Strathmiglo Pl. Sten 23 F2
Strathmore Ave. Pais 114 B2
Strathmore Ave. Udd 140 B1
Strathmore Cres. Aird 103 D1
Strathmore Cres. Stir 2 A2
Strathmore Dr. Stir 2 A2
Strathmore Gdns. Glasg ... 138 B2
Strathmore Pk. Irvine 220 A3
Strathmore Rd. Glasg 97 D4
Strathmore Rd. Ham 162 C2
Strathmungo Cres. Aird ... 102 C3
Strathord Pl. Muir 81 D2
Strathord St. Glasg 119 D2
Strathpeffer Cres. Aird 103 D1
Strathspey Cres. Aird 103 D2
Strathtay Ave. Glasg 136 C1
Strathtummel Cres. Aird ... 103 D2
Strathview Gr. Glasg 136 C1
Strathview Pk. Glasg 136 C1
Strathview Rd. Hat 141 F3
Strathy Pl. Glasg 96 B3
Strathy Pl. Kilmk 228 A3
Strathyre Gdns. Bear 76 A3
Strathyre Gdns. Glenm ... 102 C3
Strathyre Gdns. Muir 81 D2
Strathyre Pl. Ham 161 F3
Strathyre St. Glasg 136 C1
Stratton Dr. Glasg 136 A1
Strauss Ave. Clyde 74 C1
Stravaig Path. Pais 133 D4
Stravaig Wlk. Pais 133 D4
Stravanan Rd. Glasg 137 D3
Stravanan St. Glasg 137 E1
Stravenhouse Rd. Law 186 C2
Strawberry Field Rd. Hous .. 91 D1
Strawberrybank Rd. Kilmk . 223 D1
Strawhill Rd. Newt M 157 F4
Strenabey Ave. Glasg 138 B2
Stripehead. All 10 A3
Striven Cres. Wish 165 D1
Striven Dr. Falk 24 B1
Striven Gdns. Glasg 96 C2
Striven Terr. Ham 162 A1
Stroma Ave. P Glasg 69 D4
Stroma Ct. Irvine 225 E4
Stroma St. Glasg 98 A1
Stromness St. Glasg 117 D2
Strone Cres. Green 46 A2
Strone Gdns. Kils 60 A4
Strone Path. Glen 101 E3
Strone Rd. Glasg 119 D4
Stronend St. Glasg 97 D3
Stronsay Ct. Irvine 220 A1
Stronsay Pl. Bish 78 B1
Stronsay Pl. Kilmk 223 D3
Stronsay St. Glasg 98 A1
Stronsay Way. Irvine 220 A1
Stronvar Dr. Glasg 95 D2
Stroud Rd. E Kil 180 B3
Strowan Cres. Glasg 119 D2
Strowan St. Glasg 119 E2
Strowan's Rd. Dumb 50 B2
Strowan's Well Rd. Dumb .. 50 B2
Struan Ave. Glasg 136 B2
Struan Gdns. Glasg 137 D3
Struan Rd. Glasg 137 D3
Strude Howe. Alva 5 D4
Strude Mill. Alva 5 D4
Strude St. Alva 5 D4
Struie St. Glasg 120 A4
Struma Dr. Newt M 157 E4
Struther St. Lark 199 D4
Struther & Swinhill Rd. Ash 199 E3
Struther & Swinhill Rd. Lark 199 E3
Struthers Ave. Hurl 228 B4
Struthers Cres. E Kil 160 A2

285

Struthers Pl. Troon — Thornside Rd. John

Struthers Pl. Troon 229 F4
Stuart Ave. Glasg 138 A3
Stuart Ave. O Kill 73 D3
Stuart Dr. Bish 97 F4
Stuart Dr. Lan 215 D3
Stuart Dr. Lark 185 E1
Stuart Pl. Dund 225 F1
Stuart Quadrant. Wish 164 C1
Stuart Rd. Bishop 72 A2
Stuart Rd. Dumb 50 B2
Stuart Rd. E Kil 158 B4
Stuart St. E Kil 159 F1
Stuart St. O Kill 73 D3
Stuarton Pk. E Kil 159 F1
Stuckleckie Rd. Helen 17 D1
Sturrock St. Kilmk 227 F4
Succoth St. Glasg 95 F4
Sudbury Cres. E Kil 159 D1
Suffolk Rd. Gour 44 C2
Suffolk St. Glasg 117 E3
Suffolk St. Helen 16 B1
Sugworth Ave. Glasg 120 A3
Sumburgh St. Glasg 119 D4
Summer St. Glasg 117 F3
Summerfield Cotts. Glasg 95 F1
Summerfield Rd. Cumb 82 A3
Summerfield St. Glasg 118 A2
Summerford. Falk 41 E2
Summerford Gdns. Falk 41 E2
Summerford Rd. Falk 41 E2
Summerhill and
Garngibbock Rd. Glen 82 B2
Summerhill Ave. Lark 185 D1
Summerhill Rd. Glasg 75 D2
Summerhill Rd. Newt M 157 F4
Summerhill Way. Hat 141 F2
Summerlea Rd. Glasg 135 F2
Summerlea Rd. W Kil 190 A2
Summerlee Cotts. Coat 121 F4
Summerlee Rd. Lark 184 C3
Summerlee Rd. Mother 164 B2
Summerlee St. Coat 121 F4
Summerlee St. Glasg 119 E4
Summertown Rd. Glasg 116 A4
Suna Path. Shot 147 D2
Sunart Ave. Ren 94 A2
Sunart Ct. Ham 162 A1
Sunart Gdns. Bish 78 B1
Sunart Rd. Bish 78 B1
Sunart Rd. Glasg 115 F3
Sunart St. Wish 165 D1
Sunbury Ave. Newt M 157 E4
Sundale Ave. Newt M 157 E3
Sunderland Ave. Dumb 49 E2
Sunderland Ct. Kilb 170 A4
Sundrum Pl. Kilw 207 E1
Sunflower Gdns. Mother 163 F4
Sunningdale Ave. Ayr 239 D2
Sunningdale Ave. Newt M 156 C3
Sunningdale Dr. B of W 110 B3
Sunningdale Rd. Glasg 96 C4
Sunningdale Sq. Kilw 207 E2
Sunningdale Wynd. Udd 140 C2
Sunnybank Dr. Newt M 157 E4
Sunnybank Gr. Newt M 157 E3
Sunnybank Rd. Stir 7 D2
Sunnybank St. Glasg 118 A2
Sunnydale Dr. Blac 107 F2
Sunnydale Rd. Blac 107 F2
Sunnyhill. Twe 59 F2
Sunnylaw Dr. Pais 113 D1
Sunnylaw Pl. Falk 41 F2
Sunnylaw Rd. B of A 2 A4
Sunnylaw St. Glasg 97 D2
Sunnyside Ave. Holy 143 D3
Sunnyside Ave. P Glasg 69 D4
Sunnyside Ave. Udd 140 C3
Sunnyside Cres. Holy 143 D3
Sunnyside Ct. All 10 A4
Sunnyside Dr. Coat 121 D3
Sunnyside Dr. Glasg 75 D1
Sunnyside Dr. Glasg 157 E4
Sunnyside. Kilm 222 A4
Sunnyside Pl. Barr 134 A1
Sunnyside Pl. Glasg 75 D1
Sunnyside Pl. Holy 143 D3
Sunnyside Rd. All 10 A4
Sunnyside Rd. Cle 165 D4
Sunnyside Rd. Coat 122 A4
Sunnyside Rd. Falk 41 F3
Sunnyside Rd. Kilmk 227 F1
Sunnyside Rd. Lan 214 B3
Sunnyside Rd. Pais 113 E1
Sunnyside Rd. Quart 184 B2
Sunnyside Sq E. Kilmk 227 F1
Sunnyside Sq W. Kilmk 227 F1
Sunnyside St. Falk 41 F3
Sunnyside St. Lark 184 C2
Sunnyside. Stir 7 D2
Sunnyside Terr. Holy 143 D3
Surrey La. Glasg 117 D2
Surrey St. Glasg 117 D2
Susannah St. Alex 27 F3
Sussex St. Glasg 116 C3
Sutcliffe Rd. Glasg 95 F4
Sutherland Ave. All 10 B4
Sutherland Ave. Bear 75 F4
Sutherland Ave. Glasg 116 B2
Sutherland Ave. Stir 2 B1
Sutherland Dr. Aird 122 C3
Sutherland Dr. Den 39 E4
Sutherland Dr. Dumb 50 B2
Sutherland Dr. Glasg 136 B1
Sutherland Dr. Kilmk 223 E1
Sutherland La. Glasg 96 B1
Sutherland Pl. Hat 141 F1
Sutherland Rd. Clyde 74 A1
Sutherland Rd. Green 45 D2
Sutherland St. Helen 16 A1
Sutherland St. Pais 113 E3
Sutherland St. Udd 161 E3
Sutherland Way. E Kil 160 B2
Sutton Ct. Kilw 207 D2
Sutton Pk Cres. Sten 23 F2
Sutton Pl. Falk 42 B3
Swaledale. E Kil 159 E2
Swallow Rd. Dunt 74 B4
Swan Pl. John 131 E4
Swan St. Clyde 73 F2
Swan St. Glasg 97 E1
Swanson Rd. Alex 27 E4
Swanston St. Glasg 118 A1
Sween Ave. Glasg 137 D2
Sween Dr. Ham 162 A1
Sween Path. Hat 142 B2
Sweethill Terr. Coat 122 B2
Sweethill Wlk. Hat 142 B4
Sweethope Gdns. Udd 141 D1
Sweethope Pl. Udd 141 D2
Swift Bank. Ham 161 F1
Swift Pl. E Kil 179 F3
Swift Pl. John 131 E4
Swindon St. Clyde 73 F2
Swinhill Rd. Ash 199 E3
Swinstie Rd. Cle 165 E4
Swinstie View. Cle 144 B1
Swinton Ave. Glasg 120 B3
Swinton Cres. Coat 121 D2
Swinton Cres. Glasg 120 B3
Swinton Dr. Glasg 115 D3
Swinton Gdns. Glasg 120 B3
Swinton Path. Glasg 120 B3
Swinton Pl. Glasg 115 D3
Swinton Rd. Glasg 120 B3
Swinton View. Glasg 120 B3
Swisscot Ave. Ham 183 D4
Swisscot Wlk. Ham 183 D4
Switchback Rd. Bear 75 F1
Sword St. Aird 122 C4
Sword St. Glasg 117 F3
Sword's Way. Falk 24 A1
Swordale Pl. Glasg 120 A4
Sycamore Ave. Beith 150 A1
Sycamore Ave. John 112 A1
Sycamore Ave. Klrk 79 E3
Sycamore Ave. Tan 141 E4
Sycamore Cres. Aird 123 E3
Sycamore Cres. Ayr 239 E3
Sycamore Cres. E Kil 180 B3
Sycamore Ct. Beith 150 A1
Sycamore Ct. Coat 121 F2
Sycamore Ct. E Kil 180 B3
Sycamore Dr. Aird 123 E3
Sycamore Dr. Clyde 74 A2
Sycamore Dr. Ham 162 C1
Sycamore Gr. Udd 161 E4
Sycamore Pl. E Kil 180 B3
Sycamore Pl. Gour 44 B3
Sycamore Pl. Holy 143 E2
Sycamore Pl. Stir 6 C3
Sycamore Way. E Kil 158 B4
Sycamore Way. M of C 58 B3
Sycamores The. Tull 4 A1
Sydenham La. Glasg 96 B2
Sydenham Rd. Glasg 96 B2
Sydes Brae. Ham 161 D2
Sydney Dr. E Kil 180 B4
Sydney Pl. E Kil 180 B4
Sydney St. Clyde 73 E2
Sydney St. Glasg 117 F3
Sykehead Ave. Hat 142 A3
Sykes Terr. Neil 154 C4
Sykeside Rd. Aird 122 C2
Sylvania Way. Clyde 74 A1
Sylvania Way S. Clyde 74 A1
Symington Dr. Clyde 74 A1
Symington Pl. Shew 224 C4
Symington Pl. Sten 24 A2
Symington Rd N. Sym 231 E2
Symington Rd S. Sym 231 E2
Symington Sq. E Kil 180 C4
Syms La. Ayr 236 A1
Syriam Pl. Glasg 97 F2
Syriam St. Glasg 97 F3
Tabard Pl. Glasg 95 E4
Tabard Rd. Glasg 95 E4
Tabernacle La. Glasg 139 D3
Tabernacle St. Glasg 139 D3
Taggart Rd. Kils 60 C2
Taig Rd. Kirk 80 A4
Tait Ave. Barr 134 B2
Tait Dr. Lar 41 E4
Takmadoon Rd. Kils 36 C2
Talbot Dr. Glasg 95 D3
Talbot. E Kil 160 B2
Talbot Pl. Glasg 95 D3
Talbot Rd. Bonh 28 A4
Talbot Terr. Glasg 95 D3
Talbot Terr. Tan 140 C4
Talisman Ave. Dumb 49 E2
Talisman Cres. Helen 25 C4
Talisman Cres. Mother 142 B1
Talisman Rd. Glasg 95 E3
Talisman Rd. Pais 132 C4
Talisman Wlk. Salt 206 A1
Talla Rd. Glasg 115 D3
Tallant Rd. Glasg 75 D2
Tallant Terr. Glasg 75 E2
Tam O'Shanter Dr. Cowie 12 B4
Tam's Brig. Ayr 236 A2
Tamar Dr. E Kil 179 F3
Tamarack Cres. Tan 141 E4
Tambowie Ave. Miln 54 C1
Tambowie Cres. Miln 54 C1
Tambowie St. Glasg 95 F4
Tamfourhill Ave. Falk 41 E2
Tamfourhill Rd. Falk 41 E2
Tammy Dale's Rd. Kilw 207 F2
Tamshill St. Glasg 96 C3
Tanar Ave. Ren 94 C1
Tanar Way. Ren 94 C1
Tandlehill Rd. Kilbar 111 D1
Tanera Ave. Glasg 137 E2
Tanfield Pl. Glasg 119 E4
Tanfield St. Glasg 119 E4
Tankerland Rd. Glasg 137 D3
Tanna Dr. Glasg 115 F2
Tannadice Ave. Glasg 115 E2
Tannahill Cres. John 111 F1
Tannahill Dr. E Kil 160 B2
Tannahill Rd. Glasg 136 C3
Tannahill Rd. Pais 113 D3
Tannahill Terr. Pais 113 D3
Tanners Rd. Falk 42 A2
Tannery La. Stir 2 A1
Tannoch Dr. Cumb 82 C4
Tannoch Dr. Miln 55 D2
Tannoch Pl. Cumb 82 C4
Tannoch Rd. Uplaw 153 D2
Tannock St. Glasg 97 D2
Tannock St. Kilmk 227 F3
Tantallon Ave. Gour 43 F3
Tantallon Ct. Car 187 F2
Tantallon Dr. Coat 101 E1
Tantallon Dr. Pais 113 D1
Tantallon Dr. Sten 24 A2
Tantallon Pk. E Kil 159 E1
Tantallon Rd. Glasg 120 A2
Tantallon Rd. Glasg 136 C4
Tantallon Rd. Udd 141 D2
Tantera Ct. Falk 42 A1
Tanzieknowe Ave. Glasg 139 D2
Tanzieknowe Dr. Glasg 139 D2
Tanzieknowe Pl. Glasg 139 D2
Tanzieknowe Rd. Glasg 139 D2
Tappoch Pl. Lar 23 D2
Taransay St. Glasg 116 A4
Tarbert Ave. Udd 140 B1
Tarbert Ave. W Kil 190 C3
Tarbert Ave. Wish 165 D1
Tarbert Ct. Ham 162 A1
Tarbet Pl. Car 188 A1
Tarbet St. Gour 44 C4
Tarbolton Dr. Clyde 74 B2
Tarbolton. E Kil 160 B2
Tarbolton Path. Lark 184 C2
Tarbolton Rd. Cumb 62 A1
Tarbolton Rd. Dund 225 F1
Tarbolton Rd. Glasg 136 B3
Tarbolton Rd. Pres 233 F2
Tarbolton Rd. Sym 231 F3
Tarbolton Sq. Clyde 74 B2
Tarbrax Path. Shot 147 D2
Tarbrax Way. Ham 162 A2
Tarduff Pl. Duni 21 D1
Tarff Ave. Eagle 178 C3
Tarfside Ave. Glasg 115 E2
Tarfside Gdns. Glasg 115 E2
Tarfside Oval. Glasg 115 E2
Target Rd. Aird 123 D3
Tarland St. Glasg 115 F3
Tarras Dr. Ren 94 C1
Tarras Pl. Glasg 139 E3
Tarryholme Dr. Irvine 219 E1
Tasker St. Green 45 E3
Tasman Dr. E Kil 180 A4
Tasmania Quadrant. Wish 165 F2
Tassie Pl. E Kil 160 A1
Tassie St. Glasg 136 B4
Tattershall Rd. Glasg 99 E1
Tavistock Dr. Glasg 136 B3
Tay Ave. Pais 112 C1
Tay Ave. Ren 94 C2
Tay Cres. Bish 78 A1
Tay Cres. Glasg 98 C1
Tay Ct. All 10 B3
Tay Ct. E Kil 179 F4
Tay Gdns. Ham 183 D4
Tay Gr. E Kil 179 F4
Tay Loan. Holy 143 D3
Tay Pl. Dumb 50 A4
Tay Pl. E Kil 179 F4
Tay Pl. John 131 E4
Tay Pl. Kilmk 228 A3
Tay Pl. Lark 199 D4
Tay Pl. Shot 146 C3
Tay Rd. Bear 75 E1
Tay Rd. Bish 78 A1
Tay Rd. Pres 233 E2
Tay Rd. Troon 229 F2
Tay St. Coat 101 E1
Tay St. Falk 24 B1
Tay St. Green 45 D3
Tay Terr. E Kil 179 F4
Taybank Dr. Ayr 239 D2
Tayinloan Dr. Car 202 A4
Taylor Ave. Holy 143 E1
Taylor Ave. Kilbar 110 C2
Taylor Pl. Glasg 117 E4
Taylor St. Alex 27 E4
Taylor St. Ayr 235 F1
Taylor St. Clyde 94 B4
Taylor St. Glasg 117 E4
Taylor's Rd. Lar 23 E1
Taymouth Dr. Gour 43 F3
Taymouth St. Glasg 119 D2
Taynish Dr. Glasg 137 D3
Tayside. Aird 102 C1
Teak Pl. Tan 121 E1
Teal Cres. E Kil 179 F3
Teal Ct. Tan 141 F4
Tealing Ave. Glasg 115 E2
Tealing Cres. Glasg 115 E2
Teasel Ave. Glasg 135 D2
Teawell Rd. Newt M 156 B3
Teesdale. E Kil 159 E2
Teign Gr. E Kil 179 F3
Teith Ave. Ren 94 C1
Teith Dr. Bear 75 E2
Teith Pl. Glasg 139 E3
Teith Pl. Kilmk 228 A3
Teith Rd. Pres 233 E2
Teith St. Glasg 98 C1
Telegraph Rd. Cald 105 D4
Telephone La. Glasg 96 B1
Telford Ct. Bann 7 E1
Telford Ct. Clyde 74 A1
Telford Pl. Cumb 83 D4
Telford Pl. Irvine 219 F1
Telford Rd. Cumb 83 D4
Telford Rd. E Kil 180 C4
Telford Sq. Falk 41 F3
Telford St. Hat 142 A3
Telford Terr. E Kil 180 C4
Teme Pl. E Kil 179 F4
Templand Cres. Dalry 191 E4
Templand Rd. Dalry 191 E4
Templar Ave. Glasg 75 E1
Temple Denny Rd. Den 21 E1
Temple Gdns. Glasg 95 F4
Temple Rd. Glasg 96 A4
Templehill. Troon 229 D2
Templeland Rd. Glasg 115 E1
Templerigg Ct. Pres 233 E1
Templerigg St. Pres 233 E1
Templeton Bsns Ctr. Glasg 117 F3
Templeton Cres. Pres 236 B4
Templeton Gdns. Pres 236 B4
Templeton St. Glasg 117 F3
Ten Acres. N Sau 5 D1
Tennant Ave. E Kil 159 D1
Tennant
Complex The. E Kil 159 D1
Tennant Rd. Pais 113 D3
Tennant St. Ren 94 B2
Tennent St. Coat 122 A3
Tennyson Dr. Glasg 118 C2
Tern Pl. John 131 E4
Terrace Rd. Green 46 A2
Terregles Ave. Glasg 116 B1
Terregles Cres. Glasg 116 B1
Terregles Dr. Glasg 116 B1
Teviot Ave. Bish 78 A2
Teviot Ave. Pais 132 C4
Teviot Cres. Bear 75 E1
Teviot Dr. Bishop 72 B1
Teviot Pl. Glasg 139 F3
Teviot Pl. Troon 229 F2
Teviot Rd. P Glasg 68 C3
Teviot Rd. Pres 233 E2
Teviot Sq. Cumb 61 F1
Teviot St. Ayr 236 A2
Teviot St. Coat 101 E1
Teviot St. Falk 41 F2
Teviot St. Glasg 116 B4
Teviot Terr. John 131 E4
Teviot Way. Udd 161 E4
Teviotdale. Newt M 157 D3
Tewkesbury Rd. E Kil 160 B2
Thane Rd. Glasg 95 E3
Thanes Gate. Udd 140 C3
Thankerton Ave. Holy 142 C3
Thankerton Rd. Lark 185 D1
Tharsis St. Glasg 97 F1
Thimble St. Alex 27 E1
Third Ave. Bonh 27 F3
Third Ave. Dumb 50 B1
Third Ave. Glasg 137 D4
Third Ave. Irvine 224 A4
Third Ave. Ren 94 B1
Third Ave. Stepps 79 E1
Third Ave. Stepps 99 E3
Third Gdns. Glasg 116 A2
Third Rd. Ham 161 F3
Third St. Tan 140 C4
Thirdpart Cres. Clyde 94 C4
Thirdpart Pl. Kilmk 227 E4
Thirlmere. E Kil 179 F3
Thistle Ave. Duni 21 E2
Thistle Bank. Klrk 79 E2
Thistle Cres. Lark 185 D1
Thistle Gdns. Holy 143 D3
Thistle Pl. E Kil 159 E2
Thistle Quadrant. Aird 103 D1
Thistle Rd. Holy 143 D2
Thistle St. Aird 103 D1
Thistle St. All 10 B3
Thistle St. Cle 144 B1
Thistle St. Falk 42 B3
Thistle St. Glasg 117 D2
Thistle St. Glasg 117 E3
Thistle St. Klrk 79 E4
Thistle St. Pais 113 E1
Thistle Terr. Steven 206 C1
Thistle Wlk. Ayr 239 E2
Thistleeneuk. O Kill 73 D4
Thom St. Green 45 E2
Thomas Campbell St. Salt 217 D4
Thomas Muir Ave. Bish 98 A4
Thomas Muir La. Green 46 C1
Thomas Muir St. Green 46 C1
Thomas St. Alex 27 F2
Thomas St. Pais 113 D2
Thompson Ave. Klrk 79 F4
Thompson Pl. Dunt 74 B3
Thompson Pl. Slam 86 A2
Thompson St. Glasg 118 A3
Thompson St. Ren 94 B1
Thompson's Cl. Lan 215 D2
Thomson Ave. John 111 F2
Thomson Ave. Wish 164 B1
Thomson Dr. Aird 122 C3
Thomson Dr. Bear 75 F3
Thomson Dr. Tan 141 E3
Thomson Gr. Glasg 139 D4
Thomson Pl. Cam 6 B3
Thomson St. Ayr 236 B1
Thomson St. Car 187 F1
Thomson St. John 111 F1
Thomson St. Kilmk 222 C1
Thomson Terr. Shot 146 B3
Thomson Terr. Stew 211 E4
Thorn Ave. Thorn 158 B2
Thorn Brae. John 112 A2
Thorn Ct. John 112 A1
Thorn Dr. Bear 75 E3
Thorn Dr. Glasg 138 B2
Thorn Rd. Bear 75 E3
Thorn Rd. Hat 142 A3
Thorn Terr. Kilmk 223 D2
Thornbank St. Glasg 116 B4
Thornbridge Ave. Glasg 96 B3
Thornbridge Ave. Glasg 120 A3
Thornbridge Gdns. Falk 42 C2
Thornbridge Gdns. Glasg 120 A3
Thornbridge Rd. Falk 42 C3
Thornbridge Rd. Glasg 120 A3
Thornbridge Sq. Falk 42 C3
Thorncliffe Gdns. Glasg 116 C1
Thorncroft Dr. Glasg 137 E2
Thorndale Gdns. Bon 39 D1
Thorndean Ave. Hat 142 A2
Thorndean Cres. Hat 142 A2
Thornden La. Glasg 95 D2
Thorndene Ave. Holy 143 E1
Thorndene Ct. Falk 41 F1
Thorndene. John 112 A2
Thorndyke. E Kil 160 B3
Thorne Rd. All 4 C1
Thornhill Ave. John 112 A1
Thornhill Ave. Udd 161 E4
Thornhill Ct. Kilw 207 D2
Thornhill Dr. John 112 A1
Thornhill Gdns. John 112 A2
Thornhill. John 112 A1
Thornhill La. Udd 141 D2
Thornhill Path. Glasg 118 B3
Thornhill Pl. Kilmk 227 F2
Thornhill Rd. Falk 42 B3
Thornhill Rd. Ham 161 F2
Thornhill Way. Coat 122 B2
Thornhouse Ave. Irvine 219 E1
Thorniecroft Dr. Cumb 82 B3
Thorniecroft Pl. Cumb 82 B3
Thornielee. E Kil 160 A1
Thorniewood Gdns. Tan 141 D4
Thorniewood Rd. Tan 140 C4
Thornlea Dr. Glasg 136 B2
Thornlea Pl. Lan 215 F4
Thornlea St. Car 202 A4
Thornley Ave. Glasg 95 D3
Thornlie Gill. Wish 165 D1
Thornliebank Rd. Glasg 135 F1
Thornliebank Rd. Glasg 136 A3
Thornly Park Ave. Pais 133 F4
Thornly Park Dr. Pais 133 F4
Thornly Park Gdns. Pais 113 F1
Thornly Park Rd. Pais 133 F4
Thornside Rd. John 112 A2

Thornton Ave. Bon 40 A3
Thornton Ave. Cross 221 F1
Thornton La. Glasg 96 C4
Thornton Pl. Ham 183 E3
Thornton Rd. Thorn 158 B1
Thornton St. Coat 101 E1
Thornton St. Glasg 96 C4
Thorntree Ave. Beith 150 B1
Thorntree Ave. Ham 161 F3
Thorntree Way. Udd 141 D2
Thornwood Ave. Ayr 236 C1
Thornwood Ave. Glasg 96 A1
Thornwood Ave. Klrk 79 D3
Thornwood Cres. Glasg 95 F2
Thornwood Dr. B of W 110 A4
Thornwood Dr. Glasg 95 F1
Thornwood Dr. Glasg 96 A2
Thornwood Dr. Irvine 219 E1
Thornwood Dr. Pais 113 D1
Thornwood Gdns. Glasg 96 A1
Thornwood Pl. Glasg 96 A2
Thornwood Quadrant. Glasg 95 F2
Thornwood Rd. Glasg 95 F1
Thornwood Terr. Glasg 95 F1
Thornyburn Dr. Glasg 120 B2
Thornyburn Pl. Glasg 120 B2
Thornyflat Dr. Ayr 236 C1
Thornyflat Pl. Ayr 236 C1
Thornyflat St. Ayr 236 C1
Thrashbush Ave. Wish 165 E2
Thrashbush Cres. Wish 165 E2
Thrashbush Rd. Wish 165 E2
Threave Ct. Car 187 F2
Three Rivers Wlk. E Kil 180 A4
Three Stanes
    Roundabout. Shew 224 B3
Threepwood Rd. Beith 150 C1
Threestonehill Ave. Glasg . 119 E3
Threshold. E Kil 160 A1
Threshold Pk. E Kil 160 A1
Thriplee Rd. B of W 110 B4
Thrums Ave. Bish 78 B1
Thrums. E Kil 160 B3
Thrums Gdns. Bish 78 B1
Thrush Pl. John 131 E4
Thrushbush La. Aird 103 D1
Thrushbush Quadrant. Aird 103 D1
Thrushbush Rd. Aird 103 D1
Thrushcraig Cres. Pais 113 F1
Thurso St. Glasg 96 B1
Thurston Rd. Glasg 115 D3
Tibbermore Rd. Glasg 96 A2
Tig Rd. Ayr 236 C1
Tighnasheen Way. Udd 140 B1
Till St. Wish 165 D3
Tillanburn Rd. Holy 143 F2
Tillet Oval. Pais 113 E4
Tillie St. Glasg 96 C2
Tillycairn Dr. Glasg 99 E1
Tillycairn Rd. Glasg 99 E1
Tilt Rd. New 165 F3
Tilt Rd. Pres 233 E2
Tilt St. Glasg 98 C1
Timmons Pl. Den 21 E1
Timmons Terr. Chap 123 E1
Tinker's La. Mother 163 E3
Tintagel Gdns. Muir 80 C2
Tinto Cres. Kilmk 228 A2
Tinto Cres. Wish 165 E1
Tinto Dr. Barr 134 B1
Tinto Rd. Aird 123 D3
Tinto Rd. Bear 75 E3
Tinto Rd. Bish 78 B1
Tinto Rd. Glasg 136 B3
Tinto St. Wish 165 E1
Tinto View. Ham 183 F4
Tinto Way. Cle 144 A1
Tintock Dr. Kirk 58 C1
Tintock Rd. Kirk 59 D1
Tinwald Path. Glasg 115 D3
Tiree Ave. P Glasg 69 D4
Tiree Ave. Pais 133 E4
Tiree Ave. Ren 94 B1
Tiree Cres. New 165 F3
Tiree Ct. Cumb 82 B4
Tiree Ct. Irvine 225 D4
Tiree Dr. Cumb 82 B4
Tiree. E Kil 181 E4
Tiree Gdns. Bear 75 D3
Tiree Gdns. Glenm 102 C3
Tiree Pl. Falk 42 A1
Tiree Pl. Newt M 156 A3
Tiree Rd. Cumb 82 B4
Tiree St. Glasg 98 B1
Tirry Ave. Ren 94 C1
Tirry Way. Ren 94 C1
Titania. All 10 A4
Titchfield Rd. Troon 229 D1
Titchfield St. Kilmk 227 F4
Titchfield Way. Irvine 220 A3
Titwood Dr. Kilmk 222 C2
Titwood Rd. Glasg 116 B1
Titwood Rd. Newt M 156 C1
Tiverton Ave. Glasg 119 E2
Tivoli Ct. E Kil 180 C3
Tobago Pl. E Kil 159 D1
Tobago Pl. Glasg 117 F3
Tobago St. Glasg 117 F3

Tobago St. Green 45 F3
Tobermory Rd. Glasg 138 B2
Todburn Dr. Pais 133 F4
Todd St. Glasg 118 B4
Todhill Ave. Kilmk 222 C2
Todhills. E Kil 180 C4
Todhills. N E Kil 180 C4
Todhills. S E Kil 180 C4
Todholm Cres. Pais 114 A1
Todholm Rd. Pais 114 A1
Todholm Terr. Pais 114 A1
Tofthill Ave. Bish 77 F1
Tofthill Gdns. Bish 77 F1
Tofts Cres. Dalry 191 E4
Tofts. Dalry 191 E4
Togo Pl. Green 45 F2
Tolbooth St. Falk 42 A2
Toll La. Glasg 116 C3
Toll St. Mother 163 F3
Toll Wynd. Ham 183 E4
Tollbrae Ave. Aird 123 D4
Tollcross Rd. Glasg 118 C2
Tollerton Dr. Irvine 219 E2
Tollhouse Gdns. Hat 142 B2
Tollpark Cres. New 166 A3
Tollpark Pl. Cumb 62 C4
Tollpark Rd. Cumb 62 C4
Tolsta St. Glasg 76 C1
Tom-A-Mhoid. Ros 15 D2
Tomtain Brae. Cumb 81 F4
Tomtain Ct. Cumb 81 F4
Toner Gdns. Wish 186 A4
Tontine Cres. Alex 49 E4
Tontine La. Glasg 117 E3
Tontine Pk. Alex 49 E4
Tontine Pl. Glasg 138 C2
Topaz Terr. Hat 142 A2
Toppersfield. Kilbar 111 E1
Torbeg House. Pres 236 A3
Torbothie Rd. Shot 147 D2
Torbreck St. Glasg 115 F3
Torbrex Farm Rd. Stir 7 D2
Torbrex La. Stir 7 D3
Torbrex Rd. Cumb 62 A1
Torbrex Rd. Stir 6 C2
Torburn Ave. Glasg 136 A2
Torburn Ave. Plea 12 B2
Tordene Path. Cumb 61 E2
Torgyle St. Glasg 76 B1
Tormeadow Rd. Newt M ... 156 B3
Tormore St. Glasg 115 E3
Tormusk Dr. Glasg 138 A2
Tormusk Rd. Glasg 138 A2
Torness St. Glasg 96 B1
Torogay Pl. Bish 97 F4
Torogay St. Glasg 97 E4
Torogay Terr. Glasg 97 E4
Toronto Way. Glasg 139 E4
Torphin Cres. Glasg 119 D4
Torr Ave. Kil 89 F1
Torr Cres. Rhu 15 F3
Torr La. Kil 89 F1
Torr Rd. B of W 110 A4
Torr Rd. Bish 78 B1
Torr St. Glasg 97 E2
Torran Rd. Glasg 119 F4
Torrance Ave. Aird 123 E4
Torrance Rd. E Kil 159 F1
Torrance Rd. Green 46 A1
Torrance Rd. Lennox 78 B4
Torrance St. Glasg 97 F2
Torranyard Terr. Ham 161 F1
Torriden Pl. Coat 121 F3
Torriden St. Coat 121 F3
Torridon Ave. Falk 24 B1
Torridon Ave. Glasg 116 A2
Torridon Ave. Holy 143 E2
Torridon Ct. All 10 B3
Torridon Gdns. Bear 75 E4
Torridon Gdns. Newt M ... 157 D2
Torrin Loan. Shot 147 D2
Torrin Rd. Glasg 76 B1
Torrinch Dr. Bonh 19 F1
Torrington Ave. Glasg 157 D4
Torrington Cres. Glasg 119 E2
Torrisdale Pl. Coat 121 F4
Torrisdale St. Coat 121 F4
Torrisdale St. Glasg 117 D1
Torry Dr. Alva 4 C4
Torryburn Rd. Glasg 98 B2
Torwood Ave. Lar 23 D1
Torwood Brae. Ham 161 F1
Torwood La. Muir 81 D1
Torwoodhill Pl. Rhu 15 F2
Torwoodhill Rd. Rhu 15 F2
Toryglen Rd. Glasg 137 F4
Toryglen St. Glasg 117 F1
Touch Rd. Cam 6 A3
Touchhill Cres. Plea 12 B2
Tourhill Rd. Kilmk 222 C2
Tourmaline Terr. Hat 142 A2
Tournai Path. Udd 161 E4
Toward Ct. Udd 161 E4
Toward Rd. Glasg 119 E4
Tower Ave. Barr 134 B2

Tower Cres. Ren 94 A1
Tower Dr. Gour 44 B3
Tower Dr. Ren 94 A1
Tower Pl. Clack 10 C3
Tower Pl. Helen 16 B1
Tower Pl. John 112 A1
Tower Pl. Miln 55 D1
Tower Rd. Bish 56 C2
Tower Rd. Cumb 83 D3
Tower Rd. John 111 F1
Tower Rd. Lennox 56 C2
Tower St. All 10 A4
Tower St. Glasg 116 C3
Tower Terr. Pais 113 E2
Tower View. N Sau 5 F1
Towerhill Ave. Kilm 222 B3
Towerhill Rd. Glasg 75 E1
Towerlands
    Farm Rd. Irvine 220 A2
Towerlands Gate. Irvine ... 220 A1
Towerlands
    Interchange. Irvine 219 F2
Towerlands Rd. Irvine 220 B1
Towerlands Rd. Spring 220 C1
Towers Ct. Falk 42 A3
Towers Pl. Aird 123 F4
Towers Rd. Stir 2 B2
Towers Rd. Aird 123 F4
Towerside Cres. Glasg 115 D1
Towerside Rd. Glasg 115 D1
Towie Pl. Glasg 96 B3
Towie Pl. Udd 140 C3
Town House St. Den 21 F1
Townend. Kilm 222 B4
Townend La. Dalry 191 E4
Townend Rd. Dumb 50 A3
Townend Rd. Kilmk 227 F2
Townend St. Dalry 191 E4
Townend Terr. Sym 231 E2
Townfoot. Irvine 220 B1
Townhead Dr. Holy 143 F2
Townhead. Irvine 219 E1
Townhead. Kilb 149 D1
Townhead. Kilm 222 B4
Townhead. Kilw 207 E2
Townhead. Klrk 79 E4
Townhead Pl. Tan 141 D4
Townhead Rd. Coat 101 E1
Townhead Rd. Helen 17 D1
Townhead Rd. Newt M 156 B2
Townhead Rd. Salt 217 D4
Townhead St. Beith 171 D4
Townhead St. Ham 162 C2
Townhead St. Kils 60 B4
Townhead St. Steven 206 B1
Townhead St. Stone 198 C1
Townhead Terr. Pais 113 E2
Townhill Rd. Ham 161 F2
Townhill Terr. Ham 161 F2
Townholm. Kilmk 223 D1
Townmill Rd. Glasg 118 A4
Townsend St. Glasg 97 E1
Tradeston St. Glasg 117 D3
Trafalgar St. Clyde 73 F1
Trafalgar St. Glasg 117 F2
Trafalgar St. Green 45 F2
Trainard Ave. Glasg 118 C2
Tramore Cres. Pres 236 B4
Tranent Pl. Cle 144 B1
Tranent Pl. Glasg 118 C4
Traquair Ave. Pais 132 C4
Traquair Ave. Wish 165 E3
Traquair Dr. Glasg 115 D3
Traquair Wynd. Udd 161 E4
Treebank Cres. Ayr 239 E3
Treeburn Ave. Glasg 136 A2
Treemain Rd. Glasg 157 D4
Trees Park Ave. Barr 134 A2
Treesbank. Kilw 207 E1
Treesbank Rd. Kilmk 227 F2
Treeswoodhead Rd. Hurl . 228 A1
Treeswoodhead Rd. Kilmk 228 A1
Trefoil Ave. Glasg 136 B4
Trefoil Pl. Ayr 239 E2
Trelawney Terr. Steven 217 F3
Trent Pl. E Kil 179 F3
Trent St. Coat 101 E1
Tresta Rd. Glasg 96 C4
Tribboch St. Lark 184 C2
Trident Way. Ren 94 B1
Trinidad Gn. E Kil 159 D1
Trinity Ave. Glasg 115 C2
Trinity Cres. Beith 150 B1
Trinity Dr. Dalry 191 D3
Trinity Dr. Glasg 139 E2
Trinity Way. Lark 185 E1
Trinley Rd. Glasg 75 E1
Triton Pl. Holy 142 C3
Tron Ct. Tull 4 A1
Trondra Path. Glasg 119 F4
Trondra Pl. Glasg 119 F4
Trongate. Glasg 117 E3
Trongate. Stone 198 C1
Troon Ave. E Kil 180 A3
Troon Ct. E Kil 180 A3
Troon Dr. B of W 110 B4
Troon Pl. Newt M 157 D2
Troon Rd. Troon 230 A2

Troon St. Glasg 118 A2
Trossachs Ave. Holy 143 D3
Trossachs St. Glasg 97 D2
Trossachs Rd. Glasg 138 B1
Trossachs St. Glasg 97 D2
Troubridge Ave. Kilbar 111 D1
Troubridge Cres. Kilbar ... 111 D1
Trows Rd. Wish 186 A3
Truce Rd. Glasg 95 D4
Truro Ave. Muir 80 C2
Tryfield Pl. Ayr 236 A1
Tryst Rd. Cumb 61 F1
Tryst Rd. Cumb 62 A1
Tryst Rd. Sten 23 E2
Tryst Rd. Sten 23 E2
Tryst Way. Sten 23 E1
Tudhope Cres. Alex 27 E4
Tudor La. S. Glasg 95 F2
Tudor Rd. Glasg 95 F2
Tudor St. Glasg 119 F2
Tulliallan Pl. E Kil 181 D4
Tulliallan Pl. Sten 24 A2
Tullibody Rd. All 9 F4
Tullibody Rd. Tull 4 C1
Tullichewan Dr. Alex 27 E4
Tullichewan Rd. Alex 27 F4
Tulligarth Pk. All 10 A4
Tullis Ct. Glasg 117 F2
Tulloch Gdns. Mother 164 A2
Tulloch Rd. Shot 147 D2
Tulloch St. Glasg 137 D3
Tulloch-Ard Pl. Glasg 138 B2
Tullymet Rd. Ham 183 E4
Tummel Dr. Aird 102 C1
Tummel Gn. E Kil 159 F2
Tummel Pl. Sten 23 F2
Tummel St. Glasg 98 C1
Tummell Way. Pais 112 C1
Tunnel St. Glasg 116 C4
Tuphall Rd. Ham 162 B1
Turnberry Ave. Glasg 96 A2
Turnberry Ave. Gour 44 A3
Turnberry Ct. Kilw 207 D2
Turnberry Dr. B of W 110 B3
Turnberry Dr. Glasg 137 F3
Turnberry Dr. Ham 161 E1
Turnberry Dr. Kilmk 227 F2
Turnberry Dr. Newt M 157 D3
Turnberry Gdns. Chap 123 F1
Turnberry Gdns. Cumb 61 F3
Turnberry Pl. E Kil 180 A3
Turnberry Pl. Glasg 137 F2
Turnberry Rd. Glasg 96 A2
Turnberry Wynd. Udd 140 C1
Turnbull Ave. Alex 27 E2
Turnbull Cres. Alex 27 E2
Turnbull St. Glasg 117 E3
Turner Pl. Kilmk 223 D2
Turner Rd. Glasg 97 F1
Turner Rd. Pais 113 F4
Turner St. Coat 121 F3
Turnhill Ave. Inch 93 D4
Turnhill Cres. Inch 93 D4
Turnhill Dr. Inch 93 D4
Turnhill Gdns. Inch 93 D4
Turnlaw. E Kil 180 B3
Turnlaw Rd. Glasg 139 D1
Turnlaw St. Glasg 117 E2
Turquoise Terr. Hat 142 A2
Turret Cres. Glasg 95 E4
Turret Ct. All 10 B3
Turret Rd. Glasg 95 E4
Turriff St. Glasg 117 D2
Twain Ave. Sten 24 A2
Tweed Ave. Pais 112 C1
Tweed Cres. Glasg 98 C1
Tweed Cres. Kilmk 228 A3
Tweed Cres. Ren 94 C1
Tweed Cres. Wish 165 E3
Tweed Ct. Aird 123 E3
Tweed Dr. Bear 75 E2
Tweed La. Holy 143 D3
Tweed Pl. John 131 E4
Tweed Pl. Pres 233 E1
Tweed St. Ayr 236 A2
Tweed St. Coat 122 A2
Tweed St. E Kil 179 F4
Tweed St. Green 45 D3
Tweed St. Lark 185 D1
Tweedmuir Pl. Coat 122 B2
Tweedmuir. Bish 78 B1
Tweedsmuir Cres. Bear 75 F4
Tweedsmuir Pk. Ham 183 E4
Tweedsmuir Rd. Glasg 115 D3
Tweedvale Ave. Clyde 94 C3
Tweedvale Pl. Clyde 94 C3
Twinlaw St. Glasg 100 B1
Tylney Rd. Pais 114 B3
Tyndrum Rd. Bear 76 A3
Tyndrum St. Glasg 97 E1
Tyne Pl. E Kil 179 F3
Tynecastle Cres. Glasg 119 D4
Tynecastle Path. Glasg 119 D4
Tynecastle Pl. Glasg 119 D4
Tynecastle St. Glasg 119 D4
Tynron Ct. Ham 161 F1
Tynwald Ave. Glasg 138 B2

U.P. La. Kils 60 B4
U.P. Rd. Kils 60 B4
Uddingston Rd. Udd 141 D2
Udston Rd. Ham 161 F3
Udston Terr. Ham 161 F3
Uig Pl. Glasg 119 F3
Uist Ave. P Glasg 69 D4
Uist Cres. Stepps 99 D3
Uist Dr. Kirk 80 A4
Uist St. Glasg 115 F4
Uist Way. Wish 165 F3
Ulg Way. Shot 147 D2
Ullswater. E Kil 179 F3
Ulundi Rd. John 111 F1
Ulva St. Glasg 115 F3
Umberly Rd. Kilmk 227 C2
Underwood Cotts. Cam 6 B3
Underwood La. Pais 113 E3
Underwood Pl. Kilmk 227 C2
Underwood Rd. Cam 6 B3
Underwood Rd. Glasg 138 B3
Underwood Rd. Pais 113 E3
Underwood Rd. Pres 236 B4
Underwood St. Glasg 136 C4
Union Arc. Ayr 238 C4
Union Ave. Ayr 236 A2
Union Pl. Glasg 117 D4
Union Pl. Lar 23 D1
Union Rd. Falk 41 E3
Union St. All 10 A3
Union St. B of A 2 A4
Union St. Bonh 27 F2
Union St. Car 187 F1
Union St. Falk 42 A4
Union St. Glasg 117 D4
Union St. Green 45 F3
Union St. Ham 162 B2
Union St. Holy 143 D2
Union St. Hurl 228 C3
Union St. Kilmk 222 C1
Union St. Klrk 79 E4
Union St. Lark 185 D2
Union St. Pais 113 F1
Union St. Salt 216 C4
Union St. Shot 146 B3
Union St. Sten 23 F2
Union St. Stir 2 A1
Union St. Stone 198 C1
Union St. Troon 229 D2
Union Street La. Bonh 27 F2
Unitas Cres. Car 187 F1
Unitas Rd. Hat 142 B3
Unity Pk. Shot 146 B2
Unity Pl. Glasg 97 D1
Universal Rd. Gran 42 C4
University Ave. Glasg 96 B1
University Gdns. Glasg 96 B1
University Pl. Glasg 96 B1
University Rd W. B of A 2 B3
Unsted Pl. Pais 114 A2
Unthank Rd. Hat 142 B3
Uphall Pl. Glasg 118 C4
Upland La. Glasg 95 E2
Upland Rd. Glasg 95 E2
Uplawmoor Rd. Neil 154 A3
Uplawmoor Rd. Uplaw 153 F2
Upper Adelaide St. Helen .. 16 C1
Upper Arthur St. Alex 27 E4
Upper Bourtree Ct. Glasg . 138 B2
Upper Bourtree Dr. Glasg . 138 B2
Upper Bridge St. Alex 27 E4
Upper Bridge St. Stir 2 A1
Upper Cartsburn St. Green . 46 A2
Upper Castlehill. Stir 7 D4
Upper Colquhoun St. Helen 16 A2
Upper Craigs. Stir 7 D4
Upper Crofts. Ayr 238 C1
Upper Glenburn Rd. Bear .. 75 E3
Upper Glenfinlas St. Helen .. 16 C1
Upper Hall Rd. Rhu 15 E3
Upper Loaning. Ayr 238 C1
Upper Mill St. Aird 123 D4
Upper Newmarket St. Falk .. 42 A2
Upper Smollett St. Alex 27 E2
Upper
    Stoneymollan Rd. Alex .. 27 E4
Upper
    Sutherland Cres. Helen .. 16 A2
Upper Sutherland St. Helen 16 A2
Upper Torwoodhill Rd. Rhu .. 15 F2
Ure Cres. Bon 40 A3
Urquhart Cres. Ren 94 B1
Urquhart Dr. E Kil 160 A2
Urquhart Dr. Gour 43 F3
Urquhart Pl. Helen 16 B2
Urquhart Rd. Kilmk 223 E1
Urrdale Rd. Glasg 116 A3
Usmore Pl. Glasg 119 F3

Vaila Pl. Glasg 97 D4
Vaila St. Glasg 96 C4
Vale of Ieven Ind Est. Bonh . 27 F1
Vale Pl. Duni 21 F2
Valentine Cres. Tan 141 D4
Valetta Pl. Clyde 73 E2
Valeview. Lar 23 E1
Valeview Terr. Dumb 50 A3

Valeview Terr. Glasg 137 D4
Vallantine Cres. Tan 141 D4
Vallay St. Glasg 97 E4
Valley View. Glasg 139 E3
Valleybank. Kils 37 E2
Valleyfield. Cumb 60 C1
Valleyfield. E Kil 159 E1
Valleyfield. M of C 58 A3
Valleyfield Pl. Stir 7 E3
Valleyfield St. Glasg 97 F2
Valleyview Dr. Falk 42 A4
Vancouver Ct. E Kil 159 D1
Vancouver Dr. E Kil 159 D1
Vancouver La. Glasg 95 E2
Vancouver Pl. Clyde 73 E2
Vancouver Rd. Glasg 95 E2
Vanguard St. Clyde 74 B1
Vanguard Way. Ren 94 B1
Vardar Ave. Newt M 157 E4
Varna La. Glasg 95 F2
Varna Rd. Glasg 95 F2
Varnsdorf Way. Aird 123 F3
Vasart Pl. Glasg 96 C2
Vaults La. Kilw 207 F2
Veir Ter. Dumb 49 F2
Veitch Pl. Lennox 57 E4
Veitches Ct. Dunt 74 A3
Vennachar St. Shot 146 C3
Vennachar Rd. Ren 94 A2
Vennal St. Dalry 191 D4
Vennel Gdns. Glasg 116 C1
Vennel La. Stew 211 F4
Vennel St. Stew 211 F4
Vennel The. Den 21 F1
Vermont Ave. Glasg 138 A4
Vermont St. Glasg 116 C3
Vernon Bank. E Kil 159 F2
Vernon Dr. Lin 112 A3
Vernon Pl. Dund 225 F1
Vernon St. Salt 216 C4
Verona Ave. Glasg 95 E2
Verona La. Glasg 95 E2
Vesalius St. Glasg 119 D3
Viaduct Circ. Kilw 207 F3
Viaduct Rd. Newt M 157 F4
Vicar St. Falk 42 A3
Vicarfield St. Glasg 116 A4
Vicarland Pl. Glasg 139 D2
Vicarland Rd. Glasg 139 D3
Vicars Rd. Stone 198 C1
Vicars Wlk. Glasg 139 D3
Vickers St. Mother 163 D4
Victor St. Plains 104 A1
Victoria Ave. Car 187 F1
Victoria Cir. Glasg 96 B2
Victoria Cres. Aird 122 C3
Victoria Cres. Irvine 219 E1
Victoria Cres. Kils 60 A4
Victoria Cres. Mother 164 B2
Victoria Cres. Newt M 157 F4
Victoria Crescent La. Glasg . 96 B2
Victoria Crescent Pl. Glasg . 96 B2
Victoria Crescent Rd. Glasg . 96 B2
Victoria Cross. Glasg 117 D1
Victoria Dr E. Ren 94 B1
Victoria Dr. Troon 229 E1
Victoria Dr W. Ren 94 A2
Victoria Gdns. Aird 122 C4
Victoria Gdns. Barr 134 A2
Victoria Gdns. Kil 69 E1
Victoria Gdns. Pais 113 E1
Victoria Park Cnr. Glasg 95 E2
Victoria Park Dr N. Glasg ... 95 F2
Victoria Park Dr S. Glasg ... 95 F2
Victoria Park Gdns N. Glasg . 95 F2
Victoria Park Gdns S. Glasg . 95 F2
Victoria Park La N. Glasg ... 95 E2
Victoria Park La S. Glasg ... 95 E2
Victoria Park St. Glasg 95 E2
Victoria Pk. Ayr 238 C3
Victoria Pk. Kils 60 A4
Victoria Pl. Aird 122 C3
Victoria Pl. Glasg 138 A4
Victoria Pl. Hat 141 F2
Victoria Pl. Kils 60 B4
Victoria Pl. Miln 55 D1
Victoria Pl. Stir 7 D4
Victoria Quadrant. Holy 142 C3
Victoria Rd. Barr 134 A2
Victoria Rd. Cumb 61 E3
Victoria Rd. East 127 F3
Victoria Rd. Falk 42 B3
Victoria Rd. Glasg 117 D2
Victoria Rd. Glasg 138 A3
Victoria Rd. Gour 44 B4
Victoria Rd. Helen 16 C1
Victoria Rd. Kilbar 111 E3
Victoria Rd. Klrk 79 E2
Victoria Rd. Lar 23 D1
Victoria Rd. Pais 113 E1
Victoria Rd. Salt 217 D4
Victoria Rd. Stepps 99 E3
Victoria Rd. Stir 7 D4
Victoria Roundabout. Irvine 219 D1
Victoria Sq. Stir 7 D4
Victoria St. Alex 27 F2
Victoria St. All 10 A4

Victoria St. Ayr 236 A1
Victoria St. Dumb 50 A2
Victoria St. East 127 F3
Victoria St. Glasg 138 A4
Victoria St. Ham 162 A3
Victoria St. Klrk 79 E4
Victoria St. Lark 185 D2
Victoria St. New 166 A2
Victoria St. Udd 161 E4
Victoria Terr. Cumb 61 E3
Victoria Terr. Men 4 A4
Victoria Way. Stew 195 F1
Victory Dr. Kilbar 111 D2
Victory Way. Glasg 120 A2
Viewbank Ave. Calder 123 D1
Viewbank. Glasg 136 A2
Viewbank St. Glen 101 F3
Viewfield. Aird 122 C4
Viewfield Ave. Bish 97 F4
Viewfield Ave. Glasg 119 F3
Viewfield Ave. Klrk 79 E3
Viewfield Ave. Loch 129 D1
Viewfield Ave. M of C 58 A3
Viewfield Ave. Udd 140 C1
Viewfield Dr. Alva 4 C3
Viewfield Dr. Bish 97 F4
Viewfield Dr. Glasg 119 F3
Viewfield La. Glasg 96 C1
Viewfield Rd. Ayr 236 A1
Viewfield Rd. Bank 38 B2
Viewfield Rd. Bish 97 F4
Viewfield Rd. Coat 121 E2
Viewfield Rd. Hat 141 F2
Viewfield Rd. East 127 F3
Viewfield St. Stir 7 D4
Viewmount Dr. Glasg 96 B4
Viewpark Ave. Glasg 118 A4
Viewpark Ct. Glasg 138 B3
Viewpark Dr. Glasg 138 A3
Viewpark. Miln 55 D1
Viewpark Pl. Mother 163 E3
Viewpark Rd. Mother 163 E3
Viewpark
  Shopping Ctr. Tan 141 E3
Viewpoint Pl. Glasg 97 F3
Viewpoint Rd. Glasg 97 F3
Viking Cres. Hous 111 E4
Viking Rd. Aird 123 D3
Viking Terr. E Kil 180 C3
Viking Way. Ren 94 B1
Villa Bank. Den 21 F1
Villafield Ave. Bish 78 A3
Villafield Dr. Bish 78 A2
Villafield Loan. Bish 78 A2
Village Gdns. Udd 140 C1
Village Rd. Glasg 139 F2
Vine Park Ave. Kilm 222 A4
Vine Park Dr. Kilm 222 A4
Vine St. Glasg 96 A1
Vineburgh Ave. Irvine 219 E2
Vineburgh Ct. Irvine 219 D2
Vinicombe La. Glasg 96 B2
Vinicombe St. Glasg 96 B2
Vintner St. Glasg 97 E1
Viola Pl. Lennox 78 B4
Violet Gdns. Car 201 F4
Violet Pl. Holy 143 D3
Violet St. Pais 114 A2
Virginia Ct. Glasg 117 E4
Virginia Gdns. Ayr 236 A1
Virginia Gdns. Miln 76 B4
Virginia Pl. Glasg 117 E4
Virginia St. Glasg 117 E4
Virginia St. Green 46 A2
Viscount Ave. Ren 94 B1
Vivian Ave. Miln 54 C1
Voil Dr. Glasg 137 D2
Voil Rd. Stir 2 A2
Vorlich Ct. Barr 134 B1
Vorlich Dr. Shi 66 C4
Vorlich Gdns. Bear 75 E4
Vorlich Pl. Kilmk 228 A2
Vorlich Pl. Stir 2 A1
Vorlich Wynd. Holy 143 E2
Vrackie Pl. Kilmk 228 A2
Vulcan St. Glasg 97 F2
Vulcan St. Mother 163 F4

W Lodge Gdns. All 9 F4
Waddell Ave. Glenm 102 B2
Waddell Ct. Glasg 117 E3
Waddell Ct. Kilmk 222 C2
Waddell St. Aird 103 D1
Waddell St. Glasg 117 E2
Waddell St. Sten 24 B1
Waggon Rd. Ayr 235 F1
Waggon Rd. Falk 42 A4
Waid Ave. Newt M 156 B3
Waldemar Rd. Glasg 95 E4
Walden Rd. Hurl 228 C3
Waldo St. Glasg 95 F4
Walk The. All 10 A3
Walker Ave. Kilmk 228 A4
Walker Ave. Troon 229 E3
Walker Ct. Glasg 96 A1
Walker Dr. John 111 D1
Walker Path. Tan 141 D4
Walker Rd. Ayr 236 A1

Walker St. Glasg 96 A1
Walker St. Green 45 E3
Walker St. Kilb 149 D1
Walker St. Pais 113 E2
Walkerburn Dr. Wish 165 E3
Walkerburn Rd. Glasg 115 D2
Walkinshaw Cres. Pais 113 D3
Walkinshaw Rd. Inch 93 E2
Walkinshaw St. Glasg 118 A2
Walkinshaw St. John 112 A2
Wall Gdns. Falk 41 E3
Wall St. Falk 41 E3
Wallace Ave. Bishop 72 A2
Wallace Ave. Dund 225 F1
Wallace Ave. John 112 B1
Wallace Ave. Steven 206 B1
Wallace Ave. Troon 229 E3
Wallace Cres. Den 21 E1
Wallace Cres. Plea 12 B2
Wallace Ct. Pres 236 B4
Wallace Ct. Stir 2 A1
Wallace Dr. Lark 185 E1
Wallace Gdns. Lennox 57 D1
Wallace Gdns. Stir 2 B2
Wallace Pl. Cam 6 B3
Wallace Pl. Falk 42 B3
Wallace Pl. Fall 8 B2
Wallace Pl. Green 45 F3
Wallace Pl. Ham 163 D1
Wallace Pl. Udd 140 C1
Wallace Rd. Holy 143 D1
Wallace Rd. Irvine 219 E2
Wallace Rd. Ren 94 A1
Wallace St. All 10 B4
Wallace St. Bann 7 F1
Wallace St. Clyde 74 A1
Wallace St. Coat 122 A3
Wallace St. Dumb 50 A2
Wallace St. Falk 42 B3
Wallace St. Glasg 117 D3
Wallace St. Glasg 138 A4
Wallace St. Green 45 E2
Wallace St. Kilmk 227 F4
Wallace St. Mother 163 E4
Wallace St. P Glasg 47 F1
Wallace St. Pais 113 F3
Wallace St. Plains 104 A1
Wallace St. Stir 2 A1
Wallace View. Kilmk 227 F3
Wallace View. Shi 66 B4
Wallace View. Tull 4 B2
Wallace Way. Lan 215 E2
Wallacefield Rd. Troon 229 E2
Wallacehill Rd. Kilmk 227 F2
Wallacewell Cres. Glasg 98 A3
Wallacewell Pl. Glasg 98 A3
Wallacewell
  Quadrant. Glasg 98 B3
Wallacewell Rd. Glasg 98 B3
Wallbrae Rd. Cumb 83 D4
Wallneuk Rd. Pais 113 F3
Walls St. Glasg 117 E4
Wallstale Rd. Stir 7 D2
Walmer Cres. Glasg 116 B3
Walnut Cres. Glasg 97 E3
Walnut Cres. John 112 A1
Walnut Ct. M of C 58 A3
Walnut Dr. Klrk 79 D3
Walnut Pl. Glasg 97 E3
Walnut Pl. Tan 121 E1
Walnut Rd. Glasg 97 E3
Walnut Rd. Kilmk 227 E4
Walpole Pl. John 131 E4
Walter St. Glasg 118 B4
Walter St. Wish 165 E2
Walton Ave. Newt M 156 B3
Walton St. Barr 134 B2
Walton St. Glasg 136 C4
Wamba Ave. Glasg 95 F4
Wamphray Pl. E Kil 179 E4
Wandilla Ave. Clyde 74 B1
Ward St. All 10 A3
Warden Rd. Glasg 95 E4
Wardend Rd. Lennox 57 D1
Wardhill Rd. Glasg 98 A3
Wardhouse Rd. Pais 133 E4
Wardie Pl. Glasg 119 F4
Wardie Rd. Glasg 120 A4
Wardlaw Ave. Glasg 138 A4
Wardlaw Cres. E Kil 181 D4
Wardlaw Dr. Glasg 138 A4
Wardlaw Dr. Bear 75 F1
Wardlaw Rd. Fen 223 F3
Wardneuk Dr. Kilmk 223 D2
Wardneuk. Pres 236 B3
Wardpark Ct. Cumb 62 B3
Wardpark Pl. Cumb 62 B3
Wardpark Rd. Cumb 62 B3
Wardrop Pl. E Kil 159 F2
Wardrop St. Beith 171 E4
Wardrop St. Glasg 116 A4
Wardrop St. Pais 113 F2
Wardrop Terr. Beith 171 E4
Wards Cres. Coat 121 F3
Wards Pl. Kilmk 227 F4
Ware Rd. Glasg 120 A4
Warilda Ave. Clyde 74 B1
Warlock Dr. B of W 90 B1

Warlock Rd. Hous 90 B2
Warly Dr. Dund 225 F1
Warly Pl. Dund 225 F1
Warner St. Steven 217 E4
Warnock Cres. Hat 142 A2
Warnock Rd. Newt M 156 B4
Warnock St. Glasg 117 F4
Warren Rd. Ham 183 E4
Warren St. Glasg 117 D1
Warren Wlk. Lennox 57 F4
Warriston Cres. Glasg 118 C4
Warriston Pl. Glasg 119 D4
Warriston St. Glasg 118 C4
Warriston Way. Glasg 138 B2
Warrix Ave. Irvine 219 E1
Warrix Gdns. Troon 232 C4
Warrix Interchange. Irvine . 219 F1
Warroch St. Glasg 116 C4
Warwick. E Kil 160 B2
Warwick Gr. Ham 161 F3
Warwick Hill. Irvine 220 A3
Warwick Rd. Gour 45 D4
Warwickhill Rd. Kilmk 222 B1
Washington Rd. Klrk 79 D4
Washington Rd. Pais 113 F4
Washington St. Glasg 117 D4
Watchmeal Cres. Dunt 74 B4
Water La. Kilmk 227 F4
Water Rd. Barr 134 B2
Water Row. Glasg 116 A4
Water St. P Glasg 47 E1
Waterbank Rd. E Kil 158 B3
Watercut Rd. Irvine 218 C4
Watercut Rd. Kilw 219 D4
Waterfoot Ave. Glasg 135 E4
Waterfoot Rd. Newt M 157 D2
Waterfoot Row. Newt M 157 E2
Waterfoot Terr. Glasg 135 E4
Waterford Rd. Glasg 136 A2
Waterlands Gdns. Car 188 A2
Waterlands Pl. Law 187 D2
Waterloo Dr. Lan 215 D3
Waterloo Gdns. Kirk 58 B1
Waterloo La. Glasg 117 D4
Waterloo Rd. Lan 215 D3
Waterloo Rd. Pres 236 A3
Waterloo St. Glasg 117 D4
Watermill Ave. Klrk 79 E2
Watersaugh Dr. Cle 144 A1
Watersedge Ct. Rhu 15 E2
Waterside Ave. Newt M 156 B2
Waterside Ct. Kilmk 227 F4
Waterside Dr. Newt M 156 B2
Waterside Gdns. E Kil 158 B4
Waterside Gdns. Ham 162 C1
Waterside. Irvine 219 D2
Waterside Rd. E Kil 158 B4
Waterside Rd. Kilw 207 F2
Waterside Rd. Klrk 79 F4
Waterside Rd. Thorn 158 B3
Waterside St. Glasg 117 E2
Waterside St. Kilmk 227 F4
Waterslap. Fen 213 D1
Waterston Way. Loch 129 E2
Wateryetts Dr. Kil 69 E1
Watling Ave. Falk 41 E3
Watling Dr. Falk 41 E3
Watling Gdns. Falk 41 E3
Watling Pl. E Kil 159 D1
Watling St. Falk 41 E3
Watling St. Mother 142 B1
Watling St. Tan 140 C4
Watson Ave. Glasg 138 A4
Watson Ave. Lin 112 A3
Watson Ave. Stone 199 D2
Watson Cres. Kils 60 C4
Watson Pl. Bank 39 E2
Watson Pl. Udd 161 D4
Watson St. Falk 42 A3
Watson St. Glasg 117 E3
Watson St. Kilmk 228 A4
Watson St. Lark 184 C2
Watson St. Mother 163 F3
Watson St. Udd 140 C3
Watson St. Udd 161 E4
Watson Terr. Irvine 219 E1
Watsonville Pk. Mother 163 F3
Watstone Rd. Stone 199 D1
Watt Cres. Hat 142 A4
Watt Gdns. Falk 41 F3
Watt La. B of W 110 C4
Watt Low Ave. Glasg 137 F3
Watt Pl. Green 46 A3
Watt Pl. Miln 54 C2
Watt Rd. B of W 110 B4
Watt Rd. Glasg 115 D4
Watt St. Aird 103 E1
Watt St. Glasg 116 C3
Watt St. Green 45 F3
Wattfield Rd. Ayr 238 C3
Waukglen Ave. Glasg 135 D1
Waukglen Cres. Glasg 135 E2
Waukglen Dr. Glasg 135 D2
Waukglen Path. Glasg 135 D2
Waukglen Pl. Glasg 135 D2
Waukglen Rd. Glasg 135 D2
Waulking Mill Rd. Dunt 74 B4

Waulkmill Ave. Barr 134 B2
Waulkmill Pl. Kilmk 228 A4
Waulkmill St. Glasg 135 F2
Waverley Ave. Helen 25 D4
Waverley Ave. Kilmk 222 B1
Waverley Cres. Bon 40 A2
Waverley Cres. Cumb 82 B4
Waverley Cres. Ham 161 F2
Waverley Cres. Klrk 79 E4
Waverley Cres. Lan 215 E2
Waverley Cres. Stir 2 B1
Waverley Ct. Helen 16 B1
Waverley Ct. Udd 141 D1
Waverley Dr. Aird 103 D1
Waverley Dr. Glasg 138 B4
Waverley Dr. Wish 165 D2
Waverley. E Kil 160 B2
Waverley Gdns. Glasg 116 C1
Waverley Gdns. John 112 B1
Waverley Pl. Salt 205 F1
Waverley Rd. Lar 23 E1
Waverley Rd. Pais 132 C4
Waverley St. Coat 102 A1
Waverley St. Falk 42 A4
Waverley St. Glasg 116 C1
Waverley St. Green 45 E2
Waverley St. Ham 161 F2
Waverley St. Lark 199 D4
Waverley Terr. Dumb 49 D2
Waverley Terr. Lar 23 E1
Waverley Terr. Udd 161 E3
Waverley Way. Pais 132 C4
Weardale La. Glasg 119 E4
Weardale St. Glasg 119 E4
Weaver Ave. Newt M 156 B4
Weaver Cres. Aird 123 D3
Weaver La. Kilbar 111 D2
Weaver Pl. E Kil 179 E4
Weaver Row. Stir 7 D2
Weaver St. Ayr 235 F1
Weaver St. Glasg 117 E4
Weaver Terr. Pais 114 A2
Weavers Ave. Pais 113 D2
Weavers Rd. Pais 113 D2
Weavers Way. Stone 198 C1
Weavers Wlk. Lan 215 D2
Webster Ave. Sten 24 A2
Webster Groves. Wish 165 E3
Webster St. Clyde 94 C4
Webster St. Glasg 118 A2
Wedderlea Dr. Glasg 115 D3
Wee Cl. Beith 171 D4
Wee Row. Falk 42 A3
Wee Sunnyside Rd. Quart .. 184 A1
Weensmoor Rd. Glasg 134 C2
Weeple Dr. Lin 112 A3
Weighhouse Cl. Pais 113 F2
Weighhouse Rd. Car 187 F2
Weir Ave. Barr 134 B1
Weir Ave. Pres 233 E1
Weir Dr. Fall 8 B2
Weir Pl. Kilb 149 D1
Weir Pl. Law 186 C2
Weir Rd. Ard 205 E2
Weir Rd. Ayr 235 F2
Weir St. Coat 122 A4
Weir St. Falk 42 B3
Weir St. Green 46 B1
Weir St. Pais 113 F3
Weir St. Stir 1 C1
Weirston Rd. Kilw 208 A2
Weirwood Ave. Glasg 120 A3
Weirwood Gdns. Glasg 119 F2
Welbeck Cres. Troon 229 D1
Welbeck Ct. Troon 229 D1
Welbeck Mews. Troon 229 D1
Welbeck Rd. Glasg 135 D2
Welbeck St. Green 45 E4
Welbeck St. Kilmk 228 A4
Weldon Pl. Kils 60 C2
Welfare Ave. Glasg 139 E2
Well Gn. Glasg 136 B4
Well La. Lennox 57 E4
Well Rd. B of A 2 A4
Well Rd. Kilbar 111 D2
Well Rd. Lan 215 D2
Well St. Pais 113 E3
Well St. W Kil 190 B3
Welland Pl. E Kil 179 F4
Wellbank Gdns. W Kil 190 B3
Wellbank Pl. Udd 140 C3
Wellbrae. Lark 185 D1
Wellbrae Rd. Ham 162 A1
Wellbrae. Stone 198 C1
Wellbrae Terr. Muir 80 C1
Wellcroft Pl. Glasg 117 D2
Wellcroft Rd. Ham 161 F2
Wellcroft Terr. Ham 161 F2
Wellesley Cres. E Kil 179 F4
Wellesley Dr. E Kil 179 F4
Wellfield Ave. Glasg 136 A2
Wellfield St. Glasg 97 F2
Wellgate Dr. B of A 2 B4
Wellgate. Lan 215 D2
Wellgate St. Lark 185 D2
Wellgatehead. Lan 215 D2
Wellgreen. Stir 7 D3
Wellhall Ct. Ham 162 A2

Wellhall Rd. Ham 162 A2
Wellhead Ct. Lan 215 D2
Wellhouse Cres. Glasg 119 F4
Wellhouse Rd. Glasg 119 F4
Wellington Ave. Hurl 228 B4
Wellington. E Kil 180 A4
Wellington La. Ayr 238 C4
Wellington La. Glasg 117 D4
Wellington Pl. Clyde 73 E2
Wellington Pl. Coat 121 E3
Wellington Pl. Kilmk 222 C1
Wellington Pl. Wish 186 B4
Wellington Rd. Bish 78 A2
Wellington Sq. Ayr 238 C4
Wellington St. Aird 103 D1
Wellington St. Glasg 117 D4
Wellington St. Green 45 F2
Wellington St. Kilmk 222 C1
Wellington St. Mother 164 B3
Wellington St. Pais 113 E3
Wellington St. Pres 236 A3
Wellington Terr. Lan 214 C3
Wellington Way. Ren 94 B1
Wellknowe Ave. Thorn 158 B1
Wellknowe Pl. Thorn 158 B2
Wellknowe Rd. Thorn 158 B2
Wellmeadow Cl. Newt M ... 156 B3
Wellmeadow Gn. Newt M .. 156 B3
Wellmeadow Rd. Glasg 136 A3
Wellmeadow St. Pais 113 E2
Wellmeadow Way. Newt M 156 B3
Wellpark Ave. Kilmk 228 B4
Wellpark. Ayr 238 C1
Wellpark Bldgs. Green 46 A2
Wellpark Cres. Stir 6 C2
Wellpark Ct. Kilmk 228 B4
Wellpark Gr. Kilmk 228 B4
Wellpark La. Salt 216 C4
Wellpark Pl. Kilmk 228 B4
Wellpark Rd. Bank 38 B1
Wellpark Rd. Mother 163 E3
Wellpark Rd. Salt 216 C4
Wellpark St. Glasg 117 F4
Wellpark Terr. Bon 40 A3
Wellpark Terr. Neil 154 B3
Wells St. Clyde 73 F2
Wellshot Dr. Glasg 138 C3
Wellshot Rd. Glasg 118 C2
Wellside Ave. Aird 103 D1
Wellside Dr. Glasg 139 E2
Wellside La. Aird 103 D1
Wellside Pl. Falk 42 A3
Wellside Quadrant. Aird 103 D1
Wellsquarry Rd. E Kil 159 E3
Wellview Dr. Mother 163 E3
Wellwood Ave. Lan 215 D3
Wellwood. Kilw 207 E1
Wellynd. Aird 122 C4
Wellyard La. Gour 44 B2
Wellyard Way. Gour 44 B1
Wellyard Wynd. Gour 44 B1
Welsh Dr. Ham 183 E4
Welsh Dr. Udd 161 E3
Welsh Gdns. B of A 2 A4
Welsh Pl. Salt 205 F1
Wemyss Ave. Newt M 156 B4
Wemyss Bay St. Green 45 F2
Wemyss Dr. Cumb 60 C1
Wendur Way. Pais 113 E4
Wenlock Rd. Pais 113 F1
Wensleydale. E Kil 159 E2
Wentworth Dr. Glasg 76 C1
Wentworth Sq. Kilw 207 E2
Wesley St. Aird 122 C4
West Abercromby St. Helen 16 B2
West Academy St. Wish 164 C2
West Ave. Car 187 F1
West Ave. Ham 161 F3
West Ave. Holy 143 D1
West Ave. Plains 104 A2
West Ave. Ren 94 B2
West Ave. Stepps 99 E3
West Ave. Tan 141 E2
West
   Balgrochan Rd. Lennox . 57 D1
West Barmoss Ave. P Glasg 68 C3
West Benhar Rd. East 127 D2
West Blackhall St. Green 45 F3
West Boreland Rd. Den 21 E1
West Bowhouse Way. Irvine220 A3
West Bowhouse
   Workshops. Irvine 220 A3
West Brae. Pais 113 E2
West Bridge St. Falk 42 A3
West Bridgend. Dumb 49 F2
West Buchanan Pl. Pais 113 E2
West Burn Rd. Stew 195 F1
West Burn St. Green 45 F3
West Burnside St. Kils 60 B4
West Campbell St. Glasg ... 117 D4
West Campbell St. Pais 113 D2
West Canal St. Coat 121 F4
West Carmuirs Loan. Bon .. 40 C3
West Chapelton Ave. Bear .. 75 F2
West Chapelton Cres. Bear 75 F2
West Chapelton Dr. Bear 75 F2
West Chapelton La. Bear 75 F2

West Clyde St. Helen 16 B1
West Clyde St. Lark 185 D1
West Coats Rd. Glasg 138 C3
West Cres. Troon 229 F2
West Ct. Clyde 73 F2
West Dhuhill Dr. Helen 16 B2
West Doura Ave. Salt 205 F1
West Doura Way. Kilw 207 E2
West Dr. Aird 123 F3
West Dr. Lar 23 E1
West End. Dalry 191 D4
West End Dr. Hat 141 F2
West End Gdns. All 10 A3
West End Pl. Hat 141 F2
West Fairholm St. Lark 184 C3
West Faulds Rd. Lan 215 F3
West Fullarton St. Kilmk ... 222 C1
West Gate. Wish 165 E2
West George La. Glasg 117 D4
West George St. Coat 122 A4
West George St. Glasg 117 D4
West George St. Kilmk 222 C1
West Glebe Terr. Ham 162 B1
West Glen Gdns. Kil 69 F1
West Glen Rd. Kil 69 F1
West Glen Rd. Lang 70 A1
West Gr. Troon 229 F2
West Graham St. Glasg 97 D1
West Greenhill Pl. Glasg ... 116 C4
West Hamilton St. Mother . 163 F3
West High St. Kirk 58 B1
West James St. Alva 5 D3
West Johnstone St. Alva 5 D3
West Kilbride Rd. Dalry 191 D4
West King St. Helen 16 A1
West Kirk St. Aird 122 C4
West Kirklands Pl. Dalry ... 191 D4
West La. Pais 113 D2
West Langlands St. Kilmk . 222 C1
West Lennox Dr. Helen 16 B2
West Link Rd. B of A 2 B3
West Lodge Rd. Ren 94 A2
West Main St. East 127 F3
West Mains Rd. E Kil 159 E1
West Mains Rd. Gran 42 C4
West Montrose St. Helen 16 B1
West Murrayfield. Bann 7 E1
West Nemphlar Rd. Lan 214 B3
West Netherton St. Kilmk . 227 F4
West Nile St. Glasg 117 E4
West Park Cres. Kilm 222 A4
West Park Dr. Kilm 222 A4
West Pl. New 166 A3
West Port. Lan 214 C2
West Portland St. Troon ... 229 D1
West Porton Pl. Bishop 71 F2
West Prince's La. Glasg 96 C1
West Prince's St. Glasg 96 C1
West Princess St. Helen 16 B1
West Quay. P Glasg 47 E1
West Rd. Irvine 219 D2
West Rd. Kilbar 111 D2
West Rd. Lennox 57 D1
West Rd. P Glasg 68 C2
West Regent La. Glasg 117 D4
West Regent St. Glasg 117 D4
West Rossdhu Dr. Helen 16 B2
West Row. Strath 31 D2
West Sanquhar Rd. Ayr 236 A2
West Scott Terr. Ham 162 B1
West Shaw St. Green 45 F3
West Shaw St. Kilmk 227 F3
West St. Clyde 94 C4
West St. Glasg 117 D3
West St. Pais 113 E2
West Stewart St. Green 45 F3
West Stewart St. Ham 162 B2
West Stirling St. Alva 4 C4
West Thomson St. Clyde 74 A2
West Thornlie St. Wish 165 D1
West Vennel. All 10 A3
West View. Dunlop 195 D4
West View. Fen 213 F2
West Wellbrae Cres. Ham . 183 D4
West Whitby St. Glasg 118 B2
West
   Woodside Ave. P Glasg . 68 C3
West Woodstock St. Kilmk 227 F4
Westbank Ct. Glasg 96 C1
Westbank La. Glasg 96 C1
Westbank Quadrant. Glasg . 96 C1
Westborne Gdns. Helen 16 B1
Westbourn Bldgs. Green 45 F3
Westbourne Ave. Pres 236 B4
Westbourne Cres. Bear 75 E3
Westbourne Dr. Bear 75 E3
Westbourne
   Gardens La. Glasg 96 B2
Westbourne Gdns N. Glasg 96 B2
Westbourne Gdns. Pres 236 B4
Westbourne Gdns S. Glasg 96 B2
Westbourne Gdns W. Glasg 96 B2
Westbourne Rd. Glasg 96 A2
Westbourne
   Terrace La N. Glasg 96 B2
Westbourne
   Terrace La S. Glasg 96 A2
Westbrae Dr. Glasg 95 F2

Westbrae Rd. Newt M 156 C3
Westburn Ave. Falk 41 F2
Westburn Ave. Glasg 139 E3
Westburn Ave. Pais 113 D3
Westburn Cres. Dunt 74 A4
Westburn Cres. Glasg 137 F4
Westburn Farm Rd. Glasg . 139 D3
Westburn Rd. Glasg 139 E3
Westburn Rd. Glasg 140 A3
Westburn Way. Pais 113 D3
Westcliff. Dumb 49 D2
Westclyffe St. Glasg 116 C1
Westcott Pl. Lan 215 E3
Westend. Bear 76 A1
Westend Ct. Law 186 C2
Westend Park St. Glasg 96 C1
Wester Carriagehill. Pais .. 113 F1
Wester Cleddens Rd. Bish .. 78 B1
Wester Common Dr. Glasg . 97 D2
Wester Common Rd. Glasg 97 D2
Wester
   Mavisbank Ave. Aird 122 C4
Wester Moffat Ave. Aird ... 123 F4
Wester Moffat Cres. Aird .. 123 F4
Wester Myvot Rd. Glen 82 A2
Wester Rd. Glasg 119 E2
Westerburn St. Glasg 118 C3
Westercraigs. Glasg 117 F4
Westerdale. E Kil 159 E2
Westerfield Rd. E Kil 158 B2
Westerglen Rd. Falk 42 A1
Westergreens Ave. Kirk 79 E3
Westerhill Rd. Bish 78 B2
Westerhouse Ct. Car 187 E1
Westerhouse Rd. Glasg 120 A4
Westerkirk Dr. Glasg 76 C1
Westerlands Dr. Stir 7 D3
Westerlea Ct. B of A 2 A3
Westerlea Dr. B of A 2 A3
Westermains Ave. Kirk 79 D4
Western Ave. Falk 42 A3
Western Ave. Glasg 137 F4
Western Cres. Kilb 170 A4
Western Isles Rd. Clyde 73 E3
Western Rd. Glasg 138 C2
Western Rd. Kilmk 223 D2
Westerton Ave. Glasg 95 F4
Westerton Ave. Lark 185 D1
Westerton Ave. Thorn 158 A3
Westerton. Cowie 12 B4
Westerton Dr. B of A 2 A4
Westerton La. Thorn 158 A3
Westerton. Lennox 57 F4
Westerton Terr. Sten 24 B2
Westfield Ave. Glasg 137 F4
Westfield Cres. Bear 75 F1
Westfield Dr. Bear 75 F1
Westfield Dr. Cumb 81 F4
Westfield Dr. Glasg 115 D3
Westfield Dr. Green 45 E4
Westfield Dr. Kil 89 D4
Westfield. Dumb 49 E2
Westfield. Kilb 170 A4
Westfield Pl. Den 21 F1
Westfield Rd. Ayr 238 C3
Westfield Rd. Cumb 81 F4
Westfield Rd. Glasg 136 A2
Westfield Rd. Holy 143 E4
Westfield Rd. Kils 36 A1
Westfield Rd. P Glasg 68 C4
Westfield St. Falk 42 C3
Westfields. Bish 122 C4
Westgarth Pl. E Kil 159 D2
Westgate Way. Hat 141 F2
Westhouse Ave. Glasg 137 F4
Westhouse Gdns. Glasg ... 137 F4
Westland Dr. Glasg 95 D2
Westlands Gdns. Pais 113 E1
Westlea Pl. Aird 123 D3
Westminster Pl. Sten 23 F2
Westminster Terr. Glasg ... 116 C4
Westmoor Cres. Kilmk 227 E4
Westmoreland St. Glasg ... 117 D1
Westmorland Rd. Gour 44 C2
Westmuir Pl. Glasg 137 F4
Westmuir St. Glasg 118 B3
Weston Pl. Pres 236 B3
Weston Terr. W Kil 190 B3
Westpark Ct. Steven 217 E4
Westpark Dr. Pais 113 D3
Westport. E Kil 159 D1
Westport St. Kils 60 B4
Westray Ave. Newt M 156 B4
Westray Ave. P Glasg 69 D3
Westray Cir. Glasg 97 E3
Westray Ct. Cumb 82 C4
Westray Pl. Bish 78 B1
Westray Pl. Glasg 97 E3
Westray Rd. Cumb 82 C4
Westray Sq. Glasg 97 E3
Westray St. Glasg 97 E3
Westray Terr. Falk 42 B1
Westray Wynd. New 165 F3
Westside Gdns. Glasg 96 B1
Westview Cres. Tull 4 B1

Westward Way. Troon 229 F4
Westwood Ave. Ayr 236 C1
Westwood Ave. Glasg 136 A2
Westwood Cres. Ayr 236 C1
Westwood Cres. Ham 162 B1
Westwood Dr. Cle 144 C1
Westwood Gdns. Pais 113 D3
Westwood Hill. E Kil 180 A4
Westwood Quadrant. Clyde 74 B1
Westwood Rd. E Kil 180 A4
Westwood Rd. Glasg 136 A3
Westwood Rd. New 166 A3
Westwood Sq. E Kil 180 A4
Weymouth Cres. Gour 44 C3
Weymouth Dr. Glasg 96 A3
Whamflet Ave. Glasg 120 B4
Wharry Rd. Alva 4 C4
Whatriggs Rd. Kilmk 228 A2
Wheatfield Rd. Ayr 238 C4
Wheatfield Rd. Bear 75 E1
Wheatholm Cres. Aird 103 D1
Wheatholm St. Aird 103 D1
Wheatland Ave. Udd 161 E4
Wheatland Dr. Lan 214 C3
Wheatlandhead Ct. Udd 161 E4
Wheatlands Ave. Bon 40 A3
Wheatlands Dr. Kilbar 111 D2
Wheatlands
   Farm Rd. Kilbar 111 D2
Wheatlandside. Lan 214 C3
Wheatley Cres. Kils 60 B4
Wheatley Pl. Salt 206 A1
Wheatley Rd. Steven 206 C1
Wheatpark Rd. Lan 214 C2
Whifflet Ct. Coat 122 A3
Whifflet St. Coat 122 A3
Whin Ave. Barr 134 A2
Whin Hill. E Kil 160 A2
Whin Hill Rd. Ayr 239 D1
Whin Loan. Kils 59 E4
Whin Pl. E Kil 160 A2
Whin St. Clyde 74 A2
Whinfell Dr. E Kil 180 A3
Whinfell Gdns. E Kil 180 A3
Whinfield Ave. Pres 236 B3
Whinfield Rd. Glasg 135 D2
Whinfield Rd. Pres 236 A3
Whinhall Ave. Aird 102 C1
Whinhall Rd. Aird 102 C1
Whinhill Dr. Glasg 115 D2
Whinhill Rd. Green 46 A2
Whinhill Rd. Pais 114 A1
Whinknowe. Ash 199 F4
Whinney Gr. Wish 165 F2
Whinnie Knowe. Lark 184 C1
Whinpark Ave. Hat 141 F2
Whinriggs. Stone 198 B1
Whins Rd. All 10 B4
Whins Rd. Glasg 116 B1
Whins Rd. Stir 7 D1
Whins Rd. Troon 229 F4
Whinwell Rd. Stir 2 A1
Whirlie Dr. Hous 111 D4
Whirlie Rd. Hous 91 D1
Whirlies
   Roundabout The. E Kil . 160 A2
Whirlow Gdns. Glasg 120 A3
Whirlow Rd. Glasg 120 A3
Whistleberry Cres. Ham ... 162 A4
Whistleberry Dr. Ham 162 A4
Whistleberry Rd. Ham 162 A4
Whistlefield Ct. Bear 75 F2
Whitacres Path. Glasg 135 D2
Whitacres Rd. Glasg 135 D2
Whitburn St. Glasg 118 C4
White Ave. Dumb 50 A2
White Cart Rd. Pais 113 F4
White Craig Rd. Ard 205 E2
White St. Ayr 236 A2
White St. Clyde 94 B4
White St. Glasg 96 B1
Whiteadder Pl. E Kil 179 E4
Whitecraigs Pl. Glasg 96 C4
Whitecrook St. Clyde 74 B1
Whitefield Rd. Glasg 116 B3
Whitefield Terr. Lennox 33 E1
Whiteford Ave. Dumb 50 B3
Whiteford Cres. Dumb 50 B3
Whiteford Ct. Ham 183 E3
Whiteford Pl. Dumb 50 B3
Whiteford Rd. Pais 114 A1
Whiteford View. Ayr 239 E4
Whitegates Pl. Falk 41 E2
Whitehall Ave. Pres 236 B4
Whitehall St. Glasg 116 C4
Whitehaugh Ave. Pais 114 A3
Whitehaugh Cres. Glasg ... 135 D2
Whitehaugh Dr. Pais 114 A3
Whitehaugh Rd. Glasg 135 D2
Whitehill Ave. Aird 103 D1
Whitehill Ave. Cumb 61 E1
Whitehill Ave. Kirk 58 C1
Whitehill Ave. Stepps 99 E3
Whitehill Cres. Car 187 F2
Whitehill Cres. Dunt 74 A4
Whitehill Cres. Kirk 58 C1
Whitehill Cres. Lan 214 C2

Whitehill Farm Rd. Stepps .. 99 E3
Whitehill Gdns. Glasg 118 A4
Whitehill Pl. Stir 7 D3
Whitehill Rd. Bear 75 E2
Whitehill Rd. Ham 162 A3
Whitehill St. Glasg 118 A4
Whitehill Street La. Glasg .. 118 A4
Whitehill Terr. Lan 214 C2
Whitehills Dr. E Kil 180 C4
Whitehills. Ersk 73 D1
Whitehills Pl. E Kil 180 C4
Whitehills Terr. E Kil 180 C4
Whitehirst Park Rd. Kilw .. 207 D2
Whitehope Green. Irvine ... 220 A2
Whitehorse Wlk. E Kil 180 A4
Whitehouse Rd. Stir 7 E4
Whitehurst. Bear 75 E3
Whitekirk Pl. Glasg 75 D1
Whitelaw Ave. Glen 101 F3
Whitelaw Cres. Hat 142 B2
Whitelaw St. Blac 107 E1
Whitelaw St. Glasg 96 B4
Whitelaw Terr. Twe 59 F2
Whitelea Ave. Kil 89 E4
Whitelea Rd. Kil 89 E4
Whitelee Cres. Kil 89 E4
Whitelee Cres. Newt M 156 A3
Whitelee. E Kil 180 B3
Whitelee Gate. Newt M 156 A3
Whitelees Rd. Cumb 62 C3
Whitelees Rd. Green 46 C1
Whitelees Rd. Lan 203 F1
Whitelees Rd. Lan 215 E2
Whiteloans. Udd 141 D2
Whitemoss Ave. E Kil 159 F1
Whitemoss Ave. Glasg 136 C2
Whitemoss Gr. E Kil 160 A1
Whitemoss
   Roundabout. E Kil 160 A1
Whitepond Ave. Hat 141 F2
Whites' Loan. Lan 215 E3
Whitesbridge Ave. Pais 113 D3
Whitesbridge Cl. Pais 113 D3
Whiteshaw Ave. Car 187 E1
Whiteshaw Dr. Car 187 E1
Whiteshaw Rd. Law 187 D2
Whiteside Rd. Pres 236 B4
Whiteside Terr. Pres 236 B4
Whitestone Ave. Cumb 61 D1
Whitevale St. Glasg 118 A4
Whitewisp Ct. Irvine 220 A2
Whitfield Dr. Ayr 236 B2
Whithope Rd. Muir 80 C2
Whithope Terr. Glasg 134 C2
Whithorn Cres. Muir 80 C2
Whitlawburn Ave. Glasg ... 138 C2
Whitlawburn Rd. Glasg 138 C2
Whitlawburn Terr. Glasg .. 138 C2
Whitlees Cres. Ard 205 E2
Whitletts Ct. Ayr 236 C1
Whitletts Rd. Ayr 236 B1
Whitriggs Rd. Glasg 134 C2
Whitslade St. Glasg 100 A1
Whitsun Dale. E Kil 159 E2
Whittagreen Ave. Holy 143 E2
Whittagreen Cres. Holy 143 E1
Whittagreen Ct. Holy 143 E2
Whittingehame Dr. Glasg ... 96 A3
Whittingehame La. Glasg ... 95 F3
Whittington St. Coat 122 A3
Whittle Pl. Irvine 219 F1
Whittle Rd. Ayr 236 B2
Whittlemuir Ave. Glasg 136 C2
Whitton Dr. Glasg 136 C2
Whitton St. Glasg 96 B4
Whitworth Dr. Clyde 74 A1
Whitworth St. Glasg 97 D3
Whyte Ave. Glasg 138 C3
Whyte Ave. Irvine 219 E1
Whyte Cnr. Dumb 50 C1
Whyte St. East 127 F3
Wick Ave. Aird 122 C2
Wickets The. Pais 114 A2
Wickham Ave. Newt M 156 B3
Wide Cl. Lan 215 D2
Wigton Ave. Newt M 156 B4
Wigtoun Pl. Cumb 62 A2
Wildcat Rd. W Kil 190 A2
Wilderness The. Air 14 B2
Wildman Rd. Wish 187 D4
Wilfred Ave. Glasg 95 E4
Wilkie Cres. Lark 185 D1
Wilkie Loan. Hat 142 A4
Wilkie Rd. Udd 141 D3
William Booth Pl. Stir 7 D2
William Dr. Ham 183 E4
William Mann Dr. Newt M . 156 B2
William St. Coat 122 A3
William St. Dunt 74 A3
William St. Glasg 116 C4
William St. Green 46 A3
William St. Ham 162 B1
William St. Helen 16 B1
William St. John 111 F2
William St. Kilmk 222 C1
William St. Kils 60 B4
William St. P Glasg 47 D1

William St. Pais	113	E2
Williamfield Ave. Stir	7	D2
Williamfield Gr. Irvine	219	D2
Williamfield Pk. Irvine	219	D2
Williamsburgh Terr. Pais	114	A3
Williamson Ave. Dumb	50	A2
Williamson Ave. Falk	24	A1
Williamson Dr. Helen	16	C1
Williamson Pl. John	112	A1
Williamson Pl. Falk	42	B4
Williamson St. Clyde	74	A2
Williamson St. Falk	42	A2
Williamson St. Glasg	118	B2
Williamwood Dr. Glasg	136	C1
Williamwood Pk. Glasg	136	C1
Williamwood Pk W. Glasg	136	C1
Willie Mair's Brae. Kilmk	223	E1
Willie Ross Pl. Kilmk	223	E2
Willison's La. P Glasg	47	E1
Willock St. Kilmk	227	F3
Willockston Rd. Troon	229	F1
Willoughby Dr. Glasg	95	F3
Willoughby La. Glasg	95	F3
Willow Ave. Bish	98	A4
Willow Ave. John	112	B1
Willow Ave. Klrk	79	E3
Willow Cres. Coat	122	A2
Willow Ct. E Kil	180	A3
Willow Dr. Aird	123	E4
Willow Dr. Bank	38	C1
Willow Dr. John	112	A1
Willow Dr. M of C	58	B3
Willow Dr. Udd	161	E4
Willow Gdns. Irvine	219	F3
Willow Gr. Holy	143	D3
Willow La. Glasg	119	D1
Willow La. Troon	229	E2
Willow Pk. Ayr	239	E2
Willow Pl. John	112	A1
Willow Pl. Tan	141	E4
Willow Rd. Kilmk	227	E4
Willow St. Glasg	95	F4
Willow Way. Ham	162	C1
Willowbank Cres. Glasg	96	C1
Willowbank Gdns. Klrk	79	E4
Willowbank. Lark	185	D3
Willowbank St. Glasg	96	C1
Willowburn Rd. Beith	170	C4
Willowdale Cres. Glasg	120	A2
Willowdale Gdns. Glasg	120	A2
Willowford Rd. Glasg	135	D2
Willows The. E Kil	158	C4
Willows The. Tull	4	A1
Willowyard Rd. Beith	170	C4
Wills Rd. Ayr	236	B1
Willwood Dr. Wish	165	E4
Wilmot Rd. Falk	41	E3
Wilsgait St. Cle	144	B1
Wilson Ave. Den	21	E1
Wilson Ave. Falk	41	E3
Wilson Ave. Irvine	219	E2
Wilson Ave. Kilmk	228	A4
Wilson Ave. Lin	112	A3
Wilson Ave. Troon	230	A1
Wilson Dr. Bann	7	E1
Wilson Dr. Falk	41	E3
Wilson Gdns. Falk	41	E3
Wilson Pl. Bon	40	B2
Wilson Pl. Dund	225	F1
Wilson Pl. E Kil	160	A2
Wilson Pl. Newt M	156	B2
Wilson Rd. Alla	167	D4
Wilson Rd. Falk	41	E3
Wilson St. Aird	122	C4
Wilson St. Alex	27	F3
Wilson St. Ayr	236	A1
Wilson St. Beith	150	B1
Wilson St. Coat	122	B4
Wilson St. Glasg	117	E4
Wilson St. Ham	162	A4
Wilson St. Lark	185	D1
Wilson St. Mother	163	F4
Wilson St. P Glasg	47	E1
Wilson St. Pais	113	E2
Wilson St. Ren	94	B2
Wilton Crescent La. Glasg	96	C2
Wilton Dr. Glasg	96	C2
Wilton Rd. Car	202	A4
Wilton St. Coat	101	E1
Wilton St. Glasg	96	C2
Wiltonburn Path. Glasg	135	D2
Wiltonburn Rd. Glasg	135	D2
Wilverton Rd. Glasg	95	F4
Winburne Cres. Ham	162	A2
Winchester Ave. Den	21	F2
Winchester Dr. Glasg	96	A3
Windelstraw Ct. Irvine	220	A2
Windermere St. Hat	141	F2
Windermere. E Kil	179	F3
Windhill Cres. Glasg	136	A3
Windhill Pl. Glasg	136	B3
Windhill Rd. Glasg	136	B3
Windlaw Ct. Glasg	137	E1
Windlaw Gdns. Glasg	136	C2
Windlaw Park Gdns. Glasg	136	C2
Windlaw Rd. E Kil	158	B4
Windlaw Rd. Glasg	137	E1
Windmill Rd. Ham	162	B2
Windmill St. Salt	216	C4
Windmillhill St. Mother	163	F3
Windrow Terr. Wish	165	E4
Windsor Ave. Falk	41	F2
Windsor Ave. Newt M	156	C3
Windsor Cres. Clyde	74	A2
Windsor Cres. Falk	41	F2
Windsor Cres. John	112	A1
Windsor Cres. Pais	114	A3
Windsor Ct. Car	187	F1
Windsor Dr. Duni	21	E2
Windsor Dr. Falk	41	F2
Windsor Dr. Glenm	102	C2
Windsor Gdns. All	9	F4
Windsor Gdns. Falk	41	F2
Windsor Gdns. Ham	162	A3
Windsor Path. Lark	185	E1
Windsor Pl. Shot	146	C3
Windsor Pl. Stir	7	D4
Windsor Quadrant. Car	187	F1
Windsor Rd. Falk	41	F2
Windsor Rd. Holy	143	D3
Windsor Rd. Ren	94	B1
Windsor St. Coat	121	F2
Windsor St. Glasg	97	D1
Windsor St. Glasg	119	E3
Windsor St. Men	3	F3
Windsor St. Shot	146	C3
Windsor Terr. Glasg	97	D1
Windsor Wlk. Tan	141	D4
Windward Pk. Ayr	239	D1
Windward Rd. E Kil	159	D1
Windy Yetts. Twe	59	F2
Windyedge		
and Hareshaw Rd. Chap	144	B2
Windyedge Cres. Glasg	95	E3
Windyedge Pl. Glasg	95	E3
Windyhill Pk. Eagle	157	F1
Windyridge. Ham	162	C1
Windyridge Pl. Udd	161	E4
Winehouse Yett. Dund	225	F1
Winfield Ave. Glasg	138	C4
Wingate Ave. Dalry	191	D4
Wingate Cres. E Kil	160	B2
Wingate Dr. E Kil	160	B2
Wingate Pk. E Kil	160	B2
Wingate St. Mother	164	C2
Wingfaulds Ave. Dalry	191	D4
Wingfield Gdns. Udd	141	D1
Winifred St. Glasg	98	B2
Winning Ct. Udd	140	C1
Winning Quadrant. Mother	164	B2
Winning Row. Glasg	118	B3
Winnipeg Dr. E Kil	180	A4
Winstanley Wynd. Kilw	207	E3
Winston Ave. Pres	236	B4
Winston Cres. Lennox	57	E4
Winston St. Helen	17	D1
Wintergreen Dr. E Kil	159	E2
Winton Ave. Eagle	178	C2
Winton Ave. Glasg	136	B1
Winton Ave. Kilw	207	E2
Winton Cir. Salt	216	C4
Winton Cres. Udd	161	E4
Winton Ct. Ard	205	E1
Winton Dr. Glasg	96	B3
Winton Gdns. Tan	141	D4
Winton La. Ard	205	E1
Winton La. Glasg	96	B3
Winton Pk. E Kil	159	D1
Winton Pl. Ard	205	E1
Winton Rd. Irvine	219	E3
Winton St. Ard	205	E1
Winton St. Salt	216	C4
Wirran Pl. Clyde	94	C4
Wishart Ave. Dunt	74	B4
Wishart Dr. Stir	7	E2
Wishart St. Glasg	117	F4
Wishaw High Rd. Cle	165	E4
Wishaw Low Rd. Cle	165	D4
Wishaw Rd. Wish	186	C4
Wishawhill St. Wish	164	C2
Wisner Ct. Glasg	135	F2
Wisteria La. Car	201	F4
Wiston St. Glasg	139	F3
Witch Rd. Kilmk	222	C1
Witches Linn. Ard	205	D2
Witchill Pl. Kilmk	222	C1
Witchknowe Ave. Kilmk	227	F3
Witchknowe Ct. Kilmk	227	F3
Witchknowe Rd. Kilmk	227	F3
Witchwood Ct. Coat	101	E1
Woddrop St. Glasg	118	A1
Wolcott Dr. Udd	161	E4
Wolfe Ave. Newt M	156	B4
Wolfe Rd. Falk	42	B2
Wolseley St. Glasg	117	E2
Wood Aven Dr. E Kil	159	E2
Wood Avens. Tull	4	B1
Wood Cres. Kilw	207	F4
Wood Cres. Mother	142	C1
Wood Farm Rd. Glasg	136	A1
Wood Gr. Irvine	220	B1
Wood La. Bish	98	B4
Wood Pk. Ayr	239	D2
Wood Pl. Strath	31	D2
Wood Quadrant. Clyde	94	C4
Wood Rd. Troon	229	D1
Wood St. Aird	103	E1
Wood St. Coat	121	F4
Wood St. Glasg	118	A4
Wood St. Green	45	E4
Wood St. Kilw	207	F2
Wood St. Mother	163	F4
Wood St. Pais	114	A2
Wood View. Alla	166	C4
Wood View. Holy	143	D3
Woodbank Cres. John	111	F1
Woodbank Cres. Newt M	157	F3
Woodbank Ct. Alex	27	E4
Woodbank Gdns. Alex	27	E4
Woodbank Rd. Cross	221	F1
Woodburn Ave. Aird	122	C3
Woodburn Ave. Bonh	28	A4
Woodburn Ave. Kilw	207	F2
Woodburn Ave. Newt M	157	F3
Woodburn Ave. Udd	161	F4
Woodburn Cres. Bon	39	F2
Woodburn Dr. All	4	C1
Woodburn Gdns. Falk	42	C3
Woodburn Pl. Hous	111	F4
Woodburn Rd. Beith	171	E4
Woodburn Rd. Falk	42	B3
Woodburn Rd. Glasg	136	B3
Woodburn Rd. Holy	143	D4
Woodburn St. Falk	42	C3
Woodburn St. Mother	163	F4
Woodburn Terr. Lark	185	E1
Woodburn Way. Alva	5	D3
Woodburn Way. Cumb	61	E1
Woodburn Way. Miln	55	D1
Woodcroft Ave. Glasg	95	F2
Wooddale. Mother	163	E2
Woodend Ct. Glasg	119	F1
Woodend Dr. Glasg	95	F3
Woodend Dr. Pais	114	B2
Woodend Gdns. Glasg	119	E1
Woodend La. Glasg	95	F3
Woodend Oval. Coy	239	F1
Woodend Pl. John	112	A1
Woodend Rd. Ayr	239	D1
Woodend Rd. Car	188	A1
Woodend Rd. Glasg	119	F1
Woodend Rd. Glasg	138	A2
Woodend St. Helen	16	A1
Woodfield Ave. Ayr	236	A3
Woodfield Ave. Bish	98	A4
Woodfield Cres. Ayr	236	A2
Woodfield Dr. Aird	103	E1
Woodfield Rd. Ayr	236	A2
Woodfield. Tan	141	E3
Woodfoot Pl. Glasg	135	D2
Woodfoot Quadrant. Glasg	135	D2
Woodfoot Rd. Glasg	135	D2
Woodfoot Rd. Ham	162	A1
Woodford Pl. Lin	112	A3
Woodford St. Glasg	136	C4
Woodgreen Ave. Glasg	137	E3
Woodhall Ave. Calder	123	D1
Woodhall Ave. Coat	121	F4
Woodhall Ave. Ham	162	A2
Woodhall Ave. Holy	142	C3
Woodhall		
Cottage Rd. Calder	123	E1
Woodhall Mill Rd. Calder	123	D1
Woodhall Pl. Coat	121	F2
Woodhall Rd. Calder	123	D1
Woodhall Rd. Car	201	E1
Woodhall Rd. New	165	F2
Woodhall Rd. Wish	165	F2
Woodhall St. Chap	123	E1
Woodhall St. Glasg	118	A1
Woodhall Terr. P Glasg	69	D4
Woodhead Ave. Cumb	81	F4
Woodhead Ave. Udd	141	D1
Woodhead Cres. Ham	183	D4
Woodhead Cres. Tan	140	C4
Woodhead Ct. Cumb	81	F4
Woodhead Gdns. Ham	162	A4
Woodhead Gr. Cumb	81	F4
Woodhead Pl. Cumb	81	F4
Woodhead Rd. Glasg	135	D3
Woodhead Rd. Muir	100	A3
Woodhead Terr. Muir	100	A4
Woodhead View. Cumb	81	F4
Woodhill Cres. Irvine	220	A3
Woodhill Gr. Bish	98	B4
Woodhill Pl. Kilm	222	A3
Woodhill Rd. Blac	107	D2
Woodhill Rd. Glasg	98	A3
Woodhill Rd. Kilmk	222	C2
Woodholm Ave. Glasg	137	E3
Woodhouse Ct. Thorn	158	A3
Woodhouse St. Glasg	95	F4
Woodilee Cotts. Kirk	79	F3
Woodilee Rd. Holy	143	F2
Woodilee Rd. Klrk	79	F3
Woodland Ave. Aird	123	E2
Woodland Ave. Kils	79	D4
Woodland Ave. Pais	133	F4
Woodland Cres. Eagle	178	B3
Woodland Cres. Glasg	139	E2
Woodland Gdns. E Kil	158	B4
Woodland Gdns. Ham	162	C1
Woodland Pl. Ard	205	E2
Woodland Terr. Lark	185	E1
Woodland Way. Cumb	62	A2
Woodland Way. Den	39	E4
Woodlands Ave. Irvine	219	E2
Woodlands Ave. Muir	100	C3
Woodlands Ave. Udd	141	D2
Woodlands Cres. Ayr	239	D2
Woodlands Cres. Falk	42	A2
Woodlands Cres. Glasg	135	F2
Woodlands Cres. Udd	141	D2
Woodlands Ct. Alex	27	E4
Woodlands Ct. Glasg	135	F1
Woodlands Dr. Coat	121	E4
Woodlands Dr. Glasg	96	C1
Woodlands Dr. Holy	142	C3
Woodlands Gate. Glasg	96	C1
Woodlands Gdns. Glasg	135	F2
Woodlands Gdns. Udd	141	D2
Woodlands Gr. Kilmk	223	D2
Woodlands Gr. Miln	55	D2
Woodlands. N Sau	5	F1
Woodlands Pk. Glasg	135	F2
Woodlands Pl. Kilmk	223	D2
Woodlands Rd. Glasg	96	C1
Woodlands Rd. Glasg	135	F1
Woodlands Rd. Holy	143	E4
Woodlands Rd. Mother	163	F2
Woodlands St. Miln	55	D1
Woodlands St. Mother	163	F4
Woodlands St. Pres	236	A4
Woodlands Terr. Glasg	96	C1
Woodlands Terr. Udd	141	D2
Woodlands The. Hat	142	B2
Woodlea Ave. Aird	123	E2
Woodlea Cres. Cross	221	F1
Woodlea Ct. Cross	221	F1
Woodlea Dr. Glasg	136	B2
Woodlea Dr. Ham	183	E4
Woodlea Pk. N Sau	10	A4
Woodlea Pl. Aird	103	E1
Woodlea Pl. Glasg	239	D1
Woodlinn Ave. Glasg	137	D3
Woodmill Dr. Lennox	57	E1
Woodmill Gdns. Cumb	81	F3
Woodmill. Kilw	207	F1
Woodneuk La. Muir	100	C3
Woodneuk Rd. Glasg	135	D3
Woodneuk Rd. Muir	100	C3
Woodneuk St. Chap	123	E1
Woodneuk Terr. Muir	100	C3
Woodrow Ave. Holy	143	D1
Woodrow Ave. Kil	69	E1
Woodrow Cir. Glasg	116	B2
Woodrow Pl. Glasg	116	B2
Woodrow Rd. Glasg	116	B2
Woods La. Ren	94	B2
Woodside Ave. B of W	90	B1
Woodside Ave. Glasg	136	A2
Woodside Ave. Glasg	138	B4
Woodside Ave. Ham	162	C1
Woodside Ave. Kilmk	227	E3
Woodside Ave. Kils	60	C4
Woodside Ave. Klrk	79	E3
Woodside Cres. Barr	134	B1
Woodside Cres. Bonh	27	F3
Woodside Cres. Glasg	96	C1
Woodside Cres. New	166	A3
Woodside Cres. Pais	113	E2
Woodside Ct. Cam	6	B3
Woodside Dr. Calder	123	D1
Woodside Dr. Newt M	157	E1
Woodside Gdns. Coat	121	E2
Woodside Gdns. E Kil	158	B4
Woodside Gdns. Newt M	157	E4
Woodside. Hous	91	E1
Woodside La. Kilbar	111	E3
Woodside Pl. Dunlop	195	E4
Woodside Pl. Fall	8	B2
Woodside Pl. Glasg	96	C1
Woodside Pl. Tan	141	E4
Woodside Place La. Glasg	96	C1
Woodside Rd. All	4	C1
Woodside Rd. Beith	150	A1
Woodside Rd. Cald	106	A2
Woodside Rd. E Kil	158	B4
Woodside Rd. Kilbar	111	E3
Woodside Rd. Stir	2	A2
Woodside Rd. Tull	4	A1
Woodside St. Chap	123	E1
Woodside St. Coat	121	E4
Woodside St. Holy	143	D2
Woodside St. Mother	164	A2
Woodside Terr. Clack	10	C2
Woodside Terr. Falk	42	A2
Woodside Terr. Glasg	96	C1
Woodside Terrace La. Glasg	96	C1
Woodside. W Kil	190	B2
Woodside Wlk. Ham	162	C1
Woodstock Ave. Glasg	116	B3
Woodstock Ave. Klrk	79	E4
Woodstock Ave. Lan	215	D2
Woodstock Ave. Pais	132	C4
Woodstock Dr. Lan	215	D2
Woodstock Dr. Wish	165	E2
Woodstock Pl. Kilmk	222	C1
Woodstock Rd. Green	45	E1
Woodstock Rd. Lan	215	D2
Woodstock St. Kilmk	227	F4
Woodstock Way. Pais	132	C4
Woodstone Ct. Rhu	15	F2
Woodvale Ave. Aird	123	E2
Woodvale Ave. Bear	76	A1
Woodvale Ave. Glasg	157	D4
Woodvale Dr. Pais	113	D3
Woodview Dr. Aird	123	D3
Woodview Dr. Hat	142	B4
Woodview La. Aird	123	D3
Woodview Rd. Lark	199	E3
Woodview. Tan	141	E4
Woodview Terr. Ham	162	A2
Woodville Pk. Glasg	116	A3
Woodville St. Glasg	116	A3
Woodwynd. Kilw	207	F2
Woodyard Rd. Dumb	49	F2
Woodyett Pk. Thorn	157	F3
Woodyett Rd. Thorn	157	F3
Wooer St. Falk	42	A2
Wordsworth Way. Udd	141	D2
Works Ave. Glasg	139	F3
Workshops. Coat	122	A3
Worsley Cres. Newt M	156	B4
Wotherspoon Dr. Beith	150	A1
Wraes Ave. Barr	134	B2
Wraes View. Barr	133	F1
Wraisland Cres. Bishop	71	F2
Wrangholm Cres. Holy	143	D2
Wrangholm Dr. Holy	143	D2
Wren Ct. Tan	141	F4
Wren Pl. John	131	E4
Wren Rd. Green	45	D2
Wright Ave. Barr	134	A1
Wright St. Falk	42	A3
Wright St. Ren	94	A1
Wright Way. Holy	143	D2
Wrightfield Pl. Ayr	238	C1
Wrightlands Cres. Inch	93	F4
Wyburn Pl. Ayr	236	A2
Wye Cres. Coat	101	E1
Wykeham Pl. Glasg	95	E3
Wykeham Rd. Glasg	95	E3
Wylie Ave. Alex	27	E2
Wylie Ave. Newt M	156	B4
Wylie. E Kil	160	B3
Wylie St. Ham	162	B1
Wyllie Rd. Salt	217	D4
Wynd Beatson. Tan	121	D1
Wynd The. Alva	5	D4
Wynd The. Cumb	62	A3
Wyndford Dr. Glasg	96	B3
Wyndford Pl. Glasg	96	B3
Wyndford Rd. Cumb	62	B4
Wyndford Rd. Glasg	96	B3
Wyndford Terr. Tan	141	D4
Wyndham St. Glasg	96	B2
Wynyard Gn. E Kil	180	A4
Wyper Pl. Glasg	118	A3
Wyvil Ave. Glasg	75	F1
Wyvis Ave. Bear	75	E4
Wyvis Ave. Glasg	94	C4
Wyvis Gdns. Kilmk	228	A2
Wyvis Pl. Glasg	94	C4
Wyvis Pl. Irvine	220	A2
Wyvis Pl. Shot	147	D2
Wyvis Quadrant. Glasg	94	C4
Wyvis Rd. Kilmk	228	A2
Yair Dr. Glasg	115	D3
Yardley Pl. Falk	24	A1
Yardside Rd. Kilm	222	A4
Yarrow Cres. Bishop	72	B1
Yarrow Cres. Wish	165	D2
Yarrow Ct. Glasg	139	F3
Yarrow Gardens La. Glasg	96	C2
Yarrow Gdns. Glasg	96	C2
Yarrow Pk. E Kil	160	A1
Yarrow Rd. Bish	78	A2
Yarrow Way. Udd	161	E4
Yate St. Glasg	118	A3
Yerton Brae. W Kil	190	B2
Yetholm St. Glasg	94	C3
Yetholm Terr. Ham	161	F2
Yett Rd. Holy	143	E2
Yetts Ave. Kil	69	E1
Yetts Cres. Klrk	79	F4
Yetts Hole Rd. Glen	102	A3
Yetts The. Cam	6	B3
Yew Dr. Glasg	98	A2
Yew Pl. John	111	F1
Yews Cres. Ham	162	A3
Yieldshields Rd. Car	189	E2
Yoker Ferry Rd. Glasg	94	C3
Yoker Mill Gdns. Clyde	94	C4
Yoker Mill Rd. Clyde	94	C4
Yokerburn Terr. Clyde	94	B4
Yonderton Pl. W Kil	190	B2
York Dr. Falk	42	B3
York Dr. Glasg	138	B3
York Rd. Gour	44	C3
York St. Ayr	235	F1
York St. Clyde	74	B1
York St. Falk	42	B3
York St. Glasg	117	D4
York St. Wish	165	D1

York Street La. Ayr

Zetland Rd. Glasg

ORDNANCE SURVEY

STREET ATLASES

The Ordnance Survey / Philip's Street Atlases provide unique and definitive mapping of entire counties

Street Atlases available

- ◆ **Berkshire**
- ◆ **Bristol and Avon**
- ◆ **Buckinghamshire**
- ◆ **Cardiff**
- ◆ **Cheshire**
- ◆ **Derbyshire**
- ◆ **Edinburgh**
- ◆ **East Essex**
- ◆ **West Essex**
- ◆ **Glasgow**
- ◆ **North Hampshire**
- ◆ **South Hampshire**
- ◆ **Hertfordshire**
- ◆ **East Kent**
- ◆ **West Kent**
- ◆ **Nottinghamshire**
- ◆ **Oxfordshire**
- ◆ **Staffordshire**
- ◆ **Surrey**
- ◆ **East Sussex**
- ◆ **West Sussex**
- ◆ **Warwickshire**

The Street Atlases are revised and updated on a regular basis and new titles are added to the series. Many counties are now available in full-size hardback and softback editions as well as handy pocket-size versions. All contain Ordnance Survey mapping except Surrey which is by Philip's

The series is available from all good bookshops or by mail order direct from the publisher. However, the order form opposite may not reflect the complete range of titles available so it is advisable to check by telephone before placing your order. Payment can be made by credit card or cheque / postal order in the following ways:

By phone
Phone your order through on our special Credit Card Hotline on 01933 414000. Speak to our customer service team during office hours (9am to 5pm) or leave a message on the answering machine, quoting T511N99C, your full credit card number plus expiry date and your full name and address

By post
Simply fill out the order form opposite (you may photocopy it) and send it to: Cash Sales Department, Reed Book Services, PO Box 5, Rushden, Northants, NN10 6YX

O|S STREET ATLASES ORDER FORM

T511N99C

Registered office: Michelin House, 81 Fulham Road, London SW3 6RB. Registered in England No 1974080

	Hardback QUANTITY TOTAL	Softback QUANTITY TOTAL	Pocket QUANTITY TOTAL	
	£12.99	£8.99	£4.99	
Berkshire	ISBN 0-540-05992-7	ISBN 0-540-05993-5	ISBN 0-540-05994-3	➤
Buckinghamshire	ISBN 0-540-05989-7	ISBN 0-540-05990-0	ISBN 0-540-05991-9	➤
East Essex	ISBN 0-540-05848-3	ISBN 0-540-05866-1	ISBN 0-540-05850-5	➤
West Essex	ISBN 0-540-05849-1	ISBN 0-540-05867-X	ISBN 0-540-05851-3	➤
North Hampshire	ISBN 0-540-05852-1	ISBN 0-540-05853-X	ISBN 0-540-05854-8	➤
South Hampshire	ISBN 0-540-05855-6	ISBN 0-540-05856-4	ISBN 0-540-05857-2	➤
Hertfordshire	ISBN 0-540-05995-1	ISBN 0-540-05996-X	ISBN 0-540-05997-8	➤
East Kent	ISBN 0-540-06026-7	ISBN 0-540-06027-5	ISBN 0-540-06028-3	➤
West Kent	ISBN 0-540-06029-1	ISBN 0-540-06031-3	ISBN 0-540-06030-5	➤
Nottinghamshire	ISBN 0-540-05858-0	ISBN 0-540-05859-9	ISBN 0-540-05860-2	➤
Oxfordshire	ISBN 0-540-05986-2	ISBN 0-540-05987-0	ISBN 0-540-05988-9	➤
East Sussex	ISBN 0-540-05875-0	ISBN 0-540-05874-2	ISBN 0-540-05873-4	➤
West Sussex	ISBN 0-540-05876-9	ISBN 0-540-05877-7	ISBN 0-540-05878-5	➤
	£12.99	£9.99	£4.99	
Bristol and Avon	ISBN 0-540-06140-9	ISBN 0-540-06141-7	ISBN 0-540-06142-5	➤
Cardiff	ISBN 0-540-06186-7	ISBN 0-540-06187-5	ISBN 0-540-06207-3	➤
Cheshire	ISBN 0-540-06143-3	ISBN 0-540-06144-1	ISBN 0-540-06145-X	➤
Derbyshire	ISBN 0-540-06137-9	ISBN 0-540-06138-7	ISBN 0-540-06139-5	➤
Edinburgh	ISBN 0-540-06180-8	ISBN 0-540-06181-6	ISBN 0-540-06182-4	➤
Glasgow	ISBN 0-540-06183-2	ISBN 0-540-06184-0	ISBN 0-540-06185-9	➤
Staffordshire	ISBN 0-540-06134-4	ISBN 0-540-06135-2	ISBN 0-540-06136-0	➤
	£10.99	£8.99	£4.99	
Surrey	ISBN 0-540-05983-8	ISBN 0-540-05984-6	ISBN 0-540-05985-4	➤
Warwickshire	ISBN 0-540-05642-1			➤ ▼

Name _____

Address _____

_____

_____ Postcode

◆ **Free postage and packing** ◆ All available titles will normally be dispatched within 5 working days of receipt of order but please allow up to 28 days for delivery
☐ Please tick this box if you do not wish your name to be used by other carefully selected organisations that may wish to send you information about other products and services

I enclose a cheque / postal order, for a **total** of ▢
made payable to **Reed Book Services**, or please debit my
☐ Access ☐ American Express ☐ Visa
account by ▢

Account no ▢▢▢▢ ▢▢▢▢ ▢▢▢▢ ▢▢▢▢
Expiry date ▢▢ ▢▢

Signature _____